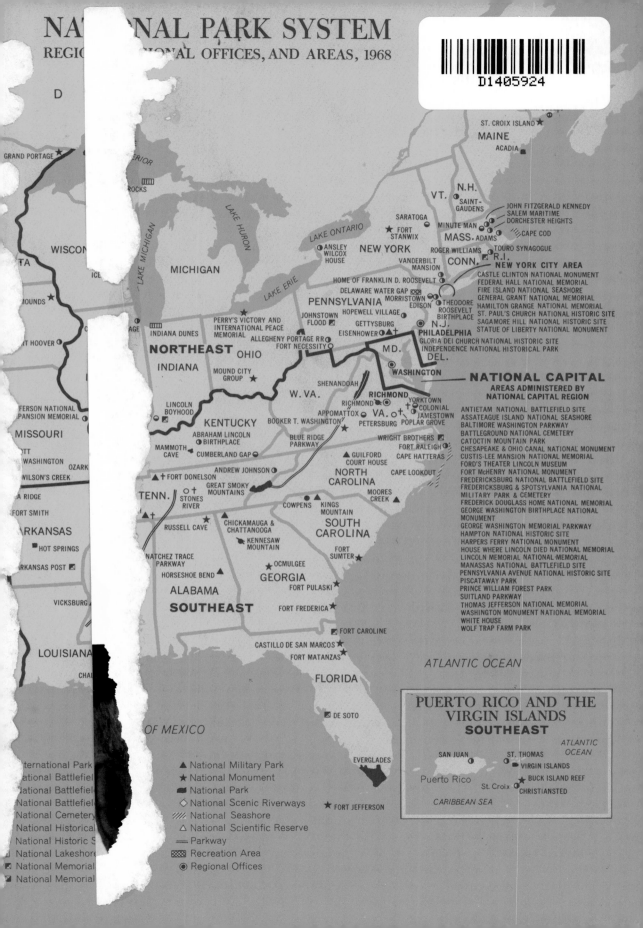

# NATIONAL PARK SYSTEM
## REGIONAL NATIONAL OFFICES, AND AREAS, 1968

D1405924

**MAINE**
ST. CROIX ISLAND ★
ACADIA

**N.H.**
VT.
SAINT-GAUDENS

SARATOGA
MINUTE MAN
FORT STANWIX

**MASS.** ADAMS
JOHN FITZGERALD KENNEDY
SALEM MARITIME
DORCHESTER HEIGHTS
CAPE COD

ANSLEY WILCOX HOUSE
**NEW YORK**
ROGER WILLIAMS
TOURO SYNAGOGUE
**R.I.**
**CONN.**

VANDERBILT MANSION
HOME OF FRANKLIN D. ROOSEVELT
DELAWARE WATER GAP
MORRISTOWN
EDISON
THEODORE ROOSEVELT BIRTHPLACE

**NEW YORK CITY AREA**
CASTLE CLINTON NATIONAL MONUMENT
FEDERAL HALL NATIONAL MEMORIAL
FIRE ISLAND NATIONAL SEASHORE
GENERAL GRANT NATIONAL MEMORIAL
HAMILTON GRANGE NATIONAL MEMORIAL
ST. PAUL'S CHURCH NATIONAL HISTORIC SITE
SAGAMORE HILL NATIONAL HISTORIC SITE
STATUE OF LIBERTY NATIONAL MONUMENT

**PENNSYLVANIA**
JOHNSTOWN FLOOD
HOPEWELL VILLAGE
GETTYSBURG
EISENHOWER
**PHILADELPHIA**
GLORIA DEI CHURCH NATIONAL HISTORIC SITE
INDEPENDENCE NATIONAL HISTORICAL PARK

**LAKE ONTARIO**
**LAKE ERIE**
**LAKE HURON**
**LAKE MICHIGAN**
**SUPERIOR**

GRAND PORTAGE ★
ROCKS
**WISCON...**
ICE...
**MICHIGAN**

PERRY'S VICTORY AND INTERNATIONAL PEACE MEMORIAL
INDIANA DUNES
ALLEGHENY PORTAGE RR
FORT NECESSITY

**NORTHEAST**
**INDIANA**
**OHIO**
MOUND CITY GROUP
LINCOLN BOYHOOD

**MD.**
**DEL.**
**N.J.**
**WASHINGTON**

# NATIONAL CAPITAL
## AREAS ADMINISTERED BY NATIONAL CAPITAL REGION

ANTIETAM NATIONAL BATTLEFIELD SITE
ASSATEAGUE ISLAND NATIONAL SEASHORE
BALTIMORE WASHINGTON PARKWAY
BATTLEGROUND NATIONAL CEMETERY
CATOCTIN MOUNTAIN PARK
CHESAPEAKE & OHIO CANAL NATIONAL MONUMENT
CUSTIS-LEE MANSION NATIONAL MEMORIAL
FORD'S THEATER LINCOLN MUSEUM
FORT McHENRY NATIONAL MONUMENT
FREDERICKSBURG NATIONAL BATTLEFIELD SITE
FREDERICKSBURG & SPOTSYLVANIA NATIONAL MILITARY PARK & CEMETERY
FREDERICK DOUGLASS HOME NATIONAL MEMORIAL
GEORGE WASHINGTON BIRTHPLACE NATIONAL MONUMENT
GEORGE WASHINGTON MEMORIAL PARKWAY
HAMPTON NATIONAL HISTORIC SITE
HARPERS FERRY NATIONAL MONUMENT
HOUSE WHERE LINCOLN DIED NATIONAL MEMORIAL
LINCOLN MEMORIAL NATIONAL MEMORIAL
MANASSAS NATIONAL BATTLEFIELD PARK
PENNSYLVANIA AVENUE NATIONAL HISTORIC SITE
PISCATAWAY PARK
PRINCE WILLIAM FOREST PARK
SUITLAND PARKWAY
THOMAS JEFFERSON NATIONAL MEMORIAL
WASHINGTON MONUMENT NATIONAL MEMORIAL
WHITE HOUSE
WOLF TRAP FARM PARK

**W. VA.**
SHENANDOAH
**RICHMOND**
RICHMOND
APPOMATTOX
BOOKER T. WASHINGTON
**VA.**
PETERSBURG
YORKTOWN
COLONIAL
JAMESTOWN
POPLAR GROVE

**KENTUCKY**
ABRAHAM LINCOLN BIRTHPLACE
MAMMOTH CAVE
CUMBERLAND GAP
BLUE RIDGE PARKWAY
WRIGHT BROTHERS
FORT RALEIGH
CAPE HATTERAS

ANDREW JOHNSON
GREAT SMOKY MOUNTAINS
**NORTH CAROLINA**
CAPE LOOKOUT

**TENN.**
STONES RIVER
RUSSELL CAVE
CHICKAMAUGA & CHATTANOOGA
KENNESAW MOUNTAIN
COWPENS
KINGS MOUNTAIN
MOORES CREEK
**SOUTH CAROLINA**
FORT SUMTER

JEFFERSON NATIONAL EXPANSION MEMORIAL
**MISSOURI**
...OTT
WASHINGTON
WILSON'S CREEK
OZARK
...A RIDGE
FORT SMITH
**ARKANSAS**
HOT SPRINGS
...RKANSAS POST
VICKSBURG
FORT DONELSON

NATCHEZ TRACE PARKWAY
HORSESHOE BEND
**ALABAMA**
OCMULGEE
**GEORGIA**
FORT PULASKI
**SOUTHEAST**
FORT FREDERICA

FORT CAROLINE
CASTILLO DE SAN MARCOS ★
FORT MATANZAS
**FLORIDA**
DE SOTO

**ATLANTIC OCEAN**

**LOUISIANA**
CHAL...
...OF MEXICO
EVERGLADES
FORT JEFFERSON ★

# PUERTO RICO AND THE VIRGIN ISLANDS
## SOUTHEAST

SAN JUAN
ST. THOMAS
VIRGIN ISLANDS
**Puerto Rico**
St. Croix
BUCK ISLAND REEF
CHRISTIANSTED
**ATLANTIC OCEAN**
**CARIBBEAN SEA**

▲ National Military Park
★ National Monument
◼ National Park
◇ National Scenic Riverways
/// National Seashore
△ National Scientific Reserve
═ Parkway
▨ Recreation Area
◉ Regional Offices

International Park
National Battlefiel...
National Battlefiel...
National Cemetery
National Historical
National Historic S...
National Lakeshore
National Memorial
National Memorial

# THE NATIONAL PARKS

*Freeman Tilden*

# The National Parks

A REVISED & ENLARGED EDITION

*of the classic book on the national parks,*

*with new information & evaluation on all of the*

NATIONAL PARKS, NATIONAL MONUMENTS,

& HISTORIC SITES

*Foreword by* George B. Hartzog, Jr.

*Director of the National Park Service*

*New York / Alfred · A · Knopf*

1 9 6 8

THIS IS A BORZOI BOOK
PUBLISHED BY ALFRED A. KNOPF, INC.

FIRST REVISED EDITION

*Frontispiece:*
*Sunset storm over Mount Moran. Grand Teton National Park. [Photo: B. D. Glaha]*

To the Interpreters
of the National Park Service,
steadfast in their efforts
to reveal the truths
that lie behind the appearances.

# FOREWORD

T HE PUBLICATION, in 1951, of the first edition of *The National Parks: What They Mean to You and Me* heralded good things for the National Park Service and the public it serves. And it was superb evidence of what has been rightly termed Alfred Knopf's "love affair" with the national parks. From the House of Knopf have come a number of fine books on conservation; and from Mr. Knopf himself, distinguished service as chairman of the Secretary of the Interior's citizen Advisory Board on National Parks, Historic Sites, Buildings and Monuments.

But primarily the book brought to a new focus the talents of a sensitive and thoughtful observer, Freeman Tilden, who approached the subject of national parks with a rare understanding. In this book, and in his other writings, Mr. Tilden has enriched our literature, helping people appreciate the National Park System and the benefits the parks can bring to the people of America, and of the world.

The 1951 edition dealt only with the natural areas of the system. This new edition includes the entire spectrum of natural, historical, and recreational areas—more than tripling the coverage and making it the most comprehensive book of its kind.

This is a book, too, that conveys the "feel" of the parks to readers who may take pleasure from simply knowing they share in park ownership, as well as to the millions who enjoy them first-hand. This creative essence of the parks is especially well conveyed through a judicious selection of new illustrations.

Regarding these, Mr. Tilden has said: "This is the first book ever published on our parks for which the pictures have been chosen, invariably, on the judgment not of whether they were pretty pictures (though most of them are) or examples of the photographer's skill (though they are mostly highly professional), but of whether they INTERPRET. For every illustration in this book I have used the criterion: Does this picture somehow contrive to convey something of the spirit, the essence, of the area? I dare not say that the results are 100 per cent, but I do think they represent a very high degree of success."

They do, indeed.

I would like also to suggest something of the enormous expansion in responsibilities that has taken place in the years since 1951. A program to save the finest of the nation's shoreline areas, given vigorous impetus under President Kennedy and President Johnson and Secretary Udall, has resulted in a network of national seashores along the Atlantic, Gulf, and Pacific coasts and national lakeshores on the Great Lakes. The Land and Water Conservation Fund Act of 1964 has enabled us to acquire lands needed for the many new parks.

Major impoundments behind the giant dams have become full-fledged recreation members of the system; they answer a need recognized as long ago as 1925, when Director Stephen Mather's annual report foretold the demand for areas that would provide specifically for healthful outdoor recreation. His concern was only that such areas be clearly differentiated from the national parks and monuments, on which the fullest protection of natural features for human enjoyment and inspiration was paramount. That distinction has been faithfully observed.

There have been other significant changes affecting the system. Now in progress is the identification of potential units of the National Wilderness Preservation System within the National Park System. The establishment of Ozark National Scenic Riverways shows the way for what many hope will be a nationwide system of national rivers—free-flowing streams in unspoiled settings, providing for a unique kind of outdoor recreation. And the Bureau of Outdoor Recreation has been established in the Department of the Interior to correlate the activities of federal and state agencies in the park and recreation field.

And our management problems have become increasingly complex as we have watched visits to the national parklands increase from 37 million in 1951 to 139 million in 1967.

And yet, the policy that governs the preservation of park resources remains essentially unchanged. We still strive to attain for the parks the goal so eloquently expressed by Director Newton B. Drury in his 1951 Introduction: "to conserve them, not for commercial use of their resources but because of their value in ministering to the human mind and spirit."

This book, which interprets so well one of the priceless cultural resources of this nation, will do much to help us keep that goal steadfastly in mind.

GEORGE B. HARTZOG, JR.
*Director, National Park Service*

# CONTENTS

# Contents

PART FOUR

# Contents

# Contents

PART FIVE

# A Note on the Illustrations

*Each of the 225 photographs is listed in the Index under the name of
the park in which it was taken.*

*A map showing the location of each of the national parks, historic sites,
and monuments is found on pages 2–3.*

# THE NATIONAL PARKS

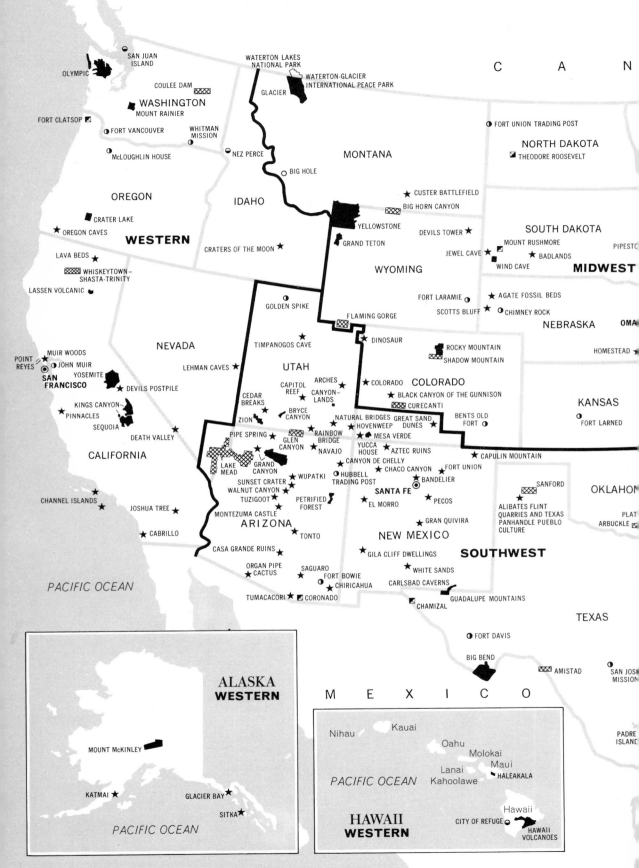

C A N
OLYMPIC
SAN JUAN ISLAND
WATERTON LAKES NATIONAL PARK
WATERTON-GLACIER INTERNATIONAL PEACE PARK
COULEE DAM
WASHINGTON
GLACIER
MOUNT RAINIER
FORT UNION TRADING POST
FORT CLATSOP
FORT VANCOUVER
WHITMAN MISSION
NORTH DAKOTA
THEODORE ROOSEVELT
McLOUGHLIN HOUSE
NEZ PERCE
MONTANA
OREGON
IDAHO
BIG HOLE
CUSTER BATTLEFIELD
BIG HORN CANYON
SOUTH DAKOTA
CRATER LAKE
OREGON CAVES
WESTERN
CRATERS OF THE MOON
YELLOWSTONE
DEVILS TOWER
MOUNT RUSHMORE
PIPESTO
LAVA BEDS
GRAND TETON
JEWEL CAVE
BADLANDS
MIDWEST
WHISKEYTOWN– SHASTA-TRINITY
WYOMING
WIND CAVE
LASSEN VOLCANIC
GOLDEN SPIKE
FLAMING GORGE
FORT LARAMIE
AGATE FOSSIL BEDS
NEBRASKA
OMA
SCOTTS BLUFF
CHIMNEY ROCK
POINT REYES
MUIR WOODS
JOHN MUIR
NEVADA
TIMPANOGOS CAVE
DINOSAUR
ROCKY MOUNTAIN
HOMESTEAD
SAN FRANCISCO
YOSEMITE
LEHMAN CAVES
UTAH
SHADOW MOUNTAIN
DEVILS POSTPILE
COLORADO
COLORADO
KANSAS
KINGS CANYON
CAPITOL REEF
ARCHES
BLACK CANYON OF THE GUNNISON
PINNACLES
CEDAR BREAKS
CANYON-LANDS
CURECANTI
SEQUOIA
BRYCE CANYON
NATURAL BRIDGES
GREAT SAND DUNES
BENTS OLD FORT
FORT LARNED
DEATH VALLEY
ZION
HOVENWEEP
RAINBOW BRIDGE
MESA VERDE
PIPE SPRING
GLEN CANYON
NAVAJO
YUCCA HOUSE
AZTEC RUINS
CALIFORNIA
LAKE MEAD
GRAND CANYON
CANYON DE CHELLY
CHACO CANYON
CAPULIN MOUNTAIN
FORT UNION
SUNSET CRATER
WUPATKI
HUBBELL TRADING POST
BANDELIER
SANFORD
OKLAHOM
CHANNEL ISLANDS
WALNUT CANYON
SANTA FE
TUZIGOOT
PETRIFIED FOREST
PECOS
JOSHUA TREE
MONTEZUMA CASTLE
EL MORRO
ALIBATES FLINT QUARRIES AND TEXAS PANHANDLE PUEBLO CULTURE
PLAT
ARBUCKLE
ARIZONA
TONTO
GRAN QUIVIRA
CABRILLO
CASA GRANDE RUINS
NEW MEXICO
SOUTHWEST
GILA CLIFF DWELLINGS
ORGAN PIPE CACTUS
SAGUARO
FORT BOWIE
WHITE SANDS
CARLSBAD CAVERNS
PACIFIC OCEAN
TUMACACORI
CORONADO
CHIRICAHUA
CHAMIZAL
GUADALUPE MOUNTAINS
TEXAS
FORT DAVIS
BIG BEND
AMISTAD
SAN JOS MISSION

ALASKA
WESTERN
M E X I C O
Nihau
Kauai
Oahu
MOUNT McKINLEY
Molokai
Maui
Lanai
PACIFIC OCEAN
Kahoolawe
HALEAKALA
KATMAI
GLACIER BAY
SITKA
Hawaii
HAWAII
WESTERN
CITY OF REFUGE
HAWAII VOLCANOES
PACIFIC OCEAN
PADRE ISLAND

J. P. TREMBLAY

# NATIONAL PARK SYSTEM
## REGIONS, REGIONAL OFFICES, AND AREAS, 1968

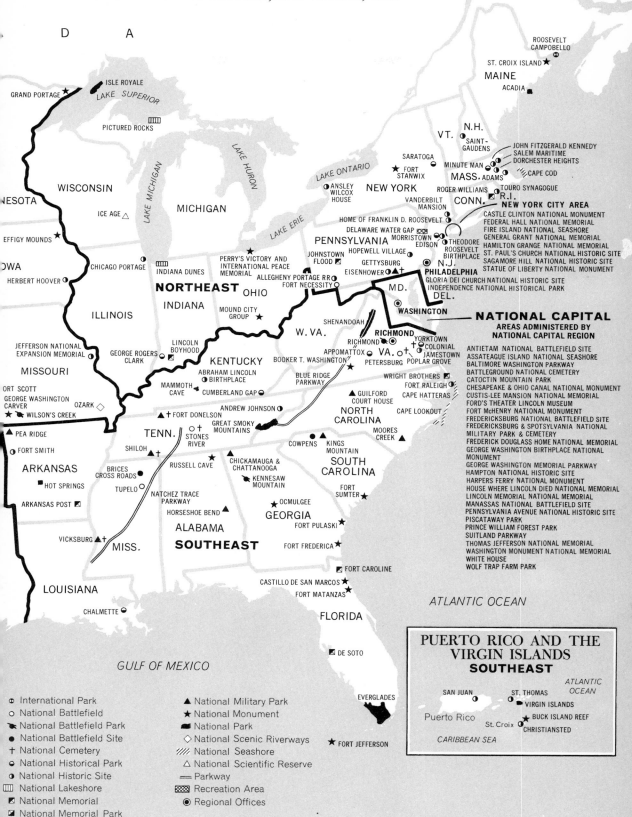

D A

ROOSEVELT CAMPOBELLO

ST. CROIX ISLAND ★

MAINE

ACADIA

ISLE ROYALE
GRAND PORTAGE ★
LAKE SUPERIOR

PICTURED ROCKS

WISCONSIN

MICHIGAN

LAKE HURON

LAKE ONTARIO

N.H.
VT.
SAINT-GAUDENS

SARATOGA
FORT STANWIX

JOHN FITZGERALD KENNEDY
SALEM MARITIME
DORCHESTER HEIGHTS
MINUTE MAN
MASS. ADAMS
CAPE COD

ICE AGE △
LAKE MICHIGAN

NESOTA

NEW YORK

ANSLEY WILCOX HOUSE

ROGER WILLIAMS
CONN. R.I.
TOURO SYNAGOGUE

EFFIGY MOUNDS ★

VANDERBILT MANSION

NEW YORK CITY AREA

CASTLE CLINTON NATIONAL MONUMENT
FEDERAL HALL NATIONAL MEMORIAL
FIRE ISLAND NATIONAL SEASHORE
GENERAL GRANT NATIONAL MEMORIAL
HAMILTON GRANGE NATIONAL MEMORIAL
ST. PAUL'S CHURCH NATIONAL HISTORIC SITE
SAGAMORE HILL NATIONAL HISTORIC SITE
STATUE OF LIBERTY NATIONAL MONUMENT

HOME OF FRANKLIN D. ROOSEVELT
DELAWARE WATER GAP
PENNSYLVANIA MORRISTOWN
EDISON
THEODORE
ROOSEVELT
BIRTHPLACE
N.J.

OWA
CHICAGO PORTAGE
INDIANA DUNES

HERBERT HOOVER

PERRY'S VICTORY AND
INTERNATIONAL PEACE
MEMORIAL

JOHNSTOWN FLOOD
HOPEWELL VILLAGE
GETTYSBURG
EISENHOWER

NORTHEAST OHIO

ILLINOIS
INDIANA

ALLEGHENY PORTAGE RR
FORT NECESSITY

PHILADELPHIA
GLORIA DEI CHURCH NATIONAL HISTORIC SITE
INDEPENDENCE NATIONAL HISTORICAL PARK

MD.
DEL.

MOUND CITY GROUP

WASHINGTON

JEFFERSON NATIONAL
EXPANSION MEMORIAL

SHENANDOAH

W. VA.
RICHMOND

NATIONAL CAPITAL
AREAS ADMINISTERED BY
NATIONAL CAPITAL REGION

GEORGE ROGERS CLARK
LINCOLN BOYHOOD

RICHMOND
APPOMATTOX
VA.
YORKTOWN
COLONIAL
JAMESTOWN
POPLAR GROVE

MISSOURI

KENTUCKY
BOOKER T. WASHINGTON
PETERSBURG

ANTIETAM NATIONAL BATTLEFIELD SITE
ASSATEAGUE ISLAND NATIONAL SEASHORE
BALTIMORE WASHINGTON PARKWAY
BATTLEGROUND NATIONAL CEMETERY
CATOCTIN MOUNTAIN PARK
CHESAPEAKE & OHIO CANAL NATIONAL MONUMENT
CUSTIS-LEE MANSION NATIONAL MEMORIAL
FORD'S THEATER LINCOLN MUSEUM
FORT McHENRY NATIONAL MONUMENT
FREDERICKSBURG NATIONAL BATTLEFIELD SITE
FREDERICKSBURG & SPOTSYLVANIA NATIONAL
MILITARY PARK & CEMETERY
FREDERICK DOUGLASS HOME NATIONAL MEMORIAL
GEORGE WASHINGTON BIRTHPLACE NATIONAL
MONUMENT
GEORGE WASHINGTON MEMORIAL PARKWAY
HAMPTON NATIONAL HISTORIC SITE
HARPERS FERRY NATIONAL MONUMENT
HOUSE WHERE LINCOLN DIED NATIONAL MEMORIAL
LINCOLN MEMORIAL NATIONAL MEMORIAL
MANASSAS NATIONAL BATTLEFIELD PARK
PENNSYLVANIA AVENUE NATIONAL HISTORIC SITE
PISCATAWAY PARK
PRINCE WILLIAM FOREST PARK
SUITLAND PARKWAY
THOMAS JEFFERSON NATIONAL MEMORIAL
WASHINGTON MONUMENT NATIONAL MEMORIAL
WHITE HOUSE
WOLF TRAP FARM PARK

ABRAHAM LINCOLN
BIRTHPLACE

BLUE RIDGE PARKWAY

WRIGHT BROTHERS
FORT RALEIGH
CAPE HATTERAS

ORT SCOTT
GEORGE WASHINGTON
CARVER
OZARK ◇

MAMMOTH CAVE
CUMBERLAND GAP

ANDREW JOHNSON

★ WILSON'S CREEK

NORTH CAROLINA

FORT DONELSON
GREAT SMOKY
MOUNTAINS

GUILFORD
COURT HOUSE
CAPE LOOKOUT

▲ PEA RIDGE
TENN.
STONES RIVER

MOORES CREEK

FORT SMITH
SHILOH

COWPENS
KINGS MOUNTAIN

ARKANSAS
RUSSELL CAVE

CHICKAMAUGA &
CHATTANOOGA

SOUTH CAROLINA

BRICES CROSS ROADS
HOT SPRINGS
TUPELO

KENNESAW MOUNTAIN

FORT SUMTER

NATCHEZ TRACE PARKWAY

ARKANSAS POST

HORSESHOE BEND

OCMULGEE

GEORGIA

VICKSBURG
MISS.
ALABAMA
SOUTHEAST

FORT PULASKI

FORT FREDERICA

LOUISIANA

CHALMETTE

FORT CAROLINE

CASTILLO DE SAN MARCOS
FORT MATANZAS

FLORIDA

ATLANTIC OCEAN

GULF OF MEXICO

DE SOTO

EVERGLADES

PUERTO RICO AND THE
VIRGIN ISLANDS
SOUTHEAST

ATLANTIC OCEAN

SAN JUAN
ST. THOMAS
VIRGIN ISLANDS

Puerto Rico
St. Croix
BUCK ISLAND REEF
CHRISTIANSTED

CARIBBEAN SEA

★ FORT JEFFERSON

- ⊕ International Park
- ○ National Battlefield
- ✹ National Battlefield Park
- ● National Battlefield Site
- † National Cemetery
- ○ National Historical Park
- ○ National Historic Site
- ⦀ National Lakeshore
- ▨ National Memorial
- ▨ National Memorial Park

- ▲ National Military Park
- ★ National Monument
- ▬ National Park
- ◇ National Scenic Riverways
- ///// National Seashore
- △ National Scientific Reserve
- ══ Parkway
- ▨ Recreation Area
- ◉ Regional Offices

# PART

---

# ONE

---

# [ I ]

# *The Life Community*

## [ 1 ]

THE VALUE OF THE NATIONAL PARKS to the scientist, the student, and the researcher is with some, perhaps not with many, a touchy subject. I sometimes meet an enthusiast who delights in the parks as "pleasuring-grounds," who squints horribly when I happen to mention the scientific importance of the wilderness areas. "I see," he says. "You are one of those fellows who wants to keep everybody out of the parks so that the long-haired, nearsighted professors can prowl around in them, working up material for a master's degree."

Now, it happens that most of the men of science with whom I am acquainted are not long-haired. Some of them are as close-cropped as a freshly sheared Angora goat, while others have had most of their hair removed permanently by nature. As for their physical condition, I recommend that anyone who doubts their stamina follow a geologist up a canyon with pack and specimen bag; or travel with a wildlife expert on a snowshoe trip in the high mountain country, with the temperature something below zero and a gale blowing. But this is aside. If there were any plot afoot to deprive me of the pure fun of loafing and inviting my soul in these lovely preserves, I should be the first to raise a howl of protest.

It so happens that park management that provides the maximum of spontaneous, lazy enjoyment to visitors is also ideal for the natural scientist and the student. What the average person loves about the primeval parks is the feeling of elbowroom, bigness, far horizon, freedom. You can get these sensations in the highest degree only when the areas are large enough; and this condition is the very one that makes them of value from the scientific

*The young moose is curious and unafraid. Isle Royale National Park. [Photo: William W. Dunmire]*

point of view. For the historian of the future, they must not be flooded out by river dams and "improvements" or by other encroachments that seem of vital importance at the moment but later may be recognized as wasted effort and money, even commercially. For the student of plant and animal life, their value depends upon their being large enough to constitute a home. Half a home may still be a home for humans; in the economy of the wilderness it is just about no home at all. Humans are able to juggle with their environment or quit it at will for another. Only to the faintest degree is this true of the animals and plants that, with the spectacular features, constitute the attraction of the national parks.

At this point I want to introduce a word not yet in common usage. The word is *ecology*. It ought not be a hard word to take, since we are already accustomed to the word *economy*, which comes from the same root. Economy, in its original meaning, was just the art of running a *home*—household management—and perhaps the political economists would do well to remember this fact before they go on star-gazing expeditions. Ecology, in our present context, is the study of animal and plant life in their *home*—in their environment—over long periods; and therefore their relationships with other forms of life which share that home. These make up a community. We used to study natural history differently; each form of life was observed for itself, or its kind, without much reference to its intricately poised habitat.

Some biologists dislike the expression "the balance of nature" because it seems to imply the desire to attain a certain status of relationship between living creatures and then to freeze that condition. It could not be done even if anyone wanted to do it; and the Park Service, in its wilderness management, does not attempt it. What is desired is that the flowers and shrubs and trees, the hoofed animals and the rodents and the insects shall have the opportunity to adapt themselves to changing natural conditions as best they may. The fittest will survive; or rather, since nobody yet knows who the fittest are or in just what sense they are fittest, at least the survivors will survive, without man's interference. And it is the maintenance of this freedom that will always be the root of the greatest pleasure to those who go to the national parks merely to see and to admire.

Letting nature take its course is, and always will be, an ideal. Once man comes into the picture, an approximation to the ideal is as near as you can get. Even if the national parks were closed to the public, which is an absurdity since they were set aside for the public, you would still not have ideally natural conditions. The people and activities on the fringe of the areas would make a difference. And park management sometimes implies a direct interference with nature. Once, when I was in Yellowstone, lightning set six forest fires raging in the dry woodlands of the park, and half the ranger force and half the naturalists were out fighting. Since it is nature's way to touch off a blaze with her celestial torch, why not let the forests burn? The answer is so obvious that the question is not worth debating. In geologic time—a few hundred million years—it would not make any difference whether Yellowstone was a smoking waste. As mankind may not be here that long, it is common sense to keep the trees if we can.

There will be interference with wildlife for the same reason, but it will be resorted to only when it is imperative, after careful study, and when a little evil is sure to prevent a greater one.

## [ 2 ]

MY MANY FRIENDS among the men of the natural sciences—the gentle sciences like zoology, botany, and geology—do not scold me when I commit an anthropomorphism. An anthropomorphism is the misdemeanor of ascribing to the lower forms of life feelings that only *Homo sapiens* is supposed to entertain. If you say that an Eastern white pine *prefers* a sandy soil, or that a yellow lady-slipper *likes* damp woods, that is anthropomorphism. Preferences and likes have nothing to do with the matter; they grow in those places because of their adaptation.

Sometimes, however, my specialist friends surprise me. Once, down in Big Bend National Park, I sat listening to a mockingbird for at least twenty minutes. Something about the bird's manner convinced me that he was deliberately trying to impress me with his virtuosity. He would stop, cock an eye at me, and then, as if to say: "Wait a minute, you haven't heard anything yet; listen to this one!" he would pour out his silver notes. Finally he jumped to another branch and said: "Don't go yet. This is the one I like best myself!" I never heard a tenor at the Metropolitan who more plainly seemed to be playing to the audience.

I told this to a park naturalist who happened to be down in the Bend. I wanted to hear that good old word *anthropomorphism*. Instead he smiled and said: "I don't know; you might be right. Anyway, I don't know *why* birds sing."

I'm not so sure I like the physicists, among the men of science. It took me thirty-five years to adjust my mind to the existence of a thing known as an atom. Just when I had it well in mind, these ferocious fellows took my atom apart, leaving me not only without my atom, but with an uncertainty about my mundane future. But among the men of unexplosive science I feel at ease. I respect their proficiency, and they envy me the ease of my amateur standing. I have an advantage: I can laugh when I make an erroneous conclusion. Nobody cares.

I will tell you a secret about the specialists. In their hearts they always carry the wistful memory of the rank amateur. They know too much. Of course, they get pleasure out of their work, just as anyone gets pleasure from work well done. But the anatomist often wishes he could look at an animal specimen without knowing where all its bones and muscles are; and I knew two accomplished biologists in Washington who regularly reverted to amateur type by going to a little island in the Potomac River, peeling off their clothes to their shorts, and becoming ignorant and happy aborigines. These fellows pay the price: the law of compensation is pitiless. They wish they could go into the national parks once in a while and say "Oh!" and "Ah!" and ask silly questions the way we visitors do.

There is a touching story about David Starr Jordan, the great ichthyologist and onetime chancellor of Stanford University. He had an astonishing memory for the names of the students and could greet them familiarly when he met them on the campus. One day, when walking with a faculty member, on meeting some undergraduates he failed to call them by name. His companion was surprised and asked Jordan if he had really forgotten. Dr. Jordan replied: "Yes, I have forgotten, deliberately. I mustn't let myself remember their names. I've found that every time I remember the names of two students, I forget the names of two fishes."

Poor man! As a specialist he was forced to choose between young men and fish, and professionally he had to choose the fish. It was the excise tax of specialism.

But the top men of the natural sciences have one great advantage over us amateurs: they have discovered humility. The smatterer prances around in his paddock of misguided opinion and hates to say "I don't know." The farther these specialists go in their knowledge, the more modest they are inclined to get. And what is more charming, as a bit of intellectual conduct, than the pronouncement made back in Darwin's time by his friend Thomas Huxley?

Men of science do not pledge themselves to creeds; they are bound by articles of no sort; there is not a single belief that it is not a bounden duty with them to hold with a light hand and to part with it, cheerfully, the moment it is

---

*A blinding flash reveals the flower stalk of the agave. Big Bend National Park. [Photo: M. Woodbridge Williams]*

really proved to be contrary to any fact, great or small. And if in course of time I see good reasons for such a proceeding, I shall have no hesitation in pointing out any change in my opinion, without the slightest blush for so doing.

Thus it is with the men who have in their care the management of the wildlife in the national parks. Ecological successions work themselves out over great periods when they are let alone. Park management implies arrangements for relatively short periods and depends upon conclusions that simply cannot be fully demonstrated. They may be verified someday. Meantime, though the principles are sound, the practice will be a common-sense best possible.

[ 3 ]

THE COMMUNITY OF LIFE in any given locality is governed by a number of factors, but chiefly by the climatic zone in which the living organisms are struggling to adapt themselves. This is the "struggle for existence" noted by Charles Darwin. But it is wrong to think of it in the sense of a fight among animals. As conditions change, those forms which cannot adjust themselves must migrate if they can; otherwise they go under. Thus there is a biological succession which ends in a balance that will be maintained, with minor fluctuations, over a long period.

If you live near a pond or lake, you have the whole picture under easy observation. Perhaps the pond was gouged out by glacial action; it may have been dammed behind a moraine; it may be the cut-off section of a meandering river which once made almost a circular detour at that point. In any event, the tendency of the pond will be to fill up and disappear. Soil will be washed in along the edges, dust will be blown in, and plants will press toward the water.

When the water in the pond was deep enough, fish could thrive in it. Along the edges frogs and salamanders lived. In the shallower water, pond lilies grew. When the soil conditions were right, cattails and rushes began to appear. Behind them in this march toward the center would come marsh grasses; and in time these would give way to meadow grass, and finally shrubs and trees might begin to take the place of the grasses. With no interference by man, in time not only will the pond disappear, but where the pond was there will be vegetation exactly like that of the surrounding country. If the pond was in a forest, trees will grow there; if in a prairie, it will become prairie. All the animal life that wholly depended upon the pond's remaining a pond will have gone, and other animals will have moved in from the surrounding country.

This illustration does not pretend to cover the whole ground, but it will suffice to suggest what is continually happening. It is a "balance of nature" in which the scales are constantly moving up and down but are heavily weighted on one side or the other only when humans introduce artificial conditions.

Does this seem remote from human affairs? On the contrary, it touches our lives at every point. In the first place, the history of mankind shows that we have been, in some respects, helpless pawns in this game. It was no accident that the first savages began to tame wild animals. They tended to exhaust their supplies of wild game and fish, and dependence on hunting and fishing became too precarious. But with the growing population even the pastured animals were not enough, and the more resourceful people supplemented them with agriculture; and these men in turn were bound to be succeeded by those who could create devices for better living, with a greater range of communication in which to think of even better tools and methods.

The farmer uses "ecological" principles all the time. If he is a graduate of an agricultural college, he uses them knowingly. But even if he has never been to college, his cut-and-try experience, in addition to what he learned from his forebears, leads him to manage his affairs in consonance with them. And he has observed one thing in particular: when you interfere with the delicate balance of nature, the result may not be exactly what was expected. Or, at least, there is a price tag attached to it, and the cost of interference may be too high.

For example, ranchmen do not like the badger because it makes big burrows on the prairie land that are a menace to horses and their riders. But if the superior rights of man are vindicated by a wholesale slaughter of the badger, it is then observed that the number of ground squirrels has greatly increased, and these animals destroy crops and compete for forage with the livestock. The badger had been keeping the number of squirrels in check.

It is not necessary to detail other similar instances. Every rural dweller can cite dozens of them that closely affect his daily life; and even the city dweller who is at all observant can add some from his own experience.

[ 4 ]

NOT SO LONG AGO predatory animals—the wolf, the cougar, the bobcat, the coyote, and such—were considered an unmitigated nuisance even in the national parks, to be either extirpated or held to a bare representation. It is easy enough to see why. A predator may be loosely described as any animal that kills game that man himself wishes to kill. The emphasis was on maintaining a good crop of game animals, and even if hunting was not permitted within the parks, the game could migrate outside. The psychology was against the cougar who pulled down a fawn, even though that was his natural right.

As late as 1918 a distinguished naturalist writing of the wild animals of Glacier National Park said in the caption on a photograph of two dead cougars: "Picture of two cougars that will kill no more game. The only good mountain lions are those gathered in by hunters and trappers. Some effective means should be taken for their destruction." Yet within ten years deer and elk were starving in great numbers, because for lack of predators they had become too numerous for their food supply.

Of the Canada lynx the naturalist wrote: "Their presence adds little of interest to the Park. They could certainly be well spared in the interest of game protection." Of bobcats: "It is fortunate that they do not reside in the Park in great numbers. They are not safe animals to have in a region where the increase of large game is to be encouraged." Of other animals he wrote: "It is to be hoped that the presence of the gray wolf may be eliminated before many years." "It would not be difficult for one or two reliable and skilful trappers to keep the number of coyotes in the Park to a practically harmless minimum." What a "practically harmless minimum" might be, the naturalist did not say. Possibly it could be represented as one castrated male specimen.

"A few martens would do no harm, but *the delicate balance of species is not easily maintained by hard and fast laws of man*." The italics are mine, because I do not know what can be made of this statement. Here we are confronted with the concept of a "balance of nature" with a deliberate plan to upset any such natural adaptation as much as possible. Apparently in 1918 it was held possible by good thinkers to maintain the "balance of nature" by putting the thumb on the scales.

One thing is certain: in the national parks there must be a striving, even if it falls below the ideal, to maintain a complete haven for all the kinds of life known to belong there and to exclude those which do not belong there, or else we should forget the whole thing and put the animals people like best on display at convenient hours, patching up the ecological holes as they occur, as the improvident farmer mends his roof. But in that case they are not wilderness parks—and Americans do seem to enjoy wilderness parks.

[ 5 ]

MUCH OF OUR EARLIER HISTORY lives today within the boundaries of the national parks. Some of our best literature has its roots there; and it is not too much to hope that some of the best to come may spring from these scenes.

But there may be a far greater consideration. Man is a trustee of animal life. "Some animals are antiques," as J. Arthur Thomson, an eminent biologist, Regius Professor of Natural History at Aberdeen, reminded us, "like the giant tortoises of the Galápagos islands," and there is an *impiety* in obliterating ancient milestones.

Some animals reveal secrets, as the New Zealand lizard disclosed the story of the pineal eye, and as the spectral tarsier the trend of brain evolution toward man, and there is an impiety in defacing our own history. Others, again, like the osprey, are simply masterpieces, and there is impiety in destroying the great works of art.

Many creatures, often humble ones, are wrapped up in the bundle of life with ourselves. Their threads enter our web, often in very subtle ways. And careless introduction may be as disastrous as ruthless elimination.

Professor Thomson would hardly be suspected of peddling treacle. So, for the final words on this subject, I am glad to lean heavily upon him. If I said the same thing, I might be charged with an amateur sentimentality.

. . . But there is an attitude even more humane than that of scientific conservation. It is the evolutionist attitude. These creatures are our kin. With Emerson, we may see the worm "mount through all the spires of form, striving to be man." We are solidary with the rest of creation, which once included our ancestors. These animals are distant collaterals of the human stock, our remote relatives.

This might explain why so many people feel a sense of ease and relief, and a contentment they cannot impart, when they are in the wilderness parks. They could be strayed members of the wild community who left home years ago and made good in the big city, now coming back to see what the old place is like.

It would be fine to have as little change as possible!

[ 15 ]

# [ II ]

# *The Meaning of the National Parks*

## [ 1 ]

I F A GREAT WATERFALL, in a setting of natural beauty, is in question, it is much easier to explain that you are going to harness it for waterpower than to explain why you are forgoing that industrial use in favor of preserving it as a thing of beauty and inspiration. If it is a mountain meadow, capable of fattening sheep, that is under discussion, the commercial use of it is obvious. Not so obvious is a proposal to let wild animals have that forage. You are inviting someone to listen to what sounds like a distant drum; and the first human impulse is always to "take the cash and let the credit go."

To understand the full scope of the purposes and activities of the National Park Service requires considerable thought. The good reasons that lie behind some of the park policies are not always instantly apparent. They need interpretation; then they become clear enough.

The word *conservation* may itself be misleading. The Park Service and the Forest Service are both dedicated to conservation, in the general sense of the term. Forest conservation was a direct answer to the atrocious greed and waste that had once characterized private exploitation of timberlands in the United States. The national forests, except for the reservation of primitive areas, are set aside for wise current use, which includes selective cutting, study of growth and plant disease, regulated grazing by domestic animals, recreational pleasures, and hunting of certain game. These multiple uses are admirable, and they have the advantage of being easily understood; everyone has some firsthand knowledge of conservation of this sort. It is primarily, though not wholly, economic. The language is that of dollars and cents.

---

*Where the sun filters through, the young redwoods get a chance. Muir Woods National Monument. [Photo: George Grant]*

Now, you need only set foot in a forest area in a park to come abruptly against a clear-cut concept of conservation. Suppose you are driving through Yellowstone. There are places along the road where you see a wild disorder of fallen trees—lodgepole pines, perhaps—so thickly intertwined that it would be hard to make your way through them. Your first thought might be, and perhaps has been: "This debris should be cleaned up. This is an awful mess." But you would be wrong. It is *not* a mess. It should *not* be cleaned up. Any such suggestion means that you have not grasped the meaning of the national parks.

When a tree falls in a national park, it will lie where it fell. Of course, if it falls across a road in such a way as to spell trouble or becomes a menace to visitors, it is removed. It is not necessary to indulge in absurdities in order to fulfill the general plan. The tree undisturbed will decay and become forest mold and supply the nourishment for future growths. It harbors sustenance for animal life. It is nature's way. Whether those trees in Yellowstone are an eyesore or something agreeable to look at depends on what you are looking for. If you like to be in a wilderness, the sprawled trees are in harmony with all else, and beautiful. If you prefer a botanical garden or a manicured private estate—both of them good as such—then there is no quarrel. But each concept must be itself.

In the national parks there is no harvesting of timber. There is at present no hunting of wild animals. There is no mining of minerals. There is, or should be, no grazing of domestic animals. There are no shows, or what are commonly known as "amusements." There is no attempt to make profits. The parks are operated on funds appropriated by Congress, and the receipts from visitors go into the miscellaneous receipts of the Federal Treasury, so that the balancing of income and outgo, common to business enterprises, does not exist.

This scheme of land use, so far removed from the average person's economic experience, may glancingly seem strange and remote. And so it is. It is a new theory in the world, of management of the public land for a superior kind of pleasure and profit; for the perpetuation of the country's natural and historic heritage, untarnished by invasion and depletion other than that of invincible time. No wonder, then, that it is a difficult story to tell. Worse, it is one of those efforts at public relations and interpretation where, by telling only a part, a false impression is almost surely created.

The meaning of the parks is known and revered by hundreds of thousands of those thoughtful Americans who spur to the defense of the integrity of the system whenever it is threatened by selfish and unimaginative private designs. The number grows every year. But so splendid is the master plan, so wide its implications, so novel in the history of civilized man, so successfully impractical—like one of the things that cannot happen, but do —that a half century is really a short time for full realization to be widespread. This book aims to be of help.

### [ 2 ]

IN TRYING to convey the ultimate meaning of the national parks, perhaps I should first explain what they are not.

The national parks are *not* merely places of spectacular scenic features and curiosities. This seems a strange statement in the face of the advertised lure of wonders like the geysers of Yellowstone, the incredible blue of Crater Lake, the unrivaled erosion picture of the Grand Canyon of the Colorado, and the falls of the Yosemite. But nearly all the national parks, and many of the wilderness monuments, would justify their existence even if they did not possess so great a scenic merit. The scenery is inspiring, unforgettable; but the meaning goes deeper.

The national parks are not merely places of physical recreation. If finer and more re-creative recreation can be found anywhere in the world, the spots have not yet been revealed. But the word *recreation* covers a host of activities, and many of them can be had in municipal, state, or other areas, in the national forests, and in similar locations. I cannot understand why anyone should travel long distances to the national parks for physical recreation as such, but if they represent a special dividend, deriving from a larger appreciation and a higher use, then visiting them becomes a most desirable thing.

The national parks are not merely attractions whereby travel facilities are stimulated; railroads, buslines, and garages made busy; hotel and other accommodations and eating places made profitable; and the hearts of local chambers of commerce made glad. I say this with no intent to reflect on any of these incidental corollaries of the system of national parks. To see and enjoy the parks, one must first get to them. There must be housing and food, or at least campgrounds and a commissary to provide for them. Inside the parks there must be concessions of many kinds; outside the gates there will be a growth of businesses that cater to visitors. Any concessioner and any owner of facilities at the gates and on the highway, who supplies the public with good wares and services at a reasonable price is doing his part toward the enjoyment of the parks. Such businesses are not only legitimate, they are absolutely necessary. But private enterprise being as eager as it is, it is sometimes necessary to issue a reminder that the national parks were not established to afford profit to anyone. That there are profits to be made is wholly adventitious.

Finally, the national parks are not in the least degree the special property of those who happen to live near them. They are national domain. Yellowstone and Yosemite belong as much to the citizens of Maine as to those of Wyoming and California; Isle Royale to the New Mexican as much as to the people of Michigan. The people of the states in which national parks happen to exist are rightly proud of them, and should normally be the first to rise against any spoliation of them; but pre-emption and settlement of land that happens to border on the present parks, or any that may be created later, imply no title to any rights in the preserved area beyond what belong to any American.

Now that I have mentioned a few things the national parks are not, it is cheerful to turn to what they are.

## [ 3 ]

WHEN YELLOWSTONE NATIONAL PARK WAS ESTABLISHED in 1872, it was as "a public park or pleasuring-ground for the benefit and enjoyment of the people." Whatever Congress meant by those words, it is fairly easy to surmise what was in the minds of men like Langford, Hedges, Hayden, and Folsom—pioneer preservationists. It occurred naturally to the exploration party that the wonders of the region were no ordinary creations of nature—that the volcanic phenomena especially were of world significance, and that consequently any private interests that could gain ownership would reap large profits. It is not likely that these men had in mind a "recreational area." The whole reach of the Rocky Mountains was a place where you could have even more physical exercise than you wanted, including running. The idea of a complete game sanctuary would not have occurred to them. They were not interested in the harboring of grizzlies, wolves, and other "varmints."

It seems clear to me that "public park or pleasuring-ground for the benefit and enjoyment of the people" meant simply the opposite of what these early conservationists feared might happen: "private park or pleasuring-ground for the financial benefit of a few." It is true that the discussions of the bill in Congress brought forth many various points of view. It was even said

*Martin Volcano. Katmai National Monument. [Photo: Lowell Sumner]*

that the forests of the region were what was most worth preserving. But I see no point in reading into the words meanings not necessarily there. The reason given was ample enough at the time.

In the the act of Congress that set up the National Park Service, some forty-five years afterward, the field of purpose was much widened. The words of the act should be well remembered, for the National Park System operates today under that organic law, which orders the conservation of "the scenery and the natural and historic objects and the wild life" in the national parks, and the provision "for the enjoyment of the same in such manner and by such means as will leave them unimpaired for the enjoyment of future generations."

This is what the national parks are for—not a part, but the whole of the stated purpose. This, with the implication of policies and methods to achieve the stated ends, is the full meaning of the national parks. It is no longer "conservation." It is *preservation.* Or it may be called conservation in another and newer sense: the conserving of resources that are not to be expressed in terms of money, but embrace the moral, spiritual, and educational welfare of the people and add to the joy of our living.

The Romans had their lares and penates—their protective and benevolent household and neighborhood gods. At the risk of being too precious about it, I should say that perhaps our American lares and penates can best be discovered in the national parks.

So we see that the national parks are really national museums. Their purpose is to *preserve,* in a condition as unaltered as is humanly possible, the wilderness that greeted the eyes of the first white men who challenged and conquered it. It is to ensure that the processes of nature can work, without artifice, upon all the living things, as well as the earth forms, within their boundaries. It is to keep intact in the wilderness areas all the historic and prehistoric evidences of occupation by our predecessors. And in doing these things, the extra reward of recreational value emerges as a matter of course.

John Muir wrote, in 1898: "Thousands of nerve-shaken, overcivilized people are beginning to find out that going to the mountains is going home; that wildness is a necessity; and that mountain parks and reservations are useful not only as fountains of timber and irrigating rivers, but as fountains of life." With every passing year, the truth of the statement is emphasized.

During one of the debates in the Senate, at a time when the fortunes of Yellowstone Park were balancing dangerously, George Vest of Missouri told his hearers that "there should be to a nation that will have a hundred millions or 150 millions of people, a park like this as a great breathing place for the national lungs." Vest, no doubt, was recalling what Lord Chatham once noted—that "the parks are the lungs of London." The Senators must have smiled sardonically when a future population of 150 million was predicted. California did not then number 600,000. Yet see where we are already!

The physical size of the preserved area in the National Park System has nothing to do with the designation. Acadia National Park, in Maine, contains only 28,000 acres. Katmai National Monument in Alaska contains more than 2,697,000 acres. Why is part of the Grand Canyon area known as a national park, while a contiguous area, dedicated to the same purposes and managed with the same ideals, is called Grand Canyon National Monument? The answer to this question is simple. A national park can be established only by act of Congress. A national monument can be set aside by Presidential proclamation. Since the lands so set aside must be already federally owned, it really means that the change is only one of new purpose and management: commercial use has been supplanted by cultural uses.

The total area of all the lands administered by the National Park Service has grown to more than 27 million acres. It sounds like a great deal, and as the Hollander or Belgian would see it, it is. But it is actually less than one per cent of the total land area of the country. By far the greater part of the territory preserved, invaluable as it is for the spiritual enjoyment of our future generations, contains little that could be used for commercial purposes, so far as anyone now knows. The great virgin forests, where they exist, are of course sources of lumber and pulp, and somebody is always eying them avidly across the fence; but the lands are not rich in minerals and are not generally suitable for agricultural production.

Sometimes, but not as often as formerly, you may hear the comment that in the management of the wilderness parks the Service has become overscrupulous, overscientific, in its zeal for preservation of all the natural features; that too much stress is placed on the good of future generations and too little on current fun and use. There is even a suggestion that the professors want to embalm the parks or preserve them in alcohol for laboratory analyses. Considering the fact that the number of visitors tends to outrun all the facilities for sheltering and feeding them, and that it is always increasing, this is amusing. But the idea of emphasizing constantly the highest uses of these places and stressing their cultural value is not new at all. It was

*Overleaf: Paradise Valley campground. Mount Rainier National Park.* [*Photo: Bob and Ira Spring*]

a long, long time ago that Senator Wilkinson Call of Florida, speaking of Yellowstone, said: "The Park and the natural curiosities there, and the game, were set aside to be preserved for future generations, for the *naturalist* and the *philosopher*. We cannot estimate the value of the preservation of the almost extinct animals of the western continent, to *science*."

An Indiana Congressman named Cobb, speaking also of Yellowstone, was even against having any large hotels in the park. "People can go there and camp out," he said. "They would delight in doing so; it is the very thing visitors would enjoy." He thought it unwise to improve the park in any way, lest its "natural charm should be destroyed."

Perhaps Cobb was a campfire man. At any rate, his comment was particularly interesting to me. I have personally tried every kind of accommodation afforded in the parks—the great hotels, cabins, and tents—and observing other visitors as well as consulting my own feelings and those of my children, I am inclined to think that the campers and hikers manage to get the most out of the experience. But there is something for every taste.

In 1885 a party of Congressmen made a junket to Yellowstone. They reported: "The Park should so far as possible be spared the vandalism of improvement. Its great and only charms are in the display of wonderful forces of nature, the ever-varying beauty of the rugged landscape and the sublimity of the scenery. *Art cannot embellish them*."

The Park Service would hesitate to use such dogmatic declarations today, for fear of being charged with too austere an attitude in its management; yet the *Congressional Records* of a long-gone period are replete with similar statements. To be sure, it must be admitted that there were plenty of legislators who, far from having such tender feelings, were for exploiting whatever natural resources there were, and having no parks at all.

World War II in particular put the parks to a great test. In a great conflict, where the very existence of a nation may be the stake, it is inevitable that the way of life and all natural resources will be subordinated to one end: the successful prosecution of the war. That the parks came through practically intact in their basic integrity, however much they may have deteriorated for lack of money and manpower, is really a heartening testimony that their meaning is understood and cherished. War is a time when the heads of the armed forces keep cool heads and the civilians run high temperatures. It is also a time when, under the color of necessity, profitable invasions into public lands may be made, which establish footholds for continued private profit.

Olympic National Park contains some magnificent virgin stands of Sitka spruce. There was a need for this kind of wood for the manufacture of certain types of aircraft, mostly in Britain. What a pleasant coincidence! How convenient! The Park Service admitted that if the sacrifice of the wonderful trees was necessary to win the war, of course they must be logged. But it asked: Is it necessary? Have all the facts been obtained? Have all the avenues been explored? It was not found necessary to destroy the trees. Other sources of the spruce were found. The Olympic trees still stand, to be seen and admired by generations to come.

A deposit of the vital mineral tungsten was known to exist in Yosemite National Park. Doubtfully, the guardians of the park gave way to the demands for a mining operation there. Was it necessary? The net result was that just fifty-five tons of ore were taken out, and the work ceased.

A demand was made that grazing of cattle should be permitted upon park lands in California as a wartime measure. Indeed, a bill was introduced in Congress that would have permitted grazing of livestock upon all national parks and monuments during the war and for "six months thereafter." It might have been a long six months. The Park Service again asked: Is it necessary? Would the amount of food produced justify the damage to the features of the parks? A similar demand had been made during World War I. It had then been found that if all the demands of California cattlemen had been met, the maximum amount of beef produced would have added less than one half of one per cent to that state's supply. So when the same challenge appeared in World War II, it was agreed that "each case would be considered on its merits." The merits were not found to be transcendent, nor the motives wholly guileless.

Throughout such dangerous periods the Park Service was sustained and fortified by public sentiment, expressed partly through the many conservation societies that are alert to the needs of the national parks and to the potential dangers. But behind those organizations perhaps there was further force. Today there is a more general understanding of the meaning of the parks by the whole people. It may be that the "public relations" of the Park Service have been, over the years, far better than it realizes.

# [ III ]

# *That Elderly Schoolma'am: Nature*

## [ 1 ]

IT HAPPENED at Crater Lake National Park, in Oregon.

Just inside the rim of the crater stands the Sinnott Memorial Observation Station, cunningly ensconced so as to give visitors the best possible view of the lake and its surroundings, which suggests the origin and subsequent geologic story of the region. And to make understanding as easy as possible, the memorial is equipped with exhibits, field glasses fixed upon key points, and a large relief map.

On this relief model, with a scale of one foot to six miles, are depicted the prominent features of the landscape—Wizard Island, the Phantom Ship, the deep glacial valleys, and other important landforms that are part of one of the finest of our preserved natural wonders.

One day in summer the park naturalist, just then inside the memorial, was introduced to a man of middle age whose appearance at once whispered: "Here is a man who is different." It was not his clothes, though he was fastidiously dressed. It was not his face, though the face lighted up with fine intelligence at the introduction. But there was something about the gloved hands, the walking stick hung by a curved handle on his arm, something about the erectness of his posture, the grip of his hand, that set the naturalist wondering. A pair of very dark glasses that the man wore forced the conclusion that the man was totally blind.

Blindness was not mentioned; it did not need to be. But when the visitor asked gently: "Will you describe Crater Lake for me?" the naturalist knew that he had a task before him. This man had come to *see* Crater Lake. Perhaps

---

*The "phantom ship," sailing in the bluest water. Crater Lake National Park.* [*Photo: Joseph Dixon*]

his friends back home had vainly tried to describe it to him; now he was here to see it for himself.

The poignancy of the situation gave a tug at the heart of the naturalist. How convey to a blind man the distances, the heights, the highlights and reflections, and the forests on the crater walls—to say nothing of that blue of the water which has no counterpart? For even we who have our normal sight fall far short of full appreciation of this picture—we see only in part and understand only in part.

The naturalist had an inspiration. Perhaps, after all, he could make his visitor see what he wished. He knew that with the blind the other senses usually become compensatingly acute. He knew, too, that the Danish poet Henrik Hertz was voicing no sentimental illusion when he wrote, in his *King René's Daughter*:

In the material eye, you think, sight lodges!
The eye is but an organ. Seeing streams
From the soul's inmost depths. The fine, perceptive nerve
Springs from the brain's mysterious workshop.

He knew that this is just a simple truth, demonstrated every day in his experience: for every park naturalist observes that of the millions of visitors with reasonably normal eyes, there are all grades of sight, from seeing astonishingly much to seeing not much at all.

"I think I can show you Crater Lake, sir," said the naturalist, "if you will take off your gloves and put your hands in mine."

The gloves came off.

As the naturalist told me: "I took his hands and moved them around the crater model in relief, trying to convey through his sensitive fingertips and through his quick, eager mental perception the general shape of the crater and the variations of its rim skyline. By putting his thumb tips together, with hands extended, the little fingers accomplished the scaled diameter of the lake.

"I asked him if he had an idea of distances. He said that he could relate distances to those he experienced in walking. It was obvious that when he knew the scale spanned by his hands, he could sense the great expanse covered by the crater and its water.

"Then we moved the fingertips up the modeled face of Llao Rock, the two inches on the model representing the sheer face of almost twenty-two hundred feet of drop. He understood that there were two thousand more feet of the crater below the surface of the water. His fingers told him the conical shape of Wizard Island. The tiny depression at the summit of the cone gave him not only that special feature, but the type of many other craters too. He could *see*, through his fingers, the lava flows that extend from the base of the island cone. And then we traced out the U-shaped glacial valleys and compared them with the V-shaped stream-cut valleys in other parts of the park. Then, with a model block, I could explain to him that perhaps—we do not certainly know—this whole mountain peak, where now the crater and lake exist, was another of the great volcanic cones that rise along this long mountain uplift—not unlike Mount Hood, Mount Rainier, and others—but that this one suffered a strange collapse. It was so evident that he saw it all.

"But then, as we finally must, we came to the great outstanding quality of Crater Lake—its color. How encompass that? How convey the importance of the reflection of the sky, the action of the wind, the refracted sunlight, and all those known and unknown factors which result in this blue to end all blues? And how suggest its crystal clearness?"

Suddenly the man said, with a little catch in his voice: "I do remember —I think—yes, I know I do remember something of the blue of the sky— when I was a little boy—it comes back to me now."

Well, the blue of Crater Lake is not that of the sky, of course. It is not the blue of anything—except Crater Lake. But *blue* he could recollect, and perhaps in that "mysterious workshop of the brain" he charted the color better than the naturalist could possibly know.

"He thanked me and was led away," said the naturalist. "He went away with a smile on his face. And I shall not forget that smile. He had not only seen Crater Lake. He had extended his power of seeing—which was an achievement beyond price."

[ 2 ]

WELL, we are all of us somewhat blind, even those who believe their eyesight is faultless. In viewing natural objects and scenes, the total amount we discern is nearly nothing compared with what there is to see. Even the trained naturalist, whose business it is to make the fullest use of his senses, will readily admit that he is living a life of constant discovery. And when it comes to understanding the why and the how of what we do manage to see, which is vital to a feeling of its reality, we all need what help we can get.

The National Park Service had scarcely come into existence before the need was felt for a program of interpretation. It can be called, and correctly enough, an educational program, but to call it so is to invite a misunderstanding of its true purposes. Very few persons visit the national parks to study. They do not want to take a course in botany or geology. They want to look at the spectacular displays, the flowers, the birds, the wild creatures; they want to idle, browse, inhale deeply, hike, go horseback riding, take pictures, mingle with folks doing all these things, and forget their jobs or their routine existence.

That is all they want. Rather, that is all they think, at first, they want. But almost all of them find that it is not enough. They see the eruption of the Old Faithful geyser at Yellowstone; or in early summer they watch the tremendous gush of water of Yosemite Falls; or at Mount Rainier they see the avalanche fawn lilies pursuing the retreating snowbanks. These things are no longer something just to look at; they are something to wonder about. The birds and the flowers ask for a little intimacy. Nature holds out a hand. There are few who do not grasp it. There are secrets. There are few who do not want to penetrate some of them.

Good books about nature, and descriptive of places and things few of us can hope to visit, are precious, and we should feel poor without them. But at best, if it remains a matter of reading or of pictures, the acquaintance is secondhand. In the national parks, whoever wishes it can greet these things in their homes; it is firsthand. Nature is the teacher; the classroom is outdoors; the textbooks are the very things you see. And what the interpreters of the National Park Service really do is to arrange an introduction to the schoolma'am and lead visitors to the place where class is in session.

The great fun is in seeing everything "in place." Mr. Squeers, master of Dotheboys Hall, in Dickens's *Nicholas Nickleby*, was a cruel, bullying, cowardly rascal; but I have always thought that his explanation of his teaching method, while selfish, had great merit. He said that he taught the boys to spell *winder* w-i-n-d-e-r, and then go and wash it! To see a natural wonder "in place," in its surroundings, with the bright sky overhead and the mountains over yonder and the good earth underfoot—that is something that cannot be had from books.

All over the Western country you are likely to come upon bits of petrified wood—not of the gorgeous hues of the logs in Petrified Forest National Park, but easily identifiable as fragments of trees that once grew in places perhaps now desert, but formerly inundated by some invading sea. One day I toiled several miles up a sweltering dry creekbed just to have a look at the stump of a petrified tree of which I had been told. It was not much to look at. What had been the trunk was hardly more than a foot above the ground, and even that part was badly broken. But the roots of the tree were there. It was *in place*. That was the very spot where it had actually sprouted, grown, and later been overwhelmed. I felt rewarded. It was a thrill. No vagrant chips could satisfy like that.

In some such way the interpretative work in the parks carries on its policy of introducing visitors to the schoolma'am, the original teacher. By means of guided trips, in the company of a naturalist ranger; by the creation of nature trails, so selected and labeled that visitors may go exploring by themselves; by campfire talks, observation stations, museums, and other devices, visitors to the parks may take as much as they please of the opportunities to observe and learn. In this school there are no marks, no examination papers.

To go on a walking trip with a naturalist guide, or better still to make a three-day trip on horses into the backcountry not accessible except in this manner, is to have an enthusiast for a companion. These naturalist rangers are all-around fellows. They must be resourceful, tactful, patient, and understanding. If the blind man who was shown the crater of ancient Mount Mazama had happened to be on the trail with a naturalist, he would have found that sight, however precious, is not the only desirable sense, for the guide would have made plants come to keen perception by their odors and tastes; trees by the feeling of their bark; birds by their call notes and songs. Even many rocks can be recognized, or guessed, by touch, especially when one knows the kind of rocks that might be expected to occur in a locality.

Many visitors to the parks prefer to wander and inspect alone or with a companion or two. For these the "self-guiding nature trails" have been created. These paths find their way along objects or to places that the average visitor is most likely to wish to see, and the labeled rocks or plants or trees answer the questions the stroller would ask a guide if one were present. They indicate, too, such features as the superb polish and striations made by the glaciers of Yosemite, or the former locations of the retreating Nisqually Glacier at Mount Rainier National Park. All the major parks have these self-guiding trails. They will never quite take the place of a guide. Animals and birds, for instance, cannot be labeled, and naturally it is impossible to identify any but salient features. But for those who dislike to join larger parties, the self-guiding nature trails are admirable.

Who can forget the campfire talks in the high country, when the blaze from burning logs sends flittering gleams and stalking shadows into the branches of the surrounding trees, and the night air has just the amount of invigorating nip to put edge on the appetite for this wilderness experience? The setting is perfect; and here is a ranger who talks from no schoolbook study, but from a rich experience with the forests, the birds and other animals, the upland streams and fish, and the threading canyons. They are informal, these naturalist talks, but they have meat in them. They are chat, but never chatter. They call for questions from the audience, and the questions seldom fail to come. Visitors who gather round some of these campfires in the larger places are not numbered in the hundreds, but in the thousands. The talks are given not only in the campgrounds, but in the hotels, lodges, and museums.

[ 3 ]

FINALLY, TO SUPPLY THE INFORMATION that will make a visit to the parks and monuments the fullest possible experience, there are museums and observation stations.

The observation stations are just what the name implies, but they may also have something of the quality of museums. The station at Yavapai Point, on the South Rim of Grand Canyon, one of the first to be erected, was the result of the most careful study. In a very real sense the whole of Grand Canyon is a museum, and so is every other park and monument. Likewise any point where you happen to be is an observation point. But for those who believe they have neither the time nor the inclination to explore the details of the canyon, the observation station at Yavapai seems to be almost ideal.

First you have a glimpse of the wide range of the great chasm and that first shock of its vastness. Then you may go out upon the parapet at Yavapai and look through the telescopes for closer views of points of special interest. Through one telescope the rushing, muddy Colorado can be seen; through another the top of Cedar Mountain; and still others show the differences in the rock structure of the walls. At hand are references to these very details. Here is a sample of the silty river water—you may see how enormous is the quantity of land material being poured toward the Gulf of California. Here is a "formation column." You have seen these formations through the glass; now they are at your fingertip, in the shape of actual slabs of rock from the canyon walls. Here is a "fossil column," which reveals the evidences of life still remaining in those stratified cliffs. And here are several large sandstone slabs showing the footprints of animals, reptiles, and land-water forms that ages ago crept along on the plastic surface which at that time—but only at that time—was the level of the land hereabouts. It will be more of an adventure, certainly, if visitors go down into the canyon and see similar footprints where these animals crawled along, on the very spot—the thing *in place*—but if not, then these sandstone fragments are the next best things.

Museums anywhere, everywhere, are a problem. The museums of the National Park Service, those of the wilderness areas and those of the historical classifications, are without doubt the finest of their kind in the world. Into them has gone superior intelligence, taste, painstaking accuracy, superb craftsmanship, and, indeed, art.

Much as they are used, and really popular as they are, the museums of Yellowstone, Yosemite, Rocky Mountain, Lassen, and the other wilderness parks and monuments should have even more visitors than they do. It is not expected that everyone who visits the parks will go to the museums. Not all who visit the parks even see the major features. I know of one man who went in by the Cody Gate of Yellowstone, spent two weeks in camp at Fishing Bridge, and saw nothing but that locality. He was well and happy all the time and said he had had a great vacation.

There is, however, such a thing as "public resistance" to museums of any kind, and it has been a source of discussion not only in this country, but in Europe as well. It has even been suggested that the name *museum* be changed to something else; and although this may sound absurd, you have to consider that the naturalists are aiming at telling the story of the parks to the greatest possible number, and the end to be achieved is the finest pleasure of the public and the noblest uses of the parks. The name is unimportant.

I understand well why some people dodge museums, especially if they have visited unfortunate samples. I have been through historical-society museums that left me dazed and dizzy. Each article displayed was valuable in its way, and possibly a treasure, but the whole setup was inchoate. It is really bewildering to find a letter from Napoleon to Josephine reposing beside a stuffed albino squirrel. If you add to those a fireman's hat just above a first edition of Fenimore Cooper, and both of these in front of a Revolutionary musket, the display becomes almost crushing.

You will not find museums of the National Park Service of that kind. They limit themselves to what is local, coherent, important, authentic. They tell a story, and having told *that* story, they stop. They tell the story in a way which requires no special knowledge to understand. Because they are the work of enthusiastic experts and artists, they stimulate the imagination without diffusion. They amplify many confidences that nature makes in low whispers.

[ 3 5 ]

# [ IV ]

# *Audit of the Treasure*

I HAVE OFTEN BEEN ASKED which are the best national parks. The answer is easy. There are no "best" parks. There are your favorite parks and mine and those of somebody else. These wilderness areas are highly individualized, and the choice is a matter of taste. If you were fortunate enough to be able to visit all of them, you would find yourself most in sympathy with one, or two, or three, perhaps without knowing exactly why.

It is true that some of the parks are more spectacular in their showing of natural elements than others. But each park is an expression in its own manner —a de luxe edition, so to speak—of some manifestation of natural forces. I believe that as visits to the areas increase, the proportion of hobbyists grows in relation to the number who come for the merely spectacular. Thousands return again and again to Mesa Verde, in Colorado, because they have developed an interest in the story of the prehistoric peoples; and for the same reason they visit as many as they can of the Southwestern monuments because they want to read other chapters of the same book.

For those who love to explore the roadless regions on horseback, there are parks that are pre-eminently trail parks. Wild-flower lovers find in the more northerly high mountain country a season-long profusion of bloom so impatient that the plants can scarcely wait until the snow recedes, but actually thrust up through the white cover. Bird lovers know which parks present the best opportunities for their favorite sport; and the hardy hikers and mountain climbers have a wide range of choice. The desert has its own following. So has the dense forest wilderness. Fishermen willing to forgo the easy armchair approach and pack back to the less-visited streams and lakes

---

*Rising from a carpet of goldenweed bloom. Joshua Tree National Monument.*
*[Photo: Josef Muench]*

will have their just reward. In a word, there is adventure for everybody. The person who wants to "see something different for a change" can draw upon an inexhaustible fund.

Our wars revealed in a touching way the love of the American people for their national parks and, in particular, the place that certain aspects of wilderness have in the hearts of those who know them. In the files of the Park Service are letters from young men and women of the armed forces, indicating the dreams they had during their exile on land and sea or at the scenes of the bloody conflict: "When I get my furlough, I want to come back and rest in Yosemite." "I'm counting the days, if I can have a little luck, before I get back to Mount Rainier. . . . I never realized before . . ."

Looking back at that period, with ordinary means of travel impeded or stopped altogether, it was a trying time in the parks—undermanned, short of funds, and faced with the threat of permanent invasion for destructive purposes—yet altogether perhaps it was a good thing. Perhaps short of such a crisis the basic mission and meaning of the national parks would not have been revealed so quickly. In that time of stress, the healing qualities and the power of mental and physical restoration inherent in the wilderness places were suddenly and sharply defined. Early in the spring of 1941 the Army recognized the tonic possibilities of wild areas for soldiers on leave; and as the war went on, the parks were used more and more for convalescence and for the recuperation of jaded, shocked, and frustrated young souls, as well as for maneuvers, tests of equipment, and training for Arctic and other climatic conditions. And the armed services authorities were, on the whole, most understanding in their attitude toward the use of the parks. Deterioration under war conditions was inevitable, but a minimum of irreparable damage was done.

Yes, there is something for every taste in the great cluster of park jewels. What will you have?

In dealing with the wilderness parks and monuments, I have decided, and not without a good deal of doubt and reflection, to group them according to what has seemed to me best presents the essential character of each one. The grouping is arbitrary, and is obviously open to some objections. But I feel that the advantages of treating the parks in this manner will outweigh any disadvantages. The categories are:

1. Primeval forests.
2. Volcanic scenes.
3. Earth-building and erosion.
4. Caves.

5. Desert and desert-mountain areas.
6. Work of the glaciers.
7. Tropics.

The defect of this grouping will appear at once. There are scarcely any areas that do not show a variety of the earth forces that have been at work over the ages. Earth-building and erosion are common to all. There is not one square foot of surface in our country where, unless hidden by human constructions, the evidences are not clear. The identical wasting powers that created the Grand Canyon are to be observed in your own back yard, if you have one. But some parks and monuments present the results of these forces on such a magnificent scale, with such overpowering color and stunning scenic drama, that it seems to me fair to exclaim: "Here is erosion!"

Mount Rainier is an extinct volcano; yet its twenty-six active glaciers form the largest single-peak glacier system in the United States, if we except Alaska. The Tetons of Wyoming owe their alpine form to the chiseling of mighty glaciers; yet they are the most dramatic, if not the greatest, example of uplift and block-faulting to be seen in the country. And though Big Bend National Park is primarily a desert picture, the Chisos Mountains, which are part of its lure, are volcanic in origin. So we could go on taking exceptions to an impertinent grouping like this.

But it seemed to me that any method was better than the usual hodge-podge of describing one park after another, leaving each to stand apart from all the rest, with no emphasis on the most arresting and stimulating fact of all: that they are all parts of the same drama; that each is a scene within the whole, and vital to appreciation and enjoyment of the whole.

So, to begin the most fascinating quest that I can imagine for any human —a journey into unity as shown in the national parks—let us go first into the primeval forests.

# PART

# TWO

# [ I ]

# *Green Sanctuaries*

IN THE WOODS, TOO, *a man casts off his years, as the snake his slough,
and at what period soever of life, is always a child. In the woods is
perpetual youth. Within these plantations of God, a decorum and
sanctity reign, a perennial festival is dressed, and the guest sees
not how he should tire of them in a thousand years. In the woods we
return to reason and faith.*

—RALPH WALDO EMERSON

## 1. APPALACHIAN ADVENTURE

IN WRITING OF THE NATIONAL PARKS and monuments, especially of those
where the wilderness aspect is most pronounced, it is easy to glide over
the human impress that gives them a part of their significance as pages in the
Book of America. It is true that man has had nothing to do with the creation
of the scenic beauty and the natural marvels we see within these areas. Indeed it is sadly true that man has done much in the past, before they became
wards of the government, to deface and alter the primitive scene. But when
all is said, our people have moved restlessly through and within and around
these places; they have fought and bled, pioneered and hungered, created
homes, raised children, laughed and wept, and lived and died—and all this
cannot well be forgotten.

We are now approaching two of the Eastern national parks where the
human story is the very woof of the fabric that delights both the eye and
the imagination. In both the Great Smokies and Shenandoah, though visitors

---

*The forested mountains seem to go on and on into infinity. Great Smoky Mountains
National Park.* [*Photo: Great Smoky Mountains Natural History Association*]

[ 4 3 ]

may easily wander into forested recesses that seem to have been untrodden, there is always the feeling that these ancient hills are still peopled with sinewy backwoodsmen, roving with squirrel guns, cultivating a tiny patch in the wilderness, and living off the land like an army on conquered ground. It is a feeling justified by the facts, for here we have the Park Service dedicated to a dual purpose of preservation: to keep the natural scene unimpaired and to keep the human story accessible and vivid.

First as to the Appalachians themselves. If there were ever historic mountains, considered either as a range or as a system, they are these. Here are some of the oldest uplands on earth. The crushed and folded formations of their oldest rocks are part of a mountain chain that once extended from Nova Scotia down into Alabama and possibly swung far southwestward of that apparent terminus. The intensity of the forces which thrust out of the Southeast and carried older rocks over younger rocks, a phenomenon similar to that which the tourist sees in Glacier National Park, is beyond human understanding. How high were the peaks of those earlier Appalachians? Impossible to know; but there is evidence that they were like the modern Alps or—not to go so far away—the Tetons of Wyoming. They could have been much higher than that, even; we do not know how rapidly they were torn down while they were still rising.

But those Appalachians passed away millions and millions of years ago; they were planed down almost to sea level; and the mountains that we now so much admire were warped up gently, with long periods of quietude, at a much more recent period. They are the highest elevations of the eastern part of the continent. From the northern end of the Appalachian Trail to the southern end, the foot traveler will find plenty of ruggedness in these deep-cut flanks, where thousands of mountain torrents pour sparkling water toward the rivers and the sea. But seen from the air, or from any distant vantage point, the Appalachians are innocently sleek, almost velvety. In the Southern mountains particularly, the climate is so bland and the rainfall so ample that even when the ancient ledges come to the surface, or where the bold face of a precipice occurs, the vegetation so clothes the whole scene that the eye sees only forests after forests, billowing away and away to the horizon.

## 2. Great Smoky Mountains National Park
### [North Carolina–Tennessee]

It is really amazing that when the twentieth century opened, part of the southern Appalachians where the mountains form a high divide between

North Carolina and Tennessee was almost an unknown land. It just does not seem possible, but so it was. Populous cities had come into being not far away. The streams that flowed through the foothills were already furnishing power for busy factories. Speaking impulsively, most people along the eastern seaboard would have told inquiring strangers that everything on their side of the Mississippi was mapped and known. But the Great Smokies were still sleeping peacefully and sending up from the lush vegetation a bluish perpetual haze, a filmy veil as mysterious as the mountains themselves. Their name was old and inevitable. The first men who ever saw them could not fail to use those words—Great Smokies.

A small group of geologists and botanists had packed their way into the dense forests. It was known that few spots in the world had a richer variety of plantlife than this. The highest peaks (sixteen within the park rise more than six thousand feet) were covered with a magnificent primeval cloak of spruce and fir. On the mountainsides was an unbroken cover of deciduous trees, permitted by a genial climate and ample moisture to attain unusual size. Growths that farther north in the Appalachians are only shrubs here become trees. The serviceberry or shadberry of my own home in the northern Appalachians is never more than a big shrub or a small tree, a thrice-welcome harbinger of spring with its lacy white early bloom. Here it reaches a massive size that makes it almost unrecognizable.

In all Europe there are not as many species of native trees as are to be seen in the Great Smokies—130 native tree species and more than 1,300 varieties. And what great flowering plants some of them are! First in the spring, the dogwood; then in May, the mountain laurel; in mid-June, the flame azalea and the rose-purple rhododendron, with the magnificent blooms of the white rhododendron to come a few weeks later. Most of the gorgeous blooming is in the forest, of course, for the forest is nearly everywhere. It is said that at least 40 per cent of the one-half million acres within the park are in the original forested condition. And this, mind you, in the "settled" East. No wonder there was a movement to preserve this wild beauty so that it could be enjoyed by all future generations!

The establishment of the park was authorized by Congress in 1926, and North Carolina and Tennessee began to acquire lands with state funds and with donations, to be matched dollar for dollar by John D. Rockefeller, Jr., through the Laura Spelman Rockefeller Memorial, in honor of his mother. There were no federally owned lands to form a nucleus in the undertaking. All was privately owned and had to be acquired the slow and hard way. But finally 461,000 acres were amassed, and the park was formally dedicated in 1940.

There are larger parks. For those who love the forest land there is none so gifted with feminine softness of outline. You feel like stroking those velvet vistas shown in a photograph taken from one of the mountain crests. And when autumn comes and the broad-leaved trees assume their brighter finery, then is the time that millions of pilgrims come to see the painting of the foliage, as millions have done before.

One of the strangest natural features in the Smokies is the presence of the unexplained "balds," mountaintops that are not forested but have a grassy and heath growth. Naturally, the views to be obtained from these spots are unobstructed and panoramic. Elevation seems to have nothing to do with the presence of the balds, for those called Andrews, Silers, and Parsons are not much higher than many of the wooded peaks.

A hike along the seventy-one-mile stretch of the Appalachian Trail, with eight trailside shelters spaced for easy one-day walks, is the high point of Appalachian adventure, but for less active visitors there are plenty of short trips leading to ingratiating corners of peacefulness and charm.

To visit this lovely national park without learning and observing something of the people who have lived in these mountains since the earliest days of America would be to lose much of the flavor of the holiday. Aside from the Cherokees, who camped and trailed in this forest fastness long before the white man came, the people of the mountains constitute a part of the oldest white immigrant stock that settled the English-speaking New World. That the Indians are still here—several thousand of them on the Qualla Reservation, adjoining the park—is an accident. They have survived from the refugees who took sanctuary in the deep woods when in 1838 their fellows were herded by the soldiers to be driven westward from their ancestral home.

The chief interest, however, is in the pioneer white stock that went into the mountains in colonial days and remained there, in remote freedom, while the rest of the eastern seaboard was achieving what is called progress. English, Scotch-Irish, and Irish most of them were, and their dialect has been sometimes described as "Elizabethan English." Probably that is too fancy a claim; but certainly the mountain folk use many words and phrases of the time of Elizabeth the Virgin that have elsewhere ceased to be current. More important, they retain the love of the spoken word, not more for bare utility than for the satisfying expression of their simple and strong emotions. They are natural singers and balladists, and I would almost say a bardic people.

*Always clouds, always that dim mystical look. Great Smoky Mountains National Park. [Photo: Josef Muench]*

*When the tension in Cade's Cove becomes too great, Uncle Dave Meyer whittles.*
*Great Smoky Mountains National Park. [Photo: Allan Rinehart]*

Love and death, the fine-pretty world around them, the seasons, the birds and beasts, their sorrows and joys are expressed with a clarity like that of an etching. I give you a sample recorded by Percy MacKaye, the distinguished poet, who has known these people well:

"Yea, Sir, hit war the first cold spell that come, right when the grapes is about all gone and the rest of the berry tribe, between the turnin' of the weeds under and the dyin' of food; and thar comes in a gang of jay-birds, and they fills the mind of the bird poetry."

Could there be a more adequate or poetic thumbnail picture than that, of the end of summer and the coming of the frost?

Now, for comparison, listen to Mistress Quickly, the hostess of Eastcheap, describing the death of Sir John Falstaff in Shakespeare's *Henry V*:

". . . A' made a finer end and went away an it had been any christom child; a' parted even just between twelve and one, even at the turning o' the tide: for after I saw him fumble with the sheets and play with flowers and smile upon his fingers' ends, I knew there was but one way; for his nose was as sharp as a pen, and a' babbled of green fields."

The dialect is not quite the same, truly; but in respect of the neat turn of phrase and the singing quality, Mistress Quickly, as I feel it, is still living in the Appalachians. I say still living, but her time will be short now. The mountaineers of today are being planed down like their mountain peaks; the impact of education, refinement, and gadgets is the eroding force. In a few years they will be ashamed to speak poetry and sing homespun songs. Better see something of them now, when it is not wholly too late! They are as hospitable and kindly to strangers as the Bedouin Arabs are alleged to be. There is no people, and there is no place, in the midst of which the life of a well-disposed person is safer.

When these people came from their cramped life in Europe and tasted the liberty of the hills, where there was no exciseman to tax their windows and no recruiting sergeant to press the King's shilling into their helpless palms, they must have thought themselves transported to the very Eden of their deeply religious imagination. Perhaps that is why they were content to remain isolated, to live a hard existence scratching a patch of hillside, to weave, to forge, to swing an adz—to do everything for themselves the laborious way —but in freedom. True, they were free to starve; but they were also free to sing, to dance, to pray, to hunt, to fish, to drowse and dream on the sunny side of the cabin—to let the world go hang.

Now, it happens, too, that they brought from the cold north of Europe a taste for certain liquids that may be distilled from grain. In the New World they discovered that the Indian corn, or maize, a plant easily raised on these hillsides, would produce a mash, and afterward a distillation, which gives a divine jolt when it passes the esophagus, going in either direction. Thus "co'n whiskey" became one of the notable products of the region. I am informed that it still is. The government thinks that such industries should be supervised and pay a tax. The mountain people do not agree. There has long been friction on this point, which after all concerns not personal but political morals, if you are so adept as to separate these. You will not be taken for a "revenooer," a revenue officer, if you keep away from any little column of smoke you should see rising from a neck of woods outside the park.

These Southern mountaineers were responsible for the defeat of the British forces under Colonel Ferguson at Kings Mountain in 1780. Equipping themselves, at their own expense, and wonderfully handy with a musket, they wasp-swarmed down from their corn patches and helped make possible the final humiliation of Cornwallis at Yorktown. They could shoot. Indeed they could. In the course of years they developed such skill that when Great Smoky Mountains National Park was established, the animals native to the region were pretty well gone. Since then, under protection, the bears and deer and smaller game-creatures have come back in good numbers. Poaching by these rugged individualists is a problem. The hill folk are not fundamentally lawless, but use and wont over the centuries are hard things to hurdle in a few years. Tact and firmness are called for on the part of the Park Service personnel, and that they show both is evidenced by the slow, sure progress in carrying the gospel of preservation to the park's border dwellers.

No, the mountain folk are not really lawless. On the contrary, when their sentiments are touched and their confidence is gained, there are no gentler people. I recall, one day at the park headquarters, pointing to a certain shrub that grew at the base of the main building, and asking the naturalist for the name of it. He gave me first its botanical name. Then he smiled and added: "But the natives call it 'hearts-a-bustin'.' That is short for 'hearts-a-bustin'-with-love.' "

*Hearts-a-bustin'! Hearts-a-bustin'-with-love!* In that name you see the sentimental side of the mountaineer. More than that, it seems to carry the fragrant essence of the wild, flowered park itself.

## 3. SHENANDOAH NATIONAL PARK
### [*Virginia*]

LIKE ITS SISTER APPALACHIAN PARK farther to the south, Shenandoah National Park was created from privately owned lands. These were bought by the state of Virginia, and contributions were received from public-spirited people everywhere in the nation. The pennies, nickels, and dimes of the schoolchildren of the Old Dominion were the mites that went to swell the funds for acquisition.

Nor were these conservation-minded donors the only ones who gave. To rid the proposed park of private owners, so that it could be properly administered according to the policies of the National Park Service, it was necessary to buy the quitclaims of six or seven hundred mountain families and relocate these people outside the boundaries. Many did not want to leave. After all, one's home is a home though it may be made of chinked logs and have pullets and pigs coursing at will through the kitchen. They came to old Hezekiah

Lam, aged eighty-three, and told him that the government wanted his land. Man and boy, Hezekiah had been in these mountains so long that he could tell you from just smelling a tumbler of new-made corn likker just what "holler" it was made in, the name of the man who made it, and the approximate date when it ran through the still.

"I ain't so crazy about leavin' these hills," said Hezekiah, rubbing his rheumatic leg, "but I never believed in bein' agin' the government. I signed the papers they asked me. No; I didn't read 'em. I reckon I could've if I hadn't lost my specs. I allus said these hills would be the heart of the world."

Bless your old heart, Hezekiah; you have gone from us, maybe to a place where a man can use Indian corn for what you thought its noblest purpose, without putting an excise stamp on it. Where Hezekiah farmed his little hillside patch, the trees are coming in now. You can still discern, from one of the outlooks on the Skyline Drive, the furrows, grassed over, where the corn was hoed. In these hills the forest moves in quickly when it has a chance. Except, of course, on those queer "balds." Big Meadows is one of them.

*The farmer shocks his corn at the forest edge. Shenandoah National Park. [Photo: M. Woodbridge Williams]*

I was wandering over Big Meadows not long ago, meditating on why trees never come up on such places. I soon gave up this mad pursuit of knowledge and went into the excellent hotel, and out on the stone rampart just in time to see a young bald eagle—an infrequent visitor—hovering overhead. It was coming autumn. The proprietor told me that the telephone was ringing frequently, people asking whether the leaves had begun to turn. He said he was booked solidly through October by people who wanted to come and see that miracle of coloring which comes to the trees of Shenandoah.

The three hundred square miles of mountain and ridge that Shenandoah National Park comprises extend from Front Royal at the north to near the entrance to the Blue Ridge Parkway on the south, at Rockfish Gap, about seventy-five miles. At no point is the park very wide, and since the idea was to include not only the spine of the range but also the infinite number of ridges that shoot out from it easterly and westerly, the surveying of the boundary must have made the engineers mildly insane. The general effect is that of tracing the skeleton of a fish—preferably a shad, that osseous labyrinth which has mortified many a diner who wished to exhibit a delicate performance at table.

Shenandoah is notably different in aspect from the Great Smokies, but the adjacent mountain people are essentially the same. Here are no great expanses of virgin forests. There are a few pockets of primeval hemlock and some very ancient oaks that have escaped the ax, but mainly it is modern growth. Oak, especially the fine chestnut oak, predominates, but there are gums and locusts, hickories and walnuts, maples and—I was going to say chestnuts. Alas, the wonderful American chestnut, once one of the most valuable and cheerful Appalachian trees, has never recovered from that fatal blight which came upon it. Not only children and squirrels in our Eastern states but especially the mountaineers who lived in the Blue Ridge country looked forward to the nutting as they longed for Christmas. All that remain of the chestnuts in Shenandoah are the ghostly trunks that rear themselves among the oaks, resisting the weathering of time, and a few hopeful sprouts that still come from the old roots, but do not long survive.

For the motorist, there is a constant succession of well-placed overlooks, now to the west, down to the foot of the ridges, into and across the Shenandoah Valley to the dimmer heights of the Alleghenies; then to the eastward, down into other hollows and ridge ends, with cultivated fields beyond. At times the road travels along on a spine so narrow that you can look off to both east and west. It is one of the most restful scenes in our country.

I know a man who tells me he greatly prefers Shenandoah to the Smokies.

"Down there," he said, "I feel shut in; I can't see anything but woods. I was born in the dense woods, up in New Brunswick, where the primeval trees were always knocking at your front door, and, for me, give me a place like that Skyline Drive where I can look off and see human habitations and feel the nearness of humankind."

Well, that is a point of view. Other folks feel that Shenandoah entirely lacks the wilderness quality they seek. It goes to prove one thing, at least: that there is something for everyone in our national parks. And not only is there something for everyone: there is even something for everyone's changing mood. The variety is unbounded.

One evening I sat in a club in Washington, talking with a group of men about Shenandoah National Park. I had just returned from a trip down there, and I was full of what I had seen. Some of the group knew the park well; some had never been there. One man sat a little aloof, with a quizzical smile, and I began to suspect he knew much more about Shenandoah National Park than any of the rest of us. I was right; he did. I think he would prefer to remain anonymous, so I will call him Smith. No; come to think of it, I can't call him Smith, because his name *is* Smith. I shall call him Jones.

Finally, when it came his turn, Jones said: "Well, I have some pleasant recollections of Shenandoah. I put in one of the best holidays of my life down there. You see, I had done the Skyline Drive many times, but I was still curious about the two hundred miles of trail that the government folders talked about. And I thought I'd better learn something about the folks that lived around there.

"I went down to a little place called Arcadia and got myself a horse. A good little Virginia mare she proved to be, with plenty of spirit and well gaited. She shied at everything from leaves and bits of paper to the mention of General Sherman, but we got along very well. Her name was Tuckie.

"My saddlebags carried what I needed for overnight stops, but I figured on eating where I could find meals. I crossed the Lee Highway one fine October afternoon and got into the park by going southward around the foot of Pine Mountain on a dirt road at the mouth of Kettle Canyon. This is the place persons going to the Skyland resort before the days of the drive used to start for the four-mile climb up the steep mountain on horseback or in carriages to an elevation of thirty-six hundred feet. George Freeman Pollock, the genial story-telling showman and host, founded Skyland, and his years of efforts to save the park from spoliation by fire and lumbering interests made the park possible. He was one of the ardent pioneers in the movement to make a national park. On horseback he used to rout out his guests with a bugle in the morning, and in the evening he would more than likely put on a rattlesnake show. I stopped off at Skyland the first night.

"Next day I crossed the Skyline Drive and the top of the Blue Ridge and went down the White Oak Canyon Trail. The canyon got its name from the magnificent stand of large white oak and the six falls, each more than fifty feet in height. The stream drops about fifteen hundred feet in falls. I also took the Limberlost Trail, which led me to the Limberlost Swamp area, in which are growing grand red spruce, Canada yew, and enormous hemlocks. Descending on down the mountain trail, you come into a vast meadow, and Old Rag Mountain comes towering into view.

"Down the Robertson River there were a lot of mountain cabins. I rode into one yard where they were having an old-fashioned apple-butter bilin'. A young couple were stirring the slow-boiling, chopped apples in a forty-gallon kettle. By an old tradition, this is a duty performed only by young courting boys and girls. A day's bilin' produces about thirty or thirty-five gallons of apple butter.

"When I got as far as Syria, it had become misty and cold, so I turned in for the night. They were picking apples in the orchards thereabouts, on hillsides so steep that you needed a ladder on one side and you had to reach down to pick them on the other. Next morning I crossed the Robertson River and came to the Rapidan road at about the place, I think, where Stonewall Jackson camped on his way to Fredericksburg. All this region is historic ground. The Confederate troops made valuable use of their familiarity with these mountain trails and passes.

"It began to get steep as I climbed up a mountain. I've forgotten the mountain's name, but I remember there was one spot where I could almost look down the stone chimney of a cabin. An old wagon trail followed the Rapidan, through a forest of mostly hemlock, and then I got directions at Graves' Mill for a section called Fletcher's Store, by way of a pass between Buzzard's Rock and Kirtley Mountain. I was up at least two thousand feet there. Coming down a steep road on this jaunt, I stopped at a house and asked a woman who was on the porch if I was on the right road. She told me I was. I hadn't gone far before I heard a horn—an automobile horn—blowing. It kept on blowing long after I was out of sight. I'm sure now, looking back on it, that the horn was to warn somebody down in the woods tending a co'n-likker still that there was a stranger in the vicinity.

"Well, that gives you a sketchy idea of the mountain country I traveled for seventy-five miles before I got back to Arcadia. I could have spent weeks on the trip if I had accepted the invitations of these hospitable mountain

*From Skyline Drive the visitor looks down. From the Great Valley the mountains loom above him. Shenandoah National Park. [Photo: M. Woodbridge Williams]*

people, wherever I stopped to ask the way, to spend the night with them and share their food, whatever it happened to be. Oftentimes when I was coming down a mountain trail, I would be seen by folks in the hollow below, and they would relay my approach, from one cabin to another, by a sort of yodeling call. One of the great views I had was from a place called Devil's Tanyard. From there I could look down into three or four 'hollers' where ridges branched off the mountain like wagon spokes."

Mr. Smith—I mean Jones—hoisted himself out of his chair and concluded: "Well, I have to go now. Hope I haven't bored you. Really, nothing exciting happened. It was just the mildest kind of adventure, in a beautiful and interesting wild country, different from anything we commonly see. But try it sometime. I think you'll like it even better than driving along on the top and looking down."

Mr. Jones went out. There was a silence. Then somebody said:

"He really knows something about those mountains. He *saw* them. We just *looked* at them."

## 4. ISLE ROYALE NATIONAL PARK
### [*Michigan*]

THE TERM WILDERNESS PARK is perforce an elastic one. Almost all the national parks are essentially primitive areas, where nature is left to go its own way; and it is true that even in places of heavy visitation like Yosemite and Yellowstone you have only to step a little aside from the spots where people congregate and the paved access roads to find yourself in a wilderness where you may cruise and meditate in a peace unbroken save for the company of the lowly creatures who enjoy it all tax-free. Still, with the necessary developments which make possible a public enjoyment, every park must be something short of a wilderness. It is obvious: it is unavoidable.

Isle Royale National Park, a rock fortress in Lake Superior, clothed with dense woods and dotted with many lakes, is perhaps the nearest thing, except for the Alaskan areas, to a true wilderness. You can reach Isle Royale only by boat, or by chartering a seaplane. When you get there, you find no roads, no wheeled vehicles, and only limited lodge facilities, concerning which it is well to inquire and make reservations in advance. There is nothing to prevent your taking your dinner jacket with you, but it will suffer the indignity of appearing alongside red sweaters and mackinaws, worn, you may find, by bank presidents, university dons, and others who know that even in summer the nights in the park get cool and the waters of Superior breathe frostily. Hiking clothes and boots are *de rigueur*.

Even the trails of Isle Royale lack the sophisticated touch. They are entirely practicable for good hikers—they are marked with metal tags, except where they cross open spaces, when stones or posts show the way. Explicit directions should be obtained from park headquarters before starting on a hiking trip. Several memorable excursions can be made by going by boat one way and returning afoot, and this is probably the ideal way to see the main island, which combines a land-and-water adventure.

The main island, for which the park is named, is about forty-five miles long and nine miles across at its widest point. The park really comprises an archipelago, for there are two hundred small islands in the group, not count-

*Quiet haven at the edge of wilderness. Isle Royale National Park.* [*Photo: Abbie Rowe*]

ing a multitude of mere rock projections from the lake. The northeastern end of Isle Royale consists of five chains of islands and peninsulas, which together form four long harbors of such deep water that they resemble fiords. On Mott Island, facing the longest of these fiords, Rock Harbor, the park headquarters, is located. The park is closer to Canada than to the nearest point in Upper Michigan, and is only one or two miles from the international boundary.

From the earliest pioneering time to the day in 1940 when the Secretary of the Interior accepted from Michigan the deed to all the hitherto privately owned land and thus created Isle Royale National Park with the addition of public domain that had been set aside in 1923, this ancient stronghold, flanked by its rock bastions and deep moat, has had a highly varied career. Long before summer cottages ever dreamed of going there, the exploiters had swarmed over it, testing its resources—first the fur traders, then the miners, lumbermen, and fishermen. At one time there were six fur-trading posts—at least one belonging to the Hudson's Bay Company, others of the American Fur Company. Intensive trapping practically exterminated the beaver and other fur-bearing animals, but under protection, now that it is a national park, they are restored to their enjoyment of the Animal Bill of Rights.

For a number of years Isle Royale has been the perfect laboratory for the study of the predator-prey relationship—in this case the moose and the wolf. Early in the twentieth century, it is known, the moose came over from the mainland before there were any timber wolves there. They found ample browse and flourished. By the mid-thirties there were as many as three thousand of the great animals. But, with no predator to keep down the exploding population the inevitable happened. They ate themselves out of house and home. A report of the Michigan Biological Survey of 1905, giving a "complete list" of mammals on the island, did not mention the moose, although it included the woodland caribou, now no longer seen.

About the time of a second starvation cycle, timber wolves crossed the fifteen-mile stretch of ice from Canada, and a new and brighter period began for the *prey*. It sounds odd to the nonscientist, but it is simply the fact. The predator, under natural conditions, corrects imbalance. Conditions such as exist in Isle Royale are, it has proved, nearly perfect, not only for the correction, but for the study of it by the biologist. L. David Mech, who was Dr. Durward L. Allen's first student when the Purdue University studies began, reports that "at this time the condition of the moose herd is health. A good measure of its health is its productivity. Aerial and ground surveys have shown that the Isle Royale moose are among the most productive in the country. No other herd bears such a high proportion of twin calves." And of course with the volunteer effort of the wolf, the browse supply is likewise in good shape. Their favorite haunts are Washington Creek, McCargo Cove, and Lake Eva. The sight of a moose on the edge of a pond at twilight, his awkward shape looming out of the still water, and his head completely hidden as he browses on succulent underwater plants, is a thrilling one. A nearer acquaintance is not suggested.

All over the main island are vestiges of the copper mining that began with aborigines who hollowed out the first open pits where they observed the metal outcropping from the rock. With only crude stone instruments, which they had brought from the mainland, they had enough rude inventiveness to break up the tough country rock with fire and water, after which they could batter out the big masses of almost pure copper for use in creating utensils. Isle Royale inherited a share of native copper, which is not common, along with the Keweenaw Peninsula of Michigan, where it was mined until the supply diminished below the profit point.

*Mama Moose and children navigating Rock Harbor. Isle Royale National Park.*
*[Photo: William W. Dunmire]*

The white man later took out enormous chunks of the metal from Isle Royale's ancient rocks. One of these masses was exhibited at the Centennial Exposition in Philadelphia in 1876. It weighed 5,720 pounds. There were periods when mining was active, but it was mainly a story of blasted hopes and hardship, like most of the mining ventures in our southwestern desert. Neither did it have any beneficent effect upon the landscape of the island, for much of the primeval forest was burned deliberately in order to expose the hoped-for metal, which might lie beneath the forest duff.

Isle Royale is one of those areas where every inch of soil is precious. The predominant rocks are extremely ancient lava flows, which may be as much as a billion years old. Whatever accumulation of soil there may have been in the hundreds of millions of years that passed before the great ice sheet moved down and overrode the island, the final retreat of the great glacier must have left it bare. And thereupon began a long series of changes in the water level of what is now Lake Superior. These changes are recorded in benches cut out by waves, and by beach lines, which show that the island was at times submerged completely, merely a reef of greenstone rock in the great body of water. As the "modern" Lake Superior found new outlets for its water, Isle Royale gradually rose higher and higher from the lake level, until it achieved its present condition. But it was all the work of lazy Time, and the years between each stage of emergence and the next, indicated by those beach lines, is difficult to grasp.

Because of that broom wielded by the ice sheet, because of the low mean annual temperature of Isle Royale and the added fact that the rainfall and snowfall are very moderate, the growth of plants on the island is not rapid, and recovery from fires is slow. Yet for the scientist, and especially the ecologist, it is one of the most interesting of all the national parks. So many questions can be raised concerning the occurrence of the plant and animal forms that now exist! How did certain mammals get there after the glacial ice had finally gone? The swamps and bogs of the earth are perhaps the most revealing testimonial areas of life-economy, and Isle Royale has its full share of them.

There were certainly caribou on the island once. A small group was seen by trappers, years ago, five miles out from the Canadian shore, headed for the island, and other men saw caribou on the ice at Rock Harbor after the ice had broken up. But how did the mice, the squirrels, and the weasels get there? Possibly by driftwood rafts? The conjectures are fascinating.

Then, too, in the dense cedar-tamarack swamps, with their low temperature at all seasons, it was once reported that "perennial ice" had been found

*Seventeen wolves on the ice—nearly the whole wolf population of the island. Isle Royale National Park. [Photo: William W. Dunmire]*

beneath a layer of turf, not in one spot, but in several. It could hardly fail to suggest the possibility of what would be called a "relict" of glacial ice, though the masses would have to be rather large, I suppose, to maintain the supposition. No doubt the existence of a glacial remnant is improbable; but the mere fact that the year-round ice was there is highly suggestive. It emphasizes the far-north aspect of the park. With an annual snowfall a quarter of that which visits Mount Olympus, in Olympic National Park, what would Isle Royale be like? Or, not to indulge in anything so fanciful, suppose the mean temperature were just a few degrees lower than it is? What new cycle of life-adaptation would ensue? A small rare fish taken from the stomachs of trout caught off Isle Royale has been described as "doubtless a relic of a former arctic marine species." There is no lack of engaging speculations in this extraordinary environment.

But the fishermen will be more interested in fishing. I have not fished in Lake Superior, nor in the lakes of Isle Royale, but from what I have heard I should imagine that this place does not prove disappointing. There are trout on the offshore reefs, and fishing boats may be rented at the developed centers. On guided trips fishing tackle is supplied. I have even seen a report somewhere that in some of the smaller inland lakes there are more fish than should be there. I suppose that means they outrun their food supply. It sounds like the dream of a devotee, but there may be a hidden drawback somewhere. Possibly these places are hard to reach. Incidentally, the ranger force at Isle Royale, engaged in protection work, is not numerous enough to undertake the interpretative services offered in many parks, but to the extent that the men have time, they will be glad to inform and to help all visitors.

Scenically, if you like the northern forest scene—that in which the immaculate canoe birch mingles with the balsam and the other evergreens; where the sugar, red, and mountain maples splash the landscape with their paintpots in autumn; where, in tramping, there is not a single three-mile path of monotony, because the forest changes are rung by stands of maples, stands of birch and poplar, cedar, and tamarack, then jack pine, then alders and willows, and back to evergreens again—if you like this scene, and love to hike in it and search for the surprises it holds, then you will find in this remote wilderness of Isle Royale exactly what you seek. You will not have to rough it much—not more, I assume, than you will prefer to.

## 5. SEQUOIA AND KINGS CANYON NATIONAL PARKS
### [California]

As a narrator, Lemuel Gulliver, a seafaring man, had the fault of letting his timidity lead him into understatement. He tempered the accounts of his adventures in strange places for fear that he might be disbelieved. This was especially true of his sojourn on the island of Brobdingnag. I have this lesson before me as I begin to write of Sequoia and Kings Canyon National Parks, which, administered as one park, present a Sierra scene that complements and emphasizes the beauties and wonders seen by so many millions in Yosemite.

Gulliver, left behind by his fleeing shipmates, found himself in a land where the wheat fields were composed of stalks forty feet high; where "the trees were so lofty that I could make no computation of their altitude." The house cats were larger than oxen; the King's kitchen was six hundred feet high; the King's horses were sixty feet tall. The human inhabitants of Brobdingnag were proportionately large. Gulliver was at first taken by them to be an insect.

We who have been in Sequoia and Kings Canyon, as well as in the backcountry of Yosemite, know well how Lemuel Gulliver felt. To enjoy it is the easiest thing in the world. To comprehend the magnitude of it all is quite another matter. The first feeling of a new visitor to this Brobdingnagian scene may well be one of puzzlement. He has heard of trees so huge that the lumber in a single one of them would be sufficient to build 100 five-room houses. He has been told of looking down from a certain rocky eminence almost a sheer mile, and of canyons whose granite walls rise abruptly 5,000 feet from a plunging river at the bottom. He has seen on a map, perhaps, that seventy-five of the mountain peaks exceed 11,000 feet in height, twenty are more than 12,000, and seven, including the master of them all, Mount Whitney, are more than 14,000 feet above sea level. He gazes about him. What about it? Is this all true? It doesn't seem so colossal as he expected.

The reason is clear. There is no effective scale. Everything is gigantic except the visitor himself and his companions; and because the human life against this background is as a mustard seed lost in a square mile, it is no scale at all. Comparisons must be made from like to like or they fail to register. This is notably true of the giant sequoias. Standing at the base of one of these trees, the newly arrived visitor has no perspective. The statistics—height, diameter, circumference—mean almost nothing at all. It is only when you have lived with these trees for a while and have seen them in their relation to the community of which they are the biggest living things but where there are other giants too—sugar and ponderosa pines, cedars and firs—it is only then that you will appreciate the grandeur and significance of the sequoia patriarchs. It is a revelation never to be forgotten.

Since these two national parks cannot adequately be pictured for those who have never visited them, we must fall back on statistics that will intimate what may be expected there. It is customary to begin with the Big Trees, and I suppose it is really necessary. Yet it would be almost tragic to leave anyone with the impression that, having seen some of the sequoia groves, he has seen all that Sequoia and Kings Canyon have to offer. On the contrary, this region, the mightiest section of the Sierra Nevada, offers trail experiences, some easy, some difficult, which go far beyond anything that can be had elsewhere if you are looking for titanic proportions. The trail enthusiast can here ride over the top of the mightiest mountain peak in the United States proper, or if he is a practiced hiker, he may cross it afoot. It is not easy, but it is done. This is really extraordinary. Here is a peak that towers 14,495 feet. Many mountaintops not nearly so high are closed to any but the most skillful alpinists.

We shall come back, a little farther on, to those 400,000 acres of unbroken wilderness which lie between the southern tip of Sequoia National Park and the northernmost limit of Kings Canyon National Park, a territory with the wildest grandeur the eye can look upon. But for the moment the Big Trees must have their say.

When John Dryden wrote that ringing line "The monarch oak, the patriarch of trees . . . ," he knew nothing of the existence, in a faraway land called California by the Spaniards, of a kind of tree that could dethrone his monarch without half trying. Dryden had in mind some English trees that were truly venerable, such as the Damorey Oak in Dorsetshire, blown down in 1703 and found to be more than 2,000 years old. But it was a comparatively young monarch. We do not know how ancient some of the greatest of the standing sequoias may be, but the rings of trees that have been cut frequently exceed 3,000, and some of the larger trees may be between 3,500 and 4,000 years old. Thus they were aged trees when Dryden's oak was an acorn. They had gone into their patriarchal period when Rome, the Eternal City, was a settlement of shepherds from the Alban Hills. They are older than any human historical reference to which we can turn with a feeling of true kinship with the men who left the record.

This *Sequoia gigantea*, growing only on the western slopes of the Sierra in central California, is one of three survivors of a genus that once flourished throughout the world. Its near relative, the coast redwood—a fine grove of which may be seen in Muir Woods National Monument—makes luxurious stands from Monterey County to Oregon. The only other species now alive, the metasequoia, or "dawn redwood," located and examined in China a few years ago by Dr. Ralph Chaney of the University of California, may possibly be the tree of which so many and such widespread fossil forms have been found. As a genus, the sequoia was certainly as abundant once as the pine is today. The roster noted above embraces all that are known to exist as living trees. What happened to them? Who knows? Probably a number of factors were involved—changes of climate and creation of desert areas, volcanic lava flows, the movement southward of polar or mountain ice sheets. For the most part they disappeared with the passing of the mighty reptiles of a moist, warm geologic period.

If the Ice Age finally put an end to most of the Big Trees, that would explain why the remnant in the Sierra escaped. It would not explain why they have never been found there as a continuous forest cover, but always in groves, living in association with other trees, and numbering in each group

*Snow comes to the giant forest. Sequoia National Park.* [*Photo: R. Badarocco*]

from as few as six to as many as several thousand. There are approximately sixty-three of these groves.

Looking back to our earliest knowledge of the presence in our country of such magnificent trees, it is rather amusing to note the almost complete ignorance of them as late as 1853 by a botanist as famous as was Dr. Jacob M. Bigelow, who was attached to the Pacific Survey party led by Lieutenant Amiel Whipple. The sequoias were known to exist, to be sure. Probably Captain Joseph Reddeford Walker saw them as early as 1833. But when Dr. Bigelow arrived in California, he found that a local amateur had taken the trouble to send specimens of bark, wood, leaves, and cone, with a full description, back to Washington by way of the Isthmus of Panama. The specimens never arrived.

Meanwhile a certain Mr. Lobb, collecting for some botanical society in Scotland, sent specimens to Dr. John Lindley in London. Lindley pronounced the tree a new genus and called it *Wellingtonia gigantea*, in honor of the Duke of Wellington. Dr. Bigelow was greatly annoyed. He had already made up his mind that it was a new genus, and proposed to call it *Washingtonia*. Bigelow had nothing against the Duke, but he wanted no foreign interloper claiming the tree of trees. He reported sourly: "Well, let England have the empty name. *We* have the tree!"

But there was no international incident. The Hungarian botanist Stephan Endlicher had studied the coast redwood and declared it to be an entirely new genus, which he called *Sequoia sempervirens*; and now a Frenchman came along and recognized the Big Tree as another species of sequoia, calling it *gigantea*. Endlicher had named the tree in honor of the Cherokee chief who created for his people a syllabary of eighty-six symbols representing each sound in the language spoken by them. There is a statue of this extraordinary Indian in the national Capitol. Well is it deserved. Uneducated, and speaking no English, Chief Sequoyah was no less touched with genius than any of his forerunners who made writing and printing possible.

But how little Bigelow knew of this tree, which he declared one of the wonders of the world! He relied upon hearsay, probably never seeing more than a small grove near the headwaters of the Calaveras. "The whole number of these trees in existence, young and old," he wrote, "does not exceed 500, and all are comprised in an area of 50 acres. I am impressed with the belief that the species will soon be extinct." (He was providentially wrong about

*Looking down into Paradise Valley. Kings Canyon National Park.* [*Photo: Weldon F. Heald*]

this; the ax and saw of the lumberman were stayed in time.) There are probably not less than twenty thousand Big Trees with a diameter of more than ten feet, and it is heartening to note that 92 per cent of these are either in national parks and national forests or in the custody of California. It would be well if the other 8 per cent should somehow come into preserves. Not a single *Sequoia gigantea* should be cut. They represent a unique survival; the patriarchs are probably the oldest living things; they belong to our remote and future histories. In a wider sense they should even be regarded as wards of the world.

Although it is unique in other respects, what makes the giant sequoia the true monarch of the plant world is its massiveness. The vast volume of wood in these trunks is caused by the fact that they rise from the ground without the taper that characterizes most trees. They are prodigious clubs rather than Brobdingnagian walking sticks; you might almost call them cylinders. Hence, though no Big Trees approach anywhere near the record of the tallest coast redwood, or even the tallest Douglas firs, in total volume they stand supreme. The General Sherman tree, in Sequoia, reaches a height of 272 feet, with a diameter at the base of 30 feet and 7 inches. But consider! At the height of 120 feet the trunk has still a diameter of 17 feet, and the first large limb, nearly 130 feet from the ground, is close to 7 feet in diameter. Even as I write these words, which are the statistics of qualified engineers, I keep asking myself if it can be really so. A tree with a limb far bigger than the trunk of any tree that grows in my own well-forested countryside?

The General Grant, in the Grant Grove section of Kings Canyon National Park, is even thicker at the base than the General Sherman, but not quite so tall. This Grant Grove section, by the way, was the first stand of sequoias to be given national-park protection, and the reason may be seen in the cut-over areas nearby. Magnificent sequoia groves, more extensive than anything now preserved, were ruthlessly destroyed before the butchery ended. Vandalism is a harsh word, and I should certainly not apply it to any ordinary deforestation, even when it has been proved to be inept and unwise; but here among the sequoias it is doubtful if the destruction even resulted in any monetary profit commensurate with the effort involved. And near Big Stump Basin you may see a tree that was nearly cut through and then abandoned, as though the children tired of their play. Strange to say, this tree refused to fall, and the cut is steadily healing. The powers of recuperation of a maimed Big Tree are a phenomenon in the plant world.

You may also see the Centennial Stump, all that remains of a huge tree that was cut up in sections and shipped to the Centennial Exposition in

Philadelphia in 1876. It was a bright idea, undoubtedly; but the promoters were rewarded by having most of those who saw it pronounce it an absurd fake. No tree like that ever existed!

At Sequoia National Park the center of activities is at Giant Forest. This was the favorite of John Muir, and a discovery of Hale Tharp, who found a huge hollow log there and fashioned himself a comfortable cabin from it. Not far away is the Crescent Meadow, likewise beloved by Muir, who esteemed it the loveliest spot in all the Sierra. Giant Forest Village has a strategic location, with easy foot trails or short drives to many things of admiration—recalling that the original meaning of the word *admiration* was "wonder." Moro Rock, Beetle Rock, Sunset Rock, the Tokopah Valley, Crystal Cave, the Muir Grove, Admiration Point—all are readily accessible.

Nine miles along the Colony Hill road from Giant Forest is the site of the lumber mill of the Kaweah Cooperative Commonwealth Colony, whose lumbering activities, oddly enough, had much to do with the establishment of Sequoia National Park. Even the site is worth visiting, and not alone for its location in the midst of grand prospects of canyon and mountain. Kaweah Colony was a belated example of an outburst of experiments in communal living which began in the early part of the last century and flourished in numbers, if not in durability, like dandelions in the commuter's lawn. Of such gestures toward the equitable life, the famous Brook Farm was a bluestocking example—Ralph Waldo Emerson, declining an invitation to join Brook Farm, said dryly that he preferred to own his real estate in Concord.

Noble as were the motives of the leaders in these communal enterprises, and undeniable as it is that the theory is sound and only lacks the existence of people who can live according to a sound theory, nearly all the communities started with clay feet. Some of the colonies were planted upon soil that was hostile even to beans; others, believing that they held the master key that would unlock all economic closets, gravely repeated all the practical errors that had preceded them, and added some of their own.

Kaweah, instituted with such high hopes in the glorious Sierra forest country, was no exception. It should have occurred to the founders, who were going to attain the upright social existence by cutting down trees— trees, by the way, that they later found they did not own—that people who depend for their thrift upon eating up a forest will have no resource when the forest is gone except to eat up each other. The colony, however, did not last long enough to experience cannibalism, for the day soon came when a detachment of U.S. cavalry came in and ordered an end to the timber operation.

That was the finish of Kaweah Commonwealth, but you may be sure that the devotees dispersed with the conviction that only bad luck prevented the consummation of a success that would have astounded and allured the world; and that many of them hastened to form or join other experiments of the kind. I once met, in the single-tax colony at Fairhope, Alabama, a number of enthusiasts who had lived successively in half a dozen such communities, dutifully remaining with each one long enough to give it a decent interment. The concept dies hard, especially among folks who are naturally good and humane; and doubtless the world stands always in need of a little Arcadian madness.

Of these two great parks, Sequoia and Kings Canyon, only a small part—but that sufficiently revealing for those who have only a few days to spend—can be reached by automobile. Beyond is the wilderness of mountain, lake, stream, flowered meadow, imposing canyon. The way to see what this fastness holds is the way pioneers saw it, and such a holiday is for those who have the time and the willingness to plod, browse, and associate with the things of the wild. To cover the longest trail trips afoot is, of course, for the most vigorous. Slightly less arduous would be to let a donkey carry the grub and the pans and bedding, as did the old-time prospectors. When you get well acquainted with a sad-faced burro and learn to speak his language, he can be an excellent companion. Behind his mournful face he conceals a fine, albeit occasionally annoying, sense of humor.

Those who want to rough it deluxe—camping out under the easiest conditions—may procure the services of seasoned guides, packers, and camp cooks. In these circumstances it will still be a retreat into the primitive.

In Sequoia the rock-carved passages of the Kaweah and the Kern, and in the neighboring park the stupendous canyons of the forks of the Kings, reach upward toward the hundreds of lakes of the Sierra and tumbling tributary streams that have wild fish in them—wild fish eager to fight when they feel the barb. Even the novice can get his fish here, but he has honestly earned them by going back where no serried ranks of highway fishermen are crowding the landscape. This statement is prompted by the fact that I have just been looking at a photograph, reproduced in a sportsmen's magazine, showing "opening day" on one of Pennsylvania's streams. The sportsmen, poor wretches, are lined up shoulder to jowl as far as the camera lens can reach. What that sort of thing would do to the "natural economy" that exists along

*Big Trees along the Generals Highway. Sequoia National Park. [Photo: National Park Service]*

a riverbank in a wilderness area requires no special scientific knowledge to understand. For real sport, with a tingle in it, the streams and lakes of the high Sierra are an Izaak Walton domain.

Then, in these backcountry places, the glimpses of the native animals come naturally and almost surely into every tramping experience. The black bear, harmless when you leave him alone, is common at about the elevation of Giant Forest. Mule deer are plentiful and, if anything, too tame. They tend to move down into places where they can be fed tidbits by sentimental people. The sentiment is a natural one; the limpid eyes of the deer are almost irresistible when he approaches for a handout; but let us resist the impulse. A toffee-fed deer is going to be a sick deer later, an easy victim for the predator. The hiker will not see bighorn and cougar, probably, but they are there. And almost surely the golden eagle will be found soaring over the craggy peaks.

The John Muir Trail, all the way from Sequoia up to Yosemite, finds its way along the ridgepole of this Sierra stronghold, seldom dropping below the 8,500-foot elevation. Lucky are those who have the time and the passion for a trail adventure like this one.

Yes, in these two magnificent parks we are all, without exception, Gullivers arrived in Brobdingnag. Yet, really, I do not wish to overemphasize the smallness of man in relation to the immensity of the natural scene in which he finds himself. The skill and daring that through his will and hand have transmuted the stubborn raw materials of earth into comfort and dominance form no less a marvel, perhaps, than any of the elements he has wrought upon. Man is able. I congratulate him, and he will think my congratulations no more than his desert.

Still, when he stands at the foot of the Grizzly and the General Sherman sequoias and considers not so much their bulk as their meaning and history, or when he gazes from the pinnacle of Moro Rock at the flowing harmony of the crests of the Kaweahs and the mountains of the Divide, or when he is engulfed in the magnificence of the canyons of the Kings, it would be no confession of weakness, but rather an affirmation of true strength, to consider a certain brief utterance set down many centuries ago. These occur in the third verse of Psalm CXLIV, in a book that may be consulted, I think, at any good public library; and before delivering it, the attendant will considerately dust it off.

6. Olympic National Park
[*Washington*]

THERE IS A LEGEND TO THE EFFECT that Jupiter, aghast at the growing skepticism of his people and angered at the gibes of scurrilous writers like Lucian, pulled up stakes from his mountain in Greece, emigrated to the New World, and took up residence in the western part of Washington State, on a peninsula fronting upon the Pacific Ocean and the Juan de Fuca Strait.

I do not vouch for this tale. But it must be said that there is some evidence to substantiate it. There certainly *is* a mountain in the peninsula—where Olympic National Park is situated—called Mount Olympus, and nothing is more natural than that Jupiter should have kept up the ancestral name and style. There is on this Mount Olympus a blue glacier of transcendent beauty, and, as every schoolgirl knows, blue was Juno's favorite color. Everything about the area suggests that it is a place a god like Jupiter would choose.

This is not all. You remember—do you not?—that the Romans paid respects to Jupiter under many titles, corresponding with his various supernatural powers. He was, among other things, Jupiter Pluvius (Rain-Bringer). If you needed rain, you resorted to the appropriate temple and asked for a shower. There was a small charge for the service. But if you wanted the weather to clear, you went to the temple of Jupiter Serenator (Fair-Weather-Bringer). If all went well (there was trifling fee), the sun began to shine. What happened when the farmers wanted rain and the rest of the people planned a pantheistic picnic, I do not know. My informant is silent.

Now, it *may* be a coincidence that the weather conditions on the Olympic Peninsula suggest that Jupiter is locally sometimes Pluvius and sometimes Serenator. On the western side of Olympic National Park the yearly precipitation may exceed 140 inches. It is the wettest winter climate in the United States. As for Mount Olympus itself, it has been estimated, from the runoff, that the total snowfall might be at least 250 feet in a season. Yet the easterly slope of the park is the driest place on the west coast outside of southern California, and even drier than some parts of that irrigated land.

The meteorologists explain this phenomenon glibly. They say that the Olympic Mountains reach up and squeeze dry the moisture-laden clouds that come in from the Pacific before they can get over to the eastern side. This

*Overleaf: Here and there the sun finds an opening in the rain forest. Olympic National Park.* [*Photo: George Grant*]

explanation would eliminate the need for Jupiter altogether and is therefore destructive modernism. I am tolerant, however. If my neighbor prefers to worship a barometer, I am content. Let us look to the results.

Olympic National Park, which has been set aside as part of the cultural wealth of the United States, for the admiration and enjoyment and education of generations to come, is indeed a wilderness. It contains a temperate-zone rain forest that is unique. There are other rain forests in the world. Darwin described the jungle of beech giants in Tierra del Fuego. There is a temperate rain forest, predominantly of a kind of yew, in New Zealand. But this forest of evergreen cone-bearing trees of the Olympic Peninsula is one of the world's wonders.

There are no words competent to picture such a forest. Photographs give merely a feeble suggestion of such plant fecundity, the result of a happy combination of climatic conditions and soil. Even actually seeing it, walking in it, observing the community life that goes on within it, leave one with a sense of unreality and incredulity. There diffuses through the forest in its heaviest portions a greenish-white light that becomes in other spots a glow of misty warm ivory when the sun strikes in upon some broad leaves like those of the maple, which have a transparent quality in comparison with the light-devouring conifers.

Pile carpets of moss cover the ground; moss dangles from the branches; ferns climb from the bases of the trees to join the mosses above; at first venture the silence is frightening. It is not only the luxuriance of the vegetation that is bewildering. There are pygmies in this forest that would be giants in many places; and the giants here are in troops, in regiments, in armies. The largest known Douglas fir, found on the Queets River, is seventeen feet eight inches in diameter four feet above the base. Here are considered to be the largest red cedar, twenty feet in diameter; the largest Western hemlock; and the largest Alaska cedar. There is a Sitka spruce that as yet has no discovered rivals for size. That any soil in any climate could support such a total of growth in the space provided for it is a challenge to belief.

It is called a rain forest, and that is just what it is. But the name suggests to the imagination a perpetual drip and driving rain, like a Gustave Doré picture, or like the weather that made the army swear so terribly in Flanders. Do not be alarmed. To be sure, there is copious rainfall, annually. How could there be a rain forest otherwise? In winter the word *copious* may be an understatement. At Quinault Lake in one twenty-four-hour period, twelve inches of rain bucketed earthward. The rivers that course to the ocean are subject

*Ruby Beach, on the log-strewn ocean strip. Olympic National Park.* [*Photo: George Grant*]

to great fluctuations, and are awe-inspiring when in flood. Even in summer the Pacific may send spongy clouds in upon the peninsula without much warning.

But in summer and early autumn there may come days upon days that smile invitingly upon those willing to take the potluck of the wilderness and follow on foot or horseback some of the five hundred miles of trail that find their scenic way through the forest and into the mountains to the choice meadows, blooming from June through October.

The hiker who wants to pack a few necessaries and a bedroll and really test his kinship with the wild can find trailside shelters at convenient points. The Oregon jay will be watching you from point to point as you plod along the trail. He will not abuse you in seven avian languages, like Steller's jay, but as soon as you strike one of these rustic shelters, a half-dozen of him will drop in on you before you have unpacked. He will propose a partnership. Beware of partnerships. If you have any success, your partner's infinite sa-

[ 7 7 ]

gacity was responsible. If you do not, it was due to *your* stupidity. You will enjoy the company of this alert bird, but you must maintain your sturdy independence.

A jay's nest found in these woods contained the portion of a Seattle newspaper that carries the dateline—April 4. Any bird that lays a cornerstone and deposits evidences of current history therein is worthy of respect and—suspicion.

There is no lack of wild animals to be seen from the roads and trails. Outstanding, of course, is the fine Roosevelt elk. In summer, these animals are in the higher country, but when snows come, they move down into the valleys to browse on the vine maple, which forms such an important undergrowth in the dense forest. The elk bulls are sturdy fellows, weighing from seven hundred to a thousand pounds. They seldom go down to tidewater and have an odd way of concentrating in some of the valleys and rarely visiting others. The Columbian black-tailed deer and the mule deer are also abundant, though the latter was introduced from the pine country of eastern Washington.

While in the rain forest, visitors should note the extraordinary features of tree growth. First of all will be observed the way in which so many of the living trees have taken root on fallen logs and old stumps. Though this habit is also characteristic of the coast redwood of California and seems to be connected with the difficulty the seeds may have in sprouting in the thick mat of moss that carpets the forest, here the adaptation may be seen in most dramatic form. For example, a Sitka spruce, three feet in diameter, and a Western hemlock may be seen making a twin growth out of the stump of a Sitka spruce that went down more than a century ago. Another instance is twenty-three trees, twenty-one of them hemlocks, one a spruce, and the other a maple, which have taken root on one giant fallen log. They line up like a platoon of soldiers.

But it is high time to leave this temperate-zone jungle and take the trail up one of the river valleys toward the cluster of mountains that rise in a scattered way—there is no definite range—in the center of the park. These rivers, most of them crystal-clear, which come plunging down from the mountains to flow into the Pacific, do not travel long distances to their goal, but they carry a surprising amount of water from the melting snow and ice of the peaks. It is not far to timberline in these mountains, generally not more than five thousand feet, which is a low timberline compared with that

*Cove of quietude. Olympic National Park.* [*Photo: Joseph Dixon*]

of most of the Western parks. At timberline are the alpine meadows, with their profusion of flowers, and from these bright spots it is no great distance to the perpetual snow. There are probably a hundred glaciers in these peaks, though many of them are small. Mount Olympus has seven major glaciers on its upper flanks.

Though one of the great charms of Olympic National Park lies precisely in its lack of "developments," and though the best things are reserved for those willing to take at least short and easy jaunts on foot, there is still much beauty and strangeness to be observed from the approach and mountain roads. Deer Park, in the northeastern section, can be reached by a road that climbs to six thousand feet and affords splendid views of the mountain cluster of the Juan de Fuca Strait and of Vancouver Island. Some of the finest of the rain forest, along the Hoh River, may be seen without leaving your car, but it would be better to put on your galoshes and get a more intimate sense of this marvel of tree growth by following some trail a short distance into the wilderness.

It is the same here in Olympic as anywhere else; good fishermen get fish, and the others say there are no fish left in this wicked world—at least, none in places where a fellow can go and get them without any inconvenience to himself. Hence has arisen the great clamor for the planting of legal-sized fish that, reared in the cloistered luxury of a hatchery, will have, when transplanted to the streams, all the desperate fighting quality of aquatic rabbits, and the high flavor of wet newspaper. These educated trout, dumped into a river to take their chances with rough-mannered wild fish, have been known to jump into a fisherman's basket and beg to be taken back to boarding school, where they were so happy with the rest of the girls, with chopped-liver hors d'oeuvres three times a day and nobody ever speaking a rude word. Sport fishermen will understand what I mean by this; others should order their fish by mail.

### 7. Muir Woods National Monument
#### [*California*]

Mount Tamalpais, in Marin County across the Golden Gate, is the holy mountain of the native San Franciscan. Hence it is that sometimes Fujiyama is spoken of (though not by Japanese) as the Mount Tamalpais of Japan. There is no likeness in appearance. It is a matter of reverence: the famous Bohemian Club performs its devotional exercises in its tutelary grove on the Russian River.

In the days before the Bay and Golden Gate bridges were built, the dwellers in Marin County who got up early to catch the Sausalito boat were regarded with some respect even by those San Franciscans who spoke sneeringly of the commuters from Oakland and Berkeley. The voyagers who came in on the Sausalito ferry had a spicy aroma, of cinnamon and cloves, like the old-time salts from the South Seas. They were all able-bodied seamen —survivors of many a dense fog. There were giant commuters in those days. Transportation is now rapid and—colorless. *¡Ay de mi!*

At the foot of Mount Tamalpais, the aforesaid holy mountain, is Muir Woods National Monument, donated to the people of the United States by Congressman William Kent and his wife, Elizabeth Thacher Kent. They tied only one string to their noble gift: that the beautiful valley of redwoods, when proclaimed as a national monument, should bear the name of John Muir, who loved these trees with all the ardor of his great Caledonian heart. A request granted before it was asked! No name could have been more fitting. Nimble John, clambering everywhere in California and seeing everything, had made the sequoias almost as much his own as Chief Sequoyah's.

These coast redwoods, which launch their great spires skyward all the way from Monterey County to just across the California-Oregon line, are cousins of the mighty giant sequoias of the High Sierra. They are called *sempervirens*—evergreen—and aside from the great difference in the manner of growth, particularly in the shape of the trunk, there are a number of other distinguishing characteristics when the two trees are more closely examined. The foliage of the *gigantea* of the Sierra somewhat resembles that of the juniper; the other is nearer to the hemlock. The bark of the giant is a bright reddish brown, while that of the coast redwood is a dull chocolate. Finally, the cones of the *sempervirens* are very small, only one third as large as those of its relative.

Which is the nobler sequoia—*sempervirens* or *gigantea?* Not Solomon himself could judge. For if the *gigantea* is one of the oldest living things on earth, and if its girth is far greater than that of the coast redwood, the latter breaks all forest records too. The *tallest* living thing known to exist is a specimen of the coast redwood.

This tallest tree is not in Muir Woods, but the trees there are quite tall enough and varied enough in their habits to afford a perfect demonstration. Here in Muir Woods, for example, you may see dramatic instances of how the coast redwood propagates itself. It does not need to spring from seed, coming up very readily from stumps, from the roots of veterans, or even obligingly from burls, as many people know who have put these lifeless-looking tree warts in a bowl of water and seen the green shoots emerge from them. You may see an albino redwood of great size, and instances of albino shoots; and circles of large trees, with a patriarch in the middle of each ring, where fire ran through these woods two centuries ago and the wounded tree made haste to send up a liberal progeny from its roots, in case the worst should arrive.

In northern California, where the redwood growth is most intense, there are great stands of these trees, almost exclusively. The giants grow so close together as seemingly to leave no room for anything else and to allow no sunlight to come through the canopy of their tops. Yet enough sun does filter through to allow a rich ground cover of ferns and flowering plants, especially the oxalis; and where the redwoods are not quite so dominating, the Douglas fir, tan oak, and madroña may add a modest companionship to the scene, as they do at Muir Woods.

To visit Muir Woods National Monument is to have an adequate sample of the typical redwood forest. If the tallest redwood there is only 246 feet, with a diameter of 17 feet, the Statue of Liberty is not much taller, and Niagara Falls nowhere near so high. It must be owned, too, that the greater forests to the north do not have quite such an intimate touch as the moderate acreage of Muir Woods. Wandering along the trail among the Muir trees, most visitors have a sense, even among these giants, of kinship and friendliness. They have this feeling, too, in driving over the Redwood Highway, which winds for many miles among the towering trees.

But in those dense uncut forests which reach from Dyerville to the Smith River, where California and the Save-the-Redwoods League have created precious reserves that will never feel the saw and ax, the wilderness is uncompromising. To go into that overpowering, silent cathedral of the Smith River redwoods—into, let us say, the National Tribute Grove, which has been set aside to honor the men and women of the armed services of World War II—is to leave human vanity in the sunlight just outside. The beauty and majesty of it is inspiring, and also a little crushing.

The wilderness, as an old friend of mine says, is "strong medicine." He knows. He has lived with it more than most men. Going into the *true* wilderness for a long sojourn alone, you had better pack in your saddlebags, besides chocolate bars and changes of socks, a maximum of character and integrity, and a willingness to go to a school of stern discipline. The wilderness can

*Sometimes the seedling redwood is an albino. Muir Woods National Monument.*
[*Photo: George Grant*]

[ 8 2 ]

ennoble the Jedediah Smiths and John Muirs; it can also disconcert and dilute.

Of course, for a holiday land cruise, the wilderness, especially in the company of a guide who has both skill and imagination, is pure tonic. At all events, singing the praises of the wilderness *merely as such* is much like congratulating the Cosmos. The Cosmos will not feel obligated. Even so good a physicist as Sir James Jeans, who patiently explained the Universe to itself, never received any acknowledgment from it while he lived. Since then his relations may have become more chummy.

So do not demand any immediate mental or spiritual profit from a visit to the wilderness. All in good time. The wilderness simply *is*. That is the best reason for preserving our finest examples of it.

Muir Woods is the best kind of introduction, I think, to the larger California State wilderness redwood preserves. It is redwoods-in-cameo.

Deer are quite common in the monument, but except in early morning and late evening you are not likely to see them till autumn, when they come down from the surrounding hills. When the winter rains have set Redwood Creek to flowing briskly, you may see mature salmon and steelheads fighting their way up the rapids to the spawning beds within the monument. Naturally, you are forbidden to catch them. It is a great sight; after a first greedy impulse, you will not want to catch them.

## 8. PETRIFIED FOREST NATIONAL PARK
### [*Arizona*]

THE FOREST THAT WAS, 135 million years ago, stood on the banks of an ancient stream in northern Arizona when the face of that now mountainous country looked very different from what it does today. In the days of the Forest That Was, it expanded as a flattish lowland, not much above sea level. On the flood plains grew ferns and rushes, and cycads that looked somewhat like modern palms; and among these floundered giant saurians and salamanders. Somewhere upstream, on slightly higher ground, grew pines. They were not wholly different from our modern pines, but were rather more like certain pines now living in South America and Australia.

The Forest That Was is now again the Forest That Is. But how changed! No longer standing upright with anchors of root and with branches and leaves. Those Triassic pines are now scattered helter-skelter—some in whole logs, some in broken sections—over an area perhaps a hundred miles from where they grew. They are now stone trees—stone of such hardness that it will scratch all but the hardest alloy steels.

## Petrified Forest National Park

Petrified trees, they are called; and this is Petrified Forest National Park, preserved first as a monument under the Antiquities Act so that Americans of the future may see and study the greatest natural phenomenon of its kind. For these are not merely fragments of petrified trees, such fragments as can be seen in many places, particularly in the Southwest, where every heavy summer rain washes them from the soil. This is the greatest and most colorful concentration of petrified wood ever yet revealed on the earth's surface. Most petrified wood is brownish or slaty in color, if not black. These stone trees are of nearly the hues of the rainbow; indeed, one of the six "forests" within the area is called the Rainbow Forest. Their colors are practically the colors of the Painted Desert, part of which is in the northern part of the park. The reason for this similarity is evident when the story of the trees is unfolded.

Are everyday folks interested in geology? They certainly are interested in the phase of geology expressed in Petrified Forest. The yearly visitation here greatly exceeds that of many other national parks, and few of the monuments

*Hansel and Gretel at doorway of the witch. Muir Woods National Monument.*
*[Photo: Donald Reeser]*

anywhere nearly approach it. It is true that the trees are near one of the most heavily traveled cross-country highways; but it is also true that the area is not near any populous cities, where people might run out merely to spend a Sunday afternoon. Visitors to Petrified Forest definitely come to see the trees; and having seen them, they wish to know more about them. In the Rainbow Forest Museum there is a fine exhibit of polished wood, revealing the coloring in all its brilliance, as well as local fossils and a diorama that graphically shows the way it all happened. In summer, a short talk is given at regular periods in this museum, and there are naturalist guided tours through the nearby forest.

There must be something especially mysterious and romantic about the petrifaction of a tree, especially when it also becomes a mineral rainbow. There seems to be no other reason why such great numbers of people are lured here. Yet, dramatic as was the occurrence that created this wonder, it was one of those natural sequences which can be traced without difficulty. These trees, when they were living things, were swept into the rivers and carried downstream, finally to be buried in the sand and mud in the spot where they are now, and will be for many thousands of years, because they will continue to be constantly exposed by erosion. Their progress downstream was probably a slow one. In that journey the pines lost their bark, their branches, and most of their roots.

If nothing further had happened, the forest giants would have decayed, or at most would have become some sort of coal, under pressure. But the something else happened. Distant volcanoes threw up vast clouds of fine cinders, which were carried by the wind and deposited upon the muds and sands in which the trees were buried. For ages this story was repeated—more trees, more burials, more volcanic ash. Indeed, hundreds of feet below where the petrified trees are seen today, there are probably hosts of others that will someday come to view.

To turn these trees to stone it was required that the ground where they lay should be flooded with waters containing silica in solution. The volcanic ash supplied this silica as it was leached. It also supplied the minerals from which the paint was mixed. Iron and manganese were in that amorphous dust which finally settled to earth to become later a kind of claylike rock called bentonite—a rock that takes up water like a sponge and becomes a fine mud that easily creates "badlands."

---

*135,000,000 years ago these stone logs were part of a great forest. Petrified Forest National Park. [Photo: George Grant]*

Out of these badlands the stone trees were washed; to the north, the wild coloring of the Painted Desert was produced. The tourist who, leaving the main highway and running up to Desert Inn, looks out for the first time upon this kaleidoscope of reds and orange, of purple, blue, and yellow, stretching away into the distance, can only gaze in silent wonder. There are rare times, in the early morning, when the rosy fingers of the dawn dabble with just such colors along the horizon; and many a cross-country motorist, getting an early start for a long day's pull, has hauled over to the side of the road and watched the shifting miracle awhile. It is something like that.

Another thing that makes this silicified wood so prized is the presence of lovely quartz crystals, which, as fluid silica, sought out the crevices in the petrifying wood and solidified as gemstones of water—clear amethyst, amber, green, black, red. The logs literally became warehouses of jewels. But the lapidary must get his gems from other sources than this park. Naturally, it is forbidden to remove any of this precious petrified wood, no matter what the size of the fragment. Does this seem stingy? Simply consider what would happen if each visitor took away a few pounds. These forests are not growing. This particular alchemy of nature has been completed. The supply is exhaustible. That is why it comes as a shock to learn that the incident which hastened the creation of the earlier monument was the erection of a mill to crush these petrified trees into abrasive material. Imagine that!

Besides the petrified trees and the Painted Desert, visitors to this park will not fail to see the evidences of an occupation, many centuries ago, of a pre-historic people. The story of these early settlers follows generally that of northern Arizona as a whole: first the rude pithouses and excavations, then the later developments of stone houses and pueblos. But these people have left behind something else—some curious picture-writing on the sandstone rocks.

In 1200 or thereabouts, there was no particular hurry in northern Arizona. A pleasant way to spend a month was to chisel geometric designs or pictures of frogs, birds, antelope, snakes, footprints on a cliff or boulder. Some of these petroglyphs seem to convey a message, and some seem quite aimless. Nobody has yet found a clear interpretation of them. One of the best examples of the picture-writing is called Newspaper Rock, found near Rainbow Forest. Do not miss it. As to what this chiseled "newspaper" means, your guess will be about as good as anyone's.

Another feature of interest is the evidence of the use of the petrified wood for tools and weapons of these aborigines. Many objects fashioned from the agatized trees have been found, and near Rainbow Forest and Third Forest are several ruins of houses that were built of blocks of petrified wood. One of these, Agate House, has been partly restored and can be reached by the Third Forest Trail.

In the First Forest is Agate Bridge. Where a great stone tree trunk lay, a gully was created by erosion, so that finally the log became what might be called, if one labored, a natural bridge. In time, if nature had her way—which, so far as is practicable, she is intended to do in the wilderness parks and monuments—this unsupported log would break under its own weight. It would therefore no longer be a bridge. By building a support under the log, it could be made to persist for many years. Eventually, however, all this scenery of northern Arizona will undergo a change. So far as the park is concerned, other logs will appear, and gullies will be created under them. The last time I was at Petrified Forest, I thought I saw something artificial supporting Agate Bridge. In such cases, however, my admiration of the National Park Service being what it is, I always conclude that my eyesight is faulty.

*In easily eroded soil the buried trees come to view over the years. Petrified Forest National Park. [Photo: George Grant]*

# [ 11 ]

# *Forge of Vulcan*

AMONG THE WONDERS *of mountains there is Etna, which always burns in the night, and for so long a period has always had materials for combustion, being in the winter buried in snow, and having the ashes it has ejected covered with frost. Nor is it in this mountain alone that Nature rages, threatening to consume the earth. . . . In so many places, and with so many fires, does Nature burn the earth.*

—PLINY THE ELDER (A.D. 77), *Natural History*

## 1. YELLOWSTONE NATIONAL PARK
### [*Wyoming–Montana–Idaho*]

### [ 1 ]

IN 1870 CHARLES SCRIBNER, a book publisher, began the issue of a monthly magazine, with Dr. J. G. Holland as editor. Illustrated throughout by wood engravings, the initial number, containing a poem eighteen pages long and a provocative article about the ocean, indicated a stern purpose to lift the morals of the reading public or, where those were too heavy to lift, at least to agitate. This worthy publication, *Scribner's Monthly*, had hardly been born when Dr. Holland began hearing tales of extraordinary discoveries in the Western states. It was related to him that a certain General Washburn, with a gentleman named Langford and others of a party escorted by soldiers, had spent more than a month in the little-known mountain wilderness that lay south of Montana Territory and had seen strange things.

---

*Old Faithful seen against its forested background. Yellowstone National Park.* [*Photo: M. Woodbridge Williams*]

Dr. Holland was no amateur editor and he had heard about strange things from the West before—things that were more strange than true. The sturdy trappers and frontiersmen who for years had been risking their scalps in the remotest spots of the Rockies, the Patties and Sublettes and Colters and Jedediah Smiths, were probably taciturn and uncommunicative men as a class; but Jim Bridger and the later comers loved to astound the tenderfoot. There was a feeling east of the Mississippi that the Ananias family had emigrated to the wide-open spaces and multiplied exceedingly. The fact, however, that this expedition of Montanans had been given a sort of official color by the presence of a cavalry lieutenant encouraged the editor to invite a contribution from Nathaniel Pitt Langford, who later was to be the first superintendent of a newly created Yellowstone National Park.

Langford, who had kept a diary of the expedition, obliged with two articles, which were published in 1871. There is evidence that the editor, mindful of his responsibility to pure and impressionable young minds, toned down the descriptions considerably. The existence of Yellowstone Lake was already known; Langford's report of its extent could be set down to bad eyesight. Such matters as a mountain of volcanic glass and a stupendous canyon with a waterfall higher than Niagara might pass muster as innocent illusions, and hot springs of a sort were entirely credible. But when the writer passed into the field of vents in the surface of the earth which suddenly shot tons of water two hundred feet into the air; one such monster that obligingly erupted every hour on the hour; fountains of boiling water that played continuously; explosions of multicolored muds that plastered the landscape; hills made of solid brimstone; ice-cold streams with hot stones on the bottom; a valley of smokes, or a hillside that looked like a New England factory town with its belching chimneys—well, it was what Artemus Ward would have called "2 mutch." A blunt reviewer said that "this Langford must be the champion liar of the Northwest," and many readers of the monthly gently reminded Dr. Holland that his prospectus had guaranteed a moral tone.

Langford was made to feel a kinship with David Folsom, who, with two companions, had seen some of the geysers in 1869 and on his return to Helena was invited to relate publicly what he had experienced. Folsom replied that up to the moment his local reputation for veracity was good; he thought it would be well not to trifle with it. He did prepare an article about his trip for the *Western Monthly* of Chicago. By some who knew its content, it was considered an act of Providence that before the magazine could mail out the issue containing the story, the building burned down. C. W. Cook, one of Folsom's companions, sent an article to *Lippincott's Magazine,* timidly report-

*In 1916 "we had our pictures taken at Jupiter Terrace." Yellowstone National Park.*
*[Photo: courtesy Marietta Sumner]*

ing what they had seen. He received a polite rejection slip: "Thank you but
we do not print fiction."

Looking back upon it, it seems strange that the marvels of the Yellowstone should have aroused such incredulity. This was no unknown land, like
the canyon of the Colorado before Powell revealed its majesty. John Colter,
the soldier of the Lewis and Clark Expedition, and afterward famous as a
trapper, had visited part of the region in the early days of the century. Other
traders and trappers knew Yellowstone Lake and had seen geysers, boiling
springs, and mudpots. Jim Bridger, with a bit of charcoal on a buffalo hide,
mapped out the general lay of the land with fair accuracy for Lieutenant
J. W. Gunnison about 1850. Father de Smet, Captain Charles Reynolds, and
Walter De Lacy either had seen some of the spectacles or knew of them from
guides. But until the definite sanction of an official report had been seen and
digested, the skeptics were unrelenting.

This official report was the work of a shavetail in the Second Cavalry,
stationed at Fort Ellis. His name was Gustavus C. Doane. He was the one

detailed, "with one sergeant and four privates," to escort the surveyor general of Montana and his party to "the falls and lakes of Yellowstone and return." The commanding officer at Ellis had not been happy about furnishing an escort for a group of wonder-seekers. The Indians were giving trouble; the Crows especially were thumping the drum. The garrison was already weakened with so many soldiers in the field. If the civilians from Helena had not been territorial bigwigs with some influence, they would have been invited to go sightseeing at their own risk and expense. It was fortunate that they had an order from General Winfield S. Hancock, describing the trip as "an important military necessity"—which it was not.

Fortunate indeed, because it resulted in the classic report of Second Lieutenant Doane, describing, day by day, what the party saw in Yellowstone. Volumes have been written since on the wonderland that became a national park, more accurate in detail, more specific in scientific observation; but there will never be anything finer, fresher, or more responsive than the military document of this young soldier. He tried to remember that, after all, he was just on a tour of duty, and that the cavalry was no place for hearts and flowers. When somebody "reckoned" that a geyser eruption, such as that of the one they called the Giantess, had reached a height of three hundred feet, he straightway triangulated, and declared it to be not more than two hundred and fifty. "Our whole party was wild with enthusiasm"—but Doane had to measure. But little by little the professional detachment began to be swept away and the lieutenant opened the floodgates of his admiration. Yet he did not strive for words and he did not reel with superlatives. It was as though nature, in some of her strangest moods and forms, was speaking to him and he was translating as best he could.

There were several men in that Washburn party who could write very acceptably. Washburn, Langford, Hedges, and Everts all published journalistic material, and no newspaper ever carried better special correspondence than the Helena *Daily Herald* during the period when that frontier newspaper was publishing their accounts. But Doane had an eye and a gift. He climbed the peak now known as Mount Washburn on a day when the pure air of the high country revealed everything with crystal clarity. He saw the snowy summits above the Gallatin Valley, and from them traced almost an unbroken circle of mountains, of which he thought the Tetons were a part. He noted that this circle was broken through in places for the passage of rivers; but he felt that he knew, at this first view, what that circle, with the great basin below him as he faced southward, meant.

"A single glance" he said in his report, "at the interior slopes of the ranges, shows that a former complete connection existed, and that the great basin has been formerly one vast crater of a now extinct volcano. The nature of the rocks, the steepness and outline of the interior walls, together with other peculiarities, render this conclusion a certainty." Well, with whatever amendments the geologists might later make, Doane had gone straight to the heart of Yellowstone. There may have been thirty or forty volcanoes. There are sixteen vents known in the Absaroka Range alone. Wherever Doane went in the next three weeks—to the hot springs, to the geysers, to the mudpots, and even to the great canyon that had eroded through volcanic material of many kinds—it all made sense. It fitted the picture he had seen from Washburn peak. The wonder of it lay behind the individual spectacles, the outbreaks of fiery force from the earth's entrails. He thought there must be "springs of all kinds in the valley to the number of at least 1500," and he was certain they had seen far less than remained to be seen.

Doane stood on the brink of the great canyon of the Yellowstone, first at a point where the upper fall could be viewed, then the lower. The wild beauty and power of the cataracts stunned him. As the dazzle of it receded, he began to think of comparisons, as we all naturally do. But Doane showed the taste that makes for the perfect enjoyment of national parks. "There can be no standard of comparison between such objects, either in beauty or grandeur," he said. His memory, however, naturally summoned up pictures of Niagara and Yosemite and the Shoshone Fall, and each one conveyed to his imagination a special quality. Niagara was "overwhelming power"; Yosemite was "altitude"; Shoshone, in the desert, was "going to waste." So he bathed his eyes with the beauty of the upper fall of the Yellowstone and decided that it embodied the conception of Momentum; and the lower fall—that was Gravitation. As a visitor to Yellowstone National Park you will rightly pay no attention to Doane at this point. Still, you see that this was a strange young second lieutenant, out West fighting Indians. If you had called him a poet, he would have been surprised and might have been annoyed, but of course that was what he was, at the moment. The Yellowstone had drawn it out of him.

For the record, it appears that the Washburn party was never in much danger from the Indians, Crows or other. One gets the impression that Indian scares were already being used to dispossess the red man from land he regarded as his own. Indeed, a multiplying gang of white desperadoes was operating in the Montana Territory who were more to be feared than the aborigines. It is also evident that there were plenty of white men who knew the Yellowstone region like survey men. These men were simply not inter-

*Sheep on Mount Washburn. Yellowstone National Park.* [*Photo: Bob and Ira Spring*]

ested in geysers, waterfalls, or gorgeous rock and hot-spring colorations. They had gold and the fur market in mind.

An incident that occurred during the Washburn exploration points up these facts. One of the party, Truman C. Everts, had very unfortunately established himself as a pathfinder by taking a short cut back to camp and reaching there before his companion arrived by the blazed trail. This convinced him, it would appear, that he was a Jedediah Smith or Kit Carson. The next thing that happened to him was that he was lost, and he remained lost in the wilderness for thirty-seven days. The Washburn party had to return to Helena without much cheer for his family and friends. Everts, by his own account—which he miraculously lived to write for a magazine—besides being handicapped by poor eyesight, was a man who could have strayed on an atoll. He entrusted all his effects, including his matches, to a

horse, and the animal departed. Had he remained where he was, he would
have been quickly found; but he started a pilgrimage on foot, which always
took him a little farther from his pursuers. They caught up with his trail,
only to find that he had gone in a new direction. He had a field glass in his
pocket, the only thing he had not confided to the horse, but it was nearly
two weeks before he remembered that you can make a fire with a lens if the
sun is shining. He slept once in a bear's den, and only the fact that the bear
was visiting and did not get home that night prevented a brutal eviction
proceeding. All this is not to belittle Everts's intelligence. It simply means
that certain men are naturally forest-wise, but most others had better stay
with the guide; and this is something all visitors to the great primeval national
parks might profitably bear in mind.

The point is this. When a reward of six hundred dollars was offered for the recovery of Everts, two experienced frontiersmen started on a search and found him, in the last stages of physical exhaustion, within a few days. No, this was no trackless wilderness, nor was it so dangerous as was commonly believed; it was simply that until Folsom, Cook, and Washburn, Hedges, Langford, and Doane went into the region with eyes for the grand qualities of it, and the ability to publish their discoveries to the world, the Yellowstone was merely a place where animals wore valuable skins, and a pushful prospector might strike it rich if he could survive the wear and tear.

## [ 2 ]

THE MARVELS OF YELLOWSTONE having been revealed to the country, there was the rush that might be expected, on the part of ambitious individuals, to capitalize and sell admission tickets. It was government domain and presumably could be filed on. It looked like good tourist country, and there was gold in those hills, or was thought to be. A railroad into the region of the spectacles was soon projected.

A little group of idealists, however, who knew the real present values and sensed greater ones not so apparent, were sure that with ruthless private exploitation these values would be degraded. There were not many of them, but what they lacked in numbers they made up for with the reiteration of whippoorwills. Led by members of the 1870 party, who themselves gave up lands and potential wealth they might well have claimed, these idealists stormed Congress, gained disciples in the House and Senate, and demanded that this region should become a national park, to be preserved forever for all the people.

The demand could hardly have been made, from the viewpoint of federal finance, at a worse time. The backwash of the Civil War was making itself felt in our economy. The public lands were regarded by otherwise respectable people as a legitimate grab bag. It was still a pioneer country, except for the selvage along the Eastern seaboard, and words like *aesthetics, natural beauty*, and *spiritual values* were received with a squint. Man must eat; man must thrive; spiritual values should be left for posterity. It was all quite natural. The unnatural thing was that such idealism prevailed.

At any rate, for once the insistent angels had their day, and on March 1, 1872, Yellowstone National Park was established by act of Congress. The area was set apart as a "pleasuring-ground for the benefit and enjoyment of the people," and the act provided for "the preservation, from injury or spoliation, of all timber, mineral deposits, natural curiosities or wonders . . . and their retention in their natural condition." True, it was many years before the legislation and the money necessary to carry out properly the noble design were forthcoming, but the course was set.

It may be said that the proponents of Yellowstone had, as leverage, the precedent of Yosemite, which was set aside by Congress in 1864 as an area to be preserved under the protection of California. There has been much heartburning over whether this was, in effect, the establishment of a national park, and therefore whether Yosemite was not the first. We may leave the matter with the historian, who will cheerfully dot all the i's and cross the t's for us. Such matters obscure the real phenomenon, which is that the concept of setting aside such places of natural beauty and geological significance had never before been carried out in any young country in recorded history. It was the Magna Charta of national cultural behavior. The few instances of zealous preservation in ancient times had only a religious background.

That was a wonderful thing: that a hustling, restless, dollar-chasing young nation, with much of its population swarming like locusts over rich virgin land, should have been able to pause long enough to look into the future with such spiritual prudence; it had not happened before.

For this forethought and insight we can thank those who made the preservation of these treasures possible. For the scenic loveliness, for the solace and healing quality of the wilderness places, and for their prodigies of form, color, and animal life—nature at her grandest and simplest, with all that belongs in the picture and as little as possible that does not—we can take no credit. We happen to be the fortunates who live in a spot on the earth's surface where nature has been notably lavish and experimental, if sometimes boisterous and explosive. So we have, taken as a whole, perhaps the best that all the world affords. But if we cannot claim authorship, at least we are trying to safeguard the rare volume—not against the ravages of time, for that would be a foolish hope; not against change, for change in nature is order, and life is adaptation; but against all but the wholly unavoidable intrusions into the book's integrity.

[ 3 ]

IF YELLOWSTONE NATIONAL PARK had no geysers and hot springs of such variety, color, and power, the great canyon and falls of the Yellowstone would still make it one of the world's most inviting attractions for tourists and for students of nature's manifestations in the grand manner. If it lacked the canyon and the plunging water, it would still be the largest of all parks for the refuge of every kind of wildlife that belongs to its type of geographical and climatic condition. But as it has all these, in addition to other allurements, the whole being maintained in as natural circumstances as the presence of humans will permit, there is no wonder that it attracts each year nearly a million people.

"In as natural circumstances as the presence of humans will permit." There, of course, is the constant challenge to the preservation of the primitive. There is the constant headache of administration. The act of Congress that established Yellowstone National Park and led to a great system of national parks and monuments was really a wonderful document, but the twin purposes it embodied are essentially in contradiction. Enjoyment and use in the present, with preservation in their natural condition for all time—how do you contrive that?

The contradiction shows its problems in all the primeval areas, in greater or less degree. But in Yellowstone nobody is to be satisfied with a telescopic view of the geysers and boiling springs. The great thrill is to stand close by them, watch for eruptions or changes, revel in the color of their craters and in the forms of their terraces, and above all to have the shocking but joyous adventure of putting your boot soles closer to the interior fires of the earth than you can do at any other spots on the globe save two. And these other places, Iceland and New Zealand, while wonderful enough, make a poor display compared with the vulcanism of Yellowstone.

But because myriads come year after year, to see and experience, what happens to the natural conditions? The sinter, or mineral deposit of the springs, is softer than that of the geysers, which is tough silica; but even the siliceous material stands no chance against the millions of feet that tread it. If you resort to wooden catwalks to keep the boots from the lovely mineral, where is your "state of nature"? The Washburn party did not record any catwalks when they saw the geysers in their time. This is but one example of a disconcerting problem of managing the national parks for the welfare of the whole people and for posterity. Again and again in visiting the other parks we come upon it; the National Park Service can only strive to approximate the ideal.

[ 4 ]

EVERYTHING THAT MEETS the eye in Yellowstone, unless you chance to be in a wooded spot away from steam vents or the sight of the rim of mountains, expresses the volcanic tumult that was here. You look upon the cliffs of black obsidian, a lava rock that either cooled so quickly as it flowed that it had no time to form crystals or was perhaps too viscous to do so. This was the favorite material of the Indians for arrowheads. You see the great depths of rhyolite, through which the canyon is partly cut, and, not being held to strict scientific account, you can fancy it as being once a granite, like that of the New England hills, being melted and poured out in a new rock-form, not pepper-and-salt, but so close-knit that only the microscope reveals the crystals.

Then you gaze up at the columns of basalt, jointed so neatly as to look like man-made architecture; and beneath and above these columns are other kinds of eruptive or flow material. Off in the distance you see the marching crests of the Absarokas—more volcanic rock, a sort of basalt. There are evidences of the belching of ash from craters—not really ash, of course, like coal or wood ashes, but finely pulverized material, which must have covered a vast terrain with dust when it was blown into the upper air. There are breccias that were hurled out of the craters when the eruptions were most explosive and were consolidated by ash showers that followed, or by later seeping waters. All are volcanic—all are the product of ferocious violence, originating in the terrific heat beneath the earth crust.

Compared with that former violence, the present activity in the form of steam, boiling pools, and geysers is vulcanism at senility, speaking in a weak voice and approaching extinction. Or is it? The geologist may know it; you may know it; does the earth know it?

Something else claims your attention as you look incredulously into the hot springs of so many shapes and temperatures. The mineral deposits have built charming encrusted basins, over the edges of which the water flows or trickles. But on the sides and along the edges of these basins something has painted colors—reds, bluish grays, browns, pinks. You surmise that they may be mineral pigments from the water; but it is not so. Living organisms have made the decorations. It seems impossible that life, as we know life, could exist at such temperatures. But microscopic forms of plant, of bacterial life, and the tiniest of one-celled creatures, diatoms, flourish in this environment. You begin to sense the community scheme of existence—algae clinging to the rock habitation, diatoms clinging to the algae. It is what impressed the young Charles Darwin when he was examining a salt lake in Patagonia. "How surprising," he said, "that any creatures should be able to exist in brine!" They were worms, crawling among crystals of sulfate of soda and lime. "And what becomes of these worms when the surface is hardened to a solid layer of salt, in summer? I saw flamingoes wading about in search of these worms, and the worms feed on infusoria or confervae. Thus we have a little living world within itself, adapted to these lakes of brine." So, here in Yellowstone, are these little worlds.

What you see in the hot pool is a miniature. The larger tapestry is hung all around you. The magnificent herd of bison in the Lamar Valley, the thousands of elk and deer, bands of mountain sheep, antelope, grizzly bears, black bears, and from these larger mammals down to the very smallest, including the animals that prey on other animals, all are included in the picture. Those that are there belong there; none are there that do not naturally inhabit that kind of country. No domestic creatures, except necessary work animals, compete with the wild for the grazing and browsing. They are living their spans, long or short, according to their ability to survive, not according to favoritism. The cougar belongs to the community as much as the deer, and so does the coyote.

There are flaws in the carrying out of this plan, no matter how good the design. Wherever the wild animals receive protection against humans, no matter how huge the domain set aside for them, some of them multiply beyond their food supply. A minimum of artifice must be resorted to, but the approximation to normal life conditions in this vast wildlife refuge is so nearly perfect that it can be said that visitors to Yellowstone see what the first pioneering intruders into the wilderness saw.

The great moment for most of us is when we come upon these animals unexpectedly. You may travel a long distance without seeing any except the ubiquitous black bear. The beasts are going about their affairs, and it gives them no thrill to have their pictures in the newspapers; so there is no guarantee, particularly if you stick to the tourist track, that you will see much of the great wild population. But you may be lucky enough to stumble suddenly into the fellowship of the primeval. That will be something to remember.

Thomas Moran painted the canyon of the Yellowstone. No artist was ever more at ease with Western scenery than Moran. But he was not satisfied with his work; he felt that he had not caught it. Its delicacy, which tends to make the observer forget its size, derives from the happy proportions of rock, tree, and water, with their color and intimacy, especially at the two favorite spots for viewing it: Artist's Point and Inspiration Point. Under a noonday sun the walls of the canyon glare in yellow and white; but actually, as is

*As the great pioneer photographer saw the Falls in 1871. Yellowstone National Park. [Photo: William Henry Jackson]*

revealed by coming closer, the volcanic gases and waters have blocked and streaked the rock with everything from the yellow of grapefruit to the mellowed brick of an ancient manse, and from pearly gray to jet black. Where the river has found tougher rock, it leaps for something easier to grind: and so, seeming to come from nowhere, with a sudden spring, the water drops more than a hundred feet at the upper falls and nearly three times that height at the lower. The falls at Tower Creek, some twenty miles to the north, would themselves be regarded as notable, anywhere. Here the drop is 132 feet, over great boulders.

While the forest growth in Yellowstone is not extraordinary, as Olympic and Sequoia and Muir Woods trees are, the park has a fine unspoiled cover, mostly of evergreens, which is permitted to go through its cycle of birth, decline, and fall without benefit of tree surgery. There are several pines, alpine and Douglas fir, Engelmann spruce, and the juniper of the Rockies. Perhaps the typical tree is the lodgepole pine, which is not a showy tree, but has one great merit: a lumber-mill operator can stand beside it without feeling obliged to estimate how many board feet of lumber it would make.

But there were once forests in Yellowstone—forests after forests, and forests after more forests—and some of them were very different from those seen now. There were pines, to be sure, but not these present pines; there were sequoias, but none exist here now; there were broad-leaved trees that must have enjoyed a much warmer climate than that of the present. These forests are gone, but they are still here: a riddle until you recollect that they are petrified trees. The original wood has disappeared, but mineral matter replaced the organic material of the tree form, ring for ring, cell for cell. There is a place in the park where a succession of twelve forests, each buried in volcanic dust, each rising on the ruins of the next older, can be studied in a vertical section of two thousand feet of rock. A fine standing specimen, readily accessible, can be seen just off the main road between Tower Junction and Mammoth. It remains just as it was overtaken by the storm of ash.

Many visitors to Yellowstone find the profusion of wild flowers one of the chief attractions of the park. The varieties, seasonally decorating the open spaces with splashes of color, are generally characteristic of the high Rocky Mountain country, but especially noteworthy is the fringed gentian. This delicately beautiful plant, whose bloom emulates the sky, has been chosen as the "park flower," not only for its appeal to the eye, but because it is to be seen throughout the entire visitor season. Beginning in June on the warm earth of the geyser basins, it is still to be enjoyed when the last visitors are leaving in late September.

## 2. HAWAII VOLCANOES NATIONAL PARK

### [*Hawaii*]

"THE PRESENT PREDICTION for Kilauea is that it is on its way to a new period of activity, which may bring back the full firelake of the great pit and pour out new flows on the mountain flanks."

So I wrote in 1950 when I was preparing the manuscript for the first edition of *The National Parks*. It was not my personal opinion, of course; I was dependent upon the prognosis of the experts in volcanology. Well, Kilauea obliged within a few years. On November 14, 1959, fire fountains began to play from a rift on Kilauea's Iki Crater. It was the most spectacular eruption ever witnessed in Hawaii—possibly in the entire world. One of these flaming fountains reached a height of 1,900 feet. Lava poured into Kilauea Iki to a depth of 414 feet. Today that lava is cool enough to walk on, but below the crust will be at high temperatures for years.

Less than a month after Kilauea Iki's fountains subsided, a new vent opened near the village of Kapoho in the Puna district, twenty-eight miles away. This flow buried most of the village, entered the ocean, and added some acreage to the island. Since 1961, eight eruptions have occurred—three in Halemaumau and five along the east rift zone.

One of the greatest flows from Mauna Loa began on the first night of June 1950. Emitted from a fissure thirteen miles long, this highly fluid lava raced to the sea at a speed of nearly six miles an hour. This outbreak lasted for twenty-three days, producing enough cubic yards of lava (quoting one of our statistically minded friends) to pave a four-lane highway four and a half times around the earth. It is consoling to feel sure that this is only a hypothetical highway. At best, highways have a way of obliterating fine landscape features.

Twelve years after Captain Cook discovered the Hawaiian Islands, a native chief of considerable ability was trying to bring the largest of the volcanic group under his sway. He had ideas about making himself king of the whole cluster of islands, and in 1791 he succeeded, becoming King Kamehameha I. But in 1790, when this story opens, the fighting was brisk on the island of Hawaii.

Whether the troops were those of Kamehameha or of the opposition, it is sure that on a certain day part of an army was on the march past Kilauea volcano. The soldiers tramped in their bare feet. It may have been a ragamuffin army, but to be in bare feet would not prove it, nor would the weapons they carried be any indication of their combat quality.

In the desert six miles southwest of Kilauea's crater you may still see the prints of those bare feet as they were imprinted in a layer of volcanic ash on that day in 1790. Most of the soldiers were killed; perhaps even those whose footprints can now be seen failed to escape. They were the victims of a surprise attack. As they were passing the home of the fire-goddess Pele —she whose delicate strands of pumice-hair are swirled up from the boiling lava lake of Kilauea—the crater let go with one of its violent steam explosions. The assault must have come without the slightest warning, for the islanders were familiar with the vagaries of their fire mountains. The blast of rock and of rock dust was lethal. Whoever the soldiers were, they had a right to expect something better from Pele. Every army, Hawaiian or other, being so undoubtedly in the right, deserves the assistance of fire-goddesses. This was treachery and ingratitude.

Hawaii National Park, which originally included both those now known as Hawaii Volcanoes and Haleakala, was voted by Congress in 1916 to preserve, free from exploitation or other abuse, the most accessible and best-studied of the areas in the world where volcanic activity is great. The craters here, both the active and the dormant, may be approached with what may be called reasonable safety. That means that there cannot be any guarantee about volcanoes; but I should think the danger about the same as that of being struck by lightning while riding in your automobile, which, as you know, is much less than that of being killed by slipping in the bathtub.

Kilauea is a low dome built up by many layers of lava erupted from the central crater, as well as from lines of craters east and southwest of the summit. Because the neighboring Mauna Loa towers so much above it, Kilauea might seem to be a crater in the side of the greater mountain. It is in fact probably older than its colossal companion. Within the broad depression at its top is the vast pit, Halemaumau. For most of the years during which this pit has been observed, the "House of Everlasting Fire" has contained a lake of active lava, sometimes rising and overflowing, sometimes sinking from sight. Always the sinking has meant the collapse of the pit walls in great avalanches. When the sinking has been so violent that water has rushed through the cracked walls, then have come tremendous explosions of steam. It was one of these that caught the native soldiers.

*Eruption fountain bursts from Kilauea Iki. Hawaii Volcanoes National Park. [Photo: National Park Service]*

The Kilauea Ridge, though not high, effects a marked difference in the scenery on the windward and leeward sides. Along and below the northeast rim and the Chain of Craters Road is a tropical rain forest watered by the copious rainfall of the trade winds. Here visitors pass through a jungle of tree ferns and ohia trees, the latter rich with scarlet pompon bloom. In the area of Twin Craters and the Thurston Lava Tube, where for many years there has been no new covering of lava, the ohias become a forest of giants. The way in which vegetation moves in, where there is plenty of moisture, may be seen along the Chain of Craters, where a young rain forest is recapturing the fields.

South and west of Kilauea is a different scene. This slope of the ridge is cut off from the trade-wind rains, though it gets a heavy general storm on occasions. The rim road enters the upper edge of the Kau desert, and except for scrubby ohia plants and the bushes of the ohelo berry, which was held by the Hawaiians to be sacred to Pele, the strange lava formations are seen in all their nakedness. From here to the seacoast is a wild expanse of the successive products of Ilauea—crusted volcanic ash, barren lava, and dunes of drifting ash and pumice. There is a road through the desert, and several long foot trails traverse it, but hikers should not set out into this waste without getting detailed information from park headquarters.

From the 4,000-odd feet of Kilauea to the 13,680 feet of Mauna Loa is a rise from tropical forest to a volcanic crater where ice remains the year round in places protected from the sun.

Mauna Loa actually rises from the Pacific Ocean floor to a height of little less than 32,000 feet—18,000 feet of its bulk is beneath sea level. So it is in truth a "mountain mass" with its lava-covered flanks extending over more than 2,000 square miles of the island surface.

Obviously it makes no difference to the furious caldron of molten rock below the earth crust—fingering here and there for a weak spot, a fissure, a new or old vent—whether that vulnerable place happens to be in an ocean deep or in an Indian's cornfield in Mexico. One can only wonder what the ocean must be like, locally, in times of great cone-building activity in its depths. A suggestion of it is seen when the lava from Mauna Loa rolls down into the sea, and the ocean becomes deep green and appears to be steaming in ever-widening areas.

The Hawaiian lava flows have given several terms to the science of volcanology. When the lava flows slowly, like cool molasses, the upper portions harden while the interior continues to move forward. This results in a field of sharp, irregular blocks that were tumbled over one another as they were carried along. The thin, fast-moving lava, which spreads out in twisted and ropy forms, with glistening surfaces, sometimes in glowing tones of blue, purple, and bronze, is called *pahoehoe* (pah-hoay-hoay), and fine examples of this are seen also at Craters of the Moon National Monument in Idaho.

Traveling clockwise from the park headquarters, visitors pass lush jungle, raw craters, and great areas of devastation; you will see pumice piled high from recent eruptions, and lava flows only a few years old. Along the road you will come to trails and overlooks—Byron Ledge Overlook and its exhibits, Thurston Lava Tube with a trail through jungle and part of a tunnel through which once rushed glowing lava, the overlook at Kilauea Iki, the boardwalk Devastation Trail, Kilauea Overlook north of the Hawaiian Volcano Observatory, and Sulfur Bank.

The Thomas A. Jaggar Memorial Museum at park headquarters has exhibits, relief models, and paintings on the story of the park. Daily programs

*The fiery breath meets cool air and vaporizes. Hawaii Volcanoes National Park.*
*[Photo: Robert T. Haugen]*

include a talk by a park naturalist and a color film of recent eruptions. The Wahaula Heiau Visitor Center contains another museum.

Hawaii Volcanoes National Park now has an entrance from the sea—a magnificent new road that rises from the Kalapana Black Sand Beach and rugged seacoast of Puna, up over the cliffs to Kilauea Crater some twenty miles distant. The National Park Service has proposed an extension of the boundaries of Hawaii Volcanoes National Park to include the summit region of Hualalai and to connect these areas with each other and with City of Refuge National Historical Park at Honaunau by a scenic parkway.

## 3. HALEAKALA NATIONAL PARK
### [*Hawaii*]

ON THE ISLAND OF MAUI, in the Hawaiian group, is the 10,000-foot Haleakala, an old volcano considered to be in its last stage of activity. Is it? Or is it just taking one of those long naps? The occurrence of earthquakes on the island suggests that someday it could renew the business under new management.

The Hawaiian natives called this mountain House of the Sun, from a legend about the demi-god Maui, who climbed to the summit of Haleakala, snared the rays of the sun, and forced it to travel more slowly in its course so that his mother, Hina, might have more sunlight each day in which to do her work. When we talk of mythology we are usually thinking of the Greeks and Romans, but the truth is that primitive people everywhere made their first timorous attempts to explain natural wonders by inventing myths.

The great depression in the summit of Haleakala is attributed partly to erosion and partly to glacial work during the Ice Age—even though Maui is but little more than twenty degrees from the equator. Subsequent eruptions have dotted the crater floor with great cinder cones and flooded the area with laval flows, some of which poured down the valleys to the sea. The tallest gaily colored cone, Puu O Maui, rises a thousand feet from the floor.

Sometimes visitors, arriving at the airport, find that thick clouds are obscuring the mountain. These trade-wind clouds drift in through the great Koolau Gap and override the high western rim. Meeting in the center of the crater, they leave the high north rim, Hanakauhi, an island in a sea of vapor. Patience. The clouds will probably blow away. Sometimes in late afternoon an observer standing on the western rim will see his shadow cast against a crater cloud and surrounded by a circular rainbow—an effect similar to the famous "specter of the Brocken" long famous in the Alps of Germany.

No roads lead into the crater, but there are well-marked trails. However,

*Lava pours into the sea. The islands were built just so. Hawaii Volcanoes National Park. [Photo: Robert T. Haugen]*

at this elevation, one must be in the pink of condition to make a one-day trip of it, even on horseback. A wiser plan is to get a permit from a park ranger and stay overnight in one of the crater cabins, each of which has twelve bunks, potable water, a woodburning cookstove with fuel, and kerosene lamps. Reservations are required, naturally.

In the northeast part of the crater, which gets as much as 150 inches of rain in a year and where soil conditions are favorable, there are luxuriant grasses, trees, and ferns, in startling contrast to the lean and hungry appearance of the rest. On the walls and within the crater the rare silversword grows. Its long, narrow leaves gleam like frosted silver, and each plant produces one flower stalk, sometimes six feet high, bearing hundreds of small purple flowers. When the seeds have matured, the plant dies, just as does the agave of the Southwest desert of our mainland. They say that fifty years ago, the silversword covered many acres of the crater floor with transcendent beauty. It was almost exterminated by visitors who thought it would look better growing somewhere else than on the islands of Maui and Hawaii, where, in all the world, it was found native. But under the protection of the National Park Service, this botanical rarity is recovering.

Near Paliku Cabin, the Hawaiian goose, the nene, which had nearly become extinct, has been reintroduced. Among the native birds are the apapane, iiwi, amakihi, pueo (Hawaiian short-eared owl), koae (white-tailed tropic bird), and kolea (American golden plover). The many other birds are species that have been introduced to the island. The only mammals are a native bat and exotic nuisances like wild pigs and goats, mongooses and rats. To migrate naturally from any mainland point to these volcanic isles of the Pacific, mammal forms would have to be hardy sailors indeed.

## 4. CITY OF REFUGE NATIONAL HISTORICAL PARK
### [Hawaii]

THE IDEA OF FLEEING to sanctuary, and thus taking advantage of the fact that a sacred shrine must not be blemished by violence, is almost as ancient as religion itself. Immediately one thinks of Orestes taking refuge from the Furies in the temple of Apollo at Delphi after he had killed his mother to avenge the murder of his father. Or, nearer to us in time, we recall that as late as the reign of James I in England, a person accused of any crime except treason could go to the nearest church or churchyard, be free from arrest there, and upon promising to quit the country from the nearest seaport, receive safe-conduct to the seaport.

The concept of such haven has been universal, but in this City of Refuge at Honaunau, on the largest of the Hawaiian islands, we see today the remains of a sanctuary that was clearly far different from anything else of its kind. Here, on a twenty-acre shelf of lava rock with the ocean front on two sides and a great wall of dry-laid stone on the other two, was an asylum which could accommodate great numbers of men, women, and children, even defeated warriors escaping the hard fate of the loser in ancient island days— extermination, root and branch.

All such sanctuaries have been violated, and no doubt the City of Refuge was no exception, since that would account for the great wall, ten feet high and seventeen feet wide. The city sometimes needed, no doubt, more than the aura of holiness to prevent invasion and vengeance. The thousand-foot-

*Giant ferns. Hawaii Volcanoes National Park. [Photo: W. W. Dunmire]*

*Growing only here, the silversword is the grand monarch of the sunflower family. Haleakala National Park. [Photo: National Park Service]*

long wall dates from the time of Chief Keawe-ku-i-ke-ka'ai, who ruled Kona about A.D. 1550, but such refuges are common to the islands and date from a much earlier period of native existence.

## 5. CRATER LAKE NATIONAL PARK
### [*Oregon*]

FIRST THE LAKE WAS CALLED Deep Blue Lake. Later it was rediscovered and named Blue Lake. Two soldiers from Fort Klamath stumbled upon it, never having heard of it, and christened it Lake Majesty. Finally it became Crater Lake. To me, this final name is the best one. "Deep Blue" does not describe its color. "Blue" does not describe its color. "Majesty" was a reverent

[ 114 ]

attempt to capture the flying perfect with a word. But where the attempt so obviously can never have fulfillment, it is better to accept defeat and resort to the accurate commonplace. It is, certainly, a lake in a crater.

Crater Lake is a thing of the spirit. It must be so, for I have never met anyone who did not express it in one way or another. Long before I ever saw it myself, I heard about it as I sat talking one day in a London club, from an Englishman who had just returned from a round-the-world trip. He was a rich sportsman, especially a dry-fly fisherman. He had been jogging in the Orient, had come over to Puget Sound and fished, and then, before returning to England, had visited Crater Lake. I recall a foolish tinge of jealousy that I, an American, should be learning of this place of beauty from a European. This man said to me: "I have seen beautiful things all over the world. I have never seen anything that touched me so strangely and deeply as Crater Lake. As I sit here, I can still see *that blue*."

The cause of the color of Crater Lake has long been a subject of speculation and inquiry. Some have thought it was due to the reflection of the sky, but it is the same whether the sky is clear or clouded. Then it was suggested that there was something peculiar about the mineral content of the water. Chemical analysis indicated no such thing. A small quantity of the water does not exhibit the color characteristic. The generally accepted theory is that a scattering of light, in this water of such clearness and depth, separates and reflects the blue rays and absorbs those of other colors. I suppose the men of science know. I suppose they have wrested the secret of the purple from the murex. But I recall a saying attributed to a wise man of the sixteenth century: "Blue is not merely a color; it is a mystery."

If the blue of Crater Lake is mysterious, not much less so is the volcanic bowl in which the water rests. There is no peculiarity about the existence of the volcano itself. It is one of many that at a fairly recent period burst into activity in the uplift known as the Cascade Range. There is a line of them stretching from northern California to Canada. Seeing them even from a distance, you have no doubt that Lassen, Shasta, Rainier, St. Helens, Baker, and Adams are the results of repeated outpouring of lava, rocks, and ashes. But something strange happened to Mount Mazama, where Crater Lake nestles, and the best geologists are puzzled.

Mount Mazama is what may be called a "theoretical" mountain. Many cubic miles of what once constituted the conical peak are not there. There is every evidence that they were once there. How high the mountain was is not certain, but it may have been twelve thousand feet above sea level at its highest. If so, it was about the same height as Mount Adams.

Did Mazama suddenly blow its head off? Volcanic peaks have done that very thing. Katmai in Alaska did, and so did Krakatao. But if Mazama did, where is the evidence? There ought to be fragments around the rim of the present crater, and the surrounding country should be well covered with the materials hurled out. They are not found.

The only conceivable explanation is that the top of the mountain collapsed, falling inward and disappearing into the pit, which is now in places almost four thousand feet deep, half of which depth is the lake itself. Vast quantities of pumice lava extend more than eight miles northeast of Mazama. This came from the heart of the volcano, and it is believed that after this eruption the crater poured out rock broth that raced down the sides of the mountain at great speed and traveled thirty-five miles to the south and southwest. If, then, during these violences cracks had appeared in the flanks and base, it is possible that the leakage of incandescent lava into these fractures drew enough material away so that there was no support for the upper part of the cone. This is the best of the theories advanced up to now, and there is much evidence to support it.

The volcano did not die at once. There must have been sufficient activity left to produce the cone called Wizard Island, which rises above the surface of the lake, and there may be other cones that do not come to the surface.

Then comes the question of the existence of the lake within this great pit. Lakes in volcanic craters are known in other places in the world, but they have nothing of the magnitude of this one, nor have any of them appeared under such conditions. It seems to have required a set of factors of exactly the right kind to create and maintain a lake of such dimension which, without inlet or outlet of stream water, would maintain its total volume with only a slight variation throughout the year and across the years. The gain from snow and rainfall and the loss by evaporation and seepage are almost perfectly balanced.

Less than fifty years ago Crater Lake was almost, if not quite, devoid of the aquatic life one expects to exist in a great body of water. It was not until Judge William Gladstone Steel, whose efforts later succeeded in having the park established, had hiked and toted minnows nearly fifty miles from the Rogue River and put them into the lake that fish of any kind have been there. Even then there was no food for them in the mysterious blue water, which lacked even vegetation. The problem was solved by planting freshwater shrimp, and when it was found that these little creatures throve, trout could be introduced. The fishing now is considered by many anglers to be the finest in all the parks.

*From the air we see the whole caldera—the collapsed volcano called Mazama. Crater Lake National Park. [Photo: Delano Photographics]*

There is much else in this lovely place to lure visitors. Of the larger animals there are black bear and Columbian black-tailed deer, as well as mule deer and elk. The smaller animals are abundant, but there are few reptiles because of the high elevation. The golden eagle and the Southern bald eagle have nesting places here, and Llao Rock is the home of falcons. California gulls and Farallon cormorants come over from the ocean.

Virgin forest, mostly of cone-bearing trees, and meadows of wild flowers are on the slopes that ascend to the rim of Crater Lake. During July and August visitors will find beautiful displays of alpine blooms on the road between park headquarters and Rim Village and along the trails on the crater rim. The flowering season is short, so there is a rapid succession of blooms during July and August. Winter sets in early and lingers; in the winter of 1932–3 there were seventy-three feet of snow—feet, not inches. Fifty feet

[ 117 ]

is about average. The suburbanite whose back creaks when he shovels a path from the front door to the street after a snowfall of some eight inches should stop his unreasonable plaints. He is enjoying an open winter.

Despite the snow upon snow, and the snow upon that, Crater Lake National Park is accessible all year, and the slopes are ideal for skiing. It is only necessary for winter visitors to take the usual precautions in motoring in the high Cascade Mountain country.

## 6. LASSEN VOLCANIC NATIONAL PARK
### [*California*]

THE ARRANGEMENTS FOR INTERNMENT of Lassen Peak as a deceased volcano were made back in the time of President Taft, when that chief executive proclaimed two national monuments in the little-known wilderness at the southern end of the Cascade Range in California. One monument was intended to preserve the peak itself, the other to preserve a perfectly formed cinder cone, colorful and symmetrical; and both were in the heart of a country clad with beautiful evergreen forests. The idea was a good one, though at that time only a little group of people had the slightest interest in it, and those were mostly Californians motivated by local interest and pride. In the rest of the country you would have found few with more than a vague notion of the location of the new monuments.

Some people knew that since the white man moved westward to the Pacific there had been volcanic activity in the chain of peaks stretching from Shasta into the state of Washington. In 1843, when Frémont pushed his way across the continent, Mount Baker and Mount St. Helens were both in mild eruption, casting a spray of volcanic dust over the surrounding country. In 1858 the clouds over Baker were seen reddened by activity from the crater. Rainier and Shasta were both known to emit hot vapors from fumaroles on their summits. But the mountain named for Peter Lassen, the Danish emigrant pioneer of Alta California, had, so far as anyone knew, slumbered peacefully so long that it was fit and proper to put up a marker: "Here sleeps . . . once a volcano . . . exact age unknown. Requiescat in pace."

One feature of the landscape might have given the mourners pause. Directly south of Lassen Peak was a basin that hot sulfuric acids had eaten out of solid lava rock. Here were steam vents, hot springs, and mudpots. Visitors to Lassen Volcanic National Park today know the place as Bumpass Hell. It somewhat resembles the thermal areas of Yellowstone National Park. Bumpass, an oldtimer of the region, discovered the basin during a hunting trip. In 1865 he took a Red Bluff editor to see it and cautioned him to step carefully, as the ground was treacherous. So saying, Bumpass broke through the thin crust and plunged his leg into the boiling mud beneath. He was so annoyed, as well as burned, that he forgot to swear. This was remarked as a pioneer phenomenon almost equal to the brilliant coloring of the basin itself. But for years few except the most adventurous climbers or the straggling homesteaders at the base of Lassen ever saw this thermal exhibit, and the mountain slept on.

At five o'clock in the morning on May 30, 1914, Mount Lassen, without the slightest warning in the way of mutterings or twitchings, woke up. The next day the forest supervisor of the area reported to a newspaper at Redding, fifty miles distant: "Mount Lassen is in eruption from a new crater on the north slope close to the summit. The new crater is 25 feet wide, 44 feet long, with deep fissures radiating in all directions. Lava and ashes have been shot up to a depth of a foot to two feet. The new volcano is in eruption today."

For several days the eruptions were heavy, though of short duration. By June 11 the crater had enlarged from about 600 to 1,500 feet, and in the ensuing months ashes and steam rose as high as 20,000 feet above the mountaintop, so that they could be seen all up and down the Sacramento Valley. For nearly a year the new Lassen crater puffed and fretted away, at no time as violent as the eruptions of the Hawaiian and Alaskan volcanoes, but doing very well for an embalmed curiosity. It still had some surprises in store for its first birthday observance.

On the night of May 19, 1915, a party was watching the volcano from the west side of the mountain when they saw a red line appear at the notch in the crater rim. With tremendous explosions, lava spilled through the notch and down the slope for a thousand feet. During that night the snow, which was still deep on the northeast side, was melted and sent a mud torrent rushing down Lost Creek and over the divide into Hat Creek, sweeping everything before it. There was no loss of life because the very few persons who lived in the valleys were warned, but in a few hours the meadowlands on both creeks were an indescribable mass of rocks, logs, uprooted trees, and other debris. In places the river of mud was at least twelve feet deep. Boulders weighing twenty tons were swept for several miles by the slippery torrent, and one of these, ever afterward called the Hot Rock, was said to have sizzled in the surrounding water for a whole day. And still old Lassen had something left to say.

In Lost Creek Valley before the 1915 eruption, there had been an estimated five million feet of primeval forest timber. Three days after the mud tore down into the creek valleys, some minor mudflows took place on the north and west flanks of the mountain. But these were not important. What was important was a sudden terrific blast that came from the crater at a low angle and swept down the northeast flank. The nature of such a blast, which in this case was perhaps like a quick puff from crusted-over soft coal when the stove lid is lifted, can hardly be realized when it comes on such a ferocious and sweeping scale. It was perhaps a little like that which overwhelmed St. Pierre, in Martinique.

The trees on the slopes of Raker Peak went down like rows of corn. They lay uniformly with their tops pointing straight away from the crater and up the hillside. Every tree had its bark on the crater side sand-blasted; trees that were broken off left stumps smoothly rounded and polished, and grains of volcanic sand were driven into the trunks a full inch. The curious thing about this prodigious blast was that no fires were kindled—or at most only one or two were reported—so that the temperature of the crater's breath must have been low. This Devastated Area is now one of the things visitors to Lassen Volcanic come to see. To view anything similar of such recent occurrence is nowhere else possible within the United States proper.

One of the great experiences in Lassen Volcanic is the climb of Cinder Cone, the velvety sides of which make the going slow, but not really difficult. Once at the edge of the crater, you look down upon a painted river of volcanic sand, which stops abruptly against a sheet of helter-skelter lava. To the southwest looms Lassen itself, serene and ermine-cloaked, posing as an innocent mountain again, but possibly harboring thoughts of further mischief later on.

Behind it all is the story of a very ancient volcano from which the Lassen scenery has stemmed. Three miles southwest of Lassen Peak once stood a mighty mountain known as Tehama, whose top towered more than four thousand feet over the present Sulphur Works, in the southwestern corner of the park. A succession of quiet lava flows had built this Tehama mountain. Later it collapsed inward, perhaps as Mazama did to form Crater Lake. Brokeoff Mountain, with its precipitous sheared side, is the largest remnant of this old crater rim.

Lassen Volcanic National Park is pre-eminently the place for people who are in no hurry. It is, truly, a relatively small area, as wilderness parks go.

*About 1980 the volcano may take up unfinished business. Lassen Volcanic National Park. [Photo: William L. Perry]*

But hikers and horseback riders will have the best of it here, and without exertion that would tax the strength of anyone in fairly good physical condition. Lassen Peak itself is not a difficult climb, and, except as a challenge to youth, there is no particular reason for climbing the craggy sections of the western side of the park. The eastern half is the reposeful place for ambling, meditating, and filling the eye with the soft beauty of little gemmy lakes in a setting of evergreen forests. Those who set up camp in one of the fine areas set aside for the purpose and who give themselves plenty of leisure to follow the trails will be as richly rewarded in Lassen as in any of our primeval parks.

We were taught in school to say that nature "abhors a vacuum." She also seems to dread nakedness, though wherever lava has issued forth or sand has blown into great dunes, the process of covering bare spots will be hard and long. Here in Lassen you can see the great clothing arrangements at work. You walk through a forest of luxuriant pines, to come abruptly against a wall of lava rock. From the bare flanks of Cinder Cone you have to go only a short distance to find parklike stands of mature pines growing up through the ash that showered from the crater fifty years ago. The charming little lakes are after all but intruding jewels set in bars of slag that came hurtling out of Vulcan's forge. The evidence of violence is at hand everywhere in Lassen, but you step aside no great distance into soothing softness.

Fishing is excellent in Lassen. The rainbow trout is the most abundant, but there are also Loch Leven and Eastern brook trout. Down at the hot pools of Devil's Kitchen it is said that you can catch a trout from the nearby mountain stream and, without removing it from the hook or moving far, toss it into the natural pot and cook it. You *can* do so, but I do not advise such blasphemy. *Boiled* brook trout! Oh, no!

As the snow melts in spring and early summer, Lassen Peak Road is cleared and skiers are able to follow the snowline to the road summit. At this time, cross-country skiing is most popular. The timber-free slopes of the high country are ideal for the sport.

## 7. HOT SPRINGS NATIONAL PARK
### [*Arkansas*]

A BELIEF IN THE THERAPEUTIC VALUE of hot springs is very ancient. It will never be known, I suppose, just where lies the borderline between the curative powers of the waters and the delightful social experience of exchanging symptoms and other personal history with a similarly minded group.

*Eruption of Lassen Peak, 1915. Lassen Volcanic National Park.* [*Photo: R. I. Meyers, copyright by B. F. Loomis*]

In England for more than a century a large segment of "society" was built up around the famous town of Bath and its thermal springs. Many a sober merchant overworked diligently to the end that he might give his wife and family the distinction of being seen for two weeks among the aggregation that "took the waters."

But our American Indians believed in the magic of hot springs, too, and there are plenty of legends to the effect that various tribes battled over the undisputed use of certain thermal localities. Among these places was undoubtedly the present Hot Springs of Arkansas, the oldest reservation set aside by act of Congress for the perpetual use and enjoyment of the people, with freedom from exploitation. So, in a sense, it may be called truly the first national park. The Indian legend continues to the effect that after warring for some years over the possession of the forty-seven springs grouped at the base of Hot Springs Mountain the tribes took a large view of the question and decided that the Great Spirit had meant the benefits for all the sick. I see no advantage in being skeptical about this, unless one is a specialist in Indian manners and customs.

Hot Springs National Park contains about a thousand acres in the region of the Ouachita Mountains of Arkansas. The climate is unusually equable, with mild winters and summers that are very tolerable owing to the low humidity. The slopes and crests of the park are traversed by excellent roadways, and there are miles of forest trails, bridlepaths, and footpaths.

One does not need to be ill to enjoy Hot Springs. It is a restful place, and if one is merely in a run-down condition, where nature needs only a bit of the feeling of partnership, one can sit on the hotel porch and consider the words of Lucretius, a poet who was very far from being cynical:

> Tis sweet when tempests roar upon the sea
> To watch from land another's deep distress
> Amongst the waves—his toil and misery:
> Not that his sorrow makes our happiness,
> But that some sweetness there must ever be
> Watching what sorrows we do not possess.

This graceful translation is W. H. Mallock's.

The government wishes it to be generally understood that while baths can be taken, on permit, at any of the bathhouses receiving water from the hot springs of the park, it is recommended that the advice of a physician be procured. The waters are not beneficial in all diseases, and the ailing are urged not to diagnose their own cases and prescribe for themselves, the principle being the same as that one often mentioned in legal cases: that he who acts as his own lawyer has a fool for a client.

## 8. PLATT NATIONAL PARK
### [Oklahoma]

NEAR THE CITY of Sulphur in southern Oklahoma is a pleasant little national park among gently rolling hills, well wooded, with a number of streams, springs, waterfalls, and cascades. This is Platt, named for a Senator Orvill H. Platt of Connecticut, who was distinguished for his interest in the Indians. Platt National Park is within the holdings of the Chickasaw Nation of the old Indian Territory.

I am in some doubt about the category in which Platt should be placed. In a way, this is a penalty I have to pay for dividing my book into arbitrary groups dealing with certain major characteristics. This area has many springs, some of sulphur and some of bromide; but they are cold springs. A hot spring falls naturally into the field of volcanism. Seemingly a cold spring does not. After some mental anguish over this point, I have evolved the pleasant theory that perhaps these springs were once hot, but the underlying fires have gone out. I do not invite any correspondence on this, especially from geologists. Can we not rely, once in a while, on pure intuition?

While the waters of the springs are for the use of all visitors, they should be taken extensively only on the advice of a competent physician. The National Park Service maintains and protects the waters according to the best possible standards, but there are no provisions in the park or in the city of Sulphur for free consultation on treatment of diseases.

Pavilion Spring, Bromide Spring, and Medicine Spring are among the best-known of the mineral waters. These springs are in the valleys along Travertine and Rock Creeks. In the eastern end of the park, along Travertine Creek, are two natural springs that together flow more than five million gallons of pure water a day. It is said that these springs, named Buffalo and Antelope, were so called because of the animal herds that formerly came there to drink.

Campgrounds, with water, lights, and other facilities, are maintained at three places in the park. There are also several attractive picnic sites, two of them capable of accommodating large parties. Within the park is a complete circuit drive of eight miles, and there are horseback trails. Saddle horses are readily available nearby.

## 9. LAVA BEDS NATIONAL MONUMENT
### [*California*]

A RAGGED BAND of Modoc Indians, never more than seventy-one in fighting strength, and without benefit of warpaint and feathers, managed to maintain a campaign against the U.S. Army for six months, during which the white men suffered two costly defeats. This was in 1872–3, in the northeastern corner of California, near the Oregon border. It was the same old story: the Indians did not want to be relegated to a reservation—and the Modocs were particularly unwilling because they were to share it with their hereditary foes, the Klamaths. So Lava Beds is historic grounds in the development of the West.

But that was not the basic purpose for the proclamation setting aside the bewildering area for preservation. This national monument presents another exhibit of the strange ways of volcanoes. And the reason why a small force of Indians was able to cope with large numbers of their enemy is the same reason why the region so well deserved to come into the National Park System. Those natural rock trenches and caves from which bullets could come so unexpectedly, those forts which did not have to be built, that wild, broken terrain where one armed man could hold off a dozen—all these had gushed and belched from flaming volcanoes centuries before. For the Indians this was a ready-made Maginot Line.

From a distance Lava Beds looks like fairly level country. The whole region is high. Symmetrical cinder cones dot the landscape, and if you come from the southwest you look toward the towering precipices that mark the front of the great Columbia River lava flow. Once you are in the monument, the scene is entirely changed. Most of the fantastic devices of flowing molten rock are to be seen here. Chasms a hundred feet deep are walled by contorted masses of lava, which as it cooled or was thrust forward by an incandescent stream pouring from behind twisted itself into every conceivable shape. Where fountains of gas-inflated lava once played like those of Kilauea in Hawaii, there are now deep "chimneys." One of these, on the main road northwest of Indian Well, is three feet in diameter and more than a hundred feet deep.

Some of the lava flowed like thick, frothy molasses from deep cracks in the earth crust. The surface hardened, but the interior continued to flow, so that when the drainage was complete, horizontal tubes were formed. Sometimes the surface of these tubes fell in and they became serpentine trenches, with bridges marking places wherever the roof remained.

After the lava tubes drained, the space between the fiery floor and the roof filled with hot gases, which remelted and glazed the ceilings and side walls with drip-pendants of many colors. Along the main road, which traverses the monument, are many large caves. At Captain Jack's Cave, named for the Modoc Indian leader, the road crosses a natural bridge of such height that from a distance an automobile on the bridge seems to be suspended in air.

Skull Cave has three levels. The roof, rising seventy-five feet above the floor, is beautifully domed. The lower story is a river of solid ice. Many skulls of bighorn and pronghorn were found here, indicating occupancy by Indians of long ago. They killed their game on the surface and took it downstairs to the freezer.

But there are no bighorn in Lava Beds now. Their trails are still visible, but before the monument was established, domestic sheep and cattle claimed the little forage that existed. During a snowy winter, however, many Rocky Mountain mule deer come to Lava Beds from the neighboring high country.

## 10. CRATERS OF THE MOON NATIONAL MONUMENT
### [Idaho]

IF THERE WERE rocket excursions to the moon (and who says there may not be?) I would not buy a ticket, even if the return trip were guaranteed. Admittedly, it would be exciting, but it would be too depressing. At less expense, and with much more pleasure, I can visit Craters of the Moon National Monument in Idaho, not far from the town of Arco, and see much of what the moon has to offer; and that same night I can get back among sweet forests and verdure such as the moon never had. The moon has an excessive supply of volcanic wreckage. The choice specimens of such hot riot included in the Park System are just about enough: a leaven sufficient to give us an understanding of those prodigious earth forces.

Some national park volcanic areas show certain features of the vagaries of eruptive work, some show other effects; Craters of the Moon has nearly everything. It is all dead now, this field of tumult which came blasting out of the Great Rift—that series of fissures in the earth crust which constituted a zone of weakness allowing the incandescent dough to well up from the depths. But what a scene of activity it must have been a thousand years ago, or even five hundred years ago, when it was sputtering out! Lava cones, cinder cones, spatter cones, and bombs! Not all volcanoes manufacture bombs. These did. Exploding lavas sent big and little blobs of magma high into the air—high enough so that some of the bombs took a streamline teardrop shape on the way down and hardened with slender tails. It rained stone pollywogs at intervals. Other bombs curiously resemble bread crusts, still others are ribbonlike.

*Overleaf: Where lava swirled over the landscape and created grotesque forms. Geologically speaking, these lava flows are recent. Craters of the Moon National Monument. [Photos: Franz Lipp]*

The lava sheets flowed down upon forests, felled the trees, and encased them. The heat consumed the wood, but the moisture of the trees had coolness enough so that the lava hardened quickly. Here are the molds that resulted. They are perfect casts of the trunks and even the roots of the overthrown trees.

It is a scene of desolation, if you like; but it is beautiful in its terrible way. If you look closely at the pahoehoe lava—the kind that has a ropy, billowy quality—you will see that some of it, notably the Blue Dragon, shows an iridescent glow in the sunlight. The curves of the billows are graceful. It flowed like a river, this lava, and in places it shows low falls such as you see in a sluggish, wide river where the water has met a tough rock dike across its path.

Then, too, vegetation has come in, even in the relatively short period since the ground was smoking. Already the limber pines and aspens and chokecherries are of fair size, and shrubs spring from the cracks where soil has accumulated.

A loop road southward along a portion of the Great Rift provides access to many points of interest. There is adequate camping space in the monument, and a limited number of tourist cabins, with provision for meal service, during the season.

## 11. Sunset Crater and Wupatki National Monuments
### [*Arizona*]

It may have been just about the time that the Normans, under William, invaded England and conquered it that Sunset Crater began pouring out lava and cinders upon the country around. As you stand at the foot of this thousand-foot cinder cone, its summit tinted with red and orange, you can imagine the terror of the Indians who lived in the vicinity. You can see the little groups of farmers and their wives and children hastily grasping whatever of their possessions came to hand and leaving their pit houses to be buried under the ashes that rained upon their heads as they fled. The imagination does not have to be stretched in creating this picture, for Sunset happens to be one volcano, of the many in the Southwest, where eruption has been very accurately dated, by a combination of tree-ring comparisons using the beams from the buried houses and archaeological evidences. It is in north-central Arizona, and is part of the great San Francisco Mountain volcano field, the highest peak of which, Humphreys Peak, rises 12,600 feet.

# Sunset Crater and Wupatki National Monuments

The prehistoric people were driven away by the firemountain, but they must have remained somewhere in the general vicinity, for it is certain that they came back. What was more natural? It had been home. They had been happy there; they had raised their families there. They felt no differently from modern Italians when Vesuvius and Etna have calmed down after a terrible outburst destroying houses, vineyards, and orchards; soon they are back again with renewed confidence. And so these prehistoric people came timidly back after the volcano seemed tired and the lava had cooled. They discovered that all was not on the debit side; the very ashes and cinders that had buried their homes had actually improved the lands they had farmed. Once they could raise crops only in favored little pockets that held moisture. Now the layer of ashes permitted rain and snow to soak into the soil and be held there. Now they could produce good crops of corn and beans almost anywhere.

Somebody has said very aptly that this started a prehistoric land rush.

*Scene of a prehistoric "land rush." Sunset Crater National Monument. [Photo: Edgar P. Bailey]*

The ancient grapevine telegraph spread the news that volcanoes were not such bad demons after all. Within a few years after the eruption as many as four thousand Indians were occupying the fields covered by ash. New customs and new arts were introduced as strangers came from long distances to settle.

But again Fortune turned her head. The same winds that had whipped the ashes from the crater of Sunset and spread it around as a mulch now began to blow it away. First from the higher places, then from the level lands, the light cover began to disappear. The farmers were back where they had started; and there were many more of them now, dependent on the crops. In the end, the coyote howled mournfully at night on the mountainside, and there was nobody to hear him.

For years after Sunset became harmless, there were still hot springs and vapors rising from the crater vents. It was these that, by the deposit of minerals, painted the crater rim with the glowing colors that suggested the mountain's name.

At the height of their most flourishing period, the villages that clustered in the cinder-blanketed area of eight hundred square miles developed a culture which is called Wupatki, the Hopi word for "tall house." From an original small pueblo this one grew to a habitation of more than a hundred rooms, capable of housing as many as three hundred persons.

In the valley below the Wupatki village was a "ball court" of stone masonry. What kind of a game was it? We can only conjecture. Was it purely a physical recreation, the pleasant use of leisure, or was there a religious element, as there was in the Olympic games of the early Greeks? Within the monument are about eight hundred ruins; notably, besides Wupatki, those of the Citadel, Lomaki, and Wukoki and the less accessible ruin of Crack-in-the-Rock near the Little Colorado River.

## 12. DEVILS TOWER NATIONAL MONUMENT
### [*Wyoming*]

THOSE WHO HAVE DRIVEN through the Black Hills to Yellowstone National Park by way of Spearfish and Sundance must have caught glimpses from the highway of a strange-looking peak rising in lonely majesty from the rolling ground along the Belle Fourche River. If they were in too much of a hurry to ask about this mountain and to discover that its significance in the American scene is so great that it was the first national monument to be established, their haste cost them a fine experience. For this fluted stone

*The Sioux called it "Grizzly Bear's Lodge." Devils Tower National Monument.*
*[Photo: Franz Lipp]*

column, rising 1,280 feet above the bed of the Belle Fourche and 865 feet above its apparent base on the hilltop, is a piece of modernistic volcanic sculpture. And it is a geological mystery.

The Sioux Indians called the tower Mateo Tepee ("Grizzly Bear's Lodge") and had a legend that the columns of the rock were the result of clawmarks of a grizzly bear that tried to climb the sheer wall to get at some Indians on the top. He was a larger bear than ordinary. The Sioux explanation does not satisfy the geologist. But neither does his own. For the tower could have been the lava neck of an old volcano, the walls of which have been weathered away; or it could have been part of a great sheet of molten rock that found its way between layers of other rock—what is called a "sill." But either way, it has to be explained how the surrounding material was disposed of so easily.

The diameter of the tower at its base, where it is surrounded by rock fragments—fallen bits of the fluting—is about a thousand feet. The flat top of the tower is about an acre and a half, on which there are not only grasses and shrubs but also mice, pack rats, and chipmunks, who must have climbed up in past days and found the place agreeable enough so that they never came down.

In the mythology of the ancient Greeks, there were two brothers, Prometheus and Epimetheus. Prometheus, as his name implies, did his thinking first, and then acted. His quarrel with Jupiter was disastrous for him, but at least he went into the venture with his eyes open. It was a calculated risk. Epimetheus was the other sort: he acted first and did his thinking afterward. He was the counterpart of the modern snagwit who sits out on a limb and saws it off between himself and the tree trunk. On his way down, it occurs to him that he should have had a plan. In practical affairs epimetheans are more deadly, to themselves and others, than smallpox.

A young parachutist, some years ago, decided to make a landing on top of Devils Tower. He made a very good landing. He then began to think of going down. He was surprised when he walked around the edge of that acre and a half and found no flight of stairs. It went straight down, like the side of the Washington Monument, so far as he could see. Actually, the tower had once been conquered by an expert who took advantage of breaks in the flutings for footholds. It had been climbed by a promethean—the kind of alpinist who takes calculated risks. Such a man may have an accident, but he tries to provide against all the contingencies.

The parachutist spent six days and five nights—thinking—on top of the tower, and was then rescued by a party that included National Park Service men and was led by the very man who had climbed the mountain before.

For most of us, Devils Tower will be much more interesting viewed from the base. There is a fine trail all around it, and a little museum at headquarters, where the volcanic mystery is framed clearly and the natural and the human history of the region are happily pictured.

## 13. Capulin Mountain National Monument
### [New Mexico]

From the top of Capulin Mountain, in the northeastern corner of New Mexico, visitors may look into four other states: Colorado, Kansas, Texas, and Oklahoma. Unusual as this experience is, it is only an incident of political geography. The real attraction is the picturesque mountain itself, an imposing example of an extinct volcano with a crater whose symmetry is almost perfectly preserved. The latter fact indicates that, as geologic time goes, the volcano was active at no very distant date. The high angles of the slopes of the mountain also attest this conclusion.

Possibly Capulin came into action during the last period of wild volcanic outbursts in western North and South America. All around it can be seen other fire-mountain peaks. Northwest of it are mesas topped with black lava. Perhaps a series of lava flows at long intervals overspread much of this country, followed by a final effort in which Capulin, among other volcanoes, began to hurl cinders and rocks. Rising from a base of already high land, the peak is about eight hundred feet high; but it was its regular form that made it a landmark, like the volcanic Spanish Peaks back of Trinidad, Colorado, eagerly sought by the eyes of the immigrant trains following both branches of the old Santa Fe Trail.

Capulin not only is beautiful in its form, but, owing to its general elevation above sea level, is clothed with lush grassland and with a forest of pine and juniper. Sometimes one may see the golden eagle hovering over the peak.

Nearby is the famous Folsom site—the spot where in 1926 a discovery was made that revolutionized the notions of the length of time humans have been on our land. Rather, it might be said that it was an additional discovery, but it was so well authenticated that it assumed major importance.

A field party from the Colorado Museum of Natural History, while excavating the fossil bones of bison, found a finely chipped stone lancepoint. This aroused the greatest interest; but on the strength of one such find, conclusions were naturally reserved. Then four more similar points were found, always, as it looked, associated closely with the bison bones. In all, nineteen of these well-formed lance-points have been discovered, and it is now reasonably supposed that the owners of the weapons killed some of the extinct bison, particularly since every one of the animal skeletons lacks the tailbone. It would seem that the ancient hunters skinned their prey and "took the tail with the hide," literally.

Capulin is accessible all through the year except when, rarely, the road to the summit may be blocked by a heavy snow. The road spirals around the cinder cone, and ends at a parking area on the western side of the crater. Near the western base there is a picnic ground, but water and supplies are not available in the monument. The towns of Capulin and Folsom, however, are nearby.

# [ III ]

# *Discipline of the Desert*

*I HAVE CROSSED wide tracts of desert, and I count the hours of undisturbed musing, of still possession of Nature unbroken by sound, and of beneficent repose that I have enjoyed there as among the happiest of my life.*

—GEORG EBERS

## 1. BIG BEND NATIONAL PARK
### [*Texas*]

MEMORIES OF OUR LAST FRONTIER, where the Rio Grande makes its big vagrant swing, dallying with the compass, wondering which way to go.

I remember the sweet, clear days in the basin of the Chisos Mountains in the latter part of May, when the agaves—or century plants, if you must call them so—came into their prodigious bloom. Outside the mountain circle the desert was already growing hot, but here, at the foot of Casa Grande, in the shade of a weeping juniper, no human lot could have been more fortunate than mine.

A miracle was taking place—a miracle worth coming thousands of miles to see. For those agaves, which had lived their term of eighteen or twenty or twenty-five years on these slopes of crumbled igneous rock, were now ready to flower, to seed, and to depart. Without warning, except perhaps to skilled botanists, a great stalk overnight begins to thrust up from the tightly clasped heart of the fleshy leaves. From that moment until the last petals have fallen, the agave is a marvel of purposeful intensity. The rate of growth of that stalk, which may measure half a foot in diameter at the base, is almost unbelievable, in a climate where the rainfall is so niggardly.

But the agave is reckless of consequences. Like a miser who has hoarded,

---

*The yucca struggles for survival against the shifting sands. White Sands National Monument. [Photo: Fritz Henle]*

skimped, haggled, and starved and then in a burst of profligacy enjoys one great moment of life, the agave goes to its end proudly and grandly. For this is the bloom of death. Almost before the seeds have rattled down, to be snatched by furry animals and birds before they have time to sprout, the leaves that were so plump and fresh in their smooth green with just a touch of blue sky in the color have turned ashen and then yellow and then sere. *Morituri salutamus!* And what an unforgettable salute when the sides of the Chisos, all the way up from Green Gulch to the foot of the bare rock faces of Casa Grande, Ward, Pulliam, and Emory, are flying the standards of the amaryllis family! Look at them from the basin and you seem to see a host of deployed giants seeking to take the heights by storm.

I would not suggest that these Big Bend agaves are finer than those of Mexico or some other place, but if you go down into that wild frontier in the loop of the Rio Grande—into this national park which was given by the people of Texas to the nation—you will find *Agave scabra* something to feast the eyes upon. Perhaps it will not be the season of bloom when you are there. No matter; the plant at any time is a triumph of symmetry. Even the stiletto that is carried on the end of each leaf, if you will examine it, is as lovely a piece of burnished carbon as ever was turned on nature's lathe. On many of the younger leaves there is a decorative motif, like tiny fingerprints, along the margin.

There is a little sister of the century plant, called the lechuguilla, which all across this rocky soil contends with the other desert plants. It is from the fibers of this plant that the native Mexicans weave ropes and harness and halters, saddlebags, and a hundred other useful things. These and the sotol and the wild pineapple and the creosote bush; the ocotillo and the allthorn; tarweed and cactuses and Mormon tea—these give the answer to the impertinence of those who ask: "What can possibly live in such a desert?" They say: "*We* do. And if you keep your domestic animals off our necks, we will settle, one day, amongst ourselves, we and the wild animals, where each of us shall live." These brave, self-reliant green things I remember.

I remember the full moon rising over Casa Grande, and the sun setting in a blaze at the Window. For there is one break in this mass of dissected lava, forming a great bowl, the very bottom of which is the basin. Looking toward the west, out across Burro Mesa and into Old Mexico, there is a V-shaped opening, with a vedette on the left, guarding the entrance. This is the Win-

*Across the desert expanse the Chisos Mountains rise, ghostlike. Big Bend National Park. [Photo: M. Woodbridge Williams]*

dow. The whole mountain mass rises abruptly from a peneplain, and when you are in the basin you are at an elevation of five thousand feet. The highest peak on the rim of the bowl, Mount Emory, is nearly eight thousand. Emory was the peak that the members of the boundary-survey party in 1852 "long and anxiously watched." It was their beacon—this and the Boquillas Finger, which sticks up above the long regular line of the Sierra del Carmen, on the east side of the park.

One winter morning I looked up at Casa Grande and Toll Mountain. From where I stood there is an apparent cleft between them, and I saw a huge waterfall—a thousand Yosemites—pouring down from that cleft. It was fog. A great bank of it had crept up the eastern side of the Chisos, found a path, and was pouring down in a cascading stream into the bowl. I remember this; and I remember coming down one afternoon through Persimmon Gap and reaching that point on the road from Marathon where the Chisos suddenly comes into view. And I saw then the Chisos rising out of a mist like a medieval walled city. You would have said it was the Cité of Carcassonne in Provence.

What simple incidents thrill us in the desert! A few weeks before, I had been standing at the corner of Broadway and 42nd Street, in Manhattan, with a mind thoroughly confused at what was going on in the world. I could make nothing of it. Whatever the mad scramble meant, I, at least, was being jostled out of the orbit. Now, in the desert, in the lovely basin of the Chisos, things began to make sense again. I remember that. And I remember what complete sense the herd of flagtail deer made. When I drove back to the cabin, I frequently met them—fifty or more—browsing quietly not far from the road. One of them had only three legs. They gazed at me with that quizzical expression from behind their black burglar masks, and then, not seeming frightened, but just for the lark of it, scampered up the mountainside, with three-legs always well to the fore. They stopped for a while, looked at me again, and then scampered a little farther up.

I remember those merry flagtails, and I remember harvesting some of the curious seeds of the mountain mahogany, which have a spiral feathery tail. The barbed seed vessels, when ripe, are blown along the ground and finally gyrate into the earth at some favorable spot. I planted some of them, to save them the trouble of so much gyrating. I wonder if any of them came up. If you go down there—or *when* you go down—please look for them, will you? I can give you the exact location. Anyway, it is pleasant to remember something of so little utility and so much good will.

Dog Canyon, too; and a little canyon that I called Puppy Canyon, be-

*The Rio Grande finds its way through these narrow slits. Big Bend National Park.*
*[Photo: M. Woodbridge Williams]*

cause it presents a geological picture you do not often see—a canyon that is just in the formative stage. Dagger Flat, where the yuccas have found a condition absolutely to their taste; and here the Giant Dagger, which will be the object of a favorite pilgrimage for visitors to the park, outdoes in size and magnificence all the other yuccas of the region. There are at least five species in all to be found there.

I remember—and who could forget?—the mouth of Santa Elena Canyon, that dark, winding slit in the Mesa de Anguila, a tilted fault-block of hard limestone through which the Rio Grande has cut a narrow channel with precipitous walls. The sheerness of the drop of Santa Elena Canyon from rim to river has scarcely any equal in the topography of the West. For nearly ten miles the river has been flowing through this great chasm. Suddenly, near where Terlingua Creek flows in, it emerges into full daylight, making a charming picnic spot, and an easily accessible one for fishermen. For there are big fish here in the Rio Grande.

Santa Elena is one of the three great canyons through which the Rio Grande has carved its way. The others are Mariscal and Boquillas. I learned from the notes of Dr. Parry, botanist with the boundary survey, that they ran the Mariscal in India-rubber boats, "one of which was capsized in shooting a sharp rapid." Santa Elena and Boquillas canyons they left alone, wisely enough, for they were on important business, not men out for adventure. All the canyons have been successfully navigated, but it is not a feat recommended for the average person.

We linger awhile at the mouth of beautiful Santa Elena, to loll under an alamo and hark back to the day in late July 1860 when a body of tired, ragged, discouraged soldiers, led by a shavetail named Echols, came down the creek now called Terlingua and gazed in wonder at the mouth of the canyon. It was a strange sight. Thirty men, some jaded packmules, and twenty camels! The native wildlife of the district must have goggled at the sight of camels in Big Bend. The camels, said Echols, had done nobly. They had stood the journey from Camp Hudson better than the mules; better even than the men. On July 3 the whole command had been in imminent danger of death from thirst; water was found on July 4, and that was a day of celebration. But all the hardships were forgotten when at last the soldiers came out upon the river and saw its rush-covered bottom lands and the trees along its banks.

It was Jefferson Davis's idea, when he was Secretary of War, to use camels for army transport across the deserts of the West. They never had a real chance to prove themselves. First the Civil War intervened. Then the transcontinental railroads pushed across the country. The last of the camels were turned loose upon the desert and finally disappeared.

The picturesque little quicksilver-mining town of Terlingua lies just outside the boundaries of Big Bend National Park. Terlingua—what does the name mean? We used to wonder about it, among the things we talked over, around a fire on a winter's night in the Bend. Some thought it meant "three languages." But what three languages could they have been? The name is not Spanish, as presently spelled. Lieutenant Echols called the creek

*Santa Elena Canyon releases its hold on the Rio Grande. Big Bend National Park.* [*Photo: M. Woodbridge Williams*]

Lates Lengua, which was the way he caught it from his guide. Was it really Las Tres Lenguas, which might mean three strips of land, as, for instance, the sand-bar tongues in a creek delta? Who cares? But it is so pleasant to speculate about unimportant matters! It is one of the enjoyments of the desert.

We must be moving down the river.

I remember Mondays at the little post office and store at Hot Springs. Monday was mail day. The nearest railroad station is at Marathon, and the postman drove the hundred miles down once a week, stopped over in Hot Springs, and went back on Tuesday. Mrs. Margaret Smith, a frontier woman who could face a cougar with equanimity, kept the store and with her son and daughter maintained a rendezvous for the scanty population in the south end of the area, as well as for the straggling denizens on the other side of the river. Monday was a great day for these latter folk. The rules were relaxed and they could come across if they had legitimate trading affairs or were expecting letters—or for no particular reason, probably, if they were known to the border men as trustworthy. For you must know that between the Rio Grande at this point and any town or city of Old Mexico is a vast expanse of land about which the average Mexican knows as little as we know of Tierra del Fuego. The Mexican border patrolmen used to come across on a Monday to get their paychecks from the U. S. Treasury, and perhaps they still do. The mail from Mexico City came round by way of Laredo or some other border station, then over to Marathon, and so down into the Bend. *That* is frontier!

For years hopeful invalids had come from other places in Texas to soak in the hot springs along the riverside. I once found a man immersed in one of these tubs. I asked him if he thought the waters did him any good. He replied that he didn't think so, but they *might*, and it gave him a chance to get away from home for a few days.

I remember footing it along an exposure of gray-white limestone where the living-rock grows. The living-rock is a cactus, and one of the queerest of the whole great family. In the crevices of this limestone it takes root. The limestone is full of fissures. So the cactus decides that it, too, will be full of fissures. The cactus resembles the rock, and the rock resembles the cactus, and I assure you you can be looking directly at one of these plants and never see it at all, so perfect is this imitation.

*Sometimes, over Casa Grande, the clouds pour like a waterfall. Big Bend National Park. [Photo: M. Woodbridge Williams]*

I remember the lime-rock hillside, not far from Hot Springs, where the resurrection plant grows. Here is a strange little fernlike growth that has learned to tailor its suit according to the amount of material on hand. One day you pass by and there is nothing on the hillside but what appears to be dried-up herbage; then comes one of the grudging rains of the desert. Two days later you pass the spot again, and the hillside is green and flourishing. A week later all may be sere once more. But the little plant can sit out the longest drought.

A few years ago we used to wonder if the pronghorn could ever return to its old home in Big Bend. Great numbers of pronghorn formerly lived in this region, feeding on the good herbs, especially the tobosa grass of Tobosa Flat and along the Tornillo creekbed. But the hunters shot them out, and a few that escaped the gun were no match for the sheep and goats and for the sheet erosion, which was partly natural and partly due to the trampling of the "hoofed locusts," as John Muir called sheep. If sheep deserve this harsh epithet, what shall we say of goats? Goats are long-haired Japanese beetles, at the very least. Anyone who has wandered around the Basin of the Chisos and seen the mountain-mahogany and the Apache plume literally torn to pieces by these terrific foragers can well believe that a few goats on the island of St. Helena, in a few years, converted a forest to a tangle of inedible sedge grass.

And, finally, I remember the way night comes to the Big Bend desert. You arrive somewhere along the Tornillo Wash late in the afternoon and busy yourself with the thousand things to do and see. You are about south of massy Chisos, and to the eastward you look, on your far left, at the Dead Horse Range, and in front of you at the regular line and banded cliffs of the Sierra del Carmen. Seemingly a part of the Carmen range, but really having nothing in common with it, is the towering Fronteriza—in Old Mexico. And what appears to be a volcanic peak—Picotena, I think it is called —is also on the alien side of the Rio Grande.

Your own shadow begins to lengthen. The dark line slowly crosses the wash, deepens the color of the vanadium yellow on the low cliffs on the eastern side, and begins to approach the foot of the Carmens. Those bands of gray and reddish yellows and brown, as seen in the full sunlight, now begin to change. First a pink flush suffuses the whole escarpment; the grays take on the tone of magenta, the reds deepen, and there seems to be a violet haze coming over all. It deepens to a purple as you watch. The lower part of the Carmen is turning a velvety black, but on top the last rays of the sun set up a riot of colors for just the flicker of a minute—and night settles down.

Creosote bushes and candelillas, etched so sharply against the yellow sands a few minutes ago, now soften into vague blurs and withdraw. It is time to be going. But you go with a rested mind and a sort of renewal of faith.

Thus I remember a few things about Big Bend, and if I have here indulged myself with a little excess of the personal pronoun, it has not been to celebrate myself, believe me. I wanted to convey the general notion that in these national parks there are so many gentle, refreshing, unspectacular experiences of eye and soul, which, taken home, are a treasury from which memories can be withdrawn, long afterward, with delight. For these recollections, though dimmed, can always be rekindled, just as I am doing now— I, who am writing these words thousands of miles from the desert and looking out a window upon a landscape so different: pines, oaks, sugar maples, and beeches and the lush tall grasses of an Eastern spring.

The national parks are operated for profit—this kind of profit.

## 2. DEATH VALLEY NATIONAL MONUMENT
[*California–Nevada*]

WHEN DEATH VALLEY, with its surrounding mountains, was proclaimed a national monument in 1933, there must have been great wonderment on the part of those who knew the region only by hearsay. Why set aside a strip of wilderness notorious for undrinkable water, uncrossable bog, billows of drifting sand, and the bleached bones of blasted hopes? If the idea was to preserve the memories of the ill-advised emigrants who suffered and died there in the great trek of '49, why not just fence off a piece and call it a national cemetery?

Fortunately, those who knew the real value of this strange page of American geography were able to have it set aside and to save it from any further commercial exploitation. For if you consider its winter climate alone, the future of Death Valley was assured. From October until May the weather conditions are as nearly ideal as nature is willing to provide. Imagine a year with 351 clear days! This, to be sure, was an exceptional year, but the average annual rainfall is slightly less than one and a half inches. *That* is true desert.

This rugged area of nearly two million acres, which lies east of the Sierra in California along the southwestern Nevada boundary, is a bundle of contradictions. Almost anything you would guess about it is either not true or only partially true. It is one of the driest spots in the United States, yet it is rather well supplied with water—though you may not like the taste of all the water. More than five hundred square miles of the valley are below the level of the Pacific Ocean, and the lowest spot, at Badwater, is 280 feet below sea level; yet not far from that very depression towers Telescope Peak, 11,325 feet above the valley floor. Telescope is therefore higher above its immediate surroundings than any other mountain in the conterminous United States—higher in this relation than Mount Whitney. The aridity would seem to forbid the existence of any considerable life of any sort; yet the fact is that not only is animal life abundant, but there is plenty of plantlife too; and under exactly the right conditions, which occur at irregular intervals, the parched soil comes to life and mantles itself with such beauty that the mass blooming will one day be an event to be teletyped over the country by the press associations.

This desert bloom occurs on the alluvial fans, in the dry washes, and in the canyons. No one can predict the flowering with certainty. The intervals recorded are somewhere between five and ten years—there was a mass blooming in 1935, again in 1940, and in 1947. In a brief period the annual plants must produce their seeds and cast them where they will lie dormant till some favorable time of moisture. The seeds not only retain their vitality, but even tend to produce too many plants in some years. A botanist, observing the crowding plants near Daylight Pass, noted that every plant developed at least one flower spike, even if it was reduced to only a single flower, and even if there were only two resulting seeds—a beautiful example in the desert of the provision for the survival of the species!

Nearly three hundred feet below the surface of the ocean you would expect there should be fish. Very well; there are. And they are salt-water fish, too; at least, they belong to an order that lives in both fresh and salt water. Desert sardines, they are called, and they are found in Salt Creek and Saratoga Springs. Are these minnows survivors fom a period, perhaps of glacial time, when the drainage of the region was altogether different and a fish could be cool and composed on a summer day? There are those who think so; and anyway, their presence here is something that needs explaining.

Let us get the overall picture of this extraordinary sink and its forbidding mountain barriers. The valley is boxed, east and west, by precipitous slopes —the Amargosa Range on the Nevada side, and the Panamints on the other. From Dante's View or Zabriskie Point, on a day when the haze permits, the High Sierra can be seen. Some optimists have believed they could make out Mount Whitney, but there is a frailty that leads folks to see what they wish to see. Certainly, so far as low humidity may help, this is the ideal place to look long distances. From a perch on the Panamints it seems impossible that the valley floor is seven thousand feet or more below the viewer. It is almost touchable with the finger.

The geologists are chary about coming to conclusions about the creation of the deep sump. One thing is certain: it was not eroded like the Grand Canyon. There is no sign of the work of glaciers. To some degree the most ancient history of the region follows the general sequence of changes that took place in the Southwest—the thrusting up and planing down, the advent of oceans, with marine life, the raging of volcanic action, and the creation of limestones and sandstones from sediments of torn-down mountains. But at some point in the dim past—yet a past nearer to our own little wafer of time—the forces that created Death Valley worked the effect we see today. Was it a stupendous folding of the earth crust that left the valley at this sunken point? Or was there a vast block that dropped down between two great fractures of the earth crust? Now that this desertland is becoming more accessible to study, the correct scientific picture will some day be drawn.

Meanwhile visitors will be more interested in the coloring. Not even in the Grand Canyon is there quite such a dazzling variety of tints and shades—the dark and jet-black volcanic masses, the red and gray granites, and sandstones that mineral pigments have painted green, red, pink, and blue. And in this almost rainless land there is one mocking relic of a time when water must have been plentiful. Not far up the canyon from Natural Bridge is an extinct waterfall. The rock is grooved to a depth of ten feet, and the fall was as much as twenty feet wide. Not a trickle ever goes down that chute now. It must have been a very different climate when cascading water wore away the stone.

Until the Bennett-Arcane party crossed the salt flats and camped for three ghastly weeks (December 22, 1849, to January 16, 1850) in the vicinity of Bennetts Well, Death Valley was a land unknown to the white people of the United States. A small tribe of the Shoshone Indian nation had lived for some centuries in the Panamints, trading a pretty meager existence for security, and migrating back and forth from the high land to the low. It is possible, too, that the Spanish freebooters from Mexico knew the locality, for they went into the byways in their search for loot; but they left no record of such knowledge. It was not until some of the forty-niners came back to look for gold and silver in the barrier mountains that any whites deliberately braved the hardships of life in the valley.

Stout-hearted, determined, and utterly self-reliant were these prospectors who crossed and recrossed the salt floor of the valley and climbed the mountainsides, with burro for companion, and hope springing eternal, looking for the rich finds alleged by gossip and campfire yarn to be awaiting them. Some of them, indeed, found pockets of gold; many of them found only happiness and death—happiness because they learned to love the absolute freedom of the nomad life, with a beckoning fortune awaiting them in the very next "porphyry"; death because they wagered too heavily upon their iron nerve, missed the waterholes, let their burros stray, or stayed too long into the hot season and were driven mad by a furnace blast that has been known to touch 134 degrees in a modern thermometer shelter.

Now this is changed. No, not all; but the valley is readily accessible to visitors, and there are enough good roads so they can see the salient features. Where the prospector prodded his burro along, and a few years ago a few adventurous souls with motorcars blew their tires and cursed their day on villainous cart tracks, now sightseers roll comfortably in buses because they are there in the proper season.

For five or six months, Death Valley is a joy and a delight. There are signs for the prudent motorist, such as: WARNING: DO NOT ATTEMPT THIS ROUTE WITHOUT AMPLE SUPPLIES OF WATER, GAS, AND OIL. There is a campground, maintained by the National Park Service near the mouth of Furnace Creek, in a side canyon surrounded by hills of high color. Restrooms, water, tables, and parking spaces are provided for tenters and trailer folk. There is no firewood, so visitors should bring an adequate supply or an oil stove for cooking.

Just inside the monument, on the new highway between Trona and Wildrose Canyon, there is a service station, with cabins, where supplies may be had. This is controlled, under franchise, by the government. All the other accommodations—the luxurious hotel and ranch at Furnace Creek, Stovepipe Wells Hotel, near the Sand Dunes, and limited accommodations at Scotty's Castle—are on private land and are not Park Service concessions.

Scotty's Castle is almost as great a paradox in this setting as the "sardines" in Salt Creek. A two-million-dollar edifice, placed in a singularly unpromising location—except for the water supply—it reflects, perhaps, the strange building whims that take possession of humans. Years ago I used to observe in Los Angeles a man who had constructed a small hut in the top of a tree; he pulled up his rope ladder at night against inconvenient visits. And once in the south of France, near the Spanish border, I saw an unfinished house in which the floors had been purposely constructed to make an angle of, say, thirty degrees. The owner was called away for examination before the place was finished, and did not return. The lady across the street told me that he was an "original."

But Scotty's Castle is certainly worth seeing. Perhaps it constitutes a study in diffidence—the desire to live in such a way as not to attract attention. If so, it is as unobtrusive as a symphony conductor's bandaged thumb.

Because you may never see them, you must not conclude, after a visit to Death Valley, that animals in this real desert are scarce. They are really abundant, but most of them get about only at night, and all of them are wary. A notable wildlife feature of the monument is the several hundred head of desert bighorn that live in the high country. In some parts of their range these wild sheep have become extinct, but under protection here they are holding their own in numbers. The wild burros you may see are of course the progeny of those brought in by prospectors, who were turned loose or escaped. They fend for themselves as burros can.

There are a dozen or more species of lizards, from the big chuckwalla to the anemic-looking gecko; and besides the rodents like the antelope ground squirrel, kangaroo rats, and pack rats, the kit fox and the coyote are sometimes seen. Then, of course, there are snakes. Somehow most of the people I know associate snakes with the desert. They are there, but personally I have seen

*A great boulder is being pushed across the slick playa by the wind. Death Valley National Monument. [Photo: Josef Muench]*

ten snakes in the East and the humid South to every one I ever saw in the Southwest. This may be merely a singular personal experience.

There are two kinds of rattlesnakes in the area, neither of which you are likely ever to see; but campers should of course take reasonable precautions against the vicious little sidewinder, which goes abroad at night. No, the dangers from venomous creatures are negligible in this desert. The great danger is to rash adventurers who might disregard sage advice and go off the trail on excursions for which they are neither practically nor mentally equipped. For, to be safe as an explorer of far corners in the desert, one must be in perfect attunement with the terrain, like the Bedouin and our own desert rats. And even then there are accidents. So be wise: learn the desert little by little, and you may come to love it so well that you will want to live nowhere else.

I have heard people, crossing the Mojave on the Santa Fe and looking from the train window, say with a shudder: "How can people live in such a place as this?" The desert dweller has an answer to that, a retort not at all impolite. He merely shrugs and says: "How can people bear to live anywhere else?"

Jim Dayton was for some years caretaker of the Furnace Creek Ranch. One August day he started, alone, on one of his periodic trips to Daggett, 160 miles away. Later he was found lying under a mesquite, his four horses dead, and his dog still alive on guard. Jim was buried where they found him.

Some years later Shorty Harris died. By his own request he lies beside Jim Dayton. There is a marker on the spot, which is worded as Shorty wanted it:

> *Here lies Shorty Harris*
> *A Single-Blanket Jackass Prospector*
> *Bury me beside Jim Dayton*
> *In the Valley*
> *We both loved*

No elegant elegy could tell better than this rude epitaph, touched with frontier humor, the affection of men for the desert.

## 3. ORGAN PIPE CACTUS NATIONAL MONUMENT
### [*Arizona*]

SOMEBODY HAS REMARKED that a "whim of Nature" placed a section of the Mexican desert on the north side of the international boundary. I doubt it. I don't think Nature cares who says he owns the land, so long as the taxes are paid. The law of compensation sees that the taxes are collected. And claims for abatement are ignored at the bureau.

I didn't mean to quarrel with the phrase, though. It does well enough. It emphasizes the odd fact that when the boundary between the United States and Mexico was finally adjusted, the northern end of the Sonoyta Valley, which belongs climatically to the Sonoran desert, was clipped off, to give us a strip of desert unlike any other we have. Here, if you are an enthusiast for desert plants, is the spot for your venture into the exotic. Here you will see that wonderful cactus, springing up with unbranched arms to a height of nearly twenty feet, in great clumps of thirty or more stalks, which has been called the organ-pipe cactus. There is, indeed, some resemblance to the pipes of a church organ.

Here, in this desert garden, and just barely over the line in our country, you will see the equally bizarre sinita cactus—the cactus with whiskers. Near the tips of the older arms long, gray, hairlike spines appear, and continue to the ends, with occasionally a bare spot that looks as though the barber had started his work and been called away. Here along moist drainage chan-

*Wearing a medieval jouster's coat of mail: the collared lizard. Organ Pipe Cactus National Monument. [Photo: M. Woodbridge Williams]*

nels you will see plants you have not seen before, flowers like the ajo, or desert lily, which in blossoming time fills the air around it with a perfume much like that of the orange tree. All this queer assemblage of subtropical life in the country of little rain has been set aside for preservation for the Americans of years to come, under the designation of Organ Pipe Cactus National Monument.

Arizona, at the southwest end of which this monument is situated, is the richest state, I think, in the variety of its cactuses. Certainly it has many that can be found nowhere else. In recent years the interest in these brave, spiny marvels of adaptation has greatly increased, so that a huge mail-order business has grown up, and even a steady demand by the five-and-ten-cent stores. They look better, like all other wild plants, where they grow naturally; yet I think it rather a delightful little hobby. One of my neighbors is an elderly lady whose windowbox of assorted cactus plants is the joy of her life. She cannot travel, and she tells me that the plants take her to the desert on a magic carpet.

Of course you will never dig up a cactus or any other plant in Organ Pipe Cactus National Monument, or in any other national monument or national park. You will be tempted to; it is very human; but then you will remember that it is an unsocial act. You are a joint owner of these preserved places. You are a partner with about 190 million others. Partners of character do not raid a jointly owned property. They are anxious to protect, not to despoil. I hate lecturing, and I hate being lectured, on the subject of duty. Just consider that I am reminding the reader of a thing that I know from my own experience is easy, in the zest of meeting new and interesting plant-life, to forget. A mere jog of the elbow, may I say?

While Organ Pipe Cactus National Monument may perhaps interest you most because it is a wild desert garden, you may see plenty of wildlife, too, if you are fortunate. The desert wild hog, sometimes called the peccary, and by the Mexicans called the javalina, lives in the brush-covered plains. There are antelope, four kinds of them; and some of the wild sheep that were nearly wiped out by hunting in the thoughtless pioneering period are still living in the higher elevations of the monument.

It is historic ground, too. The early explorer Díaz went through here on his march toward the Colorado River in the conquistador days, and many years later Father Kino set up the San Marcel Mission at what is now the

*Nature's own cactus arboretum: Santa Rosa peak in background. Organ Pipe Cactus National Monument. [Photo: Natt N. Dodge]*

town of Sonoyta, just over the border. The padre developed a route across the southwestern corner of the area, traces of which may still be seen.

Caravans of gold-seekers squeaked through these sands when the emigrants from eastern Texas and other Southern states joined in the rush toward the California diggings just about a century ago. Many forged through, after terrible hardships, and many paid the toll of Midas. The U. S. Treasury price of gold at this time is thirty-five dollars an ounce. The world's hoard of gold has cost far more than that. Far more.

When the desert poppies are in flower in Organ Pipe Cactus National Monument, they are of gold, too. And unstained.

## 4. SAGUARO NATIONAL MONUMENT
### [*Arizona*]

LONG BEFORE I ever saw the superlative stand of giant cactus near Tucson, I had formed a passing acquaintanceship with the saguaro. Of course,

*This cactus is happily named. Organ Pipe Cactus National Monument. [Photo: M. Woodbridge Williams]*

I did not then know how impressive a saguaro forest could be, for the speci-mens I saw were at the northern edge of the range of this species, and could not compare either in number or size with those farther south. But I mention that first sight of the plant because something I observed on a rocky hillside not far from Apache Junction puzzled me no end, and later I was to find the answer in Saguaro National Monument.

I was spending a gloriously idle day, in the bright sunshine, browsing over what appeared to be bleak and barren ground, but was on closer exam-ination rich in plant and animal life, like all the desert country. I was seeing the saguaros for the first time, with their leafless, fluted trunks, strange sema-phore arms, sometimes contorted into imitative forms, some healthy, some dead. The dead saguaros reminded me of skeleton steel towers, into which the vegetable concrete might be poured.

Then it occurred to me that I should like to find a small saguaro, to take home to the East and rear to such size as it might attain in alien custody. I found none. It seemed strange. Big saguaros, middle-sized saguaros, but no little ones! Plenty of other tiny cactuses, but not the ones I sought. I remem-ber that rodents were plentiful on that Arizona hillside. I had neither the wit nor the knowledge to put the facts together, and perhaps at that time there were not many biologists who could.

I know now. The great saguaro forest near Tucson is possibly a doomed forest. It is not renewing. True, it will be there for many years. But civilized human life moved in upon it. The life story of the strange plant reveals what has happened.

During the lifetime of the saguaro it scattered vast numbers of seeds over the ground, but few escaped the bright eyes of mice and other relishers or fell on a favorable spot for germination. The seedlings needed the shelter of a shrub, and even then the rodent life was thirsty and hungry for the tiny plants. Cattle had browsed off the shrubs; woodchoppers had cut down the trees for fenceposts and fuel; the stockmen had killed off the coyotes that had balanced out the rodents; and, the vegetative cover being gone, the humus and duff had been washed away.

And the saguaro has such a precarious infancy, too! About fifteen years may pass before the seedling is large enough to be noticed, and another fifteen years, maybe, before it is big enough to loom above its protective cover. Only at thirty years is it in a way to protect itself fully, with root system and spines. But in survival this object of such tender incubation becomes the greatest of all cactuses reaching a possible height of fifty feet and a weight of twelve tons. How long it can live is not accurately known. Perhaps two hundred years is its limit. It does not develop its flinging, admonitory, or knot-tying arms till it reaches a ripe age.

When the saguaro is in its prime, it is a tremendous natural storage tank for the meager rainfall of the desert where it thrives. No leaves for the saguaro! Leaves would mean a loss of precious fluid. Instead, the tough green skin of the fluted columns does the breathing, and the moisture gathered by the widespread root system is stored in the pulpy tissue between the vertical ribs. During one storm a ton of water may thus be put away by a single plant for a rainless day. As the tissue stores the water, it expands, so that when the tank is full, the huge stem puffs and rounds. Then, as the water is used, the deep-set wrinkles begin to appear.

Major William H. Emory, who ran the Mexican boundary, was astonished when he came into the neighborhood of the saguaro forests. "We encamped," he wrote, "in a grove of cacti of all kinds; amongst them the huge *pitahaya*, which was fifty feet high." To George Engelmann, the botanist of that time, Emory sent either specimens or descriptions of the various cactuses he found growing in southern Arizona. One of them was the bisnaga, or barrel cactus—the one that stores water in such a way as to furnish drink for men thirsting in the desert. This cactus, too, Engelmann told Emory, is called Pitahaya by the Californians, "but this appears to be a general name applied in Mexico and South America to all the large columnar cacti which have edible fruits."

The fruits of the saguaro are certainly tasty to birds, chipmunks, and ground squirrels, and in the early days the Pima and Papago Indians ate them fresh, dried them, and made syrup from them. The blossom, which has become the state flower of Arizona, is creamy white, appearing in clusters at the ends of the branching arms in May and early June.

In age, the giant cactus falls prey, it seems, to a strange disease, a bacterial enemy carried within the intestine of a tiny moth that flies at night. The larva of this moth lives only in the juicy pulp of the saguaro, and gnaws a tunnel that becomes the focus of the incurable rot that finally may slay the giant. Incurable? Well, not quite; for another of the natural balances here shows itself. The drone fly breeds in decaying saguaro pulp, and the bird called the gilded flicker, probing for the flies, opens the pockets of rot and clears out the lesion, thus performing what amounts to a surgical operation, enabling callusing and healing in many cases.

---

*Defiant of drought, the giant cactus draws on its water storage. Saguaro National Monument. [Photo: Roger Toll]*

The wonder of it! Bacterium to moth to larva to plant cell—spelling disease. Gilded flicker to lesion to drone fly—spelling surgery and cure. Could there be a more dramatic example of the community existence, over whose plodding, adapting course man seems to have no power except to thwart!

"It appears, however," says a well-known naturalist, "that it is only a matter of time until the famous Cactus Forest of Saguaro National Monument will gradually go down under the persistent efforts of the bacterium and the moth-carrier." If this should be so, then the preservation of the integrity of Organ Pipe Cactus National Monument becomes doubly important, for in that place there is a younger and healthy stand, not so showy as that at Saguaro, but promising well for the future.

## 5. JOSHUA TREE NATIONAL MONUMENT
### [California]

FOR THOSE who are not skilled in botany, it is hard to believe that the Joshua tree belongs to the same family as the onion. They are both lilies. And the lily is the Smith family of the plant world. The rose family represents the Joneses.

In this great lily family there is a genus known as the yucca, and the yucca also takes a variety of forms, including the dagger and the Spanish bayonet. But one of these yuccas found the conditions of a part of the Southwest desert greatly to its liking and became a sizable tree: a queer sort of plant with burly arms crooked at the elbow, and so unsymmetrical that it looks as though it were constantly asking itself the question: "What shall I do next?" Some of these Joshuas are nearly forty feet high.

It has been said that the name was given to this giant yucca by the Mormons, who saw in its extended arms a symbol pointing to the promised land they were seeking. It may be so, but the promised land must have been in all points of the compass, for the Joshua tree points everywhere, including up and down. Though the tree itself may be no thing of beauty, when blooming time comes it sends forth a cluster of creamy-white blossoms a foot long at the very ends of its branches. Visitors look up at them with the feeling that nature's ends always justify the means.

Joshua trees are well scattered throughout the Mojave, but the finest stand, a real Joshua forest, is found east of Riverside, California—or south of

*And the rocks are as bizarre as the trees. Joshua Tree National Monument. [Photo: O. F. Oldendorph]*

Amboy, or north of Indio, according to the direction of approach. Here is Joshua Tree National Monument, a fine bit of desert with a fine climate almost any time of year. It was set aside by Presidential proclamation in 1936, to preserve not only the rare Joshua trees, but other rare plants and a remarkable assortment of wild animal life. Besides a limited number of mountain sheep, which will increase under protection, the coyote, the desert fox, and the bobcat, shy creatures, but sometimes to be glimpsed, live within the monument.

Here, in Joshua Tree National Monument, the landscape is entirely different from that of Death Valley and its mountain fringes. This segment of desert receives a minimum annual rainfall of perhaps five inches—not very much, surely. But in the desert Southwest a few inches more or less of moisture may mean a very different distribution of plant and animal life. The cactus family is better represented here, for example, than in Death Valley; indeed, there is an amazing stand of a kind of cholla vulgarly known as the Teddy bear. Next to the "jumping cholla," which has a reputation of throwing its missiles similar to that of the porcupine, the Teddy bear is perhaps the most formidable member of the tribe. There is much talk of snakes and Gila monsters and scorpions and tarantulas of the desert country. For my part, I would fear accidentally walking into the embrace of one of these barbed cactus monsters more. So when you see the army of them in Pinto Basin, be respectful. After you have concluded that you are not too close to one, stand away a little farther.

From a point on the ridge of the Little San Bernardinos, known as Salton View, you may have one of the greatest desert views of the country. You are at little more than five thousand feet above sea level, but the nature of the surrounding land is such that there is a panorama of mountain, valley, and desert. You see the Salton Sea of the Imperial Valley, the date gardens of the Coachella Valley, the great escarpment of Mount San Jacinto, and on some clear days you may even look into Old Mexico.

Gold mining and cattle grazing have left their scars on this bit of desert. The jackass prospector has gophered everywhere among the hills. Some rich finds were made, but in most cases the ores were not rich enough to pay for hauling them to faraway mills for reduction. As a Colombian mine owner said to me once, "Ah, *señor*, it takes much gold to run a gold mine." After a pause he added, clinchingly: *"Sí, mucho!"*

Like other desert areas, this Joshua country once had a much wetter climate. In Pinto Basin, in the eastern end of the monument, an ancient people must have lived along the shoreline of a stream that afforded the means of subsistence for many. It may have been twenty thousand years ago that a great dryness came and drove the primitive people out. The "pinto points"—flints used on an ancient throwing stick, which probably was used long before the arrow—found at the basin take us back into a past that makes our own national history seem like a single page torn from Time's diary.

## 6. WHITE SANDS NATIONAL MONUMENT
### [*New Mexico*]

ONCE WHEN I WAS VISITING this unrivaled gypsum desert, not far from Alamogordo, and staring with renewed wonder upon the great dunes, which are not really of sand but of snow-white powdered alabaster, the superintendent led me aside and asked: "How can I tell the story of this White Sands National Monument?"

Truly, it is a nice problem in interpretation. I am glad to say that I was not flattered into trying to pull a quick rabbit out of my hat. The trick looks well, but on closer examination the rabbit is too often mangy. It was clear enough to me what the superintendent had in mind. There had been so many visitors, unprepared with a background of information, who had driven, looked around a few minutes, and then asked what the distance was to El Paso. And I thought what a pity this was. Because here is one of the choicest of the areas that have been set aside because of their notable scientific values. Relatively, too, it requires so little explanation to make it a great adventure in the mind, as well as an unforgettable picture to the eye.

Yet the question is how to condition the casual visitor so that he may look a little beyond the lovely dunes—fascinating in themselves—and give himself a full day's pleasure in contemplating this graphic example of the ebb and flow of surface which affects every living thing within its grasp. It is not easy to do. I have a few comments, which I do not value highly, but which might stimulate curiosity. Certainly I think visitors should go first to the fine museum, housed in the headquarters building. In many areas I would recommend that you first fill the eye with the scenic offering and later go to the museum. I believe White Sands is a place where the order should be reversed.

This is a great basin, stretching north and south between two ranges of mountains. There are thick beds of gypsum beneath the floor, and similar beds show themselves high up on the sides of the mountains, indicating that probably this whole section of country was once a plateau, of which the middle part sank. For a long, long time the rains and snows have carried the gypsum in solution from mountains to basin, while more gypsum "sand" is brought to the surface from the underground supply. The result is a vast alkali flat. But that is only the first result; for then the never quiet southwest winds pick up the particles and begin to whirl them into dunes—dunes that are ever on the move, assuming shapes that are never duplicated. A giant snow-white billow is here today—tomorrow it is moving on.

Whenever the drifting material encounters shrubs, like the yucca, it becomes a matter of life and death for the plants. As the sand moves in, the yucca exerts itself to keep its head above water, so to say. With each increase of an inch of sand around the stem, the plant adds another inch to the stem. Where dunes have receded from a spot, plants have been found with stems more than forty feet long. But the plants have their days of triumph, too. Sometimes when a dune has rested in one place long enough, the plantlife binds it down, as the Lilliputians tied up big Gulliver with ropes.

Observe how the animals have adapted themselves to life on this expanse of white. Obviously a dark-colored mouse or lizard would be an easy mark for an enemy against this snowy background. So in the life story of the species the survivors have been the white or pale-colored individuals. The proof of this is found in the surrounding hills. Whereas the pocket mouse of the basin floor is white, his cousin in the red strata has a reddish fur, and his relative on the beds of black lava a few miles north is nearly the color of that rock.

Incidentally, those who would like to prolong the skiing season can bring their boards to White Sands. On the steep sides of the dunes the finely pulverized gypsum offers a surface almost like that of a snow-covered slope in the northern regions.

Whenever I see the White Sands drifting, creeping, obliterating, irresistibly marching, I somehow think back to the great legendary character Kilroy, whose inscription was found in the later days of World War II in so many unexpected places in western Europe. On barns, on the sides of houses in French villages, on chunks of bomb-torn rubble in West Germany, later arrivals of the American armed forces found that classic announcement: "Kilroy was here."

Now, this has given me what I hope is a useful thought. The desire of humans to leave a record of their presence in any place of historic significance is ages old. I have no doubt that the Babylonians, visiting some site of previous human occupation, carved their names or initials on the plaster.

*Creek bed of the Medano. Great Sand Dunes National Monument. [Photo: Robert T. Haugen]*

But this *cacoëthes inscribendi*—this hankering for wall writing—is a sore trial to the National Park Service in its attempt to preserve the areas under its protection from impairment. The walls of the prehistoric Indian edifice at Casa Grande, in Arizona; the staircases of the Statue of Liberty; the stones on which the Indians, or some ancient dwellers, made their puzzling pictographs, are defaced by thoughtless people who wish to leave for posterity their names, addresses, and telephone numbers.

Here, upon the gypsum sands of this monument, is an opportunity for the satisfaction of this urge for personal inscription. With a stick or any pointed instrument, names, places, dates, and even poetic thoughts may be engraved upon the sides of the dunes. No harm will be done. No rules will be transgressed. The personnel of the Park Service will even be willing to offer suggestions for decorative motifs, including hearts impaled by arrows.

As for the permanence of these inscriptions, there is no guarantee, express or implied. But they will afford a relief not only to the desires of the inscribers, but to national parks where wall writing is sharply prohibited.

There is no proof that Kilroy was ever at White Sands, but I like to believe that Kilroy was here.

## 7. GREAT SAND DUNES NATIONAL MONUMENT
### [*Colorado*]

IF I WERE AN AMATEUR PHOTOGRAPHER aiming to get an arresting shot that might find a wall place at the next salon in my neighborhood, I would lose no time in getting to the sand dunes. "Next to nudes, sand dunes are probably the greatest delight of camera-men who like to take the arty type of pictures called salon photographs," says *Life*, the pictorial magazine. *Life* should know. "Texture, pattern, tones and mood are the ingredients readily to be found in sand dunes."

To be sure. But I cannot imagine why the qualification "next to nudes" was used. Sand dunes *are* nudes. They are nature's presentation of that very texture and tone which even the loveliest human form does not quite equal. For excellent reason you seldom see a well-composed dune photograph that does not satisfy; and you seldom see even the most brilliant picture of a forest which leaves the observer quite convinced. The dune, though really never at rest, conveys the feeling of finality. The woods are busy and diffuse, advertising growth.

Great Sand Dunes, at the eastern edge of the San Luis Valley of south-central Colorado, should be the photographer's Mecca. They are not only the highest-piled dunes in the country, but they parallel for ten miles the base of the heavily forested, snow-capped mountain range called Sangre de Cristo, whose tallest peaks attain an altitude of fourteen thousand feet above sea level. Foreground and background are ready-made. Here, for instance, is a forest of dead ponderosa pines, standing stark against the sandline and skyline, victims of the irresistible tidal wave of dune that swept into them, smothered them, and covered them to the very tops. Then, later, the dune moved on, uncovered the victims of its blanketing power: went in quest of new victory. But the dunes themselves will be stopped dead at last, for when they reach the foot of the Sangre de Cristos, the winds drop them there, to assume bizarre forms of shadow and light. The burden is too great; the wind can transport them no farther.

The soil of the San Luis Valley, material that was deposited as silt in the bed of an ancient lake, is easily picked up by the southwest winds that blow almost continually and finally funnel out through gaps in the range. For centuries the dunes have been piled, shifted, sorted, and repiled, and the crests of some of them are now eight hundred feet above the valley floor.

Dunes are strange vagabonds on the earth's surface. They give the impression of willful, powerful giants, doing as they please. Actually they do nothing as they please. Their *padrone* is the wind, and they obey the boss without question, slavishly. In the formation of a single dune you will note the typical shape: gradual slope on the windward side, and a steep declivity on the protected side. If the dune is isolated, the wind sweeps past on both flanks and builds two long, pointed arms, resulting in that beautiful crescent which, with the front in a shadow, makes the heart of the photographer glad. Such crescents are called barchans, from a Turkish word.

The beginning of the dune is easy to explain. The blown sand accumulates around some object—grasses or bushes, perhaps—which starts the formation of a pile. But many have asked themselves why, when once the dune is created at a certain spot, the whole mass goes forward on the march, moving year after year till it comes to a place, like the foot of the Sangre de Cristos, where it can move no more. The answer is that the material of the gentle slope on the windward side is never at rest. Up that slope, unceasingly, sand is being carried and dumped over the crest. Soldiers, having thrown up a breastwork along their trench lines, could similarly move their breastwork forward, by shoveling the material at the base and throwing it just over the top. That is, in theory they could; in practice the enemy would resent the operation and take strong counter measures. But the process is the same.

# [ IV ]

# *Change, the Unchanging*

Now we *have canyon gorges and deeply eroded valleys, and still the hills*
*are disappearing, the mountains themselves are wasting away, the*
*plateaus are dissolving, and the geologist, in the light of the past history*
*of the earth, makes prophecy of a time when this desolate land of Titanic*
*rocks shall become a valley of many valleys, and yet again the sea*
*will invade the land, and the coral animals build their reefs. . . . Thus ever*
*the land and sea are changing; old lands are buried, and new lands are born.*

—JOHN WESLEY POWELL, *Explorations of the Canyons of the Colorado*

### 1. GRAND CANYON NATIONAL PARK
### [*Arizona*]

THE GRAND CANYON OF THE COLORADO is probably the greatest visual
shock ever experienced by man. Only when the human observer is
wholly intimidated and his ego completely wrecked can the beauty and the
serenity of the canyon begin to work upon him. The camera, having neither
pride nor humility, and not feeling called upon to express infinitude in finite
terms, does very well. The camera says, simply: "This is what I see, of form,
color, and dimension." What it sees is, of course, very little, compared with
what is there; but at least it is not duped by the dictionary.

The best story of the impact of the canyon is that of the Texas cowboy
who had taken a job with an Arizona outfit that ran its stock on the plateau
not far from the South Rim. Nobody told him about the canyon; they
thought he knew. One day, rounding up strays, he came abruptly to the
edge and found himself staring into the abyss. He looked down, across, into.

*Angel Arch. Canyonlands National Park. [Photo: M. Woodbridge Williams]*

Then he took off his hat, wiped the sweat from his forehead, and exclaimed: "My God! Something has happened here!"

Very likely López de Cárdenas, who saw the Grand Canyon in 1540, made a similar remark. He also rode up to it in ignorance. But his thoughts were upon the loot of the Cíbola, those fabulous Indian cities so rich in gold and silver that the streets were paved with them, and Cárdenas cursed the obstruction to his march and moved on. Cárdenas had actually looked upon something far richer than the things he sought—a vein of beauty and wonder that never pinches out. But in those days the wilderness was only something to be exploited and plundered. For Coronado and his freebooters the greatest abyss in all the world was only a scenic nuisance. It is only fair to the conquistadors to say that this practical view survived them by many centuries. But the more than a million annual visitors to Grand Canyon, and the 145 million who delight in the other national parks, will witness that while the things of the flesh are necessary, the things of the spirit are important too.

When you come upon the Grand Canyon suddenly—and from the nature of the chasm you cannot otherwise come upon it—your feelings must be somewhat those of the Texas cowboy. Something has happened here! You may have seen rifts in the earth surface, from gullies to gorges of large proportion; they have prepared you for nothing like this. The normal world, the substantial footing you have felt entitled to, disappears before your stunned eyes, to pick itself up miles away. You look downward, and if you are where you can observe it, there is a straw-colored thread a mile below you, and that is a river. But unless you have been informed, you are not sure it is a river. It might be an optical illusion. Maybe the whole thing is an illusion. No matter what you have been told about it, and no matter how many pictures you have seen, you wince and instinctively look behind you to see if the earth you have had such confidence in is still there. There are mountains down there. They are in the wrong place. You should be looking up at mountains. You are looking down on their tops. It is disconcerting, when you have spent part of a lifetime establishing a metrical relationship between yourself and nature, to have the scale switched and the rules changed.

This is no doubt why your first thought when you resume thinking and ask yourself "What happened here?" is naturally in terms of a catastrophe. There was a weak spot in the earth crust, and a collapse. Maybe it was an earthquake. Of course, a geologist wouldn't think so, but you are not a geologist; you are just a puzzled observer. And you can take comfort, if you wish, in the fact that the geologists did not always know as much as they do now. There was a time when they laid great store by cataclysms—violent upheavals and submergences. Plodding study of natural phenomena has revealed the truth that the earth form is due in very minor degree to turbulence and shock. The Grand Canyon is the result of what David Starr Jordan, with a roguishness permitted to proficient men and women of science, called "the infinite laziness of nature." It has all been done without rest, but without haste.

As the feeling of sheer rebuff at the canyon fades, you begin to realize the color. Thomas Moran, whose painting of the canyon hangs in the nation's capital, was sure that no palette could approximate the endless tints and shades. He was not deterred from putting on canvas what he saw and felt, and because he was such a humble intimate of our Western scenery, many will find Moran's early pictures still the most satisfying of all interpretative attempts.

The Southwestern part of the United States is, as a whole, a region of brightness. The nature of the rocks, whether diffused as sand or in eroded sculptures, the scanty rainfall, and other natural agencies have combined to produce a color gaiety that dazzles, even at first annoys, the eye that has come from places of greens and somber browns. You do not have to go to national parks to see examples. They are nearly everywhere. There is a place on the highway west of Gallup, at about the boundary between New Mexico and Arizona, where, at a swoop, within what seems a few car lengths, the stage hands seem to have shifted the scenery. The rock forms have not greatly changed—the color has become entirely different.

But the Grand Canyon, with Bryce and Zion, goes far beyond anything else of the Southwest in this respect. Partly because you are here seeing colored forms almost in three dimensions; partly because so many differing rock formations are piled atop one another and all draped before your eyes; and perhaps mostly because of the number of ways the light from above can surround the objects in the abyss: whatever the reasons, the adventure in color here can never be forgotten. And this is so in spite of the fact that you will never have an isolated moment of coloring in memory. You could not, because though you were to remain for years at the North or the South Rim of the canyon, you would never see again what you saw a minute before. The scheme constantly changes. From the first shimmer of light that follows the darkest night, from actual sunrise in any of the infinite parts, through forenoon to noon to sunset—an infinity of sunsets, of course, all combining into the one that is sunset for the spot you stand on—never will there be a time when you can say: "There! That is it." It *was* it.

The time of day will make a difference. The time of year will make a difference. It will be different whether you are at Yavapai or Yaki or Bright Angel Point. It will certainly be something else to those who leave the rim and make the trip down into the gorge where the Colorado is now biting its way through a rock that seems to be the very root of ancient uplift. Not to make this thrilling voyage in time, space, and climate is to leave the Grand Canyon rather less than half seen. The vague novel of mountain, platform, butte, cliff, and box canyon—a mere hint so far as the poor eye can discern from the plateau above—is now to be read chapter by chapter, and the story becomes clearer. It is not an arduous trip; anyone in reasonably sound condition can make it in a guided mounted party. You had better be in prime physical form to attempt to do it afoot. Many a pedestrian sturdy in purpose but lacking in wind and muscle has gone gaily down the trail, to be humiliated on the return. It is undignified for *Homo sapiens* to have to be retrieved by a mournful-looking mule.

If you happen to go to the bottom of the canyon from the North Rim, you have dropped just about a mile in elevation above sea level, though the Colorado has still another half mile to fall before it reaches its mouth. But in this drop you have had an amazing experience in traversing the zones of organic life. Vertically you have made the equivalent of a horizontal trip from northern Mexico to the Canadian border, or nearly so.

So far as there is any accuracy or fairness in putting humans in categories, you may say that there are three classes of people who visit Grand Canyon, Yellowstone, Yosemite, or any other national park. Aside from specialists in the natural sciences, who will always resort to these places for study, these three classes are:

First, those whose interest is satisfied with visiting the famous areas, "seeing" them in the sense of looking at their outstanding natural features, seeing them in company with a lot of other people, and being able thereafter to say that they have been there, fishing or indulging in other sports where those are possible, getting out of hot lowlands in summer into cooler altitudes, getting away from a humdrum town life into something that at least stands for primitive experience—and for other similar reasons. The "seeing" is almost purely visual, and very incomplete. You could spend your whole life at Grand Canyon and not see it, even visually. Yellowstone is so vast an area that there are corners that nobody has ever looked at. But, not to chew words, the meaning is clear enough. The meaning in the instance of Grand Canyon is that you *have been there.*

Those in the second category remain unsatisfied with this kind of seeing. They ask themselves questions. How did it happen? What is the meaning of

*Looking down into the geologic past. Grand Canyon National Park. [Photo: Wayne Bryant]*

it? In what way does it touch their own existence? How does it relate to the places they come from? For such inquirers there are at every national park facilities for knowing, so far as knowing is possible. There are naturalist guides, brief lectures, museum exhibits, specimens of rocks, minerals, or organic life, explanatory maps, planned to put visitors in possession of the rudiments of the tale. The object is not so much directly to educate as to create a background that will add to the visual pleasure. Visitors can have as much or as little of it as they please. For most people, probably, a little suffices; yet a common expression heard from those who have just returned from one or more of the parks is: "I wish we had stayed longer and learned more about it."

There remains another group, who visit the national parks and make the most important discovery: they discover themselves. When they exclaim, "I didn't know there were such beautiful and interesting places!" what they are really saying is that they did not know they had within them such capacity for the realization of beauty and significance. They fall in love with the national parks, not for the spectacular features within them, but for the essence of them. They do not state this in self-conscious words, but they feel it. They cultivate the pleasurable hobby of dabbling, secondhand, in the greatest of all mysteries, partly revealed, but only partly, in the study of the natural sciences: our place in nature. Whatever can be learned of this mystery can be learned only where areas of size sufficient to preserve natural conditions in integrity are insulated from the march of utility.

These people are not geologists, or botanists, or zoologists. Whether the rock they are looking at belongs to the Ordovician or the Silurian period, or whether it was igneous or sedimentary before pressure and heat altered it, is not important to them. They will not grieve if they stumble in taxonomy. But they do want to know enough of the detailed story of the earth forces and organic life to be able to put them against the background of what they see and create a pattern. So far as they do go, it is fun, it is adventure, and it may be a passion.

To such folks the chief expression of Grand Canyon, beyond the beauty and the impact of its incredible vastness, is the geological story of how it came to be.

When you go up to the South Rim of the Grand Canyon from the town of Williams, you are making a gentle ascent up the slope of a tilted plateau. Across on the north side of the great chasm the land continues to rise, though more sharply. With the elevations at these three points in mind, you do not have to be a geologist to realize that something is wrong in the picture. The Colorado is taking its course *across* a slope instead of *down* one.

The upper reaches of the Colorado, and many of the tributaries, show the same perversity. They share this peculiarity with all the major streams in the central and southern Rockies, which seem to ignore the easy way in favor of the hard. The Arkansas, for instance, cuts profoundly through the Front Range in the Royal Gorge. The South Platte cuts through at another place. The Laramie, instead of following the lowlands north to the Platte, turns east and chisels through the mountains. And though seemingly the Green River could have passed around the Uintas, following valleys on the north side, it chose to carve a passage through them.

The answer is that the observer is now looking at a geographical picture bearing no resemblance to the one that formerly existed when the rivers began to flow. It is as though you arrived late at the theater, near the end of the play. The tag end of the action, if you lack a knowledge of what led up to it, is either misleading, or pretentious heroics with no good reason. But if you can figure in your imagination that when the Colorado, as well as these other Rocky Mountain streams, was in its infancy, the tough rocks of the deep canyons through which they now pass were buried thousands of feet below sedimentary material, you can see what has happened. The river made its bed when the bed was soft, and continues to lie in it.

As the river began to cut down, the land began to rise, responding to strange building and thrusting forces that originate far below the earth crust. And as the uplifting is never uniform, the result will be to accelerate the currents of the streams. Even as the land rises, erosion is taking place simultaneously: the washing of sand, gravel, and boulders into the river furnishes just what the water needs for cutting power. Thus it follows the course it originally found easiest, regardless of the nature of the rock that must be sawed through.

All the canyons, from Flaming Gorge on the Green down almost to the Gila River, where the Colorado is getting near to sea level, are thus explained. But impressive and colorful as these other canyons are, it is when the river enters that area which is now included in the national park that the marvels rapidly multiply. Here you come into a place that, aside from its majestic proportions, its beauty, and its almost frightening silence, is the prize geological sourcebook of the world.

To descend from the rims to the river, whose shouting increases with the snow melt in the mountains, is to go down the ladder of time, rung by rung, with each rung representing centuries, not years. And your excursion into time, tremendous as it is, is not even a true interpretation; for there must have once been a rim as much higher than the one on which you now stand as this one is now above the bottom of the canyon. If you go from the Grand Canyon to Bryce Canyon and Zion and rejoice in the flaming color of their rocks, you will see what was once superimposed upon the Grand Canyon rims, which time and the rain clouds have swept away.

But this is enough. It will be all you can safely view, and far more than anyone can comprehend. Will you descend, and thus go backward in time? Or do you prefer to climb the ladder and thus come forward toward the present year, which will have the relative importance, expressed in thickness, of a sheet of paper alongside the Empire State Building? Perhaps not that much; but let us not sink to the humility of nothingness.

We may as well begin at the river bottom and climb toward ourselves. Down there in the granite gorges the Colorado is now grinding its course

*Overleaf: Kaibab Trail, below Yaki Point. Grand Canyon National Park. [Photo: George Grant]*

through one of the oldest rocks known on this continent. It is not a granite, and perhaps was not unlike the other limestones and sandstones before the enormous pressure of an overburden, and heat from below, recrystallized and contorted it. Sedimentary rocks, miles high, once covered this schist, but they were not the rocks that lie above it today. These are recent: only a few hundred million years old. For between that dark, crumpled schist and the next layer above it occurs what the geologist calls an "unconformity." It means that this oldest visible rock had been uplifted and planed down flat by the elements before it sank beneath a sea. As it contains no fossil life, all you can say of its age is that it is even less comprehensible than what appears above it. It is possible that this rungless space in the time ladder represents a greater period than all the rocks from the Tonto platform to the rim.

But above this lowest rock appears, in wedge-shaped masses, seen near the mouth of Bright Angel Creek and elsewhere, another rock younger than the first, if the word *younger* does not become, in this relation, somewhat humorous. This tilted rock represents a deposit of something like twelve thousand feet of stratified sediments, which rested on the planed surface of the schists and gneisses. It, too, was elevated and planed down, so that between it and the next overlying rock is another unconformity—another signature torn from the record book and lost.

As from these most ancient rocks you climb the ladder to what is now the rim, you come to other missing pages, for the same reason always—that what was below the surface of a sea had been lifted up and eroded down. And about the only possible appreciation of the time involved is to keep referring it back to something now going on. If you live at the mouth of a river or at the edge of the ocean, how long, at the present rate, would it take to pile up twelve thousand feet of sand or mud? Or a thousand feet, or two hundred feet, or even ten feet? The foundation of the colossal statue of Rameses II was discovered in Memphis, Egypt, in 1854, beneath nine feet of silt deposits of the Nile. The statue being not more than three thousand years old, the rate of deposition had averaged not more than three and a half inches per hundred years. Although this is not a perfect yardstick, because the rate of erosion would not always be the same for every situation, it gives at least a feeble notion of the time element.

When you finally reach the South Rim, having come up through the layers of shales, limestones, and sandstones, some green, some gray, some red, buff, or tints that incline toward any of these colors, you reach what seems to be the end of the ladder. It is nothing of the sort. It is merely the place where the ladder has been sawed through and the upper part lost. For as you

*Without that flowing river there is no true Grand Canyon. Grand Canyon National Park.* [*Photo: Philip Hyde*]

look south from El Tovar to Red Butte, or east of Desert View to Cedar Mountain, you are looking at what remains, on this side of the canyon, of later rocks, which once had a total thickness of twice the distance from the present rim to the river.

The story, then, told by the ladder rungs on which you can put your feet is that of a succession of submergences beneath the sea and emergences from the sea; of mountain building and the tearing down of mountains; of rocks that have been ground to sand and mud and poured into oceans, to become rocks again, of a different kind, of a different color, and to take different forms in the erosion that never halts.

Years ago, when visitors to the Grand Canyon were not so numerous nor so well informed, a noted lecturer indulged his audience with this bit of feverish rhetoric: "The Grand Canyon of Arizona is Nature wounded unto death and lying stiff and ghastly, with a gash of 200 miles in length and a mile in depth in her bared breast, from which is flowing fast a stream of life-blood called the Colorado."

[ 179 ]

In a day when Barnum's press agent was describing an elephant as "the blood-sweating Behemoth of Holy Writ" this was probably not a bad funeral oration over Nature, as Nature appears at the Grand Canyon. The only trouble with it was that Nature was not even slightly wounded, her bared breast was not where the lecturer thought it was, and the funeral had to be postponed. Far from being sick, and lying stiff and ghastly, the Grand Canyon is all-beautiful, in perfect health, and possibly self-renewing. For all we know, the mountain-building forces may be still in progress here. Our time clock is built to tell hours, days, and even centuries, but it is no match for this dilatory progression. The canyon is not a passive thing: every inch of this area is pulsating with life. Gravitation is working on the walls incessantly; every rainstorm sweeps tons of material down toward the river; the weather bites into the softer rock, and the tougher rock above now overhangs; one night a great block drops and goes crashing down, but the noise is swallowed up in the vast web of silence. The Colorado moves to the Pacific.

Though it means nothing tangible to write down the symbols for a billion years, yet your excursion into time in the Grand Canyon has given you at least a sense of continuity: you have seen enough of the record to guess that it goes on and on in an orderly fashion, any appearances of disorder and catastrophic accident to the contrary. The rocks are not called organic, though something remains to be found out about that. But they are a part of the stream of life, of which you are an incident that need not be ashamed, though infinitely small.

When we remember that the national parks preserve not only the finest scenic and significant natural treasures of our country, but also the human record of discovery, occupation, and migration that has finally peopled the United States, we realize that the fullest enjoyment of visits to these areas calls for some knowledge of their first and continuing effect upon man. For this is the American story; this constitutes the richest American heritage; and valuable as are books, the actual presence in such places goes beyond reading. Here the American sees, feels, touches, and understands.

In Grand Canyon your joy and adventure are not complete unless, when you descend to the river and watch it galloping past, you can look back through the years to an August day in 1869 when a little party of battered men, under the leadership of a soldier who had lost his right arm at the Battle of Shiloh, were fighting for their lives near the end of a challenge that rates high in the drama of exploration.

These men, who had begun their river journey at Green River Station in Wyoming, were doing what could not be done. Pioneers had opened gaps in the wilderness, through which eager Americans were pouring to the Pacific—to the north, to the south, along well-set survey routes—and the railroad was fast displacing the pony express and the ox-team caravan. But the Colorado River, for many hundreds of miles, was an unknown world.

Its general course was observed well enough; trappers had been taking beaver in the lower reaches since the early years of the century, and they had trapped at accessible places in the upper tributaries. A steamboat coming from the Gulf of California had safely ascended above Callville, a Mormon outpost just below where the Virgin joins. Many a man had stood at the rims of the successive canyons, all along the line, and turned away convinced that the great stream would never be run. Lieutenant J. C. Ives, no milksop, after ascending the Colorado in 1858 to the mouth of Vegas Wash and then overland to the mouth of Diamond Creek, wrote, after a vain attempt to reach the rim: "It seems intended by nature that the Colorado River, along the greater part of its lonely and majestic way, shall be forever unvisited and undisturbed."

Captain Sitgreaves, of the Topographical Engineer Corps, some years before Ives, had been given airy instructions from Washington to "pursue the Little Colorado to its junction with the Colorado . . . and pursue the Colorado to its junction with the Gulf of California." He set out from Zuñi Pueblo, reached the Little Colorado and followed it down for some distance, and then washed his hands of the whole business as being "too hazardous." The fact was that the War Department had not the faintest idea of the country contiguous to the Colorado, or of much of the river itself.

Major John Wesley Powell started with nine men and four boats from Green River City, Wyoming, on May 24, 1869. That the venture was one of the greatest hazards, they knew. Powell did not credit the reports of trappers that there were high waterfalls and underground passages in the Colorado and its tributaries, nor was he deterred by the exhortations of friendly Indians that the Great Spirit would be affronted by this foray into his private domain; but hardships and danger were expected. One thing was certain: there would be places on the journey where, walled by precipitous canyon cliffs, there would be no turning back. Every twist of the madly plunging river would be a plunge into the unknown.

In the Canyon of Lodore one of the boats was smashed beyond repair, and a considerable part of their food supply and scientific instruments was lost. The upsetting of the boats and the hurling of the occupants into the cataracts became an incident of the day's course; for weeks their clothing was never dry. Sometimes at night they perched, or crouched, with scanty covering, on a narrow shelf of rock where sleep was impossible. There were rapids of foaming, jumping waves where the walls were vertical from the water's edge, with huge rocks in the channel. Then, by a most laborious process, the boats had to be let down, one past another, finally leaving one last man on a rock, from which he plunged into the water and was hauled out into a boat as he was being swept past farther downstream.

Whenever he could, Major Powell climbed the steep canyon walls to take observations. It seemed incredible that a man with one arm could have gone where he did. Only once, it appears, did he find himself clinging to a wall of rock and able neither to advance nor to retreat. With great difficulty he was rescued.

The party's flour was wet and dried so many times that it was in hopeless lumps, and musty. When their bacon spoiled, they boiled it and made it do; their sugar had melted away in every upset; but they always had coffee. Toward the end they were down to the thinnest rations, but they cheered themselves with each loss of food and stores by saying: "Well, the boats will be lighter, anyway, as we go on."

The final challenge came when they reached the granite canyons of the Colorado. Here they entered the positively unknown—not even a trapper professed knowledge of the next stage. The walls at their sides were more than 1 mile high. As Powell said later, "Here even the great river was insignificant in the vastness of the chasm, its angry waves were but ripples, and we were but pigmies." They had but a few days' rations left. But this last effort, which taxed their remaining strength and will, saw them through. At noon on August 29 they emerged into the Grand Wash.

*"The river rolls by us in silent majesty; the quiet of the camp is sweet; our joy is almost ecstasy."*

Major Powell and his party had the highest kind of courage when they set themselves adrift in the uncharted river: the kind of valor that is not to be confused with mere recklessness. For the adventure was long studied and the preparations as perfect as they could be, and though the drop of the Colorado from Flaming Gorge to the Virgin was known to be nearly a mile in altitude, which made it possible that there would be some place from which they could neither retreat nor go on without certain death to all, yet from what he knew of the nature of the rocks the geologist concluded that the chances were favorable.

---

*A flicker of sun lights the North Rim. Grand Canyon National Park. [Photo: Philip Hyde]*

Three men of the party died. Ironically, it was not the Colorado that caused their death. They had passed through the first granite gorge, frightfully buffeted and with provisions nearly gone. They did not know it, but they were nearly at the end of their labors. But when, after surviving the first black barrier, a second one just like it was seen, three of the men would go no farther. They were not cowards. They had not flinched from danger. But they had had enough. Their nerves were lacerated. They left the party to climb out of the canyon and make their way overland to the Mormon settlements, and were murdered by Indians on the Shivwits Plateau.

If the willful Colorado had had its choice, probably it would have preferred not to be at last humbled by a man who had only one arm. But, in return, when the game was up, the river and the canyons turned loose upon their master all their seductive loveliness and lure, forcing from him emotional outbursts that mocked at his scientific poise. In 1901, thirty-two years after his triumph, the major was writing: "The glories and the beauties of form, of color and sound unite in the Grand Canyon—forms unrivaled even by the mountains, colors that vie with the sunsets, and sounds that span the diapason from tempest to tinkling raindrop, from cataract to bubbling fountain."

## 2. CANYONLANDS NATIONAL PARK
### [Utah]

I WOULD DESCRIBE CANYONLANDS as the place where the adjective died from exhaustion. Our language, as any language, has its limitations, especially when we attempt to ascribe a quality to natural objects, according as to how we *feel* about them. In contact with the examples of scenery created by the forces of nature, we may begin confidently with such modest adjectives as *large* or *pretty*, and proceed to *vast* and *beautiful*, but the end of that word game is always in sight. Sooner or later we have to admit our incapacity. We do it with the final adjective: *indescribable*.

After that, we stick to nouns. Note how the early venturers into the Canyonlands came to the rescue of their pride. Realizing that they could not describe, they named. The erosional marvels became Doll House, Elephant Canyon, Ernie's Country, Bagpipe Butte, Devil's Lane, Bobby's Hole, and The Sewing Machine. The pygmy in the presence of a giant loses nothing by assuming the jocular, and it may give him courage.

Canyonlands National Park, though it may seem limitless in extent to urban dwellers who find themselves within its maze of strange erosional

*The Doll House. Canyonlands National Park. [Photo: M. Woodbridge Williams]*

forms, is really only a small segment of a Greater Canyonlands that may be called the Colorado River Country. The region taken as a whole, far from being "unknown" to visitors of the National Park System, has in fact been visited by many millions of them. The Colorado Plateau includes three national parks—Grand Canyon, Zion, and Bryce—and many national monuments, with a total area of more than 800,000 acres, and as a geographical unit it even embraces Mesa Verde National Park in southwestern Colorado. These individual preserves are mostly not difficult to reach. They present, each in its manner, choice examples of the mighty dissecting forces—rushing streams, wind, frost, and rain—that together slowly abrade rock of varying resistance. But now, here in the heartlands, we are invited to see the rest of the exhibition, some of it even yet unexplored: needles and arches, mesas and buttes, quiet parklike bottoms, tumultuous river rapids, breakneck scarps, standing rocks sliced thick or finny. Above all, *standing* rocks. "Standing-up country" it has been called, since some baffled venturer threw up his hands and declared, "There is more of this place standing up than there is laying

down." He may, of course, have said *lying* down, but I have the feeling that he would have been inattentive to grammar.

Stark and rigorous as this land is, it could not keep acquisitive man from making traverse of it. The prehistoric "ancient ones" lived here. The prospector for gold and silver bet his stake and his life against its hazards; and in later days, after the magic element uranium became something quite other than the source of paint color, the feverish fellow with the Geiger counter rutted the delicate landscape with lines that will be seen for half a century, unless they are painstakingly erased—and even then, we shall continue to note the erasures. It is curious that land surfaces that seem at a glance so tough and repellent should scar as easily as a baby's skin.

The problem of providing access roads, trails, and visitor centers while preserving wilderness in this new national park should not be difficult, in the opinion of Secretary of the Interior Stewart Udall. He has viewed the domain from no ivory tower in the District of Columbia. He writes with intimate knowledge of its nature:

> Here, careful development can allow visitors into the heart of the park in relative comfort without disturbing natural values, and still keep the wilderness areas accessible only by foot, boat or horseback.

> Dry camps (to which visitors must carry their own drinking water) are available throughout the park. Salt Creek, in the Needles Country, provides water for travelers on horseback. For the present, overnight accommodations are expected to be provided by motels and lodges outside the park. Tourists need four-wheel-drive vehicles to negotiate much of Canyonlands. Unpaved but passable roads allow ordinary passenger cars to go as far as Grand River Point in the Island in the Sky, or to Squaw Spring in the Needles area. In the land between the rivers, the Island in the Sky will be the primary visitor-use area. Roads, overlooks and various interpretive devices, including a visitor center, self-guiding trails and a campground are planned. The White Rim road skirting the lofty Island in the Sky will remain a trail for four-wheel-drive vehicles.

> Ultimately there will be hard-surfaced roads, but it will be a number of years before Canyonlands will be as accessible as other parks nearby. Even when the roads are built, they will not be allowed to dominate the landscape through which they pass. Where rivers and canyons divide major segments, access to the separate areas will be from outside roads, not by way of connect-

---

*This was a rugged roadway for pre-Columbian folk. Canyonlands National Park.*
*[Photo: M. Woodbridge Williams]*

ing bridges and roads which would scar the landscape. Canyonlands will always remain a wilderness park. . . .

Visitors will have a wide range of recreational opportunities. Both the Green and the Colorado Rivers are navigable and this impressive country should be seen from the bottom up. A few river runners will challenge the rapids of Cataract Canyon down to the impounded waters of Lake Powell. Most visitors will be content with floating down the Colorado from Moab to Spanish Bottom, then up the Green River via Anderson Bottom to the town of Green River.

Even those visitors who have no special interest in geology will make their way to Upheaval Dome, at the northerly end of the new park. This is a natural feature that puzzled the professionals over a long period. Was it the huge crater of a volcano—about 4,500 feet from rim to rim and 1,600 feet deep? It looked like it, certainly. But there was no sign of igneous rock, or rock of any kind that would indicate alteration by volcanic steam and gas. Was it a so-called "crypto-volcano," then—resulting from a volcano that lay beneath the center of the crater, but never giving surface indications other than the depression? Finally it has been rather generally accepted by geologists that Upheaval Dome was created by the slow action of salt-doming. Such features do occur, but not commonly, throughout the world. There is still room for speculation on the part of the experts. The lay visitor will be content to look at the phenomenon. If he has any hypothesis he can confide it to a specialist, who will receive it, I hope, with a grave politeness.

Some time ago I fell to pondering: What will be the immediate physical and psychic responses of those who for the first time find themselves in this classical erosional miniature world of rim, bench, and stream bottom? In a sense, of course, this is unfruitful speculation: all the great scenic and scientific parks are many things to many persons. But Canyonlands is, it must be admitted, rather special.

As to form, texture, and color, these rocks of the canyon heartland are wilder, less believable, and more whimsically painted than one expects even in a region of "red rock." At times they flame. The gaunt, self-sufficing loneliness is disconcerting. Practically all people will call it beautiful, but they will not all be at home with this kind of beauty. I have a friend who says that the canyonlands have for him a lure like that of the siren, and yet when he found himself within this area he had the feeling of nightmare— as though he had eaten hot mince pie and cheese for dessert and dreamed the kind of dream where one is being pursued by an ogre, fleeing into one cul-de-sac after another, always finding a dead end. Which is only another way, I suppose, of expressing what the old-timers meant when they spoke of being "rim-rocked."

There will be those who will be less delighted visually than curious about how it all came to be. Though in the minority, they will be in the best of company, for Charles Darwin said bluntly, after his voyage around the world in the *Beagle*, that "group masses of naked rock, even in the wildest forms, may for a time afford a sublime spectacle, but they will soon grow monotonous. Paint them with bright and varied colours . . . they will become fantastic; clothe them with vegetation, they must form a decent, if not a beautiful picture." Darwin would have liked the Great Smoky Mountains better, but even there his word "decent" implies that he would have found the scenery merely "pretty good." But how he would have reveled in the marvels of the canyon-cutting and in such a puzzling occurrence as Upheaval Dome! Incidentally, Darwin detested travel as such. "No doubt," he said, "it is a high satisfaction to behold various countries . . . but the pleasures gained at the time do not counterbalance the evils. It is

*Chesler Park. Canyonlands National Park. [Photo: M. Woodbridge Williams]*

necessary to look forward to a harvest, when some fruit will be reaped." Well, it must be admitted that this man, wedded to laboratory exercises, reaped a great harvest. Besides, on the *Beagle* he was seasick for a good part of five years. That could color one's opinion about travel!

Some of the early pioneers, trying to wrest a living or strike a bonanza among these stark cliffs, not only didn't think the region beautiful; they cussed it out as willful and stingy. Captain John N. Macomb, who took a party into the country in 1859, reported: "I cannot conceive of a more worthless and impracticable region than the one we now find ourselves in." Yet the geologist with that same expedition, a man named Newberry, said that the view from one rim point called out "exclamations of delight from all our party." Macomb included? Possibly, because when he spoke of the worthlessness of the region he may have had commercial exploitation in mind. The military parties were not only seeking travel routes; they were to keep an eye out for material riches.

I was amused to read, in a "proposal" for a Canyonlands National Park, printed several years before the park was actually voted by Congress, a little paragraph that now sounds excessively timid. It was feared that "some people may be repelled, and call the scenery ugly; not because it is drab or dull, but because it is so different as to be incomprehensible to them and therefore hostile." Now that we have the fine park, we find it unnecessary to be so defensive!

Yet, though all conservationists and lovers of wilderness were heartened when Canyonlands National Park came into being, there was, and still is, disappointment that the area could not have been much greater than the present 257,000 acres. The 330,000 acres first requested was extremely modest. There were 800,000 acres of mostly federally owned land that could have been set aside. But even the 330,000 shrank to 300,000, then to the present acreage. "The Governor of Utah made it clear from the start," according to the Interior Secretary, "that he was opposed to park status that would . . . 'lock up' the resources and 'damage' his state's future economy." I think America will have come to maturity when it will be possible to erect somewhere—probably it will be west of the Mississippi—a great bronze marker which will read:

*Beneath these lands which surround you there lies enormous mineral wealth. However, it is the judgment of the American people, who locked up*

---

*Fish-Eye Arch. Canyonlands National Park. [Photo: M. Woodbridge Williams]*

*this area, that these lands shall not be disturbed, because we wish posterity to know that somewhere in our country, in gratitude to nature, there was at least one material resource that we could let alone.*

## 3 · MESA VERDE NATIONAL PARK
### [*Colorado*]

IT DID NOT RAIN.

Day after day the sun beat down upon the Green Mesa. The filmy white clouds drifted lazily around the circuit of the horizon line. At times, but rarely, the sky darkened over the higher lands to the northeast, and clouds crawled without conviction in the direction of the villages of the farm people. But instead of the forked fire that should have spoken with the voice of the Great Spirit, it came to nothing but flashes across the sky. It did not rain. It seemed to have forgotten how.

Yes, surely, occasionally a few drops fell. Once there was a sharp shower, which brought back life to the firing corn, and perked up the beans and squashes, and the villagers cried with joy and ran around repeating the refrain: "The rain has come. Now, after this, we shall have rain enough!" The priests wagged their heads triumphantly and said: "See, you of little faith! We have placated the Great Spirit. Get you about your business, and leave such matters to us."

But it amounted to little. Again the sun blazed down. Again the corn fired and the squash vines drooped, and the few showers that came were only enough to leave spots like tiny anthills on the dust of the gardens.

It did not rain; and the village people of the Green Mesa despaired and trembled for the future. And in winter it was the same. There was snow, but it merely put a thin cover on the ground, to evaporate speedily.

It was 1280—the year of the death of Kublai Khan, the great founder of the Mongol Empire, on the other side of the earth from the Green Mesa. The people of the mesa knew nothing of Kublai Khan nor of the Mongols, though they could possibly have originated over there—sometime in the dim past perhaps having crossed the Aleutian bridge and found their way down to the tableland and canyon country where they now lived. They had no record of their past, not even a bardic one—simply a vague notion that they had come from the direction of certain bright stars that move together, like a band of goats, around the sky.

Four years now, there had been a shortage of rain. Rain, but not enough rain. Some of the smaller trees were dying. The Spring of the Lame Deer,

*Upheaval Dome, long a mystery to the geologist. Canyonlands National Park.*
*[Photo: M. Woodbridge Williams]*

which had run so copiously, was noticeably depleted. Several lesser springs were down to a trickle.

There were those who were cheerful and hopeful. There had always been lean years. The weather would turn, and there would be good crops again. There were those who spoke darkly of some offense to the Great Spirit. There was an old woman who, when the Big House was receiving another addition (she was a girl then), had imprinted her hand in the ceiling plaster; and now she wagged her head and said that ruin was coming to the people of the Green Mesa. The village people had become proud—too proud. Pride—human pride—the Great Spirit would not too long tolerate. These jewels of turquoise and other colored stones; this delicately woven raiment; these pots fancifully decorated with black figures on a light-gray background: it was pride, pride. Their ancestors were content with little houses, with rougher garments, with pottery more for use than for show.

In the kivas—the ceremonial rooms—the elders and the men of magic consulted, divined, chanted incantations, made offerings, pitted their prayers against the elements. There was a raid by some nomadic ruffians who came out of the east to plunder and to kill. The Green Mesa people stood them off, as they had before; but there was less and less of value to defend. At the end of another five years the springs were really drying up. Large trees were dying. For lack of feed, the deer, rabbits, squirrels, and prairie dogs were getting scarce; even the mice were departing.

The old Cassandra shook her head and muttered: "Pride. Pride. Punishment. And I heard my grandfather say that it does not do to cut down all the trees. The Great Spirit does not like it. He refuses to let it rain when you have cut down too many trees. He said that. It is true."

The end came. Twenty-four years the drought lasted. There was no food. The last of the water supply was going. By 1299 it was certain that only death awaited the villagers of this no longer green mesa if they remained. Where to go? Nobody knew. There were messengers from the southeast now and then who brought news that though conditions were also bad in that direction—toward a great river that came out of the mountains and flowed to the end of the earth—yet things were not as bad as here.

So the people of the Green Mesa—not all at once, but village by village—left their houses and their garden plots, left all but the necessary things for travel, and went off to the southeast. What became of them? It was no small migration. Many, no doubt, perished, either from hardship or from attacks by brigand people. Along the Rio Grande in New Mexico today live many tribes of Pueblo Indians. Also, to the west, are the Hopis and other Pueblos.

*Every nook and cranny among the rocks was turned to some use by these ancient dwellers. Mesa Verde National Park. [Photo: Fred Mang, Jr.]*

Perhaps the people of the Green Mesa found a haven among the ancestors of these agricultural folk. There may be Green Mesa blood among the Jamez and the Isletas and the Zias and all the rest. But there remain only the ruins of a happy life once lived on the tableland and canyons of the Mancos country.

They are fascinating ruins, for they tell the story of the development of a people who began living in this region in the first century of our era, a peaceable, agricultural people who started with rude devices, though with certain skills, and rose from culture to culture till they attained an intricate social scheme, an elaborate religious organization, and some superb craftsmanship.

Mesa Verde National Park is the only area with *park* status that was set aside for preservation primarily because of its historical importance. But more people every year are becoming interested in the story of the prehistoric inhabitants of the Southwest, and Mesa Verde is the key to the fascinating puzzle of the vanished cultures whose ruins are preserved in the Southwestern monuments.

There are hundreds of ruins in Mesa Verde, although only a few have been excavated. The passage of centuries since they were built has weakened the structures, and before they finally came under the protection of the National Park Service some were badly damaged by thoughtless people who were unaware of their value. Visitors at Mesa Verde are not permitted to enter any cliff dwelling unless accompanied by a ranger. Violation of this regulation will not be tolerated. It is always with the utmost reluctance that the Park Service makes a rule of this kind. But the reason is obvious: preservation is authorized imperatively by acts of Congress, and preserving some of the structures would be impossible without this rule. But the rule does *not* apply to the ruins on the mesa top, which visitors may inspect at any time during the daylight hours if they have registered at the park entrance station or at the museum.

Visitors to Mesa Verde should see at least one ruin of each type: pit house, pueblo, and cliff dwelling. These, in order, represent the progress of the prehistoric people during the 1,200 years of their residence. They began as farming Indians, skilled in weaving baskets, but ignorant of pottery, houses, and any weapons except the throwing stick, or *atlatl*. The baskets served all purposes for which containers were needed. The people lived in shallow caves, in which there were places for the prudent storage of the things they raised on their mesa-top fields.

About A.D. 400, the archaeologists have found, there were important developments among the Green Mesa people. They had learned to make pottery and they had acquired the bow and arrow. They still made baskets; their pottery was plain; but they had taken to houses, even though these houses were shallow pits with head-high roofs of poles and adobe. Each pit house served as the home for a single family. The population must have been on the increase, for there are hundreds of villages on the top of the mesa and in the caves of the Four Corners region.

By 700, evidences show clearly, the people showed an increased tendency to group and form compact villages. The "pueblo" period had come. Their religious observances probably became more ceremonious, for each cluster of houses around an open court had its kiva. A strange development in this period was the adoption of a baby cradle, and as a result the heads of most of the people were flattened at the back, as the exhumed skulls show.

The final period was one of prosperity, of highly skilled construction, of artistic development—and of the penalties for all these things. They now had something worth stealing, and less peaceful Indians on their flanks probably made incursions upon them. They had to fortify against these enemies. It is also possible that the population increased to the point where crowding caused disease to spread. But there is no question about the superior culture the people had attained. It was in this final period that Cliff Palace, Square Tower House, Spruce Tree House, Long House, and other great buildings were erected.

Spruce Tree House, besides being wonderfully well preserved, serves as an example of the skill of the builders and the stage of social organization they had attained. A great many of the high walls still touch the top of the cave, and many of the original roofs are still intact. There were 114 living rooms in this apartment house and eight ceremonial rooms.

The reader may say, with a skeptical rise of the eyebrow: "No doubt your archaeologists are clever. Their studies and diggings have certainly been revealing. But—these Green Mesa people left no written records. There is no evidence that they had a calendar. And yet experts talk about the year

*It was not really a square tower, standing alone, but a part of a ruined whole. Mesa Verde National Park. [Photo: Fred Mang, Jr.]*

400, or the year 1200, as though they were speaking of the Battle of Gettysburg. How do they know?"

The answer is that the story of Mesa Verde, and of the other ruins left by prehistoric Indians in the Southwest, is partly written in trees. The great work of Professor A. E. Douglass, an astronomer who worked out a "calendar" through tree rings—using freshly cut trees for comparison with the wood found in ruins—has left little doubt of the dates.

The tree-ring technique is too involved to describe here. Briefly, it is based upon the cross-identification of annual growth rings of different trees from the same forest, extended to the different timbers of a prehistoric ruin, and then to fragments of charred ceiling beams in various other ruins. The work of Douglass and his associates lengthened our American calendar by so many centuries that it made the voyage of Columbus seem like a comparatively recent event.

## 4. PAGEANT OF THE SPECTRUM

### A. ZION NATIONAL PARK
#### [*Utah*]

CAN THERE BE any better example of the way in which the demolition squads of nature produce stunning forms and revelations of color than this which greets visitors to Zion Canyon? Here is the Virgin River, the historic stream of the Southwest, which was named by the fur trader Jedediah Smith for one of his wounded comrades, and near the mouth of which the Mormon settlers planted an outpost in the days when their rugged followers were threading their way through the semidesert wilderness to the Zion of their dreams.

This Virgin, which with its numerous forks and tributaries can be a relatively innocent stream, can also be a very devil in its raging moments. At the present, the Virgin is removing three million tons per year of ground-up rock from within the boundaries of Zion National Park and pouring it into the Colorado River. It has been doing this for thousands of years. Presumably it will continue for more thousands. The river will cut its channel deeper, the precipitous walls will be wider, the colorings will be more profuse, because there will be more facets to show.

Even with such a stiff gradient—the Virgin system falls from fifty to seventy feet per mile, nine times as much as the Colorado in Grand Canyon—

you wonder, when you see the tiny creeks that act as feeders, how all this gorgeous destruction has been done. But there is a good key to the puzzle, a partial explanation. The river has able assistants in the nature of the rock and the cloudbursts of summer, but there is something else to be observed.

Suppose you have passed through the little Mormon village of Springdale and come to the south entrance of the park. For sheer surprise and the unfolding of wonders of form, this is the better way to come, though there will be no disappointment by any route. You see on either side of the Temples, the two great domes with crimson crests, and streaks of the same red down their sides. The Watchman, the Red Watchman, stands vigil over the valley. Somebody has called this other white summit, with its ruddy stains, the Altar of Sacrifice. We shall not quarrel with names, but its beauty required no gory reference. The strange white cones on the left are the broken top of the Streaked Wall.

Now, then, on your right is Bridge Mountain, called so because high up on its face there is a great flying buttress or natural bridge. In the face of that mountain, on the Pine Creek side, we are going to find the key to much of the demolition that produces gladdening sights. The famous Zion–Mount Carmel Road, after climbing almost eight hundred feet in three miles, by

*Along the Narrows Trail—a high-walled garden spot. Zion National Park.* [*Photo: Wayne Bryant*]

means of cleverly engineered switchbacks, plunges straight into the face of that canyon wall. The tunnel, much more than a mile long, has six openings, where visitors should pause and look. As the tunnel rises on a mild grade, each one of these openings forms a step in the ascent or descent.

When this spectacular tunnel was being built, the windows were cut first, and the debris from the borings was thrown into little Pine Creek below. Perhaps when you see Pine Creek almost dry and wholly innocuous, you will expect to see that rock rubbish which came out of the mountain wall. It is not there. In only a few months the floods that came down the creek as a result of rainbursts, pouring upon rock with no vegetation to hold back the water, had chewed up that rubble and whirled it on its way to Hoover Dam.

The north fork of the Virgin works upon soft material, for the most part. The amazing "architectural" shapes that everywhere greet the eye are due primarily to the attack upon the porous Navajo sandstone. A short, heavy rain on the rims above sends torrents of water pouring from the cliffs in large and small waterfalls. Frost and tree roots are forever sapping and mining. The weak sandstone itself disintegrates by chemical agencies. Over all, the Navajo formation is joined both horizontally and vertically. So the destruction, beginning at the bottom and causing great slabs and blocks to fall, results in those sheer walls, which remain precipitous even when the canyon is widening. In these circumstances it was natural that startling massive figures should result.

Somebody has called Zion Canyon a Yosemite done in oils. In the mere matter of dimension of the valley floors, there is indeed a similarity, as there is in the bare fact of overtowering walls; but to me Zion Canyon resembles only Zion Canyon. A stream-cut chasm through granite, later grooved and polished by glaciers, such as is Yosemite, does not appear like a Southwest canyon cut angularly through sandstone, whether or not it is painted in oils. This gorgeous pageant of the Utah-Arizona country, it seems to me, cannot be compared with anything else we have.

To travel up the eight miles of road from the south entrance of Zion to the oasis called the Temple of Sinawava is to follow the Virgin between high walls, widening and narrowing by turns, till the Narrows are reached. Then for a mile there is a walk into the soft twilight, cool and green, where the canyon walls become a mere slit in the rocks, but with festoons of greenery and blooming flowers high up on their moist sides. What a stroll is this! And it should be a stroll, with ample time to feel it all. This, remember—this Southwest—is a country of much time. Depend upon it, the Great White Throne will be looking down at Sinawava when you get back to that lovely spot.

There are trails to East and West Rims, and from the top, looking down, a very different Zion is revealed. The relative proportions of the great mountain masses appear. From the valley floor, naturally, one cannot gauge the variation in heights. The coloring becomes something different.

You become aware that there is a constant deception in the color scheme. Some of the rocks are fooling you. They are getting their tints and shades from reflections, from subtle changes in the atmosphere. Angel's Landing, on the West Rim, is gleaming vermilion at the moment. Over to the left the Great White Throne is *not* white. What is it, then? Heaven knows. It is every color you ever saw, all in subdued, faintest tones—because it is getting the effect of every tint and shade from its surroundings.

Everyone says that the time to see Zion Canyon is when there is a full moon. For once everyone is right. It is not only the moon; it is the night, silent, windless, full of fragrances that have gone unnoticed in the lusty sunshine. It is a great moment in anyone's life when out of the darkness a filmy cloudlike apparition touches the peak of one of the cliffs above, and then, from this first torch, the lamplighters go speedily to work. The reds, pinks, creams, and yellows make themselves felt in the moonlight like ghosts of colors—but they are there.

A sweet retreat Zion Canyon must have been for the prehistoric cliff-dwelling people who once lived there, cultivating their crops of corn and beans and vines by the river and taking refuge in the face of the cliffs when need arose. Then, so far as humans were concerned, there seems to have been a long interlude, perhaps broken by the restless journeyings of the Spaniards, certainly by the indefatigable fur trappers and traders who sought out beaver streams. Then the Mormons.

Whatever former opinion may have been concerning the earlier domestic arrangements of these indomitable people who trudged into the desert and made it fertile and rich, nobody has ever had any doubt that they were pioneers of courage, intelligence, and utter self-reliance. They nosed everywhere; when roads were lacking, they built them, even down the wall of a canyon; impediments merely whetted their insistence.

They found Zion. Or, if you wish, they refound it. The early Mormon history, like all other, has become a medley of fact and legend. It is sure that among the first Mormons in this canyon was Joseph Black. Homesteading precariously there, Black was so thrilled by the beauties and colossal

*Overleaf: A crossbedded sedimentary rock has its own austere beauty. Zion National Park. [Photo: M. Woodbridge Williams]*

forms, the colors and the delicious carpet greenery of the valley, that he tried to do it justice in messages to his friends back in Salt Lake. Now, Salt Lake has fine mountains, fine streams, and canyons at its threshold, too; but they are not like what Black saw, and the friends thought Joseph a trifle mad. With gentle sarcasm, they called it "Joseph's Glory." But when they, too, had seen it, the place became known as Zion or Little Zion.

Zion was not a term, with these stern religious folk, to be used in a offhand way. Zion was an aspiration, a promise, a prayer to be fulfilled. So Brigham Young, though he acknowledged all the beauty of the canyon, shook his head. "It is *not* Zion," he said.

There was discipline, as well as giants, in those days. For many years the canyon was dutifully called Not Zion—presumably with accent on the *not*.

## B. BRYCE CANYON NATIONAL PARK
### [*Utah*]

EBENEZER BRYCE, A MORMON CATTLEMAN, was forewarned by the example of Joseph Black. When he suddenly rode up to the brink of the "canyon" now named for him, and the dazzling color of it, and its bizarre spires and pinnacles, burst upon him like a fairy tale—and that is probably the way he stumbled to the verge of it—he kept the damper on his enthusiasm. He wanted nobody to joke about "Ebenezer's Glory" or to ask whether the hot sun had affected his head. He shifted his quid, stared at the miles of marching pink and white castellations, and murmured: "A tough place to find a stray cow." At least, that is the tale, and it sounds entirely reasonable.

The Paiutes were familiar with this great horseshoe-shaped bowl cut into the pink cliffs of the Paunsaugunt plateau. They marveled at it, possibly regarded it with a sort of religious awe. The Indian was closer to nature than we are and felt himself more a part of it than we do. I once heard a simple but affecting account from a highly educated Sioux of the way he had been accustomed as a youth to go up to the top of a neighboring hill and greet the rising sun, merely standing silently, self-effacingly, letting nature flow through him. No words, no posturing, but a perfect intimacy. I can believe that the Paiutes looked down into Bryce Bowl with that same simplicity and reverence. It is said that they called the painted amphitheater "unka-timpe-

*Naturally, somebody would waggishly call this "Wall Street." Bryce Canyon National Park. [Photo: M. Woodbridge Williams]*

wa-wince-pock-ich." Not knowing the Paiute tongue very well, I assume that this is succinct. It is translated as "red rocks standing like men in a bowl-shaped canyon." *Red* is correct: it is the master pigment. But it is pink, red, less red, more red, and white, creamy white, ivory—oh, it is of no possible use to try to tell it in words. You have to see it. The delicacy of it is melting. The domes and spires and temples carved in the rocks of Bryce are rugged, even colossal, yet I feel that there is a tenderness and gentleness about them that is not common in rocks. You may feel differently after you have gone down by one of the many trails to the floor and find yourself hemmed in by an army of gaudy jinn.

Bryce is not really a canyon, but it came into the National Park System by that name, and it really makes little difference. In an area three miles long and about two miles wide the falling rains and snows, the wind, and the changes in temperature have cut down a thousand feet into the pink and white limy sandstone. The streams of the present plateau have done little, for those watercourses fall away from the rim. But the Paria and its rapid tributaries have cut deep into the face of the Paunsaugunt. The erosion is constant. The rim of the "canyon" is receding constantly, and the forms are constantly changing—new ones appearing, old ones softening down and altering shapes —though in any brief period the difference might not be apparent. New natural bridges are destined to appear; present arches will crumble and fall; but the colors—the corals, the oranges, the roses, all those pastels which now delight the eye by changing with every hour—will, I should suppose, be even more emphasized as the gnawing at the rocks goes on.

A series of fine horseback and foot trails has been built by the Park Service in the area under the rim. Inquiry should always be made before attempting a trip, as storms sometimes make the trails unsafe. Trails lead into Queen's Garden, the Silent City, Fairyland, Wall Street, Peekaboo Canyon, and other points. Horses and guides are always available. For those who do not wish to go below the rim—and this is almost unthinkable for people who are physically able—there is a delightful walk along the rim, with benches where one can sit. By all means follow some of the trails—but also, by all means sit. Meditate awhile about the Palette on which these colors were mixed.

## C. GUADALUPE MOUNTAINS NATIONAL PARK
### [*Texas*]

IN THE DAYS when the Butterfield stages bumped and rattled through this West Texas country, and changed horses at the Pinery station in the shadow of Guadalupe Peak, there were elk and turkeys and Texas bighorn in the mountain wilderness. The cougar and the bobcat saw to it that there was no population explosion on the part of the smaller animals. The Mescalero Apaches were fighting a bitter but hopeless battle against submersion in the westward flood of the whiteman's progress.

Prehistoric Americans had occupied these canyons perhaps as long ago as ten thousand years, and had hunted animals now long extinct. The Spanish conquerors noted the existence of the Guadalupes as they passed northwest of them along the Rio Grande, or up the Pecos. In the mid-nineteenth century military expeditions were surveying possible routes to the Pacific. Captain John Pope attempted to establish a post in the lower Pecos Valley in 1855, but gave up for lack of potable water. The Butterfield Trail was used for less than a year and was located far southward. The deeply cut mountains seemed to offer slight invitation for exploitation, so they slumbered through the years while traffic moved around them. Only in recent years have the geologists and other men of science revealed the significance of this region, in some respects unique. The world's best known fossil organic reefs are found here, and the greatest of them, the Capitan, has been described as the most extensive known to exist in our world.

A marine barrier reef here? Here, in Texas and the adjoining part of New Mexico? Well, of course this phenomenon has no element of surprise for the geologist; but most of us, who are not specialists, have to peer pretty dimly back through the passages of earth's long history to imagine the invasion by the ocean, in the period called the Permian, of this part of the continent. But so it was: a vast salt-water basin in a large part of what are now Texas and New Mexico. In the shallower water tiny, lime-secreting organisms created a barrier not essentially different from that which shelters the coastline of Queensland, Australia, today. When Guadalupe Mountains National Park is ready for visitors, there will be a museum in which the geological story will be graphically interpreted.

What we shall visit is a highland area that rises from about 3,000 feet in the Pecos Valley near Carlsbad, New Mexico, to the 8,751 feet of Guadalupe Peak. This is the highest point in Texas, though Mount Emory in the Chisos Mountains of Big Bend National Park is a worthy second. This highland is the northeast arm of the Guadalupe Mountain range, which resembles a great V, with two arms extending into New Mexico. One of the arms contains Carlsbad Caverns National Park, which will be a neighbor of only a few cross-country miles.

Though the geological features of the area come first in importance, the life communities are extraordinary in their zonal range. Here, within the space of a few miles, even a nonscientific observer will clearly note that four climatic zones are represented, from the character of northern Mexico to that of southern Canada. Here are agaves and cactuses at the foot of the mountains, but as elevation is gained, and with an increase in vegetation, we reach highlands with a cover of pines, alligator juniper, even a sampling of Douglas fir and groves of quaking aspen. There are spots on the highest peaks that show decidedly Canadian attributes. Roasting pits found at all elevations indicate that the early inhabitants followed the ripening of native plants from the valley floor in spring to the highest ridges in autumn. Many pictographs are found in the caves and rock shelters.

In 1961 the federal government received from Wallace Pratt a donation of 5,632 acres of land in the fine North McKittrick Canyon area of these mountains. It was thought at that time that the gift might someday be joined with Carlsbad Caverns National Park, but something even better than that awaited the preservation. It so happened that more than 70,000 acres of ranch land adjoining the Pratt holding were owned by J. C. Hunter, Jr., of Abiline, Texas, who ran a great herd of angora goats for the production of mohair wool. When one remembers John Muir's classic definition of sheep as "hoofed locusts," and that the goat is just as remorseless a feeder, that does not sound promising. But the Hunters, father and son, had shown an unusual affection for the land and an interest in preserving the more fragile features, as well as in restoring wildlife.

Since the early 1920's, an elk herd has been established—if not the identical species that were wiped out, at least a related species. The wild turkey has been restored. The little hunting that has been done has been strictly controlled. The section of the ranch used for goal raising was not the part of the area containing the best ecological values. Particularly, J. C. Hunter has employed strict conservation practices to protect the more sensitive terrain and its vegetation. Also it was his desire that when the ranch was sold, it should be preserved and protected for cultural and recreative public use. In 1965 Congress authorized the purchase of the land and the creation of one more national park.

Not least interesting to the conservation world is the fact that this is the first national park which has been acquired by purchase of private lands. Hitherto, either the land involved was already in federal domain, or was

*Bristlecone pine may be the world's oldest living thing. Cedar Breaks National Monument. [Photo: Weldon F. Heald]*

donated. True, in the case of this park there is a donated part, but the major part was bought—and at a bargain price.

### D. CEDAR BREAKS NATIONAL MONUMENT
#### [Utah]

TWO MILES ABOVE SEA LEVEL, and still in the pink-cliffs formation, Cedar Breaks National Monument is, you might say, an appendix to the Red Book of the Utah-Arizona colorland. It is not a repetition of Bryce. There is naturally a similarity, but in this area which has been marked for preservation out of Dixie National Forest, we come upon something even more brilliantly colored, and on a greater scale, than the bowl of Ebenezer Bryce.

The climate here is superb. In summer, when the desert is seething with heat, there is perfect comfort at Cedar Breaks. The gathering clouds, though they do not gather to remain for any length of time, may bring flurries of snow in July. In July, too, there is enough moisture in the ground to provide rich displays of wild flowers. There are fine forests of fir and spruce, and meadows with carpets of blossoms that vie with the rocks of the amphitheaters—a competition for the admiration of visitors which, in July, is not common in the desert country.

Here the pink cliffs are nearly two thousand feet thick, and the rock shapes are bolder. The road skirts the rim in places, revealing from a number of outlooks the furrowed and corroded side walls, broken into massive ridges that radiate from the center like the spokes of a wheel. White or orange at the top, the cliffs, as they go down, are in rose and coral tints. There are chocolates, yellows, lavenders, and even purples. This is not one bowl, but really a series of them, or broken circles with the ends joined.

Someone has said: "If Cedar Breaks were anywhere but in this region, it would be picked as one of the world's greatest scenic wonders." It is true. It seems like the final lavish disbursement of a spendthrift of beauty.

### E. DINOSAUR NATIONAL MONUMENT
#### [Utah–Colorado]

NOBODY KNOWS who may first have seen those monstrous petrified bones which protruded from the coarse-grained rock lying upturned along the north side of the Green River where it makes its swing from Colorado over into Utah. Possibly the aboriginal Indians saw and marveled at them, for there is ample and valuable evidence that prehistoric man lived in what is now

Dinosaur National Monument. Indeed, it was about the farthest north of the early "southwestern culture," and tree-ring studies have established habitation there at about A.D. 500.

The first man to report the quarry of bones of the fossil reptiles was O. A. Peterson. That was in 1892. Earl Douglass, working the area for the Carnegie Museum of Pittsburgh, found the rich main deposit in 1909, and Dinosaur is now one of the most famous of the world storehouses where there were strange mass deaths of the creatures and they were preserved under exactly the right conditions, so that we are now able to recover and re-create the skeletons of the nightmarish reptiles that swarmed in the semi-tropical Jurassic plains more than 100 million years ago.

By 1922 the Carnegie Museum had removed a score of dinosaurs. Afterward the U. S. National Museum obtained additional specimens, and still later the University of Utah continued the exploration. It was while the Carnegie Museum was active in the quarry, in 1915, that the original area of eighty acres was set aside by Presidential proclamation for perpetual protection by the National Park Service.

In 1938 the original monument was enlarged to include about 325 square miles of federal land in Utah and Colorado. The irregular boundaries were calculated to preserve not merely the dinosaur quarry but the classic canyons of the Green River—Lodore, Whirlpool, and Split Mountain—through which Major John Wesley Powell had twice been buffeted on his way to the un-

*The bone is 135,000,000 years old. The girl is, say, 20? Dinosaur National Monument.*
*[Photo: M. Woodbridge Williams]*

charted waters of the Grand Canyon of Arizona; and included also were the canyons of the Yampa River from near Lily Park to the Green.

Now, the increase in the size of Dinosaur National Monument was no whim; nor was the National Park Service hungry for land, merely as such, to administer. With appropriations far from sufficient to do justice to the ever-growing desire of our mobile people to see their pristine America, it is hardly likely that the Service would invite additional custody of areas un-related to its well-defined purposes. Nor was the extension due to any recent discovery of the profound beauty and significance of these river reaches. Adventurous souls had been thrilled, over the years, by the colossal examples of nature's forces to be seen there. It was merely that the country had just arrived at this point in its program of preservation.

It happened that this magnificent area was placed in safekeeping none too soon. We are in a period of dam building. It might be called our national "beaver period." Perhaps that is unjust to the beaver, who may have a prescience of which I know nothing. There is no doubt that many river dams are not only justified, but most necessary. Many are valuable, but less necessary. Some are of doubtful long-range value; some pose as being for one purpose when they are really for something else; some are just dams, result-ing from the simple fact that if you are skilled in building dams, you like to build dams—in itself, if bridled, a very human and laudable trait. I admire these expert engineers no end. But I tremble for the day when they first see the trout brook behind my humble country box.

As for the extension of the boundaries of Dinosaur, it has been well said that errors in the creation of national parks have seldom been that too much land was taken but have often been that too little was taken. Let me see if I can present an analogy. It may limp a little, but I think it will do.

The reader of this chapter may be one of those who, each working day, passes through the entrance of some great office building whose portals are reared on blocks of polished granite. Perhaps you have paused beside one of those stone blocks for a moment and admired its texture. It might be, even, that you became curious about granite and got out your old geology textbook and relearned that those crystals in the stone, made brilliant by polishing, were quartz and feldspar and some kind of mica. Now, those things are good to know; but if you stop there, you really know very little about the story of granite and its place in this fascinating natural world.

*The meaning of these rock pictures is unknown; but they surely had purpose. Dino-saur National Monument.* [*Photo: M. Woodbridge Williams*]

Perhaps the quarry from which the granite block came is not very far from the place where it now rests. So one Saturday afternoon you go out to the quarry. Here, on a cliffside, is exposed the mighty jointed raw material from which the finished building blocks are broken and hewn, and there are the great cranes and derricks that swing them from their bed. Now you know more about granite, but you are still far from the whole story. How did the granite come to be there, on that spot, and not somewhere else?

So you go on a hike in the adjacent area. And soon you discover, maybe, that the outcropping rock you now find around you is not granite at all, but a kind of slaty rock, with the bedding planes turned up at a sharp angle; and in making a great circle around the dome of granite, you find that the inclination of the slate layers is such that they seem to have been thrust back by some force from the center. Thus you come to the fact that the big dome of granite was actually an intruder, which thrust up as molten rock under an older rock that had hardened from mud at the bottom of a shallow sea. It did not break through to the surface, this hardening granite, but bowed up the older rock above it.

You can get the same effect (with the housewife's permission) if you take a dozen dinner plates and slip them under the tablecloth to the center of the table. You make a dome, but the plates are not visible. In the case of the granite, it was exposed and ready for quarrying only when the surface rock had eroded away. But there is more yet to find out, and you need more travel. Your area must be extended.

Perhaps this country where the granite is quarried is mountainous. But the rivers do not flow as though they had first made their beds while coursing down steep declivities. They take meandering courses. How could that be? To determine the answer to that, you need a still wider range of observation.

Now, Dinosaur National Monument needed extension for reasons similar to those in this imperfect example I have given. To begin with, perhaps you have seen first the reconstructed skeleton of the colossal dinosaur called *Diplodocus* on exhibit at the U.S. National Museum. With infinite pains and scientific skill this skeleton was put together from the petrified bones taken from the quarry at Dinosaur National Monument. You gaze at the remains of a prodigious creature that has disappeared from earth. You are glad there are none of them to meet on the way home from work. Your imagination clothes those stony bones with flesh. But still, you know little about those reptiles and the conditions under which they throve.

When you visit the quarry at Dinosaur National Monument, you come nearer to that strange life form. You may see where the bones are adroitly taken from the rock—that rock of the "Morrison formation" which in this exact spot represents a former shifting river channel. Here the dinosaurs and other reptiles met death in a great group, for some reason not known. A museum near the quarry contains the fossilized bones of some of these reptiles, as well as explanatory maps, photographs, and paintings. Now the dinosaur becomes somewhat more real, and yet there is still much to observe on the road to knowing.

You are here in a mountainous country, but obviously these ungainly creatures were never built to climb hills. It is evident that they lumbered through lush vegetation in a region almost as flat as your hand, where the sluggish streams took winding courses through sandy or muddy plains. Here are the bones, then, of gigantic sauropods—but this is surely *not* the land-scape that, alive, they saw!

*Where Major John Wesley Powell had hardships, nowadays river-runners have thrills. Dinosaur National Monument.* [*Photo: M. Woodbridge Williams*]

The intervening millennia have brought mighty changes. To see what has happened, you must leave the bone quarry and look at the gorgeous canyons of the Green and the Yampa. There you will find not only beauty and the ferocity of swift-flowing rivers armed with abrasives, but also the explanation of what has occurred to the whole Rocky Mountain region since the dinosaurs floundered and fed there.

You will see that the Green River, instead of taking the easy way westward, has apparently plunged directly southward through the hard rocks of the Uinta uplift, creating the turbulent rapids of Split Mountain Canyon. You will see that the Yampa also has done things the impossible way. Like the Colorado at Grand Canyon, it is flowing along the flanking slope of a plateau. But a river cannot start in business that way; and so, by viewing the monument as a whole, the perception comes that this Rocky Mountain region was once a plain, or nearly so. Earth forces have raised it high above the sea and arched it into ranges. It has been crumpled, broken, deformed, and worn down. The Green and the Yampa have kept to the beds they made before the uplift came, and as a consequence are now flowing at the bottom of stupendous canyons; and the picture is considered by many even more revealing than that shown in the Grand Canyon.

The reconstructed skeletons in the great natural-history museums are the tickets to a long journey into the past; a visit to the dinosaur quarry has the thrill of approaching a little nearer to that faraway period. But it is the surrounding country—so extraordinary that it may someday gain the status of a national park—that enables us to imagine the conditions which made possible the reptilian life that once dominated the scene.

## 5. BADLANDS NATIONAL MONUMENT
### [South Dakota]

TOURISTS WHO DRIVE through the Black Hills of South Dakota on their way to Yellowstone or other Western national parks will be richly rewarded by a visit to the School of Mines in Rapid City. They will be even more surprised and delighted if, coming from the east on U. S. 16, they do *not* rush blindly through the "Mauvaises Terres," or Badlands, intent only upon the principal objects of their tour. To do so is to miss some of the strangest as well as the most beautiful scenery of the West.

*In the boiling river at Split Mountain. Dinosaur National Monument. [Photo: M. Woodbridge Williams]*

[ 216 ]

The mineral collection of the School of Mines is outstanding. There are larger exhibits and greater curiosities than those shown here, but I know of no collection that is displayed with finer taste and museum skill than this one. Perhaps it is only natural that it should be so, for right at the door of the school is, for a start, one of the most variously mineralized regions in the world. In addition to those local specimens, there are precious trophies of crystals and ores from most of the best world sources.

What may interest the average visitor most, however, is the fine exhibit of extinct animals that once roamed in grassy swamps where, in the Badlands, now stands an almost barren labyrinth of pinnacles and bizarre shapes, washed into existence first from the high levels of the ancient Black Hills, and then carved by weathering. From Cedar Pass to Pinnacles, along the road through the monument, visitors may stop their cars and view billows and peaks and valleys of delicately banded colors—colors that shift in the sunshine, reds, grays, and a thousand tints that color charts do not show. In the early morning and in the evening, when shadows are cast upon the infinite number of peaks, or on a bright moonlight night when the whole region seems a part of another world than ours, the Badlands will be an experience not easily forgotten.

Now a country almost devoid of water, this region once must have had ample moisture. The three-toed horse, the camel, the rhinoceros, the saber-toothed tiger, and all the rest of those creatures whose artfully reconstructed skeletons are to be seen at the School of Mines were snuffed out of existence for the same reason that the people of Mesa Verde were finally forced to migrate. With the people, the cause was a short-term drought; with the extinct animals the gradual climatic change went on over a myriad of lifetimes. But the change from a moist condition to one of aridity did it; and the huge titanothere, king of the grass-eating animals, part elephant and part rhinoceros, literally starved to death, to be covered by silt and sand, and 40 million years later to be washed into the light of day again.

Little by little the Badlands are disappearing. The easily eroded volcanic cinders that were spewed over this region by volcanoes when the Rocky Mountain front was being raised and all nature was in labor pains are being carried to the sea—the destiny of all raised earth surfaces—through gullies and draws to the White River, thence to the Missouri and the Mississippi.

A mere glance at this wild, barren land might convince anyone that animal and plant life would be impossible. Yet a surprising number of small animals manage an existence; birds are not scarce, and the golden eagle is sometimes seen hovering over the peaks. As for flowers, they simply cannot be sup-

*On the trail through the "open door." Badlands National Monument. [Photo: R. A. Grom]*

pressed, it would seem. For here on these inhospitable clays the gumbo lily, or evening primrose, luxuriates. The prickly pear—great fields of it—bursts into its waxy red and yellow bloom, and the Spanish dagger—that same resolute plant which battles with the shifting gypsum sands in White Sands National Monument in New Mexico—finds the Badlands to its liking.

So do not hurry through the Badlands. The Dakota Indians found it hard to travel through, and called it *makosica* (bad land); but they had no surfaced highways and no speeding carriages that go without horses. They did, however, have plenty of time. In that respect let us emulate the Dakotas.

### 6. COLORADO NATIONAL MONUMENT
### [*Colorado*]

AT A TIME when human beings were still in the blueprint stage—they were "on order," as the procurement division says—some very strange beasts were roaming the shallows and swamps that existed where the present Colorado National Monument is situated. Here in the sandstone—called by geologists the Morrison formation—are found the bones of five species of dinosaurs. They were lizards. I saw one of the modern representatives of the family the other day as I was walking a shady path in the damp woods. He was a bright-red eft, with black spots—about an inch long. The family has shrunk in size, but is probably just as happy.

These Morrison lizards were of tremendous bulk. About sixty-five of them, head to tail, in a circus parade, would stretch a mile. Brontosaurus— called the thunder-lizard because the earth might seem to have trembled under his tread—was at least sixty-seven feet long, as a well-articulated skeleton in a museum shows. Diplodocus may have reached the length of ninety feet. But Diplodocus had a brain that weighed fifteen ounces.

The ultimate in brainlessness seems to have been the Stegosaurus, the fellow with heavy armor plate over his neck. His brain weighed two and a half ounces, whereas his body weighed ten tons. It is something to speculate upon—why, at the period when these dinosaurs lived, there should have been such a tendency toward flesh and bone. Can it be that brain development keeps down one's weight? If this should be so, and your friends tell you that they are planning to reduce, you may look for some pretty handsome intellectual results.

One of the other saurians was a giraffelike wading creature, and there was a meat eater with short forelegs and long hind legs. Even in museums, stripped down to their bones, the dinosaurs have an unpleasant look, to most people; but this may be sheer prejudice. Certainly, in a world that has so many difficulties currently, we need not regret their extinction.

Colorado National Monument is an area of fantastically carved and highly colored highlands, with sheer-walled canyons, towering stone towers, and fluted columns. Weird formations come into view at every turn of the road that follows the rim of the canyons for most of its twenty-two miles. There are parking spots at particularly scenic outlooks. Devil's Kitchen, Coke Ovens, Monolith Parade, and Window Rock are a few of the examples of nature's handiwork. The monument road is open and passable all year.

## 7. BLACK CANYON OF THE GUNNISON NATIONAL MONUMENT
### [Colorado]

GOVERNMENT PUBLICATIONS are commonly regarded as desiccated fodder circulated to everybody and read by nobody. There may be some truth in this, but there was a period when some of the most stirring narratives of adventure and courage poured fom the government printing presses. It was in the middle part of the nineteenth century, when the great westward march of Americans was attaining its swing. Army engineers, supported by meager detachments of troops, were surveying the states west of the Mississippi for practicable railroad routes to the Pacific. Geologists, botanists, topographers, accompanying the surveying parties, were furnishing the reports that, for the first time, acquainted the people with the potentials of their little-known territories.

And there were tragedies in those Senate and House documents, too. These explorations were no tea parties. The reports to the Secretary of War are replete with harrowing tales of hardship—soldiers who had straggled, lost in the desert; the loss of food and transport; attacks by seemingly friendly Indians who suddenly went on the warpath.

I have before me, as I write this, Volume II of a Senate Document, which opens with the day-by-day journal of Lieutenant E. G. Beckwith, Third Artillery—the narrative of the survey for a possible railroad along the 38th and 39th parallels. The first paragraph is severely formal:

*Sir: In order that you may be put in possession . . . of the result of the investigations of the exploring party organized under your order of the 20th of May, 1853, by the lamented Captain J. W. Gunnison of the Corps of Topographical Engineers, who was barbarously massacred by the Pah Uta Indians on the Sevier River, in the Territory of Utah, I deem it my duty . . .*

The account is more thrilling than any Wild Western fiction.

*Captain Gunnison had encamped early in the afternoon. . . . It was known that a band of Indians was near him, but a recent quarrel had terminated, and an experienced citizen of the Territory, acting as guide, had considered a small escort sufficient. . . .*

*The sun had not yet risen when the surrounding quietness was broken by a volley of rifles and a shower of arrows. . . . Stepping from his tent Captain Gunnison called to his savage murderers that he was their friend; but this had no effect. . . . Only those escaped who succeeded in mounting on horseback, and even these were pursued for many miles. . . .*

And there, near the Sevier, fell Captain Gunnison, for whom is named this Gunnison River; and the thrilling Black Canyon constitutes one of the most remarkable bits of scenery of the Rocky Mountain states. Within the boundaries of the national monument lies the deepest and most spectacular ten-mile section of the gorge of the Gunnison, cut through the heart of a great plateau; it is notable for its narrowness, its sheer walls, and the extraordinary depth, which ranges from 1,730 to 2,425 feet. So narrow are some places in the canyon that the channel of the river has only forty feet of space; so deep that only at midday does the sun light up the perpetual twilight on the bottom. It was partly because of this that the canyon was called "black," but also because of the nature of the rocks through which the river has cut. These are ancient dark schists, with many intrusions of dark granite; and where they are weathered and stained, the gloomy and forbidding aspect is heightened.

Both rims of the canyon within the monument are accessible by automobile in the late spring and in summer.

The trees of the monument are of unusual interest. On the highest point on the south rim, at an elevation of 8,300 feet, is a stand of piñon patriarchs. Borings taken from some of the trees showed ages of from 467 to 742 years.

## 8. CAPITOL REEF NATIONAL MONUMENT
### [Utah]

INACCESSIBLE? Not to the prehistoric Indian, at first a "basketmaker." He seems to have lodged everywhere in the Southwestern country where there occurred a reliable trickle of water and a flat of soil that would provide sustenance. And meager though that sustenance was, he had the urge to make pictures on the surrounding rocks. The spirit of the artist budded in his soul: cornbread and snared rabbits were not all of life, and hands could do other than wield a wooden hoe. Some of these mystifying petroglyphs at Capital Reef were tinted with color obtained from minerals and the scant vegetation.

Inaccessible? Yes, so far as the white man was concerned, until very late in the exploration day. This great, brilliant escarpment, extending from Thousand Lake Mountain southeastward for 150 miles to the Colorado River, was uncharted domain until Colonel John C. Frémont looked down upon it one day in 1854. Later a band of Mormons came in and gazed at it, for they were ever seeking tillable land. But the first real study of the area waited for a member of the Powell survey of 1875.

Beautiful though the reef is—this edge of an earth-folding—it will never be described as an agricultural breadbasket. A sturdy pioneer managed a homestead here in 1880, but a few families was all it could support. Fortunate that there are places without the chance of exploitation for material ends! Visitors will come here to delight their eyes, and engage their wonder.

The present Rocky Mountains began their upheaval, rising from forces working within the earth crust. Swamps and shallow lagoons that had been the lush feeding grounds of giant reptiles (they have left footprints in the rippled shale along the base of the escarpment) were gradually elevated until it was no longer a place for such animal life. They went—or died; and finally they did both. This shale is a reddish brown; above it is another shale of many tints and shades, and then still higher the red sandstone is cut into strange pinnacles. Finally comes the capping of the white Navajo sandstone, whose domes (like those of many state capitols) give the reef its name.

From the visitor center, a road leads southward to Pleasant Creek. Off this road are spurs that can be followed into Grand Wash and Capitol Gorge. Richly rewarding is the short hike that is needed to find yourself in a narrow street with walls that tower a thousand feet on either side. Somewhat more than two miles into Capitol Gorge there is a trail that leads to the top of the reef.

The upper sections of the monument offer opportunities to do some exploring in wild country, but all except the initiated should stick closely to the trails, and should by all means tell the superintendent what they plan

*In trolley-car days someone said, "Look! The Motorman!" The name stuck. Capitol Reef National Monument.* [*Photo: George Grant*]

to do and report their return to him. It is better to be frankly prudent than to boast of a self-sufficiency that is likely to disappear when most required.

## 9. ARCHES NATIONAL MONUMENT
### [*Utah*]

NOT FAR from the old Mormon pioneer town of Moab, a great mass of buff-colored sandstone towers over the surrounding plain. Into this rock the weathering forces of nature have cut more natural stone arches, windows, spires, and pinnacles than are to be found anywhere else in the country. So far, eighty-eight openings large enough to be called arches have been discovered within the boundaries of this monument, but it is certain that others will be found hidden away in the less accessible rugged areas.

Landscape Arch, believed to be the longest natural stone span in the world, has a length of 291 feet. The lower end of Devil's Garden, a part of the monument known as the Fiery Furnace—a great jumble of vertical slabs of red rock that glows in the setting sun like a mighty fire—is such rough terrain that it has never yet been thoroughly explored. Another part that awaits full knowledge lies west of the Dark Angle portion of Devil's Garden. Tower Arch, a rock formation known as Joseph Smith and the Golden Plates, and the long rows of immense parallel sandstone fins can be seen at the end of a four-mile trail trip necessary to reach the Klondike Bluffs section.

The impressive grandeur of Delicate Arch, in its setting of precipitous cliffs and massive domes of "slickrock," with the gorge of the Colorado River beyond and the snow-capped peaks of the La Sal Mountains in the distance, may be enjoyed by taking a spur road to a point two miles away and then following a foot trail.

## 10. NATURAL BRIDGES NATIONAL MONUMENT
### [*Utah*]

FORMERLY the three great natural bridges within this monument were known by the names of Edwin, Caroline, and Augusta. These are good wholesome names, fit to be embroidered on a bath towel. But they were no more in place in this kaleidoscope-cliffed San Juan County of Utah than a Paiute Boulevard would be in the city of Liverpool.

---

*On a side gulch in Armstrong Canyon is Owachomo. Natural Bridges National Monument.* [*Photo: George Grant*]

*Hickman Natural Bridge. Capitol Reef National Monument.* [*Photo: George Grant*]

It is true that the local Indians did not have individual names for the holes in the rocks. To them any kind of bridge was simply "under the horse's belly." Quite graphic, surely; but the visiting Indian (and some of those early redfolk were tourists traveling light) might well ask: "Which horse?" Well, somebody recalled that the prehistoric inhabitants of southern Utah were possibly the ancestors of the present Hopis. Whether or not this is so, the bridges now have Hopi names. Edwin became Owachomo; Caroline is now Kachina; Augusta is Sipapu. And for excellent reasons, which I leave you to discover when you rest at the bases of these colossal arches and peruse the park folder.

Though of great size, and each possessing a marked individuality, these natural bridges are surpassed in grandeur by Rainbow Bridge, which lies in a preserved area of the National Park System about sixty miles to the southwest. Yet they are among the world's greatest; and after all, our captivation by such superlatives as biggest, highest, or fastest is rather a juvenile trait. Do you *like* it? Does it *inspire* you, more than anything else of its kind? Do you *tune* to it? These are the important matters. Of all these natural arches I somehow like Landscape best. But don't ask me why. I can't explain. There is no disputing of taste.

You are here in a country of piñon and juniper forest, and in the canyons the bighorn find food and a pleasant place to ruminate in the winter midday sun. Coyotes and bobcats move around without undue noise—though occasionally the coyote practices his song at night. Once in a while a cougar prowls through. Maybe you already know this kind of country—vast, mystic, satisfying when you come partly to feel its allure.

You won't fail to interest yourself in the origin of such natural bridges as these, wherever they exist. How the studies of the geologist and naturalist have determined that they are of various stages of maturity—some young, some old, some on the road to departure and destined to leave behind only relic abutments on the canyon walls. How swift water erosion has mostly chiseled some of them; how others are more the work of frost and sand-laden winds and rain. How varying rock material and climatic conditions may govern the type of arch. All such things. Fascinating, and wonderful

*Landscape Arch and Devils Garden. Arches National Monument.* [*Photo: Jack E. Boucher*]

considerations to think of, to take your mind off your worry about a dis-ordered world.

There are thousands of prehistoric ruins all through this painted canyon world, too.

## 11. RAINBOW BRIDGE NATIONAL MONUMENT
### [*Utah*]

PARTLY SPANNING BRIDGE CANYON, which extends from the western slope of Navajo Mountain to the Colorado River near where that stream crosses the Arizona-Utah boundary, Rainbow Bridge was long the least accessible of all the natural wonders included in the National Park System.

If I know anything about Americans, this statement was always accepted as a challenge. It is like telling the venturesome that a certain mountain peak has never been climbed. Very well; if you knew how to make your way through a desert country with no roads—unless you call *those things* roads—or if you wanted to make a six-mile hike up Bridge Canyon after having come down the Colorado River by boat, you were one of the small number of Americans who saw this phenomenon of erosion.

Worn into the salmon-pink rock of the Navajo sandstone, Rainbow Bridge is, so far as is known, the greatest natural bridge in the world. It not only is a symmetrically curved arch below, but also presents a curved surface above, thus suggesting a rainbow to the Navajos and the Paiutes, who had names for it in their own languages. Both tribes had called it Rainbow Bridge before the white man came.

The bridge is 309 feet in the clear from the bottom of the gorge, and the horizontal span from pier to pier is 287 feet. If it could be arched over the dome of the Capitol in Washington, there would still be space to spare.

Somewhere between Rainbow Bridge and Navajo National Monument the car stalled. It had been raining, though the cart track across the desert looked dried out. You never know. In a low spot, down went one of the rear wheels, and it began to spin. Well, that is nothing. You get out and look for sage or greasewood, and you finally rock the tire up on some brush —it may take some time and some brush—and off you go. But this time it didn't work. The wheel got deeper into the treacherous sand, and it looked like a long sojourn on the spot.

An old Navajo came along. He couldn't speak English or Spanish, but he was interested in the predicament. He squatted down and looked and reflected. He knew what was needed: horses. Off to the right a flash flood had left a wide, shallow "river." The Navajo peeled off his good trousers of civilization, waded across, and disappeared. More perspiring efforts with sagebrush under the wheel. No result, except to go deeper into the sand.

Then a young Navajo schoolboy came along. He knew English. He said he would try to get help, and he disappeared. Would either he or the old man bother to come back *¿Quien sabe?*—Spanish, which, in a case of growing despondency like this, means "probably not."

But after three long hours something appeared in the distance. It was a wagon. Sideless, drawn by two horses, with three passengers on the seat: the old man, the schoolboy, and another. Glory hallelujah! They had delivered their "message to Garcia." While the automobile was being dragged out, two more Navajos, gypsy-looking men, rode up and looked on.

A typical experience in the Navajo country. Something to talk over and laugh about when you get safely to port. But those incidents can be discouraging at the time!

## 12. CHIRICAHUA NATIONAL MONUMENT
### [*Arizona*]

IN MANY of the Western parks and monuments the agencies of erosion have carved the rocks into strange and imitative shapes, but to see what Nature can do when she sets out really to create a museum of "the grotesque and arabesque" (as Edgar Allan Poe called one of his collections of stories), it will perhaps be necessary to visit Chiricahua National Monument, in the southeastern part of the state. Here is the domain of whim. Here, if you get fun from finding silhouettes in stone of humans you like or don't like, of animals and edifices, of historical and legendary characters, you will find endless material.

Pinnacles are not uncommon, but here are incredibly slender ones, delicate needles reaching far skyward. Giant beasts and men you may have seen elsewhere, but these in Chiricahua are out of nightmares. Seventeen square miles on the western slope of the Chiricahua Mountains are crowded with mad sculptures.

They come into being mainly from the nature of the rock. Old lava flows, layer on layer, varying in thickness, spread out over this area. The lava shrank in cooling and vertical cracks were created, and when later the earth was slowly lifted and tilted, the forces of erosion began to work. Some of the rock layers were undercut. The great fissures were developed along lines that dimly indicated the finished work the sculptor might produce.

Massive rocks are balanced on teetering points; sometimes other rocks on top of the balanced ones; jutting rocks maintain such precarious positions that the law of gravitation seems defied. There are Punch and Judy's, China-Boys, and—but you may have more amusement in choosing your own names. Whatever you look at now will someday not be there, because the forces that created them will demolish them; but there will be others just as curious in their places, and some of the squarish blocks you see are the raw material for the shapes to come.

This is historic ground, too, which with the fine wildlife habitat gave additional reason for its preservation in the National Park System. For centuries the Chiricahua Mountains in southeastern Arizona were the home of the warlike Apaches. Living on wild animals and native plants, these people were always on the move, following the game and the seasonal supply of food, and varying their activities by raids on agricultural Indians of the desert valley.

With the coming of the white man, who introduced cattle, horses, and new foodstuffs, the Apaches waxed even more prosperous. Here was new and bigger plunder. Nor were these nomads respecters of persons. The inoffensive farmer Indians or the mail-and-passenger stages of the old Butterfield Express route—all were one to the Apaches.

Fort Bowie was established in 1862, to command the strategic Apache Pass at the end of the Chiricahua Mountains, and a troop of U.S. Cavalry was stationed there. But under the leadership of the slippery Chief Cochise the Indians continued their raids. It was not until 1886 that the famous Geronimo and his band finally surrendered, and even then a small force of Apaches led by Big Foot Massai continued to give trouble.

Because the Chiricahuas rise as a cool refuge from the semidesert grasslands of Arizona and neighboring New Mexico, there is a surprising variety of wildlife and forest cover. Whitetail deer are numerous, and among the birds are those which come from their homes in the wooded highlands of Mexico—birds like the coppery-tailed trogon and the thick-billed parrot. Dense vegetation covers the shaded canyon bottoms and the cooler northerly slopes of the high elevations.

An excellent mountain road can be followed by automobile up the Bonita Canyon to Massai Point, where there is a splendid view of the monument and the valleys to the east and west. Fourteen miles of trails enable visitors

*Lava rock was ideal for nature's sculptors. Chiricahua National Monument.* [*Photo: Wayne Bryant*]

to reach all parts of the monument on foot or horseback. When personnel is available, visitors are accompanied by park rangers, who explain the natural and historic events that have created the need for preservation of this fascinating bit of Western America.

## 13. AGATE FOSSIL BEDS NATIONAL MONUMENT
### [Nebraska]

IN THE MIOCENE EPOCH of the Tertiary Period (which is the geologic-clock division just before that in which modern man arrived to upset nature's applecart) there was a population explosion among the mammals. This evolutionary profusion has been referred to as the Golden Age of Mammals. How long ago? It isn't much use talking about millions of years, because we cannot readily comprehend the passage of even ten thousand. The geologist doesn't try. He contents himself with a scale of references governed by what he finds in the earth crust.

In these fossil beds in Sioux County, Nebraska, is a boneyard of strange creatures that came into being and passed into extinction without leaving more than the faintest characteristics associating them with the mammals of today. For example:

A two-horned rhinoceros, small but swift, about the size of a Shetland pony and presumably as numerous as later became the bison on our Western plains of the eighteenth century. A bizarre creature with a head like a horse, a suggestion of the giraffe, front legs rhinoceros-like, hind legs like a bear. Then there was the "terrible pig," a beast ten feet long and seven feet tall at the shoulder, with great tusks. Then a graceful little deerlike animal, no doubt in great numbers—some vague resemblance here to the South American guanaco.

This mammalian ossuary, called by Henry Fairfield Osborn the most remarkable deposit of the kind ever found, has long been known and studied by paleontologists, and the two grass-covered hills of the site are named University and Carnegie, for the work done in the field by parties from Nebraska University and the Carnegie Museum.

The find was on a ranch owned by Captain James H. Cook, a cattle-rancher who had been army scout, big-game hunter, and guide, and trusted friend of the Indians. He, and later his son Harold, fully understood the scientific importance of their fossil quarries, and they generously helped to preserve them for educational use and for ultimate possession by the public.

Though at the time of this description there are no exposed fossils to be seen at the two sites of the monument, the plan is that someday visitors will not only see the skeletons of these creatures of 15 million years ago, but also watch scientists working among them.

## 14. PINNACLES NATIONAL MONUMENT
### [*California*]

ASSUREDLY, this is the place for the hiker. If only to exercise the legs and fill the lungs with dry pure air, this alone is worthwhile. To get away from urban rush and conformity is better. Best of all is to follow some of the fifteen miles of trails and see an aftermath of one of nature's moments of violence. For here one views the wreckage of a lava field. Out of fissures in the crust flowed molten rock, piling up until it stood in domelike form three times as high as what is seen today. Roaring explosions of steam and gas threw liquid and solid rock into the air. A pudding was stirred—the breccia that became the common landscape base seen along the trails.

The rainfall here is scant, and comes ordinarily in winter and early spring. Then come months of dry heat. But the clothing vegetation has found

*The humble coreopsis becomes a giant on Anacapa Island. Channel Islands National Monument. [Photo: Ronald Mortimore]*

a way to creep in and get established upon this naked rock. Not trees, though you could call it a forest. These are leathery-leaved shrubs—chamise, some manzanita, some buckbrush. Altogether, this miniature forest is known as chaparral. Here in Pinnacles is perhaps the finest example of this type of vegetative cover that exists within the National Park System.

It is a curious thing that this chaparral's continuity is a matter not merely of its defenses against desert drought, but is also controlled by natural wild-fire; that is to say, not fires set by man, but usually by lightning. Long before man ever came to the scene, these fires swept the chaparral at intervals. This regular burning could be borne only by a plant adapted to it—able to restore itself from a large root crown, or to produce seeds that germinate by the very heat that kills its mother plant. It follows that, in a case like this, when man protects the chaparral by extinguishing brush fires—ordinarily a prudent thing to do—species that are less resistant to natural fires may be introduced. So you will see, for instance, the digger pine gradually spreading within the monument, and it is possible that someday it may replace the "pygmy trees."

Nevertheless, it is better for us to be careful with our matches. Don't draw unfortunate conclusions from one interesting biological fact. Don't "play Nature!"

## 15. CHANNEL ISLANDS NATIONAL MONUMENT
### [*California*]

SOMETIMES during the misty geological past the eight islands that lie off the southern California coast were part of the mainland. In relation to the land mass, the ocean level changed, so that what were the tops of mountains were alone left unsubmerged. Two of these former peaks, Santa Barbara and Anacapa—the smallest of the group—constitute the monument that was set aside in 1938 for the preservation of a plant and animal life which in the course of time has had to pursue its own special way. Whatever could adapt itself to new conditions survived, somewhat changing its form; all the rest was destined to extinction. Thus the story told here, of the results of geographical isolation by the forces of nature, is suggestive of what has happened everywhere in our world under like conditions.

Santa Barbara Island is about opposite San Pedro, thirty-eight miles away. Anacapa Island, forty miles to the north, is ten miles from the mainland. Visitors have been few in these wild domains, where the barking of sea lions is continuous and the voices of the gulls and other sea birds advertise the questing, nesting, and quarreling that goes on along the cliffs that face the sea. More frequent than human visitors are the cruising sea elephants, huge and fantastic in shape—the bull of the species has a foot-long snout that gives it its name. Occasionally one of the rare sea otters is seen. But the California sea lion, which learns circus tricks so readily, is the sure attraction.

The National Park Service has plans to provide ways for more Americans to know these interesting places which have hitherto been so near and yet so remote. Anacapa, in particular, will have means of access, camping accommodations, and the interpretive services so greatly needed for appreciation of the "way of life" in a community that is highly specialized.

For example, the giant coreopsis, seen to fullest perfection on the island of Santa Barbara, is a treelike sunflower whose thick, gray-barked "trunk" grows to a height of eight feet. It aspires to be a tree. In summer, which is rainless, coreopsis appears to be without life. It is only sleeping. With the rains, it puts forth a new growth of feathery leaves. Coreopsis reminds the botanist of the odd tendency, on islands, for the Compositae family to become shrubs and even trees. On Juan Fernández is seen an example of how even the lowly lettuce plant can be a lusty figure in the landscape.

The boatman approaching Santa Barbara Island sees from miles away the golden yellow flame of its full bloom of spring. But this is only one flower of a great number of plants that are as distinctly individual as those of the deserts of the mainland.

*Sea elephants eye the photographer with sullen suspicion. Channel Islands National Monument. [Photo: Lowell Sumner]*

# [ V ]

# *The Underground World*

BY AND BY *somebody shouted:*
*"Who's ready for the cave?"*
*Everybody was. Bundles of candles were procured, and straightway there*
*was a general scamper up the hill. The mouth of the cave was up*
*the hillside—an opening shaped like a letter A. . . . By and by the*
*procession went filing down the steep descent of the main avenue.*

—M A R K   T W A I N , *Adventures of Tom Sawyer*

## 1. CARLSBAD CAVERNS NATIONAL PARK
### [*New Mexico*]

WHEN the Spanish conquistadors forged their way northward from Mexico—a march of continuous reconnoitering in an unmapped wilderness—they probably skirted the foothills of the Guadalupe Mountains in what is now southeastern New Mexico. It is quite possible, as they searched everywhere for loot, that they saw the dragon-mouth entrance to Carlsbad Caverns.

Two and a half centuries later the Butterfield Trail, the first such route across the West, freighted more gold on one stage, from the California placers, than the Spaniards ever found in their fruitless quest; and the Butterfield wagons crossed the older trail not far from the caves. Behind the gold-rush wayfarers came the cattlemen and the permanent settlers. They knew the caverns, called them the Bat Caves, and found them rich in—what? Beauty? Mystery? Geological revelation?

Not at all. They found in them a new and valuable product: bat guano.

---

*Temple of the Sun, in the "Big Room." Carlsbad Caverns National Park.* [*Photo: George Grant*]

The occupancy of millions upon millions of bats, through at least fifteen centuries, had presented the eager exploiters of the nineteenth century with what seemed at first glance an inexhaustible supply of agricultural fertilizer, rich in nitrate, and easily mined. In twenty years, before the caverns were set aside as a national park, at least 100,000 tons of guano were taken out and mostly sold to growers of citrus fruits. Thus—and not for the qualities that attract so many visitors today—the great Carlsbad Caverns came into use.

Yearly visitors to Carlsbad Caverns are approaching the half-million mark annually, which, all things considered, is amazing. The Texan who confessed that he had never been in this great cave would be a Texan who might say that Texas was not the greatest state in the Union, and there is no such person.

But the white man was certainly not the first to see the caverns. In making trails through the caves, the Park Service men uncovered, a short distance inside the entrance, a sandal. This footgear was identified as belonging to the prehistoric Indian period of the Basketmakers who lived in the region four thousand years ago. The Indian was in such a hurry to leave that he did not stop to pick up his shoe. Somehow I feel I understand that. There were no electric lights in the caverns then.

Among the early explorers was a local cowboy, Jim White. Jim was deeply impressed by the wonders of the caverns. He saw more than guano and bats in them. He became a walking advertisement for these underground marvels, preaching them with almost religious devotion, and was an unofficial guide; and when the area was set aside by Congress for preservation, White finally became chief ranger. The name of Jim White is tied tightly to what is without prideful claim, the greatest of all known caves. And this is said without prejudice to the superlative qualities that other renowned caverns possess. A cave has an individuality, a personality almost. So, as with so many other natural wonders, you have your choice. As I have suggested before, the "best" national park is the one that is best for you.

Thoroughly to enjoy the stupendous work of engineering and artistry that nature has performed in Carlsbad Caverns, you need not have more than a smattering of the scientific facts. The history of Carlsbad goes back to a remote period. Call it 200 million years. We cannot grasp that retrospect, but it may do for vague comparison. It was perhaps in that period that the limestone, or the sediments that hardened into limestone, were laid down in a shallow sea. Later the uplifting and folding that produced the Rockies also elevated the Carlsbad country. This uplift occurred about the time the dinosaurs were taking their leave, and you may call that about 60 million years ago.

As the limy sediments settled and as the earth contortions later squeezed and bent them, cracks in the stone were made. The surface waters began to find their way along these cracks, increasing them in size, and keeping each chamber and corridor so created full of water, which hastened the dissolution. Later another series of uplifts, which brought the Guadalupes into being, allowed surface streams to cut canyons into the limestone, and this drained the caverns. Air entered the chambers and corridors, and then began the deposition by slow, evaporating seepage of the lovely sculptured decorations —the delicate mineral growth called helictites, the huge stalactites that hang from the ceilings, and the stalagmites that rise from the floors. The delicate colorings come from pigments of iron or other mineral matter.

This explanation is inadequate, but the study of caves is a complex specialty within the science of geology, and for most of us a general notion of cause and effect will suffice.

Huge as Carlsbad Caverns are known to be, nobody as yet has reached the limits. Seven miles of corridors and chambers are open to visitors, who go through in parties accompanied by a ranger guide, who explains the salient points and answers questions. But the truth is that the part of the caverns open to inspection by the public is only the 750-foot level. Below that level, at 900 feet, is another vast apartment; and below that still another at 1,320 feet. Nor is it known how far it may eventually be discovered that these passageways and rooms creep into the Guadalupe Mountains.

For the present, and for years to come, the display now offered in those seven miles will prove sufficient for visitors. Anyone in good health can make the trip, for it is not hurried, and there is a rest for lunch, just at the door of the Big Room. It may seem profane to sit down in a cafeteria and get hot coffee and a snack in such awe-inspiring surroundings, and perhaps it is; but mortals are weak, feet get tired, exercise means hunger, and I have not seen anyone decline the lunch on aesthetic grounds. We are naturally depraved. Why else would an overweight person nibble on a chocolate bar during a lecture on diet and reducing?

Am I requested to give a word picture of the architectural and sculptural masterpieces of Carlsbad? Respectfully, I decline. Even photographs, which better than words delineate these strange and charming forms, fall far short of revealing what you will see. Photography in caves is extremely difficult, as every expert knows: without artificial lighting, nothing; with it, dilution and distortion.

I once heard a lecturer trying to describe some beautiful primeval park— maybe it was Yosemite. Now and then he came to the end of his verbal rope and stammered: "It—it—*beggars* description!" He had to resort to this several times—"It *beggars* description"—and I came away with an amusing picture in my mind of a poverty-ridden *thing* known as Description, in mendicant rags, standing with a tin cup outstretched: a victim of too much natural perfection. Actually it was the lecturer who was reduced to want. I wish to avoid that fate.

The main corridor of the cavern, just beneath the yawning entrance, is enormous, but gives no indication of the beauties that will greet the journeyer as he passes through the corridors and chambers beyond. The trail through the main corridor extends for almost a mile, leading to the Green Lake Room, which gets its name from a small green pool beside the trail. Then into the King's Palace, a place of such surpassing loveliness that some cave lovers think it the finest display in all the world. A natural "keyhole" leads from the King's Palace to the Queen's Chamber; and then comes a charming little room called the Papoose Room.

After the stop for lunch, the Big Room is entered. Although not the most beautiful, this section is the most impressive chamber of the cavern. The trail around it is a mile and a quarter long, and at one place the ceiling arches 285 feet. Here the Giant Dome leans like the Tower of Pisa; the stalactites vary from delicate needles to huge chandeliers, and the stalagmites are equally of strange contour.

Carlsbad Caverns National Park is open all the year. Whether the summer temperature outside is more than 100 degrees or the winter temperature approaches zero, a constant 56 degrees always exists inside. Therefore visitors should wear clothes that suit the outside temperature, and in summer a light sweater will suffice for the walk through the cavern. For their comfort, it is recommended that women wear low-heeled shoes, though the trails and stairways make progress easy.

Thus far we have been concerned with the inanimate marvels of Carlsbad. But there is another spectacle visitors should not miss. This is the singular bat flight from the mouth of the caverns, which takes place about sundown in the summer. Pouring out from that part of the caverns known as the Bat Cave—a great chamber into which visitors do not go—these little creatures of the underground world swirl in a spiral stream through the entrance arch and over the rim toward the south. They are not in hundreds, not in thousands —they are literally in millions, when the night-flying insects on which they feed are in ample supply. The bats return before dawn the next day.

To give some notion of the incredible bat population at its height, naturalists have computed that, assuming the number to be three million, they would consume nearly twelve tons of moths, beetles, flies, and other insects during one night's foray. What a colossal amount of insect life, unseen and unsuspected, there must be in this New Mexico semidesert to support such a bat population as this!

There are five kinds of bats in the caverns, but the greater number belong to a species called Mexican free-tailed bats, the name being descriptive of a tail projecting beyond the skin that stretches between the hind legs.

Having witnessed this prodigy of massed animal flight, visitors may well ponder a little the queer, unreasonable superstitions that get indelibly fixed in the human mind and imagination over the years—notions that go unchallenged and seem to thrive on the very fact that they bear no relation to the truth.

Most people shudder even at the mention of bats. The impression is that they are unclean things, dangerous, and fit only to be present at a hellbroth-brewing ceremony conducted by witches, like that described by Shakespeare in *Macbeth*. And what is the truth about the poor little creatures who during the day hang by their hind legs, head downward, in dense clusters from the ceiling of their favorite caves? Do they suck blood? Do they get caught in people's hair, and scratch and bite their victims? Do they have a nauseating odor? All in all, are they creatures that the world would be better off without?

Poor little bat! Personally clean—though their apartment houses may have a disagreeable odor—with fragile little claws used only to hang with, the "flying mouse" is a timid thing with fine, soft fur, whose naked wings are not dry or parchmentlike, but really triumphs of silky, translucent structure, filled with those nerves which may explain their accuracy of flight. It is true there is a Southern American species that has bad manners. But the "vampire bat" is mostly a figment of the imagination and belongs with the werewolf and the basilisk. One of the tropical bats eats the bananas of the plantation owner. But what are bananas for?

The bat seems to be a leftover from some strange animal that lived in a warm and uniform climate in past ages. Unable to adapt itself to sharp climatic changes, the bat took to the uniform temperature of caves. This is what the cave bear of Europe did, and no doubt for the same reason; but the bat has made a go of it, whereas the bear died, probably of disease—arthritis, some of the European naturalists think.

The bat has been able to compromise with nature in several ways. The bats that remain in a cave all winter cluster together, head down, with their wings folded around them, and go into a sort of suspended animation. The lethargy cannot be continuous, for the bats have been found flying about the caves in midwinter. But some of the bats migrate instead of hibernating. It was long a subject of speculation where certain bats went when they disappeared from the caves of southern France. They were not seen anywhere in Europe. The answer was found after they were banded, as birds are banded. The bats spent their winters in Japan.

To witness the Carlsbad bat flight it is necessary for most visitors to stop overnight in the city of Carlsbad, after going through the caverns. There are no overnight accommodations in the park. But the whole district around Carlsbad richly deserves more time than tourists give it; and he who misses the bat flight is losing the chance of seeing one of the world's greatest sights associated with the mystery of caverns.

## 2. MAMMOTH CAVE NATIONAL PARK
### [Kentucky]

SOMEWHERE AMONG the stalagmites on the floor of a great chamber in the Mammoth Cave of Kentucky, there is an English shilling, lawful money of Her Majesty Queen Victoria. How do I know? Well, I have it on the word of "An Officer of the Royal Artillery," who honored the cavern with his presence in 1850. This British military man was a sad wag. He roguishly wedged the shilling piece into a crevice to deceive the archaeologists of 2300 and, as he put it, "to throw fresh confusion into all the chronology of American History."

Just how it would bother the archaeologists I cannot quite see. The modern archaeologist is a hard man to hoax, and he becomes less gullible as the years pass. It was not always so, and perhaps the Briton had in mind the fact that up to a century ago it was a firm conviction in England that the great stones of Stonehenge were erected by the Romans, the "proof" being that Roman coins were dug out of the surrounding turf. It seems never to have occurred to anyone that when the Romans were in Britain they were as much puzzled about these slabs of stone as any later people. They went on weekend trips to see them, just as the British officer went to see Mammoth Cave. They lolled around on the grass and dropped coins out of their pockets.

So the archaeologist of the future, discovering the Queen's shilling in Mammoth Dome floor, will say: "Ah, how interesting! Sometime during the Victorian period a visitor here dropped a coin. No; on second thought, from the position in which we find it, it was probably deliberately placed. Possibly—but not certainly—he was an English visitor to the cave. He may have been the man who dropped the monocle we found near the Giant's

Coffin. The coin, judging by the usual rate of deposition, seems to date from the same decade of the nineteenth century." Do not waste time trying to outwit the modern specialist!

One day, as I was reading the artilleryman's account of his American cave experience, in the stained pages of an old *Fraser's Magazine*, the thought came to me that Mammoth Cave is not merely a cave; it is not alone a cavern of international geological distinction: even more it is one of our historic shrines. For, long before the imagination of American people went beyond the Mississippi River, this giant cave in a region dotted with caves and sink-holes had been at least partly explored, and had played a role in stirring events.

It was from Mammoth's bowels that the new Americans gathered saltpeter —in the form of what they called "petredirt"—to make their gunpowder for the War of 1812. The ruts of cartwheels and the hoofprints of oxen remained in the clay, leading to pipes and pumps and vats, from which Archibald Miller took the vital material to Philadelphia by wagon train. Venturesome marvel seekers from all along the seaboard and visitors from Europe were threading their way through these dark corridors in a day when the great Western parks were still to be discovered. And we make a great mistake

*River of the blind fish. Mammoth Cave National Park.* [*Photo: National Park Service*]

if we imagine that our ancestors did not get around. Within the limitations of their slow, hard means of travel, they were incorrigible rovers. When they could not find a road for wheels, they went on horseback; and where they could not go on a horse, they tramped.

Our early Americans challenged the physical country and made it give over. Their eyes were always searching for the metals and the earths they needed. Every outcrop of bull quartz had to be hammered: if they couldn't find gold or silver, it might be lead or graphite, or talc or soapstone, or something else they could use. But they were not wholly material. When they found Mammoth Cave, even if it contained nothing but adventure and beauty, they reveled in those qualities also.

Very early in the last century, as is apparent from the writings of that time, Mammoth Cave was one of the things the traveler had to see. Foreign visitors went inevitably to Niagara Falls; there they were told not to fail to go to Kentucky and see "the greatest cave that ever was." Then they could go back to Europe or die; and in the estimation of these heady, boastful, insular new Americans, one fate was the same as the other.

And what a country it must have been that the first visitors to Mammoth looked upon! It was virgin forest, most of it—broad-leaved trees, with a sprinkling of conifers. The Kentucky shrubs and wild flowers made a riot of color in spring and summer; the hillsides and ravines were painted with St.-John's-wort, with the butterfly weed and blazing stars, with May apple and Solomon's-seal and the puccoon. They still are. For what is now Mammoth Cave National Park is to be enjoyed not only for the cave, but for the forest cover, the flowers, the great variety of birds that either live or visit there, and the wildlife that is now under protection.

Truth to say, it was not easy to impress upon the independent, individualistic folk who lived in this hill country that casual trespass and free and easy gunnery had gone out and a preservation policy had come in. The hill folk have many virtues, like their counterparts in the Blue Ridge and the southern Alleghenies: self-reliance, courage, and hospitality. They are of ancient stock, and probably the most colorful and uninhibited Americans that now exist. And just because they are as they are, it has not been easy to steer them from their old-time ways. But the superintendents of the national parks are chosen as much for their patience and tact and understanding as for their technical ability. Force is always reserved for last resort. But when it must be force, the men who operate the parks can use it, and will. With every passing year, however, the local conditions are a little happier in areas like Mammoth. There is finally the dawn of appreciation of what is being preserved for all of us *by* all of us. As often happens, some of the natives who were toughest are now proudest.

As long ago as 1926 Congress had authorized the establishment of Mammoth Cave National Park, and years before that many ardent conservationists had been pressing for such an act. Finally, through the acquisition of land by Kentucky and by donations from the people of the state, and further by direct purchase by the federal government, the fifty thousand acres of forest and caves were put together, and the many objects of historic, prehistoric, and scientific value will be kept in their integrity.

In general, Mammoth Cave follows the typical development of all limestone caverns, but here the more than 150 miles of explored corridors were created by a chain of geological events that took a different turn from those which left Carlsbad, for instance, as it is today. There was the same original laying down of sediments on the floor of an ancient sea, the same story of percolating surface waters along the cracks and joints of the rock; but whereas the region of southeastern New Mexico turned gradually arid, the ample rainfall of the Kentucky country has kept a live river, the Green, as an attendant of the deepening of the caverns.

The five separate levels of the Mammoth corridors are explained as corresponding to five different levels of the Green River. Whenever the river deepened its channel, the water in the cave accommodated itself to this level, following horizontally through the limestone and emptying into the nearby stream. Today Echo River, 360 feet below the ground surface, flows slowly along the fifth, or lowest, level of the cave and drains into the Green. Visitors to Mammoth Cave may have the strange sensation of boating on an underground river that contains eyeless fish and other creatures that have adapted themselves to a life of perpetual darkness.

The water that trickles down the walls of the cavern forms sheets that hang like folded draperies, and masses that resemble fountains. The largest onyx formation in the cave is called Frozen Niagara, and while some of the names given to cave formations are, as Mark Twain dryly remarked, a bit "overdescriptive," this one is no misnomer. But even more impressive to me are those gypsum formations which take the shape of flowers and coils, pendants, and grotesque shapes; some of them look like Corinthian-column decorations, while others are gargoyles. Some are so fragile as to be mere spider webs.

It is not hard to grasp the idea of the creation of stalactites and stalagmites. Sometimes you can actually *hear* them—drip, drip—being brought into existence. But what of these fairylike forms, of the same or of like mineral composition, which may rise at an acute angle, fling out tentacles, grow upward and sidewise, with the facility of plantlife? They are called helictites, and, apparently defying the laws of gravity, they have invited the puzzled speculation of many a cave expert.

Mammoth is redolent of the memories of famous visitors. At a point about half a mile from the Historic Entrance, a place now called Booth's Amphitheater, there must have been a hushed and deeply affected audience one day in 1876 when the great Edwin Booth mounted the stage of rock and recited from Shakespeare's plays. Ole Bull, the famous violinist, likewise gave his name to one of the chambers.

It is said that Mammoth was originally sold by its earliest claimant for the sum of forty dollars. It sounds like a moderate price for so valuable a property. On the other hand, in those days there were no modern facilities for printing paper money, and what there was of it went farther. The royal artilleryman who secreted his shilling on the cave floor noted the fact, in his relation, that he traveled from Buffalo to Sandusky on one of the finest little steamers he had ever seen, with commodious staterooms and beds carved of rosewood, and the fare with meals was two dollars.

The early guides of Mammoth Cave were Negroes, and one of them, Stephen Bishop, became famous. He knew and loved the cave and for many years girded on his canteen of oil every day, supplied visitors with a lamp, and bade them follow him into the gloom. It was not an easy trip in the old days. I note with some amusement that there was some early conflict between the "improvers" and those who wished to keep the caverns as rude and primitive as possible. One visitor was already writing that "electric lights would gradually illuminate the large halls and domes. Telephones would be of advantage. Tramways might be laid through the main cave and the more accessible avenues. Shafts might be opened at certain terminal points, through which the visitors might be taken up by elevators and conveyed back to the hotel in hacks." Curiously enough, when this critic mentioned his suggestions to the proprietor of the cave, he was rebuffed with the blunt remark that "it would take away the feeling of adventure, and it would be flying in the face of Nature." Possibly the proprietor was not so idealistic as the words would seem to imply; he may not have wanted to risk the expense. But nowadays when there are suggestions for more and more "facilities" and "improvements" in the national parks, more ease for visitors and more interference with the natural scene, this evidence of a former conflict in the conception of management has an enlightening touch.

### 3. WIND CAVE NATIONAL PARK
*[South Dakota]*

IN A THIRSTY MIDSUMMER DRIVE across the high plains, bound westward toward Yellowstone and the great national parks beyond, the Black Hills of South Dakota constitute an island of refuge and a pause of soothing delight. Just as the jaded wayfarer has concluded that his world has flattened to a dusty plane, scorching under a pitiless sun, just then the great bubble of granite, worn down and clothed with trees, green and refreshing, appears.

Well I remember the day when, leaving Mitchell after a night of little sleep and no restoration, we skidded along upon a road surface made slick by the crushed remains of grasshopper armies that had been on their march for several days; we threaded our course through the bare pastel-colored forms of the badlands and finally came to rest in a shady campground beside a little pond on the outskirts of Rapid City. Then we knew how Xenophon's tired Greeks felt when they had finally fought their way back from Persia and staggered to a height from which they could discern the waters of the Euxine. "The men embraced one another, wept, and cried: '*Thalatta! Thalatta! The sea! The sea!*'" We were not so dramatic. We merely pointed at the pond and feebly murmured: "It looks like real water!"

These satisfying Black Hills, upon the southeast flank of which is Wind Cave National Park, seem to have everything necessary to make them a popular resort. They present a geological phenomenon so compact and evident that it can be readily appreciated without any special knowledge of the science. It is one of the most richly mineralized spots in the United States. Custer State Park, operated according to policies that closely approximate those of the National Park Service, is adjacent to the national park and has excellent accommodations for those who want to spend some time there. It is within easy distance of a group of highly interesting national monuments—Devils Tower and Badlands.

The Black Hills came into existence as a result of one of those strange but not uncommon occurrences in the drama of mountain-building whereby the molten material below the earth crust thrusts up under the overlying rocks in the form of a great dome. It does not, when it ceases to rise, appear at the surface. It simply bows back the upper crust, just the way your tablecloth

*Overleaf: As our pioneers saw these Dakota lands. Wind Cave National Park. [Photo: Wayne Bryant]*

would be disturbed if you slipped an orange underneath it. Only when the overlying layers have been broken up and taken away by time, wind, and rain can what took place be seen. Then you find, as in the Black Hills, tilted remains of the former cover, encircling the core in concentric ridges.

Electrically lighted Wind Cave presents a formation quite unlike that of any other cave in the National Park System. Instead of stalactitic and stalagmitic growths, here was developed a series of passages, known to be at least ten miles in extent, covered with a delicately beautiful boxwork, on which newer and even more fragile crystals have been deposited. It appears that when the original limestone was cracked by earth movement, the fissures were tiny ones, just large enough to permit the calcite fillings to make finlike, interlacing shapes. The calcite was less soluble than the limestone rock. Consequently as more dissolution went on, through percolating waters, the "boxes" were left projecting, in lacy compartments.

The cave is easily accessible and both dry and clean, and anyone in reasonably good physical condition can make the trip with little fatigue. The entrance door has been artificially constructed, and for an excellent reason. You could hardly expect to get in by the passageway that Tom Bingham, an old Black Hills pioneer, discovered. It was only ten inches in diameter, and Bingham did not find it by seeing it; he found it by *hearing* it. He was deer hunting one day when he heard a strange whistling sound coming from the underbrush. No other natural opening to the cave has ever been found. The strong currents of wind that alternately blow in and out of the cave mouth are responsible for the whistling.

When the barometer is falling outside, the air from the cave is likely to blow outward; when it rises, the air rushes in, and the small size of the opening causes the sound. Many visitors like to stop at the cave entrance and post themselves on weather probabilities. Having found out, their next reflection is that they can do nothing about it anyway.

But Wind Cave National Park is much more than a cave. Here, in the 28,000 acres of range and forest land, is one of the most engaging of wildlife pictures. There is a herd of four hundred buffaloes living under—I was going to say natural conditions. No; not quite that. Their boundaries are fenced. That, of course, is artificial. Still, as visitors are never likely to see much of the fence, the impression of the primitive grazing of one of our noblest native mammals is strong. I have sat in an automobile on one of the park roadways and watched a band of fifty or sixty of the big creatures quietly feeding or lying down only a few hundred yards from me, and I had the definite sense of looking upon an unspoiled frontier scene. It was a delightful picture. Once in a while a big bull would lift up his head to scowl in my direction; then, convinced that he had me disciplined, he would go back to grazing.

By all means, see these fine animals at Wind Cave; and by all means do not disregard the signs that the Park Service has posted along the roads, warning visitors not to leave their cars and approach these herds. The buffalo is not a safe mammal to trifle with. Even if you try to flatter him by calling him a bison, which is of course his true name, you will get nowhere, or worse. Every bull buffalo believes that human visitors to the park are blood relatives of the late William F. Cody, known as Buffalo Bill, and there was an unfortunate feud between the Cody and Buffalo families many years ago, which nearly resulted in the disappearance of the bison. To avoid being involved in a recrudescence of that quarrel, be sure to obey the warnings.

The Wind Cave buffaloes prosper so well that at times they have really exceeded the capacity of their range. Custer State Park also has a fine showing of bison. Elk are numerous in the park, and there are some antelope. Deer are there too, but they usually remain in the wooded parts and are seen only when crossing the grasslands on their way from shelter to shelter.

There are two colonies of prairie dogs. And here is a queer incident that happened in the park recently, which illustrates, more forcibly than preachment, in what danger we always stand of wholly losing some of our native fauna and how vital it is to preserve enough of them to make our wilderness picture a true one. One of the Park Service men was standing beside a visitor, who had just left his car to watch the antics of the prairie dogs. There were buffaloes not far away, but the visitor was more interested in the smaller animals. He turned to the man at his side and said: "I never saw any of those before. What are those funny little critters, anyway?"

The answer was: "Those are prairie dogs."

The man went on watching, and the park official walked away. But before he left he observed the registration plate on the visitor's automobile. *Kansas.* Of all places in the world—Kansas! The state that once had prairie dogs by millions upon millions. Yet it was entirely possible. No doubt the man was a late settler in a region where the little creatures had been poisoned out of existence years before.

## 4. Jewel Cave National Monument
### [*South Dakota*]

YOUR TRUE SPELUNKER is a bibliophile who collects books with stone pages, set in crystal type and rubricated with initials of iron salts. He snorts at the cheap editions of caves run off on rotary presses for the millions. He wants the real Gutenberg—no electric lights, no elevators, and everything achieved the hard way. If you are going to make it as easy as that, he says, why not engineer a four-lane highway through the cave and set the speed limit at about fifty?

Very well: this time I give you Jewel Cave, also of the Black Hills, and not far from Wind Cave. Here the cave adventurer will not be pampered. Though perfectly safe, Jewel Cave means gasoline lanterns instead of electricity, and old clothes instead of fastidious attire. There are ladders and steps at certain points, but that is about all the modernization.

In the cave are crystals of dogtooth spar—calcite crystals which, as they grow, take on the shape of longish, slender pyramids, resembling the teeth of dogs. It is this mineral that accounts for the name Jewel Cave, for many of the chambers are solidly coated with calcite in this glittering form. Box-like cavities along the walls and ceilings are covered with minute crystals that stand in bold and dazzling relief from the mass behind them. There is an attractive color range from light brown to a deep chocolate. Some of the rooms have a peculiar light-green tint; others are darker green, or bronze.

Jewel Cave, like Wind Cave, was discovered by the whistle of wind coming from a small hole in the cliffs on the east side of Hell Canyon. Two prospectors, the Michaud brothers, found the cave opening and enlarged it in the hope of finding valuable minerals. By "valuable minerals" they would have meant, of course, gold or silver, or at least a lode of tin, which would be even better, since nature seems to have forgotten the United States when tin was parceled out. What they found was a rich jewelry display of dogtooth spar. Is that a valuable mineral? It is for the visitor to look and say.

Anyway, the Michaud brothers had found something they felt sure would attract tourists. They built a log house nearby to accommodate visitors. And though they did not prosper at this, at least their efforts made the lovely little cave known and hastened the time when it came into the preserves of the National Park System.

Within this monument is a forest of virgin ponderosa pine, one of the last remaining such stands in the Black Hills. Besides the ordinary cave bat and Say's bat, there is found in Jewel Cave the so-called pallid lump-nosed bat. With all due respect to the naturalists, no bat deserves a name like that. It sounds to me like unprovoked vituperation. After all, bats may be sensitive.

## 5. Timpanogos Cave National Monument
### [*Utah*]

FROM THE HEADQUARTERS of Timpanogos Cave National Monument a trail winds for a mile and a half up the steep side of Mount Timpanogos to the cave entrance. Along this trail are the most stirring and stimulating views of the Wasatch Mountains, Utah Valley, and American Fork Canyon. To turn from these brilliant scenes, etched against a blue sky and flooded with sunlight, and enter the cavern is to go into a strange world of the underground, not less beautiful, but so different!

Mount Timpanogos is a snow-capped giant that raises its head 12,000 feet above sea level, one of a group of peaks of the Wasatch Mountains that tower above the Great Salt Basin. The monument covers an area of 250 acres in American Fork Canyon. The cave entrance is about 1,000 feet above the canyon floor.

Much of the cave interior is covered by a filigree of pink and white translucent crystals, which glow and sparkle like an array of jewels. Feathery boas, braided wreaths, and needle stalactites are among the many smaller features, which culminate in larger forms such as the fantastic Chocolate Falls, the Jewel Box, and the Great Heart of Timpanogos. The formation of these wonders is still going on. Tiny pools of water reflect the magic of the dazzling beauties overhead.

From the tips of countless stalactites hang gleaming drops of water, each of which leaves behind its tiniest layer of lime before it drops to the floor to build up a corresponding form. So slow is this action that hundreds of years may be required to add one inch of the mineral.

At monument headquarters is a picnic ground, with water, tables, and stoves. Meals and supplies can be had from the nearby store. The cave is only a few miles from Provo or Pleasant Grove, on a paved road, which is normally free from snow between April and November.

## 6. Lehman Caves National Monument
### [*Nevada*]

THE EARTH FORCES were experimenting when the caves discovered by Ab Lehman, the Nevada pioneer homesteader, were in course of construction. No two rooms in these caverns are alike. Strange stone faces, animals, and figurines line the paths of the easy trails. A rippled curtain of stone here, gracefully tapered stalactites there; and high-arched, multicolored ceilings over all. The great artist tried almost every device that was later to bewilder the human eye.

Pools of water on the floors have built tiny, beautifully terraced dikes, or dams, around their edges, and have deposited a white, spongy, nodular growth in the pool itself. Huge fluted columns reach from floor to ceiling. Tiny needle crystals, peculiar mushroom effects, frosty incrustations in infinitely varied forms, grow on the larger shapes, or cover the walls and ceilings where the others do not occur.

Some stalactites here grew laterally in one plane, forming graceful draperies of dripstone, or translucent ribbon like partitions, or "bacon-strips." Thin round disks of dripstone were deposited on the flat bedrock ceilings, and as the lengthening stalactites that hung from them grew heavier, these plates were slowly peeled away. These strange structures, called tom-toms, because when struck they give a drum sound, are abundant throughout the caves.

The Lehman Caves are in the heart of a region of wide basins and towering mountain ranges, five miles west of Baker. The mighty Snake Range, on the eastern edge of the state, is topped by Wheeler Peak, over thirteen thousand feet high, one of the higher mountains of the Great Basin. On the eastern side of this peak the monument, one square mile in area, is found in the belt of piñon and juniper. There are mule deer in the meadows and higher forests of pine, spruce, and mountain mahogany. Cougars are not uncommon in this wilderness, but casual visitors are not likely to see them, for they have learned that the combination of man, dog, and rifle is catastrophic even to big and ferocious predators.

In a deep deposit just adjacent to the natural entrance of the caves the skeleton remains of prehistoric Indians have been found, indicating that many thousands of years ago it was used as a burial chamber.

The National Park Service maintains attractive overnight camp and picnic facilities in the headquarters area of the monument. Refreshments, limited food service, and overnight cabins are maintained near headquarters by a concessioner operating under contract with the government. There are also many beautifully situated campsites in the nearby Nevada National Forest.

## 7. OREGON CAVES NATIONAL MONUMENT
### [Oregon]

IT IS INTERESTING to note the variety of accidents that led to the discovery by modern man of those caves which are now included in the primitive areas of the National Park System. There is no doubt that prehistoric men of North America knew about most of them and used them for refuge, burial, or other purposes. The presumption is that the flight of bats from the cave entrance may have attracted the attention of the first white men to Carlsbad Caverns; but of the others, the two in South Dakota attracted notice by the whistling of the wind that rushed in and out of their small apertures. Mammoth Cave was discovered by a pioneer hunter pursuing a wounded bear; Ab Lehman was driving cattle when his horse stumbled into an opening in the ground, which thus revealed the Nevada caverns; and, finally, another hunter, pursuing another bear, is said to have found Oregon Caves.

The only natural openings of many of the great caves seem to have been so small as to escape attention. A slight rockslide or growth of brush would hide these openings effectively. This has been true in the Pyrenees, where cave hunters resort to an ingenious method of discovery. Through field glasses they watch the flight of jackdaws—birds that resemble our American grackle—on a mountainside. The jackdaw is one of the few birds known to nest and rear its young in caves, and the French speleologist Casteret tells of observing the flight of the fledglings in the chambers of a cave, where they spend an apprenticeship in lateral flying before they attempt to ascend to the mouth of the cavern.

One wonders whether in the United States there may not be vast limestone caverns as yet unknown, either because the small openings have been unobserved or because they have no visible outlets.

While the Oregon Caves are not in limestone, they are in a marble rock that represents a former limestone which became changed under terrific heat and pressure and later was raised above the sea as part of a mountain range. Marble is dissolved out by the action of surface water charged with carbonic acid from decaying vegetation, so the Oregon caves were formed in much the typical way.

The deposits in these caves assume grotesque shapes as well as pleasing forms. Here and there are miniatures of lakes or waterfalls, done in stone. Among the early visitors here was Joaquin Miller, the Poet of the Sierra, who celebrated "the Marble Hills of Oregon" in many of his writings.

There is guide service through the electrically lighted caves throughout the year, and in summer there are accommodations and meals in a mountain chateau and in cabins. There is also a picnic area, but no camping is permitted in the monument, though there are adequate facilities at the Greyback Campground, eight miles away on the approach highway.

# [ VI ]

# *The Ice Moves Down*

THE LONG SUMMER *was over. For ages a tropical climate had prevailed over
a great part of the earth, and animals whose home is now beneath
the equator roamed over the world to the very borders of the arctics. . . .
But their reign was over. A sudden intense winter, that was also to
last for ages, fell upon the globe; it spread over the very countries
where the tropical animals had their homes, and so suddenly did it
come upon them that they were embalmed beneath masses of snow and
ice, without time even for the decay which follows death.*

—LOUIS AGASSIZ, *Geological Sketches*

## 1. ACADIA NATIONAL PARK
### [*Maine*]

SOME YEARS AGO a minor poet, having visited Mount Desert Island, in Maine,
upon which the greater part of Acadia National Park is situated, referred
to it as "the most beautiful island in the world." This sort of statement, I confess, always irritates me. It is a double impertinence, a discharge of both
barrels of egotism at once. It assumes that the writer has seen all the islands
of the world—an impossibility—and it also conveys the assumption that whatever the writer considers most beautiful the reader must tamely accept as his
own standard. Let us have done with such nonsense.

Besides, even if Mount Desert Island is actually the most beautiful island
in the world, the description utterly fails to do justice to this rock-built
natural fortress which thrusts forward into the Atlantic and challenges its

*Climbers meet a great crevasse on Sperry Glacier. Glacier National Park.* [*Photo:
Jack E. Boucher*]

[ 2 5 7 ]

power. You may have affecting beauty in a meadow sprinkled with daisies and paint-flowers; in any glen where dryads frisk in the evening hours; but where can you find anything in our country to match these mountains that come down to the ocean, these granite cliffs alongside which the biggest ship could ride, these bays dotted with lovely islets clothed in hardwood and hemlock, altogether such a sweep of rugged coastline as has no parallel from Florida to the Canadian provinces?

This is the theme of Acadia—the final expression of a strange act of nature by which the ocean flooded in upon an ancient, worn-down land surface and turned its high hills into islands, its rivers into slender arms of the sea, and its wider valleys into bays and gulfs. And having done this, then all was dressed at last, in the greenest of green vegetation, soothing to the eye, hospitable to migrating birds, a kind shelter to browsing animals. Everything is here to rejoice the soul of the human visitor—the combination of summer warmth from the mainland, the fresh salt tang from the sea, cool sleepful nights, silvery dawns and the reddest of sunsets, and unforgettable pictures from any height of granite rock. Beauty, certainly, but far more. Visitors to Acadia take their place with the long line of Maine homefolk, part farmer, part sailor and fisherman, and with their summer guests, who discovered long ago that this is a place where you can stand with one foot in the brine and one on the blossomy land, fish with one hand and pick blueberries with the other—in short, be a Janus and look two ways at once.

Strange forces of nature have worked to contrive a landscape that makes Mount Desert and Acadia National Park unique. If you look at the map of Maine, you will see something very strange about its coast. From Portland across to St. Croix, drawing a straight line, is less than 200 miles. But between the two places, if you were to follow the tortuous line where the ocean touches the land, you would travel 2,500 miles, or about the distance by sea from New York City to a Venezuelan port. Good hikers, who usually carry in their pockets a topographic map, will guess what happened to produce the astonishing result. In any hilly country, if you set yourself to follow that brown contour line on your topographic map which shows a height of, say, 300 feet, you would expect to ramble a long distance, as opposed to cutting straight across country, up hill and down. The present Maine coast is precisely a contour line drawn on an upland surface by an ocean which drowned everything up to that level.

An ancient valley, then, is now the Gulf of Maine; the little valleys and rivers and smaller streams that once flowed into the big valley are now arms and fingers of the sea. Somes Sound, which nearly divides the island into two

*From the top of Cadillac the seascape writes indelibly on the memory. Acadia National Park.* [*Photo: Jack E. Boucher*]

parts, is probably one of the deeper-cut valleys that existed long before the coastline was depressed; and so sheer is the drop from mountains to the floor of the sound that the greatest ocean liner could find plenty of water near shore. And when you see the lobster-trap buoys sometimes so near the edge of the rocky promontories that you could hit them with a pebble, you realize how for ages the sea has been attacking the hard stone, undercutting the cliffs, and dropping their upper parts into the hungering maw. Brave the rocks are, and grand in their defiance of the sea, but the end is foreseen. The ocean always wins. But as a visitor, you will have ample time to enjoy the present duel.

What caused this Maine coast to sink and the sea to rush in? That goes back to another story, and the evidences of that story are everywhere you look in Acadia and on the mainland behind the park. The great ice sheet is supposed to have depressed Mount Desert Island as much as 600 feet. The

solid rocks are not so inflexible as they appear, and the outer crust of the earth will give and rebound; for after the final surge of ice from the north had melted away, the land rose again. But it never came back to the previous level, as is shown by the old sea cliffs and beaches on the mountains 250 feet above the present ocean shore. As you go along the road beneath the two smaller peaks known as The Bubbles, you will see one of the great erratic boulders dropped by the glacial ice almost on the very top. It looks precariously perched, but actually it would be hard to move.

Although the skilled geologist will laugh at my simplicity, I cannot help feeling a likeness between this great granite intrusion of the Mount Desert country and the granite that came up beneath the covering rocks of the Black Hills in South Dakota. Superficially the weathered exposures are entirely different. In the Black Hills the granite is worn down into towering pinnacles; here in Acadia all is smoothed and rounded by glacial ice, and you may see places where scratches and crescents were made by the rocks the glacier used for tools. But standing on the mushroom summit of Cadillac Mountain, and looking about on one of the greatest land-and-ocean scenes of America—so different from anything in the West—I cannot help considering how Mount Harney and its surrounding peaks would look if they had been subjected to seaboard forces like those that molded Acadia. A road winds around Cadillac till you reach the very top, with ample parking space there. And what a view is this!

Frenchman Bay on one side, with the little Porcupine Islands, which resemble amphibians swimming out to sea; Great Cranberry and Little Cranberry to the south, with the blue Atlantic behind them; and on the horizon still more islands that were once mainland mountaintops. Eastward the eye traces the jagged coast on its way to New Brunswick, and on the land side, on a clear day, Mount Katahdin and the White Hills of New Hampshire can be distinguished. And even if the day is not perfectly clear, it is a grand thing to look upon. For myself, I do not mind if a bit of fog comes wreathing in, curling among the estuaries, blotting out one marine view only to reveal another. Indeed, you may well ask for a little fog—not too much!—to complete the picture, for the fog patches here are like the clouds for which the outdoor photographer lies in wait.

If you look at a map of Acadia National Park, you will see that the boundary is very vagrant: a big block of the park east of Somes Sound, an area across Frenchman Bay on the Schoodic Peninsula, and other segments

*The cliffs fall sheer to deep water. Acadia National Park. [Photo: Jack E. Boucher]*

scattered about among private lands, not forgetting fractions on the islands. There is a reason. The Western national parks have mainly grown, you may say, from the inside out: they were federal lands diverted to the high park uses, and they try to exclude, when the money is available, sections that are still privately owned. Acadia is the opposite. It has grown from the outside in. There were no federal lands to be diverted; the park has come into existence through the generosity of heart and purse of idealists who, having tasted the beauties and joys of the region, longed to make it the protected, preserved haven of all the people. It will continue to expand that way. Meanwhile, what there is of it is superb.

Land and sea, woodland, lake, and mountain are all contained in a neat package in Acadia National Park. This, added to the fact that Mount Desert is exactly where the northern and the temperate zones meet and overlap, results in a land-and-sea bird congregation that will delight the amateur naturalist. The number of warblers that either nest on the island or visit it when migrating is exceptional. Among them are the flashing redstart, the myrtle, the black-and-white, the magnolia, the yellow palm, and the brilliant yellow.

The osprey, that expert but victimized fisherman, is always to be seen along the shore and over the lakes. Also, you may have the luck to see the bald eagle executing his airway robbery at the expense of the osprey. The black ducks, goldeneyes, and scaups and the eiders and old squaws are conspicuous in winter and spring.

Those who come from inland to see this land-and-sea national park will always be most interested in the sights of the rocky coastline. The harbor seal is frequently observed along the shore of the island and on the ledges that lie outside. The fishermen who depend on their nets and weirs for a livelihood are not so enthusiastic about the sportive harbor seal as are the rest of us. The seal refuses to admit that any fish is private property. The most he will admit is that a net may be.

At certain times of the year whales may be seen spouting close to shore or lying near the surface. Porpoises are commonly seen by those who make boat trips to the outlying islands or in the waters of Frenchman Bay. The smaller marine forms—mussels, crabs, and occasionally a lobster that gets entangled in the seaweed and washes ashore—and the sea anemones and other creatures of the changing tides are of unfailing interest to those who for the first time get the tang of the ocean in their nostrils.

I am in Acadia National Park on an afternoon in late June. One of the many sylvan footpaths and fire-control roads passes a swampy pond, a glacial

*Retreat of the ice sheet left this boulder perched on the edge of South Bubble. Acadia National Park. [Photo: M. Woodbridge Williams]*

remnant on its way to becoming dry land in time, but there still is plenty of shallow water with lush vegetation. Somebody has dumped gravel to make a dry-shod approach to the water's edge. The round-leaf sundew has come up through the gravel and, with its sticky leaves, sets a snare for tiny insects. Over at one side of the footway a single pitcher plant, the Jedediah Smith of the plant-trappers, rears its head from the water. Behind it a pair of inquiring eyes is fixed on me—those of a frog that has just dunked in.

The air is bland, but a faint breeze has zest in it, and in the open spaces among the reedy growth the sky-blue reflections are rippled. The stickwork of a beaver dam is out just in front of me. I watch awhile for a beaver to appear, but none comes. Behind me in a natural plantation of poplar, I have already seen where these tireless and inventive woodsmen have been at work. Dozens of trees as big through as my upper arm show the neat chiseling of the teeth. The bottom end of the felled trees is a cone; and where the beaver has left his felling job unfinished, the cut is in the shape of an hourglass. I wonder at just which point in the cutting the animal dodges and gets from under.

Something comes swimming straight toward me: a muskrat, making good time, half out of water, with easy strokes. He finally sees me standing there, jams his rudder hard aport, and without too much concern sets a course straight back again. There are plenty of birds flitting about, but they are unusually quiet—a chip here and a twitter there.

Nothing exciting happens. The surrounding hills shimmer a little in a filmy haze. I come away from the spot with a pleasant feeling of partnership in all the small business transactions of the wild. Several thousands of eyes have been looking at me all the while—little lives I could not see with mine. I am not a naturalist. My perception misses a good deal. I do not flatter myself that any of the creatures has overrated me; not even that they had any keen interest in me. Yet I do have the agreeable sensation that I have not, as a guest, been unwelcome.

It is now three days since I saw a newspaper headline. I feel relaxed. A little swampy pond in a national park can be a healing thing, I find.

The history of the white man on Mount Desert goes back into the earliest days of the exploration of North America. Champlain came in 1604, and nearly a century later Louis XIV gave the island to the Sieur de la Mothe Cadillac, who signed himself Seigneur des Monts Deserts. The French word did not imply what we now call a desert; it described a wild uninhabited land. It was, indeed, heavily forested.

In the early part of the nineteenth century the only settlers were fisherman farmers who sold off the virgin timber and lived an austere but healthy and self-reliant life. But about the middle of the century, Mount Desert began to be discovered. New York and Boston people—the venturesome sort for that day—came in and "roughed it," finding the native people hospitable, ungreedy, intelligent. Then, naturally, came summer homes, boardinghouses, and finally large hotels and "development." That part of the island which is outside the park is still a vacationland, for people of modest incomes as well as for the rich.

I have seen the journal kept by a New York paterfamilias who spent about six weeks on the island in the summer of 1855. It was a family of ten, with friends also; and they journeyed into what then seemed like the utter northern frontier, with some misgivings. As they felt they would need a tie to conventions and culture, they ordered a grand piano sent up from Boston, and installed it in the home of the sturdy Mr. Somes, one of the earliest natives to accept boarders. After the piano had brought unusual pleasure to the islanders, who were generously invited for miles to enjoy it, the instrument went back to Boston by schooner, being reverently loaded at Southwest Harbor.

The New York family was enraptured. The writer of the diary galloped into dithyrambs over such beauty and wildness and inspiring scenes as he had never experienced. They kept Sundays faithfully. Some Boston ladies came up to Bar Harbor for a few days. They "appeared like superior persons; but we were willing to let them go by without acquaintance because of their slack notions of Sunday-keeping." What Papa would have said if the Boston ladies had appeared in shorts and halters one shudders to consider. The schooner would have called for the grand piano at once.

Papa of the large family, back in New York, ended his diary: "The expedition has been interesting and often exciting, in a very high degree. It will be the fund of story and conversation for years to come. The children come back broader, browner and stronger than they went."

I will wager that Papa went back the following year, bought a piece of land, and built a cottage on Mount Desert; and perhaps his heirs have been among those generous souls who later gave their land to help establish Acadia National Park.

*Fog shuts down on a lobsterman. Acadia National Park.* [*Photo: Paul M. Tilden*]

## 2. GRAND TETON NATIONAL PARK
### [*Wyoming*]

THE IMPRESSION made by the Teton Range is indelible. No matter how many years afterward, if one were shown a photograph of these Wyoming mountains, just south of Yellowstone National Park, there would be not a moment's hesitation. "I know those peaks. Those are the Tetons. And *that* peak is the Grand Teton."

This is not because of their beauty, though their beauty is ravishing. Other mountains and other ranges are beautiful too. It is partly because from any point where you are likely to come to rest to look at them, the eye involuntarily puts a frame around them. Close your eyes, you who have seen the Tetons, and bring them back to mind as you saw them. Is it not a framed picture? But this surpassing individuality arises even more from the way they were created and from the forces that later worked upon them to create their aspiring peaks.

Once upon a time (perhaps all references to geological periods should have that fairy-tale beginning), when the Rockies were heaving and straining in their orogenic labor, the earth crust cracked along this forty-mile line, the "Teton fault." There came a time when the rocks on both sides of the fault began to slip, one along the other; one rising, the other going down. It was not a sharp catastrophe. How long the movement went on is not known and is really not important. But when the slip had ended and the rocks had come to rest, the Tetons were towering seven thousand feet above the basin now called Jackson Hole. In the ensuing centuries, as the Tetons were being torn down, Jackson Hole was filling up with the debris; so perhaps the relationship, in height and depth, has not greatly changed.

So you see that the Tetons, as you view them from Jackson Hole, are mountains without foothills. They rise impetuously from almost level land on the Wyoming side. On the Idaho side of the range it is different. The mountain block was tilted to the west as it rose, just as was the greater uplift of the Sierra, where it accounts for those foothills through which you wind on your way to the sequoia country. One may imagine that before the tearing-down processes began, the eastern side of the Teton block presented a colossal sheer escarpment of crystalline rocks, frowning bluntly upon the depression below. Actually such a stark wall never existed, because erosion and uplift were working in unison; but I think it aids comprehension if one pictures it that way.

[ 266 ]

## Grand Teton National Park

The wondrous jagged outline, the cirques and horns and knife-edged ridges, the headlong slopes and pinnacles that characterize the Tetons as you see them from the perfect observation point provided by Jackson Hole, were to be the later work of storm and frost, wind and sun, and chiefly of that master carver, ice. There came an age when at high elevations the snow accumulated faster than it could melt, piling up such depths that rivers of ice began to move and pluck and tear, bringing down burdens of broken rock to the lowlands. There are still impressive glaciers and snowfields in the Tetons.

Where the ancient and much greater glaciers stopped and began to retreat, embankments of debris were left, called moraines, and behind these were formed lakes. Thus came into being Jackson, Jenny, Phelps, Taggart, and Leigh Lakes, and the other bodies of water, without whose enchantment the Teton picture would be incomplete. To see the Tetons mirrored in Jackson Lake early on a clear summer morning when not a breath of wind is stirring and the image of the range is so sharply defined that its identical twin lives in the water—this is an experience never to be forgotten in discovering the real America.

*The tent is not yet secured, but little sister sends a message to someone. Acadia National Park. [Photo: M. Woodbridge Williams]*

Just as it is easy to understand the lure of this Rocky Mountain retreat for present-day Americans, so it is not hard to believe that the aesthetic quality of the surroundings was fully appreciated by the Indians in their time and by the fur traders who so well knew this ground. Can anyone suppose that the red man could look upon such a scene without a thrill, and an inner impulse of devotion? Or even that the Colters and Sublettes, Smiths and Bridgers and Fitzpatricks, though their tough muscles and iron wills were bent upon their trade, could come back to Jackson Hole after long journeys without a similar feeling? Other holes these men used for rendezvous, truly, but there was only one like Jackson Hole, which Sublette named for a fellow trapper, David E. Jackson, who was said to be especially enamored of the basin.

The winters were savage in this region then, as they usually are now. It was no place for a weakling when the first white settlers came there to home-stead, in the mid-1880's. Less stubborn men and women than those first settlers would not have remained a second year, despite the beauty of the spot. Early in 1949 three or four approaches to Jackson Hole were closed for months by continuous storms. Yet, interestingly enough, in March of that year, three men—all skillful and seasoned climbers—made the ascent of the Grand Teton, a challenging feat at any time.

Exactly here is a good place to speak of climbing 13,766-foot Grand Teton and other peaks of the range. This range is ranked by practiced moun-taineers all over the world as among the most delightfully defiant. Every year sees increasing numbers of alpinists coming from abroad to test their skill against the Tetons. There are those who regard such difficult and dangerous ventures as foolhardy. I am not one of these, though personally I shall choose easier delights. My own notion of excessive temerity goes no farther than pre-empting the favorite window chair of the oldest member of some club like the Union or the Somerset. That is danger enough for me. But I seem to see that these rugged fellows in the hobnailed boots, with their ice axes and rope, risking their necks to say no to the impossible, may after all be inheri-tors of the spirit of those undaunted primates who insisted on rearing up and walking on their hind legs at a time when swinging from branch to branch was accepted as positively a permanent condition. If Prometheus had not challenged invincible Zeus, we should have no steam heat.

It does not follow that the mere wish to scale the Teton peaks will end happily. Those who have not served the hard apprenticeship of this sport will be well advised to get the services of experienced guides who are author-ized to serve in this capacity. Of course, the tyro may find some good climb-ers to accompany, but the chances are that before the end of the bout the

*The Tetons seen from the Idaho side. Grand Teton National Park.* [*Photo: William Henry Jackson, 1879*]

adepts will wish they had left their companion at home. Under all circumstances rangers and guides should be consulted before any attempt at climbing is made, and each expedition is required to report at park headquarters or at Jenny Museum before and after the trip. Climbing alone is absolutely prohibited.

The usual climbing season embraces July, August, and September, though weather and snow conditions are uncertain, naturally. Usually two days are allowed for an ascent of Grand Teton, Moran, or Owen. For other peaks, one day may suffice.

The trails of Grand Teton National Park are truly magnificent, and most visitors will be well satisfied to leave the alpinists to their special thrill and go afoot or on saddle horses over these ninety miles of adventure, constructed

[ 269 ]

to give the very best experiences for the least possible physical exertion. For those who wish to ride these trails, a concessioner, with a fine string of saddle horses and with equipment for long or short trips, will be found at the south end of Jenny Lake.

The lakes trail parallels the mountains, following closely the base of the Tetons and skirting the shore of each large lake from Leigh to Phelps. Leigh and Jenny Lakes are completely circled by trails.

Teton Glacier Trail goes up the east slope of Grand Teton to Surprise and Amphitheater Lakes. The end of this trail is at Amphitheater Lake, which is the starting point for the climb to Teton Glacier. All along this trail are superb views of the surrounding country.

On the Indian Paintbrush Trail, which begins near the outlet of Leigh Lake, not only is there a profusion of wild flowers for gay company, but the chances are good for seeing some of the park's large animals, especially Shiras moose. What this creature lacks in beauty he duly compensates for in bulk, and, unlike some of the others of the deer family, he is not timid about being watched. You will probably see mule deer along this trail, too. This trail connects with the Cascade Canyon Trail by way of the small but exquisite Lake Solitude, and one of the finest views of the looming Tetons is to be had across this body of water.

Cascade Canyon and Death Canyon Trails pass through deep and impressive chasms, whose walls rise sheer. Death Canyon Trail, as awesome as its name, emerges finally into broad meadows. Cascade Canyon Trail leads into the deepest recesses of the mountains, along the bases of the great peaks.

Skyline Trail, from the head of South Cascade Canyon to the head of the north fork of Death Canyon, passes through a part of Alaska Basin and to the west of the Limestone Wall at the head of Avalanche Canyon.

In isolated parts of Grand Teton National Park there are small herds of Rocky Mountain sheep, or bighorn, and there are bears in the mountains and canyons, but these are not numerous, and until visitors learn not to fraternize with this animal, perhaps it is just as well. Cheerful ground squirrels and chipmunks are everywhere, and there are beavers, martens, minks, coyotes, and other small animals. More than one hundred species of birds have been identified. In a park where movement of humans is practically restricted to Mr. Shanks' or somebody else's mare, the relationship between people and wildlife tends to be on a fine basis.

The botanists tell us that the plantlife of the Tetons is in some respects unique. The high mountains have proved to be a barrier that many forms could not cross. The region is the range limit for many plants deriving from

*The classic fault: uplifted range seen from Jackson Hole. Grand Teton National Park. [Photo: George Grant]*

all four points of the compass, and there are a few known only to the Tetons. The flowering period begins in the park as soon as the ridges and flats are free from snow, usually in May, and continues until about mid-August in the higher places, so there is bloom of some sort continuously in spring and summer. Though much of the Teton Range is above timberline, the usual Rocky Mountain evergreens clothe the lower parts of the mountains and fringe the many lakes.

Jackson Hole is in every respect the complement, the fulfilling adjunct, to the Teton Range. Historically it completes the scene of discovery and pioneering. Geologically it is the other half of a story. And it supplies the sloping stadium seats, so to speak, from which the majestic mountains are witnessed in their glory. All this was understood many years ago, and among those who realized the importance of Jackson Hole to the park was John D. Rockefeller, Jr., whose keen and generous understanding had already done so much to ensure the integrity of many of the finest examples of American scenery.

Rockefeller's interest, once enlisted, went to work in the usual practical way. It was asked then, and unthinking people still ask in similar cases, why it was necessary to make a part of the National Park System an area that nobody could ever carry away and that would always provide a site for viewing the Tetons. What harm could there be in leaving it in private hands? Any sensitive visitor to the national parks can give the answer to that. One of the joys of being in these preserved spots is the consciousness and the observation that there is at least a brave attempt to keep the scenery free from the ugliness of commercial exploitation. One comes to look at the beauties of nature, not to gaze on intruding claimants for attention, some tawdry, some impudent, and even when least offensive, still out of place.

Over many years, Rockefeller, through a corporation set up for the purpose, acquired 33,562 acres of land in Jackson Hole, with the intention of presenting it to the American people at such a time as he could feel assured that the lands would be administered by the National Park Service. On March 15, 1943, President Roosevelt proclaimed an area of about 223,000 acres, 173,000 of which were already owned by the government, as Jackson Hole National Monument. This child of the National Park System, however, came into the world with a birthmark in the form of angry litigation.

It is all settled now. Today there is no Jackson Hole National Monument. The Tetons and Jackson Hole are what they should have been many years ago: one national park. There is no possible good in rehashing the sorry story of verbal violence and political maneuvering that followed upon the Presidential proclamation of 1943. Most of the participants in the outcry, in Wyoming and elsewhere, are sufficiently ashamed of having been so easily drifted across the legal landscape ahead of a small group of interested persons who were afraid of the loss of long-enjoyed benefits accruing from the use of public lands. The clamor long ago died down and was kept alive only by poking. In September 1950 President Truman signed an act of Congress that established the enlarged park.

The compromise—it had to be somewhat of a compromise—was not altogether satisfactory from the viewpoint of those who would like to see fewer rather than more management problems in the national park. For example, ever since the white man came to the Teton and Jackson Hole region the elk, or wapiti, one of our finest big-game animals, has been of the greatest impor-

*But you must know how. Grand Teton National Park. [Photo: Herb Pownall]*

tance and interest. In spring it leaves the low country and the Elk Refuge near the town of Jackson and moves into the higher lands north and east. Some small bands go into the Teton Range for the summer. When the snow falls, the elk return to the refuge.

It is on this return, in crossing open country, that the elk herd is usually thinned by a great assemblage of sportsmen, curiously and variously armed, in all stages of emotional elevation. But sometimes the elk do not come down on schedule, or they perform a quick migration before the armament can be assembled. If this occurs and the thinning does not take place, the elk tend further to outrun their natural feed.

The fishing in Grand Teton is considered very good. During most of the summer fish may be taken with artificial fly, but in Jackson and Jenny Lakes the mackinaws must be taken with heavy tackle by trolling. Cutthroats (locally known as blackspotted trout) and Eastern brooks are in the park waters.

Among the many reasons for visiting the museum at Jenny Lake is the collection devoted to mountaineering. There are also exhibits showing the history and geology and the plants and wildlife of the area. Adjacent to the museum is an open-air amphitheater where campfire talks are given. Nature walks, all-day hikes, and auto caravans are conducted regularly by naturalist guides.

### 3. ROCKY MOUNTAIN NATIONAL PARK
### [*Colorado*]

"THIS CITADEL OF EARTH; this outpost of heaven."

As a description of the Colorado Rockies, you might think this a trifle perfervid—a little on the hysterical side. But pause. Let us consider the manner of man who uttered the words. Samuel Bowles, the founder and publisher of the Springfield (Massachusetts) *Republican*, a newspaper that carried the flag of literacy to all the Eastern seaboard in the middle of the last century, was a great economist of praise. Some thought him a severe, metallic person. He had attained the reputation with himself of never being wrong about anything; therefore his newspaper could not be in error.

Tell me whether you would quarrel with the dictum of a man like that. Not I. And besides, the recollection of my own first sight of the Rockies and the journey into their magnificence is so vivid to this very day that I am not disposed to weigh any poetic flight.

Far out on the plains, east of Denver, clouds appear to be gathering in the

*Camping with elbow room. Rocky Mountain National Park.* [*Photo: M. Wood-bridge Williams*]

west. They are not clouds. Drive only a little more on your westward trend to a point, say, thirty-five miles out from the city, on what was called the Smoky Hill road, and you no longer doubt your eyes. The great Barrier Wall confronts you. You are already a mile above sea level, or somewhere near it, but on the landscape on three sides of you there is nothing to indicate it. On the remaining side, the Front Range of the Rockies, drawing a horizon line far up the sky, seems to warn you that you shall go no farther. There is more United States beyond, you know; indeed, the San Franciscan making a trip to Salt Lake City says that he is going "back east"; and you are not so naive as not to know that there are passes through the mountains that will take you into the Great Basin. Still, the impact of the first sight of the Great Barrier is stunning.

You do go on. You do find shrewdly engineered roads of fine quality, and you do easily find yourself before long in the very heart of the Front Range of the Rockies, marveling at what is one of the greatest mountain masses in

*"I took a few pictures of the park. Would you like to see some of them?" Courtesy requires a warm affirmative. Rocky Mountain National Park. [Photo: M. Woodbridge Williams]*

the world. For *mass* is the word. There are higher peaks elsewhere. The eastern escarpment of the Sierra may be even more precipitous. But for sheer sense of towering density, of closely packed mountaintops, I know of nothing like this. And today your course will probably be steered toward one of the entrances to Rocky Mountain National Park, for, of all the national parks, this one is perhaps the most accessible to the greatest number of populous states, being but a short distance from Denver and an overnight trip from most of the Midwest. But the accessibility reaches farther than this. Nowhere else can the tourist so easily attain the high mountains and achieve familiarity with them.

These majestic mountains are amiable. Even Longs Peak, 14,255 feet above sea level, is not difficult to climb for those who are properly equipped and in good condition and take the advice of a park ranger. But within the four hundred square miles of park there are sixty-five other named peaks more than ten thousand feet high; and of these, fifteen are more than thirteen thousand feet high. True, one starts from an elevation of eight thousand feet; but the real reason why these might be called the Intimate Rockies, aside from the peculiar incident of their formation by nature, is that roads and trails have been so constructed that visitors can view with ease sights that almost anywhere else would cost great physical effort.

Think of a fine, transcontinental road, of which eleven miles are above the timberline of eleven thousand feet, and four miles are above twelve thousand feet! This is Trail Ridge Road. Bear Lake Road leads to a network of trails where hikers can go on to mountain peaks or into lake-studded gorges. Old Fall River Road is narrow and one-way-controlled, the sort of challenge to good driving and the kind of path to adventure well remembered by many a motorist who navigated in the mountain country only a few years ago.

*Good morning, Miss! Yes, I'll join you in a snack. Rocky Mountain National Park.*
*[Photo: M. Woodbridge Williams]*

After winding along its steep, forest-bordered course, the one-way road joins the modern Trail Ridge Road.

Although Rocky Mountain National Park is open all year, Trail Ridge Road is normally closed to trans-mountain travel by snow about the end of October, opening again about the first of June. But, as in other primeval parks, those who can arrange to enjoy them before and after the great rush of summer travel have a real reward. A friend of mine who lives not more than seventy miles from several beautiful sea beaches said to me not long ago: "I never go down to the beaches in summer. I wait till the winy, sunny days in the fall, when the hotels and boardinghouses and cottages are closed. I have the beach to myself—along with a few others who feel as I do. It isn't that I don't like people; it's just that the things I go for are not there for me when there are crowds."

All the wild animals you expect to find in the high country are in Rocky Mountain; but the elk and the mule deer are especially abundant. Outstanding, naturally, is that noble old-time resident the Rocky Mountain bighorn. These animals are not to be seen, except accidentally, without going up into the high places where they feed and have protection from their enemies, the cat family. But those hikers who see them on Specimen Mountain or at Sheep Lake have something to tell about. The beavers are everywhere, logging and constructing. They are the army engineers of the animal world; they never see a running stream without having thoughts of a dam. But beavers are shy, and you must be patient and quiet before you can see them at their business locations.

Here, too, if you love birds, even if you are not an expert, you may meet some old friends and some new ones. Above timberline, pipits, rosy finches, horned larks, and ptarmigans are often seen, and anywhere you can strike up an expensive acquaintance with the Rocky Mountain jay, known as the camp robber, who will filch any article not weighted down. John Muir tells of his taking a cake of soap and a towel down to a brook one morning for a wash. He lathered himself, laid the soap on a rock at his feet, made one pass across his face with the towel, and saw one of these feathered kleptomaniacs swooping off with his soap, all in a split second.

Looking back through the years, it is interesting to note that this Colorado mountain fastness was one of the first to be appreciated by holiday-makers. A party from the East went into what is now part of Rocky Mountain National Park long before Yellowstone was revealed, and came to a deserted mining village. "Here we found welcome. Half the place was *pre-occupied* by a large party of men and women, some 20 to 30 in all, from the villages

*Where beavers abandoned their house. Rocky Mountain National Park.* [*Photo: Roger Contor*]

in the lower country . . . they had ox teams for their baggage, saddle animals to carry themselves, and a cow to furnish fresh milk. Thus generously equipped, they were jollily entering upon camp life for ten days or a fortnight up among the mountain tops."

Think of that! These were pioneers, already living no delicate life in the lower altitudes. But the lure of the higher places drew them; they wanted that "distinctive charm of the atmosphere, so clear and dry and pure all the while, as to be a perpetual *feeling*, rather than a vision, of beauty."

There were even forerunners of the concessioners who now serve the public in the national parks. Here were a man and wife and daughter who had driven a herd of forty or fifty milch cows up from southern Colorado and were making 150 pounds of butter a week, selling it to eager campers at seventy-five cents a pound, and paying all their expenses with the increase in their herd. And this was back in the middle part of last century, in a period when the Utes were killing four thousand antelope in a grand hunt of three weeks.

No doubt the keynote of this park is the rugged uplift picture as a whole, with its gorges, its glacial carvings and moraines; its alpine lakes, profuse and of sumptuous beauty; the flattops on which even a soft and sedentary tourist can feel himself on the world's roof; hanging valleys and plunging streams, eternal snows, even small glaciers. That is the impact on the visual sense. But against this mighty background is the loveliness and imaginative appeal of the second look. There are the flowers. All through the Rockies, it is true, you are constantly delighted with the bloom that begins when the snow has hardly begun to retreat and ends only when all is frozen and blanketed. But here in Rocky Mountain, with such a wide range of elevations, the variety of plantlife is remarkable. In the park are more than seven hundred species of flowering plants. Perhaps the best known is the blue columbine, the Colorado state flower. But the gentians and lilies, the paintbrushes and primroses are ever with you in your ascent from zone to zone, till finally, above timberline, mats of flowers spread everywhere. In June on the north slope of Twin Sisters the alpine moss campion, clinging to every space where there is nourishment between the rocks, makes a crazy quilt wonderful to look upon; and later in the season the sight is repeated on Fall River Pass, Flattop, and Longs Peak.

To many, the great dramatic moment of a visit to Rocky Mountain will be witnessing the struggle at timberline. Timberline is a mountain climatic zone, which varies, partly, according to the latitude. In the White Mountains of New Hampshire, timberline is only a few thousand feet. Here it is very high—about 11,500 feet. Timberline is the place where plantlife says: "I *will* live. I shall bend. I shall creep on hands and knees. I shall dodge, devise, join hands, and compromise; but I *will* live. Let the cruel gales blow; let the snow and ice pile up; if I cannot grow as I would like, I shall still grow."

Below that timberline you see fair-growing, luxuriant yellow pine, lodgepole and Douglas fir, Engelmann spruce and aspens, with the fine Colorado blue spruce, alder, and birch along the streams. But once at the deadline, how different! Aged trees, lacking symmetry and bent like staggering crones under a heavy burden, sometimes stand out alone; again the dwarfed trees have grown so closely packed, for mutual protection, that they appear as a woven mat in which the strands of differing trees can hardly be distinguished. In places snowdrifts mulch the creeping trees; the shoots emerging above the snow are promptly nipped, but those beneath the protecting blanket grow outward defiantly. If the ice tears and strips the bark upon the windward

*Wild sheep on McGregor Mountain. Rocky Mountain National Park. [Photo: Merlin K. Potts]*

side, no matter. Half a bark is better than none: the tree will make do. Little caves of scrub growth are formed, where the hiker, caught in one of those storms which blow so suddenly at the alpine level, can take shelter. But thrashed unmercifully though these insistent plants are, they cannot be subdued. For every one that, beaten or dying of old age, gives up the struggle, another is ready to take its place.

Above the timberline, where it would seem impossible for any vegetation to exist, much less to produce a lovely carpet of bloom, is the Alpine tundra. We associate such a meadow of grasses, lichens, mosses, and stunted plants with the Arctic regions. Indeed, to see anything resembling what is shown on the mountaintops of Rocky Mountain National Park, one would have to go, in our own country, to Alaska. There is a nature trail, beginning at the Rock Cut parking area more than twelve thousand feet above sea level, where visitors, advisedly at a slow pace, may observe this phenomenon of pygmy vegetation not merely existing, but thriving, in a mantle of moist wet soil—plants that have needed perhaps several hundred years to attain the growth one now observes. Yet these indomitable little dwarfs—forgetmenots, avens, harebells, and other species—put forth their gay flowers in July, invite the pollinating insects, and go to seed in a season that cannot be more than six weeks and is usually less. Do not tread on the plants when you walk this strange trail. Can you imagine a more delicate growth than one which may require five years to grow a quarter of an inch?

## 4. GLACIER NATIONAL PARK
### [*Montana*]

IF YOUR VACATION TRIP should happen to take you from the range of the Tetons northward through Yellowstone National Park—not hurriedly, if later you wish to tell the precious beads of reminiscence—and then on to Glacier National Park, in northwestern Montana, you would find yourself translated into what, at first glance, seems to be an entirely different scenic world. Yet there are interesting points of similarity between the Tetons and the mountains of Glacier, and the chief one is their "personality."

As, once having seen them, you will never mistake the Tetons for any other range, just so the marked characteristics of the mountains of Glacier will remain in your memory. You have gone from the vertical to the horizontal, as the eye receives it, even though you are among mountains that top ten thousand feet. Granted, such a statement has the flaw of all attempts to simplify. But as you journey through Glacier, your impression will be of mountains that are on the march. The explanation is found in the different nature of the two rock masses, and though your interest in geology may ordinarily be mild, here you are certain to be fascinated by the story revealed. As the cowboy said of Grand Canyon, "Something has happened here!" Later we shall see what it was.

First, though, another point of likeness between the Grand Teton and Glacier. The mountain part of the Wyoming park provides a thrilling trail

*The pure gothic architecture of nature. Glacier National Park.* [*Photo: George Grant*]

experience. Glacier National Park is a trail park on a much vaster plan. It is true that you can see gorgeous scenery in Glacier, traversing one of the most spectacular roads of the world, without ever getting out of your car. You can enter the park in the morning on the eastern side at St. Mary, cross the Continental Divide at Logan Pass, look out of the rock windows of the famous Going-to-the-Sun Road, follow the shore of Lake McDonald down to Belton, and by driving in your safe but fast way you could play canasta in Spokane that night, arriving a little late, with apologies for having loitered to look at the scenery.

There is a story current in Park Service circles about two young men who chugged into Yellowstone on a motorcycle one evening at dusk. One of them had evidently been there before. This conversation was overheard:

"Is there a good night club here?"

"I don't think they have 'em here."

"Well, we'll go and see a good picture."

"I don't believe they have any, except maybe some fillums of animals and flowers and that kind of stuff."

"No kiddin'? What do you know? Well, what the hell *do* they expect a feller to do here—look at *scenery*?"

Although mountain-and-forest-and-lake wilderness can never be savored to the full except by those who leave their automobiles and take to the trails, a great degree of compensation has been provided for those who must get their enjoyment from the roads. If the Going-to-the-Sun Road is not the finest and most spectacular road in the world—which individual taste must decide—nobody will question that it is one of the best. It is both an engineering and a planning triumph. Where it was necessary, in order to present the magnificent vistas, the roadway bores through rock cliffs, and the outside wall of the west tunnel has two picture windows that constitute framing in the grandest imaginable manner. The transition from the quiet loveliness of lakeside into the rock fastnesses of the Continental Divide and then down again to the limpid and tree-fringed glacial waters will remain always in your memory. Yet this trip is no stencil, for when you drive back again over the same road, as you should do, there is no sameness of impression. The wonder is not how much was seen on the first journey, but how much was missed.

Although there is but this one road that traverses Glacier National Park,

*Hikers on the knife-edge slope of Mount Lincoln. Glacier National Park. [Photo: Jack E. Boucher]*

[ 2 8 5 ]

there is another that, coasting along the Front Range of the Rockies, has its own strong attractions. At Kennedy Creek still another road leaves the Blackfeet Road, swings round the base of Chief Mountain, and crosses the international boundary to Waterton Lakes National Park.

Even if this trip were not a glorious adventure on its own natural account, it would be well worth taking for its historical significance. Here are two nations that can not only live in amity, but actually pool their scenic treasures in an International Peace Park. If someday Mexico creates a national park adjoining our own in Big Bend, we shall have on our two borders a pulsating gage of friendship such as has no counterpart in the story of nations.

Waterton-Glacier International Peace Park was established in 1932, authorized by the U.S. Congress and by the Canadian Parliament to be "forever a symbol of permanent peace and friendship." And if when you are at Waterton Park you should take the launch that goes to the southern end of the lake, you will have again crossed an invisible boundary between the two countries, and no ferocious gendarme will have held you up and demanded to see your visa, your wallet, and the lining of your briefcase.

Outside the park but much worth seeing is the Museum of the Plains Indian in the town of Browning, twelve miles east of Glacier Park Station. Here are exhibits that interpret the life and arts of the Indians of the Plains, who once roamed at large among the buffalo herds in the grasslands or hunted in the mountains where your trail trips will presently lead you.

The only other well-surfaced roads inside the park are the short spurs that lead to Many Glacier and Swiftcurrent Lake, and from Glacier Park Station to Two Medicine. From those centers, where varied overnight accommodations are available, and where visitors who are out to taste the joys of roving the wild country may get horses and guides as well as what equipment they may need, the trails take off in many directions. For horseback riders and hikers, the many trips are made as convenient as anyone would wish. Those who crave to rough it may certainly do so, but those who want the prospect of a good meal and a bed at the regular hours will be satisfied. After all, the greater number of people who visit the parks are not muscle-hard and are not saddle-wise. Unfortunately a good many thousands who would really like to follow the trails are deterred by the fear that they may fall by the wayside for lack of skill.

The truth about this is that all you have to do is be frank with yourself and with others. The first rule is that, afoot, you do not attempt more than you should, do not wander off the trails, do not try to climb peaks or go into uncharted country alone, do not attempt other kinds of stunting. As for the saddle trips, if, when you engage a mount you tell the wrangler frankly that you have not ridden or are years out of practice, if that is the case, you will make a friend of him at once. You will get special attention and end by having a better time than some dude who has been pretending to be an equestrian adept. It would be well, though, to make a few short trips and limber up before going on one of the longer jaunts.

Especially attractive in Glacier National Park are the profusion of wild flowers and the abundant wildlife. In both respects hikers and horseback riders will have the best of it, though on the Blackfeet Road there is usually an opportunity to see elk, deer, moose, and bears as well as the smaller animals; and on the Going-to-the-Sun Road, especially between Mount Cannon and Logan Pass, the automobilist will probably see, besides the ubiquitous black bear, plenty of the deer family and mountain goats and bighorn, which can be made out on the cliffs on either side of the highway or on the "fishbone" known as the Garden Wall.

These bighorn, or mountain sheep, are characteristic of the Rocky Mountain parks generally, but the goats are the distinguishing wildlife feature of Glacier. All visitors look for them and feel triumphant when they see a group close at hand, or decide through field glasses that the white spots on the side of a sheer cliff are really animals and not patches of snow.

No one can consider the story of man's ruthless attitude toward the wild game in pioneer days without a feeling of thankfulness that the creatures in Glacier, among other parks, are now protected and allowed to go their own way according to the natural law of tooth and claw. In saying this I am in no way reflecting upon those mountain men who lived on the country and shot game for their food. They were doing a logical and proper thing.

As to sport hunting, I am not a Nimrod myself, but I know many excellent people who love to try their skill with the gun, and I trust they are all as good sportsmen as was Henry Cuyler Bunner, once editor of the comic weekly *Puck*. An aspiring poet sent Bunner a sheaf of verses with a terse note asking: "What do I get for these?" The editor sent back the poems and scribbled on the contributor's letter just three words: "Ten yards start."

I merely ask that my hunting friends give as much start to their game as the editor was willing to grant a poet. But what is the truth about the hunting of animals that once went on in these delectable mountains? From the early 1880's until the establishment of the park in 1910 the wildlife must have been extraordinarily plentiful. A visitor to the region in 1895 was told by the trappers themselves that at least five hundred elk and moose, to say nothing of mountain sheep, goats, and deer, were killed every year for—what would you think! For bear bait! The trapping of grizzly bears for their furry hides was then at a peak, and the traps were baited with carcasses of these splendid animals.

Over the entrance to the Nairobi National Park in East Africa is a sign: "The wildlife of today is not ours to dispose of as we please. We have it in trust." Whenever I think of that African-refuge admonition, I somehow instantly recall the grizzly traps of Glacier in the days before it was a national park, and I feel a sense of deep satisfaction and relief that somewhere the animals have havens of trust.

As to the flowers of Glacier National Park, the showiest is undoubtedly the bear grass, which blooms almost everywhere, beginning on the valley floors and rising to the alpine meadows as the summer warmth comes. With its tall head of tiny white lily blooms, it dominates the scene, somewhat at the expense of many others of the lily family which follow the retreating snow and fill the eye with their color. There are more than a thousand species of wild flowers in Glacier, and though many of them are not advertisers of themselves, a considerable number of them are exceptionally brilliant when they form their dazzling carpets.

Then, too, one must take to the trails to see the living glaciers. There are many of these in the park, and some of them are accessible with very little trouble. Though these glaciers are not large, there are few in our country that can be visited so readily. These glaciers, in common with others in Western America, have been diminishing in recent years, making meteorologists wonder if we are entering a warm cycle that may have some far-reaching effects. Whatever may be the truth about that, the glaciers of this park should certainly be visited, for most of them display the curious features that distinguish such moving ice—tables, cones, moulins, crevasses, cirques, and all the rest. Even if the living glaciers should disappear wholly from this park—a matter of guesswork, because a series of colder and snowier winters could set the ice building up and flowing again—Glacier National Park still would be well named. Almost all of what the eye now sees, in the sculpture of these mountains and valleys and the creation of more than two hundred lovely lakes, is referable to the work of mighty glaciers of the past.

And this brings us back at last to the fascinating geological explanation of why the mountains of Glacier National Park strike the eye as they do—the reason for that uncompromising selfhood which I have compared with that

*Near the summit of Logan Pass, Lake McDonald side. Glacier National Park. [Photo: George Grant]*

of the Tetons. I remarked that they seem to be marching; or, rather, they seem to have been checked and frozen in the midst of a lateral movement. I suppose my thought in this respect is in some degree directed by the fact that I happen to know something of the geology of the region. But nearly every visitor has some comment on the peculiar Mayan-temple shape that characterizes so much of the mountain mass, and also on a certain dark arrow-band, with two light arrow-bands on each side of it, which is seen on the sides of so many of the peaks. And there are other horizontal layering lines that carry out the feeling of the lateral movement.

Glacier National Park records a colossal event in our earth history. The same thing has happened elsewhere, but nowhere in this country is there such a perfectly graphic example. First, it must be understood that all this region was under a shallow sea, not once but many times, and each time erosion brought down to the sea floor mud and sand—mostly mud. Layer upon layer, as the sea level rose and subsided, these deposits were later to be hardened into shales, sandstones, and limestones, of varying hardness. These are known as sedimentary rocks, and it is said that here in Glacier are the oldest *unaltered* rocks of this kind known on earth. Some of them retain in perfect delineation the mud cracks, ripples, raindrop dents, and casts of salt crystals that were in the original drying muds.

Then came the uplift, which strained the crust and broke it in many places; and some great force, little understood even by the experts, began to thrust a whole huge mass to the northeastward for a distance of fifteen to eighteen miles. Perhaps in that great thrust the soft rock of the Plains refused to give way before this moving mass, and as the force from behind was terrific, the rocks wrinkled just as a sheet of paper would be wrinkled by shoving it along a table against a hard object. At the finish of the movement some of the oldest rocks in the region were lying *above* the youngest rocks of the Plains. At Chief Mountain this may be seen clearly.

The identifying arrow-band of which I have spoken came from a different source. It is a sill, or intrusion of molten rock, which found its way between layers of limestone, just as the Palisades of the Hudson River on the New Jersey side once intruded horizontally into such established rocks, finally to remain the surface rock itself, in our time.

Finally came the series of glacial periods which set ice flowing down the valleys that streams of water had already cut, to gnaw on the rock cliffs, to tear and pluck and grind, build moraines, impound the lakes behind them, and at last produce the physical Glacier National Park we see today. Such a sketchy account as this is almost impudent, but the naturalist guides in Glacier will be delighted to explain fully and correctly all these things to visitors who are interested.

Identical forces working on the Teton Range produced mostly spire forms, with sides that tend to be concave. In Glacier the ice carved the rock, generally speaking, into rectangular forms, and even the horns are those of the pyramid rather than the cone. It makes a difference, you see, whether the ice is working upon sedimentary rocks or upon the crystalline kind. The great carver knows the material, and fashions accordingly.

## 5. YOSEMITE NATIONAL PARK
### [*California*]

### [ 1 ]

AT A TIME when Yellowstone could record but a scant five hundred visitors, Yosemite Valley was already a thriving tourist resort. There is doubt that any scenic locality ever enjoyed such a quick publicity and growth. Within a year from the day when the Mariposa *Gazette* published the account of the Hutchings tourist party's expedition into the area, a camp for travelers had been built on the south fork of the Merced, and trails for saddle parties were being pushed toward the valley floor. The Hutchings account was reproduced all over the country and found its way to Europe. On to Yosemite!

Horace Greeley was an early visitor. He arrived in August, when the falls, especially those of the Yosemite Creek, had almost suspended operations, according to habit. Greeley, who had come specially to see the longest leap of water, felt that he had been swindled. Besides, his riding boots hurt his feet, and his saddle chafed him. There are people today who arrive at the same time of year as did the journalist and wish the Park Service to install hydrants of some sort above the valley, so that they may see exactly what the June visitors do. It is a modest request, it would seem: like asking for the postponement of an eclipse of the moon because it coincides with an evening when one usually bowls.

But Greeley, recovering from his tantrum, became a captive of Yosemite's special beauty. He sent back to his newspaper an account that did the tourist business no harm. It was said that Editor Greeley's handwriting could be read by only one typesetter on the *Tribune*. That typesetter deciphered his employer's measured opinion that Yosemite was "the greatest marvel of the continent," that the "grandeur and sublimity" of the wondrous chasm were "overwhelming," and that it was to be hoped that California would immediately provide for the perpetual safety of the Mariposa Grove of Big Trees. The appeal was to the state because at that time the area had been so entrusted by the federal government.

Considering the fact that for twenty-three years after the Hutchings party described what they had seen, the only access to the valley was by means of horses and guides, the number of visitors in that period was remarkable. But when the wagon roads were built and it became possible for soft and timid people to make the journey in a less arduous way, then the influx really began. There was great competition among the travel agencies in San Francisco for this increasing business. One traveler of the period remarked that he was advised by a stagecoach agent to be sure to go to Yosemite by way of Mariposa. If he ventured by the Calaveras route he would be "traveling steerage."

No city was more excited by the photographs and writeups of the new place to see than was Boston. Bostonians had always been great travelers, but they had usually gone to Europe to see the Alps, or to the White Mountains, or to Mount Desert (where Acadia National Park is now) or to favorite Eastern watering places. Transcontinental travel had now become relatively easy and safe, so they turned to Yosemite, and exposed its wonders to the home folks with an infinite deluge of letters to the *Transcript*. For those accustomed to the graceful amenities of the Parker House and Young's Hotel, the hotel accommodations and cuisine of Yosemite were a trifle rugged. The first-comers especially were shocked to find that a "room" might be a space with a bed in it, surrounded by cloth curtains; and besides split infinitives there were other and more serious errors in California locution; but when all was done, and they had looked upon the valley from old Inspiration Point and seen Half Dome and Mirror Lake and the Mariposa sequoias and all the rest then accessible, there was nothing stingy in their enthusiasm. They agreed with Horace Greeley—it was grandeur and sublimity.

It was never, and is not now, "the greatest marvel of the continent," however. There is not an area among all the parks and monuments which merits that title. Each has its own kind of beauty, its own charm, its own story to tell. But it is true that Yosemite has a gemlike luster, a sort of fulfilling completeness, which makes its devotees cling to it as a first and last affection. They are lovesick swains and proud of it; and they will fight a duel with you over their superlatives.

Not all the Bostonians were weak in the muscles. Soon after the State

*Monolith. Yosemite National Park. [Photo: Ansel Adams]*

Geological Survey Corps had declared that Mount Lyell was impossible to climb, John Boies Tileston, of Beacon Street, was at the top of the highest pinnacle in two days. Tileston left his engraved card on the summit, where it was picked up by later alpinists. The card, of course, was not to be construed as an opening of social relations with the finder.

One party that journeyed from the East in the early seventies was attracted as much by the reports of the Big Trees of Mariposa Grove as by the waterfalls and towering cliffs. In this party, which entered the area by the old road to Wawona and consequently visited the sequoias first, was a man named Isaac Bromley. He recorded the experience for a magazine of the period, and it is worth passing notice for two reasons. It was, first, an uncommon bit of intellectual honesty. But, better than that, it stands as a warning to those who approach such natural phenomena as the national parks have to offer in an artificial and self-conscious spirit.

"I was in a sort prepared for the big trees," wrote Isaac, "and had worked up pretty carefully what I should probably think about them. I think I had fixed pretty nearly upon the emotions I should take down and spread out, and had arranged judiciously the profound impressions they were to convey to me. I was dismally disappointed. I supposed the spectacle of the Grizzly Giant would inspire me, and that I should think of a great many things to put down in a note book and preserve. I confess I was not inspired at all."

The truth was that Bromley had come a long way, and the end of his trip, in a coach, was irksome. He had not eaten since noon, his pampered stomach was in rebellion, and he was suddenly plumped down at the foot of a sequoia with the remark: "Well, here we are. Now go ahead and enjoy it!" He was fully prepared to attitudinize heavily. Nature does not tolerate any such posing. It was not a matter of the slightest importance to the giant trees what Bromley thought about them or felt about them, nor are the trees concerned today with what the millions of Bromleys think. A tree that was already a sturdy forest specimen when Julius Caesar was crossing the Rubicon is not to be flattered by the condescension of a few small bipeds in trousers who cannot, from its lofty top, be very well distinguished from beetles. The Grizzly Giant had been overadvertised to Bromley by those who had not the slightest conception of its deeper meaning.

Just as soon as Bromley put away his vanity and made a respectful approach to the sequoias, he began to enjoy the privilege of being near them, walking around them, looking up at their lightning-riven heads, feeling their bark, noting their fire scars, forgetting himself in the contemplation of the trees. Then, in a humbled state, he was able to say:

"And though one looks with profoundest wonder at the vast size of these monsters, it is, after all, the suggestion they give of their far reach backward into time that most impresses the beholder."

The early exploiters of the resources of the region had no such awe of the historical significance of the Big Trees. Without compunction they would have logged them all and carted them away. Curiously enough, the very thing that made them most desirable to the lumber hunters was what constituted their best defense. The Big Trees were too big. Especially were the biggest Big Trees almost invulnerable to attack. The Lafayette Tree is thirty and a half feet in diameter at the base and has a girth of ninety-six feet. Archimedes said that if he was given a fulcrum and a place to stand he would pry the earth off its foundation. A skilled axman, or two good men with a crosscut saw, have talents that cannot be laughed away; but the saw was not yet made that would not disappear before the bark of a Big Tree was penetrated; and if the assault was made with axes, where would the choppers stand?

Ingenious little man did fell at least one of the giants with pump augers. Hardly anyone nowadays knows what a pump auger was. It goes back to the time when water pipes were made from the trunks of trees; it was used to make the hole. By literally boring the tree down, the end was finally achieved. Having demonstrated the power of steel over wood, the men went away, and the prostrate tree remained to be the wonder of visitors. Other good reasons protected the sequoias from slaughter. Their weight was so great that they checked or broke when they came to earth, and the cost of transporting the logs was such that Maine pine and spruce could be brought to San Francisco by ship at no greater expense.

This is not the place to discuss the sequoias, because far more extensive groves were later to be found in the Sierra, and were to be protected in what are now Sequoia and Kings Canyon National Parks. But if you should wish the refined pleasure of driving *through* a Big Tree, you should do it while at Yosemite. The Wawona Tunnel Tree, twenty-seven and a half feet through at the base, has a hole eight feet wide cut through it. This operation, a touching tribute to age and dignity and beauty, was performed in 1881, and the tree is still alive. On the Big Oak Flat road, about seventeen miles from the Valley, there is another sequoia, of even greater diameter, through which automobiles can glide.

Eight feet cut from nearly thirty leaves ample wood for a tree to stand on and bring up its sap. The health of the giants seems not to have been prejudiced. Still, the sequoias must have wondered, if they have time for dealing with such affairs, why it would not have been possible to detour around them. For it could not possibly occur to them that anyone would want to drive through a tree just to be able to say that he had driven through a tree.

[ 2 ]

SEAMING AND GROOVING the western flank of the Sierra Nevada range are many yosemites, but there is only one Yosemite. It is difficult to say why this is. The ingredients are not different, and some of the other rock sculpturings are on just as grand a scale. You would find the same thing true of the mellow, serene landscape of the Berkshire Hills, or the Shenandoah Valley of Virginia. The ingredients that make up the scenery are the same in various spots in those places, too; yet one spot pleases the eye more than another. Perhaps it is a matter of proportion. Perhaps in Yosemite the combination of grassy floor, of trees and rocks, of dome and cliff and pinnacle, in just that relationship, under a faultless sky, fills exactly the outer and inner eye, with nothing in excess. Add one of the greatest spectacles of leaping water in the entire world—it is no wonder that yosemite means *this* Yosemite, this one of the seven falls, the Three Brothers, Cathedral Spires, and Glacier Point.

Behind all this which can be so readily seen lies the rest of Yosemite, the part of Yosemite Park that makes clear the meaning of what is commonly viewed; and just as he who remains on the rims of the Grand Canyon of the Colorado is staggered, delighted, but only half informed, so the Yosemite visitor who remains on the beaten track or with the crowds must miss the great adventure. Not everyone, certainly, has either the time or the physical equipment to take the knapsack and bedroll paths, but some access to the back country has been made available for almost everyone. For Yosemite National Park extends from El Portal to the perpetual snows of the crest of the Sierra, from the Tuolumne Grove on one side to Tioga Pass on the other, and in that great sweep of dissected rock are hundreds of icy streams, hundreds of lakes where the snow water pauses and gathers volume, again to renew its turbulent way toward the Great Valley of California. There is much more than a thousand square miles of it, and many hundreds of miles of well-built trail invite those who wish the fullest pleasure.

There is nothing in human experience that would enable us to comprehend the reaches of time in which nature works. The scientist, using observable differences connected with rock material and the evidences of life found

*For real sport, ski the Tuolumne Meadows! Yosemite National Park. [Photo: William C. Bradley]*

in it, may construct a table of periods, but they are after all only bookmarks in a volume so ponderous that nobody could read much of it. So most of us, standing on the valley floor of Yosemite and staring up at granite walls that tower three to four thousand feet above us, sometimes almost sheer, can only gasp and wonder. It was all done by water, after the uplift and tilting of the Sierra Nevada block gave the existing streams their impetus. By a flow of glacial ice later, yes; but ice is merely the mineral form of water.

The Sierra Nevada is carved out of a single "fault block," as the geologists call it, mostly composed of a granite that welled up from below the earth crust. The fissuring or fracturing to be expected when a molten mineral mass hardens and shrinks may be observed by anyone who lives where a highway has been cut through rocks. But sometimes, when the earth movement is intense, the rocks move along the fracture, the movement being greater on one side than on the other. This happened here. A block four hundred miles long and eighty miles wide moved upward and tilted toward the west. On the eastern side of the block, as you see it from Owens Valley, for instance, is a towering escarpment two miles high; it looks like a final barrier in that direction.

Probably there was a first uplift of a few thousand feet and then a long rest, one of those rests of a duration no one can imagine. Then followed another movement, which tilted the block still more westerly and sent the edge a mile higher. There were streams already established, possibly running sluggishly through a fairly flat country, when the uplift began. It is not hard to imagine what happened. The sluggish streams began to run faster, and then faster as their heads gained slope, and the increasing elevation meant increased rainfall to feed the streams. Having cut down through softer rock, which has long since disappeared, the raging torrents went to work on the granite. The result, after long enough, was a V-shaped canyon where Yosemite Valley now lies.

Afterward came the period of glaciation, when ice moved down from the highlands to finish the job water had begun. The V became a U. The glaciers are supposed to have deepened the valley 1,500 feet opposite Glacier Point, and 500 feet at the lower end; then widened the valley 1,000 feet at the lower end, and 3,600 feet in the upper part.

But how could water and ice carve their way through one of the toughest rocks? Half Dome looks as neatly cleft as though it had been machined. Tap any of the rocks with a hammer, and the sound they give forth makes them seem anything but victims of water or ice. The answer, of course, is that the water and ice used tools to do the work. Ice has a hardness, at the freezing point, of about the same as graphite, and all graphite would do in collision with granite would be to leave a smear. Well, all a granite cutter in Barre, Vermont, could do with his bare hands, too, would be less than a smear; but give him an edged tool and a mallet, and he will make the chips fly.

The mountain glaciers found their edged tools in the form of loose rock masses, breaking away on natural joints and loosened out of place by frosts and sun. Once gripped by the ice, these were tools enough, and the mallet was gravity and the push of the ice masses that lay behind. The water torrents used the same device: abrasive material, from quartz sand and pebbles to boulders, with an irresistible corroding force behind them. The tough Vishnu schist of the Grand Canyon, and many another resistant canyon bed, are being gouged out in the same way today. It is the story of earth-building and earth-tearing-down that we look at everywhere, no matter where we live; but the most startling evidences of the process, past and present, are seen in those areas set apart as national parks.

Then the visitor asks: "How about the waterfalls? What of the Yosemite Fall, which leaps first a sheer 1,430 feet, and then, after a series of cascades, another 320? What of the lovely Bridal Veil and Nevada Falls, one 620 feet and the other 594? And Vernal and Ililouette; and the Ribbon Fall, 1,612 feet straight down, a distance ten times as great as that of Niagara?" Unforgettable are these falls when the snows are melting fast in the upper Yosemite, when the Yosemite Creek is pouring such volumes of water that the ground seems to shake, and the Merced is a leaping, whirling mad thing, breathtaking to see and not to be trifled with. But how did it happen that Yosemite Creek and Bridal Veil Creek and the rest of the streams that suddenly leap into the valley from such heights—why did not these cut their way down through the granite as did the stream that carved the canyon?

Because the tributaries of the main stream were not traveling west, perhaps. They did not acquire the speed and power of the Merced because they got no benefit from the tilting of the Sierra Nevada block. They were left as "hanging valleys"—stranded far above, even higher after the glacier had plowed the canyon deeper. They flow as streams as far as they can go, and end their careers by jumping. And these prodigious leaps are known wherever photography has gone.

### [ 3 ]

NOBODY NEED WONDER, after visiting Yosemite, that Chief Tenaya and his tribe wanted no competition in their occupancy of the place. Even if their food was mostly acorns, they had one of the noblest all-year resorts to be found. Tenaya bragged on one occasion that "a small party of white men once crossed the mountains on the north side of the valley," but were deliberately prevented by the Indian guides from seeing Ahwahnee, the place of the deep grass. The comment may have referred to the Joseph Walker expedition of 1833. Walker could have been the first white man to come at least to the brink of the valley.

In this stronghold Tenaya and his people enjoyed, besides a good natural fortification, a nearly perfect climate. Not too hot in summer, not too cold in winter, and when the temperature fell lower than desirable on the southern side of the great chasm, they could bask in the sunshine by crossing over to the northern side. So it is today, and that is why winter visitors may take a choice of skiing on Glacier Point Road, near Badger Pass, or hiking in perfect comfort where the sun shines in and the towering cliffs cut off the chill winds.

Whether Joseph Walker ever saw the valley remains a little vague, but there is no doubt that Major James D. Savage did, some years later. Major Savage went out to California in 1846 with one of the overland groups from the Middle West and remained to become an almost legendary figure in the San Joaquin country. What his life lacked in duration was compensated for by high variety. Possessed of a great fund of animal courage, quick wit, ability to pick up the Indian tongues, and a cheerful pawnbroker's outlook on life, Savage was a soldier, a trader, and a professional husband. Having discovered that by taking to wife one of the squaws of the San Joaquin tribes he established a business and social alliance with the whole group, Savage married five of them in easy succession and would have gone further if he had not run out of tribes. He thus became a sort of feudal baron, with half a thousand retainers, who rendered fee by bringing him gold nuggets and dust, for which they received beads. It was not as unfair an exchange as it sounds. The Indians could not understand what anybody wanted of gold, which could be picked up anywhere, whereas bright-colored bits of glass were rare in the region and highly desirable as ornaments.

Early in 1850, after Savage had established a trading post on the south fork of the Merced, not more than fifteen miles below Yosemite Valley, a band of Indians attacked his place and plundered it. This act led to the actual discovery of the Yosemite and the revelation of its astonishing scenic

*In spring the Merced River floods. Yosemite National Park. [Photo: M. Woodbridge Williams]*

qualities. When, in the following year, Major Savage went in command of a punitive expedition against the Yosemite tribe, he took three companies of trained men, among them an impressionable youngster named Lafayette Bunnell. Savage's purpose was not to kill Indians but to force them to come out of their stronghold and give themselves up to the Indian commissioners. Tenaya and some of his followers did come into the white man's camp, but as Savage suspected that others were recalcitrant, he set off over the old Wawona Trail and went into camp near the waterfall now called Bridal Veil.

Next day the military party began exploring the Yosemite. They went above Mirror Lake and into Tanaya Canyon and up the Merced Canyon beyond Nevada Fall. The young Bunnell was ravished by the beauties and the majesty of the place. The streams above were coming into flood, and Yosemite Falls was at its wildest. The granite walls rose out of a floor lush with grasses and bordered by inviting shade. The sky was azure, except that clouds were massing for what might well be a late snowstorm. Bunnell took side trips, with full knowledge of the danger that Indians might appear from behind any pinnacle of rock and hurl stones at his head. He came into camp breathless with admiration and said to Major Savage: "Yosemite must be beautifully grand when the foliage and flowers are at their prime, and the rush of waters has subsided a little. Such cliffs and waterfalls I never saw before, and I doubt if they exist elsewhere."

The young man was horrified in the evening, around the campfire, by the party's indulging—in the presence of so much natural loveliness and mystery and the display of nature's power and craftsmanship—in coarse jokes and raucous laughter. It seemed to him like sacrilege.

But Major Savage did not share these elevated thoughts. He sat moodily considering that it was likely many Indians were still around and defiant. He thought of his trading posts, which had been sacked, and realized that, baron though he was, and generous as was his supply of wives, he was a man beset by enemies, of whom the worst were jealous white business devils. It looked like a storm.

Major Savage gazed up at the granite walls and growled. He said to Bunnell: "It looks to me just as I expected it would look. It's a hell of a place!"

[ 4 ]

FROM AMONG all the large-souled men and women who from the very first days have devoted themselves to the preservation of the integrity of Yosemite, it seems partial and ungrateful to single out one alone. Yet they all, without hesitation, would testify to the pre-eminence as an impresario of John Muir. Muir was the understanding, untiring, articulate press agent of the Sierra.

Arriving in San Francisco as a youth, Muir tarried not a needless moment in that mushroom municipality. He wanted nothing to do with cities, crowds, and marketing. He struck out for the mountains, of whose hugeness he had been hearing, and he came to Yosemite in 1868.

Soon after, he was herding sheep on the mountain meadows and spending a shepherd's leisure by exploring, botanizing, climbing, speculating, and scribbling. Nimble, observant far beyond the average man, educated in the truest sense, with much shrewdness and a pawky humor, Muir was something more than all that. He was a possessed man. He copyrighted the Sierras, all rights reserved, including those of translation. He made his way through canyon, up peak, across rivers, through woods, all alone, not foolhardy but with supreme confidence. Caught in a snowstorm, he could burrow a hole and wait it out. He was a born naturalist, always doing fieldwork for the love of it.

Muir was the Western Thoreau. They had much in common, though there were sharp differences, too. They were most alike in their capacity for incorporating themselves into any primitive natural scene—no fuss, no attitude, no tinge of strangeness, simply becoming instantly a part of what they saw. Muir was expansive—couldn't wait to tell the world about it. Thoreau chewed the end of his pencil wondering whether anybody was worthy to know, finally setting down some gnarly paragraphs on a chance. Both men wrote two languages. One language was the identic gossip of field mice and squirrels, unstudied and expressed with obvious fun. The other language was for company, for publication.

It was when John Muir was writing for the joy of setting himself down in homely particular that he could write delightfully. In 1875 he made a trip, alone, into the Sierra, and took with him a "little Brownie mule." Now listen to this:

> Many a time in the course of our journey, when he was jaded and hungry, wedged fast in rocks, or struggling in chaparral like a fly in a spiderweb, his troubles were sad to see, and I wished he would leave me and find his way home.

What a picture in those homespun strokes: of the poor beast, and of John Muir's perfect self-reliance; his instinctive humanity and tenderness; the twinkle in his eye as he thought the thoughts of a tired mule—and, over all, the tough going of a ramble in the Sierra's vastness!

When Muir was writing for the *Century*, to arouse in the minds of a nation of readers an enthusiasm and solicitude for these Sierra treasures, he was not so artless. He frequently opened the word faucet and let the flood loose—two adjectives for every noun, a verbal phalanx in which every clause was trained to march straight ahead, fire a tremendous salvo at the end, and disperse the enemy, galvanize the unappreciative, spread the good news of conservation to the world. It came out of the goodness of his great heart and from his passion to have these precious places understood and protected. Still, it is a question whether understatement and a lower temperature will not go farther. After all, the national parks, insofar as they may lack anything, do not want for rhapsodies. You can turn *Roget's Thesaurus* loose upon them, epithet on eulogy, but they will offer their deepest satisfactions when they are recognized for what they are. They are not merely scenic places in America. They are America.

[ 5 ]

JOHN MUIR HAD READ the essays and poems of Ralph Waldo Emerson and felt that here was the one man who could "interpret the sayings of these noble mountains and trees." He wrote letters to the Concord philosopher urging him to visit Yosemite and testify that justice might be done the beloved Sierra. Though Emerson was sixty-seven, and not vigorous, he came. The result was not what the impetuous Muir had wished, but at least it gave him an opportunity for one of the most charming and touching passages of auto-biography ever penned.

The scene has its humor, and it has its pathos. Here was the indefatigable, wiry, youthful Scot who could start out with a handful of rice, sleep in hollow logs, frisk up a rock-strewn canyon, camp on a glacier, and return the following week fresh as you please. He was now asking an elderly gentleman—who had, to be sure, climbed Wachusett in his youth and had been rowed up the gentle Concord by Henry David Thoreau, but had never been a physical rival of the mountain goats—to join him "in an immeasurable camping trip back in the mountains." Those are John's own words, and when he said mountains, he did not mean foothills. Said John to Emerson: "The mountains are calling! Run away, and let plans and parties and dragging low-land duties all gang tapsal-teerie. We'll go up a canyon singing your own song, 'Good-bye, proud world! I'm going home.' "

*After many years, this remains one of the noblest pictures ever taken in the parks. Yosemite National Park. [Photo: Ralph Anderson]*

Emerson—such is the power of honest enthusiasm—might have gone up a canyon, in which case it would unquestionably have been "Good-bye, proud world," for him. But Emerson was with a party of devoted friends, who had come along to see that he did not take cold or overexert himself. They sized up young Muir as a man who made overexertion a life design. So they said, as affably as possible, *no*.

John was cast down, but he made one more attempt. He proposed that the Boston gentlemen remain in a hotel while he and Emerson camped for the night in a sequoia grove. Muir promised his friend "at least one good wild memorable night"—a promise that would have been easy to keep; but again the conventional friends intervened with a *no*. Finally:

> The party mounted and rode away. . . . I followed, to the edge of the grove. Emerson lingered in the rear of the train, and when he reached the top of the ridge, after all the party were over and out of sight, took off his hat and waved me a last goodby.
>
> I felt lonely, so sure had I been that Emerson of all men would be the quickest to see the mountains and sing them. Gazing a while on the spot where he vanished, I . . . made a bed of sequoia plumes and ferns by the side of the stream, gathered a store of firewood, and then walked about till sundown. The birds, robins, thrushes, warblers, that had kept out of sight, came about me, now that all was quiet, and made cheer. After sundown, I made a great fire . . . and though lonesome for the first time in these forests, I quickly took heart again. . . . Emerson was still with me in spirit, though I never saw him again in the flesh.

The curious thing about all this is that the romantic Muir had created for himself an Emerson that did not exist.

In the presence of nature Emerson was uneasy and distrustful of himself. He revered beauty, more especially the inner beauty, which is harmony and unity. He was never unmoved; rather, he was made silent and deeply meditative in the presence of wilderness life. Muir noted that among the sequoias Emerson "hardly spoke a word . . . yet it was a great pleasure to be near him, warming in the light of his face." Again: ". . . he gazed in devout admiration, saying but little, *while his fine smile faded away*." And, truly, the *Essays* are sprinkled with pithy comments on Nature, showing how shrewdly he had appraised its aspects.

---

*The deer are unconcerned with landscape beauty—or are they? How do we know? Yosemite National Park. [Photo: Ralph Anderson]*

Nevertheless, Emerson feared Nature; and for the reason that he expounds, by indirection: he believed that man had such capacities that, if only they could be developed, Nature would not then seem so grand by comparison. Instead of marveling at a beautiful waterfall, or at the miracle of spring, he wished that someday the onlooker would almost swoon at the sight of a perfect human. So, not loving Nature less, but man more, Emerson heartily wished that the dice were not so loaded. *That* is why his fine smile faded.

When Muir said to Emerson: "You are yourself a sequoia. Stop and get acquainted with your big brethren," he meant exactly what he said. It was no flattering turn of phrase. But Emerson saw mankind as something special and removed. Perhaps lazy eons may prove him to have been right, but meanwhile many of us who visit Yosemite and the other primeval parks will conclude that John Muir, on this point, had the better part.

## 6. DEVILS POSTPILE NATIONAL MONUMENT
### [*California*]

THE DEVILS POSTPILE is a remnant of a basaltic lava flow that originated in what is now known as Mammoth Pass and extended approximately six miles down the canyon of the Middle Fork of the San Joaquin River, to a point just beyond Rainbow Fall. This outpouring took place during the later interglacial periods in the Sierra Nevada—at least 915,000 years ago. The basalt cracked into columns as it cooled.

During the thousands of years that the ice held sway, the bulk of this basaltic flow was removed, with only the more resistant parts left standing. Of these, the largest is the Devils Postpile, which is about nine hundred feet long and two hundred feet high. The top of the formation presents an unusual sight. Here the cross section of the three- to seven-sided columns has been worn smooth by the grinding action of the glacier, and the exposed surface has the appearance of a mosaic or tile inlay.

Two miles down the river trail from the Postpile, the Middle Fork of the San Joaquin makes a sheer drop of 140 feet into a deep-green pool. The dark basaltic cliffs contrast strikingly with the white water, and during the middle of the day many rainbows add to the beauty of the scene.

## 7. MOUNT RAINIER NATIONAL PARK
### [*Washington*]

SOMEWHAT LIKE a retired business executive, Mount Rainier, after many years of close application to its volcanic activity, once upon a time ceased

*The "Alpine Specialist." A mountain is about to be climbed. Mount Rainier National Park.* [Photo: Bob and Ira Spring]

operations and contemplated a pleasurable idleness. Prudently, it kept its physical plant intact and left a few fires burning, in case of a change of mind. Such impulsive retirements are always questionable. Mount Rainier, in the course of centuries, had worked itself up to a height of possibly 16,000 feet, all solid growth of rock material. It had more than a local reputation. Any eruption from this mountain was guaranteed up to standard, or lava refunded.

Also like many a tired business executive, Mount Rainier as a loafer was uneasy, fretful, undecided. Many times it quit repose and went back into active business, even with new branch operating units. There is some reason to think that, seized by a fit of renewed energy and delighted to be back at work, it once put on so much steam that it blew about two thousand feet off its top. But it was really tired. And there was competition, too. New and

*At 11,000 feet, climbers rest at an overhanging "serac." Mount Rainier National Park. [Photo: Bob and Ira Spring]*

well-furnaced volcanoes, circling the Pacific Ocean like a ring of beacons, had gone into production.

So finally Mount Rainier definitely retired. This time it did a wise thing. It acquired two hobbies. One of them was flower arrangement. The other was rock carving, with glacial ice as a tool. In both respects the mountain became pre-eminent in conterminous United States, and so remains today.

There is still fire in the old factory. In the crater at the very highest of three summits, Columbia Crest, steam vents still melt the snow. There are hot springs at the foot of the mountain. But today Mount Rainier tends its flower gardens, weaves the blooms into glorious rugs and other displays, and maintains the finest single-peak glacier system this side of the Arctic chill, with twenty-six active glaciers that radiate from a lofty white center and cover forty square miles with their slow-moving tongues.

It may seem strange, in dealing with Mount Rainier National Park, to begin with its flowers. Flowers are such small and fragile things, and the mountain is such a giant! It is the fourth-highest mountain of the continental United States, if we except Alaska. Only Mount Whitney and two peaks in Colorado top it. Its height is so great and its bulk so enormous that when one views the mountain from Puget Sound, it seems to rise abruptly from the ocean. Yet the truth is that there are ridges and crests around Rainier's base that would be considered lofty in many other regions.

This national park covers about 380 square miles, and the mountain itself occupies more than one fourth of the whole. *That* is mass! No wonder the native Indians always felt that it dominated their every puny human endeavor!

Lovers of flowers are, of all people, very sure of what they like best. It would be rash indeed to proclaim the flowers of Rainier foremost in an assembly of national parks, where the show of bloom is one of the usual great attractions. Besides, there must always be considered the mood, the moment, and the associated incidents, all three being most important in weighing our pleasures afield. But at least it can be said that the display of wild flowers in Rainier is superb, soul-satisfying, memorable; we may leave it that way.

Centuries ago the philosopher Theophrastus made a few comments about flowers and trees. He noted that "all trees grow fairer and more vigorous in their proper positions . . . some love wet and marshy ground . . . some love exposed and sunny positions, some prefer a shady place." The severe botanist shies away in professional alarm from that word *love*. "No *love* about it," says he, "it is a matter of adaptation. The plant has no choice." Of course he is right, but let us be erringly romantic and insist that plants *love* Mount Rainier and the country around it. And then we can explain the reason. It is due to the peculiar combination of climate, of soil, of topography. The flower display of Rainier is what it is because it is where it is.

You begin, for instance, with the flowering plants that grow in the forest zone from the two-thousand-foot elevation up to about four thousand feet. Here you observe some queer species—plants that live on decaying vegetation. Ghostlike plants that manufacture no green coloring matter, like the Indian pipe. But there are many others that provide their own living—the clintonia, the trillium, and the forest anemone. And here the ferns luxuriate. Many trails take you along the shaded, quiet places where you will see this sort of plant at its best.

Then you go upstairs. I cannot help thinking of this display as being like a horticultural show held upon several floors of a building. Up one flight you will find the squaw grass, the coralroot, pyrola, and salal, and the twinflowers, graceful and fragrant, draping the road embankments.

Another flight, and you will be in the glacial valleys, forest-bordered, clad in their season with the devil's-club and salmon flower, with the mertensias and stonecrops. Do not expect any arbitrary divisions, however. The flowers, according to their special situations, blend easily, variety into variety. Often in late summer where it has been shady and the melting of the snow has been tardy, a group of the "early" flowers will be found crowded by a surrounding ring of the later ones.

The grassy meadows begin at an elevation of about 4,500 feet. First we cross meadows that are moist, even swampy, and the typical plants here will be the spiraeas, cotton grass, monkey flowers, and arnicas. But a little higher up is drier ground, and interspersed with lovely tree groups the greatest floral display comes into view. This is the "subalpine garden" that John Muir described as the greatest he had ever found. "A perfect flower elysium," he said. We all make reservations about an enthusiasm like that; we want to judge for ourselves. But if any man was able to discriminate, it was that tireless tramper of the mountain wildernesses John Muir. I, for one, will take his word for it.

Winter comes early in these gorgeous "parks"—Yakima and Paradise and Van Trump and the rest—and the snow lingers late. But during June, July, and August the flowers hasten into beauty and fulfillment. There are two peaks of bloom, one coming late in June, when the avalanche lilies, the heathers and pasqueflowers arrive, and another late in July, continuing for a month or more, when the slopes are radiant with lupine, paintbrush, valerian, and bistort. These parks, between ice and dense forest, circle the great Rainier "like a wreath," as John Muir said.

Visitors who revel in color and form amidst these flower fields should bear in mind a fact that may at first seem odd. This soft volcanic soil on which the enchanting flower rugs are laid is extremely delicate. Picking the flowers without a permit is generally known to be forbidden, but what is not so well understood is that wandering off the established trails sets up tiny channels of erosion that may result in deep gullies. And tramping among the flowers is injurious to the plants, too. By all means, remain upon the provided trails. They afford as fine a view of the display as you could possibly want.

The splendid forests of Rainier follow much the same pattern in distribution as that of the flowers. The dense evergreen growths characteristic of the lower western slopes of the Cascades extend into the park in the valleys of the Nisqually, the Carbon, the Mowich, and the Ohanapecosh. These are mainly Douglas firs, red cedars, and Western hemlocks, many of them of

*Pack oufit on the trail: Tatoosh Range in the background. Mount Ranier National Park.* [*Photo: National Park Service*]

great size and age. Other species of fir occur higher up, and above 5,200 feet the dense forest growth gives way to charming tree groups.

Since the summer season is so short, one would not think that Mount Rainier forests would be especially subject to fire hazard. The truth is that, in the higher altitudes especially, there is always great susceptibility; many burns in the subalpine growth, where recovery is painfully slow, testify to the carelessness of men years before the region became a park. At lower elevations restoration after a fire is more rapid, but everywhere constant vigilance and care are imperative.

There are twenty-six active glaciers remaining on Mount Rainier. Twelve of these are major glaciers originating either in large cirques at about ten thousand feet, or in six of them possibly at the very summit. As in Glacier National Park, the glaciers have diminished rapidly in the past quarter century, and the Nisqually, on the south side, which is one of the most accessible and can be reached over a good trail a short distance from the surfaced road, has been retreating as much as seventy feet a year. The Emmons Glacier, on the northeast side of Rainier, can be best seen from Yakima Park. Of the four-teen minor glaciers, the Paradise is the easiest to inspect. It is comparatively small, but presents all the features connected with such flowing mineral masses, and at times fine ice caves can be seen where the outlet flows from beneath the snout.

In a park where the snow covers the mountainsides in winter to a depth of fifteen to twenty feet, and where large centers of population with eager ski enthusiasts are so near, you would expect a heavy use of Rainier for this rapidly growing sport. You would be right. From December until May the conditions are usually ideal for both the expert and the duffer. The annual snowfall at Paradise Valley averages about fifty feet, and the slopes provide wide-open and safe courses. Unlike skiers in the Eastern states, with their "January thaws" and eccentric winter weather, the Seattle or Tacoma folk never have to wonder whether snow conditions will be good when they start out with the boards atop their automobiles.

When Captain George Vancouver of the British Navy first glimpsed Mount Rainier, in 1792, and named it for his friend Admiral Peter Rainier, it is not recorded that he had any desire to climb the mountain. But the day was certain to come when mountaineers could not resist the challenge to their endurance and skill and their will to conquer. In 1857 Lieutenant A. V. Kautz and four companions made the first recorded attempt to achieve the summit, but the party was forced to turn back. Thirteen years later Gen. Hazard Stevens and P. B. Van Trump attacked the volcano over what is now known as the Gibraltar Route, and it is a testimony to the judgment and preparation of these men that this attack has since proved to be the safest and most con-venient.

Rainier is a difficult climb. Whether it is more arduous than the Grand Teton is a matter for the experts to decide. It is certainly very different. A large portion of the mountain flanks is covered by dangerously crevassed ice, and the sharp ridges among the ring of glaciers give a precarious footing of crumbling lava and pumice. The rock climbing of the Cowlitz Glacier and Gibraltar Rock is not for the unguided amateur. Consequently all aspirants for the conquest of the volcano must prove to the park rangers that they have the requisite stamina and experience, as well as proper equipment.

The eighty miles of paved roads in the park provide a satisfactory range of representative scenic views. In Rainier, as in so many other parks, the trails take the hiker and the horseman into a real wilderness area, with alpine meadows, waterfalls, and constantly shifting volcano prospects. There are many short trails, but the Wonderland Trail, completely encircling the mountain, with shelter cabins spaced not more than a dozen miles apart, offers a packing trip of a week or more for those who want to taste the ultimate joys of the primitive.

There is something else at Mount Rainier National Park that every visitor should see—and not only see but ask about and think about. It is a dramatic example of the inexorable law of nature by which the earth's surface—all that we see and all that we think we see—is constantly undergoing change by upbuilding and demolition. It is also, when understood, a graphic interpretation of the concept of land management that governs the setting aside of national parks for *preservation* "in their natural condition."

In October 1947, after several days of moderately heavy rains, the sky really opened and dropped nearly six inches in a few hours. At park headquarters at Longmire the ground shivered for many hours as great boulders hurtled down the Nisqually River. But to the west of the Nisqually, in the broad valley of Kautz Creek, a melodrama of the highland wilderness was in the making. High up on the slopes of Mount Rainier a part of the Kautz Glacier was being undermined and broken up by the streams of water that were pouring down upon it from the sides. Loose rock and debris of all kinds began to move down into the streambed, first creating a dam, then breaking the barrier with deafening roars and sweeping down upon the heavily wooded country below.

Trees five feet in diameter and hundreds of years old were pounded and sawed till they went down as helplessly as the ferns and other undergrowth. In building Hoover Dam, the engineers figured that they had removed eight million cubic yards of earth and rock. In about fifteen hours the waters coming down from the upper Kautz Valley moved more than six times as much material as was moved at Hoover Dam in three years with the finest modern machinery!

After the flood there were all kinds of suggestions for dealing with the situation. Some people recommended that the felled trees be salvaged for lumber, and the scarred area near the road be nicely landscaped. The standing trees, many of them partly cut through by the abrasive waters, should surely be converted into boards and planks, because they would die anyway!

Such proposals were no doubt very well meant, but how obvious it is that they could come only from people who have never realized the under-

---

*Overleaf: "The Mountain" from Marmot Point on Paradise Valley Road. Mount Rainier National Park. [Photo: C. Frank Brockman]*

lying meaning of the parks! In the life of the wilderness a flood like this one is the merest incident. It has, of course, some local importance to the plants and animals involved. For eons these petty "catastrophes" have happened and will happen. The aim of the Park Service is to preserve natural phenomena, wherever humanly possible—not to repair and reconstruct and refashion them. Whatever nature does is right. It is only the dilapidations and changes brought about by human occupation and use that have to be curbed and managed.

## 8. ALASKAN WILDERNESS

### A. MOUNT MCKINLEY NATIONAL PARK
#### [*Alaska*]

CAME MY WAY, just before I sat down to begin this chapter, the notice that John Rumohr was dead, in Anchorage, Alaska. Have you ever heard of John Rumohr? It is not likely. He was just another of those unsung rangers of the wilderness whose lives have been mainly spent in preserving the precious preserves known as national parks. He fitted into the Alaskan wilderness readily, for he came from the mountains of Norway. Stubborn of opinion was John, but a loyal public servant, if there ever was one.

From 1931, for ten years, Rumohr made the winter rounds of the park boundaries by dog sled. Some of the patrols kept him absent from his winter quarters on the Lower Toklat for six weeks at a time, carrying enough provisions for himself and team. One day he and his sled broke through the ice while crossing a deep river. His lead dog, Tige, rallied the strength of the other dogs to pull their master from the water. He was a good dog man, as they say in the north. There is plenty of courage, of a sort, left in our country, but it takes a special kind of self-reliance and relationship with nature to do this kind of job. In the early days of our history such men were so numerous that they were not remarked. There has been a softening.

And, thinking of the late chief ranger, I remembered Adolph Murie, too. Many years ago I came into possession of his book *The Wolves of Mount McKinley*, and reveled in it. Published as a government document and written in the line of duty, it is modest, professional, and purely factual; yet it has a breath of romance in it that for me is far beyond any literary confections.

*Alpine firs, Yakima Park. Mount Rainier National Park.* [*Photo: Joseph Dixon*]

*This is real wilderness. Even the dogs feel the call. Mount McKinley National Park.*
*[Photo: Bob and Ira Spring]*

When I feel the need of getting away from myself, and wonder what book will do it, *The Wolves* never fails me. I find myself interested even in the naturalist's close-up examination of animal droppings.

In 1939 I was requested to make a study of the relationships between the timber wolf and the Dall sheep in Mount McKinley National Park, Alaska. I arrived in the Park on April 14, and three days later was taken 22 miles by dog team and left at a cabin on Sanctuary River where I started my field work.

Thus, in the way of a businesslike report, Murie begins the account of studies made over a period including most of three spring and summer seasons, two autumns, and one winter. Much of the time he worked alone, afoot or on skis, and he must often have been dog-tired, hungry, frustrated; but I cannot remember that he ever said so. Aside from furthering research, his patient work emphasized that the predatory wolf has a right to live (my phrasing, not his) and to be part of the wildlife community in areas governed by such a land-use concept as that of preservation in national parks—subject, of course, to considered judgment and constantly renewed appraisal of wildlife conditions.

Of course the Dall or white Alaska mountain sheep, sometimes prey of the timber wolf, must be preserved too. One of the handsomest of our park animals, the heavily horned ram may weigh two hundred pounds. Against any but a snow background the Dall sheep looks perfectly white; only against the snow is its slightly yellowish tinge apparent. During the tourist season at McKinley, the best places to see the sheep are on the slopes of Igloo Creek and the East Fork and Toklat Rivers. The lambs, since their birth in May, have been scampering about on grassy mountain slopes in little bands under the watchful eye of an old ewe, playing the game of follow-the-leader, which gives them sureness of foot and almost incredible agility later on the rocks. It is said that even a lamb can make a vertical jump of six feet, and easily.

The principal scenic feature of the park is Mount McKinley itself. Not only is it the highest peak on the North American continent, rising to 20,300 feet, with snow two thirds of the way down from the summit all the year, but it is probably the tallest mountain in the whole world *from its base.*

*Harmony at Camp Denali, just outside the park. Mount McKinley National Park.*
*[Photo: Bob and Ira Spring]*

Everest and the peaks of the South American cordilleras thrust up from what are already very high levels. McKinley is naturally a challenge to the very toughest of the alpinists, but those who should attempt the climb are very few, and even experts have sometimes had to give up when success was close to their grasp because of weather conditions. Permission to try an ascent must always be obtained from the park superintendent.

The northward-flowing glaciers of the Alaska Range rise on the slopes of Mount McKinley and Mount Foraker. The largest of these glaciers are the Herron, the Peters, and the Muldrow, the last with a front of fifteen miles and a source in the unsurveyed heart of the range. But the greatest are those on the southern slope, which gets the moisture-laden winds of the Pacific, piling up the snow that is to become a river of ice. A strange thing is ice—so brittle, so rigid under ordinary conditions, yet, under pressure, plastic and almost fluid. The southern-slope glaciers have their sources high up in the range and extend south far beyond the boundaries of the park.

The wildlife of this national park is second only to the great mountain peak in interest; some will rate it first. Here are thousands of caribou. Or, rather, there may be and there may not. They may be grazing in the park or they may be many miles away, for they are rovers, at home equally on the high ridges and on the barrens. Almost anywhere in the park there are caribou trails through the tundra and battered trees where the animals have rubbed the velvet off their antlers.

The Alaska moose is the largest animal in McKinley. The biggest bulls weigh as much as seventeen hundred pounds with an antler spread of more than five feet. The moose is no Apollo among the ungulates. His shoulders may be nearly eight feet from the ground, and his hindquarters much less, so that, with his overhanging muzzle, he looks as though he had pushed against something so hard that he flattened his face and buckled his front end. In summer, moose will be met along the willow thickets and the margins of spruce timber growths.

The other large mammal is the grizzly bear. The most conspicuous evidence that the grizzlies have been in the vicinity is the presence of little craterlike holes on the tundra. The bears have been there digging out ground squirrels. Adolph Murie found the grizzlies unusually well behaved. "One day my companion and I met a female with three cubs. We were about 100 yards from her, far from any trees, and unarmed. . . . She stood placidly

*"Barren ground" caribou move across the tundra. Mount McKinley National Park. [Photo: Charles Ott]*

*What the well-dressed ptarmigan wears. Mount McKinley National Park.* [*Photo: Steve McCutcheon*]

watching us and soon resumed her grazing." So much for the tradition that a bear with cubs is invariably dangerous. Naturally, discretion is indicated. Murie did not press any nearer acquaintance.

The white spruce is the characteristic evergreen of Mount McKinley National Park. There are white birches in the lower valleys, and cotton-woods along the streams. The willow is common, ranging from the small trees of favored locations to the matlike growths on the mountain slopes. These willows, insistent upon survival, hide their woody stems underground, putting above the surface only the catkins of their flowers and a few leaves.

Denali Highway, the only road to the park, connects with the Richardson Highway at Paxson, about 160 miles from the park entrance. The Denali Highway is passable from about June 1 to September 15. The Alaska Rail-road provides daily passenger service in summer to McKinley Park from Fairbanks and Anchorage. It is a four-hour trip from Fairbanks, an eight-hour trip from Anchorage. A three-thousand-foot airstrip, within easy walking distance of the hotel, is available for small private and nonscheduled aircraft.

## B. Glacier Bay National Monument
### [*Alaska*]

It was John Muir, the sure-footed pedestrian of the Sierra, who let the world know about the wonders and beauties of Glacier Bay. "I decided," said John, telling of his 1879 travels, "to turn westward and go in search of the 'ice mountain' that Sitka Charley had been telling us about. Charley said that when he was a boy he had gone with his father to hunt seals in a large bay full of ice . . . he thought he could find his way to it." And Sitka Charley, Muir's guide, did find it.

> At length the clouds lifted a little, and beneath their gray fringes I saw the berg-filled expanse of the bay, and the feet of the mountains that stand about it, and the imposing fronts of five huge glaciers, the nearest being immediately beneath me. This was my first general view of Glacier Bay, a solitude of ice and snow and newborn rocks, dim, dreary, mysterious . . . breasting the snow again, crossing the shifting avalanche slopes and torrents, I reached camp about dark, wet and weary . . . and glad.

It was a sight that Muir never forgot. Passionately loyal as he was to his Sierra country, he had to share his passion with this newfound place of primitive beauty. Visitors who see it today will understand.

As late as 1700, Glacier Bay was covered with an icecap at least three thousand feet thick. It doesn't seem possible, yet we know that there is never rest in the advance or retreat of mountain glacial ice. The snowfall increases, piling up the feeding heads, and the mean temperature lowers; or the climate turns a little warmer, the air grows drier, and the front begins a retreat. The John Muir system of glaciers, originating in the southerly part of the Mount St. Elias cap, is one of the most active groups. The so-named Muir glacier has retreated approximately thirty miles since John was there with Sitka Charley, a rate of more than two fifths of a mile a year.

Here on the coast of southeastern Alaska is the unrivaled place to see the life of the glacial ice on our continent. The glaciers of Mount Rainier

---

*Overleaf, left: An ice-fall from Margerie Glacier, Tarr Inlet. [Photo: Steve McCutcheon] Right: Margerie Glacier snout. Glacier Bay National Monument. [Photo: John Kauffmann]*

*The clouds lift and there is His Majesty! Mount McKinley National Park.* [*Photo: John Kauffmann*]

and Glacier National Parks are impressive, but it is in Alaska that they may be studied and enjoyed on the grandest scale. For these glaciers come down to the sea, and when the great cliffs, some as tall as a twenty-five-story building, are broken off and sent crashing into the ocean, they put out a circle of immense waves and fill the tidal inlets with thousands of drifting bergs. Here, in the twenty tremendous glaciers and others of lesser but still great size, may be viewed all stages of activity—the fast-moving ice, the slow-moving ice, the slowly dying glacier.

The famous Muir Glacier is distinctly a lively one, moving at the rate of twenty or thirty feet a day, a rare speed indeed. It has a sheer face that rises 265 feet above the water and is nearly two miles wide. Most of the eight fiordlike inlets of Glacier Bay terminate at similar ice cliffs.

In 1899 an earthquake speeded up the downhill flows of ice. Glacier Bay became choked with floating ice, which put an end to the steamship excursions that for a number of years had brought sightseers close to the cliffs.

Following this speeding up, the ice receded rapidly. Between 1899 and 1913 Muir Glacier retreated eight miles. Tarr Inlet emerged as open water. In the following thirty-three years Muir Glacier went back another five miles, leaving the old John Muir cabin, which had formerly been near the terminus of his day, more than thirteen miles from the present face.

Wherever the glaciers recede, vegetation is not long in seizing the exposed land. It may be only mosses and lichens at first, but they prepare the way for flowers and shrubs. Then when there is sufficient soil, the trees move in: spruce and hemlock forests. The climate changes again, and again the ice is on the move down the mountain slopes. Ancient tree stumps, showing where giant trees once flourished and were overwhelmed, are being revealed by the glacial streams, which wash away the gravel that covered them. Yet still the forest moves in when it can. The retreat of the ice from stage to stage can be plainly seen in the kind of plants and trees that appear as soon as the land is unlocked.

Toward the mouth of Glacier Bay these forests are now heavy. Here visitors can go ashore, push through the dense thickets of alder near the beach, and emerge into a luxuriant mossy growth of old trees.

*Fishermen dream of a situation like this. Katmai National Monument. [Photo: Bob and Ira Spring]*

At present, transportation facilities to this monument are limited. It is certain that someday it will be a favorite objective of the millions who visit the national parks annually. The enthusiastic report on this Alaska coast written forty years ago by Dr. Henry Gannett and circulated by the Smithsonian Institution is heartily echoed by all those who have had the joy of making this visit. The Alaskan coast, said Dr. Gannett,

> is to become the showplace of the earth, and pilgrims not only from the United States but from far beyond the seas, will throng in endless procession to see it.
>
> There is one word of advice and caution to be given those intending to visit Alaska for pleasure, for sight-seeing. If you are old, go by all means; but if you are young, wait. The scenery of Alaska is much grander than anything else of the kind in the world, and it is not well to dull one's capacity for enjoyment by seeing the finest first.

The wildlife of the monument includes a number of bears—the Alaskan brown, the grizzly, the black, and the rare bluish-colored glacier bear. Then there are mink, marten, beaver, red fox, wolverine, Sitka black-tailed deer, mountain goat, and smaller land mammals, while the waters of Glacier Bay are frequented by the porpoise, whale and hair seal. Various waterfowl inhabit the coves and inlets of the bay—loons, ducks, geese, king eiders, many gulls and shorebirds, cormorants, puffins, murrelets, and guillemots. In spring and summer, during the spawning season, salmon crowd the streams.

## C. KATMAI NATIONAL MONUMENT
### [*Alaska*]

BEFORE THE FIRST WEEK of June 1912, no one would have thought of creating a national monument of 2,700,000 acres in the Alaska Peninsula. Except for one valley the whole region was an unexplored wilderness. For ages there had been a trail between a village of natives at Katmai, on the Pacific side, to Sabanoski, at the head of Naknek Lake, whence there was easy passage to the Bering Sea. Adventurous white men, Russian and American, knew the valley as a dense forest of spruce, poplar, and birch, with low spots of tundra. Herds of caribou, as well as moose and the great brown bear, added their footprints to the trail. But it was farther from New York than the moon, which is an object of interest in that city only during an electric-power failure.

In that June week Vulcan called attention to this significant and beautiful Alaskan wilderness with one of the most violent exertions of subterranean power of which we have any record. When it was over, Katmai Valley had become the Valley of Ten Thousand Smokes, and Mount Katmai, disemboweled, had collapsed with a roar that was heard hundreds of miles away. So far as is known not a single human life was lost, but the disaster to wildlife must have been pitiable. Earth shocks that preceded the eruption sent the few natives in the vicinity scurrying for safety.

*A lake thought by some to be an impact crater, but not yet so proved. Katmai National Monument. [Photo: John Kauffmann]*

*Kukak Bay. Katmai National Monument. [Photo: John Kauffmann]*

In 1918 a member of the National Geographic expedition interviewed "American Pete," the chief of the Sabanoski villagers, who was the last person to quit the valley before all organic life was blotted out. After six years Pete was still frightened. All he could recall was that, as he had been on the trail from Ukak,

the Katmai mountain blow up with lots of fire, and fire come down trail from Katmai with lot of smoke. Me go fast Sabanoski. Everybody get in bidarka [skin boat]. Helluva job! We come Naknek one day. Dark. No could see. Hot ash fall. Work like hell. Now, I go back every year, one month maybe, after fish all dry, and kill bear. Too bad! Never can go back to Sabanoski to lib. Everything ash. Good place, too, you bet! Lot moose, bear, deer; lot fish. No many mosquitoes. *Naknek no good.*

As Pete was living in Naknek when he made this final remark, it must have annoyed the local Chamber of Commerce.

The final gigantic explosion of Katmai Volcano, which blanketed the neighboring island of Kodiak with a foot of fine ash and sent eye-smarting sulfurous-acid rain for 360 miles around, actually was not quite as strange as what happened in the once placid valley. The human mind is not capable of imagining the inferno there, when innumerable holes were suddenly blown through the floor, to hurl forth ash and pumice in unthinkable quantity. The "ten thousand smokes"—seen by the first expedition to enter the area—have dwindled with the passage of years, but seven years after the eruption scientists reported a number of fumaroles sending forth heat that melted zinc (784 degrees F.) and one record of a temperature of almost 1,200 degrees F. It is estimated that a *cubic mile* of incandescent sand was spewn into the valley—a sand similar to granite dust. One cubic mile! Someone has tried to adjust our minds to that figure by imagining that all the stonecrushers in the United States were pulverizing that mass of granite. It would take them one hundred years. Vulcan did it in a week or less.

The jagged-rimmed bowl of collapsed Katmai, with its jade-green lake, is cradling a number of glaciers upon its cliffed walls. They hang below the rim, separate from the regional snowline. All of us who have seen and trodden upon glaciers have many times wondered how old they were. When fell

*Katmai Crater. Katmai National Monument.* [*Photo: Lowell Sumner*]

*Alaskan brown bear at lunch. Katmai National Monument.* [*Photo: Steve Mc-Cutcheon*]

those first snows that compacted into the ice that began to flow? Many North American glaciers are supposed to be more than four thousand years old. A five-thousand-foot core driven through the icecap in Greenland reflects nearly ten thousand years of Arctic history. But there is a more-or-less quality about these figures. Not so with the glaciers formed on the walls of Katmai. They are the youngest glaciers in the world, no doubt, and we know their birthdate. Into this crater lake, which is warmed by volcanic heat, the immaculate ice cows are already calving.

Ever since the National Geographic expeditions "opened up" the Katmai country, the ardent fisherman's mouth has watered from stories of the size, number, and hungriness of the rainbow trout, grayling, and mackinaws. During World War II military personnel came to Katmai to fish. It was a heavy drain on the supply, but there are still plenty. The great brown bear —largest of the world's carnivorous animals—has been fishing the streams there since time out of mind. When the salmon are migrating in summer, bears may be seen wading into the water and seizing fish with their front paws. In drifting down the Sabanoski River for a distance of ten miles, a park ranger from Mount McKinley saw twenty-three fishing bears. My friend Lowell Sumner, a Park Service biologist, who knows and loves the monument, reports that on one occasion a party of human fishermen came back to Brooks Camp with the story (greeted with lifted eyebrows) that they had seen bears swimming in the streams with their noses just out of water, submerging like submarines, and surfacing up with their prey. It may be that some bears do this while others do not, but this "yarn" has now been well substantiated. After all, not all human fishermen are snorkelers, either.

The elusive wolverine, the beaver, and other fur-bearing creatures are here in Katmai. In such a country of swampy forestlands, unexplored and without trails, who can say what the number of beaver may be? In the forest near the mouth of the Brooks River is a small lake formed by a beaver dam three quarters of a mile long, eight feet high, and twelve feet wide at the base. Large cottonwoods growing up through this house indicate that it is old and has been undisturbed.

Eagles are numerous along the Katmai coastline, and the second enlargement of the monument in 1942 added the coastal islets—not merely for their landscape beauty but to secure them as refuges for an ample and varied wildlife.

## D. SITKA NATIONAL MONUMENT
### [*Alaska*]

WE COMMONLY THINK of the romantic fur-trading era as exclusively a matter of British-American competition. But the Russians, too, were early arrivals in the field. There was a Russian-American Fur Company, and in 1790 Alexander Baranof, as chief manager, set up headquarters on Kodiak Island, beginning the slaughter of sea otter. Later he moved over to Sitka Sound and called a post New Archangel.

The neighboring Tlingit Indians, who wanted no white neighbors, promptly attacked the settlement and killed most of the inhabitants, ending "Old Sitka." But the Tlingit were gradually forced back by the cannon of a small warship. These Indians were not the ones who carved the classic totem poles to be seen in the monument. Most of them were made by the Haida Indians, who lived farther south. These bright-colored totem poles depict family or tribal histories and the familiar wildlife.

The Russian colonial outpost was once a busy place. In the foundries were cast some of the bells of Padre Serra's California missions. Yankee sea captains spoke of Sitka in its heyday as "the Paris of the Pacific." A replica of one of the spruce-log blockhouses tells the story of defense from the Kik-Siti Indians, who proved no friendlier than the Tlingit.

# [ VII ]

## *Savor of the Tropics*

THE WISDOME *of God receives small honour from those Vulgar Heads that
rudely stare about, and with a gross rusticity admire His works: those
highly magnifie Him whose judicious inquiry into His Acts,
and deliberate research into His Creatures, returne the duty
of a devout and learned admiration.*

—SIR THOMAS BROWNE

### 1. EVERGLADES NATIONAL PARK
### [*Florida*]

WHENEVER I visit Everglades National Park I am reminded of these
words of a seventeenth-century doctor and antiquarian. I must explain
that by "Vulgar Heads" Sir Thomas did not mean stupid or unpleasant people.
He had in mind those (a larger majority in his day) who are content merely
to gaze at natural or man-made wonders without inquiring into the manner
in which they came about. What he was extolling is exactly what we are
nowadays suggesting when we use the words "research" and "interpretation."

Of all our great national parks, none stands more in need of interpretation than this land-and-water ecological gem of southern Florida. As Dr.
William B. Robertson, park biologist, has written: "Everglades is a prisoner
of its notoriety . . . many find the real thing pale and unsatisfactory beside
the synthetic Everglades they built"—whether from overdone advertisement
or passionate romance. It is true, in my own experience, that I have heard
more expressions of disappointment from day-visitors in this park than in
any other.

---

*A fast getaway just ahead of a cruising shark. Everglades National Park.* [*Photo:
M. Woodbridge Williams*]

[ 337 ]

It is not that this preserved subtropical area has lacked for in-park interpretation. On the contrary it has had consistently fine naturalists or other communicators, who tell the story of this intricate natural order with the enthusiasm of those who themselves find new wonders every day. Nor does the park lack beauty. It is not of the spectacular kind; it is timid, subtle. Yet it has its great moments: the winter sunset, painting the Southeast, viewed across a sea of sawgrass, dotted with tree-islands, on one of which may rise a single palm, flagging down the speeding wildfowl. But truly the beauties of Everglades are chiefly of another kind, appealing to what Darwin called "the eye of the mind."

Far more beautiful than what the senses perceive is the never ending adventure of organic life itself: the creation of communities adapted for survival in whatever earthform they find existence. He who comes into such a life community with some knowledge of what he is about to find will not demand the stunning landscape. His pleasure will come from the recognition of complex relationships, from lower to higher forms, and not excluding his own position of triumphant but risky dominance.

Seen from this point of view, Everglades, one of the largest of the national parks in area, is also one of our most significant preservations of the natural scene—preservation at least insofar as possible. Here are just such complex relationships, life with life, from plankton to panther: a food chain of prey and predator in which the only incongruous link is the intrusion of a managing predator, the human.

The present park is the southernmost segment of what was, in nature, a great self-sustaining unit. Southern Florida is a flat plain, rising so little above sea level that it is nearly awash by the tides. It resembles a great pie plate, with low edge, and with a nick upon the Gulf of Mexico side. From central Florida the high annual rainfall, and streams like the Kissimmee, have been held in the Lake Okeechobee reservoir until floodtimes, and then spilled southward as a mighty marshy river moving almost imperceptibly for 120 miles to the ocean. The Seminole Indians, relative latecomers to the region, called it a river of grass—pa-hay-okee.

A flat, flat land, where a few inches of elevation make all the difference in the nature of the plant cover and the kind of animate creatures! Visitors to the park who are familiar with the mountain areas of the Western states are amused by the sign on the road to Flamingo: "Rock Reef Pass—elevation

*Young spoonbill "playing with sticks." Everglades National Park. [Photo: M. Woodbridge Williams]*

3.1 feet." At this point, where the highway eases over a gentle hump of limestone ridge, the sign is a reminder that inches, not thousands of feet, may create a zone of sharp variance. The plants and animals of the elevated or submerged parts of the Everglades—the sawgrass, hammocks, bayheads, pineland, and mangrove swamps—are all dependent on these existing or missing inches.

The self-sufficing unit, which the Seminoles and the early white explorers of this wilderness saw, no longer exists. The drainage canals that made possible the agricultural development to the north of the park and the creation of almost continuous cities of leaping population upon the coastal strips have diverted the flow of fresh water that formerly moved into what is now Everglades National Park. Of course, there had always been minor catastrophes, so far as plant and animal life were concerned. Hurricanes, natural fires, and periodic droughts and flooding were part of the order. The healing, or restoration of equilibrium, was not difficult.

The man-made threat to the continued existence of the park—to the conditions which were intended to be preserved—is entirely different. Much, in recent years, has been published on this threat, and since the study of the possibilities is in process, I shall not go farther into the matter here, except to say that competent biological opinion holds that in the long run the park cannot continue to function upon its local rainfall alone. The terra firma would still be there. The bland, inviting winter climate, yes. Much of what the visitor comes to see would finally disappear. Even the sport fishermen and the commercial shrimpers of the Gulf, might get a shock. The primitive glades were creative even beyond present knowledge.

If your idea of the tropics is that of frost-free lowlands, then south Florida is not tropical. It can be described accurately as almost but not quite. In fact there is an extraordinary mingling here of two zones. It is nearly the southern limit of certain plants and animals and the northern limit of others. The crocodile and the sea cow are here, but so is the black bear, the raccoon, and the panther, the latter making his last stand east of the Mississippi. Here are the palms, the mahogany, and the strange strangler fig, but also the hackberry and the persimmon. Willows, too; but that family feels at home almost anywhere. Where the channels of the Shark River empty into the Gulf of Mexico is a mangrove forest that is possibly the greatest in the world. But the "feel" of the region is that of the tropics, despite the cold winter winds that sometimes descend.

---

*Nesting time in the mangroves. Everglades National Park. [Photo: M. Woodbridge Williams]*

The alligator claims a larger share of the visitor's attention; perhaps more than he should, for you can find him much farther north than this. But your chances of seeing him in the Everglades, without going into a swamp, are excellent. There are usually numbers of them below you in the Pa-hay-okee when you go to the top of the elevated platform that has been built to permit a wide-sweeping view of the island-dotted, grassy ocean, a true wilderness.

But it is for its birds that southern Florida has been most famous over the years since white men came. These flooded glades with their shallow water heated by an almost tropical sun are a biological marvel of productivity of aquatic life. When the early summer flooding comes, the lower end of a long food chain sets to work with vigor. The freshwater plankton, crayfish larvae, and tadpoles quickly build up a population of small fishes, which are eaten by larger fishes, and by the end of the rainy season, when lowered water levels concentrate this supply of food, the birds, especially the waders, move to their dinner. But on this point, biologist Robertson has a word of warning to the enthusiastic bird watcher. No matter what their numbers, the birds are still "where you find them." The birds go where food is in abundance. You may find a location in a slough where the show is fantastic—waders and waterfowl of many species, including the roseate spoonbills "sweeping" in their odd fashion; and ten days later in the same spot there will be merely a few come-late janitors cleaning up.

The bird population of the Everglades is still impressive; only careful research can reveal the fluctuations and their identic causes. But if visitors now thrill at the sight of so many water birds of so many kinds—the herons and egrets and wood ibises (so-called, but really storks), spoonbills and limpkins, cormorants and anhingas—we can only wonder what were the numbers when, for instance, William Bartram was on the lower St. Johns River in 1774, and reported that "sleep was almost impossible because of the continuous noise and restlessness of the seafowl." In 1832 Audubon wrote of Sandy Key that "the flocks of birds that covered the shelly beaches and those hovering overhead so astonished us that we could for a while scarcely believe our eyes."

Even more impressive than these quotations, I think, is an extract from the diary of Charles William Pierce, who as a young lad accompanied "the old Frenchman," Chevalier—a collector and feather hunter—on a long voyage in the glades. Pierce described one nesting place as "the biggest I ever saw . . . as we went along the birds kept flying up, all kind mixed together, . . . Mr. Chevalier just sat there, pointed his gun first one way, and then another . . . at last laid down his gun and said 'Mine God, 'tis too much bird on this countrie, I cannot shoot.'"

### Everglades National Park

Pierce's trip was of that lamentable period when women had discovered that good taste required them to wear bird feathers on their bonnets. The slaughter was pitiless, especially of those birds so unlucky as to have exceptional plumage. Pierce says that Chevalier got ten dollars for the great white heron and twenty-five dollars for a flamingo, though the pelican brought only fifty cents and the least tern twenty-five. A "plume hunter," named Batty at Big Gasparilla Pass had sixty men killing birds for him on the Gulf Coast.

When I first visited the Everglades, which was not long after the park was established, there were no commodious visitor centers and only a few rough trails. Flamingo, now with its fleet of powerboats, lodge, cabins, and campgrounds, was just a collection of framehouses, rude piers, and fishermen who took fish seriously. Mahogany Hammock, to be treated so brutally by Hurricane Donna in 1960, was a dark and tropically forbidden jungle, at the door of which a group of paurotis palms invited visitors, like Chamber of Commerce professional greeters. I knew nothing then, by personal experience, of the Cuthbert Lake rookery, Whitewater Bay, and the maze of channels among the mangrove islands of the Shark River Basin.

*From the "river of grass" rise the forested "hammocks." Everglades National Park.*
*[Photo: M. Woodbridge Williams]*

But I came away from that first visit with a vivid realization, somehow like an answer to long wondering, of what the word "ecology" means, for I spent several entranced hours on Paradise Key, with its then homemade platform walk which extended a short distance out into the waters of Taylor Slough. Then, as now, it was called Anhinga Trail, but since that time, to accommodate the vastly increased number of visitors, it has been modernized and greatly enlarged. I think it will ever be one of the high spots of our park system for those who suspect their implicit kinship with all the other forms of life. I also recall that I acquired, from brushing against the shrubs on the trailside, a dozen or more "redbugs," whose chumminess made itself violently apparent next day, when I reached Fort Jefferson. Also, the mosquitoes wolfed me. But it was worth it.

I had seen many of the birds and fish and reptiles that assembled for me at Anhinga Trail, though as I recall the showy purple gallinule and the water turkey were new. But it was to be able to view, so clearly and easily, the relationship chain! I saw the spearfisherman, the anhinga, who easily runs short of oil for his feathers, leave the water and hang himself out to dry in a tree, and here was the cormorant, who dives and hooks his fish—each bird being expert in its profession. The poet Sidney Lanier, a Georgian who visited the Everglades a century ago, wrote of this "water-turkey":

The anhinga . . . is the most preposterous bird within the range of ornithology. He is not just a bird; he is a neck . . . he has just enough stomach to arrange nourishment for his neck; just enough wings to fly painfully along with his neck; and just enough legs to keep his neck from dragging on the ground.

This is good fun, albeit a shade on the heavy side. But the fact is that the anhinga, thus insulted, might have retorted that to him Lanier was a comical-looking biped with a loose outer skin and a nose ill adapted for spearing fish.

I hope that those of my readers who leave the Everglades to go north along the Gulf Coast may be able to visit the superb Corkscrew Swamp Sanctuary, maintained by the National Audubon Society. Here are more than six thousand acres of the last of the virgin bald cypress forest—the oldest trees in eastern North America—that once covered millions of acres of swamplands. Cores taken from some of these giants suggest that they were ancient trees when Columbus came ashore.

*The mangrove trees build land, and the birds build nests. Everglades National Park. [Photo: M. Woodbridge Williams]*

## 2. VIRGIN ISLANDS NATIONAL PARK
### [*Virgin Islands*]

DURING WORLD WAR I the Danes maintained a nervous neutrality; but the United States, anxiously viewing its sea approaches in the Caribbean, thought it wise to acquire the Danish holdings in the Virgin Islands, notably the three larger ones known as St. Thomas, St. Croix, and St. John. The price was 25 million dollars, and after the war ended there was considerable doubt as to the value of this real estate situated on the summits of a submerged mountain chain. There was no doubt about the delightful quality of the climate, where the northeast trade winds temper the sun's daytime heat, and the nights are blissfully cool—only a mean temperature difference of about six degrees between winter and summer.

But, 25 million dollars! One of the government civil servants wrote to his home folks in the mid-twenties that the United States had been horn-swoggled. He was wrong, just as those jeerers were mistaken when they referred to Seward's purchase of Alaska as an investment in icebergs. It did take some years to demonstrate that it was a bargain.

In the early thirties there was a minor government functionary on St. Thomas, a peppery sort of chap, who likewise took the dim view. He wrote that "the enchantment of distance turns into a commonplace reality," refer- ring to both the capitals of St. Thomas and St. Croix. But Hamilton Cochran raved about the island of St. John. He called it "a paradise of solitude." He was a lover of unspoiled nature, with a pair of legs that he used for walking. He got around; there was little he didn't see and enjoy. I quote him:

> Three miles westward from St. Thomas, across the flashing blue waters of Pillsbury Sound, lies St. John, the smallest, most romantic and best-beloved of the Virgin Isles. Best-loved, that is, by those few happy mortals whom destiny had privileged to know its charms. Strangers are rare. Occasionally some white people go over for short holidays to refresh their souls . . . aside from these the island slumbers through the years, happy, forgotten, serene in its own for- getfulness. It is as wild, detached and primitive as if it were lost somewhere on the rim of an unknown sea.

The white population of St. John in Cochran's time could be counted on the fingers of one hand. Cruz Bay was the "capital," where were ten or fif- teen board shacks, a frame cottage or two, a tiny barracks on stilts that once housed a squad of U.S. marines, and, the "White House," residence of the

*Ruins at Annaberg tell the story of sugar-cane days. Virgin Islands National Park.*
*[Photo: M. Woodbridge Williams]*

dispatching secretary. One wonders what the dispatching secretary dispatched. The five white residents were: the dispatcher and his wife, an ex-construction foreman and his wife "trying to carve an estate out of the bush," and "a lonely Dane over on Lovango Cay." About five hundred "ebony and chocolate faces" were sparsely sprinkled through the bush.

St. John was a sweet, verdant tropical isle when the Danes began sugar-cane culture there in the early part of the eighteenth century. In truth, considering the great extent of lands suitable for cane, it was not highly adaptable even for that crop. The hillsides were steep and stony. But slave labor made the competitive difference. All through the reviving landscape of today are the old boundary walls of stones, piled when the black folk from Africa cleared the slopes. It is doubtful if the Danes brought their hearts with them into these islands. Rather, they hoped to carve out a competency and go home to the Baltic and spend the money. Even with slaves, the profits were for the big operators: still, for poorer white men it was, at least, an easy life. There was, however, always the fear of an outbreak by the slaves, who so greatly outnumbered the proprietors.

The servile insurrection came in 1733, with a great loss of life on both sides. Those planters were lucky who got refuge at Durlieu's Caneel Bay plantation. A tough soldier, imported from Martinique with the consent of France, ended the rebellion mercilessly, and the few remaining mutineers rafted themselves over to British Tortola. But a letter sent to Copenhagen by Governor Gardelin of the Danish West India Company in that black year sufficiently describes the tragedy:

> Most of the planters and their families are dead. I cannot tell how many. No work is being done on the estates. The cattle are running wild . . . I myself have been ill with fever these two days. Nor have we a priest to say a burial service. He, too, is dead . . . send us a ship!

Denmark forbade any further importation of African slaves to the islands in 1802, and in 1848 slavery was abolished. In the intervening years, since the insurrection, the planters had become more prosperous than before. In 1789 the population consisted of 167 whites, 16 free Negroes, and 2,200 slaves. But the termination of slave labor sent the island back to bush. It had been gutted of most of its original beauty; now it could begin the long job of restoration. The restoration, as visitors to the park see today, is still proceeding. This, in itself, should be of great interest to observers of nature, who need not be biologists to enjoy the processes at work on a ravaged landscape. Within the boundaries of the park, nature will be allowed to proceed in her own way, except that certain exotic nuisances, like the mongoose, might be expelled.

This animal, very worthy where it belonged, which was in India, was brought to the West Indies to cope with the rat population that had escaped from shipboard. It was a typical instance of do-it-yourself treatment without consulting a doctor, who would, in this case, have been a biologist. The mongoose eats rats in India, but on these isles his range of taste expands to include a menu of delicacies we prefer to keep for ourselves.

Virgin Islands National Park was dedicated in December 1956. On the first of that month, Laurance Rockefeller, as President of Jackson Hole Preserve, Inc., presented more than five thousand acres of the island land, accumulated by purchase over a number of years, to the Secretary of the Interior, then Fred A. Seaton.

It was a happy and generous inspiration to set aside so much of this relatively unsophisticated island of St. John. Modern technology will make it possible for the other West Indian islands to become suburbs of the Atlantic coastal cities. I have a friend, an art editor, who for several years has been commuting regularly from his home on St. Thomas to his New York office, where his presence is required only one week a month. But faster planes, with an assist from helicopters, will do far better than that. It should be possible, for those in the upper income brackets, to breakfast on a veranda overlooking the tropical sea, have luncheon in the neighborhood of Madison Avenue, and arrive home with the evening newspaper in time for a cocktail—maybe even for a brief swim—before dinner. The newspaper could even be that day's London *Times*, or the Paris *Figaro*. Each of the smaller isles that were thrown in with the purchase from the Danes should bring a pretty front-foot price.

At such a time, the suburbanites of the islands will look forward to a trip over to St. John on weekends, where they can experience a tropical wilderness. Instead of the cement pavement at their front door, they can enjoy a jeep trip over the unimproved road from Cruz Bay to the Bordeaux Mountain overlook, or the Annaberg ruins. In time, the renewed native forest of mahogany, breadfruit, cinnamon bay, and the palms and mangroves and soursops, will be a relief from the nursery-stock flowering shrubs of their own front lawns. There will always be a limited number willing to walk, so a park ranger will lead groups and tell the story of the old plantations and sugar mills. At the Trunk Bay underwater trail, the snorkeling swimmer will follow a series of submerged labels describing the marine world he is invading with his fabricated fins.

This is partly a view of tomorrow, but it is not fanciful. However, if I were able to choose, I would visit St. John differently. I would leave a northern city, say New York, on some blustery winter day, preferably during a frigid spell when cakes of ice are floating down the Hudson. I would have a pardonable thrill of pleasure, having stowed myself on board ship, that there might be a blizzard next day that would tie up traffic horribly. It should be a slow boat. Six days to St. Thomas would be all right; but slow boats are hard to find nowadays, at least ones that take passengers.

The first day out would be cold: too cold for a deck chair. Walk the deck! Second day, a warming trend would come into the air. And the ocean would begin to look bluer. Lafcadio Hearn—who could have been one of our best writers, but who decided to go to Japan, marry a Japanese girl, and become a naturalized subject of the emperor—made a trip on a slow boat like

*Overleaf: A marine garden of corals. The undersea growths strangely resemble a desert scene. Virgin Islands National Park.* [*Photo: M. Woodbridge Williams*]

this on a journalistic assignment from *Harpers Weekly* back in 1887. He noticed, two days out from New York, that the water was becoming bluer. He said as much to a fellow passenger, an elderly French gentleman going home to Guadeloupe. "Blue?" was the reply, with a snort. *"This* isn't blue!"

Two days later, Hearn ventured to intimate that now the water looked blue. His French gentleman admitted that it "was *becoming* slightly blue." But not blue. Hearn resorted to the ship surgeon. "Wouldn't you say this ocean looks very blue?" "No sir, not yet. Not really blue." But there came an hour when "over the verge of the sea there is something strange growing visible, looming up like a beautiful golden-yellow cloud. It is an island, so lofty, so luminous, so phantom-like, that it seems a vision of the Island of the Seven Cities."

It was, indeed, St. Vincent, but it might have been any island in that Caribbean. The man of Guadeloupe came to Hearn and touched him on the shoulder and pointed down at the water. "That, monsieur," he said with satisfaction, "is *blue.*" And surely, those tropical waters such as in the Virgins, are blue—an indescribable blue—as distinctive in their blueness as is the blueness of Crater Lake, also not imitable on the color chart. Lafcadio Hearn put it this way: "the sea is absurdly, impossibly blue. The painter who should try to paint it would be denounced as a lunatic."

That blue, which on the coraled fringes of the islands becomes an equally incredible aquamarine, is one thing. The tropic night is another. "The Caribbean night falls with a weight and density from which it is difficult to believe that day will ever re-emerge," is the way Peter Quennell put it. It has to be experienced—that feeling of finality. You can't tell anyone about it. It is not like cave darkness. It is, at first, a disturbing feeling that you are being *left alone.* You become used to it, of course. On St. John the bats like it. Maybe their sonar equipment works better than up north, where night has a dallying, indecisive way. There are six species of bats in this national park. They are, in fact, the only native land mammals. One of them is red, and eats figs, and has been rediscovered only recently. And, incidentally, though the bird watcher may see here a great variety of land birds, there is no such show of waterfowl as one finds in Everglades. The food chain which makes possible the vast numbers of waders and shore birds of the shallow glades river does not exist here.

But to come back for a moment to the definiteness of the Antillean night: I have asked many of my friends who have taken passage on one of these cruise ships (nine fun-packed days, six ports, $395.50 and UP, go now and pay later) what they thought of the quality of night in the islands. I was at first surprised that they didn't know what I was talking about. Then it occurred to me that, of course, they had never known it was night; they had been aboard a navigable night club—a sort of Manhattan Times Square with propellers, blazing with incandescent lamps. Don't misunderstand me on this point: I not only have no objection to people having fun-packed days and nights, touching at duty-free ports and defeating inflation by getting perfume at half price; bringing triumphantly home a quart of rum free of duty—I think it a charming adventure for young, buoyant people in no need of rest. I merely say that one doesn't get intimately acquainted with the tropical isle that way. A leisurely fortnight in a cottage, or at the guest facility at Caneel Bay, or at the campground at Hawksnest Bay (equipment can be rented), is something greatly to be coveted, and will not be forgotten.

Paradise? I have before me a picture of smooth sailing water, a sloop in the foreground, waving palm fronds, and the island hills giving invitation across the blue expanse. "Island Paradise," the picture is captioned. So seductive is this that I am nearly deceived. Would it not be a joyous forever? But then I recall that Paradise is like the mirage of cool lake seen by the traveler in the desert: when you reach it, it is not there; it is farther on. People have to live with themselves, and this is as difficult in the tropics as in Norway. This sour statement out of the way, I suggest that if you shall be so lucky as to have a chance to live with the realities of St. John Island for a while, you are by no means to miss it.

### 3. BUCK ISLAND REEF NATIONAL MONUMENT
#### [*Virgin Islands*]

*WE FEEL surprised when travelers tell us of the vast dimensions of the Pyramids and other great ruins, but how utterly insignificant are the greatest of these when compared with these mountains of stone accumulated by the agency of various minute and tender animals! This is a wonder which does not at first strike the eye of the body but, after reflection, the eye of reason.*

—CHARLES DARWIN, *Voyage of the Beagle*

THE SNORKELER has a fine field for underwater adventure in the coral shrubbery at Trunk Bay, Hawksnest, Annaberg, and Lameshur on the island of St. John, but I suppose the high point of this modern educational sport will always be found on Buck Island, a mile and a half off the northeast coast of

St. Croix. For here, on an islet that looks no different from hundreds of others in the dotted West Indies, exists an unusual barrier reef which surrounds the eastern shore. The resultant lagoon is protected from the waves of the open sea by a wall of elkhorns, staghorns, and other cone forms erected by the unconscious cooperation of the countless tiny marine animals that colonize to produce a stony structure often in treelike form. It is cause for wonder, this unthinking cooperative effort. The coral polyps are architects of an undersea beauty that rivals anything of the land surface.

Each of the three main islands of the American Virgin group has its nearby "Buck" satellite. The one off St. John, to be sure, is labeled "Le Duck" on most maps, but that name is not common locally. The Buck Island that is now a national monument of our National Park System was set aside in 1961 from the rest of the island authority because of its precious natural features. It has a length of only a mile, a width of a third of a mile, and the highest point is but little more than three hundred feet above sea level, but that small package holds a world of the highest enjoyment for visitors of future years.

Deliciously clear is this lagoon which lies between the barrier reef and the shore. Even when there is a fifteen-knot wind curling the surface outside, the ocean gently laps over the barrier into this placid pool that some see as emerald green. Color is a tricky thing, even for the color-sharp. *Some* green surely is. No fresh water drains into the lagoon to discolor it or dilute its salinity. Indeed, the underwater photographer, I am told, must stir the plankton or limy cloud, lest the clarity of the undersea gardens be too much like that of a land view.

Frigate birds hover continually over Buck Island. These gliders are unrivaled in the world of wings. Circling, circling, hour after hour with no apparent expenditure of energy, they are a challenge to the technologist. With a similar rate of fuel expenditure, the fare from New York to Los Angeles should be about one dollar. But these magnificent gliders do not seem to nest now on Buck Island. If once they did, they may have changed their habits because of that "infamous mongoose," as the delinquent rat-catcher has been called. The mongoose certainly raids the sand nests of the turtles, as the raccoon does in Everglades, and also preys upon the pelican. The mongoose should be returned to India, with thanks for the loan.

I am not a skin diver or snorkeler myself, for a reason which I may explain at some opportune time, but I am quite willing to believe that it is a royal diversion, with more than mere entertainment value. Of course, it represents an impudent human invasion of marine-life sovereignty, and I am surprised that the sharks do not resent it more than they seem to do. It has its hazards,

*A spanking wind heels a pleasure craft off St. Croix. Buck Island Reef National Monument. [Photo: M. Woodbridge Williams]*

but they are not great, and it is a little gamier for that. Of course the snorkeler should know his equipment and should not go alone, but the latter injunction applies as well to the surface swimmer. In fact, with snorkel equipment you don't even need to be a good swimmer. My old friend "honest John" Lewis, who used to be superintendent of Virgin Islands National Park, said that dog-paddling would suffice. But then, John was a very accomplished dog-paddler. The main thing for the initiate is not to panic. This cautionary advice is not from me; it is from those who know. My acquaintance with the under-sea wonders comes to me secondhand, through "Woody" Williams and George Schesventer, snorkeling photographers, who went down to the Virgins for me to make some pictures for this book. I asked Woody to make some notes for me describing his operations and his sensations. He felt self-conscious about this assignment, and started in with something like this:

A rim of tossing silver split my vision of land and sea: above rose the tawny slopes of Buck Island, spotted by weird cactus; below spread diaphanous scenes of blue and green through which strange shapes drifted.

*Snorkel diver watches a school of grunts. Buck Island Reef National Monument.*
*[Photo: George F. Schesventer]*

Now *that*, Woody, is purple prose, and you know it, who are not only my favorite photographer, but my sensitive and perceptive philosopher! You weren't thinking of anything diaphanous below. Nor weird cactus above. You were quite properly thinking about your camera and your diving equipment, and wondering whether you and George Schesventer had brought enough film along, and other un-purple thoughts. And then overboard you went, like the professionals you are.

But when you tell me about the closeup experiences in that lagoon, about the dark-skinned form that suddenly came down, with cheeks puffed, hands clenched over a supply of bread-crumb chum, and how the gaily colored wrasse swarmed in like butterflies in migration, and how when the Negro's lungs could sustain him no longer he swam to the surface with the blue and yellow wrasse in hot pursuit: well, then, Woody, I am with you; I am down there underwater.

Some of the snorkelers went along above me clinging to cork rings towed by a guide. Others hung to the arms of stronger swimmers. Some gave me a wave of the hand as they passed overhead. They looked like nothing else but giant, clumsy frogs. George was watching out for sharks, and keeping an eye on me to see that my preoccupation didn't keep me under too long, and switching cameras when my film ran out.

Yes, I can see all that. I am there.

And I can see, through Woody's eyes, among the coral patches, the schools of tang—surgeonfish they are sometimes called, because of the razor blade they carry at the base of the tail—and the trunkfish that came along, black-polka-dotted on a white background and with "a snout pursed in a big sneer at me."

We can expect that the bird watchers will have a rival host, one of these

*Yellowtail and parrot fish in the antler coral. Buck Island Reef National Monument.*
*[Photo: M. Woodbridge Williams]*

days: the fish watcher. Buck Island Reef will be one of the prime locations for the hobby.

## 4. Christiansted National Historic Site
### [*Virgin Islands*]

THE SPANISH CONQUERORS who followed Columbus into the New World regarded the islands of the Lesser Antilles with slight esteem; but with an eye to the safety of the golden galleons, and the loot from the mainland, they wanted no other European settlements either. Thus for many years these islands, including St. Croix, were a sort of no man's land which the French, the Dutch, or the English could claim and try to make good the claim. Actually, we know little enough about the history of St. Croix from 1493 to 1733, when the Danish Guinea Company bought it from France. We do know, however, that it was a romantic frontier in which the pirate, the freebooter, or the buccaneer was often top dog. Interestingly enough, the word "freebooter" is from the Dutch *vrij-bueter*.

National Park Service headquarters are in Fort Christiansvaern, and guided tours are available from there every day except Saturday and Sunday; or visitors may stroll around and see Government House and the Landmarks Society Museum in the Steeple Building on their own. In any case, what is represented here is a period of prosperous Danish occupation, when, with slave labor and good prices for sugar, island plantation owners were able to build luxurious homes and public buildings, and indulge in other refinements that stemmed from a fictitious well-being.

Fictitious? Yes, because a one-crop economy, slave-worked or with free labor, has never offered true prosperity. Sugar was king for many years, but even at the best of times the cane production was running a losing race with debt. Agriculture is a good ambling nag, but compound interest is a racehorse. The Danes found it out. Better cane lands were opened up elsewhere; the slaves of St. Croix got their freedom; production costs increased; finally the Danish state took over. When the United States bought the Virgin Islands in 1917, St. Croix was on its way toward a new crop that the slave-owning planters could never have imagined: an influx of tourists eager to enjoy the climate and learn the history of the West Indies.

# PART

---

# THREE

---

# [ I ]

# *The Seashores*

## 1. Cape Cod National Seashore
### [*Massachusetts*]

Thoreau's neat description of the topography of Cape Cod could not be bettered. "Cape Cod is the bared and bended arm of Massachusetts; the shoulder is at Buzzard's Bay; the elbow, or crazy-bone, at Cape Malle-barre; the wrist at Truro; and the sandy fist at Provincetown."

In 1849, when the great migration to the California gold fields was getting under way, Thoreau and the younger William Ellery Channing packed their bags and left Concord on a treasure hunt of their own. Neither one was greedy for mineral riches; both preferred the companionship of forest and stream, of birds and animals, and both had stout and willing legs. What was this Cape like? As flew the crow, it was not very far from their homes, yet to them it was unknown land. At Orleans they stopped at Higgins' Tavern. "The inhabitants of Orleans measured their crops not only by bushels of corn but by barrels of clams." With that introduction to the fresh salty air, they began a long walk over marsh, dune, and strand.

From this first visit, followed by two other expeditions, in one of which Thoreau walked alone, emerged the book which should be in the baggage of every visitor to what is now a national seashore. There have been great changes, of course, since the Concord naturalist ventured his volume. Yet much remains the same as when the two explorers spent a memorable night with the Wellfleet oysterman, who took them for tinkers or peddlers—and was the more certain of this when Thoreau's nimble fingers set going a stubborn clock.

Already, far more than a century ago, Henry Thoreau was worried about

*The cliffs reminded Sir Francis Drake of home. Point Reyes National Seashore. [Photo: M. Woodbridge Williams]*

*The fishhook of the Pilgrim fathers: Cape Cod. Cape Cod National Seashore.* [*Photo: M. Woodbridge Williams*]

the kind of people who would sometime "discover" the Cape. He had a large contempt for the gentry who went to Newport and Saratoga Springs to be noticed by their peers and waited upon by varlets. "The time must come," said he, "when this coast will be a place of resort for those New Englanders who really wish to visit the seaside." He hoped that "fashionable people" would "always be disappointed here."

True, it was not many years before summer saw a great influx of visitors. At Eastham a vast camp-meeting ground was the scene of revivals that brought 5,000 hearers of 150 ministers, who, to the delight of the Cape Codder, as well as visitors, gave religion "in earnest," in a loud voice, plenty of swinging gesture, and no clipped syllables. The Eastham people themselves were not mumblers. They didn't say "Eastum." They said "East-ham," and you knew the word ended in h-a-m.

No, the fashionable world never did come to the Cape, but the population billows were ever coming shoreward, and more people who loved the place were seeking summer homes. The Cape Codder had shunned the ocean front: he built his house in the shelter of an inland hollow, out of the galloping winds. Folks who intended only ten weeks of occupancy could feel differently. They were not farmer-fishermen.

The wonder is not that so many mobile millions flow down the highways into the Cape nowadays: the wonder is that four wonderful sections of this alluring land could so lately have been thus redeemed from private holding and placed in the hands of the National Park Service for the pleasure of all Americans. For some years, although ardently desired by conservationists, it just didn't seem possible. But the effort proved not too tardy. Congress authorized the establishment of this national seashore in 1961.

Snug in the palm of the "sandy fist" lies old Provincetown. In the peak of the summer season the place is sufficiently frantic. It offers a humorous study of human swarming, apparently for the purpose of watching people watching other people. The dementia is highly profitable to the professional oddball, who is nobody's fool, and puts on a pretty good show. This is fun— for a while; and when you get satiated you can go up to the Ocean View lookout and see some real history.

*Browsing deer leave their footprints on the dunes. Cape Cod National Seashore.*
*[Photo: M. Woodbridge Williams]*

All Cape Cod, of course, is the creature of the great continental glacier of recent age, but the miles of dunes on this windswept front are truly impressive. Ocean currents have furnished the material and the winds have piled them; and still they do, where the sands are not anchored by vegetation. You are here within those "province lands" set aside by Plymouth Colony folks who fondly remember the "commons" of old England. You will have good protected swimming at Race Point; and this is the strip of coast where in the old days so many brave ships were torn apart by the furious sea—Cape Codders on the shore watching the fatality, usually unable to offer more help than a prayer.

The Pilgrim Heights area is just a little farther up the "arm." What a page of our history is here! The *Mayflower* reached the Cape the second week in November. The provisions of the Pilgrims were scanty; it was an unfavorable time of year to arrive. They found a spring of pure, sweet water. They had agreed, one remembers, upon setting up a government of pure communism—from each according to his ability and to each according to his need, as the Essene Christians had attempted centuries before. It failed, naturally: people are not like that, yet. The married women refused to do the laundering for bachelors, especially if they seemed shiftless. Four days the Pilgrims spent here; then they went to the mainland and hewed the timbers for their first building.

This hallowed spot, marking the first timid explorations of the immigrants, was formerly a Massachusetts state park. The nature trails present essentially the scene as the fathers viewed it: the pines on the higher ground, the heath of bearberry and shrub sloping down to the Pilgrim Lake, a "kettle" that was formed in glacial times, salt meadow and swamp. There will be surf fishermen all along Great Beach, hoping to hook one of the big, fighting striped bass.

More acres of the seashore surround the Marconi Wireless Station, where the first wireless message went out from the United States to England in 1903. The sea has moved in upon the old station, but a part of it still remains. Inland there was formerly a military reservation with its consequent disruption of the natural scene, but this area is being restored. But what was never much disturbed, thanks be, is the precious white cedar swamp. You do not look for this rare island of tree life on Cape Cod; indeed it is not usual anywhere in the latitude. A boardwalk trail leads into the very heart of it. On a

*Today's Huck Finn on Herring River. Cape Cod National Seashore.* [*Photo: M. Woodbridge Williams*]

*You can have company without being crowded . . .*
*or you can be alone with the sea and your thoughts.*
*Cape Cod National Seashore.*
*[Photos: M. Woodbridge Williams]*

*Above: This Provincetown street in summer is thronged with tourists. Cape Cod National Seashore. [Photo: M. Woodbridge Williams]*

summer day this is a cool spot. The swamp soil is cold: that's why the trees are here.

Thoreau remarked that "to an inlander" the Cape landscape is a constant mirage. He gave the instance of seeing a solitary traveler on the plains of Nauset who at a distance loomed like a giant. I wonder if this is a common phenomenon, or whether it occurs only on certain days? I had this experience on an October day, when a distant automobile loomed like a bus.

Charles S. Olcott, in 1914, wrote an introduction to a new edition of Thoreau's *Cape Cod*. He said, "The visitor who goes to Cape Cod today in the spirit of Thoreau may still avoid, as he did, most of the signs of habitation . . . observing the birds and flowers and trees, the sands and the shellfish in very much the same way Thoreau did." Well, not quite true today, for the most part; yet there are nooks: and as for the restless Atlantic and the sandy

*Left: Fresh-water ponds, legacies of the ice age. Cape Cod National Seashore. [Photo: M. Woodbridge Williams]*

'beaches, after Labor Day there are long stretches where you may walk alone.

One of the first trails in the National Park System specifically built for bicycling was opened at Cape Cod National Seashore while this volume was being prepared. One such trail, in the Province Lands, will run about eight miles. Another, in the Pilgrim Springs area, will be two and a half miles. Later, the two trails will be joined.

## 2. CAPE HATTERAS NATIONAL SEASHORE
### [North Carolina]

ATLANTIC SEABOARD WEATHER, in general, is full of sudden surprises. Hatteras weather is only a little more brusque and whimsical, perhaps. For example, I once spent the first three weeks in November in a cottage just south of Nags Head. November is a month when the prudent visitor does not set his hopes too high. Yet those three weeks, except for one two-day northeaster, gave me as perfect a run of Indian summer as I have ever known. Day after day of delight for the beachcomber, the surf fisherman, even the stout bather. And every evening the sun dropped below the Roanoke Sound horizon and left an incredible riot of color in which red was merely the major theme.

But while it lasted, that northeaster was an experience I would not have missed. Like the sedentary idiot that I was, with muscles softened by sitting at a desk, I ventured out upon the beach of the Outer Banks and plunged against that gale. It was like pushing against one of the great bronze doors of the Interior Building in the Washington I had just left. I hadn't staggered far before I was glad I had moved against the wind. With the raincoat as a sail, I could easily blow back, provided I could keep erect. In the misty rain the skittering sand hit my goggles with a force that I could hear. I had the miles to myself. There was a queer, exultant feeling about that. Just myself, a mere flyspeck between dunes and waves, facing a gale! No surf fishermen today. Not even sanderlings dancing along the margin of the ebb. Alone, but with no sense of loneliness.

No; not quite alone, because when I paused to wipe the mist from my goggles, I saw at my feet a shipwrecked loon, lying on his side in the sand. It was obvious why he was where he ought not be. He had somehow swum, or risen into, a patch of oil sludge dumped from a lawless steamship passing

*Right, above: Schooner* Kohler *high and dry on Hatteras sands in 1933.* [Photo: Roger A. Toll] *Below: All that was left of the* Kohler *in 1956. Cape Hatteras National Seashore.* [Photo: W. Verde Watson]

coastwise. He had life enough left to challenge me with an open bill. He naturally regarded me as the author of his disaster. I could do nothing for him but wish him a miracle. The patch of bones and feathers I saw at about that spot, after the storm cleared, were probably his. If it was a raccoon that found him, I wondered how the prowler liked the petroleum flavor.

But next day all was Indian summer again on the Outer Banks, and black clouds of boattail grackles were feeding on the sea oats, lighting deftly atop the straws and bending them to the dune tops, holding them down till they were stripped of seed. And a few surf fishermen were back, because the channel bass had been running well. There is wonderful fishing on the Hatteras Seashore, but of course the summer season is the time for the deep-sea trolling for marlin and tuna or less spectacular mackerel and bluefish. From Oregon Inlet and Hatteras and Ocracoke villages the charter boats go out.

This barrier bank, broken by inlets at only two places in the seventy-mile reach between Whalebone Junction and the tip of Ocracoke Island, has none of the boulder and moraine and kettle aspects of the Cape Cod Seashore of Massachusetts. Yet really it is a child of the same glacial stage, for when the melting of the polar ice loosed a vast addition into the Atlantic bowl, a former shoreline that stood some miles to the eastward of the present one was submerged, flooding the low tidewater areas and creating the "sounds," like Pamlico, that now lie between the open ocean and the mainland.

These shoals that once lay to east, together with ocean currents driving alongshore, have supplied the material for this great bow-shaped barrier, erratically widening and narrowing. Winds have created the dunes, and where feebler plantlife has been able to hold the sands for long enough, the shrubs and trees have marched in. Instead of a bare landscape, then, we have here well-carpeted flats behind the dunes—wild flowers blooming almost into winter, bright-berried yaupons, even pines and lusty live oaks. When the ponies that now roam wild on Ocracoke first came to the Banks there must have been plenty of good grazing.

Just as the shore, dunes, and ponds of Cape Cod are on the fringe of a folkway, and as the Blue Ridge Parkway pictures something of the secluded life story of the southern Appalachian people, so the Hatteras Seashore brings visitors to the doorstep of a unique human habitation. The Outer Banker came here in colonial days, recruited mainly from Virginia and Maryland. It was not what we now call the abundant life, though the sea

*Its beacon warns that these shoals are "the graveyard of ships." Cape Hatteras National Seashore. [Photo: Ralph Anderson]*

offered ample food, there was plenty of game on the mainland, and a limited amount of stock could be raised. Fishermen they became naturally, and pilots and sailors.

The villages, you will observe, are all on the Pamlico Sound shore, Rodanthe, Avon, Buxton, Ocracoke, and the four others. From time to time, as the dreaded Diamond Shoals claimed its maritime victims, a good harvest of necessaries and luxuries came ashore, or could be salvaged. Not without reason was this coastal strip called "the graveyard of the Atlantic." Buried beneath the sands are hulks that appear after a great storm, to remain in sight until the next tempest covers them again.

Blackbeard the pirate maintained a lair on Ocracoke Island. Coast Guard stations were once maintained at locations seven miles apart, and the narrative of the heroic exploits of these brave men forms one of the inspiring chapters of marine history. What a strange story is that of the five-masted *Carroll A. Deering*, which went ashore on Diamond Shoals in 1921! When the Bankers boarded her, there was not a soul on the schooner, though the ship's cat was there. The crew? They have never been heard from. And, as an instance of

*Morning plunge of the Ocracoke wild ponies. Cape Hatteras National Seashore.*

what the restless power of the sea can do, after the wreck was dynamited the bow drifted over to Ocracoke, where it remains—sometimes beneath the sands, sometimes uncovered by the storms. The story of the "men against the sea" is graphically revealed at the visitor center, situated about two miles from the Cape.

When I first went down to the Hatteras shore, the crossing of Oregon Inlet was made by automobile ferry. I boarded the good ship *Conrad L. Wirth*, and to my amazement the pilot headed straight out to sea—or so it appeared. He knew his business: he knew where the bars lay that day, and he had to keep up with his homework, because on some other crossing they might be otherwhere. There is a bridge there now. It is not so romantic, but the waxing needs of tourism will not be denied. I suppose Hatteras Inlet will be bridged too, in time, and finally the wild ponies of Ocracoke will approach visitors for handouts, like Great Smoky Mountain bears. But the need for more seashore space for the millions is imperative, and something has to give, even if conformity is the result.

One of the never-failing attractions, at the upper end of Hatteras Island,

[*Photo: H. Raymond Gregg*]

is Pea Island National Wildlife Refuge. Undisturbed, and quite aware that they are in sanctuary, here every year arrive the thousands of snowgeese and Canada geese, and all the species of ducks which favor this bit of coast. There are whistling swans; gadwall, too. Altogether, within the seashore limits, you may see forty species of shorebirds, and the area around Bodie Lighthouse is a favorite haunt of bird watchers.

At Coquina Beach, not far from park headquarters, is a day-use area for surf bathing and picnicking, and campgrounds are at Pea Island, Salvo, Frisco, and Ocracoke. The nature trail at Buxton Woods should not be missed.

### 3. Point Reyes National Seashore
#### [California]

When I first frequented San Francisco, my Golden Gate friends assured me that the afternoon fogs never came down Market Street farther than Van Ness Avenue. Therefore, when I met this invigorating fleece in the neighborhood of Grant Avenue I had my choice of believing my friends or believing my eyes. Naturally I put the thing down as due to my poor vision.

This "Bay" climate, where the mean temperatures of January and July are so phenomenally near each other, extends up the coast to this new seashore of the National Park System. Sir Francis Drake and his men simply couldn't understand this weather where, on the 38th parallel (about the same as Lisbon), they "felt cold in midsummer." They could not know that one day the people who lived inland in Alta California would flock to Point Reyes Peninsula to get away from the cloudless sky and its shimmering heat. Anyone who has come in from Sacramento on a summer day knows the galvanic effect of the whiff of air as you drop down from the rise at Pinole. (I am thinking of the "old road" as I used to drive it.)

There is history here at Point Reyes—and landscape beauty, and a botanical meeting of northern and southern California plants, and beaches and cliffed headlands, and always the reviving air that pours out of the Pacific waters. What more can the day-user and the camper wish?

Drake's *Golden Hind* was leaking badly when he put in here in 1579, at the bay that now bears his name; and from here he continued on his epic circumnavigation of the globe. He met the Indians and looked over the

*Right, above: The upland meadows are famous grazing lands. Below: Gathering succulent oysters. Point Reyes National Seashore. [Photos: M. Woodbridge Williams]*

adjacent country, seeing "hordes of Deere by 1000 in a company, being large and fat of body." On the wooded uplands today, deer can still be seen. But what were these "conies" seen by the English sailors, "with the tail of a rat, of great length?" Is it possible that they were the unique "mountain beavers" of which a few colonies are now found in the thickets?

Drake was reminded of the chalk cliffs of Dover, which come down abruptly to the English Channel just in the manner of these highlands at Point Reyes, so he called the country Nova Albion and claimed it for his mistress, the Queen; and he "set up a monument of our being there . . . namely, a plate, nailed upon a fair great post, whereupon was engraven her Majesty's name . . . together with her Highness's picture and arms in a piece of sixpence current money. . . . It seemeth that the Spaniards had never been in this part of the country."

Drake's narrator was wrong. Cabrillo had preceded the Englishmen, but had attempted no settlement. Later, Vizcaino came and gave the place its name—"Port of the Kings." In the nineteenth century the whalers out of Cape Cod and Nantucket were to know the peninsula as a resting and trading station.

Much of the land to be included in this national seashore, at present under development for outdoor recreation, is still in private ownership and likely to remain so. But the 25,000 acres of cattle and dairy ranchland offer in themselves a beautiful pastoral scene. Visitors are asked to respect the rights of these landowners.

The gradual recreational development will provide for both freshwater and ocean swimming, fishing, campgrounds, picnic sites, and interpretive trails, with campfire programs. At any time one of the great attractions will be the sea lions who gather on the rocky beach at the end of the point. Several California state parks are nearby.

## 4. PADRE ISLAND NATIONAL SEASHORE
### [Texas]

MORE THAN A CENTURY AND A HALF HAS PASSED since Padre Nicolas Balli pastured his horses and cattle on this barrier island, reaching almost to the Mexican border (as it now is) from the bay of Corpus Christi. As cattle range, there were lusher pastures. The beef animals were long on horn and short on fat, but for those who had good teeth they developed real flavor.

Later, for generations, this was a seashore wilderness visited by few. There was no bulging population in southern Texas to move in upon the

Gulf front and speckle it with cottages. Sport gunners and fishermen and adventurers came across the shallow Laguna Madre that lay between the island and mainland, but the squirrels and coyotes and rabbits had the flatland behind the dunes as mostly an undisturbed reservation. Long before Father Balli ever saw it, the island was the refuge of brown and white pelicans, innumerable gulls, and herons and egrets. The ghost crabs scratched their burrows in the glistening white sand, ignorant of what a man looked like—something for which perhaps they had reason to be thankful. For man is the Great Predator, and it is only when he suddenly becomes alarmed at what he has done to the natural scene of which he is a part that he hurries to preserve the remnant and create a sanctuary which may curb his own rapacity.

Still later, when Texas reached the point where its people began to look around for places of public recreation that would be beyond the whim of private owners, a county park was set aside at the northern end of Padre Island, and another at the southern tip. In addition, some of the 113 miles of this seashore will remain long in private ownership. But as a gift of Texas, the federal government has come into possession of the submerged lands

*Underwater tidal life. Point Reyes National Seashore. [Photo: M. Woodbridge Williams]*

*What shall I do when I retire? A suggestion. Padre Island National Seashore.* [*Photo: M. Woodbridge Williams*]

within the boundary of this superb National Seashore, and the resulting wilderness strip of coast, eighty miles long and about as wide as the island itself, constitutes the largest of the seashores administered by the National Park Service.

This is a year-round place of outdoor recreation. The climate, winter and summer, is what you would expect of a shoreside park on about the same latitude as southern Florida. The great orange and grapefruit groves of the lower Rio Grande are nearby, and even if a biting, northerly wind comes down occasionally, it does not remain long.

Most visitors will come to fish, to swim, to watch the seabirds; perhaps just for a day's picnicking, perhaps for a camping week. The surf fishermen will be rewarded with redfish, trout, drum; and boat fishermen will find sailfish, tarpon, and other gamefish in the deeper Gulf waters.

But whatever reason we give for coming down to the sea, there may lie behind this lure of the strand a vaguer impulse: hard to define, but by most people keenly felt. It may go back to our very beginnings as human beings. Of the origin of mankind, it is believed that it was "riparian"—that is, beside either fresh or salt water. If this is true, in most of us the homing instinct is strong. Carl Sauer, in his *Land and Life,* says that "when all the land will be filled with people and machines perhaps the last need and observance will be, as it was at his beginning, to come down to experience the sea."

## 5. FIRE ISLAND NATIONAL SEASHORE
### [*New York*]

IT SO HAPPENED that I was in New York City on that September day in 1938 when a West Indian hurricane, taking an eccentric course, struck the Long Island and Rhode Island coasts with lethal fury and continued through New England, even across the Canadian border. The rain in metropolitan New York was torrential, but that was all. We did not know for some hours what had happened at Fire Island and Great South Bay, at New London and at Newport. A member of my club who owned a cottage on Fire Island told me several days later that he had not only been unable to find a remnant of his structure; he couldn't even locate exactly the spot where it had stood. Had the storm come before Labor Day, when recreation was at peak, the loss of life would have been ghastly.

Some time afterward I went down there to view the shambles. I felt convinced that few persons, even of the sort that loved the relatively isolated thirty-mile stretch of delightful beach, dune, and marshland, would ever risk an investment there again. How shortsighted of me! I had forgotten that after each outpouring from Vesuvius, the Italians have always returned with vine and flock. It is a prime factor perhaps in man's advance that he will take a chance, if it looks at least fifty-fifty.

And sure enough the "developments" came back; not merely villages of summer residents, but state, county, and town parks. Nature "came back," too, healing the battered dunes, filling the breaches, planting new seed for stabilizing grasses. But meanwhile, at the edge of the greatest population concentration in the nation, the very people who loved the place because of its somewhat isolated location were faced with proposals that would make the whole of the island a Sunday edition of Jones Beach. This is no sneer at Jones Beach. For what it is, and what it must necessarily be, it is a master-piece of devoted and brilliant management. But among ardent conservation-ists, and even among many Fire Island owners, the question was: cannot Fire

Island remain something different, looking forward to future years, when a seashore retaining a virgin quality will be such a precious possession? In September 1964, the President signed an act establishing Fire Island National Seashore "for the purpose of conserving and preserving for the use of future generations" its beaches as examples of unspoiled areas near urban centers.

Here is perhaps the greatest challenge to the Department of the Interior and to the National Park Service that has yet to be faced in the acquisition of seashores for the public use. For the congressional act, properly protecting individual rights, especially where ownership is in favor of maintaining the beautiful primitive scene, the vegetation, and the wildlife, implies that the process of entire restoration will be a slow one. Toward the ideal end, however, the job has already begun. It will be expensive; it will mean a program of conservation education; but it will be worth all it costs.

It must have been a halcyon day—that day when Fire Island National Seashore became a fact—for the ardent local group of preservationists who since 1960 have been wardens of the unusual "sunken forest," financing its protection and inviting to it those who can appreciate its beauty and strangeness. Who would expect to find these large hollies and sassafras trees, or black gums or maples, springing from the sands of a barrier reef? Yet, unique as it is, it is only a part of a beautiful plant cover that can be saved to delight generations to come.

## 6. ASSATEAGUE ISLAND NATIONAL SEASHORE
### [Maryland–Virginia]

ANNE MORROW LINDBERGH, writing in her lapidary prose style, some years ago offered a little book called *Gift from the Sea*. She had herself received from the ocean and beach an experience of the spirit, and she wished to share it with others. But she had a note of warning: "The sea does not reward those who are too anxious, too greedy, or too impatient. To dig for treasures shows not only impatience and greed, but lack of faith. Patience, patience, patience, is what the sea teaches. Patience and faith. One should lie empty, open, choiceless as a beach—waiting for a gift from the sea."

Perhaps it was not exactly in Mrs. Lindbergh's sense; yet in March 1962, the people of America received a gift from the sea. It was unexpected. The sea has no publicity department. The gift came in the form of a hurricane.

*Vegetation clothes the dunes and ties them down. Fire Island National Seashore. [Photo: M. Woodbridge Williams]*

## Assateague Island National Seashore

Let us go back a little. In 1935 the National Park Service had surveyed the coastline of the Atlantic and Gulf states, searching for unspoiled seashore that could be preserved for public enjoyment. Assateague Island, off the eastern shore of Maryland, was one of the strands that possessed all the desirable natural features. But the survey party did not recommend it. Private development had reached the point where acquisition seemed impossible. A fifteen-mile stretch south of the Sinepuxent Neck Bridge had already been subdivided, and there were already three thousand private owners, and many houses built. Too late!

Then came the hurricane. When the winds died down all but the sturdiest homes were overturned, and many were driftwood. The beautiful barrier reef, thirty-three miles along the Maryland and Virginia coasts and within easy reach of 34 million people, again became a possible reservation for outdoor recreation, federally owned and administered. A gift from the sea, was it not? On August 25, 1965, President Johnson signed the congressional act by which this precious bit of shoreline became a national seashore.

The sea gives, and the sea takes. These barrier beaches, so nearly on the level of the ocean, are subject to erosion of wind and wave. Indeed, that hurricane of 1962 was but one attack in a constant recession of the shore, especially at the northern tip of the island. A cedar forest that once grew on the shore and was overwhelmed by rising waters was revealed by the great storm. The tree stumps now dot a stretch of beach as mute testimony to the changing shoreline of Assateague, and the power of the elements.

As you near the southern end of the island—the final nine miles are within the Chincoteague National Wildlife Refuge—the vegetation becomes a notable feature, and here are the marshes where the famous wild ponies fatten on the grasses and the wildfowl gather in prodigious numbers. Occasionally a sika deer is seen. A difference of a few inches in elevation determines whether the loblolly and Virginia pines can have their feet out of brackish water.

All kinds of outdoor activity will be provided for at Assateague—boating and surf fishing, swimming, and even crabbing and digging for clams. But the recreative value will always be determined not by the activities available but by the place itself. To quote Anne Lindbergh again:

Rollers on the beach, wind in the pines, the slow flapping of herons across sand dunes, drown out the hectic rhythms of city and suburb, time tables and

*White pelicans winter luxuriously. Padre Island National Seashore.* [Photo: M. Woodbridge Williams]

schedules. One falls under their spell, relaxes, stretches out prone. One becomes, in fact, like the element on which one lies, flattened by the sea; bare, open, empty as the beach, erased by today's tides of all yesterday's scribblings.

*That* is the consolation of the sea. A gift to the needy.

## 7. CAPE LOOKOUT NATIONAL SEASHORE
### [*North Carolina*]

SEVENTH, AND LATEST, of the seashores that have been set aside for the physical and spiritual comfort of the nation's people (not forgetting our foreign friends, of course!) is this barrier bank of nearly sixty miles that extends down the North Carolina coastline from Ocracoke Island to the hook of Cape Lookout, then turns westward to Beaufort Inlet. This barrier reef is a primitive one, and its existence is unsuspected even by the millions who visit the three island "banks" that constitute the seashore styled "Hatteras."

In all, nearly sixty thousand acres are involved in this acquisition—but the word "acres," in relation to a barrier reef, hardly suffices to describe. Continually widening and indenting as the natural wave and wind action has been speeded or retarded by the storms that sweep it, Core Banks especially —the stretch that lies below Portsmouth Island—stands in need of restoration. Fortunately this is something that man's skill can do almost as easily—but not quite—as it can destroy. It takes time and labor to tie the bare dunes down with vegetation; but given a chance, nature gladly takes over. North Carolina, which acted with such prudent generosity in the case of Hatteras, has already acquired four fifths of the desirable recreational area and given it to the federal government.

Unlike Fire Island, this new seashore did not pose problems of redemption from private ownership. There is a little village at Portsmouth, on the island just across Ocracoke Inlet; and at the other end the Shackleford Banks have some holly, oak, myrtle, and red cedar. But otherwise the sand bar, broken across by a number of inlets, is just dune and flat and marsh. And who wants better than that, when it is stabilized? What more does one come to do and to see and to enjoy? I understand that the director of the National Park Service, on his inspection trip to the area, kicked off his shoes, climbed barefoot over the dunes, and declared the place "simply terrific." Well, why not?

*Old Coast Guard station. Assateague Island National Seashore.* [*Photo: M. Woodbridge Williams*]

Think forward to the millions of Americans who will be able to do the same, with no signs that say, "Private Property—Keep Off."

All the delights of seashore recreation, which do not require mechanization, are here in prospect. The sea birds will come in great numbers, the sport fisherman will take part of the harvest that now goes to commerce. Such development for public use as is necessary can be confined to a hundred or more acres on the mainland, with perhaps a ferry or causeway to take visitors to a day-use area on Shackleford Banks. Core Banks and Portsmouth Island could well remain roadless, with access by boat and simple facilities for hikers and campers. It is all in the planning stage so far; but the main point is that

*Where the tides creep into the land. Assateague Island National Seashore. [Photo: M. Woodbridge Williams]*

this *is* the newest seashore, and preserved against all enemies but the sea. If the sea, in partnership with the wind, makes an occasional foray—well, that is a part of the natural history we really aim to keep alive.

Nor, in spite of its remoteness today, does this strip of seashore lack historical interest. The huts of whale fishermen once were frequent along Core Banks, built not only by the hardy men who made homes here on the Carolina coast, but by eager New Bedford and Nantucket sea hunters, too. Portsmouth was once a place of more than five hundred "frontier" folks. Now it has more houses than people. In the mid-18th century, corsairs, sniffing loot, cruised along these lower banks.

*An overwhelmed cedar grove once grew here. Assateague Island National Seashore.*
[*Photo: Robert K. Bergman*]

# [ I I ]

# *The Parkways*

## 1. BLUE RIDGE PARKWAY
### [*Virginia–North Carolina*]

A COMPUTER IS . . . A COMPUTER. Far be it from me to let myself become involved in a discussion of the qualities and possibilities of a mechanism which I do not understand, or to venture into a field where I have no place. Some of my friends have told me, in a kind of awed ecstasy, that this truly wonderful device "almost thinks." It may be so. That makes me want to defend mankind against the menace of a potential monster; and thus I reply that the difference between almost-thinking and thinking is so great that it can be expressed only in terms of light-years. It seems to me akin to the difference between a contract and a quasi-contract. The latter isn't a contract. It is just a quasi, as has been frequently and annoyingly revealed.

The computer, I hazard to assume, makes no decisions. It does not declare war; it does not get married; it does not go into debt. It ponders no abstractions: justice, beauty, good. If you want those parameters in, put them in if you think you can. What comes out will supply the basis on which somebody can make a decision. The speed with which the output pours forth is the amazing, the revolutionary, thing. Already commerce is a changed affair, and the politician views the computer with fearful respect.

These modest reflections come to me because I lately heard that a certain Western municipality, planning a highway, used the computer to lighten the chores. Relative cost of land acquisition, exit roads, population factors, traffic considerations: all those engineering details that had formerly exhausted so much time and patience. The machine did a fine job. It is inherent in it that it should. It was not the computer's fault that when the highway was completed, it had cut right through the city's finest park. That vital parameter,

---

*Tidewater creeps up through the marshes along the way to Yorktown. Colonial Parkway. [Photo: M. Woodbridge Williams]*

*Mabry Mill—the word "photogenic" could have originated here. Blue Ridge Parkway. [Photo: M. Woodbridge Williams]*

of the value of the preservation of beauty, had not been part of the input. Almost-thinking proved an illusion. Thinking will remain, for some time at least, the activity of persons. And, more than thinking, feeling.

I had such thoughts in mind on an April day, going down the Blue Ridge Parkway, when I stopped at one of the overlooks where a self-guided trail takes off into the forest. The wind was northerly and chill, but I found a place where I could beg a backrest from a matronly tulip poplar, shielded from the breeze. "Pardon me, madam; may I recline against your warm back?"

My mind went back a good many years, to the day when I first drove a section of this Appalachian avenue. I don't remember how many miles of it had then been opened. I do recall that about 1950 I wrote that about two thirds of it could be traversed. Now, as I write again, only a few miles of the total project remain to be completed. I said formerly that it would be one of the great scenic highways of the world. It is. Four hundred and sixty-nine miles of ribbon park.

The thought came to me that for most of the years of construction the engineers must have had to do a tremendous amount of time-consuming figuring. The only computer in those earlier days was an adding machine. I suppose, in a sense, the modern marvel is still an adding machine, but with an incredible extension of powers.

But it seemed good to realize that those landscape architects and other planners and doers of this parkway had in their minds primarily that though this was to be recreation, this journey into human and natural history, it was never to be forgotten that it was also to be a sojourn in an outdoor museum where all that was beautiful could remain so, and that nothing of disharmony should creep in. To what an astonishing degree this ideal has been achieved!

I wonder how many people had used any part of the Blue Ridge Parkway when I was writing about it in 1950? My statistical computer-user tells me that "approximately *eight million* visits were made to it in 1965." It led all

*Tranquil resting spot near the Peaks of Otter. Blue Ridge Parkway. [Photo: W. E. Dutton]*

but the numerous attractions offered by the great National Capital Parks complex.

Again I look back to what I wrote. "Connecting Great Smoky Mountains National Park, which sits astride the Tennessee and North Carolina boundary, with Shenandoah National Park, in Virginia, is the Blue Ridge Parkway." Very crisply said, sir; go on from there!

Distinctly, this is not a highway for anyone who wishes to go somewhere in a hurry. It is not like the highways that have been advantageously built as access roads to our great cities. This is a road the holiday-maker will browse upon, like a booklover among rare and beautiful volumes, stopping every little while to look upon a scene that has no counterpart in America. These are the Southern Highlands, and for miles upon miles you pass the fences of split rails, the weathered cabins, the livestock, and the barns of the people who have lived here so long.

Where the road has been engineered to offer as much interest and beauty as possible, the cuts and fills have been and are being planted with the native shrubs and trees—the white pine, azaleas, rhododendrons. This is one road where, because the highway is protected by a buffer strip, the traveler will not be importuned to use any particular shaving cream, dentifrice, or chewing gum. There are no signs suggesting that you come in just as you are and eat at a restaurant that went out of business several years ago. If you wish advice on what pills to take for your special misery, you will have to leave the Blue Ridge Parkway and use one of the older routes.

Well, retrospectively, I believe this wasn't bad. It had a good measure of enthusiasm. But as I now see it, and now go up or down the parkway, that chapter sounds a bit stingy. I suppose I may have felt cramped for space. That is a ready escape hatch for an author. I certainly didn't give Linnville Falls—the gift of a lover of beauty, John D. Rockefeller, Jr.—their due notice. I did not mention the Moses H. Cone Memorial Park, mile 292 on the log, with its twenty-five miles of horse and carriage trails. And Mabry Mill! How could I have neglected that masterpiece, so photogenic that the worst duffer with a camera has been unable to make a failure of it, unless he superimposed it on a picture of Uncle James?

Forgivable was the lack of mention of certain other features of the parkway, because they hadn't then come into existence; at least as part of the present scene. Well, the Blue Ridge Parkway is so well known (eight million visitors in one year!) now that it doesn't need the advertising I rather skimpily gave it in 1950 or thereabouts.

[394]

## 2. NATCHEZ TRACE PARKWAY
### [*Mississippi–Tennessee–Alabama*]

NASHVILLE WAS THE POINT to which the footsore or muleback travelers of the old Natchez Trace were used to look with eager expectation. My friend and I, one early spring day when the redbud and the dogwood were blended upon the hillsides, were also following the Trace, but we were going in the opposite direction. They had it hard; we were pampered wayfarers with benefit of rubber tires. Yet, even in an automobile you may encounter discomfort; it looked like rain after we had left Cunningham's Ridge, just south of Leiper's Fork, and county roads, though good enough when dry, can become well greased under a drizzle.

At Cunningham's Ridge, not far from the home of Thomas Hart Benton, statesman and historian, we had left the car and footed it with great joy along a stretch of the very ground where so many thousands of pioneer travelers had slogged. That, my friends, is a real thrill, for American history is walking with you. You bunt your booted toes against the stones of the ancient trail just as did the Kentucky boatmen when they toiled, cursing their pedestrian fate, toward home. The French traders went along this ancient path; so did the missionaries whose zeal to bring the Light to the Indians led them to become bedfellows of roisterers and thieves; and long, long before all these the ancestors of our historic Indians went bartering for the exotic things they craved from far-off tribes. No road is fuller of romance than this—the Natchez Trace.

When the French first explored and mapped this land they saw a trail running from the home of the Natchez Indians to the villages of the Choctaws and the Chickasaws in northeast Mississippi. And horrible was the vengeance taken by the armed French against these Natchez in 1729, following the massacre of their compatriots who had settled on the river bluffs and in the St. Catherine Creek valley. The Indians had grievances and struck with blind rage, killing men, women, and children. The French replied in kind, and when it was over, all who were left of the Natchez nation were sold into slavery or managed to escape to the Chickasaw people, who received them with a hospitality that was to make trouble for the hosts in later time.

Before we go forward toward Natchez, let us pause a moment to consider what this Natchez Trace Parkway really is, or will be when it is completed. You may call it, if you like, an elongated National Park. For about 450 miles it will be a motor road with ample space upon either side to preserve

*Sunken road near the southern end of the trail. Natchez Trace Parkway. [Photo: M. Woodbridge Williams]*

the natural scenery of the route. Here it will show a meadow; there a copse of native trees, some perhaps dating from Indian-treaty time; over there a hillside farm, its natural operations undisturbed.

The parkway does not, of course, follow the identical ancient trail. It crosses and recrosses it, giving easy access to the historic spots along the route —the "stands" where travelers got bed and board at the end of their day, the ferry sites, the Indian mounds, and many spots where the native plantlife may be studied and enjoyed. Now and again the parkway traveler will see the Trace where it moves furtively off into the underbrush—always unmistakably the old Trace, however, even though nobody pursues it today.

Distinctly this is not a parkway for speeding or for local convenience in going places. In its finest aspect, it will endure for future generations as an outdoor museum of human history, of quietly beautiful scenery and of the

*The plodding "Kaintuck" boatmen were near home at this part of the trail. Natchez Trace Parkway. [Photo: Tennessee Conservation Department]*

ways of nature. Happiest, to my mind, of all the visitors to the region will be those who leave their automobiles at some proper point and follow a piece of the Trace afoot. That is the ideal journey into the past, and in some shaded spot, on a genial day, thoughtful ones will sit on a fallen tree and meditate upon the ways of men, weaving their own short experience into the tapestry of time and change.

So, at some point along the Natchez Trace, we re-create the motley procession passing by, following the ridges, even though steep and stony, to avoid the swamps and streams. First the aboriginal people, the excavations of whose ceremonial and burial mounds telling us how they lived; then their descendants, either on the warpath or on a peaceful trading journey; next the hardy explorers—Spanish, French, English; and after them our own colonials, engaged in that westward push which so many of our National Monuments commemorate. We see the boatmen of Kaintuck, who floated their rude boats down the Ohio and Mississippi into New Orleans and there broke them up for the lumber they contained. The steamboat had not come to the Great River, and against its current they could not return home the way they came. This Trace they took.

First, after leaving Natchez, they made their way upon the soft, loose, easily eroded soil; and that is why, today, if you leave your car and tramp awhile, you will go along sunken roads with high vertical sides, walking on a level below even the tree roots of the forest. Not at all like the thin, stony path the Trace becomes farther north, when sometimes it goes upon a limestone outcrop supporting only scrubby growth.

And here, as we watch, comes "Old Hickory," Andrew Jackson, indignantly marching his stalwart followers back from Natchez when he was ordered to disband them; and again we see Jackson's men returning victorious from the Battle of New Orleans; and with Jackson comes a circuit rider, a government official, and sundry vagrants who have attached themselves to the troop for security and the chance to mooch their rations. And then there is the ill-starred Meriwether Lewis, friend of Thomas Jefferson and co-leader with Clark on the epic journey to the Pacific Northwest. His violent death, for many years thought to have been a murder, occurred at Grinder's Stand— one of the rough taverns of the Trace, in Tennessee.

Not least among the shadowy figures that haunt the Trace are those vigorous missionaries, either sent forth by established churches to carry the gospel to the benighted or evangelizing by personal inspiration: James Hall, the Presbyterian on horseback in 1801; the eccentric Methodist Lorenzo Dow, the "crazy preacher" from Connecticut, sallow, lean and hard, holding forth to the sinners of the grogshops; Jacob Young with his band of five, undeterred by reports from the white tavernkeepers that the Indians "would be unimpressed by preaching."

The American settlers were moving in, meanwhile, and so came demands for regular mail service along the Trace. At first the Washington authorities were doubtful; the Postmaster General complained that the Natchez Trace was only "an Indian footpath, very devious and narrow." Well, so it was, until the United States troops were called upon to clear a wagon road and bridge the creeks, finally shortening the distance from the Mississippi terminus to Nashville by at least a hundred miles.

One thing remains of the Choctaw culture. Perhaps because their language was more adaptable than that of the neighboring tribes and so became in a modified form a sort of trading tongue along the lower Mississippi region,

*A ruin can be beautiful. Tower of the brick church at Jamestown. Colonial Parkway.*
[*Photo: M. Woodbridge Williams*]

this country along the Natchez Trace abounds with a delightful and racy nomenclature. Bogue Chitto, so common in Mississippi, is Big Creek. Shocka-loo Creek is really Cypress Creek. And that Dancing Rabbit Creek, the scene of an Indian treaty, was Chukfi Ahihla Bok, and in the words you can almost see what the Choctaw observer one day saw there—an Uncle Remus rabbit doing a jig.

But the whites, after they took possession were also quite able to give challenging names. By-wy Creek, Sugar-tree Hollow, Coon Box, Buzzard's Roost, Crippled Deer Creek, Many Panther Creek, Trimcane Creek (the

kind of cane growing here was woven into baskets by the Choctaw women)
—these are a few of the names that delighted my companion and me as we
went across, around, and along the Natchez Trace on those delightful April
days.

### 3. COLONIAL PARKWAY AND COLONIAL NATIONAL
### HISTORICAL PARK
#### [*Virginia*]

IN COMPARISON WITH THE BLUE RIDGE PARKWAY and Natchez Trace Parkway, this one is short indeed. But its twenty-two miles represent a gentle
conspiracy between the historian and the landscape architect to the end that
the traveler in the classic triangle that includes Jamestown, Colonial Williamsburg, and Yorktown shall have the fairest possible experience with the beauty
of the Tidewater Virginia into which Englishmen first came for permanent
settlement. From planning to execution to maintenance this highroad has
always been a labor of love. It follows no pathways of early days. Rather, it
traverses an unspoiled ribbon of countryside and brings one to the gates of
cherished historic memorials.

Jamestown, Williamsburg, Yorktown—one chapter of our national story
led inevitably to the next. So we begin the journey into the past at Jamestown
Island. It was close to the shore of the James River that the newcomers built
their stockaded fort. For health it was not the wisest choice. But at their
backs were an uncharted wilderness and a savage people. They were unweaned
from their homeland; and so long as they were at the waterside they were
assured that the way back to the white cliffs of Dover was open.

The parkway runs across Powhatan Creek and eastward along the James
for a few miles, then turns off into the woods. The forest is not spectacular,
but soothing. Of course there will be no billboards. You will not miss them.
Then a tunnel lets you pass under Williamsburg: an excellent idea because
the restored city does not need more traffic, and you will do best to see it
afoot.

The Williamsburg Information Center is just beyond the tunnel. Williamsburg advertises itself. You may have seen the advertising—restrained yet
alluring, messages that make one want to march for a moment in this procession of people and events. Thanks to the generosity and wisdom of John D.
Rockefeller, Jr., this restoration is not for profit. It therefore advertises not
for customers but for beneficiaries. The interpretation of life as it was lived
in this second provincial capital is here admirably done, and of course the

felicity with which the restoration work was accomplished is known wherever taste and talent exist.

Your destination is Yorktown. From the woodsy surroundings the way comes out on blue water—the York River, really an estuary at this point. Six miles, along which there are pleasant overlooks and instructive historical markers, and then you are at the city, which in the eighteenth century was a busy mart and port, and where the American Revolution came virtually to its close in 1781. In this famous spot where Cornwallis surrendered to Washington and his French allies, a self-guided motor trip will take you from the visitor center (where Washington's actual military tents can be seen) to the Siege Line and the redoubts with old cannon in place. Thence you will wish to go about the present-day Yorktown, where there is not much that is of Washington's day, but that little remainder is precious.

Preserved as a part of Colonial National Historical Park is Cape Henry Memorial, where the emigrant Englishmen saw the "Land of Virginia," "about foure o'clock in the morning" of April 26, 1607, and rejoiced that their voyage in their three small ships had been fortunate. Here they remained for four days, after claiming the country for God and king. It was 174 years before one of these proprietors was eliminated.

# [ I I I ]

# *National Recreation Areas*

## 1. LAKE MEAD NATIONAL RECREATION AREA
### [*Arizona–Nevada*]

WITHIN THE VAST AREA, land and water, where two lakes were created by the damming of the scouring Colorado River, visitors may swim, boat, fish, water ski, skin dive, camp, hike, or just drive the hundreds of miles of road. But, also, they may observe and study extraordinary rock formations; delight their eyes with the red and yellow splendor such as that in Iceberg Canyon; or watch the great variety of birds from hummingbirds to eagles. Wild burros, desert bighorn, and a number of smaller mammals make their homes here; the great forest of Joshua trees is found on the Pierce Ferry road; on the high plateaus of Shivwits and Hualpai is piñon and juniper wilderness.

With these facts in mind the reader may well ask, "How does this differ from a national park? Why do you call it a national recreation area?" Good questions; and since we fortunate Americans should not only know our parks, but also have awareness of the management policies that govern them in preservation and use, this seems a favorable moment for explanation.

In midsummer of 1964 a Secretary of the Interior sent to the director of the National Park Service a memorandum titled "Management of the National Park System." It was not a revolutionary document, but it was a highly important one. It was based upon long and careful studies of the great changes that had taken place in American life since the Park Service came into being half a century before. This means the phenomenal mobility, the increase of leisure, the greatly increased take-home income, and the consequent urgent need for more and more opportunities for outdoor recreation for the exploding population growth.

---

*Lake life: aquatic forms. Lake Mead National Recreation Area. [Photo: Fred Mang, Jr.]*

The memorandum was a study within a study. It sought not only a reassessment with a view toward necessary changes; it studied the older principles and policies to see how much could be retained and even emphasized. And much remains as it was. The natural areas will be, as was stated by Secretary Lane in 1918, "maintained in absolutely unimpaired form for the use of future generations." In historical areas the memorial purpose is paramount, but use of natural resources can be made when it offers no detriment. But in the recreational areas the emphasis will be upon "outdoor recreation." The area has a "recreation mission." There may be other values within the area, and these may be utilized for public enjoyment. But they are a plus. Outdoor recreation is the dominant resource.

Also you find another plus, not mentioned in the memorandum but inherent, that will apply in cases where dams like Hoover and Davis have created these manmade places of outdoor recreation. The dam itself becomes part of the enjoyment offered. Man cannot hope to rival nature's wonders, but he can produce a work of gigantic skill. Though built in the period 1931–5, Hoover Dam remains the tallest dam in the western hemisphere. From the road across the top visitors look down 726 feet to the base rock. The entire flow of the Colorado River for two whole years can be stored behind this wall. Davis Dam, behind which Lake Mohave forms, is not so high, but has a longer span. Indeed, these dams are memorials of American technology. So it is three-way: physical recreation, history, the grand natural scene.

Nobody has yet found a satisfactory definition for the word *recreation*. However, it isn't necessary to define it. Observing the way visitors to these two manmade lakes find and constantly change their diversions would provide a better definition than any word. For example, the fisherman comes here. He may think he is interested only in fishing. But he finds himself using a boat for water adventuring. The tourist, perhaps on his way to Grand Canyon or Yosemite, stops to have a look at the dams. The clear, clean, and buoyant nature of the surroundings exercise their allure, and you find him back as a camper, in one of the many designated campgrounds or even in an isolated spot on the lakeside.

Or the weekender, usually from one of the adjoining states, who comes in "just to have a look" finds so much to interest him that when the summer heat has subsided he returns with a trailer. Just to relax and forget the naughty, irritating world? That is what he tells himself, but he hears a campground slide talk, or sees an exhibit at a visitor center, and decides he wants to know more about the wildlife, the geology, or the prehistoric people who

*Uncrowded spaces for the fisherman. Lake Mead National Recreation Area. [Photo: R. C. Middleton, Bureau of Reclamation]*

left their picture stories on the canyon walls along the shore of Lake Mohave.

Without a doubt, it is the great area of water surface which forms the primary attraction. "Our folks down this way have a hunger for water," a park director told me once in Oklahoma. "Or maybe I should say 'thirst.' " I replied that I thought his word *hunger* was the better, because it really wasn't that they lacked water to drink. Their craving was for the feeling, the eye-soothing presence of a hill-bordered lake, an invitation to swim in it, or skim over it. Yes, *hunger* is the word. Even those of us who come from the regions of glacier-formed lakes feel the ceaseless urge to return and refresh.

It was within the Lake Mead–Lake Mohave area that some of the significant events of the famous expeditions of Major John Wesley Powell occurred. Much has been learned of the geology of the country through which this river takes its winding course. Yet there are still baffling mysteries. My favorite geologist tells me that it is in the Lake Mead region and below that answers to questions about the Colorado River will be found.

## 2. COULEE DAM NATIONAL RECREATION AREA
### [*Washington*]

FROM MAY THROUGH OCTOBER this is a region of almost continuous sunshine. There may be morning mists, but they burn off just as the unaccustomed visitor had resigned himself to a cloudy day. A wind begins to blow down over Lake Roosevelt from the surrounding hills and fills the sails of those who regard this kind of boating as the sport of kings. But there are other kinds of craft, too; and there is no restriction on the size of them, though they must be handled with respect for the rights of others. Swimming, of course, is the favorite sport on the twelve developed beaches along the shore of the lake and in many other places.

Fishing, yes; and improving each year. At the mouths of the creeks you may get trout, though the Kamloops breed will be found farther out in the colder waters. Up the creeks and in Banks Lake are rainbows, bass, pike, and crappies.

A good way to begin acquaintance with this huge manmade body of water, created by halting and harnessing the Columbia River, is to see the dam and the impoundment from the lookout point about two miles from the town of Coulee Dam. Here is the dam from above; on one side the immense concrete face and on the other the blue waters of the lake. The Bureau of Reclamation, which operates the dam, offers free sightseeing tours on a self-guiding basis. During the long summer season, lights play a variety of color combinations upon the water that curtains down the face of the massive structure.

Even though the emphasis may be on the various kinds of physical recreation, visitors can hardly fail to be aware that the natural surroundings are most unusual. What is the meaning of this prodigious gorge, with its columnar cliffs that so plainly indicate that they were built up a little at a time? The many layers are clearly delineated from any point in the bottom of the canyon. To the geologist it is all relatively simple. With a little interpretation, the whole story is not hard for the layman to grasp. And in terms of

*On the Trinity Division. Whiskeytown-Shasta-Trinity National Recreation Area.* [*Photo: L. K. Noonan, Bureau of Reclamation*]

geologic time it all took place just a short time ago. In all the western hemisphere there is nothing comparable in magnitude to the flows of lava out of which the present scene was created.

The lava squeezed out of earth rifts that developed in the regions to the south. Not as one great flow—there were long inactive periods. But the lava kept coming until it piled up a plateau that in places reached a height of four thousand feet. That was the first chapter. As the lava surface rose, it naturally blocked the rivers in its path, and the great Columbia was forced out of its course.

The latest advance of the ice age arrived, and thousand-foot sheets moved southwesterly out of the Canadian mountains. This time, the new blocking created a glacial lake about where Franklin D. Roosevelt Lake now spreads, though it was much larger. The cutting of the coulee was done by the immense volume of water, made abrasive with sand and pebbles, which spilled over the edge of this glacial lake.

A short distance south of Banks Lake is Dry Falls State Park. Visitors who wish to understand the geological story will do well to visit that area. One could call it a preface to the recreation area.

## 3. GLEN CANYON NATIONAL RECREATION AREA
### [*Arizona–Utah*]

CONSIDERING THE VAST EXTENT and variety of the areas included under the administration of the National Park Service, visitors encounter surprisingly few "don'ts" in their recreational enjoyments. Wherever such warnings appear, they relate either to normal good social conduct with a regard for the rights and welfare of all, or to the safety of the individual.

Here is an example of what I mean. The folder that invites us to make use of the recreational facilities which have been created by the Glen Canyon Dam and its resultant Lake Powell has a word of caution. "The water of the lake is deep, right to the shoreline in most places, and—especially in side canyons—the smooth vertical cliff walls offer a swimmer no handholds . . . swimming in Lake Powell is not for the beginner . . . taking these warnings into account you will find some delightful coves such as those in Last Chance Canyon."

One incidentally gets from this warning a pretty clear picture of what

*Major John Wesley Powell gave the canyon its name. Glen Canyon National Recreation Area. [Photo: W. L. Rusho, Bureau of Reclamation]*

this part of the Colorado River looked like before the waters were impounded: the deep, sheer walls of the brick-red Navajo sandstone that represent wind-blown sand dunes, and the sedimentary rocks at Wahweap that tell of an ancient sea which once covered the region. With Major Powell on his second trip down the great river was Frederick S. Dellenbaugh. It was in October, he said, that Powell came to this labyrinth, then called Mound, but later consolidated with the part below called Monument, and "altogether now standing as Glen Canyon."

"The walls," said Dellenbaugh, "were strangely cut up by narrow side canyons, some not more than twenty feet wide, and twisting back a quarter of a mile where they expanded into huge amphitheaters, domes and cave-like." Now, deeply covered by the water of the lake (and obviously with no handholds for a swimmer), these side canyons form mystically beautiful avenues of adventure for the prudent man with a boat.

The Navajo Reservation forms the southern boundary of Glen Canyon National Recreation Area. The Indians, conservation-minded, with tribal parks of their own, invite all visitors to see their way of life, their flocks of sheep and goats, and their round houses called hogans.

For fishermen there have been plantings in the lake of rainbow trout, kokanee salmon, and largemouth bass. Catfish needed no introduction. They have ruled the river over the centuries; and speaking only for himself, the present writer finds them the best eating of all. Perhaps a plebeian taste, but my own.

Just as the catfish has so long called this entrancingly lovely country his own, so did the beaver. It is hoped that this competent rodent will adapt to the fluctuations of a manmade lake, and return to build his houses.

From Wahweap Campground, where there are campsites for both tents and trailers, it is now less than sixty miles by boat and trail to Rainbow Bridge National Monument.

### 4. WHISKEYTOWN-SHASTA-TRINITY NATIONAL RECREATION AREA
#### [California]

IF THE NAME Whiskeytown brings into your mind an image of the bearded and wool-shirted miners of the California gold rush, you will not be in error.

*The breeze is 'long shore. Shadow Mountain National Recreation Area. [Photo: L. C. Axthelme, Bureau of Reclamation]*

It was not long after the strike at Sutter's Mill that Clear Creek began to yield its placer wealth. Whiskey Creek flows into one side of the recreation area and Brandy Creek on the other. The strength of the stimulant reflected, perhaps, the relative size of the nuggets that were panned from the gravel in those feverish days.

The coarse gold played out. You could still get a "showing" in any of those creekbeds, but it would be a tough way to make a living. Instead, people are now coming here from San Francisco, Portland, and Sacramento to make use of the golden opportunities to camp and picnic and fish, surrounded by some of the most charming scenery in northern California.

The dam and reservoir are features of the Trinity River section of the Bureau of Reclamation's Central Valley project, making multiple use of the excess waters of a stream that formerly raced to the ocean. First stored behind Trinity Dam for a powerplant, later carried in a tunnel through the Hadley Peaks and down to another source of electric energy, the water finally enters Whiskeytown Lake to create a surface area of 3,600 acres. Before the needs of man are satisfied, the same water will have joined the Sacramento River for irrigation and other purposes. Altogether an elaborate and carefully studied engineering project!

The movement of earth incident to the building of a huge dam—this one is 272 feet above the streambed—necessarily effects a disturbing change upon the local landscape. As restoration gradually takes place, however, some of the working trails of the constructors will be maintained for hiking and horseback riding, leading through thickets of toyon and manzanita and offering fine views of the lake.

Not the least interesting thing about the Whiskeytown Dam is the fact that the water is released through two outlets of different levels, blending the warmer and cold waters of the impoundment, just as you would turn on both faucets in your washbowl. The reason is (as you may have guessed already) that the salmon and steelhead trout which use Clear Creek as a spawning ground require a certain water temperature for their reproductory process. Since fish are not notably communicative to man, they have only one way to signal whether the temperature is right or wrong: they either spawn or they don't. Here is where preliminary research pays off. We don't have to find out the hard way.

## 5. SHADOW MOUNTAIN NATIONAL RECREATION AREA
### [*Colorado*]

IT HAS GENERALLY BEEN TAUGHT that the Continental Divide decides whether the precipitation that falls in the Rocky Mountains shall wend toward the Pacific or the Atlantic Ocean. This information remains accurate, but with the addition of the clause: "provided man's applied scientific ability does not rule otherwise." The Colorado–Big Thompson reclamation project takes surplus water from the Colorado River Valley west of the Divide, flows it through a thirteen-mile tunnel underneath the towering peaks, and turns it into the valley of the South Platte in eastern Colorado.

Apparently nature is not hastily vengeful, even though this impertinence comes close to being the unforgivable pride which the ancient Greeks called *hubris*. Nothing serious has happened yet. On the contrary, in the progress of this water diversion several other diversions have come into existence: ample facilities for boating and fishing, picnicking, camping, and hiking in the recreational area thus created. Grand Lake is, of course, a natural body of water, long known and enjoyed; but now there are two manmade lakes, Shadow Mountain and Granby, both of them much larger than the glacial one. Intensive use of the area, which even at present offers many possibilities for the vacationer, is planned by the National Park Service by agreement with the Bureau of Reclamation and Bureau of Land Management.

These three lakes in the valley of the Colorado are in the high region that was torn and reshaped during the most recent period of geologic history when ice covered much of the North American continent. Many of the islands in the lakes are the tops of hills which represent the accumulation of rock and sand plucked and milled by the irresistibly flowing ice sheet. The forest is not varied, being for the most part lodgepole pine and aspen—quaking aspen, the tree that flutters its leaves when there is not a noticeable breath of wind. Curious lovers of trees—I don't mean professional botanists but just outdoor folks—have discovered by examining the leaf stem just how the quaking comes about.

The lakes are open to fishing all the year, but regulations and permits are those of Colorado. There are brook trout as well as cutthroat, rainbow, and brown; in the manmade lakes the kokanee, or landlock sockeye, salmon is caught.

Visitors have a choice of several fine campgrounds, where housetrailers are accommodated. Picnic anywhere you like in the areas open to public use—

*With a dog as pilot. Flaming Gorge National Recreation Area. [Photo: Stan Rasmussen, Bureau of Reclamation]*

but be a good housekeeper! Riding horses may be rented in the town of Grand Lake. As to hunting, the laws of Colorado apply.

There are many privately owned boat docks where rentals can be arranged, or if you bring your own you can launch it at no cost.

## 6. Flaming Gorge National Recreation Area
### [*Utah–Wyoming*]

The impounded waters of the Colorado River at Flaming Gorge have created a lake that extends upstream for ninety miles, almost reaching the city of Green River, Wyoming. You are in truly historic country here. It was about at this point that Major John Wesley Powell put his boats in the stream in 1869. The hardy one-armed Civil War veteran began his voyage into the unknown, literally betting his life upon a generalization he had made from his knowledge of geological processes. Many intelligent men avowed that there *must* be great falls in the Colorado. They said it was inevitable. If there were, Powell and his companions would not have a chance. They could not retreat, once they entered the canyon.

Powell said no; there were no falls. Rough waters, undoubtedly; not falls. He later told Dr. William H. Brewer of Yale that he was perfectly convinced that a river so loaded with silt and abrasive material would have long since scoured its bed down to almost an even grade. But he felt sure also that it would be a wild journey.

Again, two years later, and better equipped, Powell essayed the second conquest of the river. Dellenbaugh, who was with him this time and who wrote the story of the expedition, says that when they left Green River

there was a gale . . . filling the eyes with sharp sand. But we could see high up before us some bright red rocks, making the first canyon of the wonderful series that separates this river from the common world.

From these bright rocks, glowing in the sunlight like a flame above the grey-green of the ridge, the major [Powell] had bestowed on this place the name of Flaming Gorge. We were now at the beginning of the battle with the "sunken river."

This recreational area is under the joint administration of the National Park Service and the Forest Service. The southern part, the most scenic canyon sector, is within Ashley National Forest. To the north, centering around Green River city, the rolling rangelands with their typical wildlife are bulging with memories of the pioneers like Jim Bridger—the roguish trader who invented fantastic fables to tell the tenderfeet in revenge for their disbelief in his true stories of the wilderness marvels. Jim was here, and many other mountain men ranged this territory where Indians fished, trapped, and hunted.

# [ I V ]

# *Wild Rivers*

Toward the end of the eighteenth century Samuel Taylor Coleridge, the English poet-philosopher, went to Germany. He has left us a bitter epigram in verse, descriptive of what humans achieve when they congregate in large numbers upon a river that nature offered as a clean, sparkling, and free-flowing stream:

> In Köln, a town of monks and bones,
> And pavements fanged with murderous stones,
> And rags, and hags and hideous wenches
> I counted two-and-seventy stenches,
> All well-defined and separate stinks!
> Ye nymphs that reign o'er sewers and sinks
> The river Rhine, it is well known,
> Doth wash your city of Cologne,
> But tell me, nymphs, what power divine
> Shall henceforth wash the river Rhine?

Yet, at about the time that Coleridge was venting his disgust, a substantial citizen of the young American republic, living in New Hampshire just south of Concord, was noting in his diary that "three of us went down to the river today and catched a good lot of fish which is just now helpful and the Lord continue his mercy." And what were these helpful fish? They were the delectable Atlantic salmon, running up the Merrimack River toward its headwaters. Not only up the Merrimack they swam, but the Maine rivers,

---

*Unpolluted, serene, a river preserved for the delight of posterity. Ozark National Scenic Riverways. [Photo: Gerald R. Massie]*

and the Connecticut, and even the Hudson. And now? What self-respecting salmon would be found in those nauseous corrupted streams?

The story is old; it repeats itself with the insistence of a whippoorwill. When Caesar was in Gaul the Rhine was one of those unpolluted rivers, and so was the Seine, and the Loire and the Thames and the Danube. Still, nobody today would wish to return to the age of the Roman republic, when the life expectancy was about thirty-five years and the luxuries of the rich were less in quantity and quality than what the modern man now considers a minimum requirement. Every technical advance in the creation of economic welfare, save perhaps the use of the oceans as highroads, is necessarily an attack upon the landscape and upon nonrenewable resources. The diminution of natural beauty, and the effect of that aesthetic loss on humans, is the price paid for easier labor, for conveniences, for longer if less placid lives, for mobility and its various rewards. It becomes a question of preserving the benefits of exploitation while curbing the losses. A fast-growing nation is not likely to make much effort toward a discreet balance in this respect. "Take the cash and let the credit go." There are always a few farsighted thinkers, like Dr. George P. Marsh, who in 1874 published a warning book with the clumsy title: "The Earth as Modified by Human Action." The volume had few readers. But within the past few years more and more people have realized the importance of checking the prodigal and dangerous pollution and abuse of those precious resources, the American rivers.

In early 1961 the Senate Select Committee on National Water Resources recommended that "certain streams be preserved in their free-flowing condition because their natural scenic, scientific, aesthetic and recreational value outweigh their value for water development and control purposes now and in the future." The Secretary of the Interior and Secretary of Agriculture joined to appoint a study team to determine what rivers might be suitable in a nationwide system. Such a study was made. It was a fine start, but like all such innovations, it needed the voice of the highest authority. When President Johnson, on February 8, 1965, transmitted to the Congress his message "On Natural Beauty of Our Country," he said in blunt terms ". . . the time has come to identify and preserve free-flowing stretches of our great scenic rivers before growth and development make the beauty of the unspoiled waterway a memory. To this end I will shortly send to Congress a bill to establish a *national wild rivers system*." The hour had struck.

---

*Where the layman becomes interested in geology. Flaming Gorge National Recreation Area.* [*Photo: Stan Rasmussen, Bureau of Reclamation*]

Whether these wild river preserves are administered by the National Park Service or by the Forest Service is not important. They would be well served by either agency. It is true, as Interior Secretary Udall said in his letter to the Chief Executive, that "a truly wild river is a rare thing today in the United States. But there are still many free-flowing rivers, or parts of such, that retain much of their original character and beauty." They speak to the spirit. They can even cure melancholy, according to the old Oxford vicar Richard Burton, who wrote: "Fishing is good . . . and if so be the angler catch no fish, yet he hath a wholesome walk and pleasant shade by the sweet silver streams."

Theodora Kroeber, in her "Story of Ishi," goes deeper into that yearning of urbanized man for an association with the waters of an unspoiled stream. "Perhaps," she comments, "creek and river continue to draw old and young to their quiet pools, to fish, because it is restful and healing to re-enact an age-old craft. No other occupation today brings modern man so close to his stone-age ancestors."

## 1. Ozark National Scenic Riverways
### [*Missouri*]

As a prototype of the elongated parks that are planned to preserve the un-stained wild river, no better location could be found than the Ozarks, and no finer free-flowing streams than the Current and the Jacks Fork of south-eastern Missouri. Much of this country has the aspect of being unpeopled. I recall that, driving down from St. Louis, I felt that I had never been over so long a stretch of forest where so few habitations could be glimpsed along the highway. Not virgin, to be sure. Much of this was once pine-clad, and lumbered off; but the succeeding oak-hickory growth is dense and appealing, and dogwood and redbud announce themselves boldly in the spring, and then modestly withdraw into forest anonymity.

This is a country of extraordinary variety in its plantlife. The Ozarks saw nothing of the ice of the period of continental glaciation, but they felt the effect of it; and here you have an amazing mingling of northern plants that migrated southward away from the arctic breath; of southern species that moved north when a warm stage renewed; and finally of plants that have moved in from both east and west. With such forest cover it is no wonder

---

*From a ledge of limestone Big Spring boils out its vast supply of water. Ozark National Scenic Riverways.* [*Photo: Don Wooldridge*]

that the wide variety of animals has persisted, despite constant hunting. Even the rare red wolf is here. Birdlife is abundant. This must once have been a great ground for the wild turkey which Ben Franklin thought should be our national bird instead of the eagle. The species has been exterminated here, but has been reintroduced and is making a good comeback.

But of course the most notable feature of this Ozark region is what is known to the geologist as the "karst" topography, quite like the type of formation on the eastern side of the Adriatic Sea. That sounds pretty special and scientific. But no; the delight of visitors in this scenic riverway will spring wholly from the fact that the region *is* karst. How else the fascinating caves, with their dripstone creations, like Round Spring Cavern? How else the rugged limestone bluffs, and the clear cold springs with their phenomenal output of water? Big Spring, four miles south of Van Buren, alone could supply the needs of the city of St. Louis. It has had years when it could do far more than that; 840 million gallons in one day, if the figures mean anything to you. Other springs, like Welch and Blue Springs on the Current River and Alley Spring on the Jacks Fork, may seem small in comparison, but they would be sensational almost anywhere else.

All this adds up to fishing—the Current and Jacks Fork are famous for their bass—and for boating, swimming, and camping. The National Park Service has plans for a comprehensive program of outdoor recreation, but the natural and human history that make the region unique will definitely be preserved.

Other riverways on the list presently discussed for legislative action that will preserve them in their wilderness state are the Salmon and Clearwater in Idaho; the Rogue in Oregon; the Rio Grande in New Mexico; the Eleven Point in Missouri; and the Capacon and Shenandoah in West Virginia.

# PART

---

# FOUR

---

# [ I ]

# *Americans Before Columbus*

## 1. CHACO CANYON NATIONAL MONUMENT
### [*New Mexico*]

THE ENGLISH ARCHAEOLOGIST GEOFFREY BIBBY, in his book *The Testimony of the Spade*, asserts that archaeology is meaningless without asking the question: "What did it *feel like* to be prehistoric?"

As stated, the question is rather absurd, because one may as well ask the question: "What does it feel like to be a human being?" We are all descendants and progenitors of people. Did anyone ever think of himself as a prehistoric person? And if not, how could he have any feelings about it?

But I think I know what Bibby had in mind. He probably meant, and justly, that in viewing what was left behind by a vanished people such as those who lived at Chaco Canyon for so many centuries before Columbus sailed, we are not to consider them as exhibits like the showcase of animal bones, charcoal, weapons, and pottery dug from ruins, but as working, wondering, striving, loving, quarreling, progressing human beings with basic emotions and problems not essentially different from our own. Were it not for the printed word our latest generation would find it hard to conjecture a world without the electric lamp. Equally, the late Basketmakers must have put the question: "How do you suppose our ancestors got along before (as some of our old folks say) there weren't any bows and arrows?" There *was* just such a time. And there was a Golden Age, to be sure—to which a grandfather in the *kiva* looked back sorrowfully. "In my time the teenagers were disciplined; now look at them!"

Probably about 600 A.D., about the time Pope Gregory was sending Augustine into England to carry the word of God to its pagan inhabitants, a farming people known to the archaeologist as Basketmakers were planting

*From mesa top to the ancient dwellings is sheer fall. Canyon de Chelly National Monument. [Photo: Fred E. Mang, Jr.]*

maize and squash on the floor of Chaco Canyon, watering their gardens with carefully hoarded summer rainstorms, and eking out a subsistence with edible wild plants and such small animals as they could trap or shoot.

The early Basketmakers, living in pit houses and thinking themselves pretty well off—possibly pitying those who lacked nice pithouses like theirs—developed thinkers and visionaries who said: "We can do even better than a hole in the ground!" Thus developed the laying up of blocks of sandstone, mortared to create structures to house many families under one roof. Other innovators began to weave from the fibers of the plentiful yucca around them, and not only to make pottery but to decorate it so that the eye might be pleased as well as the stomach. The aesthetic urge had arrived. And then, in that transition period when Basketmaker became pueblo dweller, we find that it became modish to flatten the heads of infants by laying them on their backs on hard cradleboards. If your children did not have flattened skulls, they were not "in." From that sort of thing to the society pages of the newspaper is not, after all, too long a jump.

This desirable luxury and modernity of the Chaco people would attract immigration—a human flow toward the affluent society. So they began really to build. Pueblo Bonito (Spanish for "beautiful village") went up to a height of five stories on a floor plan that covered three acres. Eight hundred or more rooms could shelter twelve hundred persons; and the developers of this high-rise included thirty-two *kivas* which served as ceremonial chambers or men's clubrooms. Perhaps the *kivas* were a sentimental memory of the days when the earliest Basketmakers burrowed into the ground for shelter.

And then? The Chaco people began to leave for parts unknown. Why? Also unknown. Drought, internal politics, enemies—perhaps a combination of these factors. Before the fourteenth century, rabbits and other game stared at tenantless dwellings and wondered at the stillness.

## 2. CANYON DE CHELLY NATIONAL MONUMENT
### [*Arizona*]

ACCORDING TO THE TIME OF DAY, the color of these canyon walls changes, but always there is redness of some sort. In some places there is a sheer drop of a thousand feet from the mesa to the river—a meandering stream which has come out of the mountains to the east and ends in the Chinle Wash. The water that was so precious to the prehistoric Indians who lived here for a thousand years still is at the whim of stingy rainfall or snow-melt. It is a land in which primitive people simply must have a rain god to be propitiated.

Some years ago I started out over the mesa with a Navajo who, because he apparently had conceived a liking for me, said that he was going to take me to a spot where we could see some ruins of ancient dwellings that "even the folks at headquarters don't know about." Alas, I never saw them. Just as we neared the edge of the canyon one of those blizzardy late-spring snowstorms came down upon us. Visibility dropped almost to zero. So we sat in the truck and tried to wait the weather out. And we talked—of many things.

"No," said Tom, in answer to a question, "I don't feel any closer to those old people than you do. They were not Diné [Navajo]. Some ways, I think, they were smarter than we are today; some ways not."

We discussed the pictographs that are seen on the cliff faces. When I told Tom that some people think they were just "doodling," to while the time away, he snorted. "That's foolish. I don't know what they mean, but they mean something."

R. J. C. Atkinson, an English archaeologist, would agree. He thought there was too strict an appeal to the canons of archaeological evidence, which in fact may "merely serve to conceal a lack of imagination."

## 3. RUSSELL CAVE NATIONAL MONUMENT
### [*Alabama*]

UNTIL A FEW YEARS AGO, Russell Cave was just another cave; and the United States has no paucity of caves. In 1953 a group of members of the Tennessee Archaeological Society began digging here, not far west of Bridgeport, Alabama, and uncovered the evidence that archaic man was an occupant nine thousand years before our time. It was an exciting discovery. If indeed our first immigrants came from Asia across Bering Straits "ten thousand years ago," a view commonly held, they must have moved fast across North America at a period when motion would presumably be slow.

But they were here; and curiously enough they began to take refuge in Russell Cave rather soon after it became habitable, for there had been a stream running through it, and only a fall of rock from the roof had created a dry flooring. On this slabby foundation the firstcomers camped and began to leave for the archaeologist the tell-tale charcoal from which the time clock can be approximately read by measuring the radioactive carbon.

The first occupants were "hunters and gatherers." Nuts and seeds were plentiful, and so were game animals—deer, turkey, squirrel, fox, and skunk—and then even the porcupine, now found only much farther north. The tough chert that occurred in the surrounding limestone was the perfect material from which to fashion spearpoints. We can see them in the colder weather, well protected from the elements, sitting beside their fires smithing a good supply of weaponry against the coming hunts. They fished with hooks made from bone. The nearby great river furnished a pleasant diet-variety item of fish and mollusk.

Ornaments they seem not to have had. Was time for leisure not sufficient? Nor did they make pottery. That appears only at the much later period when the Woodland Indian began his occupancy of the cave. Maybe the early ones were conservatives—even reactionaries.

## 4. Montezuma Castle National Monument
### [Arizona]

Except for two bothersome facts, Montezuma Castle was aptly named. It never was a castle, and Montezuma's Aztecs had nothing to do with it. The information of the early settlers who christened it was outpaced by their enthusiasm. Still, should we cavil too strongly at a touch of romanticism in a too-drab world?

Called by any name, this ancient tenement house, built into a naturally eroded hollow of the northside cliff of Beaver Creek, will delight those who have interest in our prehistoric Americans. In almost pristine condition, a few miles up a tributary from the Verde Valley, it gives to visitors an impression of a relatively happy life lived by the folks who occupied its twenty rooms, in five stories. Farming the valley by day for their corn and squash, coming back in the evening to climb the ladders and enjoy happy security from raiding enemies, these cliff dwellers should have been envied by the other inhabitants of the region, who had to cluster for protection.

Part of this monument preserves Montezuma Well, about seven miles by road northeast of the "castle." Out of this sink in the limestone flows the great quantity of water that was used by the aboriginal farmer for his irrigated land below. The ditches are still to be seen.

## 5. Tonto National Monument
### [Arizona]

Before the Roosevelt Dam was built, the irrigation ditches of the Salado people could still be seen in the valley of the Salt River, though the pre-

*They chose a safe location for their apartment house. Montezuma Castle National Monument. [Photo: Bob Bradshaw]*

historic Indians who built them left their cave-shelter homes six centuries ago. Why did these early farming folk live so far from their croplands, toiling with their burdens several miles, and climbing uphill a thousand feet of elevation? Certainly for protection against the incursion of freebooters hovering on their flanks, ready to seize the opportunity to loot and enslave. From the visitor center, a trail winds up the steep hillside through the plant cover, which thrives now, as it did then, in desert conditions—the cholla and other cactuses, jojoba, ocotillo, yucca, and sotol—to the "lower ruin." Familiar enough to those who live in the Southwest, this is a plant world strange indeed to all who come from regions where the rainfall is more generous.

Apparently these Salado people were not only well advanced potters and weavers, but they traded widely. Since they could not raise cotton the fibers they wove so artfully must have come from farmers farther south; and in the ruins were found ornaments—pendants, bracelets, and beads—made from shells brought in from the Gulf of California.

## 6. Pipestone National Monument
### [*Minnesota*]

WELL ETCHED IN MY RECOLLECTIONS is my first visit to this monument in southwestern Minnesota. Looking across the grassy plain that stretches endlessly toward a straight-line horizon, I saw a single tepee, and beside it seated on a campstool an Indian. As I approached, I saw that the Sioux was working on a piece of the clay rock called catlinite, rough-shaping it into what might be a pipe bowl. His remote ancestors would have done it with stone tools; he had saw and knife of steel.

The scene was idyllic—except for one detail. At his side the Indian had a battery radio, which was blurting forth a nauseating cacophony. Thus the white man's technology was completing the job that the white man's bad whiskey had failed to finish.

Yet, as I remained in this preservation of prehistoric and historic Indian life and habit, the place became ever more satisfying. What a story is told here! The odd lithogenetic puzzle of this bed of red indurated clay between two layers of sandstone that became quartzite. The decision of primitive man that this was the superlative material from which to fashion ceremonial smoking bowls and sculptured ornaments. The trading of this most-esteemed rock

*Standing Eagle, a Chippewa, shapes a peace pipe of "catlinite" rock. Pipestone National Monument. [Photo: Thomas Roll]*

wherever calumets or figurines were shaped. (A beautiful piece of art by the hand of a Rodin of ancient days, unquestionably made from this very Pipe-stone catlinite, was found in a mound on Shiloh battlefield.)

## 7. Mound City Group National Monument
### [Ohio]

These so-called "Hopewell" people lived for at least a thousand years in the Middle West. Here, in the valley of the Scioto, in southern Ohio, early explorers had observed a group of mounds that they perhaps thought to be merely a feature of the local landscape. But in 1846 the two pioneer archaelogists Squier and Davis began excavating the prehistoric earthworks. Out of them they took a surprising collection of artifacts, including stone tobacco pipes artistically carved in the shapes of human heads, birds, and animals. The British Museum now has these first trophies.

It seems certain that these primitive Americans, laboring with rude picks and shovels and baskets, reared the mounds as memorials for their high-ranking dead. Borrow pits from which the earth was gathered can still be seen within the monument. From far and wide this vanished people, who developed the arts to such a high point, obtained the materials with which they worked. They had obsidian (from Yellowstone?), mica from North Carolina, native copper that could have come down only from Lake Superior, shells gathered from the Mexican Gulf, and the teeth of grizzly bears. Fine objects taken from these and similar mounds throughout southern Ohio are to be seen at Chilicothe and at the State Museum in Columbus.

## 8. Effigy Mounds National Monument
### [Iowa]

There is a bonus for those who come here to see the unusual work of a mound-building people who had novel ideas as to the way in which their distinguished dead should be honored. In scenic quality, the monument, situated on the high bluffs across the Mississippi River from Prairie du Chien, Wisconsin, is outstanding. Even if there were no important prehistoric evidences here, the forests, wild-flower displays, and interesting animal community would still qualify the place as a delightful parkland. You have the feeling that the first primitive occupants of this region were in a well-chosen spot where game-food abounded.

Within the boundaries, enclosing about two square miles, there are known to be 183 burial mounds. Most of them, like those seen in other areas, are conical or linear. But twenty-seven of the mounds are an astonishing departure from the rule. Working with the crudest of instruments, this group of people created barrows in the shapes of birds and animals—the hawk, the eagle, the bear, the fox, the deer, and the dog. One of these mounds—the Great Bear—is 137 feet long and 70 feet across the shoulders. The persistence of these low mounds of pictorial earthworks over the centuries is hardly less remarkable than their ethnic origin.

## 9. Ocmulgee National Monument
### [*Georgia*]

A FAITHFUL DIORAMA, to be seen in the museum, reconstructs for visitors a council of the religious and governing elders of the farming Indians who lived here more than ten centuries ago on the outskirts of what is now the city of Macon. Here, over the original clay floor, is a reconstruction of one of the earth lodges of these mound-building people.

In the center is the sunken pit where the town's sacred flame was kept alight. Around the red-clay walls is a bench containing forty-seven seats. Opposite the door is a platform shaped like an eagle, and three seats are here—for the bigwigs. To purify the body, to cleanse it for the reception of advice from supernatural powers, the leaders first drank cassina, an emetic made from stewing the leaves of the yaupon shrub. The Egyptians had the same idea, but they used castor oil. Those of us who have been dosed with castor oil will prefer cassina—provided we have never tasted cassina.

Such an earthlodge was probably used in winter. Just north of this reconstruction is the Cornfield Mound, perhaps built in a field of holy maize seed. The prehistoric town was protected by two big ditches, indicating, perhaps, that successful farmers in those days had frequently to fight to keep what they raised.

## 10. Bandelier National Monument
### [*New Mexico*]

LIFE WAS NOT ALL ROSES for the prehistoric peoples of North America, especially among the farming folk, with whom maize was a staple of diet. They had trouble with their teeth—they had toothache—and we wonder what they did about it. Did the shaman, or medicine man, offer anything better than consolatory words?

[ 433 ]

You might happen to be one of a group at Bandelier someday when the ranger is demonstrating, with the very utensils the ancients used, how the corn was ground in a *metate* (hollowed stone) with a stone *mano* (literally, a hand, in Spanish). Nothing more flavorful than this fresh-ground grain, and nothing worse for the teeth, for in the grinding, particles of grit are rubbed off the stones into the meal.

This monument was named for the Swiss-American ethnologist Adolph F. A. Bandelier, who studied these ruins, and entered into the life of the Pueblo Indians around Santa Fe, in the early 1880's. Bandelier set the scene of his novel *The Delight Makers*, in this Frijoles Canyon, where cliff ruins extend along the base of the northern wall for two miles. The Pajarito Plateau, in the tuff canyons of which the dwellers cut their houses, is of great geological interest. At any given spot in the Jemez Mountains it is hard to realize that you are on the rim of one of the world's greatest calderas—a gigantic saucer created by the collapsed summit of a volcano.

## 11. TUZIGOOT NATIONAL MONUMENT
### [*Arizona*]

WHEN the Spanish adventurer Espejo came into the Verde Valley in 1583 he found Yavapai Indians living in thatched shelters amid the many ruins of old pueblo masonry houses. Actually it was an instance of a settlement "reverting to type," although the Yavapais did not know it, and probably cared less. Long before those crumbled stone dwellings had been built, there had been another people here in the valley, also living in pole-and-brush huts. These first settlers were related to a group that farmed the irrigated terraces near what is now the city of Phoenix.

The Tuzigoot settlers had been here somewhat more than a century when they were visited by Indians from the north, who liked the region and decided to stay. Perhaps the union of the two was peaceful—we cannot know that; but as always happened, new customs came in with the immigrants. The archaeologist finds that cremation of the dead gave way to burials: adults on the hillsides below the dwellings that were now built of stone; young children beneath the house floors.

In 1933 and 1934 the University of Arizona began to work upon the heaps of scattered rock, revealing enough of the original town so that, with

---

*The Indians ground their corn this way, with* mano *and* metate. *Bandelier National Monument.* [*Photo: Robert W. Gage*]

a partial reconstruction, visitors receive a good idea of what it looked like in its flourishing days.

## 12. GILA CLIFF DWELLINGS NATIONAL MONUMENT
### [*New Mexico*]

IN THE FACE of a high cliff on a stream that flows into the west fork of the Gila River, some prehistoric Indians, looking for a home easily defended against marauders, found one ready-made by nature. The year-round water in the canyon, though not of great volume, was treasure-trove, too. More than thirty-five rooms, some of them large, were built into the cavities of the rock. From the largest shelter, natural archways led into two other sites suitable for rooms, separated by walls built of flat stones and adobe. The adobe is in such a good state of preservation that fingerprints can still be seen.

These ruins are in a rough country to which the only access is through Silver City to the Sapillo on the Forest Service road, and up Copperas Canyon truck trail to the head of Copperas. The last fourteen miles of the road are passable only to trucks with four-wheel drive, or to jeeps. The trip from Silver City to the ruins, by trail, takes about three hours. Therefore, anyone wishing to visit this area should get in touch, at least two or three weeks in advance, with the National Park Service superintendent, Box 1320, Silver City, New Mexico 88061.

## 13. WALNUT CANYON NATIONAL MONUMENT
### [*Arizona*]

IMAGINE YOURSELF to be one of a band wandering across the semiarid lands of our Southwest looking for a likely place to create a community. Perhaps your group has swarmed out of a home which could no longer contain so many people, as bees leave the hive under a new leader. The place you are looking for must have, above all things, a dependable supply of water. It should have fuel—if not for warmth, surely for cooking. There are unfriendly nomads not far away; you seek a place not too hard to defend. Finally, since you are peaceable farming people, there must be fertile soil for your beans and corn and pumpkins. If the spot should be pleasing to the eye, so much the better.

*Tyuonyi Ruins. Bandelier National Monument.* [*Photo: John V. Young*]

Eureka! Happy discovery! Here is the place of your dreams. A canyon with sufficient all-year water; farmland on the rim above. Not being geologists you do not know how it happened, but there are ready-made shelters in the rock, where the top of the cliff projects over the lower part. What a roof over which to build a series of one-room homes! Good hunting here, too—almost every game creature from pack rat to cougar. You have only stone tools to work with, but these will suffice.

You and your descendants live here for many years. The time comes when for some reason your people decide to go. But you leave behind the testimony that you were there: your walls, your refuse dump, your pots and trinkets. Centuries later a people who call themselves American will come to look and to wonder. They will call the place Walnut Canyon.

## 14. Casa Grande Ruins National Monument
### [Arizona]

IF YOU LIVED in a flat country, subject to raids from your enemies, and if you had the wit and skill, you would build yourself a watchtower high enough to see the invaders before they came too close. This is precisely what these Gila Valley pueblo people did. From the top of Casa Grande's four stories the watchmen could look far out over the desertland.

The archaeologists found here a fascinating story of prehistoric building methods. The lime clay found on the scene was good material for the purpose. Since they had not been intended to house anyone, after the walls had gone up seven feet above ground level, the first rooms that had been formed were filled in. That made a stout foundation for the next two stories and furnished a brace for the inner walls. As the archaeologist interprets: "They built an artificial seven-foot hill, then constructed a three-story house upon it." The upstairs apartments probably accommodated eleven families, and if the pueblo folk were like later Americans, those apartments were reserved for the elite. "I live in the Tower Apartments; my father has an official position."

It was the Jesuit missionary Father Kino who provided the name Casa Grande—"Big House." Did these pueblo people waterlog their lands by excessive irrigation? Why did they drift off—some of them to become, as is thought, ancestors of the present Pima Indians? The Pimas speak of them as the Hohokam, meaning "ancient ones."

*The "sheltered life" in one respect. Navajo National Monument. [Photo: Fred Mang, Jr.]*

## 15. NAVAJO NATIONAL MONUMENT
### [*Arizona*]

JUST AS the Pima Indians refer to their supposed ancestors as "the ancient ones," so do the Navajos called the vanished pueblo people of the San Juan River region Anasazi—which means the same thing. Actually the tie of kinship is vague. The Navajo people are almost as awed by the ruins of Betatakin and Keet Seel as were Byron Cummings and the Wetherills when they stumbled upon them and gazed in astonishment.

In time three prehistoric cultural centers developed in this Four Corners region where the boundaries of Colorado, Utah, New Mexico, and Arizona meet: the Mesa Verde of southwestern Colorado, the Chaco Canyon people of northwestern New Mexico, and the Kayenta in northeastern Arizona. The three cliff dwellings of this monument represent the life and arts of the Kayenta.

Betatakin was built on the floor of a great cave, the roof of which projected far out over the dwellings. It once had nearly 150 rooms, and tree-ring dating indicates that it was occupied between 1242 and 1300 A.D. Keet Seel, which can be reached from Betatakin on horseback over a primitive trail, is the largest cliff ruin in Arizona, and was the last one to be abandoned in the Segi Canyon region. Visitors are not allowed to enter those two ruins unless accompanied by a guide. But you are free to make an unannounced journey to Inscription House, the smallest of the three communities.

## 16. AZTEC RUINS NATIONAL MONUMENT
### [*New Mexico*]

THE "ANCIENT ONES" here built large stone houses and farmed on nearby lands which are still in cultivation, irrigated with water from the Animas River. Situated as these people were, between Chaco Canyon to the south and Mesa Verde to the north, it was natural that they should, at different periods, be influenced by the culture of both. For instance, the large pueblo, built during the time of Chaco dominance, reflects the pattern and large size characteristic of those builders. Later came a change to the thin walls and low ceilings of smaller structures similar to those of Mesa Verde.

It must have been hard going at first for the settlers at Aztec. With only stone and wooden tools the irrigation ditches were dug. They hauled sand-

*Only a pile of stones, where a people once lived. Hovenweep National Monument.*
*[Photo: Fred Mang, Jr.]*

stone blocks for a considerable distance without benefit of wheeled vehicles or beasts of burden. Their roof timbers, too, had to be brought in. Yet the time came when they touched a high level in the arts and crafts. Their intricately woven cotton cloth was noteworthy, though they cultivated no cotton themselves. The Great Kiva, excavated and restored by Earl H.

Morris and similar to those at Chaco Canyon, has an inside diameter of forty-eight feet.

## 17. Hovenweep National Monument
### [*Utah–Colorado*]

It was William Henry Jackson, the pioneer "wet-plate" photographer accompanying the Hayden Survey party into Yellowstone, who gave Hovenweep its name. He was here in 1874, and used the Ute Indian word meaning "the deserted valley."

This is the off-beat adventure for those who find a satisfaction in following the fortunes of the pre-Columbian inhabitants of our country. To explore the vast, lonely region which lies north of the San Juan, and to see the extraordinary groups of defensive towers—square, oval, circular and D-shaped—is a delight reserved only for the hardy, those who thrill at overcoming difficulties. Hovenweep is almost off the map. You don't approach it over paved roads. Timid souls will think they have gone out of the world. There are no sleeping or eating accommodations, no gas stations, no food stores nearby. No wood for fires, and no water that you can wisely drink. And yet—of course you can get there. If it hasn't been storming recently, the approach roads are not so bad. And when you do arrive at the monument, and when you do see some or all of the ruins clustered at the heads of wild canyons—what a feeling of triumph!

The reason for so many defensive rock-towers? The people here had a vital water supply to protect.

## 18. Pecos National Monument
### [*New Mexico*]

The tall tales about the wondrously rich Seven Cities, which had led Francisco de Coronado north from Mexico, were proving to be a complete hoax. But there was one liar who had not yet had his inning—an Indian called by the Spaniards El Turco. The Turk peddled a yarn of new marvels "a long distance to the east." He told of the wonderful golden bracelets of which he had been robbed by the natives of Cicuyé.

This Cicuyé was in the valley of the upper Pecos River and at the foot of the Santa Fe Mountains. Coronado sent Hernando de Alvarado back to the Indian village, where shortly before he had been treated with hospitality, to demand the Turk's bracelets. The Indians replied that there were no such bracelets. Alvarado put the head chief in chains; other abuses followed; finally there was insurrection. The Spaniards were able to put down the Indians, but Pecos, or Cicuyé, was to be an important milestone in the advance of the conquistadors. Wherever Coronado or his lieutenants went thereafter, their promises of peace were jeered. The pueblos could be "pacified"; the Indians could be plundered; but implacable enmity had been established.

Pecos National Monument, twenty-six miles southeast of Santa Fe, has been a site administered by the Museum of New Mexico and known as Pecos State Monument. The area embraces the remains of two Indian villages dating from the thirteenth century, and two mission churches established by the Spaniards—one early in the seventeenth century, the other, about a hundred years later. On June 28, 1965, the National Park Service was authorized to assume administration of the area.

# [ 11 ]

# *Struggle for the Continent*

## 1. SAN JUAN NATIONAL HISTORIC SITE
### [*Puerto Rico*]

"THREE THINGS SAN JUAN HAS, that Madrid has not: El Morro, San Cristóbal, and the sight of the ships coming in from sea." Thus speaks the Puerto Rican with pardonable satisfaction, not esteeming Madrid less, but loving San Juan more.

Historic ground, indeed. And if there comes into the voice of the interpreter at this historic site something different of fervor and flavor, it is somewhat like the effect of the illuminated initial on the page of an ancient manuscript. For here was an outpost and a fortification that had to exist, if the convoys of Spain, laden with silver from Mexico and treasure from Cartagena and Puerto Bello, were to reach their destination. Without this keeper of the gate on one side and St. Augustine on the other, the pirates and privateers (it was not easy to distinguish) would have had Spain in the position of a gull fishing for the profit of a man-of-war bird: the plunderer plundered.

Nor was it only that. Puerto Rico, in the hands of another European power, would have been a fatal menace. Juan Ponce de León saw this when he made a settlement at Caparra in 1508. From here he went to explore the North American mainland—not, you may be sure, because he indulged in any silly notion of a "fountain of youth," but because the glowing picture of new treasures was in his eyes.

To protect the sea route something better than Caparra was required, and something much stronger than the Casa Blanca of Ponce de León, or even the Fortaleza (fortress), of which Gonzalo de Oviedo remarked that

---

"*Queen of the Spanish Missions.*" *San José Mission National Historic Site.* [*Photo: Harvey Patteson*]

*Señor Morales tells the story of the "Castle." San Juan National Historic Site. [Photo: M. Woodbridge Williams]*

"only blind men could have chosen such a site for a fort." There was certainly a better site. At the west end of San Juan was a *morro*, or headland, rising from the sea 120 feet. Here Morro Castle was reared, and it was none too soon. Havana had been sacked by corsairs, who were becoming even bolder. It was a time of conflict among European powers, too, and hardy mariners of many nations hungered for prize money as jackals eye a lion feasting on his kill. El Morro was still young when the English adventurer Drake came with a fleet of ships and three thousand men to test its worth. He very nearly succeeded in taking the town, but at the last moment, fortune deserted him. But then came George Clifford, Earl of Cumberland. Rather strangely, in this time of war, San Juan had been left with a mere skeleton force. An English warship proved too well armored for the shore guns at the point of attack, and its siege guns smashed the landward wall of El Morro. His Britannic Majesty's flag flew triumphantly over Puerto Rico, and Spain's domination in the New World seemed near an end. But San Juan was harder to hold than to gain. The Earl of Cumberland, his men weakened by disease, finally set sail for home.

[ 446 ]

But now Spain and the Netherlands were at each other's throats, and in 1625, after San Juan's defenses had been strengthened, the Dutchman Hendrick confidently entered the harbor, seemingly undisturbed by fire from the fort. For more than a month there were attacks and counterattacks.

El Morro, Cristóbal, La Casa Blanca, El Cañuelo—magic names with music in them. The last scene of all: Admiral Sampson with an American flotilla exchanging fire with the batteries of El Morro, without great damage on either side. Four centuries of Spain in the New World: the last page of this volume of Puerto Rican history was turned.

## 2. FORT RALEIGH NATIONAL HISTORIC SITE
### [*North Carolina*]

"A MOST PLEASANT AND FERTILE GROUND" was Roanoke Island in the eyes of Sir Walter Raleigh's agents, who explored the coast of what is now North Carolina when England was seeking a foothold in the New World. The year was 1584. The following spring, Sir Richard Grenville, Raleigh's cousin, brought more than a hundred colonists to these shores and set up "the new fort in Virginia," the land being named in honor of the so-called virgin queen, Elizabeth. But these transplanted hopefuls were homesick and discouraged, and when Sir Francis Drake anchored nearby, bringing them supplies in 1586, they had had enough of the wilderness.

Raleigh, wedded to his dream of an English empire in North America, was persistent. A second colony, with 150 men, women, and children, was begun in the summer of 1587, under sounder auspices. The fort was improved, the old houses repaired and new ones constructed. Manteo, the nearby Indian chief, welcomed the settlers. In return, he was baptized and created Lord of Roanoke. John White was governor, and one of his assistants, Ananias Dare, who had apparently overcome the handicap of his Christian name, was his son-in-law. The Dare's daughter, born soon after their arrival, was named "Virginia"—the first English child born in the new colony. But again there was dissension. Supplies ran short; Indian rations did not take the place of the good things of the old country. So White returned to England to arrange for the colonials' return.

But England was now at war with Spain and feared an invasion by a mighty hostile fleet. Two small ships were all that were sent out, and these

*Overleaf: The "Castle" guarded the sealanes for Spain. San Juan National Historic Site. [Photo: M. Woodbridge Williams]*

never arrived. It was not until 1590 that the governor could return to Roanoke Island. To his consternation, the colony had utterly disappeared. The houses had been dismantled, and high palisades had been erected. On a tree, of which the bark had been peeled, was written a single word: CROATAN. Croatan Island (part of what are now Ocracoke Island and Hatteras Island) was searched, and the Croatan Indian village visited. Never a trace of the colonists was found. The mystery has never been solved. Every summer, at this historic site, a pageant, *The Lost Colony*, is performed under the auspices of the Roanoke Island Historical Association.

## 3. JAMESTOWN NATIONAL HISTORIC SITE
### [*Virginia*]

BY THE HAPPIEST of arrangements, the scene of the first permanent English settlement in America is preserved jointly by the National Park Service and the Association for the Preservation of Virginia Antiquities. Except for the historic site, the island where the colonists disembarked from three small ships in May 1607 is preserved as part of Colonial National Historical Park, with headquarters at Yorktown, Virginia. Inquiries relating to the work of the association should be addressed to it at Jamestown.

The day came, of course, when its distinction passed to Williamsburg, but for nearly a century Jamestown held its place as the political as well as the social and economic center of Virginia Colony. From the viewpoint of health there could have been far better locations. As in Raleigh's colonies, there were loneliness and inexperience, and here was added inevitable sickness coming out of the Pitch and Tar Swamp that lay behind. Only the will and resourcefulness of the redoubtable Captain John Smith and a few others held it together. And when Smith, disabled, sailed for England, there were threats of desertion. With the coming of Lord Delaware and a competent governor, Sir Thomas Dale, and not least with the arrival of English lasses to soften the rigors of bachelor life on the edge of a wild continent, a degree of prosperity came.

Admirably interpreted, the life of early Jamestown comes clearly to visitors today. It was never more than a country town, really, however important, and its appearance constantly changed according to needs and taste. Of seventeenth-century Jamestown nothing remains standing except the ivy-covered Old Tower, presumably part of the brick church of 1639. The landing place and the site of that "James Fort," which in the first years was the whole town, were long ago devoured by river floods.

*"Happy are the painters, for they shall not be lonely."—Sir Winston Churchill. Fort Caroline National Memorial. [Photo: Barry Mackintosh]*

There is no more charming self-guiding tour than this, which takes visitors around a colonial capital which not only ceased to exist at the time of the American Revolution, but actually became plowed ground. Yet the historian and the archaeologist have worked together to bring Jamestown back to the imagination. Not to be missed is a visit to the working glass furnace, where glassblowing is done as the colonists, with similar equipment, did it three and a half centuries ago.

## 4. Fort Caroline National Memorial
### [Florida]

ON A JUNE DAY in 1564 the Timucua Indians who lived along the St. Johns River, in what the Spaniards had vaguely termed "Florida," saw three small ships put down their anchors at a point about five miles from the mouth. About three hundred white men came ashore. The Indians could not suspect it, but it was an important day in the story of fluctuating empires. France was knocking at the door of this treasure house, the New World, intending to claim a share in the vast riches that had been pouring into Spain from Mexico and tropical America.

Gold! Silver! Pearls! Loot from thousands of "savage" towns and cities. Spain's monopoly in middle America was fairly secure. But to the north was a great expanse untouched.

René de Laudonnière, commander of this expedition, built an earth fort and named it Caroline, in honor of his king. In truth, though it might not seem to be in competition, this was a sword pointed at Spain. The treasure ships would have to pass the mouth of the St. Johns when they followed the Gulf Stream on their way home. Menéndez, the Spanish admiral, got orders to drive out such settlers "by what means you see fit."

The clash came without delay. The French were willing to fight, and decided to attack. But Ribaut's fleet was caught in a hurricane and wrecked. This was the chance for Menéndez. He marched straight for Fort Caroline, most of whose fighting men were in the wrecked fleet. In one hour it was over; the men in the garrison were slaughtered and the women and children taken prisoner.

What of the Frenchmen on the wrecked ships? That part of the story is told at another area of the National Park System—Fort Matanzas.

### 5. FORT MATANZAS NATIONAL MONUMENT
#### [*Florida*]

THE WORD *matanza*, in Spanish, means "slaughter." It is a befitting name for what took place on September 29, 1565, at this spot where visitors today come to the inlet south of Anastasia Island, just below St. Augustine.

The shipwrecked men of Jean Ribaut, more than 500, managed to scramble and swim ashore through the surf. In two groups they began a march up the coast back to Fort Caroline, not knowing its fate. The swift waters of Matanzas Inlet halted them. Menéndez, with a small force artfully deployed, trapped the first group into a surrender. Ten at a time they were taken across the inlet, herded together as though to be marched, and then pitilessly butchered. Of 208 men, only 8 were spared.

Part of the second group of Frenchmen, perhaps 350 in all, met the same fate when, about a week later, they straggled up to the inlet. After a talk between Menéndez and Ribaut, and in sight of the unburied bodies of their compatriots, more than half the Frenchmen turned and trusted themselves to the wilderness rather than to the Spaniard. The others were led across the inlet, where another cold-blooded butchery took place. And gradually

Menéndez rounded up the remaining enemies. France's first attempt to share New World riches had failed. But she was to have better fortune at a later time far to the north—in Canada.

## 6. Castillo de San Marcos National Monument
### [*Florida*]

GRIM, VITAL, defiant of time, this monument of Spain's hours of greatness seems still to be peering defensively out upon the Gulf Stream, seems still to be guarding the homegoing galleons from the corsair. To touch its gray outer walls, to wander among its rooms, to climb its ramp and to look out upon the blue waters of Matanzas Bay, is to wish to know the story of Spain in America; and here a part of it is beautifully told.

The short-lived colony of France at Fort Caroline was a warning to the Spanish realm. Hungry predators had their eyes upon the prosperous sheepfold. Hardly more than two decades after the Spanish colonized at St. Augustine, England, in the person of Sir Francis Drake, was ready to test supremacy. Piracy? Official policy? In those stirring times the difference was not always apparent. In 1670 England was moving closer, with a settlement at Charleston.

The Castillo you see now was begun in 1672, and it required almost twenty-five years to complete. The walls were thirty feet high and, in places, twelve feet thick, built of the shellrock called coquina, conveniently quarried on Anastasia Island nearby. St. Augustine was raided and sacked many times, but the Castillo was impregnable against any cannon of the period. The British general James Oglethorpe set out from Fort Frederica in 1740 swearing to take this outpost "or leave his bones before its walls." Oglethorpe returned to Frederica discomfited, but still in possession of his bones.

## 7. Fort Frederica National Monument
### [*Georgia*]

IF YOU WILL COMPARE the Spanish settlement at Fort Caroline with that of Oglethorpe's Britishers on St. Simon's Island in Georgia, you will perceive at least one important reason why England finally dominated North America, instead of France or Spain. Of the three hundred persons who landed with de Laudonnière, all but seventy were soldiers or sailors. There was not a farmer among them. The artisans were mainly chosen for their ability to construct defenses.

*Outpost of Spain at St. Augustine, Florida. Castillo de San Marcos National Monument. [Photo: M. Woodbridge Williams]*

Although Oglethorpe's Frederica, for reasons of state, lasted only thirteen years, it was a true settlement. It was designed with the greatest care by an intelligent group who actually aimed at reproducing a typical English village in the New World. Tailor, weaver, tanner, shoemaker . . . all the important trades were represented in that roster. There were doctor, preacher, midwife, also. They were not adventurers for gold and pearls. They came over the ocean to *live*.

They needed a fort, of course, and hurriedly built one; and they needed soldiers, because Spain did not want them there. Built of tabby (a mortar made of sand, lime, and oystershells), Frederica was soon a well-designed and prosperous town, with shops lining the principal street. After an attack by the Spaniards, Oglethorpe planned a full-scale invasion of Florida by taking the Castillo at St. Augustine. When this failed, Spain made the inevitable reprisal. Three thousand men in fifty-one ships got past the batteries of Fort St. Simons, but after being routed in a land fight they returned to St. Augustine. It was Spain's last attempt to control Georgia.

## 8. DE SOTO NATIONAL MEMORIAL
### [*Florida*]

CRUEL, RAPACIOUS, UNSCRUPULOUS—call them any unpleasant adjective you please; but there was one word these conquistadors of Spain did not seem to have in their vocabulary: fear. In 1528, Narváez landed upon the west coast of Florida—and was swallowed up by the wilderness. True, the incredible Cabeza de Vaca and a few others of that party survived, to appear years later. Did such a mischance deter Don Hernando de Soto, Knight of Santiago, when he was commissioned by King Charles to conquer, pacify, and populate the great unknown North America, supposed to contain riches far beyond those of Mexico and Peru?

No whit. We see him in 1539 landing somewhere on Florida's coast between Tampa and Estero Bays, and with six hundred or more stout warriors and a dozen equally fearless priests plunging into an unknown land. Up through Georgia and Carolina, across the Great Smokies, down almost to the Gulf of Mexico, up north again nearly to Tennessee, then to the Mississippi River, a stream so wide that "if a man stood still on the other side, it could not be discerned whether he were a man or no."

There, on the bank of the "Father of Waters," De Soto fevered and died, and his followers, sorrowing mostly for the loss of his leadership, sank his coffin in the river. Doña Isabel de Soto, who was in Havana awaiting the return of her husband with news of the discovery of vast riches, received news indeed, months later. But it was that the Don was not returning to her.

## 9. CORONADO NATIONAL MEMORIAL
### [*Arizona*]

AT THE VERY MOMENT when De Soto was in his winter camp near Apalachee Bay in Florida, surrounded by hostile Indians, another Spanish worthy was moving out of Compostela in Mexico into unmapped wilds. Francisco Vásquez de Coronado, with a strong force, aimed to search out and conquer the Seven Cities of Cíbola, reported to be richer by far than anything Peru had yielded. Here, according to a credulous investigator, Fray Marcos de Niza, were great populations with such wealth in gold and silver that they studded their doorways with turquoise and emeralds. It was the first exploration into what is now our American Southwest.

From Coronado Peak, visitors today look out over the great Sonoran Plain of Mexico. The borderline between Mexico and the United States lies just beneath him. It requires no great stretch of the imagination to see those lusting armed soldiers of the advance party coming into view, riding or walking beside their horses, mules heavily loaded with supplies. They come to a spot where two cuts in the mountain barrier indicate valleys. They choose one and press forward.

It is a thrilling story, this mad rush for wealth into a country where there were only poor Indian pueblo folk getting a meager subsistence by farming desert patches. Lured on and on by an artistic Plains Indian liar they called El Turco, they probably got as far as what is now Kansas. The finest thing they discovered was the Grand Canyon of the Colorado. But they were not looking for beauty; it halted them, and they were annoyed.

## 10. SAN JOSÉ MISSION NATIONAL HISTORIC SITE
### [*Texas*]

IN 1777, Father Morfi came up from Mexico to San Antonio to report on the condition of Mission San José y Miguel de Aguayo. He was ravished both by the beauty of its structures and by its success as a converter of savage souls. In his eyes, it was "the Queen of all the missions in New Spain . . . a symbol of the faith, courage and vigor of the Franciscan Fathers." This noble mission is still queenly, for in spite of years of neglect, when parts of it became ruin and the cut stone was requarried by unsentimental settlers, there were those who would, a century later, restore the church and other structures to much of their former condition.

The administration of the mission today is rather unusual. On the operations board are representatives of the Texas State Parks, the Archdiocese of San Antonio, and the San Antonio Conservation Society. The Advisory Board also includes representatives of the National Park Service and the county of Bexar. Its welfare and future are in good hands.

In the old days what delighted the resident Indians and the mission folk were the bright colors that decorated the plastered walls of the church on three sides. The lovely rose windows were the work of Pedro Huizar, whose ancestors had chiseled the delicate tracery of the Alhambra in Spain.

## 11. EL MORRO NATIONAL MONUMENT
### [*New Mexico*]

OÑATE WAS HERE. And lest ensuing generations should forget the fact, he incised upon a rocky bluff, rising two hundred feet above the plain, the record of his passage. "Passed by here the Adelantado Don Juan de Oñate, from the discovery of the Sea of the South, the 16th of April of 1605." The "Sea of the South" was the Gulf of California. As other explorers passed this same "Inscription Rock" they too left their names and sentiments. There is even a verse in praise of Governor Don Francisco Manuel de Silva Nieto, who "made it possible to carry the Christian faith to the Zuñi Indians." The Zuñis had their own ideas about this reported achievement.

The courageous and devoted padres had a stormy time of it for many years among the pueblo people. Often, when the neophytes seemed on the way to conversion and discipline, they suddenly reconsidered. At Acoma they slew fifteen Spanish soldiers. Many priests suffered martyrdom. We read today on the face of El Morro that one party passed the rock on the mission to "avenge the death of Father Letrado."

Many years after the Spanish had engraved their names, a camel train, conducted by Lieutenant Edward Beale, camped overnight at the rock. Of course his men duly added their signatures.

No further names, addresses, or telephone numbers, either on El Morro or an any other natural or manmade feature in the National Park System, are desired. This may seem odd to today's aspirants for immortality. They must remember that they are not Don Oñates, and the year is not 1605. Requirements and values shift with the years.

## 12. GRAN QUIVIRA NATIONAL MONUMENT
### [*New Mexico*]

AS EARLY AS A.D. 800 in the territory that lay between the Chupadera Mesa of central New Mexico and about the present Mexican border, there were a people known as Mogollons (pronounced Mug-ee-yowns), gaining a sparse subsistence by farming the dry country as best they could and adding wild plants and game to their food supply. Three hundred years later their early crude brown pottery changed to one of black-on-white, because they had been influenced by contact with the pueblo people farther west, and the kiva, or underground ceremonial chamber, had been adopted.

By the early part of the seventeenth century this people had achieved the largest pueblo village in the region, the *pueblo de las Humanas,* as it was called by the visiting Spanish.

The Franciscan fathers arrived with the Cross and the Spanish language, to replace the way of life with one that would weld the Mogollons into loyal subjects of the Crown, besides endowing them with the unquestioned superiority of European civilization. Very discerning, as well as wonderfully effective, were these missionaries. They built churches, but they did not try to expel the kivas. If the natives believed that the forces of nature could be propitiated by old-time rituals, they were gently led to see that this was not necessarily inconsistent with the worship of Catholic saints.

But the Apache Indians, with whom the Mogollon people had traded for generations, were raiders, and warlike beyond the nature of pueblo folk. Sometime between 1672 and 1675 the pueblo was abandoned.

## 13. TUMACACORI NATIONAL MONUMENT
### [*Arizona*]

WHAT MORE CONSOLING SPOT, where one can rest in a shaded patio, surrounded by cactus and other native plants, can possibly exist? Never oppressively hot nor bitingly cold, and bathed in sunshine, Father Eusebio Kino must have loved this place when he came in 1691 and said the first Christian mass under a shelter of brush in a little Pima Indian village. The Jesuit father was a man of practical good sense. No doubt the Pimas invited him to visit them because they wondered how these people of Spain had been able to acquire so many of the material good things of existence. Father Kino showed them. In a few years Tumacacori had fields of wheat, cattle, sheep, and goats.

The church we see here, however, dates from a later period. The Jesuits were expelled from all Spanish dominions in 1767, and the Franciscans took over the Sonoran chain of missions that had once been the charge of Father Kino. Although it was never wholly completed, as the unfinished bell tower shows, it had a period of prosperity and a body of Indian converts more than ordinarily devout. In the museum of the monument is a charming diorama which brings to the visitor the very spirit of the mission in its flourishing day.

## 14. CABRILLO NATIONAL MONUMENT
### [*California*]

THE INDIANS of North America had their news services, though the transmission facilities may have been slow. The people of the Zuñi pueblo were

well aware that there was a great ocean far to their east, over which the
sun rose. And the Indians on Point Loma in San Diego Bay, when Juan
Cabrillo went ashore, had already heard about white men of great strength
but bad manners, who had mistreated pueblo folks in their search for precious
metals. So, on the principle that the best defense is to shoot first, they shot
a few arrows into the strangers.

Only fifty years had passed since Columbus had stumbled across a world
new to Europe. But events had been swift in following. Balboa had found
the "South Sea" in 1513. Cortes had gone from Mexico City to the Pacific.
Lower California had been well explored. In 1542 the question remained:
What lay to the north? What peoples? What vast riches?

Cabrillo was of Portugal, but he sailed for Spain. His two small ships
came out of Navidad, on Mexico's west coast, went cautiously up the shoreline, asking questions of the natives along the way, and on September 28,
1542, saw the fires of Indian camps. Cabrillo National Monument marks
the spot where they landed, remained a few days, and then continued northward until they had passed Point Reyes, above present-day San Francisco.
At the death of Cabrillo, his successor got as far as Oregon.

*Inscription Rock, where history was written by many hands. El Morro National
Monument. [Photo: George Grant]*

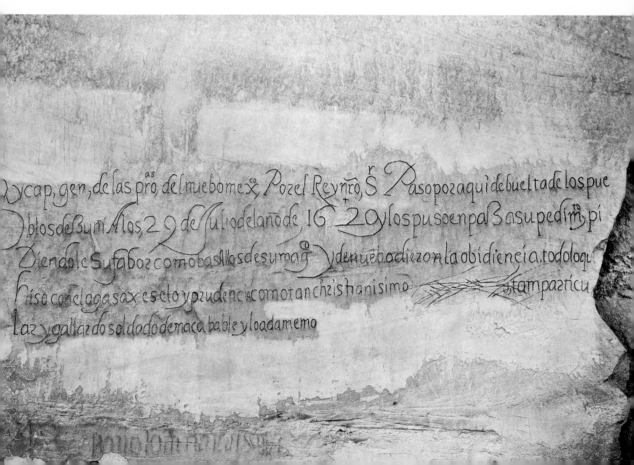

# [ I I I ]

# *Our Early Days*

## 1. INDEPENDENCE NATIONAL HISTORICAL PARK
### [*Pennsylvania*]

ABRAHAM LINCOLN, speaking in Baltimore in 1864, remarked that "the world has never had a good definition of the word 'liberty'." So true it is: there are emotions and ideas for which the revealing word is not in language. But here in Philadelphia, lovingly preserved not only for Americans but for the world's peoples, you come into the presence of liberty itself. Independence Hall, Carpenters' Hall, the Liberty Bell: these are superior to definition. You see; you touch; you understand.

The colonial delegates who met at Carpenters' Hall in 1774 had all been schooled by Montesquieu. From him, and from their own keen observation, they well knew this truth: that "in constitutional states liberty is but a compensation for the heaviness of taxation; in despotic states the equivalent liberty is the lightness of taxation." The taxes levied on the American colonies by the Crown were not onerous, but they were the tokens of vassalage when political voice was denied. The colonials decided to pay the heavier taxes of independence.

And the bell. What an odd life it has had! "Life" is a permissible word, for in the course of years this metal has become nearly animate. From the first it "proclaimed liberty," but this was merely a reference to the charter of William Penn. One suspects that they got a cut-rate price from the London bell founders, for when it was tested, it cracked. Two "ingenious local workmen" recast it, and then it tintinnabulated hoarsely. Again it was recast, this time by workmen perhaps less ingenious, but more skillful. Now it had a

---

*The bell called the Indians (sometimes reluctant) to prayer. Tumacacori National Monument.* [*Photo: George Grant*]

pleasing tone and rang on proper occasions, and this is the very bell we so reverence today. The British having occupied Philadelphia, the bell was in hiding for a year, then returned to Independence Hall. Perhaps it was when it tolled for the funeral of Chief Justice John Marshall that it once more cracked. In silence it speaks with more meaning as years pass. Generations of Americans say: "I have seen the Liberty Bell." And still schoolchildren swarm to be near it and go home with that something the schoolroom and book cannot impart.

All that brilliant planning and skilled craftsmanship can perform, all that patriotic and generous cooperation can achieve, has been contributed to the end of placing this choice memorial of the nation's birth and infancy into safe deposit. In 1818 the city of Philadelphia bought Independence Hall from the Commonwealth of Pennsylvania, which now is developing a mall in the three blocks just north. Congress provided that with the agreement of the three groups which own the surrounding historic buildings, and with added sites to the east, all this should be preserved and interpreted for posterity. A lesson in history: not to be forgotten.

And to what end is recorded history? Emerson has given us the sufficient reason: "The world exists for the education of each man. There is no age, or state of society, or mode of action in history, to which there is not somewhat corresponding in *his* life." The study of history is not a deterrent of mass error: that is plain. It satisfies curiosity; but that is a meaner use. Not merely at Independence National Historical Park, but in every other historic or prehistoric unit of the great National Park System, the thinking visitor is revealed to himself. His ideals, his fears, his hopes, his loves. He asks himself the questions: "What would *I* have done? How, there and then, wherever and whenever, would *I* have measured up to need and opportunity?"

## 2. MINUTE MAN NATIONAL HISTORICAL PARK
### [*Massachusetts*]

SUBURBAN BOSTON now lumbers out over the old Battle Road where, on April 19, 1775, Gage's British troopers marched to teach a lesson to defiant provincials. The precipitate return of the punitive expedition is one of the large facts of history. Today, embattled non-farmers struggle over crowded

*The word "liberty" defines itself here for all Americans. Independence National Historical Park. [Photo: Ralph Anderson]*

roads to get to work and back again without having the fenders of their motor cars bashed. East of where Mass. 128 makes its arc from the South Shore to the North Shore, there is no hope of restoring the original scene, though interpretive markers will identify the way taken by the threatening drums. But a considerable acreage in Lexington and Concord is still restorable, and by order of Congress this is being done. The interested visitor, however, need not wait till the long job is completed. This is ingratiating countryside at any time.

General Gage, you remember, had been stationed in Boston to quell a spreading "sedition." Through his spies (and there was no lack of them, for loyalists were many) he heard that military stores were being collected in Concord. What he did not know was that Paul Revere and his "patriot patrol" were hawk-eyed and keen of ear. The moment the redcoats crossed the Charles River the alarm was spread.

When the British soldiers come into Lexington Green they face Captain John Parker's unshowy muster of Minute Men. "Stand your ground," Parker tells his men. "Don't fire unless fired upon. But if they mean to have a war, let it begin here!" It began there.

The British did very well to get back to the shelter of Boston without greater discomfort than they suffered. It was unlike a European battlefield. From behind trees and stone walls came shots that speeded the quickstep. The minutemen were untrained but indignant.

## 3. YORKTOWN BATTLEFIELD, COLONIAL NATIONAL HISTORICAL PARK
### [*Virginia*]

THE YEARS have been kinder to Yorktown and Gloucester on the lower Chesapeake than to the farmlands that surrounded Boston in the days of the minutemen. Indeed, Yorktown is not as populous today as when Lord Cornwallis surrendered there in 1781. This is fortunate for the lover of historic places, for still to be seen are structures of colonial times—the Customhouse, the Nelson House, two Digges homes, and the Somerwell and Sessions houses. Grace Episcopal Church originated in 1697. There are others.

The Moore House! In this historic home of a Yorktown merchant the

---

*"By the rude bridge that arched the flood . . ." Minute Man National Historical Park. [Photo: M. Woodbridge Williams]*

Revolutionary War came, virtually, to a close. The house has been restored to its original condition and furnished in period style by patriotic groups. It is easy to picture the agents of the British, French, and American commanders sitting here, debating the articles of capitulation. One wonders about the thoughts of Washington, who awaited the results in camp, and the Right Honorable Earl Cornwallis, who rested in a Yorktown residence. For Washington, it was the end of his long service as commander in chief, during which he had coped with treachery and ingratitude within his ranks. For Cornwallis, it was naturally humiliating, but, in truth, few of the English people, and not many of the British generals, had any great bitterness against their transplanted cousins. They frowned on this passion for freedom and felt that revolutions had to be scotched, but some felt that if His Majesty George III had been wisely advised, it wouldn't have happened anyway. At least, not at that epoch.

## 4. MORRISTOWN NATIONAL HISTORICAL PARK
### [New Jersey]

AT A CERTAIN DESK in the Ford Mansion visitors today may feel the very presence of General George Washington, writing his letters and military orders during that bitter winter of 1779–80, when the British command had possession of New York City. For the Continentals, Morristown was a shrewdly chosen site. Only thirty miles from the enemy lines, it was behind the barrier Watchung Hills. This historical park is beautifully maintained, with a high degree of the original appearance, and is one of the gems of National Park Service preservation.

In lovely Jockey Hollow there were sometimes ten thousand patriot soldiers encamped in log huts. Go into one of these reconstructed shelters; meditate. Had you been one of these soldiers, you would often have been ill fed, homesick, cold, ailing, with only confidence in your devoted commander in chief to buoy your sinking spirit. Would help come from France, as Ben Franklin deemed possible? Yes; on a May day in 1780 Lafayette arrived with the cheering news of a second French expedition on its way.

Go into the Historical Museum and view the carefully prepared exhibits that tell the story of the Morristown winter and its relation to what went before in our Revolutionary period—and to what followed as a result of the stubborn courage and wise strategy displayed. An unforgettable page in the American story!

## 5. MOORES CREEK NATIONAL MILITARY PARK
### [*North Carolina*]

WHEN NEWS of the clash of arms at Lexington and Concord came belatedly to North Carolina, there was rejoicing among the provincials there, at least among those who had become convinced that only separation from the mother country would end their subjection to royal whim. But in numbers these insurgents were not an easy majority. Martin, the Crown's governor, though opposed by the provincial legislature and later forced to flee, yet held strong cards against this "most daring, horrid and unnatural rebellion." He gathered a formidable well-armed force of Highland Scots and other loyalists and set about to reconquer the province.

About twenty miles above Wilmington there was a bridge across "Widow Moore's Creek." The creek, as you see it today in this military park, is not wide, but it runs deep and dark. Martin's troops had to cross it to get to the

*The winter of 1776–7 was a bitter one in Jockey Hollow. Morristown National Historical Park. [Photo: M. Woodbridge Williams]*

coast and provisions. The surrounding land was swamp. Who would get first to that vital crossing?

The loyalists lost this race, and when they camped six miles away, Lillington and Caswell were ready for them. They took up the bridge floor, applied a coat of grease to the girders, and covered the approach with their guns. When the attack came, it took three minutes to cut the King's forces down and send them flying. The "rebels" lost one man. Perhaps he had carelessly exposed himself.

## 6. KINGS MOUNTAIN NATIONAL MILITARY PARK
### [South Carolina]

MAJOR PATRICK FERGUSON, head of a scouting force for Lord Cornwallis in South Carolina, was a doughty marksman and the inventor, in 1776, of the first breech-loading rifle carried by warring troops. But his invention was better than his judgment, for he potshotted a wasps' nest. When he threatened the Appalachian mountaineers, mostly Scotch-Irish, that he would "march an army over the mountains, hang their leaders and lay their country waste," they replied that they would see about that. So they took their hunting rifles, knapsacks, and blankets, mounted their horses (those who had horses), and went after Ferguson.

It was 1780. For two years the Crown had had doubtful success in the Northern colonies, but now a new plan, to conquer the South seemed likely to succeed. It was a gloomy prospect for the patriots. An American army under Benjamin Lincoln had surrendered Charleston; Gates had been badly thrashed at Camden. Cornwallis had occupied Charlotte, North Carolina.

In the heavily wooded and rocky battlefield ridge of Kings Mountain, still possessing a wilderness quality, Major Ferguson's force was surrounded by the angry mountaineers and either captured or killed. Ferguson himself was a game one. The shrill note of his whistle, urging his men, could be heard above the shouting and crack of rifles. It took at least eight bullets from the backwoods sharpshooters to eliminate him. The tablet over his grave in the park does him justice.

## 7. COWPENS NATIONAL BATTLEFIELD SITE
### [South Carolina]

ANOTHER VICTORY for the Americans followed the Moores Creek engagement. The numbers engaged were not great, but the effect was to depress the loyalists, to enhearten the colonial revolutionaries, and to move Cornwallis northward toward his ultimate surrender at Yorktown.

There was a new commander of the Americans in the South—General Nathanael Greene. Hearing that Greene had divided his forces, the British general sent a force to defeat Daniel Morgan in northwestern South Carolina, while he moved out of Winnsboro to get between Greene and Morgan. Learning that his pursuers were near, Morgan picked a spot near the North Carolina line to stand and fight, and his leadership and quick thinking were mainly responsible for the signal rout and capture of most of the troopers of his opponent, Banastre Tarleton.

## 8. SARATOGA NATIONAL HISTORICAL PARK
### [*New York*]

THE FRENCH KING, eager enough to humiliate Great Britain, had been hesitant about intervention in this revolution of British subjects in America. In 1777, when Burgoyne's army moved down from Canada to unite with forces moving from the west and south, even the rebellious colonists were far from confident of their chances of success. The battle of Saratoga was a turning point in both respects.

The threat of Burgoyne was formidable. He had 4,200 British regulars and 4,000 German mercenaries, besides some Canadians and Indians. Fort Ticonderoga stood in his way only a few days. After that, the going was rougher. Some small engagements left him in the air; but instead of pulling back to Canada, he decided to risk all to reach Albany. September 13, 1777, found him moving down the west bank of the Hudson at Saratoga to a point four miles from Stillwater Village, where General Horatio Gates, newly selected commander of the American army, was entrenched and ready to receive him.

Kosciuszko, the Polish engineer who had come to assist the colonies in their fight for liberty, had selected this narrow defile where the road squeezed between river and hills. In the notable fighting that led to the final surrender of Burgoyne, Benedict Arnold, later to become villain rather than hero in Revolutionary annals, was one of the most brilliant figures.

All this is charming countryside in and around the battlefield area, and there is much to be seen, besides the famous Schuyler House, that recreates the time and occasion.

## 9. GEORGE WASHINGTON BIRTHPLACE NATIONAL MONUMENT
### [*Virginia*]

IN A CODICIL to his last will and testament Benjamin Franklin wrote: "My fine crabtree walking stick, with a gold head curiously wrought in the form of the cap of Liberty, I give to my friend, and the friend of mankind, *General Washington*. If it were a sceptre he has merited it; and would become it."

The estimation of George Washington as one of the world's greatest men came early. The shock of the loss of the American colonies was scarcely over when perceptive Englishmen were ready to claim this man as an illustrious transplant from home soil. When Ralph Waldo Emerson, in 1833, visited Walter Savage Landor, he heard from that stout Briton the opinion that "three of the greatest men were Washington, Phocion, and Timoleon"— no hesitation in placing Washington first. The few paltry attempts to diminish the stature of this Virginia planter have merely served to enlarge him.

There is no pretense that the tidewater mansion called Wakefield, on Pope's Creek in Westmoreland County, is the identical house in which Washington was born. It is merely a memorial building that represents the eighteenth-century home of a plantation owner such as was Augustine, the father of George. But here, on the high bank of the creek, and near the sandy Potomac shore, a little boy of destiny spun his top and romped, and later, as a youth, returned to take his lessons. Here he learned surveying. At eighteen, he mapped the Bridges Creek area. And before his death, he was to survey a vast political area.

## 10. FORT NECESSITY NATIONAL BATTLEFIELD
### [*Pennsylvania*]

AT THE AGE of twenty-one, George Washington, surveyor and officer of the Virginia militia, was sent with a small force to warn the French to withdraw from the upper Ohio Valley, to which Colonial Governor Dinwiddie and a Virginia corporation laid claim. The French, operating out of Fort Niagara, were harassing English traders on that side of the Alleghenies. The mission failed, and at the place which is now Pittsburgh, where Dinwiddie planned an English stronghold, the French hurriedly built Fort Duquesne.

In April 1754, Washington, now a lieutenant colonel, went out again, and became commander of the Virginia force when his colonel died at Wills Creek. After a skirmish in which a French camp was taken, Washington built a palisaded fort at a spot known as Great Meadows. In his diary he spoke of it as Fort Necessity. But the position could not be held. Coming down from Fort Duquesne, the French, with Indian allies, forced a capitulation. It was the first and last time Washington ever surrendered. The terms were honorable—the colonials gave up only their swivel guns and withdrew with honors. There is now a replica of the palisaded fort on Great Meadows, well worth visiting, and the nearby museum contains relics of the subsequent Braddock defeat.

## 11. PERRY'S VICTORY AND INTERNATIONAL PEACE MEMORIAL NATIONAL MONUMENT
### [*Ohio*]

IN LAKE ERIE, a few miles from the mainland of Ohio, is South Bass Island. During the summer holidays, ferries are busy transporting visitors to this resort, where one of the "musts" is to ascend the memorial shaft and look out over the lake, the shore, and the nearby islands. About ten miles out in the lake is the spot where Oliver Hazard Perry scored a victory over a British naval squadron during the War of 1812. From the deck of the brig *Niagara*, 110 feet long, Perry wrote to William Henry Harrison, commander of the land forces, the famous message: "We have met the enemy and they are ours. Two ships, two brigs, one schooner & one sloop."

The pink granite of the memorial was brought from Milford, Massachusetts. The shaft, a Doric fluted column 352 feet high, has a rotunda made of marble, limestone, and granite. Besides commemorating the naval engagement, this national monument also serves to announce a cheerful fact: that the long boundary between the United States and Canada requires no armed forces to maintain; that the two nations are good friends and intend to remain so.

## 12. FORT McHENRY NATIONAL MONUMENT AND HISTORIC SHRINE
### [*Maryland*]

WHEN ONE of our National Park Service Historians wrote that "on land, during the first part of the war [of 1812] American military operations left much to be desired," he achieved a nice piece of understatement. It was really messier than that. There was a baddish lot of running away by the young republic's troops. Still it must be said that the Americans didn't claim to be a military people, and the British army had the advantage that, after Waterloo, they could detach some of their best veterans from the European sphere. Besides, they had experts at arson among them, as shown by the burning of the White House in Washington—an incident that now makes English gentlemen blush and turn the conversation to the weather.

After an easy victory at Bladensburg the British took the capital city and then turned toward Baltimore—commercially much more important. Fort McHenry had to be reduced, of course. So sixteen warships anchored about two miles down river and started a bombardment that lasted more than a full day and night. Francis Scott Key was a witness of the action. Thrilled, after such a cannonade, to see the "star-spangled banner" still flying, he wrote the words of the song, fitted to the music of the English "To Anacreon in Heaven." Nearly all Americans know the first verse, though singing it has pitfalls for the unskilled.

## 13. CHALMETTE NATIONAL HISTORICAL PARK
### [Louisiana]

THE TREATY OF PEACE, to end the War of 1812, had been signed the day before Christmas, 1814. It had not been ratified. A battle took place on a plantation near New Orleans, on the following 8th of January, that may have hurried a laggard British decision. More than five thousand crack troops, commanded by no less a personage than Sir Edward Pakenham, the Duke of Wellington's brother-in-law, met an incredible motley of volunteer riflemen from adjoining states, some regular soldiers, Creoles, Negroes, Indians, sailors, pirates, and disorderlies just released from jail. The result was astonishing. The British casualties were more than two thousand; American losses, seven killed and six wounded. It sounds like a myth, but it actually happened. How? Why?

Perhaps because Wellington's distinguished brother-in-law had a contempt for these overseas cousins. Perhaps because he was of the old school: you don't hide behind a mud rampart like a cowardly blighter; you form in a solid line, step forward three paces and fire, then repeat. Pakenham's troopers, nothing lacking in courage, so trained and led, came across canefield stubble against a murderous fire and were mowed down. Pakenham himself died of wounds; but the star of Andrew Jackson, credited with this stunning victory, was ascendant. He was on the road to the White House.

## 14. HORSESHOE BEND NATIONAL MILITARY PARK
### [*Alabama*]

NINE MONTHS BEFORE ANDREW JACKSON defeated the British army at Chalmette, he had acquired a reputation for grim determination in his campaign against the "Red Sticks"—that part of the Indian Creek nation which warred upon the white colonial Americans during the War of 1812. The Creeks were divided by a sort of civil war among themselves. Jackson was one of five volunteer generals defending the Southern frontier.

At Horseshoe Bend, a hundred-acre peninsula in the Tallapoosa River in Alabama, the Red Sticks were completely crushed by the army led by our vigorous Tennesseean, who followed his success with a hard peace. More than 20 million acres—half the territory of the Creeks—were ceded to the whites, opening for peaceable settlement a rich country extending from

*Where the Star-Spangled Banner yet waved. Fort McHenry National Monument and Historic Shrine. [Photo: M. Woodbridge Williams]*

Georgia to Mobile. The natural features of the battlefield look about the same as in Jackson's time, but the log barricade and the Indian huts were destroyed after the battle. A stone monument records the victory.

## 15. ADAMS NATIONAL HISTORIC SITE
### [*Massachusetts*]

MANY CUSTODIANS of historic ancient houses have remarked to me that there is one question almost invariably asked by visitors: "Is this place still in the hands of the *same* family?" May this thought somehow be a reflection of a longing to discover some sign, even if a pale one, of a *continuity* which each life may hope to share? Whether or not, this Adams house in Quincy, Massachusetts, is a satisfying memorial to four generations of a family famous in American history. The very walls breathe the Adams rugged individuality: intellectual, unspectacular, nonconformist, and, to be truthful, with something of the acidity of the crab apple. What a breed!

True, the oldest part of this home was not built by an Adams. But when John Adams bought it in 1787, he named it Peacefield, and he and his successors built additions as needs arose. The remarkable Abigail Adams, wife of one President and mother of another, was its first mistress, and her housekeeping eye was no doubt as sharp as her descriptive pen. Then came John Quincy Adams, who served one term as President and later went to the House of Representatives for seventeen years. His son, Charles Francis Adams, as Minister to Great Britain during the Civil War, had the delicate job of preventing a recognition of the Confederacy. Finally, all four of his sons were men of great ability, three of them distinguished in the world of literature. Henry Adams, in his *Education*, has left us fragrant memories of "The Old House."

## 16. SALEM MARITIME NATIONAL HISTORIC SITE
### [*Massachusetts*]

THOSE SALEM SHIPMASTERS went everywhere upon the seven seas. In the earliest days of the port it was usually to the West Indian islands for sugar and molasses, from which the good rum was made, which buoyed the spirits of colonial men. Then, during the Revolution and the War of 1812, they built and manned swift privateers, roaming like killer whales in the lanes of enemy shipping. Salem was the one important American port that never fell into British hands in those wars, perhaps because of the shallowness of the water in her snugly placed harbor; but the time came, in peace, when bigger ships of deeper draft could not be accommodated, and then Derby Wharf, which visitors walk today, went slowly to seed.

But what great days those were when the Derbys, father and son, were building such rovers as the *Light Horse* and the *Grand Turk* and sending them on voyages to the East Indies and China Seas! Eager buyers of the cargoes gathered among the Derby warehouses, and the Custom House, opposite the long wharf, was a busy and exciting place. Here in later years sat, at a desk you may still inspect, a young aspirant for literary fame, Nathaniel Hawthorne. He was Surveyor of the Port from 1846 to 1849. Surveying the port was not then exacting, but he wandered much in the vicinity and developed plot and scene for *The Scarlet Letter,* a novel that has weathered well.

## 17. HOPEWELL VILLAGE NATIONAL HISTORIC SITE
### [*Pennsylvania*]

IN THE EARLY DAYS of colonial development the need for iron increased rapidly—more rapidly than the colonists could accumulate the money necessary to import the metal from Europe. It was no wonder, then, that especially in the Northeastern states the ruins of old furnaces are plentiful, and many place names on the map end with "Furnace." Good sources of the ore, and of limestone, were not hard to find, and the plentiful hardwood forests were nearby to furnish the charcoal fuel to create the "bloom" of wrought iron. For nearly a century these small enterprises, requiring little capital and no year-round operation, supplied the demands.

When Mark Bird built Hopewell Furnace in 1770, to furnish cast iron for his forges, the industry had become big business, requiring ample capital, mines of high-grade ore, and a shrewdly directed organization of skilled workers. The ironmaster had arrived. In Hopewell Village, beautifully preserved within the National Park System, visitors learn what a self-sufficient operation this Hopewell Furnace was. An easy walking tour leads along historic village roads, past charcoal sheds, water-wheel and blast machinery, the casting house, the blacksmith shop, and other relics, to the house of the ironmaster, where may be seen the very furnishings that were there when the freshly baked bread was brought to hungry workers in the Big House.

## 18. HAMPTON NATIONAL HISTORIC SITE
### [*Maryland*]

IT WAS FROM THE PROFITS of an iron furnace that Charles Ridgely, "Charles the Builder," constructed the elegant Georgian mansion known as Hampton. Who was the architect of this stately stone pile, with its wide porticoes set off by balanced wings, its big cupola and fancy dormers, and its urnlike roof decorations? It may have been a local carpenter, one Jehu Howell, for there were artisans in those days who could respond to the order of a rich man: "Build me the finest house that money can buy."

Furnishing this mansion with the proper pieces to display such a center of social life of that Maryland period was aided by the fact that much of the Ridgely furniture had never been alienated. A nephew of Charles the Builder, who became Governor of Maryland in 1816, added the formal gardens described at the time as "an object of beauty and renown." The Governor was said to keep the best table in America; fast horses munched their oats in his stables; and Charles Carroll spoke of a party there when three hundred of the county notables were entertained.

The daughter of Governor Ridgely played the harp, as visitors see from the copy of Sully's *Lady with the Harp* that hangs over the piano in the Great Hall. In the midst of all this beauty, it is impossible to believe that the lady handled the instrument other than well. Next best thing to having received a dinner invitation from the master of Hampton is to visit the place today.

## 19. FEDERAL HALL NATIONAL MEMORIAL
### [*New York*]

BY 1840 THE ANCIENT NEW YORK CITY HALL, which had housed the convention of our first Congress under the Constitution, was in a ruinous condition. It had known great events. On its balcony George Washington had been inaugurated as our first President. Here was adopted the Bill of Rights. It was the first Capitol of the Republic, though not for long. Here Andrew Hamilton defended Peter Zenger in the famous trial that led to a free press in America.

The present Federal Hall, on the site of the older, is an outstanding example of Greek Revival architecture. Here visitors will find themselves in the presence of many historic objects and documents associated with the people and events of our nation's first days. The presentation of the Peter Zenger story has always seemed to me one of the chief gems turned out by those talented artists, unknown to the public, who produce the dioramas and other interpretive displays for National Park Service museums.

*"Send these, the homeless, tempest-tost, to me, I lift my lamp beside the golden door!"*
*Statue of Liberty National Monument.* [*Photo: M. Woodbridge Williams*]

### 20. Statue of Liberty National Monument
### [New York–New Jersey]

What American, returning from abroad and coming into New York harbor, has not felt a quickening of pulse at the sight of this great lady of Liberty with the beckoning torch? A monument designed to commemorate the alliance of France and the United States during the War for Independence, the statue has over the years taken a meaning far beyond its original one. To generations of people, fleeing oppression from other parts of the world, it has been a beacon of welcome and promise.

The French historian Edouard de Laboulaye conceived the idea of this pledge of friendship, and he found an imaginative Alsatian sculptor, Frederic Auguste Bartholdi, to put it into this bold and classic form. The French people, notably frugal, raised by popular subscription the money to defray the cost of the gift; the cost of the pedestal on which the colossal figure stands was met by American subscribers. The security of the statue in a position where high winds often sweep was a great engineering accomplishment.

As modern lighting systems have improved since the torch first shone, its illumination has increased, so that now, if you multiply the light of the full moon by 2,500, you arrive at the gleam that goes out to sea from the little island of Bedloe—now known as Liberty Island.

### 21. St. Paul's Church National Historic Site
### [New York]

Anne Hutchinson believed that we are saved by our personal intuition of God's grace rather than by obedience to church laws. It wouldn't make much of a ripple now, but in Puritan Boston of 1637 it was a scandal: besides, Anne's velvet tongue was corrupting even some of the ministers. So she was banished and asked not to come back. First she went to Rhode Island, then to the north side of Long Island Sound, near Pelham Bay, where she founded the church body of which the present edifice, built of brick and stone in 1760 and ensuing years, is her memorial. Its Freedom Bell is the twin of the one at Independence Hall—cast by the same founders in England.

### 22. Touro Synagogue National Historic Site
### [Rhode Island]

George Washington, when President, told the members of the Newport Congregation that his government "gives to bigotry no sanction, to persecution no assistance." For nearly two centuries the small synagogue on a Newport street has "testified that men may seek eternal truths in their own particular ways without hindrance from the civil government that embraces them all." In December 1763, four years after laying of the cornerstone, the synagogue was dedicated, Isaac Touro then being the spiritual leader. Peter Harrison, the dean of colonial architects, was the designer—in the Georgian style, but modified to accommodate the Sephardic ritual. A plain brick exterior; no hint of the riches within.

## 23. GLORIA DEI (OLD SWEDES') CHURCH NATIONAL HISTORIC SITE
### [*Pennsylvania*]

THERE WERE SWEDISH SETTLERS in the Philadelphia region before the arrival of William Penn with his land grant. Gloria Dei (Old Swedes') was founded in 1677, but the present structure dates from about 1700. The Swedish origins are apparent in the steep gable roof, the square belfry, and the small spire. The church still operates in the section of South Philadelphia that was early known to settlers as Wicaco, but in the pressure of modern life and commerce the surroundings have lost a good deal of their primitive charm. An ironic understatement, visitors will perceive.

## 24. DORCHESTER HEIGHTS NATIONAL HISTORIC SITE
### [*Massachusetts*]

THE BRITISH COMMANDER GENERAL HOWE looked out upon the fortifications that toiling patriots had created on the night of March 4, 1776, on the two highest hilltops of Dorchester Heights, and sourly remarked: "The rebels have done more in one night than my whole army would have done in a month." Well, he should not have been surprised. The provincials were working for their independence.

Washington's strategy paid off. The British were forced to evacuate Boston. The heights are now solidly built up with residences, but a white marble shaft at the summit is evidence that this spot was a formidable position.

# [ IV ]

# *Westward Expansion*

## 1. JEFFERSON NATIONAL EXPANSION MEMORIAL NATIONAL HISTORIC SITE
### [*Missouri*]

HARDLY HAD PIERRE LACLÈDE of New Orleans received a patent from Louïs XV of France granting a monopoly of the fur trade "between the Missouri and St. Peter's Rivers" when a secret treaty ceded the whole Colony of Louisiana to Spain. It was two years before Laclède knew he had a dead contract. But by that time he had picked a strategic location on the Mississippi sixteen miles below the junction with the Missouri, built a house, and made the brash prediction that this place would "become one of the finest cities in America." From Fort Chartres he sent a thirteen-year-old youth, Auguste Chouteau, to clear a way for the settlement. Thirteen years old! Maturity came early then.

A band of Missouri Indians arrived, when the house foundations were being laid, to help and to stay to dinner. The warriors restricted their help to giving advice, but the squaws actually shoveled. When Chouteau politely asked his guests to go home, they laughed and replied blithely, "We are like the ducks and the geese. When we see quiet water, we light on it, rest, feast and enjoy life." A poetic garment for a happy philosophy!

On a bluff above the river floods and convenient to other river approaches, St. Louis was to become truly the Gateway of the American West. Wise Napoleon knew that France could not hold this unmapped inland empire and sold it to an even wiser buyer, Thomas Jefferson. The mighty stainless-steel arch of Eero Saarinen, rising 630 feet in the cleared space below the old Courthouse of Dred Scott memory, symbolizes the epic flow of America toward its "manifest destiny."

---

*Gateway to the West. Jefferson National Expansion Memorial National Historic Site. [Photo: M. Woodbridge Williams]*

Figuratively, through this shining gate passed the mountain men of the fur trade, the covered wagons of the Oregon emigrants, the eager rushers toward the California diggings, the traders of the Santa Fe Trail, homesteaders and cowboys headed for a vast extent of free cattle range—all, indeed, that we associate with the "winning of the West." Along this riverfront were docked the famous Mississippi steamboats, belching black clouds from their stacks when they fired up; and alongside were the smaller craft that went out to serve the developing towns of the upper Mississippi and Missouri Rivers. The historian Hiram Chittenden said: "It is doubtful if history affords the example of another city which has been the exclusive mart for so vast an extent of country as that which was tributary to St. Louis."

When visitors come to see what modern technology has done, to ascend the arch and gaze out upon the surrounding city and countryside, or, when it is completed, to visit the great museum which the National Park Service will create beneath the arch, they should not forget that there is much of precious history not far from the city itself. Who could fail to be charmed, for instance, by the dreamy allurement of Ste. Genevieve, with its fine old Creole Bolduc house? One can see how the early builders, having first followed the Norman or French Canada design, then added their wide West Indian galleries to fend off the burning summer sun. Or, on the Illinois side of the river, one can visit the Pierre Menard home, the sweet retreat of a man who had made his fortune from the skins of animals, in company with the Chouteaus, Andrew Henry, and other partners.

## 2. CUMBERLAND GAP NATIONAL HISTORICAL PARK
### [Kentucky–Tennessee–Virginia]

THEIR GRACIOUS MAJESTIES (*dei gratia*, etc.) had a quaint way, in the colonial times of North America, of issuing grants of land to those who had influence at court. We grant; you go and find out where it is. It cost the Crown nothing, and it might bring in some pounds sterling in the way of taxes.

Employed by one of these "proprietors" in 1750, Dr. Thomas Walker set out from Albemarle County in Virginia, with five fellow walkers, to locate 800,000 acres of desirable real estate in a wilderness the Indians called Kentucky. Report had it that the grazing lands were incredibly rich, and abounding in bison, deer, and other game. The Cherokees of North Carolina used to cross the Alleghenies and battle with other red men for the hunting rights. That journey was all very well for Indian warriors traveling afoot. But these

*Bolduc House. Ste. Genevieve, Missouri. [Photo: M. Woodbridge Williams]*

same Alleghenies loomed like an impassable barrier against white men with carts and oxen, which required roads. Was there a natural cut somewhere that the "Loyal Land Company" could find and use?

Walker never did discover the rich grazing lands. He did come upon the "levil" gateway to the West that he named "Cave Gap." It was destined to become the main artery through which poured the migrating colonists, first into the Northwest Territory, and finally to the Mississippi River and beyond. And he found a large river which he named the Cumberland in honor of the son of George II. Later the gap was so named too.

It remained for Daniel Boone and his hardy band to reach the "dark and bloody ground," and to blaze a trail. In March 1775, Judge Richard Henderson bought "twenty million acres of land south of the Kentucky River" from the Cherokee Indians. Whatever the Indians got for it was pure velvet, because they didn't own it. But less than two decades afterward, when Ken-

*Through this cut in the Alleghenies, America moved westward. Cumberland Gap National Historical Park. [Photo: National Park Service]*

tucky became a state, it had a population of 100,000. The end of the Revolutionary War had sent venturesome Americans on a great westward trek.

### 3. FORT LARAMIE NATIONAL HISTORIC SITE
#### [*Wyoming*]

IN THE ANGLE formed by the junction of the North Platte and a tributary creek there was a fine location for a voyageur of the fur-trading days. Jacques La Ramie spotted it first, hence the later name of Fort Laramie. He was soon erased by the Indians, but Sublette and Campbell set up a post on the spot, calling it Fort William. The competition in the fur trade was keen, even bitter. The trading posts changed hands oftener than the traders changed shirts, and with less ceremonial observance. Thomas Fitzpatrick, the great mountain man, took over for the American Fur Company in 1836.

When Francis Parkman saw Fort Laramie in 1846 it was a rare sight for a Bostonian. Near the post were clusters of Indian lodges—Cheyennes, Arapahoes, Sioux—ready to trade their coats for doctored alcohol. In the late summer would come bands of bison hunters. The fur trade was declining, and the era of the "buffalo-robe" was waxing.

Here, on the parade ground of the army fort that was abandoned in 1890, visitors can reconstruct in their minds the stirring scenes of its past. It is a long time since the last soldiers had their farewell roaring party, with the officers tilting their glasses to "Old Bedlam." Old Bedlam had well earned its name. There was, among other memories, the memorable Christmas night when the dance was on. Suddenly came "Portugee" Phillips, a veteran scout, out of a wild ride through a blizzard, to summon aid for the besieged troops at Fort Phil Kearny, at the foot of the Bighorns.

Visitors to this monument should push onward over the trail of the Oregonian emigrants to Guernsey, Wyoming—a matter of ten miles or so— and see Register Cliff, on whose chalky face the covered-wagon folks cut their names and left messages for those laboring behind. And nearby are those historic deep ruts in the surface rock cut by the iron-shod wheels of the pioneer wagons. We hear much about the toils of the emigrants, and truly they were heroic souls; but has anyone mentioned the draft animals that here sweated and strained to pull their loads up, up, over this bare limestone rock?

## 4. Scotts Bluff National Monument
### [*Nebraska*]

THE COVERED WAGONS of the Oregonians had not proceeded far beyond Chimney Rock when a peculiar geologic formation halted them, saying, "What's your hurry, little men?" The little men well knew what their hurry was. They knew that time was of the essence; they had to pass through the western mountains before the deep snows came. But the badlands, coming right down to the south bank of the North Platte, were not negotiable for wagons. There was a choice: a deep slit at an imposing headland known as Scotts Bluff, and a pass between two ridges named for the squaw-man Roubideaux.

The bluff, looming up eight hundred feet above the river, had received its name from a tragic event of the early trapping days. According to Washington Irving's "Captain Benneville," a pioneer named Hiram Scott, with several other men, had been descending the North Platte in canoes. Caught in eddying currents, their craft overturned, and supplies and ammunition went. Living upon wild fruits and roots, they finally reached Laramie Fork, where Scott was taken sick. A generally accepted story is that Scott was left to die by his companions. It is hard to believe, but the tradition goes on to state that the abandoned man actually crawled and tottered for sixty miles to the base of this bluff, where his skeleton was later found.

From the summit of the bluff there is a revealing view of the badlands which forced the emigrants away from the Platte; to the west can sometimes be seen Laramie Peak, 120 miles distant.

## 5. CHIMNEY ROCK NATIONAL HISTORIC SITE
### [*Nebraska*]

WILLIAM HENRY JACKSON, a photographer in Vermont, heard the call of the roseate West. With camera and painter's easel he roamed it most widely of all limners. He loved it, to the last days of his ninety-ninth year. Maybe while you were in the museum at Scotts Bluff National Monument you saw Jackson's watercolors, painted in his ripe years from sketches made when he was a muleskinner with a caravan heading west along the Oregon trail.

Once, when I was going down the long but not steep hill near Gering, Nebraska, I came into view of that "earthy sandstone" pinnacle called Chimney Rock (how could it have had any other name!). I happened to have with me a reproduction of Jackson's watercolor of the very scene. In his picture the hill was steeper than now, as the highway engineers of today make easier grades. But there are the covered wagons at the foot of the hill, drawn up in circle for protection; the golden-yellow sunset puts a violet light upon the hills, and I am sure the bullwhacker in the foreground, twirling a rawhide, can be none other than William himself. That's the way Jackson saw Chimney Rock in 1866; the way I see it with the inner eye; the way you and millions of other tourists will picture it till Chimney Rock, inevitably crumbling, shall be a heap of angular blocks.

## 6. FORT CLATSOP NATIONAL MEMORIAL
### [*Oregon*]

HAVING SEEN AT LAST the blue water of the Pacific, Lewis and Clark looked for a suitable location for fortified winter quarters. They chose a place near

*From a distance it is almost like a ruin of the classic age. Fort Laramie National Historic Site.* [*Photo: Carl Degen*]

the river which now bears the name of the two Jeffersonian explorers, on a bay, said Clark in his journal, "which I call Meriwether's Bay, the Christian name of Captain Meriwether who no doubt was the first white man who ever surveyed this Bay."

Most of their supplies exhausted, the party settled down to a lean winter diet of fish and "pore elk," with wild roots for vegetables. Lacking salt, they set up a camp on the ocean beach and boiled out three bushels from the sea-water. Some families of "Killamuck" Indians made them a friendly gift of "a considerable quantity of the blubber of a whale which had perished on the coast . . . it was white and not unlike the fat of Poark."

There is an Oregon state park at Ecola, "the place of the whale." When I was there, on one occasion, I remembered with delight the story of how little Sacajawea, the Shoshone squaw who had made the long trip with the explorers, begged to be allowed to see that whale. When Clark at first declined to have her go with the group, she said that "she had traveled a long way with us to see the great waters, and now that monstrous fish was to be seen, she thought it very hard that she could not be permitted." Sacajawea had

[ 4 8 7 ]

her way. She saw the whale. But the explorers did not get much meat from it to take back to Clatsop. The Indians liked blubber, too.

## 7. FORT UNION NATIONAL MONUMENT
### [*New Mexico*]

WHEN COLONEL EDWIN V. SUMNER selected a spot on the west bank of Coyote Creek as a place where the military could serve and protect the great traffic that was moving over the Santa Fe Trail, one of his purposes was to seek an isolation that would keep the enlisted man from the temptations of the town. What the soldiers thought of this we may conjecture, since a freedom from temptation made life so dull in a frontier post that, lacking activity against the Indians, a new temptation arose: to shoot themselves.

But it was a well-chosen spot nevertheless. Strange indeed how the cobweb of wagon ruts made a century ago are so clear on the face of the land today. As the fort was at the division point of the trails, Fort Union was a welcome haven where travelers could rest and refit. It was the principal quartermaster depot of the Southwest.

All in all, the dragoons and mounted riflemen were not called upon for large-scale operations. They had to knock out Chief Chacon and his Jicarilla Apaches in 1854 and the southern Utes the following year; in 1860 the Kiowas and Comanches were restless, and the following January a column from the fort killed a few rebellious ones and otherwise discouraged them. Yet if Fort Union hadn't been where it was . . . it would have been a different story!

## 8. BENT'S OLD FORT NATIONAL HISTORIC SITE
### [*Colorado*]

THERE WERE MANY TRADERS who set up posts in the Indian country to do a lucrative and often reprehensible business, but none had the phenomenal success of Bent, St. Vrain and Company. Gray Thunder, a potent chief of the Cheyennes, was not loth to give his comely daughter, Owl Woman, in marriage to William Bent. William's brother Charles was the credit man of the firm; St. Vrain was the merchandiser; but the magic touch of friendly relations with the tribes resided in the finesse and fair dealing of William. It was said: "These were mighty men, whose will was prairie law."

On the north bank of the Arkansas River in southeastern Colorado one sees the remains of the way station erected in 1833, which became headquarters for trappers and Indians and the chief point of contact between the whites and their neighbors. Here, springing up from the prairie land like a legendary sky castle, the Bents reared a fortress of mud bricks, fireproof and impregnable. It was a self-contained little barony. If your caravan needed the service of gunsmith, wheelwright, carpenter, or blacksmith, they were here. From this stronghold went General Kearny to Santa Fe in 1846, to raise the American flag over that Mexican possession.

Overtaken by reverses, William Bent abandoned the adobe structure in 1849 and set up a new fort farther down the Arkansas.

## 9. Fort Davis National Historic Site
### [*Texas*]

NOT THE LEAST COLORFUL of the memories connected with this best preserved of the Southwestern forts is the experiment with camel transportation from

*Century-old wagon ruts are clearly seen around this Santa Fe Trail post. Fort Union National Monument.* [*Photo: G. S. Cattanack, Jr.*]

1857 to 1860. It was Jefferson Davis's pet idea to use these burden beasts to cross the desert country—a sound scheme that came to nought when the Civil War changed all things.

The rush of emigration to the goldfields of California sent a horde of eager Easterners toward the West, and thousands chose the most southerly route to avoid the winter snows. The San Antonio–El Paso road had just been opened. The Indians made this a dangerous trip, for the trail crossed the trails of the Comanches and the Mescalero Apaches, raiders who had long plundered the villages in northern Mexico. Fort Davis was the answer.

The ardor of the Comanches was finally chilled by the United States Army in the Red River War, though troops from Fort Davis were not engaged there; but as late as 1880 the Apaches were making the El Paso road hazardous. It was then that Chief Victorio came up out of Mexico and found Colonel Benjamin H. Grierson and his Fort Davis troopers blocking his progress. There was some hard fighting, but the death of Victorio brought peace at last to West Texas.

## 10. Fort Smith National Historic Site
### [*Arkansas*]

MAJOR WILLIAM BRADFORD reached Belle Point, a rocky bluff at the junction of the Arkansas and Poteau Rivers, on Christmas Day, 1817. Though white men habitually encroached upon Indian lands, the immediate need here happened to be to quell the warfare between the Osages and the Cherokee invaders, who had come from North Carolina to get a share of the good hunting. The frontier shifted, and this first post gradually melted away. Later another installation was built, and it is of this later Fort Smith that visitors today see the barracks and commissary buildings.

The fort's military career was never impressive. The real drama began when the U.S. District Court moved into the abandoned barracks in 1871 and began sternly to deal with the lawlessness and violence that existed in the territory to which the dispossessed Indian tribes of the East had been moved by that kindly old gentleman Uncle Sam. Here, for more than twenty years, the fearless and upright Judge Isaac C. Parker dispensed justice with a capital J. Three hundred and forty-four men stood before the bar accused of major crimes: seventy-nine were hanged. Hanging having such a strong touch of finality about it, conditions in the region steadily improved.

## 11. HOMESTEAD NATIONAL MONUMENT OF AMERICA
### [*Nebraska*]

DANIEL FREEMAN WAS A MAN who knew a good piece of land when he saw it. He was serving in the Union Army in 1862 when the Homestead Act was passed by Congress. Not far from Beatrice, Nebraska, there was a sweet portion of turf. Cub Creek ran through it, providing an unfailing water supply, as well as a fringe of cottonwood and oak.

I happened to be a visitor at this monument soon after it was established. In the makeshift office of a newly arrived superintendent, I saw Daniel Freeman's "Entry Number One," the classic of homesteading, hanging on the wall. I saw also a cracked and weathered wooden spade, a relic from somewhere in the vicinity, dating back to those days of filing on the land. It was not that steel spades didn't exist; many of the homesteaders just didn't have the cash, so they whittled their own. There were hardships.

But the homesteaders could say: "This is only a little cabin, but it is our own. We have only one skillet and we honestly are tired of flapjacks, and come night our muscles are sore . . . but someday we'll have a brick house and Ma will have a hired girl." I doubt if we should pity the pioneers more than they pitied themselves, and I am guessing that wasn't much.

## 12. WHITMAN MISSION NATIONAL HISTORIC SITE
### [*Washington*]

ABOUT THE THIRD DECADE of the nineteenth century there was a great searching of hearts among church folk about carrying the gospel to the benighted. The Indians of the Far West were in this category. Not only were their notions of personal hygiene faulty, but they were inclined toward superstitions. It happened that a delegation of Nez Perces and Flatheads had visited St. Louis and suggested that they would like to hear more about the white man's Truth. The Commissioners for Foreign Missions gave ear. They sent Marcus Whitman, a doctor not of divinity but of medicine, to found a mission in the Columbia River Valley. The location, in Cayuse tongue, was Waiilatpu—"The Place Where the Rye Grass Grows."

What a man was this Marcus Whitman! A stubborn and devoted dynamo, he raised the standard of living and the health of the Indians around him. When the fur-trade rivalry was acrimonious and the Hudson's Bay Company was for the moment getting the better of it, someone said, seeing Marcus pass by, "*There* goes a man the British can't drive out of Oregon!" But a sudden burst of primitive passion on the part of the Cayuses spent itself on their benefactors on a night in November 1847, though none of the Christianized Indians were involved. The mission was destroyed; Dr. Whitman, his wife, and fourteen other persons were murdered.

### 13. McLoughlin House National Historic Site
### [*Oregon*]

Sir George Simpson was a Scotsman with a cold gray eye, a boundless energy, and a dislike of deficits. He came into the fur-trade picture in 1821 when the Hudson's Bay stockholders discovered a situation not unknown to-day: that gross sales may be large, business brisk, but net profits nonexistent. The trading posts, remote from London, were staffed by young men with a vast appetite for comforts and delicacies. To Sir George's horror, he found in the warehouses such things as ostrich plumes and coats of mail. His eye fell upon an apprentice surgeon out of Montreal, by name John McLoughlin, a very giant of a man with a booming voice, liable to sudden rages, but scrupulously honest and big hearted. This man, Simpson's manager, was to become "the father of Oregon."

Simpson was a dapper man who felt uncomfortable in the company of this Goliath whose clothing was usually in tatters and who had "a beard that was like the chin of a grizzly bear." He wrote that "McLoughlin is such a figure as I should not like to meet on a dark night in one of the byelanes of London." Yet this was the same man whose hospitality and aid to the missionaries and stranded emigrants was unfailing. When the people of the United States set up a "provisional government" in Oregon, he joined them, and the Hudson's Bay Company lost an irreplaceable servitor.

### 14. Fort Vancouver National Historic Site
### [*Washington*]

The original Fort Vancouver was built on a lovely point of land on the north bank of the Columbia above the confluence of the Willamette. Even so stern a businessman as Sir George Simpson of the Hudson's Bay Company was ravished by the beauty that surrounded it. "I have rarely seen a Gentleman's seat in England," he said, "possessing so many natural advantages."

In 1829 it was decided to shift the location farther west and four hundred yards from the river. This later Fort Vancouver was the one to which American settlers turned for aid against Indian malcontents; it recovered the abducted women and children of the Whitman Mission at Waiilatpu. After the fur trade declined, the post was still conducting a booming business, especially during the California gold rush. It was, in effect, the terminus of the Oregon Trail.

Though the Oregon Treaty gave the Hudson's Bay people "possessory rights," the end of its occupancy could be foreseen. On June 14, 1860, the last load of the company's property was aboard a ship and headed for Victoria on Vancouver Island.

So ended the life of Fort Vancouver—until the day came when the importance of the old post caused it to be "rediscovered." The site was excavated, careful research began, and Fort Vancouver's place in the National Park System was secured.

## 15. GOLDEN SPIKE NATIONAL HISTORIC SITE
### [*Utah*]

"THE LAST RAIL IS LAID, the last spike driven, the Pacific Railroad is completed."

So flashed a telegraphic message to the Associated Press on May 10, 1869, from Promontory Summit, Utah. Two railroad companies—the Union Pacific building from Omaha westward, and the Central Pacific laying rail eastward from Sacramento—had met. The dream of transcontinental direct transportation was now realized.

On the western face of the Promontory Range, the Central Pacific, using Chinese labor, laid down ten miles of track in one day—a record in the history of railroad building that has probably never been equaled.

## 16. PIPE SPRING NATIONAL MONUMENT
### [*Arizona*]

WHEN JOSEPH SMITH, founder of the Church of Jesus Christ of Latter-Day Saints, was murdered by a mob at Nauvoo, Illinois, the embattled Mormon people chose Brigham Young as successor. They could not have found a more resourceful and energetic man. Young's executive force, diverted to profane purposes, would have made him one of the commercial giants. By his sagacity and iron will the Saints achieved their "land of the honey-bee," Deseret, and made it bloom like a rich June meadow. "If the Gentiles will let us alone for ten years," Young had said, "I'll ask no odds of them." On the shores of the Great Salt Lake of Utah the Mormons asked no odds, as their descendants do not today.

They had not long been seated at Deseret when they began to fan out into the adjoining country. Their outposts reached to the Grand Wash of the Colorado River. In 1856 the Jacob Hamblin party, sent out to explore the Navajo country, make friends of the Indians, and set up tithing cattle ranches for the church, came upon a spring about fifteen miles southwest of present-day Fredonia. From a dugout of earth and juniper logs, this settlement finally had two red sandstone buildings of two stories each, constituting a fort.

Clothed with juniper, piñon, cottonwood, willow, and desert plants, this national monument is just about a mile above sea level. You will see Lombardy poplars here, too, but they are not native. The Mormons brought them in.

## 17. BIG HOLE NATIONAL BATTLEFIELD
### [*Montana*]

DURING THE WHOLE SOMBER HISTORY of the expulsion of the Indian peoples from their ancestral homes, the Nez Perces of the Northwest had been singularly docile. They had even joined with the whites against their own color, on occasion, as when they covered Colonel Steptoe's retreat in the "Oregon War." Their intelligent Chief Joseph, not because he loved the whites but because he saw the futility of trying to broom back the ocean, was pacific and yielding.

In early August 1877 the Nez Perces were about to receive their reward for cooperation. It was the old story. The white settlers had moved in upon the fertile lands of the Willowa Valley which, by treaty, were to belong to these Indians in perpetuity. "Perpetuity," in a treaty with the Indians, meant "till we change our minds." Now the Nez Perces were to be moved out to places "just as good." A sarcastic chief once said to an army commander, "You have moved us five times. Why don't you put us on wheels? You could move us with less trouble."

The Indians, planning to migrate to Canada, promised to do so peaceably and were so doing when they arrived at their old campground at Big Hole. There they were attacked by federal troops at night. They rallied and counterattacked with such courage that when they moved on the troops dared not pursue them.

*Here Custer's men made their "last stand." Custer Battlefield National Monument.*
*[Photo: Andrew M. Loveless]*

But of course the end was certain. The Nez Perces finally surrendered in the Bearpaw Mountains and became government wards.

## 18. Custer Battlefield National Monument
### [*Montana*]

LET US SAY AT ONCE that the whole truth about the slaughter into which the 7th U.S. Cavalry rode can never be known. Custer died; of his surrounded men on the ridge above the Little Bighorn not one survived. One wounded horse, Comanche, survived to become an army pet while he lived—and then was stuffed and preserved to the present day. A century after that battle, military buffs will be shouting vehement opinions at each other at the visitor center of the monument.

For myself, I can never look upon certain widely separated white markers rising from the ungrazed prairie grass without an unashamed tug at the heart, even more than when viewing the fenced cemetery. White slabs that tell where troopers fell upon this uneven ground—the very markers seeming to flee toward a hoped-for refuge. Here one man. Over yonder two men, close together. Two stumbled and died over there . . . that black and white bird just winging past us is a lark bunting . . . what a fluttering of lark buntings there must have been on that June day in 1876!

In death, color differences are washed out. In the cemetery you see headstones that read: Coyote, Indian scout; Bad Heart; Hunts-the-Enemy; Chippewa Indian Woman. Chippewa? So far from home? And one marker says, simply: An Indian Child.

## 19. CHICAGO PORTAGE NATIONAL HISTORIC SITE
### [*Illinois*]

MILO M. QUAIFE, the historian, wrote: "It is no exaggeration to say that Chicago owes her very existence to the fact of her strategic location on one of the most important water routes of North America . . . Chicago Portage was one of the five great 'keys of the continent.' "

The explorer Louis Jolliet had suggested as early as 1673 that it would only be necessary to cut a canal through a mile and a half of prairie "to go in a bark by easy navigation from lake Erie to the Gulf of Mexico." He had reason to know. With Père Marquette, in their return from the Mississippi voyage, he had reached the Great Lakes by way of a little creek and Mud Lake, "portaging" over this very mile and a half of land barrier.

## 20. THEODORE ROOSEVELT NATIONAL MEMORIAL PARK
### [*North Dakota*]

WHEN THE FRENCH VOYAGEURS called these strangely eroded "vast silent spaces" badlands, they did not mean that they might not someday be productive. They merely meant that this country was hard to travel through. Teddy Roosevelt's cattle found good sweet grazing here on the Little Missouri when their owner came from the East and set up as a ranchman in 1883. The Northwest was still a frontier. Only the year before had the Northern Pacific Railroad finally put a bridge across the Missouri at Bismarck.

---

*Totem poles tell a family and tribal story. Sitka National Monument. [Photo: Josef Muench]*

In the sense that Roosevelt did not have to get his bread and butter from the cattle industry, we shall have to regard the Maltese Cross brand as a dude undertaking. He was there partly for his health, partly because it was a wilderness region of the kind he loved to the end of his life. Nevertheless he aimed to make the business prosperous, and he came through one bad winter without great loss. But the winter of 1886–7 was the most terrible that the white man had ever recorded in the Northwest. It ended the "open-range" delusion which, it must be confessed, had stood up well for a good many years. Roosevelt lost more than half his cattle. He did not give up, and though he was now enjoying his political successes back East, he returned to the Little Missouri nearly every year, until in 1898 he disposed of the dwindled stock before going to Cuba with his colorful Rough Riders. He always regarded his losses as money well spent.

## 21. Chesapeake and Ohio Canal National Monument
### [Maryland–West Virginia–District of Columbia]

On the Fourth of July 1828, President John Quincy Adams raised the first shovelful of earth to initiate the digging of a canal that was planned to connect the federal capital on the Potomac with Pittsburgh on the Ohio. It was that boom period of canal building when the Eastern states were feverishly attempting to capture the trade of the fast-growing West. Stock-company speculations found ready capital, and this plan of the Chesapeake and Ohio Canal Company for water transport between 360 miles of artificial banks was at first greeted with enthusiasm. George Washington as a young man had been among the first Americans to promote such projects.

Various difficulties, ultimately financial ones, prevented the completion of this ambitious design. At Cumberland, where the canal was to cross the Alleghenies, the stockholders decided to quit. It took twenty-two years to reach that point, and by that time the frenzy for building steam railroads was in full swing. Nevertheless this canal continued to carry freight in its barges until 1924, and in its most active period, in the 1870's, as many as 540 boats were in use.

The right-of-way of the canal is now owned by the government. The western division, from Seneca to Cumberland, constitutes this monument, where the towpath can be walked in surroundings of great beauty and interest. The twenty-two miles from Georgetown to Seneca may be enjoyed by visitors to Washington.

## 22. GRAND PORTAGE NATIONAL MONUMENT
### [*Minnesota*]

*Stalwart* IS THE WORD for those Canadian French voyageurs—picturesque wilderness figures in their deerskin leggings, moccasins, and red woolen caps—who came paddling out of Montreal in canoes laden with trade goods for the North West Company posts. The word originally meant "with a firm foundation." These indefatigable men with full chests and muscular legs could tote two ninety-pound packs over the "big carry" to the rendezvous on the Pigeon River, undaunted by rocky ledges or trails that turned to grease in the rain and sleet.

They had come from France when Canada was French. The British victories at Quebec and Montreal had changed all that. The names of the fur-trade enterprisers were now McTavish, McGill, Mackenzie, and the like; but the carriers were still Jacques and Armand and Louis.

In July and August the guns and kettles, axes and beads, tobacco and rum were exchanged for beaver and other furs brought to the North West post by other canoe brigades. Along this highway of the voyageurs were many of these carries, and this Grand Portage of nine miles was neither the longest nor the most laborious, but it was at the point where the trading company maintained its Great Hall, held its annual meetings, feasted and bickered, and kept the payrolls. Sometimes a thousand workers were paid off. And then . . . what an odor of West Indian rum!

## 23. NEZ PERCE NATIONAL HISTORICAL PARK
### [*Idaho*]

HERE IS A REGION in our Northwest not only rich in history but still retaining much of its frontier natural beauty. Here is the Lolo Trail of Lewis and Clark; here are told the stories of the fur traders, the gold seekers, the work of the missionaries, and the Nez Perce War of 1877. The area marks rather a departure from the usual in the National Park System. It is a coordination of related sites, in which the large land areas separating those sites will remain under present ownership and control.

Two of the separated historic units deal with the conflict between the Nez Perces and the federal troops: Whitebird Canyon and Clearwater River. These engagements forced the crucial battle at Big Hole.

## 24. Hubbell Trading Post National Historic Site
### [*Arizona*]

It was after the Indian of the Western plains and mountains had been subdued and brought into reservations that a new kind of trader came into existence, to run the necessary post exchange where the government wards could dispose of their articles of craftsmanship and obtain the needed goods of white man's fabrication. The Indian trader came to exercise far more influence upon the lives and ways of the native people than could the federal agents, who usually came and went with political change.

These traders might be good or bad; usually those who did business in Navajo lands were genuinely interested in the welfare of their clients—even to a fatherly attitude. Perhaps the greatest and most influential was John Lorenzo Hubbell, whose post at Ganado had distinguished visitors from all over the country and from foreign lands. In the house Don Lorenzo built in

*Inside the great wall on Honaunau Bay was sanctuary. City of Refuge National Historical Park. [Photo: Walter Horchler]*

1900, next to the trading post, the walls of the big living room and the bedrooms are covered with the works of famous artists who thus showed their appreciation of the Hubbell hospitality.

## 25. ARKANSAS POST NATIONAL MEMORIAL
### [*Arkansas*]

TERRITORIAL CAPITAL of Arkansas in 1819, this military and commercial lodgement in the wilderness then looked back upon a tempestuous career since "Iron Hand" Tonti, the vigorous lieutenant of the adventurer La Salle, had founded it in 1686. Those were the days of the Great Triangle—the struggle among England, France, and Spain for supremacy in the rich new world. The moves on the European chessboard were sudden and sly. Commanders at the post, in a day of tardy communication, were never sure whether they were governors or intruders.

Altogether, the history of this outpost of empire, besides being a reflection of the turbulent struggle for power, reveals a picture of men at their best and worst. You wonder how such a post could be governed at all. There were humorous aspects too. An English traveler, in 1766, found the place a rendezvous for undesirables, including one chap "whose only cargo in his pirogue was a pack of cards by which, and by his skill, he stripped hunters of their possessions." The perennial cardsharp!

## 26. FORT LARNED NATIONAL HISTORIC SITE
### [*Kansas*]

SINCE IT IS the best preserved of all the military posts that protected the Southwestern frontier, Fort Larned is certain to have many visitors, now that it has become part of the National Park System. For years since its abandonment by the army it has been preserved as a ranch headquarters, in parts of which the Fort Larned Historical Society has maintained a museum.

The location of the post in 1859 was strategic. First known as the Camp on the Pawnee Fork and later as Camp Alert, it was the northern anchor of the military protective line. The following year, a new location three miles west was chosen and a sod-and-adobe Fort Larned was built, later to be replaced by stone structures, of which nine are still standing. In 1864 the fort became the agency for the Kiowas and Comanche Indians, and later for the Cheyennes, Arapahoes, and Kiowa-Apaches. Traders flocked in for a rich harvest. When the Santa Fe Railroad was being built, this fort provided protection for the laborers.

# [ V ]

# *The Civil War*

## 1. Appomattox Court House National Historical Park
### [*Virginia*]

THE UNION VICTORY at Five Forks on April 1, 1865, forced General Robert E. Lee to evacuate the long-besieged town of Petersburg, which in turn had so effectively protected the Confederate capital from that quarter. With Richmond doomed, the Confederacy had one last chance of continuing the war. Lee headed his Army of Northern Virginia toward Danville with the hope of uniting his remaining forces with those of General Johnston in North Carolina.

Hot in pursuit, General Grant followed the retreating army. The Union forces cut Lee's line before he could reach Amelia Courthouse, and forced him northward toward Farmville. Downhearted, many of Lee's soldiers left the ranks and took the muddy roads for home. They were no longer even called deserters. Appomattox Station on the Southside Railroad was the last chance of escape. When daylight came on the morning of April 8, at Appomattox Court House, the Confederates found Union infantry in front of them. In the quiet of an informal truce, Lee then arranged a meeting with the Union commander to discuss terms of the surrender of his army.

The two great military leaders met in the red-brick home of Wilmer McLean, who, oddly enough, had seen the battle at Manassas rage around his house in the first days of the war. After the war this Appomattox building was taken down with the idea of making it a museum. Later it was faithfully reconstructed by the National Park Service. In the parlor of this house the two men, who had served in the Mexican War together, began by amiably discussing their old army days. As to the terms of surrender, Grant's attitude

---

*. . . Enshrined forever: the Lincoln Memorial. National Capital Parks. [Photo: W. E. Dutton]*

was one of greatness of spirit. The generous concession by which the common soldiers of the Confederacy were allowed to keep their own horses or mules "to work their little farms" caused Lee to remark: "This will have the best possible effect upon the men. It . . . will do much toward conciliating our people."

The civil strife between North and South was now virtually at an end. But it was necessary for Lee's troops to march past their conquerors, to lay down their weapons, and to receive paroles. Three days later, as eighty thousand Union soldiers quietly watched, the men in gray filed up the side of Clover Hill. Grant had left this final ceremony in the hands of the tough, bullet-scarred Maine schoolmaster General Joshua L. Chamberlain, who proved not less magnanimous in victory than his chief. As the defeated soldiers came opposite the receiving group, with General Gordon at the head, a bugle sounded, and the marching salute, from "order arms" to the old "carry," was given.

And later, Chamberlain was to record a strange aspect of this surrender, as moving as the scene in the McLean house. With the dispersion of the disarmed men in gray, "we are left alone, and *lonesome*. We miss our spirited antagonists . . . and lose interest. Never are we less gay. It was dull, on our march homeward, to plod along . . . without scouts and skirmishers ahead, and reckless of our flanks. It was dreary to lie down and sleep at night without a vigilant picket out . . ."

Thus it was; that four years of savage conflict had created for the armies a way of life, and they found the stillness and the freedom from danger tame.

## 2. GETTYSBURG NATIONAL MILITARY PARK
### [Pennsylvania]

THE GREAT NUMBER of Americans who yearly visit the battlefield of Gettysburg is an expression of the consummate interest this engagement will always have for students of our history. Though no immediate military aims were achieved by either side, it still was the great battle of the greatest of civil wars. Here, on the first three days of July 1863, more soldiers died than before or since in an encounter in the Western Hemisphere. More than 172,000 men were involved. It was rightly called "the high water mark" of the efforts of the Confederate States to break away from the Union. Not only that, but

---

*The famous cyclorama is beautifully housed. Gettysburg National Military Park. [Photo: M. Woodbridge Williams]*

*Warren's figure still surveys that sanguinary field. Gettysburg National Military Park. [Photo: M. Woodbridge Williams]*

the imperishable Gettysburg Address of Abraham Lincoln was delivered here.

Once before—in September 1862—General Robert E. Lee had taken an army north of the Potomac River. A salient reason then was that a successful invasion could well have resulted in the recognition of the South by the European powers. The resulting battle at Antietam was a stalemate and a disappointment to the South, but the opportunity of a negotiated peace was still alive. Besides, Vicksburg was in danger of falling to the hammering of Grant, and a single victory might relieve the pressure there.

From early June, Lee's army had been moving through the gaps in the Blue Ridge and into Pennsylvania. It left the back door of Richmond vulnerable, but Lincoln chose to send an army in pursuit of Lee. That the opposing forces met and fought at Gettysburg was really accidental, but a chance contact having been made, the great armies were soon locked in a gigantic struggle in which the fortunes swayed dramatically in favor first of one and then of the other, ending with the magnificent but tragic charge of fifteen thousand Confederates against the Union center. The costly effort failed, and with it went the last hope of a successful invasion of the North.

Lee's Army of Northern Virginia retreated across the Potomac, unpursued by the Union forces; but it was a bitter day for the Confederacy, for on that very Fourth of July came news that Vicksburg had been surrendered.

### 3. VICKSBURG NATIONAL MILITARY PARK
#### [*Mississippi*]

FARRAGUT'S NAVAL FORCES in the spring of 1862 had been able to clear the lower Mississippi River and capture New Orleans, Baton Rouge, and Natchez. Union forces could move up the Tennessee and Cumberland Rivers into the very heart of the Southland. But so long as the Confederacy held Vicksburg, with big guns lining the waterfront and the steep bluffs, the problem of dividing the seceding states, East and West, was unsolved. The task of reducing this formidable bastion had been given to Ulysses S. Grant, as commander of the Union Army of Tennessee. And through no fault of his, but

*An unusual monument—a pup tent of 1863. Gettysburg National Military Park.* [*Photo: M. Woodbridge Williams*]

rather because of dismal failures in the eastern theaters of the war, the North was discouraged.

When Farragut took his fleet back to New Orleans and the Union gunboats withdrew to Memphis, it became certain in Grant's mind that the city could not be taken by amphibious operations through the swamps and bayous of the riverfront. Among several possibilities of taking the city from the land side, Grant chose to fix a bridgehead to the south on the west bank, and with the help of Porter's gunboats ferrying them across, to move his troops eastward against the Confederates under General John C. Pemberton, hoping not only to capture Vicksburg but to destroy Pemberton's army. A quick change of plan enabled him to defeat Johnston's forces, which were aiming at a juncture with Pemberton, and to take the vital rail center of Jackson. By the middle of May, Pemberton was besieged in Vicksburg, and the Union forces were ready to storm the city.

Vicksburg finally fell, not to the several costly assaults that were made, but to hunger and lack of supplies. Stubbornly as the city was defended, the net was drawn ever tighter. Cornmeal was gone, and mule meat took the place of salt pork. No help came; and on the morning of July 4, 1863, the Confederates marched out and stacked their arms. There was a tinge of irony in the fact that Vicksburg was surrendered by a Confederate general who had been a West Pointer from Philadelphia and who, following his sentiments at the cost of lifetime friendships, had thrown in his fortunes with the South.

### 4. MANASSAS (BULL RUN) NATIONAL BATTLEFIELD PARK
#### [*Virginia*]

TWO IMPORTANT BATTLES were fought on almost the identical ground at what was an important railroad junction near the little stream of Bull Run, not far from Washington. The green troops on both Union and Confederate sides were not lacking in courage, but panicked easily on the first occasion they clashed in July 1861. There was no conception of the magnitude the civil struggle would attain. The North clamored for a quick finish of the war by the capture of Richmond; and Manassas, on the Orange and Alexandria Railway, was the only direct connection between the two capitals. Quickly after the firing on Fort Sumter this junction had been fortified for defense. A final attack by the Southerners routed the federals and sent them straggling back to Washington. It was in this battle that General Thomas J. Jackson won his famous nickname "Stonewall."

The second battle here, a little more than a year later, was even more of

*The Yazoo has changed its course many times since 1863. Vicksburg National Military Park. [Photo: M. Woodbridge Williams]*

a crushing defeat for the Union; so much so that General Robert E. Lee now saw the possibilities of a bold invasion north of the Potomac. Only a steady stand by federal troops on that same Henry House Hill where in the first battle the Confederates had put them to rout enabled Pope's army to get back to the shelter of Washington defenses. McClellan's Peninsular Campaign had failed to take Richmond. Now another setback. The clouds in the North looked sullen.

## 5. CHICKAMAUGA AND CHATTANOOGA NATIONAL MILITARY PARK
### [*Georgia–Tennessee*]

WITH VICKSBURG FALLEN, in July 1863, the major Union strategy next called for creating another dividing line among the states of the Confederacy. The aim now was possession of the great rail center of Chattanooga, in eastern Tennessee. In expectation of this move, the Southern general Braxton Bragg, with a large force of seasoned men, was dug in for its defense. The battle at Stones River, six months earlier, had opened this campaign. Bragg was facing Rosecrans, and both generals showed a good deal of skill in their tactics. Fighting for the key city began with a skirmish on September 18, 1863, and quickly developed into a general battle party in open fields, partly in dense woods, and sometimes waged hand to hand. The first day was indecisive, but on the day following, Rosecrans's army was nearly cut in half and destroyed by a sudden thrust by Longstreet. Only the Union left, on Snodgrass Hill, held its position. It was then that General George H. Thomas, the Union field commander, earned for himself a title somewhat similar to that of Stonewall Jackson. With stubborn determination the "Rock of Chicka-mauga" held against every assault and covered the Union retreat. But now the Union army was trapped in Chattanooga, reduced to near starvation, and it was only later, near the end of November, that Grant, now overall com-mander, after bitter fighting, succeeded in raising the siege and opening the way for Sherman's campaign through Georgia. The famous "battle in the clouds" on Lookout Mountain occurred during the last days of the engage-ment.

## 6. PETERSBURG NATIONAL BATTLEFIELD
### [*Virginia*]

MANY OF THE MEN of the 48th Pennsylvania, the army of Grant at the siege of Petersburg, had been coal miners in civilian life. Though against the city defenders of 50,000 the Union troops numbered at least 112,000, this vital back door of Richmond was so heavily armed against a frontal attack by troops as to make that idea unthinkable. "But," said the miners, "let us drive a tunnel under the Confederate battery opposite us, and let the infantry pour through the breach we shall make." The idea was accepted, and on July 30, 1864, four tons of powder were exploded, leaving a great crater, 170 feet long, 60 feet wide, and 30 feet deep. But this mine, which could have meant the capture of the city, not only failed of its purpose, but because of incompetence and blunders, cost the Union army dearly in killed, disabled, and prisoners.

Most visitors who come to Petersburg Battlefield first ask, "Where is the crater?" Naturally enough: it was a dramatic event. Yet really the great story here is the matching of skill and power of the two great generals, Grant and Lee, from the Wilderness struggle in May 1864 until Petersburg—and therefore the capital of the Confederacy—fell. Every Grant move, to the end, had brought him closer to Richmond, by way of its outpost on the south. In the ten-month siege, the Union losses were far heavier than those of the defenders—but the war was won. Petersburg was the war's largest single battlefield—approximately 170 square miles.

## 7. FORT DONELSON NATIONAL MILITARY PARK
### [*Tennessee*]

IT WAS HERE that Ulysses S. Grant came into national prominence as a bold and able military leader. At this time a brigadier general, he worked out a plan to break the eleven-mile line between Fort Henry and Fort Donelson, part of the Confederate front which now stretched from Columbus on the Mississippi River to Cumberland Gap. With seventeen thousand men, he moved up the Tennessee River on transports supported by gunboats. Fort Henry, a mudhole at best, could not be defended, and its garrison moved to Fort Donelson.

Grant had twenty-seven thousand men when he arrived before the fort. There were twenty-one thousand men within Donelson, and they were well supplied—except with leaders who could face a man like Grant. Indeed, Grant's position was precarious after the Confederate batteries had knocked out Foote's supporting gunboats. But the Confederate commander, Floyd, was timid, and his associate, Pillow, feared falling into federal clutches. Finally, on the night of February 15, 1862, the decision was made to have the junior commander, Simon Buckner, ask Grant for surrender terms. Pillow and Floyd escaped up the Cumberland River, and the cavalry leader, Nathan Bed-

---

*Overleaf: Lookout Mountain stood in Sherman's path. Chickamauga and Chattanooga National Military Park. [Photo: M. Woodbridge Williams]*

ford Forrest, who would have no part in the shady business, took his men out safely. When Buckner asked for terms, Grant's reply was: Unconditional and immediate surrender. "Unconditional Surrender Grant" was a slogan that brought fresh spirit to the drooping Union. But in Richmond it was dismal news.

## 8. KENNESAW MOUNTAIN NATIONAL BATTLEFIELD PARK
### [Georgia]

WROTE GENERAL SHERMAN, when he was making his drive toward Atlanta and the sea in early May 1864: "Kennesaw, the bold and striking twin mountain, lay before us . . . the scene was enchanting; too beautiful to be disturbed by the harsh clamor of war; but the Chattahoochee lay beyond, and I had to reach it."

Sensitive writing, this, on the part of a military man, who could perceive the loveliness of the north Georgia countryside at a time when he was facing the master of Fabian tactics, Joseph E. Johnston. Sherman had 100,000 well-supplied troops against the Confederates of half that number, but he was in hostile country and had always to take the offensive against adroitly chosen positions. Not till Sherman found Kennesaw Mountain looming between him and his objective, Atlanta, did the Union general decide upon a direct attack.

Up the steep grades of the mountain the federal troops pushed against formidable Confederate breastworks and the deadly rifle fire. Two hours and a half of this vain attempt, and the fighting ended. The breakthrough had failed, with great Union losses. Sherman went back to his flanking tactics that were forcing Johnston steadily, if slowly, back upon Atlanta. Then the Richmond government, tired of retreat, retreat, and wanting something more dashing, replaced the patient Johnston with the eager General Hood. It was what Sherman had wanted. The capture of Atlanta soon followed.

## 9. ANTIETAM NATIONAL BATTLEFIELD SITE
### [Maryland]

WHILE THE BLOODY BATTLE that took place here at Antietam Creek and Sharpsburg was not a Union victory, it was essentially a defeat for the Confederacy. Lee's hope of swinging Maryland to the Southern side, and the possibility of getting Great Britain (hit hard in its economy by the lack of American cotton for its mills) to declare the Confederacy a sovereign nation, had to be relinquished for the moment.

It is said that more men were killed and wounded at this battle than on any other single day's fighting during the entire war. Of the 87,000 federal troops under General McClellan the losses were more than 15 per cent. Lee had about 41,000 men in the fight, and 26 per cent were lost. So desperate was the conflict at many points that the soldiers quit from sheer exhaustion. The terrible effectiveness of the firepower can be imagined from what General Hooker wrote of the action north of the town of Sharpsburg: "in the time I am writing every stalk of corn in the greater part of the field was cut as closely as could have been done with a knife, and the slain lay in rows [Jackson's troops] precisely as they had stood in their ranks a few moments before."

The timely arrival of Confederates from Harpers Ferry prevented a Union victory here.

## 10. SHILOH NATIONAL MILITARY PARK
### [*Tennessee*]

THE CAPTURE of Fort Henry and Fort Donelson by Grant forced the Confederate commander, Albert Sidney Johnston, to fall back from Kentucky and that part of Tennessee north of the all-important railroad that ran from Memphis to Chattanooga. The possession of this supply line was to become the reason not only for the battle at Shiloh, but for much sanguinary fighting afterward.

The Tennessee River was now open to Union gunboats and transport. Up to Pittsburg Landing, only a short distance from the Confederate railroad center at Corinth, Mississippi, came 40,000 of Grant's soldiers, and Buell, with 25,000 more, left Nashville to join Grant. Before these reinforcements could arrive, Johnston moved out of Corinth to get between the Union forces and their supply base at Pittsburg Landing. Before daybreak on April 6, 1862, the Southerners made an attack upon the federal camp, which apparently was unaware that Johnston was so near them. It touched off the bloody encounters between the unseasoned but courageous men on both sides, which caused Grant to write in his memoirs that "Shiloh . . . was a case of Southern dash against Northern pluck and endurance . . . the troops on both sides were Americans . . . united they need not fear any foreign foe."

Albert Sidney Johnston died from a wound received in this battle, as he sat on his horse under the oak tree still seen by visitors. And peaches still bloom in the part of the battlefield where some of the fiercest combat took place.

[ 5 1 5 ]

## 11. RICHMOND NATIONAL BATTLEFIELD PARK
### [*Virginia*]

ONLY A LITTLE MORE than one hundred miles separated the capital of the Confederacy from the federal city of Washington. This geographical location constituted a military liability to the seceding states from the first; yet it is easy to understand why the old seat of government of Virginia was chosen. Richmond, on the James, naturally became the symbol of secession. The Northern slogan "On to Richmond!" meant "Put down the rebellion!"

In spite of seven distinct drives to capture Richmond, the city was never actually taken. It fell because Petersburg fell, and only at the very end of the war. It did, though, have two narrow escapes: once during McClellan's Peninsular Campaign in 1862, and again two years later when Grant crossed the Rapidan and came to the very edge of the city. But all the terrific hammering of Grant's forces would not break down the defenses that had been created against the chance of just such a frontal attack. The final effort, at Cold Harbor on June 3, 1864, lasted less than half an hour, but left seven thousand soldiers dead and dying. Grant himself said that the attack was an error of judgment.

As would be expected, the battlefield park, as preserved and administered by the National Park Service, consists of ten different parcels of land, and a complete tour of the battlefields is about fifty-seven miles.

## 12. FREDERICKSBURG AND SPOTSYLVANIA COUNTY BATTLEFIELDS MEMORIAL NATIONAL MILITARY PARK
### [*Virginia*]

FOUR MAJOR BATTLES of the Civil War are represented in this military park— Fredericksburg, the Wilderness, Chancellorsville, and Spotsylvania Court House. As Petersburg was the back door of the capital of the Confederacy, so was Fredericksburg the front door. At the falls of the Rappahannock River, just about halfway between Richmond and Washington, the possession of this city was of the utmost importance. The wide river was a barrier against attack from the Union.

In November 1862, President Lincoln had wearied of McClellan's super-caution and slow movement and replaced him with General Ambrose Burnside. After a long delay while pontoon bridges were procured, Burnside crossed the Rappahannock successfully and captured the city in street fight-

*More than a memorial: a heartbreak in stone and bronze. Shiloh National Military Park. [Photo: George Grant]*

[ 5 1 7 ]

ing. But the later attack upon Marye's Heights, despite heroic efforts, was a disaster. There was a long lull on this front until Hooker succeeded Burnside and made an attempt to get behind Fredericksburg. The ensuing Chancellorsville was a Confederate victory, but their great leader Stonewall Jackson was killed during the fighting.

In May 1864, Grant, now in supreme command of the Union forces, sent the army of Meade across the Rapidan, and the battle of the Wilderness followed, west of Fredericksburg. The bitter fighting here was indecisive, but the struggle moved on to Spotsylvania Court House, where Lee formed a new strong line which Grant decided not to attack.

## 13. STONES RIVER NATIONAL BATTLEFIELD
### [Tennessee]

THE HOPE OF THE CONFEDERACY, to bring Kentucky under the banner of secession, vanished when the army of General Braxton Bragg was defeated by Buell at Perryville in October 1862. Indeed, with Nashville in Union hands, Bragg needed all his strength to frustrate the clear intention of the northern leaders to cleave the upper from the lower South by thrusting along the line of the west-east rails into Chattanooga from Memphis.

Bragg selected a base at Murfreesboro and placed his troops along the stream called Stones River. Thirty miles northwest was the Union Army of the Cumberland, commanded by Rosecrans. Late in December the two armies were facing each other, and the opposing generals had developed almost identical plans. Each intended to assault the other's right wing and bend it back into the river. The three days of desperate fighting that took place here ended with a sudden reversal of fortunes at the moment when the Confederates were about to achieve a victory. Eight batteries of guns, assembled with astonishing speed and massed on the heights to meet the Confederate all-out attack, poured out a devastating fire of a hundred rounds a minute. An almost certain success changed to a rout in a matter of minutes.

Bragg's soldiers had captured Union cannon in this fighting, as well as more than three thousand prisoners. But it was hardly a victory. The Union troops held the field, and Bragg had to seek another base.

## 14. FORT SUMTER NATIONAL MONUMENT
### [South Carolina]

ON DECEMBER 20, 1860, South Carolina seceded from the Union, and this example, so long threatened and feared, was soon followed by the formation of a Confederate government, with Jefferson Davis of Mississippi as President. Virginia, North Carolina, Tennessee, and Arkansas, though generally sympathetic with the other Southern states, hesitated to make the break. By March 1861 nearly all the forts and navy yards in the seceding states had been seized by the Confederates, but Fort Sumter, in Charleston harbor, remained in federal possession.

Major Robert Anderson, in command of the small garrison at Fort Moultrie on the mainland, moved over to Sumter "to prevent the effusion of blood," as he reported to Washington. The Charlestonians immediately occupied Moultrie and prepared to bombard the harbor fort if necessary. Anderson had only a few months' provisions, and Buchanan, then President of the United States, sent a supply ship to his aid. But it was turned back by the shore batteries. After Abraham Lincoln became President he notified the Governor of South Carolina that Fort Sumter would be supplied and defended.

The Confederate officers did not wait. At four thirty a.m. on April 12 a shell burst over the fort. By daybreak other shore cannon opened fire. A hot shot started a fire. In the afternoon, "the magazines surrounded by flames," Major Anderson agreed to a surrender.

On April 15, Lincoln issued his call for 75,000 volunteers, and Civil War had begun. The reluctant Southern states, including Virginia, now threw in their fortunes with the Confederacy.

## 15. FORT PULASKI NATIONAL MONUMENT
### [*Georgia*]

AFTER THE WAR OF 1812 the young United States, realizing the vulnerability of its long coastline against a possible invasion by a European power, began the construction of a chain of forts, of which this one, named for its Polish friend of Revolutionary days and located on Cockspur Island, near Savannah, was nearly twenty years in the building. In its massive walls were 25 million bricks, and the superb masonry had not only utility, but also a touch of elegance. One military authority said that "you might as well cannonade the Rocky Mountains as Fort Pulaski."

At the outbreak of the Civil War, Pulaski was not garrisoned by the federal government, and Governor Brown of Georgia ordered it seized just before Georgia joined the Confederacy. Early in November 1861, Robert E. Lee, then in command of defenses in the Southeast, considered the possibility that the fort might be attacked from batteries on nearby Tybee Island.

About eight hundred yards was then considered the distance from which a brick fort could be breached by cannon. Lee said to the fort's chief: "They can make it very warm for you, Colonel, with shells from that point, but they cannot breach you at that distance."

It was true when Lee said it, but the war soon brought refinements of old means, and when federal batteries did open up from Tybee, early in 1862, rifled cannon were used. A thirty-hour bombardment brought about its surrender.

## 16. BRICES CROSS ROADS NATIONAL BATTLEFIELD SITE
### [Mississippi]

AS THE CIVIL WAR dethroned some military idols, so it also unexpectedly created others. Not the least surprising of the latter was Nathan Bedford Forrest, who entered the Confederate service in a humble capacity and proved to be one of the greatest of cavalry commanders. Forrest had no formal military training whatever. He was original, daring, and a natural leader of men. There was a legend that when Forrest was once asked for the secret of his success he replied, "To git thar fustest with mostest." Even if he never said it, this actually described his tactics on many a field.

Brices Cross Roads was the scene of a spectacular victory by this swift-moving leader over a Union force more than twice his numbers. As Sherman was moving toward Atlanta in mid-1864, his supply line, the railway from Nashville to Chattanooga, was in danger from attack by the Confederates located in Mississippi. Sherman ordered: "Hold Forrest . . . until we can strike Johnston." So General Sturgis came out of Memphis headed for Corinth, Mississippi. Forrest attacked him with such swift energy at Brices that soon there was confusion in the Union ranks, then panic. The attempted orderly retreat of Sturgis to Memphis became a rout. Most of the Union artillery and more than 1,500 soldiers fell into Forrest's hands. At points of his own selection, the unschooled tactician had struck first with the most.

## 17. TUPELO NATIONAL BATTLEFIELD
### [Mississippi]

ALTHOUGH IT WAS a vain attempt on the part of the Confederates to keep Sherman from Atlanta—and the ocean—the battle at Tupelo was fought with the courage usual to both combatants, but produced no real honors for anyone. General Stephen D. Lee, the senior commander, had come to the scene without troops. Forrest, the Confederate cavalry genius, had 9,400 horsemen to defend the rich prairie part of eastern Mississippi from an advance by a Union force of 14,000. Actually the Union thrust was aimed to destroy Forrest. After the fight at Brices Cross Roads, where Forrest had humiliated a Union general with a classic display of skill, Sherman had cried: "There will be no peace until Forrest is dead. Follow him to the death, if it cost ten thousand lives and breaks the Treasury."

So Sherman picked two commanders he thought might have better luck and possibly more ability. "Forrest whipped Sturgis fair and square," said Sherman with wry frankness. "Now I will put him against A. J. Smith and Mower." Smith was an old hand with real soldier quality. Mower was "a young and game officer." Together they might finish off this terrible gadfly.

They did not, but neither did they come off badly. The battle, fought in wilting heat, swayed back and forth evenly. The Union forces were turned back, but Sherman's command of his supply line was safe. And that was his main aim.

## 18. Fort Jefferson National Monument
### [*Florida*]

On one of the coral key islands called the Dry Tortugas, about seventy miles into the Gulf of Mexico from Key West, was built the largest of the brick forts intended to secure the nation from invasion. It covered most of sixteen-acre Garden Key. The plan provided for 450 guns, in three tiers, but although thirty years' work was done on it, it was never completed.

Actually Fort Jefferson played no part in the Civil War, save that it was hurriedly garrisoned at the outbreak and was used to imprison Dr. Samuel A. Mudd and others accused of complicity in the assassination of President Lincoln. An insecure foundation and hurricanes gradually made a ruin of this "guardian of the Gulf ports."

What Fort Jefferson lacks in military significance is far outweighed by the amazing wildlife picture presented here. Nesting of the thousands of sooty terns between May and September (with some hundreds of noddy terns among them) is an unforgettable spectacle. Then come in the man-of-war, or frigate, birds to live a life of ease by robbing the terns of their hard-earned catches of fish. Around and around, without moving a wing, these seven-foot-spread soarers circle above the fort, gliders without parallel. Wonderful, too, is the underwater plant and animal life seen in the crystal-clear waters.

## 19. HARPERS FERRY NATIONAL HISTORICAL PARK
### [West Virginia–Maryland]

"THE PASSAGE of the Potomac through the Blue Ridge is perhaps one of the most stupendous scenes in nature . . . this is worth a voyage across the Atlantic." So wrote Thomas Jefferson after many a visit. Peter's Hole, the place was first called. Robert Harper built a mill here, and ferried folks across the river. Then came canal and railroad, and the lower part of the gap, less beautiful than before, was busy and important. Occasionally flood waters of the Shenandoah and Potomac, joining their streams here, scoured the lower town. But Harpers Ferry hung itself out to dry, and trade went on.

It was inevitable that when the Civil War came, both sides in the struggle should covet the possession of this stragetic point. Even before, the place had been dramatically awakened to the coming conflict by the raid of the abolitionist John Brown, who swooped down upon the armory there to obtain weapons for a Negro insurrection. When Brown was hanged at Charles Town, there was a man present, in charge of a state guard, named Thomas J. Jackson. Less than two years later Stonewall Jackson, now a Confederate colonel, would lead a column to capture the entire Union garrison.

Fought over continuously, burned, looted, reduced to a ghost town, Harpers Ferry still retained the spark of life. The loveliness of the surrounding mountains and the inspiring view of the great marrying rivers were beyond the malice of man to spoil.

## 20. GENERAL GRANT NATIONAL MEMORIAL
### [New York]

THIS RUGGED SOLDIER, Ulysses S. Grant, who emerged from the obscurity of a country store in Illinois when the Civil War came and was to be the answer to the harassed Lincoln's prayer for a general who "would do something," lies buried in a gray granite monument on a bluff overlooking the Hudson River. He was, indeed, a West Point graduate, and had served throughout the Mexican War, but he had resigned from the army and was so little considered by the War Department that when he offered his services to the Union he was ignored.

Grant's indomitable drive and tenacity, first demonstrated at Fort Donelson, took him to the supreme command of the Union armies, to the surrender at Appomattox, and inevitably, as a war hero, to the White House in 1868. We like to recall his generous terms to the defeated Lee, his personal integrity, and the frank fairness of his *Personal Memoirs*, written in his final days in an effort to pay off his debts and provide for his family.

In the center of the marble-lined interior of "Grant's Tomb" is an open crypt containing the sarcophagi of Grant and his wife. In niches around the walls of the crypt are bronze busts of his old field comrades Sherman, Sheridan, Thomas, Ord, and McPherson.

## 21. Abraham Lincoln Birthplace National Historic Site
### [*Kentucky*]

In the winter of 1808, when Kentucky was still "dark and bloody ground," and only the resolute could endure the pioneer hardship, Thomas Lincoln and his wife Nancy Hanks paid $200 in cash for a three-hundred-acre farm, a few miles south of Hodgen's Mill. There was a one-room log cabin there, near the Sinking Spring. Here, February 12, 1809, was born Abraham Lincoln, destined to have many memorials of his great life and tragic death, but none that will be so enduring as the love and hope he inspired in the hearts of people of good will, wherever men exist.

The precise history of that log cabin, now seen within a memorial building that was erected with funds raised by popular subscription and including the pennies of schoolchildren throughout the nation, will always be open to controversy. It makes little difference. The multitude of yearly visitors are not interested in the neatness of historiography. They come to do reverence to the great American who, with patience and humor and steadfastness, saw their country through four years of bitter civil strife, and himself remained with malice toward none, and charity for all.

Since Dr. George Rodman bought this log cabin which stood upon the birthplace farm and moved it to his own property nearby, it has seen long travels. Dismantled, and carefully marked for reassembly, it was exhibited at many expositions throughout the country. In 1909, it came back to a spot near Sinking Spring at last.

## 22. Pea Ridge National Military Park
### [*Arkansas*]

Nowhere were fiercer passions engendered by the issues of slavery and secession than in Missouri. Sixty per cent of all Missourians of military age served in the Civil War—109,000 in the Union armies and 30,000 with the Confederacy. But these numbers did not tell the whole story. Bitter hatreds arose from internal dissension, political and otherwise. The possession of St. Louis alone, as a base for operations in the West, would be a rich prize for either side.

When General John C. Frémont, fresh from an interview with Lincoln, arrived in St. Louis in July 1861, he found himself, as he said, "in an enemy's country, enemy's flag displayed from houses and recruiting offices . . . St. Louis was in sympathy with the South, and the state was in actual rebellion against the national authority." The fiasco at Bull Run had been a damaging blow to Union prestige.

At Christmas, General Samuel Curtis was given the mission to drive the pro-Confederate forces out of Missouri. His opponent was General Sterling Price, former governor, who, like many Missourians, had been utterly opposed to secession, but also opposed to the invasion of the South. Price, with state troops that had not become part of the Confederate Army, had to pull back across the Arkansas line, where he could join the regular forces. The ensuing two-day battle of Pea Ridge, bitterly contested, with both sides having their successes, was a decisive defeat for the Confederacy. Missouri was saved for the Union. Yet the state continued to be ravaged by guerrilla warfare throughout the war.

## 23. Andrew Johnson National Historic Site
### [Tennessee]

THE NATION has had many prominent leaders who rose from humble beginnings, but none whose climb was quite as steep as that of Andrew Johnson, who became President at the death of Abraham Lincoln. When still a boy, in order to help support his family, he became apprentice to a tailor instead of attending school. But, with a devoted wife and invincible determination, he achieved an education, created a prosperous business, and entered politics, rising steadily from mayor of his city to the United States Senate.

A holder of slaves himself, Johnson took his stand with the Union at the outbreak of the Civil War. "I intend to stand by the Constitution as it is," he declared, "insisting upon a compliance with all its guarantees . . . it is the last hope of human freedom." Thus an ideal choice to run with Lincoln in 1864, he became Vice President, and so was called upon to face the vast problems of Reconstruction.

Like the martyred President, Johnson held that the Southern states had never been out of the Union; the secession was a nullity; the Union was indissoluble; so when resistance ended, they could resume their functions. This brought him in conflict with the program of a Congress that aimed to punish rather than to heal. He became the first President (and the last) ever to be impeached. One vote saved him from conviction.

In Greenville are preserved the tailoring shop that saw his lowly beginning, the home in which he later lived, and a monument that records his devotion to his country's Constitution.

## 24. Lincoln Boyhood National Memorial
### [*Indiana*]

Sometime in December 1816, a seven-year-old boy was trudging into the wilderness in southern Indiana with his emigrating family. The Lincolns were moving again. Indiana was just at that time assuming statehood, but the locality into which Thomas Lincoln was taking his wife and family was wild, and Abraham remembered that they had to make their own road for the final four miles of the trek.

There was land to clear, and a cabin to build, and the boy was expected to help. On the frontier there were no teen-age problems due to idleness. And here Abraham Lincoln went to school, developed a taste for reading worthwhile books, fell in love, fell out again, collected the salty anecdotes of rural life that he narrated with such telling results in political life in the days to come. He read *Pilgrim's Progress*, Ben Franklin's *Autobiography*, and—best guide of all to the use of simple vibrant language—the King James version of the Bible. Out of reading like this came the monosyllabic trenchant quality of the Gettysburg address.

Other than that he was more studious than most of his companions, this youthful Abraham Lincoln of southern Indiana days was not remarkable. At sixteen he was an odd-job worker, earning money by slaughtering hogs or ferrying passengers out into the Ohio River to board a passing steamboat. A few years afterward he came into New Salem, Illinois, "like a piece of driftwood," as he said. His boyhood and youthful years in Indiana were ended.

## 25. Booker T. Washington National Monument
### [*Virginia*]

That two-hundred-acre piece of land of James Burroughs, situated south of Roanoke, must have been, when he was cropping it in Civil War days, what Shakespeare called a pelting farm. To get tobacco, corn, and oats out of the worn-down Piedmont soil, it is said that Burroughs himself worked side by side with his slaves. Of these there were at one time ten, inventoried for tax purposes at something over $7,000. A Negro boy named Booker was listed as having a fair-sale value of $400.

Little Booker had just turned nine when the day came in 1865 that the war was over and there were no more slaves. At first a burst of joy: then, as with so many others, came the somber feeling that a fixed and certain way of life was being exchanged for a cloudy unknown. But Jane Ferguson and her children went to West Virginia, where for the first time Booker met the alphabet. "Your full name? Booker what?" asked the schoolteacher. "Booker . . . *Washington*," was the reply. He chose a name for himself; chose gravely.

Hardship could not gravel this Negro youth. Working in the salt furnace, in the coal mine, as a houseboy, as a waiter, he got his education. The time came when he had a college under his own administration and was writing widely read books, the best known being *Up from Slavery*. This memorial to a great man, who helped so many of his people to help themselves, preserves the Burroughs "plantation," with a reproduction of the kind of cabin in which Booker Washington was born.

## 26. GEORGE WASHINGTON CARVER NATIONAL MONUMENT
### [*Missouri*]

IT SO HAPPENS that another Negro who pulled himself up by indomitable will, achieving a distinction in the sciences that warranted his birthplace being made a national monument, also had in his name a memory of the first President. Although the date of his birth is uncertain, George Washington Carver was probably about five years old when the Civil War ended. He and his mother were the property of Moses Carver, who lived in Diamond Grove in southern Missouri. At the outbreak of the Civil War that region was the scene of merciless guerrilla raiding. George, his mother, and a baby sister were kidnapped. Later, Carver recovered only the boy, who, now orphaned, continued to live with the white family and went to school in the nearby town of Neosho. As he grew, he showed remarkable versatility. Music, painting, mathematics, the natural sciences—he was proficient in all; but he finally devoted himself to agricultural chemistry. Booker Washington had the inspiration to bring Carver to Tuskegee in Alabama, where he produced many bulletins aimed at teaching Negro farmers how to raise their standard of living.

George Washington Carver once said: "I like to think of nature as an unlimited broadcasting system, through which God speaks to us every hour, if we will only tune in." Carver himself tuned in, effectively for himself and for those who had less skill in listening.

## 27. WILSON'S CREEK BATTLEFIELD NATIONAL PARK
### [*Missouri*]

ACCORDING TO one Civil War buff, there were more surprises at the battle of Wilson's Creek than at any other engagement during the war. "The initial attack of both Lyon and Sigel were complete surprises. In turn, Sigel was completely surprised and defeated by McCulloch. But possibly the greatest surprise was that of Lyon when he encountered the Missouri Militia under Price. These troops were fresh from the farm, without drill or organization . . . but they had led a frontier life . . . and had great skill in marksmanship."

In 1938, at the seventy-seventh anniversary of this battle, it was reported that there were no important changes since '61. "Bloody Hill remains untouched and on its rocky side many bullet-scarred oaks still are mute witnesses. A pile of native stones marks the spot where General Lyon fell . . . across the valley on the east side is the old farmhouse where Lyon lay."

# [ VI ]

# *March of America*

## 1. Sagamore Hill National Historic Site
### [*New York*]

"I wished a big piazza . . . where we could sit in rocking chairs and look at the sunset," wrote Theodore Roosevelt when he was describing the home he had built, as a young man, at Cove Neck on Long Island. He had it, as he had most things that he wanted during his life of sixty years. The piazza looked out over Oyster Bay and Long Island Sound. Though he ranched in Dakota for several years, traveled widely, and occupied the White House in Washington, this was his home, and visitors today, especially older visitors, feel his presence in it. "There isn't any place in the world like home—like Sagamore Hill, where things are our own."

The Roosevelt children felt that way about it, too. Father was an out-doorsman, and he carried to them his healthy notion of the vigorous enjoyment of simple pastimes. He said, "They swam, they tramped, they boated, they coasted and skated in winter, they were the intimate friends with the cows, chickens, pigs and other livestock." He saw to it that they could manage a pony or horse as soon as they could sit one. He called his fellow Americans to "the strenuous life," and set the example.

This solidly constructed Victorian house at Cove Neck, with its ample acreage, became a summer White House where newspapermen could always find copy that had country-wide appeal. If there was a touch of the flamboyant in his activities, it endeared him the more to the millions who still retained a feeling that a frontier, and frontier virtues, still existed. They called him, affectionately, Teddy. Of course, as might be expected, he was called other things by those he denounced, in political life, as "malefactors of great wealth."

---

*"Teddy's" family had a happy childhood. Sagamore Hill National Historic Site. [Photo: M. Woodbridge Williams]*

Though there were not many dull domestic moments during his years at the White House, perhaps Theodore Roosevelt's participation in the international field was even more important. After the war with Spain, in which he had led a cavalry regiment of Rough Riders, his doctrine "Speak softly, and carry a big stick" began to have expression in important ways. An American fleet went around the world, as an advertisement of our naval strength; the Panama Canal was built; the Russian and Japanese envoys had discussed peace on the porch at Sagamore Hill; and Roosevelt had a frank talk with the German Kaiser, which resulted in neither of them becoming fond of the other.

Notwithstanding all this prominence in the affairs of state, somehow visitors to Sagamore Hill leave with the feeling that here was a home where domestic virtues were the normal thing; where children "were never allowed to be disobedient or to shirk lessons or work," but where "they were encouraged to have all the fun possible." Old-fashioned, perhaps. If the idea is to suffer the fate of the dodo, all the better reason for preserving Sagamore Hill, as we preserve the bones of the dinosaur.

## 2. THEODORE ROOSEVELT BIRTHPLACE NATIONAL HISTORIC SITE
### [New York]

NOT AT ALL like Sagamore Hill was the house on 20th Street in New York City where Theodore Roosevelt was born in 1858. It was one of those narrow-fronted dwellings where the first floor was really a basement, English-fashion, and you climbed up a stoop to make a social entrance. Very respectable place for a couple, newly married and of moderate means; and to it Theodore Roosevelt, Sr., brought his Southern bride, Martha Bullock. There was a porch on the rear of the house overlooking the fine gardens of rich Mr. Goelet—almost as good as having gardens of your own, and less upkeep.

The first child born to the Roosevelts was sickly, weak of eyes, not even rugged enough to attend school. His parents called him Teedie, and there is something about that very nickname which suggests weakness. How strange it is that these weaklings sometimes grow up to be so energetic that it is exhausting to the less robust merely to be in their presence. So it was with little Theodore; but it was not until manhood, after he had deliberately sought health and strength by coming in close relation to the raw nature of the Western range, that he really became the Teddy of an admiring public, instead of the Teedie of his childhood.

Roosevelt's own recollection of this middle-class house on 20th Street is graphic enough. "The black haircloth furniture in the dining-room scratched the bare legs of the children as they sat on it. The middle room was a library, with tables, chairs and bookcases of gloomy respectability."

## 3. HOME OF FRANKLIN D. ROOSEVELT NATIONAL HISTORIC SITE
### [New York]

THERE IS NOTHING UNCOMMON, in our succession of Presidents, about election for a second term. Indeed, it has almost been a tacit expectation. Franklin Delano Roosevelt was not only elected President for a third term but a fourth, and the November returns suggested that he could have remained in the White House as long as he chose to do so. From the time he was sent to the New York Assembly by his Hyde Park neighbors in 1911, his political career sustained but one setback—an unsuccessful campaign for the Vice Presidency. He was twice elected governor of his state.

In this, his ancestral home overlooking the Hudson River, visited by millions of his fellow Americans, there is a museum label that never fails to elicit a warm and intimate response. It reproduces a telegram sent by the happy father, James Roosevelt, announcing the arrival at Hyde Park on a January day in 1882 "of a bouncing boy, weight 9½ pounds, this morning." He was to be an only son, but a famous one.

Unlike the first Roosevelt in the White House, this boy had a healthy playtime in the woods and fields of a lovely countryside. But in 1921, in the full vigor of manhood, he was struck down by infantile paralysis, which his own courageous battle to overcome resulted in so much benefit to other sufferers.

The shock wave of the sudden death of Franklin Roosevelt in April 1945, at Warm Springs, Georgia, will long be remembered. The month before, he had been at Hyde Park for what was to be his final visit. Perhaps the room in the house that seizes most visitors is the bedroom, in the stone wing over the living room, where the President was at ease among his naval prints, his pictures and family photographs. Scattered about are the books and magazines, just as they were left when he was last there; and the chair and leash and blanket of the scottie Fala, who, in Washington days, was a character better known than many members of Congress.

In the rose garden, nearly surrounded by an ancient hedge of hemlock, Franklin Roosevelt was buried, and beside his grave is that of his wife Eleanor, who survived him by many years. A rose garden was traditional with the family, since the name Roosevelt is Dutch for "field of roses." The white marble tombstone is from the Vermont quarry that supplied the beautiful material that went into the Thomas Jefferson Memorial in Washington.

Next to the site is the Franklin D. Roosevelt Library, administered by the Archivist of the United States.

### 4. Vanderbilt Mansion National Historic Site
#### [New York]

How DIFFERENT from the ample but unostentatious Roosevelt homes at Sagamore Hill and Hyde Park is this "royal palace" almost literally transported from Europe, one of the finest examples of Italian Renaissance architecture in the United States! Rightly it has been called "A Monument to an Era." The era was that of vast fortunes created by the spectacular growth of the nation in the days following the Civil War. It was the "country home" of Frederick W. Vanderbilt, a grandson of Commodore Cornelius Vanderbilt of steamboat and railroad fame. These giants of commerce seldom went into active political life, choosing to remain silent partners in the art of governing.

When Frederick Vanderbilt bought this imposing site, with its magnificent outlook across the Hudson River to the Shawangunk Range on the west and the Catskills to the north, it was already a place of great distinction. It had been the scene, since early in the eighteenth century, of development and experimentation in gardening and horticulture. The rare and exotic flora seen on lawns and park were the work of a Belgian landscape gardener as early as 1828. And there was a fine mansion there, which was demolished to make a place for the present one, erected at a cost of $660,000, not counting furnishings. Visitors wonder at the elegance, and usually conclude that, for themselves, they would like something simpler.

### 5. Herbert Hoover National Historic Site
#### [Iowa]

IT WAS THE ILL LUCK of Herbert Hoover, who had acquitted himself so nobly in relief work during and after World War I, to be elected President of the United States just as the economic roof of the country was about to collapse,

*Having climbed to great wealth one may climb a staircase like this. Vanderbilt Mansion National Historic Site. [Photo: M. Woodbridge Williams]*

due to several years of unbridled popular capitalization of assets that existed only on paper. It was hardly to be expected that a whole generation of eager young people, stunned and disillusioned, would realize the truth that any other Chief Executive in office would have shared the same fate. Hence it was many years before Hoover emerged from eclipse and his great abilities and patriotic devotion were again recognized.

This historic site preserves the cottage in which the President was born in West Branch, and restores, with some minor changes, the neighborhood atmosphere of 1874. Hoover was a great mining engineer, but his scholarship is not so well advertised. With his wife, Lou Henry Hoover, he translated the Latin text of the great *De Re Metallica* of Georgius Agricola, rendering clearly into modern terms the often baffling references to mining and metallurgy of the fifteenth century.

## 6. SAINT-GAUDENS NATIONAL HISTORIC SITE
### [New Hampshire]

IT WAS IN 1876 that Augustus Saint-Gaudens, one of America's foremost sculptors, established his home in the lovely region on the Connecticut River in New Hampshire where one looks westward toward smooth-shouldered Mount Ascutney. Other artists loved this spot, too: Maxfield Parrish, the painter whose blue skies rivaled the blue water of Crater Lake; and Percy MacKaye, the poet-dramatist. This significant cultural memorial, administered by the National Park Service, is the donation of the Saint-Gaudens trustees for the use and inspiration of the public.

Among the most important of Saint-Gaudens's works are the Farragut Monument in New York City; the Shaw Memorial in Boston; the Adams Memorial in Rock Creek Park, Washington, D.C.; and statues of General Sherman and Abraham Lincoln. Not so often seen by the public nowadays is the Saint-Gaudens gold double eagle, considered by some the most beautiful coin ever minted in this country. Aside from its artistic merit, the sight of this gold piece arouses wistfulness.

## 7. EDISON NATIONAL HISTORIC SITE
### [New Jersey]

BENJAMIN FRANKLIN snatched the lightning from the sky and Thomas Alva Edison put it to work. This is a tickling manner of speaking, so obviously an oversimplification that it can be ignored. But one thing is certain about these two great inventive geniuses: they both had the sketchiest kind of conventional education, and each went to work for his living at the age of twelve. Neither had to be baited with the carrot of opportunity. They went looking.

This inspiring historic site presents two phases of Edison's life and work at Menlo Park and West Orange. In the large library of Glenmont, the estate purchased in 1886, was the inventor's "thought bench," where ideas (whence? how?) came into that diligent searching mind. Not far distant is the "work bench"—the laboratory buildings where the new devices got shape and substance.

"The greatest adventure of my life," according to Edison, was on September 4, 1882, when New York City began the commercial distribution of electricity for light and power over a system designed by him and built under his supervision. "As darkness fell, that day, in the financial district of Manhattan hundreds of little incandescent lamps went on." When you return home after visiting the Edison site and push the button beside the front door, you have brought, so to say, a great man home with you.

Of course Edison was famous for many other inventions that have changed the course of our lives. The phonograph, the motion-picture development, with addition of sound to sight . . . the display of objects at the laboratory-headquarters gives a fascinating picture of the man at work and the almost incredible range of his proficiency.

## 8. WRIGHT BROTHERS NATIONAL MEMORIAL
### [*North Carolina*]

IT FLEW. It flew only twelve seconds; but in the words of Orville Wright, "it was the first [flight] in history in which a machine carrying a man had raised itself by its own power into the air in full flight, had sailed forward without reduction of speed, and finally landed at a point as high as that from which it started." The conquest of the means of air travel, dreamed of by Leonardo da Vinci and perhaps by other engineering minds before his, had arrived. The year was 1903; and today the upper air is so full of transport that the planes are subject to collision.

The scene of the event was Kitty Hawk, on the sand dunes of the North Carolina coast, below Norfolk. The brothers Wright, Wilbur and Orville, had built a camp just north of Kill Devil Hill in 1900, to test a man-carrying glider. Two years later, having solved important problems of equilibrium, they were ready to test a powered machine. They built both *The Flyer*, the craft with a wingspan of some forty feet, and the power plant, a twelve-horsepower engine weighing 170 pounds. The first attempt was unsuccessful, but two days later the plane took off, from a spot visitors now see marked by a granite boulder, and went 120 feet.

The Wright Memorial shaft is a sixty-foot pylon of North Carolina granite on a high dune whose normally shifting sands have been partly tied down by shoreline grasses.

## 9. CASTLE CLINTON NATIONAL MONUMENT
### [New York]

BEGINNING AS A FORT for the protection of New York City and its harbor, but never called upon to do serious shooting, Castle Clinton has had a strange and varied life. When its military use ceased it was converted to a place of public entertainment. Band concerts, exhibits, an occasional balloon ascension, receptions for distinguished visitors, grand opera; name the type of amusement, and it was there. Here, in 1850, New Yorkers jostled and outbid each other to hear the first concert in America of Jenny Lind, "the Swedish nightingale." In the middle part of the nineteenth century, during the great surge of immigration, the garden was a landing depot, where the newcomers had a shade of protection from the human predators that swarmed for prey at the arrival of each shipload. Then it became a famous aquarium. In 1941 there were plans to destroy the historic building, but an act of Congress preserved it as a sample of our fast-moving development since the time when the guns of the West Battery celebrated the evacuation of New York by the British.

## 10. MOUNT RUSHMORE NATIONAL MEMORIAL
### [South Dakota]

A FEW MILES to the north of Wind Cave National Park is Mount Rushmore National Memorial. Here, carved out of the solid granite of one of the pinnacles that characterize the Black Hills Dome, are the colossal portraits of Washington, Jefferson, Lincoln, and Theodore Roosevelt.

Concerning this astonishing feat, which, in the immensity of the undertaking, compares with the carving of the Great Sphinx of Egypt or the rock sculptures of Babylonia, I confess that, for myself, I was for a number of years a skeptic. I was so sure that art had become enmeshed in engineering, and that the audacity of the conception bordered on pertness, that I would not even go and look at it. Finally I did, however, and found reasons to revise my snap judgment. That it is impressive there is no doubt. There could be no better testimony to its assault on the imagination—which is just what the sculptor, Gutzon Borglum, intended—than the fact that on the day when I was there, when the area was thronged with visitors, there was an unmistakable hushed and reverential attitude noticeable in every group that stood viewing the work from different angles.

Whatever else one may think of it, the memorial now seems to me an unforgettable example of man's will to force nature to take him into at least a junior partnership. He may be a relatively feeble thing on the face of the earth, but he insists on making his presence felt. He may be expelled from the garden at any moment, but he will leave his initials carved on the fig tree.

## 11. JOHN MUIR NATIONAL HISTORIC SITE
### [*California*]

DURING THE LAST twenty-four years of the life of the man who has been described as "the father of our national parks and forest reservations," the old library den on the second floor of this Muir home was the place where most of his published writings originated. Leaders in the conservation field met here with Muir and planned with him many a move toward the saving of precious spots of natural beauty. They were generally successful, though they lost the fight for the Hetch Hetchy in Yosemite—a butchery that we now look back upon as profitless and witless.

In the mid-nineteenth century, Dr. John Strentzel came from Poland to the Alhamora Valley and established a ranch. His daughter became Muir's wife. The "big house," which is being preserved, along with the Vicente Martinez Adobe, is the one John and Louie Muir occupied by invitation of Mrs. Strentzel after her husband's death. The nearby adobe was built about 1849 by a son of the original grantee of Rancho El Pinole.

In 1912, a lonely widower, Muir wrote in a letter to a friend: "I'm in my old library den, the house desolate, nobody living in it save a hungry mouse or two . . . dearly cherished memories [I have] about it and the fine garden grounds full of trees and bushes and flowers that my wife and father-in-law and I planted—fine things from every land."

The place is little changed from Muir's lifetime. It will certainly be a mecca for preservationists who regard him as "one of the great few who have won title to remembrance as prophets and interpreters of nature."

# PART

## FIVE

# [ I ]

# *National Capital Parks*

*"Born of compromise—witness to history—reflection of culture."*

PROGENY OF COMPROMISE between Thomas Jefferson and Alexander Hamilton, the Capital of the United States rose from the Potomac flatlands.

With watchwords of order, beauty, and vision, its planner, Pierre Charles L'Enfant, said: "I would not plan for thirteen States and three million people but for a republic of fifty States and five hundred million; not for a single century, but for a thousand years."

In the L'Enfant Plan of 1791, Washington was intended as a city of parks or a city in a park. To L'Enfant, the crown jewel was the Grand Mall stretching from the Capitol to the proposed site for a monument to George Washington. It was envisioned as a formal park, bordered by a canal with broad basins and imposing fountains.

As the public buildings and parks took shape, there came the inescapable association between the city and George Washington. Its name, its monuments, its origin, its importance as the capstone of our representative system of government bespoke of his leadership and his example. This association gave something very special to the Capital, for Daniel Webster once remarked: "America has furnished to the world the character of Washington! And if our American institutions had done nothing else, that alone would have entitled them to the respect of mankind."

As the Capital's parks matured, three principal responsibilities, each significant and together forming an interrelated whole, emerged. These three responsibilities were reflected by the role of the parks as (1) settings for public buildings and national memorials; (2) areas for public recreation; (3) elements in forming the character of the city.

---

*Picture without a title. National Capital Parks.* [*Photo: W. E. Dutton*]

The key to the impact of the L'Enfant Plan was the site selection of the public buildings and their enhancement by complementary park settings. The site for the Capitol was selected as the radial center of the plan; the site for the White House chosen; and both structures linked by a broad avenue named for the "Keystone" State. A line was drawn west from the Capitol and south from the White House; at its intersection, a monument to George Washington was proposed. Between that memorial site eastward to the Capitol lay the Grand Mall. Completing the final arm of the cross was a site for a memorial to a second national leader at a point directly south of the Washington Memorial site. The resulting cross—joining living government with heroes of the past—is the heart of the Washington park system. In 1901, the McMillan Park Commission reaffirmed the soundness of the L'Enfant Plan and added a major refinement—an extension of the Mall vista west of the Washington Monument to the Potomac River, where a third memorial, the Lincoln Memorial, rose to enshrine the memory of Abraham Lincoln in the hearts of the people.

Today the mall complex with its east-west, north-south axes epitomizes the initial purpose of the parks as settings for the public buildings and national memorials; and yet, these formal parks are much more. They are places where 16 million Americans and foreign visitors converge each year to feel the impress of this setting—the center of what some call the most beautiful city in the world.

Washington, more than any other city in the nation, reflects the past achievements of our country. First and foremost, as its symbol, stands the Washington Monument, 555 feet tall. The eager eyes of millions of young Americans see this monument. If they but pause to reflect upon its purpose, they will see in its granite the nation's resolve to honor the man who helped to forge the United States of America.

Not far from the Washington Monument, through the green-swathed parks, aglow with pale, misty pink and white cherry blossoms in early April, they will visit the Thomas Jefferson Memorial. Here they can read and absorb the words of a great architect of democratic thought: "I have sworn upon the altar of God eternal hostility against every form of tyranny over the mind of man." And nestled deep in the heart of downtown Washington is the House Where Lincoln Died—the smallest unit of the vast National Park System. Within its walls a brave heart stopped at 7:22 on the morning of

*Iwo Jima (the flag half-staffed for ex-President Hoover). National Capital Parks. [Photo: W. E. Dutton]*

April 15, 1865. Young citizens of the Union which he saved now come to pay their respect.

It would be difficult to envision many of the great moments in the history of the United States without the historic background of Washington's streets, circles, and parks. Hardly a single period in our proud national history did not have its origin in Washington. Here for almost 170 years the leaders of government and the private leaders of America's economic, social, and cultural development have wrestled with the problems of their times. Many of their actions took place in the historical parks of the Capital—the prime example is Lafayette Park across from the White House, which throughout the nineteenth century was the residential setting for the homes of the great and the near-great. Center of social, literary, and political life, it might have been called Cabinet Park, for around it have lived at different times members of the official families of seventeen Presidents.

"The mission of parks is to make urban life not just bearable but happy" —hence the second major responsibility, to provide active programs to build healthy bodies and nourish eager minds. The parks of Washington appeal to a wide variety of interests and tastes. More than 100 million visitor days per year are spent by people engaged in picnics, hiking, fishing, horseback riding, sailing, organized baseball, football, tennis, soccer, cricket, and just sitting on a park bench as Bernard Baruch so often did in Lafayette Park across from the White House. There are also a host of cultural attractions in the parks—art shows, bands from every branch of the armed services in concerts at the Watergate, Shakespeare on the Washington Monument grounds, and a variegated program of Broadway entertainment at the Carter Barron Amphitheatre in Rock Creek Park. Parks—particularly metropolitan parks—are for the people. As people use them, they bring refreshment to mind and body, awaken interest in nature's omnipresence, and foster greater community spirit as citizens take increased pride in the appearance of their city.

Because of the urban character of many parks in Washington and the geographical features of the area, one would not expect to find exemplary natural parks of outstanding scenic quality. Yet, there are few metropolitan areas in the country that possess an array of natural wooded parks which offer so much in the way of contrast for the city dweller. In them children, who have not known anything but city life, are introduced to the wonders

*Just as our ancestors traveled on the Chesapeake and Ohio Canal. National Capital Parks. [Photo: M. Woodbridge Williams]*

*No pollution in this laughing mountain stream at Catoctin. National Capital Parks.*
*[Photo: M. Woodbridge Williams]*

of the natural world and to the "beautiful," which Goethe said "is a manifestation of secret laws of Nature, which, but for this appearance, had been forever concealed from us."

The third responsibility of the Washington parks stems from the historical legacy of the parks themselves—as basic elements in forming the character of the city. There is the Grand Mall, which impresses because of its monumental character and its broad vista; there are the small circles and triangles which break the boredom of concrete, offering greenery and treating the eye to pleasant floral colors. There are the larger squares where thousands of office workers find welcome respite from their confinement and shaded repose while they listen to a high school band from Ames, Iowa, or some other home-town group in Washington to participate in one of the big parades which are so much a part of the city scene.

And finally, there are Washington's large natural retreats—the 1,700-acre Rock Creek Park, winding its sylvan path along the stream valley of the creek from its mouth northward to Maryland. Established in 1890 as a national park, its charter was worded much the same as that of Yellowstone National Park, created eighteen years earlier and the first national park in the world. Rock Creek Park, with its thickly wooded slopes, shaded glens, and wild flowers, was a favorite haunt of Theodore Roosevelt and his family and has been frequented by statesmen, ambassadors, and millions of plain citizens. Speaking of Rock Creek Park, Teddy Roosevelt said:

> When our children were little . . . each Sunday afternoon the whole family spent in Rock Creek Park . . . I would drag one of the children's wagons; and when the very smallest pairs of feet grew tired of trudging bravely after us, or racing on rapturous side trips after flowers, and other treasures, the owners would climb in the wagon . . .

Bringing visitors and nearby residents into the city are several expressively landscaped parkways. The most spectacular is the George Washington Memorial Parkway—a ribbonlike park passing the high bluffs of the Potomac along the Virginia shoreline, and giving panoramas of Washington. Not far away is Great Falls Park, Virginia, a more recent addition to the National Capital Park System and the site of the remains of the old locks of the Potomack Canal Company, the first corporate work in America, chartered by George Washington in 1785.

Thus parks of many kinds and with many purposes form the character of Washington. And the larger natural parks—changing ecological communities surrounded by man's proud achievements of urban living—bring smiles to little faces as they watch ducks swimming in Rock Creek or turtles sunning themselves on a log along the old canal.

# [ I I ]

# L'Envoi: Vistas of Beauty

TRUTH, *and goodness, and beauty, are but different faces of the same All.*
*Beauty in nature is not ultimate. It is the herald of inward and*
*eternal beauty . . . it must stand as a part and not yet as the last or highest*
*expression of the final cause of Nature.*

—RALPH WALDO EMERSON

## [ 1 ]

IN FEBRUARY 1965, President Johnson sent to the Congress of the United States a message "On the Natural Beauty of Our Country." It was a state paper probably unique in the history of government. Can anyone recall a similar instance, when a nation's leader has proclaimed the vital importance of beauty in human welfare, and moved to salvage what remains of the lovely heritage which a thrusting, feverish, ruthless technology has dilapidated to the point of ugliness? This is a Great Chart. And the time to preserve, to repair, to cease being a nation of prosperous slovens, is now.

The German poet Goethe said: "We should do our utmost to encourage the Beautiful, for the Useful encourages itself." Indeed, utility needs nothing other than its physical materials to work upon. We need not quarrel with that. And it was inevitable that the primeval landscape of America would be vastly altered; that the rich resources would be eagerly tapped and exploited; that rivers should be harnessed, prairies plowed; that roads should scar the land surface; that virgin forests should fall. Nor could it be expected that, except for a few souls gifted with insight, a people aiming at a fuller and more comfortable existence would exercise a philosophic restraint.

---

*Twins are twice as much trouble: white-tailed deer. Blue Ridge Parkway.* [*Photo: Leonard Lee Rue III*]

*Prancing coyote, Mount McKinley. Mount McKinley National Park. [Photo: National Park Service]*

There is no deep villain in this very human drama. There is only a saddening imbalance that was bound to ensue. Man does not live by bread and gadgets alone. Take beauty out of his life: a googol of dollars and a Lucullan luxury will not fill the void.

The imbalance is here. It is shockingly manifest. With an erupting population, we see the places of natural beauty retreating from the millions as fast as they seek and move toward them; urban slums where people feebly degenerate; roadways lined with the horrible corpses of junked automobiles, and with the vulgarities of clamoring commerce; our air polluted with fumes and our rivers and lakes and estuaries so laden with filth and chemicals that fish are killed and humans endangered. The whole drab picture is outlined in President Johnson's message, in measured terms.

Will the President's appeal be effective? There are already signs that it will. The regeneration will take time. Nature repairs ills of the abused human body by slow processes; ills of the spirit even more slowly. There are signs of awakening on all political levels. But it is a warning that must come into

the realization of every citizen. Josiah Royce said that the philosopher Immanuel Kant "had small interest in noble sentiments, but very great natural
respect for large and connected personal and social undertakings, when
guided by ideas." The point is timely. The appeal for the restoration of
Beauty to her rightful eminence cannot remain merely a "noble sentiment."
It needs action, and not merely in the field of legislation. It must enter the
understanding of all of us.

## [ 2 ]

BUT THE MESSAGE to the Congress has far wider significance than appears
upon its surface, or in its words. What *is* natural beauty? What, indeed, is
*beauty?*

The wisest philosophers have failed to define or to explain this human
emotion to which, in our English language, is given the name of beauty.
There is an equivalent word in every language. Paul Shorey, reflecting his
study of Plato, said that feeling for beauty is "a touch of noble unrest; the

*Falling through thin ice, these creatures are in mortal danger. Grand Teton National
Park. [Photo: National Park Service]*

reaching for something of finer quality than the dailiness of life." The love of beauty, he added, becomes the guide toward the perception of the good and the true. Vague as this may sound, at first glance, it will serve as the path along which our quest for understanding must go. Surely we deal with an essence that is beyond our powers of expression. But we can, and we do, feel its reality.

In the realm of natural beauty, apprehended mainly through the sense of sight, but also by the other organs, we are first overwhelmed by the more spectacular forms. "Breath-taking" is a hackneyed expression; yet it is accurate. The pulse reflects the surge. Beyond that impact, we can come to understand that what we have sensed is only a gorgeous greeting. Behind that curtain lies an infinite world of detailed beauties. As we develop realization of those composing elements, we know that there can be nothing ugly in nature. Nothing. The seeming exceptions are simply facets of beauty we have not yet grasped.

Sometimes we think, in our egotism, that nature has provided these beauties as a special act on our behalf. If I may be allowed a harmless bit of fantasy, I shall imagine a conversation you might have with nature on this point. After hearing you patiently on the subject of Beauty, nature would perhaps say something like this: "I see the source of your error. It derives from your very limited knowledge. You are thinking that I have a Department of Beauty—that I deal with beauty as one of my activities. Really, I do not *intend* beauty. I *am* beauty. I am beauty and many other things, such as you are trying to express by your abstractions like order, harmony, truth, love. What you see in my scenic manifestations is the glamour behind which lies an absolute beauty of which I myself am an expressive part. You do not understand? Naturally it is difficult. But you are trying: I do like *that* in you, little man."

No, we can only shadowly comprehend, and perhaps the mystery will always tantalize us. But fortunately for our spiritual welfare we live with the fact. And this fact is that in the presence of unsullied, unexploited "raw" nature, we are lifted to a height beyond ourselves. Our first physical contact with Yosemite, the Tetons, the redwood groves, the Alps, the falls of the

*Above, left: Some summer fur shows on this "snowshoe rabbit." Mount McKinley National Park. [Photo: Charles Ott] Right: The raccoon is a resourceful and impudent masked bandit . . . and charming. Great Smoky Mountains National Park. [Photo: Leonard Lee Rue III] Below, left: Mountain goat youngsters. Glacier National Park. [Photo: Leonard Lee Rue III] Right: Nine ounces of shrill defiance. Isle Royale National Park. [Photo: W. W. Dunmire]*

## L'Envoi: Vistas of Beauty

Iguazu—with such spectacles wherever they exist—leaves us with an indelible coloring such as has not dominated our thoughts and feelings before. That is the fact. The metaphysical reasoning about it is more engaging than important. We grow in dimension and capacity. Not only that. We become more sensitive to the opposites of beauty: ugliness, defacement, disharmony.

Although the purely aesthetic aspect of this absolute beauty is but the prologue to a whole, its importance must not be minimized. It is as basic as the letters of the alphabet. Without those letters there are no words; and without words, no communication.

### [ 3 ]

WHILE OUR PEOPLE have been remiss in the sacrifice of beauty to utility, and the time has come to take account of stock, as the President asked, there is still much to our credit. In a period of explosive growth such as few nations have known, possessors of a technological skill which has finally become more than a little frightening, we have yet managed to set aside and wisely to administer a system of national parks that evokes the admiration of the world. It is true that we had rare advantages, and time was on our side. But it is also true that we had from our earliest days a large and articulate group of forward-thinking men and women alive to the need for preserving the treasures of our culture and the integrity of our inheritance before, as in other lands, it was too late. So that, as the case stands, it is not so much that we have been unmindful of spiritual and moral values: we have not been sufficiently alert to the somber truth that "the Useful encourages itself," while the preservation and affirmation of beauty needs a constant renewal of faith and the watchful devotion of a shepherd. Nor can our preserved places of natural beauty and memorials of the historic past prosper and remain inspirational if they become islands in an environment of sanctioned ugliness. This is a very nullification of our reverence for beauty. To paraphrase Lincoln: our cultural and spiritual aspirations must shrivel in a world half beautiful, half loathsome. We shall not expect the impossible. But there must be in our mechanized and controlled ecology, while we confess that we have violated much natural beauty physically, and defend it as unavoidable, a mani-

---

*Above, left: The brown pelican. Everglades National Park. [Photo: M. Woodbridge Williams] Right: Big-eared bat. Jewel Cave National Monument. [Photo: Jack E. Boucher] Below, left: Blacksnake—harmless friend of man. Shenandoah National Park. [Photo: William M. Taylor] Right: The anhinga spears his victim. Everglades National Park. [Photo: M. Woodbridge Williams]*

festation that we still retain the spirit, and show it in our national house-keeping. That is where we have failed.

## [ 4 ]

As I HAVE SAID, this message is something not merely for legislation, though that is imperatively desirable, but for all of us to meditate. What are its implications, for example, in the work of the National Park Service, where so much natural beauty, majestic and awe-inspiring, and so many less obvious beauties, even hidden ones, are the current stock in trade? The very business of the National Park Service is the custodianship and interpretation of beauty. How could it be otherwise? The interpreter, whether naturalist or ranger or historian or mechanic, is a middleman of this precious cultural wealth.

Viewed as an absolute, beauty has numberless aspects. For the purpose of the interpreter I think we need be directly concerned with but four:

1. The park visitor's sensuous contact with scenic or landscape beauty —with "wildness."

2. The beauty of the adventure of the mind: the revelation of the order of nature.

3. The beauty of the artifact: man's aspiration to create beautiful things.

4. The beauty of human conduct, or behavior, of which man has shown himself capable.

It is axiomatic that natural beauty, as perceived by the organs of sense, needs no interpretation: it interprets itself. Here the interpreter acts only as a scout and a guide. He leads his groups to the most alluring scenes he has discovered, and is silent. Would you varnish the orchid? He refrains even from using the word "beauty." To suggest that his visitors are to consider either the scene or the song of the hermit thrush as beautiful is even an affront. They *know*. In this aspect beauty is a precious personal possession. It is the individual's shock, *his* apprehension, *his* discovery: and what he discovers is more than what he sees or hears. He has discovered something of himself, hitherto unrealized. No; we do not interpret that aspect of beauty. It is an exhibit.

Exactly at this point is where the office of the interpreter begins. There is a concealed beauty that does not appear to the senses. Indeed, this aspect takes two forms. It involves a revelation of the natural beauty we think of as order—nature at work—and the beauty of that development of the human

*A boxing match; most of the does are unimpressed. Glacier National Park. [Photo: Channing T. Howell]*

mind which makes it possible for man partly to understand it. What are the forces that created what one sees, and feels as beautiful?

Whether we call it so or not, the interpreter is engaged in a kind of education. It is not the classroom kind. It is, if you will, a proffer of teaching; but it is not the professorial sort. It aims not to *do something* to the listener, but *to provoke the listener to do something to himself.* It is a delicate job, requiring the greatest discretion. The man on holiday does not wish to be lectured; he did not come to a park to be educated. Even the most discerning, and therefore successful, interpreter must feel conscious of the fact that the materials upon which he works are by their very nature—what shall I say? not *cold,* but certainly *cool.* We appeal to the head, to the mind.

Can we not infuse into this worthy activity an appeal to the heart: to attain something of that impact which nature does so easily and implicitly by presenting the beautiful landscape? Erosion and mountain building, the adaptation of life to its environment, the grand and vital organic community of which man is only a species, however a dominant one; all these entertaining revelations of man's place in nature are at last a presentation of an aspect

[ 5 5 7 ]

of the beautiful. If the interpreter feels this to be so, he can project that feeling. Not by a preachment about it. Heavens, no. It is something to be felt, not analyzed. If deeply felt, it can be communicated.

The scenes upon which you have looked, and the natural sounds you have heard, you regard as beauty. How did it all come about? By a process which science aims to know more and more about; but whatever we may discover, one thing is sure about that process—it is even more beautiful than what the eye or ear perceives. This is an appeal to the heart, the soul, or what you wish to call it, whichever yearns to be satisfied. It is warmth. Added to understanding, it is the objective of interpretation.

The other day, a great American chemist, Robert S. Mulliken, received a Nobel prize. This man once wrote something which has deeply affected my thinking about this world of natural beauties. The italics are mine:

> The scientist must develop enormous tolerance in seeking for ideas which *may please nature*, and enormous patience, self-restraint and humility when his ideas over and over again are rejected by nature before he arrives at one to *please her*. When the scientist does finally find such an idea, there is something very intimate in his feeling of communion with nature.

When the non-scientist understands what Mulliken meant when he talked of "pleasing nature" he will be on his way to understanding the scientific mind. He will realize what the pure scientist means when he talks of a "beautiful equation"—the statement of an idea in artistic form with an economy of means. We "please nature" when we search for, find, and *feel* beauty. It is as simple as that: and yet it is not simply attained and maintained in a world where the marketplace dominates.

When we come to the beauty of the artifact—man's inspiration to produce with his own hands something of the quality which he has observed in his natural surroundings—we are in a complex and baffling domain. Much we must guess. A paleolithic artist incised on the wall of a cave at Altamira the figure of a running deer. The draughtsmanship, resulting from the acute observation of this prehistoric man, is by modern standards a beautiful thing. But did he intend beauty, or was it a propitiation of the spirit of the chase —a magical device to procure meat, and therefore a matter of utility? We cannot know: surely there is no harm in concluding that it could have been both. I have held in my hand the bowl of a ceremonial pipe made of the red Catlinite claystone which came from southwestern Minnesota, but taken from a mound in northern Mississippi, the work of one of our prehistoric

*Left: Prairie dog, almost exterminated by predatory man. Wind Cave National Park.
[Photo: Wayne Bryant] Right: The almost extinct blackfooted ferret. Badlands
National Monument. [Photo: Robert Powell]*

Indian artists. It is the figure of a man sitting and thinking—a forerunner of
the famous Rodin sculpture, and not a whit less impressive. Did this early
artist intend beauty? I think he did; perhaps also religious significance.

But clearly we are here in a region of taste, tradition, changing standards
of judgment. The interpreter of the story of the artifact is not dealing with
beauty as such, but with man's attitude toward beauty; and this can be made
warmly appealing, for it is an appeal to the heart even more than to the mind.
The standards of judgment in architecture change. The filigree gingerbread
of the Victorian period is today a matter of mild amusement. Structures that
were considered beautiful in their time cause pained surprise now. Yet,
worldwide, there are not many people who do not thrill at the classic beauty
of the Parthenon, the Maison Carré at Nîmes, or the Lincoln Memorial in
Washington. And all of us are sensitive to harmony of structure and environment. The humble adobe dwelling arising from our southwestern desert,
created from the desert soil itself and roofed with rush or with tiles shaped
on the thigh of the builder, violates no principle of art. The most expensive
structure, of architectural merit in itself, but alien to its environment, may be
an excrescence—almost an ugliness. Hence the fine current effort around
Washington to procure scenic easements. The objection is not so much to the

artifacts themselves: in relation to the greater natural beauty they may be in the wrong place.

One could go on endlessly in a discussion of the opportunity for the interpretation of man's aspiration to produce beautiful objects. More to the point at the moment is the effort to restore some of the natural beauty we have blighted, and to make resurgent an innate delight in the beauty of our environment: the aim of the program of beautification to which the wife of the President, Lady Bird Johnson, has given her enthusiasm and the prestige of her position.

As the interpreter, in or out of the National Park Service, is not needed to define or explain scenic beauty, neither does its opposite require interpretation. When Alice was in Wonderland, the Mock Turtle told her that he went to school with an old turtle who taught Uglification.

"I never heard of 'Uglification,'" Alice ventured to say. The Gryphon lifted up both its paws in surprise.

"Never heard of uglifying," it exclaimed. "You know what to beautify is, I suppose?"

"Yes," said Alice, doubtfully. "It means to make anything prettier."

"Well, then," the Gryphon went on, "if you don't know what to uglify is, you *are* a simpleton."

Well we know what ugliness is, and the processes that create it. In the haste to gain material welfare we have forgotten, or chosen to forget; and the bill has now come due. To live willingly in tawdry surroundings is to become numb to their baleful influence upon us; they tend to seem as inevitable as climate. It is not so. It is already proved, in city, state, county, and town, that the feeling for beauty can be dramatized and renewed by *beautifying*. The start has been made.

What interpreters can do is to communicate, from their own conviction, *by indirection but with warmth*, this appeal to an always receptive human heart.

In the interpretation of the beauty of conduct of which the human being is capable, we come under the leering squint of the pessimist. We read in Emerson that "the beauty of nature must always seem unreal and mocking, until the landscape has human figures that are as good as itself."

"Perhaps," replies the cynic, "but tell me just when that will be?"

We do not have to go back to antiquity—to Socrates, Jesus, or the Roman general Regulus—for the answer to that. It is here and now, just as it was

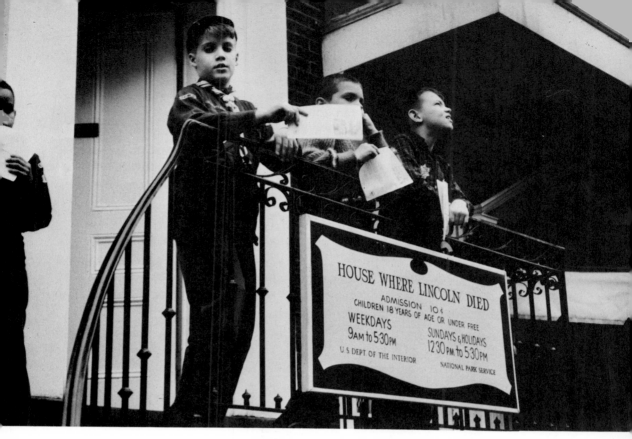

*That the young may realize the past. National Capital Parks. [Photo: M. Woodbridge Williams]*

yesterday and the day before. The National Park System includes scores of historic memorials, the truest interpretation of which is the evidence that our country has possessed men and women of great moral beauty. And for each one of those a myriad of the humbler unknowns have lived and passed. The birthplace of Washington; the several areas that keep in memory the great-heartedness of Lincoln; the house at Appomattox where Grant and Lee revealed beautiful magnanimity on the one side and a nobility in the acceptance of defeat on the other; the farmer soldiers at the bridge in Concord; an ample preservation of the Civil War battlefields—what are all these but the testimonials that man does transcend his animal boundary?

Just the other day, in Vietnam, a soldier threw himself upon a hand grenade, saving the lives of his comrades. War is a terrible thing; the hope of mankind is that it will cease to be; yet it cannot be denied that out of its shambles have emerged valor and fortitude and self-sacrifice on the part of the individual man and woman. William James, the Harvard philosopher, had this undeniable truth in mind when he wrote his "Moral Equivalent for War"—an attempt to find some other agent in life that would perform the same service to human character. That he failed is less important than that he showed his own beauty of conduct in the failure.

The interpreter in a monument or battlefield of war may thrill his hearer with the account of the mass action, the losses and gains in a swaying conflict, the skill of leadership. This can be made dramatic stuff, exciting the imagination, a capsuled fragment of the national past that must not be forgotten. But these things are an appeal to the mind, to logic and imagination. The appeal to the heart is the story of how in such tragic environment the human being finds the path to beauty of behavior.

The appeal for a renaissance of the appreciation of beauty—in the abstract and in its particular aspects—must not be allowed to falter. It is vital to our moral growth. It is a program of education. Perhaps it is truer to say that it is a program of re-education, for we have always known, in our innermost recesses, our dependence upon beauty for the courage to face the problems of life. We have let ourselves forget. It is the duty of the interpreter to jog our memories.

# INDEX

[iii]

# Index

# Index

# About the Author

FREEMAN TILDEN, a native of Massachusetts, quit a successful career as a writer of fiction and plays to devote his talents to the cause of conservation, with particular reference to the role of the National Park System in American life. He has served as consultant to four Directors of the National Parks. Beginning with his standard work *The National Parks*, of which this present volume is a completely revised and enlarged edition, Mr. Tilden has produced a series of books devoted to the preservation and interpretation of natural and historic places: *The State Parks, The Fifth Essence, Interpreting Our Heritage*. Part of his volume *Following the Frontier* deals with the early days in Yellowstone National Park. When he is not traveling in the parks Mr. Tilden continues a pleasant association with nature in the woods and fields of his farm in Warren, Maine.

# A NOTE ON THE TYPE

THE TEXT of this book was set on the Linotype in Janson, a recutting made direct from type cast from matrices long thought to have been made by the Dutchman Anton Janson, who was a practicing type founder in Leipzig during the years 1668–87. However, it has been conclusively demonstrated that these types are actually the work of Nicholas Kis (1650–1702), a Hungarian, who most probably learned his trade from the master Dutch type founder Kirk Voskens. The type is an excellent example of the influential and sturdy Dutch types that prevailed in England up to the time William Caslon developed his own incomparable designs from these Dutch faces.

*Typography and binding design by*
GUY FLEMING

# COMPUTERS TODAY

As an additional learning tool, McGraw-Hill also publishes a study guide to supplement your understanding of this textbook. Here is the information your bookstore manager will need to order it for you: 54704-1   STUDY GUIDE TO ACCOMPANY COMPUTERS TODAY, 2/e

**Second Edition**

# COMPUTERS TODAY

## Donald H. Sanders
Educational Consultant

**McGraw-Hill Book Company**

New York   St. Louis   San Francisco   Auckland   Bogotá   Hamburg
Johannesburg   London   Madrid   Mexico   Montreal   New Delhi
Panama   Paris   São Paulo   Singapore   Sydney   Tokyo   Toronto

COMPUTERS TODAY

1234567890  KGPKGP   898765

ISBN 0-07-054701-7

This book was set in Times Roman by York Graphic Services, Inc.
The editors were Christina Mediate, Barbara Brooks, and Edwin Hanson;
the designer was Merrill Haber;
the production supervisor was Phil Galea.
New drawings were done by Fine Line Illustrations, Inc.
The cover photographs were taken by Joe Ruskin;
cover computer model constructed by Bob Schein.
Kingsport Press, Inc., was printer and binder.

Photo research was performed by Lorinda Morris/ Photoquest, Inc.
Module-opening photographs © Digital Effects, Inc. (DEI)

Photo credits for the timeline (from left to right)
**Page 31:** IBM Corporation; The Granger Collection; IBM Corporation; The Granger Collection. **Page 32:** The Bettmann Archive, Inc.; The Granger Collection; IBM Corporation. **Page 33:** Wide World Photos; IBM Corporation; Iowa State University Information Service; IBM Corporation; IBM Corporation; United Press International Photo. **Page 34 (from top):** The Bettmann Archive, Inc.; IBM Corporation; IBM Corporation; Sperry Univac; United Press International Photo; Dartmouth College News Service; Intel Corporation; Intel Corporation. **Page 35:** Apple Computer, Inc.; Microsoft Corporation; AT&T Technology.

**Library of Congress Cataloging in Publication Data**

Sanders, Donald H.
    Computers today.

    Includes index.
    1. Electronic data processing.   2. Computers.
I. Title.
QA76.S289  1985    001.64    84-15473
ISBN 0-07-054701-7

# About the Author

DONALD H. SANDERS is the author of six books about computers—their uses and their impact—spanning 25 years. His books have been widely used by training programs in industry and government as well as by colleges and universities.

After receiving degrees from Texas A & M University and the University of Arkansas, Dr. Sanders was a professor at the University of Texas at Arlington, at Memphis State University, and at Texas Christian University. In addition to his books, Dr. Sanders has contributed articles to journals such as *Data Management, Automation, Banking, Journal of Small Business Management, Journal of Retailing,* and *Advanced Management Journal.* He has also encouraged his graduate students to contribute computer-related articles to national periodicals, and over 70 of these articles have been published. Dr. Sanders chairs the "Computers and Data Processing" Subject Examination Committee, CLEP Program, College Entrance Examination Board, Princeton, N.J.

# Contents in Brief

# Contents

Photo courtesy Hewlett-Packard Company.

Photo courtesy General Electric Information Systems Company.

Photo courtesy International Business Machines Corporation.

# Module 2   Hardware

Photo courtesy NCR Corporation.

Photo courtesy Datakey, Minneapolis, Minn.

Photo courtesy Fujitsu Microelectronics, Inc., Professional Microsystems Division.

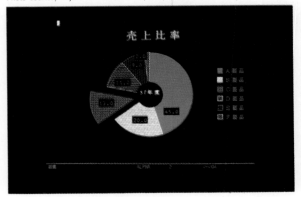

# Module 3   Systems and Software

Photo reproduced with permission of AT&T.

Photo courtesy Honeywell, Inc.

# Module 4   Social Impact

Photo © Chuck O'Rear/West Light.

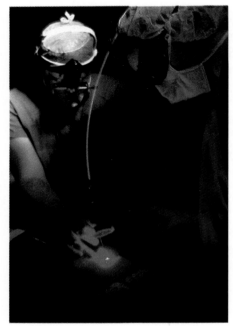

# Module 5    Programming

Photo courtesy International Business Machines Incorporated.

# Preface

Remember . . . when you thought a silicon
chip was a new kind of snack food?
Does it seem like only yesterday? It
was.

*Inc.* magazine, April 1984.

In a figurative sense, it *was* only yesterday that components
such as silicon chips were first introduced into strange machines called computers. But now it's today, and the pace
from yesterday to today has been frenetic. In Lewis Carroll's
*Through the Looking Glass,* Alice met the Red Queen in the
garden. "Faster! faster!" the Queen urged, but "however
fast they went they never seemed to pass anything." Finally,
Alice observed that "in our country, . . . you'd generally
get to somewhere else—if you ran very fast for a long time as
we've been doing." "A slow sort of country!" replied the
Queen. "Now, here, you see, it takes all the running you can
do to keep in the same place. If you want to get somewhere
else, you must run at least twice as fast as that."

Computer scientists and users have been running many
times faster than that in the last few years, and we've now
entered what has been termed the Information Age or the Age
of the Computer. Computers, like automobiles and electricity, are now exerting a daily—and rapidly growing—influence on all of us. Thus, an essential outcome of the educational process today must be computer literacy. Computer
literacy is "knowing" computers. It's knowing what they
are, what they can and cannot do, how they are put to work,
and how their use in homes, schools, and workplaces can
affect society. It's vital, of course, to continue to educate the
many thousands of people who will become computer specialists. And this book certainly contains the information required to introduce these future specialists to the subject of
computers and data processing. But computer literacy is now
needed by *all* students so that they will not be intimidated by

daily life, but will instead feel a sense of belonging in a
computer-rich society.

## THE DEVELOPMENT AND PURPOSE OF THIS EDITION

To paraphrase the Red Queen, it takes a significant effort or
"run" in today's computing environment just to keep a text
in the same relative place. But to move forward and make
improvements, an author and publisher may need to "run at
least twice as fast as that."

Work on the *development* of this edition of *Computers
Today* began almost immediately with the release of the first
edition. Research was carried out and plans were made to
produce a new text—one that would not only move forward
with the technology, but would also be improved in other
ways. For example, the new chapter on personal computers
has been acclaimed by reviewers for the thorough way it considers hardware capabilities and software packages. But personal computer concepts are also integrated throughout the
text, and an extensive new art program featuring the use of
personal computer systems has been created. Many other
improvements are detailed later in this Preface. These improvements were required by the technology, demanded by
the title of this book, and expected by its readers. The Red
Queen would understand the need to thoroughly update a
best-selling text in just two years!

*Computers Today* is designed for use in the introductory

one-term course in computer data processing that's now taught throughout the world. Thus, it's suitable for computer literacy courses, for technically oriented programming courses, and for courses that attempt to strike a balance. This is true because the *purpose* of this book is to acquaint readers with *all four* of the following related areas of knowledge required for computer literacy:

1. **Computers themselves.** The organization, function, capabilities, and limitations of the equipment in modern computer systems of *all sizes* (personal, mini, mainframe, and supercomputer) are presented.

2. **What computers do.** Common data processing uses or applications of computers in today's society are treated. The focus is generally on business data processing applications, but many of the selected applications are also processed by not-for-profit organizations such as governments, hospitals, and schools.

3. **How computers are put to work.** The techniques used in the analysis and design of information systems are explained, and the procedures that are used to prepare programs are outlined. Programs for a number of the common data processing applications that have been identified earlier are then coded using the constructs of the BASIC language.

4. **The social impact of computers at work.** The ways in which people and organizations may be affected by present and future computer applications are presented.

## FLEXIBLE ORGANIZATION AND INTEGRATED PROGRAMMING EXAMPLES

Two popular features unique to the first edition have been carried over to this revision. The *first* of these is the *modular organization* that permits the book to meet the needs of courses with different subject emphases and with different presentation sequences. This flexibility is possible because *Computers Today* is organized into five modules. An overview of the four areas of knowledge mentioned above is presented in the four chapters of the first Background Module. Students should read these chapters (1 through 4) in sequence, but once they have completed them, they can turn *immediately to any of the remaining modules* to meet whatever sequence and depth requirements are needed in a particular course (see the chart below). For example, after completing Chapter 4 they can then go directly to the Programming Module chapters (18 through 21) that are conveniently placed in this edition at the back of the book. Or, readers may be more motivated to study computer data processing if some time is spent on the Social Impact chapters (15 through 17) after Chapter 4 is completed. Of course, it's also logical to consider computing equipment in more detail (Chapters 5 through 9) and then move to the Systems and Software Module (Chapters 10 through 14) prior to studying programming concepts.

But you get the idea: *Computers Today* gives you the flexibility to choose the sequence that is best for your needs. It also permits you to vary the depth of the material covered in a one-term course. Although it's unlikely that you'll be

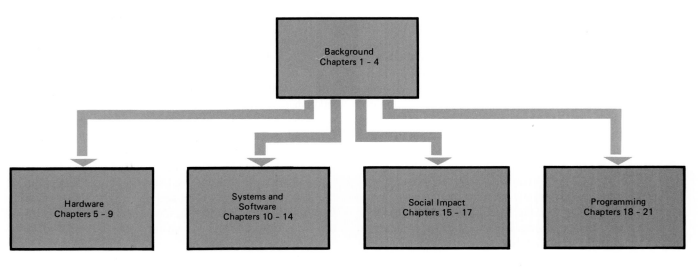

able to cover all 21 chapters in a single term, you'll have the freedom to select those topics that are most appropriate for your needs.

A *second* unique feature of *Computers Today* retained in this edition is the use of *integrated programming examples*. This innovative approach introduces readers to the methodology and techniques of computer programming. The programming examples used in most texts involve a series of unrelated data processing applications at a number of separate organizations. Since readers are often unfamiliar with common data processing systems and with the interrelated nature of the outputs produced by those systems, these examples are often viewed as random and boring exercises. To counter this problem, an enterprise created by two college students is presented and discussed in the early chapters. Some of the information needs of this business—R-K Enterprises—are outlined in a number of applications examples in Chapter 2. This theme of an "actual" business with realistic interrelated data processing needs is then carried to Chapters 18 through 21 in the Programming Module. Readers will see in Chapters 18 and 20 how the R-K Enterprises' applications presented in Chapter 2 are analyzed, flowcharted, and coded in the BASIC language. Chapter 20 provides sufficient material so that students can develop BASIC programming skills at a fundamental level. But if further development of programming skills is an objective of the course, additional R-K Enterprises' applications are then analyzed, flowcharted, and coded in an all-new Chapter 21 that explains more advanced features of the BASIC language. And *over two-dozen new end-of-chapter flowcharting/programming problems* built around R-K Enterprises' processing needs have been created for this edition. In fact, there's now a total of *over 50* BASIC programs tied to the R-K theme. Creating a realistic enterprise that students can identify with, discussing a number of the most common applications that such a business must process, and then carrying these interrelated applications through the analysis, flowcharting, and BASIC coding steps is unique to *Computers Today*.

## ADDITIONAL REVISION FEATURES AND AIDS TO LEARNING

Included among the numerous revision features and learning aids found in this edition are:

- A careful reorganization of chapters and modules has been carried out to meet changing conditions.

For example, the chapters dealing with data communications and word processing/electronic mail systems have been moved to a restructured Systems and Software Module. The Social Impact Module has been repositioned, and, as noted earlier, the Programming Module is located at the back of the book.

- Hundreds of *full-color* photographs, drawings, and illustrations are provided, and a high percentage of these are new. For example, new photo galleries are presented in a number of chapters (e.g., 1, 8, 9), new drawings featuring the use of a personal computer system to process R-K Enterprises' applications are found in Chapter 2, and new art depicting the spreadsheet, graphic, word processing, and data base capabilities of integrated software packages are found in Chapter 4 and elsewhere.

- Although there are still 21 chapters in the book, some earlier material has been condensed, reorganized, and repositioned to make room for *four* new chapter titles. These new chapters are "Personal Computers: The Micro Miracles" (8), "Minis, Mainframes, and 'Monsters'" (9), "System Software Packages: Operating Systems and Data Base Management Systems" (13), and "More about BASIC" (21).

- A wealth of new and up-to-the-minute material has been added on dozens of topics including integrated software packages, primary and secondary storage components, I/O devices, the selection of personal computer applications programs, the international race to develop "fifth-generation" supercomputers, telecommuting systems, voice mail, local-area and digital PBX networks, expert systems, organizational information centers, micro-to-mainframe linkages, artificial intelligence research—this list could go on and on!

- Most of the following aids to learning are either all new or substantially revised: (1) The *vignettes* used to open a chapter and highlight some aspect of its contents; (2) the *boxed inserts* included in each chapter to provide applications, cases, and items of interest to support chapter material and stimulate discussions; (3) the *Closer Look* reading following each chapter that provides additional information on selected topics.

■ A new *Projects to Look Into* section has been added at the end of most chapters to suggest student research topics that are based on material presented in the chapters. Some projects may be completed at a library, while others require visits to computer stores and/or computer-using organizations.

■ Learning aids carried over from the first edition include *Chapter Outlines, Looking Ahead learning objectives, Feedback and Review sections* with answers, *Looking Back chapter summaries,* listings of *Key Terms and Concepts, Topics for Review and Discussion,* and a *Glossary.*

## SUPPLEMENTS FOR THIS EDITION

Numerous supplements have been prepared to make the *Computers Today* package a complete teaching/learning tool. They include:

■ *Inside Computers Today.* This student Study Guide is designed to provide extensive self-tests for each corresponding chapter in *Computers Today.* Each Study Guide chapter contains learning objectives; a chapter overview and summary; and varied self-test sections including key term matching, multiple choice, true or false, and completion exercises. Answers for all exercises are included in the Study Guide. *Inside Computers Today* is an instrument planned to reinforce and integrate text concepts. It is designed for success—no "tricky" questions have been included intentionally. Successfully completing the Study Guide exercises should increase the confidence of all levels of students. It is a straightforward, no-frills, self-testing implement written for students, not for teachers.

■ *The Computers Today Software Supplement.* This new applications software is designed to give students hands-on experience with an integrated software package. Using examples from R-K Enterprises, students learn word processing, database management, spreadsheeting, and graphics. In addition to the student disks, McGraw-Hill will provide adopters with an instructor's gradebook disk. Features of the gradebook include checking attendance and computing grades.

■ *Instructor's Resource Kit.* The components of this Kit provide instructors with extensive support materials for teaching a course with *Computers Today.* The following supplements are included:

1. *Instructor's Manual.* Beyond supplying resource material for each chapter of the text, this Manual contains FORTRAN, COBOL, and Pascal programs dealing with R-K Enterprises applications. (The logic of each program is analyzed in text Chapter 18.) These programs use the same input data and produce the same output results as the BASIC programs discussed in Chapter 20 of the text. The Manual also supplies transparency masters and a bibliography of selected references.

2. *Overhead Transparencies.* A set of 64 color transparencies serves as a visual classroom aid which can be used to further explain text concepts.

3. *Test Bank.* This completely reworked set of more than 2,600 questions covers the important ideas and definitions in *Computers Today.* For your convenience the test bank is available for use with the computer. *MicroExaminer* allows you to generate tests using your Apple IIc or II+, IBM PC, or TRS 80 microcomputer. Questions can be scrambled into two versions, allowing you to create alternative exams for multiple sections of the same course. You also have the option of adding your own questions to the test bank. *The EXAMINER System* contains a magnetic tape which can be installed in your computer center, and offers the same features as *MicroExaminer.*

■ *Structured COBOL: A Beginner's Guide.* This revised manual is intended to be a beginner's guide to solving and coding COBOL programs. The revision covers most of the basic formats and commands recommended by the American National Standards Institute (ANSI), with modifications for the beginning student. The authors of this manual are Frederick R. Prisco and Charles J. McNerney, both of Bergen Community College.

■ *Pascal Supplement.* This supplement to accompany *Computers Today* parallels wherever possible the material presented in text chapters 20 (Programming with BASIC) and 21 (More about BASIC). All the programs appearing in these chapters are rewritten in Pascal. The author of this manual is Philip Drummond of Queens College.

- **Slide Package.** This set of 36 color slides will give your students a visual orientation to the course. This package contains new photographs, many not found in the text, that introduce your students to computers.

- **BASICard.** This convenient pocket-sized card enables students to have important BASIC commands and codes always at their fingertips. A great aid for student programming.

## ACKNOWLEDGMENTS

It's customary for authors to conclude a preface by acknowledging the contributions and suggestions received from numerous sources. This is particularly appropriate in the case of *Computers Today* because a colorful package of this scope just doesn't happen without the input of many people.

The authorities who responded to a research study and helped reshape the content and organization of *Computers Today,* and the professionals who reviewed the manuscript and made many helpful suggestions are acknowledged separately following this Preface.

Another word of thanks must go to the equipment manufacturers, publishers, and photo agencies who furnished materials, excerpts, and photographs for this text. Their individual contributions are acknowledged in the body of the book.

The final tribute and greatest appreciation, however, is reserved for these few: to Barbara Brooks, who somehow found time in the midst of new responsibilities to turn in another incredible developmental editing job—her inspired ideas and creative talents are visible on almost every page; to Mel Haber, whose last design, you're convinced, can't be topped—and then you see his next one; to Phil Galea and Lorinda Morris, whose production and photo research efforts continue to surprise a critical author; to Ed Hanson, who efficiently manages complex projects without a hitch; to Eric Munson and Christina Mediate for their editorial support; to Rob Fry for his efforts on the supplements; to Hal Sackman for his time and efforts on the test manual; to Anne Green for her artistic talents; to Gary D. Sanders, University of Illinois, for his additional program contributions and suggestions; and to Joyce Sanders for her continuing suggestions and encouragement.

Donald H. Sanders

# Acknowledgments

Professor Lawrence W. Arp
*Indiana State University-Evansville*

Mr. James J. Basl
*American Institute of Banking*

Professor Robert D. Brown
*University of Georgia*

Professor Jean Burgess
*Charles County Community College*

Professor William R. Cornette
*Southwest Missouri State University*

Professor Jay Edwards
*Crafton Hills College*

Professor John Egloff
*Westchester Business Institute*

Professor Rich Fleming
*North Lake College*

Professor Jon Fults
*Cerritos College*

Professor David Godderz
*Lakewood Community College*

Mr. Larry Greenhaw
*Texas Department of Human
Resources*

Professor Marilyn Jussel
*Kearney State College*

Professor John W. McCarty
*Wichita Area Vocational-Technical
School*

Professor Laurence Madeo
*The University of Iowa*

Professor George C. Moore
*Oklahoma City University*

Professor Paul J. Mulcahy
*Morehead State University*

Professor Jack Oakes
*Missouri Southern State College*

Professor Harold Sackman
*California State University,
Los Angeles*

Professor Sharon Sipe
*Prince Georges' Community College*

Professor David Wen
*Diablo Valley College*

Professor Laurie Werth
*University of Nevada-Las Vegas*

Professor Fatemeh Zahedi
*University of Massachusetts-Boston
Harbor Campus*

# Background

# module 1

To be an educated citizen today, you must be acquainted not only with computers themselves, but also with what computers do, how they are put to work, and the impact of their use on individuals and organizations in a society. An overview of all these topics is presented in the chapters of this Background Module. Each of the four remaining modules in the book will then consider one of these topics in greater detail.

The chapters included in this Background Module are:

1. Hardware, Systems, and Software Concepts: Introduction and Impact
2. Computers at Work: An Overview of Applications
3. Putting the Computer to Work: Systems and Software Development
4. The Impact of Computers at Work: A Preview

# Hardware, Systems, and Software Concepts
## *introduction and impact*

## IT'S A WHOLE NEW WORLD

As each year draws to a close, the editors of *Time* magazine review the year's newsmakers and select one as representative of the year just passing. This selected newsmaker is then featured in a cover story in the year's final issue. A politician, a chief of state, a scientist—perhaps these are the people you'd expect to see featured in the special issue. If so, you might have been as surprised as were millions of others a few years ago to find that *Time*'s "Man of the Year" wasn't a person at all. It was a machine: the computer.

*Time*'s editors noted that sales of small personal-sized computers—numbering in the millions—had virtually doubled the preceding year. Additional millions of these **personal computers** have been sold since. It appears that the affection that many Americans have for their automobiles and television sets has now expanded to include their personal computers.

But think back. Have you always taken computers for granted as an everyday part of life, or do you remember your first specific "encounter" with a computer? If you were born in the 1950s or earlier, you might have grown up thinking of the few computers in existence as enormous and expensive machines, used mostly for special scientific purposes. They had little direct impact on your life or the lives of most people. Only a handful of pioneers had first-hand knowledge of them, and the rest of the population probably expected to live happy lives

Computers have changed the way we do business with powerful portable units (*top left*), electronic systems for information such as travel reservations (*bottom left*), and new technologies for manufacturing (*above*). (Photos courtesy The Bohle Company, Sperry Corporation, and reproduced with permission of AT&T)

3

without ever using—or ever touching—these laboratory curiosities. (An in-depth study that traces the evolution of computer development and identifies many of the early pioneers is presented in the Closer Look reading at the end of this chapter.)

If you grew up in the 1960s, though, you probably acquired a different perspective about computers. Although you marveled at their role in sending people to the moon and back, you also knew that these former curiosities were regularly used to process your bills and checks. Each year during the 1960s and 1970s, new computers were announced that were more compact, more powerful, and much less expensive than their predecessors. And

during these decades, millions of people joined the early pioneers in gaining first-hand knowledge of computer capabilities and limitations.

Now, in the 1980s, millions of personal computers (as well as hundreds of thousands of larger machines) have come to inhabit offices, factories, schools, homes, hospitals, government agencies, banks, and retail stores as well as laboratories. Computers of all sizes, like automobiles and electricity, exert a daily influence on your life. It's now almost impossible to avoid reading, seeing, or hearing about computers; their presence in your daily life simply cannot be denied or ignored. Some computer uses, or *applications,* offer benefits (you make travel arrangements quickly and efficiently, your credit card is readily accepted, and your paycheck is on time and accurate). But other computer uses may make you uneasy (you may feel that you are being numerically coded and molded to meet the needs of computer systems, and you may be concerned about how personal information about you that has been entered into these systems may be used).

The fact that a revolutionary invention like the computer can have both good and bad uses should not come as a surprise. After all, automobiles give us mobility and freedom, but they also kill us by the thousands. Computer

Fast-paced innovation within the computer industry offers increasingly sophisticated ways of using information. (Photos courtesy Apple Computer, Inc., top; Gould Inc., above far left; reproduced with permission of AT&T, above left, above; Texas Instruments Incorporated, left)

Computer-created images advertise automobiles (*above*); computer hardware gives us the option of banking by car (*right*). (Photos courtesy MAGI Synthavision, Inc. and International Business Machines Corporation) Increasing amounts of information are conveyed by quality computer graphics (*below*).

applications will grow even faster in the years ahead. And as *Time*'s editors noted, with the expanded use of computers there will be vast potential for widespread benefits as well as undesirable results. Educated citizens should not rely solely on computer specialists to prevent the possible dangers and bring about the positive potential. Rather, each citizen should learn about computers to better participate in the benefits and to insist that the designers of ill-conceived computer systems assume the responsibility for the effects these systems have on people. Your need for **computer literacy** is a fact. It's also the purpose of this book.

(Photos reprinted with permission from Computervision Corporation, Bedford, Mass., above; courtesy Image Resource Corporation, above right; Viewdata Corporation of America, Inc., above far right; Ashton-Tate, right; and Spinnaker Software Corp., far right)

## LOOKING AHEAD

The information in this chapter will enable you to:

- Understand your need for computer literacy

- Define the term "computer" and outline some of its capabilities

- Outline the activities involved in data processing and the data processing operations that computers can perform

- Identify the hardware components in a basic computer system and describe the functions of each component

- Explain how a computer can accept and process data, and produce output results, by following the detailed set of instructions contained in a stored program

- Describe some ways in which computer systems may differ

- Discuss some limiting factors in the use of computers

## WHAT TO EXPECT

*Computers Today* is an ambitious title for a book. It suggests a breadth of contemporary computer information that's usually not found within a single text. But a broad familiarity with computers is just what you'll need in the years ahead. Thus, the *purpose of this book* is to acquaint you with *all four* of the following related areas of knowledge required for computer literacy:

## Chapter Outline

1. ***Knowing what computers are.*** You should understand the organization, capabilities, and limitations of the various machines, or **hardware,** that make up a modern computer system.

2. ***Knowing what computers do.*** You should be familiar with some of the more common uses or **applications** of computers in today's society. The focus in this book will be primarily on business data processing applications.

3. ***Knowing how computer systems are put to work.*** You need to know the analysis, design, and program preparation procedures that must be carried out in order to produce written programs of instructions, or **software.** These programs cause the hardware to function in a desired way to process applications. Like television programs, computer programs turn lifeless machines into something useful.

4. ***Understanding their impact.*** You should be aware of how individuals and organizations may be affected by present and future computer applications.

**How This Book Is Organized**

To provide a well-rounded introduction to the field of data processing, *Computers Today* is organized into five modules. An overview of *all four areas* of knowledge mentioned above is presented in the four chapters of this Background Module. You should read Chapters 1 through 4 in sequence, but once you've completed them you can then turn immediately to *any of the other modules*. Figure 1-1 shows this flexible organization. Let's begin now by picking up some background information about the computer itself. You'll be surprised at how much you know already and by what you'll learn.

**Figure 1-1** How *Computers Today* is organized. After reading the first four chapters, you will then have the background needed to permit you to go immediately to any of the other modules.

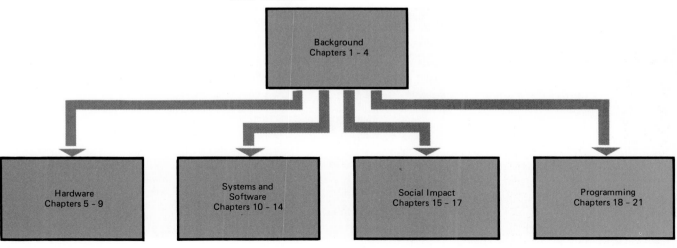

# INTRODUCING THE COMPUTER

Most people are aware that a computer is a machine that can perform arithmetic operations. But it's much more than just a fast arithmetic device. It's also a machine that can choose, copy, move, compare, and perform other nonarithmetic operations on the many alphabetic, numeric, and other symbols that humans use to represent things. The computer manipulates these symbols in the desired way by following an "intellectual map" called a program. A **program,** then, is a detailed set of humanly prepared instructions that directs the computer to function in a specific way to produce a desired result. And a **computer** is a fast and accurate electronic symbol (or data) manipulating system that's designed and organized to automatically accept and store input data, process them, and produce output results under the direction of a detailed step-by-step stored program of instructions. In the following pages we'll examine the elements in this not-so-simple definition in more detail. At the same time, we'll cover some important computer and data processing concepts.

## Computer Capabilities: Speed and Accuracy

A computer works one step at a time. It can add and subtract numbers, compare letters to determine alphabetic sequence, and move and copy numbers and letters. There's certainly nothing profound in these operations. What's significant is the computer's *speed*. Measured in the units shown in Figure 1-2, the time required for computers to execute a basic operation—e.g., add—varies from a few **microseconds** for the smallest machines to 80 **nanoseconds** or less for the larger ones. Thus, the slowest computers can perform hundreds of thousands of additions in a second while the largest systems can complete many millions.

The benefit of the computer's speed is that we humans are freed to use our time more creatively. Our time dimension has been broadened. We can now often obtain information that could not have been produced at all a few years ago or that could

Figure 1-2 The minuscule units used to measure computer speed.

| Unit of time | Part of a Second | Interpretation |
|---|---|---|
| Millisecond (ms) | One-thousandth (1/1000) | A baseball pitched at a speed of 95 miles-per-hour (mph) would move less than 2 inches in a millisecond. |
| Microsecond ($\mu$s) | One-millionth (1/1,000,000) | A spaceship traveling toward the moon at 100,000 mph would move less than 2 inches in a microsecond. |
| Nanosecond (ns) | One-billionth (1/1,000,000,000) | There are as many nanoseconds in one second as there are seconds in 30 years, or as many nanoseconds in a minute as there are minutes in 1,100 centuries. |
| Picosecond (ps) | One-trillionth (1/1,000,000,000,000) | Electricity (and light) travels at 186,000 miles-per-second or about 1 foot in a nanosecond. In a picosecond, electricity would move less than 1/50th of an inch. A picosecond is to a second what a second is to 31,710 years. |

have been prepared only after great human effort. John Kemeny, former President of Dartmouth College and an author of BASIC, a popular language used to prepare computer programs, has noted that in 1945 it took many people a full year of working around the clock to complete certain calculations at the atomic laboratories at Los Alamos. The same calculations, Kemeny observes, could now be done in one afternoon by a single undergraduate student while sharing a computer's time with dozens of others. Of course, as you'll see in Chapter 2, some jobs are gathered into batches and are then processed by the computer only at scheduled times. When this approach is used, the delay required to accumulate the jobs for processing may seem excessive to impatient computer users.

In addition to being very fast, computers are also very *accurate*. It's estimated that you or I would make one error in every 500 to 1,000 operations with a calculator. But the circuits in a computer require no human intervention between processing operations and have no mechanical parts to wear and malfunction. These circuits can perform hundreds of thousands (or millions) of operations every second and can run errorless for hours and days at a time. Beyond this, computers also have built-in, self-checking capabilities that permit them to monitor the accuracy of their *internal* operations. *If* the input data entering the computer are correct and relevant and *if* the program of processing instructions is reliable, *then* we can expect that the computer generally will produce accurate output. Perhaps you've heard the phrase **"garbage in–garbage out,"** or GIGO. (GIGO is an **acronym**—a term formed from the first letters of related words.) Used often by people who work with computers, GIGO implies that "computer errors" can usually be traced to incorrect input data or unreliable programs—and both are usually caused by human and not computer frailties.

**The Computer's Processing Abilities**

**Computer processing** involves manipulating the symbols that people use to represent things. The first computers were built to manipulate *numbers* in order to solve arithmetic problems. But as Figure 1-3 shows, we create, use, and manipulate many

Figure 1-3 A few of the symbols people use to communicate facts and concepts.

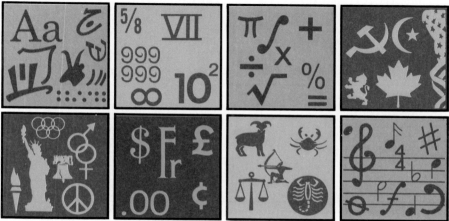

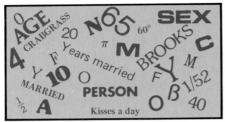

(a) Raw data input

| Person | A | B | C |
|---|---|---|---|
| Age | 10 | 65 | 20 |
| Kisses a day | 0 | 4 | 40 |
| Sex | M | M | F |
| Married | N | Y | Y |
| Years married | 0 | 40 | 1/52 |

(b) Selected data have been arranged (processed) in an ordered form to produce information

**Figure 1-4** Processing converts raw data into information. All information consists of data, but not all data produce specific and meaningful information. The accumulation of additional data can often add new dimensions to existing information, but the interpretation of the information generally requires human judgment and may vary from person to person.

*other symbols* that represent the facts of our lives. Luckily for us, early computer experts soon made the important discovery that a machine that can accept, store, and process numbers can also manipulate nonnumerical symbols. Manipulating these familiar symbols is possible if an identifying code number is assigned to the symbol to be stored and processed. Thus, the letter A can be represented by a code, as can the letter B, the addition symbol (+), and so on. Of course, someone must give the computer instructions if it is to manipulate the coded and stored symbols in a desired way. Instructions are needed, for example, to put a stored list of names into an alphabetical sequence.

**Data versus Information.** The word "data" is the plural of datum, which means "fact." **Data,** then, are facts, the raw material of information. Data are represented by symbols, but they are *not* information except in a limited sense. As used here, information is data arranged in ordered and useful form. That is, **information** is relevant knowledge produced as output of data processing operations and acquired by people to enhance understanding and to achieve specific purposes. Figure 1-4 illustrates the distinction between data and information. You can see that information is the result of a transformation process in Figure 1-5. Just as raw materials are transformed into finished products by a manufacturing process, raw data are transformed into information by data processing.

**Data Processing Activities.** **Data processing** consists of gathering the raw data input, evaluating and bringing order to it, and placing it in proper perspective so that useful information will be produced. All data processing, whether done by hand or by the latest computer system, consists of three basic activities: capturing the input data, manipulating the data, and managing the output results.

**Figure 1-5** Information is the result of a transformation process. Products produced by a manufacturing process (part a) have little value until they are used; similarly, information produced by data processing (part b) is of little value unless it supports meaningful human decisions and actions.

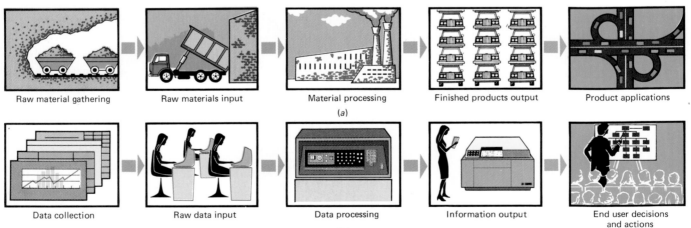

Raw material gathering    Raw materials input    Material processing    Finished products output    Product applications

(a)

Data collection    Raw data input    Data processing    Information output    End user decisions and actions

(b)

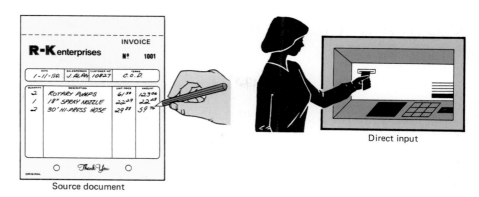

Source document

Direct input

**Capturing the Input Data.** Data must be *originated* in some form and *verified* for accuracy prior to further processing. They may initially be recorded on paper **source documents** and then converted into a machine-usable form for processing. Or they may be captured by a **direct input device** in a paperless machine-readable form.

**Manipulating the Data.** One or more of the following operations may then have to be performed on the gathered data:

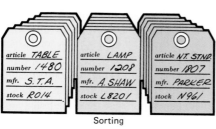

Classifying

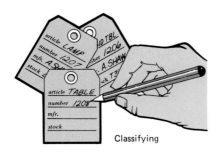

Sorting

1. *Classifying.* Organizing similar items into groups or classes is called **classifying.** Data taken from a retail store's sales ticket, for example, may be classified by product sold, sales department, salesperson, or any other classification useful to store managers. Classifying is usually accomplished by assigning predetermined abbreviations or codes to the items being arranged. The three types of codes used are *numeric* (postal Zip codes used for geographic classification), *alphabetic* (persons A, B, and C in Figure 1-4), and **alphanumeric** (letters and numbers, like the identification codes used to classify General Motors trucks by type of engine, chassis, body, and assembly location).

2. *Sorting.* Usually, it's easier to work with data if they are arranged in a logical sequence. Examples include first to last, biggest to smallest, oldest to newest. Arranging classified data in such a sequence is called **sorting.** Retail sales tickets may be sorted by the name or number of the salesperson. Numeric sorting is common in computer-based processing systems because it's usually faster than alphabetic sorting.

3. *Calculating.* Arithmetic manipulation of the data is called **calculating.** In calculating a salesperson's pay, for example, the hours worked multiplied by the hourly wage rate gives the total earnings. Payroll deductions such as taxes are then calculated and subtracted from total earnings to arrive at the salesperson's take-home pay.

4. *Summarizing.* Reducing masses of data to a more concise and usable form is called **summarizing.** For example, the general manager of a retail store is interested only in a summary of the total sales of each department. A summary report would give only total sales information. Department man-

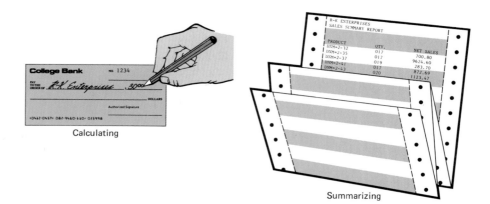

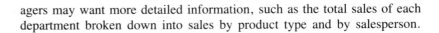
Calculating

Summarizing

agers may want more detailed information, such as the total sales of each department broken down into sales by product type and by salesperson.

*Managing the Output Results.* Once data have been captured and manipulated, one or more of the following operations may be needed:

Storing and retrieving

1. *Storing and retrieving.* Retaining data for future reference is **storing.** Of course, facts should be stored only if the value of having them in the future exceeds the storage cost. Storage media such as paper, microfilm, or magnetizeable disks and tapes are generally used. Recovering stored data and/or information is the **retrieving** activity. Retrieval methods vary. One slow approach is for people to search file cabinets. A much faster method is to use electronic inquiry devices that are connected directly to a computer which, in turn, is connected directly to a mass-storage unit containing the data.

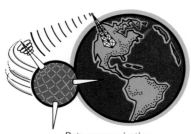

Data communication

2. *Communicating and reproducing.* Transferring data from one location or operation to another for use or for further processing is **data communication**—a process that continues until information, in a usable form, reaches the final user. Sometimes, of course, it's necessary to copy or duplicate data. This **reproduction** activity may be done by hand or by machine.

**Processing by Computer.** There's nothing new about the data processing steps just outlined. They've been performed down through the ages, first by hand, then by machine-assisted manual and electromechanical punched card methods, and now by computers. You can take a closer look at the evolution of data processing in the reading that follows this chapter. The four function categories which follow are all that a computer can perform, but they include most data processing steps.

1. *Input/output operations.* A computer can accept data (input) from and supply processed data (output) to a wide range of input/output devices. Such devices as keyboards and display screens make human/machine communicating possible. Multiple output documents may be reproduced by computer-controlled printers.

**Figure 1-6** (a) A computer can compare two items and then take an appropriate action branch depending on the outcome. By using combinations of these simple comparisons, the computer is able to perform sophisticated procedures and answer complicated questions. (b) Let's assume that the data in a large listing have been organized in some logical order (alphabetically or in numerical sequence) on a computer-readable medium. The computer can be programmed to search for a specific data item (A) by looking first at the middle item in the listing (M). If, as a result of a comparison, the value of A is alphabetically or numerically less than M, the last half of the listing can be quickly eliminated. Thus, this one comparison has cut the search problem in half. An additional comparison using the middle item of the remaining half of the listing can now be made, and this search procedure can be continued until the desired item is either located or shown to be missing from the listing.

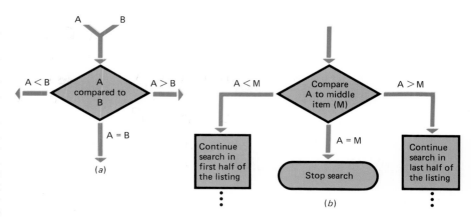

2. **Calculation operations.** The circuits in a computer are designed to permit addition, subtraction, multiplication, and division. Such operations, of course, make calculating possible.

3. **Logic/comparison operations.** The computer also has the ability to perform logic operations. For example, when we compare two data items represented by the symbols A and B, there are only three possible outcomes: (1) A is *equal to* B (A = B); (2) A is *greater than* B (A>B); or (3) A is *less than* B (A<B). The computer is able to perform a simple comparison and then, depending on the result, follow a *predetermined branch*, or course of action, to complete its work (see Figure 1-6). This comparison ability thus makes it possible to *classify* item A as having or not having the characteristic of B, to determine the sequence between A and B for *sorting* purposes, or to determine if A meets the selection criterion of B for *summarizing* purposes. This simple ability to compare is an important computer property because more sophisticated questions can be answered by using combinations of comparison decisions.

4. **Storage and retrieval operations.** Both data and program instructions are stored internally in a computer. And once stored, both may be quickly called up, or retrieved, for use. The time required for data or instructions to be retrieved is measured in micro- or nanoseconds.

## Feedback and Review 1-1

So far, we've seen that a computer is a very fast and accurate machine. Computers can accept input data in the form of numeric and nonnumeric symbols, manipulate these data through a series of data processing activities, and arrange the output results in order to produce useful information. Now is a good time to pause so that you can test and reinforce your understanding of these concepts. This "pause that reinforces" will occur from time to time in each chapter. The *crossword puzzle* is one of a variety of formats you'll see. You'll find the answers to each exercise at the end of the chapter. Fill in the puzzle form using the sentences and definitions found on page 14.

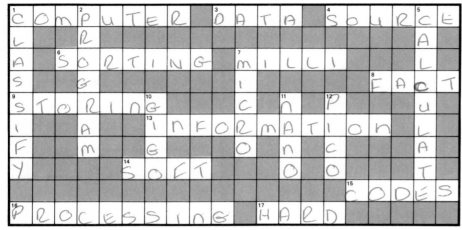

## Across

**1.** A _____ is a fast and accurate electronic symbol (or data) manipulating system that will accept and store input data, process them, and produce output results under the direction of a stored program of instructions.

**3.** _____ are facts or informational raw materials represented by symbols.

**4.** Data may first be recorded on paper _____ documents and then converted into a machine-usable form for processing.

**6.** Arranging classified data in a predetermined sequence to facilitate processing is called _____.

**7.** A unit of time equal to one-thousandth of a second is a _____ -second.

**8.** The word ''data'' is the plural of datum, which means _____.

**9.** Retaining data for future reference is _____.

**13.** _____ is relevant knowledge produced as output of data processing operations and acquired by people to enhance understanding and to achieve specific purposes.

**14.** _____ -ware is the name given to the programs that have been written to cause computers to function in a desired way.

**15.** The three types of _____ used to classify data items are numeric, alphabetic, and alphanumeric.

**16.** The purpose of data _____ is to capture raw input data, evaluate and bring order to them, and place them in proper perspective so that useful information will be produced.

**17.** _____ -ware is the name given to the various machines that make up a computer system.

## Down

**1.** To _____ is to organize data items with like characteristics into groups or classes.

**2.** A _____ is a detailed step-by-step set of instructions that cause a computer to function in a desired way.

**5.** To _____ is to perform arithmetic manipulations on data.

**7.** A _____ -second is one-millionth of a second.

**10.** _____ is an acronym that recognizes the fact that ''computer errors'' can usually be traced to incorrect input data or unreliable programs.

**11.** A _____ -second is one-billionth of a second.

**12.** A _____ -second is one-trillionth of a second.

# COMPUTER SYSTEM ORGANIZATION

Now that we've examined what computers do, let's look again at our computer definition: A computer is a fast and accurate symbol manipulating *system* that is organized to accept, store, and process data and produce output results under the direction of a stored program of instructions. This section explains why a computer is a system and how a computer system is organized.

**The System Concept**

The term ''system'' is used often in many different ways. For example, everyone is familiar with expressions such as ''Professor Nastie has an impossible grading system,'' or ''Marty has a system for betting on the horses.'' But for our purposes, a **system** is a group of integrated parts that have the common purpose of achieving some objective(s). The three following characteristics are key:

1. *A group of parts.* A system has more than one element. A steel ball is not a system, but it might be part of a bearing assembly that could be combined with other components to produce an irrigation system.

Coleco's Adam is a microcomputer sold as a system for use in the home. (Photo courtesty Coleco Industries, Inc.)

2. ***Integrated parts.*** A logical relationship must exist between the parts of a system. Mechanical and electronic systems such as washing machines and video games have components that work together. And a personnel management system may consist of integrated procedures for recruiting, training, and evaluating employees.

3. ***Common purpose of achieving some objective(s).*** The system is designed to accomplish one or more objectives. All system elements should be controlled so that the system goal is achieved. Totally automated systems have tightly controlled operations; systems operated by people sometimes manage to get out of control. (Humans regularly lose control of those mechanical systems called cars and wind up in body shops or hospitals.)

A computer is a group of integrated parts that have the common purpose of performing the operations called for in the program being executed: It qualifies as a system. Now any system may be comprised of smaller systems or subsystems. A **subsystem** is a smaller system contained within a larger one. Some of the component parts found in most computer systems—e.g., printers—are systems in their own right. And computers, in turn, may be considered subsystems in larger **supersystems** such as the air traffic control system used to monitor flights of the nation's aircraft.

## Organization of Computer System Components

Figure 1-7 shows the basic organization of a computer system. Key elements in this system include input, processing, and output devices. Let's examine each component of the system in more detail.

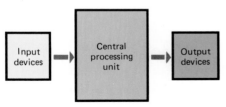

**Figure 1-7** The basic organization of a computer system.

**Input Devices.** Computer systems use many devices for input purposes. As shown in Figure 1-8, some **input devices** allow direct human/machine communication, while some first require data to be recorded on an input medium such as a magnetizeable material. Devices that read data magnetically recorded on specially coated plastic tapes or flexible or *floppy* plastic disks are popular. The keyboard of a workstation connected directly to—or **online** to—a computer is an example of a direct input device. Additional direct input devices—e.g., the mouse, input pen, touch screen, and microphone—are discussed in Chapter 6. Regardless of the type of device used, all are components for interpretation and communication between people and computer systems.

**Central Processing Unit.** The heart of any computer system is the **central processing unit** (CPU). As Figure 1-9 shows, there are three main sections found in the CPU of a typical personal computer system. But these three sections aren't unique to personal computers: They are found in CPUs of all sizes.

■ ***The primary storage section.*** The **primary storage section** is used for four purposes. Three of these relate to the data being processed (see Figure 1-9):

(1) Data are fed into an **input storage area** where they are held until ready to be processed.

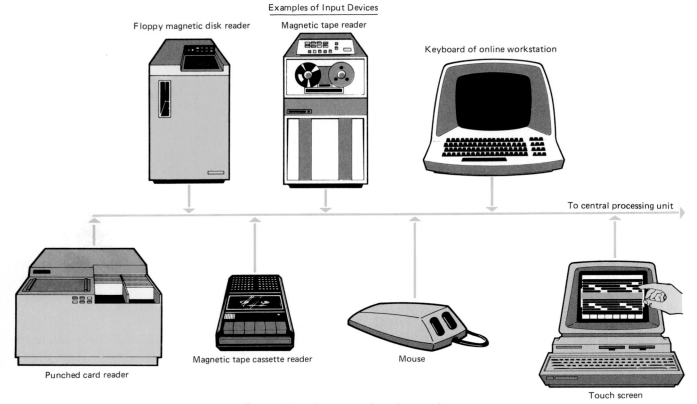

Examples of Input Devices

Floppy magnetic disk reader | Magnetic tape reader

Keyboard of online workstation

To central processing unit

Punched card reader

Magnetic tape cassette reader

Mouse

Touch screen

Figure 1-8 A few examples of input devices.

**(2)** A **working storage space** that's like a sheet of scratch paper is used to hold the data being processed and the intermediate results of such processing.

**(3)** An **output storage area** holds the finished results of the processing operations until they can be released.

**(4)** In addition to these data-related purposes, the primary storage section also contains a **program storage area** that holds the processing instructions.

The separate areas used for these four general purposes are not fixed by built-in physical boundaries in the storage section. Rather, they can vary from one application to another. Thus, a specific physical space may be used to store input data in one application, output results in another, and processing instructions in a third. The programmer writing the application instructions (or ''housekeeping'' software prepared by other programmers) determines how the space will be used for each job.

In addition to the primary storage or **main memory** section, most computers also have **secondary** (sometimes called **auxiliary** or **external**)

**storage** capabilities. Secondary storage devices are machines that are generally connected *online* to the CPU where they serve as reference libraries by accepting data directly from and returning data directly to the CPU without human intervention. In Figure 1-9, these devices are built into the system cabinet of the personal computer. Computer-usable data are also retained outside the CPU on paper and magnetizeable secondary storage

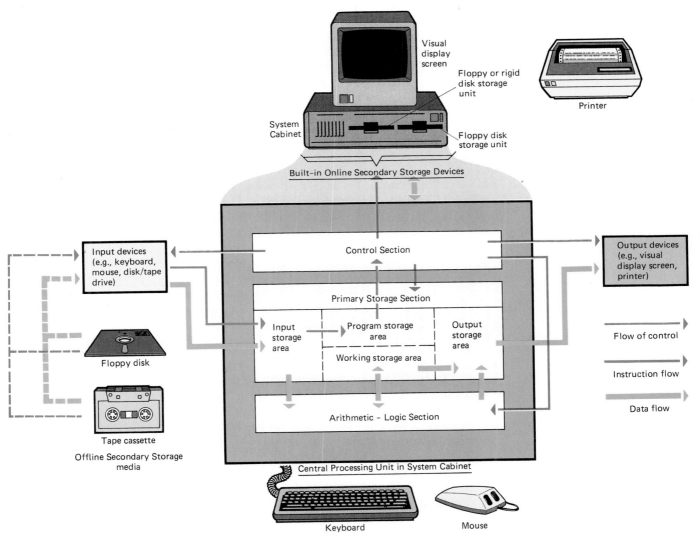

**Figure 1-9** The components in the CPU of a personal computer system. Primary storage, arithmetic-logic and control sections are found in CPUs of all sizes. The specific areas of primary storage used for a particular purpose (input storage, program storage, etc.) are *not* physically fixed. Rather, they vary depending on the application program. The dashed lines in the storage section are used to indicate this boundary flexibility.

media. However, these facts are frequently **offline,** that is, the CPU doesn't have direct and unassisted access to them (see Figure 1-9).

■ *The arithmetic-logic section.* All calculations are performed and all comparisons (decisions) are made in the **arithmetic-logic section** of the CPU (see Figure 1-9). Once data are fed into primary storage from input devices, they are held and transferred as needed to the arithmetic-logic section where processing takes place. No processing occurs in primary storage. Intermediate results generated in the arithmetic-logic unit are temporarily placed in a designated working storage area until needed at a later time. Data may thus move from primary storage to the arithmetic-logic unit and back again to storage many times before the processing is finished. Once completed, the final results are released to an output storage section and from there to an output device. The type and number of arithmetic and logic operations a computer can perform are determined by the engineering design of the CPU

■ *The control section.* How does the input device know when to feed data into storage? How does the arithmetic-logic section know what should be done with the data once they are received? And how is the output device able to obtain finished rather than intermediate results? It's by selecting, interpreting, and seeing to the execution of the program instructions that the **control section** of the CPU is able to maintain order and direct the operation of the entire system. Although it doesn't perform any actual processing on the data, the control unit acts as a central nervous system for the other components of the computer (see Figure 1-9). At the beginning of processing, the first program instruction is selected and fed into the control section from the program storage area. There it's interpreted, and from there signals are sent to other components to execute the necessary action(s). Other program instructions are then selected and executed in a sequential fashion until the processing is completed.

**Output Devices.** Like input units, **output devices** are instruments of interpretation and communication between humans and computer systems of all sizes. These devices take output results from the CPU in machine-coded form and convert them into a form that can be used (*a*) by people (e.g., a printed and/or displayed report) or (*b*) as machine input in another processing cycle (e.g., a series of magnetized spots on tapes or disks).

In personal computer systems (Figure 1-9), display screens and desktop printers are popular output devices. Larger and faster printers, many online workstations, and magnetic tape drives are commonly found in larger systems (Figure 1-10). Additional output devices such as microfilm recorders are presented in Chapter 7.

The input/output and secondary storage units shown in Figures 1-9 and 1-10 are sometimes called **peripheral devices** (or just *peripherals*). This terminology refers to the fact that although these devices are not a part of the CPU, they are often located near it.

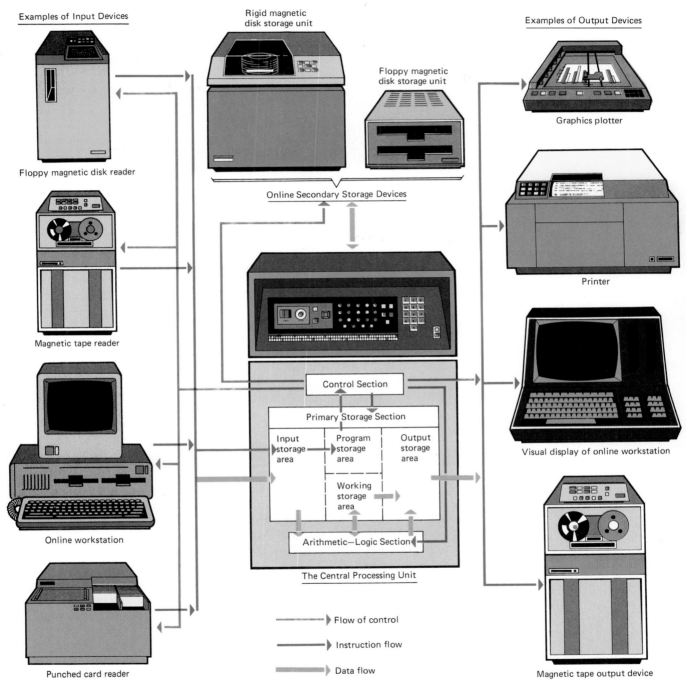

Examples of Input Devices

Floppy magnetic disk reader

Magnetic tape reader

Online workstation

Punched card reader

Rigid magnetic disk storage unit

Floppy magnetic disk storage unit

Online Secondary Storage Devices

Examples of Output Devices

Graphics plotter

Printer

Visual display of online workstation

Magnetic tape output device

Control Section

Primary Storage Section

Input storage area

Program storage area

Output storage area

Working storage area

Arithmetic—Logic Section

The Central Processing Unit

Flow of control

Instruction flow

Data flow

**Figure 1-10** A summary of some components found in the larger computer systems used in organizations.

## Feedback and Review 1-2

Now that you've seen how computer systems may be organized, try the *scrambled words* format below to test and reinforce your understanding of this section. Rearrange the letters to spell out the correct word for the space indicated in the corresponding sentence.

**1.** A group of integrated parts that have the common purpose of achieving some objective is a _System_
Ⓣ Ⓔ Ⓢ Ⓢ Ⓨ Ⓜ

**2.** The heart of any computer system is the _central_ processing unit.
Ⓣ Ⓛ Ⓝ Ⓒ Ⓐ Ⓔ Ⓡ

**3.** The _working_ storage area of the primary storage section of a CPU is used to hold the intermediate results of data processing.
Ⓚ Ⓞ Ⓡ Ⓖ Ⓝ Ⓘ Ⓦ

**4.** CPUs of all sizes have primary storage, arithmetic-logic, and _con Tra_ sections.
Ⓛ Ⓞ Ⓞ Ⓝ Ⓡ Ⓒ Ⓣ

**5.** The input, output, and working storage areas in the primary storage section of a CPU are used for data-related purposes, but the _prog_ storage area is used to hold instructions.
Ⓜ Ⓐ Ⓡ Ⓡ Ⓞ Ⓖ Ⓟ

**6.** Input and _output_ devices are combined with a CPU in a typical computer system.
Ⓤ Ⓤ Ⓣ Ⓣ Ⓞ Ⓟ

**7.** Actual data processing operations are performed in the arithmetic-logic section, but not in the _prim._ storage section or the control section of a central processor.
Ⓡ Ⓡ Ⓨ Ⓘ Ⓟ Ⓐ Ⓜ

**8.** The control section of a computer _Selects_, interprets, and sees to the execution of program instructions.
Ⓔ Ⓔ Ⓢ Ⓢ Ⓛ Ⓣ Ⓒ

**9.** In addition to a primary storage section, most computers also have secondary storage devices that are connected _online_ to the CPU and are thus able to accept data directly from, and return data directly to, the CPU without human intervention.
Ⓝ Ⓞ Ⓔ Ⓛ Ⓝ Ⓘ

**10.** The locations used to store input data, intermediate and output results, and program instructions in the CPU can _vary_ from one application to the next.
Ⓨ Ⓐ Ⓥ Ⓡ

# THE STORED PROGRAM CONCEPT: AN EXAMPLE

The computer system components just described are able to accept data, process it, and produce output results *only* by following the detailed set of instructions contained in a stored program. Let's now see how such a program might be used to process an application. In our example, let's assume that it's time for Longhorn College to issue checks to the part-time student workers that it employs. Follow the process shown in Figure 1-11 as you read the explanation here. Input data for each student are first entered on time sheets. As shown in Figure 1-11, these data are then keyboarded from the source documents to a computer-readable input medium, in this case a floppy magnetic disk. The first student to be paid is Rob Brooks, who works part-time as a groundskeeper at the college.

**Processing the Payroll Application**

The program required to process the payroll data for Rob and other students must first be entered into the Longhorn computer's CPU through an appropriate input device. Let's assume that the 11 steps in this program are now stored in a program storage area shown in Figure 1-11. Next, the computer operator places the floppy disk containing the payroll data in a disk reader. Then the operator sets the computer

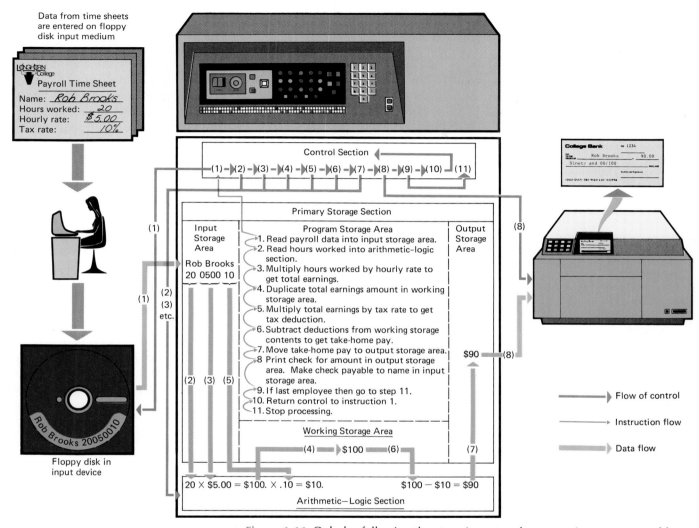

Figure 1-11 Only by following the steps in a stored program is a computer able to accept and process data and produce output results. The program is held in primary storage, data to be processed are supplied to an input device, the computer is set to the location of the first program instruction, and the processing begins. The program steps are executed automatically and without human intervention. Unless directed by a specific instruction to do otherwise, the computer executes the program steps in sequence.

to the location in the program storage area that contains the first instruction and the processing starts. Longhorn College uses its central computer to perform this processing. But these same 11 instructions can be executed in the same way by a personal computer system to produce identical results.

The initial control setting feeds the first program instruction (''Read payroll data into input storage area'') into the control section of the CPU where it is interpreted. Control signals are then sent to the input device which executes the instruc-

**SOFTWARE IS THE DRIVING FORCE**

In the old days, five years ago at least, you sold a computer on the basis of its power—bits, bytes, storage capacity, and a raft of similar statistics. Today all that is changing. With hardware from a wide variety of manufacturers looking more and more alike, the action is heating up on a different front: software—the instructions that tell the computer what to do.

There is now an overwhelming demand on the part of computer users for software packages that allow them to apply their computer's power to an entire range of tasks, from processing a payroll to booting up educational games for the kids. At the organizational level, companies are finding that they simply do not have the internal resources necessary for writing the programs they need. And so, many large businesses have stopped writing all their own software and started buying standard packaged products.

At the personal computer level, the name of the game is shelf space. Software houses are trying out sophisticated marketing techniques to win precious shelf space in retail outlets. There certainly appears no lack of products for any application.

But on the larger level, software producers have been hard pressed to keep up with the demands of ever-more-powerful hardware. As the shakeout in hardware helps to calm the rush of innovation, then, the software vendors look forward to some breathing space to catch up and to supply organizations with packages for the varied uses they find for their computer systems.

—Source of data: *Business Week*, Feb. 27, 1984.

tion and transfers Rob's payroll data to an input storage area of the CPU. (See the lines labeled 1 in Figure 1-11 for the interpretation and execution of this first step. Other program steps are similarly shown, but some lines have been omitted to simplify the figure.)

The control section automatically selects program instructions *in sequence* after the initial control setting unless specifically instructed to do otherwise. Thus, as soon as the first instruction has been dealt with, the control unit automatically begins interpreting the second step. This instruction directs the control unit to "Read hours worked into arithmetic-logic section." The control section is not concerned that Rob has worked 20 hours (the next student's hours may differ). It merely carries out program orders, and so places 20 hours in the arithmetic-logic section.

And so the processing continues in sequence: The 20-hour figure is multiplied by the $5 hourly rate to get Rob's total earnings of $100 (step 3); this total earnings figure is duplicated in the working storage area (step 4); the tax deduction is found by multiplying the $100 earnings by the 10 percent tax rate to get a $10 deduction (step 5); and this deduction is subtracted from the $100 total earnings figure that was temporarily stored in the working storage area to get Rob's take-home pay (step 6). After this take-home pay has been computed, the amount is transferred to the output storage area (step 7) and sent to a printer which is instructed to print Rob's check (step 8).

At this point in the program a **branchpoint** is reached and a decision must be made. Is Rob the last student to be paid? The computer follows an appropriate logic/comparison technique, which we'll discuss in the next chapter, to answer this question. If Rob is the last to be paid, then program control jumps to step 11 and the processing will stop. Since he is not the last student, however, program control moves to the next instruction in the sequence (step 10). This step directs the control section to reset itself to instruction 1 so the processing may be repeated for the next student. Thus, the same instructions will be executed over and over again until the repetitive payroll task is completed. As the data for the next student are read into the input storage area, they will erase and replace Rob's data just as recording music on a sound tape recorder erases any music that may have previously been stored on the tape.

This payroll example demonstrates most of the computer concepts and capabilities discussed in this chapter. To review:

■ The various components of a computer system can manipulate and process data automatically and without human intervention by following the directions contained in a stored program of instructions.

■ A computer has the built-in ability to obey different types of commands such as READ, PRINT, MULTIPLY, and MOVE. (Every computer is designed with a particular set or **repertoire** of these instruction types.)

■ A computer follows the steps in a program in sequence until explicitly told to do otherwise.

■ A change in the sequence of steps can result from the computer's ability to follow different paths depending on the answer to a simple question.

As noted earlier, there's nothing difficult about these computer capabilities. What's impressive, however, is the speed with which computer operations are performed and the accuracy of the resulting output.

## Feedback and Review 1-3

Understanding the stored program concept is a basic part of the knowledge required for computer literacy. In the chapters of the Programming Module, we'll return to this important subject. For now, place a T or F in the space provided in the following *true-false* questions to test and reinforce your understanding of the concepts presented:

**1.** It's only by following the steps in a stored program that computer hardware is able to accept and process data and produce output results.

**2.** Both data and program instructions are entered into the CPU through an input device and are stored in primary storage.

**3.** Processing begins when the control unit is set to the last instruction stored in the program storage area.

**4.** The control section interprets and then executes all processing instructions.

**5.** The control section automatically selects program steps in sequence unless specifically instructed to do otherwise.

**6.** All data processing is done in the control and arithmetic-logic sections of the CPU.

**7.** The working storage area is used to accept output results and the program instructions that actually do the processing work.

**8.** The computer can be programmed to consider simple questions and then follow different program paths depending on the answer.

**9.** A computer can be programmed to return program control to an earlier step to repeat operations, but it cannot jump ahead and bypass steps in the sequence.

# SOME COMPUTER SYSTEM DIFFERENCES

All computer systems of interest to us are similar in that they contain hardware components for input, central processing, and output. They all perform basic machine operations under the direction of stored programs which can be quickly changed to permit the processing of a stream of different applications. Of course, widely different sorts of applications require different system resources to process them. In other words, the personal computer used in the home to play Space Invaders would hardly be used in a NASA mission control center to monitor an actual space shuttle launch.

**Size Differences**  Modern computers vary in physical size from those that fill rooms to those with CPUs the size of a dime. Generally, the larger the system the greater is its processing speed, storage capacity, and cost. Also, the larger systems are better equipped to handle a greater number of more powerful input and output devices.

Systems on the low end of the size scale are called microcomputers or minicomputers. **Microcomputers** or *personal computers* (Figure 1-12) are the smallest general-purpose systems. But they may perform the same operations and use the same program instructions as much larger computers. **Minicomputers** (Figure 1-13) are also small general-purpose systems. They are typically more powerful and more expensive than micros, although the performance of some newer micros may

**Figure 1-12** Microcomputer industry leaders Apple Computer (*above left*) and International Business Machines Corporation (*above*) offer a full range of personal computers for use at home, at work, and at school. Innovative new computers, such as portable machines (*left*), are the result of fast-paced technology combined with continuing study of users' needs. (Photos courtesy Apple Computer, Inc., International Business Machines Corporation, and Hewlett-Packard Company)

**Figure 1-13** (*left*) Digital Equipment Corporation's VAX series of minicomputers are among the most widely installed computer systems used by organizations. (*right*) Minicomputer applications often involve the shared use of a powerful CPU by a number of interconnected individual workstations. (Photos courtesy Digital Equipment Corporation and Honeywell, Inc.)

**Figure 1-14** (*left*) A mainframe model from the Honeywell DPS8 family of computers. There are at least six different DPS8 processors in this mainframe family. (Courtesy Honeywell, Inc.) (*right*) One of several computers available in IBM's 4300 series of mainframes, this 4341 processor is considered to be a medium-sized mainframe model. (Courtesy International Business Machines Corporation)

surpass the capabilities of some older minis. In physical size, minis can vary from a desktop model to a unit the size of a small file cabinet.

Continuing up the size scale, **mainframe computers** (Figure 1-14) are systems that may offer faster processing speeds and greater storage capacity than a typical mini. A whole series of mainframe models ranging in size from small to very large are generally lumped together under a *family designation* by mainframe manufacturers. There's quite a bit of overlap possible in the cost, speed, and storage capacity of larger minis and smaller mainframes.

Finally come the **supercomputers** (Figure 1-15), designed to process complex scientific applications. These systems are the largest, fastest, and most expensive computers in the world. You'll find more information on computers in each size category in Chapters 8 and 9.

**Architectural Differences** Most small and medium-sized computers follow the traditional design approach of using single control, primary storage, and arithmetic-logic sections in the CPU. But there are several ways this design, or **architecture,** can be changed. For example, by adding additional control and arithmetic-logic sections (see Figure 1-16), several instructions can be processed at the same instant. Such a **multiprocessor** architecture makes it possible for the system to work *simultaneously* on several program segments. This design represents, in effect, a system with two or more central processors.

Another variation from traditional design involves separating the arithmetic-logic section into several parts. While one part is performing addition other elements can, at the same time, be multiplying and making comparisons. Such variations from traditional design result in faster computing speeds and are used in some larger systems such as the IBM 3084 (Figure 1-17).

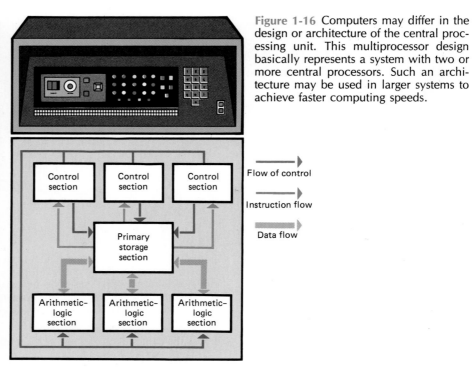

Figure 1-16 Computers may differ in the design or architecture of the central processing unit. This multiprocessor design basically represents a system with two or more central processors. Such an architecture may be used in larger systems to achieve faster computing speeds.

Control section

Control section

Control section

→ Flow of control

Primary storage section

→ Instruction flow

Arithmetic-logic section

Arithmetic-logic section

Arithmetic-logic section

→ Data flow

Figure 1-15 The Cray 2 supercomputer (*foreground*) is right at home in its liquid coolant bath. The machine's circuits must constantly be supercooled to dissipate high heat generated by their density. In the background are John Rollwagen, Cray Research president, and Seymour Cray, inventor. (Photo by Joe Gianetti, courtesy Cray Research, Inc.)

Figure 1-17 A large-scale mainframe, the IBM 3084 has four processors that share a large main memory and a system control unit. (Courtesy International Business Machines Corporation)

# SOME COMPUTER LIMITATIONS

By now you know that computers are capable of processing data accurately and at very high speeds. Further, they have the important ability to compare data items and then perform alternative operations based on the results of the comparison. These easy-to-grasp capabilities make the computer one of the most powerful tools ever developed. But we've all read newspaper articles similar to the one about a woman who was billed $26,000 for a set of tires by a computer system, or the one that told how a man was treated for pneumonia and then charged by the hospital's computer system for the use of the delivery room and nursery. Such "computer failures" may be amusing, but in most cases the blame for the foul-up can be laid at the feet of people who failed to give proper attention to some basic computer limitations. Without reliable programs, sound logic, and suitable applications, no computer system will perform adequately.

**Programs Must Be Reliable**

As a machine, the computer does what it's programmed to do and *nothing else*. This doesn't mean that it must be stupid. Clever programs can be written to direct the computer to store the results of previous decisions. Then, by using the branching ability designed into the program, the computer may be able to modify its behavior according to the success or failure of past decisions. But a seemingly flawless program that has operated without a problem for months can suddenly produce nonsense. Perhaps some rare combination of events has presented the system with a situation *(a)* for which there's *no* programmed course of action, or *(b)* where the course of action provided by the programmer contains an error that's just being discovered. Of course, a reliable program that's supplied with incorrect data may also produce nonsense.

**Application Logic Must Be Understood**

The computer can only process applications which can be expressed in a finite number of steps leading to a precisely defined goal. Each step must be specifically and clearly defined. If the steps in the problem solution cannot be precisely stated, the job cannot be done. The computer may not be of much help to people in areas where qualitative material, or evaluations, are important. The computer will not, for example, tell you how to "get rich quick" in the stock market, and it may not tell a sales manager if a new product will be successful. The market decision may be of a qualitative nature because sales volume data may rest on future social, political, technological, and economic events. However, the computer *can* let the manager know how the product will fare under *assumed* price, cost, and sales volume conditions. These assumed values can be fed into the computer. A program can then manipulate them in response to a series of "what if" questions to project the effects that the manager's questions will have on profits.

Even if program steps are finite and understood, there are still some tasks whose execution could take millions of years, even on a giant computer. Joseph Weizenbaum, a computer scientist at MIT, has observed that a program could be written "to try every legal move in a certain chess situation; for each move try every possible response; for each response try its response; and so on until the computer has found a move which, if suitably pursued, would guarantee it a win. Such a program would surely be finite, but the length of time required by a computer to execute it would be unimaginably large. In principle, then, a computer could carry out such behavior: in fact, it cannot."[1]

**Applications Must Be Suitable** Just because a computer can be programmed to do a job does not always mean that it should. Writing programs is a human task. It can be time consuming and expensive. Thus, nonrecurring jobs are often not efficient areas for business data processing applications. Rather, as a general rule it's most economical to prepare business programs for large-volume, repetitive applications, such as payrolls, that will be used many times. As with most general rules, there are exceptions to this statement about business applications. We'll see some exceptions later on in the book. Also, in engineering and scientific computing, the importance of a nonrecurring task often warrants the necessary investment in programming time. An example might be the engineering planning and construction scheduling, by computer, of a single multi-million-dollar office building. Then too, a person who spends many hours writing a personal computer program to successfully process a nonrecurring job may feel that the effort was justified by the knowledge and satisfaction that was gained.

[1]Joseph Weizenbaum, "The Last Dream," *Across the Board*, July 1977, p. 39. The term "combinatorial explosion" is given to this type of problem where a finite number of steps generates an impossibly large number of computer operations.

# LOOKING BACK

**1.** The use of computers—particularly personal computers—has expanded so rapidly that their presence can no longer be denied or ignored. Everyone needs to feel comfortable with these machines in order to function in a modern society. To be a computer-literate person, you need to know about computers themselves, the *hardware;* what they do, their *applications;* how they are applied through *software;* and the *social impact* of their use. Providing knowledge in these four areas is the purpose of this book.

**2.** A computer is a fast and accurate electronic symbol (data) manipulating system that's designed and organized to automatically accept and store input data, process them, and produce output results under the direction of a detailed stored program of instructions.

**3.** Computers perform at very high speeds. The time required to execute a basic operation such as addition is usually measured in *microseconds* (one-millionth of a second) for the smallest computers, and in *nanoseconds* (one-billionth of a second) for larger machines. The reliability of computer circuits enables them to run errorless for hours and days at a time. Computer "errors" can usually be traced to faulty programs or inaccurate input data—both generally caused by human and not computer frailties.

**4.** Computers can manipulate both numeric and nonnumeric symbols. *Data* are facts or informational raw materials represented by these symbols. *Information* is the relevant knowledge that results from the processing and arranging of data in an ordered and useful form.

**5.** *Data processing* consists of (a) capturing the raw input data; (b) manipulating it by using classifying, sorting, calculating, and summarizing techniques; and (c) storing, retrieving, communicating, and reproducing the output results of the manipulation.

**6.** These data processing activities are readily carried out by computers. A computer can accept input data from, and communicate processed output to, a large number of devices. The circuits in a computer are designed to facilitate calculating. Classifying, sorting, and summarizing are made possible by the computer's ability to perform simple comparisons and then, depending on the result, follow a predetermined course of action. And split-second storage and retrieval activities are possible through the use of primary and secondary storage devices.

**7.** A *system* is a group of integrated parts that have the common purpose of achieving some objective(s). Since a computer is made up of integrated components that work together to perform the steps called for in the program being executed, it is a system. A basic computer system is comprised of input and output devices and a central processing unit (CPU). CPUs of all sizes contain primary storage, arithmetic-logic, and control sections.

**8.** The space in the primary storage section is divided into four areas: input, where data are held for processing; working storage, where intermediate processing results are kept; output, where finished results are kept prior to release; and program storage, which holds the processing steps. In addition to primary storage components, most computers also have secondary storage devices. These devices are usually connected online to the CPU where they can accept data directly from, and return data directly to, the CPU without human intervention.

**9.** All calculations and comparisons are made in the arithmetic-logic section of the CPU. Engineering design determines the type and number of arithmetic and logic operations that can be performed. The control section of the CPU maintains order among the system components and selects, interprets, and sees to the execution of program steps. After an initial control setting, it automatically selects program instructions in sequence until specifically instructed to do otherwise.

**10.** Computers have the built-in ability to obey different types of instructions. Once problem-solving or job instructions are stored in a computer, the system can process data automatically and without human intervention until the problem is solved or the job is completed.

**11.** Computer systems differ in size and in design. Sizes vary from the smallest microcomputers to minis, mainframes, and supercomputers. And the architecture can vary from systems that use single arithmetic-logic and control sections to those that use multiple sections in order to work simultaneously on several program segments and thus speed up processing.

**12.** Computers have impressive capabilities, but they also have a few important limitations. Programs must be reliable, applications logic must be understood, and applications must be suitable.

## KEY TERMS AND CONCEPTS

**personal computer 3**
**computer literacy 5**
**hardware 7**
**applications 7**
**software 7**
**program 8**
**computer 8**
**millisecond (ms) 8**
**microsecond (μs) 8**
**nanosecond (ns) 8**
**picosecond (ps) 8**
**garbage in–garbage out (GIGO) 9**
**acronym 9**
**computer processing 9**
**data 10**
**information 10**
**data processing 10**
**source documents 11**
**direct input device 11**

**classifying 11**
**alphanumeric 11**
**sorting 11**
**calculating 11**
**summarizing 11**
**storing 12**
**retrieving 12**
**data communication 12**
**reproduction 12**
**system 14**
**subsystem 15**
**supersystems 15**
**input devices 15**
**online 15**
**central processing unit (CPU) 15**
**primary storage section 15**
**input storage area 15**
**working storage space 16**
**output storage area 16**

**program storage area 16**
**main memory 16**
**secondary (auxiliary, external) storage 16**
**offline 18**
**arithmetic-logic section 18**
**control section 18**
**output devices 18**
**peripheral devices 18**
**branchpoint 22**
**repertoire 22**
**microcomputer 23**
**minicomputer 23**
**mainframe computer 25**
**supercomputer 25**
**architecture 25**
**multiprocessor 25**

# TOPICS FOR REVIEW AND DISCUSSION

**1.** If computer literacy was a rare skill 20 years ago, why do you need it today?

**2.** *(a)* What is a computer program? *(b)* Why can a computer program be described as an "intellectual map?"

**3.** *(a)* What is a computer? *(b)* What capabilities does a computer possess?

**4.** *(a)* Discuss the different views that people may have of computers as they are reflected in cartoons, magazines, newspapers, movies, television, and science fiction. *(b)* Discuss four ways that computers have affected your life.

**5.** Electricity can travel about one foot in a nanosecond. Does this fact place any upper limits on computer operating speed?

**6.** Discuss this statement: "If computers are so accurate, why is the phrase "garbage in–garbage out" associated with their use?"

**7.** *(a)* What are data? *(b)* What is information? *(c)* What's the difference between these two terms?

**8.** What additional facts could be supplied to transform the data item "102.2" into useful information?

**9.** *(a)* What is data processing? *(b)* Identify and explain the basic data processing activities.

**10.** In order to classify data, codes are assigned to the items being arranged. Light trucks are classified with an alphanumeric identification code by General Motors. A code for a particular vehicle is CCL247F153278. How might this code be interpreted and used for classification purposes?

**11.** Why is the computer's ability to make a simple comparison between two data items important?

**12.** *(a)* What is a system? *(b)* What three hardware components are required in a computer system?

**13.** "The primary storage section of the CPU is used for four purposes." What are these four purposes?

**14.** What's the difference between primary and secondary storage devices?

**15.** *(a)* What's the function of the arithmetic-logic section of the CPU? *(b)* What's the function of the control section?

**16.** What's the typical data flow pattern in a computer system?

**17.** What's the stored program concept and why is it important?

**18.** How may computers be classified according to size?

**19.** Discuss some limitations of computer usage.

# PROJECTS TO LOOK INTO

**1.** Visit your local computer store or other retail outlets that sell computers and write a report describing the hardware characteristics of four of the models you've seen on display.

**2.** At this writing there are over 150 manufacturers of personal computers. Dozens of these vendors advertise on television and radio and in magazines and newspapers. Make a list of 15 of these vendors you've identified from their ads. You may want to visit your library to check personal computing magazines or other specific sources.

# ANSWERS TO FEEDBACK AND REVIEW SECTIONS

**1-1**
The solution to the crossword puzzle is shown at the right.

| 1-2 | 1-3 |
|-----|-----|
| 1. system | 1. T |
| 2. central | 2. T |
| 3. working | 3. F |
| 4. control | 4. F |
| 5. program | 5. T |
| 6. output | 6. F |
| 7. primary | 7. F |
| 8. selects | 8. T |
| 9. online | 9. F |
| 10. vary | |

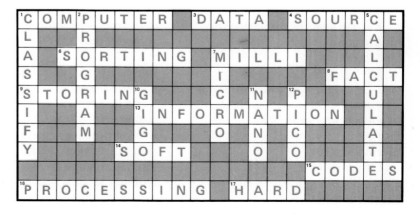

# Our Debt to the Past
## The Evolution of Data Processing

It has taken thousands of years for data processing to evolve from the use of notches in sticks to the application of the latest computer system. In fact, written history really began when people started keeping records. Let's look now at the highlights of this historical path.

### The First Record Keepers

For centuries, people lived on the earth without keeping records, but as social organizations such as tribes began to form, records became necessary. The complexities of tribal life required that more details be remembered. Methods of counting based on the biological fact that people have 10 fingers developed this way. However, the limited number of fingers combined with the need to remember more facts posed problems. For example, if a shepherd was tending a large tribal flock and had a short memory, how could that shepherd keep control of the inventory? Problems bring solutions, and the shepherd's solution might have been to let a stone, a stick, a scratch on a rock, or a knot in a string represent each sheep in the flock.

As tribes grew into nations, trade and commerce developed. Stones and sticks no longer met the needs of early traders. By 3500 B.C., ancient Babylonian merchants were keeping records on clay tablets. An early manual calculating device was the *abacus*. Although it's over 2,000 years old, the abacus is still widely used.

### The First Record-Keeping Machines

Manual record-keeping techniques continued to develop through the centuries, with such innovations as record audits (the Greeks) and banking systems and budgets (the Romans). Machines were introduced in Europe over 300 years ago to improve the performance of *single* data processing steps. In 1642, for example, the first mechanical calculating machine was developed by Blaise Pascal, a brilliant young Frenchman. About 30 years later, Gottfried von Leibniz, a German mathematician, improved upon Pascal's invention by producing a calculating machine which could add, subtract, multiply, divide, and extract roots.

But in the 20 years following the Civil War, the main tools of data processing in the United States were pencils, pens, and rulers. Work sheets were used for classifying, calculating, and summarizing; journals for storing; and ledgers for storing and communicating.

The volume of business and government records during this period was expanding rapidly, and, as you might expect, such complete reliance on manual methods resulted in information that was relatively inaccurate and often late. To the consternation of the Census Bureau, for example, the 1880 census was not finished until it was almost time to begin the 1890 count! Fortunately for the Bu-

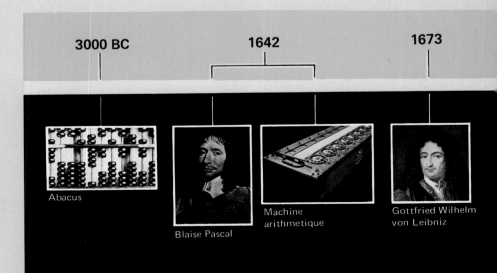

**3000 BC**  **1642**  **1673**

Abacus

Blaise Pascal

Machine arithmetique

Gottfried Wilhelm von Leibniz

reau and for others with a need for improved data processing methods, a number of new machines were introduced at about this time. For example, the typewriter was introduced in the 1880s as a recording aid that improved legibility and doubled writing speeds. And machines that could calculate and print the results were produced around 1890. These devices *combined* calculating, summarizing, and recording steps, and produced a printed tape record suitable for storing data. The most important breakthrough at this time, however, was the development of electromechanical punched card equipment.

## The Weaver, the Statistician, and Their Cards

The history of the punched card dates back to about the end of the American Revolution, when a French weaver named Joseph Marie Jacquárd used them to control his looms. Although they continued as a means of process control, it was not until the use of manual methods resulted in the problem of completing the 1880 census count that cards began to be looked at as a medium for data processing. The inventor of modern punched card techniques was Dr. Herman Hollerith, a statistician. He was hired by the Census Bureau as a special agent to help find a solution to the census problem. In 1887, Hollerith developed his machine-readable card concept and designed a device known as the "census machine." Tabulating time with Hollerith's methods was only one-eighth of the time previously required, and so his techniques were adopted for use in the 1890 count. Although population had increased from 50 to 63 million in the decade after 1880, the 1890 count was completed in less than 3 years. (Of course, this would be considered intolerably slow by today's standards. The 1950 census, using punched card equipment, took about 2 years to produce; the 1980 census yielded figures in a few months.)

After the 1890 census, Hollerith converted his equipment to business use and set up freight statistics systems for two railroads. In 1896 he founded the Tabulating Machine Company to make and sell his invention. Later, this firm merged with others to form what is now known as International Business Machines Corporation (IBM).

Punched card processing is based on a simple idea: Input data are first recorded in a coded form by punching holes into cards. These cards are then fed into a number of electromechanical machines that perform processing steps. The early Hollerith cards measured 3 by 5 inches; different sizes are used today, and different coding schemes are employed. You'll find more information on modern cards and their codes in Chapter 6.

It's obvious that punched card data processing was a significant improvement over the manual methods that went before. Gains in speed and accuracy were made. Punched card equipment proved effective in performing many of the individual steps necessary. But it was still necessary to have people handle trays of cards between each step. Separate machines had to be fed, started, and stopped. This need for human intervention between processing stages was a major disadvantage. With the computer, of course, this disadvantage disappears: human intervention is not required between each step.

## Computer Development

About 50 years before Hollerith's efforts, Charles Babbage, Lucasian Professor of Mathematics at Cambridge University in England, had proposed a machine, which he named the "analytical engine." Babbage was an eccentric and colorful individual who spent much of his life working in vain to build his machine. Babbage's dream—to many of his contemporaries it was "Babbage's folly"—would have incorporated a punched card input; a memory unit, or *store*; an arithmetic unit, or *mill*; automatic printout; sequential program control; and 20-place accuracy. In short,

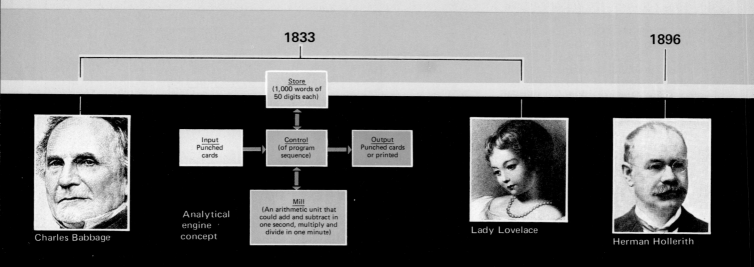

1833                   1896

Store
(1,000 words of
50 digits each)

Input
Punched
cards

Control
(of program
sequence)

Output
Punched cards
or printed

Mill
(An arithmetic unit that
could add and subtract in
one second, multiply and
divide in one minute)

Charles Babbage

Analytical
engine
concept

Lady Lovelace

Herman Hollerith

Babbage had designed a machine that was a prototype computer and that was 100 years ahead of its time. Assisting Babbage in his efforts was Ada Augusta Byron, the daughter of Lord Byron, the English poet. Ada corrected some errors in Babbage's work. She is often referred to as the first computer programmer. After Babbage's death in 1871, little progress was made until 1937.

Beginning in 1937, Harvard professor Howard Aiken set out to build an automatic calculating machine that would combine established technology with Hollerith's punched cards. With the help of graduate students and IBM engineers, the project was completed in 1944. The completed device was known as the Mark I digital computer. Internal operations were controlled automatically with electromagnetic relays; arithmetic counters were mechanical. The Mark I was thus not an *electronic* computer but was rather an *electromechanical* one. In many respects the Mark I was the realization of Babbage's dream. Appropriately, this "medieval" machine is now on display at Harvard University.

The first prototype *electronic* computer was conceived in the winter of 1937–1938 by Dr. John Vincent Atanasoff, a professor of physics and mathematics at Iowa State College. After concluding that none of the calculating devices then available was adequate for

his needs, Atanasoff decided to build his own machine. Using design concepts that crystalized in his mind late one winter night in a small roadside tavern in Illinois, Atanasoff teamed up with Clifford Berry, his graduate assistant, and began the task of building the first electronic computer. This computer was called the "Atanasoff-Berry computer" (ABC). The ABC used vacuum tubes for storage and arithmetic-logic functions.

During 1940 and 1941, Atanasoff and Berry met with John W. Mauchly and showed him their work. Mauchly, working at the Moore School of Electrical Engineering of the University of Pennsylvania, then began formulating his own ideas on how a general-purpose computer might be built. (The ABC was designed for the special purpose of solving systems of simultaneous equations.) Mauchly's ideas came to the attention of J. Presper Eckert, Jr., a graduate engineering student at the Moore School, and the team of Mauchly and Eckert was formed. This team was responsible for the construction of ENIAC in the early 1940s.

ENIAC was the first electronic general-purpose computer to be put into full operation. It was funded by the U.S. Army, and was built as a secret wartime project at the Moore School (the Army was interested in the rapid preparation of artillery trajectory tables). Vacuum tubes

(18,000 of them!) were also used in ENIAC. It could do 300 multiplications per second, making it 300 times faster than any other device of the day. Operating instructions for ENIAC were not stored internally; rather they were fed through externally located plugboards and switches. ENIAC was used by the Army until 1955 and was then placed in the Smithsonian Institution.

In the mid-1940s, in collaboration with H. H. Goldstine and A. W. Burks, John von Neumann, a mathematical genius and member of the Institute for Advanced Study in Princeton, New Jersey, wrote a paper in which he suggested that (1) *binary* numbering systems be used in building computers and (2) computer *instructions* as well as the *data* being manipulated could be stored internally in the machine. The origin of these ideas is disputed, but they became a basic part of the philosophy of computer design. The binary numbering system is represented by only 2 digits (0 and 1) rather than the 10 digits (0 to 9) of the familiar decimal system. Since electronic components are typically in one of two conditions ("on" or "off," conducting or not conducting), the binary concept facilitated computer equipment design.

Although these design concepts came too late to be incorporated in ENIAC, Mauchly, Eckert, and others at

**1937 — 1947**

Howard Aiken

John Atanasoff

Vacuum Tubes

ENIAC

Bardeen
Shockley
Brattain

Thomas Watson, Sr.

Thomas Watson, Jr.

UNIVAC I

Grace M. Hopper,
COBOL

**1948**

about
**1950**

**1951**

**1959**

**1963**

**1971**

about
**1974**

Ted Hoff

the Moore School set out to build a machine with stored-program capability. This machine—the EDVAC—was not completed until several years later. To the EDSAC, finished in 1949 at Cambridge University, must go the distinction of being the first *stored program electronic computer.*

One reason for the delay in EDVAC was that Eckert and Mauchly founded their own company in 1946 and began to work on the Universal Automatic Computer, or UNIVAC. In 1949, Remington Rand acquired the Eckert-Mauchly Computer Corporation, and in early 1951 the first UNIVAC-1 became operational at the Census Bureau. In 1963, it too was retired to the Smithsonian Institution—a historical relic after just 12 years! The first UNIVAC-1 displaced IBM punched card equipment at the Census Bureau, but Thomas J. Watson, Jr., the son of IBM's founder, reacted quickly to move IBM into the computer age.

**Computers in Business**
The first computer acquired for data processing and record keeping by a business organization was another UNIVAC-1, which was installed in 1954 at General Electric's Appliance Park in Louisville, Kentucky. The IBM 650 first

saw service in Boston in late 1954. It was a comparatively inexpensive machine for that time and it was widely accepted. It gave IBM the leadership in computer production in 1955.

In the period from 1954 to 1959, many organizations acquired computers for data processing purposes, even though these *first-generation* machines had been designed for scientific uses. Managers generally considered the computer to be an accounting tool, and the first applications were designed to process routine tasks such as payrolls. The potential of the computer was frequently underestimated, and more than a few were acquired for no reason other than prestige.

But we shouldn't judge the early users of computers too harshly. They were pioneering in the use of a new tool; they had to staff their computer installations with a new breed of workers; and they initially had to cope with the necessity of preparing programs in a tedious machine language. In spite of these obstacles, the computer was found to be a fast, accurate, and untiring processor of mountains of paper.

The computers of the *second generation* were introduced around 1959 to 1960 and were made smaller, faster, and with greater computing capacity. The vacuum tube, with its relatively short life, gave way to compact *solid-state* components such as the transistors that had been developed at Bell Laboratories by John Bardeen, William Shockley, and Walter Brattain. And the practice of writing applications programs in machine-oriented languages gave way to *higher-level languages* that are easier for humans to use and understand. (Only a few of the software pioneers of yesterday and today can be mentioned on the timeline accompanying this reading.) Unlike earlier computers, some second-generation machines were designed with nonscientific processing requirements in mind.

In 1964, IBM ushered in a *third-generation* of computing hardware when it announced its System/360 family of mainframe computers. During the 1970s and early 1980s, many manufacturers introduced new equipment lines. For example, IBM first announced its System/370 line and then later introduced newer mainframe models in the 4300 series and the 3080 series. Dozens of new minicomputers were unveiled during this period, and the entire personal computer industry was created to produce hundreds of thousands of machines each month. Hardware of all sizes continued the trend toward miniaturization of circuit components. Improvements in speed, cost, and storage capacity were realized. In Chapter 4 we'll look at some recent developments in computer technology.

## The Computer Industry

In 1950, the developers of the first computers agreed that eight or 10 of these machines would satisfy the entire demand for such devices for years to come. We now know that this was a monumental forecasting blunder. By 1956, over 600 computer systems (worth about $350 million) had been installed. Today, the theme of a recent computer conference—"Computers . . . by the millions, for the millions"—characterizes the size and scope of the computer industry.

Today there are hundreds of computer manufacturers. Many small firms specialize in assembling small scientific and/or process-control machines, or produce the even smaller personal computers used by individuals. The growth of some of these microcomputer manufacturers has been phenomenal. Apple Computer, which began by assembling its product in a garage in the late 1970s, was reporting sales of over $100 million just 3 years later. Another company producing portable personal computers that can operate with the software prepared for use with IBM personal computers did even better: It achieved sales of over $100 million in its first year in business!

Although much of their effort in the past was devoted to supplying organizations with families of mainframe and minicomputers, many of the largest computer manufacturers have rushed to become personal computer suppliers in recent years. Of the larger companies, most were initially business-machine manufacturers (IBM, Burroughs Corporation, Sperry UNIVAC, and NCR Corporation), or they manufactured electronic controls (Honeywell). Exceptions are Control Data Corporation and Digital Equipment Corporation which were founded to produce computers. The industry leader is IBM with annual revenues of well over $40 billion.

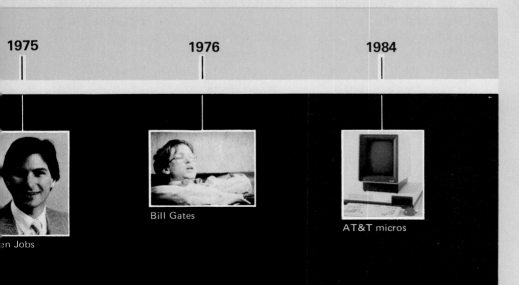

**1975**

**1976**

**1984**

en Jobs

Bill Gates

AT&T micros

# Computers at Work
*an overview of applications*

### Giving Business Growth a Computerized Push

Keeping a business healthy is much like keeping a body healthy—you have to work at it. When you work out, you carefully choose particular exercises to firm up certain parts of your body. When you want to strengthen your business, you similarly learn, and choose, which facts and figures will help you reach your goal. By using an IBM Personal Computer to keep track of such customer trends as the demographic information of current members, the staff of the Nautilus Fitness Centers in the Washington, D.C. area can now keep their business as healthy as their members.

"With the computer we're able to accomplish in a few minutes what used to take hours," says Jeff Neuburg, president of the Centers. "Most important, we can now keep records we couldn't keep before because they required too many man-hours to maintain."

The staff at Nautilus has used the computer and custom-designed database management software to compile information about members who have joined the centers over the past five years. Examining the information, Neuburg has learned members' average ages, incomes, and terms of membership. . . .

The demographic data Neuburg has collected . . . helps him determine what forms of advertising would be most effective in reaching his specific audience. Knowing the average age of the people who are currently joining the centers allows him to place radio spots on appropriate stations. For example, if he wants to reach people in the 40- to 50-year-old age group, he can choose a station whose listeners fall into that demographic category. "Now, we can tailor our advertising and measure the results," he says.

—"People in Computing," reprinted with permission from *Personal Computing,* May 1983, p. 45. Copyright 1983, Hayden Publishing Company. Photo courtesy Spinnaker Software Company.

In this chapter, you will first learn how data are organized for processing. Then, you'll learn about the data processing applications most commonly used in businesses as well as nonprofit organizations such as schools, hospitals, and government agencies. The information in this chapter will enable you to:

■ Describe how data are organized into logical groupings to facilitate computer processing

■ Discuss the computer applications presented in this chapter

■ Outline two ways in which files may be organized and processed

■ Identify the applications that account for the greatest use of business computing resources

# ORGANIZING DATA FOR COMPUTER PROCESSING

Computers operate on data. They accept and process data and communicate results. They cannot directly carry out any physical activities. They cannot bend metal, for example, but they *can* control metal-bending machines.

Data fed to the computer are organized into logical groupings to ensure effective processing and useful output. The smallest logical data entity is a **field,** or **data item.**[1] A field consists of a group of related characters treated as a single unit. Think back to the Longhorn College payroll example discussed in the last chapter. There was a name field (containing "Rob Brooks"), an hours-worked field, an hourly-pay-rate field, and a tax-rate-deduction field.

---

[1] Some make the distinction that a field is a designated physical location for a data item on a storage medium while the data item itself represents whatever might be contained in the location. This may be a valid distinction, but the terms tend to be used interchangeably.

## Chapter Outline

**Figure 2-1** Longhorn College's student payroll file. The record for each student consists of four fields, and all student records make up this file. Thousands of records can be stored on this one small floppy disk. Files are also maintained on other media such as punched cards and magnetic tape. In a card file, each card may represent a record; in a magnetic tape file, a record is stored on a short length of the tape.

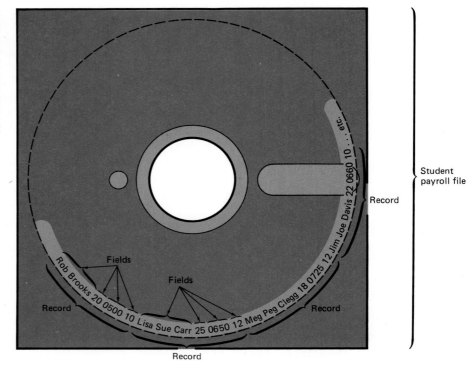

During processing, the data characters in each of these fields were treated collectively and as a single unit. Such a collection of related fields or data items treated as a single unit is called a **record.** Thus, there is a record made up of four fields for each of the student workers at Longhorn College.

Records are grouped to form files. A **file** is a number of related records that are treated as a unit. The student payroll file at Longhorn College consists of the records of all student employees (see Figure 2-1). Finally, a **data base** is a collection of

**Figure 2-2** Data are normally organized into a hierarchy for computer processing. The field is the smallest entity to be processed as a single unit. Related fields are grouped to form records, and related records are combined to form files. The highest level in the data organization hierarchy is the data base, which is a collection of logically related data elements that may be structured in various ways and used for multiple purposes.

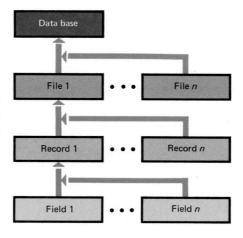

logically related data elements that may be structured in various ways to meet the multiple processing and retrieval needs of organizations and individuals. Figure 2-2 summarizes this data organization hierarchy used by computer-based processing systems.

# WHAT COMPUTERS DO: AN INTRODUCTION TO APPLICATIONS

As you'll recall from the last chapter, the operations which computers perform on data are classified into four categories:

1. Input/output

2. Calculation

3. Logic/comparison

4. Storage and retrieval

It is simply because computers can do these four types of operations that they are being put to work performing the thousands of different applications you saw a sampling of in Chapter 1. In this chapter, you'll learn about computer applications in business through a series of processing tasks that emphasize each of the four categories. Since most of the examples in this chapter relate to one particular business, let's pause briefly here for some background information on that business.

**R-K Enterprises**

You know that Rob Brooks is a student and part-time groundskeeper at Longhorn College. But he's much more than that. He's also a founder and partner in R-K Enterprises. The idea for what was to become R-K Enterprises' first product came to Rob some months ago while he was reading a newspaper. The article that caught his eye told about a state legislator who, after fighting a losing battle with swarms of large mosquitos at a family picnic, had introduced a bill in the legislature to make the mosquito the official state bird.[2] Intrigued by this account, Rob decided to paint a picture of a ''mosquito bird'' and an appropriate slogan on one of his tee shirts to show his support for the lawmaker's bill. To his surprise, dozens of students tried to buy the shirt right off his back.

Realizing then that he had a marketable product, Rob made arrangements with a manufacturer for a supply of the shirts. It wasn't long before they became the latest fad. Demand spread far beyond the Longhorn campus. After hiring some fellow students to help sell the shirts, Rob began to think about further ways to exploit the mosquito bird fad. His friend, Kay Oss, is a music major, and so Rob asked her to write a song in support of the mosquito bird movement. When he heard

The initial product of R-K Enterprises.

[2]This is not entirely fiction. Such a bill was actually introduced by a fun-loving legislator in a southern state.

Kay sing her song (accompanied by guitar and kazoo) he decided to market a record and a tape cassette of "The Mosquito Bird Song." Since Kay created these products and helped finance their introduction, she became an equal partner in the newly formed R-K Enterprises. The success of these products led to others that will be discussed in later chapters.

Any successful business must perform data processing tasks, and R-K Enterprises is no exception. Drawing on their experience in a computer data processing course, the partners decided to use a personal computer to handle certain input/output, calculation, logic/comparison, and storage/retrieval operations. Let's now look at these applications and at other ways in which a computer can be used.

## An Input/Output Application: The Mailing List

Computers are often used to print the names and addresses of prospective customers on gummed labels to ease the mailing of a large volume of promotional material. Since the partners at R-K use mailings to introduce and advertise their products, they developed a mailing label application right away. Input data for this application are contained in a file of prospect records. Each record has fields for the prospect's name, address, city, state, and Zip code.

The data needed to develop this file were gathered from the first orders received, from the letters and calls of prospective customers, and from responses to a few small newspaper ads. After these facts were captured, they were logically organized on a machine-readable medium to create the master prospect file. Since then, the computer has been used periodically to add, delete, and change records through a **file maintenance** or **file updating** operation (see Figure 2-3).

To process this mailing list application and produce the gummed labels, the computer system follows the procedure shown in Figure 2-4. Let's assume that the program instructions needed to prepare the mailing labels are stored on one floppy magnetic disk, and the input data in the prospect master file are stored on another. Instructions and data are represented by tiny magnetically formed patterns that are invisible to our eyes.

The computer operator places the program disk in one disk drive and inserts the prospect master file into a second drive. A few keystrokes are used to duplicate instructions on the program disk in the program storage area of the CPU. Under program control, a data record from the prospect file disk is read into the input storage area, the record fields are arranged in the desired format and moved to the output storage area, and the mailing label is then printed. If additional records are contained on the disk, program control will branch back to step 1 and the next record will be processed. After the last record has been printed, the processing will stop. Another way to produce mailing labels is presented in this chapter's Closer Look.

Computers are often used for such basic input/output purposes. And they are not only used by businesses. Political, religious, and charitable organizations solicit support and contributions with the help of computer-produced labels. Also, computer listings of personnel and products are sometimes extracted from personnel and product files for management purposes.

ED'S CULTURAL CENTER
822 PHILHARMONIC AVENUE
CRAMPS, TEXAS 77786

PIERRE'S RECORD SHOP
6453 ORLEANS STREET
BOOGIE, LOUISIANA 54321

ROCKY COLLEGE STORE
1563 BEETHOVEN DRIVE
ROCKTOWN, MARYLAND 20765

WYNN D. TOOTS, INC.
120 BROWNING STREET
GONG, CALIFORNIA 98765

## Calculation Applications

You may have noticed that no calculation activities were performed in the mailing label example. Alphanumeric data were merely entered in one form and reproduced as output in another. But some calculations are usually needed in computer applica-

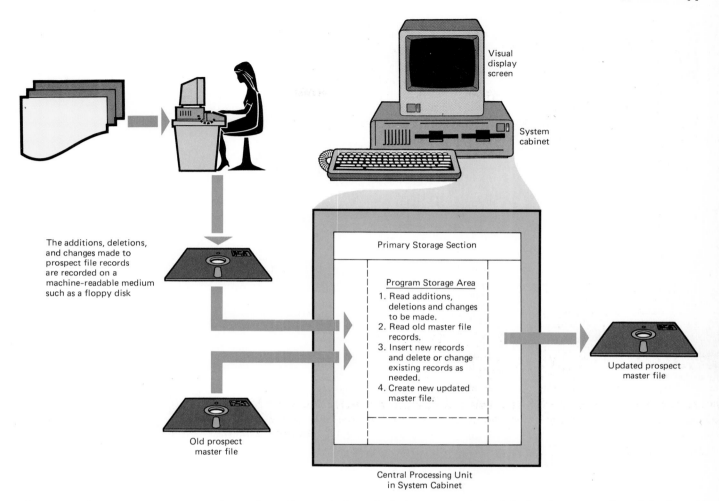

The additions, deletions, and changes made to prospect file records are recorded on a machine-readable medium such as a floppy disk

Old prospect master file

Primary Storage Section

Program Storage Area
1. Read additions, deletions and changes to be made.
2. Read old master file records.
3. Insert new records and delete or change existing records as needed.
4. Create new updated master file.

Central Processing Unit in System Cabinet

Visual display screen

System cabinet

Updated prospect master file

**Figure 2-3** File maintenance is required to add new records and delete or make changes to existing records. A maintenance program stored in the computer can cause the system to (1) read additions, deletions, and changes to be made from one input device; (2) read the old master file records from another input device; (3) insert new records and delete or change existing records as needed; and (4) produce as output an updated master file.

tions. For example, calculations were required during the preparation of the Longhorn College payroll application discussed in Chapter 1. They are also needed in a report that Rob and Kay use.

**Sales Compensation Report.** One of the partners' reports is a sales compensation document that shows the amount of sales and earnings for each salesperson during a 4-week period. The salespeople are paid a percentage of their total sales for the period. Figure 2-5 illustrates how this report can be prepared.

The input data are first transferred from the sales reporting forms to a floppy disk. After instructions stored on a program disk have been loaded into the program storage area, records from the data disk are entered (one at a time) into the input storage area of the CPU under program control. The first calculation involves adding the four weekly sales figures in a record to determine the *total sales amount* for the salesperson. The second computation consists of multiplying this total sales amount figure by a 10 percent commission rate to get the salesperson's *earnings* for the period. Finally, the salesperson's name, total sales amount, and earnings are

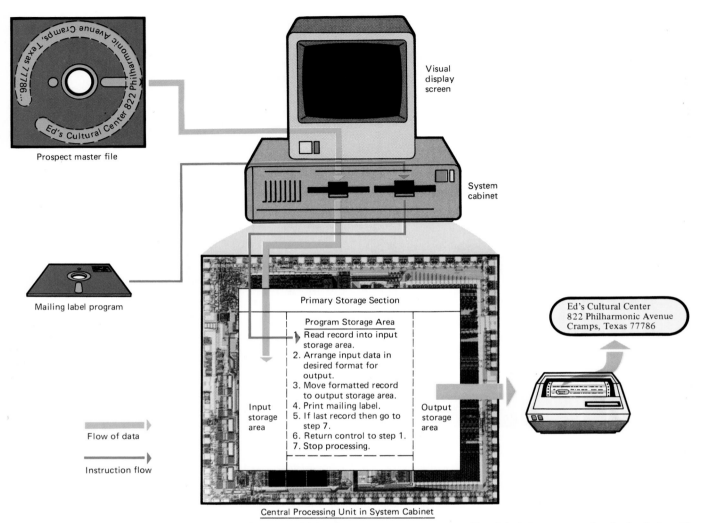

Prospect master file

Visual display screen

System cabinet

Mailing label program

Primary Storage Section

Program Storage Area

1. Read record into input storage area.
2. Arrange input data in desired format for output.
3. Move formatted record to output storage area.
4. Print mailing label.
5. If last record then go to step 7.
6. Return control to step 1.
7. Stop processing.

Input storage area

Output storage area

Ed's Cultural Center
822 Philharmonic Avenue
Cramps, Texas 77786

Flow of data

Instruction flow

Central Processing Unit in System Cabinet

**Figure 2-4** Using a computer to prepare mailing labels is an example of a basic input/output application. The following steps are taken during the processing of this application: (1) A record from a prospect master file is read into the input storage area of the CPU under program control; (2) the record fields are arranged in the desired format; (3) the formatted record is moved to the output storage area in the CPU; and (4) the mailing label is printed. These steps are repeated until all input records have been processed.

printed on the output report. This report can then be used to evaluate salesperson performance and to prepare paychecks.

**Updating Savings Account Records.** Most of us have deposited and withdrawn money from a savings account at a bank, savings and loan, or other financial institution. Such transactions require calculations and are now usually handled by computer systems. Let's assume that Rob has decided to deposit in his savings

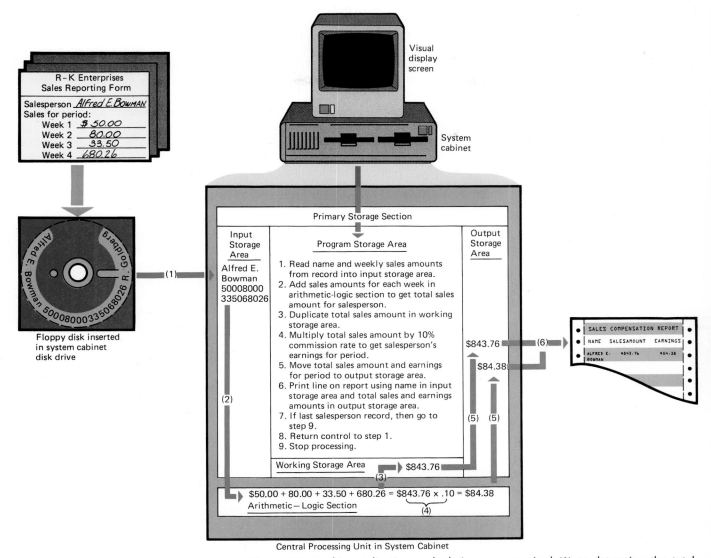

**Figure 2-5** In this application, calculations are required (1) to determine the total amount of sales made by each salesperson over a four-week period, and then (2) to determine the salesperson's earnings for the same period. The *nine* program steps required to process the input data and produce the output sales compensation report are shown in the program storage area of the CPU. The numbers in parentheses in this diagram refer to the program steps.

account the $90 paycheck he received from Longhorn College in Chapter 1. After filling out a deposit ticket, Rob presents the ticket, his savings account passbook, and his paycheck to a teller. The teller inserts the passbook into an online transaction terminal (see Figure 2-6) and keys in the transaction data in response to questions displayed on the terminal screen. The data are then sent to the input storage area of the CPU. In Rob's case, a transaction code "*D*" is entered. *D* indicates that a deposit is being made. However, the instructions in the program storage area of the CPU are also capable of handling withdrawal transactions.

After the input data have been entered, the computer then quickly retrieves Rob's savings account record from an online secondary storage device and adds the $90 deposit to his previous balance of $810. The account number, customer name, and new balance of $900 are then moved to the output storage area. From that location the updated record is used to (1) replace the old account record in online secondary storage and (2) print an updated account balance in Rob's passbook that is inserted in the teller's terminal. This entire input/process/output operation takes only a few seconds.

## Sequential and Direct-Access Processing

Implicit in the applications that we've now discussed is the fact that a file must be *organized* in some way to facilitate processing. File organization requires the use of some **record key** or unique identifying value that's found in every record in the file. The key value must be unique for each record; duplications would cause serious problems. In the sales compensation example, the record key was the salesperson's last name, and in the savings account application, the record key was the customer's account number. Numbers are used far more often than names to avoid the confusion that results when different people have the same name.

**Sequential Processing.** A **sequential file organization** typically consists of storing records one after another in a file in an ascending or descending order determined by the record key. The sales compensation application organizes the sales records by the salesperson's last name in an alphabetical sequence. Sequentially organized files that are processed by computer systems are typically kept on storage media such as magnetic tape and magnetic disks. **Sequential processing** (also called **serial** processing) consists of reading and processing the first record in the file sequence, then the second record, and so on. The processing of Rob's paycheck discussed in Chapter 1 (Figure 1-11) and the mailing label and sales compensation applications described in this chapter (Figures 2-4 and 2-5) are all examples of sequential processing, as is the preparation of the monthly bills sent to credit-card customers.

Sequential processing is quite suitable for such applications because it's not necessary to prepare employee paychecks or customer bills every few hours. Rather, data on employee earnings and customer purchases are often accumulated into batches of transactions (thus the name **batch processing**) and processed only at scheduled intervals. The processing delay that results presents no problems. And sequential processing is efficient and economical if there are a large number of file records to be updated during a processing run. Since most employee records will be updated during each payroll run, the processing cost per record is very low.

In spite of these advantages, there are also some limitations to sequential processing. As Figure 2-7 shows, when a sequential file is updated, the transactions (additions, deletions, or changes) that affect the records in the old master file must first be sorted into the same sequence as the master file before processing can begin. A separate computer program written specifically to sort data into numeric or alpha-

On another day, Rob might use an automated teller to do his banking. (Photo courtesy NCR Corporation)

**Figure 2-6** A computer system may be used to update savings account balances by following the program steps outlined in the program storage area. Data from a deposit or withdrawal ticket are entered directly into the input storage area of the CPU from an online financial transaction terminal. The computer then quickly retrieves the customer's account record from an online secondary storage device and determines whether a deposit or withdrawal calculation is called for. If the transaction code is "D" (for deposit), program control branches to step 6 and the new deposit amount is added to the old account balance. If the transaction is *not* a deposit, then it is assumed here to be a withdrawal, and the transaction amount is subtracted from the old balance. After the computer has performed the necessary processing, the customer's updated record is placed in online secondary storage and the updated account balance is printed on the customer's passbook by the online terminal. The entire transaction takes just a few seconds. (The figures in parentheses refer to effects of numbered program steps.)

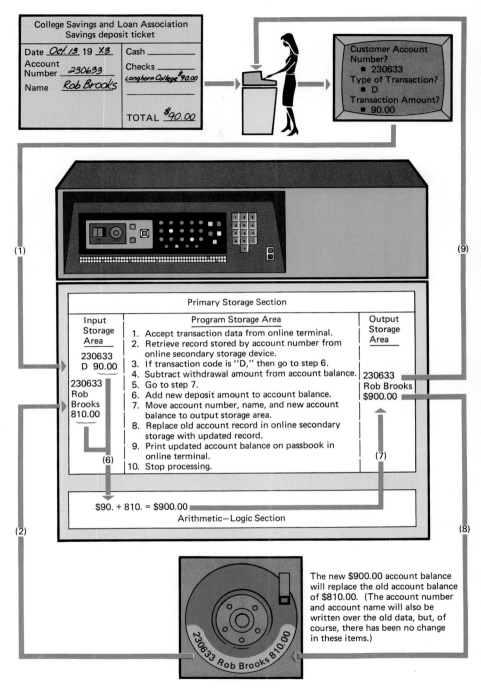

College Savings and Loan Association
Savings deposit ticket

Date _Oct. 13_ 19 _X3_    Cash _____
Account
Number    _230633_       Checks _____
Name     _Rob Brooks_    _Longhorn College_ $90.00

TOTAL $90.00

Customer Account Number?
■ 230633
Type of Transaction?
■ D
Transaction Amount?
■ 90.00

(1)                                                        (9)

Primary Storage Section

| Input Storage Area | Program Storage Area | Output Storage Area |
|---|---|---|
| 230633 D 90.00 | 1. Accept transaction data from online terminal. | |
| | 2. Retrieve record stored by account number from online secondary storage device. | |
| | 3. If transaction code is "D," then go to step 6. | 230633 |
| 230633 Rob Brooks 810.00 | 4. Subtract withdrawal amount from account balance. | Rob Brooks $900.00 |
| | 5. Go to step 7. | |
| | 6. Add new deposit amount to account balance. | |
| | 7. Move account number, name, and new account balance to output storage area. | |
| | 8. Replace old account record in online secondary storage with updated record. | |
| | 9. Print updated account balance on passbook in online terminal. | |
| (6) | 10. Stop processing. | (7) |

$90. + 810. = $900.00
Arithmetic—Logic Section

(2)                                                        (8)

The new $900.00 account balance will replace the old account balance of $810.00. (The account number and account name will also be written over the old data, but, of course, there has been no change in these items.)

230633 Rob Brooks 810.00

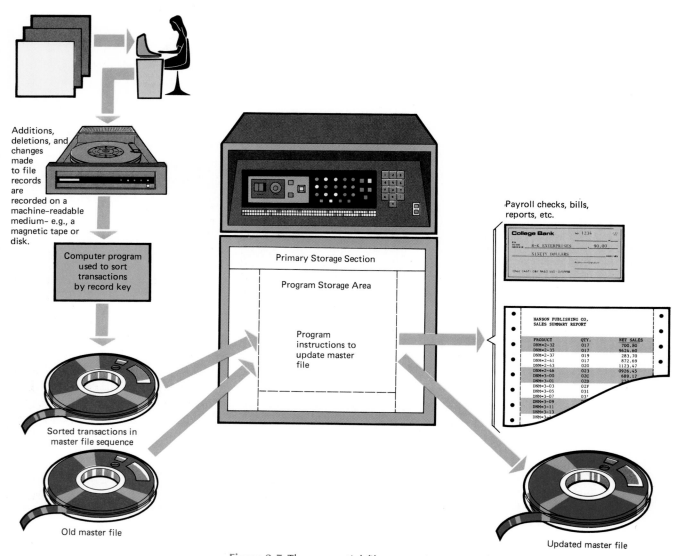

Additions, deletions, and changes made to file records are recorded on a machine-readable medium- e.g., a magnetic tape or disk.

Computer program used to sort transactions by record key

Sorted transactions in master file sequence

Old master file

Primary Storage Section

Program Storage Area

Program instructions to update master file

Payroll checks, bills, reports, etc.

College Bank

Updated master file

**Figure 2-7** The sequential file processing approach. Transactions affecting file records must be identified by a record key, and these transactions must be arranged into the same ascending or descending sequence as the master file before processing can begin. Transaction data and old master file records are then read into the CPU. The record key is used to match a new transaction with the appropriate old file record. The old record is updated by program instructions and a new file record is created and written on an output medium. Various documents such as checks, bills, and reports may also be prepared during the processing.

betic sequence by comparing items to determine which is greater is typically used. (A sorting program is presented in Chapter 21). And when processing a sequential file, records near the end of the file cannot be accessed until all preceding records in the sequence have been read into the CPU. Thus, if there's a need to update only a few records near the end of the file, these records cannot be retrieved until all earlier records have been read. Finally, for some applications the delay caused by accumulating the input data into batches prior to updating can be a serious problem. For example, if Rob needed to withdraw his recently deposited funds because of some emergency, he would be understandably upset if he were told that a 2-week wait would be required before the file could be updated to show if he did indeed have the needed funds on deposit.

**Direct-Access Processing.** Fortunately for all of us with bank accounts, processing alternatives exist to overcome sequential processing limitations. A **direct file organization** (also called a **random file organization**) consists of storing records in such a way that the computer can go directly to the key or identifying value of the record needed without having to search through a sequence of other records. The records in directly organized files must be kept in an online secondary storage device such as a rigid or flexible disk unit.

**Direct-access processing** (also called **online** or **random-access** processing) consists of directly locating and updating any record in a file without the need to read preceding file records. When a computer system is performing direct-access processing, it typically accepts input data from an online keyboard or from some other online data-collection or transaction-recording device. This was what was done in our savings account application. The record(s) being updated is then retrieved by the appropriate record key. (Rob's savings account number in our example). Accessing and retrieving the record is quick and direct. It's located and retrieved in a fraction of a second, and it's obtained without the need for a sequential search of the file. Once the record has been updated, it's returned to the **direct-access storage device** (DASD).

In addition to quickly and directly updating records without the need to sort transactions, direct-access processing can also provide up-to-the-minute information in response to inquiries from the keyboard of a personal computer (Figure 2-8a). And in larger systems, inquiries may be received from many *simultaneously usable* online stations (Figure 2-8b). The speed of the larger system allows the CPU to switch from one using station to another and to do a part of each job in the allocated "time slice" until the work is completed. The speed is such that each user often has the illusion that no one else is using the CPU. Thus, a teller can quickly determine the exact balance in Rob's savings account at any instant. Also, any airline ticket agent can have immediate access to reservation system records to see if seats are currently available on particular flights. If you purchase a ticket for flight 205 to Boston, the agent can quickly update the appropriate record and reduce by one the number of available seats.

**Figure 2-8** The direct-access processing approach. Transactions and inquiries about the current status of records are entered into the CPU from keyboards and online workstations. Sorting of transactions is not required. The access to, and retrieval of, a file record stored in an online secondary storage device is accomplished through the use of a record key in a fraction of a second and without the need for a sequential search of the file. Once the record has been updated or has provided up-to-the-minute information about its contents to the inquiry station, it is returned directly to a designated location in the direct-access storage device.

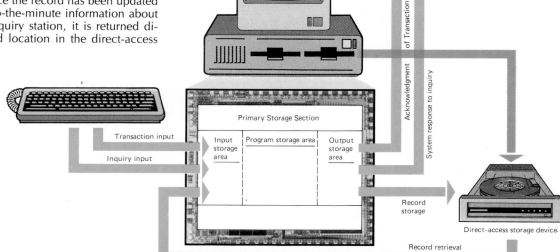

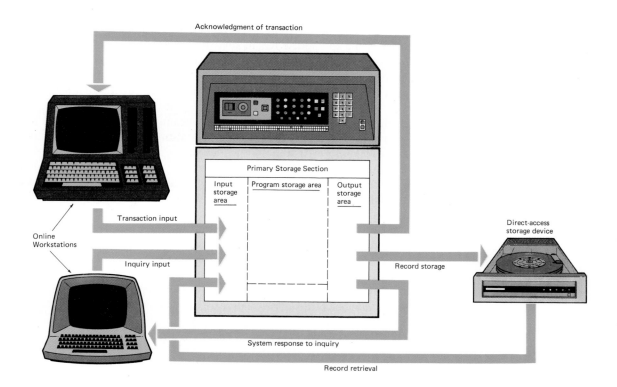

## Feedback and Review 2-1

In the preceding section you've seen how data may be organized for computer processing. You've seen how a computer can be used to process a mailing label application that emphasizes input/output operations. And you've looked at two applications that were used to illustrate the calculation operations performed by computers. In the first sales compensation application, the file of the partners' sales force was sequentially organized and sequentially processed. In the second application to update Rob's savings account record, a direct file organization approach was used and direct-access processing was employed. You can test your understanding of these concepts by using the following sentences and definitions to fill in the *crossword puzzle* form.

### Across

**1.** Sequential processing is also called _____ processing.

**2.** A _____ is a collection of related fields that are treated as a unit.

**10.** _____ file organization consists of storing records one after another in a file in an ascending or descending order determined by the record key.

**11.** When updating a sequential file, the transactions that affect the records in the old master file must first be _____ into the same sequence as the master file before processing can begin.

**13.** A _____ file organization consists of storing records in an online storage device in such a way that the computer can go directly to the key or identifying value of the record needed without having to search through a sequence of other records.

**15.** A _____ base is a collection of logically related data elements that can be used for multiple processing needs.

**17.** The first product of R-K Enterprises was a _____ shirt.

**20.** Computers cannot directly carry out any _____ activities. For example, they cannot bend metal, but they can supply the information needed to control metal-bending machines.

**21.** Computers are able to _____ and retrieve data.

**22.** Direct or _____ -access processing consists of directly locating and updating any file record without the need to read preceding file records.

### Down

**1.** One of the applications illustrating the calculating capabilities of a computer was a _____ compensation example.

**3.** When _____ -access processing is used, up-to-the-minute information about record contents can be provided to answer inquiries from operators of online stations.

**4.** The _____ caused by accumulating the input data into batches prior to file updating can be a problem when sequential processing is used.

**5.** A limitation of sequential processing is that records near the end of the file cannot be accessed until all preceding records have been read into the _____ .

**6.** File organization requires the use of some record _____ or identifying value that's found in every record in the file.

**7.** In sequential processing, transactions are typically accumulated into _____ and processed only at scheduled intervals.

**8.** A tee shirt promoting the mosquito as the state _____ was the initial product of R-K Enterprises.

**9.** A _____ consists of a group of related characters that are treated as a single unit.

**12.** _____ maintenance is required to add new records and delete or make changes to the existing records in a file.

**14.** _____ is the acronym for direct-access storage device.

**16.** The master files used in sequential processing are often stored on magnetic _____ .

**18.** Rob's partner in R-K Enterprises is Kay _____ .

**19.** A file update program can cause the system to read new record transactions from one input device, read the _____ master file records from another input device, change the existing records as needed, and produce an updated master file as output.

## A Logic/Comparison Application

You saw in Chapter 1 that a computer system is able to perform logical operations by first comparing numbers, letters, or other symbols, and then by following a prescribed course of action determined by the result of the comparison. Although they've not been spelled out in detail, logical operations have played a part in several of our earlier applications programs. In the mailing label application, for

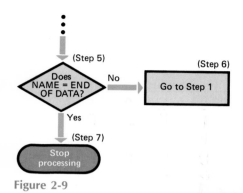

Figure 2-9

example, step 5 in the program is "If last record, then go to step 7." The purpose of this step is to determine if the last prospect record has been processed. If the last record has not been processed, program control goes to the next step in the sequence and from there it branches back to the first program step and the next label is printed. If the last record has been processed, the computer is instructed to go to step 7 and stop the processing.

How does the computer know when the last valid record has been processed? One approach is to place a **dummy record** at the *end* of the prospect master file. In the record field reserved for the prospect's name, the contents in the last dummy record could be END OF DATA. The computer instruction in step 5 could then be revised to read: "If name = END OF DATA, then go to step 7." The computer will then compare each prospect name to "END OF DATA" and continue the processing until the dummy record is finally read after all valid data have been processed (see Figure 2-9).

The same approach could also be used in the program that processes the sales compensation report. Step 7 in that program (see Figure 2-5) reads: "If last salesperson record, then go to step 9." The salesperson's name in a dummy record at the end of the file could again be END OF DATA. Step 7 could then be revised to read: "If name = END OF DATA, then go to step 9." A comparison of each salesperson's name to "END OF DATA" will continue the processing until the dummy record is finally read.

**Billing Application for R-K Enterprises.** Rob followed a "cash-only" policy in his initial sales of mosquito bird tee shirts. But after R-K Enterprises was created and the sale of mosquito bird products spread beyond the Longhorn College campus, it became profitable to accept orders from, and then make shipments to, selected customers without receiving immediate payment. This delayed payment policy made it necessary to design an *order entry, shipping,* and *billing system* for credit customers.

Orders from customers may result from the visits of salespersons, from telephone contacts, or from other sources. The **sales order** (or **customer order**) is the first document generated in the order entry process. Typically prepared by a salesperson or an order clerk, this document provides the data needed to produce the **shipping order.** Multiple copies of the shipping order are generally made. One copy is needed by the employee(s) filling and shipping the order. Another copy may be sent to the customer to acknowledge receipt of the order. A third may be packed with the shipment. A fourth may be kept in the files.

After the order has been shipped, a **bill** or **invoice** must be prepared and sent to the customer. Bills must be sent out promptly to minimize the amount of money that a business has tied up in unpaid shipments. It's also very important that these bills be accurate: Overcharges irritate customers and undercharges can mean lost revenues. Because of this need for speed and accuracy, and because of the mountains of bills that many organizations must prepare each month, billing has long been a major computer application.

As shown in Figure 2-10, the data from the shipping order usually provide the input for the billing application. These data may be transferred to an input storage

## HOW THEY KEEP SMURFS UNDER CONTROL

Along with any meteoric rise in sales comes the blizzard of orders which, if uncontrolled, can prevent a company from servicing its customers efficiently and keep management from knowing the sales information needed to control the business.

Such a prospect faced Wallace Berrie & Co., the Van Nuys, CA, gift distributor, when it latched onto Smurfs. Since purchasing U.S. rights to the famous Belgian cartoon characters in 1979, sales have doubled each year, soaring to $700 million from its nearly 100 licensees plus another $100 million from its own Smurf products.

"When you have over one thousand stockkeeping units [SKUs] in your product lines," says Gary Trumbo, vice president of marketing, who joined the company 12 years ago when sales hovered around $1 million, "and you're involved in what I call disciplines, such as ceramics, seasonal items, and stuffed animals, it's impossible to keep track of all those things without a data base system that tracks every SKU and sale." Adds William Gootnick, vice president of operations, "We handle over 150,000 orders, from 2,500 customers, a year. There's no way we can keep track of the orders without computers."

Keeping track starts with order entry at Van Nuys, where operators edit the sales orders sent in daily on printed forms by the company's 170 salespeople. After checking for errors in titles, descriptions, categories, or prices, they enter the information into an IBM System/38.

The information is sped to two warehouses in Edison, NJ, and Woodland Hills, CA, via data link. After the order is filled, a tabulation of shipment and inventory information is transmitted back to Van Nuys where it is again checked for accuracy and re-entered into the computer.

The data are no different from what salespeople have been forwarding to home offices for years. The difference is that, rather than getting lost in cubbyholes or scattered in a dozen or so different offices, they instantly are combined in one unified data base which can be accessed. This capability is vital to Trumbo and his product managers who constantly analyze the information.

—Source: *Sales & Marketing Management* magazine. Copyright Dec. 5, 1983. Photo courtesy Viewdata Corporation of America, Inc.

medium. From there they are read into the CPU under program control during a billing run. The steps required to process R-K Enterprises' bills are shown in the program storage area in Figure 2-10 and explained in detail. For our present purposes, it's not necessary to grasp fully all the program details presented in the CPU storage area and in the caption of Figure 2-10. But a careful study of this figure should give you some insights into several of the examples presented in the chapters of the Programming Module.

It is important here to point out that two logic/comparison operations are carried out in Figure 2-10. After step 1 in the program storage area of the CPU has been followed to read in the data from an input record, the *first* logic/comparison operation is set up by step 2. The value stored in the quantity-shipped field of the input

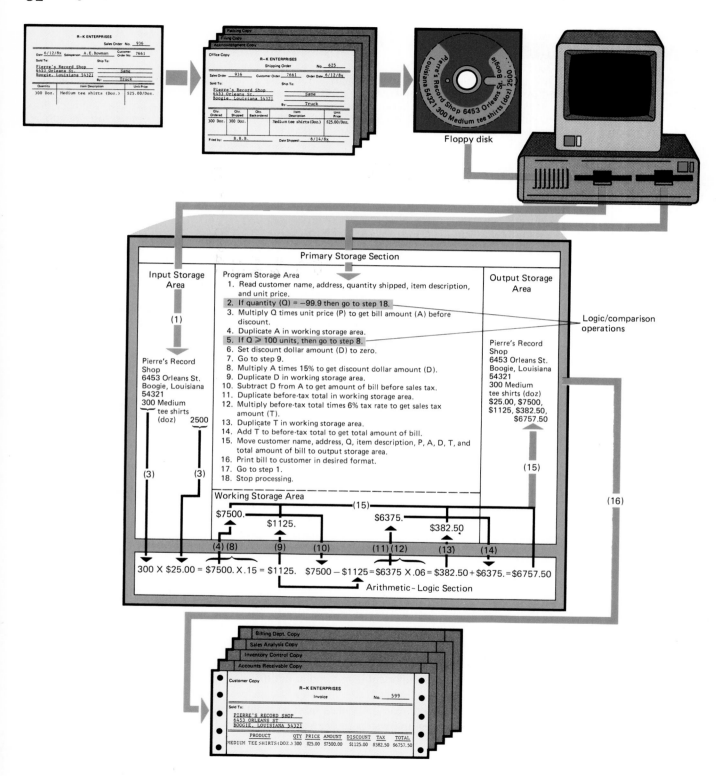

Floppy disk

Primary Storage Section

Input Storage Area

Program Storage Area

1. Read customer name, address, quantity shipped, item description, and unit price.
2. If quantity (Q) = −99.9 then go to step 18.
3. Multiply Q times unit price (P) to get bill amount (A) before discount.
4. Duplicate A in working storage area.
5. If Q ≥ 100 units, then go to step 8.
6. Set discount dollar amount (D) to zero.
7. Go to step 9.
8. Multiply A times 15% to get discount dollar amount (D).
9. Duplicate D in working storage area.
10. Subtract D from A to get amount of bill before sales tax.
11. Duplicate before-tax total in working storage area.
12. Multiply before-tax total times 6% tax rate to get sales tax amount (T).
13. Duplicate T in working storage area.
14. Add T to before-tax total to get total amount of bill.
15. Move customer name, address, Q, item description, P, A, D, T, and total amount of bill to output storage area.
16. Print bill to customer in desired format.
17. Go to step 1.
18. Stop processing.

Logic/comparison operations

Output Storage Area

Pierre's Record Shop
6453 Orleans St.
Boogie, Louisiana
54321
300 Medium
tee shirts (doz)
$25.00, $7500,
$1125, $382.50,
$6757.50

(15)

(1)

Pierre's Record Shop
6453 Orleans St.
Boogie, Louisiana
54321
300 Medium
tee shirts
(doz)      2500

(3)      (3)

(16)

Working Storage Area

(15)

$7500.          $6375.

$1125.               $382.50

(4) (8)        (9)        (10)        (11)(12)        (13)        (14)

300 X $25.00 = $7500. X .15 = $1125.    $7500 − $1125 = $6375 X .06 = $382.50 + $6375. = $6757.50

Arithmetic–Logic Section

R-K ENTERPRISES
Sales Order No. 936
Date 6/12/8x   Salesperson A.E. Bowman   Customer Order No. 7661
Sold To:   Ship To:
Pierre's Record Shop
6453 Orleans St.   Same
Boogie, Louisiana 54321   By:   Truck
Quantity | Item Description | Unit Price
300 Doz. | Medium tee shirts (Doz.) | $25.00/Doz.

Packing Copy
Filing Copy
Acknowledgment Copy
Office Copy
R-K ENTERPRISES
Shipping Order   No. 625
Sales Order 936   Customer Order 7661   Order Date 6/12/8x
Sold To:   Ship To:
Pierre's Record Shop
6453 Orleans St.   Same
Boogie, Louisiana 54321   By:   Truck
Qty. Ordered | Qty. Shipped | Qty. Backordered | Item Description | Unit Price
300 Doz. | 300 Doz. | | Medium tee shirts (Doz.) | $25.00/Doz.
Filed by:   B.B.B.   Date Shipped:   6/14/8x

Billing Dept. Copy
Sales Analysis Copy
Inventory Control Copy
Accounts Receivable Copy
Customer Copy
R-K ENTERPRISES
Invoice   No. 599
Sold To:
PIERRE'S RECORD SHOP
6453 ORLEANS ST
BOOGIE, LOUISIANA 54321
PRODUCT | QTY | PRICE | AMOUNT | DISCOUNT | TAX | TOTAL
MEDIUM TEE SHIRTS (DOZ.) 300 | $25.00 | $7500.00 | $1125.00 | $382.50 | $6757.50

**Figure 2-10** This illustration shows a system that may be used to accept and fill customer orders and prepare customer bills. An order from a customer is entered on a sales order form. The sales order data are then used to produce the shipping order which is used (*a*) to fill the order and (*b*) to supply the input data for the billing application. The input data are transferred to an input storage medium from where they are read under program control into the CPU during a billing run. The steps required to process R-K's bills are shown in the program storage area. The numbers in parentheses refer to the actions taken in response to numbered program steps. After reading in the input data (step 1), the program sets up the first logic/comparison operation (step 2). If the value of the quantity (Q) field in the input record is equal to $-99.9$, processing will stop. (This will occur when the last dummy record at the end of the file which has a quantity of $-99.9$ is read.) If Q is not $-99.9$, the program moves to the next step. To encourage large purchases, a 15 percent discount is given if the shipment quantity is equal to or greater than ($\geqslant$) 100 units. The dollar amount of the bill before any discount is applied is computed first by multiplying the units shipped times the unit price (step 3). This amount (A) is stored for future use in the working storage area (step 4). The computer next compares the value of Q to 100 (step 5). If Q is 100 units or more, as it is in our example transaction to Pierre's Record Shop, program control branches to step 8 and a 15 percent discount amount (D) is calculated and then duplicated in working storage (step 9). If Q is less than 100 units, the program moves to step 6 and no discount amount is applied. Once the discount amount is determined, it is subtracted from the total amount previously calculated to get the amount of the bill before a 6 percent sales tax is applied (step 10). Since this before-tax total will need to be preserved for later use, it is duplicated in a working storage area location (step 11). The amount of the sales tax (T) is then found by multiplying the before-tax total times the 6 percent tax rate (step 12). This value of T is also preserved in working storage (step 13). The next step is to add T to the before-tax total to get the total amount of the customer's bill (step 14). Finally, all the information that is needed to prepare the bill is moved to the output storage area of the CPU (step 15), and is then used to print the customer's bill in the desired format (step 16). The computer then resets itself to begin processing the next customer's bill (step 17).

record is compared to a value of $-99.9$. If the quantity (Q) is not $-99.9$, the processing continues in sequence. If Q is $-99.9$, program control will branch to step 18 and the processing will stop. A quantity of $-99.9$ dozen tee shirts will never be shipped, but such a value is used in a last dummy record at the end of the billing run to indicate that all valid data have been processed.

The second logic/comparison operation is accomplished in step 5. To encourage large purchases, Rob and Kay offer a 15 percent discount on shipments with a quantity equal to or greater than ($\geqslant$) 100 units. (Each unit is one-dozen tee shirts in our example.) In step 5, the computer is instructed to compare the value in the quantity-shipped field of the input record to 100. If the input value is 100 units or more (as it is in our example transaction to Pierre's Record Shop in Figure 2-10), program control branches to step 8 and a 15 percent discount amount is calculated. If the input quantity is less than 100 units, however, the program continues to step 6 which specifies that there should be no discount applied (see Figure 2-11).

The processing of the billing application continues in a step-by-step fashion in Figure 2-10 until all the needed information for the customer's bill has been prepared and moved to the output storage area of the CPU. From there the information is sent to a printer which prepares the customer's bill in the desired format. Program control then branches back to step 1 and processing begins on the next customer record.

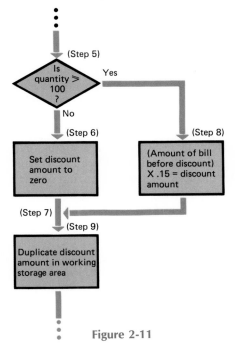

**Figure 2-11**

## After Billing: Some Important Follow-Up Applications

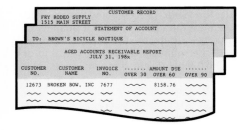

As we've just seen, it's a common business data processing practice to use the data found in the sales order to prepare the shipping order. The shipping order becomes the source of input data for the billing application. And it's common to use the data found in a customer bill as input to several other important business applications. As shown in Figure 2-10, multiple copies of the invoice are often prepared. Copies may then be forwarded to employees who are responsible for accounts receivable, inventory control, and sales analysis applications.

**Accounts Receivable.** A business that grants credit to its customers must maintain an **accounts receivable** (A/R) operation to keep track of the amounts owed by, and the payments received from, these customers' accounts. Thus, the primary *input* documents for the A/R application are customer invoices (showing amounts owed by customers) and payment vouchers (showing payments received from customers). The *output* results produced by the A/R application include:

■ Updated records of individual customers showing charges and payments for a period and the present amount owed

■ Monthly summary statements to remind customers of their debts

■ Management reports that give information about the amounts owed and the ages of the unpaid accounts.

The A/R application is obviously an important follow-up to the billing application. Accuracy of customer records and statements is required to avoid loss of revenue and/or customer irritation. And speed of processing is needed since delays in preparing statements can result in slow collections and can tie up excessive amounts of capital in unpaid accounts.

**Inventory Control.** The **inventory control** application is a second important follow-up to the order entry/shipping/billing system. A business generally has two objectives in maintaining an inventory control operation. The first goal is to keep a low level of inventory on hand to minimize the amount of money invested and to reduce the costs associated with storing, handling, and insuring a large quantity of goods. The second goal is to maintain good customer relations by having the goods on hand when they are ordered. Unfortunately, these two goals are at cross-purposes. Stockouts and customer backorders can usually be avoided by carrying large inventories, but this is contradictory to the financial goal of minimizing carrying costs. The purpose of the inventory control application, then, is to give managers the information they need to strike a profitable balance between the two goals— i.e., to allow them to keep stock levels reasonably low while still giving good customer service.

The input documents for the inventory control application may include receiving reports (showing goods initially received or goods that customers have returned) and customer invoices (showing goods sold). The output results produced by the inventory control application include:

**Figure 2-12** R-K's inventory control report. (The program that has been written to allow the computer system to prepare this report is discussed in Programming Module Chapter 18.)

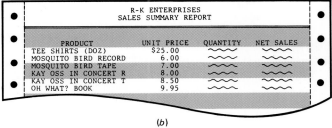

R-K ENTERPRISES
INVENTORY CONTROL REPORT

| PRODUCT | BEGINNING INVENTORY | QUANTITY RECEIVED | QUANTITY SOLD | ENDING INVENTORY |
|---|---|---|---|---|
| TEE SHIRTS (DOZ) | 50.00 | 10.00 | 30.75 | 29.25 |
| MOSQUITO BIRD R | | | | |
| MOSQUITO BIRD T | | | | |
| KAY OSS IN CONCERT R | | | | |
| KAY OSS IN CONCERT T | | | | |
| OH WHAT? BOOK | | | | |

■ Updated records of individual inventory items

■ Management reports used to determine what items to reorder or discontinue, how much to reorder, and which items have experienced unusual changes in demand

In later chapters you'll see that an inventory control report is prepared for R-K Enterprises. This report (see Figure 2-12) shows the partners the quantities of each product on hand at the beginning of a period such as the first of the month, how many of each product were received and how many were sold during the period, and the quantities of each product that remain at the end of the period.

**Sales Analysis.** The preparation of **sales analysis** reports is a *third* important follow-up activity to the order entry/shipping/billing system. The *input* documents that provide the sales analysis data include the customer invoices (showing who is buying, what they are buying, how much they are buying, where they are located, etc.) and the receiving slips (showing goods returned by customers). The *output* reports may provide information to answer questions such as: Who are our best customers? Which of our products are selling and which should we drop? Where are sales brisk and where are they lagging? Later on you'll see that two sales analysis

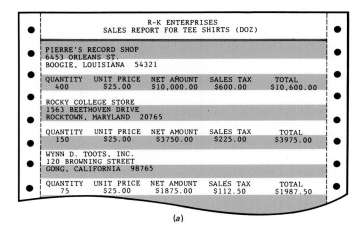

(a)

R-K ENTERPRISES
SALES SUMMARY REPORT

| PRODUCT | UNIT PRICE | QUANTITY | NET SALES |
|---|---|---|---|
| TEE SHIRTS (DOZ) | $25.00 | | |
| MOSQUITO BIRD RECORD | 6.00 | | |
| MOSQUITO BIRD TAPE | 7.00 | | |
| KAY OSS IN CONCERT R | 8.00 | | |
| KAY OSS IN CONCERT T | 8.50 | | |
| OH WHAT? BOOK | 9.95 | | |

(b)

**Figure 2-13** In the sales report (a), purchases are *classified* by the type of product sold. (The program that produces this report is discussed in Chapter 18.) Sales of all products are *summarized* in a periodic report (b). By comparing this report with those of earlier periods, Rob and Kay can spot unusual sales patterns and then take appropriate action. (The program that makes this report possible is discussed in Chapter 18.)

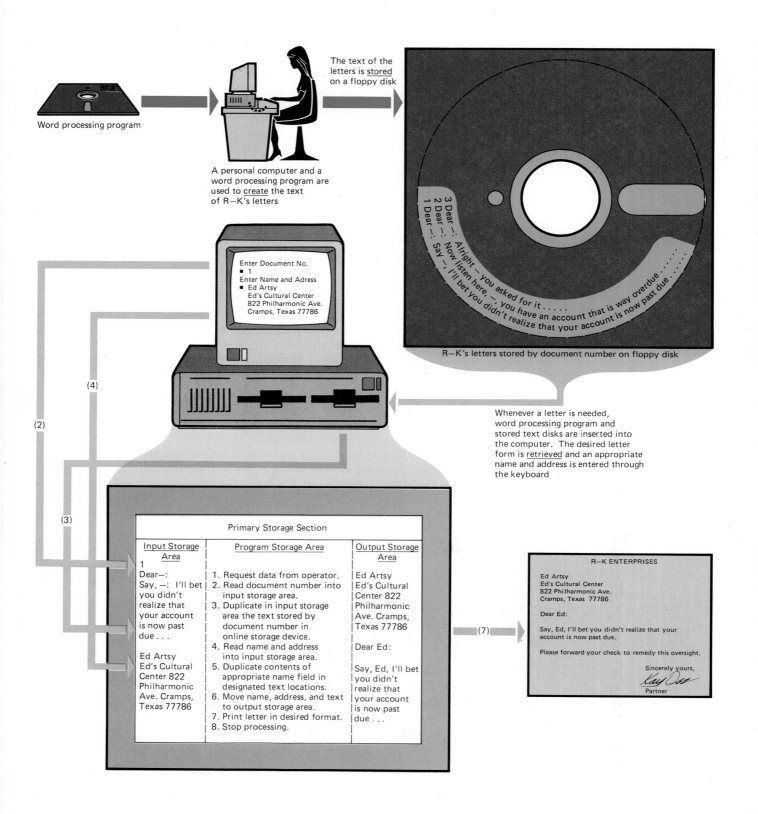

Word processing program

A personal computer and a
word processing program are
used to create the text
of R—K's letters

The text of the
letters is stored
on a floppy disk

3 Dear —:
2 Dear —:
1 Dear —:
Alright — you asked for it . . . . .
Now listen here, —: you have an account that is way overdue . . . . .
Say —, I'll bet you didn't realize that your account is now past due . . . .

R—K's letters stored by document number on floppy disk

Enter Document No.
■ 1
Enter Name and Adress
■ Ed Artsy
   Ed's Cultural Center
   822 Philharmonic Ave.
   Cramps, Texas 77786

(4)

(2)

(3)

Whenever a letter is needed,
word processing program and
stored text disks are inserted into
the computer. The desired letter
form is retrieved and an appropriate
name and address is entered through
the keyboard

## Primary Storage Section

| Input Storage Area | Program Storage Area | Output Storage Area |
|---|---|---|
| 1 | | |
| Dear—:<br>Say, —: I'll bet you didn't realize that your account is now past due . . . | 1. Request data from operator.<br>2. Read document number into input storage area.<br>3. Duplicate in input storage area the text stored by document number in online storage device.<br>4. Read name and address into input storage area.<br>5. Duplicate contents of appropriate name field in designated text locations.<br>6. Move name, address, and text to output storage area.<br>7. Print letter in desired format.<br>8. Stop processing. | Ed Artsy<br>Ed's Cultural Center 822 Philharmonic Ave. Cramps, Texas 77786<br><br>Dear Ed:<br><br>Say, Ed, I'll bet you didn't realize that your account is now past due . . . |
| Ed Artsy<br>Ed's Cultural Center 822 Philharmonic Ave. Cramps, Texas 77786 | | |

(7)

R—K ENTERPRISES

Ed Artsy
Ed's Cultural Center
822 Philharmonic Ave.
Cramps, Texas 77786

Dear Ed:

Say, Ed, I'll bet you didn't realize that your
account is now past due.

Please forward your check to remedy this oversight.

Sincerely yours,

Kay Oss

Partner

reports help Rob and Kay manage their empire. One of these reports *classifies* the purchases made during a period by a named customer according to the type of product shipped (see Figure 2-13*a*). The other report *summarizes* the total sales for each product during the period (Figure 2-13*b*).

The computer's ability to perform the logic/comparison operations spelled out in a program makes it possible for it automatically to control its own operations during the repetitive processing of records in a file. This same logic/comparison ability makes it possible for a computer system to *sort* data into numeric or alphabetic sequence by comparing two items to determine which is greater. Finally, this logic/comparison ability enables the system to *classify* and *summarize* data and records to produce useful information.

## A Storage and Retrieval Application: Word Processing

We've already seen how direct-access systems can be used by airlines, banks, and other organizations to provide up-to-the-minute information instantly in response to inquiries from online workstations. Such storage and retrieval applications depend on the ability of a computer system to store huge quantities of data in a direct-access storage device and to directly retrieve and update any of the thousands of stored records in a fraction of a second. Another important application that depends on the ability of a computer system to store and then quickly retrieve large quantities of data is word processing.

**Word processing** is the use of computers to create, view, edit, store, retrieve, and print text material. In the days before word processing became commonplace in offices, preparing the volumes of written communications was a time-consuming and expensive process. Office productivity gains lagged far behind the gains achieved in other business areas. But today, as you'll see in Chapter 11, millions of computers with word processing capabilities are used in offices and homes to improve efficiency by streamlining the creation and production of letters, reports, and other documents.

For example, routine letters may be prepared by accounts receivable employees and sent to customers to remind them when their accounts are past due. Of course, these letters could be preprinted, but such form letters are often ignored. To personalize each letter, and to create an original copy for each customer, a word processing system can be used. Let's assume that Kay and Rob want to use a personal computer–based system to send out collection letters to their slow-paying accounts. The first requirement would be to create a series of collection letters using the keyboard and a word processing program (see Figure 2-14). The first letter in the series could be a pleasant reminder that the account is past due. If no response is received to this message, the partners could follow it up with a second sober letter and then, if necessary, with a third notification that the account is being turned over to a bill collection agency. The second requirement would then be to store these three letters on a floppy disk as shown in Figure 2-14. For call-up purposes, each letter is given a number in our example.

After a letter has been created and stored, it can be easily retrieved by the operator of the word processing system. Following the insertion of the disks containing the word processing program and the stored text, the operator uses a few keystrokes to notify the word processing program in the CPU that a particular stored document is needed. The program then locates the needed text and duplicates it in the primary storage section. The operator then keys in the name and address of the

◀

**Figure 2-14** A word processing system. Here the text is created at a personal computer and stored on a floppy disk. When a specific letter is needed, the operator keys in the document number, which is read into the input storage area (see step 2 in the program storage area of the CPU). The program then duplicates the stored text in the input storage area (program step 3). Thus, although the text has been retrieved from online storage, it has not been erased. (Reading data *from* a magnetizeable storage medium such as a disk does not destroy the original data; entering data *into* a disk storage location, however, does erase the previous contents of the location.) Once the letter has been retrieved, the program reads the keyed name and address of the person to whom the letter should be sent (step 4). The letter is then "personalized" by inserting an appropriate name field into the text at designated places (step 5). After the name, address, and text message have been moved to output storage (step 6), the letter is printed (step 7), signed by Rob or Kay, and mailed to the customer.

person to whom the letter should be sent, and these facts are also read into primary storage. Finally, under program control the name of the recipient of the letter is inserted into the text at appropriate places to ''personalize'' the message, and the letter is automatically printed. Figure 2-14 gives the program details of this text storage and retrieval application. It's obvious how the efficiency and productivity of office workers are enhanced by the use of word processing systems.

### The Most Common Business Applications

You've now seen just a few of the thousands of computer system applications that exist. We classified these few examples rather arbitrarily according to one of the functions that they performed: input/output, calculation, logic/comparison, and storage/retrieval. But you can see, too, that in most applications the computer system will execute more than one of these functions.

Although our selected applications are limited, they are not random. Rather, our selection includes the applications that account for the greatest use of business computing resources. Figure 2-15 shows that a typical business computer operates an average of 81.5 hours each week. Over 9 hours or 11.5 percent of that time is spent on processing accounting applications. We've already discussed one of these tasks—updating accounts receivable records and preparing summary statements to remind customers of their debts. Another accounting application, **accounts payable** (A/P), keeps track of debts owed to suppliers for goods and services. One of its goals is to make sure that the discounts given for prompt payment are not lost. (A 2 percent discount is often given if a bill is paid within 10 days of receipt.) It may not be desirable to pay bills too early, however, because the organization would lose the use of the money for several days. Thus, an A/P system is designed to verify the accuracy of incoming bills, to make sure that discounts are not lost, and to issue payment checks toward the end of the discount period. We will discuss A/P applications in later chapters, and you may even try your skill at writing an A/P program for R-K Enterprises.

Figure 2-15 also shows that *inventory control, billing, payroll,* and *sales analysis* applications are among the most common in business. You saw how billing, accounts receivable, inventory control, and sales analysis applications were tied together earlier. You also saw examples of a payroll application in Chapter 1 and a report that computed sales compensation early in this chapter. Several billing, inventory control, sales analysis, and sales compensation computer programs for R-K Enterprises will be discussed in later chapters.

The other applications that have been presented are also quite common. Businesses such as savings associations, airlines, hotels, and car rental agencies use direct-access processing and have up-to-the-minute information available to answer inquiries from online stations. And a survey of businesses already using or considering small computer systems showed that about 40 percent were interested in word processing capability, and more than 20 percent were present or potential users of mailing list applications.[3]

And remember, business firms are not the only ones that process popular commercial applications. Nonprofit organizations such as schools, hospitals, and government agencies also produce payrolls, control inventories, prepare mailing labels, pay bills, and handle word processing.

**Figure 2-15** The five application areas that represent the greatest use of business computing resources. Nearly 36 percent of a computer's operation time each week is spent on applications in these five areas. (Adapted from G. A. Champine, ''Perspectives on Business Data Processing,'' *Computer,* November 1980, p. 86)

Percent of computer operation time

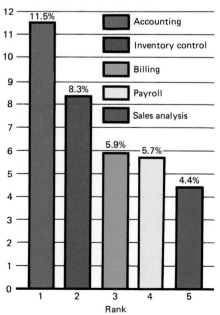

Average computer operation time = 81.5 hours per week

[3] See Karen E. Rosenfeld, ''Small Users Value Maintenance, Ease of Use,'' *Computerworld,* Aug. 25, 1980, Special Report section, p. 3.

## Feedback and Review 2-2

As you now know, computers are easily able to perform logic/comparison and storage/retrieval operations. The R-K billing application was used to illustrate logic/comparison operations, and the word processing application showed the storage/retrieval capabilities of computers. The examples in Chapters 1 and 2 represent the most common business applications, and they account for the greatest use of business computing resources. You can test your understanding of the concepts that have just been presented by answering the following questions. Place the letter of the best response in the space provided.

___**1.** A computer can determine when the last valid record in a file has been processed by comparing the contents of a designated field in each record to the contents of the same field in a dummy record placed
a) at the beginning of a file.
b) in the middle of a file.
c) at the end of a file.
d) at the end of the middle record.

___**2.** In an order entry, shipping, and billing system,
a) the sales order is the last document to be produced.
b) the sales order provides the data needed to produce the shipping order.
c) only a single copy of the shipping order is usually needed.
d) the invoice generally provides the input data needed for the sales order.

___**3.** The data found in a customer invoice are commonly used as input in the preparation of
a) accounts receivable statements.
b) inventory control reports.

c) sales analysis reports.
d) all of the above.

___**4.** In an accounts receivable application,
a) there's no reason to avoid delays in preparing statements.
b) the goal is to tie up excessive amounts of capital in unpaid accounts.
c) payments received from customers can be ignored.
d) management reports showing the ages of unpaid accounts are often produced.

___**5.** In an inventory control application,
a) an objective is to keep a high level of inventory on hand.
b) an objective is to maintain good customer relations by having the goods on hand when they are ordered.
c) there's generally no conflict in the goals that are pursued.
d) management reports are useless since the inventory is constantly changing.

___**6.** The use of computers for word processing
a) has increased the expense of written communications in all cases.
b) has caused a decline in office productivity.
c) is an application that makes use of the computer's ability to create, store, retrieve, and print text material.
d) requires that written communications be rigid and depersonalized.

___**7.** Which of the following is not one of the most common business computer applications?
a) accounts postponable
b) billing
c) inventory control
d) sales analysis

## LOOKING BACK

**1.** All that computers do is operate on data, and these data are organized into logical groupings. The smallest data entity is a *field* consisting of related characters that are treated as a unit. Fields are grouped together to form *records,* and related records are then grouped to produce a *file.* A collection of logically related elements may then be organized into a *data base.*

**2.** Computers are able to perform operations on data that can be classified into input/output, calculation, logic/comparison, and storage/retrieval categories. Example applications

emphasizing each of these types of operations have been presented in this chapter.

**3.** The preparation of mailing labels for R-K Enterprises was the application used to emphasize basic input/output operations. A file of prospective customers was created and maintained on a machine-readable medium. Under program control, a customer record was read into the CPU. The record fields were arranged in the desired format, and the mailing label was then printed.

**4.** Two example applications were used to illustrate the calculation operations performed by computers. The first was the preparation of a sales compensation report for Rob and Kay, and the second was the updating of Rob's savings account record. In the first application, the file of the sales force was organized sequentially using the salesperson's last name as the *record key*. In the second application, a direct file organization approach was used with the savings account number being the record key. File organization requires the use of some key or identifying value that is unique and is found in every record in the file.

**5.** If records are stored in an ascending or descending order determined by the record key, then a *sequential file organization* approach is being used. Sequential files are typically stored on such media as magnetic tape and magnetic disks. *Sequential processing* consists of reading and processing the first record in the file sequence, then the second record in the order, and so on. Such processing is suitable for applications such as payroll and customer billing, but when a sequential file is updated, the transactions that affect the records in the old master file must first be sorted into the same sequence as the master file before processing can begin. Also, it's not possible to quickly access a particular record in a file until all preceding records have been read into the CPU.

**6.** When a *direct file organization* approach is used, the computer can go directly to a key of the record needed without having to search through a sequence of other records. Directly organized files must be stored in an online secondary storage device such as a magnetic disk unit. When *direct-access (random-access* or *online) processing* is used, the desired record is retrieved in a fraction of a second and without the need for a sequential search of the file. Such processing can provide up-to-the-minute information in response to inquiries.

**7.** The billing application for R-K Enterprises was used to illustrate the logic/comparison operations performed by computers. After an order from a customer was entered on a sales order form, the sales data were then used to produce the shipping order. This shipping order, in turn, supplied the input data for the billing application. Under program control, the input data were read into the CPU a record at a time. In our example, a logic/comparison operation was used to recognize the appearance of a final *dummy record* and to thus determine when the processing should stop. After processing a record, the output information was used to print the customer invoice. Multiple copies of customer invoices are often prepared. In addition to the customer's copy, other copies are forwarded to those responsible for accounts receivable, inventory control, and sales analysis applications.

**8.** A word processing application was used to illustrate the storage/retrieval capabilities of computers. A series of collection letters was created and stored on a magnetic disk. Once stored, the desired letter can be retrieved on demand by the operator of a word processing system. Such an application can greatly improve the productivity of office workers.

**9.** The greatest uses of business computing resources are represented by accounts receivable, accounts payable, inventory control, billing, payroll, and sales analysis applications. All these applications were discussed at length in this chapter. Direct-access processing, word processing, and mailing list applications are also among the most common of business applications which we have also considered. Computer programs for many of these applications will appear in later chapters.

## KEY TERMS AND CONCEPTS

field 37
data item 37
record 38
file 38
data base 38
file maintenance/file updating 40
record key 44
sequential file organization 44
batch processing 44

sequential (or serial) processing 44
direct (random) file organization 47
direct-access (online or random-access) processing 47
direct-access storage device (DASD) 47
dummy record 50
sales/customer order 50
shipping order 50

bill/invoice 50
accounts receivable (A/R) 54
inventory control 54
sales analysis 55
word processing 56
accounts payable (A/P) 58

## TOPICS FOR REVIEW AND DISCUSSION

**1.** "When computers operate on data, the data will normally be organized into logical groupings so that processing will be effective and output results will be useful." Identify these logical groupings and discuss the relationship that exists between them.

**2.** Computers are able to perform operations on data that can be classified into four categories. What are they?

**3.** After a master file has been created, why is it necessary to periodically perform file maintenance or file updating?

**4.** (a) How was a computer used to prepare the mailing labels for R-K Enterprises? (b) Have you received any mail recently that made use of computer-prepared labels? (c) Have you received any that didn't?

**5.** (a) How was a computer used to prepare a sales compensation report for Rob and Kay? (b) To update Rob's savings account record?

**6.** "A file must be organized in some way to facilitate processing." Identify, define, and discuss two ways in which files may be organized.

**7.** (a) What is sequential processing? (b) What are the strengths and limitations of this processing approach?

**8.** (a) What is direct-access processing? (b) What are the strengths and limitations of this processing approach?

**9.** How may a "dummy" record be used to indicate to a computer that the last valid record has been processed?

**10.** (a) How was a computer used to prepare bills for R-K Enterprises? (b) Discuss the flow of data from the time they are entered on the sales order form until they appear on the customer's invoice.

**11.** Identify and discuss the important business data processing applications that use input data taken from customer invoices.

**12.** (a) How was a computer used in the R-K word processing application? (b) Have you received any letters recently that were produced by a computer? (c) What was your reaction to these letters?

**13.** What applications account for the greatest use of business computing resources?

**14.** What is the purpose of an accounts payable application?

## PROJECTS TO LOOK INTO

**1.** Contact a business or nonprofit organization in your area and see how the organization uses a computer to process one of the applications discussed in this chapter. Summarize your findings in a report to the class. Prepare drawings to show the class how the organization processes the selected application.

**2.** Thousands of brand-name, prewritten applications programs are currently offered for sale by equipment manufacturers and independent software firms, who advertise their products in magazines and newspapers. Many of these programs are designed to process the types of applications discussed in this chapter. Visit your library or a retail computer store and identify three program products that can process the types of applications discussed in this chapter. Prepare a report for the class that summarizes some of the features of the programs you've selected.

## ANSWERS TO FEEDBACK AND REVIEW SECTIONS

**2-1**
The solution to the crossword puzzle is shown at the right.

**2-2**
1. C
2. B
3. D
4. D
5. B
6. C
7. A

# An Application for a DBMS Package

You saw in Figure 2-4, page 42, that the R-K partners developed their own program to produce gummed mailing labels. But many individuals and organizations prefer to buy a specialized set of programs called a *data base management system (DBMS)* to handle mailing list processing and countless other activities. Thus, the prospect master file could be treated as a data base, and the partners could respond to menu prompts (Figure 2-A) and/or use the relatively simple and understandable commands provided by the DBMS package to tell the computer what

they want it to do. These instructions are then automatically translated and executed by the DBMS software.

For example, Rob and Kay could use a DBMS package to *add records* to their prospect master file, to *make changes* to existing records stored in the file, and to *delete records* from the file when they are no longer needed (Figure 2-B). We'll come back to this mailing label application and to the many other uses of DBMS packages in Chapter 13.

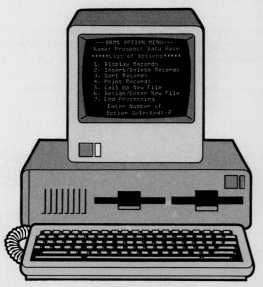

**Figure 2-A** Option 2 is selected here to add, change, or delete records.

**Figure 2-B** Data maintenance activities and many other operations are controlled by the DBMS software.

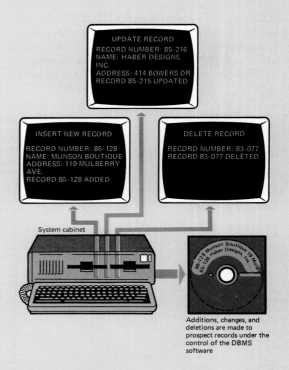

Additions, changes, and deletions are made to prospect records under the control of the DBMS software

# Putting the Computer to Work
## *systems and software development*

### Getting the Sales Force to Think about Computers

Six years ago, when . . . business at Leegin Creative Leather Products started growing at the rate of 50% a year, the paper blitz became a blizzard. Form shuffling in the office got out-of-hand and the sales force was inundated with paper work.

The answer was computerization of the whole operation in two major steps: (1) home office and (2) sales force. . . . [Company president Jerry] Kohl took a long look before leaping into electronics. He made a list of all the tasks he wanted a system to perform, read every piece of computer literature he could lay his hands on, and hired a consultant to research his company's needs and find the hardware.

The consulting company . . . spent six months interviewing office employees and key people of other departments. Analyzing the information it had gathered, [the consultant] prepared flowcharts on paperwork procedures. A 100-page proposal request was prepared and submitted to four companies, who were asked to provide information on their systems' capabilities . . .

Once four [hardware] systems were installed and six months of programming and reprogramming completed, the statistics started to flow in an orderly fashion, giving information for such tasks as sales trends projections.

With the home office operation running smoothly, Kohl decided six months ago to extend computerization to field selling. He asked himself, "What can I do to help my sales representatives do more business?" His answer: provide them with quicker retrieval of data. This meant giving each salesperson a portable computer with on-line inquiry capabilities to the home office data base. This would help them to organize their activities and make them better prepared to make sales calls.

—Source: *Sales & Marketing Management* magazine. Copyright Dec. 5, 1983. Photo courtesy The Bohle Company.

It's *people* who put the computer to work to perform useful tasks. People in an organization must work together to complete a step-by-step system study process that will first identify and then develop needed informational improvements. Each of the steps in this process is outlined in this chapter. The information in this chapter will enable you to:

- Discuss why people are motivated to introduce new computer-based systems or to modify existing ones
- Outline the steps in the system study process, and identify the steps that may be bypassed when suitable software packages are purchased
- Explain the purpose of system analysis and system design, and outline the uses of a system flowchart
- Understand the purpose of programming analysis, program preparation, and program implementation and maintenance

# THE DATA PROCESSING SYSTEM: INTRODUCTION AND REVIEW

In Chapter 1 we described a system as a group of integrated elements that have the common purpose of achieving some goal(s). Essential elements in a computer-based data processing system include the necessary *input data*, the proper *hardware*, the processing *procedures* designed to convert the input data into the desired output, and the various *computer programs* that allow the hardware to accept the input data and follow the procedures. But something is still missing, and that something is people. The central and most important element in any computer-based system is *people*.

## Chapter Outline

**Figure 3-1** All elements of a computer system revolve around the people in the system. Some of these people are specialists in data processing. But many other nonspecialists provide the input data needed, make suggestions for appropriate data processing procedures, and use the output results. (Photos courtesy Apple Computer, Inc.; Hewlett-Packard Company; and reprinted by permission of Nixdorf Computer Corporation, Burlington, Mass.)

*It's people who put the computer to work: It's people working together who determine processing needs, provide input data, design processing procedures, select hardware and software, write computer programs, and use processed output.* In organizations, some of these people are data processing specialists. But contributions from nonspecialists such as clerks, secretaries and assistants, and managers who enter the data and use the output are equally essential to the creation of a successful system (Figure 3-1). When people create a clever system, the credit often goes to the machine that processes the data. And when people produce a flawed effort, the machine may get unreasonable blame for the results.

With machines capturing much of the credit and most of the blame, why are people motivated to introduce new computer-based systems or to modify existing ones? Generally speaking, people in organizations introduce or change systems in order to deal with the changing operating conditions that they face. The motive for adding to or changing a system might result from changes inside or outside the organization. Consider these four examples:

1. New government regulations change the accounting for employee pension plans.

2. Top managers decide to acquire or merge with another organization.

3. A billing department manager wants to reduce the recent increase in billing errors.

4. A data processing specialist is convinced that new or existing data can be used in a more creative way to produce better information in a particular area of the organization.

Whatever the motivation, new computer systems are not overnight creations. Computer hardware will not by some miracle automatically begin to produce output results that will satisfy changing conditions. Once again, people must first go to work to complete a series of steps called a *system study*. In the following sections, we'll trace through the steps that people in organizations use to put the computer to work. But you'll also find that these same steps can help you produce useful results with a personal computer. Keep in mind as you read, too, that both organizations and individuals may be able to bypass some steps if software packages are available that will meet their needs. A **software package** is a prewritten set of program instructions prepared by equipment manufacturers and software vendors to perform specific tasks. Some guidelines that people can use to identify and then select suitable software packages are outlined in Chapter 8.

# THE STEPS IN A SYSTEM STUDY

A formal definition: The **system study** is a step-by-step process used to identify and then develop specific improvements in an organization's information system(s). The steps or stages in the system study process are outlined in Figure 3-2 and briefly summarized below. Later chapters in the Systems and Software and Programming Modules will discuss all these steps in greater detail.

## Step 1: Defining the Need

To create a new system and/or improve or modify an existing one, people first have to recognize that a problem or need exists. As you've just seen, this problem or need may result from changing operating conditions. Managers, employees of departments that are affected by changing conditions, and data processing personnel often participate in requirements sessions until the problem has been defined and specific study goals have been outlined. These goals should then be put in writing and approved by all concerned. This first step cannot be bypassed even if a software package is used to put the computer to work. After all, how can people identify and select a suitable package if they don't have a clear understanding of exactly what they want the package to do?

## Step 2: System Analysis

After users and specialists have identified the need for specific changes, a *study team* gathers and then analyzes data about current data processing operations. The people in this study team are often selected for the offsetting talents they can bring to the job. At least one member usually represents (and has a knowledge of the information needs of) the departments affected by the study. Another is a **systems analyst**—an information specialist who is knowledgeable about the technical aspects of analyzing, designing, and implementing computer-based processing systems. And a third may be an auditor who can see to it that proper accuracy and security controls are built into a new system.

**Data Collection.** The team's first job is to *gather data* about current data processing operations. These facts must be accurate, up-to-date, and sufficiently complete, for they will become the input to later study stages. Gathering such data can be difficult because a system may cut across several departments and involve many people using dozens of documents. Furthermore, *accurate* written statements outlining exactly what is done are usually missing. Procedure descriptions often

Courtesy Honeywell, Inc.

The first step in the system study is to clearly *identify the particular problem* to be solved or the tasks to be accomplished. Managers, departmental employees, and data processing personnel jointly participate in determining the problem and setting system goals.

The second step involves *system analysis.* After the problem has been identified, a study team works closely together to *gather* and then *analyze* data about current data processing operations.

The third stage is *system design.* After analyzing the procedures currently being followed, the people in the study team must then cooperate in the design of any new systems or applications that may be required to satisfy the need. As a part of the system design phase, people must settle on the most feasible design alternative to achieve the study goals. And they must prepare new design specifications that include the output desired, the input data needed, and the processing procedures required to convert the input data into the output results.

The fourth step is *programming analysis.* The new system or application specifications may be turned over to one or more programmers. These specifications are then broken down into the specific input/output, calculating, logic/comparison, and storage/retrieval operations required to satisfy the need.

The fifth step is *program preparation.* At this stage, one or more programmers translate or code the required operations into a language and form acceptable to the computer hardware.

The sixth stage involves the *implementation* and *maintenance* of the system or application. People must first make sure that the coded program(s) is checked for errors and tested prior to being used on a routine basis. After programs appear to be running properly and producing correct results, the changeover to the new approach is made. The cooperation of the many people who may be involved in the preparation of input data and the use of output results is needed at this time if the new approach is to be successfully implemented. Finally, implemented systems and programs are usually subject to continual change and must therefore be maintained. This modification and improvement must be a cooperative effort between those served by the system or program and those responsible for maintaining it.

**Figure 3-2** A summary of the system study process. This process must be people-oriented for a successful system or application to be created. And it should be a joint effort between those served by the system or application and those who create it. As this figure shows, computer hardware, by itself, cannot solve a single problem. (Photos courtesy Hewlett-Packard Company; Honeywell, Inc.; Teletype Corporation; General Electric Information Systems Company; Edith G. Haun Stock, Boston; and Control Data Corporation)

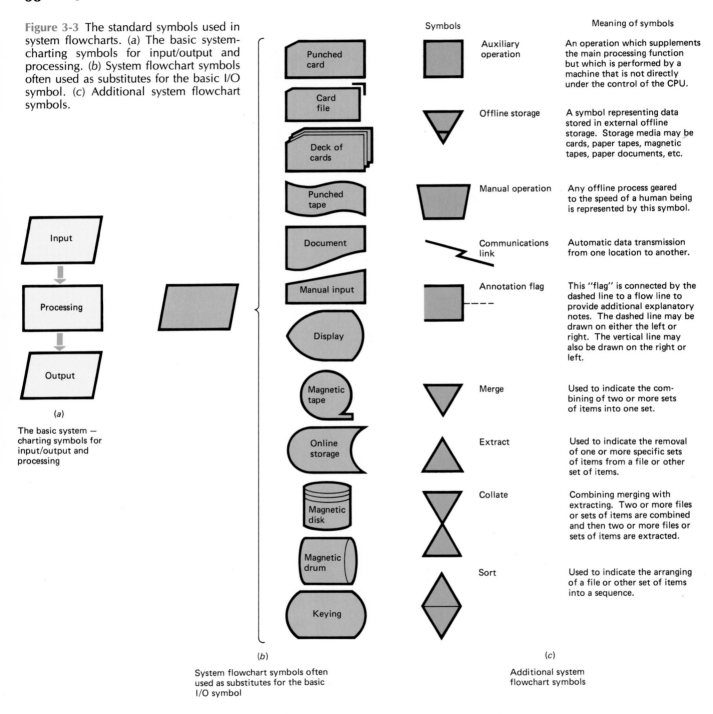

**Figure 3-3** The standard symbols used in system flowcharts. (a) The basic system-charting symbols for input/output and processing. (b) System flowchart symbols often used as substitutes for the basic I/O symbol. (c) Additional system flowchart symbols.

Input

Processing

Output

(a)

The basic system — charting symbols for input/output and processing

Punched card

Card file

Deck of cards

Punched tape

Document

Manual input

Display

Magnetic tape

Online storage

Magnetic disk

Magnetic drum

Keying

(b)

System flowchart symbols often used as substitutes for the basic I/O symbol

Symbols

Meaning of symbols

Auxiliary operation

An operation which supplements the main processing function but which is performed by a machine that is not directly under the control of the CPU.

Offline storage

A symbol representing data stored in external offline storage. Storage media may be cards, paper tapes, magnetic tapes, paper documents, etc.

Manual operation

Any offline process geared to the speed of a human being is represented by this symbol.

Communications link

Automatic data transmission from one location to another.

Annotation flag

This "flag" is connected by the dashed line to a flow line to provide additional explanatory notes. The dashed line may be drawn on either the left or right. The vertical line may also be drawn on the right or left.

Merge

Used to indicate the combining of two or more sets of items into one set.

Extract

Used to indicate the removal of one or more specific sets of items from a file or other set of items.

Collate

Combining merging with extracting. Two or more files or sets of items are combined and then two or more files or sets of items are extracted.

Sort

Used to indicate the arranging of a file or other set of items into a sequence.

(c)

Additional system flowchart symbols

exist, but they tend not to reflect the most current methods. Thus, a number of data-gathering tools and techniques must often be employed. Among these are questionnaires, interviews and observations, and system flowcharts.

**Flowchart Preparation.** A **system flowchart** is a diagram that shows a broad overview of the data flow and sequence of operations in a system. The emphasis is placed on input documents and output reports. Only limited detail is furnished about how a workstation or machine converts the input data into the desired output. Standard symbols are used in all flowcharts to clearly record and communicate information. The basic symbols representing input/output and processing are shown in Figure 3-3a. Although the input/output (I/O) symbol may be used to show any type of media or device, it's often replaced in system charts by other symbols whose shape suggests the particular medium or device being used (Figure 3-3b). Additional symbols are shown in Figure 3-3c.

Preparing flowcharts can help the study team gather data on current operations. Beginning with source-document inputs, each operation step is charted, using the

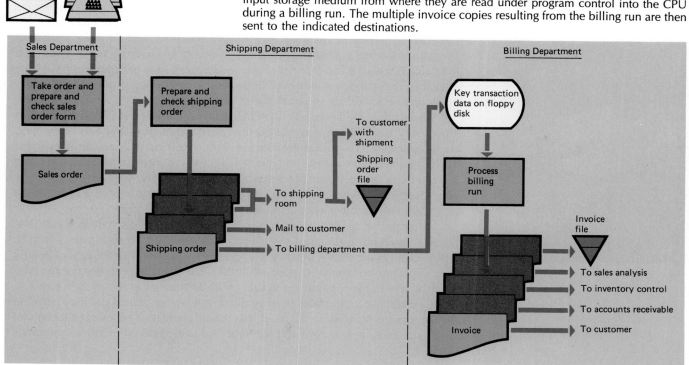

**Figure 3-4** As you saw in Chapter 2, R-K Enterprises' order-entry/shipping/billing system begins in the sales department when an order from a customer is entered on a sales order form. The sales order data are then used to produce the shipping order which, in turn, is used to fill the order, acknowledge the order to the customer, and provide the input data for the billing department. Data from the shipping order are keyed onto an input storage medium from where they are read under program control into the CPU during a billing run. The multiple invoice copies resulting from the billing run are then sent to the indicated destinations.

proper symbols. Files and equipment being used are identified, the processing sequence is described, the departments involved are located, and the output results are shown. For example, R-K Enterprises' current order entry/shipping/billing system described in Chapter 2 and shown in Figure 2-10 can be charted as shown in Figure 3-4, page 69. Notice that the arrows connecting the symbols show the direction of data flow. The main flow is usually charted from top to bottom and from left to right. Notes within the symbol further explain what's being done.

**Analyzing the Findings.** After the data about current operations have been gathered, the team members must then analyze their findings. **System analysis** is the study of existing operations to learn what they accomplish, why they work as they do, and what role (if any) they may have in future processing activities. In analyzing the current system, it's necessary to identify the essential data and procedures required for a new approach. It's also necessary to pinpoint current weaknesses and problems so that they will not be carried over to the new system. As part of this process, the system flowchart can be a helpful analysis tool. It's risky for organizations to try to bypass this system analysis step even though they expect to buy a software package.

## Step 3: System Design

Courtesy Teletype Corporation

**System design** is the process of creating alternative solutions to satisfy the study goals, evaluating the choices, and then drawing up the specifications for the chosen alternative. Design begins after the people in the study team have analyzed the current procedures. Since many factors have a bearing on the design process, it can be a complex and challenging task. For example, the design team must consider the personnel and financial resources of the organization, the different procedures that can often be used to carry out a single business operation, and the many equipment alternatives that are available to perform a given data processing job. Also, the team must consider what effects changes made in one application or department will have on related applications. A proposed improvement in a billing system, for example, might require a redesign of accounts receivable and inventory control procedures.

To illustrate the system design challenge, let's assume that R-K Enterprises grows very fast.[1] When they started their partnership, Rob and Kay knew their credit customers. They were not worried about receiving payment for shipments. Their current system shown in Figure 3-4 has worked well. But let's assume now that too many shipments are being made to newer customers who are proving to be poor credit risks. Also, the increased business volume has caused a delay in the preparation of customer statements and inventory control reports.

After analyzing the current system and studying the flowchart in Figure 3-4, the R-K study team designed the alternative system shown in Figure 3-5. (The design changes are shown in white in Figure 3-5.) To deal with the lack of control over shipments being made to poor credit risks, the team has proposed that the sales order be sent to the accounts receivable (A/R) department as shown in Figure 3-5. After a credit check, the sales order is either approved or denied and then routed to the appropriate department. Although this design alternative provides better control over shipments, it also increases the time and cost required to fill a customer's

---

[1] Alas, as you'll see in the Programming Module, this is a false assumption.

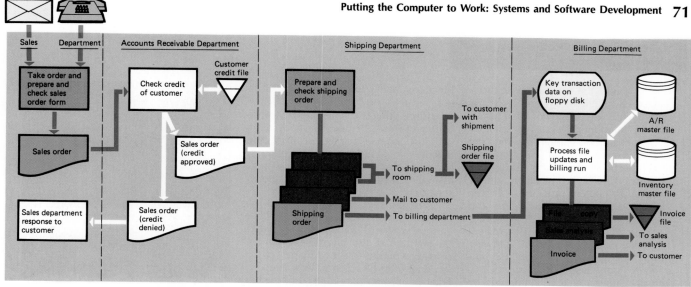

**Figure 3-5** A possible redesign of R-K's current order-entry/shipping/billing system shown in Figure 3-4 to provide better control over shipments being made to poor credit risks, and to improve the timeliness of customer statements and inventory control reports.

order. In judging alternatives, system designers must constantly make such trade-offs. No system alternative can be the best in every category. One with better control and greater accuracy may also be one that's more expensive and/or requires more processing time.

To improve the system for customer statements and inventory control reports in our example, the team has proposed that the A/R and inventory master files be stored in an online secondary storage device, and that a computer program be prepared to update these files at the same time the customer bills are being prepared (see Figure 3-5). This alternative involves tradeoffs:

| Possible Benefits | Possible Costs |
|---|---|
| Faster statement preparation | Preparing at least one new |
| Faster bill collection | computer program |
| Better inventory control | Purchasing new system hardware |
| Reduced manual processing of copies | |

It's the job of the designers to decide whether the benefits and possible savings expected from a design alternative outweigh the costs. (And, of course, it's up to Rob and Kay to approve design changes.)

After the team members have settled on the approach they consider best to meet the study goals, they must then prepare new design specifications. These specifications include the output desired, the input data needed, and the processing procedures required to convert input data into output results.

When people complete the system design step, they are in a position to identify and then select software packages that may meet their needs. For example, they can

## SOFTWARE, SOFTWARE EVERYWHERE

By one count, the number of software packages available for systems large and small is quickly approaching 35,000. Add the number of separate versions each package may offer for different hardware systems, and the total approaches 100,000 products. About half the software packages available are for personal computers, and the split between games or hobby programs and business programs is roughly 40/60.

Ease of use is the prime ingredient for launching a successful software product. In the future it's likely that programs for popular functions such as financial planning or text editing will be built into the hardware itself. For the present, one heated race in the competition for software sales is being run around packages featuring integrated functions and "windowing" capabilities.

Computing with integrated software allows the user to perform many tasks with just one package. For example, the Symphony^tm Window Management System combines five functions: word processing, database, communications, spreadsheet, and business graphics.

Programs like Symphony allow the easy transfer of information among their various programs. While the user works on one part of the job, other parts are displayed on the screen. Any part of the job may then be inserted into a report, letter or other document to be printed or transferred electronically to another computer.

—Photos courtesy Lotus Development Corporation and © Ashton-Tate, 1984.

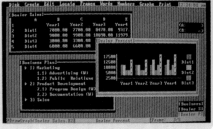

now determine if the output produced by a package is suitable, if the package will accept the necessary input data, and if the files created by the package are acceptable in terms of size and content. If a satisfactory package can be purchased, the next two steps in the system study may be skipped. If suitable software isn't available, custom-made programs must be created.

### Step 4: Programming Analysis

Courtesy General Electric Information Systems Company.

### Step 5: Program Preparation

After top managers give their approval to create custom-made software, the design specifications provide the input for the programming analysis phase of the system study process. **Programming analysis** is the process of breaking down the design specifications into the specific input/output, calculation, logic/comparison, and storage/retrieval operations required to satisfy the study goals. One or more programmers will perform this important task. Analysis tools such as program flowcharts may be used at this time. The **program flowchart** evolves from the system flowchart: It's a detailed diagram showing how individual processing steps will be performed within the computer to convert the input data into the desired output. Chapter 18 deals with this process in detail.

The detailed input/output, calculation, logic/comparison, and storage/retrieval operations identified during the programming analysis stage provide the input for program preparation. One or more programmers convert the required operations into a program (or programs) of instructions written in a language and form acceptable to the computer hardware. Further details on this activity appear in Chapters 19 through 21 in the Programming Module.

### Step 6: Implementation and Maintenance

Courtesy Control Data Corporation.

After software selection and/or program preparation is complete, the new system must be checked for errors and tested before it can be used on a routine basis. When the software appears to be running properly, changeover is made. During this period, those who prepare input data and use output results must cooperate with the data processing specialists if the new system is to be successful. Resistance to change can cause many system implementation difficulties. Such resistance may be reduced when a people-oriented system study approach is followed. This topic will be considered again in the last three modules of the book.

Finally, systems and programs that have been successfully implemented are usually subject to continual change. Just as R-K's system might need to be modified and improved to meet changing conditions, so, too, must other systems continually be maintained. A first-class maintenance effort requires the cooperation of those people served by the system/program and those responsible for maintaining it. Of course, the need for a major change could trigger a new system study effort.

## Feedback and Review 3-1

You've seen in this short overview that computer hardware, by itself, doesn't solve a single business problem. It's people—both data processing specialists and operating department members—who put the computer to work. Hardware is merely one or more boxes of electronic parts. By working together during all phases of a system study, however, people can transform these boxes into an exciting tool whose use is limited only by human ingenuity and imagination. Test yourself by doing this puzzle.

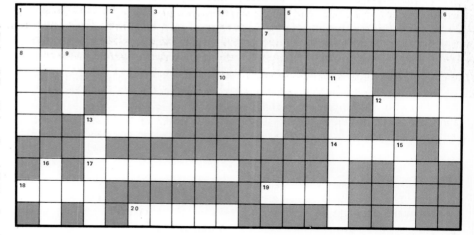

### Across

**1.** In a computer-based data processing system, computer hardware is just one of a _____ of integrated elements that have the common purpose of achieving some goal(s).

**3.** A system _____ is a step-by-step process to identify and then develop specific informational improvements in an organization.

**5.** A system flow- _____ is a diagram that shows a broad overview of the data flow and sequence of operations in a system.

**8.** Step number _____ in the system study process is the system analysis stage.

**10.** A systems _____ is an information specialist who is knowledgeable about the technical aspects of analyzing, designing, and implementing computer-based processing systems.

**12.** Step number _____ in the system study involves programming analysis.

**13.** The people on a system study _____ are often selected for the offsetting talents they can bring to the job.

**14.** In evaluating alternatives, system designers must constantly make tradeoffs because no alternative can be the _____ in every category of interest.

**17.** System difficulties can occur when people who prepare input data and use output results resist the use of new approaches. But this resistance may be _____ when a people-oriented system study approach is used.

**18.** Step number _____ in the system study involves program preparation.

**19.** A system flowchart can be a helpful analysis _____.

**20.** The same basic flowcharting symbol is used to represent both _____ and output.

### Down

**1.** The first job of the system study team during the system analysis stage is to _____ data about current processing operations.

**2.** The central and most important element in any computer-based system is _____.

**3.** Information users and data processing specialists must work together to complete a series of steps in a _____ study.

**4.** One element in a computer-based processing system is the input _____.

**6.** The _____ flowchart is a detailed diagram showing how each processing step will be performed within the computer.

**7.** In evaluating possible processing alternatives, system designers must constantly make _____ -offs.

**9.** Step number _____ in the system study is to define the problem or need.

**11.** Standard _____ are used in all flowcharts to clearly record and communicate information.

**13.** Step number _____ in the system study is the system design stage.

**15.** System design can be a challenging _____ because there are many factors that have a bearing on the design process.

**16.** Step number _____ in the system study process is to implement and then maintain the new approach.

# LOOKING BACK

**1.** Computer hardware is just one element in a broader data processing system that also includes input data, processing procedures, computer programs, and people.

**2.** The central and most important element in any computer-based system is people. It's people who put the computer to work. Some of these people are data processing specialists. But the contributions of many others in the organization who enter the data and use the output are essential to create and maintain a successful data processing system.

**3.** People are often motivated to introduce computer-based systems in order to deal with the changing operating conditions they face. Before a computer can be put to work, however, system users and data processing specialists must work together to complete a *system study*. The system study is a step-by-step process used to identify and develop specific informational improvements in an organization.

**4.** The first step in this study process is to define the problem or need. Next, a study team gathers and then analyzes data about current operations in a *system analysis* stage. A *system flowchart* is a diagram that shows a broad overview of the data flow and sequence of operations in a system. Such a flowchart is one of many data-gathering and analysis tools that may be used.

**5.** After the team has analyzed current procedures, the third step in the study approach is to design any new systems or applications that may be needed to satisfy the study goals. *System design* can be a challenging task because of the many fac-

tors that have a bearing on the design process. In evaluating design alternatives, system designers must constantly make tradeoffs. Higher processing costs, for example, may accompany design changes that offer the benefits of better control and greater accuracy.

**6.** Many people prefer to use existing software packages to put the computer to work whenever possible. The information gathered in the first three steps of a system study is generally needed before a suitable package can be identified and selected. If a satisfactory package can be purchased, the fourth and fifth steps in the system study process may be bypassed.

**7.** The specifications prepared during system design provide the input to the *programming analysis* stage—the fourth step in the system study process. The specific input/output, calculation, logic/comparison, and storage/retrieval operations required to satisfy the design specifications are established at this time.

**8.** These specific operations are then converted into one or more computer programs in the fifth stage, *program preparation*. The programs are written in a language and form acceptable to the computer hardware.

**9.** The final step in the study approach is to implement and maintain the new software packages and/or custom-made programs. These packages/programs must be checked for errors and tested before they are put to routine use. After implementation, they must be maintained to meet changing conditions.

## KEY TERMS AND CONCEPTS

software package 66
system study 66
systems analyst 66

system flowchart 69
system analysis 70
system design 70

programming analysis 72
program flowchart 72

## TOPICS FOR REVIEW AND DISCUSSION

**1.** *(a)* Identify five elements found in any computer-based data processing system. *(b)* Which of these elements plays a central role in the development and operation of such a system?

**2.** "The computer is usually at fault when a ridiculous bill is sent to a customer." Discuss this statement.

**3.** Why are people motivated to introduce new computer-based systems or to modify existing ones?

**4.** *(a)* What is a system study? *(b)* What is the first step in such a study?

**5.** "Since systems users may resist change, data processing specialists should be in charge of all phases of a system study." Discuss this statement.

**6.** "The people on a system study team are often selected for the offsetting talents they can bring to the job." Discuss the talents that may be needed.

**7.** *(a)* What is a system flowchart? *(b)* For what purpose is it used?

**8.** Explain the difference between system analysis and system design.

**9.** *(a)* What questions might the study team consider during the system analysis stage? *(b)* During the system design stage?

**10.** "System design can be challenging because there are many considerations that have a bearing on the design process." What are three such considerations?

**11.** "No alternative system design can be the best in every category." Discuss this statement.

**12.** *(a)* What is programming analysis? *(b)* What is a program flowchart?

**13.** *(a)* What is the purpose of the program preparation stage? *(b)* Of the implementation and maintenance stage?

**14.** "Organizations and individuals may be able to bypass some steps in a system study if software packages are available that meet their needs." Discuss this statement.

## PROJECTS TO LOOK INTO

**1.** Chances are your favorite magazines and newspapers contain many conflicting articles describing the work done by computers. Cartoons and movies also present different views about computer output. Write a report that identifies three of the ways that people view computers in our society.

**2.** Visit an organization (a business, your school's administrative offices, a hospital, a government agency) and ask about the system changes that have recently been implemented. Write a report to present your findings. If possible, use a flowchart to illustrate the implemented system.

## ANSWERS TO FEEDBACK AND REVIEW SECTION

**3-1**

| ¹G | R | O | U | ²P | | ³S | T | U | ⁴D | Y | | ⁵C | H | A | R | T | | | ⁶P |
| A | | | | E | | Y | | | A | | ⁷T | | | | | | | | R |
| ⁸T | W | ⁹O | | O | | S | | | T | | R | | | | | | | | O |
| H | | N | | P | | T | | ¹⁰A | N | A | L | Y | ¹¹S | T | | | | | G |
| E | | E | | L | | E | | | D | | | | Y | | ¹²F | O | U | | R |
| R | | | ¹³T | E | A | M | | | E | | | | M | | | | | | A |
| | | | H | | | | | | | | | ¹⁴B | E | S | ¹⁵T | | M |
| | ¹⁶S | | ¹⁷R | E | D | U | C | E | D | | | | O | | | A | | |
| ¹⁸F | I | V | E | | | | | | | ¹⁹T | O | O | L | | | S | | |
| | X | | E | | ²⁰I | N | P | U | T | | | | S | | | K | | |

# A Closer Look

# IBM's Information Center

In 1973, IBM Canada in Toronto dedicated several systems analysts to go into the user community to help users write reports rather than having them march through the regular systems function. By 1974, this operation was named an "information center," an idea ready to spread across Canada and south of the border.

"Our stated goal at the beginning," said Gwen Warlow, the information center manager, "was to provide education, consultation, minimal environment support and problem resolution. We were trying to assist our users to become self-sufficient, that's always been our goal. That user self-sufficiency goal has not changed, but some of the subsets under it have. We've grown and deepened our involvement with user planning, resource management and office systems. We work with users much more, help them with any of their personal computing needs."

Two thousand regular end users are served by the information staff of 25.

"We're looking at a broader user population now," Warlow said. "Initially, we had people who had learned tools and coded for themselves. Later on, there were users who were prepared to work with tools and could make extracts and reports for themselves. Now many people are using menus and program function keys only. They want things programmed for them."

Warlow's background is in marketing and administration in information systems. Her staff includes some from marketing, some from information systems and others from customer service.

"I think the information center works best under information systems," she said. "I think of information systems as neutral, not in finance, administration, marketing or customer service."

Warlow believes the information center has improved the overall quality of projects submitted to systems development because end users are more sophisticated. "Now that they know how to use the tools, they are more realistic about the system they want," she said.

"Before, they would put a request in and prepare to go through the enhancement cycle. Now they build what they want right into the original request. They count on using end-user tools. The information center has achieved that."

—"Information Centers," *Computerworld,* Dec. 26, 1983/Jan. 2, 1984, p. 73. Copyright 1984 by CW Communications, Inc., Framingham, Mass.

Effective implementation of the information center concept may aid the effective use of microcomputers within organizations. (Photo courtesy Hewlett-Packard Company)

## chapter 4

# The Impact of Computers at Work
## a preview

### Computers Unnerve Americans

Pollster Louis Harris warned Congress recently that while 45% of adult Americans claim to know how to use a computer, a big majority—77%—are worried about threats that computers pose to their privacy.

These fears about privacy have grown substantially in the last five years, as the use of computers to maintain credit card accounts, monitor loans and administer credit has grown, Harris told the House Subcommittee on Government Information April 4.

"By a massive 84% to 15%, most people are convinced that it would be easy—no problem at all—to put together a file on them that contains their credit information, employment records, phone calls, where they have lived over the past 10 years, their buying habits, their payment records on debts and the trips they've taken," he said.

Harris said that the poll he took . . . showed that people fear institutions that possess personal information do not treat it confidentially and are inclined to share it with other institutions.

According to Harris, the public favors the enactment of laws by Congress to regulate the future use of computers. "This indicates once again that the people, in recognizing that restrictions on the use of computers are an important objective, are well ahead of their leaders in the precious subject of freedom and privacy in an open society."

Harris characterized the results of the poll as "startling, to say the least. They must be taken as a warning shot across the bow of the establishment in this country that the people are in a no-nonsense mood about the vast and sweeping changes they see coming."

Computer technology and computer usage are making an impact on people and organizations throughout our society. In this chapter, we'll first look at some of the advances in computer technology that are causing significant social change. We'll then discuss some of the positive and negative effects that computer-driven change is having on people and organizations. The information in this chapter will enable you to:

- Explain the advances in computer technology that are contributing to an information revolution

- Discuss the impact that computer usage may have on each of us

- Describe the impact that computer usage may have on the organizations that function in our society

# THE TECHNOLOGICAL UNDERPINNINGS

You've seen a few examples of what computers can do in Chapter 2. But it's not enough just to be familiar with a few specific applications. You should also be aware of the broad impact that computer usage is having on society right now.

In the eighteenth century, the development of the steam engine encouraged the use of large-scale factory production facilities as replacements for cottage industries, or home manufacturing units. An *industrial revolution* followed this harnessing of steam power. In the past few years, developments in computer technology have acquired a force and significance comparable to that of the steam engine. And our society is now in the throes of an **information revolution** that has been brought on by these advances in computer technology. The steam-powered industrial revolution removed many tedious tasks from human muscles, produced huge gains in productivity, and brought significant social and economic changes to the world.

## Chapter Outline

| Hardware Development Factors | 1950 | 1960 | 1970 | 1975 | 1980's |
|---|---|---|---|---|---|
| **Size factor** — Number of circuits per cubic foot | 1,000 | 100,000 | 10 million | 1 billion | Many billions |
| **Speed factor** — Time to execute an instruction in the central processor | 300 microseconds | 5 microseconds | 80 nanoseconds | 25 nanoseconds | 5 nanoseconds or less |
| **Cost factors** — Cost (in cents) to process 1 million basic computer instructions | 2,800 | 100 | 2 | .1 | Less than .01 |
| Cost (in cents) to provide storage for one binary number in the central processor | 261 | 85 | 5 | .1 | Less than .01 |
| **Storage capacity factors** — Primary storage capacity (in characters) of the central processor | 20,000 | 120,000 | 1 million | 10 million | Greater than 100 million |
| Characters of secondary online storage | | 20 million | Over 100 billion | Virtually unlimited | Virtually unlimited |
| **Reliability factor** — Mean (average) time between failures of some central processors | Hours | Tens of hours | Hundreds of hours | Thousands of hours | Years |

**Figure 4-1** A summary of hardware advances.

Today's computer-powered information revolution is removing burdens of drudgery from human brains, producing further gains in productivity, and bringing about significant changes in employment, competition, and social attitudes.

You'll find a brief outline of the impact that computer usage may have on individuals and organizations later in this chapter. Further discussion is left to the chapters in the Social Impact Module. Before examining these computer-usage effects, though, we should first pause and consider the cause. That is, we should consider the technological developments that underlie the information revolution. Let's begin with the rapid advances which are occurring in computer *hardware, software,* and *information systems technology.*

**Hardware Advances**   Figure 4-1 summarizes the gains that have been made in computer hardware. As you can see, there have been dramatic reductions in computer *size.* A number of separate electronic components such as transistors and diodes are combined to form computer circuits. Thousands of these circuits are now integrated and packaged on a single **silicon chip** (Figure 4-2) that measures perhaps a quarter of an inch square. Since the average number of chip components has doubled each year since 1965, it's now possible through such **large-scale integration** (LSI) to squeeze billions of

**Figure 4-2** A silicon chip rests on a dime with plenty of room to spare. (Reprinted with permission from Motorola, Inc.)

circuits into a cubic foot of space. Nor is there any end in sight to these size reductions. Just as yesterday's room-sized computers have been replaced by today's single LSI chips, so will the multiple boards that make up a large computer today be replaced in the next decade by a single *superchip*. Through the use of **very large-scale integration** (VLSI) techniques, tomorrow's circuits will be many times more compact than those in use now. For example, the chip that now stores over 256,000 bits of information is made up of a half-million electronic devices. By the early 1990s, however, it's expected that there will be 15 to 20 million devices on a similar chip.

As the size of computers has been reduced, their operating *speed* has increased (see Figure 4-1). In part, this is because size reduction means shorter distances for electric pulses to travel. Figure 4-1 also shows some of the incredible *cost* reductions associated with computer usage. If automobile costs and technological developments had matched the trends in computer hardware, you would now be able to buy a Rolls-Royce for $2.75, and you could drive it 3 million miles on a gallon of gas. The cost as well as the size of many basic computer components will continue to decline in the future while their speed increases. Cheaper, smaller, and more powerful computers will cause significant social change. Marvelous tools and gadgets will be built, and communications facilities and leisure activities will be affected. But employment disturbances and organizational stress may also occur.

Finally, Figure 4-1 gives you an idea of what has happened to computer *storage capacity* and *reliability* in the last few decades. The storage capacity of both primary and online secondary storage units has increased thousands of times over the years. And the early computers that used to break down every few hours have been replaced by processors that can run for years without failure. Some modern processors have self-diagnostic circuitry built within them to monitor hardware operations and pinpoint the cause of any failure that may occur. **Self-repairing computers** were designed in the 1970s for the unmanned space missions that last many years (Figure 4-3). These space computers have built-in spare parts that can automatically take over the tasks of any original components that fail during the mission. The concept of self-repair has now been applied to some commercial computers. Vital components—e.g., circuit chips—are duplicated in these systems. Some components are used for processing immediately, while others serve as standby spares. A failure occurring in a chip is detected by a status-sensing device, and the chip is electronically and automatically replaced with its spare.

## Software Advances

Significant gains have also been made in the development of computer software. In the early 1950s, computer programmers had to write their problem-solving program instructions in the special machine code numbers that computer circuits can recognize (e.g., the number 21 might mean "add"). These strings of numbers were tedious to prepare, and they often contained errors. Special **programming languages** were then developed to permit the programmer to write instructions in a form easier for humans to understand. For example, a language might permit the word ADD or the plus (**+**) symbol to be used in place of the number 21. Unfortunately, the computer's circuitry only recognizes the number 21 as the instruction to add.

Figure 4-3 Possible variations in chemical composition from one part of Saturn's ring system to another are visible in this Voyager 2 picture which shows subtle variations that can be recorded with special computer-processing techniques. This highly enhanced color view was transmitted from a distance of 5.5 million miles. (Photo courtesy National Aeronautics and Space Administration)

How, then, can the machine execute instructions if they are in a language it cannot understand? Just as an American and a German can communicate if one of them uses a translating dictionary, so too can the programmer and computer communicate if a separate translation program is employed. A **translation program** is one that transforms the instructions prepared by people using a convenient language into the machine language codes required by computers. Almost all problem-solving programs prepared today are first written in languages preferred by people and are then translated by special software or hardware into the equivalent machine codes. (The translating process will be discussed in detail in Chapter 19 of the Programming Module.) The impact that computers are having on society today is due in no small measure to this easing of human-machine communication.

Another factor that's contributing to increased computer usage is the greater availability of applications programs. An **application program** is one that has been written to control the processing of a particular task. Although many applications programs must be custom-made for unique jobs, there are thousands of widely used applications—ranging from business functions to games—for which generalized programs may be written. Computer users may now choose from tens of thousands of these types of prewritten software packages (also called **applications packages** or **packaged programs**) offered by equipment manufacturers and independent software firms. Packaged programs for personal computers may also be found at thousands of retail computer stores and other retail outlets (Figure 4-4).

Most packages for personal computers and larger machines perform *single* functions (examples are word processing,—see Figure 2-14, page 57—the management of online data files, or the processing of accounting records). Since running these prewritten programs isn't nearly as painstaking as writing them, many people have found that a careful selection of available single-function programs has helped in their conversion to computer usage.

Figure 4-4 Computer retailers are well stocked both with hardware and with the packaged programs which make micro-computers an increasingly useful tool. (Photo courtesy ComputerLand)

▶

Figure 4-5 (a) Text of a sales report prepared with a word processing program. (b) Sales data and formulas are entered by the user, and the spreadsheet program calculates the "year total" column and the "Qtr. Total" row. (c) A graphics software program can use the results produced by the spreadsheet program to generate pie charts, bar charts, and other easy-to-understand graphic presentations. (d) The screen can be separated into windows to permit the simultaneous display of the output produced by different programs in the integrated software package. (e) Printout of the completed report.

In addition to single-function programs, more and more software products are now appearing that integrate *several* functions in a single package. Among the popular **integrated software packages** available to users of personal computers are the Lotus 1-2-3 (Lotus Development Corporation), Context MBA (Context Management Systems), VisiOn (VisiCorp), the Lisa software (Apple Computer, Inc.), and Microsoft Windows (Microsoft Corp.). These integrated packages make it possible to share data and move material among several applications.

For example, a manager can write and display the text of a sales report using the word processing program in the integrated package (Figure 4-5a). Sales data organized in columns and rows can be manipulated and analyzed by the use of the package's electronic worksheet or **spreadsheet program,** and the desired results can also be displayed (Figure 4-5b). A graphics program in the package can also use spreadsheet data to produce appropriate sales charts which are then displayed (Figure 4-5c). Furthermore, the current status of each application of interest can be shown *simultaneously* in separate **windows** or portions of the visual display screen as shown in Figure 4-5d. Since it's possible to copy information from window to window, the manager can move the desired figures and drawings from the spreadsheet and graphics windows to designated locations in the text window. A hard copy of the assembled report may then be printed (Figure 4-5e).

In addition to the advances made in translation programs and applications packages, a third factor that has helped increase computer productivity and has thus contributed to a greater use of computers in society is the use of operating system programs. An **operating system** (OS) is an organized collection of software that controls the overall operation of a computer. The OS was initially a set of programs designed to help computer operators perform such "housekeeping" tasks as erasing the contents of CPU storage locations after the completion of a job and then loading the next program into the program storage area from an input device. Since the computer could do these tasks quickly, both human and machine time was saved. The objective of a current OS is still to operate the computer with a minimum of idle time during the processing of jobs, but the OS software is now much more complex. A further discussion of the functions of a modern OS will be presented in the Systems and Software Module, Chapter 13.

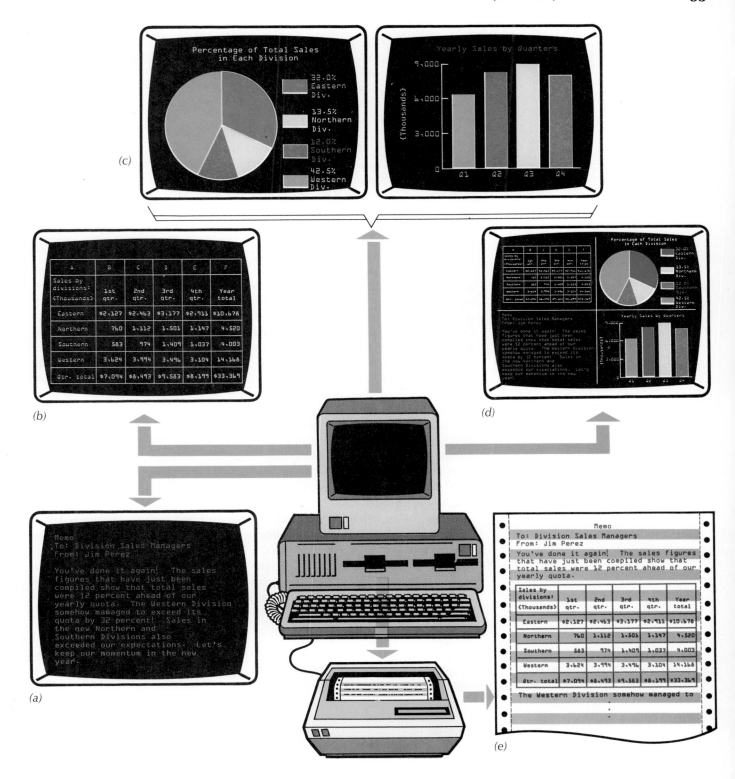

(a)

(b)

(c)

(d)

(e)

**Advances in Information Systems**

We need information to organize our vacation activities, plan meals, make intelligent purchases, vote for a candidate, select a factory location, pick an investment, and study for a test. In short, information is power: It's needed every day by decision makers—all of us—both in our private lives and in our occupations. Information that is accurate, timely, and complete should improve the quality of our decisions. If our information does not possess these characteristics, however, the quality of our decisions may suffer.

Information systems have existed in organizations for centuries. But these traditional systems often supplied information that was inaccurate, out of date, or incomplete. Historians tell us, for example, that if the data that were available in bits and pieces at scattered points had been assembled in a timely manner in the early days of December 1941, the United States would have been prepared for the Japanese attack on Pearl Harbor. It's not surprising, then, that newer computer-based concepts have been designed and developed to improve information system performance. These new concepts may be characterized as being quicker responding and broader in scope than traditional systems.

Many **quick-response systems** have been developed to increase the timeliness and availability of information. You've seen examples of how savings associations, airlines, and other organizations use direct-access processing techniques to provide up-to-the-minute information to inquiry stations. These stations may be near the CPU, or there may be a **distributed network** of stations located at many distant points. Some quick-response systems are also taking a *broader data base approach* to provide information that's more complete and relevant. In this approach, the system is designed around a collection of logically related data elements (the data base) that is maintained in a direct-access storage device. Data elements are introduced into the system only once and are then available as needed to all users of the data base. With the proper software to select and process the necessary data elements, a decision maker at an online terminal can use the data base system to search and query file contents in order to extract answers to nonrecurring and unplanned questions that are not covered by regular reports. Increasingly, the "online terminal" used by decision makers is a personal computer that can be used to retrieve facts from a personal or an organizational data base. The decision maker then uses microcomputer applications packages to manipulate and analyze the retrieved data. Many organizations are now attempting to integrate personal computers into their larger computer system environments.

Further discussions about quick-response and data base systems are presented in the Hardware and Systems and Software Modules. As you'll see in the next sections, their use can have an impact on individuals as well as on the organizations that use them.

# THE IMPACT OF COMPUTERS ON PEOPLE

The technological advances just presented have made the computer one of the most powerful forces in society today. They've made it possible for computer usage to spread into homes and organizations of all sizes. No one can doubt that the use of computers has had a strong impact on many people. But the computer is the driving force behind an information revolution, and as in any revolution some innocent people may be harmed. Let's briefly outline here some of the positive and negative effects that computer usage may have on individuals. (The chapters in the Social Impact Module deal with this topic in greater detail.)

### Positive Implications

People may benefit from computers in many ways. Among the benefits are the following:

Figure 4-6 Robots at work on an automated assembly line. Workers can control productivity at a safe, comfortable distance from the factory floor. (© Dick Durrance II/Woodfin Camp & Associates)

Figure 4-7 Making friends with the computer at school: This computer-based system is designed to help students develop their reading and writing skills. (Photo courtesy International Business Machines Corporation)

1. *New job opportunities.* Hundreds of thousands of new jobs have been created in such areas as programming, computer operations, and information systems management. Current demand for persons qualified for these jobs exceeds the current supply.

2. *Greater job satisfaction.* Scientists and engineers can tackle interesting problems that they could not have considered without computer help. And lawyers, teachers, clerical workers, and others can turn over repetitive and boring tasks to computer processing and then concentrate on the more challenging aspects of their work.

3. *Use by businesses.* The use of computers by businesses to avoid waste and improve efficiency may result in lower product prices and/or better service to individuals. In addition, the computer-controlled **robots,** shown in Figure 4-6, along with other automated tools, can precisely carry out the dreary, dirty, and dangerous tasks that cause worker discontent. The net result of using these machines may be to improve the quality of the products assembled and sold to customers. Finally, computer-controlled products built by commercial firms can contribute to improved personal safety and can provide aid to the handicapped. Computer-controlled aircraft braking systems improve passenger safety, and to aid the sightless, computer-controlled reading machines are available that will read printed material and produce the corresponding speech sounds.

4. *Use by public organizations.* Avoiding waste and improving efficiency in government agencies, school districts, and hospital units can also result in better service and a reduced tax burden for citizens. Without computers, for example, the Social Security Administration could not keep up with the payment of benefits to widows, orphans, and retired persons. The quality of education can be improved by the use of games, simulations, and computer-assisted instruction techniques (Figure 4-7). And better personal health may result from a hospital's use of computers to provide better control of laboratory tests.

5. *Use in the home.* Millions of microcomputers have been acquired for home use (see box). Such personal systems are used for entertainment and hobby purposes, for educational uses, for family financial applications, and for countless other tasks. The benefits of **personal computing** are limited only by human ingenuity and imagination.

## BANKING ON PERSONAL COMPUTERS

Impressed by the increasing number of customers owning personal computers, Chemical Bank in New York and Bank of America in San Francisco are now offering a special service: banking by personal computer. Customers who have computers and modems can call the banks and use their computers to check on accounts, transfer funds from one account to another, and even pay bills.

Chemical Bank's service, called Pronto, has been available to New York metropolitan area bank customers since September 1983. Bank of America's HomeBanking service has been operating in Northern California since November 1983. . . .

Like HomeBanking, Chemical Bank's Pronto system—which costs $12 per month [versus $8 monthly for HomeBanking]—hooks up through Tymnet. Users must also have a modem and a push-button phone. But unlike HomeBanking, Pronto uses special software, designed to ease log-on procedures and improve security.

Sergio Sedita, a vice-president at Chemical, says, "The aim was to make the system very user-friendly and secure." Through use of the software disk, some log-on procedures are eliminated. To hook up with the bank, the Pronto customer enters the local Tymnet number of the disk, which then dials Tymnet automatically. The customer enters the identification numbers for the bank, and then the software takes over to complete the hookup.

Once hooked up with the bank, the customer gets into his account by using the disk's identification codes, which include a six-digit number unique to the customer and not known by the bank. The customer inputs the number into the software himself, and for increased security, the number never appears on the customer's screen.

Pronto customers can transfer funds, check account balances, do home budgeting, and send electronic mail to the bank or to other Pronto customers. As with HomeBanking, customers can also pay bills.

—"Banking on Personal Computers." Reprinted with permission from *Personal Computing*, April 1984, pp. 45 and 47. Copyright 1984. Photo courtesy Chemical Bank.

**Potential Problems**   In spite of the countless benefits that people receive from computer usage, such usage can also lead to potential dangers and problems. Some of these problem areas are:

1. *The threat of unemployment.* The greater efficiency made possible by computer usage can result in job obsolescence and displacement for some workers. For example, the computer-controlled robots pictured earlier can sense the need for a specified task, and can then take the actions necessary to perform the task. In the auto manufacturing and supply industries alone, it's expected that tens of thousands of jobs will be eliminated by robots during the 1980s.

2. *The use of questionable data processing practices.* Input data about individuals are routinely captured by many organizations and entered into

computer-processed files. In some cases, these facts have been compiled by those who have no valid reason to gather them. In other cases, inaccurate and incomplete data about people have been placed in computer system files. Finally, human errors in preparing input data and in designing and preparing programs have resulted in system miscalculations that have harmed people.

3. ***The trend toward depersonalization.*** In most computer-based systems, the record key used to identify a person is a number—e.g., a social security, student, employee, or credit customer number. As people have come into contact with more computer systems, they have been identified by more numerical codes. Although many understand that being treated as a number results in efficient computer processing, they would prefer that systems be designed so that they are treated as persons rather than numbers.

4. ***The systems security issue.*** The lack of control over data security in a computer system has resulted in the destruction of an individual's records in some cases. The lack of control has also led to the accidental or intentional disclosure to unauthorized persons of confidential information of a very personal nature. Clever individuals have had no difficulty in the past in breaking through the security provisions of online computer systems in order to gain direct access to this confidential information. For example, a gang of Milwaukee teenagers was able to gain access into over 50 systems, including one at the Los Alamos Scientific Laboratory.

5. ***The privacy issue.*** Lack of control over data storage, retrieval, and communication has led to abuses of a person's legitimate **right to privacy**— i.e., the right to keep private (or have kept on a confidential basis) those facts, beliefs, and feelings which one does not wish to publicly reveal. In at least one state, the records of patients hospitalized for psychiatric treatment were sent to the Department of Mental Health—and were then made available to insurance companies, police departments, the motor vehicle department, and all other licensing agencies.

# THE IMPACT OF COMPUTERS ON ORGANIZATIONS

After noting that ''The world is too much with us, late and soon,'' William Wordsworth took a stroll along a sandy beach to calm his ruffled sensibilities. What he could not know was that tiny silicon chips made from the sand he was walking on would cause feverish activity 200 years later. These chips have dropped into our midst like small stones into a lake, but they are causing waves rather than ripples! And the waves caused by computers are having both positive and negative effects on the organizations that use them. A few of these effects are outlined below. (The chapters in the Social Impact Module provide further information on these effects.)

**Positive Implications**     We've seen that organizations may benefit from computers. Those benefits include the following:

1. *Better planning and decision making.* **Planning** is deciding in advance on a future course of action. Computer-based information systems that are quicker-responding and broader in scope than those previously available can have a positive impact on the planning and decision making that occurs in a business or nonprofit organization. Planning can be improved with the help of information systems that quickly notify managers of problems and opportunities. These same systems can then be used by managers to evaluate many alternative solutions and to then implement the final choice. Many of these systems cross national boundaries to link together the units of multinational organizations.

2. *Better control of resources.* **Control** is a follow-up to planning. It's the check on performance to see if planned goals are being achieved. Computer systems can be used to measure actual performance levels, compare these levels against planned standards, and then carry out preprogrammed decisions. For example, in an inventory control application the program can determine the current inventory level of a basic item, compare this level against a minimum acceptable quantity, and then produce an output reorder message when the quantity drops below the desired level.

3. *Greater efficiency of operations.* You've seen how greater efficiency may benefit individuals. But greater efficiency resulting from computer usage also benefits organizations. In addition to realizing operating efficiencies through their use of computerized reservation systems, American and United Airlines have also gained a larger share of the market by permitting travel agents to tap into their systems. Banks and other financial institutions have improved their operating efficiency by using computers for the electronic transfer of money on a national and international scale. And supermarkets and other retailing outlets use automated checkout stations to improve efficiency (Figure 4-8). These stations read the special codes and symbols attached to products and then transmit the coded data to a computer. The computer looks up prices, possibly updates inventory and sales records, and then forwards prices and description information back to the stations. Computer systems are also used to save energy and improve the efficiency of heating and cooling offices, factories, hospitals, and schools. Without a strong commitment to improve efficiency through computer usage, many businesses will be unable in the future to successfully compete with foreign firms in national and world markets.

Figure 4-8 An automated checkout station in a supermarket. (Courtesy NCR Corporation)

**Potential Problems**     The following brief listing identifies some of the challenges that computer-using organizations may face:

1. *The problems in information system design.* The design of new computer-based information systems can be a very complex and challenging task. In some cases, past designs have produced disappointing internal results and a bad public image for the sponsoring organizations.

2. ***The system security issue.*** The failure to secure the information systems being used has threatened organizations as well as individuals. Assets have been stolen from organizations through system manipulation. Secrets have been copied and sold to competitors. And systems penetrators have repeatedly broken through the existing security controls of large direct-access systems to gain access to sensitive information. Furthermore, as personal computers proliferate in organizations there's the fear that when these units are linked with larger systems the security and accuracy of the organization's valuable data bases will be placed in further jeopardy.

3. ***The challenge to organizational structure.*** When new computer systems are introduced, work groups in an organization may be created, disbanded, or realigned. Existing departments may be added to or eliminated. Such changes can lead to employee resistance and organizational stress.

4. ***The access to information issue.*** Organizations with limited computing resources may have more difficulty competing against organizations with much greater sophistication in the use of computers. For example, competitors believe that by offering their reservation systems to travel agents American and United have an unfair advantage because the availability of the two airlines' flights is displayed most prominently on the agents' terminals. Industry regulators are now looking into this issue.

## Feedback and Review 4-1

The preceding pages have provided you with a basic understanding of the technological advances that underlie the information revolution and the effects these developments can have on individuals and organizations. The scrambled words format used below will test and reinforce your understanding of these topics. Rearrange the letters to spell out the correct word for the space indicated in the sentence.

**1.** An industrial revolution began in the eighteenth century with the harnessing of _____ power, and society is now in the throes of an information revolution that has been brought on by advances in computer technology.

Ⓜ Ⓣ Ⓢ Ⓔ Ⓐ

**2.** Thousands of computer circuits are now integrated and packaged on tiny chips of _____.

Ⓛ Ⓘ Ⓞ Ⓝ Ⓢ Ⓘ Ⓒ

**3.** It's expected that the large computer of today may be replaced by a _____ superchip in the next decade.

Ⓝ Ⓘ Ⓢ Ⓔ Ⓛ Ⓖ

**4.** A translation program is one that transforms the instructions prepared by people using a convenient programming language into the machine language _____ required by computers.

Ⓞ Ⓢ Ⓔ Ⓒ Ⓓ

**5.** Computer users may now obtain thousands of generalized _____ programs for widely used applications from equipment vendors and independent software firms.

Ⓖ Ⓐ Ⓔ Ⓒ Ⓚ Ⓟ Ⓐ Ⓓ

**6.** An _____ system is a collection of software that controls the overall operation of a computer.

Ⓣ Ⓡ Ⓐ Ⓞ Ⓘ Ⓔ Ⓟ Ⓖ Ⓝ

**7.** A system using direct-access processing techniques is an example of a _____-response system.

Ⓒ Ⓤ Ⓘ Ⓚ Ⓠ

**8.** Some information systems are taking a broader _____-_____ approach to provide information that's more complete and relevant.

Ⓐ Ⓣ Ⓓ Ⓐ    Ⓐ Ⓑ Ⓔ Ⓢ

**9.** Computer-controlled _____ and other automated tools can be used to improve the quality of the products assembled and sold to individuals.

Ⓑ Ⓞ Ⓡ Ⓣ Ⓞ Ⓢ

**10.** Lack of control over data storage, retrieval, and communication has led to abuses of a person's legitimate right to _____.

Ⓡ Ⓟ Ⓨ Ⓐ Ⓘ Ⓥ Ⓒ

# A RECAP OF THIS BACKGROUND MODULE

You've come a long way in just four chapters. In Chapter 1, you were introduced to the computer itself. You saw that it's a very fast and accurate machine with the ability to handle input/output, calculation, logic/comparison, and storage/retrieval operations. You saw the types of hardware components that are organized to make up a working computer system. You saw how a detailed set of instructions could be stored within the CPU to cause it to accept input data and produce the desired output results. And you saw that computer systems can differ widely in size and design and that they are subject to certain limitations.

In Chapter 2, you gained a better understanding of what computers actually do. You saw how data are organized for computer processing, and many examples showed you how computer systems process the most common business applications.

In Chapter 3, you saw that a computer is but one element in a broader data processing system. It's only through the efforts of people that a computer is able to do anything at all. By completing a series of steps in a system study to produce new applications programs, or by locating prewritten applications packages that meet specific needs, people are able to put the computer to work doing useful tasks.

Finally, in this chapter you've learned that what computers do has a profound impact on the people and organizations in a society. Because you've learned all this, you're not restricted now to following all the remaining chapters in sequence. Instead, with the background you now have, you can turn immediately to the first chapter of *any* of the remaining four modules in this book (Figure 4-9). Each of these remaining modules builds on what you've already learned.

**Figure 4-9** How *Computers Today* is organized. You are now ready to turn to the first chapter of any of the four remaining modules.

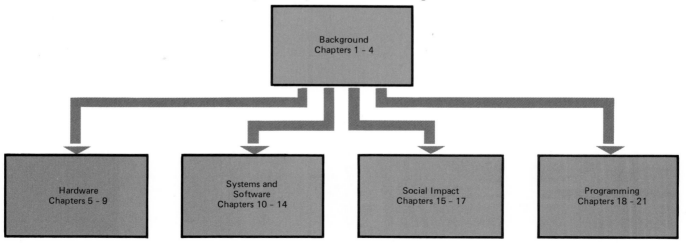

## LOOKING BACK

**1.** It's not enough just to be familiar with hardware, software, and applications concepts. You should also be aware of the impact that computer usage is having on society today. The rapid advances occurring in computer hardware, software, and information systems technology underlie the *information revolution* that's now under way.

**2.** There have been dramatic reductions in the size and cost of computer components and equally impressive gains in the speed, storage capacity, and reliability of these same components. In the software area, advances have occurred in the development of *programming languages* and *translation programs*. Thousands of *applications packages* are now readily available. And *operating system programs* have helped increase computer system productivity. Finally, information systems that are quicker responding and broader in scope have been designed to give decision makers information that is timely and complete.

**3.** These hardware, software, and systems advances have made the computer one of the most powerful forces in society. Computer usage has spread into homes and into organizational units of all sizes. As the last few pages of this chapter indicate, the impact of this spread of computer usage has both positive and negative effects for individuals and organizations.

## KEY TERMS AND CONCEPTS

**information revolution** 78
**silicon chip** 79
**large-scale integration (LSI)** 79
**very large-scale integration (VLSI)** 80
**self-repairing computers** 80
**programming languages** 80

**translation program** 81
**applications program/package** 81
**integrated software packages** 82
**spreadsheet program** 82
**windows** 82
**operating system (OS)** 82
**quick-response system** 84

**distributed network** 84
**robots** 85
**personal computing** 85
**right to privacy** 87
**planning** 88
**control** 88

## TOPICS FOR REVIEW AND DISCUSSION

**1.** "Society is now in the throes of an information revolution that has been brought on by advances in computer technology." Discuss the advances in *(a)* hardware, *(b)* software, and *(c)* information systems that underlie this information revolution.

**2.** *(a)* Discuss four ways that individuals may benefit from computer usage. *(b)* Identify four ways in which computer usage may have negative effects on people.

**3.** *(a)* Identify two ways that organizations may benefit from computer usage. *(b)* Discuss two challenges that computer-using organizations may face.

**4.** On the night of the 1980 presidential election, computer-aided projections based on models of "key precincts" were used by television announcers to declare President Reagan the winner. Only 1 percent of the vote had actually been counted, and the polls were still open in the western states. (In fact, Jimmy Carter made his television concession speech before the polls had closed on the West Coast.) How do you view this use of computers?

**5.** The following account is found on page 94 of the August 22, 1983, issue of *Business Week:*

> Few financial service companies are planning an information management system as comprehensive as Sears'. Using information as a weapon is the backbone of the No. 1 retailer's strategy to become the leader in consumer financial services. The company employs computerized information on its 40 million retail customers to reach such targeted groups as appliance buyers, gardening enthusiasts, and mothers-to-be. Sears plans to use the same data to provide sales leads to other subsidiaries—including Allstate Insurance, brokerage house Dean Witter Reynolds, and real estate brokers Coldwell Banker. "The core of Sears customers is a tremendous source that we can now tap for the [other businesses]," says Donald F. Craib Jr., chairman of the Allstate Group.

> *(a)* What impact do you think such plans will have on individuals? *(b)* On other organizations?

## PROJECT TO LOOK INTO

**1.** Articles reporting new developments in computer technology appear daily in magazines and newspapers. Select a topic from the following list and locate three recent articles that deal with your subject. Bring your articles to class and be prepared to summarize their contents.

*Topic List:* the information revolution; developments in integrated circuits; computer hardware advances; computer software developments; advances in information systems; ways that people benefit from computer usage; problems that people encounter because of computer usage; the impact of computers on organizations.

## ANSWERS TO FEEDBACK AND REVIEW SECTION

**4-1**
1. steam
2. silicon
3. single
4. codes
5. packaged
6. operating
7. quick
8. data-base
9. robots
10. privacy

# The 'Whatchamacallit'

Talk about dreams coming true—and happy ones to boot. Before our very eyes, the TV set, the hi-fi, the movie camera, the videocassette recorder, the telephone, the typewriter and the personal computer are fast becoming components of an integrated personal multipurpose thing, which—for lack of a better name—we can call the "watchamacallit."

Thus, our need to acquire the whatchamacallit's components as discrete consumer items is diminishing; and as our whatchamacallit's capabilities improve, so will our needs diminish for such items as desk calculators, still cameras, voice-recording telephone answering machines, ham radio equipment—all the electronic doodads you can think of.

Other tried-and-true gadgetry are to see immediate obsolescence, as though swept away in a tidal wave of replacement technology; electrical light switches, electric outlets, cable connectors and other such physical devices are disappearing. . . .

It's fascinating that as the whatchamacallit is taking shape in microland, mammoth macroland computer/communications systems are being developed. These Integrated Services Digital Networks (ISDN) are impersonal multipurpose things that will nourish and be nourished by our whatachamacallits.

The ISDN suggests the vision of a computer system so large it possesses electronic broadcast and cables "buses" to pipeline data swiftly coast to coast, while servicing massive clusters of systems en route—"transistors," warehouse-size lattices of high-voltage gear and "capacitors" office-building size. These further inspire a vision of America as a giant computer room, with corners in Seattle, Los Angeles, Miami and Boston.

Vested in each ISDN may be the power of a billion personal computers.

While this idea is knee weakening, the knowledge that these awe-inspiring titans will serve to nourish our little personal whatchamacallits—sending them their life's blood, data, and converting this into every conceivable use—is beautiful and offers great promise for improving the quality of our lives. Access to the massive external facilities, with their enormous power and memory capacities, allows us to enjoy the powers that computer systems provide as mixtures of that possible within our whatchamacallit's local environment, and that found in the ISDNS. . . .

Consider, for example, the possibility of the heretofore unimaginable luxury of a personal videostation, capable of communicating pictures, sound and text anywhere in the world—a personal National Aeronautics and Space Administration-like mission control for the orbit of your life.

Possessing all manner of sensing devices to obtain signals from alarm to video and anything in between, capable of processing these and displaying results in user-friendly media, the terminal of the decades ahead will provide users with creative opportunities of mind-boggling proportions.

The technically inclined will revel in the possibilities this kind of environment allows for tinkering, and the entertainment seeker will have his hedonistic wishes fulfilled and then some.

—Charles P. Lecht, "The 'Whatchamacallit,'" *Computerworld*, Mar. 19, 1984, p. 5. Reproduced with the permission of Charles P. Lecht, Lecht Sciences, Inc.

# Hardware

# module 2

In the Background Module you were introduced to the computer itself. You saw that the key elements in the basic organization of a computer system include input, central processing, and output devices.

The purpose of this module is to examine these hardware devices in greater detail and to consider some other related topics. The chapters included in this Hardware Module are:

5. Central Processor Concepts, Codes, and Components
6. Data Entry
7. Secondary Storage and Output
8. Personal Computers: The Micro Miracles
9. Minis, Mainframes, and "Monsters"

# chapter 5

# Central Processor Concepts, Codes, and Components

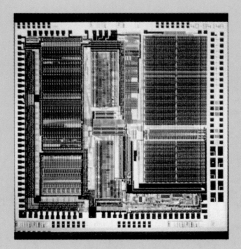

## Closer and Faster

It's become a technological imperative that each generation of electronic devices packs more elements per square millimeter than the last. The benefits of such compacting are twofold: It gives more processing power (or memory) per chip to allow miniaturization, and, because the electrons don't have to travel as far, it permits faster operation.

In the past decade, the number of elements per chip has doubled roughly every two years—from about 100 in 1970 to over 100,000 in many of today's circuits. This remarkable progress is largely due to the steady parade of refinements in lithography—the pattern-printing method by which circuit patterns are produced on silicon wafers. But traditional methods of ultraviolet photolithography probably won't be much help for the coming generations of circuits, which will consist of elements smaller than one micrometer (micron). To punch through to the submicron regime, new lithographic technology is needed. The bad news: None of the advanced techniques now under development—x-rays, electron beams, lasers, or ion beams—has proved able to make submicron circuits in a factory setting.

The crisis isn't immediate; present mass-produced circuits like the 64K RAM (65,536-bit random-access memory) require pattern resolution of only 1.5–2 microns. But for the semiconductor industry to maintain its rapid technical advancement, submicron lithography must be available for production by the late 1980s.

—Herb Brody, "The Bumpy Road to Submicron Lithography," reprinted with permission from the March 1983 issue of *High Technology* magazine. Copyright © 1983 by High Technology Publishing Corporation, 38 Commercial Wharf, Boston, Mass. 02110.

The heart of any computer hardware system is its central processor. This chapter explains what the CPU is and how it works. The information in this chapter will enable you to:

- Outline how computers are classified

- Explain how storage locations are identified, then used during processing

- Discuss the capacity of storage locations, understand how data are coded in storage, and identify the types of storage components used in a CPU

- Describe the operations of the arithmetic-logic and control sections in a CPU

# HOW COMPUTERS ARE CLASSIFIED

The word "computer" was defined and used many times in the Background Module. And in every case, we used the word to refer to a particular type of general-purpose system. While we'll continue to focus our attention almost solely on such general systems, you should also know about other, more specialized types of computers.

## Chapter Outline

## Digital, Analog, and Hybrid Computers

A digital processor, such as the scoreboard pictured here, directly counts discrete values—in this case the time left to play and the scores for each team. (Terry Wacher/Photo Researchers)

Computers are classified by the type of data they are designed to process. Data may be obtained either as a result of *counting* or through the use of some *measuring* instrument. Data that are obtained by counting are called **discrete data.** Examples of discrete data are the total number of students in a classroom or the total amount of an invoice. Data that must be obtained through measurement are called **continuous data.** Examples of continuous data are the speed of an automobile as measured by a speedometer, or the temperature of a patient as measured by a thermometer.

A **digital computer** is a counting device that operates on discrete data. It operates by directly counting numbers (or digits) that represent numerals, letters, or other special symbols. Just as digital watches directly count off the seconds and minutes in an hour, digital processors also count discrete values to achieve the desired output results.

In contrast to digital processors, however, there are also **analog computers** that do not compute directly with numbers. Rather, they deal with variables that are measured along a continuous scale and are recorded to some predetermined degree of accuracy. Temperature, for example, may be measured to the nearest tenth of a degree on the Celsius scale, voltage may be measured to the nearest hundredth of a volt, and pressure may be measured to the nearest "pounds per square inch" value. A service station gasoline pump may contain an analog processor. This processor converts the flow of pumped fuel into two measurements—the price of the delivered gas to the nearest penny, and the quantity of fuel to the nearest tenth or hundredth of a gallon or liter. Analog computing systems are frequently used to

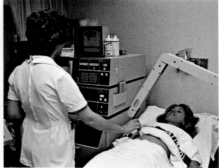

Hybrid computing systems combine the features of digital and analog machines. (Russ Kinne/Photo Researchers)

Analog computers, such as used in this postal scale, convert the weight of a package into the cost of postage needed for mailing. (Dick Durrance/Woodfin Camp & Associates)

control processes such as those found in an oil refinery where flow and temperature measurements are important.

Analog computers may be accurate to within 0.1 percent of the correct value. But digital computers can obtain whatever degree of accuracy is required simply by calculating additional places to the right of the decimal point. To illustrate, anyone who has worked arithmetic problems dealing with circles knows that pi ($\pi$) has a value of 3.1416. Actually, however, the true value is 3.14159 . . . . . (this number could go on for pages). In fact, a digital computer once worked the value of pi out to 500,000 decimal places. Now that's more accuracy than most of us care to consider!

Desirable features of analog and digital machines are sometimes combined to create a **hybrid** computing system. In a hospital intensive-care unit, for example, analog devices may measure a patient's heart function, temperature, and other vital signs. These measurements may then be converted into numbers and supplied to a digital component in the system. This component is used to monitor the patient's vital signs and to send an immediate signal to a nurse's station if any abnormal readings are detected.

Analog and hybrid processors obviously perform important specialized tasks. But the overwhelming majority of all computers used for business and scientific applications are digital devices.

## Special-Purpose and General-Purpose Digital Computers

Digital computers are made for both special and general uses. As the name suggests, a **special-purpose computer** is one that's designed to perform only one specific task. The program of instructions is wired into or permanently stored in such a machine. Although it lacks versatility, it does its single task quickly and efficiently. Special-purpose processors designed just to solve complex navigational problems are installed aboard U.S. atomic submarines. Not too long ago, however, special-purpose computers were too expensive for most applications. Only a few might be needed by one organization, and the specialized model might not do anyone else any good. But today, customized microcomputers are produced in large quantities to perform tasks such as monitoring household appliances and controlling the fuel, ignition, and instrument systems in automobiles. Furthermore, rapid progress is now being made in developing the automated design tools that engineers can use to economically build small quantities of complex microcomputer chips for specialized purposes.

A **general-purpose computer** is one that can store different programs and can thus be used in countless applications. You've seen that by using different instructions such a machine can process a payroll one minute and a billing application the next. New programs can be written, and old programs can be changed or dropped. The versatility of a general-purpose system is limited only by human imagination. And so, unless otherwise noted, all our future discussions of ''computers'' will be about general-purpose digital systems. Let's now become better acquainted with the primary storage, arithmetic-logic, and control sections found in the central processors of such systems.

# PRIMARY STORAGE CONCEPTS

You learned in Chapter 1 that primary storage is used for four purposes. Data are fed into an *input storage* area. A *working storage* space is used to hold intermediate processing results. An *output storage* area holds the final processing results. And a *program storage* area contains the processing instructions. You also saw that the separate locations used for these four purposes don't have built-in physical boundaries. Rather, a specific storage location can be used to hold input data in one application and output results or program instructions in another. Now let's take a closer look at these storage locations.

## Storage Locations and Addresses

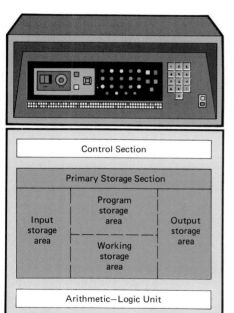

An analogy between primary storage and post office mailboxes is often used. In your local post office, each mailbox is identified by a specific number. Each box can hold different items. A letter containing instructions on how to tune an engine may have been placed in the box yesterday, and an electric bill for $46.18 may be put there today. Instructions are stored one day and data the next. The contents change, but the box and its number remain the same. A post office may have many such boxes that differ only in their identification numbers.

The primary storage section of a computer also has many small storage areas. Each one is assigned an **address**—a built-in and unique number that identifies the location. Like a mailbox, a storage location can hold either a data item or an instruction, and its identifying number remains the same regardless of its contents.

Comparing storage locations with mailboxes is convenient, but *this analogy breaks down in several important ways*. For one thing, a mailbox can hold several different messages at once while an address location only holds one item at a time. Another difference is that when a new item is placed in a mailbox the previous contents remain undisturbed. But when new data are stored in an address location the previous contents are erased and replaced. Finally, when the contents of a mailbox are retrieved the box is emptied. But when a computer system needs an item in a storage location, it merely reads and then duplicates the item elsewhere; it does not remove the item from its original location.

There are 65,536 storage locations in the primary storage sections of many personal computers. The addresses in such a computer are numbered from 00000 to 65,535. Thus, one unique address is designated 00017. There's an important difference between the address number and the contents of the address. Suppose that $90 is the data item stored in address 00017. If the programmer wants that amount printed, she will *not* instruct the computer to print $90. Rather, the machine will be ordered to Print 00017, and it will interpret this instruction to mean that it should *print the contents of address 00017*. Just as you can locate friends in a strange city if you know that their home address is 4009 Sarita Drive, so too can the computer locate the desired data item if it knows the location number.

**Use of Storage Locations**

To get a general idea of how storage locations are used, let's take another look at the Longhorn College payroll application discussed in Chapter 1. You'll recall that input data for each part-time student employee are first entered on time sheets and are then transferred to a computer-readable floppy magnetic disk. The first input record was for Rob Brooks. The processing of this application was shown in Figure 1-11, page 21. But that figure showed the stored program concept in only the most general way. It made no reference to addressable storage locations.

Figure 5-1 presents a more realistic version of the Longhorn College CPU shown in Figure 1-11 because it does illustrate the use of storage addresses. You'll read about other characteristics of Longhorn's CPU in this chapter, but keep in mind that personal computer systems possess these same characteristics. The program steps shown in Figure 5-1 are identical in purpose to those discussed in Chapter 1. These instructions have been read into addresses 04 through 14[1] in the primary storage section of Figure 5-1. This choice of addresses for the *program storage* area is arbitrary; any space in primary storage could have been used.[2] Let's now trace through the program steps shown in Figure 5-1 to see how storage locations are used to prepare Rob's paycheck. (The circled address numbers shown in the figure indicate how the computer responds to the instruction stored in that address. Some flow lines have been omitted to simplify the figure.)

After the computer operator has loaded the payroll data in a disk reader and has set the computer to the first instruction in address 04, the processing starts. The first instruction (04) is fed into the control section of the CPU where it's interpreted. Control signals are sent to the disk reader which executes the instruction and transfers a record to the *input storage* area identified in the instruction. Thus, Rob's payroll data are read into addresses 00, 01, 02, and 03.[3] The data could easily have been assigned to other unused addresses, and so this is also an arbitrary choice.

As you know, the control unit will interpret the instructions automatically and in sequence after the initial control setting until directed to do otherwise. Thus, after the instruction in address 04 has been executed, the control unit begins to interpret the instruction in address 05. This instruction sets up a type of logic/comparison operation discussed in Chapter 2. It requires that the contents of address 01 be compared to a value of −99 hours. This value of −99 hours is placed in a last dummy record at the end of the payroll run to indicate that all valid data have been processed. If the contents do not equal −99 hours, the processing continues in sequence. If, on the other hand, the quantity in the hours-worked field does equal −99, program control will branch to address 14 and processing will stop. Since Rob has worked 20 hours, program control moves on to address 06. This instruction tells the control unit that the contents of address 01 are to be copied into the arithmetic-logic section, and so 20 hours is duplicated there.

By now you should be able to trace through the remaining program steps in Figure 5-1. The 20-hour figure in the arithmetic-logic section is multiplied by the $5

---

[1] Leading zeros—e.g., 00004 or 00014—in the address numbers have been deleted here to simplify the figure. And the 18 addresses used—00 to 17—are a much smaller number than actually exist in the primary storage area but are enough to illustrate the concept.

[2] Programmers who write applications instructions in higher-level languages do not worry about address selection. Instead, they use prewritten, specialized programs provided by computer manufacturers and others to assign storage locations to the different possible purposes.

[3] As you'll see in the next section, the capacity of storage locations can vary. A few additional storage locations would probably be needed to hold all our input data. This would be no problem for the computer, but it would add unnecessary detail to our example.

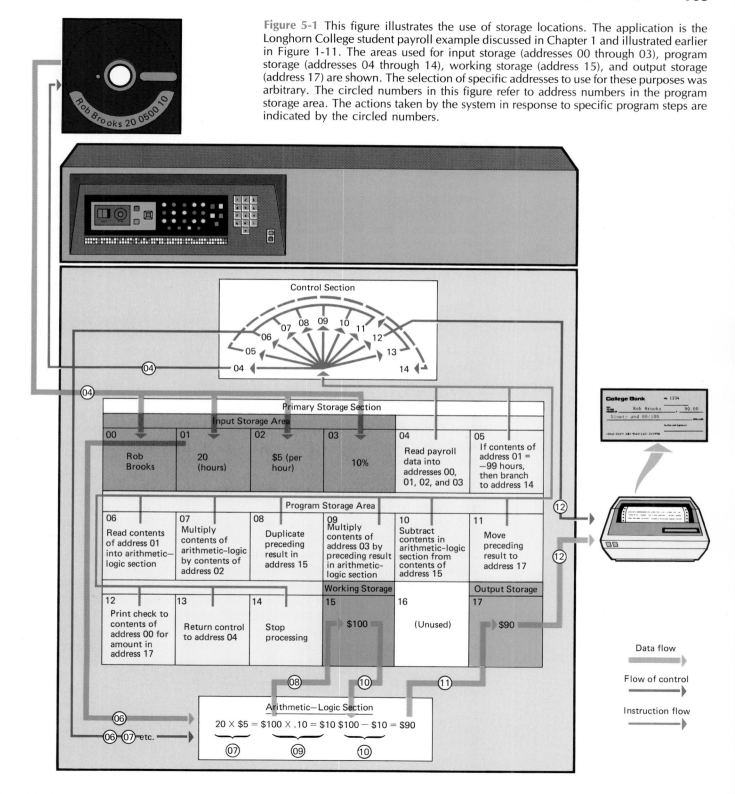

**Figure 5-1** This figure illustrates the use of storage locations. The application is the Longhorn College student payroll example discussed in Chapter 1 and illustrated earlier in Figure 1-11. The areas used for input storage (addresses 00 through 03), program storage (addresses 04 through 14), working storage (address 15), and output storage (address 17) are shown. The selection of specific addresses to use for these purposes was arbitrary. The circled numbers in this figure refer to address numbers in the program storage area. The actions taken by the system in response to specific program steps are indicated by the circled numbers.

hourly rate stored in address 02 to get total earnings (instruction in address 07). This total earnings figure is copied (instruction, 08) in address 15, which is the *working storage* area.[4] The amount of the tax deduction is computed (instruction, 09) and subtracted from the total earnings figure that was temporarily stored in the working storage area (instruction, 10) to get Rob's $90 take-home pay. This $90 is then moved to address 17 which is the *output storage* area.[5] From there, the amount is sent to a printer which is directed to print Rob's check (instruction, 12). Finally, the control unit is directed to reset itself to address 04 (instruction, 13), and the processing is repeated for the next student.

When the payroll data for the next student are entered into addresses 00 through 03, they will erase Rob's data. This example thus illustrates a basic characteristic of computer storage: Entering data *into* a storage location is **destructive** of previous contents, but retrieving data *from* a location is **nondestructive.** Various terms are associated with entering new data into storage, and with retrieving existing data from storage. The act of *entering* new data into storage is called *read in, read into,* or *write.* The act of *retrieving* existing data from storage is called *read out, read from,* or simply *read.*

## Capacity of Storage Locations

We've not yet considered the storage capacity of *each address.* All we've seen is that an address holds a specific data or program element. Actually, the storage capacity of an address is *built into* the computer. Over the years, computer manufacturers have used several different design approaches to partition the primary storage section into addresses.

One approach is to design the primary storage section to store a *fixed number of characters* in each numbered address location. These characters are then treated as a single entity or **word.** Thus, BROOKS might be treated as a single data word, and MULTIPLY might be a single instruction word. Machines built to store a fixed number of characters in each address are said to be **word addressable,** and they employ a **fixed word-length storage** approach.[6]

The primary storage section can also be organized so that *each* numbered address can only store a *single character* (8, B, $). Machines designed in this way are said to be **character addressable.** Thus, a sequence of characters such as BROOKS would require six storage addresses while $90 would occupy three addresses. Character-addressable machines are said to employ a **variable word-length storage** approach. Figure 5-2 summarizes the difference between the fixed-length and variable-length storage approaches.

Each of these ways of organizing the primary storage section has advantages and limitations. For example, variable word-length processors generally make the most efficient use of the available storage space, since a character can be placed in every storage cell. But if the storage capacity in each address of a fixed word-length processor is eight characters, and if many data words containing only two or three characters are placed in each address, then many of the storage cells cannot be used.

---

[4]Why address 15 instead of 16 or some other unused location? Again, the choice is arbitrary.

[5]You guessed it: Any unused location would have been acceptable.

[6]The number of characters that can be stored in each address varies depending on the make of computer. One modern design (the Control Data Corporation Cyber 170) can hold 10 alphanumeric characters in each address. Other machines have fixed word-lengths of two, four, six, and eight characters.

**Figure 5-2** Fixed word-length storage compared with variable word-length storage. Each approach has distinct advantages. (a) Fixed-length words of eight characters each, occupying three address locations. (b) Variable-length words of varying lengths. (Some leading zeros have been deleted in the address numbers.)

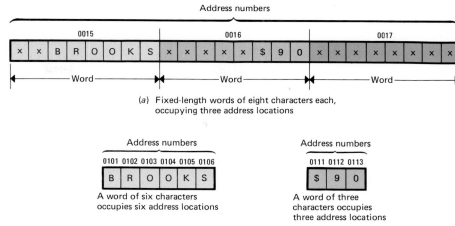

(a) Fixed-length words of eight characters each, occupying three address locations

Address numbers
0101 0102 0103 0104 0105 0106

| B | R | O | O | K | S |

A word of six characters occupies six address locations

Address numbers
0111 0112 0113

| $ | 9 | 0 |

A word of three characters occupies three address locations

(b) Variable-length words of varying lengths

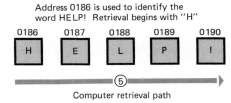

Address 0186 is used to identify the word HELP! Retrieval begins with "H"

| 0186 | 0187 | 0188 | 0189 | 0190 |
| H | E | L | P | ! |

Computer retrieval path

**Figure 5-3** A variable-length word in a byte-addressable computer is identified by the address number of the *first* character in the word. The number of characters included in the word must also be specified in a program instruction. (Some leading zeros have been deleted in the address numbers.)

On the other hand, fixed word-length machines have faster calculating capabilities. Such a machine can add two data words in a single operation. If the fixed-length word is eight characters, two eight-digit numbers can be added in a single operation. With a character-addressable processor, however, only one digit in each number is added during a single machine operation, and eight steps would thus be needed to complete the calculation.

Some of the largest and most powerful modern computers use *only* a fixed word-length storage approach. These giant processors are used primarily for scientific calculations and need the faster calculating capability of the fixed word-length design. Many personal computers, on the other hand, are variable word-length machines that operate *only* on one character at a time during processing. In between these two size extremes are the hundreds of existing microcomputer, minicomputer, and mainframe models that have built-in flexibility.

Most of today's business and scientific processing is handled by these flexible machines that can be operated as *either* variable *or* fixed word-length computers. Available program instructions permit these models to operate on either single characters or fixed-length words.

Let's first look at how a flexible computer operates as a variable word-length machine. Each address in this type of computer holds one alphanumeric character. Each character is represented in a storage location by a string of binary numbers (0s and 1s) that are treated as a unit. This unit or set of *bi*nary digi*ts*, or **bits,** is called a **byte.** Since a byte usually represents a single alphanumeric character, a flexible computer is often said to be **byte addressable.** By using an appropriate set of instructions, a programmer working with such a machine can retrieve a stored data item by identifying the address of the first character in the data word and by then indicating the number of address locations to be included in the word (see Figure 5-3). Since variable-length data words are common in business, instructions of this type are frequently used for business applications.

But bytes representing characters can also be grouped together in a flexible computer and operated on as a unit. Let's assume that a scientific application calling

**Figure 5-4** Word formats permitted with many byte-addressable computers.

1 byte = 1 coded alphanumeric character

(a) *Variable word format: a variable number of bytes make up a word*

2 bytes

(This is the only fixed word format available with many minicomputers)

4 bytes

(This is the standard word size used by many mainframe models)

8 bytes

(This is a "doubleword" size used by many mainframe models)

(b) *Fixed word formats permitted*

for numerous calculations is to be processed. To achieve faster calculating speeds, programmers can choose other available instructions that will cause the computer to automatically retrieve, manipulate, and store as a single unit a fixed word of 4 bytes. Or, they may choose to group 8 bytes into a single unit and have the machine function in this fixed-word format. Figure 5-4 illustrates the word arrangements possible with many of today's computers.

## Feedback and Review 5-1

Thus far in this chapter, you've seen (a) how computers are classified, (b) how primary storage locations are identified by address numbers, (c) how these addressable storage locations are used during processing, and (d) how the storage capacity of an address varies depending on the built-in design of the computer. To test and reinforce your understanding of this material, fill in the crossword puzzle with the words needed to complete the sentences and definitions found below.

### Across

**1.** A _____ computer is a device that operates by directly counting numbers.

**2.** Computers designed to store only a single character in each numbered address are said to be character-_____.

**7.** Fixed word-length processors are _____ calculators, but they may not make the most efficient use of storage space.

**8.** Word-addressable computers employ a _____ word-length storage approach.

**10.** A digital computer has worked the value of _____ out to 500,000 decimal places.

**11.** A computer _____ is a group of characters that are treated as a single entity.

**12.** A string of binary digits treated as a unit is called a _____.

**13.** A group of binary digits, or _____ is used to represent a character in primary storage.

**16.** An _____ is a built-in number that identifies a location in storage.

**17.** Each address in storage must have a _____ number.

**18.** A _____-addressable computer can store one alphanumeric character in each numbered storage location.

**19.** Writing data *into* a computer storage location will _____ the previous contents, but reading data *from* a location is nondestructive.

**20.** A _____ computer system is one that combines desirable features taken from analog and digital machines.

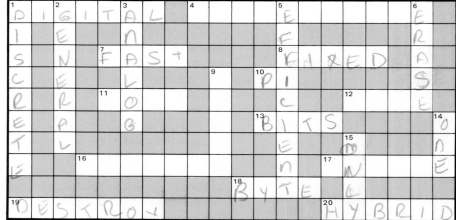

### Down

**1.** Data that are obtained by counting are called _____ data.

**2.** A _____-purpose computer is one that can store different programs.

**3.** _____ computers do not compute directly with numbers; rather, they measure continuously variable physical magnitudes.

**5.** An advantage of variable word-length computers is that they make _____ use of the available primary storage space.

**6.** Storing new data in an address location will _____ the previous contents.

**9.** A special-purpose computer performs only one specific task and thus _____ versatility.

**14.** An address location holds only _____ data item at a time.

**15.** Some of the largest and most powerful modern computers use _____ a fixed word-length storage approach.

# CODING DATA IN STORAGE

Although the capacity of their storage locations can vary, every computer stores numbers, letters, and other characters in a coded form. As you saw in the last section, every character in storage is represented by a string of 0s and 1s—the only digits found in the binary numbering system. Let's see how it's possible to use just two digits to represent any character.

## The Binary Numbering System

"Cecily, she's a genius—she's already mastered the binary system!"

There's nothing mysterious about numbering systems. The first ones used an *additive* approach. That is, they consisted of symbols such as I for 1, II for 2, III for 3, etc. Each symbol represented the *same value* regardless of its position in the number. Since arithmetic is difficult when such systems are used, *positional* numbering systems were developed as the centuries passed. In a positional system, there are only a few symbols, and these symbols represent different values depending on the position they occupy in the number. For example, 5 equals the Roman numeral V, but 51 does not equal VI because the meaning of 5 has changed with the change in its position. The actual number of symbols used in a positional system depends on its *base*. The familiar decimal system has a base of 10, and it thus has 10 symbols (0 to 9). The *highest* numerical symbol always has a value of *one less* than the base.

Any number can be represented by arranging symbols in various positions. You know that in the decimal system the successive positions to the left of the decimal point represent units, tens, hundreds, thousands, etc. But you may not have given much thought to the fact that *each position represents a specific power of the base*. For example, the decimal number 1,684 (written $1,684_{10}$) represents:[7]

$$\underbrace{(1 \times 10^3)}_{1000} + \underbrace{(6 \times 10^2)}_{600} + \underbrace{(8 \times 10^1)}_{80} + \underbrace{(4 \times 10^0)}_{4}. \leftarrow \text{decimal point}$$
$$. = 1,684$$

The principles that apply to the decimal system apply in *any other* positional system. An *octal* numbering system, for example, is one with a base of 8. In such a system, the possible symbols are 0 to 7 (8 and 9 don't exist in this case). Since each position in the octal number 463 (written $463_8$) represents a power of the base, the decimal equivalent of $463_8$ is:

$$\underbrace{(4 \times 8^2)}_{256} + \underbrace{(6 \times 8^1)}_{48} + \underbrace{(3 \times 8^0)}_{3}. \leftarrow \text{octal point}$$
$$. = 307_{10} \text{ the decimal equivalent}$$

Similarly, the **binary numbering system** uses a base of 2. The possible symbols, therefore, are just 0 and 1. Again, each position in a binary number represents a power of the base, and the decimal equivalent of the binary number 1001 (written $1001_2$) is:

---

[7] Just in case you've forgotten, $n^0$ is, by definition, 1. That is, any number raised to the zero power equals 1.

$$\underbrace{(1 \times 2^3)}_{8} + \underbrace{(0 \times 2^2)}_{0} + \underbrace{(0 \times 2^1)}_{0} + \underbrace{(1 \times 2^0)}_{1}. \leftarrow \text{binary point}$$

. $= 9_{10}$ the decimal equivalent

And the decimal number 202 is represented in binary as:

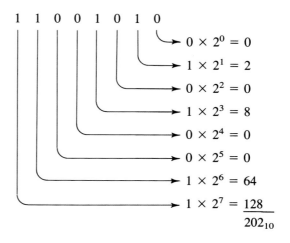

1  1  0  0  1  0  1  0

$0 \times 2^0 = 0$
$1 \times 2^1 = 2$
$0 \times 2^2 = 0$
$1 \times 2^3 = 8$
$0 \times 2^4 = 0$
$0 \times 2^5 = 0$
$1 \times 2^6 = 64$
$1 \times 2^7 = \underline{128}$
$202_{10}$

or:

| Binary number | 1 | 1 | 0 | 0 | 1 | 0 | 1 | 0 |
|---|---|---|---|---|---|---|---|---|
| Power of base | $2^7$ | $2^6$ | $2^5$ | $2^4$ | $2^3$ | $2^2$ | $2^1$ | $2^0$ |
| Decimal equivalent | 128 | 64 | 32 | 16 | 8 | 4 | 2 | 1 |

As you can see, the use of a smaller base may require more positions to represent a given value ($1001_2 = 9_{10}$). In spite of this fact, however, all but the very first computers have been designed to use binary numbers. Why the rush to binary? *One* reason is that computer circuits only have to handle 2 binary digits (bits) rather than 10. Design is simplified, cost is reduced, and reliability is improved. A *second* reason that computers use the binary system is that electronic components, by their very nature, operate in a binary mode. A switch is either open (0 state) or closed (1 state); a transistor is either not conducting (0) or is conducting (1). *Finally,* the binary system is used because everything that can be done with a base of 10 can also be done in binary.

On

Off

1  1  0  0  1  0  1  0 = $202_{10}$

**Computer Codes**  Up to now we've been discussing true or "pure" binary numbers. But most computers use a *coded* version of true binary to represent decimal numbers. Although many coding schemes have been developed over the years, the most popular of these use a **binary coded decimal (BCD) approach.**

Place Value

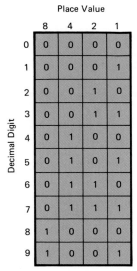

Figure 5-5 BCD numeric bit configurations and their decimal equivalent.

**The BCD Approach.** With BCD, it's possible to convert *each* decimal number into its binary equivalent rather than convert the entire decimal value into a pure binary form. The BCD equivalent of each possible decimal symbol is shown in Figure 5-5. Since 8 and 9 require 4 bits, *all* decimal digits are represented in BCD by 4 bits. You've just seen that $202_{10}$ is equal to $11001010_2$ in a pure binary form. Converting $202_{10}$ into BCD, however, produces the following result:

$$202_{10} \text{ in BCD} = \underbrace{0010}_{2}\ \underbrace{0000}_{0}\ \underbrace{0010}_{2} \quad \text{or} \quad 001000000010$$

When 4 bits are used, there are only 16 possible configurations ($2^4$). As you saw in Figure 5-5, the first 10 of these combinations are used to represent decimal digits. The other six arrangements (1010, 1011, 1100, 1101, 1110, and 1111) have decimal values from 10 to 15. These arrangements *aren't used* in BCD coding. That is, 1111 doesn't represent $15_{10}$ in BCD. Instead, the proper BCD code for $15_{10}$ is 0001/0101.

**Six-Bit BCD Code.** Instead of using 4 bits with only 16 possible characters, computer designers commonly use 6, 7, or 8 bits to represent characters in alphanumeric versions of BCD. In the **6-bit code,** the four BCD *numeric* place positions (1, 2, 4, and 8) are retained, but two additional *zone* positions are included (Figure 5-6a). With 6 bits, it's possible to represent 64 different characters ($2^6$). This is a sufficient number to code the decimal digits (10), capital letters (26), and other special characters and punctuation marks (28). Figure 5-6b shows you how a few of the 64 possible characters are represented in a standard 6-bit BCD code.

Figure 5-6 The 6-bit BCD code.

| Zone bits | | Numeric bits | | | |
|---|---|---|---|---|---|
| B | A | 8 | 4 | 2 | 1 |

(a) Format for 6-bit BCD code

| Character | Standard BCD interchange code |
|---|---|
| 0 | 00 1010 |
| 1 | 00 0001 |
| 2 | 00 0010 |
| 3 | 00 0011 |
| 4 | 00 0100 |
| 5 | 00 0101 |
| 6 | 00 0110 |
| 7 | 00 0111 |
| A | 11 0001 |
| B | 11 0010 |
| C | 11 0011 |
| D | 11 0100 |
| E | 11 0101 |

(b) The coding used to represent selected characters in a standard 6-bit code

**Seven- and Eight-Bit Codes.** Since 64 possible bit combinations isn't sufficient to provide decimal numbers (10), lower-case letters (26), capital letters (26), and a large number of other characters (28+), designers have extended the 6-bit BCD code to 7 and 8 bits. With 7 bits, it's possible to provide 128 different arrangements ($2^7$); with 8 bits, 256 variations are possible ($2^8$). In addition to the four numeric place positions, there are three zone bit positions in a **7-bit code,** and four zone bit positions in an **8-bit code.** The 7-bit American Standard Code for Information Interchange **(ASCII)** is widely used in data communications work and is by far the most popular code used to represent data internally in personal computers. The ASCII format and the coding used to represent selected characters are shown in Figure 5-7.

There are also two popular 8-bit codes in common use. One is the Extended Binary Coded Decimal Interchange Code **(EBCDIC).** This code is used in IBM mainframe models and in similar machines produced by other manufacturers. The other 8-bit code is **ASCII-8,** an 8-bit version of ASCII that is frequently used in the larger machines produced by some vendors. Figure 5-8 presents the 8-bit format and shows how selected characters are represented in these 8-bit codes. The main difference is in the selection of bit patterns to use in the zone positions.

| Zone bits | | | Numeric bits | | | |
|---|---|---|---|---|---|---|
| Z | Z | Z | 8 | 4 | 2 | 1 |

(a) Format for 7-bit ASCII code.

| Character | ASCII |
|---|---|
| 0 | 011 0000 |
| 1 | 011 0001 |
| 2 | 011 0010 |
| 3 | 011 0011 |
| 4 | 011 0100 |
| 5 | 011 0101 |
| 6 | 011 0110 |
| 7 | 011 0111 |
| A | 100 0001 |
| B | 100 0010 |
| C | 100 0011 |
| D | 100 0100 |
| E | 100 0101 |

(b) The coding used to represent selected characters in the ASCII 7-bit code.

**Figure 5-7** The 7-bit ASCII format and selected ASCII character codes.

| Zone bits | | | | Numeric bits | | | |
|---|---|---|---|---|---|---|---|
| Z | Z | Z | Z | 8 | 4 | 2 | 1 |

(a) Format for 8-bit EBCDIC and ASCII-8 codes.

| Character | Extended BCD interchange code (EBCDIC) | ASCII-8 |
|---|---|---|
| 0 | 1111 0000 | 0101 0000 |
| 1 | 1111 0001 | 0101 0001 |
| 2 | 1111 0010 | 0101 0010 |
| 3 | 1111 0011 | 0101 0011 |
| 4 | 1111 0100 | 0101 0100 |
| 5 | 1111 0101 | 0101 0101 |
| 6 | 1111 0110 | 0101 0110 |
| 7 | 1111 0111 | 0101 0111 |
| A | 1100 0001 | 1010 0001 |
| B | 1100 0010 | 1010 0010 |
| C | 1100 0011 | 1010 0011 |
| D | 1100 0100 | 1010 0100 |
| E | 1100 0101 | 1010 0101 |

(b) The coding used to represent selected characters in the EBCDIC and ASCII-8 8-bit codes.

**Figure 5-8** The format for EBCDIC and ASCII-8 8-bit codes and selected characters represented by these codes. Each 8-bit unit used to code data is called a byte.

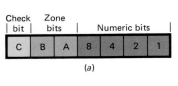

| Check bit | Zone bits | | Numeric bits | | | |
|---|---|---|---|---|---|---|
| C | B | A | 8 | 4 | 2 | 1 |

(a)

| Check bit | Zone bits | | | Numeric bits | | | |
|---|---|---|---|---|---|---|---|
| C | Z | Z | Z | 8 | 4 | 2 | 1 |

(b)

| Check bit | Zone bits | | | | Numeric bits | | | |
|---|---|---|---|---|---|---|---|---|
| C | Z | Z | Z | Z | 8 | 4 | 2 | 1 |

(c)

**Figure 5-9** (a) Format of 6-bit BCD code with check bit included. (b) Format of 7-bit ASCII code with check bit included. (c) Format of 8-bit codes with check bit included.

| Character | Check bit | Zone bits | | Numeric bits | | | |
|---|---|---|---|---|---|---|---|
| 1 | 1 | 0 | 0 | 0 | 0 | 0 | 1 |
| 2 | 1 | 0 | 0 | 0 | 0 | 1 | 0 |
| 3 | 0 | 0 | 0 | 0 | 0 | 1 | 1 |
| A | 1 | 1 | 1 | 0 | 0 | 0 | 1 |

An even number of 1 bits are found in the code for every character when even parity is used

**Figure 5-10** Using the check bit to make sure that every character has an even number of 1 bits. This is an example of the use of an even-parity format. Other computers are also designed to have the check bit produce an odd-parity format.

**Detecting Code Errors.** Computers are very reliable, but they're not infallible. If just one bit in a string of 6, 7, or 8 bits is lost during data input, processing, or output operations, an incorrect character code will be created. Such an error can be caused by dust particles on storage media, by improper humidity levels near the computer, or by many other factors.

Fortunately, however, computer designers have developed a method for detecting such errors by adding an extra *check bit* or *parity bit* to each 6, 7, or 8-bit character represented in storage. Thus, as you can see in Figure 5-9, a total of 7, 8, or 9 bits may actually be stored. The designers of a particular computer model may then use the check bit to make sure that every valid character code will *always* have an *even* number of 1 bits. The 6-bit coding used to represent selected characters was presented earlier in Figure 5-6. Several of these characters have been reproduced in Figure 5-10. You'll notice that if the *basic code* for a character such as 1, 2, or A requires an odd number of 1 bits, an additional 1 bit is added in the check-bit location so that there will always be an *even* number of such bits. This is an example of an **even-parity** format, but other computers use the check bit to produce an **odd parity.** Since every valid character in a computer that uses even parity must always have an even number of 1 bits, circuits for **parity checking** are built into the computer to constantly monitor the data moving through the system. The computer operator is notified if a bit is lost and a parity error is detected. Of course, parity checking will only detect coding errors. It cannot signal the fact that incorrect data have been entered into the system if the data are properly coded.

## Feedback and Review 5-2

You've seen in this section that computers store numbers, letters, and other characters in a coded form that's related to the binary numbering system. You've also seen that several different coding formats are used in modern computers. To test and reinforce your understanding of the material in this section, place a T or F in the space provided in the following true-false questions:

___**1.** The first numbering systems used a positional approach.

___**2.** In a positional numbering system, the highest numerical symbol always has a value of one less than the base.

___**3.** Each position to the left of the decimal point in the decimal numbering system represents a specific power of the base of 10.

___**4.** The possible symbols in the binary numbering system are 0 to 9.

___**5.** The decimal equivalent of the true binary value of $110010_2$ is $50_{10}$.

___**6.** The decimal value of $16_{10}$ is represented in pure binary as $100000_2$.

___**7.** The decimal value of $16_{10}$ is represented in 4-bit BCD as 00010101.

___**8.** Alphanumeric versions of BCD commonly use 6, 7, or 8 bits to represent characters.

___**9.** A 6-bit alphanumeric code can represent 128 different characters.

___**10.** There are four 8-bit codes in current use.

___**11.** Each 8-bit unit used to code data is called a byte.

___**12.** Eight-bit codes are limited to representing 128 different characters.

___**13.** An extra check (or parity) bit is often added to each 6-, 7-, or 8-bit character represented in storage so that it will be possible to detect coding errors that may occur.

___**14.** If a computer uses an odd-parity format to detect errors in character codes, then every valid character code will always have an odd number of 1 bits.

# STORAGE COMPONENTS IN THE CPU

**Primary Storage Components of the Past**

The first general-purpose electronic computer built in the 1940s (the ENIAC) used vacuum tubes. These tubes were relatively large and each was able to hold only a single bit. Storage capacity was thus tiny by present standards. The most popular computer in the mid-1950s (the IBM 650) used a rotating drum coated with a magnetizeable material as the primary storage instrument.

During the 15 years between 1960 and 1975, however, the dominant approach was to use the tiny rings or *cores* (Figure 5-11) of magnetizeable material in the primary storage section. Several tiny wires were threaded through each doughnut-shaped core. If a sufficiently strong electric current passed through these wires, the core was magnetized by the magnetic field created by the current. Current flowing in one direction produced a 0-bit magnetic state; flow in the opposite direction caused a 1-bit state. Since the core permanently retained its magnetic state in the absence of current, it was a **nonvolatile storage** medium. Many cores were strung on a screen of wires to form a *core plane*. These planes, resembling small square tennis rackets, were then arranged vertically to represent data, as shown in Figure 5-11. Core storage was popular for 15 years because it was safe, durable, and reasonably fast. But the new storage devices that appeared in the 1970s offered even faster performance at a lower cost, and so the popularity of cores quickly faded.

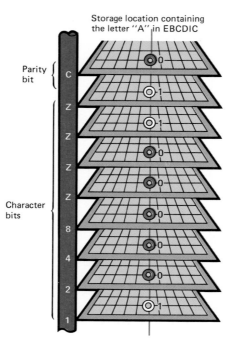

Figure 5-11 The letter A represented in core storage. The EBCDIC 8-bit code and an odd-parity format is used.

## Primary Storage Components of the Present

Virtually all computers made today use semiconductor elements in their primary storage sections. **Semiconductor storage** elements are tiny integrated circuits. Both the storage cell circuits and the support circuitry needed for data writing and reading are packaged on chips of silicon. There are several semiconductor storage technologies currently in use. It's not necessary to consider the physics of these different approaches in any detail. It's enough just to mention that faster and more expensive *bipolar semiconductor* chips are often used in the arithmetic-logic and certain other sections of the CPU, while slower and less expensive chips that employ *metal-oxide semiconductor (MOS)* technology are usually used in the primary storage section. These primary storage components are often referred to as random access memory **(RAM)** chips because a programmer can randomly select and use any of the storage locations on a chip to directly store and retrieve data and instructions, and because any of these locations may be accessed (written to or read from) in the same amount of time.

RAM chips may be classified as dynamic or static. The storage cell circuits in **dynamic RAM chips** contain (1) a transistor that acts in much the same way as a mechanical on-off light switch and (2) a capacitor that's capable of storing an electrical charge. Depending on the switching action of the transistor, the capacitor either contains no charge (0 bit) or does hold a charge (1 bit). Figure 5-12 shows how 64 bits might be arranged in a section of a chip. To locate a particular cell for writing or reading, row and column addresses (in binary) are needed. The storage location of the shaded cell in Figure 5-12 is the row numbered 0011 (3) and the column numbered 0101 (5). Since the charge on the capacitor tends to "leak off," provision is made to periodically "regenerate" or refresh the storage charge. Unlike

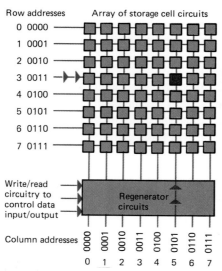

Figure 5-12 Dynamic RAM storage concepts.

a magnetic core, then, a dynamic RAM chip provides **volatile storage.** That is, the data stored are lost in the event of a power failure.

**Static RAM chips** are also volatile storage devices, but as long as they are supplied with power they need no special regenerator circuits to retain the stored data. Since it takes a total of six transistors and other devices to store a bit in a static RAM, these chips are more complicated and take up more space for a given storage capacity than do dynamic RAMs. Static RAMs are thus used in specialized applications while dynamic RAMs are used in the primary storage sections of most computers. Because of the volatile nature of these storage elements, a backup **uninterruptible power system** (UPS) is often found in larger computer installations. Personal computer users can also invest a few hundred dollars and get a small battery-powered UPS. This device will supply current for a period long enough for users to save data on a disk and then shut down the system in an orderly way.

Semiconductor memory chips have found their way into modern computers for several good reasons:

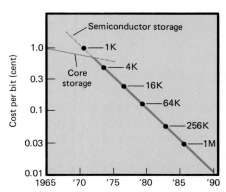

Figure 5-13 The number of bits that can be stored on a silicon chip has quadrupled every 3 years, and the cost per bit of storage has been cut in half every 3 years. This trend in semiconductor storage is expected to continue.

1. ***Economic factors.*** For the last decade, the number of bits that can be stored on a chip has quadrupled every 3 years. During the same period, the cost per bit of storage has been cut in half every 3 years. There seems to be no end in sight to these cost reductions. The symbol **K** is often used when the storage capacity of chips is discussed. One K represents $2^{10}$ or 1,024 units. Today, many chips are able to store 256K or 262,144 bits. But as you can see in Figure 5-13, these chips will soon be surpassed by others that will each store 1 megabit (or 1.048 million bits), and the cost per bit will drop once again. It's then anticipated that the trend will continue with the development of a 4-megabit chip.

2. ***Compact size.*** Semiconductor chips require a small fraction of the space needed by core storage devices of similar capacity.

3. ***Faster performance.*** Semiconductor devices are capable of faster performance than core storage units. Their more compact size contributes to this faster speed. However, the fastest core memories could outperform some of the slowest storage chips.

## Primary Storage Components of the Future

Scientists in the United States, Japan, and Europe are working on several primary storage approaches that promise to be much more compact and much faster than anything in current use. One approach is the use of the **Josephson junction**—named for British Nobel Prize winner Brian Josephson. This junction is simply a superconducting switch that can change from a 1-bit to a 0-bit state at least 10 times faster than is possible with the circuits used in today's machines. To achieve this speed, however, Josephson circuits must be wrapped in a jacket containing liquid helium so that they will be cooled to within a few degrees of absolute zero (more than 400 degrees below zero on the Fahrenheit scale). At that temperature, barriers that would ordinarily restrain the flow of electricity lose their resistive ability. But this low-temperature requirement has proven to be a serious obstacle to the use of Josephson circuits. Thus, IBM, Bell Laboratories, Sperry Corporation, and other organizations have scaled down their Josephson research efforts and are now looking at other approaches.

It has been found, for example, that if conventional devices can just be made small enough they'll enter an ultra-high-speed conducting state called **ballistic transport.** Experiments with ballistic transport are being made with devices that replace silicon with a semiconductor material called gallium arsenide. If perfected, the ballistic transport approach could provide Josephson performance at room temperature with circuits that could be easier to fabricate.

**Specialized Storage Elements in the CPU**

You know that every CPU has a primary storage section that holds the active program(s) and data being processed. In addition to this *general-purpose* storage section, however, many CPUs also have built-in *specialized* storage elements that are used for specific processing and control purposes (Figure 5-14).

One element used during *processing* operations is a **high-speed buffer** (or **cache**) memory that's both faster and more expensive per character stored than primary storage. This high-speed element is used as a "scratch pad" to temporarily store data and instructions that are likely to be retrieved many times during processing. Processing speed can thus be improved. Data may be transferred automatically between the buffer and primary storage so that the buffer is usually invisible to the application programmer. Once found only in larger systems, cache memory is now available in some of the tiny microprocessor chips used in personal computers.

Other specialized storage elements found in many CPUs are used for *control* purposes. The most basic computer functions are carried out by wired circuits. Additional circuits may then be used to combine these very basic functions into somewhat higher-level operations (e.g., to subtract values, move data, etc.). But it's also possible to perform these same higher-level operations with a series of special programs. These programs—called **microprograms** because they deal with low-level machine functions—are thus essentially substitutes for additional hardware.

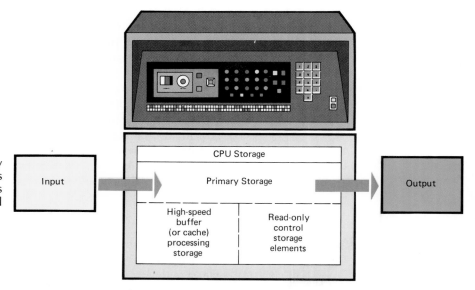

Figure 5-14 In addition to the primary storage section, many central processors also contain specialized storage elements that are used for processing and control purposes.

Scientists are developing processes for fabricating circuit patterns with micron- and submicronwide lines on gallium arsenide and related materials in the search for ultra-high-speed conductors. (Photo courtesy Honeywell, Inc.)

Microprograms are typically held in the CPU in special control storage elements called read-only memory **(ROM) chips.** Unlike RAM chips, which are volatile, ROM chips retain stored data when the power goes off. Microprogram control instructions that cause the machine to perform certain operations can be repeatedly read from a ROM chip as needed, but the chip will not accept any input data or instructions from computer users.

The most basic type of ROM chip is supplied by the computer manufacturer as part of the computer system and it can't be changed or altered by users. Such chips have found wide application as a program storage medium in video games and personal computers. Of course, it's possible for a user to "customize" a system by choosing the machine functions that will be performed by microprograms and by then using a second type of ROM chip. For example, critical or lengthy operations that have been slowly carried out by software can be converted into microprograms and fused into a programmable read-only memory **(PROM) chip.** Once they are in a hardware form, these tasks can usually be executed in a fraction of the time previously required.

PROM chips are supplied by computer manufacturers and custom ROM vendors. Once operations have been written into a PROM chip, they are permanent and cannot be altered. There are other types of ROM control chips available, however, that *can* be erased and reprogrammed. Since one type of erasable and programmable read-only memory **(EPROM) chip** needs to be removed from the CPU and exposed for some time to ultraviolet light before it can accept new contents, it's hardly suitable for use by application programmers. Another type of electrically erasable programmable read-only memory **(EEPROM) chip** is also available that can be reprogrammed with special electrical pulses. Regardless of the type of ROM chip used, however, they all serve to increase the efficiency of a CPU by controlling the performance of a few specialized tasks. A generalized CPU can be made to meet the unique needs of different users merely by changing microprograms. Figure 5-15 summarizes the list of semiconductor storage chips that we've now encountered.

Figure 5-15 Semiconductor storage chips and their use.

| Memory type | | Some applications |
|---|---|---|
| Random-access memories (RAMs) | Dynamic RAM | Main primary storage device for mainframes, minicomputers, and personal computers. |
| | Static RAM | Microcomputers requiring a small storage capacity; high-speed versions for minicomputuer buffer storage; low-power versions for portable computers. |
| Read-only memory categories (ROMs) | ROM | Program storage for personal computers; character set storage for visual displays and printers. |
| | PROM | Microprogram control instructions for minicomputers; military and automobile uses. |
| | EPROM | Same as for ROM. Ability to reprogram makes it easier to correct errors during software development. |
| | EEPROM | ROM and EPROM applications needing occasional program or data modifications. |

## A BRIEF HISTORY OF THE EEPROM

EEPROMs date back to the mid-1970s, but the early versions could store only low levels of memory. In 1980, however, Intel Corp. introduced a model of the chip with 16,000 bits of memory, and the circuit was hailed as having limitless potential. Intel's chip, the 2816, seemed to represent an ingenious solution to a basic problem with computer memory.

Random access memory, or RAM, which stores programs and data in most computers, goes blank when the computer's power is turned off or fails. An alternate type—called ROM, or read only memory—does retain its contents when the power goes off. But until recently the contents couldn't be changed. ROM chips were used when a power loss was a constant risk and reprogramming usually wasn't necessary—in video games, for example.

During the late 1970s, however, chips were developed that brought ROM closer to the versatility of RAM. First came programmable ROM or PROM, which a user could fill with information—but only once. An erasable PROM, or EPROM, could be reprogrammed repeatedly, but only by bathing it in ultraviolet light in a time-consuming procedure.

The chip that came the closest to combining the ROM's permanence and

the RAM's flexibility was the EEPROM, which could be reprogrammed with electric signals without removing it from the computer. In addition to Intel's much-heralded version, two competitors—both Intel spinoffs—brought out EEPROMs of their own. SEEQ Technology Inc. made a chip that ran on five volts, the standard for most small computers. (Intel's chip required additional circuitry to convert it to five volts.) And Xicor Inc. developed a semiconductor it called a nonvolatile RAM, or NOVRAM, which puts RAM and EEPROM on the same chip. The RAM does the high-speed processing of programs and data and then transfers its contents to the EEPROM before the power is shut off.

At the start, the industry was bullish about the EEPROM. A poll of semiconductor makers by Electronics magazine at the end of 1981 predicted that $87 million of the chips would be sold to U.S. customers that year and $141 million in 1982. "They were going hog wild," recalls Rod Beresford, an editor who worked on the poll. "Meanwhile, the designers were scratching their heads and saying 'Let's see what this thing does.'"

The next year's poll told a different story. EEPROM consumption for 1981 was estimated at only $36.6 million, and

the figure for 1982 was reduced to $63.3 million.

What happened? "Talking about using the part is just a far cry from actually using it," says A.A. LaFountain III, who follows the semiconductor industry for Shearson/American Express Inc.

But now the EEPROM seems to have overcome that problem. Several manufacturers offer the more convenient five-volt version, and the chip's top memory level has been increased to 64,000 bits, with 128,000 on the way. Prices have plummeted, too. Intel's 1980 chip cost about $120. Today, the average price for a 16,000-bit version is about $8, and market researchers guess it will be half that in 1985.

As a result, a lot of companies plan to use the chip in their new products, and most analysts predict the EEPROM will reach half a billion dollars in sales in 1986. "It's a reality, now," says Dan Sowin, the marketing director for memories at National Semiconductor Corp., which entered the EEPROM market a year ago. "It isn't just a topic of conversation anymore."

—Michael W. Miller, "Chip Breaks 'Catch-22' Cycle in the Semiconductor Industry," *The Wall Street Journal*, Sept. 2, 1983, p. 15. Reprinted by permission of *The Wall Street Journal*. © *Dow Jones & Company 1983. All Rights Reserved.*

## Feedback and Review 5-3

To test and reinforce your understanding of the types of storage components found in a central processor, *match* the letter of the appropriate key term to the definition or concept to which it belongs. (Place the correct letter in the space provided.)

a) K  b) nonvolatile  c) nine  d) microprograms  e) Josephson junction  f) transistors  g) RAM chip  h) magnetic cores  i) four  j) volatile  k) high-speed buffer  l) vacuum tubes  m) ROM chip

___1. The type of primary storage device used in the 1940s by the ENIAC computer

___2. The dominant primary storage device between 1960 and 1975.

___3. A _____ storage medium retains its magnetic state in the absence of electrical power.

___4. A _____ storage medium loses the data stored in the event of a power failure.

___5. The number of bits needed in a storage unit to code 8-bit bytes and provide for a parity check.

___6. The most popular primary storage device used today, the _____ permits users to randomly select and use any of its storage locations, and it provides access to any of these locations in the same amount of time.

___7. The storage cell circuits in some semiconductor storage chips contain capacitors and _____.

___8. A symbol used to represent $2^{10}$ or 1,024 units.

___9. During the last decade, the number of bits that can be stored on a chip has increased _____ times every 3 years.

___10. The _____ is a superconducting switch that may be found in future primary storage components.

___11. A specialized storage element found in the CPU and used during processing operations as a "scratch pad."

___12. Special programs dealing with very low-level machine functions that can be substituted for additional hardware circuits.

___13. A specialized read-only storage device used for control purposes that cannot be changed or altered by users.

# EXECUTING STORED INSTRUCTIONS: THE ARITHMETIC-LOGIC AND CONTROL FUNCTIONS

Up to now, we've concentrated almost exclusively on the storage function of the CPU. It's logical to spend so much time on this function because the data that people are interested in must be stored in a coded form before they can be processed. But you know that to process data every computer must have components to perform the arithmetic-logic and general control functions. Let's now take a quick look at these components.

### The Arithmetic-Logic Section

You'll recall that the arithmetic-logic section is where the actual data processing occurs. All calculations are made and all comparisons take place in this section (also called the arithmetic-logic unit or **ALU**). To see how an ALU operates on data, let's look once again at the Longhorn College payroll application presented earlier in the chapter. We won't need all the program instructions from the payroll application to demonstrate ALU operation. The ones from Figure 5-1 that we *will* need are reproduced in Figure 5-16a. These instructions are written so that we can understand them, but they cannot be interpreted in this form by the computer. A version of these same instructions that *would* permit machine interpretation is shown in Figure 5-16b.

| 06 Read contents of address 01 into arithmetic—logic section | 07 Multiply contents of arithmetic—logic section by contents of address 02 | 08 Duplicate preceding result in address 15 | 09 Multiply contents of address 03 by preceding result in arithmetic—logic section | 10 Subtract contents in arithmetic—logic section from contents of address 15 |
|---|---|---|---|---|

(a)

| 06 CLA 01 | 07 MUL 02 | 08 STO 15 | 09 MUL 03 | 10 SUB 15 |
|---|---|---|---|---|

(b)

**Figure 5-16** (a) Five of the program steps needed to prepare the Longhorn College payroll application illustrated in Figure 5-1. (b) The five program steps presented in Figure 5-1 in a form the computer can interpret.

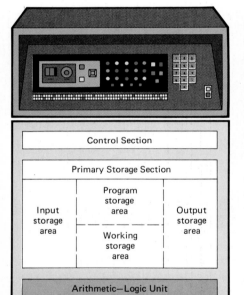

Control Section

Primary Storage Section

Input storage area | Program storage area | Working storage area | Output storage area

Arithmetic—Logic Unit

The instruction in address 06—CLA 01—calls for the computer to first CLear the ALU of all previously stored data and then Add (store) the contents of address 01 to that section. Both the ALU and the control section have special-purpose storage locations called **registers.** The number of registers varies among computers as does the data-flow pattern. In Longhorn College's computer, the contents of address 01 are entered into an ALU register known as the **accumulator.** Thus, as Figure 5-17 illustrates, Rob's 20 hours worked—the contents of address 01—are now held in both address 01 and in the accumulator. (Once again, the circled address numbers shown in the figure indicate how the computer responds to the instruction stored in that address.)

The next instruction in address 07 is MUL 02. This is interpreted to mean that the contents of address 02 ($5 per hour) are to be MULtiplied by the contents in the accumulator (20 hours) to get Rob's gross pay. The following steps are carried out in the execution of this instruction (see Figure 5-17a):

■ The contents of address 02 are read into a *storage register* in the ALU.

■ The data that are now in the accumulator (20 hours) and the storage register ($5 per hour) are copied in the **adder**—the arithmetic element in the ALU that also performs subtractions, multiplications, and divisions on binary digits.

■ The multiplication is executed in the adder and the $100 result is *entered into the accumulator*. As you know, the act of writing the $100 result into the accumulator erases the 20 hours that was previously stored in that register.

**Figure 5-17** (a) The operation of an arithmetic-logic section in a CPU. Every arithmetic-logic section uses special storage locations or registers. In this example, two such registers—the accumulator and storage register—are used to hold the data items being processed. All arithmetic functions are handled by the adder. The adder is also used in logic operations involving comparisons. By subtracting one value from another, the adder can tell if the first value is equal to, less than, or greater than the second value. The circled address numbers in the data flow lines indicate how the computer responds to the instructions stored in those addresses. (b) The execution of the instruction found in address 09. (c) The execution of the instruction found in address 10.

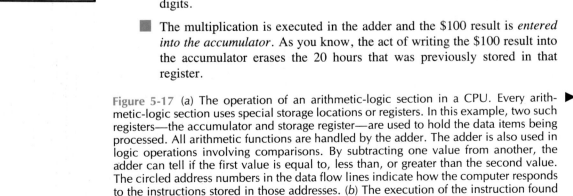

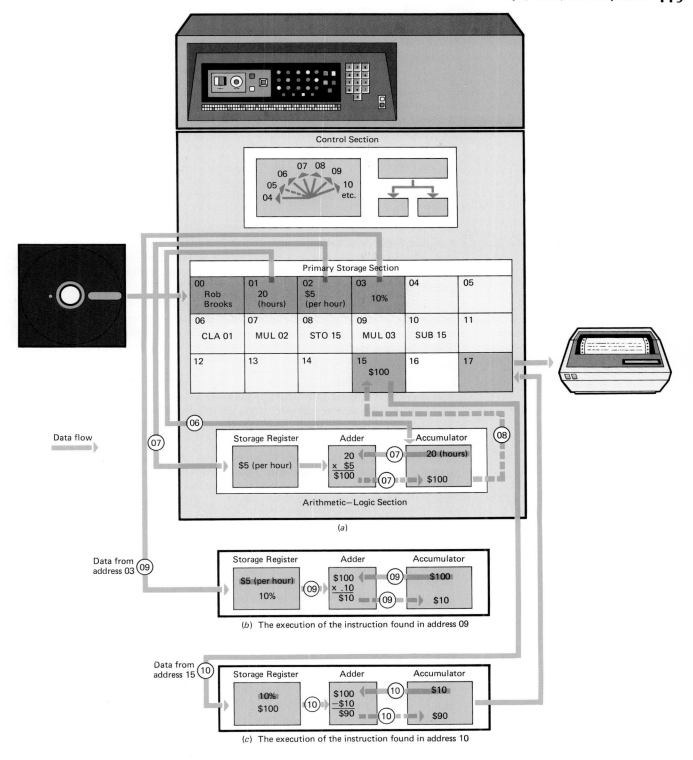

Control Section

07  08
06        09
05            10
04          etc.

Primary Storage Section

| 00 Rob Brooks | 01 20 (hours) | 02 $5 (per hour) | 03 10% | 04 | 05 |
| 06 CLA 01 | 07 MUL 02 | 08 STO 15 | 09 MUL 03 | 10 SUB 15 | 11 |
| 12 | 13 | 14 | 15 $100 | 16 | 17 |

Data flow

(06)

(07)

| Storage Register | Adder | Accumulator |
| $5 (per hour) | 20 <br> × $5 <br> $100 | 20 (hours) <br> $100 |

(07)  (08)

(07)

Arithmetic—Logic Section

(a)

Data from address 03 (09)

| Storage Register | Adder | Accumulator |
| $5 (per hour) <br> 10% | $100 <br> × .10 <br> $10 | $100 <br> $10 |

(09)  (09)

(09)

(b) The execution of the instruction found in address 09

Data from address 15 (10)

| Storage Register | Adder | Accumulator |
| 10% <br> $100 | $100 <br> −$10 <br> $90 | $10 <br> $90 |

(10)  (10)

(10)

(c) The execution of the instruction found in address 10

After executing the instruction in address 07, the computer moves to the one in address 08. This instruction—STO 15—tells the machine to *STO*re the *contents of the accumulator* in address 15. Entering the $100 amount into address 15 is destructive to any previous data that might be there, but the readout from the accumulator is nondestructive.

Figures 5-17*b* and 5-17*c* show how the ALU will execute the instructions found in addresses 09 and 10. In Figure 5-17*b*, the MUL 03 instruction in address 09 causes the data from address 03 (10 percent) to be entered into the storage register, thereby destroying the previous contents of $5 per hour. The contents of the accumulator ($100) and the storage register (10 percent) are now multiplied in the adder. The $10 result is entered back into the accumulator, thereby erasing the $100 amount. Figure 5-17*c* shows what happens when the instruction in address 10—SUB 15— is executed. The data stored in address 15 ($100) are read into the storage register and you know what this does to the 10 percent figure that was there. The adder then *SUB*tracts the $10 in the accumulator from this $100 amount in the storage register to get Rob's $90 take-home pay, which is entered back into the accumulator. From there, the $90 amount is first read into address 17 and then printed on Rob's paycheck.

By tracing through the operations of an ALU, you've seen that every arithmetic step requires two numbers and produces a result. Multiplication, for example, uses a multiplicand and a multiplier to get a product. Although *every* ALU must be able to manage the two data words and the result, different processing and storage techniques are used in different models.

In addition to arithmetic functions, the ALU also handles logic operations. You've seen that logic operations usually involve comparisons. The adder in the ALU is generally used to compare two numbers by subtracting one from the other. The sign (negative or positive) and the value of the difference tell the processor that the first number is equal to, less than, or greater than the second number. Branches are provided in the program for the computer to follow, depending on the result of such a comparison. Alphabetic data may also be compared according to an assigned order sequence. Some processors have a *comparer* in the ALU. Data from an accumulator and a storage register may be examined by the comparer to yield the logic decision.

**The Control Section**

The control section of the CPU selects and interprets program instructions and then sees that they are executed. The ALU responds to commands coming from the control section. You've just seen that a basic instruction that can be interpreted by a computer generally has at least two parts. The first part is the *operation* or *command* that is to be followed (MUL, STO, SUB, etc.). The second part is the *address* which locates the data or instructions to be manipulated. The basic components contained in the control section of Longhorn College's computer (shown once again in Figure 5-18) are the *instruction register, sequence register, address register,* and *decoder.*

Let's follow an instruction from the Longhorn payroll application through the control section to see how it's handled. We'll assume that the CLA 01 instruction in address 06 has just been executed and that 20 hours is stored in the accumulator of the ALU. The following steps are then carried out (the circled letters in the lines in Figure 5-18 correspond to these steps):

(a) The instruction in address 07 (MUL 02) is selected by the **sequence register** and read into the **instruction register** in the control section. [We'll have more to say about the sequence register in step *(e)* below.]

(b) The operation part (MUL) and the address part (02) of the instruction are separated. The operation is sent to the **decoder,** where it is *interpreted.* The computer is designed to respond to a number of commands, and it now knows that it's to multiply.

(c) The address part of the instruction is sent to the **address register.**

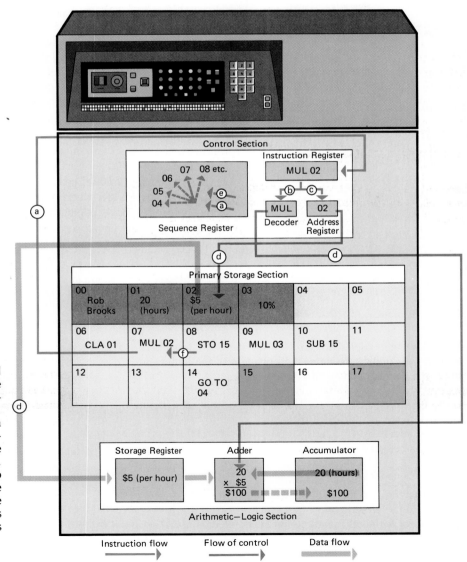

Figure 5-18 The operation of a control section in a CPU. An instruction to be executed is selected by a sequence register and read into an instruction register. The function to be performed is sent to a decoder where it is interpreted. The location of the data or other instruction to be manipulated is sent to an address register. A signal may then be sent to the ALU to execute the specified function using the contents of the specified address. These steps occur as each program instruction is considered. The circled letters in the lines refer to the steps discussed in the text.

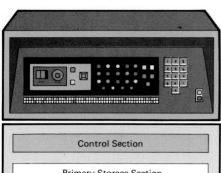

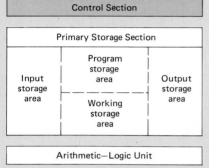

(d) The signal is sent to enter the contents of address 02 into the ALU. The command to multiply also goes to the ALU where the instruction is *executed*.

(e) The processing began when the sequence register was set to address 04, the location of the first program instruction. As each earlier instruction was executed, the sequence register automatically moved to the next instruction in the processing sequence. Now as the multiplication in address 07 is being executed, the sequence register is again automatically moved to address 08. Note, however, that when the sequence register gets to address 14, it encounters an instruction that reads GO TO 04. This instruction alters the advance of the sequence register and resets it to address 04.

(f) The instruction in address 08 moves into the instruction register, and the above steps are repeated.

There are two cycles or phases that occur as each program instruction is considered. Step *d* is the **execution cycle.** The other steps comprise the **instruction cycle.** Although the operations of the ALU and the control unit may seem cumbersome, we know that they are performed with incredible speed. Most computers are *synchronous* machines. That is, the steps mentioned above are synchronized by an electronic clock that emits millions of regularly spaced electrical pulses each second. Commands are interpreted and then executed at proper intervals, and the intervals are timed by a specific number of these pulses. Thus, the speed with which an instruction is executed is directly related to the computer's built-in **clock speed—** that is, the number of pulses produced each second. This clock speed is measured in **megahertz (or MHz),** where mega means million and Hertz means times per second. Most of today's popular personal computers have clock speeds in the 2- to 8-MHz range. But microprocessors are now being designed with a rating of 10 MHz or more. Larger machines are even faster.

# Feedback and Review 5-4

The following multiple-choice review questions will test and reinforce your understanding of the operation of the arithmetic-logic and control sections of a CPU:

___1. Both the ALU and the control section have special-purpose storage locations called
a) adders.
b) registers.
c) accumulators.
d) decoders.

___2. The adder in the ALU is used
a) only for addition.
b) for arithmetic functions but never for logic operations.

c) to store the results of addition, but it cannot store other arithmetic results.
d) to perform all arithmetic functions.

___3. The act of reading new data into a register
a) erases the previous contents of the register.
b) is nondestructive to existing contents.
c) is possible only when the register is an accumulator.
d) is possible only when the register is an accumulator or instruction register.

___4. Although different computers use different processing techniques, the ALU in every computer must be able to
a) select and interpret instructions.
b) advance the sequence register.
c) manage two data words and the result.
d) control the decoder.

_____5. A basic instruction that can be interpreted by a computer generally has
  a) a decoder and an accumulator.
  b) an operation and an address.
  c) an instruction register and an address register.
  d) none of the above.

_____6. "An instruction is selected by the _____ register, read into the _____ register, and interpreted by the _____." The terms to complete this sentence are:
  a) sequence, instruction, decoder.

  b) instruction, address, decoder.
  c) decoder, address, accumulator.
  d) address, storage, accumulator.

_____7. The two cycles or phases that occur as each program instruction is considered are:
  a) synchronous and clocking.
  b) clocking and execution.
  c) pulsating and clocking.
  d) instruction and execution.

 ## LOOKING BACK

**1.** Computers are classified by the type of data they are designed to process. A _digital computer_ is one that directly counts discrete values, while an _analog_ computer measures continuously variable physical magnitudes that are analogous to the numbers being considered. Most computers are digital devices that are designed for special or general use. The emphasis in this book is on general-purpose digital systems.

**2.** Storage locations in the primary storage section of a CPU are identified by _address numbers_. These locations are able to hold either data or program instructions. When the contents of an address are needed by a program, the machine must be given the address number so that it can locate the desired item. The act of retrieving existing data or instructions from an address is nondestructive, but entering new contents into an address will erase the previous contents.

**3.** The storage capacity of an address is built into a computer. Some computers can only store a _fixed number of characters_ in each numbered address location. They then treat these characters as a single entity or _word_. Such systems are said to be _word addressable,_ and they use a _fixed word-length storage_ approach. Other computers can only store a _single character_ in each address location. These machines are said to be _character addressable,_ and they employ a _variable word-length storage_ approach. There are advantages and limitations to each of these approaches. Many of today's computers have been built with the flexibility to operate on either single characters or fixed-length words. Such systems are said to be _byte addressable._

**4.** Every computer stores numbers, letters, and other characters in a coded form. Each character is represented by a coded string of binary digits _(bits)_ that are treated as a unit. Binary numbers (0s and 1s) are used to simplify computer design. A 4-bit _binary coded decimal_ (BCD) coding system can be used to

represent decimal numbers, but 6-, 7-, or 8-bit codes are used to represent characters in _alphanumeric versions_ of BCD. Since the 64 possible characters permitted by the standard 6-bit BCD format isn't enough for many applications, the 7- and 8-bit formats are generally used. The _ASCII_ 7-bit code is used in personal computers, and two popular 8-bit codes (_EBCDIC_ and _ASCII-8_) are used in many larger machines.

**5.** To detect any code errors that may occur, an extra _check bit_ or _parity bit_ may be added to each 6-, 7-, or 8-bit character represented in storage. The check bit is used to make sure that every valid character in a computer that uses even parity will always have an even number of 1 bits. Parity checking circuits in the computer can then notify the computer operator if a bit is lost.

**6.** Many types of primary storage devices have been used. Between 1960 and 1975, the dominant storage medium was _magnetic cores_. Since then, however, volatile RAM _semiconductor storage chips_ have been used because of economic and performance factors. And future storage devices promise to be much more compact and faster than anything in current use.

**7.** In addition to the primary storage section, many CPUs also have built-in specialized storage elements that are used for specific processing and control purposes. A _high-speed buffer_ or _cache_ memory may be used to improve processing speed. And _microprograms_ that deal with special machine functions may be held in nonvolatile read-only memory _(ROM)_ chips. Microprogram instructions are repeatedly called on to control the CPU as it performs certain basic operations.

**8.** The arithmetic-logic section does the actual processing under program control. During the execution cycle, stored data may be moved to registers in the _ALU_. From there they are manipulated by _adder_ circuits to yield a result that may be stored in a *register* (e.g., the *accumulator*) or transferred to some other storage location. The adder may also be used to compare values for logic purposes.

9. The control section selects, interprets, and sees to the execution of program instructions in their proper sequence. Several basic registers are required to perform the control function. The speed with which an instruction is executed is directly related to the computer's built-in clock speed.

## KEY TERMS AND CONCEPTS

discrete data 99
continuous data 99
digital computer 99
analog computer 99
hybrid computer 100
special-purpose computer 100
general-purpose computer 100
address 101
destructive read-in (or write) 104
nondestructive read-out 104
word 104
word-addressable computer 104
fixed word-length storage 104
character-addressable computer 104
variable word-length storage 104
bit 105
byte 105
byte-addressable computer 105
binary numbering system 107
the binary coded decimal (BCD) approach 108

6-bit BCD code 109
7-bit BCD code 109
8-bit BCD code 109
ASCII 109
EBCDIC 109
ASCII-8 109
even parity 110
odd parity 110
parity checking 110
nonvolatile storage 111
semiconductor storage 112
RAM (random access memory) chip 112
dynamic RAM chips 112
volatile storage 113
static RAM chips 113
uninterruptible power system (UPS) 113
K 113
Josephson junction 113
ballistic transport 114
high-speed buffer (or cache) storage 114

microprogram 114
ROM (read-only memory) chip 115
PROM (programmable read-only memory) chip 115
EPROM (erasable and programmable read-only memory) chip 115
EEPROM (electrically erasable and programmable read-only memory) chip 115
ALU 117
register 118
accumulator 118
adder 118
sequence register 121
instruction register 121
decoder 121
address register 121
execution cycle 122
instruction cycle 122
clock speed 122
megahertz (MHz) 122

## TOPICS FOR REVIEW AND DISCUSSION

**1.** *(a)* What's a digital computer? *(b)* An analog computer? *(c)* A hybrid computer?

**2.** How does a special-purpose computer differ from a general-purpose machine?

**3.** *(a)* How is an addressable storage location similar to a post office box? *(b)* How do storage locations differ from mailboxes?

**4.** Discuss how storage locations are used during the processing of an application.

**5.** Discuss this statement: "Over the years, computer manufacturers have used several different design approaches to partition the primary storage section into addresses."

**6.** *(a)* Distinguish between word-addressable and character-addressable computers. *(b)* What is an advantage of each of these computer types?

**7.** *(a)* What is a byte-addressable computer? *(b)* How does it achieve its flexibility?

**8.** *(a)* What is the difference between an additive and a positional numbering system? *(b)* Give examples of both types of numbering systems.

**9.** Identify two principles that apply to any positional numbering system.

**10.** Why have computers been designed to use the binary numbering system?

**11.** (a) What is the decimal equivalent of $1101011_2$? (b) Of $11010_2$?

**12.** (a) What is $150_{10}$ in 4-bit BCD code? (b) What is $75_{10}$ in BCD?

**13.** Why has the standard 6-bit BCD code been extended to 8 bits?

**14.** Identify and discuss (a) the 7-bit BCD code and (b) the two popular 8-bit codes.

**15.** How can a computer detect whether a bit in a character code is lost during processing?

**16.** (a) What types of primary storage devices have been used in the past? (b) What is the dominant primary storage technology at the present time? (c) What technology may emerge in the future?

**17.** Why are semiconductor chips popular as storage devices?

**18.** (a) Identify the specialized storage elements that may be found in a CPU. (b) How may these elements be used?

**19.** Discuss the operation of the arithmetic-logic section in a CPU.

**20.** Discuss the operation of the control section in a CPU.

## PROJECT TO LOOK INTO

**1.** Let's assume that you have a friend who is the owner of a small business. Your friend is thinking about buying a personal computer for business use and asks you to help identify some models that might be suitable. Identify three possible personal computer candidates and determine the following characteristics for each: word length; type of primary storage; minimum capacity of primary storage; maximum capacity of primary storage; ROM storage available (if any); type of microprocessor chip used; clock speed of the microprocessor; purchase price range. Prepare a report outlining your findings.

## ANSWERS TO FEEDBACK AND REVIEW SECTIONS

**5-1**

The solution to the crossword puzzle is shown below:

| 1 D | I | 2 G | I | 3 T | A | L | | 4 A | D | D | R | 5 E | S | S | A | B | L | 6 E |
|---|---|---|---|---|---|---|---|---|---|---|---|---|---|---|---|---|---|---|
| I | | E | | N | | | | | | | | F | | | | | | R |
| S | | 7 F | A | S | T | | | | | 8 F | I | X | E | D | | | | A |
| C | | E | | L | | | 9 L | | 10 P | I | | | | | | | | S |
| R | | R | 11 W | O | R | D | A | | | C | | | 12 B | Y | T | E | | |
| E | | A | | G | | | C | 13 B | I | T | S | | | | | | 14 O | |
| T | | L | | | | | K | | E | | | 15 O | | | | | N | |
| E | | 16 A | D | D | R | E | S | S | | N | 17 U | N | I | Q | U | E | | |
| | | | | | | 18 B | Y | T | E | | L | | | | | | | |
| 19 D | E | S | T | R | O | Y | | | | | 20 H | Y | B | R | I | D | | |

**5-2**
1. F
2. T
3. T
4. F
5. T
6. F
7. F
8. T
9. F
10. F
11. T
12. F
13. T
14. T

**5-3**
1. l
2. h
3. b
4. j
5. c
6. g
7. f
8. a
9. i
10. e
11. k
12. d
13. m

**5-4**
1. b
2. d
3. a
4. c
5. b
6. a
7. d

# Silicon Compilers Ease
# Design of Computer Circuits

. . . Today's microelectronic circuits already crowd a half-million transistors on a piece of metal no larger than a fingernail, and it will soon be possible to build chips that contain a million or more transistors. But as the number of transistors on a chip rises, so does the difficulty of finding a market large enough to justify the cost of building the circuit.

Perhaps more important, the time required to design

Engineers design chips with the aid of computer software, which may be used to customize the circuits or to design entire chips for standard functions. (Photo courtesy Calma Company, a wholly owned subsidiary of the General Electric Company)

Purified silicon is melted and shaped into ingots, and the ingots are then sliced into thin wafers on which chips are fabricated. (© Chuck O'Rear/ West Light)

the chip also increases so that the market could be gone before the chip is ready. In fact, designing a new integrated circuit other than a microprocessor or a memory is today more of a feat than manufacturing it.

Computer programs, however, are coming to the rescue. The latest class of programs, called silicon compilers, enables designers to specify what a circuit should do and, in a general way, how it should be done. The computer takes it from there.

As yet, there are few silicon compilers. The programs can design only a limited variety of chips at present. And some large makers of integrated circuits are skeptical. "The compilers are interesting toys that aren't all that useful yet," says Stephen P. Nachtsheim, director of design automation at Intel Corp.

But the programs have devised circuits that work and are being produced. A half-dozen companies have been founded recently to exploit the technology, and such prestigious research organizations as American Telephone & Telegraph Corp.'s Bell Laboratories believe it holds considerable promise. Says Edmund Lien, a manager at Bell Labs, "The course of the industry is clear; we have to have smarter tools like silicon compilers." Bell researchers have devised a compiler called Plex that designs computer circuits. "Even with all the computer aids we have now, it takes too many people and too much time to design chips," says Mr. Lien.

To reduce design time, new types of integrated circuits—called gate arrays and standard cells—have been developed. Both types offer the designer a choice of standard circuit elements that a computer automatically connects once the designer specifies what job the circuit is to perform. Silicon compilers go further, not only doing the wiring for the designer but also selecting the circuit elements on his behalf. In the argot of semiconductor manufacturing, the result of gate-array and standard-cell

Wafers are chemically etched and exposed to ultraviolet light in repeated steps which build successive layers of circuits on the chips. (Photo courtesy Teletype Corporation)

After a process called "doping"—implanting wafers with chemical impurities which form positive and negative conducting zones in the circuits—the chips are heated in furnaces to allow the dopants to sink into the layers of circuitry. (Photo courtesy Digital Equipment Corporation)

technologies is semi-custom chips. Silicon compilers produce full-custom chips.

Demand for custom chips is rising rapidly, and some industry experts predict that by the end of the decade, custom circuits will account for more than half of the $40 billion world market for integrated circuits. At present, less than 20% are custom circuits.

Silicon compilers could be as important to the growth of custom circuits as standard circuits like microprocessors have been to the recent growth of electronic equipment in general, according to Frank Garofalo, president of MetaLogic Inc., a Cambridge, Mass., company that is developing a compiler. . . .

The early achievements of silicon compilers are impressive. For example, in collaboration with Seeq Technology, San Jose, Calif., Silicon Compilers designed a communications chip in seven months that ordinarily would have taken about three years and many more people.

Although compilers are fast, one disadvantage is inefficiency. The programs aren't yet able to use the space on a chip as economically as the best human designers can do with only minimal help from a computer.

And advanced as they are, compilers aren't the last word in integrated circuit automation. At Carnegie-Mellon University, researchers are trying to replace circuit designers, not merely provide computer programs to help them. Already one program, a so-called expert system named VTCAD, has devised a new way to build IBM's model 370 computer. "For years people have said that the circuit-design process can't be automated because it involves too much creativity," says Donald E. Thomas Jr., a professor of electrical and computer engineering at Carnegie-Mellon. "It's true that our 370 design wasn't quite as good as an expert would have produced. But IBM called the design 'above average,' and the program did it all on its own."

Once removed from the furnaces, wafers are cut up into chips with diamond saws and tested by technicians. (Photo courtesy Honeywell, Inc.)

Fewer than half the chips on a wafer typically survive the manufacturing process. (Photo courtesy Calma Company, a wholly owned subsidiary of the General Electric Company)

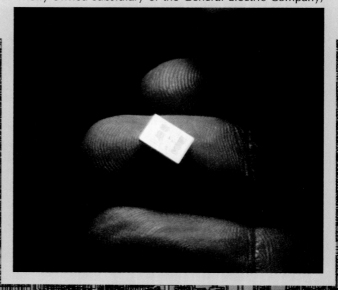

# Data Entry

### Becoming Your Own Operator

The history of the telephone provides an instructive example of what happens as a technology becomes widespread. Anyone over the age of fifty can probably remember when telephones had no dials. To make a call, you picked up the receiver and waited until an operator came on the line. You told the operator the number you wanted, and the call was placed for you. If you placed a long-distance call to some other city—a very exotic undertaking—you'd hear the operators talking to each other in their regional accents, arranging to route your call through their individual switchboards.

By the 1940s, this charming system was breaking down. There simply weren't enough operators to work the switchboards. In fact, projections of future telephone growth suggested that there weren't enough women in America—even if they all became telephone operators—to make the system run.

The solution was direct-dial telephones, which demanded all sorts of automatic switching devices and complex thingamajigs. This flashy new technology obscured a basic truth. The telephone company had actually solved the problem of insufficient operators by making everyone into his own operator. The number of operators now equaled the telephone-using population.

For nearly everyone, the telephone provided the first experience of direct interaction with a computing machine. People had to learn the harsh rules of computer interaction: numbers only, and numbers presented in a specific order. The telephone responded to exactly what you dialed, whether you'd made an error or not. There was no human to catch your mistakes. . . .

Computers are now going through the same series of transformations. Everyone is becoming his own operator. Direct access means power; and it's becoming a necessary skill for everyday life.

Chapter 6 gives you an overview of the input media and devices used to enter data into computer processing systems in both sequential (batch) processing applications and direct-access (online) processing applications. The information in this chapter will enable you to:

- Describe the data entry approaches used in sequential and direct-access processing
- Recognize the importance of input accuracy
- Discuss the characteristics of sequential processing media and describe the input devices used with these media
- Outline the characteristics and applications of the several types of data entry devices used in direct-access processing

# DATA ENTRY: SOME BASIC CONCEPTS

You'll remember from Chapter 1 that the information that people need to support their decisions and actions is produced by a series of data processing activities. The first of these activities is to capture the raw input data. In computer data processing, these facts must either be originated in a machine-readable form or they must be converted into such a form before they can be entered into the computer. Once in

## Chapter Outline

the CPU, of course, they are manipulated and managed to produce the desired information. Much of this chapter deals with the media and devices used to enter data into computer systems. But before we look at media and devices, let's briefly consider some important concepts associated with the data entry function.

## Sources of Input Data

The input data used by an organization are obtained from internal and external sources. The *internal* sources are the people and departments in an organization that produce the facts that must be processed. You've seen in Chapters 2 and 3, for example, that the data contained on the invoices produced by the billing department in an organization are used to provide the input for the organization's sales analysis, inventory control, and accounts receivable reports.

*External* sources of input data include individuals and groups located outside the organization. These sources include customers, suppliers, and competitors. The input data for the sales order, for example, must come from a customer. Business publications, trade associations, and government agencies are good sources of environmental statistics such as per capita income and consumer spending that can be used for planning purposes.

## Data Entry Approaches

You saw in Chapter 2 that files are organized and then processed by the use of *sequential* or *direct-access (online)* techniques. Sequential processing, you'll recall, consists of reading and processing the first record in the file sequence, then the second record in the order, and so on. Direct-access processing, on the other hand, consists of directly locating and updating any record in the file without the need to search through a lengthy sequence of other records. The type of processing employed in a particular application has an important bearing on the data entry approach that's used.

**Data Entry for Sequential Processing.** In a sequential processing application, the raw data to be processed are typically captured on *source documents* such as sales tickets, customer invoices, and payroll time sheets. Data can be recorded directly in a machine-readable form at the source of the transaction through the use of devices such as the imprinters that enter credit card data on sales tickets. Or, the data on the documents may be entered on input media such as magnetic tape or floppy disks by data entry operators. Since customer statements, employee paychecks, and many types of reports need not be prepared on an hourly or daily basis, the invoice, payroll, and other data are accumulated into batches, sorted into the proper processing sequence, and then processed only at scheduled intervals. Data were entered into batch processing applications in several ways in Chapter 2. Figure 6-1 illustrates some common data entry approaches used in large-volume sequential processing applications. A section on the direct data entry devices used for sequential processing is presented later in the chapter.

A large amount of input data is usually prepared and processed in batch applications. Many organizations have one or more data entry departments that are responsible for the preparation of this mass of data. In some organizations, a single data entry group is located near the computer room. The data recorded on the input medium are then easily loaded into a nearby input device. In other organizations, data entry personnel may be found in outlying offices. In this case, the data may be

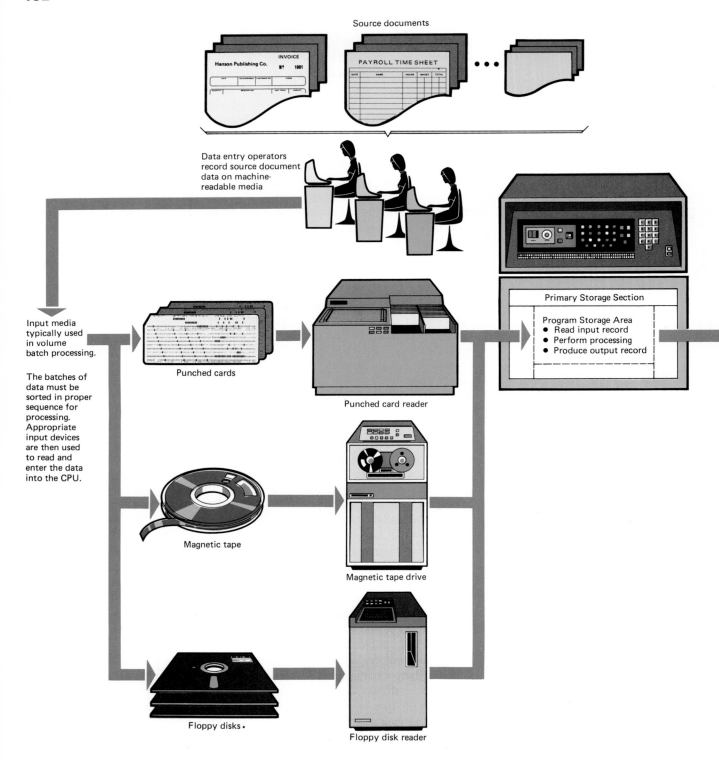

Source documents

Hanson Publishing Co. INVOICE № 1001

PAYROLL TIME SHEET

Data entry operators record source document data on machine-readable media

Input media typically used in volume batch processing.

The batches of data must be sorted in proper sequence for processing. Appropriate input devices are then used to read and enter the data into the CPU.

Punched cards

Punched card reader

Magnetic tape

Magnetic tape drive

Floppy disks .

Floppy disk reader

Primary Storage Section

Program Storage Area
● Read input record
● Perform processing
● Produce output record

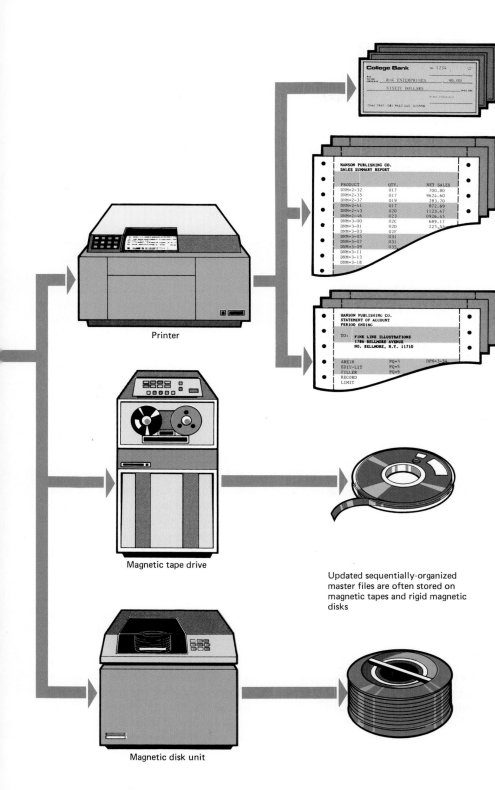

Updated sequentially-organized master files are often stored on magnetic tapes and rigid magnetic disks

Printer

Magnetic tape drive

Magnetic disk unit

**Figure 6-1** Data entry in large-volume sequential processing applications. Transaction data affecting many of the records and files of an organization are captured on source documents. Data entry operators may then record these facts on a suitable input medium. Batches of transaction data are periodically arranged in the same sequence as the master file and are then read into the CPU for processing. As shown here, the result of batch processing is to create updated records in master files and produce various documents such as payroll checks, customer statements, and management reports.

loaded into an input device at a **remote batch station** at the outlying office and sent to the CPU over telephone lines or other data communication channels. As soon as the processing has been completed, the results can be transmitted back to the remote job entry station and printed at that location.

**Data Entry for Direct-Access Processing.** In a direct-access processing application, the records affected by the introduction of new input data are kept in a direct-access storage device (DASD). Input facts are entered from the keyboard of an online data entry device or from some other online instrument at the time the transaction occurs. Source documents may not be used. Because data entry often occurs at the transaction-origination point, online data entry is also called **source data entry,** and direct-access processing is sometimes referred to as **transaction-oriented processing.**

In direct-access processing, the file record(s) affected by the input data is quickly retrieved from the DASD without the need for a sequential file search. After the new transaction data have been processed, the updated record is returned to the DASD. Since DASD records are constantly being updated, system users at online stations can enter inquiries and receive up-to-the-minute reports about the current status of these records. Online processing eliminates the need to accumulate and then sort batches of transactions into a master file sequence prior to processing. However, online processing may require the use of relatively expensive hardware and software resources, and it's not as efficient as batch processing for some applications.

One example of data being entered in an online processing application was presented in Chapter 2 when Rob Brooks made a deposit to his savings account. Another example of online data entry in a factory setting is shown in Figure 6-2. Let's assume that a manufacturer receives an order from a customer to build 100 engine braces. These braces are made out of strips of steel that are cut to length, shaped, drilled, and painted. After the job has been authorized, a shop order is prepared and the identical order data are entered into a work-in-process file in a DASD. A job control number is used to identify the order in the DASD. A copy of the shop order is sent to a shop supervisor and the job is scheduled.

When production begins, and as each activity is completed, data collecting stations located on the shop floor are used by workers to *interact* with a computer program in order to update the job record in the DASD. Messages may be flashed under program control to a screen at the data collection station to guide the worker through the data entry activity. You'll notice in our example in Figure 6-2 that in the first message the worker is asked to enter an employee number and the job control number. The job control number is used to retrieve the job record from the DASD. A **menu** of possible activities related to the particular job is the next message displayed on the station screen. The worker need only key in the correct activity number (the completion of a job task in our example). The program then reads the job record and displays another menu of the different operations required to finish the job. (A different menu would have been displayed if a different activity number had been entered.) In our example, the worker has indicated that the steel for the engine braces has now been cut to length and bent into the proper shape. As a check on the accuracy of the data received, the program sends an acknowledgment mes-

Enter Employee Number:
▮ 1564
Enter Job Control Number:
▮ 1620

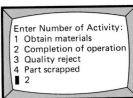

Enter Number of Activity:
1 Obtain materials
2 Completion of operation
3 Quality reject
4 Part scrapped
▮ 2

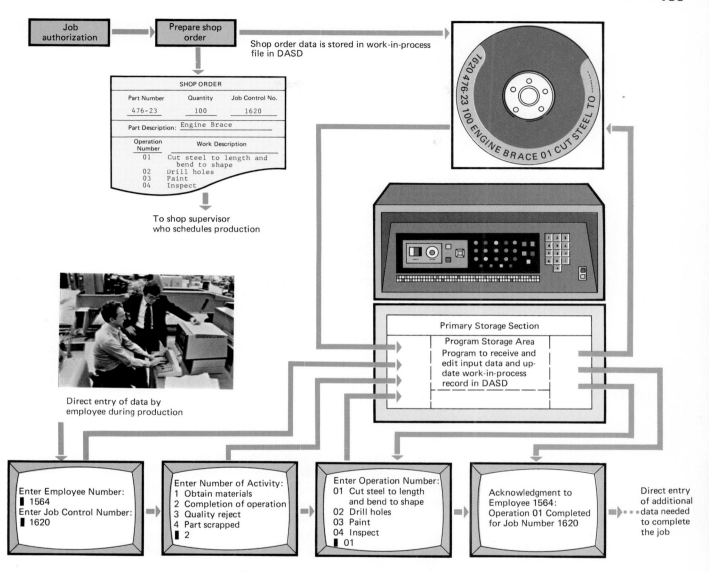

Figure 6-2 Data entry in a direct-access processing application used by manufacturing firms. The initial production order data are entered on a shop order and are stored in a work-in-process file in a DASD. When production begins, data collection stations on the plant floor are used by workers to update the job record in the work-in-process file. The production status of each job is tracked, and each job record is directly updated by workers when an activity has been completed. (Photo courtesy Raytheon Data Systems Company)

sage to the worker who then has a chance to correct any errors. The same **interactive data entry** procedure is followed as additional tasks are completed.

Such a system permits an up-to-the-minute account of the production status of each job in the work-in-process file. It can also be used to assign labor and material costs to each job. Managers can thus use the information produced by such a system to plan and control work flow, and to analyze how efficiently people and machines are being utilized.

## Costs of Data Entry

You've probably noticed that data entry often involves copying facts that have originally been captured on source documents. The transactions on these documents are converted into a machine-readable form and checked for accuracy. Such transcribing activities are expensive since they may require the efforts of many data entry operators. One estimate—made by the U.S. Commerce Department's Institute for Computer Sciences & Technology—put the cost of data entry at 30 to 50 percent of the entire data processing budget of a typical computer-using business.

Some progress has been made in controlling data entry costs by capturing data at the transaction source. You've just seen that data from a shop floor can be entered directly into a computer-based manufacturing system. Since task-completion documents are not used, the need to transcribe facts from such documents is eliminated. However, the progress that has been made in controlling data entry costs is quite modest when compared with the gains made in reducing the costs of processing within the CPU. Thus, as you'll see in later sections of this chapter, developing new direct data entry approaches that eliminate the need to recopy transaction data is a top priority of managers today.

## Importance of Input Accuracy

People have a greater effect on the quality of output of a data processing system than do the data processing machines. It's people who prepare the input data for the machines and thus determine the output quality. You've seen that if reliable programs are used, processors, storage units, and output devices can generally be expected to produce predictable results. But these results will be correct only if the input prepared by people is accurate. The term GIGO (*garbage in–garbage out*), introduced in Chapter 1, emphasizes this fact and indirectly points out the important role people play in a computer system.

People can introduce data errors into a computer system in at least two ways. One way is to record data incorrectly on source documents. Suppose a customer orders an item with a code number of 6783, and the sales order is written to ship product number 6873. If this transposition error is not caught in time, the wrong item will be shipped and an unhappy customer may be billed for an unwanted product. Errors with similar consequences can also be introduced when data entry operators make keying mistakes while copying accurate source document data on an input medium, or when employees strike the wrong keys at an online transaction-recording station.

It's important to catch these errors as early as possible. The Institute of Computer Sciences & Technology of the U.S. Commerce Department estimates that an error detected at the time of data entry can be corrected at a cost of about 10 cents per character in error. Mistakes that are not found until after they are entered into a file, however, may cost $2 or more per character to correct. Of course, if errors cause people to ship the wrong product or if they cause other inappropriate actions, the possible costs can be much greater.

**Detecting Errors in Data Entry**  Input data are normally checked for errors before they are used in a processing application. The goal of an error-checking system is control. That is, the goal is to make sure that all transactions are identified, that these transactions are accurately recorded at the right time, and that all recorded transactions are then entered into the system.[1] A few of the possible error-detecting procedures are:

- ■ *Accounting for prenumbered source documents.* A missing number in a batch of consecutively numbered source documents signals a missing form.

- ■ *Using control totals.* After knowledgeable people have inspected and edited source documents, a **control total** can be prepared for each batch that is to be entered into the system. For example, the total number of items shipped to all customers can be computed for a batch of shipping orders before the orders are recorded on an input medium. The same total can then be obtained from the input medium to see if the figures match. This procedure allows people to detect the presence of one or more transcription errors.

- ■ *Using programmed tests.* Instructions can be written in applications programs to check on the reasonableness of data as they enter the processing operation. The number of such checks is limited only by the programmer's imagination. In the manufacturing example shown in Figure 6-2, for example, **edit checks** can be made to ensure that workers don't enter letters in numeric data spaces, don't use inactive job control numbers, or don't indicate that engine braces have been painted *before* the steel has been cut or the holes have been drilled. **Range checks** can also be written to ensure that numbers fall within an acceptable range of values. If a worker in Figure 6-2 entered an operation number of 14 for a job that only has 4 acceptable operations, a range check would cause an error message to be displayed on the screen of the data collection station. Finally, programmed **limit checks** can be used to verify that input data don't exceed reasonable upper or lower values. Such a check can catch inexcusable errors such as the one that resulted in a high school student in Utah receiving a state tax refund check for $800,014.39 when the correct amount should have been $14.39.

**Feedback and Review 6-1**

You've seen in this section that input data are obtained from internal and external sources. You've also been reminded that the approaches used to enter these data into a computer system can differ depending on whether an application is to be processed by sequential or direct-access methods. Finally, you've learned that data entry costs can be high, that input accuracy is vital, and that error-detecting procedures are normally used to catch mistakes before they are entered into a file. To test and reinforce your understanding of these data entry concepts, place a T or F in the space provided in the following true-false questions:

---

[1] Most organizations must try to strike a balance between input accuracy and cost control. From a control standpoint, an ideal system would catch every error. But such a system (assuming it could be built) would be slow and expensive. The total costs of operating this "errorless" system might easily top the costs required to operate a less-accurate system and then correct at a later time the few errors that managed to slip through.

___1. The first activity in data processing is to capture the raw input data.

___2. An internal source of input data is the purchasing department located within a customer's organization.

___3. The Census Bureau in Washington is an external source of input data for many organizations.

___4. In a sequential processing application, the data to be processed are typically captured by using online terminals.

___5. Source documents are never used with direct-access processing applications.

___6. A telephone line may be used to communicate data from a remote batch station to a CPU.

___7. In a direct-processing application, a DASD is used to store the records that are to be updated.

___8. Manufacturing companies can keep track of their work in process by installing online data collection stations on the shop floor and allowing workers to directly update job records.

___9. When data are entered directly into a CPU from an online data collection station, the application program will generally contain instructions to ensure that the data entered are reasonable.

___10. Greater progress has been made in controlling data costs than in reducing the costs of processing within the CPU.

___11. Computers are primarily responsible for the quality of the output of an application.

___12. In a batch processing application, if the source documents are accurate, then the data entering the computer must also be accurate.

___13. It's better to let errors enter files so that they can all be corrected at once.

___14. A control total can be used to detect transcription errors.

___15. Edit checks, range checks, and limit checks can be written in applications programs to test the reasonableness of data entering the CPU.

# INPUT MEDIA AND DEVICES FOR SEQUENTIAL PROCESSING

You've already encountered examples of the input media and devices that are used in sequential processing in your reading. In Chapter 2, the use of magnetic tape was illustrated in Figure 2-7. And in Chapter 1, you'll recall, the Longhorn College payroll data were entered and read via a floppy disk input medium. In the following sections, we'll examine these and other input media and hardware in more detail.

## Punched Cards and Punched Paper Tape: Two Fading Media

**Punched cards** are the "Old Faithfuls" of data processing.[2] The demise of cards as a viable input medium has been predicted for some time, and their importance is certainly declining. But some are still made and used each year to enter data into computer systems. There are two types of punched cards. One has 80 columns (Figure 6-3) and the other has 96 columns (Figure 6-4). These figures show the setup of punched cards in detail. While the **Hollerith Code** is used to represent data on 80-column cards, you can recognize the standard 6-bit BCD coding system on the 96-column card.

---

[2] An historical account of the development of punched card data processing is included in the "Closer Look" reading following Chapter 1, page 32.

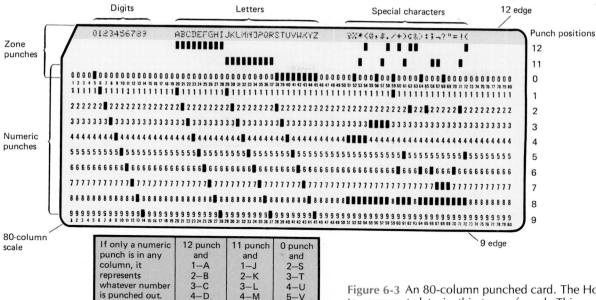

Figure 6-3 An 80-column punched card. The Hollerith Code is used to represent data in this type of card. This coding approach was named after Herman Hollerith, a statistician who developed modern punched card techniques in the late 1800s. Corners of punched cards are often trimmed to help maintain proper positioning during processing.

| If only a numeric punch is in any column, it represents whatever number is punched out. | 12 punch and | 11 punch and | 0 punch and |
|---|---|---|---|
| | 1—A | 1—J | 2—S |
| | 2—B | 2—K | 3—T |
| | 3—C | 3—L | 4—U |
| | 4—D | 4—M | 5—V |
| | 5—E | 5—N | 6—W |
| | 6—F | 6—O | 7—X |
| | 7—G | 7—P | 8—Y |
| | 8—H | 8—Q | 9—Z |
| | 9—I | 9—R | |

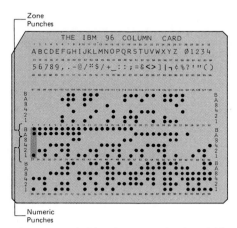

Figure 6-4 A 96-column card using 6-bit BCD coding to represent data.

**Punched Card Equipment.** Figure 6-5 shows in detail how cards are used in a typical application, in this case to prepare one type of sales analysis report. **Card punch** (or **keypunch**) machines are used to enter the invoice data. When a data entry operator depresses a key, the correct combination of holes is punched in a card. After punching, a machine called a *verifier* may be used to ensure that the invoice data have been correctly entered. The cards are loaded into the verifier, and an operator rekeys the invoice data. The verifier senses the facts being keyed and compares them with the data punched in the cards. If a mismatch occurs, the operator is notified to take corrective action. From this discussion, you can see why punched card data entry can be expensive.

The third card machine shown in Figure 6-5 is a *sorter*. Its job is to put the verified cards in some desired order or sequence. In our example the output report is a sales summary for each sales branch showing the amount of each product that has been sold. Thus, for this report the sorter might first put the cards into a sales branch sequence (branch 1, branch 2, etc.) Then, within each sales branch, the cards might be sorted into a product number sequence. After the cards have been sorted in the correct order, they are placed in the input hopper of a *card reader* and individually fed to a read station under the control of the program in the CPU. Photoelectric cells or metal brushes at the read station will detect and then convert the presence or absence of holes in a card into coded electrical pulses that the CPU can accept. Once the invoice data enter the CPU, they are processed according to the instructions in the program to produce the sales reports as output.

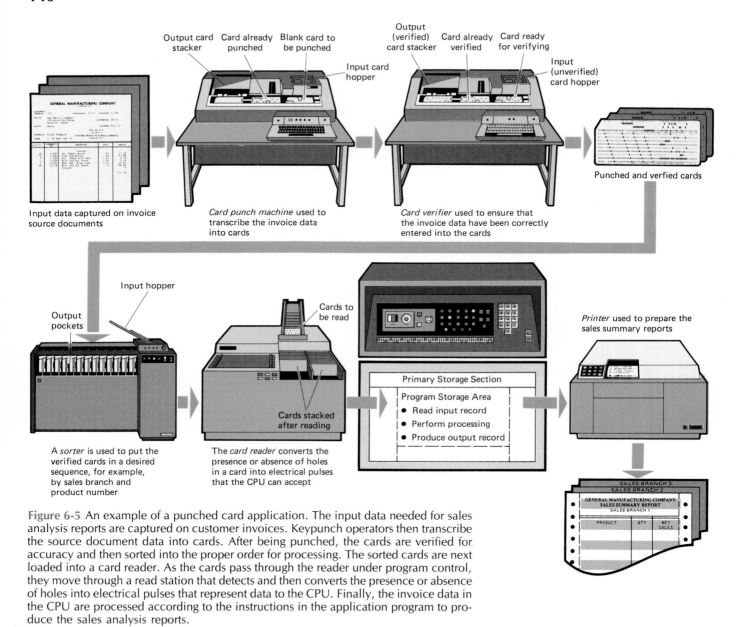

**Figure 6-5** An example of a punched card application. The input data needed for sales analysis reports are captured on customer invoices. Keypunch operators then transcribe the source document data into cards. After being punched, the cards are verified for accuracy and then sorted into the proper order for processing. The sorted cards are next loaded into a card reader. As the cards pass through the reader under program control, they move through a read station that detects and then converts the presence or absence of holes into electrical pulses that represent data to the CPU. Finally, the invoice data in the CPU are processed according to the instructions in the application program to produce the sales analysis reports.

**Advantages and Limitations of Card Input.** The following *advantages* are possible when punched card data entry is used:

- Cards are standardized and can thus be used to enter data into different hardware systems.

■ Records in a card file can be updated simply by inserting, removing, or replacing individual cards.

■ Cards are humanly readable and are easy to handle. It's easy to write on cards and send them through the mail.

In spite of these advantages, however, the following *limitations* are responsible for the fading popularity of punched card data entry:

■ The term **data density** refers to the number of characters that can be stored in a given physical space. Even when all columns are punched, the data density of a card is quite low. (Many more characters can be typed on the card with a typewriter than can be punched into it.)

■ Because of this low density, card files are bulky. They are also slow to process since a lot of paper must be moved to gain access to the punched data.

■ Cards can be misplaced or separated from their proper file deck. And as everyone knows, they can't be folded, stapled, or mutilated. A bent or warped card can jam equipment and further slow the processing.

■ Cards must be sorted and processed in a designated order, and they can't be erased and used to enter new data.

**Punched Paper Tape.** Another fading medium that has also been used for decades is **punched paper tape.** Small paper tape attachments are sometimes found on the typewriterlike terminals that are used to prepare source documents or other messages. The input data and output information being produced by the terminal can be punched into a paper tape and then later entered into a computer by a *paper tape reader*. The 6-bit BCD code discussed in Chapter 5 is used to represent data. Paper tape provides greater data density than punched cards and is cheaper than cards. But it's harder to delete or add records to tapes (splicing is often necessary), and paper tapes are also easily torn and mutilated.

Magnetic Tape

The **transfer rate** of an input medium is the speed with which data can be copied from the medium to CPU storage. Since **magnetic tape** has a much faster transfer rate than cards or paper tape—it's at least five times faster and usually hundreds of times faster—it's a preferred medium for high-speed, large-volume batch processing applications.

You'll notice in Figure 6-6 that the tape itself may be in a large **reel** or a small **cartridge** or **cassette.** However packaged, the tape is similar to the kind used in a sound tape recorder. It's a plastic ribbon coated on one side with an iron-oxide material that can be magnetized. Tiny invisible spots representing data are recorded by electromagnetic pulses on the iron-oxide side of the tape, just as sound waves form magnetic patterns on the tape of a sound recorder. Both the data and the sound can be played back many times. Like recorder tape, computer tape can be erased and reused indefinitely. Old data on a tape are automatically erased as new data are recorded in the same location.

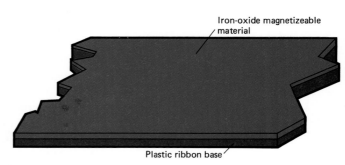

Iron-oxide magnetizeable material

Plastic ribbon base

(*a*) The tape in large reels is used in mainframe computer systems. This tape is usually ½ inch wide and 2,400 feet long. (Lengths of 300, 600, and 1,200 feet are also available.) The iron-oxide coating is applied to one side of the plastic ribbon base.

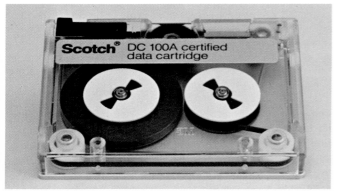

(*b*) Magnetic tape cartridges are used in minicomputers and data entry stations. This tape is ¼ inch wide and varies from 140 to 450 feet in length.

(*c*) Magnetic tape cassettes are used in microcomputers and data entry stations. This tape is either 150 or 300 feet long.

**Figure 6-6** The magnetic tape input medium is packaged in different ways. (Photos courtesy 3M)

**Data Entry Approaches.** Data are entered on magnetic tape in several ways. In one approach, the data used to update a tape file may be written on the tape by the computer during a processing run. Often, however, the following data entry devices are used to record source document data directly on the tape:

1. ***Single-station key-to-tape devices.*** Many of these **key-to-tape devices** were installed in the late 1960s and early 1970s. They enable an operator to key data directly onto a tape. Keyed data are verified by first writing a record stored on tape into a storage section of the machine. The data are then reentered from the source document and a comparison is made to detect errors. Different-size tape is used with different machines. Data recorded in cartridges or cassettes may need to be copied onto larger reels prior to computer entry.

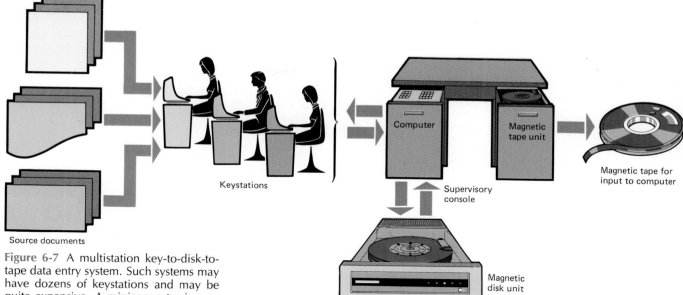

Keystations

Computer

Magnetic tape unit

Supervisory console

Magnetic tape for input to computer

Magnetic disk unit

Source documents

**Figure 6-7** A multistation key-to-disk-to-tape data entry system. Such systems may have dozens of keystations and may be quite expensive. A minicomputer is usually located in a supervisory console to control the system operation. In addition to its editing, storage, and retrieval functions, this minicomputer can also keep track of such statistics as records keyed, number and types of errors detected, and so on.

2. *Multistation key-to-tape devices.* In this approach, there are several keyboards connected to one or more magnetic tape units by a central controlling device. This controller consolidates the data coming from the keyboards.

3. *Multistation key-to-disk-to-tape devices.* As you can see in Figure 6-7, operators also key source document data into this type of system. A minicomputer controls the input coming from the keystations. As data are keyed and displayed at the stations, the types of programmed checks mentioned earlier may be made to ensure that the data are reasonable. Data that pass the programmed tests are temporarily stored on a rigid magnetic disk. Frequently used data fields can also be stored on a disk and called up by an operator to eliminate unnecessary keying. For example, the names and addresses of customers can be stored on a disk by their account number. The operator keying data from customer invoices can then call up this information merely by entering the customer number. After all source documents for a particular processing job have been keyed, the minicomputer program transfers the data on the disk to a magnetic tape for later computer processing. **Key-to-disk-to-tape systems** have replaced many of the earlier key-to-tape devices.

**Data Representation on Magnetic Tape.** Magnetic tape is divided into vertical columns (or *frames*) and horizontal rows (called *channels* or *tracks*). An 8-bit BCD code is used with a **nine-track magnetic tape** format in most magnetic tape systems. This nine-track scheme uses four tracks for the 8, 4, 2, and 1 numeric bit positions, and a fifth track for a parity bit. And as you saw in Chapter 5, the 8-bit

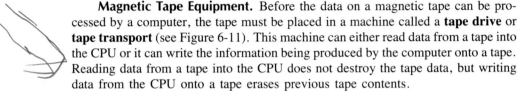

Figure 6-8 A nine-track tape code used with many modern computers. An 8-bit EBCDIC format is used in this example.

*The check position here produces odd parity.

BCD code also has four zone positions. Figure 6-8 shows a few characters coded in a nine-track arrangement. This arrangement has a peculiar appearance because the most frequently used tracks are grouped near the center of the tape. In Chapter 5, the letter A was shown to be represented by a code of 1100 0001 in the 8-bit EBCDIC format. You'll notice in Figure 6-8 that this is the code used to represent A in our example. You can also see that an odd-parity code is used in this example. It's expected that the nine tracks now recorded on standard ½-inch-wide tape will be increased to 18 or more tracks in future tape systems.

Since magnetic tape is a continuous-length medium, how can different file records be identified on a tape? The answer is that records may be separated by blank spaces on the tape called **interrecord gaps.** These gaps are automatically created when data are written on the tape. When record data are read from a moving tape into the CPU, the movement will stop when a gap is reached. The tape remains motionless until the record has been processed and then moves again to enter the next record into the computer. This procedure is repeated until the file has been processed. Figure 6-9 shows how a file of prospective customers could be represented on tape. Of course, tape records can be of varying lengths. If a tape contains a large number of very short records, and if each record is separated by an interrecord gap, then more than half of the tape could be blank and there would be a constant interruption in tape movement. To avoid this inefficient situation, several short records can be combined into a tape **block** (see Figure 6-10).

**Magnetic Tape Equipment.** Before the data on a magnetic tape can be processed by a computer, the tape must be placed in a machine called a **tape drive** or **tape transport** (see Figure 6-11). This machine can either read data from a tape into the CPU or it can write the information being produced by the computer onto a tape. Reading data from a tape into the CPU does not destroy the tape data, but writing data from the CPU onto a tape erases previous tape contents.

You can see in Figure 6-12 that the tape on a reel moves through a tape drive in much the same way that a film moves through a movie projector. The tape movement during processing is from the supply reel past a read/write head assembly to the take-up reel. There's a **read/write head** in the tape drive for each tape track.

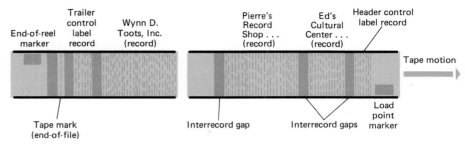

Figure 6-9 A file of prospective customers. The first several feet of tape are unrecorded to allow for threading on the equipment. A reflective marker known as the *load point* indicates to the equipment the beginning of usable tape, while a similar *end-of-reel* marker signals the end of usable tape. The markers are placed on opposite edges of the tape for machine identification purposes. Between the load-point marker and the first data record is a *header control label*, which identifies the tape contents, gives the number of the program to be used when the tape is processed, and supplies other control information that helps to prevent an important tape from accidently being erased. Following the last data record in a file is a *trailer control label*, which may contain a count of the number of records in a file. A comparison between the number of records processed and the number in the file may be made to determine that all have been accounted for. The end of a file may be signaled by a special one-character record. This special character is called a *tape mark*.

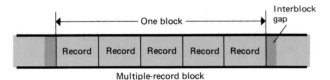

Figure 6-10 Several short records are commonly combined into a block and read into the CPU as a single unit to save tape space and speed data input. The program of instructions in the CPU separates the records within a block for processing.

Figure 6-11 A bank of tape drives in a large installation. (Courtesy Radio Shack, A Division of Tandy Corporation)

Figure 6-13 shows that each head is a small electromagnet with tiny gaps between the poles.

There are usually several tape drives used in an installation. In most applications, a tape is either read or written in a single pass. Therefore, to update a file of prospective customers, one unit may read in the old master file while another feeds in update transactions and a third writes the updated master file. If the update program is kept on tape, a fourth drive will be needed to enter the processing instructions.

**Advantages and Limitations of Magnetic Tape Input.** The following *advantages* are possible with magnetic tape data entry:

- ■ *Unlimited length of records.* The fixed size of punched cards tends to limit record length, but any number of characters can be placed in a magnetic tape record. Sequentially organized files can be as long as necessary.

- ■ *High data density.* A typical $10\frac{1}{2}$-inch reel of magnetic tape is 2,400 feet long and is able to hold 800, 1,600, or 6,250 characters in each *inch* of this length. (The actual number of characters per inch depends on the tape drive used.) Thus, if 6,250 characters are held in each inch of tape, and if the tape is 28,800 inches long (2,400 feet times 12 inches), then the maximum capacity of the tape is 180 million characters. It would take over 2 million punched cards to record an equivalent amount of data. That's a stack of cards a quarter of a mile high! Furthermore, it's expected that when new tape drives are introduced that can place 18 or more tracks on a standard $\frac{1}{2}$-inch-wide reel, it will be possible to double or even triple the current data density of magnetic tape.

- ■ *Low cost and ease of handling.* A $10\frac{1}{2}$-inch reel of tape costs less than $20. This is much less than the hundreds of thousands (and even millions) of cards that it can replace. An additional cost benefit is that tape can be

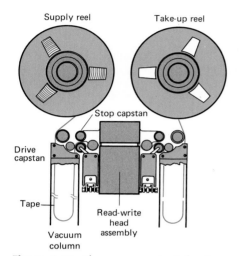

**Figure 6-12** The movement of the tape during processing is from the supply reel to the take-up reel. Tapes may move at speeds up to 200 inches per second, and they achieve this rate in a few milliseconds. Several methods are used to prevent tape damage from sudden bursts of speed. One such method is to use vacuum columns to hold slack tape.

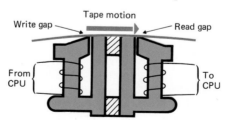

**Figure 6-13** A read/write head. There are nine read/write heads in a nine-track tape drive. When a tape is being read, the magnetized patterns on the tape induce pulses of current in the read coils and these pulses are transmitted as data into the CPU. In the writing operation, electrical pulses flow through the write coils at the appropriate tracks causing the iron-oxide coating of the tape to be magnetized in the proper pattern.

erased and reused many times. Since the reel is compact and weighs less than 3 pounds, it obviously takes up much less storage space and is much easier to handle than the equivalent number of cards.

■ *Rapid transfer rate.* Neither cards nor punched tape can compare with magnetic tape in the speed with which data can be copied into (or received from) the CPU. A tape drive can enter data into the CPU hundreds of times faster than the fastest card reader.

But there are *limitations* to the use of magnetic tape for data entry. Included among these are:

■ *Lack of direct access to records.* Magnetic tape is a batch processing medium. The entire tape must be read and processed to update the sequentially organized records in the file. If frequent access to file records is needed on a rapid and random basis, then the file should not be stored on magnetic tape. Too much operator time would be required to load and unload tapes, and too much machine time would be wasted in reading records that aren't needed.

■ *Need for machine interpretation.* Since the magnetized spots on a tape can't be seen by people, a printing run must be made if the accuracy of tape data is questioned.

■ *Environmental problems.* Specks of dust and uncontrolled humidity or temperature levels can cause tape-reading errors. Tapes and reel containers must be carefully labeled and controlled so that an important file is not erased by mistake.

Figure 6-14 The IBM 3740 data entry system. Source document data are keyed directly onto the floppy magnetic disk. (Courtesy International Business Machines Corporation)

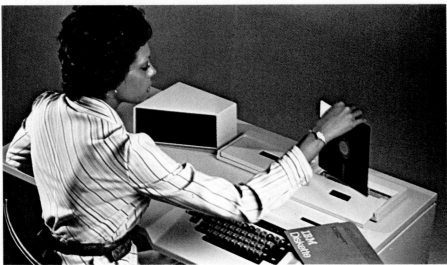

## Floppy Disks

**Figure 6-15** An 8-inch floppy disk (or diskette) packaged in a protective envelope. (Courtesy International Business Machines Corporation)

The IBM 3740 data entry system (see Figure 6-14) allows source document data to be keyed directly onto a floppy magnetic disk. The **floppy disk** (also called a **diskette**) gets its name from the fact that it is made out of a flexible plastic material (see Figure 6-15). This plastic base is coated with an iron-oxide recording substance that's similar to the material applied to the plastic ribbon of a magnetic tape. Data are recorded as tiny invisible magnetic spots on this coating. Each data entry disk in this system is 8 inches in diameter and is packaged in a protective paper or plastic envelope from which it is never removed. The contents of 3,000 punched cards can be recorded on a single disk.

A **key-to-diskette** data entry station records the keyed data directly onto a floppy disk. The disk is loaded in this station in its protective envelope. As the disk is rotated inside the envelope, a read/write head assembly accesses the disk surface through a slot in the jacket to record the data. A small display screen shows the data being entered and helps the operator perform data editing and verification functions.

Once the data have been recorded, a **floppy disk reader** can be used to enter the data into the CPU. Again, the disk is loaded and rotated inside its envelope. Tiny electromagnetic heads in the disk reader access the data through the slot in the jacket.

Just like magnetic tape, a diskette is inexpensive and can be erased and reused many times. The erasable feature makes it easy to make changes and corrections during data entry. When compared with punched cards, the floppy disk offers a much faster transfer rate and much greater data density.

In addition to being an input medium for sequential processing, the floppy disk has also become the predominant online secondary storage medium used with microcomputers and with some of the data entry devices used for direct-access processing. In many cases, the storage disk is a scaled-down $5\frac{1}{4}$-inch (or smaller) version of the original 8-inch floppy.

## Direct Data Entry Devices for Sequential Processing

The sequential processing media that we've now studied have one thing in common: Data from source documents are keyed on these media in a machine-acceptable form by operators of data entry machines. Although some improvements have been made in these input media and devices, you've seen that the transcribing activities carried out by data entry operators are still expensive and time consuming. To eliminate the need to recopy transaction data, several devices have been built to read the characters printed on the source documents and to then convert these facts *directly* into computer-usable input. Let's now examine some of these character readers that are used in high-volume sequential processing applications.

**Magnetic Ink Character Readers. Magnetic ink character recognition (MICR)** is widely used by banks to process the tremendous volume of checks being written each day. The sample check in Figure 6-16 is precoded along the bottom with the bank's identification number and with the depositor's account number. These numbers and other special symbols are printed with a special ink that contains magnetizeable particles of iron oxide. Employees at the first bank to receive the check after it has been written use the same ink to encode the amount in the lower right corner. The check can then be processed by machines as a punched card is processed.

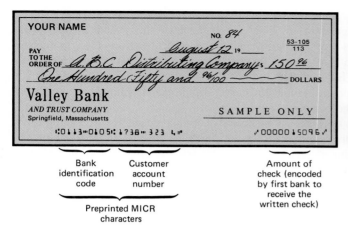

Bank
identification
code

Customer
account
number

Amount of
check (encoded
by first bank to
receive the
written check)

Preprinted MICR
characters

**Figure 6-16** A sample check encoded with MICR characters. These characters are printed with a special ink that contains particles of magnetizeable material.

**Figure 6-17** MICR reader-sorter unit. (Courtesy Burroughs Corporation)

Checks are accumulated into batches and placed in the input hopper of a **reader-sorter unit** (see Figure 6-17). As they enter the reading unit, the checks pass through a magnetic field which causes the particles in the ink to become magnetized. Read heads are then able to interpret the characters as the checks pass through the reading unit. The data being read can be entered directly into a CPU, or they can be transferred to magnetic tape for later processing. As up to 2,600 checks pass through the machine each minute, they are also sorted into pockets according to their identification code numbers. Several sortings may be required to move a check from (1) the initial bank receiving the check to, perhaps, (2) a Federal Reserve Bank, to (3) the depositor's bank, to (4) the depositor's account.

There are several *advantages* associated with the use of MICR:

- Checks may be roughly handled, folded, smeared, and stamped, but they can still be read with a high degree of accuracy.

- Processing is speeded because checks can be fed directly into the input device.

- People can easily read the magnetic ink characters.

The main *limitation* of MICR is that only the 10 digits and 4 special characters needed for bank processing are used. No alphabetic characters are available.

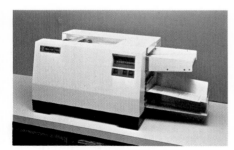

**Figure 6-18** Optical character reading systems range in size from the compact machine shown here to large systems which are linked to minicomputers. The system pictured is self-contained because it houses a programmable microprocessor. (Courtesy National Computer Systems)

**Optical Character Readers.** Unlike MICR, **optical character recognition (OCR)** (see Figure 6-18) techniques permit the direct reading of any printed character (not just 14). No special ink is required. This OCR flexibility makes it possible for organizations to eliminate or reduce the input keying bottleneck. **Optical character readers** are designed to interpret *handmade marks and characters, machine-printed characters,* and special *bar codes.*

| 1 5 8 6 3 | , 5 8 6 3 |
|:---:|:---:|
| Correct and readable | Incorrect and probably unreadable |

(b) Handprinted numeric characters

**Figure 6-19** Machine-readable handmade marks and characters.

You've probably taken tests and marked your answers to questions on a special test-scoring sheet (Figure 6-19a). Your answer sheet was then scanned by an *optical mark reader* that was used to grade the test. Optical scanners can also read certain handmade letters and numbers, but these characters must usually be precisely written (Figure 6-19b). The automatic reading of handwritten script is still some years in the future. (Your penmanship is undoubtedly beautiful, but mine presents a formidable challenge to the equipment designers.)

Figure 6-20 shows an optical reading system that's capable of scanning handmade characters. This system also has the flexibility to read entire pages of machine-printed alphanumeric symbols. These symbols are often printed in the standard type font shown in Figure 6-21. Most optical character readers of this type scan the printed matter with a photoelectric device that recognizes characters by the absorption or reflectance of light on the document (characters to be read are nonreflective). Reflected light patterns are converted into electrical pulses and then transmitted to recognition logic circuits. There they are compared with the characters the machine has been programmed to recognize. If a suitable comparison is made, the data may be recorded for input into the CPU. If a mismatch occurs, the document may be rejected.

Such readers are used in many large-volume processing applications. For example, the computer-printed bills sent to customers by many public utilities, credit card companies, and other businesses are prepared with characters that can be read by optical scanners. When customers make their monthly payments, they are instructed to return the bill or a remittance stub with their checks. These documents are then entered directly into optical readers to update accounts receivable records. Little or no human keying is needed. Other large-volume applications of scanners

**Figure 6-20** An optical page reading system. Several thousand machine-printed characters, and up to 1,200 handprinted characters, can be read each second by this type of data entry system. (Courtesy Recognition Equipment, Inc.)

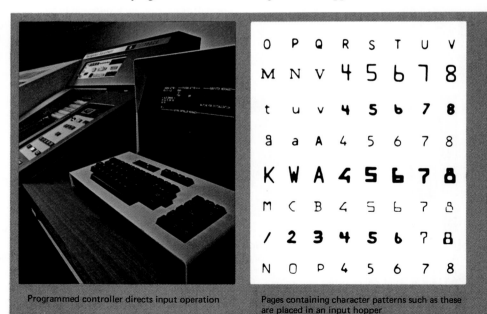

Programmed controller directs input operation

Pages containing character patterns such as these are placed in an input hopper

ABCDEFGHIJKLMNOPQRSTUVWXYZ
1234567890:;ſ=⊣?"$%|&'{}*+-

**Figure 6-21** This standard type font (designated OCR-A) is currently used in about three-fourths of the applications that rely on optical character reading for data entry.

include the reading of Zip codes by the U.S. Postal Service, the reading of passenger tickets and freight bills by airlines, and the processing of social security forms and motor vehicle registrations by governments.

In addition to marks and alphanumeric characters, optical readers can also recognize data coded in the form of light and dark bars. First used by railroads in the 1960s for the automatic tracking of freight cars, **bar codes** are most commonly used today to identify merchandise in retail stores. For example, manufacturers print a **Universal Product Code (UPC)** on most items sold in grocery stores. The next time you spring out of bed at 6 A.M. to have a hearty breakfast before your eight o-clock class, be sure to notice that your cereal box has a code similar to the one shown in Figure 6-22. When bar-coded items are received at a merchant's automated checkout stand, they are read by hand-held "wands" or they are pulled across a fixed scanning window (see Figure 6-23). As items are scanned, the bars are decoded and the data are transmitted to a computer that looks up the price, possibly updates inventory and sales records, and forwards price and description information back to the check stand. Besides using OCR readers at check stands, store personnel can also use wands attached to portable recording devices to replenish the store's inventory (see Figure 6-24). When an item must be restocked, the wand is used to read the item's bar code that's fastened on the shelf where the item is displayed. This reading accurately enters the item description into the recorder. The quantity needed is then keyed into the recorder. The recorder may later be connected by telecommunications lines to a warehouse computer system to complete the reordering procedure.

The primary *advantage* of OCR is that it eliminates some of the duplication of human effort required to get data into the computer. This reduction in effort can

After moving beneath a reading system, the character data are transmitted to integrated circuit chips for recognition. The data may then be recorded on magnetic tape.

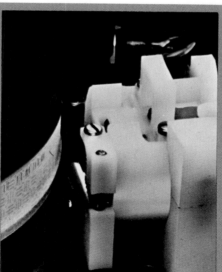

As each document is processed, a high-speed ink-jet printer capable of spraying 106,000 droplets of ink per second may be used to imprint a control code on the document.

Documents may then be directed to output pockets.

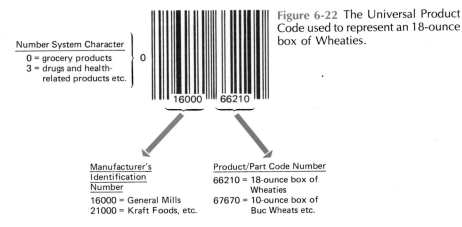

Number System Character

0 = grocery products
3 = drugs and health-
related products etc.

> 0

**Figure 6-22** The Universal Product Code used to represent an 18-ounce box of Wheaties.

16000    66210

Manufacturer's
Identification
Number

16000 = General Mills
21000 = Kraft Foods, etc.

Product/Part Code Number

66210 = 18-ounce box of
Wheaties
67670 = 10-ounce box of
Buc Wheats etc.

**Figure 6-23** Supermarket scanning. UPC bar-coded products may be pulled across a fixed scanning window at an automated checkout stand. (Courtesy International Business Machines Corporation)

improve data accuracy and can increase the timeliness of the information processed. However, *difficulties* in using OCR equipment may be encountered when documents to be read are poorly typed or have strikeovers or erasures. Also, form design and ink specifications may become more critical than is the case when people key the data from the forms. Finally, many optical readers are not economically feasible unless the daily volume of transactions is relatively high.

Many organizations find that most of their processing needs are being met quite satisfactorily through the use of the data entry media and devices that we've now examined. After all, Figure 6-25 shows that these media and devices can provide a wide range of possible input speeds. And sequential processing is acceptable—perhaps even preferable—for the types of applications these organizations process. But we've also seen that there are other applications where quick and direct access to file records is needed. In the remainder of this chapter, we'll look at the data entry devices that are used for direct-access processing.

**Figure 6-24** Portable recording devices are used to restock store inventory. (Courtesy MSI Data Corporation)

| Medium | Input Device Used | Typical Data Entry Speed Ranges (CPS) |
|---|---|---|
| Punched card | Card reader | 150–2,667 |
| Paper tape | Tape reader | 50–1,800 |
| Magnetic tape | Tape drive | 15,000–1,250,000 |
| Floppy disk | Disk reader | 12,500–60,000 |
| Magnetic ink | MICR reader | 700–3,200 |
| Paper documents | OCR reader | 100–3,600 |

**Figure 6-25** A summary of the input speeds obtained with the media and devices used in sequential processing.

## Feedback and Review 6-2

You've now learned that input data for sequential processing may be keyed from source documents onto such media as punched cards, punched paper tape, magnetic tape, and floppy disks. You've also seen that MICR and OCR devices can be used to read the characters printed on the source documents and to then convert these facts directly into computer-usable input. To test and reinforce your understanding of these input media and devices, match the letter of the appropriate term to the definition or concept to which it belongs. (Place the correct letter in the space provided.)

a) magnetic tape b) transfer rate c) 8-bit BCD code d) read/write heads e) Universal Product Code f) interrecord gap g) data density h) iron oxide i) Hollerith j) minicomputer k) block l) floppy disk m) optical character reader n) MICR reader-sorter

___1. The name of the code used to represent data in an 80-column punched card.

___2. A term that refers to the number of characters that can be stored in a given physical space.

___3. The _____ of an input medium is the speed with which data can be copied from the medium to CPU storage.

___4. A preferred medium for high-speed, large-volume batch processing applications.

___5. The type of magnetizeable material used to coat magnetic tapes and floppy disks.

___6. Used in key-to-disk-to-tape data entry systems to control the input coming from the keystations.

___7. The type of code used to represent data on a nine-track magnetic tape.

___8. Used to separate records on a magnetic tape file.

___9. Several short records on a magnetic tape are commonly combined into a _____ and read into the CPU as a single unit.

___10. Small electromagnets that are used to enter data into, and receive output from, magnetic tapes and floppy disks.

___11. A popular online secondary storage medium for small computers as well as an input medium for sequential processing.

___12. A direct data entry device designed for use in financial institutions.

___13. Devices designed to interpret handmade marks, machine-printed characters, and bar codes.

___14. A code used to identify merchandise in retail stores.

# DATA ENTRY DEVICES FOR DIRECT-ACCESS PROCESSING

Online devices are being installed at an amazing rate. One recent study estimated that the nearly 8 million online stations that were installed in 1983 will grow to almost 22 million by 1987. You've already encountered several types of online data entry stations in this book. In Chapter 2, an online financial transaction terminal was used to update Rob Brooks' savings account. And earlier in this chapter, an online data collection station in a factory was used to keep track of the production status of each job in a work-in-process file.

Online processing devices, which we'll examine now, have the following characteristics:

■ They are able to enter data directly into the CPU; data recording media are not required.

■ They are generally located at or near the data source, and this can be far away from the CPU.

■ They create a direct interactive relationship between people and computers.

■ They handle economically a low and/or irregular volume of input data.

### Teleprinter Terminals

A **teleprinter terminal** has a typewriterlike keyboard for data entry and a built-in printer to record what has been typed (see Figure 6-26 *left*). The terminal can also receive and print output information from the CPU. Some of the earliest teleprinter terminals were designed to communicate telegraph messages. Other early stations were essentially electric typewriters that had been adapted for use in a direct-access processing environment. Many of these older terminals are still in operation. Updated desktop versions using microprocessor technology and the latest printing techniques are selling briskly. And tens of thousands of small portable teleprinters (Figure 6-26 *right*) are being used today by salespeople, managers, newspaper reporters, engineers, and others on the move.

### Portable Data Entry Terminals

The portable teleprinter, in effect, lets these people take a computer with them wherever they go. For example, a salesperson can attach the terminal to a customer's telephone, dial in to a company computer system, key in questions about the availability of stock, and receive immediate confirmation on the terminal printer that if the customer places an order it can be filled. If a sale is then made, the sales order can be keyed directly into the system from the customer's office. Similarly, a manager can carry a terminal along on a business trip and keep up with office work during airport layovers or hotel stays. And a reporter can type and file a story into a computer system from a remote location.

Some other portable terminals are battery-powered, weigh less than 2 pounds, and are small enough to fit in the palm of your hand. These terminals have small keyboards and are used to send data to a computer, but they often have little or no

Figure 6-26 (*left*) A teleprinter terminal used in a direct-access processing environment. (Courtesy Teletype Corporation) (*right*) A portable teleprinter may be used by people on the move to enter data into and receive output from distant computer systems. (Photo courtesy Digital Equipment Corporation)

**Figure 6-27** A portable bar-code reader. (Courtesy Norand Corporation)

ability to receive information from the CPU. Such devices are often used by sales-people as electronic order books (see Figure 6-27). For example, a route salesperson calling on retailers can carry a terminal through a customer's store. When items are found to be in short supply, the salesperson can key in the product number and quantity needed into the terminal. (Or, as we've seen, bar codes may be read by a penlike optical reading wand that may be attached to the terminal.) Semiconductor storage chips are then generally used to hold the data that have been entered in the terminal. Every few hours, or at the end of the day, the salesperson can attach the terminal to a telephone and send the order(s) in to a company computer system. In 1980, about $250 million was spent on all types of portable terminals. By 1990, this market is expected to be 12 times larger, with the sales figure placed at $3 billion.

**Point-of-Sale Terminals**

You've seen that **point-of-sale (POS) terminals** equipped with optical scanners that read UPC symbols are replacing cash registers in supermarkets. Similar equipment is also being used at the checkout counters of other retail stores. Hand-held wands are used by clerks in department stores to speed up the checkout process. By passing the wand across a special tag attached to the merchandise, the clerk reads the item description and price into the terminal. Under computer control, the terminal may display the scanned data and then print an itemized sales receipt that shows the total amount of the purchase including taxes. If a credit card is used to complete the transaction, the wand can read and enter the numbers on the credit card into the computer to update the customer's credit account. Transaction data can also be used to update inventory records and provide sales analysis information to managers (see Figure 6-28). Fully automated gas stations also permit customers to insert a special credit card into a POS terminal, enter a personal identification code, and fill up their own gas tanks. The terminal gives the customer a receipt, and a monthly bill is prepared by the system.

**Figure 6-28** Just as POS terminals are improving service in many other retail industries, hotels and motels are turning to front-desk terminals to improve their transaction control and customer service. (Courtesy NCR Corporation)

**Financial Transaction Terminals**

In addition to the online teller terminals used to handle customer deposits and withdrawals, there are also several other types of **financial transaction terminals** in common use. Some of these devices are used in the electronic transfer of funds. One such **electronic funds transfer (EFT)** station is the **automated teller machine** (or **ATM**) shown in Figure 6-29.

**Figure 6-29** ATMs are the visible tip of the giant electronic payment network which permits more sophisticated consumer money management and a more efficient banking industry. Since 1980 thousands of auto tellers have been installed in banks, stores, and airports worldwide. (Courtesy International Business Machines Corporation)

An ATM is an *unattended* device that's located on or off the financial institution's premises to receive and dispense cash and to handle routine financial transactions 24 hours a day. To date more than 70 million plastic "currency" or "debit" cards have been issued for use in ATMs. Your account number and credit limit are magnetically encoded on a strip of tape on the back of the card. When it's inserted into the ATM, the terminal reads and then transmits the tape data to a CPU which activates your account. By following instructions displayed on a screen, and by pushing a few keys, you then direct the computer to carry out transaction(s).

A technological alternative to the use of ATMs is being developed in Europe. Instead of using a magnetic strip (or stripe), the card is made with a built-in microcomputer chip. This chip can store a considerable amount of information. Data representing a specific amount of cash can be encoded in the chips before the cards are issued to customers. As the cards are used to make purchases, bits of the stored data are destroyed by special electronic registers used by merchants. These electronic registers are not connected to a CPU. In effect, customers gradually "cash in their chips" and use up their electronic money. These "smart cards" are also able to keep a stored record of more than 100 purchases. Look for competition between ATM/magnetic stripe technology and smart cards in the future.

An ATM isn't the only type of EFT station that's connected directly to financial computers. Other stations owned by financial institutions are located at the checkout counters of stores, hotels, hospitals, and in railroad and airline terminals. These EFT stations are used to verify that a customer's check or credit card transaction will be honored. They can also be used to electronically transfer funds from a shopper's account to a merchant's account. A Touch-Tone telephone can also become an EFT terminal. A depositor can call up a bank computer, enter data through the telephone buttons, and transfer funds to or from an account.

**Visual Display Terminals**    The most popular input devices used today in direct-access processing applications are **visual display terminals** (see Figure 6-30). A terminal keyboard is used to enter data into a CPU, and a **cathode ray tube (CRT)** that looks like a television picture tube is used to display the input data and receive messages and processed information from the computer. Many display terminals are designed primarily for *alphanumeric* applications and are used to enter and retrieve letters, numbers, and special characters. Other display terminals also possess alphanumeric capabilities but are designed primarily for *graphics* applications. What's the difference between alphanumeric and graphics terminals? Without going into the technical details, a sophisticated graphics terminal is likely to need faster and more complex circuitry and a different type of display tube so that very precise lines can be quickly drawn on the screen. Such a terminal system may cost tens of thousands of dollars while a much simpler alphanumeric terminal may be available for a few hundred dollars. Let's look at a few of the ways that these display terminals are used.

**Alphanumeric Display Applications.** You've already seen how alphanumeric display stations are used by shop employees to update production records and by tellers to update savings account records. In each of these applications, the terminal operator carried on an interactive "conversation" with the computer program by supplying data in response to displayed questions and instructions. In the

**Figure 6-30** Visual display terminals are the most popular input devices used today in direct-access processing applications. (Courtesy Raytheon Data Systems Company)

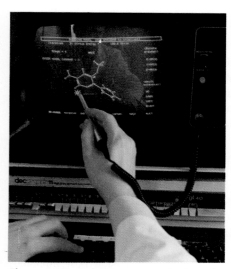

**Figure 6-31** A light pen attached to the display station may be used to choose a displayed response or to request further information. (Courtesy BASF America Corporation)

factory application, the employee merely keyed in the correct response number from a menu of displayed responses. In office applications, the user sometimes uses a **light pen** attached to the terminal, rather than the terminal keyboard, to choose a displayed response or to request further information (see Figure 6-31). The light pen is a photocell placed in a small tube. When the user moves the pen over the screen, the pen is able to detect the light coming from a limited field of view. The light from the CRT causes the photocell to respond when the pen is pointed directly at a lighted area. This electrical response is transmitted to the computer, which is able to determine that part of the displayed item which is triggering the photocell.

Since alphanumeric display stations can provide a window into a computer's data base, they are commonly used to provide quick response to operator inquiries. The status of a customer's credit, the availability of airline seats, hotel rooms, or inventory items, the addresses and telephone numbers of college students—these and many other facts are kept current in online files and are instantly available for display when an inquiry message is entered. The keyboard can then be used to update these files to reflect any transaction that's made at a display station. For example, an airline ticket agent can reduce by one the number of seats available on a flight when a ticket is sold.

More and more *color* CRT terminals are now being used for alphanumeric data entry and inquiry purposes. The increasing popularity of color CRTs is partly explained by the dramatic price reductions in these terminals in recent years. In addition, many users prefer them and report fewer instances of fatigue and eyestrain. Another advantage of color CRTs is that contrasting colors can be used to highlight errors or call the operator's attention to important entries.

Alphanumeric display stations are also being used by programmers to prepare and/or maintain computer programs. Pencils and coding sheets are giving way to these **programming workstations.** New program instructions are entered at the keyboard. A special program in the computer interacts with the programmer to edit the programmer's efforts and to detect any errors that may have been made in the syntax of a programming language. A constantly changing menu of admissible instructions may be displayed during program preparation to guide the programmer. The use of these workstations has improved programmer productivity.

**Graphical Display Applications.** Several years ago, designers and architects made preliminary sketches to get an idea down on paper. As the idea was developed, additional drawings were made. And when the final design or plan was finished, further detailed drawings were prepared. Much of this drawing-preparation time can now be saved by instruments that enable computers to directly receive human graphic input (see Figure 6-32).

The light pen is a useful instrument for graphics work. The user "draws" directly on the screen with the pen. By using the pen and a keypad attached to the terminal, the user can select different colors and line thicknesses, can reduce or enlarge drawings, and can add or erase lines. Another instrument is the **input tablet,**[3] as shown in Figure 6-32, which comes in different sizes. The tablet is a

[3] A *digitizer* is an input instrument that is similar in function to the input tablet. It has a small reading device that can be used to trace over the lines in drawings, X-ray images, or other graphic representations. The digitizer then sends precise numeric descriptions of these lines or images to a CPU for analysis and processing.

Figure 6-32 Architects use color workstations for structural layouts and floor plan designs. This system's multicolor capability enables users to more readily distinguish among elements such as structural columns, walls, and furniture groupings. Note the input tablet at the lower right in the photo. (Courtesy Sanders Associates, Inc.)

work surface that typically contains hundreds of copper lines that form a grid. This grid is connected to a computer. Each copper line receives electrical impulses. A special pen or stylus attached to the tablet is sensitive to these impulses and is used to form the drawings. However, the pen does not mark directly on the tablet. Instead, a designer, architect, or other user draws on a piece of paper placed on the tablet. The tablet grid then senses the exact position of the stylus as it is moved and transmits this information to the CPU.

The developing sketch may be displayed on the CRT. But there's a difference between the drawings and the display. Poorly sketched lines are displayed as straight; poor lettering is replaced by neat printing; and poorly formed corners become mathematically precise. Changes and modifications in the drawing can be quickly made. For example, a line can be ''erased'' from, or shifted on, the display unit with a movement of the stylus. Once the initial sketching is finished and satisfactorily displayed on the CRT, the computer may then be instructed to analyze the design and report on certain characteristics. For example, the computer might be asked to work out the acoustical characteristics of a theater design, or evaluate the flight characteristics of an aircraft design. The user may then modify the sketch on the basis of the computer analysis. This interactive graphics capability helps people save valuable time for more creative work.

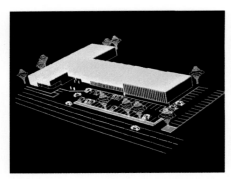

Figure 6-33 A 3-D structural design of a building as the designer would see it on a color terminal. (Reprinted with permission from Computervision Corporation, Bedford, Mass.)

**Computer graphics** are currently being used in the design of ships, highways, aircraft, electronic circuits, and buildings (see Figure 6-33).[4] They are also being used to present business financial and operating data in graphical form so that managers can spot trends and relationships and can then make faster and better decisions. Pages of computer printouts detailing the performance of product lines and sales divisions can be replaced by a few colorful charts, graphs, and maps. These visual presentations are first created on the CRT screen through human-machine interaction. They can then be copied onto paper by various printing devices, or they can be photographed from the screen. This business management use of computer graphics is expected to outpace other uses in the 1980s.

Many managers are now using personal computer systems and available graphics software packages to produce the graphs and charts they need for analysis and presentation purposes. Some personal computer models can only create monochrome (one-color) graphics by using the regular alphanumeric characters and the few special graphics characters that may be available. But many other models have an available graphics mode of operation that permits the display screen to be divided (or "mapped") into thousands of picture elements (Figure 6-34). Each picture element, or **pixel,** is controlled by the contents of a specific location in storage. By turning each pixel on or off, the CPU is able to paint a graphic image. Although the quality is generally not as good as that produced by a professional graphics terminal, a personal computer system with a large number of pixels (and a screen capable of distinctly displaying them) can produce high-resolution images in multiple colors. Of course, more pixels and more colors require more storage and a color CRT, which increases system costs.

## Intelligent Terminals

There are more than 500 terminal models that are currently being offered by more than 150 manufacturers. Most of these models can be classified into the teleprinter, visual display, and special-purpose categories that we've now used. In an attempt to classify the bewildering range of products that are available, however, the computer industry has also divided terminals into dumb, smart, and intelligent categories.

A simple teleprinter or alphanumeric display device is generally classified as a **dumb terminal.** These units have keyboards for input, a means of communicating with a CPU, and a printer or screen to receive output. They remain popular because of their low cost and reliable service. **Smart terminals** have additional features. They usually contain a microprocessor and some internal storage. They have data editing capability and the ability to consolidate input data prior to sending them to the CPU. However, smart terminals cannot be programmed by users.

**Intelligent terminals** combine terminal hardware with built-in microcomputers that *can* be programmed by users. Being programmable, they can be used in many ways. Small data processing jobs can be handled by the terminal without the need to interact with a larger CPU. Online secondary floppy disk storage devices are often used during the processing of these small jobs. Programmed error-detection

Figure 6-34 The constantly improving quality of computer graphics is keeping pace with its high demand. (Photo courtesy NEC Corporation)

[4]In one interesting application, architects use display stations to prepare sketches of a proposed building. The computer is then instructed to draw a whole series of sketches, each from a slightly different angle. These sketches are then assembled into an animated film. When the film is shown to clients, it gives them the impression that they are walking through the proposed building!

tests can also be stored in the terminal to check on the validity of input data. The input data being edited may be entered at the intelligent terminal, or they may be entered at dumb terminals that are linked to the intelligent station. After the data have been collected and edited, they can be stored for later transmission to a larger computer. Many of the terminals discussed in this section are smart or intelligent devices. And since it now costs very little more to add microcomputer components to a terminal, future terminals will have smart or intelligent features to help make data entry and retrieval easier for people.

If you think that intelligent terminals sound like personal computers, you're right. The keyboards, visual displays, internal storage/processing chips, and online secondary floppy disk storage devices are the same type components used in many personal computers. The intelligent terminal is designed with circuits that permit it to communicate with other terminals and with larger CPUs while most personal computers have been designed primarily to operate alone. But plug-in hardware and/or appropriate software packages are available to allow interaction between mainframes and some popular personal computers. And other plug-in modules are available to convert existing dumb alphanumeric display terminals into full-fledged microcomputers. For example, Digital Equipment Corporation produces a slide-in circuit board that turns its VT100 terminal into a micro, and IBM has an attachment that gives its 3278 terminals many of the capabilities of its Personal Computer. Technology is blurring the distinctions that once existed between some types of terminals and personal computers.

## Executive Workstations

"Knowledge work" consists of locating, retrieving, manipulating, analyzing, distributing, and storing information, and this describes much of what a manager does. **Executive workstations** are special desktop units designed for the busy manager who may not like to type. They have special function keys and may accept input by allowing the user to merely *touch* a menu response option on the screen. An input control mechanism called a mouse is often used. A **mouse** (Figure 6-35) is a pointing device about the size of a tape cassette. It usually rolls on a small bearing and has one or more buttons on the top. When a user rolls the mouse across a flat surface, the movement guides a pointer on the video screen—which is called a **cursor**—in the direction of the mouse's movement. Because the cursor on the screen gives a direct response to the way the user's hand moves the mouse, the user has a sense of pointing at something on the screen. Positioning a cursor with a mouse is easier for nontypists than pressing various key combinations, and is similar to using the **joystick** game controllers found in video arcades and home computer systems.

Although the functions carried out by executive workstations vary depending on the needs of their users, it's generally accepted that such stations should have the ability to:

**Figure 6-35** It's easy to see how the mouse got its name. (Photo courtesy Microsoft Corporation)

■ Perform word and data processing

■ File and retrieve information from private and organizational data bases, and access information from outside information services

■ Receive, store, and transmit messages by electronic means

■ Produce appropriate charts and graphs from data supplied by users

■ Support management activities with programs to schedule meetings and maintain appointment calendars, telephone directories, address lists, and status files

The Xerox Star multifunction terminal was one of the first executive workstations to be introduced, but its price tag of over $15,000 limited its acceptance. With advantages such as lower prices, wide availability, and ease of use, personal computers have now become the executive workstations of choice in most organizations. Apple Computer's Lisa, with its integrated software, was discussed in Chapter 4. Lisa lets the user (1) control cursor movement with a mouse, and (2) select menu options by pressing a button on the mouse. A Lisa station also has the ability to communicate with a network of other Lisa stations and with a range of mainframes and minicomputers. It's also possible to equip an IBM Personal Computer (or a similar machine) with a mouse, a choice of multifunction integrated software packages from a number of vendors (see Figure 4-5, page 83), and an option to permit communication with mainframes and other terminals. The number of these workstation configurations that have been assembled is large and is growing rapidly.

**Voice Input Systems**

Input devices, basically, do nothing more than convert human language into machine language. Why, then, doesn't someone invent a machine that will let a person talk to the computer in English? As a matter of fact, a few manufacturers have done just that (see box). A *microphone* or telephone is used to convert human speech into electrical signals. The signal patterns are then transmitted to a computer where they are compared to a "dictionary" of patterns that have been previously placed in storage. When a close match is found, a word is "recognized" and the computer then produces the appropriate output.

Most voice recognition systems are **speaker-dependent.** That is, they can't be used until after the speaker has repeated a word several times to "train" the system to recognize his or her particular voice pattern. Recently, however, **speaker-independent** systems have been developed that can recognize words spoken by anyone. But no existing system can recognize an unlimited number of words spoken in a continuous stream. Vocabularies of all systems are very limited, users must speak distinctly, and they must pause between each word or each short phrase. In one experiment, the words "recognize speech" were interpreted as "wreck a nice beach" by the computer. And the words "half fast" were . . . well, you get the idea. Other problems in speech recognition are caused by speaker accents and dialects (people's voice prints are as unique as their fingerprints), and the fact that the meaning of words can vary depending on the context in which they are used.[5]

Although speech recognition is now in its infancy, it's likely to be used much more often in future executive workstations and in situations where a person's hands are busy, where a worker's eyes must remain fixed on a display or measuring instrument, or where telephone input is desirable. Some current applications of voice recognition include:

[5] Scientists from IBM have been working for nearly a decade on a word processing system that can take dictation. However, it's believed that a commercial product that can do this is still at least another decade away.

## TALK TO YOUR COMPUTER

Every once in a while, a product comes along with the word "Future" stamped on it. Supersoft's ScratchPad with VoiceDrive—the first practical voice-driven spreadsheet designed for use on a personal computer—promises and delivers the future *now*.

Linked to a plug-in voice recognition board, VoiceDrive gives either an IBM Personal Computer or the Texas Instruments Professional Computer the ability to recognize speech and translate it into commands which the system's spreadsheet "understands." The user, in effect, talks to the computer, enters data, moves the cursor, and fills in most of the details of the spreadsheet without touching the keyboard. How's that for science fiction?

Wasn't it only 15 years ago that two fictional astronauts were gabbing with the mainframe computer HAL in "2001"? Now Supersoft comes along with a speech recognition program for the personal computer—"the first applications software product fully integrated with voice-driven hardware," says Supersoft's president Herb Schildt.

In developing the VoiceDrive system, Schildt has attempted to make something that is very complex seem simple. "The VoiceDrive integrated package sits between the voice-recognition hardware and the applications (spreadsheet) software," he explains. "The voice-recognition software tailors the spreadsheet program to the human voice."

As a speaker provides vocal input—

distinctly pronounced words or commands—the input "activates" a part of the program so the computer appears to be responding to verbal instructions. This happens because the software and hardware system together allow the user to record a "voice print" or sampling of necessary words and commands; these can be stored on disk and booted into memory at any time.

The computer uses the "prints" as a template by which to compare any incoming voice signal. In this way, it matches, through a complex series of statistical calculations, the sound of a command it "hears" with the closest sound pattern it has recorded on voice

print. When the match is close enough— or if no match occurs—the hardware sends out a signal to the program, which responds either by executing the voice command or ignoring it until an appropriate match is made. Sometimes, this boils down to a user *repeating* a command until the system recognizes the sound as familiar—that is, matching it with the voice print of the command made earlier.

Experts in the field call such a system "speaker-dependent." This means that a specific voice must "train" the system one or more times so that a template can be made. During this process, the computer extracts certain parameters from the human voice—including the unique pattern of "formants," or resonances, in the words we speak (these vary according to the individual)— which then can be used to compare succeeding voice samples.

Another, though less common, form of speech recognition is "speaker-independent." This means that the manufacturer installs the template so that the system can recognize anyone within a large group of people. The most sophisticated systems, however, currently tend to be speaker-dependent, according to Schildt; they offer the most reliable performance.

—Arielle Emmett, "Talk to Your Computer and Get a Professional-Looking Spreadsheet." Reprinted with permission from *Personal Computing,* April 1984, p. 24. Copyright 1984, Hayden Publishing Company. Photo courtesy Texas Instruments.

■ A "hand's busy" loading dock employee at a Ford Motor Company warehouse can pick up a package, read the package destination into a microphone, and then put the package on a conveyor belt. The system then moves the package to the correct storage location. A similar United Parcel system zips packages into the right trucks as workers read destinations aloud.

■ As Lockheed Aircraft Company assembly workers use hands and eyes to build components for the Trident missile system, they also use a microphone to enter inventory data into a computer system.

■ A state employee in Illinois gets clearance to make a long-distance phone call on the state's private lines by calling a computer and reciting his or her authorization number into the system. If the number is accepted, the computer then switches the employee to the next available long-distance line.

■ A shareholder in one of the 22 mutual funds managed by Fidelity Management & Research Company can dial a computer, supply a fund number, and get information about the current yield and value of the shares owned. If more information is needed, the shareholder can request human help.

## Feedback and Review 6-3

As you've seen in this section, there are different types of data entry devices that can be used for direct-access processing. The following multiple-choice questions will help you test and reinforce your understanding of these devices. (Put the letter of the most-correct response in the space provided.)

___1. Which of the following is *not* a characteristic of the data entry devices used in direct-access processing:
   a) They create a direct interaction between people and computers.
   b) They are economical even when input data volume is low or irregular.
   c) They require the use of data recording media.
   d) They are generally located at the data source.

___2. Teleprinter terminals
   a) are all intelligent devices.
   b) are of very recent origin.
   c) cannot be portable.
   d) have keyboards, printers, and the ability to communicate with distant CPUs.

___3. POS terminals
   a) are general-purpose devices capable of handling more applications than teleprinter terminals.
   b) are used only in supermarkets.
   c) may use optical scanners to read tags, bar codes, and credit cards.
   d) cannot be used in conjunction with financial transaction devices.

___4. An automated teller machine
   a) is operated by a skilled teller.
   b) transmits data coded on a plastic card to a CPU.
   c) can be used only during banking hours.
   d) generally reads data from a microcomputer chip embedded in a plastic card.

___5. A visual display terminal
   a) is, by definition, a dumb terminal.

   b) can possess either graphic or alphanumeric capabilities, but not both.
   c) must be located at the site of the CPU.
   d) is the most popular input device used today in direct-access processing.

___6. A visual display terminal generally does *not* receive input data from
   a) a felt-tip pen.　　c) a keyboard.
   b) an input tablet.　　d) a light pen.

___7. Computer graphic techniques
   a) have declined in popularity in recent years.
   b) are currently being used in the design of airplanes and buildings, but they are of little use to business decision makers.
   c) have increased the time required to complete final engineering drawings.
   d) make it possible for a designer to make quick changes and modifications to preliminary drawings.

___8. An intelligent terminal
   a) has a microprocessor, but it can't be programmed by the user.
   b) can be used for small data processing jobs without the need to interact with a larger CPU.
   c) carries on a conversation in English with the user.
   d) cannot edit data originating at dumb terminals.

___9. An executive workstation
   a) may use an input device called a mole to control cursor movement.
   b) cannot communicate with other terminals or CPUs.
   c) has the ability to use integrated software to perform multiple functions.
   d) uses packaged software and cannot be programmed by users.

___10. Voice input systems
   a) must be speaker-dependent.
   b) must be speaker-independent.
   c) have limited vocabularies and can't accept words spoken in a continuous stream.
   d) can take dictation and produce finished letters.

# LOOKING BACK

**1.** Input data must either be originated in a machine-readable form or they must be converted into such a form before they can be used by a CPU. Data used by organizations are obtained from both internal and external sources. The data entry approach followed in a given application is determined to a large extent by the processing method that's used. In a typical sequential processing application, the raw data are captured on source documents and are then copied at considerable expense onto cards, tape, or floppy disks by data entry operators. The transcribed data are accumulated into batches, sorted into a sequence, and then processed at scheduled intervals. In a direct-access processing application, however, the records affected by transactions are kept in a direct-access storage device (DASD). Input data are then entered from online terminals at (or near) the data source to immediately update the records in the DASD. An example of direct data entry in a manufacturing application was presented in this chapter.

**2.** The quality of output of a data processing system is more dependent on people than on machines. This is because people prepare the data input (and programs) for the machines. Mistakes entered on source documents or errors made during keying are not uncommon, and it's important to catch them as early as possible. Several error-detecting techniques are described in this chapter.

**3.** Punched cards, magnetic tape, and floppy disks are input media used in sequential processing. Cards are an old and reliable medium, but they have a very low data density. Card files are thus bulky and slow to process. The 80-column card uses the Hollerith Code to represent data, while the 96-column card uses a 6-bit BCD code. Data pertaining to a particular transaction are keyed into a card by a card punch operator. A verifier may be used to ensure that data have been correctly entered. The verified cards are sorted and then placed in a card reader which converts the presence or absence of holes into electrical pulses that the CPU can accept.

**4.** Data can be transferred from magnetic tape to CPU storage at a much faster rate than from cards. This is due, in part, to the fact that the data density of magnetic tape is much greater. Magnetic tape is packaged in reels, cartridges, or cassettes. Data are generally entered from source documents by key-to-tape devices, or by multistation key-to-disk-to-tape systems. An 8-bit BCD code is generally used to represent data on magnetic tape. Interrecord gaps may be used to identify different tape records. Frequently, however, several records are combined into a block and read into the CPU as a single unit to save tape space and

speed data input. A tape drive is used to read data from a magnetic tape into the CPU. In spite of its high data density, rapid transfer rate, and low cost, magnetic tape can't provide rapid and random access to file records, and it can't be read directly by people.

**5.** A key-to-diskette station is used to enter source document data on a floppy disk. A floppy disk reader is then used to enter the data into a CPU. Like magnetic tape, a disk is inexpensive and can be erased and reused many times. When compared to cards, the floppy disk offers a much faster transfer rate and much greater data density. The floppy disk is also the predominant online secondary storage medium used with microcomputers.

**6.** Magnetic ink and optical character readers have been developed to eliminate the need to recopy transaction data from source documents. Magnetic ink reader-sorter units are special-purpose devices used to process checks in the banking system. They only recognize the 14 characters needed for check processing. Optical character readers, on the other hand, can directly read handmade and machine-printed letters, numbers, and special characters, as well as bar codes and handmade marks. Such readers are often used in large-volume processing applications such as billing. They are also frequently used at point-of-sale stations to scan the items marked with the bars of the Universal Product Code.

**7.** Millions of new data entry devices used for direct-access processing are now being produced each year. The trend is to distribute these devices to data origination points. These locations can be far away from the CPU that processes the data. Online terminals create a direct interactive relationship between people and computers. Some of the earliest terminals were teleprinters, and these devices are still popular. Portable teleprinters are particularly useful to people who do a great deal of traveling. The use of other types of portable data entry devices is also expanding rapidly.

**8.** Point-of-sale (POS) and financial transaction terminals are special-purpose devices used by retail stores and financial institutions. POS terminals can reduce customer waiting time at checkout counters and can directly update the online files used in accounts receivable, inventory control, and sales analysis applications. Automated teller machines can handle routine financial transactions 24 hours a day. Other electronic funds transfer terminals can be used by stores and hotels to verify that a customer's check is good.

**9.** Visual display terminals are the most popular type of data entry devices used in direct-access processing applications. Some visual display units are only used to enter and retrieve alphanumeric characters, while others possess graphic as well as alphanumeric capabilities. Several alphanumeric and graphic uses of display terminals are discussed in the chapter. Keyboards, light pens, and input tablets are the data entry instruments that are used with visual display stations. Personal computers and graphics software packages are often used to produce business graphs and charts.

**10.** Unlike terminals classified as dumb or smart, intelligent terminals have built-in microcomputers that are user-programmable. These terminals are thus able to do small data processing jobs without having to interact with a larger CPU. They often use floppy disk devices for the online secondary storage of data and programs. Outlying dumb terminals may be linked to an intelligent station. The intelligent terminal can then accept input data from the outlying devices, use programmed error-detection tests to check on the validity of the data being received, and then store the data for later transmission to a larger CPU.

There may be little difference between an intelligent terminal and a personal computer. An intelligent terminal has the ability to communicate with other terminals and larger computers. Personal computers may initially lack this ability, but many can be upgraded with communications hardware/software packages.

**11.** An executive workstation is usually a personal computer that's designed or configured so that it may be used by busy managers who may not like to use keyboards. Touchscreen systems, mouse pointers, and menu response options are input approaches that are frequently used. Such a workstation should be able to perform word and data processing, file and retrieve data base information, produce appropriate graphics, and support other management functions.

**12.** Voice input systems have been implemented to convert human speech into electrical signals that a computer can recognize. Although speech recognition technology is in its infancy, and many problems remain to be solved, it's now being used in a number of interesting ways.

## KEY TERMS AND CONCEPTS

# TOPICS FOR REVIEW AND DISCUSSION

**1.** "The input data used by an organization are obtained from internal and external sources." Discuss this statement.

**2.** *(a)* Describe the data entry approach that is typically used in a batch processing application. *(b)* Describe the approach used in direct-access processing.

**3.** What advantages are there to capturing data at the transaction source?

**4.** "People have a greater effect on the quality of output of a data processing system than do the data processing machines." Discuss this statement.

**5.** *(a)* How are data errors introduced into a computer system? *(b)* Why is it important to catch these errors as early as possible?

**6.** How can errors be detected in input data?

**7.** Explain the different methods used to code data in 80-column and 96-column punched cards.

**8.** Describe how punched cards and punched card equipment can be used in a data processing application.

**9.** Discuss the advantages and limitations of punched cards.

**10.** How does punched paper tape differ from punched cards?

**11.** *(a)* How is magnetic tape packaged? *(b)* How are data entered on magnetic tape? *(c)* How are data represented on tape?

**12.** *(a)* How can different file records be represented on a magnetic tape? *(b)* Why are short records commonly combined into a block?

**13.** Discuss the advantages and limitations of magnetic tape?

**14.** *(a)* How are data recorded on a floppy disk? *(b)* How are floppy disks similar to magnetic tape? *(c)* How are they different?

**15.** MICR and OCR devices are similar in that both types of machines convert source document data directly into computer-usable input. How do these machines differ?

**16.** *(a)* What is the Universal Product Code? *(b)* How is it used?

**17.** Discuss the general characteristics of the data entry devices used for direct-access processing.

**18.** *(a)* What is a teleprinter terminal? *(b)* How may teleprinters be used?

**19.** *(a)* What's the purpose of a POS terminal? *(b)* Of transaction recording stations?

**20.** *(a)* What is a visual display terminal? *(b)* How may visual display units be used? *(c)* How may data be entered at such terminals?

**21.** *(a)* What is an intelligent terminal? *(b)* How may intelligent terminals be used? *(c)* What's the difference between an intelligent terminal and a personal computer?

**22.** *(a)* What's an executive workstation? *(b)* What functions should such stations be able to carry out?

**23.** "Voice input systems may be speaker-dependent or speaker-independent." How do these systems differ?

# PROJECTS TO LOOK INTO

**1.** Identify and prepare a class presentation on four sources of input data used by an organization that you know about, belong to, and/or work for. Include in your presentation a report on the input media and/or devices used to enter the data into the organization's computer system.

**2.** Go to the library and/or a computer store and identify by brand name four data entry devices used with personal computers. Prepare a report describing the characteristics of the devices you select.

# ANSWERS TO FEEDBACK AND REVIEW SECTIONS

| 5-1 | | 5-2 | | 5-3 | |
|---|---|---|---|---|---|
| 1. T | 10. F | 1. i | 10. d | 1. C | 6. A |
| 2. F | 11. F | 2. g | 11. l | 2. D | 7. D |
| 3. T | 12. F | 3. b | 12. n | 3. C | 8. B |
| 4. F | 13. F | 4. a | 13. m | 4. B | 9. C |
| 5. F | 14. T | 5. h | 14. e | 5. D | 10. C |
| 6. T | 15. T | 6. j | | | |
| 7. T | | 7. c | | | |
| 8. T | | 8. f | | | |
| 9. T | | 9. k | | | |

# Smart Card— Makes Smart Sense

Telepayment may well be tomorrow's buzzword. At least, we're going to be hearing it more and more often. Briefly, the word describes a set of financial transactions in which no money is exchanged between the purchaser and the seller.

Already in use in Minnesota and New York, "Smart Card," or Carte a' Memoire as it's called in its French patent, allows buyers to bypass the need to be billed.

The Smart Card is the key that unlocks a complex system combining the telephone, television, data transmission and processing techniques. There are two types of cards: pre-paid and post-paid. Whichever type is employed, it essentially eliminates the need to go to one's bank except to deposit money. From then on, any transaction can be done from the home or at the point of purchase.

The Smart Card itself resembles the credit cards now issued by the various credit services throughout the world. It has the same measurements with one very important difference. The Smart Card has a tiny chip imbedded within the plastic in the upper left-hand corner. The chip is similar to those found in computers and calculators. It's a microprocessor which makes the card a palm-sized dedicated microcomputer: There is another unique aspect that differentiates the Smart Card from the typical credit card. A four-digit code identifies the owner of the card. If the card were to be stolen and three successive wrong digits were entered, the card would self-destruct.

The pre-paid card is employed to pay for telephone calls from public phones. The card, which can be bought at a newsstand, has a variable value—five to ten dollars. It's inserted into the card reader on the telephone. A readout shows instantly the amount of money available on the card. As the call progresses, the caller can observe how much the call costs and how much credit remains on the card. Once the credit is used up, the card is thrown away. Another plus to the telephone company is that a telephone equipped with a card reader cannot be vandalized since there is no money to be stolen. If lost or stolen, the pre-paid Smart Card can be used by anyone who obtains it, but there is a subscriber telephone Smart Card that is personalized to eliminate this possibility. It's issued by a bank and charges are recorded on the card until a predetermined limit is reached. The accumulated charges are then transferred to a billing center. Some 12,000 telephone Smart Cards are currently being tested in France, with more than 400,000 on order by the French government.

The post-paid Smart Card also resembles the typical credit card except that it has an internal computer with an uneraseable memory. A confidential code protects the owner, as well as the bank, from fraud. The card is credited with a monthly buying power—a credit line based on the owner's accounts—that allows the owner to make purchases up to that limit. In this way, the card becomes an electronic check book. With it, the card owner can conduct a variety of transactions that would ordinarily require trips to the bank.

The card can be used from the home with the aid of a terminal. Merchandise from a participating store can be called up on the monitor. The card is inserted into the reader and the code identifying the owner is typed in with the merchandise desired.

Within a department store, the same process takes place. The card goes into the card reader at the counter with the owner's code typed in by the owner. Whether at home or at the point of purchase, the amount of the transaction is moved from the bank directly to the store. At the end of a certain period, all of the transactions can be called up on the home monitor showing the reserve on the credit limit as well as each purchase and its cost.

The field of medicine has also found an adaptation of the Smart Card. Developed by Cii Honeywell Bull, the memory card is designed for pacemaker carriers. With its 4K of memory, the card can be presented to any European doctor. A cartridge acts as the link between the encoded information about the patient and its expression by the doctor in any language he uses. Entering the card into the reader presents all of the pertinent information on the screen including dates of previous visits with implant data plus many other medical parameters and permanent data as well.

The First Bank of Minneapolis and Chase Manhattan of New York City are conducting experiments with the Smart Card now. The U.S. Department of Defense is looking into the use of the Smart Card as a substitute for the present paper ID carried by members of the Armed Services. As a result of the frauds discovered in the food stamp program, the U.S. Department of Agriculture is planning to test the card to be used as an alternative to food stamps.

Will the Smart Card eliminate money? It's hard to tell at this point, but it's proven that it can eliminate at least some of the hassles of money. Now only time will tell—n'est-ce pas?

—George Leon, "Smart Card—Makes Smart Sense." Reprinted by permission of *Electronic Education*, vol. 3, no. 5, February 1984, p. 61. Photos courtesy Schlumberger Limited and SmartCard International Inc.

Electronic payment systems reach from the home to the store to your neighborhood public telephone.

The Smart Card is a multifunctional microprocessor and memory on a computer chip embedded in a plastic card—literally a "computer in a card" for your wallet. This specimen card has the inner workings—the computer—exposed for you to see.

# Secondary Storage and Output

### The Electronic Dog Tag

Faced with 4 million pounds of paper records—and that's in Europe alone—you'd suspect that the U.S. Army would want to find a way to streamline its records storage systems. Paper records take up lots of space and lots of time for lots of Army clerks, not to mention creating lots of delays in processing information.

Enter Datakey, a Minneapolis-based company best known for its electronic key security systems. The Army is now in the process of testing Datakey's Data Tag, a plastic card that features 64,000 bits of storage and looks something like the conventional metal dog tag.

If present testing proves successful, Army troops will be issued Data Tags with an embedded microchip which carries each soldier's complete training and medical histories along with the standard name, rank, and serial number. The Army's goal, of course, is to speed access to personnel records and avoid those troublesome paperwork delays.

Access via portable terminals enables data collection in the field. With a serviceperson's medical information immediately accessible, the cards could act as a catalyst in treating the wounded and in manifesting troops, that is, deploying individual expertise efficiently when and where it's needed. The Army estimates that paperless recordkeeping with Data Tags could trim by as much as half the number of personnel clerks required in this branch of the armed services.

—Photo courtesy Datakey, Minneapolis, Minn.

Chapter 7 explains secondary storage and output concepts. You'll learn first that most computer systems use a series of different storage elements, which are usually selected for different tasks on the basis of retrieval speed, storage capacity, and storage cost. After examining secondary storage media and devices, the focus shifts to computer output, and you'll learn about output media and devices that are used to print, film, display, and capture in other ways the information computer systems produce. The information in this chapter will enable you to:

- Identify the elements in the storage hierarchy and discuss the factors to be considered in storage selection

- Summarize the characteristics of the secondary media used to store data that are sequentially organized and processed, and those which provide quick and direct access to stored records

- Summarize the types of computer output that may be produced and the devices used to prepare it

## Chapter Outline

# THE STORAGE HIERARCHY: AN OVERVIEW

By now you know that all computers must be able to store and retrieve data. Some small personal systems may need to store only a few thousand characters. But large systems need access to billions of characters stored in a computer-readable form. When computer specialists refer to the **storage hierarchy** of a particular computer system, they have in mind a series of different storage elements. These different elements are found in all but the smallest computer systems and are likely to be ranked according to the following criteria:

1. *Retrieval speed.* The **access time** of a storage element is the time it takes to locate and retrieve stored data in response to a program instruction. A fast access time is preferred.

2. *Storage capacity.* An element's ability to store the amount of data needed now and in the future must be considered. A large capacity is desired.

3. *Cost per bit of capacity.* An obvious goal is to minimize this cost.

Figure 7-1 gives you a general idea of how different storage elements rank. At the top of the storage hierarchy pyramid are the *primary storage* components found in the CPU. The principal element is the primary storage section which was discussed in Chapter 5 along with other specialized processing and control storage elements that may be found in the CPU. The semiconductor storage chips commonly used in the CPU have the fastest access times. Relative to other available storage elements, however, chips have the smallest storage capacity and the highest cost per bit of capacity.

**Secondary** (or **auxiliary**) **storage** elements supplement primary storage in most computer systems. Included in the secondary storage classification, and located below primary storage in the hierarchy of Figure 7-1, are *direct-access storage devices* (DASDs). The data retained in these secondary storage units are *online* and are available to the CPU at all times. Compared with primary storage, the storage capacity of a DASD is larger and the cost per bit stored is lower. Although the access time of a DASD may be only a few milliseconds, primary storage speed is thousands of times faster. Different DASDs provide different levels of cost and performance, as you'll see later in this chapter.

At the base of the storage hierarchy is another type of secondary storage. The data retained on **sequential-access storage media** are periodically accessed and updated by the sequential processing techniques discussed in earlier chapters. These stored data are *offline* from the CPU except when loaded on an input device. The storage capacity of these media is virtually unlimited, and the storage cost is very low. But before the CPU can gain access to a particular record, a computer operator must locate the sequential file and load it on an input device. The CPU must then read all preceding records until the desired one is found. This procedure alone takes several minutes.

## Elements in the Storage Hierarchy

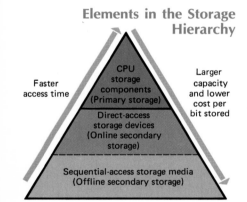

Figure 7-1 The storage hierarchy pyramid. A faster access time is obtained by moving up the pyramid. A larger storage capacity and a lower cost per bit stored are the results of moving down the pyramid. Thus, CPU storage components generally have the *fastest* access times, the *smallest* storage capacity, and the *highest* cost per bit stored. The *primary storage* of a computer system consists of the components in the CPU. Supplementing primary storage is the *secondary* (or *auxiliary*) *storage* of a computer system. This broader classification includes all the online direct-access storage devices and all the offline sequential-access storage media that hold data in a computer-readable form.

**Storage Selection**    If a single storage element were superior in speed, capacity, and cost, there would be no need for a storage hierarchy. Since this isn't the case, computer system designers must study each application and then choose the best storage approach for the job. That is, the way the data are organized and processed determines the approach they select. If a file can be organized sequentially, and if records require only periodic updating, then the lowest-cost option is likely to be the use of a sequential-access secondary storage medium. On the other hand, the need for quick access to any file record requires direct-access processing, and a DASD must be used.

In selecting a DASD, designers must usually make compromises between performance and cost. For example, in specialized scientific applications where processing speed is paramount and cost is secondary, the system selected may have a large primary storage section linked to a very fast DASD. In business applications, a slower DASD with larger capacity may be picked over a faster and more expensive device that has less capacity.

# SECONDARY STORAGE FOR SEQUENTIAL ACCESS

Punched paper media, magnetic tape, and portable magnetic disks are used to store data that are sequentially organized and accessed. You'll remember from Chapter 2 that the records in a sequentially organized file are stored one after the other in an ascending or descending order determined by the record key. To access records, the computer starts with the first one in the sequence. This record is read and is either processed or passed over. The second record is then accessed, followed by the third, and so on.

**Punched Paper Media Storage**    In addition to being used for data entry, *punched cards* and *punched paper tape* also provide offline secondary storage of data. Once the holes have been punched, of course, the data are as permanent as the paper media. The number of characters that can be stored in a given physical space is low for both cards and paper tape. However, the storage capacity of punched paper media is virtually unlimited, and the cost per bit stored is low.

**Magnetic Tape Storage**    Magnetic tape is a popular storage medium for large files that are sequentially accessed and processed. Thousands of reels of stored data are maintained in the magnetic tape libraries of large computer systems (see Figure 7-3).

Data are stored as tiny invisible magnetized spots on an iron-oxide material that coats one side of the plastic tape. The stored facts can be read many times. They will remain for years or until erased by the recording of new data. Magnetic tape has a high data density (over 6,000 characters can be stored on an inch of tape). Thus, it's possible to store over 100 million characters on a single $10\frac{1}{2}$-inch reel of tape that costs less than $20. The cost per bit stored is obviously microscopic. Tape sales have experienced renewed growth in recent years because tape is being used for the backup storage of information recorded on certain types of magnetic disk systems, as you'll see later.

**Figure 7-2** To retrieve data stored offline on a sequential-access medium, the computer operator must locate the appropriate file and load it on an input device. (Photo used with permission of Nixdorf Computer Corporation, Burlington, Mass.)

**Figure 7-3** Large computer systems make use of extensive tape libraries, which contain thousands and thousands of reels of stored information and may occupy entire rooms in an organization. (Reproduced with permission of AT&T)

## Disk Storage for Sequential Access

A magnetic disk is a metal or plastic platter that resembles a grooveless phonograph record. As you saw in Chapter 6, data can be recorded and stored on the surface of a floppy disk in the form of tiny invisible magnetic spots. These and other portable magnetic disks can be used to provide sequential-access secondary storage in much the same way that magnetic tape is used. But as the following analogy shows, magnetic disks are not limited to storing records that must be organized and retrieved according to sequence.

Let's assume that you have both a sound tape player and a record player. Let's also suppose that 10 songs are recorded on your favorite tape, and your favorite record has seven pieces of music. Now what must you do if you only want to listen to (or access) the sixth song on the tape and the fourth song on the record? To get to the sixth tape song, you must put the tape on the player and wait until the tape used to record the first five songs has moved through the player. Although your player may "fast forward" the tape quickly past the first five pieces, there's still a delay of several seconds. To get to the fourth song on the record, you can follow either of two approaches. You can place the record on the player, position the pickup arm at the beginning of the first song, and wait until the arm has played the first three pieces. (Following the stored sequence in this way is logically similar to accessing the music on a tape.) Or, you can *directly* move the pickup arm across the record to the groove where the fourth song begins.

Like the songs on a sound tape, the data records organized on a magnetic tape must be retrieved according to the storage sequence. And like the music, the data recorded on a magnetic disk can be accessed in sequence if they have been orga-

**Figure 7-4** Portable packs of rigid magnetic storage disks ready for loading into multiple disk storage devices. (Photo courtesy Sperry Corporation)

**Figure 7-5** Removable rigid disks are packaged in a number of ways. There are three sizes of disk packs shown here in front of two types of disk cartridges. (Courtesy Memorex)

nized in a way that supports such retrieval. When the data records on a disk are sequentially accessed to support batch processing applications, the direct-access capability of the disk really isn't used. The first record may be directly retrieved, but all others are then read in sequence as if they were stored on a magnetic tape.

The facts stored on a disk can be read many times. They will remain indefinitely or until the disk surface is erased and reused. The storage capacity of a floppy disk varies depending on its size and on other factors that we'll consider later. Well over a million characters can be stored on a diskette that costs less than $10. The cost per bit stored is thus very low. In addition to plastic floppies, other types of disks used in sequential processing applications are made of thin metal plates coated with a magnetizeable material. Some of these rigid disks can also be removed from their disk storage devices (see Figure 7-4). They come in different sizes and are packaged in various ways. Removable disk devices use one- or two-disk **cartridges,** or **packs** of three or more disks mounted on a single shaft (see Figure 7-5). The storage capacity of single cartridges usually varies from about 5 million to 28 million characters. For a single disk pack, the storage capacity usually ranges from about 30 million to 300 million characters. A disk pack equal in storage capacity to a reel of magnetic tape may be about 25 times more expensive. However, the cost per bit stored is still modest.

## SECONDARY STORAGE FOR DIRECT ACCESS

Even though records stored on magnetic disks are often sequentially organized and processed like tape records, the popularity of disk storage devices is largely due to their direct-access capabilities. Let's now consider disk and other direct-access secondary storage devices in more detail.

## Disk Storage for Direct Access

**Figure 7-6** Winchester was the code name used by IBM during the development of this technology. The story is told that IBM designers originally planned to use dual disk drives to introduce the new concepts. Each drive was to have a storage capacity of 30 million characters. The product was thus expected to be a "30-30." Since that was the caliber of a famous rifle, the new product was nicknamed "Winchester." The dual-drive plans were later dropped, but the name stuck. There's no extra charge for this bit of computing trivia. Many other vendors now make Winchester disk drives. (Photo courtesy Seagate)

Magnetic disks are the most popular medium for direct-access secondary storage. All magnetic disks are round platters coated with a magnetizeable recording material, but their similarities end there. As the following listing shows, they come in different sizes. They can be portable or permanently mounted in their storage devices (called **disk drives**). And they can be made of rigid metal or flexible plastic.

**Types of Magnetic Disks.** Here are some of the possible options:

■ *Larger (14-inch) metal disks permanently housed in sealed, contamination-free containers. Read/write* heads are also permanently sealed with the disks they serve. These disks are used in all but the smallest computer systems. Their containers are usually not removed from the disk drive. High-capacity systems using these sealed housings are said to employ **Winchester technology.**

■ *Other 14-inch metal disks packaged in removable cartridges or disk packs* (discussed a few paragraphs earlier). These are also used in all but the smallest systems, but they aren't sealed in contamination-free containers. Multiple disk storage devices, each capable of holding one or more cartridges or packs, may be connected to a CPU.

■ *Smaller 8-inch and $5\frac{1}{4}$-inch rigid disks permanently housed in Winchester disk devices.* These are used in mini- and microcomputer systems (see Figure 7-6). Some smaller rigid disk drives are also available with sealed but removable Winchester-type cartridges.

■ *Small 8-inch and $5\frac{1}{4}$-inch portable floppy (flexible) disks individually packaged in protective envelopes* (see Figure 7-7). In addition to their data entry uses, these diskettes are currently the most popular online secondary storage medium used in personal computer and intelligent terminal systems (see Figure 7-8).

**Figure 7-8** Personal computer systems often use floppy disks for online secondary storage as well as for data entry. (Photo courtesy International Business Machines Corporation)

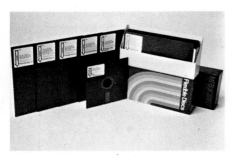

**Figure 7-7** Most floppy disks now come in these 8-inch and $5\frac{1}{4}$-inch sizes, but smaller sizes are available. (Photo courtesy Memorex)

■ *Even more compact floppy and rigid disks measuring 4 inches or less in diameter.* There are several competing floppy sizes. Offerings of 3-inch, $3\frac{1}{4}$-inch, at least three incompatible $3\frac{1}{2}$-inch, 3.9-inch, and 4-inch versions have led to a confusing "aflopalypse now" situation with several vendors vying for position. But all the floppy versions are individually packaged in a nonbendable shirt-pocket-sized plastic case. This hard case has a dust-sealing and fingerproof shutter that opens automatically after the case is inserted in its disk drive. These disks are used in desktop and portable personal computers and word processing units. For example, Apple Computer uses a $3\frac{1}{2}$-inch version in its Macintosh and Lisa 2 models. Rigid disk drives with sealed but removable Winchester-type cartridges have also been developed in these compact sizes.

**Storing Data on Magnetic Disks.** Music is stored on a phonograph record in a continuous groove that spirals into the center of the record. But there are no grooves on a magnetic disk. Instead, data are stored on all disks in a number of invisible concentric circles called **tracks.** These tracks, like the rings in a tree, begin at the outer edge of the disk and continue toward the center without ever touching (see Figure 7-9). Each track has a designated number.

A motor rotates the disk at a constant and rapid speed.[1] Data are recorded on the tracks of a spinning disk surface and read from the surface by one or more read/write heads. If a floppy disk is used, the head is in contact with the disk. If hard disks are used, the heads "fly" on a cushion of air a few micro-inches (or millionths of an inch) above the surface. When multiple disks are packaged together, a number of **access arms** and read/write heads are used (see Figures 7-10 and 7-11). Data are written as tiny magnetic spots on the disk surface. A 1-spot is magnetized in one direction, a 0-spot in another. Seven- or eight-bit BCD codes are generally used to represent data. The writing of new data on a disk erases data previously stored at the location. The new magnetic spots remain indefinitely or until they too are erased at

---

[1] The rotational speed of floppies is usually between 300 and 400 revolutions per minute (rpm). Hard disks rotate from 2,400 to 4,700 rpm, with 3,600 being a common speed.

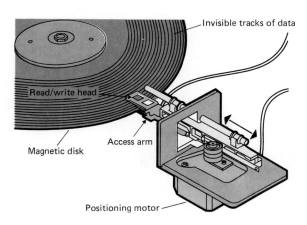

Invisible tracks of data

Read/write head

Magnetic disk

Access arm

Positioning motor

**Figure 7-9** Data are stored on invisible tracks on the surface of a disk. There may be from 35 to over 100 tracks on a floppy disk surface, and from about 200 to over 800 on hard-disk surfaces. Both the top and bottom of a hard disk are generally used for data storage, but only one surface of a floppy disk may be used. One or more read/write heads are assigned to each storage surface to record and retrieve data. These heads are fastened to access arms or actuators which are moved in and out over the spinning disk surfaces by positioning motors. The heads can thus be quickly located over any track to read or write data.

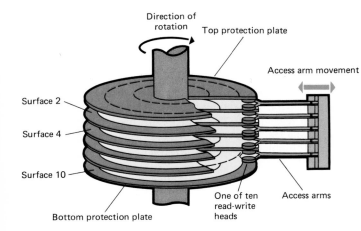

Direction of rotation

Top protection plate

Access arm movement

Surface 2

Surface 4

Surface 10

Bottom protection plate

One of ten read-write heads

Access arms

**Figure 7-10** Multiple access arms and read/write heads are used with disk packs. The arms move in and out in unison among the individual disks. Two heads are frequently mounted on each arm to access two surfaces. In this example, the heads on the top arm access the bottom of the top disk and the top of the second disk. Data aren't stored on the top surface of the top disk or the bottom surface of the bottom disk because these surfaces are easily scratched. In this illustration, the pack has ten recording and two protective surfaces.

a future time. Reading of recorded data is accomplished as the magnetized spots pass under a read head and induce electrical pulses in it.

The more disk surfaces a particular system has, the greater its storage capacity will be. But the storage capacity of a disk system also depends on the **bits per inch of track** and the **tracks per inch of surface.** That is, the storage capacity depends on the number of bits that can be stored on an inch of track, and the number of tracks that can be placed on an inch of surface (see Figure 7-12). A constant goal of disk-drive designers is to increase the data density of a disk surface by increasing the number of tracks. To accomplish this goal, it's necessary to reduce the distance between the read/write head and the disk surface so that smaller magnetized spots can be precisely written and then retrieved. But as designers gradually found ways to reduce this distance and improve the data density, they ran into a problem. As Figure 7-13 shows, they moved the read/write head so close to the disk surface that

**Figure 7-11** (*left*) A head-arm assembly used in a hard-disk drive. (*right*) One of the four thin-film read/write heads on the arm assembly shown next to a needle's eye for perspective. (Courtesy Memorex)

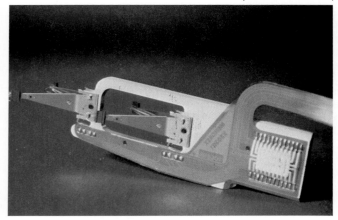

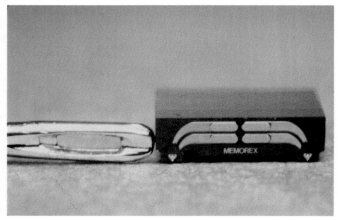

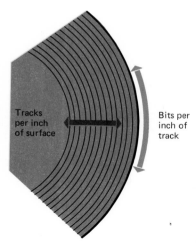

**Figure 7-12** Factors determining the storage capacity of a magnetic disk system include bits per inch of track, and tracks per inch of surface. Some Winchester hard-disk systems can store well over 10,000 bits on an inch of track and have over 400 tracks on an inch of disk surface. Their high data density permits compact 3.9-inch Winchester-type disk devices to store over 6 megabytes (a *megabyte* is a million bytes or characters). Some 5¼-inch Winchester systems can store over 40 megabytes. Similar 8-inch systems can store over 100 megabytes, and up to one gigabyte ( *gigabyte* is a billion bytes or characters) can be held on a 14-inch Winchester disk system. The 14-inch disks packaged in removable cartridges and packs usually have a lower data density than Winchester disks. Floppy disk systems come in either single- or double-density versions and record on one or both surfaces of a diskette. Thus, the capacity of an earlier system using a single-sided 5¼-inch diskette may only be a little over 100 kilobytes (a *kilobyte* is a thousand bytes or characters), while the capacity of a later system using a double-density, dual-sized 5¼-inch diskette may be over 1 megabyte.

**Figure 7-13** Data density can be improved and storage capacity can be increased by reducing the flying height of read/write heads over disk surfaces. Each reduction in height allows an increase in bits per inch of track and tracks per inch of surface. The reason Winchester technology was developed to control the disk environment is obvious in this illustration. A smoke particle 250 millionths of an inch in diameter can't begin to fit in the space between head and disk. And a human hair looks like Pike's Peak to the flying head. The head flies 20 millionths of an inch above the disk at speeds of over 100 miles per hour. That's comparable to an airplane flying 600 miles per hour around the circumference of a lake at an altitude of ¼ inch.

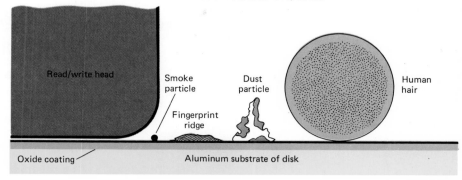

a human hair or a dust particle on the disk loomed like a mountain in the path of the flying head. The resulting collision caused the head to bounce up and then **crash** on the far side of the particle. This often damaged the head, the disk, and the data.

Winchester technology was developed to reduce this problem. Sealing the disks and their heads in contamination-free containers reduced head crashes, permitted smaller distances between head and disk, and increased disk storage capacity. Of course, disk problems can't be totally eliminated. And if there's a failure, let's say, in a Winchester device with a permanently mounted disk, the information stored isn't available for some time or it may even be lost. Thus, backup copies of the information stored on the fixed Winchester disk need to be saved periodically. As mentioned earlier, one popular approach is to make backups using magnetic tape media and devices. Another approach is to write the Winchester information onto the removable disks used with other disk drives. For example, the information on a personal computer's Winchester disk can be transferred to the computer's floppy disk system and saved on diskettes. The problem encountered in using diskettes, however, is that it may take from a dozen to well over 100 5¼-inch floppies to hold the information stored on a single 5¼-inch Winchester disk.

**Accessing Data on Magnetic Disks.** Just as the pickup arm of a record player can move directly to the location of a specific song without playing other music, an access arm can move a read/write head directly to the track that contains the desired data without reading other tracks. Before this direct access can be accomplished, however, the program instructions that control the disk drive must specify the **disk address** of the desired data. This disk address information specifies the track number, surface number, and so on, to enable the access mechanism to pinpoint the exact location of the data.

Figure 7-14 When data are organized by cylinders, the cylinder number, surface number, and record number are needed to access the stored data. All tracks with the same number in a disk pack form a cylinder with the same number. Each invisible cylinder passes vertically through the pack.

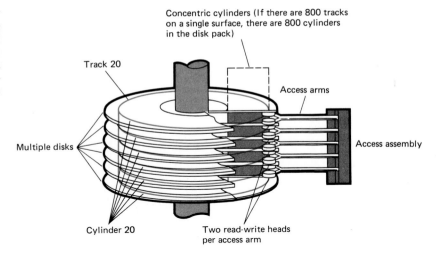

Disk-drive manufacturers use either the *cylinder method* or the *sector method* to organize and physically store disk data. Figure 7-14 shows the cylinder approach used with packs of removable disks. Access arms move in unison in and out of a disk pack. Thus, if the read/write head that serves the top recording surface is positioned over the twentieth track, each of the heads on the arms that serve other surfaces are similarly positioned over the same track. All the twentieth tracks together comprise the twentieth **cylinder** of the disks. If there are 200 or more tracks on a single hard-disk surface, there are also 200 or more cylinders in a multiple stack of the disks. Before a disk drive can access a cylinder record, a computer program must provide the record's disk address. This address supplies the cylinder number, the surface number, and the record number. Thus, a desired record might be on cylinder (track) 20, on surface 1, in record location 5. If a large number of related records are typically processed in sequence after record 5, they can be organized to follow record 5 on this same track and surface and can then be continued on the same track of other surfaces in the cylinder. In one revolution of the disk the data on track 20 of surface 1 is read. In the next revolution, control is instantly switched to the read/write head over surface 2 and a full track of data can be read in a single revolution. This procedure can continue down the cylinder without any delays caused by the movement of access arms.

The sector approach to organizing disk data is used with single disks (including floppies) as well as with cartridges or packs of multiple disks. As shown in Figure 7-15, a disk surface is divided into pie-shaped segments or **sectors.** (The number of sectors varies with the disk system used.) Each sector holds a specific number of characters and records. Before a record can be accessed, a computer program must again give the disk drive the record's address. This disk address specifies the track number, the surface number, and the sector number of the record. One or more read/write heads are then moved to the proper track, the head over the specified surface is activated, and data are read from the designated sector as it spins under the head.

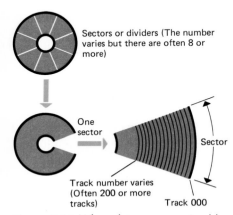

Figure 7-15 When data are organized by sectors, the track number, surface number, and sector number are needed to access the stored data. The outside track is generally numbered 000 (or 00 in the case of most floppies). The inside track on a disk with 800 tracks is numbered 799.

The access time for data stored on a disk is basically determined by:

1. The **seek time**—the time required to position a head over the proper track

2. The **search** (or **latency**) **time**—the time required to spin the needed data under the head

The average access time for most hard-disk storage systems is usually between 10 and 100 milliseconds.[2] For floppy disk systems, the average time usually ranges from 70 to 600 milliseconds.[3] Most disk drives have a single read/write head for each disk surface. But some of the faster hard-disk systems either have a *fixed-head* for *each* track of a surface, or they use *multiple heads* on each movable access arm to service a number of adjacent tracks. A **fixed-head-per-track device** has *no* seek time delay, and multiple heads reduce the average length of horizontal movement of the access arms and thus decrease the seek time. Of course, these faster systems are more expensive than the single-head-per-arm devices.

Once the data have been accessed, they are copied from the disk to the CPU. The transfer rate depends on the density of the stored data and the rotational speed of the disk. For floppy systems, the maximum transfer rate is typically between 30,000 and 150,000 characters per second. For hard-disk systems, the maximum rate usually ranges between 200,000 and 2 million characters per second.

**Advantages and Limitations of Magnetic Disks.** When compared to magnetic tape, disks have the following *advantages:*

■ Disk records can be stored sequentially and processed like magnetic tape records, or they can be stored for direct-access processing.

■ Online disk records can be accessed and updated in a few milliseconds. No sorting of transactions is necessary.

■ A single input transaction can be used to simultaneously update the online disk records of several related files.

But disks also have *limitations* when compared to magnetic tape:

■ Sequential processing using disks may be slower and less efficient than when tapes are used.

■ Removable disk media equal in storage capacity to a reel of magnetic tape may be about 25 times more expensive. On a cost-per-bit basis, the cost of disks is low. But the cost of magnetic tape is even less.

---

[2] Technically speaking, disk drives have *direct* but not *random* access to records. Random access refers to a storage device in which the access time is independent of the physical location of the data. Since the disk access time does vary with the data location, it's more correct to say that disks provide direct access. This distinction is not always observed, however, and disk drives are sometimes referred to as random access units.

[3] Floppy disks rotate much more slowly than hard disks and so their search time is much longer. A floppy can't turn too fast or centrifugal force will bend it out of shape and damage the stored data. A rigid metal disk doesn't have this problem.

■ When a tape file is updated, the old master tape remains unchanged and available in case of system malfunctions. When the records in a disk file are updated, however, the old records may be erased when the new records are written on the disk. And information stored on a fixed Winchester disk could be unavailable or lost if there's a drive failure. Special backup procedures are thus required to protect disk records from malfunctions.

■ People have broken through security provisions and gained access to sensitive online disk files from remote terminals. These files have been manipulated and destroyed. It's easier to maintain the security of tape files.

### Direct Access with RAM "Disks" and Magnetic Bubbles

"Watch where you walk in here, Howard—they dropped a storage chip and you may destroy the entire literature of the 18th century!"

**RAM "Disk" Storage.** In this direct-access storage approach used with personal computers, a block of semiconductor RAM chips is used as a *simulated* "disk" to replace the mechanical operations of rotating disks. Sometimes referred to as a *silicon disk* or a *pseudo-disk*, a **RAM disk** isn't really a disk at all, and it has no moving parts. Rather, it's a bank of RAM chips set up to look like a disk drive to the computer. The extra RAM chips may be placed on add-on circuit boards that fit inside the computer, or they may be housed in separate cabinets. Either way, these extra chips look just like a disk drive to the control programs used in the personal computer's operating system. The main advantage of a RAM disk is its speed; it turns a slow processor into a "hot rod." Instead of waiting seconds while data or instructions are loaded from a floppy disk, RAM disk users have nearly instant access. Even Winchester disks are slow by comparison. The main problem with the volatile RAM chips commonly used, of course, is that the stored contents are lost when power is removed. Thus, users often store and then access their programs from a RAM disk (these programs are backed up on floppies or some other permanent medium). The data files produced during a processing session are stored on a permanent disk.

**Magnetic Bubble Storage. Magnetic bubble storage** devices are also semiconductor chips that have no moving parts and are thus reliable (see Figure 7-16). But unlike the chips used for RAM disk storage, bubble chips retain their stored contents when power is removed. When they were introduced in the late 1970s, some researchers expected that they would eventually replace many magnetic disk systems. But bubble devices have so far failed to live up to these optimistic expectations. Disk storage costs fell much faster than expected while bubble storage costs remained higher than predicted.

Still, large numbers of bubble chips are now being used in specialized areas. They are found in portable computers. Portable terminals use bubble devices to store data until they can be transmitted to a larger system. And bubble chips are also being used in machine tools, robots, and military computers. The data density of these chips is high. About 240 typewritten pages of information can be stored on a chip the size of the one shown in Figure 7-16.

### Direct Access with Optical Disks and Tape Strips

**Optical Disk Technology.** You're probably aware that **optical disks** are now used by consumer electronics companies to record movies, concerts, sporting events, and other audio/visual presentations for playback on television sets. Some of these platters are grooveless "videodisks" that are created by **laser recording**

Figure 7-16 Magnetic bubble chip. (Courtesy Intel Corporation)

Figure 7-17 A single Hitachi optical disk provides the same memory capacity as 15 magnetic tapes. (Photo courtesy Hitachi, Ltd.)

systems.[4] A beam of laser light is used to burn tiny holes (or pits) into a thin coating of metal or other material deposited on a spinning disk. Visible only under a powerful microscope, these holes are used to represent images and sounds. Of course, they can't be erased and the disk can't be reused. At a later time, a less-powerful laser light beam in a videodisk player is used to read the hole patterns, convert these patterns into audio/visual signals, and transmit the signals to a television set.[5]

The same technology that's used to record and play back sound and images can also be used to store and retrieve data. The storage density of optical disks is enormous (100 or more times greater than a typical rigid magnetic disk of the same size), the storage cost is extremely low, and the access time is relatively fast. Laboratory systems with the potential to store on a single disk the contents of a library of several thousand volumes have already been demonstrated. Permanent archives now stored on microfilm and magnetic tape may in the future be placed on optical disks. One small inexpensive disk can already replace 15 reels of magnetic tape (Figure 7-17). And the future storage capacity of a single disk is expected to be much greater. Disk players will be able to access any data on these disks in a few milliseconds. And newer techniques have been developed to permit optical disks to be erased and reused.

**Mass Storage with Tape Strips.** Wouldn't it be nice to combine the magnetic tape advantages of low cost and high storage capacity with the advantages of direct record accessibility? This is essentially the objective of **tape strip devices** used for mass storage. The storage medium may be considered to be a length of flexible plastic material upon which short strips of magnetic tape have been mounted. These strips are then placed in cartridges, and the cartridges are loaded into a storage device that's online to the CPU. These mass storage devices employ the same techniques used to read and write data on magnetic tape. An example of such a device is the IBM Mass Storage System (see Figure 7-18). Honeycomb storage compartments are used to hold the data cartridges. It requires several seconds for

[4]Not all videodisk systems use laser optical technology. The RCA Selecta Vision system has grooved disks that are stamped out much like phonograph records.
[5]In the Magnavision system, for example, variations in the length of holes modulate the laser beam to produce a video signal.

Figure 7-18 (*left*) IBM mass storage system. (*right*) Honeycomb storage compartments are used in this system to hold data cartridges. Over 400,000 books the size of this one can be stored in this system. (Courtesy International Business Machines Corporation)

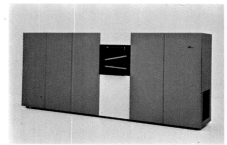

this device to locate the cartridge specified by an instruction from the CPU. Once the cartridge has been located and placed in a position to be read, several more seconds are needed to transfer the data to a magnetic disk and then to the CPU. That's an eternity compared to other online devices in the storage hierarchy. But the storage capacity is huge and the cost per bit stored is very small.

## Feedback and Review 7-1

You now know that most computer systems have a storage hierarchy. At the top of this hierarchy are the primary storage components found in the CPU. Supplementing primary storage is the secondary storage of a computer system. This broad classification includes the offline sequential-access storage media and the online direct-access storage media and devices presented in this chapter. To test and reinforce your understanding of this material, fill in the crossword puzzle form presented below.

### Across

**1.** A series of different storage elements are found in most computer systems. These different elements are called the storage _____.

**3.** The _____ time of a storage element is the time it takes to locate and retrieve stored data in response to a program instruction.

**8.** A beam of _____ light is used to record and retrieve data on optical disks.

**10.** Data retained in a DASD are _____ to the CPU, but the data stored on sequential-access storage media are offline except when loaded on an input device.

**12.** The _____ or latency time is the time required to spin the needed data under a read/write head in a disk drive.

**13.** A _____ disk is a portable storage medium that is packaged in a protective envelope.

**14.** In studying applications and choosing storage approaches to use, system designers must usually make _____ -offs between access time, storage capacity, cost, and record accessibility.

**16.** In many magnetic disk storage systems, a disk surface is divided into pie-shaped segments called _____.

**17.** Data stored on disks can be accessed in either a sequential or _____ way.

**18.** The _____ storage of a computer system includes all the online DASDs and all the offline sequential-access storage media that hold data in a computer-readable form.

**19.** A magnetic _____ chip is a serial-access memory that is used in portable terminals and robots.

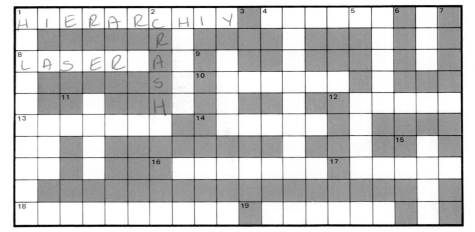

### Down

**2.** A dust particle on a magnetic disk can cause a flying head to bounce up and then _____ on the disk surface.

**4.** Disk drive manufacturers use either the _____ method or the sector method to organize and physically store disk data.

**5.** Portable magnetic disk cartridges and packs can be used to _____ data online or offline.

**6.** A _____ "disk" is a bank of semiconductor storage chips set up to look like a disk drive to a personal computer.

**7.** The generic name given to high-performance storage systems that use metal magnetic disks permanently housed in contamination-free containers is _____.

**9.** As online storage capacity increases, the _____ per bit stored tends to decrease.

**11.** Paper secondary storage media are easily _____ and mutilated.

**12.** Read/write heads are used to _____ data to and from magnetic media.

**13.** Read/write heads _____ on a cushion of air a few micro-inches above the surfaces of rigid magnetic disks.

**15.** The _____ time is the time required to position a head over the proper track on a magnetic disk.

# COMPUTER OUTPUT: SOME BASIC CONCEPTS

You'll recall that most of Chapter 6 dealt with the input media and devices used to translate human language and symbols into the codes used by CPUs. The rest of this chapter deals with the output media and devices used to convert digital codes into a humanly usable form. But just as it was necessary to pause at the beginning of Chapter 6 to discuss some basic data entry matters, so, too, is it necessary here to summarize some basic computer output concepts.

## Why Computer Output Is Needed

Early in Chapter 1 you saw that computer data processing transforms input data into output information. This output information can give people the knowledge they need to improve their understanding of issues and achieve specific goals. For example, the output of personal computers is helping many people analyze investments, prepare tax returns, monitor home energy usage, and so on.

Besides being helpful to individuals who use it to achieve personal ends, computer output is also used by decision makers in most organizations. These people must perform certain tasks to achieve organizational goals. Although different goals are pursued, the basic tasks generally involve:

1. *Planning* for the future use of scarce human and capital resources. (Capital is money and the things money can buy.)

2. *Organizing* these resources into logical and efficient units.

3. *Controlling* these resources.

The success of any organization is determined by how well its people perform these three tasks. And how well these tasks are carried out often depends, in part, on the quality of the available computer output. This is true because each task involves decision making, and decision making must generally be supported by output information that's as accurate, timely, complete, concise, and relevant as possible. If the output information doesn't possess these characteristics, the quality of the decisions will probably suffer, and the organization (at best) will likely not achieve the success it might otherwise have had.

In summary, as Figure 7-19 shows, good output information in the hands of those who can effectively use it will support good decisions. Good decisions will lead to the effective performance of organizational tasks, and effective task performance will lead to success in reaching the organization's goals. Of course, decision makers must often use important information that's not produced by their organization's computer(s). But as Figure 7-19 suggests, computer output is now an important bonding agent that helps hold many organizations together.

**Figure 7-19** The success of an organization may depend on its output information.

## Types of Computer Output

You've seen in Chapter 6 that the processing method used in an application has an important bearing on computer input. Not surprisingly, the processing method also plays an important role in computer output.

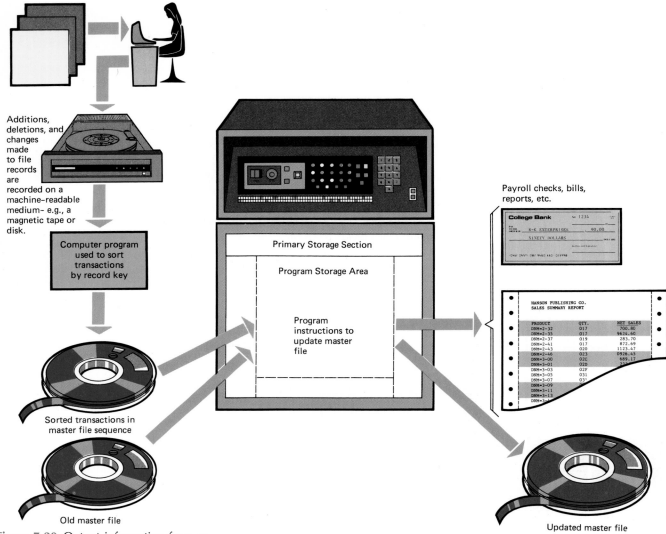

Additions, deletions, and changes made to file records are recorded on a machine-readable medium- e.g., a magnetic tape or disk.

Computer program used to sort transactions by record key

Sorted transactions in master file sequence

Old master file

Primary Storage Section

Program Storage Area

Program instructions to update master file

Payroll checks, bills, reports, etc.

Updated master file

**Figure 7-20** Output information from sequential file processing may be in the form of updated master files and various documents.

**Output from Sequential Processing.** Computer output can be grouped into internal and external categories. **Internal output** is information that's intended for use solely within an organization. The magnetic tape and magnetic disks used in sequential processing applications are **triple-purpose media.** In addition to their *data entry* and *secondary storage* functions, they also receive *output* from the CPU. (The same tape and disk drives used to enter data into the CPU are also used to write output information onto tapes and disks.) Figure 7-20 repeats an application from Chapter 2. The records intended for internal use are stored on a master file and are read into the CPU along with recent transaction data. The old master file records are revised by the recent transactions, and an updated master file is written as output on a medium such as magnetic tape. The internal information in the updated master file is reentered into the computer at a later date.

**Figure 7-21** Printed reports can provide detailed and/or summarized information. They can also point out exceptions to expected results to alert managers to the need for decisions and/or actions. (Courtesy International Business Machines Corporation)

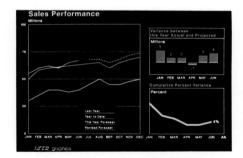

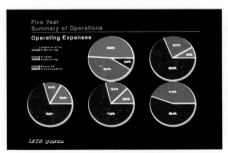

**Figure 7-22** Output created by using graphic software packages makes mountains of data easier to understand. (Reprinted with permission from ISSCO, San Diego, Calif.)

As Figure 7-20 shows, output reports and other documents may be prepared at the same time a master file is updated. Of course, internal reports that help decision makers do a better job must be in a humanly readable form (see Figure 7-21). When the information is to be retained for some time, the output from the CPU can be recorded directly on *microfilm*. In most cases, however, a *printed* report is prepared. Any format that meets the needs of the designated users is acceptable. For example, **detailed reports** that show the amount of a particular product that each customer has purchased might help salespeople and others make day-to-day operating decisions. However, decision makers at higher levels don't need (and probably won't use) reports that contain an excessive amount of detailed information. For these people, the output information should be presented in the form of summary reports and exception reports.

A **summary report** condenses and sifts the detailed data so that managers can spot patterns and trends and then take appropriate action. The same information printed in summary reports is also frequently presented in the form of **computer graphic output** (see Figure 7-22). It's thus often possible to further condense several pages of summary information into a few pictures.

Unlike detailed and summary reports that are prepared at regularly scheduled intervals, **exception reports** are usually triggered to supply computer output to managers only when operating data fall outside the normal limits specified in a program. The purpose of an exception report is to alert a manager to the need for decisions and/or actions. For example, such a report can be triggered to tell a manager when certain inventory items fall below a specified level, when a customer's charges reach a credit limit, or when sales of products fall outside the normal ranges. Exception reports save human time by permitting managers to concentrate

```
      THANK   YOU
  FOR SHOPPING AᴅP
     MONTCLAIR NJ
 STORE #864   05/06/84


 GEN              1.99X
 GEN              1.80X
 NBC COOKIES      1.39F
 SCHP GINGER      1.39E
 7UP DT 6PK C     1.99E
      6/1.99
 PF BREAD         1.05F
 AP ORANG JCE      .59F
 AP ORANG JCE      .59F
 AP ORANG JCE      .59F
 P GRP NUTS       1.59F
 COFF FILTER       .99N
 FIGARO CT FD      .43X
 FIGARO CT FD      .43X
 ST PZA BREAD     2.83F
 MILK SKIMMED     1.89F
 9LIVE CAT FD      .39X
 9LIVE CAT FD      .39X
 BRSN SPC CHS     2.69F
 TAX               .53N

    TOTAL        23.54

    CASH         30.00

    CHANGE        6.46

 3715   62 3   6.21PM
```

**Figure 7-23** Cash register tapes have become user-friendly by itemizing purchases for the customer.

their attentions on the important exceptions. Computer time and printer paper are also saved since there's no need to print lengthy reports that would merely show that most operating data fall within the normal limits.

**External output** is information that will be used outside the organization. In sequential processing applications, this output can be the invoices and statements sent to customers, the checks issued to employees and suppliers, or the income-tax withholding forms sent to the Internal Revenue Service. These and other output documents issued by the organization must often be prepared on designated forms. Colorful trademarks and other attractive symbols are often preprinted on many of these forms by the paper suppliers to present a favorable image of the organization. You can see in Figure 7-20 that output for both external and internal use can be produced in a single sequential file processing operation.

**Output from Direct-Access Processing.** As you know from Chapter 6, online terminals are used in direct-access processing applications to create a direct interactive relationship between people and computers. People use terminals to enter data into computer systems and to request and receive information from the systems. When online teleprinters, point-of-sale terminals, or financial transaction terminals are used, a computer often responds with a *printed output* produced by the terminal. This output can be intended solely for the use of the members of an organization. For example, the output sent to a portable teleprinter in response to a salesperson's inquiry about the availability of parts can include part code numbers that a customer wouldn't understand.

But the printed response sent to a terminal may also be external output intended for the use of people outside the organization. Such a response, of course, should not include unidentified code numbers. For example, the itemized sales receipt printed by a point-of-sale terminal and given to a customer should furnish clearly worded item descriptions rather than item code numbers. It's important for online systems to be "user-friendly" to those who receive the computer output (see Figure 7-23).

**Visual display** terminals are the most popular devices used today to receive output during direct-access processing (see Figure 7-24). Output messages and processed information are displayed on the screen of a CRT. You saw in Chapter 6 how an alphanumeric display station on a shop floor was used to update production records. A shop employee carried on a "conversation" with the computer program by supplying data in response to the output messages shown on the screen. The employee merely keyed in the correct response number from a menu of displayed messages. Graphic display terminals can also be used to produce output in the form of graphs, maps, and drawings. Information displayed on CRT screens is often printed if permanent copies are needed.

As you know, word processing operators can prepare letters by calling up stored messages, adding appropriate text, and then printing the information shown on their screens. Although most displayed messages and information are intended for internal use, some screen output is used by people who aren't members of the organization. Automated teller machines, for example, often display instructions to help bank customers carry out transactions.

Figure 7-24 Visual display terminals create a direct, interactive relationship between people and computers. (Photo courtesy Sperry Corporation)

In addition to presenting output information from direct-access processing in a printed or visual display format, computer systems can also prepare *voice responses* to inquiries. Voice response techniques are routinely used to supply internal and external output information.

Let's now take a closer look at the media and devices mentioned in this section that are used to produce computer output.

# PRINTED AND FILMED OUTPUT

When the output of sequential processing applications is to be used by people rather than reentered into computers, it's usually printed or filmed. Of course, as we've seen, printed output is also common in direct-access processing applications.

**Printed Output**   Printers are the primary output devices used to prepare permanent documents for human use, and the competition among printer manufacturers is fierce. The printers being produced today can generally be classified by how they print and by how fast they operate.

**Character (or Serial) Printers.** **Character (serial) printers** are one-character-at-a-time devices used with microcomputers, minicomputers, and teleprinter terminals for low-volume printing jobs. The techniques used to print characters vary

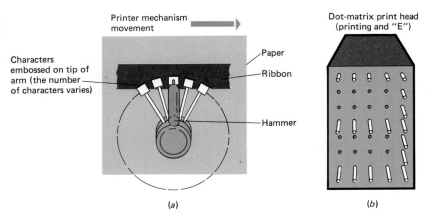

Printer mechanism movement

Characters embossed on tip of arm (the number of characters varies)

Paper

Ribbon

Hammer

Dot-matrix print head (printing and "E")

(a)

(b)

**Figure 7-26** Some of the mechanisms used in character printers. (a) The daisy-wheel approach. Daisy print wheels are easily removed and replaced with wheels having different type fonts. The speed of a daisy-wheel printer is usually in the 12 to 60 characters-per-second (cps) range. (b) The dot-matrix approach. Dot-matrix printer speeds usually range between 30 and 350 cps. A 5 × 7 matrix is shown here, but many other matrix sizes are used. Printers using these approaches are available for personal computer systems at prices beginning at less than $500.

**Figure 7-25** Print elements for (top) daisy-wheel and (bottom) dot-matrix character printers. (Photos supplied by Dataproducts Corporation, Woodland Hills, Calif.)

widely. **Impact methods** use the familiar typewriter approach of pressing a typeface against paper and inked ribbon. Serial impact printers often use a **daisy-wheel** or a **dot-matrix** printing mechanism (see Figure 7-25).

In the daisy-wheel approach (Figure 7-26a), each "petal" of the wheel has a character embossed on it. A motor spins the wheel rapidly, and when the desired character spins to the correct position, a print hammer strikes it to produce the output. (Some printers substitute print "thimbles" or "cups" for print wheels, but their operation is essentially the same.) In the dot-matrix approach (Figure 7-26b), an arrangement of tiny hammers strikes to produce the desired characters. Each hammer prints a small dot on the paper. Thus, the letter E would be formed as shown in Figure 7-26b.

Dot-matrix printers are usually faster than daisy-wheel devices and are often less expensive, but their print quality isn't as good. Thus, some organizations use dot-matrix printers for internal reports and daisy-wheel devices for the external output generated by word processing and other systems. Figure 7-27 shows the print quality possible with dot-matrix and daisy-wheel models. All impact printers can produce multiple copies by using carbon paper or its equivalent.

There are also **nonimpact** character printers available that use thermal, electrostatic, chemical, and inkjet technologies. With the **inkjet** approach, for example, droplets of ink are electrically charged after leaving a nozzle (Figure 7-28). The droplets are then guided to the proper position on the paper by electrically charged deflection plates. The print quality is good because the character is formed by dozens of tiny ink dots. If a droplet isn't needed for the particular character being formed, it's recycled back to the input jet. Inkjet and other nonimpact printers can't produce multiple copies of a document in a single printing.

! " # $ % & ´ ( ) * + , - . /
0 1 2 3 4 5 6 7 8 9 : ; < = > ?
@ A B C D E F G H I J K L M N O
P Q R S T U V W X Y Z [ \ ] ^ _
` a b c d e f g h i j k l m n o
p q r s t u v w x y z { | } ~

*(a)*

Get sharp and smart letter quality characters using a high
density 40x18 dot array matrix font. You may think this was
printed with an office typewriter or a daisy wheel printer,
but it is actually dot matrix.

*(b)*

THIS IS NORMAL.
*THIS IS NORMAL.ITALICS.*
THIS IS NORMAL,DOUBLESTRIKE.
*THIS IS NORMAL,DOUBLESTRIKE,ITALICS.*
**THIS IS NORMAL,EMPHASIZED,DOUBLESTRIKE.**
***THIS IS NORMAL,EMPHASIZED,DOUBLESTRIKE,ITALICS.***
THIS IS SUPERSCRIPT.
*THIS IS SUPERSCRIPT.ITALICS.*

*(c)*

A B C D E F G H I J K L M N O P Q R S T U V W X Y Z
a b c d e f g h i j k l m n o p q r s t u v w x y z
1234567890 ¼ ½            [ ( !@#$%¢&*+=?/_-"':;,.) ]

*(d)*

**Figure 7-27** Which print quality is right for you? Impact character printers now offer quite a range. (a) Printing produced by a basic 5 × 7 dot-matrix printer priced under $300. (b) Much better quality can be produced with a 40 × 18 dot-matrix array formed by the $800 Mannesmann Tally MT 160 printer with two passes of its print head. (c) Dot-matrix printers such as the Epson MX models can easily vary the appearance of the printed characters. (d) The highest quality comes from the fully formed characters produced by a daisy-wheel printer. (From ''The Top 40 Low-Cost Printers,'' by David B. Powell, appearing in the July 1983 issue of *Popular Computing* magazine. Copyright © 1983 Byte Publications, Inc. Used with the permission of Byte Publications, Inc.)

The speed of any character printer is incredibly slow compared with the processing speed of the computer to which it's connected. Even though the slowest personal computer is loafing along while it's sending text to a character printer, it can't normally be used for any other productive work until the printing operation is completed. But two approaches used by larger systems for years are now available to allow users to continue to operate their personal computers while printing is in progress. One option is a **spooler program** that allows the CPU to alternate be-

**Figure 7-28** The inkjet approach. Inkjet printer speeds are around 90 cps. Inkjet printers are also available for personal computer systems at prices beginning at less than $800.

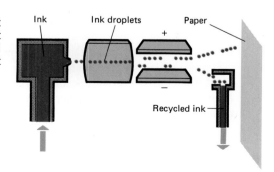

 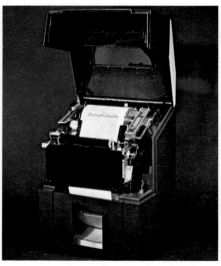 

Figure 7-29 A scalloped steel print band (*left*) is used in a high-speed impact band printer (*middle*). The print drum (*right*) used in a high-speed drum printer. (Photos supplied by Dataproducts Corporation, Woodland Hills, Calif.)

tween processing a user's ongoing activity and controlling the printing process. Of course, disk space or a dedicated block of primary storage must be available to store the text to be printed by the spooler. If the ongoing activity uses most of the system storage, there may be none left for the spooler to use. To overcome this possibility, a second option is **printer buffer** hardware. This buffer is an additional storage device that can accept text to be printed as fast as the computer can send it. As far as the computer is concerned, the printing process is completed in a few seconds. The buffer then slowly releases the text data to match the printer's speed while the computer is free to do other things.

**High-Speed Impact Line Printers. High-speed line printers** use impact methods to produce *line-at-a-time* printed output. They typically use rapidly moving *chains* or *bands* of print characters or some form of a print *drum* to print lines of information on paper (see Figure 7-29). From 300 to over 2,000 lines can be printed each minute depending on the printer used. Figure 7-30*a* illustrates the concept of a **print chain.** The links in the chain are engraved character-printing slugs. The chain moves at a rapid speed past the printing positions. Hammers behind the paper are timed to force the paper against the proper print slugs. A **band printer** (Figure 7-30*b*) is similar in operation to a chain printer. But instead of using a print chain, a band printer has a rotating scalloped steel print band. Hammers force the paper against the proper print characters. Speeds of up to 2,000 lines per minute are also possible with band printers.

In the **drum printer,** raised characters extend the length of the drum (Figure 7-30*c*). There are as many bands of type as there are printing positions. Each band contains all the possible characters. The drum rotates rapidly, and one revolution is

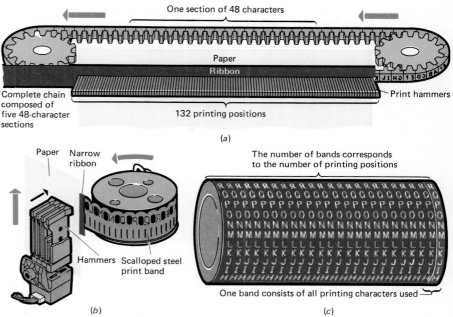

Figure 7-30 Some of the mechanisms used with impact line printers. (a) The print chain approach. Print hammers are located at each print position. Speeds of over 2,000 lines per minute are reached with chain printers. (b) The band printer approach. Similar in operation to a chain printer, a band or belt printer uses a rotating scalloped steel print band rather than a print chain. The print bands can be removed and replaced with bands using different type fonts. Speeds of up to 2,000 lines per minute are possible. (c) The print drum approach. Print hammers are located opposite each print band. Speeds of over 2,000 lines per minute are possible with drum printers.

Figure 7-31 A high-speed laser page printer. (Photo courtesy of Hewlett-Packard Company)

required to print each line. A fast-acting hammer opposite each band strikes the paper against the proper character as its passes. Thus, in one rotation, hammers of several positions may ''fire'' when the A row appears, several others may strike to imprint D's, etc. At the end of the rotation, the line has been printed.

**High-Speed Nonimpact Page Printers. A high-speed page printer,** as shown in Figure 7-31, can produce documents at speeds of over 20,000 lines per minute. (That 's fast enough to print this entire book in about one minute!) Electronics, xerography, lasers, and other technologies have made these high-volume systems possible. Each page is an original since there are no carbon copies. Although they come with a five- or six-figure price tag and thus cost more than many entire computer systems, high-speed printers can be economical when hundreds of thousands of pages are printed each month. The costs of special report forms can also be reduced since these devices can print both the form layout and the form contents at the same time.

**Filmed Output**

We've seen that organizations prepare reports for internal use. These reports and any other documents that may need to be filed away for future reference can be

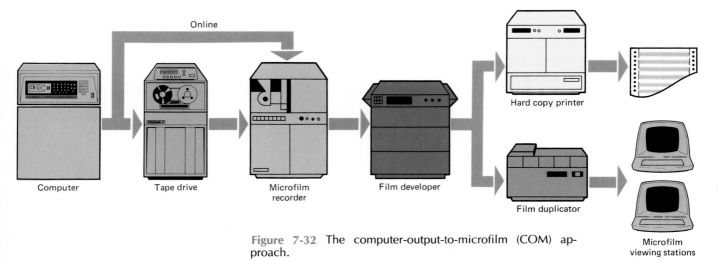

Computer     Tape drive     Microfilm recorder     Film developer     Hard copy printer     Film duplicator     Microfilm viewing stations

**Figure 7-32** The computer-output-to-microfilm (COM) approach.

**Figure 7-33** A computer-assisted retrieval system. (Courtesy 3M)

printed on paper or they can be prepared on film. **Computer-output-to-microfilm (COM)** technology is used to record computer output information as microscopic filmed images. The information that can be printed on a page of paper can be reduced in size 48 or more times and recorded on a sheet or roll of microfilm. A 4-by-6-inch sheet of film is called a **microfiche.** (Fiche is a French word meaning ''card,'' and is pronounced ''fish'' as in ''fiche or cut byte.'') A typical microfiche reproduces up to 270 page-sized images, but some ultrafiche systems can store 1,000 standard pages in the same space. Rolls of 16- and 35-millimeter film packaged in cartridges are also used.

The COM approach is shown in Figure 7-32. Output information may be read onto magnetic tape and then, in an offline operation, entered on film by a **microfilm recorder.** Or, the recorder may receive the information directly from the CPU. Most recorders project the characters of output information onto the screen of a CRT. A high-speed camera then takes a picture of the displayed information at speeds of up to 32,000 lines per minute. In some systems, the recorder processes the film from the camera; in other systems, a separate automated film developer is used. Film duplicators can make as many copies of the developed film as needed.

The information on the sheets or rolls of film is read by users from the screens of small desktop **microfilm viewing stations.** In some COM systems, users must locate and then manually search through the film cartridge or card to find the needed information. In other COM systems, however, a **computer-assisted retrieval (CAR)** approach is used (see Figure 7-33). Each microfilmed document is assigned an ''address'' that gives its cartridge or fiche drawer location. An index of document locations is stored in the memory of a small computer connected to the viewer stations. To retrieve a document, a user calls up this index, quickly locates the correct film magazine, and waits a few seconds for the viewing station to pick out the correct document from the thousands of pages that may be recorded on the film. If a paper copy of the document is needed, a reader-printer is used to provide full-size prints. This may be the first time the output information has been placed on paper.

Banking and insurance companies, government agencies, public utilities, and many other types of organizations are regular users of COM. The *advantages of COM are:*

■ *Relatively fast output.* A COM system can film information 10 to 20 times faster than a high-speed impact printer can print it. Thus, a single COM recorder can do the work of a dozen line printers.

■ *Relatively low film costs.* The cost of the paper needed to print a 1,000-page, three-copy report is about 30 times greater than the cost of the film needed to do the same job. Also, since a 1-ounce microfiche can hold the equivalent of 10 pounds of computer paper, the mailing and storage costs of filmed documents are much less than paper documents.

However, some possible *COM disadvantages are:*

■ *Relatively high system costs.* A COM recorder is an expensive piece of equipment. To justify the cost, a high-volume workload is usually needed.

■ *The limitations of film.* People who like to write notes on the margins of printed reports may feel uncomfortable when using a COM system. Also, the loss or misplacement of a few microfiche can create a significant gap in an organization's records.

# DISPLAYED OUTPUT, COMPUTER GRAPHICS, AND VOICE RESPONSE

The output from direct-access processing usually comes from character printers or from terminals with visual display screens. Computer-prepared voice responses are also used to reply to inquiries entered from online terminals.

## Displayed Output and Computer Graphics

**Alphanumeric Output.** Many of the visual terminals in use today are **alphanumeric display devices** that are used only to enter data and receive output in the form of letters, numbers, and special characters. The number of characters that can be shown at any one time varies among terminals. A frequently used display format consists of 24 lines with up to 80 characters on a line. A maximum of 1,920 characters can thus be displayed. Personal computer screens often use a reduced format. For example, a 16-line-by-64-characters/line display is used in some popular systems. Some microcomputer systems will display only uppercase letters. A number of uses for alphanumeric display devices were discussed in Chapter 6. By providing a window into a computer's data base, a terminal screen or personal computer monitor can quickly display information in response to operator inquiries.

**Graphic Output.** A study made by a computer manufacturer indicates that people communicate with words at a rate of 1,200 per minute. When pictures are

Rock-'n'-Roll Drummer Mickey Hart of the Grateful Dead takes one along on road trips, tapping out messages between performances. Space Shuttle Trainee Loren Acton has his along when he leaves Sunnyvale, Calif., for the Kennedy Space Center, using it to draft memos and read mail. New York Photographer Rick Smolan carries one on photo assignments, putting him in contact with cameramen all around the world. Physician Andrew Bern relies on his to get patient information in medical emergencies. Says Bern: "I don't go anywhere without it. Some day it will save lives."

What do doctor, drummer, photographer and astronaut have in common? None of them would leave home without his portable computer. Propped on knees and laps and fold-down trays, these marvels of miniaturization are turning up in the most familiar places: planes, buses, restaurants, at the track and on the campaign trail. Portable computers have shrunk in three years from the size of sewing machines to no bigger than a TV dinner, and in some circles they have become as ubiquitous as wristwatch calculators, headphone stereos and beepers. According to Dataquest, a California research firm, Americans this year will pay $400 to $3,000 each for some 470,000 lap-size computers, up from 10,000 two years ago. Within four years, says Dataquest, sales of portables will be growing faster than those of their desktop big brothers.

Until now, truly portable computers have been too limited or too expensive to attract a mass market. Early hand-held machines were glorified calculators with one-line screens. The first full-screen model, Grid Systems' Compass computer, cost $8,150 when it was introduced in 1982. But falling prices for both flat-panel display screens and computer chips that require little energy have made lap-size computers affordable. Last year Seattle-based Microsoft and Japan's Kyocera came up with the first winner: an eight-line screen with a full-size keyboard that could be sold with built-in software for less than $800. Marketed in slightly different models by

Limited storage capacity and display screen features have not held back sales of portable computers. They travel easily, and that's what counts.

Radio Shack, NEC and Olivetti, the machine was an instant hit. Hewlett-Packard and Epson have already introduced "laptops" that boast even more advanced features, and Data General is set to launch a machine that shows 25 lines of text. . . .

Lightweight machines that can be used for writing and telephone communications have caught on with at least one group of influential users: the press. According to some estimates, as many as half of Radio Shack's bestselling TRS-80 Model 100 portables have been sold to journalists. This year, laptops are being issued to reporters at nearly every U.S. news organization, including United Press International, Associated Press, the New York *Times,* the Washington *Post, Time* and *Newsweek.*

The popularity of portables among working reporters is easy to explain. Most models are sufficiently rugged to pack in briefcases and shoulder bags. Battery powered, they can be used anywhere, from bleachers to battlefields. And many come equipped with built-in phone jacks to send copy directly to newsroom computers. Says U.P.I. Reporter David Armon: "I used to have to write stories in longhand and dictate them over the phone. Now I just bang them out, press a button and off they go." . . .

Even reporters, though, complain that the machines have their drawbacks. Some models hold only ten pages of text

at a time, and most lack printers and disc drives for storing longer stories. All have dim screens that require good lighting conditions, and their clicking keys are far more distracting than the scratching of pen on paper. Seattle Writer Hal Glatzer was nearly thrown out of a seminar on portable computers when he refused to muffle the noise of his note taking.

But most people show more interest than irritation, especially in their first encounters with microchip technology. "There is a lot of prestige attached to the machines," says Glatzer. "When you reach into your briefcase and pull out a little computer, people know you are really plugged into high technology."

When reporters covering Jesse Jackson's trip to Cuba last June brought their portables to Havana, Cubans clustered around the keyboards with undisguised fascination. Americans are no less intrigued, reports Travel Writer Steve Roberts. He has pedaled 6,800 miles around the U.S. on a custom-built reclining bicycle that he calls his Winnebiko. Roberts first wrote his stories on a Radio Shack portable but recently switched to a Hewlett-Packard model. He also uses the machine to send his reports to magazines and newspapers. At every stop, the curious gather to gawk. Says he: "I have become an agent of future shock."

—Philip Elmer-DeWitt, "Taking It on the Road," *Time,* Sept. 17, 1984, p. 59. Copyright 1984 Time, Inc. Reprinted by permission from *Time.* Photo courtesy Hewlett-Packard Company.

used, however, the rate of comprehension leaps. Maybe the old saying that one picture is worth a thousand words understated the true ratio! Graphs, charts, maps, and other visual presentations prepared from pages of statistical data are better able to capture and hold the interest of a user. Data showing the relationships, changes, and trends that are often buried in piles of alphanumeric reports can be highlighted with a few graphic presentations. Although a loss of precision may result when tabular information is presented in graphic form, this is usually not a problem.

You'll recall from Chapter 6 how **graphic display terminals** are used by designers, engineers, and architects to display preliminary sketches. Computers can be programmed to analyze the sketches and report on certain characteristics. Designers can then interact with their computers to produce finished drawings. A booming market for graphic terminals and personal computers capable of producing high-resolution images in multiple colors has also developed in business offices. Using alphanumeric data as input, managers can use graphic software packages to create colorful and informative pictures on the screens of their terminals and personal computers. After design drawings or business graphic presentations have been displayed on a screen to a user's satisfaction, permanent copies can be prepared using the following graphics devices:

Figure 7-34 (above) Many inexpensive dot-matrix printers used with personal computers can produce effective graphics. This example was prepared using a horizontal resolution of 160 dots per inch and a vertical resolution of 144 dots per inch. The price of the printer used is less than $600. Although this printer can't produce color images, others are available for less than $600 that *do* have the ability to use four-color ribbons. (From ''The Top 40 Low-Cost Printers,'' by David B. Powell, appearing in the July 1983 issue of *Popular Computing* magazine. Copyright © 1983 Byte Publications, Inc. Used with the permission of Byte Publications, Inc.) (below) This ink-jet printer can print 120 dots per inch and is capable of producing seven colors. (Courtesy Diablo Systems, Incorporated)

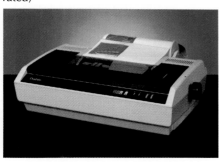

- ■ *Printers.* A **dot-matrix printer/plotter** can produce effective pictures through its ability to generate over 200 lines of tiny dots on an inch of paper. Even many of the inexpensive dot-matrix printers used with personal computers have **dot-addressable graphics capability.** That is, with the help of appropriate software, users can control each wire in the print head and thus determine where each dot is printed (see Figure 7-34*a*). Furthermore, when the print head can handle multicolor ribbons it's possible to produce color images. Nonimpact **electrostatic printer/plotters** using processes similar to photocopying are also available, and some **inkjet printer/plotters** have impressive multicolor graphics capabilities (Figure 7-34*b*).

- ■ *Plotters.* In addition to the dot-matrix, electrostatic, and inkjet printing devices that have graphics capabilities, other types of special plotters are also available that use pen or inkjet approaches. **Pen plotters** use either drum or flat-bed paper holders (see Figure 7-35). When a **drum device** is used, the paper is placed over a drum that rotates back and forth to produce an up-and-down motion. A carriage holding one or more pens is mounted horizontally across the drum, and the pen(s) can move along this carriage to produce motion across the paper. Under computer control, the carriage and drum movements act together to produce a picture. When several pens are mounted on a carriage, each pen can be filled with a different ink color. Since each pen is program-selectable, the plotter has the ability to produce color pictures. When a **flat-bed** (table) **plotter** is used, the paper doesn't move and the pen-holding mechanism must provide all the motion. **Inkjet plotters** are able to produce large drawings containing many colors. The paper is again placed on a drum, and jets with different-colored ink are mounted on a carriage. The computer program controls the color and amount of ink placed on the paper.

**Figure 7-35** *(left)* This electrostatic color plotter can produce complex, full-color plots in a matter of minutes. *(right)* Closeup view of a high-speed plotter in action. (Photos courtesy Xerox Corporation; The Bohle Company)

■ *Film Recorders.* The screen of the CRT can be photographed with black and white or color film to produce prints and 35-millimeter slides. Videotape copies can also be made.

**Voice Response**

Just as a voice recognition system will allow you to talk to a computer, so, too, will a **voice response system** permit a computer to talk back to you. In fact, a computer has probably "talked" to you many times. For example, when you try to call a telephone number that has been changed, a signal is sent to a telephone company computer. You then hear: "The number you have dialed has been changed to 9-2-6-2-5-6-3." The first part of this response is a conventional recording, but the new number is given in the "voice" of the computer's audio-response unit. This voice may be choppy and unnatural, but it's easily understood.

Many other organizations use audio-response systems to respond to human inquiries that are transmitted over telephone lines to a central computer. All the sounds needed to process the possible inquiries are prerecorded on a storage medium. Each sound is given a code. When inquiries are received, the processor follows a set of rules to create a reply message in a coded form. This coded message is then transmitted to an audio-response device, which assembles the sounds in the proper sequence and transmits the audio message back to the station requesting the information.

Audio-response techniques, combined with briefcase-sized (or smaller) terminals, turn every telephone into a potential computer I/O device. A traveling engineer, for example, can check on a project's status by keying an inquiry directly into the home-office computer. A computer-compiled audio response then gives the engineer the necessary output information. Similarly, construction personnel can enter and receive labor, material, and equipment information.

Audio-response systems can be inexpensive. Many are available now for use with personal computers. Such a system is also used in Texas Instruments' Speak &

Spell product to teach children to spell and pronounce over 200 basic words. A single integrated circuit chip costing a few dollars synthesizes the selected sounds that are used for audio response. Thus, the spoken word in machine-usable form is now very cheap—cheap enough, in fact, to be installed in your future microwave oven or washing machine if you want talking appliances.

## Feedback and Review 7-2

You've now learned that people in many organizations need computer output to carry out planning, organizing, and controlling functions. The output from sequential processing is usually written on magnetic media, on microfilm, or on printer paper. Printed detail, summary, and/or exception reports are prepared for decision makers. Teleprinter terminals receive and print the output from direct-access processing in many applications. However, visual display terminals are the most popular devices used today to directly receive alphanumeric and/or graphic output. The use of computer graphics is growing rapidly. Graphic output can be reproduced by plotters and film recorders. Systems are also available to permit computers to send back voice responses to direct human inquiries.

To test and reinforce your understanding of this output material, rearrange the scrambled words to spell out the correct word for the space indicated in the following sentences:

**1.** Good output information in the hands of those who can effectively use it will support good decisions; good decisions will lead to the effective performance of tasks; and effective task performance will lead to success in reaching an organization's _____.

Ⓐ Ⓛ Ⓖ Ⓞ Ⓢ

**2.** _____ output is information that's intended for use solely within an organization, while external output is information that will be used outside the organization.

Ⓣ Ⓔ Ⓘ Ⓝ Ⓡ Ⓛ Ⓝ Ⓐ

**3.** A _____ report condenses detailed data to help decision makers spot patterns and trends.

Ⓜ Ⓐ Ⓡ Ⓨ Ⓢ Ⓤ Ⓜ

**4.** _____ reports are triggered to supply information only when operating data fall outside specified limits.

Ⓒ Ⓔ Ⓔ Ⓧ Ⓞ Ⓝ Ⓟ Ⓣ Ⓘ

**5.** _____ output is used in both sequential and direct-access processing applications.

Ⓣ Ⓓ Ⓟ Ⓡ Ⓔ Ⓘ Ⓝ

**6.** Magnetic tape and portable magnetic disks are _____-purpose media.

Ⓘ Ⓟ Ⓣ Ⓡ Ⓛ Ⓔ

**7.** _____ are the primary output devices used to prepare permanent documents for human use.

Ⓘ Ⓔ Ⓟ Ⓡ Ⓡ Ⓢ Ⓝ Ⓣ

**8.** Unlike inkjet printers, daisy-wheel and dot-matrix printers are character-at-a-time devices that use _____ methods to produce printed characters.

Ⓟ Ⓐ Ⓘ Ⓒ Ⓣ Ⓜ

**9.** High-speed impact line printers typically use rapidly moving chains or bands of print characters or some form of a print _____ to print lines of information on paper.

Ⓓ Ⓤ Ⓜ Ⓡ

**10.** High-speed nonimpact _____ printers are fast enough to print this entire book in about one minute.

Ⓐ Ⓟ Ⓔ Ⓖ

**11.** After COM technology is used to record computer output as microscopic filmed images, these images can be displayed on the screens of desktop _____ stations.

Ⓘ Ⓥ Ⓝ Ⓖ Ⓔ Ⓦ Ⓘ

**12.** Although a single microfilm recorder can do the work of a dozen line printers, and the cost of the film needed to record large documents is much less than the paper that would be required, a _____-volume workload is usually needed to justify the cost of a recorder.

Ⓗ Ⓗ Ⓘ Ⓖ

**13.** _____ plotters are computer graphics devices that use either drum or flat-bed paper holders.

Ⓔ Ⓟ Ⓝ

**14.** Some organizations use _____-response systems that directly respond to human inquiries that are transmitted to a central computer over telephone lines.

Ⓘ Ⓒ Ⓥ Ⓞ Ⓔ

**15.** The use of spooler programs and/or _____ hardware allows personal computer operators to do other processing work at the same time a printing operation is in progress.

Ⓔ Ⓤ Ⓕ Ⓡ Ⓑ Ⓕ

# LOOKING BACK

**1.** Most computer systems have a storage hierarchy. The different components in the hierarchy are usually ranked according to their access time, storage capacity, and cost per bit of capacity. Primary storage generally has the fastest access time, the smallest storage capacity, and the highest cost per bit stored. Supplementing primary storage is the secondary storage of a computer system. This classification includes the online DASDs and the offline storage media that hold data in a computer-readable form.

**2.** Computer system designers must study each application to be processed and then select a storage approach to use. This approach is determined by the way the data are to be organized and processed. Sequentially organized files that require only periodic updating can be stored on an offline secondary storage medium. But if quick access to any file record may be needed at any time, a DASD must be used. In selecting an appropriate DASD, designers must usually make compromises between performance and cost.

**3.** Punched paper media, magnetic tape, and magnetic disks are used to store data that are sequentially organized and processed. But even though magnetic disks can be used for sequential processing, their popularity is largely due to their direct-access capabilities. Disks come in different sizes, are either portable or permanently mounted in their disk drives, and are made of rigid metal or flexible plastic. Disk storage systems come in a wide price range, and provide an equally wide range of access times, storage capacities, and transfer rates.

**4.** Data are stored on the surface of all magnetic disks in a number of invisible concentric circles called tracks. Tiny magnetic spots representing data are recorded on, and read from, these tracks by one or more read/write heads. The data density is determined by the bits per inch of track and the number of tracks that can be placed on each disk surface. Winchester disk systems have very high densities. Program instructions specify the disk address of a needed record. Cylinder and sector methods are used to organize and physically store disk data. A read/write head is then moved directly to the specified address to access the data. The access time is determined by the seek time needed to position the head over the proper track, and the search time needed to spin the needed data under the head.

**5.** The advantages of magnetic disk storage are that records can be processed sequentially or directly. Direct-access time is fast, and single transactions can be used to update the online disk records of several related files. However, sequential processing with disks may be slower than when magnetic tapes are used. A disk pack costs much more than a tape reel of equal storage capacity, and special backup procedures are required to protect disk records from malfunctions. Also, it's harder to secure disk files from unauthorized persons.

**6.** Other devices used for direct-access secondary storage include RAM "disks," magnetic bubble chips, optical disks, and magnetic tape strips. Each of these storage approaches has been briefly outlined in the chapter.

**7.** Computer output is vital for decision makers who must perform planning, organizing, and controlling functions in order to achieve goals. Output can be grouped into internal and external categories. Internal output is information that's intended for use within an organization, while external output is meant for outside use. In sequential processing applications, internal output can be written on magnetic media, printed on paper, or recorded on microfilm. Different types of reports (detail, summary, exception) are printed or filmed to meet the needs of decision makers. Of course, sequential processing also generates invoices, checks, and other printed documents that are sent outside an organization.

**8.** Online terminals are used to request and receive output information during direct-access processing applications. Printed output is produced by teleprinter, point-of-sale, and financial transaction terminals. Depending on the application, this printed output is used by people both within and outside an organization. Internal and external output is also shown on the screens of visual display terminals during direct-access processing.

**9.** Printers are the primary output devices used to prepare permanent documents for human use. Impact or nonimpact character-at-a-time printers are used for low-volume printing jobs. When impact mechanisms are used, a typeface strikes against paper and inked ribbon to create a character. Daisy-wheel and dot-matrix devices are examples of serial impact printers. Nonimpact printers use thermal, electrostatic, chemical, and inkjet technologies to produce their output. High-speed impact line printers typically use rapidly moving chains or bands of print characters, or some form of print drum, to print at speeds that can exceed 2,000 lines per minute. And even faster nonimpact page printers use xerography, lasers, and other technologies to produce output at speeds that can exceed 20,000 lines/minute.

**10.** Internal documents that are examined briefly and then filed away for possible future reference are sometimes recorded on film by a computer-output-to-microfilm process. Hundreds of page-size images can be recorded on a single 4-by-6-inch microfiche. Once information has been placed on film, it can be recovered by people using desktop viewing stations and manual search or computer-assisted retrieval techniques. Full-sized documents can be printed from the filmed images. A COM system is faster than a printing system, and film costs much less than an equivalent amount of paper. But a high-volume workload is a must to realize the significant savings that are possible.

11. Visual display stations are used to receive alphanumeric and graphic output information. Many stations are used only for alphanumeric purposes, but a booming market has now developed for terminals and personal computers with graphic

capabilities. In addition to displaying design drawings, graphic terminals and personal computers can also show the relationships, changes, and trends that often lie buried in piles of alphanumeric reports through the use of graphs, charts, maps, and other visual presentations. And when graphic presentations are displayed on a screen to a user's satisfaction, permanent copies can be prepared using printers, plotters, and film recorders.

12. Voice response systems permit computers to talk to people. In many cases, such a system is used to respond directly to human inquiries that are transmitted to a central computer over telephone lines.

## KEY TERMS AND CONCEPTS

storage hierarchy 172
access time 172
secondary (auxiliary) storage 172
sequential-access storage media 172
disk cartridge 175
disk pack 175
disk drive 176
Winchester technology 176
tracks 177
access arm 177
bits per inch of track 178
tracks per inch of surface 178
head crash 179
disk address 179
cylinder 180
sector 180
seek time 181
search (latency) time 181
fixed-head-per-track device 181
RAM disk 182
magnetic bubble storage 182
optical disk 182

laser recording systems 182
tape strip devices 183
internal output 186
triple-purpose media 186
detailed reports 187
summary report 187
computer graphic output 187
exception reports 187
external output 188
visual display 188
character (serial) printers 189
impact methods 190
daisy-wheel printer 190
dot-matrix printer 190
nonimpact printer 190
inkjet printer 190
spooler program 191
printer buffer 192
high-speed line printers 192
print chain 192
band printer 192
drum printer 192

high-speed page printers 193
computer-output-to-microfilm (COM) 194
microfiche 194
microfilm recorder 194
microfilm viewing stations 194
computer-assisted retrieval (CAR) 194
alphanumeric display devices 195
graphic display terminals 197
dot-matrix printer/plotter 197
dot-addressable graphics capability 197
electrostatic printer/plotters 197
inkjet printer/plotters 197
pen plotters 197
drum device 197
flat-bed plotter 197
inkjet plotters 197
voice response system 198

## TOPICS FOR REVIEW AND DISCUSSION

1. "In a storage hierarchy, it's generally necessary to make compromises between retrieval speed on the one hand, and storage capacity and cost per character stored on the other." Explain this statement and give examples to support it.

2. What components make up the storage hierarchy of your school's computer system?

3. What storage elements are included in the secondary storage classification?

4. "The storage approach selected for a particular application is determined by the way the data are organized and processed." Discuss this statement.

5. (a) Identify the offline secondary media used to store sequentially organized files. (b) Discuss some of the characteristics of these media.

6. Identify and discuss the types of magnetic disks used for direct-access secondary storage.

**7.** *(a)* How are data stored on magnetic disks? *(b)* What factors determine the storage capacity of disks?

**8.** *(a)* What causes head crashes? *(b)* How can Winchester technology reduce the head crash problem?

**9.** *(a)* How can data stored on magnetic disks be accessed? *(b)* What determines the time required to access the needed data?

**10.** What are the advantages and limitations of magnetic disks?

**11.** *(a)* What's a RAM "disk"? *(b)* How is a RAM disk used?

**12.** What are the characteristics of magnetic bubble storage?

**13.** What are the potential storage benefits of optical disk technology?

**14.** *(a)* How can computer output benefit the users of personal computers? *(b)* Why is computer output likely to be needed by decision makers in most organizations?

**15.** *(a)* What's the difference between internal and external output? *(b)* What should a system designer consider when planning the type of output to be produced by a computer?

**16.** Identify and discuss the three types of output reports mentioned in this chapter.

**17.** *(a)* Identify four output devices used in sequential-processing applications. *(b)* Identify four output devices used in direct-access processing.

**18.** Why is computer output entered on magnetic media?

**19.** *(a)* What's an impact printer? *(b)* Identify and discuss two types of impact character printers. *(c)* Identify and discuss three types of impact line printers.

**20.** *(a)* What's a nonimpact printer? *(b)* Identify and discuss the inkjet approach to nonimpact printing.

**21.** *(a)* What types of internal documents are typically placed on microfilm? *(b)* How is computer output placed on microfilm? *(c)* How are microfilm images retrieved?

**22.** Identify and discuss the advantages and limitations of COM.

**23.** *(a)* What's the display format of a CRT screen available to you? *(b)* What's the maximum number of characters that can be displayed?

**24.** Why has the use of computer graphics become so popular in recent years?

**25.** How can pictures displayed on a screen be permanently preserved?

**26.** How are voice response systems used?

## PROJECTS TO LOOK INTO

**1.** Visit a computer store and/or your library's periodical section and identify three suppliers of products in each of the following categories: Winchester disk drives; 5¼" floppy disk drives; 5¼" floppy disks; disk drives for disks measuring 4" or less in size; daisy-wheel printers; dot-matrix printers; inkjet printers; plotters. Prepare a summary of your findings for the class.

**2.** Collect your junk mail for a few weeks and then examine each document to see what type of printer was used in its preparation. Present your findings to the class.

**3.** Identify a business or some other organization you're familiar with (e.g., a bank, newspaper, clinic, library, admissions office, etc.) and determine how some of the organization's records are stored and maintained. Prepare a report of your investigation.

## ANSWERS TO FEEDBACK AND REVIEW SECTIONS

7-1

| | | | | | | | | | | | | | | |
|---|---|---|---|---|---|---|---|---|---|---|---|---|---|---|
| ¹H | I | E | R | A | R | ²C | H | Y | | ³A | ⁴C | C | E | ⁵S | ⁶R | | ⁷W |
| | | | | | | R | | | | | Y | | | T | A | | I |
| ⁸L | A | S | E | R | | A | | ⁹C | | | L | | | O | M | | N |
| | | | | | | S | | ¹⁰O | N | L | I | N | E | | R | | C |
| | | ¹¹T | | | | H | | S | | | N | | ¹²S | E | A | R | C | H |
| ¹³F | L | O | P | P | Y | | | ¹⁴T | R | A | D | E | | E | | | E |
| L | | R | | | | | | | | E | | N | | | ¹⁵S | | S |
| Y | | N | | ¹⁶S | E | C | T | O | R | S | | ¹⁷D | I | R | E | C | T |
| | | | | | | | | | | E | | | | | E | | E |
| ¹⁸S | E | C | O | N | D | A | R | Y | | ¹⁹B | U | B | B | L | E | | K | R |

7-2

| | |
|---|---|
| 1. goals | 9. drum |
| 2. internal | 10. page |
| 3. summary | 11. viewing |
| 4. exception | 12. high |
| 5. printed | 13. pen |
| 6. triple | 14. voice |
| 7. printers | 15. buffer |
| 8. impact | |

# Beware of "Visiknowledge"

Companies must become aware of the increasing potential for "Visisnowing" inherent in the skyrocketing use of business microcomputers, warned Stephen Caswell, president of Network Innovations, Inc. of Ottawa and a project director for International Resource Development, Inc. (IRD).

"Visisnowing" is simply a "snow job" as applied to microcomputing, Caswell explained in a recent interview. A recent IRD report asserts that "because [financial spreadsheet and scheduling] programs produce highly polished output, at least in terms of appearance, they can easily give the impression that the level of assurance surrounding the projection is far greater than in reality." . . .

[The report] notes that microcomputers are being shipped at an annualized rate of four million machines worldwide, [and] projects that the 1982 estimate of $3.7 billion spent on microcomputers and peripherals will swell to $18 billion by 1986 and $45 billion by 1991.

With such a volatile and burgeoning market, "we've seen a great amount of information about how these machines will be everywhere," Caswell observed. "But there's been very little discussion about what they'll actually do in organizations in terms of impact."

One of the major impacts will call for adjustments in the way we regard computer output, according to Caswell. "Today, typically the cost of producing a lot of charts and graphs and the time required to do market projections is such that very few people really go out and actually do it on a regular basis," he noted.

Currently, before numbers are transformed into graphics form, "they've been consulted on by a team of people and the group involved in producing the report has all pretty much signed off on it," he continued.

Therefore, the graphs and slides produced constitute an "official view of the company, although they may not be accurate in relationship to the real world," he noted.

With a microcomputer, on the other hand, Caswell pointed out, "any one individual who happens to be working with a personal computer will be able to go out and produce the same official-looking [product] and these official-looking graphs and charts will be entered into the [planning] process before everyone agrees upon them."

While the past 20 or 30 years have conditioned business people to regard computer-generated charts and graphs as output of the planning process," with the personal computer's charts, what you're really looking at is the input," he added.

One of the major advantages of computerized sched-

uling and accounting is, of course, that relationships and projections that could not normally be handled in one's head or with pencil and paper can now be undertaken, IRD noted. However, these programs are only as good as the relationships that they correlate and the information supplied by the managers.

"I don't want to say that people's view of numbers will become more jaundiced, but they'll have to become more aware of the source of numbers," Caswell warned. "The computer allows enormous flights of 'what-if' fantasy, and it becomes increasingly easy to crank out official-looking but entirely hypothetical documents."

—Marguerite Zientara, "IRD Exec: Micro Boom to Spark False Assurance, Computerworld, Feb. 14, 1983, p. 35. Copyright 1983 by CW Communications, Framingham, Mass. Reprinted from Computerworld. Photo courtesy ITT Information Systems.

## Computer Graphics: From Numbers To Pictures To People

In many business areas and professions, color computer graphics are moving into the mainstream of data processing. Business people are finding that computer graphics improves productivity because it speeds the communication of important information. The strategic use of pies, bars, horizontal bars, lines, points and areas can transform stacks of data sheets into clearly visible representations that facilitate quicker comparison of relevant data. . . .

With a graphics display system, changes in material can be input and viewed instantly. Group response time is reduced to seconds. For example, a manager or team leader using a decision support software package to make "what if" projections in a group presentation can input suggestions as they arise. The results of the changes and their impact are viewed immediately.

Graphics display systems have a multitude of other applications, including training and education, design engineering, group performance evaluation, diagnostic imaging, sales analysis, marketing and teleconferencing. Some more examples include:

Business meetings in which financial data is developed and discussed and used for group decision making.

Education for classroom presentations in science, engineering, business or computer training.

Technical presentations in which a group of engineers meet to review designs and group input is needed.

Sales presentations, where new products and services need to be evaluated and compared.

Teleconferenced meetings.

Internal evaluation meetings, where a division or department's performance needs to be reviewed.

Diagnostic imaging in which CRT terminals play a major role in radiology, nuclear medicine and ultrasound diagnosis.

—From Bart Van Cromvoirt, "Graphics Display Systems: A Major Step Forward," Computerworld, July 25, 1983, pp. 47–49. Copyright 1983 by CW Communications, Framingham, Mass. Reprinted from Computerworld. Photo courtesy Computer Sciences Corp.

A sampling of the sophisticated charts and graphs being produced via computer today. Photos courtesy Fujitsu Microelectronics, Inc., Professional Microsystems Division *(right)*; and Image Resource Corporation *(below)*.

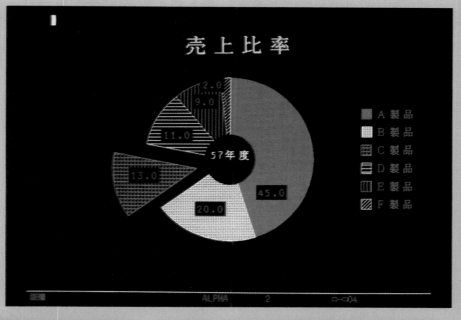

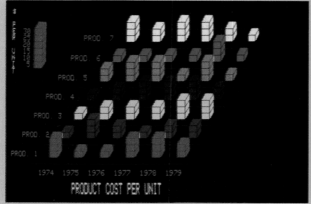

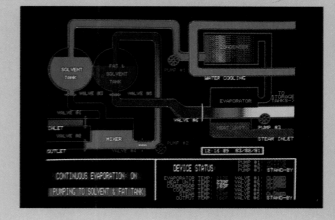

# Personal Computers
## *the micro miracles*

### Outmoded

Nothing prevents people from getting involved with computers more than the fear that whatever they learn or buy will soon be obsolete. Such concerns are heightened by reports emphasizing the rapidity with which machines and programs are changing. Advertisers promote the newness and the relentless pace of advance.

In fact, fear of obsolescence is a largely groundless concern. People imagine quantum jumps in machine development that simply don't occur. While it is true that machines become ever smaller, cheaper, and easier to use, they are not *that much* smaller, cheaper, or easier to use. It's more to the point to think about computers as you think about cars or refrigerators: subsequent models will always be better, but a sensible purchase will not look like a Model T by the time you get it home.

If you have a use for a computer now, then buy a machine that fills your needs and don't worry about the future. In three or five years, you may want a newer computer, but in the meantime you will have had the benefit of your present machine. This is especially so for small-business applications, where a computer will often pay for itself in the first year.

Chapters 5 through 7 in this Hardware Module gave you a general introduction to the CPU, to I/O, and to information storage. Now Chapters 8 and 9 will give you more specific information about real computer systems, beginning with personal or microcomputers, the smallest of the four general classes of computers. The information in this chapter will enable you to:

- Explain what personal computers are and why they were developed
- Describe general characteristics of personal computers
- Identify representative "home" and "professional" personal computer systems
- Discuss the functions that applications packages can perform in homes and offices, and outline criteria for identifying and selecting suitable software packages

# THE CLASSIFICATION DILEMMA

In Chapters 8 and 9, we classify computers as *personal, minis, mainframes,* and *supercomputers*. The classifications used here, and anywhere else, are arbitrary because the cost and performance capability of machines in different classifications are likely to overlap. As Figure 8-1 indicates, for example, a surprisingly powerful model sold as a personal microcomputer by its maker may have more processing capability (and cost more) than a machine sold as a small mini.

## Chapter Outline

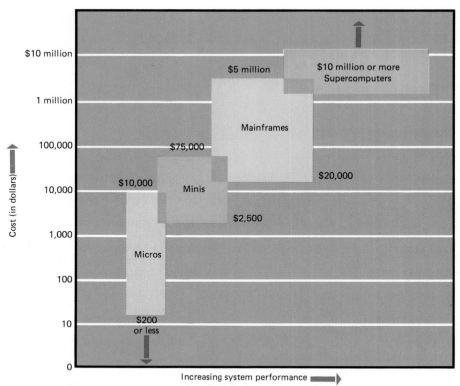

**Figure 8-1** Computer systems may be classified into personal (micro), mini, mainframe, and supercomputer ("monster") categories depending on size, cost, and system performance. Any such classification is arbitrary. Since categories overlap, the most powerful systems in one category may exceed the capabilities (and cost) of the least powerful systems in another.

In fact, if you conducted a survey now among a dozen computer experts, asking each of them to tell you the difference between personal computers and minicomputers, or between minis and mainframe family models, you would likely get a dozen very different answers. The problem is how to *classify* this broad range of available machine sizes and capabilities. Many organizations have central-site computers and "smaller" systems in outlying branches. These systems can be assembled with a wide range of peripheral I/O devices and "add-on" CPU components. Similar variations are also available for the systems individuals buy for personal use. The result is that there's a great overlap in system size, cost, and performance.

And computer technology is changing fast. Within a matter of months after a new computer model comes on the market, it's faced with two potential successors. One costs the same and has a much higher performance; the other has the same performance and costs much less. Thus, a recently introduced small system can outperform the large models of a few years ago, and a new personal computer can do the work of an earlier minicomputer at a much lower cost. This rapid technological pace plays havoc with classification schemes.

# PERSONAL COMPUTER SYSTEMS

**Personal Computer Development**

A **personal computer (pc)** is the smallest general-purpose processing system that can execute program instructions to perform a wide variety of tasks. A pc has all the functional elements found in any larger system. That is, it's organized to perform the input, storage, arithmetic-logic, control, and output functions. Although some complete microcomputer CPUs are packaged on a *single* silicon chip (Figure 8-2), most personal computers are larger and employ *several* chips. A **microprocessor chip,** for example, performs the arithmetic-logic and control functions (see Figure 8-3). Several *random access memory (RAM) chips* are available to handle the primary storage function. And additional *read-only memory (ROM) chips* may be used to permanently store preprogrammed data or instructions. Most personal computers are self-contained units which are light enough to be moved easily, and many are truly portable. They are designed to be used by one person at a time; that is, they are **single-user oriented.** Connected to the CPU of a typical pc are a limited number of peripheral devices to perform input, secondary storage, and output functions.

In studying the potential U.S. market for personal computers, analysts note that over 80 million homes have TV sets, over 50 million white-collar employees and over 25 million professionals are in the workforce, and over 4 million small businesses process data. Anticipating that every home and desktop represents a potential pc site, some analysts expect that in 10 years there will be 80 million personal computers in use in the United States. A decade ago, however, there were only a few crude systems in the hands of hobbyists. Let's briefly look at the origins and development of the pc phenomenon.

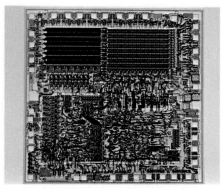

Figure 8-2 An 8-bit microcomputer, complete on one silicon chip. (Courtesy Intel Corporation)

Figure 8-3 Two sophisticated microprocessor chips. (Courtesy Western Electric and Intel Corporation)

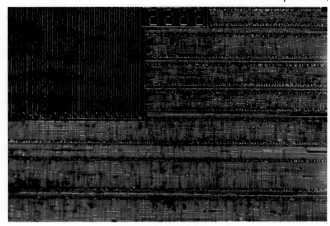 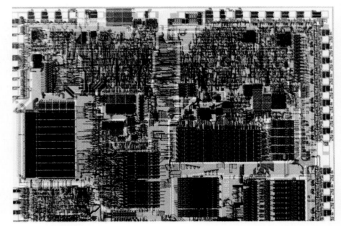

During the 1960s, Victor Poor, a Datapoint Corporation electronics engineer, had worked on the design and development of special-purpose computers. Each time a custom-designed device was needed, Poor and other engineers started the design effort with a blank sheet of paper. Designing each processor from scratch seemed a big waste of time to Poor. Instead, he reasoned, if the basic arithmetic-logic and control elements of a computer could be placed on a single silicon chip, the chip could be mass produced and then programmed in different ways to perform the special jobs for which it would be used.

In 1969, Poor and Harry Pyle, another young Datapoint engineer, developed a model of a microprocessor chip. Since Datapoint Corporation used electronic components made by others to build finished computer systems for its customers, Poor took his ''chip processor'' model to two component manufacturers—Texas Instruments and Intel Corporation—in hopes they would manufacture the chip for Datapoint. No immediate decisions came from these meetings, but the component manufacturers were free to use the microprocessor chip concept at a later time. And they did.

In the early 1970s, engineers at Intel built the first microprocessor chip for a Japanese maker of desk calculators. At the time, calculators were being built from specialized circuit chips that could perform only a single function. However, this first microprocessor chip could be programmed to perform multiple specialized calculator functions. This chip—the Intel 4004—was very limited in the number of instructions it could execute, and it could manipulate only 4-bit ''nibbles'' of data at one time.

But it wasn't long before the engineers at Intel and other companies produced more powerful microprocessors that could operate on **8 bits.** This development, in turn, led to the introduction in 1974 of personal-sized systems for the hobbyist market. The first such pc was the ALTAIR 8800, which used an 8-bit Intel microprocessor and was originally offered in kit form at a price under $400. The lead article in the January 1975 issue of *Popular Electronics* featured this machine. That article introduced many people to the beginning of the pc explosion. Later in 1975, the first retail store devoted exclusively to selling and servicing personal computers opened in Santa Monica, California.

Although the ALTAIR model was the first entry, dominant machines of the late 1970s included several versions of the Apple II from Apple Computer, Inc., the TRS-80 models from the Radio Shack Division of Tandy Corporation, and the dozens of machines that adopted the S-100 interface bus originally used in the ALTAIR computer. A system **interface bus** is a device that serves as the electrical interconnection between the CPU and the various peripherals. As more S-100 personal computers were sold, new businesses were created to build plug-in circuit boards for them. These boards allowed S-100 owners to customize their systems to fit their needs. As you might expect, most application programs prepared during the late 1970s were written for use with Apple, Radio Shack, or S-100 systems.

The leading machines of this period were used everywhere—in homes, offices, schools, and other places. But as the 1980s began, lower-cost systems intended primarily for home use were designed by companies such as Atari, Coleco, Commodore, and Sinclair. And the names of the scores of firms introducing desktop models for professionals, businesses, and other organizations ranged across the alphabet from A (Altos) to Z (Zenith). Over 150 manufacturers have entered the pc market!

The systems sold in the late 1970s and early 1980s were 8-bit machines. But a new generation of pc models was also introduced in the early 1980s. These systems are built around microprocessor chips that can operate on **16 bits** at a time. By far the most popular model is the IBM Personal Computer, but dozens of the other suppliers are also producing desktop and portable 16-bit machines. Thousands of applications programs are now available for the IBM PC and its family models. In order to be able to use this wealth of software, designers of many competitive brands have elected to use the same microprocessor and operating instructions used by IBM. The result has been the swift creation of an IBM PC-compatible industry. Hundreds of firms in this sector are churning out programs and products that work with, look like, or plug into IBM's PC and the many similar systems of other suppliers.

# GENERAL CHARACTERISTICS OF PERSONAL COMPUTERS

You've seen that personal computers may be classified as general-interest systems designed either for home use or for use in the offices of organizations and professionals. These systems can also be grouped into desktop and portable categories. (The portables even come in several classes: the pocket-sized versions, the 5- to 10-pound briefcase-sized models, and the 15- to 40-pound transportables.) Regardless of the classification scheme, most personal computers share a number of common characteristics.

## CPU Characteristics

All 8-bit personal computers are built around a few popular microprocessor chip designs. These chips—Zilog's Z80, MOS Technology's 6502, Intel's 8080, and Motorola's 6809—have built-in 8-line data paths or **data buses.** This means that these chips can only retrieve from storage, manipulate, and process a single 8-bit byte of data at a time. A 16-line **address bus** is also built into these chips to determine the primary storage locations of the instructions and data that are needed. With 16 address lines, it's possible for these chips to identify a maximum of $2^{16}$ or 65,536 separate storage locations. That's a maximum of 64K bytes in pc lingo.

All 16-bit personal computers are also built around a few popular microprocessors. The Intel 8088 is found in IBM's PC, PCjr, and many other brands. The data path between the 8088 and primary storage is only 8 bits wide and so all operations to and from storage are done 8 bits (1 byte) at a time. Once retrieved, however, data are processed 16 bits at a time internally in the 8088. The 8088 is thus referred to as an **8/16-bit chip;** it functions like a fast 8-bit microprocessor with an extended set of instructions. A stablemate of the 8088 is Intel's 8086. Unlike the 8088, the internal and external data paths of the 8086 are all 16 bits wide. The 8086 is thus a true **16/16-bit chip.** An expanded built-in address bus with 20 lines permits both the 8088 and the 8086 to identify about a million separate primary storage locations ($2^{20} = 1,048,576$ bytes or 1 megabyte).

A third popular microprocessor used in systems produced by Apple, Cromemco, Radio Shack, and many other vendors is the Motorola 68000 (Figure 8-4). A 16-bit external bus is used to move data between this chip and primary storage, but processing is done internally 32 bits at a time. The 68000 is thus a

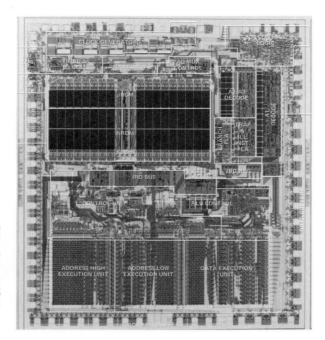

**Figure 8-4** The data path between this Motorola 68000 microprocessor chip and primary storage is 16 bits wide. Once data are retrieved, they may be processed 32 bits at a time. The 68000 chip is used in the systems of many vendors including Apple Computer's Macintosh and Lisa models, and Radio Shack's TRS-80, model 16. (Courtesy Motorola, Inc.)

Single chip 32-bit microprocessor. (Courtesy Intel Corporation)

**16/32-bit chip** and is more powerful (and more expensive) than the 8088 or 8086. The 68000's address bus has 24 lines and permits a primary storage capacity of up to 16 megabytes ($2^{24}$ = 16,777,216 bytes).

Enhanced versions of the Intel and Motorola 16-bit chips discussed above are also available. For example, Tandy Corporation's Model 2000 pc system uses an Intel 80186 chip that is a more powerful version of the 8086. Other suppliers such as Zilog (with the Z8000 chip) and National Semiconductor (with the 16000 chip) are in the 16-bit market. And engineers are hard at work on the **32/32-bit chips** that will power the next generation of personal computers. In 1981, Intel announced a 32-bit "micromainframe" processor packaged on three chips. Since then, *single-chip* 32-bit processors have been designed by firms such as Western Electric (a division of AT&T), Hewlett-Packard, NCR, National Semiconductor, Zilog, Motorola, and Intel. Digital Equipment Corporation also plans to squeeze the processor of its VAX 11/780, a powerful 32-bit minicomputer, onto a single chip. Thus, the head of microprocessor design at Bell Laboratories estimates that by 1990 the equivalent of the processor in a $20,000 VAX CPU will be available on a chip costing less than $1.

**Factors Affecting CPU Performance**

A number of factors determine the performance characteristics of all pc systems. You can get an idea of the processing capability of a particular model by answering the following questions:

■ *Is an 8-, 16-, or 32-bit microprocessor used?* An 8-bit processor can manipulate only a single 8-bit byte of data in a given period. A 16-bit chip can handle 2 bytes in the same unit of time while a 32-bit chip can deal with 4 bytes. If short program segments dealing only with *calculations* are being processed, the execution speed of a 16-bit machine may be two or more times faster than that of an 8-bit model. In processing program segments involving I/O, logic/comparison, and storage/retrieval operations, however, the 16-bit model may have less of an advantage. In general, then, a 16-bit pc will be faster than an 8-bit system, but it won't be twice as fast except under ideal situations. A 32-bit machine, of course, will have an edge over 8- and 16-bit models.

■ *What's the clock speed of the CPU?* It's noted in Chapter 5 that there are two cycles that occur during the processing of each program instruction. These *instruction* and *execution* cycles are synchronized by a specific number of electrical pulses produced by an electronic clock that's built into the microprocessor chip. Thus, the speed with which an instruction is executed is also directly related to the chip's *clock speed* or number of pulses produced each second. Different versions of a particular chip—e.g., the Motorola 68000—can be produced with different clock speeds. One version of the 68000 used in Apple's Macintosh system runs at 7.83 million pulses per second (that's 7.83 megahertz or 7.83 MHz). This chip, of course, is faster than the 6 MHz version of the 68000 used in Radio Shack's TRS-80, model 16. The Intel 8088 used in IBM's PC and PCjr has a slower clock speed of 4.77 MHz. Although most of today's pc models function in the 2- to 8-MHz range, the newest chips can operate at speeds up to 25 MHz.

■ *How much primary storage capacity is available?* The more data and program segments that can be kept in primary storage, the fewer time-consuming disk operations may be necessary. Processing speeds up. Even when a Winchester disk drive is used, it's 1,000 times faster to access data located in primary storage. More sophisticated word processing, data base management, and scientific programs can thus be processed on a pc without lengthy waits. And as you saw in Chapter 6, a larger storage capacity is also needed to produce high resolution color graphics. You know that a 16-line address bus is used with 8-bit microprocessors to provide a maximum of 64K bytes of primary storage. But you might not know that it's possible to increase the *apparent* size of primary storage in an 8-bit pc by using software-controlled switches and additional banks of RAM chips. Memory-management software is then used to keep track of the location of needed data items. The microprocessor is always directly connected to only 64K bytes of storage, but there may be 128K bytes of data in the storage blocks (see Figure 8-5). Of course, the time used by the microprocessor to execute the instructions needed to support this **bank-switched memory** approach is time that's not available for other processing tasks. With 20 or 24 lines in its address bus, a 16-bit chip doesn't have to resort to bank switching since it's able to directly address from 1 to 16 megabytes of primary storage. Although many 16-bit systems are currently equipped

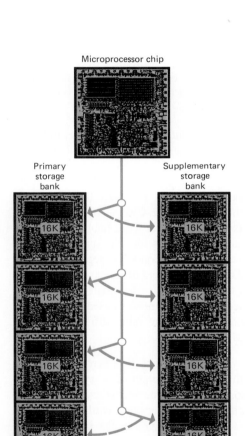

Microprocessor chip

Primary storage bank — Supplementary storage bank

16K 16K
16K 16K
16K 16K
16K 16K

Software-controlled switches determine which blocks are active at any given time

**Figure 8-5** The bank-switched memory approach found in some 8-bit personal computers. Blocks of 16K-byte RAM chips are often used. A combination of hardware and software additions is needed to "trick" the 8-bit microprocessor into accepting data from additional storage blocks.

with 256K bytes of primary storage, additional capacity can easily be added as needed.

■ *What instruction sets are available?* Every microprocessor has the built-in ability to respond to a particular set of machine instructions. These instructions are quite similar in 8-bit chips. In fact, the designers of the Zilog Z80 chip incorporated the Intel 8080 instruction set into their design and then extended the Z80 set to include other functions. But incredible as it may seem, these and other 8-bit chips have no single built-in multiplication or division instruction. Rather, these arithmetic functions are carried out at the most basic machine level by a programmed series of other instructions. In contrast, 16-bit processors *do have* single built-in multiplication and division instructions and are able to perform these operations 10 to 20 times faster than 8-bit chips. Thus, the composition of the instruction set (and the efficiency of the software used to manage the pc system) can have a significant effect on pc performance.

## Characteristics of Peripherals

**Input.** Whatever other devices are used for input—perhaps a mouse, light pen or joystick, microphone or touch-sensitive display screen, all discussed in Chapter 6—virtually all personal computers include an operator *keyboard* for data entry. And all of these keyboards follow the typewriter pattern of placing the letters QWERTY . . . in the top row of alphabetic characters. But there the similarities stop. Some keyboards are permanently housed with the CPU and display screen while others are detachable and adapt easily to individual work habits. Most have individual keys, but others substitute plastic membranes for keys and are suitable only for hunt-and-peck typing. Some have special-function keys, separate numeric keypads, and adequate spacing between keys, while others don't have any of these features. Some have more than 100 keys while others have less than half as many. And there are no standard locations for the placement of the keys used to control the location of the cursor on the display screen. These and other differences create problems for people who use several different keyboards.

Most microcomputer models offer a variety of input devices ranging from the keyboard to the mouse or joystick, light pen, or touch screen. (Courtesy Apple Computer, Inc.)

**Storage.** Magnetic tape cassette players and/or floppy disk drives are used to enter data and programs and to receive the processed output of pc systems. Small magnetic tapes and floppy disks are also used for offline secondary storage, and small rigid disk drives employing Winchester technology are available to vastly enlarge online secondary storage. Online secondary storage can also be provided by a RAM disk—a bank of RAM chips set up to look like a disk drive to the pc. All these storage concepts are discussed in Chapter 7.

**Output.** The visual display screens, character printers, plotters, and speakers that are also considered in Chapter 7 are among the devices used to produce output in a humanly usable form. A cathode ray tube (CRT) is used in most pc display monitors. Some screens are monochrome (one-color) while others produce many colors. You saw in Chapter 6 that some pc systems have a graphics mode of operation that permits the display screen to be mapped into thousands of picture elements or *pixels*. When a pc system with a large number of pixels is connected to a high-resolution color CRT, it can produce quality color graphics. A CRT is reliable, flexible, and easy to use. But it's also bulky and consumes a lot of power. Thus, some battery-powered portable personal computers use a **liquid-crystal display (LCD)**—the same type of display found in some pocket calculators and digital watches. These portable LCDs are compact, lightweight, durable, and use little power. But only a few lines of characters are displayed with current LCD systems, and the LCD graphics capability is poor because the individual pixels aren't small enough to give sharp definition.

## The Issue of Hardware Standards

Let's suppose that you want to assemble a pc system that will fit your budget and meet your needs. If all of your pc components come from the same manufacturer, there may be no problems with the shared connections or *interfaces* between various pieces of equipment. But if you want to connect a brand M printer to a brand N computer, you may run into trouble.

Printer M may not work with Computer N because of a lack of **interface compatibility**—i.e., the ability to plug various components together and have them function in an acceptable way. Stereo components from different manufacturers have this compatibility, but pc components often don't because many pc makers have developed proprietary standards that are unique to their own products. (Of course, this may help them shut out competitors and sell complete systems.) Uniform and industrywide interface standards such as those that exist for stereo equipment are needed by pc users, but they've been slow to appear. Some of the official and *de facto* (unofficial but industry-acknowledged) standards that have emerged for pc hardware over the years are discussed below.

### MICRO INTERNATIONAL

From the People's Republic of China comes the Great Wall 100, a 16-bit machine compatible with the IBM/PC. The leading microcomputer manufacturer in Brazil is Scopus, which was started in a garage by three young engineers tinkering with ideas for a personal computer.

These are but two relatively new entrants into the international computer club, joining Japan, Germany, and Great Britain, among others, and led by the United States. There is increasing awareness worldwide that not too far in the future nations will be segmented into those which produce information and those which consume it. By encouraging an indigenous data processing industry, the Brazilian government intends to keep up with the information suppliers but has no dreams of leading the international race.

Brazil's computer industry is thriving, thanks in large part to government protection, which discourages foreign competition but also has had the effect of boosting prices for micros in an already highly inflationary economy. The $6,000 Scopus micro, for example, is far out of reach of the typical Brazilian family, where wages average $160 per month. In fact, the banking and manufacturing businesses form the bulk of the market in Brazil. But the market is beginning to broaden into some other industries such as shrimp farming and to the government itself.

—Photos courtesy CPT Corporation and Hewlett-Packard Company.

**Parallel Interface Standards.** A **parallel interface** is one that moves information 8 or more bits at a time. (We've seen that a pc can also operate internally on 16 or 32 bits at a time depending on the microprocessor.) The S-100 interface bus discussed earlier was originally a *de facto* parallel standard that has now been officially designated as the *IEEE-696* by the Institute of Electrical and Electronics Engineers. Another official interface—the *IEEE-488*—was developed by Hewlett-Packard in the early 1970s to connect a computer with as many as 14 other devices on a single cable or bus. Standard cables and sockets are used.

Another *de facto* parallel standard is the *Centronics printer interface*. In the early 1970s, Centronics Data Computer Corporation developed this interface for its popular Series 100 printers. As more Centronics printers were sold, other vendors designed their printers to be compatible with the Centronics interface in order to gain greater market acceptability. (These competitors sometimes used the term ''industry standard parallel interface'' to avoid the Centronics name.) Many of today's pc systems have a built-in Centronics parallel printer connection. If both the computer and the printer that a user selects have compatible Centronics parallel connections or ports, then a hardware link-up can be made. But problems can still be encountered if the program instructions (or **driver program**) used by the computer to communicate with a printer cannot be recognized by the selected printer. It's thus wise for a purchaser to insist on a demonstration to prove that the selected computer, printer, and programs will work together.

**Serial Interface Standards.** Unlike a parallel *printer interface* that uses eight wires to transmit all 8 bits in a byte at the same time, a **serial interface** transfers the various bits in sequence over a single wire. When a pc uses an output serial interface port, the 8-bit bytes produced in parallel by the pc are then lined up into a single stream of bits for serial transmission to a printer or other device.

The most popular serial interface is the *RS-232C*, a standard originally established by the Electronic Industries Association to facilitate the transmission of data over telephone lines. Most of the serial ports installed on the CPUs, printers, and some other devices found in a pc system follow this RS-232C standard.[1] But about all this ''standard'' guarantees is that a cable connecting two devices will usually plug into both units. Problems associated with synchronizing the number of bits transmitted per second, with letting the computer know when to slow down to avoid overrunning the printer, and with assorted software incompatibilities are frequently encountered. Again, a demonstration prior to purchase is needed to prove that selected hardware and software will work together.

## The Issue of Operating System Standards

An *operating system (OS)* is the overall set of program instructions that are needed to manage and coordinate the various parts of a computer system. As you'll learn in Chapter 13, an OS controls I/O housekeeping operations, keeps track of where facts are stored, and orchestrates in other ways the operation of each pc component. After an OS is loaded into a pc, the user communicates with it, supplies applications programs designed to run with the particular OS in use, furnishes input data, and receives output results. From the user's viewpoint, it would be desirable to have access to a few pc operating systems that conformed to official industry standards, but these *official* standards don't exist.

---

[1] Later and less-popular revisions of the RS-232C standard are the *RS-422* and the *RS-449*.

Operating system disk

There are numerous *proprietary operating systems* just as there are many proprietary hardware standards. For example, Apple's DOS (Disk Operating System) and Radio Shack's TRSDOS (TRS Disk Operating System) are intended for use only with specific machines. Since applications programs must work in harmony with a pc's OS, software written for an Apple II running DOS can't be used with a TRS-80 running TRSDOS. Thus, the thousands of programs that have been written to run on these two operating systems can't be used without modification on other operating systems.

**The CP/M-80 de facto Standard.** Because of its widespread acceptance, Digital Research's **CP/M-80** (Control Program/Microprocessors) is a *de facto* OS standard for 8-bit pc systems using Z80 and 8080 microprocessors. Developed in the early 1970s, CP/M-80 has been updated several times.[2] The CP/M-80 OS was adopted for use by dozens of pc manufacturers in the 1970s. As these brands poured into the marketplace, independent software suppliers saw an opportunity and developed thousands of applications programs for the pc systems running CP/M-80. The wealth of 8-bit software that's compatible with CP/M-80 has, in turn, forced the builders of later 8-bit machines to make the OS available to their customers. Plug-in hardware kits are even available to allow the users of some Apple and Radio Shack models to run software written for this OS.

**The MS-DOS de facto Standard.** Applications programs are still being prepared for 8-bit machines, but the earlier flood has now become a trickle. Most independent software suppliers have now turned their attention to writing programs for 16- and 32-bit models. And the 16-bit machines that have received the most attention in the mid-1980s are those designed around Intel's 8088 and 8086 microprocessors. The dominant OS for these machines, and one whose acceptance has also made it a *de facto* standard, is **MS-DOS** developed by Microsoft Corporation. The popularity of MS-DOS is due to the fact that it's the one IBM selected to use with its popular Personal Computer (IBM calls it PC-DOS). After IBM selected MS-DOS, more than 50 other hardware manufacturers also picked it. Many of the popular programs first written for 8-bit CP/M systems have now been adapted to a 16-bit MS-DOS environment. And much of the best new business and professional software prepared by independent suppliers is written for this environment first. Other machines get the programs later, if at all.

**UNIX and other Important Operating Systems.** The **UNIX** OS was first developed at Bell Laboratories in 1969 for larger machines. It was later adapted for pc systems, and its recent acceptance is rapidly turning it into another *de facto* standard. Other 16-bit OSs include the proprietary versions offered by some pc makers, the CP/M-86 version developed by Digital Research for 8088/8086 microprocessors, the Oasis-16 from Phase One Systems, the Pick OS from Pick Systems Inc., and the p-System developed at the University of California at San Diego.

[2] A 1976 upgrade (version 1.4) improved on the original bare-bones disk OS, a 1979 revision (version 2.0) made further improvements, and a 1982 update (version 3.0, also called CP/M-Plus) was designed to be used with bank-switched memory systems.

# PERSONAL COMPUTER SYSTEMS

Now that we've considered some of the general hardware and software characteristics of pc systems, let's quickly examine a few examples of the systems found in homes and offices.

## Personal Computing Systems in the Home

General-interest pc systems are usually found in the home. They are used to entertain, educate, and increase personal productivity. Millions of these systems have been produced by manufacturers such as Apple, Atari, Coleco, Commodore, IBM, and Radio Shack. Prices range from less than $100 to about $2,000. The least-expensive models have limited keyboards, and the user's TV set is generally used to display output. Primary storage capacity is relatively limited, although 64K bytes are available in machines selling for less than $300. Cassette tape is often used for offline secondary storage of programs and data. It's a slow process to write output onto a cassette tape and to read programs and data from a tape, but cassette recorder/players and tapes are inexpensive. Dot matrix and nonimpact character printers, and connections that permit communication over telephone lines, are available options for many of these systems.

Since most home systems use the same microprocessor chips found in many larger systems, they can perform complex computations. Many early systems were bought simply to run available game programs. But they also allowed users to achieve a measure of computer literacy by giving them "hands-on" computer operating experience and by enabling them to become familiar with the rudiments of computer programming.

Personal computers, as shown on these pages, contain all the elements found in any larger system, and individuals are taking advantage of the technology in every imaginable way. At home, at school, or on the road, more and more Americans are expanding the pc marketplace, which the experts see as totaling at least 80 million homes. Photos courtesy Apple Computer, Inc. and International Business Machines Corporation *(above)* and Commodore Electronics, Limited *(right)*.

Personal computer systems today come in a variety of configurations, from self-contained units *(above)* to central processors you can use with your television and tape cassette player *(below)*. Photos courtesy Radio Shack, A Division of Tandy Corporation *(above)* and © 1983 Atari, Inc. All Rights Reserved *(below)*.

## Personal Computing Systems in the Office

The costs of the additional hardware and software usually needed in an organizational and/or professional setting generally means that the price of office pc systems will range between $2,000 and $10,000. For example, better keyboards, larger primary storage sections, significant online secondary storage in the form of floppy and, perhaps, Winchester disk drives, easy to read display screens, and letter-quality printers are needed with *desktop* systems designed to do serious word processing, spreadsheet calculating, and data base managing. The *portable* pc systems used by professionals also need most of these same features. Either 8- or 16-bit machines can be effective in a working system. Many thousands of business-type programs are written for the Apple DOS, CP/M-80, TRSDOS, and the other operating systems used with 8-bit models. These 8-bit programs generally perform *single functions* such as controlling inventory or creating graphic presentations.

With rare exceptions, all of the important 8-bit single-function programs have now been adapted for use on

16-bit pc systems. And as we've seen, much of the best new organizational/professional software is being single-mindedly written first for the IBM-PC and other similar 16-bit machines using MS-DOS. These newer programs often *integrate several functions* in a single package. You saw in Chapter 4 that these integrated packages allow users to simultaneously show the current status of several ongoing applications in separate "windows" on the display screen. One window can show the preparation of text, another can show the results of manipulating columns and rows of figures, and a third can show work being done to create graphic images. Data can be moved from window to window (and from application to application) as needed. Expensive resources such as 256K bytes of primary storage, floppy and Winchester disk drives, a system that permits the display screen to be divided into tens of thousands of addressable picture elements, and a printing/plotting output device are often needed to support these more sophisticated software packages.

No matter what size the organization, businesspeople and professionals with pc systems have found that the computer often pays for itself within its first year. Photos courtesy Apple Computer, Inc. *(page 219);* Radio Shack, A Division of Tandy Corporation *(above);* © Ashton-Tate, 1984. All Rights Reserved and Hewlett-Packard Company *(right);* and International Business Machines Corporation *(below).*

# PERSONAL COMPUTER APPLICATIONS PACKAGES

The OS software controls the overall operation of a computer, but application programs must be available to control the processing of a particular task. Many application programs are custom-made for unique jobs, but countless other programs have been written and packaged for pc users. Tens of thousands of these *applications packages* exist. Simply look at the ads in any of the magazines listed in Figure 8-6, and you'll get an idea of the scope and variety of available pc software packages.

## Applications Packages in the Home

Like all computers, the millions of pc systems installed in homes are general-purpose symbol manipulators. And symbols can be manipulated in countless ways to entertain, educate, and serve people. Thus, there's virtually no limit to the number of possible applications that can be developed. Since the demand for good home software is large and growing, it's no wonder that many package suppliers are working hard to serve this market.

For example, with the right applications packages, your home pc system can be used to:

- ■ Entertain you with hundreds of challenging games, many of which have impressive graphic and sound features.

- ■ Balance your budget and checkbook.

- ■ Monitor your home's energy usage.

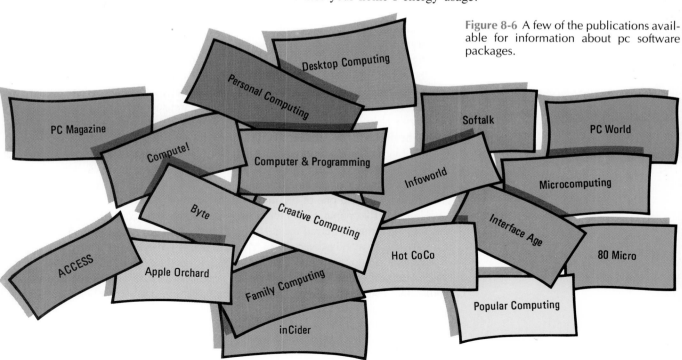

**Figure 8-6** A few of the publications available for information about pc software packages.

■ Help you learn a new subject, e.g., a foreign language or auto repair techniques. Game strategies are being incorporated into educational software to increase student motivation.

■ Help you compose music.

■ Produce better typed documents through the use of word processing programs.

■ Maintain automobile and other expense records, and accumulate income data by categories.

■ Keep track of the performance of your investments by categories, monitor the coverages and costs of your insurance policies, and prepare your tax returns.

■ Compute and keep track of your installment payments.

■ Control your household appliances and security devices.

■ File for easy retrieval and reference such information as recipes, price lists, names and addresses, telephone numbers, and dates of birthdays and anniversaries.

■ Give you information from the data bases of a number of information retrieval networks. For example, you can call a local telephone number, connect your personal computer to one of the information networks discussed in Chapter 10, and access up-to-the-minute information from a wide variety of data banks.

## Organizational/Professional Applications Packages

Personal computers are flooding into offices in unprecedented numbers. In some of the largest business and government organizations, managers have grown tired of waiting for the computer center to process their applications, have taken matters into their own hands, and have bought their own pc systems to do the work. And the relatively low cost of a pc system has meant that even the smallest organizations can now afford one. There are thousands of business and accounting packages available for use on pc systems. And this doesn't count the additional thousands of educational, health-care, and scientific software packages that are available.

Among the most important business software packages are those that provide quick answers to "what if" questions by manipulating the columns and rows of data that have been created on an electronic spreadsheet. The first pc **spreadsheet program** to appear, and one of the most popular programs ever written, is VisiCorp's **VisiCalc.** (It's so popular, in fact, that it has spawned a score of similar packages that are sometimes referred to as "visiclones" or "calc-alikes.") You can get an idea of what the standard version of VisiCalc does by visualizing a huge blackboard divided into 63 columns and 254 rows. There are thus thousands of intersections where columns and rows meet. At each intersection in this VisiCalc matrix is a "box" that can be filled with letters, mathematical symbols, numbers, and formulas. For example, box C10 is at the intersection of column C and row 10, while box D125 is found where column D and row 125 meet. A user can position the display screen cursor on a particular box in the VisiCalc blackboard and enter a title, number, or formula.

Each *standard-size* box is set to display nine characters, but box sizes can be expanded or reduced. A box will be a *value box* or a *label box* in any given application depending on the first character that's entered into the box. Numbers and mathematical symbols create value boxes; letters and quotations produce label boxes. Value boxes do the calculating; label boxes are used for titles and descriptions. With a few keystrokes a user can tell a VisiCalc program to add boxes C7, C8, and C9, and store the total in box C10. Many other mathematical functions can be performed on other identified value boxes. The data in boxes C7, C8, and C9 may change in response to different ''what if'' assumptions made by the user, and the total in box C10 will automatically be adjusted to reflect these changes. To plan for the introduction of a new product, a manager often wants to consider what will happen if different raw material prices, labor costs, and sales volume figures are assumed. The assumed figures are fed into a pc, and VisiCalc can then manipulate them to project the effect that different values will have on profits.

Spreadsheet programs can be used in dozens of ways, but they represent only one of the software categories available to pc users. With the right applications packages, a pc system can also be used in an office to:

■ Compute payrolls and process orders; maintain student, patient, customer, or client records; pay debts and collect receipts; analyze sales and market research data; and process other necessary general accounting tasks.

■ Keep track of appointments, schedule meetings, plan daily activities, and maintain an online alphabetical and subject file showing office locations of original letters and documents.

■ Schedule production, route jobs, analyze production costs, and control machine tools and other production equipment.

■ Control inventory levels of thousands of different items.

■ Produce personalized letters, mailing labels, and other documents through the use of word processing software (see Figure 2-14, page 57). And then use other software to check the spelling in the documents prior to printing.

■ Supply students and employees with educational opportunities through the use of innovative computer-assisted instruction techniques.

■ Monitor and compare the costs of fuel, oil, and repairs for many vehicles, prepare maintenance schedules for these vehicles, and produce vehicle cost reports.

■ Prepare the graphic images that are used (to cite just a few examples) by (1) managers to analyze financial data, (2) engineers for stress analysis and interactive design, (3) clinical laboratory technicians to plot quality-control data, and (4) anthropologists to plot the length of bones of prehistoric humanoids.

This listing of tasks performed by applications packages could go on and on, but you get the idea: The actual and potential uses of pc systems in homes and offices can be as numerous and varied as human ingenuity and imagination will permit.

## Identifying and Selecting Software Packages

Let's assume that you have a problem to be solved or a need to be satisfied. Let's further assume that you have a clear understanding of the nature of this problem or need. Let's suppose next that you suspect that the problem or need can best be handled through the use of a pc system. And let's finally assume that you believe that the most economical solution to the problem or need lies in acquiring one or more applications packages.

Unless you're already locked into a particular hardware system, your best bet is probably to follow the **software-first approach.** That is, you should find the applications package(s) that will do exactly what you want to do and then acquire the hardware needed to run the package(s). But how do you go about identifying prospective packages and then deciding on the "best" selection? That's not a trivial question given the past and expected growth in the pc software market shown in Figure 8-7. Some guidelines are given in the following pages to help you identify a list of possible packages, narrow the field to a few suitable choices, and then make the final purchase decision. But you should remember that even the pros have trouble picking software for themselves because programs are complicated products.

**1. Identify Suitable Applications Packages.** Some of the sources of information you can use in this first step are outlined below:

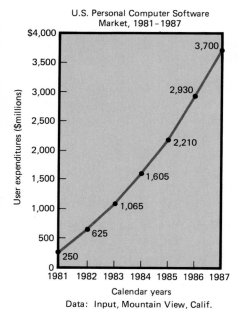

U.S. Personal Computer Software Market, 1981–1987

Calendar years

Data: Input, Mountain View, Calif.

**Figure 8-7** The sales of pc software packages are climbing rapidly. (Source: Mary-Beth Santarelli, "'Expert' Forecasts Vary for 1983," *Software News,* January 1983, p. 22.)

- The advertisements published in pc magazines and software mail-order catalogs can give general descriptions of packages, and the members of local *computer clubs* can give specific accounts of the performance of competitive products. (There are hundreds of these clubs, and some have many knowledgeable members. The Southern California Computer Club alone has over 20,000 members.)

- The reviews of software products published in many of the pc magazines go beyond the advertising descriptions and give more information on the functions and features of selected packages. The reviews in *Infoworld,* for example, are usually thorough and balanced.

- People in the retail stores that carry software packages should be able to demonstrate their products, answer questions, and furnish promotional literature. Most retail outlets also sell pc hardware, but *software-only* stores are springing up around the country.

- Vendors of software packages can often supply literature and documentation on their products. It's usually possible, for example, to buy the manual that explains the use of a package. If the package is popular, it's likely that independent publishers will also offer books specifically aimed at present and potential users. (These books are often better written than the vendor's manuals.) But if you do buy a vendor's manual and then later order the complete package, most vendors will then give you credit for the price of the manual. The problem with this data-gathering approach is that manuals and books can be expensive.

■ Computer consultants and acquaintances with problems similar to yours can answer questions and make package recommendations.

■ Several *software-searching firms* have appeared. Some are selling directories that catalog thousands of packages. Others such as Softsearch International use computers to store and retrieve information on more than 30,000 packages. This electronic library is available for a fee to pc users, retailers, and consultants.

**2. Narrow the Field.** Once you've identified suitable package candidates, use this *selection* checklist to further narrow the field:

■ Is the *output* produced by the package suitable in form and content?

■ Can the package accept the *input data* you need to process in the format that you need to use?

■ Can the package support an acceptable range of I/O devices?

■ Are the *files* created and/or processed acceptable in terms of size, contents, storage media, record formats, access restrictions, and degree of permanency?

■ Does the package have an *adequate response time,* or must you wait for lengthy periods while the program digests your last data entry?

■ What's the quality of the *documentation?* That is, are the manuals and other documents in the package complete, clearly written, and well organized?

■ Does the package have good *error-handling controls?* Are system errors reported to the user in clear messages or cryptic codes?

■ If multiple packages are needed, will they all run on the same hardware using the same operating system? Can an integrated software package be substituted for several single-function programs?

**3. Make the Final Decisions.** The following questions may help you make the best package choice:

■ Can it be *demonstrated* to *your* satisfaction that the package works with *your* data, in the format *you* use, to solve the problem that *you* specified?

■ What's the *level of support* you can expect to receive from the vendor and/or the vendor's representative? Is some knowledgeable person able and willing to help you with any problems that may develop as you use the package?

Once you've decided on a package, where do you go to buy it? There are likely to be three outlets for the software. The *first* source is a *retail store*. Although stores vary in the amount of software they carry, they *should* be familiar with the packages they sell. When that's true, they should also be able to demonstrate the program, answer your questions about it, and provide support for it. Obviously, though, a dealer can't begin to carry all the packages that are available. And perhaps what isn't carried is exactly what you need. In that case, the dealer may be able to order the package for you. The price charged by the retailer for a package is likely to be close to the list price, but this is reasonable *if* you can depend on the retailer for help before and after the sale.

A *second* possible package source is a *mail-order distributor*. If you're buying a relatively simple package and don't need any support help, then you can usually save money by ordering it from this source. And a *third* way to buy the selected package is to order it *directly from the producer*. This may be about the only way to get a copy of a program supplied by the firm whose only office is located above the owner's garage. Prices are often negotiated, and the firm may not be around later if you need help.

## Feedback and Review 8-1

The subject of this chapter is personal computers. You've seen how they were developed, you've learned about some of their general characteristics, you've studied some of the representative systems used in homes and offices, and you've read about the applications packages that are available for these home and office systems. To test and reinforce your understanding of these concepts, answer the following multiple-choice questions by placing the letter of the most nearly correct answer in the space provided.

——**1.** A recently introduced personal computer system
   a) can often do the work of an earlier minicomputer, but it costs much more.
   b) may cost the same as an earlier pc system, but it's likely to offer improved performance.
   c) differs very little from earlier pc systems in terms of cost and performance.
   d) is defined to be a personal computer by rigid industry standards.

——**2.** The first personal computer was
   a) placed on a single silicon chip.
   b) produced by Datapoint Corporation.
   c) originally offered to hobbyists in kit form.
   d) a 16-bit machine.

——**3.** A microprocessor chip used in a pc system
   a) performs the arithmetic-logic and control functions.

   b) is the only chip found in most pc models.
   c) almost always operates on 64 bits of data at a time.
   d) performs the primary storage function.

——**4.** The first microprocessor chip was built by
   a) Datapoint Corporation.
   b) a Japanese calculator firm.
   c) Texas Instruments.
   d) Intel Corporation.

——**5.** Most of the popular pc systems produced in the late 1970s
   a) were made by Intel Corporation.
   b) use 16-bit microprocessor chips.
   c) use 8-line data buses and 16-line address buses.
   d) are able to identify a maximum of 32,000 separate primary storage locations.

——**6.** All 16-bit pc systems
   a) are built around a few popular microprocessor chips.
   b) can identify a maximum of 1 megabyte of primary storage.
   c) use the microprocessor chip designed by IBM for its Personal Computer.
   d) use a true "16/16-bit" chip.

——**7.** Which of the following is not a factor affecting the processing capability or performance of a pc system:
   a) the clock speed of the CPU.
   b) the revolutions per minute of the printer disk.
   c) the primary storage capacity of the CPU.
   d) the built-in instruction set available to the CPU.

___8. A set of official industrywide standards has been approved
   a) for the layout of pc keyboards.
   b) to permit any printer to interface with any pc.
   c) for pc operating systems.
   d) for none of the choices mentioned above.

___9. A parallel interface
   a) is one that moves information one bit at a time over a single wire.
   b) is used with the RS-232C standard.
   c) moves information 8 or more bits at a time.
   d) is never used to connect printers to personal computers.

___10. Two of the most popular operating systems for 8- and 16-bit personal computers are (in 8- and 16-bit order):
   a) MOSES and ADAM.
   b) MOS and CMOS.
   c) CP/M-80 and MS-DOS.
   d) CP/M-86 and TRSDOS.

___11. Most pc systems designed for home use
   a) are 8-bit machines with inexpensive peripherals.

   b) are 16-bit models with Winchester disk drives.
   c) come equipped with display screens and letter-quality printers.
   d) are priced above $2,000.

___12. Most pc systems designed for office use
   a) use a TV set to display output.
   b) are limited to the use of programs that are only able to perform single functions.
   c) need a significant amount of online secondary storage capacity.
   d) are unable to produce graphic images.

___13. Suitable applications packages
   a) are available for home use, but office programs must be custom-made.
   b) such as VisiCalc are designed to manipulate columns and rows of data in order to answer the "what if" questions posed by managers.
   c) are easy to identify and select because of the limited number of such packages.
   d) should be considered only after you've acquired the hardware you'll need to do the work.

# LOOKING BACK

**1.** Technological changes are occurring so rapidly in the computer industry that it's now very difficult to classify the broad range of available machines on the basis of size and computing capabilities. The models discussed in this chapter are arbitrarily classified as personal computers. Larger machines are considered in Chapter 9.

**2.** Developed in the 1970s, pc systems are the smallest general-purpose symbol manipulators that can be programmed to process a countless number of applications. Built around a single microprocessor chip (which is an 8-, 16-, or 32-bit device), a pc also uses RAM and ROM storage chips in the CPU. The 8-bit pc systems have built-in 8-bit data buses and are thus able to process a single 8-bit byte of data at a time. They also have 16-line address buses, and so they can directly identify a maximum of about 65,000 separate storage locations. The built-in data paths between primary storage and the microprocessors used in 16-bit machines are either 8 or 16 bits wide, and data are processed internally 16 or 32 bits at a time depending on the microprocessor. The 20- or 24-line address buses permit primary storage capacities of 1 megabyte and 16 megabytes. A superior performance may be expected from a pc system that has a 16- or 32-bit microprocessor running at a high clock speed, a large primary storage capacity, and an efficient instruction set.

**3.** A variety of I/O and secondary storage devices are available for pc systems. Most of these devices are discussed in detail in Chapters 6 and 7. But combining the I/O and storage components made by several vendors to produce a pc system can lead to problems because of a lack of interface compatibility. Some official and *de facto* parallel and serial interface standards do exist, but they don't guarantee that selected hardware and software will work together.

**4.** An OS is the overall set of program instructions that are needed to manage and coordinate the various parts of a computer system. The user of a pc interacts with an OS, supplies applications programs designed to run with that particular OS, furnishes input data, and receives output results. There are many proprietary OS packages such as Apple's DOS and Radio Shack's TRSDOS. And because of its widespread usage, CP/M-80 has become a *de facto* OS standard for 8-bit systems. Likewise, MS-DOS has become a *de facto* standard because of its use in most 16-bit systems.

**5.** Several representative pc systems and their applications are classified into home and office categories. Some of the ways to identify suitable applications packages have been noted, and some questions to consider in selecting a specific package have been presented.

## KEY TERMS AND CONCEPTS

| | | |
|---|---|---|
| personal computer (pc) 209 | 8/16-bit chip 211 | driver program 216 |
| microprocessor chip 209 | 16/16-bit chip 211 | serial interface 216 |
| single-user oriented 209 | 16/32-bit chip 212 | CP/M-80 217 |
| 8-bit microprocessors 210 | 32/32-bit chip 212 | MS-DOS 217 |
| interface bus 210 | bank-switched memory 213 | UNIX 217 |
| 16-bit microprocessors 211 | liquid-crystal display (LCD) 215 | spreadsheet program 222 |
| data buses 211 | interface compatibility 215 | VisiCalc 222 |
| address bus 211 | parallel interface 216 | software-first approach 224 |

## TOPICS FOR REVIEW AND DISCUSSION

**1.** (a) What is a personal computer? (b) Why was it developed? (c) What's the difference between a microcomputer and a microprocessor?

**2.** "Most personal computers are stand-alone, single-user-oriented machines used by people at work and at play." Discuss this statement.

**3.** (a) What's an 8/16-bit microprocessor chip? (b) What's a 16/32-bit chip? (c) Can the microprocessor in an 8-bit pc be considered to be an 8/8-bit chip?

**4.** Why do some 16-bit pc systems have a maximum primary storage capacity of 1 megabyte while others can manage up to 16 megabytes?

**5.** Identify and discuss the factors that affect CPU performance in a pc system.

**6.** (a) Identify four ways to supply input data to a pc system. (b) Identify four ways that output may be received from a pc system. (c) Identify three devices that may be used to provide a pc system with secondary storage capabilities. (You may want to review the I/O and storage media and devices discussed in Chapters 6 and 7 to answer this question.)

**7.** (a) What is meant by the term "interface compatibility"? (b) What's the difference between a parallel interface and a serial interface?

**8.** (a) What's an operating system? (b) Identify three operating systems used with 8-bit machines and three used with 16-bit models.

**9.** (a) Give three examples of pc systems used primarily in the home, and provide three examples of professional pc models. (b) Discuss four ways that applications packages may be used in the home, and four ways that these packages may be of use in organizations.

**10.** (a) What sources are available to help you identify suitable pc applications packages? (b) What questions should be considered in selecting a specific package?

## PROJECTS TO LOOK INTO

**1.** Conduct a survey among five people in the computer/data processing field and ask them these two questions: (a) How would you differentiate between a pc and a minicomputer? (b) How would you differentiate between a minicomputer and a small mainframe model? Present the results of your survey to the class.

**2.** Select a type of application of interest to you (e.g., word processing, accounting, entertainment, educational, scientific, and so on). Identify three possible packages that could be used to process your application. List the features and hardware requirements of each package. Which package would you buy and how would you buy it?

## ANSWERS TO FEEDBACK AND REVIEW SECTION

**8-1**

| | | |
|---|---|---|
| 1. b | 5. c | 10. c |
| 2. c | 6. a | 11. a |
| 3. a | 7. b | 12. c |
| 4. d | 8. d | 13. b |
| | 9. c | |

# Supermicros

A step behind the massive invasion of corporate America by personal computers, the more powerful machines broadly defined as supermicrocomputers are finding new applications well beyond their starting niches in small businesses and scientific/engineering work.

There is no agreement on exactly what combination of characteristics defines a supermicrocomputer, and vendors and industry analysts often contradict each other on which systems to include in this grouping of processors. Nevertheless, these are higher end systems built around microprocessor CPUs that fall into two main categories: multiuser systems and dedicated professional workstations.

Each category features tremendous diversity among vendors, systems and target markets. Additionally, the two overlap. AT&T's 3B2/300, for example, can be configured either as a multiuser or dedicated system.

Although supermicros may sell against personal computers or other systems, most sales come at the expense of minicomputers. Built around today's powerful and inexpensive microprocessors, supermicros hold a strong price/performance edge over traditional minicomputers.

One notable price/performance comparison can be made between Digital Equipment Corp.'s VAX-11/785 supermini and Intel Corp.'s 80286 chip. According to Lew Glendenning, director of information systems research at Strategic, Inc. in San Jose, Calif., the VAX works at between 1.5 million instructions per second (Mips) and 2 Mips, while the 80286 is a 1-Mips machine. But some new 80286-based systems cost less than one-sixth the nearly $195,000 starting price of the VAX-11/785. . . .

Supermicrocomputers will benefit from hard disk

There is little agreement among the experts on the hardware category to choose for supermicro systems. The new machines fall somewhere between desktop personal computers and superminis.

drives' plummeting prices, the introduction of new integrated software packages, emerging communications and graphics standards and other communications advances that are helping to integrate the new systems within larger data processing environments.

However, other factors are equally crucial to market success, and Glendenning noted that supermicros make up "a much smaller market than you would think, hearing the price/performance."

Among the gaps, the most important may be a limited choice of applications software. "A supermicro is a high-performance minicomputer with no software," Glendenning joked. Other problems facing the acceptance of supermicros include the loyalty of users to their minis and the unwillingness of many systems houses and OEMs to work within much lower price margins.

—Eric Bender, "Supermicros Pushing beyond Original Small Business, Scientific Niches into New Application Areas," *Computerworld,* May 21, 1984, pp. 10–12. Copyright 1984 by CW Communications, Framingham, Mass. Photos courtesy Digital Equipment Corporation (page 229), NCR Corporation (below left), and AT&T (below).

Supermicros, the new generation of desktop computers, process information in the same way as minicomputers but cost far less.

## chapter 9

# Minis, Mainframes, and "Monsters"

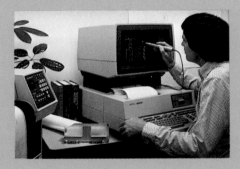

### But, Will There Always Be a Mainframe?

With the advance of personal computing and refinement of specific issues and processing problems, we can lose sight of the real needs for processing vast quantities of data and the networking communication requirements that can only be answered by the central processing mainframe. These environments require the processing power and centralized control that can *only* be effected through a centralized processor.

Summarizing information for a single personal or job related requirement is one problem. Summarizing information for an agency or a company, the Commonwealth of Massachusetts or the Internal Revenue Service is quite another.

The central processing mainframe is here to stay. The mainframe will continue to control the ever larger data, information and processing needs of most companies and agencies. As data filters into the mainframe it will begin to originate from "smart" terminals and micros which will increasingly interact with the mainframes. Data will both originate and terminate at the micro. It is clear that a common software vocabulary will be necessary.

The last few years have seen an explosion in the use of the micro and personal computers and corresponding personal computing software. Spreadsheet and reporting and graphics are now all in one package. As the mainframe and micro interact to analyze, report and coordinate from common data bases, they will be forced to use common languages, tools and software.

Mainframes today use a jumble of confusing, "hard-to-use" and "hard-to-understand" software. The micros offer their jumble of "easy-to-use" and "easy-to-understand" software. Through this decade there will be a blending of software which can be used on both the micro and the mainframe.

—Michael H. Pomerantz, ". . . But, Will There Always Be a Mainframe?" Reprinted from *Infosystems*, November 1983. Copyright Hitchcock Publishing Company. Photo courtesy Hewlett-Packard Company.

You know from Chapter 8 that computer systems may be arbitrarily classified into four categories on the basis of size, cost, and system performance. Now we turn our attention from actual microcomputer systems to currently available machines ranging upward in size from minicomputers to mainframes and then to supercomputers. The information in this chapter will enable you to:

- Define the minicomputer, tell why minis were developed, outline some of their hardware/software characteristics, recall examples of representative minis, and discuss ways they may be used

- Differentiate between a mainframe and a smaller computer, point out some characteristics and uses of mainframe models, and give examples of mainframe families

- Outline the characteristics of supercomputers that make them different from other machines, and discuss the types of applications for which they are designed

# MINICOMPUTER SYSTEMS

In spite of the fact that it's almost impossible to define a minicomputer anymore, we'll resort to an arbitrary definition. A **minicomputer** is a small general-purpose computer ranging in price from about $2,500 to $75,000. It can vary in size from a small desktop model to a unit about the size of a four-drawer file cabinet. There's obviously an overlap between the more powerful personal computer systems and the low-end minicomputers in terms of cost and processing capability. The same overlap also exists between the most expensive minis and small mainframe models. In fact, the makers of minicomputers are finding that their traditional market is being attacked on the low end by pc vendors and is being squeezed on the high side by mainframe builders.

## Chapter Outline

## The Development of Minicomputers

The development of personal computers in the early 1970s is a case of history repeating itself. A few years earlier, the first minis were also created for single specialized applications or for a few small general applications. The trend among established computer manufacturers in the early 1960s was to build larger and faster systems that could provide at a central location all the processing power needed by an entire organization. Although this approach served the needs of some organizations, others were either unable to afford the larger systems or they had specialized applications that a large centralized machine did not process effectively.

A need existed for low-cost *mini*mal computers that could fill the gaps left by the bigger, faster centralized approach. Several innovators recognized this need and formed new firms in the 1960s to produce these minimal machines. The first processors called minicomputers were developed and built by Digital Equipment Corporation (DEC)—now the largest producer of minis. Other major vendors include Hewlett-Packard, Data General, Wang Laboratories, Honeywell, IBM, Datapoint, Texas Instruments, Prime Computer, Tandem Computers, and Perkin-Elmer.

Most of the minis produced in the 1970s are **16-bit machines.** They are able to simultaneously move and manipulate data words consisting of two 8-bit bytes. This 16-bit capability gave minis an edge in performance over the 8-bit personal computers that were also introduced in the 1970s. Of course, much of the performance advantage enjoyed by the older 16-bit minis was lost when 16-bit pc systems were introduced early in the 1980s.

But the mini makers did not rest on their 16-bit designs and wait for the pc vendors to catch up. Rather, many of them were busy in the 1970s developing a new generation of 32-bit **supermini** models. Able to operate on four bytes at a time rather than two, these superminis gave users the performance of small mainframe models in less-expensive packages. The supermini market was launched early in 1975 when Systems Engineering Laboratories (now a division of Gould Inc.) introduced its 32 series, and Interdata (now Perkin-Elmer Computer Systems) quickly followed with its 8/32 model. And when DEC announced its VAX-11/780 in October 1977, the supermini market really began to take off. Since then, entire families of superminis have been developed by DEC, Data General, Four-Phase, Gould, Hewlett-Packard, Honeywell, Perkin-Elmer, Prime, Wang, and others.

It's likely that the supermini of the early 1980s will become the typical-sized mini in the years ahead. As Figure 9-1 indicates, industry sources expect that the annual sales of minicomputers will continue to grow for the next decade. The competitive situation today is that mainframe makers are bringing out lower-priced models to counter the supermini threat, both mini and mainframe suppliers are producing personal computers in an effort to ward off the advances of other pc builders, and users are benefiting from the competitive dogfight.

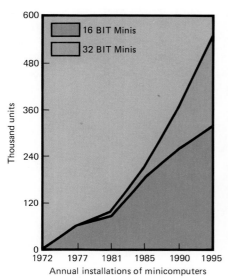

**Figure 9-1** Industry sources believe that the annual sales of minicomputers will continue to grow through 1995. The percentage of sales coming from the 32-bit supermini sector will increase in the future. Tom Henkel, "Tech Advances Put Future of 16-Bit Minis in Doubt," *Computerworld,* May 23, 1983, p. 4.

## Some Characteristics of Typical Minis

Today's typical mini system carries a higher price tag and will surpass the typical pc in storage capacity, speed of arithmetic operations, and ability to support a greater variety of faster-operating peripheral devices. For example, the larger hard-disk units used for online secondary storage in some mini systems have a much greater capacity and are faster operating than the small Winchester and/or floppy devices used in most professional pc systems.

While most pc systems remain oriented toward single users, mini systems are usually designed to simultaneously handle the processing needs of *multiple* users.

# Minicomputer Gallery

Most minis were originally 16-bit machines, as shown here, and have filled the data processing needs of business since the 1970s. Minicomputers originally gained popularity by filling a gap created by a move toward centralized processing facilities geared to large organizations which could afford mainframe power. (Photos reproduced by permission of Data General Corporation, Westboro, Mass., and courtesy Wang Laboratories, Inc.)

Some 16-bit traditional models and some 32-bit super-minis are represented in the Minicomputer Gallery. As mini systems get larger, primary and online secondary storage capacities increase, the peripheral devices that can be supported become more numerous and more powerful, and there's an increase in the number of users that can be simultaneously supported.

## Many Uses for Minis

It's obvious that organizations have found varied uses for minicomputers. The early minis were used primarily for single specialized applications—e.g., to monitor instruments and test equipment in a laboratory or to control a machine tool or a flow process in a factory—or they were used to process a number of general applications in a small organization. They are still widely used for these purposes. In addition, dedicated minicomputers are also used to control the data input received from multiple key-to-disk encoding stations (see Figure 6-7, page 143).

Although pages could be filled with other examples of minicomputer uses, perhaps one more very important type of application will be enough. Over the years many organizations have decided to establish **distributed data processing (DDP) networks.** Typically, in a DDP network, a larger central **host computer** communicates with, and exercises some control over, **satellite** (or **node**) **processors.** A satellite may, in turn, act as a host to subordinate processors and/or terminals. The satellite processors are likely to be minicomputers that handle much of the data processing done locally in offices and on factory floors. Connected to these satellite minis may be other subordinate minis, personal computers, intelligent terminals, and/or dumb terminals. And in addition to the dozens of minis that are used in some large DDP networks to process data, still more minis are used to control the flow of communications between network stations. We'll look at DDP networks in more detail in Chapter 10.

Minicomputers perform a vast array of applications, from data processing for a small organization to controlling production processes to high-speed transaction processing in the financial industry. Many newer mini systems are 32-bit machines which provide for increased processing power and multiuser capabilities. (Photos courtesy Hewlett-Packard Company and Digital Equipment Corporation *(top)*; provided by Datapoint Corporation, All Rights Reserved, and courtesy AccuRay Corporation *(above)*; and courtesy Perkin-Elmer Corporation *(right)*.

Minis may support dozens or even hundreds of terminals. Thus, they are almost always found in organizations. And in addition to processing the tasks submitted from multiple workstations, minis can also serve as a communications link between these stations and a central mainframe. One of the first mini applications was to handle the flow of information between mainframes and outlying terminals. Thus, early minis were designed to interact with mainframes, and this capability has been improved over the years. Current pc systems generally lack the communications hardware/software resources available to minis.

Some of the more advanced 16-bit minis, and many of the superminis, achieve faster processing speeds by employing a special *high-speed buffer,* or *cache,* storage section in the CPU. As noted in Chapter 5, the cache temporarily stores very active data and instructions during processing. Since the cache storage unit is faster than the primary storage section, the processing speed is increased. The capacity of this high-speed buffer typically ranges from 4K to 128K bytes. But it's interesting to note, too, that the newest microprocessor designs now include a small cache unit on the chip.

Because minis have been around longer than personal computers, mini manufacturers have built up larger libraries of applications programs of interest to organizations. More high-level programming languages are likely to be available for minis than for pc's, and mini operating system programs are likely to be more sophisticated.

# MAINFRAME FAMILY MODELS

In the 1960s, when the emphasis was on building larger and faster central computers to handle all the processing needs of an organization, the word "mainframe" was used to mean the same thing as "central processor" or "CPU." Although the words may still be used synonymously, "mainframe" took on an added meaning in the literature of computers and data processing during the 1970s. A computer that's generally *more powerful* than a typical mini is now often called a **mainframe.** Models carrying the mainframe designation vary widely in cost and performance capability. And we've already seen that there's considerable overlap possible in the cost and performance of large minis and small mainframes. The historical development of computers discussed in the reading following Chapter 1 dealt primarily with mainframes.

**Some Characteristics of Typical Mainframes**

A whole series of mainframe models ranging in size from small to very large are typically lumped together under a *family designation* by mainframe manufacturers. It's usually possible to run programs prepared for one machine on other models in the same family with little or no modification. This **software compatibility** between family models makes it easy for users to move up to larger systems in the same family if they outgrow their smaller machines. However, it's usually not as easy to convert programs to a larger system in a different product line, a fact that helps maintain the stability of a mainframe manufacturer's customer base. Unlike

# Mainframe Gallery

Mainframes are available in models that fill rooms—the IBM 4300 series shown above—or that take up only a desktop—the NCR 9300 system shown at the left and below. Regardless of their physical size, mainframes will continue to play a vital role in information processing in the coming years. (Photos courtesy International Business Machines Corporation and NCR Corporation.)

Well over half of all the mainframes installed in the 1970s were IBM System/370 machines. The 370 line consisted of about a dozen models. Although thousands of 370 machines are still in use, IBM is now concentrating its efforts on several newer mainframe families. One family of small- to medium-sized systems—the IBM 4300 series—also has about a dozen models. Another IBM family—the 308X series—currently includes seven large-scale systems. Prices of CPUs in the 4300 series range from about $60,000 to $500,000, while prices for the 308X series processors start at $1.2 million and go to $8.7 million.

Note that these and other figures given in this section don't include the price of peripherals. But for an idea of the cost/performance improvements that have occurred in the last decade, consider this: A medium-sized System/370 model (the 158) with 1 megabyte of primary storage was priced at about $1.6 million in the mid-1970s. A 4300 series processor (the 4341-1) with about the same performance and four times as much storage now costs about $200,000. Other mainframe vendors pictured here can point to similar cost/performance improvements.

## Mainframe Uses and Applications

For years, virtually everything that was done with computers was done on mainframes. Even as late as 1975, 83 percent of the money spent for computers went to buy mainframes. By 1988, however, it's expected that only 30 percent of industry sales will be for these models. Some observers have studied these figures and have concluded that mainframes are becoming obsolete and will be replaced by minis and pc systems. What they fail to notice, though, is that mainframe sales haven't declined. In fact, they've continued to grow—from about $10.6 billion in 1975 to an expected $26 billion in 1988. The confusion results from the fact that sales of smaller systems have also been growing, but at a much faster rate.

Although there are a number of major processing categories that will require mainframe capabilities for an indefinite period, we'll mention just three. The *first* category is the processing of periodic *high-volume batch applications*. Most medium-sized and larger organizations in the country with a history of computer usage have one or more mainframes to prepare thousands (and even millions) of paychecks, invoices, welfare checks, mailing labels, and so on. Mainframes are designed to control the

multiple printers and banks of disk and tape drives that are needed for large-scale batch jobs. A *second* type of application that calls for mainframe capabilities is the *management of very large centralized data bases*. Scores of people in many locations may need access to all or part of the data for update and/or inquiry purposes. The power of a mainframe is needed to control access, interpret queries, and retrieve and update records. And a *third* mainframe use is as the *central host computer in a large DDP network*. The mainframe communicates with, and exercises some control over, smaller satellite processors and workstations. At **Blue** Cross Insurance Company of Virginia, for example, a large mainframe is used for claims processing. Over 200 workstations in hospitals and doctors' offices are used to enter medical claims into the computer. The system prompts users on how to enter claims, notifies them immediately of any errors, and tells them when to expect payment.

Mainframe systems supply the processing power many organizations need to get their work done—running high-volume batch jobs, managing large centralized data bases, or acting as a front-end processor in a large distributed data processing network. (Photos courtesy Social Security Administration, *above;* Honeywell, Inc., *above right;* and Cray Research, Inc., photo by Joe Gianetti, *right.*

personal computers and minis, which are usually purchased, mainframes are often rented or leased.

What was true of the other computer categories we've now considered remains true of mainframe families: Primary and online secondary storage capacities increase as the systems get larger. Furthermore, in the larger mainframe models it's likely that an alternative computer system architecture will be substituted for the **single processor** (or **uniprocessor**) **approach** in design used in smaller machines. For example, several arithmetic-logic and control units may be used in a larger **multiprocessor mainframe** to process several tasks at the same instant in time. A multiprocessor design, in effect, creates a system with two or more CPUs. Also, high-speed cache storage sections with large capacities are routinely used in the more powerful mainframes. The result of these and other features, of course, is that larger mainframes can process applications faster than smaller computers.

Another characteristic that improves their performance is the fact that most of the *smaller* mainframes are basically **32-bit machines** and can manipulate 4-byte words in a single machine cycle. In *larger* mainframes, the length of the data word that can be manipulated in a given instant is increased to 48, 60, or 64 bits, depending on the model. Most mainframes also have large instruction sets that give them the flexibility to automatically operate on from 2 to 8 bytes in the same unit of time. Of course, we've seen that superminis now use a 32-bit design, and 32-bit microprocessor chips are beginning to appear in personal-sized computers. The trend toward cheaper, smaller, and more powerful systems continues unabated!

Mainframe vendors have *much larger* libraries of applications programs that may be of interest to organizations than do other computer manufacturers. Furthermore, most of the applications packages designed in the past by the larger software development firms have been written for mainframe computers. All popular (and some not-so-popular) high-level programming languages are available for mainframes, and their operating system programs are at a very high level of sophistication. Mainframe vendors can also provide customers with a high level of applications design support and maintenance service.

# SUPERCOMPUTER SYSTEMS

As you've probably guessed, **supercomputers** are the most powerful and most expensive computers made. Only a few of these computing monsters are produced each year because only a few organizations need (and can afford) their processing capabilities. But supercomputers are far more important to a nation than their numbers would indicate. They are a national resource. The calculations needed in some scientific research and development areas simply can't be managed without supercomputers. A nation's leadership role in energy, space exploration, medicine, industry, and other critical areas is unlikely to continue if its scientists must use computers that are less powerful than those available to their counterparts in other lands. For example, today's supercomputers aren't fast enough to simulate the

## SUPER COMPUTERS HEAD FOR THE MASS MARKET

A wave of technological change is poised to sweep over the computer industry. Faster and cheaper computers will allow users to do things they can't today—operate a typewriter by voice, for example. Companies and nations alike will face the opportunities and dangers that always accompany a major innovation. The stakes are high: the new technology will affect all information-age businesses, ranging from electronic mail networks to computer manufacturing, which are expected to have worldwide revenues, in today's dollars, of up to $500 billion a year by 1993.

The transformation will be based on one fundamental idea: that the way to speed up computers is to divide the labor among many inexpensive data-processing devices rather than continue the present quest for ever faster single processors made with ever more exotic materials and techniques. Called parallel processing, the new approach is analogous to mass-producing shoes with unskilled labor on assembly lines instead of handcrafting them with skilled workmen one by one. Over the next few years, U.S., Japanese, and European industry and governments will spend some $10 billion on advanced computer research, including parallel processing.

The demand for faster but cheaper computers grows continuously. Sales of "supercomputers"—fast, specialized, handbuilt, and expensive number-crunchers—have been taking off. Cray Research Inc., a Minneapolis company (1983 sales: $170 million), got orders for 25 supercomputers last year vs. 16 in 1982. The burst of sales was ignited by technological advances that made possible deep price cuts—as much as $5 million on a $10-million Cray—and put the machines within the reach of more users.

Aircraft and auto manufacturers have begun to use simulations performed on supercomputers in place of wind tunnels and machines that smash parts to determine their strength and durability. Pharmaceutical companies are using computers to develop new drugs with molecules derived from quantum theory, which predicts how atoms will interact, instead of relying on the random mixing and testing of substances. Oil companies are constructing computerized 3-D models of underground oil and water movements to determine how to exploit oil fields. Digital Productions, a Los Angeles company that turns out feature films and TV commercials, used a Cray to simulate in vivid detail the surfaces of alien planets that appear in an upcoming movie.

—Tom Alexander, "Reinventing the Computer," *Fortune*, March 5, 1984, p. 86. © 1984 Time, Inc. All rights reserved. Photo courtesy Gould, Inc.

airflow around an entire aircraft. Builders of new airplanes must therefore simulate the passage of air around separate pieces of the plane and then combine the results to produce an effective aerodynamic design. Scientists at the National Science Foundation (NSF) believe that the first nation to build a supercomputer capable of simulating the airflow around a complete airplane will be the country that develops planes with superior performance.

Recognizing the importance of supercomputers, Japanese leaders have launched a high-priority national effort to develop by 1989 a machine that will be 1,000 times faster than current United States models. Several responses have been made in the United States to this effort. Research and development consortiums funded by companies in private industry and supported by universities have been created to do basic research. Government agencies such as the Advanced Research Projects Agency of the Defense Department, the NSF, and the National Aeronautics

# Supercomputer Gallery

Cray Research and Control Data Corporation (CDC), two firms located in the Minneapolis/St. Paul area, are the primary builders of supercomputers in the United States. Cray has sold about 55 of its Cray-1 and X-MP models while CDC has installed about 15 of its CYBER 205 systems. In one recent year, Cray sales totaled—are you ready for this?—six systems! But Cray received about $50 million for these half-dozen machines. Cray, CDC, and the Japanese are planning new efforts in the supercomputer field. Cray is building a new Cray-2 model that is one-tenth the size of its current line, and at least six times faster. Control Data Chairman William Norris has announced a new subsidiary—ETA Systems, Inc.—that will concentrate on supercomputers, and the Japanese are expected to offer competitive models in the years ahead.

## Supercomputer Applications

Some of the supercomputers that have been delivered are making top-secret weapons-research calculations for the federal government at the Los Alamos Scientific Laboratory in New Mexico and at the Lawrence Livermore Laboratory in California. (There are five Cray-1s at Los Alamos.) A Cray-1 is providing complex calculations for petroleum and engineering companies at a Kansas City data processing service. Still other Cray-1s are working on weather-forecasting problems at the European Center for Medium Range Weather Forecasts in England and at the National Center for Atmospheric Research in Boulder, Colorado. The National Weather Service has also bought a CYBER 205.

In weather forecasting and in research involving the

Over the past 10 years, electronic design engineers have pushed the state of the art to produce faster and faster computers. Once the sole province of United States firms, advanced supercomputer technology gave the U.S. advantages in, for example, weapons research *(left)*. Now the Japanese are entering the supercomputer market with machines that challenge their American counterparts *(right)*. (Photos courtesy Los Alamos National Laboratory and Toshiba America, Inc., OEM Division)

earth's atmosphere, weather data supplied by a worldwide network of space satellites, airplanes, and ground stations are fed into supercomputers. These data are analyzed by a series of computer programs to arrive at forecasts. Although current programs certainly provide forecasts that are generally more accurate than unaided human guesses, there's still room for considerable improvement. It's not that scientists don't understand the principles involved well enough to be able to prepare programs that *could* provide much better forecasts. Rather, the problem is that even with the power of a Cray or CDC machine, the thousands of variables involved cannot now be evaluated to the satisfaction of scientists in the time available for forecasting. Nobody cares if a computer produces a storm warning hours after the storm has hit. In short, the current forecast programs being run on supercomputers are crude models of what meteorologists would use if much more powerful computers were available. This is just another incentive for supercomputer builders to make ever-larger machines.

But not all supercomputer applications involve serious scientific work. Digital Productions Inc., a Hollywood filmmaker, uses a Cray X-MP to produce computer-generated images that can be incorporated into its movies. When smaller machines were used, it took Digital Productions about a year to produce the images needed to fill a 2-minute strip of film. Now they are able to produce 4 minutes of film each month and thus substantially compress the time needed to produce a feature-length movie.

Today's supercomputers can perform in hours simulations that only a few years ago took weeks to complete. But users continue to devise tasks more complex than even the fastest computers can readily handle. (Photos courtesy Cray Research, Inc., by Joe Gianetti, and Control Data Corporation)

and Space Administration have taken renewed interest in supercomputer projects. And conferences, such as the one sponsored late in 1983 by the National Security Agency and Los Alamos National Laboratory, have been called to allow the exchange of views between supercomputer makers and users.

**Some Characteristics of Supercomputers**

Since supercomputers are designed to process complex scientific applications, the computational speed of the system is most important. To maximize the speed of computations, each address location in a supercomputer holds 64 bits of information. Thus, in a single machine cycle, two 64-bit data words can be added together. The **cycle time**—the time required to execute a basic operation—may be as low as 4 nanoseconds (billionths of a second). That's about six times faster than the largest mainframes considered in the last section. One of today's supercomputers has the computing capability of approximately 40,000 IBM Personal Computers. And as we've seen, efforts are underway in the United States and Japan to produce a machine with the power of 40 *million* IBM PCs.

The entire primary storage section of some supercomputers makes exclusive use of the types of expensive components that are generally reserved *only* for a high-speed cache section in less powerful machines. This usage, combined with the large number of circuit chips required to process the large (64-bit) fixed-length words, makes a supercomputer very expensive. Prices range from about $4 million to about $15 million.

## Feedback and Review 9-1

You've learned about real computer systems ranging in size from small minis to huge supercomputers in this chapter. To test and reinforce your understanding of the material, answer the following true-false questions by placing a T or F in the space provided:

___**1.** A recently introduced minicomputer can often do the work of an earlier small mainframe at a much lower cost.

___**2.** Computer experts agree on the definition of a minicomputer.

___**3.** The computer classifications used in this chapter are the standards of the computer industry.

___**4.** A minicomputer can have more processing capability than a mainframe model.

___**5.** A mainframe processor is generally placed on a single silicon chip.

___**6.** A supermini is designed specifically for use in supermarkets.

___**7.** The first 32-bit superminis were introduced in the mid-1960s.

___**8.** Mini systems are designed to simultaneously handle the processing needs of multiple users.

___**9.** Output from a mini is not available in humanly readable form.

___**10.** It's expected that the annual sales of minis will continue to grow for the next decade.

___**11.** Minicomputer usage is limited to less than 500 applications.

___**12.** Many minicomputers in service are 16-bit machines, but 32-bit minis are also common.

___**13.** Minicomputers can't use high-speed buffer storage components and are thus always slower than mainframe models.

___**14.** Minicomputers often serve as satellite processors to a larger central host computer.

___**15.** Mainframe models are typically given a family designation by their makers, and they can range in size from small to very large.

___**16.** Mainframes may have multiprocessor components that permit several tasks to be processed at the same instant in time.

___**17.** Most small mainframes are 32-bit machines, but many larger systems can manipulate 48, 60, or 64 bits depending on the model.

___**18.** IBM and two other vendors are the only ones that produce mainframes.

___**19.** Mainframes are becoming obsolete and will soon be replaced by minis and personal computers.

___**20.** Mainframes are poorly equipped to process high-volume batch applications.

___**21.** Finland has launched a high-priority national effort to build supercomputers.

___**22.** The Cray-1 is a micro that fits on a chip.

___**23.** Thousands of supercomputers are now in use.

___**24.** Supercomputers are usually designed to process accounting applications.

___**25.** You thought you were never going to get to the end of this review section.

# LOOKING BACK

**1.** A minicomputer is a small general-purpose machine ranging in price from about $2,500 to $75,000. There's considerable overlap between small minis and large pc systems. Minis were first developed in the 1960s to fill the gaps left by the bigger and faster central computers in an organization. Most minis produced during the 1970s are 16-bit machines, but 32-bit superminis now share the market with the 16-bit models.

**2.** Representative small, medium-scale, and supermini systems have been identified in the chapter. Minis have always been used for specialized control purposes and for general data processing applications. Organizations also use thousands of them today as satellite processors in DDP networks.

**3.** A mainframe computer is generally more powerful (and more expensive) than a mini, but again, considerable overlap may occur between large superminis and small mainframes. Mainframes, ranging in size from small to very large, are typically lumped together under family designations.

**4.** Representative mainframe families have been identified in the chapter. Most small mainframes are basically 32-bit machines, but larger systems may manipulate 48, 60, or 64 bits at a time depending on the model. Larger libraries of business and scientific programs are available for mainframe computers than for smaller systems. Mainframes are used to process high-volume batch applications, to manage large data bases, to act as central host computers in distributed systems, and to perform thousands of other tasks.

**5.** Supercomputers are the largest, fastest, and most expensive computing monsters in existence. Although they are few in number, supercomputers are a national resource because they are designed to process important and complex scientific applications. Cray Research and Control Data Corporation are the primary U.S. builders of supercomputers, but the Japanese are expected to be future competitors.

## KEY TERMS AND CONCEPTS

**minicomputer 232**
**16-bit machines 233**
**supermini computers 233**
**distributed data processing (DDP)**
  **networks 234**

**host computer 234**
**satellite (or node) processors 234**
**mainframe computer 236**
**software compatibility 236**
**single processor (or uniprocessor)**
  **approach 239**

**multiprocessor mainframe 239**
**32-bit machine 239**
**supercomputers 239**
**cycle time 243**

## TOPICS FOR REVIEW AND DISCUSSION

**1.** *(a)* What is a minicomputer? *(b)* Why were minis developed? *(c)* How may minis be used?

**2.** *(a)* What is a mainframe computer? *(b)* How may mainframes be used?

**3.** Give four examples of representative *(a)* minicomputers and *(b)* mainframe computers.

**4.** Identify and discuss three characteristics of *(a)* minicomputers, *(b)* mainframe computers, and *(c)* supercomputers.

**5.** "A large mainframe is generally software-compatible with the smaller computers in the same family." Explain this statement.

**6.** *(a)* What is a supercomputer? *(b)* How does a supercomputer differ from other machines? *(c)* How are supercomputers used?

**7.** "Supercomputers represent a national resource." Discuss this statement.

## PROJECT TO LOOK INTO

**1.** Several manufacturers of minis and mainframes are identified in this chapter, but there are other suppliers competing in these markets. Go to the library and identify one mainframe and two minicomputer vendors not mentioned here. Write a brief report describing their products.

## ANSWERS TO FEEDBACK AND REVIEW SECTION

**9-1**

| | | |
|---|---|---|
| 1. T | 10. T | 19. F |
| 2. F | 11. F | 20. F |
| 3. F | 12. T | 21. F |
| 4. T | 13. F | 22. F |
| 5. F | 14. T | 23. F |
| 6. F | 15. T | 24. F |
| 7. F | 16. T | 25. T |
| 8. T | 17. T | |
| 9. F | 18. F | |

# Linking Micros to Mainframes

When they get their first personal computers at the office, many novices assume that they'll be able to tap corporate files to do department budgeting, evaluate sales people, calculate returns on assets or track trends.

But many personal computers can't communicate adequately with the main company computers. Mary Adair, a purchasing administrator at Polaroid Corp., has been using an Apple computer to develop graphs showing what Polaroid spends on such items as fuel oil, utilities and consultants. Data on all those matters are contained in the company's mainframe, but she can't hook into it. Instead, she must use printouts from the mainframe and type the numbers she needs into her Apple.

Her personal computer can communicate with the mainframe, but it doesn't have the software that would let it easily obtain the particular information she needs from the vast amount stored by Polaroid.

To deal with gaps like that, corporate data-processing departments and independent software companies are starting to produce programs that will link personal computers and mainframes, giving more people access to the reservoir of information about customers, suppliers and employees that every company accumulates. Instead of having to ask a programmer to get information that's needed, a user will be able to go directly to the source.

## Private Corporate Data

Many personal-computer users already can easily hook up with commercial data bases. It is the private corporate data that is unavailable. Data-processing experts, though, predict that nearly all corporate personal computers will be linked to mainframes within a few years. "I don't know that there's a topic commanding more attention," says

William Rosser, who studies the personal-computer market for Gartner Group, a Stamford, Conn., research firm.

The links may produce an entirely new set of problems, however.

A data-processing manager worries about "people messing up the corporate data base" if they can easily send files into it. Security problems also grow when personal computers are hooked into mainframes. An easily concealed computer disk could hold a company's computer list or other valuable information.

And greater communications capabilities will ultimately increase the cost of personal computers to a company. While the basic machine may cost only $5,000, extra demands on the mainframe, additional software and more data-processing-department time could increase the cost to more than $20,000, Gartner Group estimates.

Nevertheless, experts agree the links are coming. "They make all that information on the mainframe more useful and powerful than it has ever been," says Betty Feezor, manager of personal-computer products for Management Science America, Inc., a software company in Atlanta that sells a link product. . . .

Links between individuals and mainframes will change the way businesses deal with information and handle computer tasks. Today, at most companies, obtaining specific information from a mainframe requires a user to ask the data-processing department to write a special program. "Traditionally, the data-processing department says that it would take six months and $100,000, and the person gives up," says Ronald G. Parkes, an assistant vice president of European American Bank in New York. He is studying ways to connect the bank's 80 personal computers with its mainframe.

A micro-mainframe link was developed to automate the distribution network of a food-processing firm by handling the administrative and accounting needs of distributors and communicating with the mainframe at corporate headquarters.

With a personal computer linked to software in a mainframe that responds to questions, an employee can get the information himself. William Harris, director of management information systems at Kendall Corp., a unit of Colgate-Palmolive Co., says he hopes to be a pilot user of a link program being developed by Cullinet Software of Westwood, Mass., because he thinks it will be the best way to reduce a 10-year backlog of user requests for pro-grams. "Within five years, instead of our data-processing department doing 90% of the programming, it will do 30% and end users will do 70%," he predicts.

—William M. Bulkeley, "Firms Linking More Users to Mainframes," *The Wall Street Journal,* Sept. 19, 1983, pp. 1 and 41. Reprinted by permission of *The Wall Street Journal,* © Dow Jones & Company 1983. All Rights Reserved. Photo courtesy Honeywell, Inc.

# Systems and

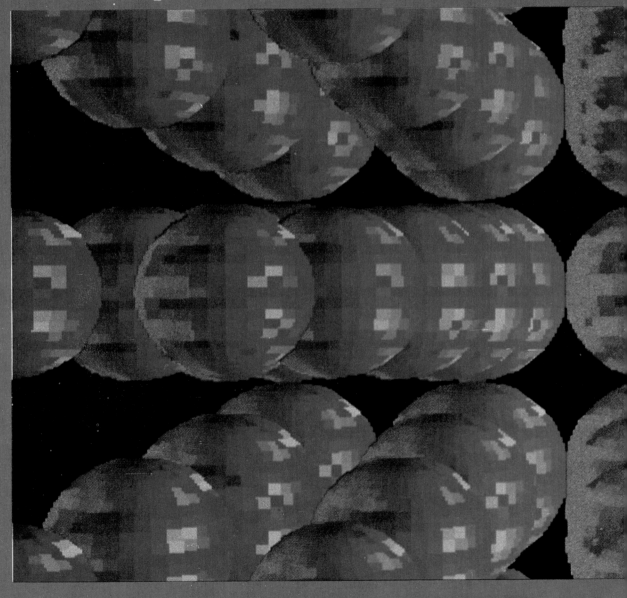

# Software

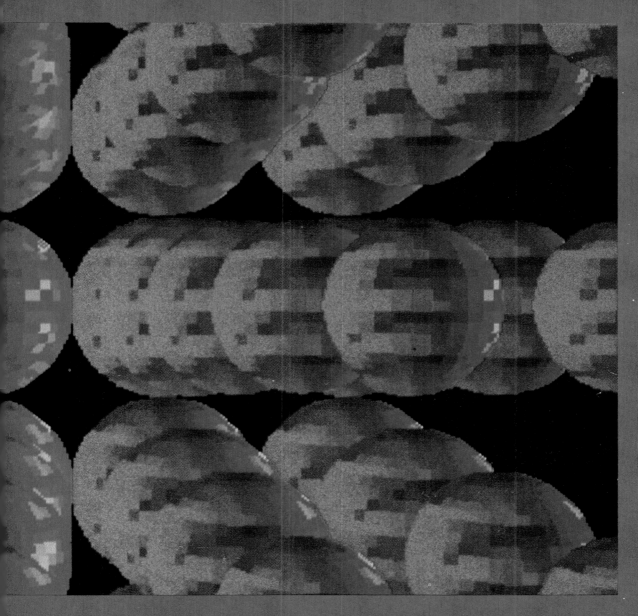

# module 3

An information system is a group of integrated elements—e.g., people, procedures, equipment—working together to support decision making and operations within an organization or in a personal setting. In this Systems and Software Module, we'll begin with two chapters that give examples of some real systems that people rely on for the information they need. We'll then take a general look at the development of computer-based information systems, including operating system and data base management system software packages, and management information systems.

The chapters included in this Systems and Software Module are:

10. Data Communications Systems and Distributed Data Processing Networks
11. Word Processing and Electronic Mail/Message Systems
12. System Analysis, Design, and Implementation Considerations
13. System Software Packages: Operating Systems and Data Base Management Systems
14. Management Information Systems

# chapter 10

# Data Communications Systems and Distributed Data Processing Networks

### Network

Interest in personal computers has usually focused on the individual's use of a so-called stand-alone machine. But within a few years, this may be less important than the fact that users around the country can be linked together over telephone lines in a network.

What's the advantage over simply making a call? Voice transmission is excellent for conveying emotional states, or limited amounts of hard data. But if you have ever listened as someone described a graphic image over the phone, you quickly realized that a picture is worth much more than a thousand words. And if anyone has tried to engage you in a complex discussion involving a lot of text or a great many figures, you probably found yourself postponing the conversation until you had a copy of the information in front of you. Furthermore, telephone calls must be arranged at a time suited to both parties. And you cannot just "put information out there"; you must call a particular person.

Computer networks have none of these disadvantages. You can transmit text or graphics at your convenience; the receiver can review the information at his. You can put information out onto a network "bulletin board" and whoever is interested (including people you don't know) can pick it up and use it, and communicate back to you.

Computer conferencing and specialized user groups of all sorts are springing up. Small computers may ultimately be as ubiquitous as telephones, because they are as useful as telephones—for communicating with other people.

—From *Electronic Life* by Michael Crichton. Copyright © 1983 by Michael Crichton. Reprinted by permission of Alfred A. Knopf, Inc. Photo reproduced with permission of AT&T.

Just as the component parts of a particular hardware system may be systems in their own right, information systems are built of smaller component systems. Data communications is an integral part of many information systems. And while communications systems date back to the beginning of history, we'll focus in this chapter on rapidly emerging data communications systems that are vital to any modern society. The information in this chapter will enable you to:

- Understand the converging computing/communications setting

- Describe the data transmission techniques and channels, and identify the types of organizations that provide these services for groups and individuals

- Outline the components used to coordinate a complex computing/communications network

- Give specific examples of information systems supported by data communications

- Present the characteristics of distributed data processing networks, and give examples of these types of networks

## Chapter Outline

# THE COMPUTING/COMMUNICATIONS SETTING

You've become familiar with the term direct-access processing in many earlier chapters. This type of processing, as shown in Figure 10-1, generally involves online terminals located at or near the data sources, and these sources can be far away from the CPU. To cite just a few examples, teller and point-of-sale terminals are spotted in locations away from computers; airline, car rental, and hotel reservation systems have thousands of terminals located many miles from their CPUs; factory data entry stations may not be near a processor; and intelligent terminals and subordinate minicomputers may be great distances away from a central host computer. **Data communication** refers to the means and methods whereby data are transferred between such processing locations. It makes possible the I/O operations that take place between remote online terminals and CPUs. It's the ''glue'' that permits a direct interactive bond between the people at these terminals and the central processing systems.

## Data Communications Background

There's nothing new about data communications. The ancient Greek runner carrying the message of victory on the plains of Marathon inspired a present-day athletic event. Pony Express riders carried messages and won the admiration of a nation in the brief period before they were replaced by telegraph service. For 30 years, telegraph companies enjoyed a monopoly on the use of electrical impulses to transmit data between distant stations. But in 1876, Alexander Graham Bell demonstrated that electrical signals could be used to transmit voice messages along telephone lines, and so a second data communications, or **telecommunications,** channel was established.

In the 75 years after the introduction of the telephone, a complex network of telecommunications systems was established to link locations throughout the world. The first linkage of computing and communication devices occurred in 1940 when

Figure 10-1 Two types of transaction-oriented processing: *(left)* hotel reservation system; *(right)* shop control at a factory. (Photos courtesy Bunker Ramo Information Systems and NCR Corporation)

Dr. George Stibitz used telegraph lines to send data from Dartmouth College in New Hampshire to a Bell Laboratories calculator in New York City. But it wasn't until the late 1950s that the computing/communications linkage began in earnest. Telegraph lines were used first to connect teleprinter terminals with computers, but telephone lines were quickly pressed into service. An early large-scale business application was the Sabre passenger reservation system developed in the late 1950s and early 1960s by American Airlines and IBM. Hundreds of scattered terminals were linked to a central processing center. Communications usage has grown steadily since then. Today, most minis and larger machines are able to communicate with outlying terminals. And with available attachments, most personal computers can use telephone lines to access the data bases maintained by information retrieval services.

## The Converging Computing/ Communications Picture

Twenty years ago computing capability was obtained from computer vendors, and communications service was supplied by telecommunications firms. The communications firms used some computer-controlled message-switching devices to improve their services, and the computer vendors offered limited communications packages to sell data processing services. But it wasn't difficult to differentiate between the two groups.

As the years passed, however, computer vendors began to offer a larger package of communications services to their customers while telecommunications suppliers furnished more computing resources to those who used their networks. Prior to this convergence of computing and communications technologies, government regulation of the many organizations that offered computing and communications services was reasonably clear. An *unregulated* legal status applied to organizations whose communications offerings were only incidental to their competitive computing services. And a *regulated* legal status generally applied to firms whose data processing services were only incidental to their furnishing of communications channels. But as many "hybrid" organizations arose to offer expanded computing and communications services, regulatory status became an uncertain—and often heated—issue (Figure 10-2).

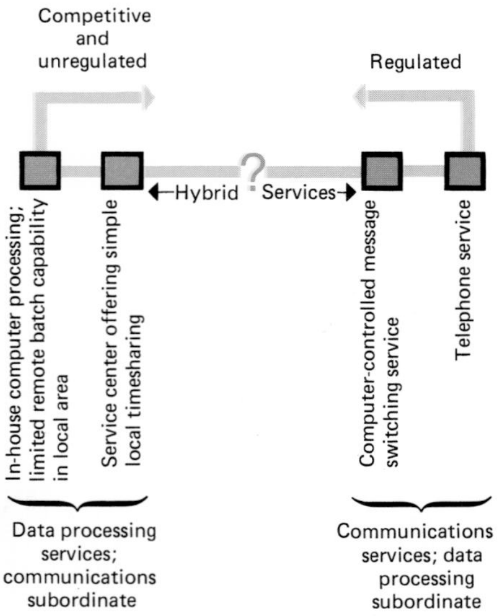

Attempting to keep up with technological advances and perform regulatory functions, Federal Communications Commission (FCC) actions served to pit rich and powerful organizations in the unregulated computing industry against equally rich and powerful regulated communications groups. Federal antitrust lawsuits brought against the largest firms in each sector—IBM and American Telephone and Telegraph Company (AT&T)—dragged on for years.

Recent FCC rulings tend to favor a greater degree of unregulated competition in the evolving data communications field. Settlements were also reached in the antitrust suits. The suit against IBM was dropped. And after agreeing to split off its regulated Bell Telephone subsidiaries into separate companies, AT&T has now entered the competitive and unregulated computing/communications environment.

Today computers are an essential part of a modern communications network, and such a network is vital to the operation of many modern computer-based information systems. Many of the same electronic circuit chips are now used in both computing and communications devices. Computer vendors can offer a large package of communications services, and they are committing more research and devel-

**Figure 10-2** As computing and communications technologies converged, the issue of government regulation in the data communications field became unclear.

Competitive and unregulated — Regulated

←Hybrid Services→

In-house computer processing; limited remote batch capability in local area

Service center offering simple local timesharing

Computer-controlled message switching service

Telephone service

Data processing services; communications subordinate

Communications services; data processing subordinate

opment funds to communications technology. Not to be outdone, suppliers who formerly concentrated on telecommunications equipment are now offering storage chips, workstations, software, and many other products.

Several new terms have been coined to reflect this merger of computing and communications technology. (The French use the word "telematique," the English use "telematics," and "compunications" has been suggested by a Harvard professor.) As more personal computers are attached to communications networks, and as more of the equipment in an organizational setting is linked together by the glue of data communications, the distinctions between computing and communications will become even more blurred.

# DATA COMMUNICATIONS CONCEPTS

In a simple data communications system, terminals and other remote I/O devices are linked with one or more central processors to capture input data and receive output information. Connecting equipment and software, sometimes referred to as **interface elements,** are used to bridge the different physical and operating environments that exist between I/O devices and central processors. And a variety of data transmission channels are available to carry data from one location to another. In the next few pages we'll concentrate on some interface elements, data transmission channels, and related data communications concepts. You'll find detailed discussions of the I/O devices and central processors found in a data communications environment in Chapters 5 through 9 of the Hardware Module.

## Data Transmission Techniques

You'll notice that an interface element called a modem is shown at *each* end of the data transmission channels in Figure 10-3. A **modem** is a *mo*dulation-*dem*odulation device that converts the discrete stream of digital "on-off" electrical pulses used by computing equipment into the type of continuously variable analog wave patterns used to transmit the human voice. Digital pulses cannot effectively travel any distance over the transmission network that was designed years ago for voice communications. Thus, a modem is needed to *modulate* or convert the digital pulses into analog wave patterns when telephone lines are used to transmit data. For example, when data from a terminal are sent over telephone lines to a CPU, a modem is needed at the transmitting end to convert the digital pulses into analog signals. And another modem is needed at the receiving end to *demodulate* or recover the digital data from the transmitted signal. Of course, when output from the CPU is sent back to the remote site the process is reversed. The modem at the CPU location modulates the output, and the modem at the remote location demodulates the transmitted signal.

The I/O equipment shown at the remote station in Figure 10-3 is not likely to be moved, and so the modem is "hard-wired" to this equipment and is referred to as a **direct-connect modem.** Some newer direct-connect modems have built-in microprocessors, storage chips, and specialized communications chips. These **intelligent modems** can be programmed to automatically perform dialing, answering,

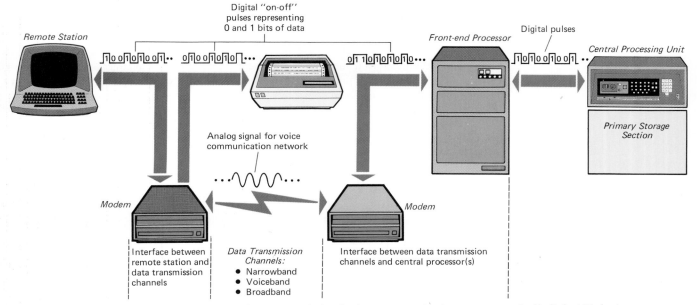

Digital "on-off" pulses representing 0 and 1 bits of data

Remote Station

Front-end Processor

Digital pulses

Central Processing Unit

Primary Storage Section

Analog signal for voice communication network

Modem

Modem

Interface between remote station and data transmission channels

Data Transmission Channels:
- Narrowband
- Voiceband
- Broadband

Interface between data transmission channels and central processor(s)

**Figure 10-3** A simple data communications system typically links I/O devices at remote locations with one or more central processors. Interface elements such as modems and front-end processors are used to bridge and control the different data communications environments. Modems are used to permit the system to switch back and forth from computer digital data to analog signals that can be transmitted on voice communication lines. A front-end processor is a computer used to monitor and control the data transmission channels and the data being transmitted. In this system, data to be sent to a CPU are entered into a workstation through a keyboard. On command from the operator, the data in digital form are sent in a serial (one bit at a time) fashion to a nearby modem to be converted into an analog signal. The converted data are then transmitted over telephone lines to another modem located near the CPU. This modem converts the analog signal back to a digital form. The data in digital form are then sent to a front-end processor which may check them for possible errors and then temporarily store them or route them to the CPU for immediate processing. The same route is followed when output information is sent from the CPU back to the remote location. The entire data communications activity is under the control of program instructions stored in communications processors and/or CPUs.

and disconnecting functions. But not all modems are hard-wired. If you've read Chapter 6, you'll recall that large numbers of portable terminals are now used by salespersons, managers, engineers, and others to communicate with distant CPUs. A special type of modem called an **acoustic coupler** is used in these situations to provide the necessary interface. The acoustic coupler is attached to (or built into) a portable terminal, and a standard telephone handset is then usually placed in rubber cups located on the coupler. The digital pulses produced by the terminal are converted into audible tones that are picked up by the handset receiver. The signals from these tones are then sent to the CPU location where another modem converts them back to digital pulses. Figure 10-4 shows how direct-connect modems and acoustic couplers can be used to effect a linkage between distant personal computers.

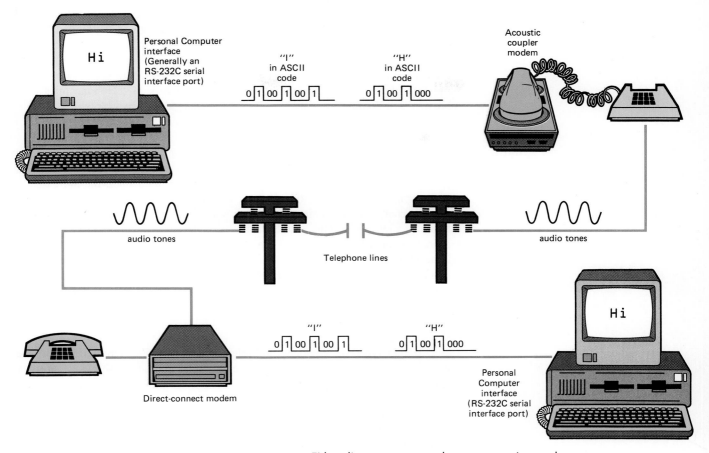

**Figure 10-4** Either direct-connect modems or acoustic couplers can be used to link personal computers. Data are transmitted as a serial stream of bits using the ASCII code (Chapter 5). An RS-232C serial interface connection (Chapter 8) is generally used to link the personal computers to the modems. In addition to the data bits, each character transmitted may also be accompanied by a "start" bit and a "stop" bit. When start and stop bits are used to coordinate communications, an *asynchronous* transmission mode is being used. *Synchronous* transmissions are also possible through the use of special codes and equipment that carefully time the data flow to the receiving computer. Start and stop bits for each character are then unnecessary. Most pc systems use asynchronous transmission because the necessary communications equipment is simpler and less expensive. If asynchronous transmission is used, 10 bits may be sent over the telephone lines for each character transmitted. Data may be transmitted at various speeds. Some standard rates are 110, 300, 600, 1200, 2400, 4800, and 9600 *baud*. For most pc users, the baud rate is effectively the same as "bits per second." Thus, a 300 baud transmission rate gives 30 characters per second, while a 1200 baud rate represents 120 characters/second. The slower baud rates (1200 and under) are normally used with pc systems.

The need to transmit large volumes of computer data over long distances has developed in a relatively short period of time. Organizations in the United States, Japan, and most of Europe are currently making large investments to build communications networks designed for *all-digital transmission*. Such networks eliminate the need for modems because analog signals aren't used. Until these systems are more fully developed, however, the vast public network of telephone lines (and modems) will continue to handle much of the transmission workload.

## Data Transmission Channels

Figure 10-3 indicates that the **data transmission channels** or "highways" used to carry data from one location to another are classified into narrowband, voiceband, and broadband categories. The wider the bandwidth of a channel, the more data it can transmit in a given period of time. *Telegraph lines,* for example, are **narrowband** channels, and their transmission rate is slow [from about 5 to 30 characters per second (cps)]. This is adequate to directly accept data being keyed into a terminal. Standard *telephone lines* are **voiceband** channels that have a wider bandwidth. They are able to speed up the transmission rate to over 1,000 cps.

In many cases, a terminal operator at a remote location uses the regular dial-up telephone switching network, calls a number at the CPU location, and enters the data. When data volume is sufficient, however, it's often more economical for an organization to acquire a **dedicated** or **leased line** which can be used for both voice and data purposes.

Different types of telephone and telegraph transmission circuits can also be selected to meet the needs of an organization. As Figure 10-5 shows, a **simplex** circuit permits data to flow in *only one* direction. A terminal connected to such a circuit is either a *send-only* or a *receive-only* device. Simplex circuits are seldom used because a return path is generally needed to send acknowledgement, control, or error signals. Thus, a **half-duplex** line that can *alternately* send and receive data, or a **full-duplex** connection that can *simultaneously* transmit and receive, is usually used. A full-duplex line is faster since it avoids the delay that occurs in a half-duplex circuit each time the direction of transmission is changed.

**Broadband** channels are used when large data volumes must be transmitted at high speeds (over 100,000 cps is possible). Coaxial cables, microwave circuits, and communications satellites are commonly used to provide these channels. **Coaxial cables** are groups of specially wrapped and insulated wire lines that are able to transmit data at high rates. **Microwave systems** use very high frequency radio signals to transmit data through space. When microwave facilities are used, the data may be transmitted along a ground route by repeater stations that are located, on the average, about 25 miles apart. The data signals are received, amplified, and retransmitted by each station along a route. Or, the data may be beamed to a **communications satellite** that acts as a reflector by accepting signals from one point on earth and returning the same signals to some other point on earth. The satellite appears from the earth to be a stationary target for the microwave signals because it's precisely positioned 22,300 miles above the equator with an orbit speed that matches the earth's rotation. Dozens of satellites are now in orbit to handle international and domestic data, voice, and video communications. Figure 10-6 lists some of these satellite systems.

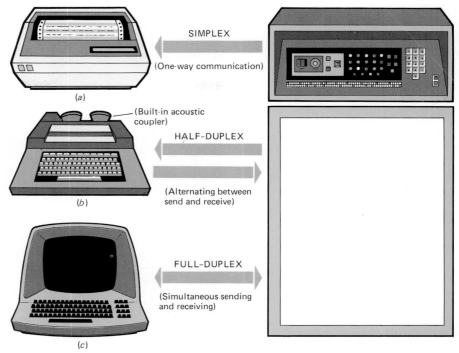

SIMPLEX

(One-way communication)

(a)

(Built-in acoustic coupler)

HALF-DUPLEX

(Alternating between send and receive)

(b)

FULL-DUPLEX

(Simultaneous sending and receiving)

(c)

Figure 10-5 Data transmission circuits. (a) A simplex line permits communication in only one direction. That direction may be from the CPU to an I/O device as shown here, or it may be from a terminal to a CPU. (b) A half-duplex circuit permits data to be sent in both directions, but not at the same time. (c) A full-duplex connection does permit the simultaneous sending and receiving of data.

Existing broadband channels are expensive and are generally used only by large organizations. However, it's expected that the rapidly maturing use of **fiber optic-cables** and **laser technology** will soon permit huge amounts of data to be routinely transmitted at the speed of light through tiny threads of glass or plastic such as those shown at the beginning of this chapter. Teamed with a laser, a single glass fiber the size of a human hair may be used to transmit across the country in a single second all the characters in dozens of books the size of this one. Since thousands of these fibers can be packaged in a single cable, the future cost of broadband transmission capability should be within the reach of small organizations and individuals. It's expected that by 1990 30 percent of the metropolitan transmissions in the United States will be over fiber-optic links.

**Data Communications Service Organizations**

The data transmission channels that we've just examined are furnished by a number of data communications organizations. You're familiar, of course, with the large public telephone and telegraph networks offered for use by **common carriers.** These carriers include the local and regional facilities of the seven ''Bell Telephone'' operating companies, the long-distance network of the AT&T Communications division (formerly the Long-Lines Division), and the networks maintained by General Telephone and Electronics and Western Union.

# INTERNATIONAL

**INTELSAT system.** This International Telecommunications Satellite Consortium includes about 130 member nations on six continents. INTELSAT is headquartered in Washington D.C., which is also the home of the Communications Satellite Corporation (COMSAT), an organization that was chartered by Congress in 1962 to be the United States representative to INTELSAT. COMSAT performs a management function for INTELSAT. Beginning with Early Bird in 1965, several generations of satellites have now been launched by INTELSAT, and these now form a global communications system that accounts for a major proportion of all long-distance international communications.

# DOMESTIC

**RCA Americom system.** The first to offer domestic satellite service, RCA has several SATCOM satellites in orbit. Major transmitting/receiving stations are located in large cities from New York to California.

**Western Union system.** The first satellite in Western Union's Westar system was launched in 1974. Several more have now been placed in orbit, and additional "Advanced Westar" satellites are now planned. Western Union has major ground stations in several cities and, of course, a nationwide network of telegraph lines.

**American Telephone & Telegraph system.** AT&T currently leases several COMSTAR satellites from COMSAT. The system also plans to launch its own satellites.

**General Telephone and Electronics system.** GTE also has access to COMSTAR satellites and has plans to launch its own units.

**Satellite Business Systems.** SBS is likely to be a major force in future data communications. Developed by IBM, Aetna Life and Casualty Insurance Company, and COMSAT at a cost of $400 million, SBS provides all-digital transmission services at very high speeds. SBS began operations in 1981 after a successful satellite launch late in 1980.

**American Satellite Company.** Jointly owned by Fairchild Industries and Continental Telephone Company, American Satellite provides high-speed, all-digital transmission services. It leases satellite capacity from Western Union, owns a 20 percent interest in the existing Westar system, and has contracted for 50 percent ownership of the Advanced Westar satellites.

**Future Participants.** Several other firms such as Hughes Communications and Southern Pacific Communications Corporation have received FCC approval to enter the domestic market.

Figure 10-6 Satellite data transmission systems. (Photo courtesy Western Union Corporation)

In addition to these common carriers that offer a broad range of facilities, there are also **specialized common carriers** whose public networks are often restricted to a more limited number of services. Included in the specialized carrier category are several of the satellite-using organizations listed in Figure 10-6 as well as:

■ *MCI Communications Corporation.* MCI is a long-distance carrier that employs microwave, fiber-optic, and satellite facilities to serve business users. It offers dedicated leased lines that are arranged exclusively for data transmission. It also offers long-distance voice communications between selected domestic cities, and has acquired Western Union International Inc. to gain entry into the international communications market.

■ *Southern Pacific Communications Corporation.* A subsidiary of the railroad company, the original SPC network followed the right-of-way of the tracks from San Francisco through Dallas. SPC now offers a nation-wide private line service to 80 metropolitan areas. Microwave stations and broadband cables are used, and a future satellite is planned.

■ *ITT World Communications.* ITT Worldcom offers long-distance circuits between 88 cities in the United States. Services between the United States and other countries are also provided.

Another type of data communications service organization is the **value-added carrier.** This type of carrier offers specialized services, but it may not have its own transmission facilities. For example, GTE Telenet and Tymnet, Inc., both have computer networks that receive customer data coming in over telephone lines. These data are temporarily stored and organized into "packets" of characters. These packets are then computer-routed and transmitted at high speed over dedi-cated common carrier channels to Telenet and Tymnet offices near the final data destination. At these offices, data in the packets are reassembled into the complete message for transmission to the final destination (Figure 10-7). The transmission cost of a **value-added network (VAN)** is frequently less than directly utilizing common carrier channels, which are often less efficient. Telenet and Tymnet are also sometimes referred to as **packet-switching networks,** and each serves over 250 cities in more than 35 countries. The Uninet system of United Telecom Com-munications Inc. is another VAN that serves over 200 cities in the United States.

Finally, there are data communications organizations that can provide a wealth of on-demand information services to *people at home.* Customers of these organiza-tions use special terminals with their TV sets and/or personal computers to receive the information requested. Two types of services—teletext and videotext—may be

**Figure 10-7** When packet switching is used, the packets of data originating at one source can be efficiently routed through different network lines. The pack-ets are then reassembled in their original order when they reach their destination. (Adapted from John G. Posa, "Phone Net Going Digital," *High Technology,* May 1983, p. 45.)

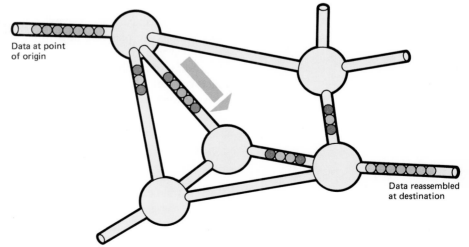

Data at point of origin

Data reassembled at destination

This videotex home information system links home video terminals to computerized data banks providing information ranging from stock market reports and news to theater reviews and advertising. The system can also be used for shopping and banking from home. (Photo reproduced with permission of AT&T)

received. A **teletext system** continuously transfers information in one direction only, and the information is generally received on a TV set. An example of teletext usage is the closed-caption system supported by some television networks that displays words on a TV screen so that hearing-impaired viewers can follow the program. A **videotex system** is one that (1) stores a vast amount of graphic and alphanumeric information at a central computer facility, (2) receives customer requests for stored information over telephone lines and other channels, and (3) retrieves the requested information and forwards it electronically to customers equipped to receive it. Videotex is thus an *interactive* (two-way), graphics-rich service that permits users to select what they want. Predictions are that videotex home information networks will experience explosive growth in the next decade, and many large organizations are planning now to participate in this growth.

But if you've read Chapter 8, you'll recall that personal computer users can already transmit and receive electronic mail messages and can participate in many other videotex services through the facilities of personal computing/communications networks. Included among these networks are:

■ **The Source.** This is a network of Source Telecomputing Corporation, a subsidiary of *Reader's Digest*. Its Source Mail service allows an individual to use his or her personal computer to exchange messages with any other Source subscriber. Instant access to over 1,000 other information and communications services is available. A $100 one-time subscription fee is charged, and an hourly hookup rate is levied that varies according to the time of day. Transmission is over local telephone lines and the GTE Telenet and Tymnet value-added networks.

■ *CompuServe Information Service.* CompuServe is owned by H&R Block Inc., the income tax service firm. It's similar to The Source, offering an electronic mail system and access to scores of large data bases. (A detailed description of what's available from The Source and CompuServe would fill up the rest of this book!) Subscriptions to the service are sold at many computer stores, and subscribers may hook into the network by using readily available software. A variable hourly hookup fee is charged. Transmission is over local telephone lines and the Tymnet network.

■ *Dow Jones News/Retrieval.* This service, offered by the publisher of *The Wall Street Journal,* gives subscribers business and economic news, historical and current stock market quotations, and other investment information.

You can take a closer look at some other representative videotex systems in the reading found at the end of this chapter.

**Coordinating the Data Communications Environment**

The simple data communications system shown in Figure 10-3 was typical of the types used in the late 1960s, and it's still appropriate for many organizations. But the data communications environment has changed rapidly since then. As Figure 10-8 indicates, much larger computing/communications networks are now in service, and the coordination required for efficient network use is complex. Such networks may have hundreds of terminals and many small processors located at dozens of dispersed sites. These sites, in turn, may be linked by different transmission channels to larger host computers. The task of network designers is to select and coordinate the network components so that the necessary data are moved to the right place, at the right time, with a minimum of errors, and at the lowest possible cost.

**Communications Processors.** Figure 10-8 shows that a number of **communications processors** (typically micro- or minicomputers) are used by network designers to achieve their goals. These processors are used for the following purposes:

1. *Remote concentration of messages.* The **remote concentrator** reduces transmission costs by receiving terminal input from many low-speed lines and then concentrating and transmitting a compressed and smooth stream of data on a higher-speed and more efficient transmission channel (Figure 10-9). Although faster communications channels are more expensive, they can do more work, and thus the cost per character transmitted may well be reduced. Devices called **multiplexers** also perform this concentration function. Multiplexers are less expensive than concentrators, but many of the earlier ones weren't programmable and thus didn't have the flexibility of concentrators. However, microprocessor-equipped multiplexers have been introduced that perform much like concentrators.

2. *Message switching.* The **message switcher** receives and analyzes data messages from points in the network, determines the destination and the proper routing, and then forwards the messages to other network locations. If necessary, a message may be stored until an appropriate outgoing line is available.

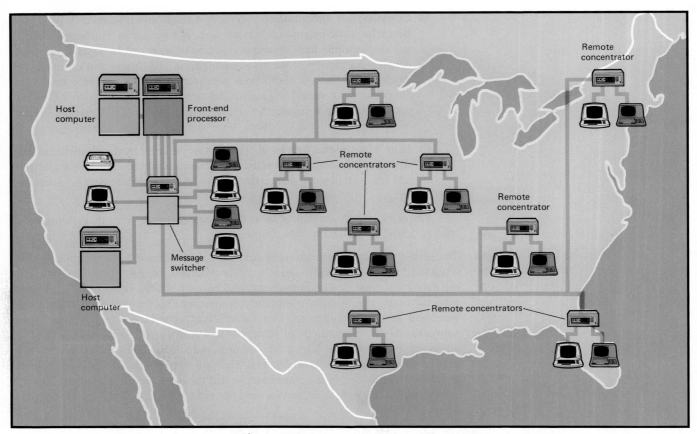

**Figure 10-8** A computing/communications network. The remote concentrators, message switchers, and front-end processors in such networks are typically micro- or minicomputers used for communications purposes.

**Figure 10-9** The function of a remote concentrator or multiplexer is to concentrate the output from many low-speed terminals into a single data stream that can be transmitted over a higher-speed channel. (Adapted from John G. Posa, "Phone Net Going Digital," *High Technology*, May 1983, p. 45.)

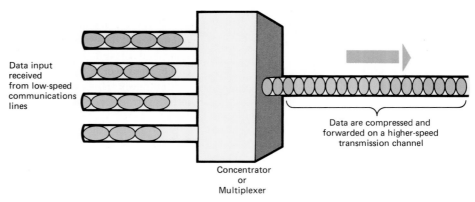

Data input received from low-speed communications lines

Data are compressed and forwarded on a higher-speed transmission channel

Concentrator or Multiplexer

3. *Front-end processing.* The **front-end processor** is usually located at a central computer site. Its purpose is to relieve a main computer—i.e., a **host computer**—of a number of the functions required to interact with and control the communications network.

The functions of communications processors differ from one network to another, and there may be an overlapping of functions. A message-switching processor, for example, may also function as a remote concentrator; a front-end processor may perform message-switching functions; and, in less complete networks, the host computer may perform most or all the functions of the front-end processor.

**Local-Area Networks.** Up to now we've been looking at communications situations in which data are transmitted between sites that are far apart. But in many organizations data are also transmitted between computers, terminals, word processing stations, and other devices that are all located within a compact area such as an office building or a campus. The communications system used to link these nearby devices together is referred to as a **local-area network (LAN).** A LAN is owned by the using organization, and most LANs use a star or bus physical configuration. A **star LAN** has a central controller, and all network station hookups radiate out from this central node like the points of a star (Figure 10-10*a*). In a **bus LAN,** however, a single cable (or ''bus'') is routed from station to station to provide the network linkage (Figure 10-10*b*).

Transmission channels may use everything from pairs of twisted wires to coaxial and fiber-optic cables. Special hardware/software elements are used in place of modems and outside telephone lines. The speed of transmission and the network cost varies widely depending on the type of LAN used. Some LANs allow the integration of peripherals and computers made by different vendors, while others are restricted to the components made by a single supplier.

Although there are dozens of LAN offerings available to organizations, most of them can be placed in one of the following categories:

■ *High-speed networks.* Over 20 million bits per second (MBps) can be transmitted over these LANs that are designed to provide links between large mainframes. Examples of these high-speed networks are Control Data Corporation's *Loosely Coupled Network* and Network Systems Corporation's *Hyperchannel*. It costs about $40,000 to attach each mainframe to the Hyperchannel LAN.

■ *Medium-speed networks.* The transmission speed of these LANs varies between 1 MBps and 20 MBps. Suitable for use with smaller mainframes and minicomputers, some of these LANs can support a few hundred workstations and other devices, while others can theoretically accommodate tens of thousands of these peripherals. The cost of attaching each device averages a few hundred dollars. One example of these medium-speed LANs is *Ethernet*. Developed by Xerox, this 10 MBps network uses a coaxial cable in a bus configuration for data transmission. Special integrated circuit chips called controllers are used to connect equipment to the

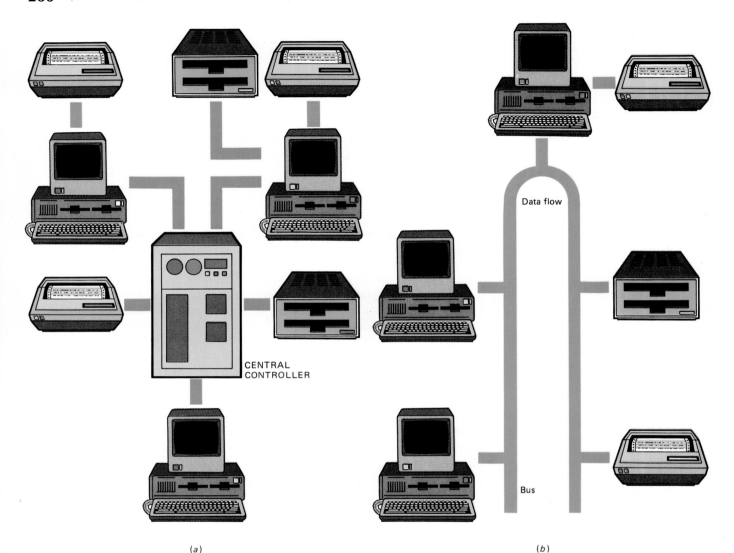

*(a)*

*(b)*

Figure 10-10 Two common LAN configurations. *(a)* A star LAN has a central controller that provides the hardware/software interface resources needed by the network stations. Thus, a failure at the central controller site may force a shutdown of the network. *(b)* A bus LAN has no central controller and so each network component must be equipped to handle interface problems. The network vendor generally supplies these hardware/software interface elements for specific types of equipment.

cable, and small boxes called transceivers transmit and receive cable data at each workstation. Each station can exchange data with any other station or group of stations. Other medium-speed bus-type LANs are Datapoint Corporation's *ARCnet,* Wang Laboratories' *Wangnet,* Sytek's *LocalNet 40,* Ungermann-Bass' *Net/One,* and Amdax's *CableNet.*

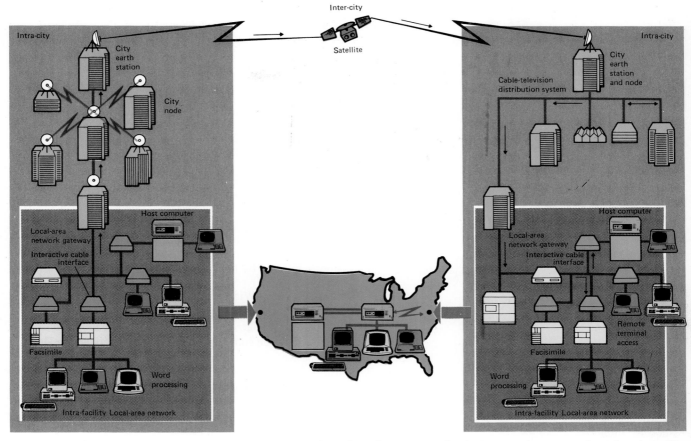

**Figure 10-11** A modern data communications network may use broadband satellite transmission channels to link the major East and West Coast offices of an organization. Various intracity data channels may include ground microwave stations, telephone and telegraph circuits, and the coaxial cables furnished by cable television companies. Within each major office, data may move over intrafacility local-area networks. Telephone and telegraph channels may be used to connect smaller offices to one or both of the major facilities.

# ADDITIONAL SYSTEMS SUPPORTED BY DATA COMMUNICATIONS

You're already familiar with many direct-access processing applications supported by data communications. To cite one example, a teller at a branch bank may update online savings account records stored at a central computer site through the use of data communications facilities. Let's take a brief look at a few additional examples of important systems supported by telecommunications.

## Real Time Processing Systems

The words "real time" have been defined in over 30 ways. However, the consensus is that a **real time processing system** is in a parallel time relationship with an ongoing activity and is producing information quickly enough to be useful in controlling this current live and dynamic activity. Thus, the words "real time" describe a direct-access or online processing system with severe time limitations. A real time system uses direct-access processing, but a direct-access system need not be operating in real time. The difference is that real time processing requires *immediate* transaction input from all input-originating terminals. Many stations are tied directly by high-speed telecommunications lines into one or more CPUs. Several stations can operate at the same time. Files are updated each minute and inquiries are answered by split-second access to up-to-the-minute records. But it's possible to have a direct-access system that combines immediate access to records for inquiry purposes with *periodic* (perhaps daily) transaction input and updating of records from a central collecting source. Such a direct-access system would meet many needs and would be simpler and less expensive than a real time system.

The reservation systems used by airlines, hotels, and car rental agencies are examples of real time systems that have been mentioned earlier. A few other examples of real time systems supported by telecommunications are:

**Figure 10-12** This U.S. Air Force air traffic control system covers air space in a 4,000 square mile area. (Photo courtesy Sanders Associates, Inc.)

■ *Military systems.* A World Wide Military Command and Control System has been developed for U.S. military commanders from the President on down. The system links 35 large computers at 26 command posts around the world. And over a dozen computers at the North American Air Defense Command accept, store, and constantly update masses of data from worldwide radar installations. Every humanly produced object in earth orbit is tracked. If a rocket is launched, the computers quickly calculate its trajectory.

■ *Air traffic control systems.* Millions of aircraft flights are tracked across the nation each year by air traffic controllers. These flights are monitored by computers and are switched to different control jurisdictions as they move across the continent (Figure 10-12). When a flight approaches Chicago's O'Hare International Airport, for example, a control system sends out special "beacon" signals. Answering signals from the aircraft give the plane's identity, altitude, and speed. These data are processed by computer and are instantly displayed on a controller's screen next to a "blip" of light that represents the plane. Over 100 aircraft can be tracked and controlled simultaneously by the system.

## Timesharing and Remote Computing Service Systems

**Timesharing** is a general term used to describe a processing system with a number of independent, relatively low-speed, online, and simultaneously usable stations. Each station, of course, provides direct access to the CPU. The use of special programs allows the CPU to switch from one station to another and to do a part of each job in an allocated "time slice" until the work is completed. The speed is frequently (but not always) such that the user has the illusion that nobody else is using the computer.

A number of organizations sell timesharing and remote computing services to their customers. These organizations may install terminals or personal computers in customer offices and then use telecommunications channels to link these workstations to their central processors. Or, they may link their processors to customer-owned personal computers. A broad range of jobs may be processed, or the service organization may specialize in the needs of a particular group. In recent years, for example, the pharmacy operations in retail drugstores have been swamped with paperwork resulting from insurance billings and government legislation. Thousands of drugstores have thus turned to a number of timesharing services that supply total hardware, software, and communications packages geared to the needs of pharmacists. Other remote computing services (sometimes referred to as *service bureaus*) may accept a customer's input data over telecommunications lines, do custom batch processing for the customer, and then transmit the output information back to the customer's terminal.

Timesharing and remote computing service organizations generally offer a library of online applications programs to their clients who need only supply the input data and access the programs to obtain the desired information. Customers pay for the processing service in much the same way they pay for telephone service: There's an initial installation charge, there are certain basic monthly charges, and there are transaction charges (like long-distance calls) that vary according to usage. Some timesharing firms also sell applications programs to former customers who decide to acquire their own small hardware systems.

## Electronic Mail/Message Systems

The ability to use telecommunications lines to send electronic messages between distant points obviously isn't limited to personal computer users. Organizations can use services such as Telemail provided by GTE Telenet, or On Tyme-II supplied by Tymnet, to send intracompany or intercompany messages. These messages may begin and end at communicating word processors or other I/O devices. Network computers are used to temporarily store and route the messages. We'll get into this subject in more detail in Chapter 11.

## Banking Service Systems

Banks communicate with each other and send funds-transfer instructions over telecommunications networks. The Fed Wire transfer network, for example, is operated by the Federal Reserve System for use by member banks. Hundreds of member banks and the Federal Reserve banks are linked together. Dozens of computers and hundreds of terminals are used to handle over 25 million messages each year. Over $50 *trillion* is annually transmitted by Fed Wire. A cooperative funds-transfer network called BankWire also serves several hundred banks in the United States. And a cooperative international network called SWIFT (*S*ociety for *W*orldwide *I*nterbank *F*inancial *T*elecommunications) links banks in over 20 countries.

**Bank-at-home** systems also use telecommunications lines to permit people to interact with their individual banks (Figure 10-13). Personal computers or special input devices attached to television sets use telephone or two-way cable TV lines to access a bank computer. After a sign-on procedure has been followed, bank customers can:

1. Display the current values of their checking and savings accounts.

2. Display the balances owed on their mortgage, installment loan, and credit card accounts.

**Figure 10-13** Bank-at-home systems enable users to check on their accounts, transfer funds, and even pay bills. (Photo courtesy Chemical Bank)

3. Obtain information from a financial advisory service.

4. Apply for loans.

5. Display what they owe to creditors, and then enter the amounts they want the bank to pay on each bill.

**Data Base Retrieval Systems**

You'll recall from Chapter 2 that a data base is a collection of logically related data elements. Organizations and individuals maintain a countless number of these data bases in a computer-accessible form for their own *private* uses. But there are also many data base producers that amass and update information on specific subjects for *public* use. Some producers of these public data bases set up their own online computer/communications systems to electronically distribute specialized information to their subscribers. But many other producers choose to sell the distribution rights to an online service organization. The service organization typically enters a data base into its computer storage facilities, provides instructions to online users on how to access it, and pays the producer royalties when subscribers use it.

Over 1,400 of these public data bases are stored and maintained in online computer systems in the United States. You've seen that The Source and CompuServe are online service organizations that enable people to retrieve information *in their homes* from scores of these data bases. And there are many videotex systems that give people online access to:

■ Weather and traffic updates, article summaries from magazines, and news accounts from radio, United Press International, and Associated Press sources.

■ Electronic shopping catalogs from retailers such as J. C. Penney and Sears, and electronic real estate listings from brokers.

■ Classified advertising and community "bulletin-board" information.

People at work also have telecommunications access to electronic libraries of information that are stored in central computers. These **data banks** tend to fall into statistical, bibliographic, and computational categories. *Statistical* data banks are compilations of numeric data. Included in this category are The Conference Board Data Base that provides information on capital spending and purchasing power for 20 different industries, the Standard & Poor's *Compustat* service that gives online access to financial statistics on U.S. and Canadian firms, and the American Statistics Index that furnishes citations and abstracts about U.S. government statistical documents.

*Bibliographic* data banks contain text-based information abstracted from books, newspapers, magazines, and professional journals. Hundreds of these data banks are maintained by their producers. Most of the important ones are then indexed and stored on computers by a few large distributors. The distributors also provide the telecommunications links to their customers. Some of the largest information retrieval distributors are:

■ *Dialog Information Services.* A division of the Lockheed Corporation, the *Dialog* system provides online access to over 170 data bases in such fields as government, health, education, social and physical sciences, humanities, and business. Many of the resources of the Dialog system are available at reduced rates to personal computer users after business hours and on weekends. The name of this pc-oriented service is *Knowledge Index.*

■ *System Development Corporation.* SDC's *Orbit Search Service* has over 70 online data bases, many of which are also found in the Dialog system.

■ *Bibliographic Retrieval Services.* BRS/*Search* offers over 60 different online data bases. Its *BRS/After Dark* service is aimed at pc users and is similar to Dialog's Knowledge Index.

■ *Mead Data Central.* Unlike the distributors above, Mead is both the producer and distributor of its LEXIS and NEXIS services. LEXIS is a vast library of legal information including federal and state codes and millions of court opinions. NEXIS, shown in Figure 10-14, is a computerized news research service that carries information produced by over 100 major publications and news services.

*Computational* data banks allow users to manipulate raw data in order to produce economic models and forecasts. These data banks are prepared with data supplied by Standard & Poor's, Chase Econometric Associates, Data Resources, Inc. (DRI), and others. DRI, a division of McGraw-Hill, Inc., has joined with VisiCorp, the producer of the popular VisiCalc spreadsheet program and other pc software, to give pc users access to DRI resources. A user can supply data to the

Figure 10-14 Subscribers to the NEXIS system enjoy access to a vast news research data base. (Courtesy Mead Data Central)

VisiCalc program from over 50 DRI data bases and then use the program to manipulate the data. (For more details on VisiCalc use, see p. 222.)

**Telecommuting Systems**

There are millions of people who do much of their work on desktop devices such as word processors and personal computers. And we've seen that these devices can be located in the home and linked to outside office systems by telecommunications networks. Thus, a growing number of people are questioning the need to commute to downtown office buildings to perform tasks they could easily do at home. In fact, tens of thousands of professionals are now doing some or all of their work in home and neighborhood work centers and are then forwarding the results in an electronic form to the office of an employer or client. This **telecommuting** approach isn't for everyone, of course, and some people prefer the social life found in an office environment. But telecommuting benefits those who prefer flexible working hours and regular days at home. In the years ahead, it's expected that millions of telecommuters will be working in "electronic cottages" and forwarding their results to other sites.

# DISTRIBUTED DATA PROCESSING NETWORKS

A little earlier we used the word "timesharing" because it's commonly applied to multistation systems that make interleaved use of the time of a computer. We saw that a service organization can install terminals in the offices of many customers and then use telecommunications to link these terminals to its CPU. It's also quite possible for a single business to set up its own timesharing system using terminals linked to its own hardware. Timesharing isn't new. The relatively high cost of computer hardware in the 1960s spurred many organizations to establish a large central computer system and to then achieve economies of scale by sharing the time of that system among many users.

When one or two processors handle the workload of all outlying terminals, the word "timesharing" is probably still accurate. But as you know, it's possible now for an organization to buy many computers for the price of just one earlier large machine. And when *many* geographically dispersed or *distributed* independent computer systems are connected by a telecommunications network, and when messages, processing tasks, programs, data, and other resources are transmitted between cooperating processors and terminals, the timesharing term may no longer be broad enough.

**Distributed data processing (DDP) network** is the term often used today to describe this extension of timesharing. For our purposes, a DDP arrangement may be defined as one that places the needed data, along with the computing and communications resources necessary to process these data, at the end-user's location. Such an arrangement (Figure 10-15) may result in many computers and significant software resources being shared among dozens of users.

## Examples of DDP Networks in Use

A distributed data processing network, like a timesharing system, may be intended for the use of a *single* organization, or it may be available for use by *many* organizations.

**Single-Organization DDP Networks.** Some examples of private DDP networks have been developed by the following organizations:

**Figure 10-15** Minicomputers in DDP networks process data and control communications among workstations. (Courtesy Hewlett-Packard Company)

■ *Hewlett-Packard Company.* Figure 10-16 shows the worldwide DDP network that Hewlett-Packard has developed for its internal business applications. Ten mainframes and several hundred Hewlett-Packard micro- and minicomputers are scattered around the network to handle processing, data entry/retrieval, and telecommunications work. About 2,500 visual display terminals are used. This network links manufacturing facilities and sales offices at over 100 sites to corporate offices in California and Switzerland. Although overall control of the network is maintained by the California center, division computers operate autonomously to process local jobs.

■ *Texas Instruments Incorporated.* Over 7,000 terminals and hundreds of computers are now included in TI's expanding network. There are several computing levels in the network hierarchy. At the top of the hierarchy are five large mainframes located at the corporate information center in Dallas. Next in the hierarchy come the medium-sized mainframes located at major sites around the world. A third level of TI minicomputers serves clusters of departmental terminals, and a fourth level of TI personal computers and intelligent terminals serves individual employees.

■ *Bank of America.* The Bank of America in California has a network of over 50 minicomputers to support online inquiries from 6,000 teller terminals located in the 1,000 branch offices in the state.

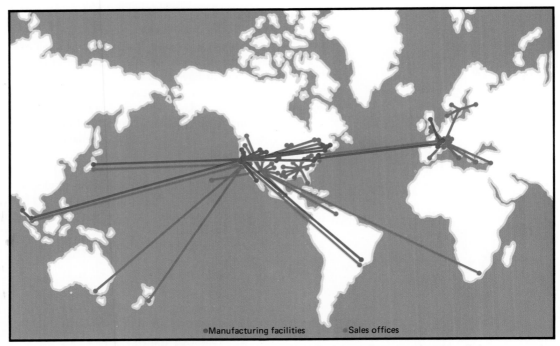

Figure 10-16 Single-organization DDP network. Hewlett Packard Company's distributed data processing network links hundreds of computers and terminals at over 100 manufacturing plants and sales offices to corporate centers in Palo Alto, Calif. and Geneva, Switzerland.

■ **Otis Elevator Company.** One medium-sized mainframe, six minicomputers, and about 40 visual display terminals are used to link offices in Massachusetts, New Jersey, Illinois, Texas, and California with the corporate headquarters in Connecticut.

**Multiple-Organization DDP Networks.** A few examples of DDP networks that serve a number of organizations are:

■ **Travel reservation networks.** United Airlines' Apollo system, American Airlines' Sabre system, and similar distributed data processing nets are in use by most airlines. In the last few years, more than half the nation's 17,000 travel agencies have tied into these computerized travel reservation systems.

■ **The ARPA Network.** Figure 10-17a shows the network of the Advanced Research Projects Agency of the U.S. Department of Defense. This net connects about 40 universities and research institutions throughout the United States and Europe with about 50 computers ranging in size from minis to supercomputers. A few of the schools included are Harvard, MIT, Carnegie-Mellon, Illinois, Utah, Stanford, UCLA, and USC.

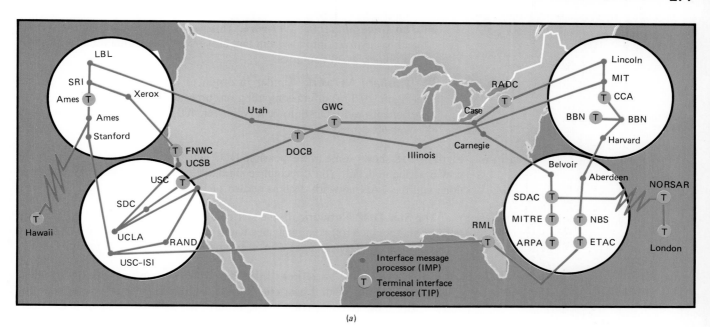

(a)

(b)

**Figure 10-17** Multiple-organization DDP networks. (a) The DDP network of the Advanced Research Projects Agency of the Department of Defense. (b) The DDP network of Tymshare, Inc.

■ *The General Electric Network.* This net began as a timesharing service and has evolved into a system that uses over 50 large mainframes to serve 750 cities in 30 countries.

■ *Tymshare Network.* Similar in origin to the GE network, this system (Figure 10-17*b*) offers computing resources to customers in business, government, and education. It serves over 400 cities and 40 countries with over 60 computers.

## Network Configurations

Figure 10-18 shows some of the possible DDP network configurations which we'll now describe in detail. You'll recognize similarities between these DDP configurations and the LAN network designs shown in Figure 10-10.

**The Star DDP Network.** In the star configuration (Figure 10-18*a*), a central host, or star computer(s) communicates with and controls a second level of satellite or node processors. These nodes, in turn, communicate with I/O terminals.

**The Hierarchical Variation of the Star DDP Network.** In this arrangement (Figure 10-18*b*), the central host computer(s) is still linked to regional node processors. But these regional nodes may, in turn, act as hosts to subordinate small district processors. In addition to processing local applications, the small third-level processors in the hierarchy (usually minicomputers) may support local-level intelligent terminals and personal computers that are also able to independently process small jobs. The higher-level computers in the hierarchy are used to manage large data bases and to serve the lower-level processors by executing jobs that require extensive computations. The Hewlett-Packard and Texas Instruments networks mentioned above are basically hierarchical variations of the star configuration. Most current DDP networks, in fact, use the star arrangement or some hierarchical variation of it.

**The Ring DDP Network.** This configuration (Figure 10-18*c*) is a "no-host" or ring arrangement of communicating equals. Each ring processor may have communicating subordinates, but within the ring there's no master computer.

## Advantages and Limitations of DDP Networks

As you might expect, there are both advantages and disadvantages today to the sharing of computing resources through the use of DDP networks. Some of the advantages are:

■ Sophisticated computers and a growing library of applications programs can be immediately available to end users whenever needed. Small local processors can often be used to quickly get local applications up and running, but large central systems are also available to do big number-crunching and batch processing jobs.

■ Skilled computer/communications specialists can be available to help network users develop their own specialized applications.

■ The availability of multiple processors in the network permits peakload sharing and provides backup facilities in the event of equipment failure.

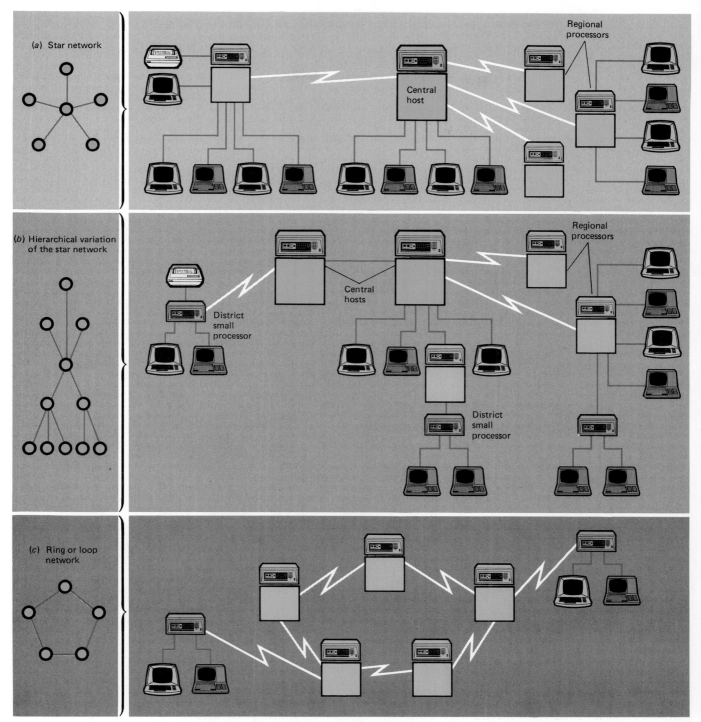

**Figure 10-18** Possible DDP network configurations. Countless variations of these themes are being implemented.

■ Users with access to nearby computers and data bases may be able to react more rapidly to new developments, and they may be able to interact with the other network resources to seek solutions to unusual problems.

■ Telecommunication costs can be lower when much of the local processing is handled by on-site minis and personal computers rather than by distant central mainframes.

Unfortunately, however, some of the possible limitations to the use of DDP networks are:

■ The reliability and cost of the telecommunications facilities used and the cost and quality of the computing service received from other network sites may disappoint users in some cases.

■ Security provisions for protecting the confidentiality and integrity of the user programs and data that are stored online and transmitted over network channels are generally ineffective today against a skilled person intent on penetrating the network.

■ Today's DDP network environment is dynamic and turbulent, and the lack of adequate computing/communications standards has often made it difficult to merge the equipment produced by different vendors into a smoothly functioning entity.

## Feedback and Review 10-1

This chapter has introduced you to a number of data communications concepts and DDP network examples. To test and reinforce your understanding of the material, use the following clues to fill in the crossword puzzle form presented below.

### Across

**1.** _____ communication refers to the means and methods whereby data are transferred between processing locations.

**2.** A _____ is an interface device that converts the stream of "on-off" electrical pulses used by computing equipment into the type of analog wave patterns used to transmit the human voice over telephone lines.

**5.** Another name for the computing/communications networks that provide information retrieval services to personal computer users is _____ systems.

**7.** "Value-added" telecommunications carriers that receive customer data over telephone lines and then organize these data into groups for transmission over high-speed channels are sometimes referred to as _____ -switching networks.

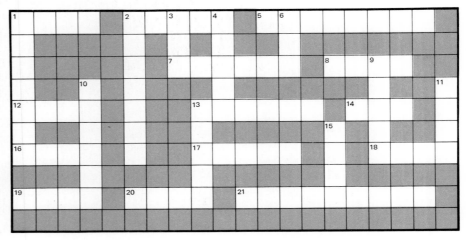

**8.** A _____ -duplex transmission circuit is one that can simultaneously transmit and receive messages.

**12.** Data communications by means of electrical signals is also referred to as _____ -communications.

**13.** The companies that offer a broad range of telegraph and telephone services to the general public are referred to as _____ carriers.

**14.** _____ is the acronym for the government agency that has held hearings to determine the extent of regulation and competition that will be permitted in the telecommunications industry.

**16.** Customers often pay for timesharing services in much the same way they pay for _____ -distance telephone service.

**17.** _____ -band transmission channels use coaxial cables, microwave systems and satellites, and fiber optic cables to transmit large volumes of data at high speeds.

**18.** A standard telephone _____ is a voiceband channel that has a wider bandwidth and a faster transmission rate than a telegraph line.

**19.** In the _____ type of DDP network configuration, a central host computer communicates with and controls a second level of node processors.

**20.** _____ -sharing is a term used to describe a processing system with a number of independent, relatively low-speed, online, and simultaneously usable stations.

**21.** A communications _____ is precisely positioned in space and acts as a reflector by accepting signals from one point on earth and returning the same signals to other points on earth.

### Down

**1.** Modems convert _____ "on-off" pulses into analog wave patterns.

**2.** _____ switchers are communications processors that receive and analyze data from points in a network, determine the destination and routing, and then forward the data to other network locations.

**3.** A _____ network is an extension of timesharing that employs many geographically dispersed computers and a telecommunications system to place data and computing resources at end-user locations.

**4.** _____ -wave transmission systems use radio signals to transmit data through space.

**6.** A specialized common carrier that offers long-distance circuits to 88 U.S. cities and to other countries is _____ World Communications.

**9.** A _____ -area network is used to transmit data between computers and I/O devices that are all located within a compact area such as an office building.

**10.** A _____ is taking place today between computing and communications technology.

**11.** Data _____ retrieval organizations tend to supply data that fall into statistical, bibliographic, and computational categories.

**13.** A coaxial or fiber optic _____ can be used to transmit data at high speeds.

**15.** _____ time processing systems are in a parallel time relationship with ongoing activities and are producing information quickly enough to be useful in controlling these current live and dynamic activities.

## LOOKING BACK

**1.** Data communication refers to the means and methods whereby data are transferred between processing locations. There's nothing new about telecommunications. Telephones, for example, have been around for over 100 years. What's relatively recent, though, is the merging of computing and telecommunications technology and the increased competition permitted in the data communications field.

**2.** When voice-grade telephone lines are used to transmit computer data, one modem must be used at the sending station to modulate the digital "on-off" pulses into the analog wave patterns used to transmit the human voice. And a second modem is needed at the receiving location to demodulate or recover the digital data from the transmitted signal. A special type of modem called an acoustic coupler is often used with portable machines.

**3.** In addition to medium-speed telephone lines, narrowband telegraph channels and high-speed broadband channels are also used to transmit data. The broadband channels use coaxial or fiber-optic cables, and microwave/satellite systems. Transmitted data can move along simplex, half-duplex, or full-duplex lines depending on the needs of the user.

**4.** Most organizations offering telecommunications services can be classified into common carrier, specialized common carrier, or value-added carrier categories. Common carriers provide large public telephone and telegraph networks and a broad range of services. Specialized common carriers often use broadband facilities such as satellites to offer public networks that are restricted to a limited number of services. Value-added carriers generally use the telephone lines and transmission facilities of other carriers. Customer data are received, temporarily stored and organized into packets of characters, and then routed over high-speed leased channels to their destinations. There are also service firms that offer computing/communications networks or videotex systems for home use.

**5.** Large computing/communications networks use a number of communications processors to coordinate network components. Remote concentrators or multiplexers receive terminal input from low-speed lines and then concentrate and transmit the data on higher-speed facilities. Message switchers receive data from points in the network, determine destination and proper routing, and then forward the data to other locations. And front-end processors are used to relieve main computers of a number of the functions required to interact with and control the network.

**6.** Local-area networks (LANs) are communications systems that are used to link the terminals, computers, word processing stations, and other devices located within a compact area. LANs typically follow a star or bus configuration, and they can be classified into high-, medium-, and low-speed categories. Some low-speed LANs designed for use with personal computers use special cables, while other low-speed networks use telephone wires and digital PBX controllers. Regardless of the type of LAN used at a local site, it must often be coordinated with the communications elements that link geographically dispersed processing centers.

**7.** A real time processing system is in a parallel time relationship with an ongoing activity and is producing information quickly enough to be useful in controlling this current live activity. A real time system uses direct-access processing, but a direct-access system need not be operating under the severe time limitations of a real time system.

**8.** Timesharing is a general term used to describe the interleaved use of the time of a processor by a number of independent, online, simultaneously usable stations. A number of firms sell timesharing services to their customers.

**9.** In addition to supporting real time and timesharing systems, telecommunications has also made it possible to develop systems to transmit electronic mail, provide banking services, and retrieve information from numerous statistical, bibliographic, and computational data bases. Some people may also enjoy the benefits of telecommuting through the use of telecommunications networks.

**10.** A distributed data processing network consists of many geographically dispersed independent computer systems connected by a telecommunications network. It places the needed data, along with the computing/communications resources necessary to process these data, at the end-user's location. As examples in the chapter show, DDP networks may be intended for the use of a single organization, or they may be available for use by multiple organizations. The possible DDP network configurations include the star, a hierarchical variation of the star, and the ring arrangements. Several advantages and limitations to DDP networks are listed in the chapter.

## KEY TERMS AND CONCEPTS

data communication 253
telecommunications 253
interface elements 255
modem 255
direct-connect modem 255
intelligent modem 255
acoustic coupler 256
data transmission channels 258
narrowband channel 258
voiceband channel 258
dedicated (leased) lines 258
simplex line 258
half-duplex circuit 258
full-duplex circuit 258
broadband channel 258
coaxial cable 258
microwave system 258

communications satellite 258
fiber-optic cable/laser technology 259
common carriers 259
specialized common carriers 260
value-added carriers 261
value-added network (VAN) 261
packet-switching networks 261
teletext system 262
videotex system 262
communications processors 263
remote concentrator 263
multiplexer 263
message switcher 263
front-end processor 265
host computer 265
local-area network (LAN) 265

star LAN 265
bus LAN 265
digital PBX 268
real time processing system 270
timesharing 270
bank-at-home systems 271
data base retrieval systems/data banks 272
telecommuting 274
distributed data processing (DDP) network 275
star DDP network 278
hierarchical variation of star DDP network 278
ring DDP network 278

## TOPICS FOR REVIEW AND DISCUSSION

**1.** *(a)* What is data communication? *(b)* What can you tell a friend who is under the impression that data communications is a new phenomenon?

**2.** *(a)* Why are computing and communications technologies merging? *(b)* What are likely to be some of the effects of this merger? *(c)* In your opinion, which computing/communications services should be regulated, and which should be open to unregulated competition?

**3.** What components are typically found in a simple data communications system?

**4.** *(a)* What's a modem and why is it needed? *(b)* What's an acoustic coupler?

**5.** Identify and discuss the three basic types of data transmission channels.

**6.** "A full-duplex line is faster since it avoids the delay that occurs in a half-duplex circuit." Explain this sentence.

**7.** *(a)* How are communications satellites used? *(b)* Identify four domestic satellite data transmission systems.

**8.** Identify, discuss, and give examples of three types of organizations that offer data communications services.

**9.** "A giant home information industry is being built around the development of videotex systems." Discuss this statement.

**10.** Identify and indicate the purpose of the communications processors used to coordinate the operations of a data communications network.

**11.** *(a)* What is a local-area network? *(b)* What's the difference between a star LAN and a bus LAN? *(c)* Identify and discuss three types of LAN offerings.

**12.** *(a)* Explain this sentence: "A real time system uses direct-access processing, but a direct-access system need not be operating in real time." *(b)* Give some examples of a real time system.

**13.** *(a)* What is timesharing? *(b)* Give an example of the use of timesharing.

**14.** Identify three banking service systems that use telecommunications networks.

**15.** "People at work may use public electronic libraries of information that are stored in central computers. These libraries tend to fall into three categories." Identify these categories and give three examples of organizations that supply data bank information.

**16.** *(a)* What's a DDP network? *(b)* Give three examples of DDP networks used by single organizations. *(c)* Give three examples of DDP networks used by multiple organizations.

**17.** Identify and discuss the possible DDP network configurations.

**18.** *(a)* What are three possible advantages of DDP? *(b)* What are two possible limitations?

## PROJECTS TO LOOK INTO

**1.** Investigate a data base retrieval system—one whose services interest you—and research the current charges it makes for *(a)* initial hookup and *(b)* delivery of information. Write a brief report of your findings and explain how you would make use of the selected service.

**2.** Identify an organization (your school, a business, a hospital, a government agency) that uses a LAN or some other communications network during its data processing operations. Outline the results of your study in a report to the class.

## ANSWERS TO FEEDBACK AND REVIEW SECTION

**10-1**

The solution for the crossword puzzle is shown at the right.

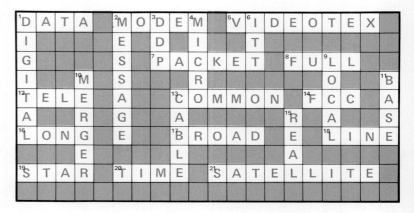

# Computer Users Make Beeline to Get On-line

Not long ago, Debbie Fuhrman from Tolleson, Ariz., and George Stickles from Dallas got married.

They got married on CompuServe, the giant public access database in Columbus, Ohio. The bride's parents tuned in on their Radio Shack computer at home in Phoenix. CompuServe's gossip columnist watched from her terminal in Valley Stream, N.Y. (and confessed that she cried throughout). Electronic friends and acquaintances watched through their own computers and filled the screen with commas and asterisks—the computer equivalent of rice—after the ceremony.

Near as anyone who follows these things can tell, there will be several hundred marriages this year as a result of computer meetings. As the headline on a recent story in New York's *Village Voice* put it: "Reach out and access someone."

About 100,000 people are "on line," as they call it, on one of the two major public databases, CompuServe and The Source. About 200,000 or so are on line with other databases, such as the Dow Jones News Retrieval, Dialog, Nexis, etc. Ninety percent of the subscribers are men, with an income twice the national average.

The number of people who are plugged into one or more networks is growing at a phenomenal rate. Early next year it will be more than a million people; in two years it should be close to 10 million. Someday (and not too far off at that) it will be the world.

It is not overstating the situation to say that the potential for this network technology is awesome. Already you can plug into one of these large databases at 2 o'clock in the morning and it is electronic Grand Central. There are tens of thousands of people on line, and they are all busily

Videotex systems offer services that range from shopping at home (*left*) to conducting electronic research on any topic (*right*). (Photos reproduced with permission of AT&T and courtesy Microtaure, Inc.)

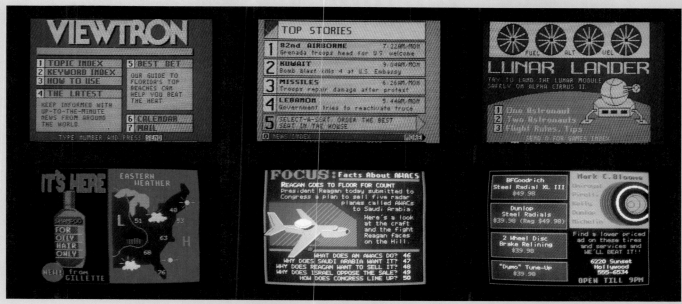

Representative screens from two videotex services offer a sample of the kinds of information available to subscribers (Courtesy Viewdata Corporation of America, Inc., and VSA—Videographic Systems of America)

chatting away with one another and conducting business.

They form themselves into interest groups: cars, computers, gardening, aviation, gourmet cooking, fine wines, computer shopping, swap meets, banking, stock market clubs, poetry, electronic art and animation . . . Sometimes they just "chat," which is its own category.

The Source alone has nearly a thousand topics, including such oddities as a program that automatically calculates the diameter of any molecule in angstroms, and another that randomly generates Elizabethan sonnets (pretty well, too).

CompuServe has nearly as many, including one called "Kinky Komputer." (You know: "Attractive male programmer desires to meet similar female with compatible terminal," etc.) Both have hundreds of games.

Maybe this isn't enough for you. There are about 1,500 other databases to choose from. These all charge an initial membership fee of from $35 to several hundred dollars, and then an hourly use fee. (The Source and CompuServe charge about $7 an hour for evening and weekend use, more during business hours.)

Then there are 500 or so "community bulletin boards." These are maintained for free by someone who loves doing it. It is on these bulletin boards that the "hackers" you have been reading about recently, the ones who gain illegal access to restricted military computers and such, share their information. The wires are alive with electronic intrigue.

All right. If you're alive, you're interested. Just what is out there, and how does one go about plugging into it?

Well, first of all, one of the nicest things about the electronic ether is that it is very democratic. It doesn't matter whether you plug in with a $5,000 IBM or a $39 Timex Sinclair; whatever you got, it works for this.

What you do need is a "modem," which is short for a "modulator-demodulator." This is a device that attaches to your computer and sends and receives information in digital form.

Modem prices range from $70 to $700. In general, find out from a dealer or your manual which one is right for your computer, and then get the best you can afford. The top of the line is the Hayes Smartmodem 1200; other big names in modems are Novation, SSM and U.S. Robotics.

—Bob Schwabach, "Computer Users Make Beeline to Get On-line," courtesy *Fort Worth Star-Telegram* News Services.

# Word Processing and Electronic Mail/Message Systems

## Micros and "E-Mail"

The coming decade will likely bring the marriage of personal computers with communications technology, producing the healthy offspring of electronic mail.

Electronic mail systems have grown slowly in today's tough economic climate because of the high cost of terminals, according to a report from International Resource Development, Inc. (IRD). . . .

However, personal computers generally procured for noncommunications reasons—word processing, games or education—"are likely to provide an unanticipated, but ideal, solution to the problem," the report projected.

Communications capabilities can be added to a personal computer today for as low as $150 on many systems, including hardware and software, and that price is expected to drop, the report pointed out. By 1992, there are expected to be 117 million installed personal computers, 60 million of which are expected to have communications capabilities.

Also by that time, microcomputers are projected to have penetrated 70 million homes or approximately 70% of U.S. households.

All told, this will comprise "an enormous base of potential terminals, freeing communications service companies to develop sophisticated services for this base," the report noted. "With the problem of communications terminals solved, personal computer-driven electronic mail is likely to flourish."

—Marguerite Zientara, "Wedlock of Micros and E-Mail Predicted," *Computerworld*, Mar. 28, 1983, p. 95. Copyright 1983 by CW Communications, Framingham, Mass., 01701. Reprinted from *Computerworld*. Photo courtesy ITT.

Word processing and electronic mail/message systems are two of the basic building blocks for the automated office. Chapter 11 gives you a better understanding of these rapidly growing systems and how they'll likely affect your future. The information in this chapter will enable you to:

- Explain why new office technology is needed and expected.

- Discuss the current developments in word processing systems, identify the types of word processing systems in use today, and outline some uses of word processing.

- Understand why electronic mail/message systems were developed, and identify the functions they perform.

# TECHNOLOGY IN THE OFFICE: AN OVERVIEW

The phrases "office automation," "office of the future," and "electronic office" have been coined to describe the use of computing/communications technology to perform many office functions. We'll discuss some of the latest applications in office technology in this chapter, but before we do, let's pause briefly here to examine traditional office functions and the status of the technology found in most offices today.

## The Traditional Office

The functions performed in offices match the data processing activities you learned about in Chapter 1. In a traditionally organized office, data in the form of numerical symbols and/or text material are typically written or typed on source documents. These documents are then read, classified, and sorted. Calculations are performed on appropriate data, and facts may be summarized. Documents are often mailed between offices within an organization as well as between offices of separate organizations. This material—generally in the form of letters, memos, bills, purchase orders, and other documents—must be dealt with in an orderly way. Once the data have been manipulated and communicated, they frequently must be filed in a safe place, and they must be available for retrieval and reproduction when needed. Typewriters, desk calculators, file cabinets, and copying machines are among the traditional tools of office workers.

Although the necessary data processing work is accomplished in offices that follow these traditional methods, several problems have developed in recent years, among them:

1. ***Low productivity of office workers relative to other groups.*** In the past decade, American farmers have invested about $50,000 per worker in equipment to increase the productivity of each worker about 185 percent. American industrial workers, aided by an investment of $35,000 per worker, have boosted productivity about 90 percent. But during the same period, office workers have been supported by equipment worth less than $3,000 on the average, and their productivity has increased by only 4 percent.

2. ***Rising costs in the typical office.*** While the costs of preparing, mailing, storing, and duplicating documents have escalated in recent years, the cost of office labor has skyrocketed. For example, IBM estimates that a typical one-page letter will cost a business over $6 to dictate, type, and correct. Most of this cost is for labor. Slightly over half of the people employed in

## THE WRONG FURNITURE CAN BE PAIN IN THE NECK

No matter how "user friendly" your business's computers may be, they can literally give you or the person using them a pain in the neck if proper attention isn't paid to ergonomics, the study of how to adapt machines and equipment to human needs. . . .

According to ergonomic researchers, how comfortable you are with your computer depends on a number of factors. Proper lighting is important. The color and size of the letters on the screen can affect the length of time you can comfortably read from a VDT. How the keyboard is designed can also make a difference.

Another critical element is computer-support furniture—what both you and your computer sit on. This should be flexible, highly adjustable and adaptable to the user's needs. . . .

Here are some tips on how the user can make himself more comfortable:

GROUND YOURSELF. Sit back in your chair and adjust the chair height so your feet rest flat on the floor and knees are at a comfortable angle. Be sure the front edge of the seat doesn't restrict blood flow to your thighs and knees. (The seat angle of your chair should be adjustable.)

GET SUPPORT. A chair with a seat and back contoured to your body will reduce muscle strain. You should be able to adjust the tension of the chair back so that it's most comfortable for you.

LEAN BACK. Back strain can be reduced by leaning back in your chair until you find a comfortable position for working. Use a chair that locks in different positions.

POSITION THE KEYBOARD. First, place the keyboard or keyboard shelf about two inches above your knees. Position it so you don't have to hunch over or reach for the keys. Next, tilt the keyboard slightly toward you. (If you can't tilt the keyboard, you might want to consider palm rests offered by many manufacturers of computer accessories.)

FINALLY, ADJUST THE DISPLAY SCREEN. With the VDT screen illuminated, find the distance from the screen where reading is most comfortable. For people with normal eyesight, this is usually 18–22 inches. It's important to have a computer stand that allows you to raise and lower the VDT and tilt the screen. A correct line of sight reduces neck and shoulder tension. Tilt the screen to minimize eye strain from glare and reflection.

—Reprinted with permission from *Computer Living,* New York, "The Wrong Furniture Can Be Pain in the Neck," June 1984.

the United States work in offices. And office overhead costs now account for over half of the total operating costs in a typical organization.

3. **Misfiling of documents.** People may be unable to locate records in large files because the records may have been stored under a number of different classification schemes.

4. **Personnel problems.** Monotonous job specialization can lead to boredom, frequent errors, high personnel turnover, and high training costs.

Low productivity, rising costs, and monotonous jobs are not confined to offices. Many traditional "smokestack" industries in the United States have also been afflicted with these problems in recent years. Production managers in these industries are investing today in automated tools and other high-technology products to improve their worldwide competitive position. And office managers are also turning to new technology to improve worker productivity and reduce costs.

## The Introduction of New Technology

Since a computer is a fast electronic symbol manipulating device, and since office work basically involves symbol manipulation, it's only natural that organizations have turned to computers and other technology for help. Widespread use of automated office technology has been predicted for at least the last 10 years, but progress has not yet lived up to these predictions. (This has led one observer to substitute the acronym OOF for office of the future!)

But things are beginning to change. Several factors are likely to lead to the introduction of new technology and applications in the office environments of many organizations in the next few years. Two of these factors are:

■ The costs of electronic office equipment have been falling 30 percent per year. Executives are now more receptive to the idea of investing in new office technology in order to reduce rising labor costs and improve productivity. They're also encouraged by studies made by consultants such as Booz, Allen & Hamilton, Inc., that project large potential savings through the effective use of new office technology (see Figure 11-1).

■ Dozens of office equipment suppliers believe that the time is now ripe for the huge new automated office market they envision, and they are working feverishly to develop new products.

In most organizations, the change from the traditional office setting to the electronic office environment is evolving through several development stages. In the early stages, a limited amount of equipment is introduced to perform specific office tasks (Figure 11-2). For example, one or more of these functions is likely to receive early attention:

■ **Word processing.** The efficient creation, editing, and printing of documents are supported by word processing equipment.

■ **Message distribution.** Electronic mail/message systems accept messages addressed to one or more persons from a sending station and transmit them over communications channels to the station(s) of the recipient(s).

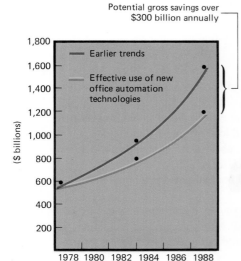

**Figure 11-1** Projected direct cost of U.S. office-based white-collar workers ($ in billions). Substantial savings can be achieved in the 1980s and beyond if new office technology is introduced and effectively used. (Estimates made by Harvey L. Poppel, Booz, Allen & Hamilton, Inc.)

Figure 11-2 In this office, the typewriter has taken a back seat to the word processor as a first step in office automation. (Courtesy Wang Laboratories, Inc.)

■ *Document transmission and reproduction.* A special device scans documents, graphs, pictures, etc., at a sending location, and then transmits the data representing the scanned document over telecommunications lines to a similar machine at the receiving end that reproduces the document.

■ *Computer conferencing.* People at different locations are using their workstations to attend conferences without ever leaving their offices.

Although products are available today to implement all these functions, few, if any, organizations have put them all together. One good reason for this lack of integration is that the products won't all *work* together. No dominant supplier has as yet developed a complete product line that encompasses all automated office functions. Rather, each major vendor has tried to develop its own market niche with its own hardware and software designs. The absence of industrywide standards in the office automation field has produced a technological Tower of Babel. Word processors A and B can't talk to each other, and neither can produce the desired output on printer C.

But this situation isn't likely to persist. As noted above, some large suppliers are working hard to broaden their product offerings, and as these lines are developed and accepted, other vendors will build equipment that will interface with the dominant lines. In the meantime, office users will become more familiar with computing/communications equipment and technology and will gradually automate more office functions. In future stages of development, the "office" may become an integrated network of compatible computing/communications systems that electronically ties the entire organization together.

Although this office of the future is still in the future, let's take a closer look now at the present-day applications that we've identified with the concept.

# WORD PROCESSING

Word processing is often the "backbone" application for office automation. It's the key that opens office doors to the introduction of other automated equipment. Once communicating word processing stations are in place, it's relatively easy to implement some other automated office functions. As used here, **word processing** describes the use of electronic equipment to create, view, edit, manipulate, transmit, store, retrieve, and print text material. Since you were first introduced to word processing (WP) concepts in Chapter 2, this topic isn't new to you. What you may not realize, however, is the speed with which WP equipment is now being introduced into offices. International Resource Development Inc., a market research firm, predicts that spending for office automation will triple between 1983 and 1990, with much of the spending for WP products.

## WORD PROCESSING SYSTEMS TODAY

In recent years, WP systems with keyboards for text input, visual display screens for text viewing and editing, floppy disks and small hard disks for text storage and retrieval, and various kinds of printers and data communications attachments for text output have been produced by dozens of vendors. If you've read Chapters 8 and 9, and if you think this description of a WP system sounds very much like the personal computer and minicomputer systems discussed in those chapters, you're right.

A **dedicated word processor**—i.e., a device that's used exclusively for WP—is basically a disguised computer that perpetually runs a program to process text material. Thus, many dedicated word processors are spin-offs of small computers and intelligent terminals that have received a few hardware modifications and/or specialized software. And although they're not dedicated exclusively to the task, most pc's and minicomputers (as well as larger processors) can also be used as word processors simply by loading an appropriate WP program into the system. For example, popular personal computer WP software packages such as Wordstar, Peachtext, Scripsit, Apple Writer, Easywriter, Perfect Writer, and many others can be purchased from their suppliers in the form of floppy disks. Once a WP program diskette is loaded into a pc system, the computer effectively becomes

## Some Uses of Word Processing

A modern WP system is an amazingly flexible tool. As text is keyed into the system, it's displayed on the screen and can easily be recorded on a storage medium such as a floppy disk. Carriage returns are automatic and corrections are easy. Sentences, paragraphs, and larger blocks of text can be added, deleted, or moved around in the document being prepared. When the displayed text is correct, instructions about output format can be added. For example, the system can be instructed to automatically put headings and numbers on each page of a report, center headings on the page, and produce specified top, bottom, left, and right margins. Finally, the document or report can be printed at the local station, or it can be transmitted electronically to a word processor located at a separate point via data communications channels. Thus, in the automated office, letters and reports need not be mailed but can be printed for the first time on receiving equipment in a nearby office or at a distant location. A printed copy may not be needed at the sending station since the text is available in an electronic file.

In addition, as we've seen, several prerecorded paragraphs can be called up from the dozens that are in storage and can then be assembled to create a new

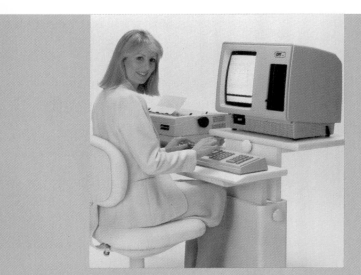

a word processor, something like the one that was used to write this book.

A pc system running *early* WP software was no match for a dedicated WP machine. On the pc, hard-to-remember codes and multiple keystrokes often performed the same operation available with the touch of a single special function key on a dedicated WP station. Furthermore, most pc keyboards and display screens weren't as well-suited for text creation and editing as were the similar components found on a WP machine.

But there seem to be as many different WP packages announced each year as there are words on this page, and some of the latest offerings are far superior to the earlier packages. Since these WP programs can make effective use of the special function keys and other hardware improvements found in some pc systems, they now provide an attractive pc alternative to the dedicated WP station.

Today's *dedicated* WP systems generally fall into stand-alone, shared-logic, or shared-resource categories. A **stand-alone WP station** is a small system that contains all the components needed to perform text processing. Electronic typewriters are sometimes considered to be *low-level* stand-alone systems. These devices can record and store a few pages of text in a small internal memory. Corrections can be

document. Then a "dictionary" or "spelling checker" program can be called up that will check every word in the document against a list of correctly spelled words. Words that don't match any of the tens of thousands stored in the dictionary are flagged with a special character. The entire document can then be searched for the special character and each flagged word automatically presented to the operator for action. (If the word is spelled correctly, it can be added to the dictionary list; if it's misspelled, it can be corrected.) This **global search** capability can also be used to search for words or phrases specified by the operator. When found, they can be deleted or replaced with other words or phrases. This **search-and-replace** feature can be used, for example, to substitute names in contracts or replace an abbreviation or acronym with a longer phrase.

A few examples of WP at work include:

- Continental Illinois Bank and Trust Company of Chicago has offices in Europe and New York. A proposal to a customer in Belgium can be prepared on the Brussels WP equipment and relayed to New York, where it's

made in the stored text before it's automatically printed in final form. A one- or two-line visual display provides a "thin window" into the internal memory of many electronic typewriters. A *higher-level* stand-alone WP system has the components mentioned at the beginning of this section and is able to display text over the entire surface of a CRT screen. Such a system is ideally suited to the small office, and many stand-alone models can be equipped with communications capabilities.

A **shared-logic WP system** has a number of keyboard workstations that share the logic and storage sections of a single central computer. This computer is typically a minicomputer. Peripheral units such as printers are also shared by the workstations. Although it's economical to share system components among multiple workstations, a major disadvantage is that if the central computer fails, none of the workstations can be used.

The **shared-resource WP system** also has multiple workstations, but each station has its own processor logic and storage sections. The failure of the computer at one station, of course, does not affect the processors at other workstations. Even though the stations can be individual stand-alone units, they share certain expensive resources such as printers and large-capacity disk drives.

Photos of word processors on these pages are courtesy Zenith Data Systems, a subsidiary of Zenith Radio Corporation and Wang Laboratories, Inc. (page 291); CPT Corporation and A. B. Dick Company (page 292); and Honeywell, Inc. (above).

Figure 11-3 The use of a WP/OCR system.

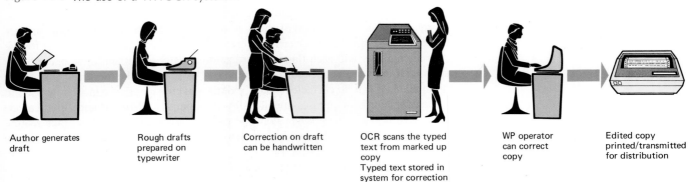

| Author generates draft | Rough drafts prepared on typewriter | Correction on draft can be handwritten | OCR scans the typed text from marked up copy Typed text stored in system for correction | WP operator can correct copy | Edited copy printed/transmitted for distribution |

It is my heart-warm and world-embracing Christmas hope and aspiration that all of us— the high, the low, the rich, the poor, the admired, the despised, the loved, the hated, the civilized, the savage—may eventually be gathered together in a heaven of everlasting rest and peace and bliss—except the inventor of the telephone.

Mark Twain

printed and studied. Changes may be made to the proposal in New York before it's sent to Chicago, and additional changes may be made in Chicago. Finally, the proposal can be forwarded back to Brussels, where it's printed and delivered to the customer. All this can be done in a single day.

■ Reporters for a major national magazine use WP stations to compose and edit their articles. After photos for the articles are scanned by special input devices, the magazine pages are then prepared right on the WP display screen. Text and photos are arranged in an attractive layout. Any last-minute changes are made at the display screens. Broadband transmission channels are then used to send the magnetically stored edition of the magazine from the magazine's editorial offices to a printing company located hundreds of miles away. The printer's computerized system makes printing plates from the transmitted signals, and then uses these plates to print the magazine issue. The first time a paper copy of the magazine is prepared is when the printing press is finally used.

■ Some word processors are teamed with optical character readers so that existing office typewriters can ''talk'' directly to the WP equipment (see Figure 11-3). An original text draft is prepared at a typewriter. After the draft has been examined, the OCR reader scans this text and automatically enters it into the WP system. The WP system is then used to edit, correct, and print or transmit the stored text. In such a WP/OCR system, every typewriter becomes an inexpensive wireless input terminal to the word processor(s). And in the absence of office equipment standards, an OCR reader can also be used as the interface between incompatible WP systems. Of course, in a totally integrated electronic office of the future, an OCR device wouldn't be needed because all keystrokes would be captured electronically. But there are 30 million IBM Selectric typewriters and millions of other models at work today, and they aren't going to disappear overnight.

# ELECTRONIC MAIL/MESSAGE SYSTEMS

There's no general agreement on what is meant by the term "electronic mail." Some define it as any kind of message system that uses computer technology. We'll be a little more specific and say that an **electronic mail/message system (EMMS)** is one that can store and deliver, by electronic means, messages that would otherwise probably be forwarded through the postal service or sent verbally over telephone lines. As Figure 11-4 shows, the cost of sending a message over an EMMS has been steadily dropping, and this trend will likely continue. The costs for traditional postal and telephone use, however, continue to rise.

### Mailroom Drag and Telephone Tag

It's estimated that most large businesses in the United States will have advanced EMMSs up and running by the late 1980s. Why this rapid movement to EMMS? One reason is the declining EMMS message costs mentioned earlier. But an EMMS can also overcome some of the limitations found in the message delivery systems provided by the postal service and telephone companies.

As you know, the postal service is relatively slow and messages are sometimes lost. The term "mailroom drag" describes the delays encountered in using this message delivery system. And using the telephone requires that (1) the message recipient can be located, and (2) the recipient is willing to be interrupted to take the call. Surprisingly enough, studies have shown that only about one in four calls made to people in organizations goes through on the first try. Three out of four times, then, people are either away from their phones or they are involved in activities where they don't want interruptions. In the cases when a call isn't completed, a frustrating game of **telephone tag** may then begin. Ms. Johnson leaves a message requesting that Mr. Burke return her call; Burke calls back to find that Johnson is in a meeting; Johnson tries again and learns that Burke has been called away from his desk. And so it goes—sometimes for days.

EMMS concepts have been developed in response to the shortcomings in other message delivery systems. An EMMS can perform a number of functions. It can, for example, provide:

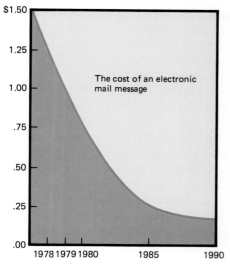

Figure 11-4 The cost of an EMMS message has been steadily dropping.

- Message distribution services.
- Transmission of documents and pictures.
- Computerized conferences.
- Follow-up services.

### Message Distribution Services

A keyed or spoken message is sent on the first try, and at any time of the day or night, to a *specified individual* who has a storage "mailbox" in the message system. (And it's just as easy for the sender to transmit a message to an identified *group of people* as it is to send it to a single person.) It's not necessary to locate the receiver(s) or interrupt him or her at a bad time. Rather, the receiver can periodically review stored messages at a time that *is* convenient.

Some EMMSs handle *spoken* messages, while others are designed to manage *keyed* text. When a **voice mail** approach is used, the sender calls the system's phone number, logs into the system, and then transmits the message to one or more recipients. The spoken sound waves produced by the sender are converted into digital pulses and are then stored on a hard disk for later retrieval. When message recipients call the **voice store-and-forward system,** they are notified that messages are waiting. After listening to the messages produced as reconstituted speech, they can then delete them, save them for future reference, or forward them to other parties.

Teleprinter and visual display terminals, and executive workstations, are generally used to enter and receive keyed messages. If you've read Chapter 6, you know that an *executive workstation* is a desktop unit—often a specially equipped personal computer—that's designed for the busy user. It includes special function keys, and it may accept input from a mouse and/or from touch-screen menus and voice recognition circuits. After reading (not listening to) the stored messages, a receiver can fire off responses and other messages, and, *if necessary,* make a printed copy of the communication (see Figure 11-5).

Users of EMMSs can also receive and send messages at home during the evening, or during business trips, by using a portable pc or terminal and/or a telephone. Beyond reducing interruptions, message distribution systems also provide *other benefits.* For example, people at remote sites no longer feel isolated because they can and do receive messages from headquarters as easily and quickly as do those who are located in the headquarters building. And people in different time zones can often communicate more easily since widely scattered offices may not be open at the same times. Another possible benefit is that EMMS messages tend to be brief and to the point, thus saving time.

Individuals and groups using the message system may be members of a *single* organization or they may belong to several *different* organizations. Many computer manufacturers—e.g., Wang Laboratories and Datapoint Corporation to name just two—offer message distribution systems to the users of their equipment. And, as you saw in Chapter 10, data communications service organizations such as GTE Telenet, Tymnet, The Source, and CompuServe provide facilities to support message distribution systems. A few examples of message distribution system users are:

- *Texas Instruments, Incorporated.* TI's DDP network discussed in Chapter 10 distributes more than 4 million messages each year. The average message is 600 to 800 characters in length and goes to four destinations.

- *Hewlett-Packard Company.* Also described in Chapter 10, H-P's DDP network carries 25 million messages a year.

- *Continental Illinois Bank and Trust Company of Chicago.* About 2,000 employees are linked by this bank's EMMS, and electronic mail can be delivered around the world in seconds. A message is sent as soon as keying is completed. The next time the recipient (perhaps in Europe or the Far East) checks his or her mailbox, the message will be waiting. In fact, if the recipient's terminal has been left on, the message will be immediately printed or displayed.

Figure 11-5 Using electronic mail (a) within an organization and (b) with the aid of an information service. (Adapted from Kevin Strehlo, "Mail Call, Mail Call!" *Personal Computing*, December 1983, pp. 126ff.)

- *University of Alaska.* Students, professors, and staff members scattered around the state are able to freely exchange messages through the MAIL System that has been developed for the university's computer network.

- *Attorneys and their clients.* Some lawyers and their clients communicate through a service called ELLA, an acronym for Electronic Legal Advice. To use this message system, a client dials a Tymnet phone number, gains access to the Tymnet network, keys in an account number and an access password, and then sends or receives messages. An attorney communicates with clients in the same way. After receiving a client's request, for example, the lawyer can draft a legal document and send it back to be printed at the client's terminal.

Figure 11-6 This tabletop digital facsimile machine can transmit high-resolution copies worldwide in as fast as 35 seconds. (Courtesy Business Communication Products Division/3M)

**Transmission of Documents and Pictures**

In this EMMS function, an original document can be placed in a sending **facsimile,** or **fax, machine** (see Figure 11-6). A communications link-up is then made with a receiving fax device at another location. As the sending machine scans the document, the receiving device reproduces the scanned image. Thus, when the transmission is completed, the receiving device has produced a duplicate, or "facsimile," of the original. The use of fax machines isn't new, but a great deal of emphasis is currently being placed on improving fax systems by increasing transmission speeds, by reducing transmission costs, and by integrating fax equipment into an automated office setting. A number of data communications service companies also provide fax transmission facilities. Satellite Business Systems, for example, offers high-speed fax services, and the Domestic Transmission Systems unit of ITT offers a Faxpak service for users. Faxpak rates permit users to send a page anywhere in the United States for a few cents.

Of course, copies of printed documents can also be sent electronically between intelligent copying machines or between communicating WP stations. In one case, for example, a Digital Equipment Corporation salesperson on the west coast sat down with a customer in front of a visual display. As sections of a proposed contract were displayed on the screen, changes were agreed on and then entered into the document stored in a WP station. After the contract had been revised, the communicating WP station forwarded it to a similar station at DEC's headquarters on the east coast. Corporate lawyers made a few alterations and then sent the contract back to the west coast. This contract was printed by the west coast WP station and signed by the salesperson and customer. The entire transaction was completed in less than one afternoon.

**Computerized Conferences**

A computer-based EMMS permits "conferences" to be held at the convenience of the participants. Since the conference dialog may be stored, it's *not* necessary for all participants to be online at their terminals *at the same time*. And, of course, it's also not necessary that they be physically present at the same place. Instead, a person can sit down at a terminal at a convenient time, call up any conversations she or he hasn't seen, make additional comments, respond to questions, etc., and then sign off. Several conference participants can "talk" at the same time. Once again, interruptions of other important work can be avoided. And a permanent history of all conference discussions can be recorded.

Infomedia Corporation of Palo Alto, California, offers two computer conferencing services called Planet and Notepad. To use these services, a group member dials a Tymnet local-access telephone number, couples the telephone to a terminal, and accesses a central computer file that's shared by all group members. Another computer conferencing network is the Electronic Information Exchange System sponsored by the New Jersey Institute of Technology. Subscribers are organized into groups devoted to specific topics such as technology for the handicapped. Many subscribers belong to more than one group, and they're encouraged to communicate with as many groups as they have time and interest for. Group members come from corporations, governments, and nonprofit foundations. Access is generally through the GTE Telenet system.

The term **computer conferencing** refers to the types of EMMSs that we've just considered that permit people to participate at *different* times. An alternative to computer conferencing is **teleconferencing**—a term that refers to the electronic linking of geographically scattered people who are all participating at the *same* time. Facsimile devices, electronic blackboards that can cause chalk markings to be reproduced on distant TV monitors, the Picturephone Meeting Service supplied by AT&T—these and other technologies allow people to communicate over wide distances in real time. Of course, there are advantages in face-to-face meetings that teleconferencing can't replace. Facial expressions and "body language" can convey information that might be missed with teleconferencing. But time, energy, and money are saved when people don't have to travel long distances to conduct a meeting. Organizations using teleconferencing include:

■ *Exxon Corporation.* If a problem had occurred a few years ago at a remote oil drilling site—e.g., in western Canada—a team of troubleshooting specialists would have been sent from Houston to Calgary to deal with the problem. Today, however, the Houston engineers and managers may "travel" to a Houston conference room to confer with people at Calgary on both a visual and audio basis. Instead of flying three engineers to Calgary in hopes that they can quickly resolve the problem, Exxon can assemble 20 Houston experts for a brainstorming session.

■ *Holiday Inns.* This large chain offers a HI-Net electronic meeting service. Conference speakers go to a Cleveland Holiday Inn and other participants go to their local Holiday Inn facility. In one recent conference, 2,000 salespeople went to 33 Holiday Inn locations to participate in a convention.

**Follow-up Services**  In this EMMS function, the message system provides additional services to help the recipient take appropriate action after the message has been delivered. For example, the receiver may:

- ■ Forward the message to others with or without further comments.

- ■ Store the message in a "personal attention needed" electronic file.

- ■ Store the message in a subordinate's electronic file with instructions for the subordinate to take the necessary action.

## Feedback and Review 11-1

This chapter has introduced you to word processing and electronic mail/message systems—two of the fastest-growing areas of computer usage today. To test and reinforce your understanding of these dynamic forces in the office of the future, answer the following multiple-choice questions by placing the letter of the most nearly correct answer in the space provided.

___1. The activities performed in most offices today
    a) are supported by an equipment investment of $50,000 per worker.
    b) are being performed with fewer and fewer total workers.
    c) consist of such data processing activities as originating-recording, classifying, sorting, calculating, summarizing, communicating, storing, and retrieving.
    d) would be impossible without WP and EMMS equipment.

___2. Which of the following is not a problem in many of today's offices:
    a) low productivity of office workers relative to other groups.
    b) too many skilled office workers for the declining number of jobs available.
    c) escalation of costs.
    d) misfiling of documents.

___3. Progress toward the "office of the future" has
    a) virtually stopped in recent years.
    b) been hampered by the rapidly increasing costs of electronic office equipment.
    c) been hampered by the lack of interest among equipment vendors in developing new products.
    d) not yet lived up to predictions.

___4. A modern WP system
    a) is basically a disguised computer that's programmed to do word processing.

    b) must be dedicated to performing only WP functions.
    c) cannot be implemented using micro- or minicomputer components.
    d) is always a shared-logic device.

___5. A shared-resource WP system
    a) has only a single station that contains all the components needed to perform text processing.
    b) has multiple stations that share the logic and storage sections of a single central computer.
    c) has only a one- or two-line visual display.
    d) has not been described by any of the above responses.

___6. Word processors can be used to
    a) relay text messages between communicating stations.
    b) prepare issues of magazines.
    c) accept input from an OCR reader.
    d) do all the above tasks.

___7. Electronic mail
    a) is a frequently used term that has no generally accepted definition.
    b) cannot be used to compete with the postal service.
    c) costs have been increasing in recent years.
    d) cannot be substituted for telephone messages.

___8. Which, if any, of the following functions cannot be performed by an EMMS:
    a) provide message distribution services.
    b) transmit copies of documents and pictures.
    c) provide computerized conference services.
    d) perform all the functions described above.

___9. Messages sent over a message distribution system
    a) can be used by individuals but not by groups.
    b) can be periodically reviewed by the recipient at a convenient time.
    c) must be printed or keyed.
    d) tend to give a feeling of isolation to people at remote sites.

___10. A facsimile machine
    a) cannot be used in an EMMS.
    b) is needed at both the sending and receiving stations.

c) requires low-speed communication channels.
d) is the only device that can send copies of documents over telecommunications channels.

——**11.** Computer conferencing and teleconferencing
a) are terms that mean the same thing.

b) both require that people participate in conferences at the same time.
c) are both used to link geographically scattered people.
d) both permit people to participate at whatever times are convenient for them.

## LOOKING BACK

**1.** The functions performed in offices consist of such data processing activities as originating-recording, classifying, sorting, calculating, summarizing, communicating, storing, and retrieving. Traditional office tools and techniques are still often followed to perform these tasks. But the relatively low productivity of office workers, rising costs, and other problems are resulting in the introduction of new electronic technology into offices.

**2.** The change from the traditional office setting to an electronic office environment is likely to evolve through several development stages. Most organizations today are in the early stages of development and are introducing equipment to perform specific tasks such as word processing, message distribution, document transmission and reproduction, and computer conferencing.

**3.** Word processing is the rapidly growing use of electronic equipment to create, view, edit, manipulate, transmit, store, retrieve, and print text material. Word processors are basically computers that are programmed to process text material. Dedicated word processors perpetually run their WP programs, and small general-purpose computers can be temporarily converted into word processors merely by loading a WP program into storage.

**4.** Dedicated word processing systems can be classified into stand-alone, shared-logic, and shared-resource categories. A stand-alone WP station is a single unit that contains all the components needed to perform text processing. A shared-logic system has multiple keystations that share the logic and storage sections of a single central processor. A shared-resource system

also has multiple stations, but each station has its own computer. These multiple stations simply share certain expensive resources such as printers and large-capacity disk drives. A number of examples of the uses of WP are presented in the chapter.

**5.** An electronic mail/message system is defined here to be one that can store and deliver, by electronic means, messages that would otherwise probably be forwarded through the postal service or sent verbally over telephone lines. The use of EMMS is growing rapidly, and this is partly due to postal service delays and the frustrations caused by "telephone tag."

**6.** An EMMS can provide electronic message distribution services, a means of transmitting copies of documents and pictures, computerized conference functions, and other services. A message distribution system allows messages to be sent at any time to specified individuals or groups. Recipients periodically review stored voice or keyed-text messages at convenient times. Interruptions are reduced, people may feel less isolated, and communication between time zones is facilitated. Many computer vendors and data communications services offer message distribution systems. Several examples of the uses of these systems are presented in the chapter. The use of facsimile machines to transmit copies of documents and pictures and a discussion of computer conferencing and teleconferencing are also presented. Computer conferencing and teleconferencing are both used to link people who are geographically separated, but computer conferencing permits people to participate at different times while teleconferencing requires participants to be online at the same time.

## KEY TERMS AND CONCEPTS

**word processing (WP) 291**
**dedicated word processor 291**
**stand-alone WP station 292**
**shared-logic WP system 293**
**shared-resource WP system 293**

**global search 293**
**search and replace 293**
**electronic mail/message system (EMMS) 295**
**telephone tag 295**

**voice mail 296**
**voice store-and-forward system 296**
**facsimile (fax) machine 298**
**computer conferencing 299**
**teleconferencing 299**

## TOPICS FOR REVIEW AND DISCUSSION

**1.** *(a)* What functions are performed in offices? *(b)* Identify and discuss the problems that have developed in recent years in offices that have followed traditional office practices.

**2.** Discuss two factors that are likely to lead to the introduction of new technology and applications in the offices of many organizations in the next few years.

**3.** "Most organizations today are in the early stages of developing an automated office and are now introducing equipment to perform a few specific tasks." What are these tasks?

**4.** *(a)* What is word processing? *(b)* How did it develop?

**5.** "A dedicated word processor is basically a disguised computer that perpetually runs a program to process text material." Discuss this statement.

**6.** Dedicated word processing systems today generally fall into three categories. Identify and discuss these categories.

**7.** Give three examples of how WP can be used.

**8.** *(a)* What's an EMMS? *(b)* What are the limitations of the alternatives to an EMMS?

**9.** *(a)* What are the benefits of an electronic message distribution system? *(b)* How are such systems used?

**10.** *(a)* How are fax machines used? *(b)* Can other devices perform the same function?

**11.** *(a)* What is computerized conferencing? *(b)* What is teleconferencing? *(c)* Give an example of each type of service.

## PROJECTS TO LOOK INTO

**1.** Identify an office setting of interest to you and make a study of how word processing and/or other office automation techniques have been/are being implemented. Present your findings to the class.

**2.** Visit your library and research the early developments in word processing. Write a report outlining your findings.

## ANSWERS TO FEEDBACK AND REVIEW SECTION

**11-1**

1. c
2. b
3. d
4. a
5. d
6. d
7. a
8. d
9. b
10. b
11. c

# What It Costs to Get into Teleconferencing

Tandem Computers, Cupterino, CA, known for its innovative management style, is one of the companies setting up its own videoconferencing capabilities. Here is how the company describes what is involved:

## Equipment Rental per Teleconference
Uplink (dish antenna)
$2,500 for first day; $1,500 for additional consecutive days (per site). Tandem currently broadcasts to 16 sites.
Satellite time
$340 per hour with one-hour minimum. Available for $170 per half hour after the initial hour.
Monitoring and switching service
$85 per broadcast.

## Company Resources Used in Teleconference
Downlink (TV receive-only dish antenna; i.e., earth station)
Downlinks cost $6,835 for a permanent unit. Tandem currently owns six. Mobile units cost $9,000 apiece, because of the trailer. Tandem owns 10; more units are being set up.
Production equipment
Production staff
TV studio with cameras, lights, and all other necessary equipment.
Permanent video staff of 14 people who spend approximately 50%–65% of their time producing teleconferences. Staff includes camera operators, producer, director, technical director, software engineers, and others. People are also brought in from other departments to handle incoming queries on teleconference materials. Some technical positions are filled through a local college internship program. Approximately 30 people are needed to produce a teleconference.

## Approximate Cost of Disseminating Information without a Teleconference
The cost factors involved in conventional classes or seminars are the travel costs for each person, including air fare, hotel, and meals. In the case of new product announcements, salespeople are flown to four or five central locations. Thus, travel costs of corporate staff to make the presentations must be taken into account, too. Such costs, naturally, vary with the length of the trip and accommodations provided. A conservative estimate for a three- to four-day trip involving a flight out of state is $1,000 per person. To give this figure some meaning, the smallest number that has viewed a Tandem teleconference is 50, the largest, more than 3,000. This results in a minimum conventional cost of $50,000 in disseminating the information. Of course, there is no way to calculate the potential revenue loss of taking salespeople out of the field for one or more days of presentations.

## Cost of a One-Hour Teleconference Once the Initial Equipment Has Been Obtained

| | |
|---|---:|
| Uplink | $2,500 |
| Satellite time | 340 |
| Monitoring and switching | 85 |
| Total | $2,925 |
| | +personnel and equipment overhead |

The teleconference is proving an alternative to face-to-face meetings. While there are advantages which teleconferencing can't replace, its capabilities are expanding while its costs are dropping. And savings in time, energy, and money mount up when people don't have to travel to conduct business. (Courtesy Fujitsu Microelectronics, Inc., Professional Microsystems Division)

## Sales Meetings Enter the Electronic Age

Advances in communications technology and falling prices are persuading more companies to use teleconferences for sales meetings. A survey by Runzheimer and Co., Rochester, WI, reveals that 15% of U.S. companies used video to cut business travel costs. A new study by Quantum Science Corp., New York City, predicts that the number of business teleconferences will explode from 89,400 in 1981 to 1.8 million by 1986, says Christine H. Ehrenbard, associate director of the consulting company's communications and teleconferencing strategy program.

Gary Badoud, president, Video-Net, Woodland Hills, CA, a producer of teleconferences, says that costs of teleconferences have dropped from 23% to 29% between 1980 and 1982, depending upon the number of cities used. He says costs are being pushed down by the increased availability of satellite receiving equipment, expanding supply of portable equipment, installation of permanent receiving facilities at more major hotels, and adaptation of cable TV for teleconferences.

### Average Teleconference Costs

|      | 10 Cities | 20 Cities | 30 Cities |
|------|-----------|-----------|-----------|
| 1980 | $40,500   | $65,500   | $75,500   |
| 1981 | 33,500    | 53,500    | 63,500    |
| 1982 | 28,500    | 46,500    | 57,500    |

Note: Teleconferencing costs, based on average costs of a management presentation to sales force members in the number of cities designated, include: TV equipment, satellite transmission, reception at all sites, meeting-room charges, one-way video/two-way audio, and a 6-ft. screen at each location.
Source: VideoNet.

### How Teleconferencing Cuts Allied Van Lines' Meeting Costs

|                     | 1980 Road Show | 1981 Video Conference |
|---------------------|----------------|-----------------------|
| Cities              | 6              | 27                    |
| People              | 650            | 1,300                 |
| Employee expenses   | $ 54,000       | $13,000               |
| Facilities expenses | 44,000         | 42,000                |
| Production expenses | 89,000         | 37,000                |
| Total expenses      | $187,000       | $92,000               |
| Cost per attendee   | $288.00        | $71.00                |

Note: Data are for Allied Van Lines' annual presentation for dealers and distributors. A travelling road show that visited 6 cities in 1980 was replaced in 1981 with a single video conference that was beamed to more cities (27) and at a cheaper total cost.
Source: VideoNet.

"What It Costs to Get into Teleconferencing," *Sales and Marketing Management,* Feb. 21, 1983, pp. 24–25.

# System Analysis, Design, and Implementation Considerations

## Systems Synergy

Companies assign their data processing managers to take charge of two divergent missions: to support high-volume production systems as well as tactical and strategic business planning.

It is not unusual for a production system to spend two to three years in development and then be used by the business for the following 10 to 15 years.

Tactical and strategic systems, on the other hand, are characterized by short lead times and short life spans. A manager may request an analysis in the afternoon and expect the results on his desk the next morning. After reviewing the result, he often tosses it out and requests a totally different analysis. The functional manager can ask for any data from any source at any time. This unpredictability can be particularly unnerving to the DP professional unprepared to cope with it. However, this unpredictability is a critical part of tactical and strategic analysis; the DP professional must learn to handle it.

During the last decade, a number of technologies emerged to help companies develop a "total solution" to their information systems problems, encompassing the production area, as well as strategic and tactical planning.

Package software, data base management systems (DBMS), fourth-generation languages and structured systems design and development are unquestionably major accomplishments in the effort to deliver information systems to modern businesses. However, proponents often mislead users in presenting these aids individually as complete solutions to the information system problem.

The first step in building a truly "synergistic" systems environment is to recognize those four technologies as tools to achieving the business' system objectives. Each tool must be used in a framework that maximizes its advantages while minimizing disadvantages.

—Mike Ruggera, "Four Tools to Build Systems Synergy," *Computerworld* In Depth, Oct. 31, 1983, p. 11. Copyright 1983 by CW Communications, Framingham, Mass. Photo courtesy Honeywell, Inc.

Chapters 10 and 11 provided examples of some real computer-based systems that people rely on for information. Chapter 12 looks at the steps people take to develop and implement such systems. A brief sketch of the material discussed here was first presented in Chapter 3. We'll flesh out that outline now and give you more details. The information in this chapter will enable you to:

- Outline the procedures that may be followed during the problem definition step.

- Describe how data are gathered and then analyzed during the system analysis step.

- Discuss some issues that may affect system design choices, and summarize the types of system specifications produced during the design step.

- Discuss factors to be considered in acquiring new equipment, and outline some of the general system implementation activities required to replace an old system with a new one.

# A SYSTEM STUDY REVIEW

As you saw in Chapter 3, information users and data processing specialists must often work together to complete a series of steps in a system study. The object of such a study is to develop and/or acquire the software needed to control the processing of specific applications. Although some study steps may be bypassed if suitable software packages are available, the six steps shown in Figure 12-1 are needed when custom-made programs are written. The first three steps are generally needed before a suitable software package can be identified, so we'll consider these steps

**Figure 12-1** The six steps people must follow in order to use computers for useful purposes may be classified into system analysis/design and programming stages. The chapters in this module deal with the three steps in the system analysis/design stage. Details of the programming process are presented in Module 5. (Photos courtesy Hewlett-Packard Company; Honeywell, Inc.; Teletype Corporation; General Electric Information Systems Company; Edith G. Haun/Stock, Boston; and Control Data Corporation)

along with some system implementation concepts in this chapter. (Steps 4 through 6 are treated in detail in Chapters 18 through 21 of the Programming Module.)

System studies are needed because people must constantly adapt to change. Opportunities come and go. Problems arise and must be solved. In organizations, many of the changes that lead to a system study effort can be traced to the following interrelated **system change factors:**

1. *Technological factors.* The ancient Greeks had several dreams. One of these was the Promethean dream of stealing fire from the gods. Another was the dream of soaring away from Earth and beyond the planets. After remaining unrealized for thousands of years, both dreams have been achieved in just the last few decades. The fires of atomic furnaces have been ignited, and people and their machines have moved out into space. People have never before lived in a time when the scope of scientific inquiry was so broad, or when the speed of applying new discoveries was so swift. The application of new technology accounts for many changes in organizations.

2. *Social and economic factors.* A wave of social and economic changes often follows in the wake of new technology. New opportunities may arise to improve on a production process or to do something that was previously not possible. Changes in the ways individuals are organized into groups may then be necessary, and new groups may compete for economic resources with established units.

3. *High-level decisions and operating pressures.* In response to technological, social, and economic factors, top-level managers may decide to reorganize operations and introduce new products. Or they may implement new budgeting procedures to help bring operating problems under control. And lower-level managers of operating departments often initiate changes in order to gain recognition and receive tangible and intangible rewards.

Regardless of the reason, however, frequent changes create conditions or problems that managers and other people must deal with.

## PROBLEM DEFINITION

**Problem definition** is the first and perhaps the most important step in the system study. After all, people must recognize that a need or problem exists before they can create a solution. A clear and accurate problem definition—one that's not open to misinterpretation by people with different backgrounds—isn't easy to prepare. But since it's the foundation for all the system study steps that follow, such a definition must be created.

**The Problem Definition Survey**    A preliminary **problem definition survey** is often conducted to identify the problem or need. There's certainly nothing new about such surveys. In the Bible in chapter 13 of the Book of Numbers, Moses sent out a team to survey the Promised Land and report back their findings. Three important prerequisite principles were observed in this early survey:

1. *The survey had support at the highest levels.* God told Moses: "Send men to spy out the land of Canaan . . . from each tribe of their fathers shall you send a man, every one a leader among them." Moses certainly had support at the highest level! Although requests for system changes or additions may originate from many sources, top-level management support is important to the success of the change effort.

2. *The survey team consisted of highly respected people.* Only tribal leaders were sent on the mission. Members of the team seeking to define the problem should also be qualified people selected for the offsetting talents they can bring to the job. At least one member (and very possibly the leader of the survey team) represents the interests of the end users of any new system that will be developed. Another member should be familiar with system development and the technical side of data processing. An auditor may also be included to evaluate the effects of any proposed changes on existing data integrity and system security controls.

3. *The scope and objectives of the survey were clearly stated.* Moses specifically told his team to investigate the richness of the land and the strength of the occupants. In a problem definition survey, the nature of the operation(s) that is (are) to be investigated, and the objectives that are to be pursued, should be specifically stated. The organizational units that are to be included should also be identified.

The biblical survey team returned to Moses after 40 days. The team members agreed on the richness of the land, but not on the strength of the occupants. Sessions were held to present the differing viewpoints. It's also usually necessary for the problem definition team to hold preliminary sessions with those who are likely to be affected by any changes. These **requirements sessions** allow people to participate in setting or revising specific system goals. Such participation allows those who are most familiar with existing methods to make suggestions for improvement and to personally benefit from the change.

A repeating (or *iterative*) process may be necessary before the problem definition step is completed. There's no definite procedure to be followed before detailed system analysis can begin. A top executive may believe that informational deficiencies exist. He or she may prepare a general statement of objectives and then appoint a manager to conduct a survey. A number of requirements sessions may be held to translate general desires into more specific goals. The scope of the survey may be enlarged or reduced, and objectives may also change as facts are gathered. When it appears that approval has been reached on the problem definition, the survey team should put the detailed definition *in writing* and send it to all concerned for written approval. If differences remain, they should be resolved in additional

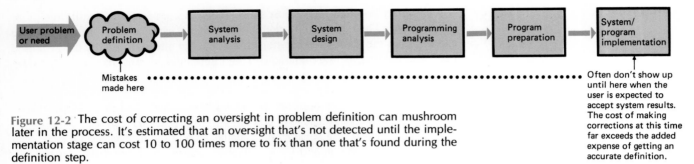

Figure 12-2 The cost of correcting an oversight in problem definition can mushroom later in the process. It's estimated that an oversight that's not detected until the implementation stage can cost 10 to 100 times more to fix than one that's found during the definition step.

requirements sessions. There are those who may become impatient with the "delays" in system development caused by these additional sessions. But wiser heads know that the really lengthy and expensive delays occur when users discover very late in the development process that the designed system is unsatisfactory because of earlier requirements oversights (see Figure 12-2).

The System Study Charter

As a final act before the detailed system analysis step begins, the survey leader should prepare a *written charter* for approval by a high-level executive or steering committee. This **system study charter** should include:

■ A detailed statement of the scope and objectives of the system study.

■ A list of those who should be assigned to the system study team.

■ A grant of authority to permit this team to use some of the working time of specified individuals.

■ A development schedule giving a target date for the completion of the study, and interim "checkpoint" dates for the presentation of progress reports to interested parties. (These progress reports give users, managers, and auditors a chance to determine the accuracy and completeness of the study effort.)

# SYSTEM ANALYSIS

Since most new systems in organizations are based to some extent on existing procedures, a first step for the study team analysts is often to gather data on current operations. In short, they must find out where they are before they can figure out where they want to go.

Data Gathering

It's likely that preliminary facts were gathered during the problem definition step. But more details are now needed to determine the strengths and weaknesses of current procedures. The data to be collected will vary, of course, from one study to another. But in most cases the study team members should answer the following general questions about current operations:

1. *What output results are currently being achieved?* The content, purpose, and use of reports and other output results should be determined, and the accuracy and timeliness of the output should be checked.
2. *What processing procedures and resources are being used to produce this output?* The records and files being processed, the frequency, volume, and accuracy of this processing, the sequence of steps being followed, the people and departments doing the work, the processing and storage equipment being used, the cost of the processing—these and other matters should be checked.
3. *What input data are used to produce output results?* The source, form, and volume of input data should be understood. The frequency of input, the accuracy of the input, and the input cost should also be known.

You recognize that these questions refer to the input/processing/output components found in any data processing system. But the input to output sequence is often reversed during system analysis because the analysts need an early understanding of current output before they can properly separate and analyze the processing and input functions that are relevant to the output.

**Data-Gathering Aids.** The following tools and techniques are often used during data-gathering operations:

- *Organization charts and organization standards.* An **organization chart** indicates by position titles the formal place in the organization of each job. Such a chart can give analysts a better picture of the people and departments that may be affected by expected changes. Some organizations have developed **standards manuals** that spell out the steps to be completed during (and after) the data-gathering phase. These manuals benefit the organization by helping produce studies that are more thorough and more consistent. They also help analysts answer such questions as: What's the next step? How should this procedure be documented? When have we gathered enough data?

- *System flowcharts.* The system flowcharts discussed in Chapter 3 are often drawn up during the data-gathering stage. They are used to record the flow of data in a current procedure from the originating source, through a number of processing operations and machines, to the output report. The flowchart may help an analyst acquire a better understanding of the procedure than would otherwise be possible. It can also help point out possible bottlenecks in the data flow of the system. In complex systems, there's likely to be an overall ''macro chart'' that describes the general input/processing/output components of the system. There may then be a hierarchy of more detailed ''micro charts,'' each of which describes a module in a higher-level chart. This decomposition of a system into a series of detailed input/processing/output graphics is a frequently used analysis technique. For example, SofTech's SADT (Structured Analysis and Design Technique) and IBM's HIPO (Hierarchy plus Input-Process-Output) are both techniques that follow this approach.

■ **Questionnaires and special-purpose forms.** A printed form can be used by analysts to obtain answers to commonly asked questions. These questionnaires and other specialized data-gathering forms are often keyed to the activities presented in a system flowchart. They supply the details about processing frequencies, I/O volumes and materials, and the time needed to perform each activity. One forms-driven approach to data gathering is shown in Figure 12-3.

You can observe a lot just by watching.

Yogi Berra

■ **Interviews and observations.** Interviews are needed to gather data, prepare charts, and fill in questionnaires and forms. Analysts can watch as people perform the tasks required by the system being studied. An analyst can also take an input document and "walk it through" the processing procedure. Such a walkthrough gives the analyst a chance to obtain suggestions from people about ways in which a procedure can be improved.

Figure 12-3 In IBM's *Study Organization Plan* (SOP), five data-gathering forms are used to describe the existing system. When completed, the *message sheets* provide detailed facts on current output and input. The *file forms* show the data stored in the system. And the *operation sheets* present the detailed processing steps performed by the system. A separate operation sheet is typically keyed to each step outlined by the system flowchart on the *activity sheet*. Finally, the organizational environment of the current system and the costs of the system are presented on the *resource usage sheet*. (Courtesy International Business Machines Corporation)

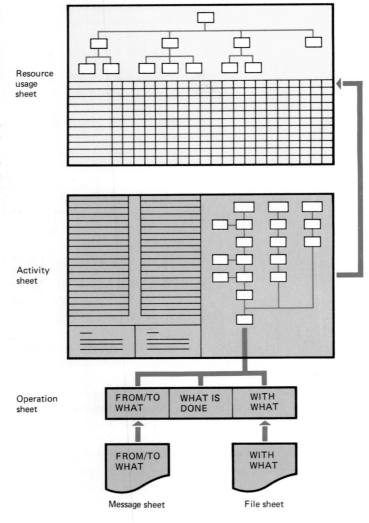

**Analysis of the Problem**    After the necessary data have been gathered, the analysts must study their findings to determine the strengths and weaknesses of the existing procedures. During data gathering, the emphasis was on learning *what* was being done. Now, the focus is on learning *why* the system operates as it does. The purpose of this analysis is to develop suggestions on how the study goals may best be achieved.

**Analysis Aids.** The following tools and techniques may be used to analyze the current system and develop suggestions for improvement:

■ *Checklist of questions.* Questions dealing with procedural, personnel, organizational, and economic considerations should be answered. A few representative questions are shown in Figure 12-4.

---

**Procedural considerations**

- Is faster reporting desired?  Is faster reporting necessary?  Can the processing sequence be improved?  What would happen if any documents were eliminated?

- Is greater accuracy needed?

- What monetary value do users place on the output?  Are they willing to have their budgets charged with all or part of the cost of preparation?

- Is the output in a useful form?  Has writing been minimized?

- Does an output document cause action when it's sent to a manager?  If not, why is it sent?

- Is the output stored?  If so, for how long?  How often is it referred to?

- Can documents be combined?  Is the same information duplicated on other reports?  In other departments?  If so, can procedures be integrated?

- Is unnecessary output generated?  Do current reports clearly point out exceptions?

- Is system capacity adequate?  Do bottlenecks exist?  Is customer service adequate?

**Personnel and organizational considerations**

- Is the output being prepared in the proper departments?  By the right people?  Could departments be combined?  What effects would organizational change have on people?

- What effect would any procedural changes have on people?  What would have to be done to reduce resistance to change?  What would be done with those whose jobs would be eliminated or changed?  If new jobs were created, what consideration would have to be given to selecting and training workers to staff these vacancies?

**Economic considerations**

- What is the cost of the present system?  What would be the cost of processing with revised current procedures?  Approximately what would it cost to satisfy needs using other alternatives?

Figure 12-4  Questions for analysis.

---

■ *System flowchart analysis.* Charts can be examined to help locate essential data and files. And they can also be used to identify bottlenecks and unnecessary files. For example, a chart may show a file where information is being stored, but from which little or nothing is being retrieved.

■ *Forms analysis.* The input/processing/output forms such as those shown in Figure 12-3 that describe I/O documents and processing logic are also helpful both in identifying key data items and in uncovering those items that are processed and stored but are seldom used.

■ *Grid charts.* Special grid (or **input/output**) **charts** may be used to show the relationship that exists between system inputs and outputs. Input documents are listed in rows on the left of the chart (see Figure 12-5), while the output reports produced by the system are identified in the chart columns. An "x" is placed at the intersection of a row and column when a particular document is used to prepare a specific report. For example, in Figure 12-5 form A is used to prepare reports 1 and 4. The chart enables the analyst to identify independent subsystems for further study. This is done by

| Input source documents | Output reports | | | | | | | |
|---|---|---|---|---|---|---|---|---|
| | 1 | 2 | 3 | 4 | 5 | 6 | 7 | 8 |
| Form A | x | | | x | | | | |
| Form B | | x | | x | | | | |
| Form C | | | x | | | | | |
| Form D | | | | | | x | | |
| Form E | | x | | x | | | | |
| Form F | | | x | | | | | x |
| Form G | | | | | x | | x | |

Figure 12-5 An example of a grid chart.

(a) drawing a vertical line down any single report column and then (b) drawing a horizontal line across any row with a covered x, etc., until further vertical and horizontal lines are impossible. For example, if we. draw a line down column 1, we cover only one x—the one indicating that form A is used in preparing report 1. If we then draw a horizontal line along the form A row, we cover the x in column 4. We then draw a vertical line down column 4 and a horizontal line along any row with a covered x. The result of this procedure is that forms A, B, and E and reports 1, 2, and 4 combine to form an independent subsystem.

■ **The top-down analysis methodology.** If the system being analyzed is complex, a "divide and conquer" methodology is often used to break the system down into smaller components. A top-level function is identified, analyzed, and then broken down into a series of second-level components. Each of these components, in turn, may be further reduced into still lower-level elements. A hierarchy of understandable subfunctions may be the result of this **top-down analysis methodology.**

**The Analysis Report**

Regardless of the aids used, the final product of the system analysis step should be a *documentation package* and a report of the analysts' findings. The documentation package should include copies of all forms, charts, questionnaires, I/O documents, and written procedural descriptions that have been gathered and analyzed. The **analysis report** should include:

■ A restatement of the problem.

■ A summary of current procedures and a statement of present problems or opportunities.

■ A listing of the general specifications needed to solve the problem along with some preliminary suggestions for solution alternatives that could be considered.

■ An evaluation of the operational feasibility of the project from a personnel and organizational standpoint.

■ An estimate of the economic feasibility of the project.

After evaluating the analysis report, responsible managers may decide to revise the study goals, cancel the project, postpone development until later, or proceed to the system design phase.

# SYSTEM DESIGN

During the system design phase, designers must decide *how* to produce an efficient (economical) and effective (relevant and useful) system. To do this, they must first *determine feasible alternatives* and then settle on a single set of *detailed specifications* for the problem solution. This isn't easy! As Figure 12-6 shows, many factors have a bearing on the design task. These factors present practical limits to the number of system alternatives that can actually be evaluated.

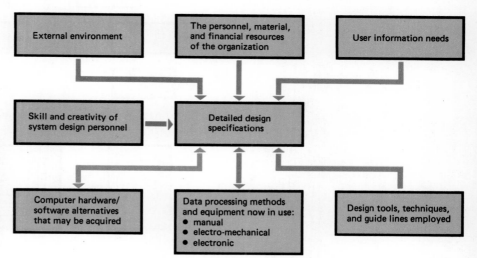

**Figure 12-6** Some factors having a bearing on the design process. The detailed design specifications depend on such input factors as user needs, the skill of system designers and the tools they use, the external environment, and the organization's resources. Design specifications may also depend on existing methods and equipment and on the hardware/software alternatives that may be obtained.

## Design Tools and Techniques

The following tools and techniques are among those used during system design:

■ *Organization standards.* Some organizations have standards manuals that specify a consistent design approach. The procedures to follow in designing output reports, input forms, and processing logic may also be spelled out.

■ *Top-down design methodology.* The **top-down design** technique requires the early identification of the top-level functions in the proposed system. Each function is then broken down into a hierarchy of understandable lower-level modules and components as shown in the **hierarchical charts** in Figure 12-7. After a top-level chart showing the total structure of the system is prepared, lower-level diagrams are created to show the input/processing/output details of each function, module, and component. Sev-

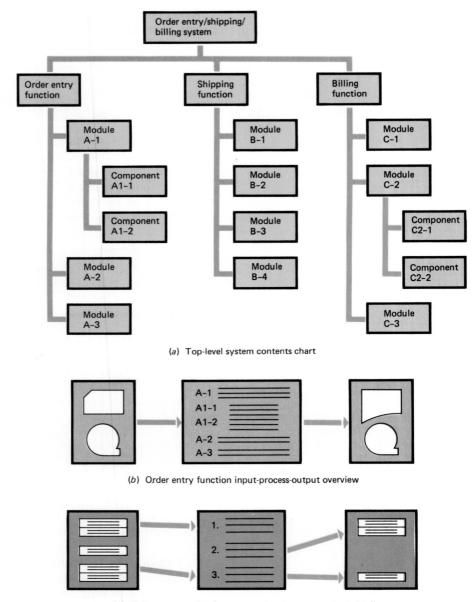

(a) Top-level system contents chart

(b) Order entry function input-process-output overview

(c) Order entry module/component input-process-output detail

Figure 12-7 Hierarchical charts used in top-down design.

eral iterations will usually occur in this design and charting process. Designers may start with simple diagrams showing general solutions. This first effort is then refined to produce more complete charts as the design requirements become clearer.

■ *Design reviews and walkthroughs.* Periodic sessions may be held so that interested users can review the design progress. Designers can present sample outputs and "walk through" the input and processing operations to describe the handling of data. Users can be encouraged to look for errors and to make comments during this **design walkthrough.**

■ *Special charts and forms.* The charts and forms prepared during the system analysis phase are very helpful in the design stage. Weaknesses spotted during analysis can now be corrected. And the existing input/processing/ output relationships may now be used to design a more integrated system.

■ *Automated design approaches.* The computer itself may also be used in the system development process. The ISDOS (Information Systems Design and Optimization System) project at the University of Michigan is working on a software package that will design systems in accordance with stated criteria. Special computer programs can be used to evaluate various hardware/software alternatives during the design stage. Processing requirements can be supplied, and a computer program can then determine how efficiently these requirements can be processed using different equipment alternatives.

## Determining Alternatives: Some Design Issues

Issues involving methodology and the use of resources usually have a bearing on the alternatives that are selected. Included in these issues are questions about:

1. *The long-range design plans that are followed.* Many organizations have developed conceptual models or long-range plans for the evolution of their information systems. These models or plans usually allow for the gradual integration of the information-producing systems in the organization. The alternatives that designers can consider in implementing specific projects must conform to the overall design plan that has been adopted.

2. *The flexibility that should be designed into the system.* Designers must decide how adaptable the new system should be to changing circumstances. An organization in a stable industry that sells only a few staple products to a reliable group of customers need not be as concerned with **system flexibility** as one in a dynamic industry that sells many products that are vulnerable to changing demand and competitive pressures. In most cases, systems will need to be changed several times during their useful life. And these changes are often unpredictable. Designers may thus face a dilemma: They can produce a relatively inflexible system that has (perhaps) lower design costs, and then incur the high costs required to periodically rebuild the system. Or, they can initially spend the extra time (and money) to produce a flexible design that may require fewer future changes. As Figure 12-8 shows, the *total cost* over the life of the system may well turn out to be less when flexibility is a design goal. Different degrees of flexibility can be created by using different approaches to *organize, access,* and *process* files. You can review the data organization hierarchy and the file processing alternatives open to system designers by reading the chapter's Closer Look.

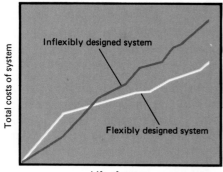

Figure 12-8 The total system cost over the life of the system may be less when flexibility is a design goal.

## ALL I WANTED WAS TO BUY A BAG OF GROCERIES

The other day I wrote out a check to pay for groceries. The clerk told me, while looking over my check, that in the near future, the store was starting a new computerized check-approval system. I would have to make a new application if I wanted to keep paying for food with a check.

After over five years of biweekly or triweekly visits to this particular store, I didn't understand why I had to make out a brand-new application. But curious, I asked for a blank application.

The old system simply kept track of bad checks. If a person wanted to continue to cash checks, he had better not write checks he couldn't cover. It was simple. Apparently, it was too simple.

The new application form demanded that I tell them my social security number (are they going to attach my old age pension?), my drivers license number (which is the same), how old and fat I am, who is silly enough to employ me and where that silly employer does business—all of that in addition to the normal address and phone numbers.

Why, I asked, did I have to give out all this information just to continue to buy groceries as I have been doing for five years? "Because the old system didn't work well enough," the manager explained. I persisted a bit, though the manager looked increasingly uneasy and exasperated. "But why pick on me? I've never written a bad check?"

You don't seem to understand," he said (this phrase became pretty familiar the more I pursued the matter). "The old system let too many bad check writers write bad checks."

Now that, of course, makes sense. Because of the normal float and other delays, unscrupulous or careless people can go on for a long time before their bad check records catch up with them. I'm sure that the new computerized check approval system will be more effective at catching bad checks than the old one was. All that data about how old and fat I am could be useful in tracking me down, if need be. And to store and retrieve that extra information only takes a few more fields on the computer record—pretty trivial, from the technical standpoint.

There is only one problem. It takes me—a person with an unblemished record of trustworthiness (at least from the standpoint of my checking account)—and dumps me into a pot with the worst thieves in the country. For the store's ease of screening out crooks, I am presumed to be a crook until proven otherwise. That's just fine for the store and for the data processing processors. But what about me?

—Terril J. Steicher, "All I Wanted Was to Buy a Bag of Groceries," *Computerworld*, Jan. 16, 1984. p. 34. Copyright 1984 by CW Communications, Inc, Farmingham, Mass.

3. *The control provisions that should be included.* Designers must make sure that procedures and controls are built into any alternative to ensure that the integrity of the data and the security of the system are not impaired. An "audit trail" that permits the tracing of transactions through the system from input to output must be included in the design. A basic issue facing designers is how to balance the control need against the possibility of creating an "overcontrolled" system that's expensive to operate and that produces delays in getting information into the hands of users.

4. *The advisability of "making" the system in-house or of "buying" it from an outside supplier.* Designers must often choose between creating a new in-house design or buying an existing applications package or custom-built system from an outside supplier. The pros and cons of this choice are discussed in Chapter 19, page 513.

5. *The attention that should be given to human factors.* Will the proposed alternatives be easy for people to understand and use? Will the alternatives give prompt response, relieve people of unnecessary chores, and be pleasant to use? These and many other questions bearing on the operational

feasibility of a system must be considered. A nonresponsive design that harasses users and wastes their time will be resisted.

6. ***The economic tradeoffs that should be made.*** The question of economic feasibility underlies the whole system development effort. The decisions made by designers in considering all the above issues can be reached only after a careful study has been made of the available economic resources. A very flexible real time system that can immediately update and retrieve all records might be nice to have, but the designers may elect to settle for a less expensive online system that gives immediate access to records that are only periodically updated using batch processing techniques.

There are so many variables bearing on the design process that it's impossible to establish exact rules to follow in selecting alternatives. The issues we've now examined are resolved in different ways by different designers using different resources in different environments.

**Choosing an Alternative**     It's assumed at this point that the designers have prepared a detailed set of written and documented system specifications to achieve the system study goals. These specifications should include:

1. ***Output requirements.*** The form, content, and frequency of output is needed.

2. ***Input requirements.*** The necessary new input data should be identified along with the stored file data that are required.

3. ***File and storage requirements.*** The size, contents, storage media, record formats, access restrictions, and degree of permanency of any affected files should be known.

4. ***Processing specifications.*** The procedures needed for the computer to convert input data into desired output results should be indicated. Manual processing procedures should also be noted.

5. ***Control provisions.*** The steps required to achieve system control should be specified, and the later system testing and implementation procedures should be outlined.

6. ***Cost estimates.*** Preliminary estimates of the costs of different alternatives should be made.

We've seen that there are no exact rules to follow in selecting alternatives. Likewise, there aren't any precise guidelines to follow in choosing from among the alternatives selected. In some situations, study results may indicate that the use of a **remote computing service** (or *service bureau*) is the best choice. Such outside firms can do the programming and processing that's required. In other situations, the system can be implemented using existing equipment. And in some system development projects, implementation may call for the acquisition of new hardware.

**Hardware Evaluation, Selection, and Acquisition Factors.** If new hardware is needed to implement the selected alternative (and it *is* often needed), the study team must then consider a whole new set of questions:

■ Which computer and/or peripheral device, when combined with its supporting software, is best suited for our needs?

■ Which hardware/software package is the most economical?

■ How should we acquire the equipment?

In answering the first question, teams have often considered the **equipment selection factors** listed in Figure 12-9 to limit the choices, and have then followed one of the **equipment selection approaches** listed in Figure 12-10. In answering the second question, the costs associated with each option are compared with the benefits produced. Both costs and benefits must be quantified. Since many benefits tend to be *intangible*, however, it's often hard to assign a value to them. (Machine A costs more than machine B, but it's also faster so it will reduce the time needed to process customer orders. What value is then assigned to the benefit of better customer service?)

The answer to the third question depends on the type of equipment being acquired. Most personal computers and minicomputers are purchased. Mainframe systems, however, are obtained in the following ways:

**Economic factor**

1. Cost comparisons

**Hardware factors**

1. Hardware performance, reliability, capacity, and price
2. Number and accessibility of backup facilities
3. Firmness of delivery date
4. Effective remaining life of proposed hardware
5. Compatibility with existing systems

**Software factors**

1. Software performance and price
2. Efficiency and reliability of available software
3. Programming languages available (not promised)

4. Availability of useful and well-documented packaged programs, program libraries, and user groups
5. Firmness of delivery date on promised software
6. Ease of use and modification

**Service factors**

1. Facilities provided by manufacturer for checking new programs
2. Training facilities offered and the quality of training provided
3. Programming assistance and conversion assistance offered
4. Maintenance terms and quality

**Reputation of manufacturer**

1. Financial stability
2. Record of keeping promises

Figure 12-9 Equipment selection factors.

1. **Single-source approach.** This noncompetetitive approach merely consists of choosing the hardware/software package from among those available from a selected vendor. There's a lack of objectivity in this approach, and poor results have been produced. But it's often used.

2. **Competitive-bidding approach.** System specifications are submitted to vendors with a request that they prepare bids. Included in the bid request may be a requirement that cost and performance figures be prepared for a specified *benchmark* processing run. The vendors select what they believe to be the most appropriate hardware/software packages from their lines and submit proposals.

3. **Consultant-evaluation approach.** Qualified data processing consultants can assist organizations in selecting the hardware/software package. Consultants can bring specialized knowledge and experience and an objective point of view to bear on the evaluation and selection problem.

4. **Simulation approach.** Specialized computer programs are available from a number of organizations to simulate the performance of selected hardware/software alternatives. Simulation programs are capable of comparing the input, output, and computing times required by each alternative to process specific applications.

Figure 12-10 Equipment selection approaches.

1. *Renting.* Mainframes are often rented from the manufacturer. This is a flexible method that doesn't require a large initial investment. It's also the most expensive method if the equipment meets company needs for 4 or 5 years or longer.

2. *Purchasing.* Many mainframes are purchased because it's the least expensive acquisition method when hardware is kept for several years. But there's also the risk of technological obsolescence—of being ''locked-in'' to a system that doesn't meet changing needs.

3. *Leasing.* Under one leasing arrangement (many others are possible), the mainframe user tells the leasing company what equipment is needed. This company arranges for the purchase of the equipment and then leases it to the user for a period (usually 3 to 5 years). This method eliminates the large purchase price and is less expensive than renting over the life of the lease. But, of course, the user has contracted to keep the machine for a relatively long period.

**The Design Report**     Guided by a written charter which defined the problem, people have analyzed relevant facts. The design of a detailed set of system specifications has evolved from this analysis, and the team has settled on the alternative that it thinks will result in the ''best'' problem solution. The team has made many decisions. But the final decisions are made by top-level managers. It's now the team's job to prepare a system **design report** and make recommendations. It's the responsibility of top executives to decide on system implementation.

The report of the study team should include the following points:

- A restatement of study scope and objectives.

- The design specifications for procedures and operations that will be changed.

- The anticipated effects of such changes on organizational structure, physical facilities, and company information.

- The anticipated effects on people, and the personnel resources available to implement the change.

- The hardware/software package chosen (if needed), the reasons for the choice, and the alternatives considered.

- The economic effects of the change, including a cost/benefit analysis and an analysis of acquisition methods (if needed).

- A summary of the expected problems and benefits arising from the change.

# SYSTEM IMPLEMENTATION

Figure 12-11 shows that after top executives have evaluated the design report and have decided to implement the design specifications, the next steps in the system project are programming analysis and program preparation. Since these steps are discussed in detail in Chapters 18 through 21 of the Programming Module, we'll not consider them here. We'll also not repeat the *program* implementation procedures presented in Chapter 19. But there are some general **system implementation** concepts associated with the task of replacing an old system with a new one, and we'll examine those now.

**The Consequences of Earlier Decisions**

The time and effort required to implement a system depends largely on the quality of the work that's done earlier in the system study. We've seen in Figure 12-2, for example, that oversights during problem definition are difficult to correct at the time of implementation. On the other hand, the implementation phase is often simplified as a result of the following preinstallation decisions:

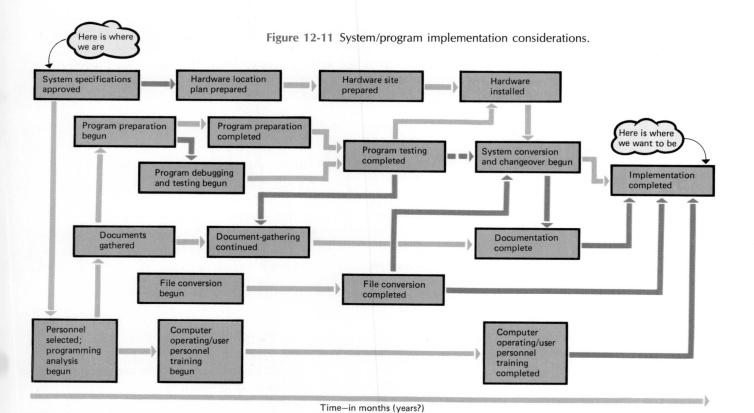

Figure 12-11 System/program implementation considerations.

■ *Decision to follow standard rules and procedures.* The job of testing systems is made easier when procedures are consistently applied, when data items are consistently defined, and when documentation rules are consistently followed.

■ *Decision to use a modular design approach.* Dividing complex systems and programs into smaller modules simplifies testing and implementation efforts.

■ *Decision to use tested applications packages.* Buying proven software, where appropriate, may make it possible to bypass many implementation problems.

## Equipment Implementation

We've seen that it's sometimes necessary to acquire new hardware or upgrade existing equipment in order to implement a new system. If only a few personal computers and/or I/O devices are added, then little time or effort may be needed. But if a large new computer system must be installed, then a great deal of planning may be required in preparing a suitable site to receive the new hardware. Some of the factors that are considered during site planning for larger installations are:

■ *Location.* The physical security of the site and its access to users must be evaluated.

■ *Space and layout.* The size of the equipment, the location and length of power and connecting cables, the room needed to service the equipment and store I/O media and supplies, the room needed for offices—these and other factors must be evaluated in determining the space requirements and site layout.

■ *Site utilities.* Provisions must be made for air conditioning, electrical power, and lighting. A fire protection system using heat and smoke detectors, emergency power cutoffs, and appropriate Halon gas and other fire prevention devices may be needed.

## System Conversion and Changeover

After programs appear to be producing correct results, the system conversion and changeover may begin. This conversion period is almost always a period of personnel and organizational strain. Data processing people may work long hours and be subjected to pressure to complete the conversion. Unforeseen problems, last-minute corrections, and the disruption of data processing services to using departments, customers, suppliers, etc., may contribute to these pressures. It's at this time that cooperation is badly needed between data processing specialists and the people in affected departments. Yet it's precisely at this time that cooperation frequently breaks down because of preoccupation with technical conversion matters at the expense of good human relations.

Everyone who will be affected by the new system should receive some training prior to the conversion period to become familiar with the changes. This training is likely to become more intense now, however, as new procedures are phased into operation, as old forms are replaced by new ones, as old input devices are retired in favor of new hardware, and as last-minute changes are made in manual methods and personnel assignments.

During system conversion, current files must be changed into a form acceptable to the processor. This can be a tremendous task, and it's one that's often underestimated. Files should be consolidated and duplicate records eliminated. Errors in current files must be detected and removed. And file inconsistencies must be found *before* the changeover rather than later when they can cause system malfunctions.

There's frequently a transitional changeover or shakedown period during which applications are processed by both currently used and new procedures as a final check before the cutover to the new system occurs. A **parallel running** conversion involves the processing of *current* input data by old and new methods. If a significant difference appears, the cause must be located. Various **pilot testing** approaches may also be used during conversion. For example, input data for a *previous* month's operations may be processed using new methods, and the results may be compared with the results obtained from existing operations. If new hardware is being acquired, preliminary pilot tests can be run on the vendor's equipment prior to delivery of the user's hardware. Thus, testing may be facilitated through the use of actual input data, and it may be possible to reduce the time (and costs) associated with maintaining two different systems at a later date. Also, a pilot conversion approach is often used when a system is to be installed in a number of different locations over a period of time. One location—say a regional warehouse—may be selected for the initial conversion effort. Once the start-up problems have been solved and the system has been proven under actual operating conditions, the organization can then convert other warehouses to the new procedures.

Regardless of the conversion approach, final changeover to computer production runs comes from satisfactory performance during this shakedown period.

## Post-Implementation Review

Once the system is implemented and in operation, a thorough audit or **post-implementation review** should be made. This follow-up is commonly conducted by people who have an independent viewpoint and are not responsible for the development and maintenance of the system. Some of the questions that should be considered in the audit are:

- How useful is the system to decision makers? How enthusiastic are they about the services they receive? Do they receive output in time to take action?

- Are planned processing procedures being followed? Are all new procedures being processed on the computer? Have old procedures been eliminated? If not, why not?

- Are responsibilities of data processing people defined and understood? Are training programs of acceptable quality?

- Are system controls being observed? Is documentation complete? Have procedures to control program changes been established? Are any modifications or refinements indicated as a result of operating experience? If so, are they being made?

- How do operating results compare with original goals and expectations? Are economic benefits being obtained? If variations exist, what's the cause? What can be done to achieve expected results?

## Feedback and Review 12-1

This chapter has introduced you to a number of concepts associated with the analysis, design, and implementation of an information system. To test and reinforce your understanding of these concepts, answer the following multiple-choice questions by placing the letter of the most nearly correct answer in the space provided.

___1. The changes that occur in organizations are due to
a) technological factors.
b) social and economic factors.
c) operating problems.
d) all of the above reasons.

___2. The sequence of steps followed in a system study is
a) problem definition, system design, system analysis, programming, and implementation.
b) problem definition, system analysis, programming, and implementation.
c) system analysis, system design, and system implementation.
d) problem definition, system analysis, system design, programming analysis, program preparation, and implementation.

___3. Which of the following activities *doesn't* usually belong in the problem definition step:
a) a preliminary survey is conducted by unbiased people who have no interest in the problem.
b) a series of requirements sessions may be held.
c) the problem definition is put in writing and approved by system users.
d) all the above activities belong in the problem definition step.

___4. During the data-gathering phase of the system analysis step,
a) program flowcharts are often prepared.
b) the system design specifications are outlined.
c) a number of specialized forms may be prepared.
d) a standards manual is of little use.

___5. Which of the following tools is *not* normally used during system analysis:
a) system flowchart.
b) question checklist.
c) grid chart.
d) program flowchart.

___6. The approach used in top-down analysis and design is to
a) identify the top-level functions by combining many smaller components into a single entity.
b) identify a top-level function, and then create a hierarchy of lower-level modules and components.
c) prepare flowcharts after programming has been completed.
d) none of the above.

___7. Which of the following tools is *not* normally used during system design:
a) program reviews and walkthroughs.
b) hierarchical charts.
c) standards manual.
d) all the above are used.

___8. Design specifications *don't* normally include
a) output requirements.
b) input and storage requirements.
c) control provisions.
d) blueprints showing the layout of hardware.

___9. In acquiring new hardware, an organization
a) may choose to rent a machine since this is the least expensive acquisition method.
b) may buy the equipment to reduce the risk of technological obsolescence.
c) may lease a machine in order to avoid a large purchase price.
d) may choose to build its own system from bins of integrated circuits.

___10. Which of the following is *not* likely to be a system implementation consideration:
a) preparing a site plan for new equipment.
b) using parallel running or pilot testing conversion techniques.
c) having enough work to keep data processing people busy.
d) training those who will use the new system.

# LOOKING BACK

**1.** The initiative for many changes in the information systems of an organization may be traced to the technical, social, and economic changes occurring in society. Executives, information users, and data processing specialists in an organization may respond to these external forces, and to other internal factors, by seeking to develop better computer-based applications. The six steps followed in the system development process are *(a)* problem definition, *(b)* system analysis, *(c)* system design, *(d)* programming analysis, *(e)* program preparation, and *(f)* system/program implementation and maintenance.

**2.** A preliminary system survey is often conducted during the problem definition stage to identify the need. This survey should have high-level support and should be conducted by qualified people. A number of requirements sessions are often held to allow people to participate in setting or revising system goals. At the conclusion of the problem definition step, the team should prepare a detailed written statement of the scope and objectives of the study.

**3.** Analysts gather data on current operations during the system analysis stage. Some of the tools they use during data gathering are organization charts, standards manuals, system flowcharts, questionnaires, special-purpose forms, and interviews. After data have been gathered, analysts study these facts to develop suggestions on how the study goals may be achieved. The analysis tools they may use include checklists of questions, a hierarchy of system flowcharts, and grid charts. An analysis report is written at the end of this step.

**4.** During the system design phase, designers decide how to produce an efficient and effective system. Feasible alternatives are identified, and a set of detailed specifications for the problem solution is prepared. Issues involving methodology and the use of resources surface at this time. Six of these issues are discussed in the chapter. Design tools such as organization standards, the top-down design approach, special charts and forms, and design walkthroughs are used. Since there are so many variables bearing on the design process, however, it's impossible to establish exact rules to follow in selecting alternatives or in choosing from among the alternatives selected. If new equipment is needed to implement a system design, the study team recommends a hardware/software package and the acquisition approach to use in obtaining this package.

**5.** After considering the design report prepared by the study team, top executives decide on system implementation. If the design specifications are implemented, programs are prepared and tested. After programs appear to be running properly and producing correct results, the system conversion and changeover may begin. There's frequently a transition period during which applications are processed by both the old and new procedures before the cutover to a new system occurs. After the new system is implemented, a thorough follow-up appraisal or audit is often conducted.

## KEY TERMS AND CONCEPTS

system change factors 308
problem definition 308
problem definition survey 309
requirements sessions 309
system study charter 310
organization chart 311
standards manuals 312
grid (input/output) chart 313

top-down analysis methodology 314
analysis report 314
top-down design 315
hierarchical charts 315
design walkthrough 317
system flexibility 317
remote computing service 319
equipment selection factors 320

equipment selection approaches 320
design report 321
system implementation 322
parallel running 324
pilot testing 324
post-implementation review 324

# TOPICS FOR REVIEW AND DISCUSSION

**1.** *(a)* How may pressures from sources external to a business create the need for changes in the firm's information systems? *(b)* How can decisions made by top executives, department managers, and information system specialists lead to changes in the firm's information systems?

**2.** *(a)* What are the steps in the system development process? *(b)* Which step do you think is most important?

**3.** What principles should be observed in conducting a problem definition survey?

**4.** Why is it important to not become impatient with "delays" that occur during problem definition?

**5.** *(a)* What tools and techniques may be used to gather data about current operations? *(b)* To analyze the current system and develop suggestions for improvements?

**6.** "There are a number of issues that have a bearing on the design alternatives that are finally selected." What are five of these issues?

**7.** What tools and techniques are used during system design?

**8.** What should be included in the written design specifications?

**9.** *(a)* What factors should be considered in selecting equipment? *(b)* What selection approaches may be used?

**10.** Discuss the methods that are often used to acquire mainframe computers.

**11.** "The conversion from an old system to a new one is almost always a time of personnel and organizational strain." Discuss this comment.

**12.** *(a)* What's a parallel running conversion? *(b)* What's meant by the pilot testing approach to system conversion?

# PROJECTS TO LOOK INTO

**1.** Visit your library and locate some articles on system analysis tools and/or system design techniques. Select a tool or technique of interest to you for further research, and then prepare a summary report of your research findings.

**2.** Identify a system you're involved with at school, work, or home. Analyze this system and point out ways that it could be redesigned to serve you better. Present your analysis and redesign thoughts to the class.

# ANSWERS TO FEEDBACK AND REVIEW SECTION

**12-1**
1. d
2. d
3. a
4. c
5. d
6. b
7. a
8. d
9. c
10. c

# System Design Considerations
## Organizing Data And Selecting File Processing Alternatives

You've seen in this chapter that it's the job of system designers to create a system solution that will satisfy the information needs of users. To do this job, designers determine feasible alternatives and then settle on a single set of detailed specifications for the new application or system. Before detailed input, processing, and output specifications can be prepared, however, the data to be processed must first be organized or grouped in some logical arrangement.

### Organizing Data: A Review

You'll recall from Chapter 2 that system designers typically organize data into different levels ranging upward from data fields to records, files, and data bases. Let's briefly look at these levels or groupings of data in the context of the billing and accounts receivable (A/R) applications outlined in Chapter 2.

Designers know that the objects of billing-A/R processing are to:

**1.** Send bills or invoices to credit customers as purchases are made during a period.

**2.** Keep track of all purchases made during the period.

**3.** Send periodic summary statements to customers to remind them of their debts.

**4.** Stay abreast of credit purchase trends, delinquent accounts, and other relevant information.

Each bill will contain *several* data items or fields. The customer's name and account number will be two fields. Other fields will include the customer's address, the date of purchase, and item(s) purchased. A *field*, then, is a group of related characters that are treated as a single unit.

Related fields are grouped to form a single entity called a *record*. This record contains all the necessary data about some object. An A/R record, for example, pertains to a credit customer and includes such data as the customer's name, account number, address, and credit limit.

A *file* is a collection of related records that are treated as a unit. Designers identify each record in a file by a *record key*. This key is a value found in every record in the file, and this value must be *unique* for each record. In a simple, *manually processed* A/R file, for example, the key could be the last name of customers, and record folders could be organized and filed in alphabetical sequence in a file cabinet. Between statement preparation dates, copies of customer bills can be used to update record folders in a **transaction file** drawer as shown in Figure 12-A. When statements are prepared, the copies of the bills are removed from the transaction file drawer. Calculations are made to determine total purchase amounts, the transaction file data are transferred to the **master file** in the bottom drawers of the cabinet, and statements are sent to customers.

In a *computer-processed* A/R application, on the other hand, the primary key selected by designers to organize records in the file is likely to be the customer account number. Transaction and master file records will be stored on computer-readable media, and these records may be processed in a numerical sequence during statement preparation (see Figure 12-B). Designers may also

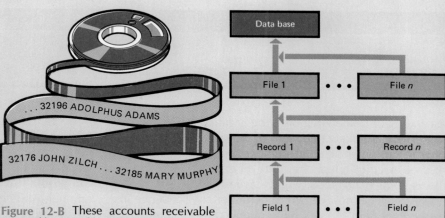

Figure 12-A Transaction and master files in a simple manual accounts receivable system.

Figure 12-B These accounts receivable master file records are organized on magnetic tape by using an ascending sequence of customer account numbers.

Figure 12-C Data are normally organized into a hierarchy for computer processing. The field is the smallest entity to be processed as a single unit. Related fields are grouped to form records, and related records are combined to form files. The highest level in the data organization hierarchy is the data base which is a collection of logically related data elements that may be structured in various ways and used for multiple purposes.

restructure files around "secondary keys" for different retrieval and processing uses. The customer account number key used for statement preparation might be replaced by a customer name key in a second file of the same data when the file is to be used by employees responding to customer complaints and inquiries.

Finally, a *data base* is a collection of logically related data elements that are structured in various ways today to reduce such duplication of data items and to provide improved access to the needed facts. Designers may link records in an A/R file, for example, with sales, shipping, contract pricing, and payment records that might be located in other files. Figure 12-C summarizes the data organization hierarchy used in data processing systems.

## Some File Processing Alternatives Open to System Designers

You saw in the chapter that there are many variables affecting the ways that designers choose to deal with the records and files that will be used in a new system. One such variable, you'll recall, concerns the amount of flexibility to build into a system. Different degrees of flexibility *can* be created by using different approaches to *organize,* *access,* and *process* files. For example, designers can elect to use sequentially organized files and batch processing techniques. Or, they may choose to follow a more flexible (and initially more expensive) approach and use a direct or indexed sequential file organization for some applications.

As Figure 12-D indicates, *sequential, direct,* and *indexed sequential* are classification terms that refer to some of the file and processing alternatives available to system designers as they consider how to meet the needs of users.

## Sequential Files

As you read in Chapter 2, **sequential files** may be *organized* so that records are stored one after another in an

| File organization | Record access method | Processing approach |
|---|---|---|
| 1. Sequential | 1. Sequential | 1. Sequential |
| 2. Direct (or random) | 2. Direct | 2. Direct (or online) |
| 3. Sequential (but with an index) | 3. Indexed sequential | 3. Indexed sequential |

Figure 12-D System designers can choose to organize, access, and process records and files in different ways depending on the type of application and the needs of users.

ascending or descending order determined by the record key. There are likely to be tens of thousands of these records in customer account number sequence in the A/R files of electric, telephone, and oil companies. Once a file is sequenced according to a designated key field, however, it's almost certain to be out of any sequence in every other field. An A/R file sequenced by customer account number, for example, will not be in a Zip code sequence or an alphabetical sequence. We've seen that other files could be sequenced on these record keys, but maintaining multiple files of duplicate data can be expensive.

When computer processing is used, the stored records in a sequential file are usually kept on magnetic tape, magnetic disk, or punched paper media. To *access* these records, the computer must read the file in sequence from the beginning. To locate a particular record, the computer program must read in each record in sequence and compare its record key to the one that's needed. Only when the record keys match will the retrieval search end and processing begin. If only a single record in a sequential file is needed, the computer would read, on the average, about half the file before it found the one it wanted.

Since an entire sequential file may need to be read just to retrieve and update a few records, it's desirable to accumulate transactions of a similar type into batches, sort these batches into the record key sequence used in the file, and then *process* the entire batch in a single pass through the file (see Figure 2-7, page 46). Designers have found that this is a very efficient processing approach to use when a high proportion of the file records in an application need to be updated at regularly scheduled intervals. Applications such as payroll processing, billing and statement preparation, and bank check processing meet these conditions.

## Direct Files

There are many other applications, however, that don't meet these conditions. In these applications, the proportion of file records to be processed is often low, the timing of record transactions and/or inquiries is often unpredictable, and the processing delays caused by accumulating transactions into batches is often unacceptable. One such application illustrated in Chapter 2 was the updating of Rob Brooks' savings account record from an online teller terminal. Another application illustrated in Chapter 6 was the updating of production records by factory workers using data collection stations located on the plant floor.

When a **direct file** (also called a **random** or **relative** file) organization approach is used, the computer can directly locate the key of the needed record without having to search through a sequence of other records. This means that the time required for online inquiry and updating of a few records is much faster than when batch techniques are used. Of course, this also means that direct file records must be kept in a direct-access storage device (DASD). A record is stored in a direct file by its key field. Although it might be possible to use the storage location numbers in a DASD as the keys for the records stored in those locations, this is seldom done. Instead, an arithmetic procedure called a **transform** is frequently used to convert the record key number into a DASD storage location number. For example, the record key number might be divided by a value determined by the transform. The record could then be stored in the DASD location that corresponds to a value calculated by the division operation. Sometimes a transform produces **synonyms**—i.e., two or more records whose keys generate the same DASD location number. Several methods are followed to overcome this difficulty when it occurs. One approach is to include a **pointer** field at the location calculated by the transform. This field points to the DASD location of another record that has the same calculated transform value.

When the computer is given the key of a record to be processed at a later date, it reuses the transform to locate the stored record. If the record is at the location calculated by the transform, the search is over and the record is *directly accessed* for processing. If the record at the calculated location does not have the correct key, the computer looks at the pointer field to continue the search.

Thus, direct files are direct accessed and *directly processed* (see Figure 2-8, page 48). It's also possible to process direct file records in a record key sequence. But if a large number of file records need to be processed in sequence, the computer may have to repeatedly use the transform algorithm and constantly reposition the reading mechanism of the DASD to retrieve and process these records. When compared to sequential processing procedures, this would be an inefficient and expensive approach to use.

| Account number key | Storage area for customer data |
|---|---|
| 1492 | 10 |
| 1776 | 11 |
| 1945 | 12 |
| 2232 | 13 |
| 2565 | 14 |
| • | • |
| • | • |
| • | • |

Figure 12-E

## Indexed Sequential Files

You've now seen that there are some processing situations that are best suited to the use of sequential files, and there are others that need the benefits to be obtained from a direct file organization. To further complicate the lot of system designers, there are also some files that are commonly used to support both sequential and online processing operations. An inventory file, for example, may be updated each week. Transactions involving quantities of parts received and quantities sold may be batched, sorted by part number, and used to produce a new report each week of the inventory available for sale. The purchasing department may use this report for reordering purposes. However, the same inventory file may also be used to provide availability data in response to inquiries coming from online terminals in the sales department. Similarly, an organization may want to use batch techniques to update an A/R file and at the same time use that file to give quick answers to customer inquiries.

When both batch and online processing must be supported, an **indexed sequential file** may be used. The records in this type of file are *organized in sequence* for the efficient processing of large batch jobs, but an **index** is also used to speed up access to the records. This file organization is thus a compromise approach that combines some of the advantages (and avoids some of the limitations) of both the sequential and direct approaches. Records are stored sequentially by a record key in a DASD. When these records are periodically updated during a batch run, the direct-access capability of the DASD really isn't used. The *first* record may be directly *accessed*, but all others are then read in sequence as if they were stored on a magnetic tape.

Figure 12-F Factors to consider in evaluating file alternatives.

### SEQUENTIAL FILES

**Advantages**
- Simple-to-understand approach
- Locating a record requires only the record key
- Efficient and economical if the *activity rate* — i.e., the proportion of file records to be processed — is high
- Relatively inexpensive I/O media and devices may be used
- Files may be relatively easy to reconstruct since a good measure of built-in backup is usually available

**Disadvantages**
- Entire file must be processed even when the activity rate is very low
- Transactions must be sorted and placed in sequence prior to processing
- Timeliness of data in the file deteriorates while batches are being accumulated
- Data redundancy is typically high since the same data may be stored in several files sequenced on different keys

### DIRECT FILES

**Advantages**
- Immediate access to records for inquiry and updating purposes is possible

**Disadvantages**
- Records in the online file may be exposed to the risks of a loss of accuracy and a breach of security; special backup and reconstruction procedures must be established
- May be less efficient in the use of storage space than sequentially organized files
- More difficult to add and delete records than with sequential files
- Relatively expensive hardware and software resources are required

- Immediate updating of several files as a result of a single transaction is possible
- Transactions need not be sorted

### INDEXED SEQUENTIAL FILES

**Advantages**
- Permits the efficient and economical use of sequential processing techniques when the activity rate is high
- Permits quick access to records in a relatively efficient way when this activity is a small fraction of the total workload

**Disadvantages**
- Less efficient in the use of storage space than some other alternatives
- Access to records may be slower using indexes than when transform algorithms are used
- Relatively expensive hardware and software resources are required

Indexes are used to permit access to selected records without requiring a search of the *entire* file. The use of an index is already familiar to you. If you wanted to find information on one or a few topics in this book, you would not begin on page 1 and read every page until you came across the topic(s) of interest. Rather, you would find the subject by turning to the index at the back of the book to locate the page number, and then by turning directly to that page to begin reading. In the same way, a computer can use an **indexed sequential access method (ISAM)** to locate a record by using an index rather than by starting every search at the beginning of the file. In an A/R file, for example, customer records may be sequentially organized by account number. One or more indexes of these account numbers can then be stored in the DASD as shown in Figure 12-E. The account number key represents the *highest* customer account number in the storage area. Thus, to locate customer number 1932, the computer is instructed to access storage area 12. Another index for storage area 12 would probably then be used to further pinpoint the location of the record. A sequential search, involving only a tiny fraction of the entire file, may then be made to retrieve the desired record. In summary, then, records in indexed sequential files can be batch processed or accessed quickly through the use of indexes.

### Advantages and Limitations of These File Approaches

Which of the above file organization approaches should system designers use? There's no single answer to this question, of course, unless the answer is "all of them." The best approach to use in a given application is the one that happens to meet the user's needs in the most effective and economical manner. In making the choice for an application, designers must evaluate the distinct strengths and weaknesses of each approach. These advantages and limitations are summarized in Figure 12-F.

# System Software Packages

## *operating systems and data base management systems*

### Operating Systems for Personal Computers

Operating systems direct the flow of instructions, data, and results from one part of a computer system to another, working in much the same way as a waiter in a restaurant: The waiter places orders with the kitchen, serves the meals to the diners, and then handles housekeeping chores, such as cleaning the table and totaling the tab.

In the late 1970s, Digital Research opened the market for personal computer operating systems with CP/M. But CP/M's popularity faded in the early 1980s when IBM launched its Personal Computer family and chose to use the MS/DOS operating system developed by Microsoft Corporation. More recently, as AT&T has expanded from communications into the computing industry, its own Unix operating system has commanded significant attention, even though a relatively small percentage of microcomputers—fewer than 150,000 by one estimate—run it.

AT&T is counting on Unix becoming widely accepted because it is versatile: Unix handles multiple tasks simultaneously and runs on computers that range in size from micros to mainframes. Early micro operating systems are much simpler and were made for much simpler machines. With CP/M, a user can perform only one task at a time; for instance, you cannot reformat a spreadsheet while you print a letter. But newer micros are more powerful and can handle several chores at once. Users want to take advantage of this multitasking capability, and Unix suits their needs.

—Source of data: Business Week, Apr. 16, 1984. Photo courtesy Stratus Computer, Inc.

You saw in Chapter 12 how information needs are identified and how new computer-based systems are then developed to satisfy these needs. The emphasis there was on designing and/or identifying new software to control the processing of specific applications. Our focus now shifts from applications software to two types of software packages used to operate, control, and extend the processing capabilities of computer hardware systems. The information in this chapter will enable you to:

■ Define an operating system and tell when and why such systems were developed

■ Outline the role of the operating system supervisor, describe the functions of the control programs in an operating system, and identify the types of programs that can be called up by an operating system in order to simplify processing operations

■ Discuss the possible problems that may occur with departmental applications, and describe how the data base concept alleviates these problems

■ Explain how data base management systems can be used, and outline their structuring techniques, benefits, and limitations

# OPERATING SYSTEMS

A **system software package** is a collection of programs designed to operate, control, and extend the processing capabilities of the computer itself. Unlike applications programs, which are often written by computer users to meet their own specific information needs, system software packages are generally prepared today by computer manufacturers and independent software suppliers. An important system software package found in almost all computer installations is the operating system. An **operating system (OS)** is an integrated set of specialized programs that's used to manage the resources and overall operations of a computer. The OS permits the computer to supervise its own operations by automatically calling in the applications programs, translating any other special service programs, and managing the data needed to produce the output desired by users. Thus, as Figure 13-1 indicates, the OS tends to isolate the hardware from the user. The user communicates with the OS, supplies applications programs and input data that are in a language and format acceptable to the OS, and receives output results. But the user is usually not too concerned with the hardware specifics of the system, or with how the OS will direct the hardware to handle certain tasks.

## The Development of Operating Systems

The computer systems running under OS control today range in size from small personal computers to the largest mainframes and supercomputers. But it wasn't always that way. It's generally conceded that one of the first elementary operating systems was produced in the early 1950s at the General Motors Research Laboratories for use with an IBM 701 computer. Then, in 1955, programmers at GM and North American Aviation joined forces to write an OS for the IBM 704—one of the most powerful scientific processors of that time. Many other OSs were produced for larger machines during the late 1950s and early 1960s by other users, computer manufacturers, and university researchers. These OSs were rather primitive by today's standards. They were limited in use to sequential (batch) processing applications, and they were generally designed to run on only one type of machine.

Minicomputers and their operating systems also came along in the 1960s, and the first personal computers equipped with floppy disk drives were introduced in the mid-1970s. If you've read Chapter 8, you know that Digital Research's Control Program/Microprocessor (CP/M) was written to manage those early disk-equipped personal computers that were built around the Intel 8080 (and later the Zilog Z80) microprocessor chip. A 1976 upgrade quickly improved on the original bare-bones disk OS, and several later revisions have been made to what is now usually referred to as CP/M-80. This has become one of the most popular OSs for 8-bit personal computers, while Microsoft's MS-DOS and AT&T's UNIX are currently the choices of most builders of 16-bit microcomputers. The OSs produced by independent software firms such as Digital Research and Microsoft now run on hundreds of different personal computer (pc) models, but many pc makers and most manufacturers of larger systems have developed proprietary OSs that are intended for use only with their machines. Regardless of their origin, OSs for machines of all sizes have now evolved from primitive programs to sophisticated software packages that can support direct-access processing in critical real time situations.

Beginning in the 1950s (and continuing up to the present time), the general goal of OS developers has been to devise ways to operate a computer with a minimum of idle time and in the most efficient and economical way during the execution of user programs. In pre-OS days, computer operators would go through the same ritual to process each job. The job program and input data would be loaded on input devices, the storage locations in the CPU would be cleared of any data remaining from the previous job, appropriate switches would be set, and the job would run alone in the CPU until it was completed. After completion, the job program, input data, and output results would be unloaded by the operator, and the entire ritual would begin again for the next job.

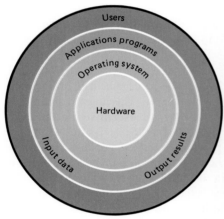

**Figure 13-1** An OS is a set of programs that, in a sense, disguises the hardware being used. For example, popular OSs used with personal computers are Digital Research's CP/M-80, Microsoft's MS-DOS, and AT&T's UNIX. (For more information about personal computer OSs, see Chapter 8, pages 216–217.) A person who knows how to communicate with CP/M-80, MS-DOS, or UNIX may be able to process applications programs written to run on these OSs on a number of personal computers without being concerned about the hardware specifics of the various machines. Likewise, programs written for use with CP/M-80, MS-DOS, or UNIX can often be run on the systems produced by many different manufacturers whose machines will accept these operating systems.

Because the computer sat idle while the operator loaded and unloaded jobs, a great deal of processing time was lost. The OSs of the late 1950s and early 1960s reduced this idle time by allowing jobs to be stacked up in a waiting line. When one job was finished, system control would branch back to OS software which would automatically perform the housekeeping duties needed to load and run the next job. This automatic job-to-job transition is still one of the major functions performed by a modern OS.

Although there are numerous programs in an OS today, most OS elements can be classified as either *control* or *processing* programs.

## Control Programs in an OS

You've just seen that one of the functions of an OS is to control *input/output housekeeping operations*. By shifting the control of these operations from human operators to specially prepared programs, the earlier OSs reduced operator drudgery. They also cut down on the need for programmers to rewrite certain I/O instructions for each program, provided relatively nonstop operation (operators could load tapes and cards for the next job while the current job was being processed), and therefore speeded up the amount of processing that could be accomplished. But a modern OS does much more than just control I/O housekeeping activities. Other sophisticated control programs are required to keep ever-faster and more powerful hardware occupied.

**The Role of the OS Supervisor.** The overall management of a computer system is under the control of an OS master program. This master program is referred to by such names as **supervisor, monitor,** or **executive routine.** The supervisor program coordinates all other parts of the OS, and it resides in the primary storage section of the CPU. Other programs in the OS are kept in an online **system residence device** (usually a magnetic disk drive) so that the supervisor can call them up and temporarily store them in the CPU when they are needed.

In many pc systems, the OS supervisor, other specialized OS programs, and one or more applications programs selected by the user are all stored on a single floppy disk. This disk is inserted into a disk drive (let's call it drive A) and the OS supervisor is automatically loaded into primary storage (Figure 13-2*a*). The other specialized OS programs on this disk are called into primary storage as needed. For example, the user can first request that a specialized program that translates instructions written in a programming language be loaded from the disk in drive A into primary storage. The OS supervisor oversees this operation (Figure 13-2*b*). Then, the user can instruct the supervisor to copy into primary storage a billing application program that's stored on the same disk with the OS software (Figure 13-2*c*). The supervisor consults a specialized file directory to determine the size of the billing program, and the primary storage section is checked to see if enough storage space is available. If so, the supervisor calls in and then turns control over to a specialized basic input/output system (BIOS) program that sees to the loading of the billing program. This billing program may then be modified, or it may be used to process data stored in disk drive B.

After a specialized task has been completed, system control branches back to the supervisor. The following discussion of the use of job control programs illustrates this fact and shows the supervisor's role in maintaining system control in a larger installation.

(a) The operating system and a billing program are stored on a floppy disk. This disk is inserted into disk drive "A." A "bootstrap" program permanently located in ROM storage may be used to automatically load the OS supervisor into the primary storage section of the CPU

A disk containing the "Billing" application data may be inserted into a second, or "B," drive

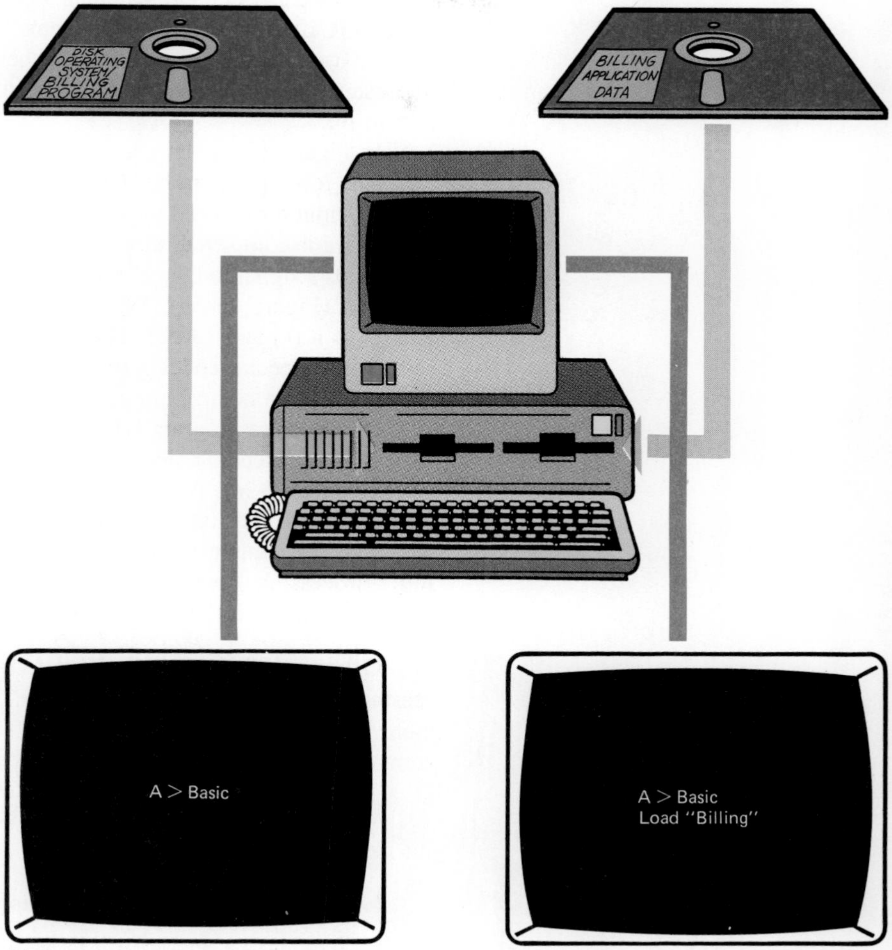

A > Basic

A > Basic
Load "Billing"

(b) The user requests a program on the OS disk that translates instructions written in a programming language, and the OS supervisor sees that the program is loaded into primary storage

(c) Next, the user instructs the OS supervisor to copy the billing program stored in drive A into primary storage. After determining from a file directory program that enough space is available, the supervisor calls up another special OS program that sees to the loading of the billing software. Control over the processing of the billing application data stored in drive B is then turned over to the billing program

**Figure 13-2** The operating system software controls the overall management of a personal computer.

**Job Control Programs.** Let's consider once again the OS function of providing automatic job-to-job linkages during the processing of applications programs. These linkages are handled by a job control program. When a number of jobs are to be run in a *batch processing* (or **stacked job**) environment, a deck of **job control cards** may be assembled by the computer operator and placed in a card reader. The job control cards contain statements presented in the codes of a **job control language (JCL).** These coded statements tell the OS such things as the name of the job, the user's name and account number, the I/O devices to use during processing, the assembler or compiler to use if language translation is needed (see Chapter 19), and so on.

In Figure 13-3a, let's assume that the job control cards for Job 1 have been read, the Job 1 program has been loaded into the CPU from a magnetic disk drive, and the input data stored on a reel of magnetic tape are being processed. When the processing is completed, system control branches back to the OS supervisor which then sends a signal to the OS residence device to load the **job control program** into the CPU (Figure 13-3b). When this program is loaded, the supervisor branches control to it (Figure 13-3c). The *function of the job control program* is to read and process the special codes written in the JCL that are found on the Job 2 control cards. The job control program then returns control to the supervisor (Figure 13-3d). Since the program for Job 2 also happens to be stored on a magnetic disk, the supervisor sends a signal to the disk drive to load the Job 2 program into the CPU (Figure 13-3e). After this operation is completed, the supervisor turns system control over to the Job 2 program which then begins to read and process the input data found on a magnetic tape mounted on a tape drive (Figure 13-3f). At the end of Job 2 processing, control is returned to the supervisor, which calls the job control program, which reads the Job 3 control cards . . . and so it goes.

**Other Job/Resource Control Activities.** Figure 13-3 showed the CPU processing one job at a time. But since CPUs of almost any size today can process far more data in a second than a single set of I/O devices can supply or receive, it's common to **overlap** processing jobs. When this happens, the OS must be ready to:

■ Perform *system scheduling* tasks.

■ Handle *system interruptions*.

■ *Monitor system status* and supply appropriate messages to people.

*System Scheduling.* Whenever possible, multiple jobs are scheduled to balance I/O and processing requirements. As noted above, this often involves overlapping I/O and processing operations. The channels shown in Figure 13-4 are used to facilitate overlapped processing.

A **channel** consists of hardware that, along with other associated monitoring and connecting elements, controls and provides the path for the movement of data between relatively slow I/O devices and the high-speed CPU. A channel may be a separate, small, special-purpose control computer located near the CPU, or it can be a physical part of the CPU which is accessible to both I/O devices and other CPU elements. Once a channel has received appropriate instruction signals from the OS, it can operate independently and without supervision while the CPU is engaged in performing computations.

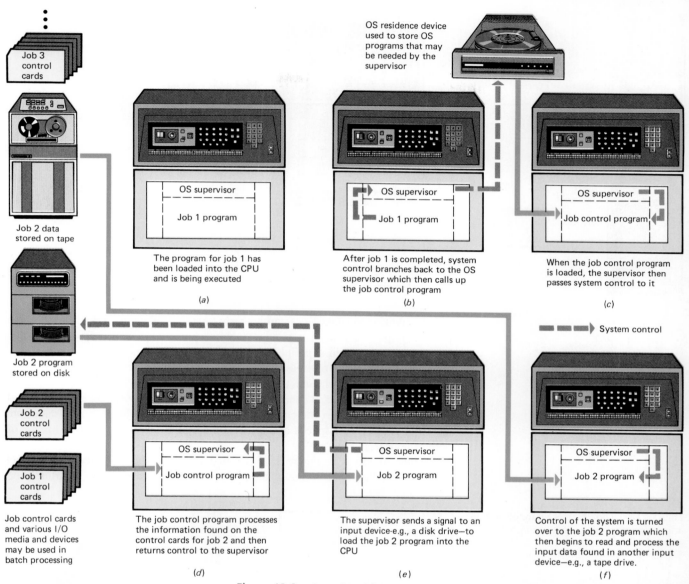

**Figure 13-3** The role of the OS supervisor and the job control program in providing job-to-job linkages.

For example, Figure 13-5 shows that in **time slice** 5 when the CPU is processing the record labeled 2 for Job A, Channel 1 can be accepting another Job A input record, Channel 2 can be receiving processed information from Job A for an output device, Channel 3 can be accepting an input record for Job B, and Channel 4 can be transmitting Job B information to an output device. The OS switches control back and forth between Jobs A and B (and, perhaps, between Jobs C, D, . . .) throughout their execution. You'll notice in Figure 13-5 that the CPU would be idle in time slice 6 if it did not branch to Job B.

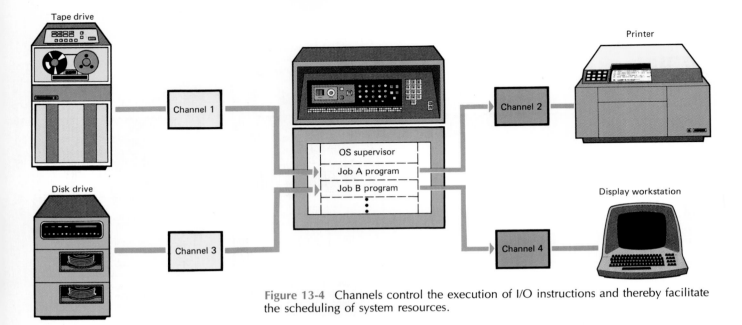

**Figure 13-4** Channels control the execution of I/O instructions and thereby facilitate the scheduling of system resources.

In addition to channels, small high-speed storage elements called **buffers** also play an important role in overlapping input, processing, and output operations. Buffers may be located in peripheral devices (printer buffers are discussed in Chapter 7), or they may be reserved sections of CPU primary storage. Data from input devices are fed under channel control into an *input buffer*. This input buffer has an important characteristic: It can accept data at slow input speeds and release them at electronic CPU speeds. (The reverse is true of the *output buffer*: It accepts data from the CPU at electronic speeds and releases them at the slower operating speeds of output devices.)

Thus, in Job A in Figure 13-5 the first two time slices are required to read record 1 into the input buffer. Once in the buffer, however, there is virtually *no*

**Figure 13-5** The OS uses channels to balance system input, output, and processing capabilities.

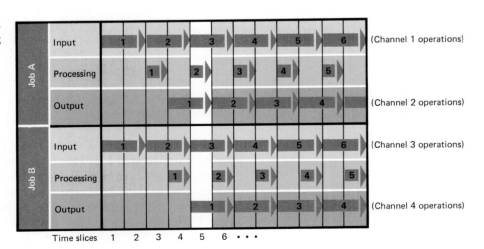

*delay* in releasing record 1 to the CPU for processing in time slice 3. While the first record is being processed, a second record starts to enter the input buffer. As soon as the first record is processed, it's *immediately* transferred under channel control to the output buffer. Two more time slices are then required before the output device can complete the writing operation. But during this time (see slices 4 and 5), the CPU processed a Job B record and another Job A record.

**Multiprogramming** is the name given to what we've been examining in Figure 13-5. It is the *interleaved* execution of two or more different and independent programs by the same computer. Notice, however, that multiprogramming is *not* defined as the execution of instructions from several programs at the *same instant* in time. Rather, it *does* mean that there are a number of programs available to the CPU and that a portion of one is executed, then a portion of another, and so on. As we've seen, the OS switches control from one program to another almost instantly. The CPU can thus keep busy while channels and buffers are occupied with the job of bringing in data and writing out information.

If a number of programs are being processed, the OS may allocate only a small amount of time—say 150 milliseconds per second—to each program being executed. Fifteen-hundredths of a second may not seem like much time to you, but that's enough to calculate the amounts owed to hundreds of employees for a given pay period. The result of such speed is that those whose programs are being processed may feel that they have the undivided attention of the computer. In some multiprogramming systems, only a *fixed* number of jobs can be processed concurrently (multiprogramming with a fixed number of tasks, or MFT), while in others the number of jobs can *vary* (multiprogramming with a variable number of tasks, or MVT).

**Multiprocessing** is the term used to describe a processing approach in which two or more independent CPUs are linked together in a coordinated system. In such a system, instructions from different and independent programs can be processed at the same instant in time by different CPUs. Or the CPUs may simultaneously execute different instructions from the same program. Again, it's the job of the OS to schedule and balance the input, output, and processing capabilities of these systems. This is no easy task! In fact, in distributed data processing networks with multiple processors, small CPUs called *front-end processors* are often dedicated to the single function of scheduling and controlling all work entering the system from remote terminals and other input devices. The front-end processor(s) thus permit one or more larger *host computers* to devote their time to processing large and complex applications programs. (If you've read Chapter 10, you already know about distributed data processing networks and front-end processors.)

The larger CPUs in a multiprocessing system may have separate primary storage sections, they may share a common primary storage unit, or they may have access to both separate and common memories. A common OS may control all or part of the operations of each CPU. Each CPU may be dedicated to specific types of applications. For example, one can process direct-access jobs while another is concentrating on batch applications. However, it's common for one CPU to be able to take over the workload of another malfunctioning machine until repairs are made.

As you would expect, scheduling and coordinating the input/processing/output activities of multiple CPUs requires a very sophisticated OS. In fact, the *largest*

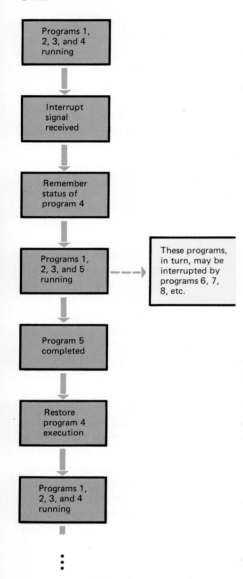

Figure 13-6 Handling system interruptions is a function of the OS.

OSs need a primary storage size of between 4 and 6 million bytes before they can get out of their own way and allow the system to produce results for users.

*Handling System Interruptions.* Priorities are typically assigned to the programs in a multiprogramming system. A high priority is given to the programs used in direct-access processing that manipulate data and respond to inquiries coming from people at online terminals. A lower priority is assigned to batch processing programs that don't require such quick response. Thus, it often happens that a high-priority program will interrupt the processing of a lower-priority program. When a **program interrupt** occurs, the OS must see to it that the data, instructions, and intermediate processing results of the interrupted program are kept separate from any other job. The storage *partitions* reserved for each job must be properly handled, shifted, and protected. After the higher-priority program(s) have been processed, the OS must restore the interrupted program and continue with its processing (Figure 13-6).

In addition to protecting and restoring interrupted low-priority programs, the OS in many installations is also able to partition the programs being executed into primary and online secondary storage portions. This is an important capability. For many years, the size of an application program was effectively limited by the size of the computer's primary storage section because the complete program was held in primary storage during its entire execution. If the program size didn't exceed the limited primary storage capacity, then there was no problem. But if, on the other hand, the task required thousands of instructions, then the programmer might be forced to find ways to trim the program or to divide it into separate jobs. This can be a tedious and time-consuming chore.

To avoid this situation, OSs with **virtual storage** capability have been developed. The basic approach is to divide total programs into small sequences of instructions called either **pages** or **segments.** Then, only those program pages or segments that are actually required at a particular time in the processing need be in the primary (or *real*) storage. The remaining pages or segments may be kept temporarily in online (or *virtual*) storage, from where they can be rapidly retrieved as needed following a program interruption (see Figure 13-7). The OS handles the swapping of program pages or segments between primary and online secondary storage units. Thus, from the applications programmer's point of view, the effective (or "virtual") size of the available primary storage may appear to be unlimited.

*Monitoring System Status.* The OS constantly monitors the status of the computer system during processing operations. It may respond to user "HELP" commands and supply information about its functions and operation. It also directs the computer to send messages to an operator's station when I/O devices need attention, when errors occur in the job stream, or when other abnormal conditions arise. When an error in a job is detected in a larger computer system, however, the computer usually doesn't stop and wait for the operator to take appropriate action. Rather, the message is printed and control passes on to the next job without delay.

The OS also keeps a log of the jobs that have been run in larger systems. These jobs are clocked in and out of the system. The elapsed time required to run programs may be recorded and printed. The security of the system may also be monitored. The attempt to use unauthorized passwords from online terminals may be noted. And messages may be printed if suspicious activity is occurring at one or more terminal sites.

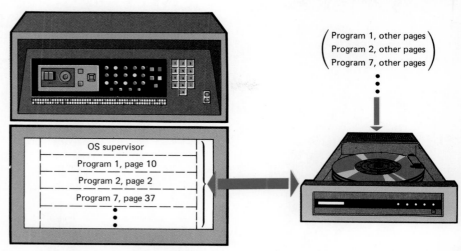

**Figure 13-7** Virtual storage capability.

In addition to control routines, an OS also includes or has access to a number of programs designed to simplify *processing* operations. These programs can reduce the time and expense of program preparation.

**Processing Programs in an OS**

The **program call-up capability** of an OS gives it access to a number of programs that can simplify processing operations. Translating programs, utility (or service) programs, and library programs are examples of OS-controlled software that can reduce the time and expense of preparing applications programs. You may recall from Chapter 4 that *translating programs* transform the instructions written in a humanly convenient form by applications programmers into the machine language codes required by computers. These translating programs are loaded into the computer where they control the translation process. As you saw in Figure 13-2, they are often stored in a direct-access storage device (DASD) and are called up when the user informs the OS supervisor of what's needed. (See Chapter 19 for more details on the use of translating programs.)

**Utility (service) programs** are generally supplied by the computer manufacturer, and are also available for call-up by the OS. These routines perform needed services such as sorting records into a particular sequence for processing, merging several sorted files into a single large updated file, or transferring data from one I/O device to another. Job control statements again tell the OS supervisor which utility programs are needed.

A library of frequently used subroutines supplied by users and computer vendors can also be stored on a DASD. These tested **library programs** are stored in a machine language form. They are then called up by the OS whenever they are required in the processing of other programs. This eliminates the need for a programmer to rewrite these modules every time they are used. A **librarian program** controls the storage and use of the programs in the system library. The "librarian" maintains a program directory. It also spells out the procedures used to add and delete programs from the library.

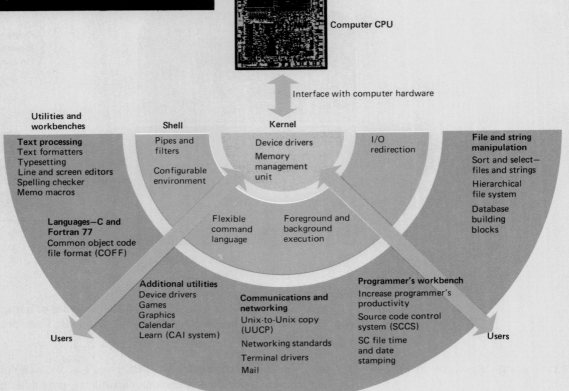

Computer CPU

Interface with computer hardware

**Utilities and workbenches**

Shell

Kernel

**Text processing**
Text formatters
Typesetting
Line and screen editors
Spelling checker
Memo macros

Pipes and filters

Configurable environment

Device drivers

Memory management unit

I/O redirection

**File and string manipulation**
Sort and select—files and strings

Hierarchical file system

Database building blocks

**Languages—C and Fortran 77**
Common object code file format (COFF)

Flexible command language

Foreground and background execution

**Additional utilities**
Device drivers
Games
Graphics
Calendar
Learn (CAI system)

**Communications and networking**
Unix-to-Unix copy (UUCP)

Networking standards

Terminal drivers

Mail

**Programmer's workbench**
Increase programmer's productivity

Source code control system (SCCS)

SC file time and date stamping

Users

Users

The multiuser, multitasking Unix operating system from Bell Labs is a layered system. The *kernel* interfaces directly to the computer's central processing unit (a microprocessor chip, in the case of supermicros) and is modified to run on different CPUs and to alter hardware-related operations such as memory management. Because Unix is written in C, a high-level language, it is less hardware-dependent than operating systems written in lower-level machine language. This trait makes Unix easy to

transport from one system to another. Surrounding the kernel is the *shell*, which serves as a programming language and as a command language interpreter, reading lines typed by the user and interpreting them as requests to execute certain programs. Around the shell are various *utilities* and *workbenches* such as text processing and support for the C and Fortran 77 languages. Some parts of Unix, such as the *programmer's workbench*, which helps software developers, aren't required by all users and

are sometimes dropped in Unix-derived systems sold by companies that license the operating system. These firms also modify parts of Unix to meet different requirements. The kernel might be changed to run on different chips, for instance, or menus might be added to help novice users interact with Unix.

—Reprinted with permission, *High Technology* magazine, December 1983. Copyright © 1983 by High Technology Publishing Company, 38 Commercial Wharf, Boston, Mass. 02110.

# DATA BASE MANAGEMENT SYSTEMS

You know that a *data base* is a collection of logically related data elements that may be structured in various ways to meet the multiple processing and retrieval needs of organizations and individuals. There's nothing new about data bases—early ones were chiseled in stone, penned on scrolls, and written on index cards. But now data bases are commonly recorded on magnetizeable media, and computer programs are required to perform the necessary storage and retrieval operations.

You'll see in the following pages that complex data relationships and linkages may be found in all but the simplest data bases. The system software package that handles the difficult tasks associated with creating, accessing, and maintaining data base records is called a **data base management system (DBMS).** The programs in a DBMS package establish an interface between the data base itself and the users of the data base. (These users may be applications programmers, managers and others with information needs, and various OS programs.)

Most DBMS packages are purchased from computer manufacturers and independent software vendors. They are available for machines of all sizes. Some mainframe packages may cost tens of thousands of dollars. (Examples of mainframe DBMSs include Cincom's TOTAL, Cullinet's IDMS, IBM's IMS, and Software AG's ADABAS.) Prices of personal computer DBMSs start at a few hundred dollars and go up to a few thousand dollars, but they usually lack many of the features found in the larger packages. (Examples of pc packages include Ashton-Tate's dBASEII, Condor Computer's Condor III, DJR Associates' FMS-80, International Software Enterprises' MDBS, Micro-AP's Selector V, and O'Hanlon Computer Systems' The Sensible Solution.)

The market for DBMS packages is growing rapidly because they can *alleviate certain types of problems* and can be used to *give fast response to users* with special information needs. Let's look at each of these topics.

Possible Problems with
Departmental Applications

Data processing activities in organizations have traditionally been grouped by departments and by applications. Most of the early computers used in organizations were installed to process a few large-volume jobs in a small number of departments. As you saw in Chapter 2, preparing customer bills and maintaining accounts receivable (A/R) files are these types of applications. Other applications, treated independently, were added over the years. Each separate application had its own master file organized in a sequential, direct, or indexed sequential fashion. (These file-organization approaches are discussed in the Closer Look reading at the end of Chapter 12.) The records in each file were organized according to a single key field. Each application also had its own input data, and its own processing program to update the file and supply information.

When the key field of the file wasn't relevant to the information that was needed, the entire file would have to be searched. For example, to get the names of employees with a certain educational background from a personnel file organized by employee number would require a search of all file records. If the personnel department's need for such "exception" information became routine, a new file structured on an educational background key would be created and a new program would be written to process this file. Of course, this second file would duplicate much of the data stored in the first personnel file.

At the same time that new files were being created and data were being duplicated *within* a department, the same duplication of related data was occurring *between different departments*. This comes as no surprise to you. After all, you've seen in Chapters 2 and 3 that many of the same data items are often kept in different files and used in different ways by people in sales, shipping, billing, A/R, and inventory control departments. Each department's applications and files were often created as the need arose without any serious thought given to the total information needs of the organization. Several problems were also created by this departmental file-oriented approach:

1. *Data redundancy.* The same basic data fields are included in many different files. For example, a great deal of redundant data on a bank customer (e.g., home address, age, and credit rating) might be contained in separate checking account, savings account, automobile loan, and personal loan files. The cost of entering and storing the same data in many files can be quite expensive.

2. *File updating problems.* When changes occur in a data item, every file which contains that field should be updated to reflect the change. Confusion can result when one file is updated while another isn't (an all too common occurrence). For instance, the credit rating of Charlie Brown, account number 1234 in the auto loan department, may be changed to reflect the fact that Charlie's car had to be repossessed. But this change in credit status may not be carried over to the file in the personal loan department that contains the record of Charles M. Brown, account number 5678. And, of course, the cost of running different updating programs can be high.

3. *Lack of program/data independence.* The programs used with file-oriented applications usually contain "picture," "format," or "data" statements that precisely define each data field to be processed. A brief survey at one university showed that the data element "student name" was stored in 13 different files and in five different formats. Anytime there's a need to add, delete, or change data formats, the application program must also be changed. Likewise, a significant revision in a program may require a restructuring of the data file processed by the program. Changing programs to accommodate data format changes is a major maintenance activity in many data processing installations today.

Dissatisfied with the problems caused by the departmental file-oriented approach, some system designers began looking in the late 1960s for ways to consolidate activities by using a data base approach. Although there are differences in opinion about what constitutes a data base system, the most prevalent view is that such systems are designed around a centralized and integrated shared data file (or data base) that emphasizes the independence of programs and data. This data base is located in a DASD. Data transactions are introduced into the system only once. These data are now a neutral resource with respect to any particular program, and specific data elements are readily available as needed to all authorized applications and users of the data base. All data base records that transactions affect may be updated at the time of input.

The data base concept requires that input data be commonly defined and consistently organized and presented throughout the organization. And this requirement, in turn, calls for rigid input discipline. In many organizations, a **data base administrator (DBA)** has the overall authority to establish and control the data definitions and standards that are used throughout the organization. A **data diction-ary** is used to document and maintain the data definitions. The DBA is also respon-sible for determining the relationships among data elements, and for designing the data base security system to guard against unauthorized use.

**Some Uses of DBMS Packages**

A DBMS can organize, process, and present selected data elements from the data base. This capability enables decision makers to search, probe, and query data base contents in order to extract answers to nonrecurring and unplanned questions that aren't available in regular reports. These questions might initially be vague and/or poorly defined, but people can ''browse'' through the data base until they have the needed information. In short, the DBMS will ''manage'' the stored data items and assemble the needed items from the common data base in response to the queries of those who aren't programmers. In a file-oriented system, users needing special information may communicate their needs to a programmer, who, when time per-mits, will write one or more programs to extract the data and prepare the informa-tion. The availability of a DBMS, however, offers users a much faster alternative communications path (see Figure 13-8).

**Figure 13-8** A data base management system can give fast response to users with special information needs.

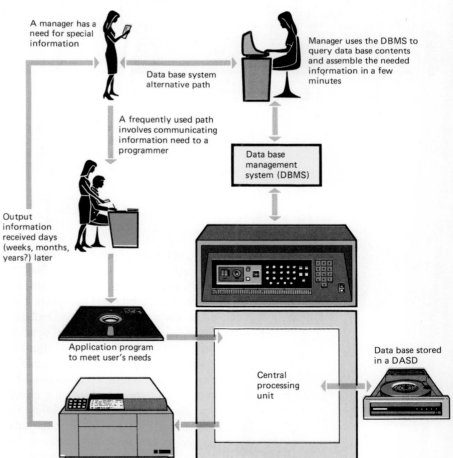

A manager has a need for special information

Data base system alternative path

Manager uses the DBMS to query data base contents and assemble the needed information in a few minutes

A frequently used path involves communicating information need to a programmer

Data base management system (DBMS)

Output information received days (weeks, months, years?) later

Application program to meet user's needs

Central processing unit

Data base stored in a DASD

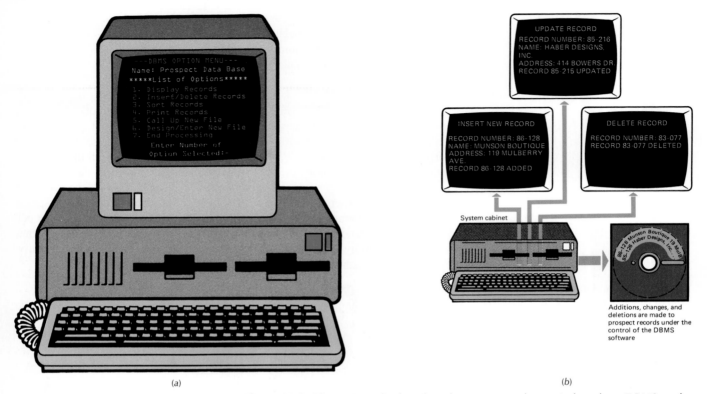

(a)

(b)

**Figure 13-9** The options displayed on the screen can be carried out by a DBMS package. The pc user selects the option(s) needed, and then interacts with the DBMS software to achieve the desired results. For example, option 3 can be selected to single out prospect records with specified zip code values, and option 4 can be used to print labels for these prospects.

Personal computer operators can use a DBMS package to create and maintain files and records. You saw in Chapter 2 (Figure 2-4, page 42) that R-K Enterprises uses a pc, a mailing label program, and a prospect master file to produce gummed labels. But the prospect master file can be treated as a data base, and the contents of each customer record can be entered on a disk under the control of the DBMS software. The DBMS menu of options shown in Figure 13-9 still allows the user to print mailing labels (option 4). But the package also allows the operator to perform many other operations. For example, records with specified zip code values can be singled out and retrieved. Gummed labels of just these records can then be printed to support a special advertising effort in a designated area.

And to illustrate the flexibility of a DBMS in a larger setting, let's assume that a personnel manager of a large multinational corporation has just received an urgent request to send an employee to a foreign country to effect an emergency repair of a hydraulic pump that the company stopped making 6 years ago. The employee needed must be a mechanical engineer, must have knowledge of the particular pump (and therefore, let's assume, must have been with the corporation for at least 8 years), must be able to speak French, and must be willing to accept an overseas assignment. Obviously, there's not likely to be a report available that will have the names of engineers with just these characteristics. But the records on each employee stored in the data base do contain information on educational background, date of employment, work experience, and language capability.

It might have been necessary in the past for the personnel manager to spend hours going through a lengthy printout of the entire personnel file in order to locate employees who match the requirements. With a DBMS, however, it's now possible for the manager to use an online station to request that personnel records be searched for the names and locations of French-speaking engineers with 8 or more years of company experience. Armed with such information obtained by the DBMS in a few minutes, the manager can then contact the named employees to fill the overseas assignment. You can take a closer look at the time-saving advantages of the DBMS in the reading that follows this chapter.

In addition to having direct access to data generated *within* the organization, a decision maker may also have *externally produced* data in his or her data base that can be readily accessible by the DBMS. Data suppliers may make external data available to users in several ways. In the least restrictive form, data may be *sold outright* by vendors on some medium such as magnetic tape, and buyers may then store these facts in their data bases in almost any way they choose. Economic statistics and United States census data, for example, may be purchased on tapes from government agencies for use in this way. Some organizations offer data on a *rental basis* to subscribers. Users then access these facts from terminals and pay for the resources used according to the pricing scheme employed by the supplier. A somewhat similar service is offered by firms that maintain *information retrieval data bases*. Many libraries, for example, use retrieval services that can access tens of millions of worldwide document references to quickly supply their users with sources of information on practically any subject. Finally, a user may buy special reports prepared from a data base owned by an outside supplier.

**DBMS Structuring Techniques**  Sequential, direct, and other file processing approaches are used to organize and structure data in *single* files. But a DBMS is able to integrate data elements from *several* files to answer specific user inquiries for information. This means that the DBMS is able to access and retrieve data from nonkey record fields. That is, the DBMS is able to structure and tie together the logically related data from several large files.

**Logical Structures.** Identifying these logical relationships is a job of the data administrator. A **data definition language** is used for this purpose. The DBMS may then employ one of the following logical structuring techniques during storage, access, and retrieval operations:

1. *List structures.* In this logical approach, records are linked together by the use of pointers. A **pointer** is a data item in one record that identifies the storage location of another logically related record. Records in a customer

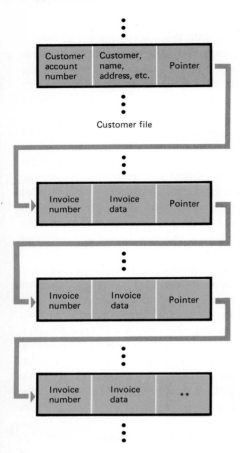

Figure 13-10 List structure.

master file, for example, will contain the name and address of each customer, and each record in this file is identified by an account number. During an accounting period, a customer may buy a number of items on different days. Thus, the company may maintain an invoice file to reflect these transactions. A **list structure** could be used in this situation to show the unpaid invoices at any given time. Each record in the customer file would contain a field that would point to the record location of the first invoice for that customer in the invoice file (Figure 13-10). This invoice record, in turn, would be linked to later invoices for the customer. The last invoice in the chain would be identified by the use of a special character as a pointer.

2. **Hierarchical (tree) structures.** In this logical approach, data units are structured in multiple levels that graphically resemble an "upside down" tree with the root at the top and the branches formed below. There's a superior-subordinate relationship in a **hierarchical (tree) structure.** Below the single-root data component are subordinate elements or nodes, each of which, in turn, "own" one or more other elements (or none). Each element or branch in this structure below the root has only a single owner. Thus, as we see in Figure 13-11, a customer owns an invoice, and the invoice has subordinate items. The branches in a tree structure are not connected.

3. **Network structures.** Unlike the tree approach, which does not permit the connection of branches, the **network structure** permits the connection of the nodes in a multidirectional manner (see Figure 13-12). Thus, each node may have several owners and may, in turn, own any number of other data units. Data management software permits the extraction of the needed information from such a structure by beginning with any record in a file.

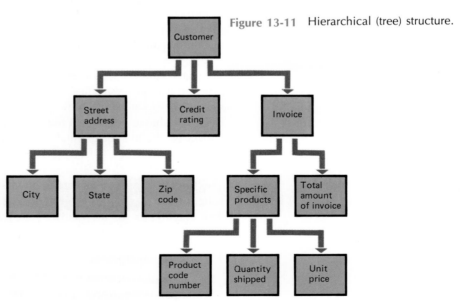

Figure 13-11 Hierarchical (tree) structure.

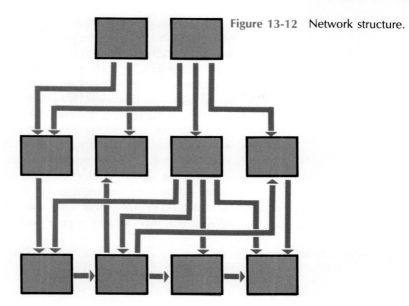

Figure 13-12 Network structure.

4. *Relational structures.* A **relational structure** is made up of many tables. The data are stored in the form of "relations" in these tables. For example, relation tables could be established to link a college course with the instructor of the course, and with the location of the class (see Figure 13-13). To find the name of the instructor and the location of the English class, the course/instructor relation is searched to get the name ("Fitt"), and the course/location relation is searched to get the class location ("Main 142"). Many other relations are, of course, possible. This is a relatively new data base structuring approach that's expected to be widely implemented in the future.

**Physical Structures.** People visualize or structure data in logical ways for their own purposes. Thus, records $R_1$ and $R_2$ may always be logically linked and processed in sequence in one particular application. However, in a computer system it's quite possible that these records that are logically contiguous in one application are not physically stored together. Rather, the **physical structure** of the records in media and hardware may depend not only on the I/O and storage devices and techniques used, but also on the different logical relationships that users may assign

Figure 13-13 Relational structure.

| Course/instructor relation | | Course/location relation | | Other relations |
|---|---|---|---|---|
| COURSE | INSTRUCTOR | COURSE | LOCATION | For example, course related to time of meeting, days of meeting, hours of credit, etc. |
| ENGLISH 103 | FITT | ENGLISH 103 | MAIN 142 | |
| SCIENCE 116 | GOMEZ | MATH 101 | SCIENCE 125 | |
| MATH 101 | PIRELLI | SCIENCE 116 | SCIENCE 111 | |
| ⋮ | ⋮ | ⋮ | ⋮ | |

to the data found in $R_1$ and $R_2$. For example, $R_1$ and $R_2$ may be records of credit customers who have shipments sent to the same block in the same city every 2 weeks. From the shipping department manager's perspective, then, $R_1$ and $R_2$ are sequential entries on a geographically organized shipping report. But in the A/R application, the customers represented by $R_1$ and $R_2$ may be identified, and their accounts may be processed, according to their account numbers which are widely separated. In short, then, the physical location of the stored records in many computer-based information systems is invisible to users.

Of course, the extent to which the logical structure of the most frequently processed applications corresponds to the physical storage techniques used may determine the amount of processing the system software must perform to reassemble the data to meet user requests. As you might expect, trying to design systems to efficiently serve many users while minimizing the use of computing resources is a difficult task that involves complex tradeoffs.

## Advantages and Limitations of DBMS Packages

The advantages and disadvantages of DBMS software packages are summarized in the following list:

| Advantages | Limitations |
|---|---|
| Fewer applications programs and lengthy regular reports containing reference data may be needed when users can directly access the data base. | More complex and expensive hardware and software are needed. |
| Better integration (and less duplication) of data originating at different points is feasible. | A lengthy conversion period may be needed, higher personnel training costs may be incurred, and more sophisticated skills are needed by those responsible for the data base system. |
| Faster preparation of information to support nonrecurring tasks and changing conditions is possible. | People may be reluctant to adapt to significant changes in data processing procedures. |
| Savings in the cost of developing new applications, and in data entry and data storage costs, may be possible. | Sensitive data in online storage might find its way into unauthorized hands. |
| Fewer errors (and thus an increase in data integrity) may result when several records may be updated simultaneously. | Hardware or software failures might result in the destruction of vital data base contents. |

## Feedback and Review 13-1

The purpose and functions of computer OSs and DBMSs have been discussed in this chapter. To test and reinforce your understanding of these system software packages, answer the following true-false questions by placing a T or F in the space provided.

___1. An operating system is an integrated set of programs that's used to manage the resources and overall operations of a computer system.

___2. An OS tends to isolate the hardware from the user.

___3. The first operating system was produced by IBM for multiprogramming applications.

___4. A modern OS is restricted to running on a single machine model.

___5. A goal of OS developers is to devise ways to operate a computer with a minimum of idle time.

___6. Automatic job-to-job transitions were performed by early OSs, but are no longer needed in a modern system.

___7. Most OS elements can be classified as either control or processing programs.

___8. The overall management of a computer system is under the control of an OS master program called the Job Controller.

___9. The OS supervisor resides in primary storage while other OS programs are kept in an online system residence device.

___10. The OS supervisor calls up a job control program to read and process the special codes written in a job control statement.

___11. Whenever possible, jobs to be processed are scheduled to balance I/O and processing requirements.

___12. Only one channel is needed for multiprogramming systems.

___13. Small high-speed storage elements called buffers play a role in overlapping input, processing, and output operations.

___14. Multiprogramming is defined to mean the execution of instructions from several programs at the same instant in time.

___15. A multiprocessing system can execute instructions from several programs at the same instant in time.

___16. In a multiprogramming system, a higher priority is assigned to batch processing than to direct-access processing.

___17. The effective size of the primary storage available for programs may appear to be unlimited when virtual storage concepts are used.

___18. The program call-up capability of an OS gives it access to programs that can simplify processing.

___19. A data base is a collection of logically related data elements that are structured in various ways to meet the multiple processing and retrieval needs of organizations and individuals.

___20. Problems created when each department develops its own applications and files include data redundancy, file updating difficulties, and a lack of independence between data and programs.

___21. A Webster's dictionary is used by a data base administrator to document and maintain the definitions of the input data used in an organization.

___22. A collection of programs used to manage a data base is identified by the initials DASD.

___23. Logical structuring techniques used by DBMSs are limited to list, hierarchical, and relational approaches.

___24. Each element or branch in a hierarchical DBMS structure may have several owners, and may, in turn, own any number of other data units.

___25. A pointer is a data item in one record that identifies the storage location of another logically related record.

___26. An advantage of the use of a DBMS package is that sensitive data in online storage cannot find its way into unauthorized hands.

# LOOKING BACK

**1.** An operating system (OS) is an integrated set of programs that's used to manage the resources and overall operations of a computer system. Users communicate with an OS, supply input data and applications programs, and receive output results. The first OSs were developed in the mid-1950s to reduce CPU waiting time between jobs. An automatic job-to-job transition procedure was devised then, and this is still one of the major functions performed by a modern OS. Other activities carried out by an OS can generally be placed in control or processing categories.

**2.** The OS supervisor controls and coordinates all other parts of the OS, and it resides in primary storage. Other programs in the OS are kept in an online system residence device so that the supervisor can retrieve them when they are needed. In a large batch processing (stacked job) environment, a deck of job control cards may contain statements telling the OS the name of the job, the I/O devices to use, etc. The statements are presented in the codes of a job control language. A job control program in the OS is then used to read and execute these codes.

**3.** It's a common practice now to overlap processing jobs in larger systems. Whenever possible, multiple jobs are scheduled to balance I/O and processing requirements. Channels and buffers facilitate the overlapping of processing tasks. Multiprogramming is the interleaved or concurrent execution of two or more different and independent programs by the same computer. Multiprocessing describes a system in which two or more CPUs are linked together in a coordinated way. Instructions from two or more programs can be processed at the same instant in time in a multiprocessing system, but not in a multiprogramming environment. Priorities are typically assigned to the programs in a multiprogramming system. When a high-priority program interrupts the processing of a lower-priority program, the OS must see to it that the data, instructions, and intermediate processing results of the interrupted program are kept separate from other jobs. The execution of the interrupted program must then be restored at a later time.

**4.** A computer with virtual storage capability keeps active program pages or segments in primary storage and assigns other program parts to an online storage device. The OS handles the swapping of program pages between primary and online secondary storage units as needed. The program call-up capability of an OS gives it access to a number of translating programs, utility programs, and library programs that can be used to simplify processing operations.

**5.** The system software package that handles the difficult tasks associated with creating, accessing, and maintaining data base records is called a data base management system (DBMS). The programs in a DBMS package establish an interface be-tween the data base itself and the users of the data base. Problems are often created in an organization when each department independently develops its own applications and files. There's considerable duplication of data, all this redundant data may not be updated to accurately reflect the changes that occur, and the programs that process the data must usually be revised anytime there's a change in data format.

**6.** The data base concept was developed to reduce these difficulties. A data base system is designed around an integrated data file that emphasizes the independence of data and programs. Data transactions are introduced into the system only once. These data are then available as needed to all authorized applications and users of the data base. A data base administrator is often responsible for establishing and controlling the data definitions and standards used by an organization. He or she is also responsible for determining the relationships among data elements.

**7.** A DBMS package can organize, process, and present selected data elements from the data base in response to queries from users. This permits users to "browse" through the data base until they have answers to nonrecurring questions. It also adds a great deal of flexibility to the information resources of an individual or an organization.

**8.** A DBMS may employ list, hierarchical, network, or relational structuring techniques to perform its functions. Each of these techniques is briefly summarized in the chapter. Some of the advantages and disadvantages of DBMS packages are also summarized at the end of the chapter.

## KEY TERMS AND CONCEPTS

system software package 334
operating system (OS) 334
OS supervisor, monitor, or
   executive routine 336
system residence device 336
stacked job processing 338
job control cards 338
job control language (JCL) 338
job control program 338
overlap processing 338
channel 338

time slice 339
buffers 340
multiprogramming 341
multiprocessing 341
program interrupt 342
virtual storage 342
program pages or segments 342
program call-up capability 343
utility (service) programs 343
library programs 343
librarian program 343

data base management system
   (DBMS) 345
data base administrator (DBA) 346
data dictionary 347
data definition language 349
pointer 349
list structure 350
hierarchical (tree) structure 350
network structure 350
relational structure 351
physical structure 351

# TOPICS FOR REVIEW AND DISCUSSION

**1.** *(a)* What's an operating system? *(b)* When were operating systems developed? *(c)* Why were they developed?

**2.** "The OS tends to isolate the hardware from the user." Discuss this comment.

**3.** *(a)* Into what two categories can most OS programs be classified? *(b)* Give an example of an OS program from each category.

**4.** Explain the role of the OS supervisor.

**5.** Discuss how job control cards, a job control language, and a job control program are used to provide job-to-job linkages in a batch (stacked job) environment.

**6.** *(a)* How are channels used to facilitate overlapped processing? *(b)* How are buffers used?

**7.** *(a)* What is multiprogramming? *(b)* What is multiprocessing?

**8.** Why must an OS be prepared to handle system interruptions in a multiprogramming environment?

**9.** *(a)* What is virtual storage? *(b)* Why was it developed?

**10.** How can the program call-up capability of an OS be used to simplify processing operations?

**11.** *(a)* What's a data base management system? *(b)* Discuss how a DBMS package can be used.

**12.** "Several problems are often created when different departments independently develop their own applications and files." Identify and discuss three of these problems.

**13.** How does the data base concept alleviate the problems identified in the previous question?

**14.** Why is the job of a data base administrator important?

**15.** Identify and discuss the logical structuring techniques used by DBMSs.

**16.** *(a)* What are the advantages of DBMS packages? *(b)* The limitations?

# PROJECTS TO LOOK INTO

**1.** Visit your library and/or a computer/software store to identify three OS packages. Gather the following information on each package: *(a)* name and supplier of the package, *(b)* primary storage requirements of the package, *(c)* price of the package.

**2.** Make another trip to your library and/or a computer/software store to identify three DBMS packages. Gather the following information on each of these packages: *(a)* name and supplier of the package, *(b)* hardware needed to run the package, *(c)* OS required to run the package, *(d)* price of the package.

# ANSWERS TO FEEDBACK AND REVIEW SECTION

**13-1**

| | | |
|---|---|---|
| 1. T | 10. T | 19. T |
| 2. T | 11. T | 20. T |
| 3. F | 12. F | 21. F |
| 4. F | 13. T | 22. F |
| 5. T | 14. F | 23. F |
| 6. F | 15. T | 24. F |
| 7. T | 16. F | 25. T |
| 8. F | 17. T | 26. F |
| 9. T | 18. T | |

# Is 'Relational' Just a New Buzzword?

Why is there so much excitement over relational data base management systems (DBMS)?

Is "relational" just a new buzzword or are there significant differences between relational, network and hierarchical DBMS?

To answer these questions, contrast the primary characteristics of the three technologies. The hallmarks of a relational DBMS are its table data structure, ease of use, data independence and theoretical foundation. Relational DBMS use a simple table structure rather than a complex network or hierarchical structure. It is not necessary to navigate through a table or between tables since there are no pointers connecting the tables.

This is in contrast to a network in which it is necessary to know in which set one is working, who the owner and members of the set are and how the sets relate to each other. A hierarchy is a simpler structure than a network, but it is still necessary to maintain position in a hierarchy when performing most operations. A relational DBMS derives its ease of use from its simple table data structure and its language.

The three true [relational, large-scale] DBMS on the market have remarkably similar languages. The language of IBM's SQL/DS is Structured Query Language; Oracle, Inc.'s Oracle is Structured English Query Language (Sequel 2); and Relational Technology, Inc.'s Ingres is Query English Language (Quel).

The relational languages are unified languages that are easily used by both end users and systems professionals. The same statements that were designed for end users are embedded in Cobol, Fortran, PL/I or assembler language by systems professionals when developing an application system.

The unified language extends beyond the retrieval and update facilities to the creation, indexing and maintenance of the system. . . .

The relational DBMS are based on a theoretical relational model. This is in contrast to the network structure that was borrowed from telecommunications and the hierarchical structure that was borrowed from bill of material systems. Network and hierarchical DBMS were developed in a heuristic fashion and have evolved over the years to accommodate as many requirements as possible.

Most DBMS began with a data definition language and a data manipulation language. Typically, the date definition language was a customized set of assembler macros and the data manipulation language was a customized set of call statements to be embedded in a host language.

As demand dictated, DBMS developers added a report writer that had no similarity to the data definition and data manipulation languages. Requirements for a query language developed. Some free-form report writers were enhanced into query languages. Data dictionaries were developed with languages that had little similarity to the other languages in the DBMS.

The developers of relational DBMS needed a language to perform the functions of relational algebra and relational calculus in a manner that was suitable for application systems development and end-user query. They learned from the proliferation of languages in DBMS on the market and developed a unified language that accomplished all the required functions in one consistent and easily learned language.

The result has been well-planned, developed and implemented DBMS that gain their power and flexibility from a theoretical foundation and experience accumulated over a decade.

—From Gabrielle Wiorkowski, "Is 'Relational' Just a New Buzzword?" *Computerworld*, April 4, 1983, p. 51. Reprinted courtesy of Gabrielle Wiorkowski.

# Management Information Systems

## High-Speed Management

Rapidly changing technology, quick market saturation, unexpected competition—these all make succeeding in business, particularly a high-tech business, harder than ever today. . . .

At the heart of the current need for change is the fact that product life cycles are getting shorter. "I can't document it, but every industry we look at seems to be undergoing shorter cycles," says Joel Goldhar, dean of the business school at the Illinois Institute of Technology. "All of a sudden, industrial products are like Hula-Hoops." The microcomputer was almost unheard of seven years ago. The first commercially successful machine could process only eight bits of information at a time—a bit being a one or a zero in binary code. But no sooner did the eight-bit micro come to market in 1977 than the 16-bit micro was on its way in 1981, followed by the 32-bit in 1983. Eventually the market for micros will mature, and the time between new products will stretch out again. This is exactly what happened with electronic calculators. . . .

Dominique Hanssens, a professor at UCLA's Graduate School of Management, has studied the life cycles of electric appliances. Years ago, he says, the market for refrigerators, say, took over 30 years to mature; the market for newer appliances like microwave ovens has taken about ten years. "Manufacturers face the end of a growth era much sooner than they used to," says Hanssens. Why? The rapid rate of technological change, plus the easy availability of credit and the power of mass communications and advertising. "In the old days," Hanssens says, "people who bought new products were what we call 'innovators'—the wealthy and well educated. It took a while for something to diffuse through the population. Today, very soon after a product hits the market, Mr. Everybody has it."

—Susan Fraker, "High-Speed Management for the High-Tech Age," *Fortune*, Mar. 5, 1984, p. 62. © 1984 Time Inc. All rights reserved. Photo courtesy Hewlett-Packard Company.

This chapter introduces you to some general management information concepts and shows you why management information systems (MIS) are needed. You'll then consider some of the issues involved in planning, organizing, and controlling an MIS, and in using an MIS for decision making. The information in this chapter will enable you to:

■ Explain why different types of information are needed by managers at different levels in an organization

■ Define the MIS concept and discuss the issues that must be considered in planning, organizing, and controlling an MIS

■ Describe how an MIS can help improve managerial planning and decision making

# MANAGEMENT INFORMATION CONCEPTS

As long as an important resource is supplied to us when and where we need it, in the right quantity and quality, and at a reasonable cost, we tend to take it for granted. It's only when the cost increases and/or the supply and quality of the resource seems to deteriorate that we recognize its importance. So it has been with management information. Previously acceptable information systems have seemed to deteriorate in recent years. In simpler times, many of the systems that have been discarded in the last decade were considered models of efficiency. But times are not simple today for managers. The growing size of many organizations, and the speed with which new technological discoveries are now being applied for competitive purposes combine to produce a complex and challenging management environment.

At the beginning of this century, for example, there was an average wait of 33 years between an invention and its application. But the laser was invented in 1958 and was being used just 7 years later for manufacturing and surgical purposes. And as this application rate continues to accelerate, less reaction time is available to managers (see Figure 14-1). Thus, as pressures increase from domestic and foreign competitors, managers have found that previously acceptable systems are no longer adequate to meet their information needs.

## Information Needs of Managers

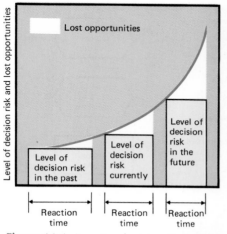

Figure 14-1 A major decision that might have taken several years to implement 10 years ago must now be carried out in a shorter period if the organization is to remain competitive. But while the available management reaction time is shrinking, each decision may carry a greater risk and be valid for a shorter time period. Furthermore, as reaction time shrinks, profitable opportunities are lost because preoccupied managers fail to recognize them.

What information does a manager need to manage effectively? A common need basic to all managers is an understanding of the purpose of the organization, i.e., its policies, its programs, its plans, and its goals. But beyond these basic informational requirements, the question of what information is needed can be answered only in broad general terms because individual managers differ in the ways in which they view information, in their analytical approaches to using it, and in their conceptual organization of relevant facts.

An additional factor that complicates the subject of the information needed by managers is the *organizational level* of the managerial job. In the smallest organizations, there are few managerial levels, and the managers tend to be generalists. That is, they are knowledgeable about most (if not all) of the group's activities. But as organizations grow in size, people with specialized knowledge are hired and additional managerial levels are created. Information that's satisfactory for generalists (who can often use their overall knowledge to fill in the missing gaps) is often not acceptable when supplied to specialists. It thus becomes necessary to supply different types of information to people at different levels.

*Top-level managers* still must have a general understanding of the organization's activities. Since they are charged with weighing risks and making major policy decisions on such matters as new product development, new plant authorizations, and so on, they need the type of information that will support these long-range **strategic plans and decisions.** *Middle-level managers* are responsible for making the **tactical decisions** that will allocate the resources and establish the controls needed to implement the top-level plans. And *lower-level managers* make the day-to-day **operational decisions** to schedule and control specific tasks. The actual results of an operation may be checked daily against planned expectations, and corrective actions may be taken as needed. In short, as Figure 14-2 shows, managers use their time differently, need internal information with varying degrees of detail, and need different mixes of internal and external information in order to make their decisions.

## Properties of Useful Management Information

As a general rule, the more information serves to reduce the element of uncertainty in the decisions made by managers at all levels, the greater is its value. But like other basic resources available to managers, information is usually not free. The cost of acquiring information must usually be compared with the benefits to be obtained from its use. Just as it's economically foolish to spend $100 to mine $75 worth of coal, so, too, is it unsound to produce information costing $100 if this information doesn't lead to actions that yield a greater return. Generally speaking, information that possesses the properties of *accuracy, timeliness, completeness,* and *conciseness* will be more valuable than information lacking one or more of these

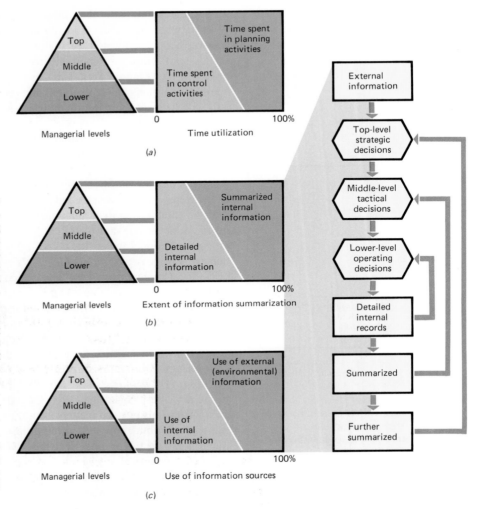

Figure 14-2 *(a)* More time is generally spent at the lower managerial levels performing control activities (e.g., checking to make sure that production schedules are being met), while at the upper levels more time is spent on planning (e.g., determining the location and specifications of a new production plant). *(b)* Lower-level managers need detailed information relating to daily operations of specific departments, but top executives are best served with information that summarizes trends and indicates exceptions to what was expected. *(c)* The higher a manager is in an organization, the more likely it is that he or she will use information obtained from external sources. A supervisor uses internally generated feedback information to control production processes, but a president studying the feasibility of a new plant needs external information about customer product acceptance, pollution control, local tax structures, and labor availability.

characteristics. However, compromises are often made in one or more of these properties for economic reasons.

**Accuracy. Accuracy** is the ratio of correct information to the total amount of information produced over a period. If 1,000 items of information are produced and 950 of these items give a correct report of the actual situation, then the accuracy level is 0.95. Whether this level is high enough depends on the information being produced. Fifty incorrect bank balances in a mailing of 1,000 bank statements are intolerable. But if physical inventory records kept on large quantities of inexpensive parts achieve an accuracy level of 0.95, this might be acceptable. In the case of bank statements, greater accuracy *must* be obtained. In the case of the parts inventory, greater accuracy *could* be achieved, but the additional value to managers of having a more accurate inventory might be less than the additional costs required to gather it.

**Timeliness. Timeliness** is another important information characteristic. It's of little consolation to a manager to know that information that arrived too late to be of use was accurate. Accuracy alone isn't enough. How fast must be the response time of the information system? Unfortunately, it's once again impossible to give an answer which will satisfy all situations. In the case of regular reports, an immediate response time following each transaction would involve a steady outpouring of documents. The result would be a costly avalanche of paper that would bury managers. Thus, a compromise is often required. The response time should be short enough so that the information does not lose its freshness and value, but it should be long enough to reduce volume (and costs) and reveal important trends that signal the need for action. Of course, when instant access to "time critical" information is needed, quick-response online systems must be used.

**Completeness.** Most managers faced with a decision to make have been frustrated at some time by having supporting information that's accurate, timely—and incomplete. An example of the consequences of failure to consolidate related pieces of information occurred at Pearl Harbor in 1941. Historians tell us that data available, in bits and pieces and at scattered points, if integrated, would have signaled the danger of a Japanese attack. Better integration of the facts available at scattered points in a business for the purpose of furnishing managers with more **complete information** is a goal of information systems designers.

**Conciseness.** Many traditional information systems have been designed on the assumption that lack of completeness is the most critical problem facing managers. This assumption has often led designers to employ an ineffective shotgun approach, peppering managers with more information than they can possibly use. Important information, along with relatively useless data, is often buried in stacks of detailed reports. Managers are then faced with the problem of extracting those items of information that they need. **Concise information** that summarizes the relevant data and points out areas of exception to normal or planned activities is what is often needed by—but less often supplied to—today's managers.

**An MIS Orientation**

In the late 1960s and early 1970s, many managers began to realize that they weren't able to cope with rapidly changing conditions merely by using the routine reports that their traditional systems were producing. Their information didn't possess the properties mentioned above, and it was no longer adequate to meet their needs. Responding to these management needs, system designers began to develop new computer-oriented management information systems that were more responsive and more comprehensive than those that had existed just a few years earlier. There was initially talk of designing a completely integrated "total system" built around a single online data base that would instantly give managers all the information they needed to make their decisions. As you might expect, this proved to be an unrealistic goal that failed to recognize the complexities of operating a modern organization. Few, if any, total system designs were actually attempted. Instead, the system designers in an organization developed a long-range conceptual model of a management information system for their organization and then gradually began to integrate the existing information-producing systems in the organization into their long-range plan. This integration continues today.

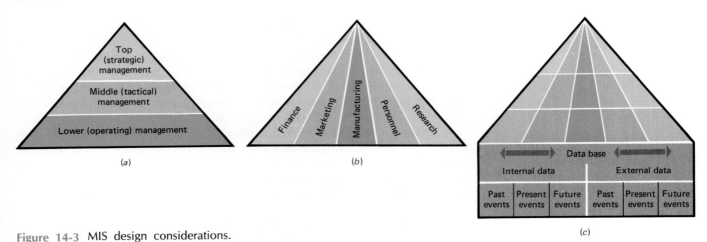

Figure 14-3 MIS design considerations.

The **management information system (MIS)** concept has been defined in dozens of ways. Since one organization's model of an MIS is likely to differ from that of another, its not surprising that their MIS definitions would also vary in scope and breadth. For our purposes, an MIS can be defined as a network of computer-based data processing procedures developed in an organization and integrated as necessary with manual and other procedures for the purpose of providing timely and effective information to support decision making and other necessary management functions.

Although MIS models differ, most of them recognize the concepts shown in Figure 14-3. In addition to what might be termed the *horizontal* management structure shown in Figure 14-3a, an organization is also divided *vertically* into different specialties and functions which require separate information flows (see Figure 14-3b). Combining the horizontal managerial levels with the vertical specialties produces the complex organizational structure shown in Figure 14-3c. Underlying this structure is a data base consisting, ideally, of internally and externally produced data relating to past, present, and predicted future events.

The formidable task of the MIS designer is to develop the information flow needed to support decision making (see Figure 14-4). Generally speaking, much of the information needed by managers who occupy different levels and who have different responsibilities is obtained from a collection of existing information systems (or subsystems). These systems may be tied together very closely in an MIS. More often, however, they are more loosely coupled.

# PLANNING ISSUES AND THE MIS

To ''plan'' is to decide in advance on a course of action. *Planning* involves making decisions about long-term goals, and about the procedures and controls needed to achieve these goals. An MIS affects the planning function in at least two ways. *First,* MIS designers must consider a number of issues as they make plans to create

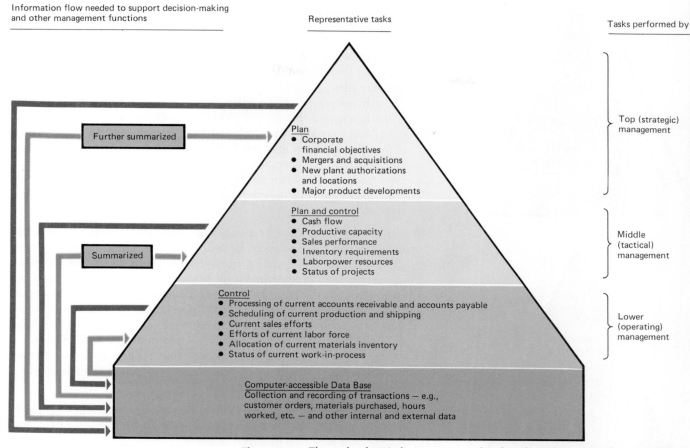

Information flow needed to support decision-making and other management functions

Representative tasks

Tasks performed by

**Plan**
- Corporate financial objectives
- Mergers and acquisitions
- New plant authorizations and locations
- Major product developments

Top (strategic) management

Further summarized

**Plan and control**
- Cash flow
- Productive capacity
- Sales performance
- Inventory requirements
- Laborpower resources
- Status of projects

Middle (tactical) management

Summarized

**Control**
- Processing of current accounts receivable and accounts payable
- Scheduling of current production and shipping
- Current sales efforts
- Efforts of current labor force
- Allocation of current materials inventory
- Status of current work-in-process

Lower (operating) management

**Computer-accessible Data Base**
Collection and recording of transactions — e.g., customer orders, materials purchased, hours worked, etc. — and other internal and external data

**Figure 14-4** The task of MIS designers is to develop the information flow needed to support decision making.

and implement an MIS in an organization. *Second,* the use of an evolving MIS is likely to have an impact on the quality of the plans managers make.

**Issues Involved in Planning for an MIS**

Figures 14-3 and 14-4 may have given you a *general* idea of the task MIS designers face as they draw up long-range plans for an organization's MIS. But some of the more *specific* issues that may be considered during the planning for an MIS are:

■ *Should MIS development be "top-down" or "bottom-up"?* In fact, MIS designers often attempt to use the best attribute of each approach. The **top-down approach** begins with studies of organizational goals and the types of decisions managers make. From these studies comes a model of the information flow in the organization and the design requirements for the system. The *advantage* of this approach is that it's a logical and sensible way to attack a problem (buildings and airplanes are essentially designed in this way), and it can make it easier to integrate system elements.

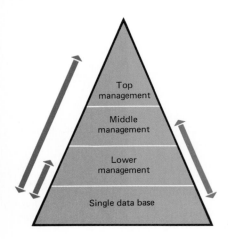

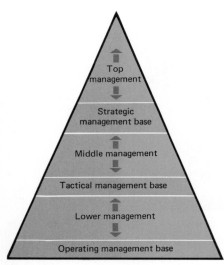

**Figure 14-5** MIS design alternatives.

The *disadvantage* is that it's difficult to define organizational goals and the decision-making activities of managers in the precise terms required for MIS design. There's a risk of building a large and expensive system that's not effective. The **bottom-up approach,** on the other hand, begins at the operating level with the existing procedures for processing transactions and updating files. The add-on modules to support planning, controlling, and decision-making activities are then built as they are needed. The *advantage* of this approach is that smaller "bites" of work are tackled, and the danger of building a complex and ineffective MIS is minimized. The *disadvantage* is that this approach may not lead to the development of high-potential systems above the operating level. And if such higher-level systems are attempted, it's then often necessary to redesign the existing programs and procedures to provide the integration of information that higher-level managers require.

■ *Can a single data base be created to satisfy the differing information needs of the three managerial levels?* Most information systems today serve the needs of operating managers and, to a lesser extent, middle managers. They provide internally produced data dealing with past and current activities. However, a growing number of MISs are now using internal data and carefully developed planning models incorporating assumptions about external conditions to simulate responses to the "what if?" questions of top executives. A problem facing MIS planners is whether to attempt to organize and structure a *single* data base to meet varying needs or to create *different* bases for different *horizontal* levels. Figure 14-5 shows the alternatives.

■ *Can different specialties share the same data base?* Can the MIS supply from a single data base the information needed by marketing, production, finance, and personnel managers at different levels, or must separate *vertically* oriented data bases be designed for each specialty? Different functions have traditionally had their own information systems. Attempting to integrate these separate systems into one or more corporate data bases that will serve the broader needs of many managers is a formidable challenge, but the effort is being made.

■ *Can externally produced data be incorporated into a data base?* To be of value to higher-level managers, an MIS must supply information about the external world. The growing availability of external data in machine-sensible form and/or the use of external data banks (see Chapter 10) makes more data available to the firm's MIS. It's the designer's responsibility to see that these new facts are incorporated into an MIS in meaningful ways.

■ *To what extent should an attempt be made to "solve the triangle"?* That is, to what extent should designers attempt to create an overall MIS that would simultaneously satisfy the information needs of most or all the segments shown in Figure 14-3c? The complexity of the problems involved usually dictates that designers take a gradual and conservative approach.

## How an MIS Can Help Managerial Planning

When compared with earlier information systems, an MIS can have an impact on the quality of a manager's plans by:

- ■ *Causing faster awareness of problems and opportunities.* An MIS can quickly signal out-of-control conditions requiring corrective action when actual performance deviates from what was originally planned. New plans can then be implemented to correct the situation(s). Masses of current and historical internal and external data can be analyzed statistically in order to detect opportunities. And data stored online may permit managers to probe and query a data base to receive quick replies to their planning questions (Figure 14-6).

- ■ *Enabling managers to devote more time to planning.* An MIS can reduce paperwork. More attention may then be given to analytical and intellectual matters associated with planning.

- ■ *Permitting managers to give timely consideration to more complex relationships.* An MIS gives the manager the ability to evaluate more possible alternatives and to consider the internal and external variables that may have a bearing on their outcome. Managers can do a better job of identifying and assessing the probable economic and social effects of different courses of action. In the past, oversimplified assumptions had to be made if resulting decisions were to be timely. More complex relationships can now be considered and evaluated through the use of tools such as *spreadsheet software packages* that provide quick answers to the "what if" questions posed by managers. (See Chapters 4 and 8, pages 82–83 and 222–223, for discussions of how spreadsheet programs can manipulate

**Figure 14-6** A data base query facility allows managers to react effectively to quick-changing business conditions. (Courtesy Honeywell, Inc.)

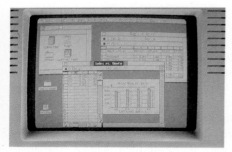

**Figure 14-7** Sophisticated software enables managers to plan more effectively. (Courtesy Apple Computer, Inc.)

columns and rows of data in response to different planning assumptions.) The important relationships that are identified are increasingly being highlighted through the use of charts, maps, and other visual presentations displayed by the *graphic devices* discussed in Chapters 6 and 7 (Figure 14-7). In short, an MIS can furnish managers with planning information that couldn't have been produced at all a few years ago or that couldn't have been produced in time to be of any value.

■ *Assisting in decision implementation.* An MIS can assist in the development of the subordinate plans needed to implement decisions. Computer-based techniques to schedule project activities have been developed and are now widely used. One such project planning program—MacProject—is included in Apple Computer's software package for its Macintosh system. Through the use of such techniques, labor, materials, and other resources can be utilized and controlled effectively.

**Planning and Decision-Making Practices Supported by an MIS**

Computer-based MISs now regularly back up the planning and decision-making activities of managers in a number of business areas (see Figure 14-8). The components of an MIS that assist managers in these activities are often called **decision support systems (DSS).** Included among the planning and decision-making practices that may be supported are the uses of *simulation, expert systems,* and *information centers.*

**Figure 14-8** An MIS supports the planning and decision-making activities of many managers.

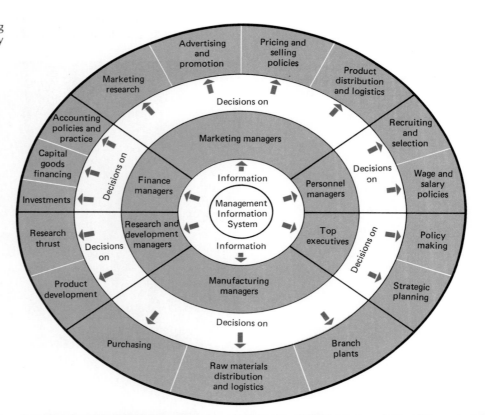

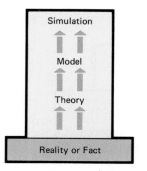

**Figure 14-9** The simulation concept.

**The Use of Simulation.** As Figure 14-9 shows, the simulation concept rests on reality or fact. Few people (if any) fully understand every aspect of a complex situation. Theories are thus developed which may focus attention on only part of the complex whole. In some situations models may then be built in order to test or represent a theory. Finally, **simulation** is the use of a model in the attempt to identify and/or reflect the behavior of a real person, process, or system. In business, for example, managers may evaluate proposed projects or strategies by constructing theoretical models. They can then determine what happens to these models when certain conditions are given or when certain assumptions are tested. Simulation is thus a trial-and-error problem-solving approach that's very useful in planning.

Simulation models have helped *top executives* decide, for example, whether or not to acquire a new plant. Among the dozens of complicating variables that would have to be incorporated into such models are facts and assumptions about the present and potential size of the total market, and the present and potential company share of this total market.

Simulation is also helpful to *middle-level managers*. For example, simulation models are used to improve inventory management. The problem of managing inventories is complicated because there are conflicting desires among organizational units. To illustrate, the purchasing department may prefer to buy large quantities of materials in order to get lower prices. The production department also likes to have large inventories on hand to eliminate shortages and make possible long—and efficient—production runs. And the sales department prefers large finished-goods inventories so that sales will not be lost because of out-of-stock conditions. But the finance department is opposed to large inventory levels because storage expense is increased and funds are tied up for longer periods of time. Through the use of simulated inventory amounts and simulated assumptions about such factors as reorder lead times and cost of being out of stock, managers can experiment with various approaches to arrive at more profitable inventory levels.

Simulation models serving managers at different levels may also be integrated into an overall **corporate modeling** approach to planning and decision making. Of course, the output of simulation models is only as good as the facts and assumptions that people feed into the computer.

*An Example.* Potlatch Forests, Inc., a producer of lumber and wood pulp products, has a corporate planning staff that has developed an overall corporate financial model. Given assumptions from top executives about economic conditions, capital expenditures, etc., for a 5-year future period, simulation runs produce estimated financial statements for each of the 5 years. Executives then analyze the simulated financial statements. If results are judged to be disappointing, executives may change variables in the model that are under their control—e.g., future capital expenditures—and the simulations are repeated.

When acceptable financial results are obtained, they become the targets for planning at lower levels in the company. When feasible, lower-level plans are formulated (again, simulation models are used), and they are assembled into an overall corporate plan. In summary, then, the planning and decision process followed by many managers may resemble the one shown in Figure 14-10.

**The Use of Expert Systems.** An **expert system** is a software package that includes (1) a stored base of knowledge in a specialized area, and (2) the capability

Figure 14-10 The strategies, goals, and economic assumptions of managers serve as the basis for *market forecasts*. This expectation of how many items can be sold then becomes the basis for determining (1) how and when to acquire materials and make the items (the *production plans*), (2) how and when to have the money on hand to pay for the acquired materials and produced items (the *financial plans*), and (3) how and when to promote and distribute the items (the *marketing plans*). And these plans are then used in simulations to estimate such variables as profit and return on investment. Of course, the results of these simulations may bring about changes in established plans and/or the results may cause changes in strategies and assumptions. Once initial simulations have been concluded and high-level plans have been made, operational plans at lower levels are often needed to implement the decisions.

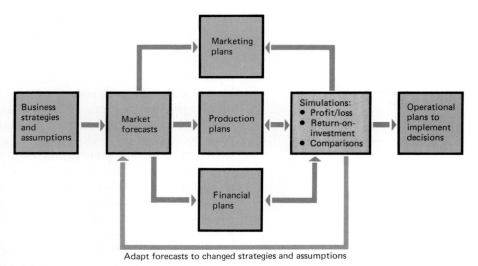

Adapt forecasts to changed strategies and assumptions

to probe this knowledge base and make decision recommendations. The products of years of research in the field of *artificial intelligence (AI)*, expert systems are only now beginning to appear in a few selected areas, but their future applications seem almost limitless, as you know if you've read Chapter 15.

To develop the knowledge base for an expert system, AI researchers spend many months picking the brains of specialists to extract and structure the knowledge that is the basis for the specialists' expertise. Once a knowledge base is created and the software needed to manipulate the stored facts and ideas is in place, the expert system can take on the role of consultant to the system user. As the user supplies input facts, the expert system responds as an intelligent assistant by giving advice and suggesting possible decisions.

*An Example.* An expert system called *Prospector* asks the user about an area's geologic formations and then gives advice on the possible location of mineral deposits. Prospector has accurately predicted the location of a multimillion-dollar molybdenum deposit in Washington state. Another expert system is *Caduceus*, a medical diagnostic program developed by Drs. Jack Myers and Harry Pople at the University of Pittsburgh. Caduceus uses a sophisticated decision-making process as it gradually moves toward its diagnosis of a medical problem. During this process, it requests and receives symptoms and other information from the using doctor.

**The Use of Information Centers.** Many organizations with large mainframe computers have established information centers to support the planning and decision-making activities of their employees. Generally set up as a service branch of an MIS department, an **information center** gives its users a direct online path into the organization's data bases to retrieve the facts they need (see the section on ''Uses of DBMS Packages'' in Chapter 13). Center personnel show managers how to employ available user-friendly software to develop their own applications and generate their own reports. Instead of channeling their information requests through analysts and programmers in the MIS department, end users produce their own output to support their planning and decision-making activities. Since analysts and programmers are often trying to cope with a huge backlog of applications requests, this "do-it-yourself" approach allows managers to cut through the backlog and get a quick response to their needs. The fast response also gives them more time to test various plans and options.

In addition to showing end users how to achieve a degree of self-sufficiency in accessing the organization's mainframe data bases, information center personnel may also function as internal *personal computer* (pc) *consultants*. Many larger organizations are developing networks that will allow managers to use their personal computers to access mainframe data. But if you've read Chapter 8, you know that the pc equipment produced by different vendors often won't work together because of hardware and software incompatibilities. Center personnel can advise managers on the pc hardware/software products that are likely to work together now, and on those that are likely to be supported by the organization's future **micro-to-mainframe linkages** (see the Closer Look reading following Chapter 9). In the absence of such guidance, an organization may find itself with a confusing variety of desktop units that are unable to talk to each other or to the organization's mainframe(s).

# ORGANIZING ISSUES AND THE MIS

The **organizing** function involves the grouping of people and other resources into logical and efficient units in order to carry out plans and achieve goals. In a manufacturing company, for example, people may be grouped by *type of work* (production, marketing), by *geographic area* (district sales offices), and by *product line* produced or sold. As MISs are designed and implemented, there's often a need to reconsider the answers to several important and interrelated organizing questions. Included in these questions are:

■ Will decision making be centralized or decentralized?

■ Will data processing be centrally located or dispersed?

■ Will the data itself be centrally stored or dispersed?

■ Where will computing resources be located?

■ How will the MIS function be organized?

As is often the case, the "right" answers to these questions for one organization may be very wrong for another. We can, however, look at some of the general implications of these MIS issues.

**The Centralization/
Decentralization
of Authority**

"Authority" is the right to give orders and the power to see that they're carried out. **Centralization of authority** in an organization refers to a concentration of the important decision-making powers in the hands of a relatively few executives. **De-**

centralization of authority, on the other hand, refers to the extent to which significant decisions are made at lower levels. In very small organizations, *all* decision-making power is likely to be centralized in the hands of the owner. In larger organizations the amount of authority that's held at different levels can vary.

An MIS can support a greater degree of centralized control because top executives can be given information from dispersed departments in time to decide on appropriate action. Without an MIS, action must often be taken at lower levels because of time, distance, and familiarity factors. An MIS may thus permit top executives to exercise decision-making options that were previously not feasible. Note, though, that the fact that an MIS reduces the necessity for decentralization of authority doesn't mean that authority should now be centralized. What it does mean is that the degree to which authority is centralized or decentralized in an organization is now often determined more by managerial philosophy and judgment than by necessity.

## The Centralization/Dispersal of Data Processing Activities

In precomputer days, data processing activities were handled by each department on a separate and thus decentralized basis. When computers first appeared, however, the tendency was to maximize the use of expensive hardware by establishing one or more central processing centers to serve the organization's needs. Today, the rapid reduction in hardware costs and the improvements being made in data communications services make it possible for organizations to structure their MIS around either a centralized or a more dispersed approach to data processing. They can still use a **centralized data processing** approach to process data originating at all using points. They can decide to use **decentralized data processing** by placing small and inexpensive computers in the hands of every using group. Or they can choose to follow some alternative *distributed data processing (DDP)* approach between these centralized and decentralized extremes. As Figure 14-11 indicates, there are a countless number of alternative DDP possibilities available today along the continuum between centralization and decentralization. If you've read Chapter 10, you're already familiar with some of the *star, hierarchical,* and *ring* variations that are possible when DDP approaches are used. If you've not yet read Chapter 10, a quick glance now through the illustrations in that chapter will give you a general idea of some of the possibilities.

**Figure 14-11** Data processing activities can be totally centralized, totally decentralized, or distributed in different degrees and in countless ways to meet the needs of the organizations they serve. Chapter 10, "Data Communications Systems and Distributed Data Processing Networks," discusses and illustrates some of the distributed alternatives. The number of DDP installations is growing rapidly today.

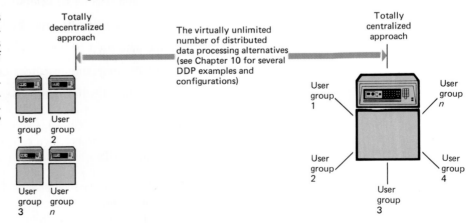

"I brought this computer in to do an efficiency study, and the first thing it suggested was to get rid of *me!*"

The closer an organization positions its data processing activities to the *centralized approach* on the continuum shown in Figure 14-11, the more likely it is to achieve the following *benefits:*

■ ***Economies of scale.*** With adequate processing volume, the use of larger and more powerful computers may result in lower record processing costs. Duplications in record storage and program preparation may be reduced.

■ ***Better systems integration.*** Developing common customer account numbers is necessary to integrate the various files in which customers may be included. Such development may be easier when all customer-related files are processed at a central site. Standards and security provisions may also be easier to implement and enforce.

■ ***Effective personnel management.*** It may be possible to concentrate fewer skilled programmers at a central site and make better use of their talents. A larger computer center that utilizes the latest data base management system and sophisticated MIS concepts may also be more challenging and appealing to computer professionals.

And as an organization moves on the continuum shown in Figure 14-11 toward the *decentralized approach,* it's more likely to receive the following *benefits:*

■ ***Greater interest and motivation at user levels.*** Users in control of their own computers and MIS programs may be more likely to maintain the accuracy of input data and use the equipment in ways that best meet their particular needs. (Of course, if a totally decentralized approach is used, it's unlikely that much progress can be achieved in developing an integrated MIS.)

■ *Better response to user needs.* The standardization that's typically required for a centralized MIS may not be equally suitable for all users. With a more dispersed approach, special programs may be written to meet exact user needs. In addition, although small hardware will probably be slower than centralized equipment, it doesn't have to be allocated to the needs of several users groups. Information considered important to one group doesn't have to be delayed because higher priority is given to the jobs of others. Thus, prompt processing of a job by a small machine may provide users with faster *turnaround* time.

■ *Less downtime risk.* A breakdown in centralized equipment or communications links may leave the entire MIS inoperative. A similar breakdown in one user group, however, doesn't affect other operations.

There's no general answer to the question of where data *should* be processed. Some small organizations may "centralize" their data processing activities and run them on a pc or minicomputer because their departments lack the volume to justify separate systems. Some businesses made up of autonomous "companies within a company" follow a decentralized approach.

But most larger organizations today are following some type of DDP approach. They are buying hundreds of thousands of personal computers to disperse some processing capability to individuals and/or small user groups in order to achieve the benefits just outlined. And as we've seen, many organizations are investing in micro-to-mainframe linkages to allow pc users access to central data bases. But the overall coordination and control of the data communication network, and the development of companywide MIS plans, are still often handled at one or a few central sites.

## The Centralization/Dispersal of Stored Data

In precomputer days, detailed data were typically stored in using departments, and summarized facts needed to prepare companywide reports were sent to central offices. When the first centralized computer centers were established to maximize the use of expensive hardware, the tendency was then to transfer much of the storage of the detailed data to magnetic tapes and other media kept at a central computer site.

Data with companywide significance continue to be stored at a central site. But hardware cost reductions, data communications improvements, and DDP network designs now make it possible to return files with local significance to user departments for storage and maintenance. Thus, many organizations are now in the process of deciding to what extent (if any) they will relocate previously centralized computer-based data to user groups. Questions involving such factors as data redundancy, file security, file updating problems, and data communications costs must be considered in these data storage decisions.

When micro-to-mainframe linkages are used, data items relevant to the needs of pc users can be copied from central data bases and stored on floppy disks at many different locations. Examples of the linkage systems that make this dispersal of data possible are On-Line Software International's Omnilink, and VisiAnswer, a software package jointly developed by Informatics General Corporation and VisiCorp. VisiAnswer allows users with IBM Personal Computers to selectively access any type of mainframe data. The data are then delivered to the user's pc in a format that's immediately usable with all "Visi" software packages including the VisiCalc spreadsheet program. Users can enter this "real data" into a VisiCalc model and then manipulate it for planning and decision-making purposes. Serious problems could develop, however, if pc users are allowed to change (add to, delete, or modify) the contents of important central data files. Maintaining the security and integrity of those files is a major concern for any organization. Thus, linkage packages such as VisiAnswer must provide close control over which pc users can access specific data. And to protect against the contamination of sensitive central data files, linkage programs generally must not allow the entry of data from the pc to those mainframe files.

**The Location of Computing Resources in the Organization**

Our focus here is *not* on the millions of personal computers located today on the desks of professionals, but rather, the location of a main computing facility in an organization. Let's look at three possibilities for a typical manufacturing firm as shown in Figure 14-12.

**Location Number One.** Historically, people in finance and accounting departments were often the first to see that a computer could be used to process large-volume applications such as customer billing. Thus, the computer was most often placed under the control of financial managers. It still remains in this traditional location in many organizations in spite of the following possible drawbacks:

■ Computer center people are likely to give a higher priority to accounting applications at the expense of important nonfinancial jobs.

■ Buried several management levels down in one functional area of the business, computer people lack organizational status and have a limited view of how to develop an overall MIS.

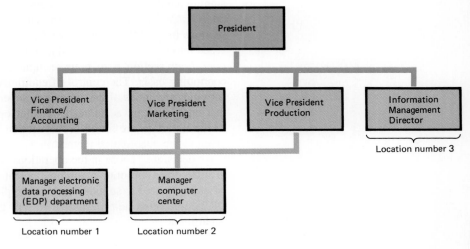

Figure 14-12 Alternative locations for computing resources.

**Location Number Two.** An approach that can avoid the lack of objectivity in setting job priorities is to establish a company "service center" to handle applications. The computer center manager may report to a neutral top-level executive or an executive committee. The center basically occupies a position that's outside the mainstream of the organization. The center manager thus has limited influence. Little attempt is usually made to initiate system improvements or develop an integrated MIS plan.

**Location Number Three.** Overcoming the limitations of the other alternatives, location three:

- **Confers organizational status.** A high-level location is needed to give impartial service to all groups that receive processed information. The top computer executive (holding such titles as "Information Management Director," "Director, MIS," "Vice President, Information Management," and so on) has a strong voice in determining suitable new applications. He or she is also responsible for studying existing corporatewide systems and for developing the MIS model that will permit better integration of information resources.

- **Encourages innovation.** People in an independent department can be encouraged to recommend improvement and change whenever and wherever the opportunity arises.

## Organizing the MIS Department

The organization of the MIS department itself can take many forms depending on how an organization responds to the issues presented earlier in this section. Recognizing, then, that other logical arrangements are possible, Figure 14-13 gives us a framework from which combinations or further subdivisions may be made as needed.

The *data base administrator* function discussed in the last chapter is usually found in an MIS department. The activities of the DBA include establishing and controlling data definitions, defining the relationships between data items, and designing the data base security system to guard against unauthorized use. The *system analysis/design* section acts as the vital interface between user groups and the other sections in the MIS department. The *program preparation* function is often subdivided into new applications and maintenance groups. The function of the *computer-operations* section is to prepare input data and produce output information on a continuing basis. The control of equipment time and the scheduling of processing activities are duties of the operations supervisor. Controls are also needed to ensure that input data are accurate. Computer operators, operators of input devices, and media librarians are found in this section. **Operations research (OR)** is the name given to the quantitative methodology and knowledge that's used to help managers make decisions. Those in the operations research section may logically be assigned to some other corporate planning element. But since the use of computers and data bases is required to support many of the planning and decision support systems that OR people often help design, there are good reasons to include them in an MIS department.

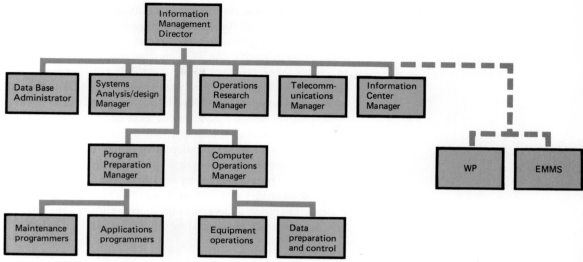

Figure 14-13 Possible functional organization of an MIS department. Dashed lines are functions that may be included when an information resource management (IRM) approach is followed. These functions may be incorporated under telecommunications or some other area, or they may be independent.

The *telecommunications* function can also logically be placed elsewhere. However, there's a growing tendency to place the responsibility for both computing and telecommunications services under a single information management executive. In smaller firms, an analyst or programmer might be able to make the necessary telecommunications decisions. But as the knowledge needed to manage the complex data communications networks discussed in Chapter 10 becomes more specialized, the need for a separate telecommunications function becomes acute. Finally, the *information center* may be a unit of the MIS department that provides the end-user services mentioned earlier. The information center may also be in charge of implementing and maintaining the micro-to-mainframe network.

Figure 14-14 Possible project organization of an MIS department.

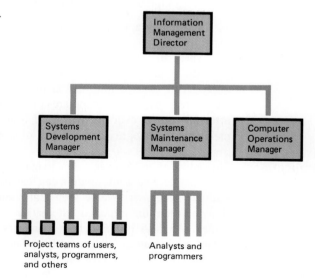

The term **information resource management (IRM)** is now being used to emphasize the belief that all the fragmented and overlapping information functions in an organization should be combined and placed under the control of a senior information executive. An IRM emphasis would thus also likely include in Figure 14-13 the *word processing and electronic mail/message office system functions* discussed in Chapter 11. Few organizations have taken this step beyond the MIS organization presented in Figure 14-13, but there's little doubt that many organizational changes will be made in the next decade as the distinctions between data processing, telecommunications, and office technologies become more blurred.

Figure 14-14 shows an alternative to the **functional organization** of the MIS department presented in Figure 14-13. Special system study teams of users, analysts, programmers, and others are often assigned the responsibility for designing and implementing a new system. Under this type of **project organization,** a project leader might report to a systems development manager. When tasks are completed, team members are reassigned to different projects.

# CONTROL ISSUES AND THE MIS

Unlike planning which looks to the future, the *control* function looks at the past and the present. It's a follow-up to planning and a check on past and current performance to see if planned goals are being achieved. The **control process** is thus based on the following steps:

1. Establishing predetermined goals or standards.

2. Measuring actual performance.

3. Comparing actual performance to the standards.

4. Making appropriate control decisions.

There are numerous control implications and issues associated with the use of an MIS. A primary concern of managers is that the MIS supply them with the **managerial control** information they need to monitor the operations for which they're responsible. A second area of vital concern to managers is to ensure that the **internal control** over the MIS itself is adequate so that it operates efficiently and maintains the integrity and security of data, records, and other assets.

**Managerial Control Implications**

The output of an MIS can help a manager carry out the control steps in many ways. For example, better information can lead to better planning and the creation of *more realistic standards*. We've seen that simulation can help managers set goals by showing them the effects of alternative decisions when certain conditions are assumed. An MIS can also help managers control by gathering and summarizing *actual performance data* promptly and accurately. Once performance data are read into the computer, it's possible for the machine to *compare* the actual performance with the established standards. Periodic reports showing this comparison can be

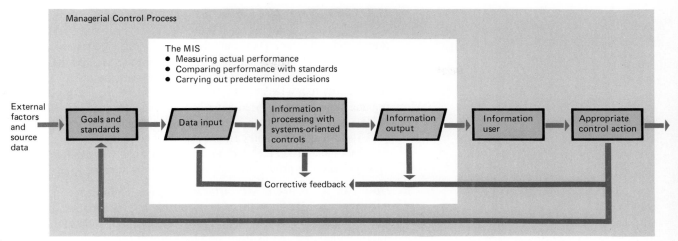

**Figure 14-15** Managerial control and the MIS.

prepared. And triggered exception reports may be furnished to managers only when variations fall outside certain programmed limits.

It's also possible for an MIS to signal when *predetermined decisions* should be carried out. For example, a program may specify that when the inventory of a basic part falls below a given level, an output message signals the need to reorder and indicates the reorder quantity. By thus relieving managers of many of the routine control tasks, the MIS frees them to devote more time to planning and leading the all-important human resources of the organization. Figure 14-15 shows the place of an MIS in the overall managerial control process.

**Internal Control Issues**

In some systems, data processing is typically separated into several departments, with a number of employees being responsible for some portion of the total activity. For example, in the processing of a customer order, credit approval may come from one location, control of the inventory of ordered items may reside in another department, customer billing may be handled by a third group, and receipt of payment for items shipped may be in a fourth location.

The organizational structure separates those who initiate the order from those who record and carry out the transaction. And both of these groups are separated from those who receive payment. Such a division of activities makes it difficult for fraud to go undetected since several people from different groups would have to be a party to any deception. Also, people in each department can check on the accuracy of others in the course of their routine activities. Thus, internal control has been achieved by departmental reviews and cross-checks.

But the use of an MIS makes it possible for processing steps to be integrated so that they may all be performed by only one or two groups. With fewer departments involved, however, it may appear that the use of an MIS reduces internal control. Managers have sometimes been distressed to learn that such a reduction can occur in a poorly controlled MIS. The issues and risks involved in controlling an MIS can be expressed in the following series of questions. The threats and problems that MIS designers must counter are suggested in the discussion of each question.

■ *How can we safeguard assets?* In the absence of proper internal controls, knowledgeable employees (or a skilled outsider) can steal data and/or programs and sell them. They can add, delete, or change transactions in the data for fraud or embezzlement purposes. And they can do these things at the computer site or at a remote station. Thieves are interested in computerized records today because the job of accounting for the assets of many organizations has now been entrusted to computer systems. When paper money was introduced, thieves used presses. Now plastic money (credit cards) and magnetic money (money cards with magnetic strips, and magnetic tapes and disks) are used, and thieves are using computers. Measures must be taken to protect the system against the theft of assets.

■ *How can we prevent MIS attack and penetration?* As Figure 14-16 indicates, an MIS is vulnerable to attack and penetration from many sources if adequate controls aren't provided. The motivation for such penetration sometimes comes from simple curiosity and the challenge of solving a puzzle or playing a joke. (This type of thinking may be a carryover from a penetrator's school days when he or she played the disturbing "game" of penetrating the control programs of the school's computer.) Or the purpose may be to steal the secrets of an individual or competitor, or to cause a competitor's MIS to "crash"—i.e., become inoperable. Regardless of the motivation, one authority has observed that penetrating today's MIS is about as difficult as solving the crossword puzzle in a Sunday paper. The ease with which 12 Milwaukee teenagers—dubbed the "414 hackers" because of Milwaukee's Area Code—gained access into over 50 systems, including one at the Los Alamos Scientific Laboratory and another at the Memorial Sloan-Kettering Cancer Center, tends to support that claim. Obviously, controls must be designed to make attack and penetration more difficult than that.

■ *How can we protect privacy rights of people?* Organizations keep records on those with whom they come in contact. Records maintained in large, integrated data bases may thus prove worthy targets for those seeking to ferret out private and confidential facts. Seemingly innocent data recorded at one time can be correlated with other data collected from different sources to reveal potentially damaging information about people. Thus, an MIS must be designed to safeguard the privacy rights of those whose records are stored in it.

■ *How can we maintain the physical security of the computer site?* The preceding internal control questions dealt with the general subject of **data integrity** and **data security.** Another internal control issue involves **physical security.** That is, it concerns the issue of how to *physically protect* the MIS hardware and software against damage or destruction from such hazards as *fire, flood,* and *sabotage.* Thousands of military records were destroyed in a fire at the Army Records Center in St. Louis. A severe tropical storm flooded numerous computer centers in the Eastern United States. And computers have been bombed, shot, knifed, and bathed with milk shakes by radical students, disgruntled employees, and frustrated program-

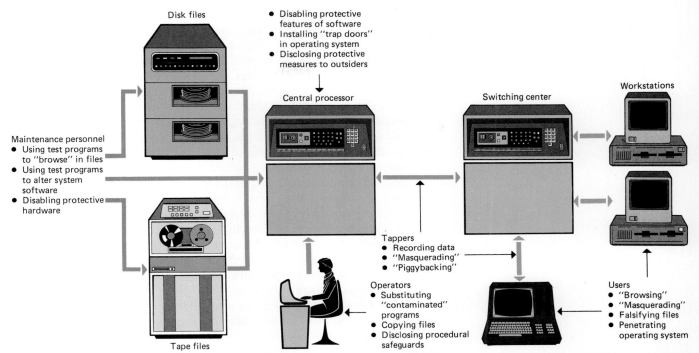

**Figure 14-16** Programmers, operators, maintenance people, and online users often have the opportunity to penetrate system security. Programmers, for example, may insert instructions into operating system programs in such a way that they provide a "trap door" for penetration at any convenient future date. Unscrupulous outsiders may also attack online systems by using the techniques of "masquerading" or "piggybacking." Penetrators can obtain the passwords of legitimate users by wiretapping or other means, and can then use these passwords to *masquerade* as authorized users to browse in a data base. In one case, for example, a minicomputer was hooked to a wiretapped line and was used to "impersonate" a central computer. The mini intercepted user calls to the legitimate processor, obtained a record of user passwords, and then informed users that the system was overloaded and requested that they call back in an hour. The identification of many users was thus obtained. The *piggybacking* approach is similar in that a small "bootleg" processor or terminal is attached to a tapped line to intercept and modify legitimate messages. Transmissions between branch banks could be intercepted, for example, and additional credits to the tapper's account could be added to the message. Numerous other techniques that don't require wiretapping are also available to the penetrator.

mers. Provisions must be made to store important programs and data at a backup site, and to protect the computer site against disasters of this type.

◼ *How can we maintain the audit trail?* Periodic examinations or *audits* of an MIS are conducted by company auditors and by independent certified public accountants to evaluate internal control arrangements. As they examine the safeguards created to maintain data integrity and security, auditors check to see if there's a proper separation of duties within the MIS department between those who prepare the programs and those who run them. They also trace processed transactions through the system to monitor activity and to determine whether integrity/security controls are effective. Such an **audit trail** begins with the recording of all transactions, winds through all the processing steps, and ends with the production of output results and updated records. By selecting sample transactions and following the audit trail, the auditor traces the transactions effects to their final destinations as a means of testing MIS controls. A readily traceable paper trail is found in a manual system. In an MIS, however, the form of the trail has changed. (It can't be eliminated since it's required by the Internal Revenue Service.) No paper source documents may be prepared when input data are entered through online terminals. And intermediate steps that were previously visible have *seemed to vanish* into magnetizeable and erasable media. It's the job of the MIS designers to satisfy auditors that adequate controls are built into the MIS to prevent unintentional or deliberate damage to "invisible" files and records stored in an erasable data base.

In spite of the threats and problems that we've now considered, *there's no reason why a company should have less internal control because of computer usage.* On the contrary, there's no reason why *system-oriented controls,* in the form of computer programs, can't be substituted for the employee-oriented controls of manual systems. Also, there's no reason why the separation of duties and responsibilities can't be maintained *within* the MIS department to safeguard the integrity of the system-oriented controls. In fact, there's no reason why a firm can't achieve better control because of:

■ The computer's ability to execute processing procedures uniformly.

■ The difficulty of changing and manipulating, without detection, properly programmed MIS controls.

■ The computer's accuracy advantage when given correct input data.

## Controlling the MIS Department

An MIS manager is responsible for safeguarding data integrity and system security, and for controlling the operating efficiency of his or her department.

**Data Integrity Controls.** The purpose of these controls is to see that all input data are correctly recorded, all authorized transactions are processed without additions or omissions, and all output is accurate, timely, and distributed only to those authorized to receive it. A number of *input controls* are identified and discussed in Chapter 6, page 137. Programmed *processing controls* are established to determine when valid data are lost, or when invalid or unauthorized data are entered for processing. Techniques involving the use of record counts, sequence checks, reasonableness checks, and so on, are used. The number of possible processing controls is limited only by the programmer's imagination. *Output controls* are established as final checks on the accuracy and propriety of the processed information. Feedback from users and a variety of techniques are used.

**System Security Controls.** Easy access to the computer(s) by people with the skills needed to manipulate or destroy the system is a primary reason for the difficulty in maintaining data security and physical security. Thus, an important step in achieving a more secure system is to limit access to the computer site. Analysts and programmers shouldn't be involved with day-to-day production runs, and computer operators shouldn't participate in the preparation of data or programs. Included in the controls designed to achieve system security are:

## CREATING A FINANCIAL MODEL

Financial modeling can be as simple as scribbling profit-and-loss estimates on scrap paper or as complex as solving matrices on large computers. To create a business model, you must define the situation to be analyzed, determine the logical relationships between variables, and input your particular data. Needless to say, the process requires a thorough understanding of the business situation you are simulating. Even a straightforward budget projection requires detailed knowledge of sales levels, fixed and variable costs, overhead, and other information.

The final product of decision-support programs should be clear, well-formatted reports offering quantitative backup for important decisions. Thus, you should start by listing in logical order all relevant business factors, with descriptions of numerical quantities ("Net Sales" or "Operating Expenses," for example) written in the rows of the first column, and variables (usually as a function of monthly or yearly periods) indicated across succeeding columns. Often you can do this by merely following existing company forms or consulting standard business reference books.

Once you know what quantities you want to consider, you must specify how they relate (for instance, "Price = SUM of rows 5, 7, and 11"). The "rules" linking different variables in your model might be arithmetic, logical, trigonometric, or financial functions. The more rules or functions available, the more sophisticated the analyses that can be set

up. Even simple arithmetic functions can be useful for testing what-if assumptions.

To use the model you have sketched out, you need data of sufficient quality to generate significant results. Remember, the best financial model is only as accurate as the figures fed into it. By substituting different values (perhaps assuming a change in costs or in interest rates), you can test the possible effects of various planning decisions without jeopardizing your firm. Yes, number-crunching can save you the indignity of getting crunched by the economy!

Financial-planning programs for personal computers automate the creation of models by integrating the design, rules, and data that you have specified, then automatically performing calculations that would otherwise have to be done tediously with a calculator and pencil.

—From "Visicalc and 'Visiclones'" appearing in the October 1982 issue of *Popular Computing* magazine. Copyright 1982 Popular Computing, Inc. Used with permission of Popular Computing, Inc. Photo © Ashton-Tate, 1984. dBASE III(TM) is a registered trademark of Ashton-Tate. All rights reserved.

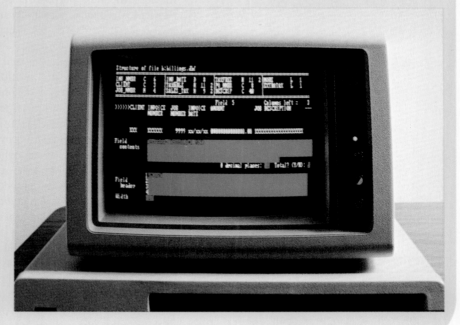

■ *Control over console intervention.* It's possible for computer operators to bypass program controls. They have the ability to interrupt a program run and introduce data manually into the processor through the console keyboard. With organizational separation of program preparation and computer operation, it's unlikely that an operator will have enough knowledge of a program's details to manipulate it successfully for improper purposes. However, the possibility of unauthorized intervention can be reduced in a number of ways. For example, a microcomputer can be used to record and analyze the processing actions performed by the host computer as well as any interventions in the host's operation. That is, the micro can be used like a flight recorder in an airplane. The recorder monitors the performance of the plane and its crew, but it's not accessible to the crew. Additional control techniques include rotating the duties of computer operators (or others in sensitive positions) and having them account for computer operating time. Manual intervention is slow, and manipulation can thus result in processing times that are longer than necessary for affected runs.

■ *Control over the use of online workstations.* Control procedures to identify authorized users of the system should obviously be given special attention. Such identification is typically based on something that users *know* (e.g., a password), something they *have* (e.g., special cards and keys with magnetically coded identification numbers or embedded microprocessor chips), some *personal quality* they possess (e.g., fingerprint or "voice print" characteristics that can be stored by the computer system and used for identification purposes), or some combination of these elements. Passwords are most commonly used, but when used frequently (and carelessly) these words lose their security value. Passwords should be changed regularly. Each password may also be combined with some bit of personal information about the authorized user (e.g., a birth date or employee identification number). A thief would have more difficulty in identifying such a combination. To deter password guessing, the system should limit the number of attempts at access permitted from an online source. Once an authorized user has been identified and has gained access to the system, various techniques employing **cryptography**—that is, "hidden writing"—are available to thwart those who would intercept the messages traveling between the computer and the remote station. For example, data encryption techniques for coding and decoding messages can be implemented on silicon chips located in the stations and host computers. If an authorized user wants to access or send sensitive data, the host computer may generate a random **session key**—a key to be used only for that exchange. This session key is sent to the station encrypt/decrypt circuitry and a copy is retained at the host. Any data passing from a host program to the station are automatically encrypted by the host, transmitted, and then decrypted by the station. (Of course, the reverse occurs when the message originates at the station.) This coding/decoding process is invisible to the user. At the end of the session, the session key disappears. The data that have been transmitted would be unintelligible to anyone without the one-time session key.

■ *The creation of a physical security program.* Definite controls should be established to safeguard programs and data from fire and water damage or destruction. Duplicate programs and master files may have to be kept at a location away from the computer site. A fireproof storage vault at the computer site is a wise precaution. Control over library tapes, cards, disks, and blank forms is necessary. Adequate insurance protection should be provided. And a waste-disposal procedure to destroy carbon papers and other media containing sensitive information should be followed.

**Control of Operating Efficiency.** The same steps used to control any activity are used to control the efficiency of the MIS function. Departmental standards should be established for people and machines. Actual performance should then be measured. Measuring the performance of creative people is more an art than a science, and the approaches vary from one MIS facility to another. It's easier to measure hardware performance because special monitors are available for this purpose. Overworked (or underutilized) components and bottleneck situations can be identified through the use of these evaluation tools. Once performance measurements are available, they are compared to the standards, and appropriate control decisions are made as needed.

## Feedback and Review 14-1

You've covered a lot of material in this chapter on management information, the systems that produce it, and the issues associated with the use of MIS. To test and reinforce your understanding of MIS concepts, place a T or F in the space provided in the following true-false questions:

___1. Managers at different organizational levels need the same kinds of information since they do the same kinds of planning.

___2. Lower-level managers need information to support strategic planning.

___3. Accuracy is the ratio of incorrect information to the total amount of information produced.

___4. Regular reports should be prepared on an hourly basis.

___5. Traditional information systems seem to have been designed on the assumption that lack of completeness is the most critical problem facing managers.

___6. Numerous "total systems" were designed in the late 1960s.

___7. An MIS is a network of computer-based data processing procedures developed in an organization and integrated as necessary to provide timely and effective information to support decision making.

___8. In planning for an MIS, designers are in agreement that the "bottom-up" approach is best.

___9. Most MISs today serve the needs of top-level managers and, to a lesser extent, the needs of operating managers.

___10. An MIS can give managers more time to devote to planning.

___11. Simulation models can be used to improve inventory planning.

___12. As defined in this chapter, an expert system is a payroll program written by an expert programmer.

___13. Employees of an information center show managers how to use MIS resources to develop their own applications and generate their own reports.

___14. A decentralized data processing approach results in reduced interest and motivation at user levels.

___15. There are only two distributed data processing alternatives available today.

___16. The main computing facility in an organization must be headed by an MIS director.

___17. An MIS department is likely to be the organizational home of a data base administrator.

___**18.** "Information resource management" is a term used by those who want to place all the overlapping information functions in an organization under the control of a senior information executive.

___**19.** The control process is based on establishing standards, measuring performance, comparing performance against standards, and then taking appropriate action.

___**20.** An MIS is of little help to a production manager in controlling production activities.

___**21.** Internal control is concerned with the integrity and security of data, and with the physical security of MIS hardware and software.

___**22.** An MIS is invulnerable to attack and penetration by outsiders.

___**23.** Privacy rights of people are of no concern to MIS designers.

___**24.** An audit trail can be eliminated only in the interests of improving efficiency.

___**25.** Authorized users of online systems may be identified by what they know, by what they have, or by a personal quality they possess.

___**26.** Cryptography can be used to improve the security of messages traveling between CPUs and terminals, but users have to enter data in complex codes.

 # LOOKING BACK

**1.** Different types of information are needed by people at different levels in an organization. Top-level managers need information to support long-range strategic planning, middle-level managers need information for tactical decisions, and lower-level supervisors need information to support their day-to-day operational functions. Regardless of the level, however, the information provided should be accurate, timely, complete, and concise.

**2.** An MIS is a network of computer-based data processing procedures developed in an organization and integrated as necessary with manual and other procedures for the purpose of providing timely and effective information to support decision making and other necessary management functions. The formidable task of the MIS designer is to develop the information flow needed to support decision making. This isn't an easy task since there are a number of unresolved issues to consider during the planning for an MIS. These issues are outlined in the chapter.

**3.** An MIS can help improve managerial planning by giving managers *(a)* faster signals of problems, *(b)* more time to devote to planning, and *(c)* the ability to evaluate more alternatives. The components of an MIS that help improve planning are often called decision support systems. Simulation is a trial-and-error problem-solving technique that's also very useful in planning. Simulation models can be used by managers to evaluate pro-

posed projects or strategies. Managers can see what happens to these models when certain conditions are given or when certain assumptions are tested. An expert system is a software package that includes a stored base of knowledge in a specialized field. As a user supplies input data, an expert system responds as an intelligent assistant by giving advice and suggesting possible courses of action. And information centers can give users a direct online path into an organization's data base(s) to retrieve the facts they need to make plans and decisions.

**4.** There are generally a number of organizing issues that must be considered when an MIS is installed. These issues involve questions about the degree of centralization or decentralization of authority, data processing activities, data storage, organizational location of computing resources, and the composition of the MIS department.

**5.** The control process involves establishing standards, measuring actual performance, comparing performance to standards, and taking appropriate action. A primary concern of managers is that the MIS supply them with the managerial control information they need to monitor their activities. A second area of vital concern is that the internal control over the MIS itself is adequate to maintain the integrity and security of data, software, and hardware.

## KEY TERMS AND CONCEPTS

## TOPICS FOR REVIEW AND DISCUSSION

**1.** Why have traditional information systems failed to meet the needs of managers?

**2.** "A factor that complicates the subject of the information needed by managers is the organizational level of the managerial job." Discuss this statement.

**3.** Identify and discuss the properties that management information should possess.

**4.** *(a)* What is an MIS? *(b)* Identify and discuss four issues involved in planning for an MIS.

**5.** How can an MIS affect the quality of a manager's plans?

**6.** *(a)* What is simulation? *(b)* How can it be used in planning and decision making?

**7.** *(a)* What is an expert system? *(b)* Identify and discuss one example of such a system.

**8.** *(a)* What is an information center? *(b)* What functions may be performed by such a center?

**9.** Identify and discuss four organizing issues that need to be considered when MISs are designed and implemented.

**10.** *(a)* Discuss the benefits that may be obtained from a centralized approach to data processing. *(b)* From a decentralized approach.

**11.** *(a)* Identify three locations for a main computing facility in a business. *(b)* Which is likely to best support an integrated MIS?

**12.** *(a)* Identify and discuss the functions that may be included in an MIS department. *(b)* How can an MIS department be organized along project lines?

**13.** *(a)* What are the steps in the control process? *(b)* What are the managerial control implications of an MIS?

**14.** Identify and discuss four internal control issues arising out of the use of a computer-based MIS.

**15.** Identify and give examples of the types of controls needed within an MIS department.

## PROJECTS TO LOOK INTO

**1.** Visit an organization with a central computing facility (your school, your job, a nearby business, a hospital, a government facility). Prepare a class report outlining *(a)* two ways that the facility supports the planning and decision-making activities of people in the organization, *(b)* the location in the organization of the central computing facility, and *(c)* the organization within the computing facility itself.

**2.** Visit your library and identify and then research three cases of computer-related fraud or embezzlement. Write a report about your findings.

## ANSWERS TO FEEDBACK AND REVIEW SECTION

**14-1**

| | | | | |
|---|---|---|---|---|
| 1. F | 7. T | 12. F | 17. T | 22. F |
| 2. F | 8. F | 13. T | 18. T | 23. F |
| 3. F | 9. F | 14. F | 19. T | 24. F |
| 4. F | 10. T | 15. F | 20. F | 25. T |
| 5. T | 11. T | 16. F | 21. T | 26. F |
| 6. F | | | | |

# A Case for the 'Personal Info Center'

Early this year I got a call from a friend who is a division chief financial officer of a Fortune 500-size company. "I just came from a planning meeting where two of our managers made presentations," he said. "Both used spreadsheet programs on their personal computers to produce the numbers, and each of them came up with a completely different prediction."

My friend continued, "The problem occurred when the analysts entered the actual results into their models by copying data from printouts—one used a week-old report, the other used a revised report he got that day. To make it worse, there were at least two data entry errors in the copying. Maybe the only real solution to problems like this is to take away all the personal computers and software used in our organization."

"No, I don't agree," I told him. "Your story isn't an argument against using personal computers; it's proof that they haven't been used enough."

This situation is typical in many companies. The most common problem new personal computer users have encountered is that while they may be using the same spreadsheets, they are not necessarily working with the same data.

We recently surveyed MIS directors at 30 of the largest corporate computer users in the U.S. Seventy percent of the companies we talked to said they were involved with information centers and that they felt these efforts were important and well-accepted in their organizations.

But when we talked to the same companies about personal computers, we came up with a different picture. Very few formal plans had been laid out. More importantly, we believe the MIS managers dramatically underestimated the number of personal computers in use in their companies. If we totaled up answers from 30 of the largest companies in the U.S., we came up with about 6,000 personal computers. Estimates vary, but the consensus is that there are at least 500,000 personal computers installed in the top 1,000 companies.

We have discovered that the information center user tends to be very computer-literate. Personal computer users, on the other hand, tend to be managers, analysts or other professionals whose personal computers are adjuncts to their jobs.

Through the information center, MIS has been able to deliver information to more people than ever before. However, most of the personal computer group members in our study were "Visicalcing" away, without MIS sponsorship. The end users were getting the micro-based tools they wanted, but they wanted access to the corporate data bases, too.

The information center and the personal computer are both incomplete solutions. The information center is controlled, secure and elitist, and the personal computer is spreading wildly. Information center growth is limited by tight coupling to mainframes. Micro users are stymied by the unavailability of information from corporate data bases.

These two worlds must be brought together into a better concept called the Personal Information Center. The Personal Information Center gives users the choice between using personal reporting systems on IBM 3270-type terminals and using personal computers with direct access to corporate data bases. It must be under the control of MIS because data base access must be protected by a high level of security. MIS also must control priorities on the mainframe.

The coming of the Personal Information Center has been accelerated by some important product announcements. On the hardware side, the IBM 3270-PC physically combines the 3278 and 3279 terminals and the IBM Personal Computer in one box. It offers application developers the opportunity to build more friendly applications.

It does not, however, offer direct downloading from data bases to personal computer applications. For that capability, MIS directors will have to turn to software companies.

As the Personal Information Center evolves, we think it will display a number of characteristics:

• Hardware and software will be engineered for strategic use. MIS will reject hot products which can't demonstrate staying power, extensibility and high quality.

• Data base access will be well-secured but also timely and available to all qualified users, whether from a personal computer or terminal.

• Mainframe software will be able to extract data from all pertinent data bases while allowing users to select only the data they need. Users will not have to download entire files when they only want selected records from these files.

• Personal computer users will insist on extraction software that works naturally and automatically with their favorite micro programs.

It's been almost a year since my friend's call. During that time a lot has happened, including a series of meetings he's had with his division MIS director. My friend hasn't thrown away his calculator and 13-column pads. He's now working with MIS to develop a Personal Information Center, and the two analysts will be among the center's first users.

—Richard Hannes, "Reconciling MIS, Micros: A Case for the 'Personal Info Center'," *Computerworld*, Mar. 19, 1984, p. 83. Courtesy Richard Hannes, Informatics General Corporation.

# module 4

# Social Impact

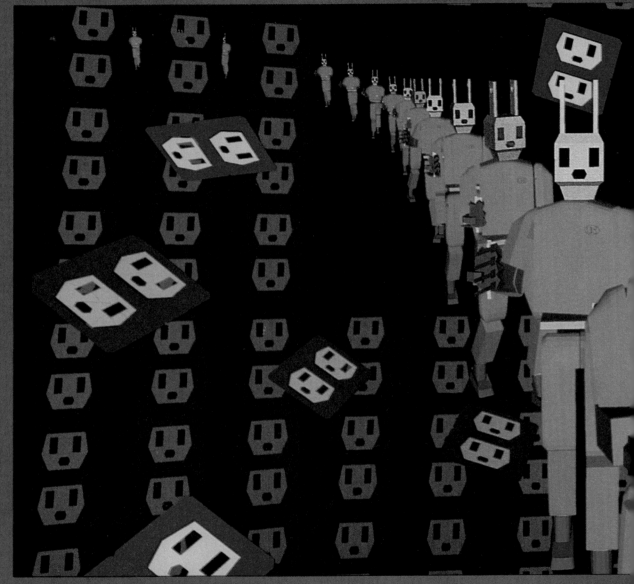

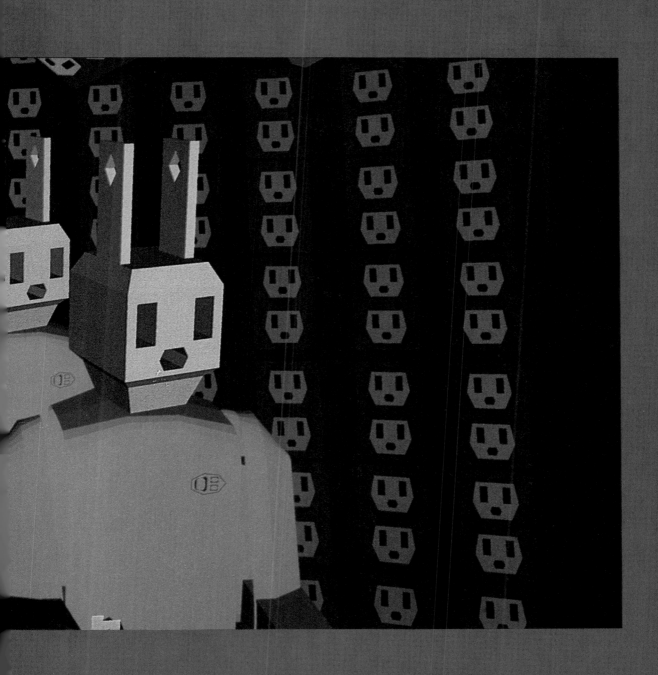

# module 4

Computers have become highly visible tools in our modern society. And people relate to these tools with an extraordinary range of views and emotions. Of course, computers aren't the only machines capable of evoking strong feelings, for people also develop positive or negative attachments to cars, stereos, and recreational vehicles. But computers touch on a sphere that people have always regarded as uniquely human: That sphere is intelligence. Thus, peoples' feelings about computers involve a higher order of hopes and fears. Throughout this module we'll look closely at some of the benefits and potential dangers of computer usage that prompt these hopes and fears.

The chapters included in this Social Impact Module are:

# The Impact of Computers on People

## Artificial Intelligence Is on the Way

Geologists were convinced as far back as World War I that a rich deposit of molybdenum ore was buried deep under Mount Tolman in eastern Washington. But after digging dozens of small mines and drilling hundreds of test borings, they were still hunting for the elusive metal 60 years later. Then, just a couple of years ago, miners hit pay dirt. They were guided not by a geologist wielding his rock hammer, but by a computer located hundreds of miles to the south in Menlo Park, Calif.

The computer was equipped with an expert system known as Prospector. This dramatic demonstration of the revolutionaly potential for commercial applications of artificial intelligence, or AI, has helped to move such research out of the "laboratory curiosity" stage and into the category of "hot new technology."

The secret lies in developing computers that can think and learn the way we humans do. In its prior 30-year history, AI research had produced little of concrete worth beyond a passable mechanical chess partner or two. AI critics viewed such creations as little more than scientific con games, but expert systems such as the electronic geologist have made AI research look considerably less "flaky."

While nowhere near their creators' goals of humanlike reasoning, expert systems do have the ability to transform computers from dumb machines into systems capable of drawing conclusions from stored data in much the way you and I think and make decisions.

—Source of data: *Business Week,* July 9, 1984. Photo, cover for *Backstage* magazine, © Digital Effects, Inc., animators, David Cox and Dennis Hermanson.

In this chapter, you'll see how people react to and may be affected by computer usage. You may find your own ideas on the subject reinforced, or you may be forced to rethink your opinions and perhaps to form new ones. The information in this chapter will enable you to:

- Comment on some of the developments that have taken place in the field of artificial intelligence
- Explain how people may benefit from the use of computers by organizations
- Outline how people can benefit from their use of personal computers
- Summarize the employment opportunities and problems that computer usage may create
- Describe some questionable data processing practices that affect peoples' private lives and personal privacy

# HUMAN THINKING AND ARTIFICIAL INTELLIGENCE

The superhuman computers found in science fiction don't exist. But science fiction often has a way of becoming science fact. Experimenters are now studying the ways in which computers may be used to solve unstructured problems—the types of problems that we assume only human intelligence can solve. These research efforts are usually classified under the heading of **artificial intelligence (AI).** They combine concepts found in disciplines such as psychology, linguistics, and computer science, and are aimed at learning how to prepare programs or construct systems that can do tasks that have never been done automatically by machines before.

## Chapter Outline

**Figure 15-1** A robot hand machine connected to a special-purpose computer plays chess with a human. (Dan McCoy from Rainbow)

For example, computers have been programmed to play checkers and to modify their programs on the basis of success and failure with moves used in the past against human opponents. In one such program, the computer has continually improved its game to the point where it easily defeats the author of the program. Thus, the machine has "learned" what not to do through trial and error.

Hundreds of chess-playing programs have been written that can run on machines ranging from micro-sized personal computers to very large supercomputers (see Figure 15-1). As you learned in Chapter 1, the possible number of moves in a chess game is so large that all the moves could not possibly be stored or analyzed by any computer. Thus, the only feasible approach is to program the computer to play the game by evaluating possible moves and formulating a playing strategy.

At the *beginning* of a chess game, proven approaches to minimize losses and, perhaps, to create openings are often followed for the first seven to 10 moves. Much less predictable is the *middle part* of the game. Good chess players must adopt a strategy and "look ahead" to determine the future consequences of a move. (Chess masters can accurately foresee the consequences 12 to 15 moves later; the author's vision is good for about $1\frac{1}{2}$ moves.) If the middle game is complicated, the *end game* is absolutely mind-blowing. Each player may have six or seven pieces left. The sides of the board have generally lost their meaning, and the pieces may be positioned in ways that have *never occurred before* in the history of the game. In a few moves, a strong attack can result in an impossible defense. People may develop new strategies at this time. A computer program, of course, must also try to adapt to end-game situations.

Given this brief summary of chess, a natural question is: How have computer programs fared against humans in this very intellectual game? This question can be answered by looking at the "Levy challenge." In 1968, David Levy, a Scottish chess champion with an international master ranking (that's one rank below the top grandmaster rank), beat John McCarthy, a Stanford University professor of AI in a chess game. McCarthy remarked that although he couldn't beat Levy, there would be within 10 years a computer program that could. A bet of 250 British pounds ($625) was made between Levy and McCarthy. Levy would win the bet unless a computer program won a match against him before the end of August 1978.

During the next few years, other AI professors and computer programmers joined McCarthy in betting against Levy. In 1977, Levy played a match against a Northwestern University program named Chess 4.5 that had just won the Minnesota Open championship against human opponents. Levy won the match and later in the year beat Kaissa, a Russian program. As the 1978 deadline approached, a final six-game match was arranged between Levy and Northwestern's Chess 4.7 (a successor to Chess 4.5). The first game was a draw (each side received $\frac{1}{2}$ point). Levy won the second and third games, the computer won the fourth game, and Levy won the fifth game. (A sixth game was unnecessary since Levy had scored $3\frac{1}{2}$ points out of a possible 6.) Although the human won this round, the Levy challenge continues, with a new bet totaling $10,000 to be decided by a future match. There's also a prize of $100,000 being offered through Carnegie-Mellon University to the creator of the first computer program to wrest the world chess champion title from a human. Carnegie-Mellon professor Hans Berliner recently wrote a program that defeated the world backgammon champion. Berliner believes there's a 50-50 chance that a program will be the chess champion by 1990. By the year 2000, he says, a program is almost sure to win.

**Can Computers Think?**  Much has been written pro and con about whether computers can be programmed to "think" and "learn." Most of the controversy probably stems from (1) a lack of understanding about the processes involved in human thinking and learning, and (2) the absence of acceptable definitions of such words as *think* and *learn*.

One test—a game—to find out if a computer might be considered to possess intelligence and the ability to think was proposed by Alan Turing, a British mathematician. Participants in the game would be two respondents—a machine and a human—and a human interrogator who tries to determine which of the unseen respondents is the human. Communications terminals are used to answer questions posed by the interrogator. The machine tries to deceive while the human tries to convince the interrogator of his or her true identity. Intelligence and the ability to think would, according to **Turing's test,** be demonstrated by the machine's success in fooling the interrogator.

Have machines passed Turing's test? Not yet, but the machines *have* passed incomplete versions. For example, several years ago Joseph Weizenbaum, an MIT professor, wrote a program with which one could "converse" in English. The program—Weizenbaum named it *Eliza*—plays the role of a psychotherapist engaged in an interview with a patient. A hypothetical conversation between patient and "doctor" might go like this (computer entries are in capital letters):

DO YOU HAVE ANY PROBLEMS?
Yes, I am depressed
I AM SORRY TO HEAR YOU ARE DEPRESSED
My boyfriend makes me unhappy
TELL ME ABOUT YOUR BOYFRIEND

In a variation of Turing's test (people tested didn't know it was a test, and the program wasn't competing with a human), staff members at Massachusetts General Hospital let a number of people "talk" to Weizenbaum's program for a time. When they were asked if they had been talking with a human or a machine, a majority thought they had been in contact with a human. David Levy, the chess master, believes that since the Chess 4.7 program he competed against is stronger than 99.5 percent of all human chess players, it has already reached and passed the stage where he could correctly identify it as a human or computer opponent under Turing-test conditions.

Where's the current research in AI likely to lead us? No one knows. Researchers use the term **heuristic** (pronounced hew-ris'-tik) to describe the judgmental, or *commonsense,* part of problem-solving. That is, it describes that part of problem-solving which deals with the definition of the problem, the selection of reasonable strategies to be followed, and the formulation of hypotheses and hunches. Human beings are now *far superior* to the computer in the heuristic area of intellectual work. As people's thinking and learning processes become better understood, however, it will be possible to develop new programs and machines with improved heuristic abilities. Certainly, some very able researchers are working toward this end.

## AI in Action: Expert Systems

In fact, some earlier results of heuristic problem-solving research projects are already moving out of AI laboratories and into commercial products. If you've read Chapter 14, you've seen that an *expert system* is a software package that has the capability to probe a stored base of knowledge in a specialized area in order to recommend solutions to specific problems. AI researchers pick the brains of specialists to extract and structure a base of knowledge in a field. Programmed techniques for efficiently representing and processing the stored facts and ideas are then used to probe the knowledge base. Different approaches are used by different expert system packages to deduce factual relationships and arrive at conclusions. But knowledge may be expressed in a natural language (English, French, Spanish), and a series of exchanges between the user and the expert system is usually needed. This give-and-take process continues with the system responding as an intelligent assistant able to give advice and suggest possible decisions.

**Example.** The *Caduceus* package is an expert system used for medical diagnosis. Developed by Drs. Jack Myers and Harry Pople at the University of Pittsburgh, Caduceus is programmed to evaluate over 4,000 symptoms and recognize over 500 diseases. *Statistical techniques* are used for diagnostic purposes. Caduceus maintains a listing of the associated symptoms that are known to occur with each disease, along with a statistical estimate of the disease's frequency of occurrence. Using Caduceus, a doctor can sit at a terminal and provide data on a patient. After considering the initial data, the program begins asking questions about the patient. During this questioning, Caduceus tells the doctor what diagnosis it's considering and what data it's temporarily disregarding. The program may provide its diagnosis for the doctor in a few minutes. In order to save the patient money by avoiding unnecessary lab tests, Caduceus is programmed to consider the least costly diseases first. Other diagnostic expert systems are *Mycin,* which specializes in blood diseases, and *Puff,* which measures lung functions.

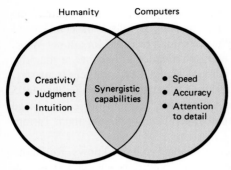

Figure 15-2 The strengths of humans and computers differ.

Much of the earlier work in expert systems has occurred in the United States, but Japan plans to spend hundreds of millions of dollars over the next decade to develop an advanced "fifth generation" computer aimed specifically at AI applications. Before the year 2000, the Japanese expect to achieve a leadership position in AI technology with a supercomputer capable of storing a knowledge base of up to 20,000 rules and 100 million data items. On a much smaller scale, owners of personal computers will soon have access to packages that will give them expert advice in legal, financial, and other categories.

For the foreseeable future, however, the role of the computer should continue to be that of an intelligence amplifier in an alliance with humanity. This alliance would combine the current superiority of the human brain in matters involving creativity, judgment, and intuition with the computer's superiority in matters involving processing speed, accuracy, and tireless attention to detail. The word **synergy** refers to the ability of two entities to achieve together what each is incapable of achieving alone. As Figure 15-2 indicates, the alliance between humans and computers could produce a synergistic effect. While the potential achievements of such an alliance are not unlimited, they also cannot be restricted in any way we can now anticipate.

# PEOPLE AND COMPUTERS: POTENTIAL BENEFITS

As you'll see in "A Closer Look" at the end of this chapter, many people enjoy challenging careers in the computing field. But each of us benefits from the use of computers in organizations. We benefit *on the job* even though we aren't computer specialists. We benefit as the *consumers* of the goods and services provided by computer-using organizations. And we benefit *at home* by using personal computers for work and for play.

## Employment Benefits

**Benefits to Managers.** The primary role of *top managers* lies in formulating policies and planning and guiding overall organizational strategy. As noted in Chapter 14, computer-based systems (MISs) have, through the use of improved simulation techniques, data bases, and computer graphics, helped remove some of the uncertainties from the usually unique and ill-structured problems that top executives face. And Chapter 11 describes how executives may use electronic mail/message systems to reduce telephone interruptions, improve the dissemination of messages to subordinates, and reduce the time required for scheduled meetings through the use of computerized conferencing techniques.

An important role of *lower-level supervisors* is to provide face-to-face communication, direction, and leadership to operating employees. By permitting supervisors to (1) schedule operations more efficiently, (2) maintain better control over economic resources, and (3) cope with a generally increasing level of paperwork, computers have made it possible for them to give more attention to this important personnel administration aspect of their work.

Some *middle-level managers* no longer need to spend as much time in controlling because the computer can be programmed to take over many clerical control activities. For example, it can signal with a triggered report whenever actual performance varies from what was planned. Time saved in controlling has enabled some middle managers to devote more attention to planning and directing the work of subordinates. More accurate and timely organizationwide information supplied from a central data base has also given them the opportunity to spend more time identifying problems, recognizing opportunities, and planning alternate courses of action. In some cases, a middle manager can use a personal computer (pc) and a micro-to-mainframe data communications link to retrieve relevant information stored in a central data base. This information can then be manipulated by a spreadsheet software package loaded in the pc to arrive at answers to planning questions. In many ways, then, the jobs of middle managers have become more challenging and more nearly resemble those of chief executives. With managers having more time to devote to departmental employee matters, improved morale may be expected. And the more timely information that's now available to some middle managers puts them in a position to be able to react more rapidly to external changes.

**Benefits to the Entire Workforce.** *Scientists* are now able to use computers to conduct research into complex problem areas that could not otherwise be considered. *Design engineers* and *architects* are now using computers to simplify design work and increase the alternatives that can be studied. *Structural engineers* are using computer models to predict the effect of stresses on different structural configurations. *Lawyers* are using legal data banks to locate precedent cases in order to serve clients better. *Sales personnel* can now receive more timely information about customers and product inventories, can promise more efficient handling of sales orders in order to serve their customers better, and can thus improve their sales performance because of computer systems. And the job duties of some *clerical employees* and *factory workers* have changed from routine, repetitive operations to more varied and appealing tasks through computer usage.

## Benefits from Organizations Using Computers

We all know that the federal government provides to individuals many services that require the use of computers. Without computers, for example, the Social Security Administration could not keep up the payment of benefits to widows, orphans, and retired persons. But we sometimes fail to realize the extent to which we benefit as consumers from the use of computers by businesses. Some (but certainly not all) of the possible benefits that people may receive from their dealings with computer-using organizations are discussed below.

**Greater Efficiency.** To the extent that public and private organizations have avoided waste and improved efficiency through the use of computers, the *prices and the taxes we now pay—high as they are—may be less than they would otherwise have been*. Edmund Berkeley, editor of *Computers and People,* has estimated that the use of computers has reduced prices by 10 to 30 percent, and often much more, of what they would be without computers. For example, about one-third of all the dairy cows in the nation are now bred, fed, milked, and monitored for productivity with the help of computers. The average ''computerized'' cow will produce 30 percent more milk than a typical cow that's not subject to computer analysis. By applying the latest knowledge, the dairy industry today can produce all the milk that was supplied 15 years ago with only half as many cows. If computer use can

# THINK OF LEONARDO WIELDING A PIXEL AND A MOUSE

Imagine: Leonardo da Vinci, without a paintbrush, subtly shading the elusive smile on the "Mona Lisa" by turning a knob; or Georges Seurat creating his impressions of French life by using a keyboard to establish the dot-by-dot technique of Pointillism; or Pablo Picasso sketching the five *demoiselles* of Avignon, their figures angular and jagged, with an electronic pen.

Sheer piffle, you say? Not if those masters were alive and working today. Unlikely as it may seem, increasing numbers of artists, art students and their teachers are converging on, of all things, the computer. The art world is beginning to resound with hitherto arcane computer terms, such as "pixel," "cursor" and "mouse."

"Put simply, the computer is becoming a hot item in the art world," said Joan Darragh, an administrator of the Brooklyn Museum Art School. "I find its acceptance extremely exciting—the way it must have been in the 19th century when people first began looking at photography and questioning its relationship to art."

Almost any mode of artistic expression can be developed and refined on a sophisticated computer, argue the addicts of what is called "the 21st-century paint." Once the prized gadget of technocrats, the apparatus that artists earlier scorned as anti-art is now being taken seriously as an electronic tool in the studio. . . .

For some years the computer's closest approach to the visual arts was as a device for achieving spectacular animation and cinematic effects, particularly in movies such as "Tron." It has been used to simulate military maneuvers and as a visual "text" for flight training.

Now, adventurous artists, realizing that they can employ a computer to devise complex and powerful images of dazzling intensity, whether for pure experimentation or for the creating of electronic art, are finding its lure irresistible.

With a computer scrupulously programmed, an artist can select from an almost infinite range of colors and, with the push of a button, change hues and intensity instantly. Sketches can be erased or stored in the computer's memory bank. A sculptor, rotating his design on a monitor, can study his labors from any angle, from any distance. And all the work on the screen, or just one segment of it, can be photographed and sold as a computer-made print. . . .

All right. But is it really *art*? "Is it art?" repeated Nam June Paik, the iconoclastic artist and composer who makes electronic "paintings" by tinkering with TV sets. "Ten years ago people ask, can video be an art form. It depends on who does it. Art is what *artists* do."

—Paul Gardner, "Think of Leonardo Wielding a Pixel and a Mouse," *The New York Times,* Apr. 22, 1984, p. H 1. Copyright © 1984 by The New York Times Company. Reprinted by permission. Photos courtesy Pacific Data Image (top) and New York Institute of Technology (right and below), imaging by Carter Burwell and Ned Greene.

significantly improve **productivity**—i.e., the amount of goods or services possessing economic value that people and machines can produce in a given time period— then these productivity gains may lead to higher levels of real income for an increased number of people.

**Higher-Quality Products.** Computers may also help improve the quality of the products and services we receive. For example, microcomputers are now installed in cars to provide a more efficient means of controlling the engine's fuel mixture, ignition timing, and exhaust emissions. If you're late for an appointment and low on gas, and if there's a deserted stretch of highway ahead, an on-board micro can monitor the gas consumption, rate of speed, and miles to destination to tell you if you should take the time to look for an open service station. The microcomputer can also perform engine diagnostic functions and pinpoint problems.

In other areas, computer-controlled tools can produce machined parts with closer tolerances than were feasible with previously used equipment. Computer-controlled manipulators or *robots* can be used to assemble products or components in a precise way. And process-control computers can be used to carefully monitor the flow of chemical raw materials into a blending tank so that the finished product is of a more uniform quality.

**Better Service.** Individuals may now receive *better service* from *government agencies*. The Los Angeles County welfare system can process new applicants quickly and keep records updated on a daily basis so that recipients can receive their checks on time and at the right address. In contrast to the bureaucratic runaround that often accompanies a call to city hall, a Long Beach, California, system enables citizens calling city hall with an inquiry or complaint to dial a single number, get the right department, and be guaranteed a response. The computer creates a record of each call, prints a letter to the caller, and sends a copy to the appropriate city council representative. If a final disposition on a call is not received within a given period of time, a follow-up procedure is initiated.

*Businesses* also use computers to improve the services they provide to customers. Computer processing techniques, for example, make possible:

- Shorter waiting lines at banks and airline ticket offices and at the reservation desks of hotels, motels, and car-rental agencies, and the option of banking and shopping at home via electronic services.

- Faster and more accurate answers to the inquiries of people served by the business.

- More efficient customer service and control of inventory in retail outlets.

Benefits from computers in *health care* include:

- Faster and more thorough approaches to the preparation and analysis of medical histories (Figure 15-3*a*).

- Faster and more thorough testing to detect and identify disease (Figure 15-3*b*).

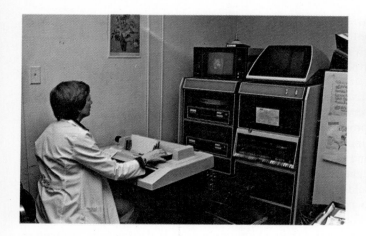

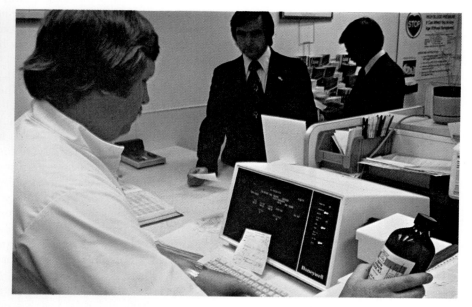

**Figure 15-3** (*a, above left*) People benefit when health-care organizations use computers to aid in the preparation and analysis of medical histories. (*b, above right*) A computerized blood analyzer that automatically tests for 25 separate factors in a blood sample. (Both courtesy Russ Kinne/ Photo Researchers) (*c, below left*) A computer-monitor provides an anesthesiologist with continual digital and waveform display of vital signs, including electrocardiogram, heart rate, blood pressure, and temperature. (Courtesy Gould, Inc.) (*d, below right*) This pharmacist is using Honeywell's COMPASS system to improve his services. (Courtesy Honeywell, Inc.)

■ More accurate methods of physiological monitoring (Figure 15-3*c*).

■ Better control of lab test results and pharmacy services (Figure 15-3*d*).

Still other computers are used to train doctors and other health-care personnel by simulating a patient with an emergency condition. The student is given the symptoms and is challenged to save the patient before time runs out by using a logical progression of diagnostic tests and treatments. Student errors are pointed out immediately by the computer.

**Recreational and Educational Benefits.** Some organizations are using computers solely to amuse and entertain people. And the potential for computers in education has barely been tapped. For example, entertaining personal computer game programs are being prepared by hundreds of producers (Figure 15-4a). And personal computers are being used to help preschool and older children learn how to write (Figure 15-4b). Some Arizona tots of preschool age use a computer to write their first words. The computer displays and then speaks the words they type. And *Bank Street Writer*, a word processing program designed for children in the elementary grades, has become an overnight best-seller and is popular with adults as well as children. **Computer animation** (Figure 15-4c) is being used to give the illusion of movement to inanimate objects. The results of computer animation are now seen regularly in movies and on TV. For example, a briefing-room scene in the movie *Star Wars* was accomplished by means of computer animation. And **computer photography** techniques developed for the U.S. space program are being used to amuse people. A TV camera captures the desired image from a photograph or a live subject. The image is frozen and is then transferred by computer to a tee-shirt, handbag, or other object.

**Aid to the Handicapped.** Microcomputers can be used to control devices that permit severely handicapped persons to feed themselves even though they have no upper limb responses. Also, the New York University Medical Center is using computer-controlled video games to help stroke victims regain use of their limbs. Computer-based human/machine analyses are making it possible for businesses to develop more effective artificial limbs for amputees (Figure 15-5). And the trend toward *telecommuting* (discussed in Chapter 10) expands job opportunities for handicapped people.

**Improved Safety.** Computer usage can contribute to personal safety in a number of ways. Computer-controlled braking systems in aircraft and in future cars may help prevent dangerous skids and produce the optimum stopping distance in all weather conditions. Minicomputer systems in pharmacies can be used to check a

Figure 15-4 Fun with computers— *(a)* playing, *(b)* learning, *(c)* viewing. (Courtesy Sperry Corporation, International Business Machines Corporation, and © Lucasfilm Ltd (LFL) 1977, All rights reserved)

**Figure 15-5** Electronic arms and shoulders are activated by motion sensors and electrical signals from the skin. The circuitry in these artificial limbs may be as small as a neuron. (Photo © Chuck O'Rear/West Light)

patient's medical profile against possible reactions to any ingredients in a new prescription or to determine the possibility of dangerous interactions between the ingredients in old prescriptions and those in the new prescription. Computers permit gas utility companies to do a better job of managing and controlling the pipeline leaks that can seriously jeopardize public safety. Dispatchers can provide work crews with information about an area, including work-history details of prior gas leaks. New leaks can be identified and old leaks analyzed through online terminals. State and local governments are using computers to design safer roads and control air and water pollution. And the federal government maintains a computerized air traffic control and navigation system that monitors over 30 million flights each year.

**Better Information Retrieval.** A New York surgeon contacted a medical library when a near-term pregnant woman lapsed into a hepatic coma. He needed immediate information on exchange blood transfusions for the woman. Using a computer terminal and an information retrieval program, the librarian was able to search more than a half-million medical documents in a few minutes to get the information needed by the surgeon to perform an emergency blood transfusion. The patient recovered fully from the hepatitis. Although most information retrieval projects obviously don't involve life-or-death situations, quick computer-assisted retrieval can save time and aggravation for many individuals. People whose interests range from the hobbyist looking for information on a particular coin to the citizen seeking information on congressional hearings can locate sources quickly by using the online information services offered by many businesses. A number of these retrieval organizations are identified, and their services are discussed, in Chapter 10. The use by individuals of *videotex systems* for information retrieval is also discussed in that chapter.

### Benefits from Personal Computing

If you've read Chapter 8, you know that a pc can be used in the home for entertainment and other applications. Since the uses of a pc are as numerous and varied as human ingenuity and imagination will permit, the benefits of personal computing are also limited only by ingenuity and imagination. The following examples reflect the detailed treatment you'll find on pages 221–222:

- **Entertainment and hobby benefits.** A pc can entertain you with hundreds of challenging games. Storehouses of information for the pc owner are available from the videotex systems discussed in Chapter 10. And pc users can compose music, store and maintain stamp and coin collection records, and polish their foreign language and programming skills.

- **Educational benefits.** Games can be educational as well as entertaining. Educators agree that the home pc can be a powerful motivating and learning tool. When children (and adults) use a pc, they have some real control over what they learn, how they learn, and how fast they learn. Making a sophisticated machine do one's bidding is fun for many people, and writing a computer program requires a person to analyze and understand the subject being studied. And you've seen that using word processing software with a pc encourages people to polish their writing skills because changes and corrections are made easily.

■ *Personal finance benefits.* A pc could help you prepare your budget and balance your checkbook, control your installment purchases, control your home's energy use, and analyze your investments and prepare your tax returns. If you wanted information on current stock prices, you could call the toll-free number of one videotex service, obtain access to the data base of Dow-Jones & Company, and use the service's programs to obtain quotes and other information on any stock listed on any of the six major exchanges in the United States. If you were trying to decide whether to buy a home, you could load an available program into your computer, supply the necessary input data (e.g., purchase price, down payment, loan term, taxes, utility costs, mortgage interest rate, etc.), and find out exactly what the costs and financial benefits are.

■ *Benefits of greater personal efficiency.* A pc can help people save time and/or use time more efficiently. For example, a pc can support the telecommuting activities of employees who work at home and thus save the time spent in getting to and from a central office; track and manage personal projects and appointments so that everything is done on time, on schedule, and within budget; and even help individuals put up a better fight for their social concerns against well-heeled bureaucracies. With his wife and neighbors, Richard Bach, author of *Jonathan Livingston Seagull,* forced the U.S. Bureau of Land Management to cancel a timber sale in Oregon that they felt would have damaged the environment by using pc's as terminals to gather information from public data banks and as word processors to help organize and analyze the raw information which was used to prepare documents for their successful protest.

# PEOPLE AND COMPUTERS: POTENTIAL DANGERS

You've seen in this chapter that people may indeed benefit from an organization's use of computers. The people who initiate changes in computer-based information systems often rush forward in the reasonable belief that such changes will increase employee productivity and improve the organization's efficiency. But they sometimes fail to appreciate the effects their decisions may have on social groups, on human skills and feelings, and on existing jobs.

**Employment Problems: Resistance, Displacement, and Unemployment**

**Resistance to Change.** In their desire to create and lead in the use of new techniques, change initiators may ignore the natural **resistance to system change** that people often feel. Resistance is often the rule rather than the exception because the changes may appear to others to be a threat—a threat that may take one or more of the following paths:

1. *The threat to job security.* Computers have a reputation for replacing people. Thus, there's the understandable fear of loss of employment and/or of reduction in salary.

"The computer says it recorded our Christmas party last week and will consider selling the tapes at very reasonable prices."

2. ***The reduction in social satisfaction.*** The introduction of a computer system often calls for a reorganization of departments and work groups. When change causes a breaking up of friendly groups and a realigning of personnel, it may also cause a reduction in job satisfaction. Resistance to such a proposed change may be expected.

3. ***The reduction in self-esteem and reputation.*** People need to feel self-confident. But self-confidence may be shaken by the lack of knowledge about and experience with a computer system. The equipment may be strange to them, and they may fear that they'll be unable to acquire the skills necessary to work with it. In short, their self-esteem may suffer as a result of the change, and so the change may be resisted. Fear of loss of status and/or prestige is also an important reason for resistance by both managers and employees. Department managers, for example, may oppose a change because to admit that the change is needed may imply that they have tolerated inefficiency—an admission that can hardly enhance their reputations. And employees knowledgeable in the ways of the old system may also suffer a loss of prestige because when new procedures are installed they may no longer be looked to for information.

People resist change in different ways. At one extreme, they may temporarily feel threatened by a change, but after a brief adjustment period they resume their previous behavior. At the other extreme, reaction may result in open opposition and even destruction. Between these extremes are a number of other symptoms including withholding facts, providing inaccurate data, and displaying an attitude of indifference. Although people are responsible for successfully putting the computer to work, resistant employees and managers have also been able to scuttle a number of computer system efforts in the past.

To reduce their chances of failure, change initiators should:

1. ***Keep people informed.*** Information relating to the effects of the change on their jobs should be periodically presented to people at all levels. Topics discussed should include loss of jobs, transfers, the extent of necessary retraining, the reasons for (and the benefits of) the change, the effect on various departments, and what is being done to alleviate employee hardships.

2. ***Seek employee participation.*** People are more likely to support and accept changes that they've had a hand in creating. The participation of knowledgeable people yields valuable information. Participation also helps these people satisfy ego and self-fulfillment needs, gives them some degree of control over the change and thus contributes to a greater feeling of security, and removes their fear of the unknown. Of course, people asked to participate must be respected and treated with dignity, and their suggestions must be carefully considered.

**Displacement and Unemployment.** Displacement and unemployment aren't the same. **Unemployment** refers to the total number of people involuntarily out of work. **Displacement** occurs when jobs are eliminated as a result of technological change. *If* displaced workers can't find similar jobs elsewhere and *if* they can't find work in other occupations, then there is, indeed, an increase in the unemployment figures. Optimists and pessimists disagree on the long-range effects of computers and automated tools on total employment. But both groups agree that to the employee being displaced, the future consequences are of secondary importance.

Some middle-level managers whose decisions were structured and repetitive have found that those decisions were programmable on a computer. The information systems have therefore taken over those duties, and the need for as many administrators to perform the remainder of the job duties has been reduced. During the first half of the 1980s, there was a significant reduction in the middle-management ranks of many large organizations. In some organizations, those who were not displaced found their jobs less challenging because, although they retained the duties that required less judgment, their other tasks that called for the skilled interpretation of systems information were moved upward in the organization. And some lower-level supervisors have suffered because their departments have been eliminated or reduced in scope and status as a result of the installation of computer information systems. Of course, when computers displace employees, the supervisors of those employees may no longer be needed.

Clerical employees have often been displaced by computers. For example, Los Angeles County expects to save $10 million annually through the use of its Welfare Case Management Information System. However, much of the expected savings will come from the elimination of 900 jobs over a 3-year period. The extent to which clerical displacement actually occurs and the significance of the problem in particular cases may depend in large measure on the following factors:

- ▪ *The rate of growth of the organization and the economy.* If the organization is growing rapidly so that more work must be done to handle the expanding volume, there may be little or no effect on the number of workers employed.

- ▪ *The objectives sought.* Is the organization introducing a computer system for processing purposes that couldn't otherwise be considered? Or is it to save money by eliminating existing jobs?

- ▪ *The types of occupations threatened.* In the past, few clerical workers were laid off in larger organizations when job reductions occurred. This was possible because workers in affected departments who quit during the many months required to implement a system were simply not replaced.

When the affected jobs are not of the clerical type, the displacement problem may be more severe. The affected workers may be older managers whose skills are no longer needed. They're not as likely to quit, and so attrition may not be of much help.

Displacement is occurring in some skilled production-oriented occupations, such as those which involve the operation of certain metal-working tools and typesetting devices, as a result of the installation of computer-controlled machines. A more serious displacement problem, however, is likely to result from the increased use of computer-controlled robots in assembly operations. The automobile industry is a leading user of robots that for several years have performed such production tasks as stamping, heat-treating, welding, and spray painting. Robots perform these dreary, dirty, and/or dangerous tasks without complaint, and "first-generation" robots have usually been applied in such areas of worker discontent. But production techniques are now changing rapidly in the automobile industry. In the $80 billion retooling program required to build smaller cars that will meet foreign competition and the mileage and emission standards of the late 1980s, auto manufacturers are replacing old machines with a new generation of robots. According to the Society of Manufacturing Engineers, 20 percent of the direct labor formerly needed in automobile final assembly has already been replaced by programmable robots. An additional 30 percent may be displaced by 1995. By 1988, half of the direct labor formerly needed to assemble small components such as starters will also be replaced.

And the trend toward fewer production workers isn't limited to the automobile industry. Today, there are about 25 million manufacturing workers in the United States. But Raj Reddy, Director of the Robotics Institute at Carnegie-Mellon University, expects this number to drop to less than 3 million by the year 2010. According to Robert Lund, a researcher at MIT's Center for Policy Alternatives, the result of this creation of robotized plants will be a substantial permanent sector of unemployment. The forthcoming changes, Lund believes, will divide workers into high-skilled and low-skilled categories, wiping out the intermediate skill range vital for a sense of upward mobility.

Nor are employees in the professions immune from the effects of computer usage. The advancement in scientific and engineering knowledge (which may be attributed in part to the expanding use of computers) makes it increasingly difficult for scientists and engineers to keep abreast of their fields. They must have the ability and willingness to learn about computing, adopt new techniques, and, perhaps, go through several "retreading" periods in their careers simply to retain marketable skills. Otherwise, as one expert has observed, they may become, over time, uneducated and therefore incompetent at a level at which they once performed quite adequately. The possible suffering and anxiety associated with the conviction that technical obsolescence is likely in a relatively short time is thus something that certain professionals may have to learn to live with.

## Questionable Practices Affecting Private Lives

Since computer systems are now performing vital functions in society, it's essential that the data affecting people aren't lost or stolen, errors aren't introduced, and facts aren't originated, stored, retrieved, or communicated without proper justification. Unfortunately, questionable data processing practices have caused some computer systems to fall short of these standards.

**Data Originating/Recording: A Lack of Control?** A staggering volume of information of a highly personal nature has been collected by government agencies and private organizations. In the government sector, for example, a study conducted a few years ago by the Senate Subcommittee on Constitutional Rights found that 858 data banks in 54 federal agencies contained a total of more than 1.25 *billion* records and dossiers on individuals—and these figures understated the actual situation at the time. These hundreds of federal data banks, when combined with more than 600 others operated by the states and more than 1,700 others operated by cities and counties, provide governments with specific information on virtually every citizen. And in addition, there are hundreds of private organizations—e.g., credit bureaus—that engage in investigative reporting for a fee.

Several problems associated with all this data gathering have been identified. These problems are:

■ *Gathering data without a valid need to know.* For years, the Justice Department maintained a computer-based Inter-Divisional Information System (IDIS) to gather data about the "agitational activities" of political dissidents. In the early 1970s, at Senate hearings on federal data banks, an assistant attorney general defended the IDIS and gave assurances that it was used only on a "need to know" basis. However, after examining IDIS files, Senate investigators concluded that "massive amounts of irrelevant information had been compiled on innocent individuals." Another example of questionable data-gathering activities involves the private firms that collect personal data about people for insurance companies, employers, and credit grantors. It's common practice for insurance companies to ask a private agency to investigate a policy applicant's background to help determine the sort of underwriting risk he or she would be. This is understandable since certain personal habits—e.g., heavy drinking or participation in a hazardous sport—may involve obvious health risks. The problem is that the data gathered may go beyond those which have probable risk value to an insurance company. These data are frequently gathered by an interviewer from two or three of the applicant's neighbors or acquaintances. In about 20 minutes, the interviewer will ask a respondent questions about the applicant's use of alcohol or narcotics, whether there's anything adverse about his or her reputation, life-style, and home environment, and if there's any news of domestic troubles or reports of dubious business practices. Questions calling for such detailed, subjective, and impressionistic responses in such a short time are an open invitation to gossip and faulty moral assessments. Furthermore, some of these questions may have little bearing on the applicant's insurability. But this is a data-gathering method that has been used by a large consumer reporting service. Once stored in a computer data bank, the contents of an applicant's file may then be available to others, such as credit grantors and potential employers, for a small fee.

■ *Gathering inaccurate and incomplete data.* We've just seen that questionable methods can permit inaccuracies to be introduced into a computer data bank. Unintentional mistakes in filling out input forms and keying records are common enough in any record-keeping system. But the consequences may be more serious in a computer-based system because there may be fewer people to catch errors and because the speed with which inaccurate information is made available to system users may be much faster than the speed with which errors are detected and corrected. For example, in converting data on a questionnaire into machine-readable form, a data entry operator may hit the 1 key instead of the 2 key (where the 1 is the code for "yes" and the 2 is the code for "no") on a question concerning a felony conviction, a prior bankruptcy, or a history of mental disorder or venereal disease. You can appreciate the possible consequences of this simple unintentional mistake! Deliberate errors have also been introduced into data banks which are so important to people. For example, a former interviewer told a Senate banking committee that he had completely invented 25 percent of his reports, and that he was far from alone in doing so. Finally, input data are also subject to serious errors of omission. If, for example, an individual is arrested and accused of, say, auto theft, this fact will probably be entered into several law enforcement data banks. But if the person is found to be innocent of the charges, this very important fact that's needed to complete the record may *not* be entered into the data banks. It's estimated that 70 percent of the arrest records stored in the FBI's National Crime Information Center (NCIC) contain no information about the final outcome of the cases.

■ *Problems of confusion and bewilderment associated with data gathering.* People are often confused and bewildered by computer data-input procedures. A significant cause of this confusion is that people aren't told what the system does or how it works. The result may be the belief on the part of people that they have been tricked or deceived by the system. For example, in signing application forms for insurance policies, individuals may not know that a fine-print statement at the bottom of a form authorizes a firm representing an insurance company to quiz neighbors and acquaintances for "any and all information" about them. People also may not realize that the supplied data may be entered into third-party data banks and used in rather secretive ways. Individuals may also find it confusing to operate the computer input devices that are replacing more familiar forms and procedures. Automated voting systems, for example, have confused voters and have produced questionable tallys.

**Standardization and Depersonalization.** A **standard** defines or specifies something so that people and machines that must use it and/or produce it do so in a uniform and efficient way. Entering input data according to some standard coding scheme can contribute to an economical and efficient system. But **standardization** may also lead to unwanted depersonalization. As we come in contact with a growing number of computer systems, the use of numerical codes for identification purposes may increase. We may understand that being treated as numbers can lead to standardized and efficient computer usage by organizations, but we may wish that it were not so. Instead of being numerically coded and molded to meet the computer's needs, we might prefer that computer systems be designed so that we will be treated as persons rather than numbers. *This isn't likely to happen.* The social security number is now being used as the personal identifier in numerous large data systems. The Internal Revenue Service, the U.S. Army, colleges and universities, state driver's license departments, insurance companies, banks—these and many other organizations may know you as 353-27-2345. The threat of an eventual ''universal identifier,'' of course, is that the separate data records you've established for particular purposes can more easily be consolidated through the use of the common number, and the combined data can be merged into a large personal dossier.

In addition to treating people as numbers, standardized procedures, once established, may tend to become inflexible. Thus, if a person's needs don't conform to the ''norms'' of the system, there may be difficulty in getting the system to deal properly with the exception. This tendency to try to force everyone into the same mold may naturally give the individual a feeling of helplessness in trying to cope with a cold, impersonal, and remote organization.

**System Mistakes.** System mistakes are primarily due to human errors in preparing input data and in designing and preparing programs. Thus, when the computer itself is blamed for some foul-up, it's frequently being used as a convenient ''scapegoat'' to cover up human error, carelessness, or indifference. Of course, the unfortunate fact remains that numerous ''computer'' foul-ups *have occurred*. We can conclude this section with a few pitiful examples of computer-system atrocities that have had a negative impact on people.

- Some voters in areas using computerized vote-counting systems may have been disenfranchised. For example, the validity of the count of the computer-processed ballots in Washington, D.C., and Austin, Texas, in past elections is subject to question.

- A New York City employee failed to get his check for three pay periods after a computer payroll system was installed. Finally, after the employee had initiated legal action against the city, a program bug was discovered and removed, and Mr. Void was at last paid.

- People have been arrested for ''stealing'' their own cars. The sequence of events goes something like this: The car is stolen, the theft is reported to a law enforcement data bank, and the car is recovered (perhaps in another jurisdiction) and returned to its owner. The recovery is not entered into the data bank, and the owner is then picked up while driving his or her recovered property. Since the arrest may also be entered into the data bank, but the final disposition may not be, the owner may wind up with an arrest record for ''grand theft—auto.'' If you don't think this can be serious, you should consider the plight of the ex-Marine from Illinois who has been jailed several times for desertion because of incorrect information stored in the FBI's computerized National Crime Information Center.

**The Systems Security Issue**

If input data important to people are accurate and complete when they enter a computer system, are processed correctly, don't become inaccurate through subsequent errors, and aren't distorted or lost through system mistakes, we could be confident about the integrity of the data. But even if we were successful in controlling **data integrity,** this wouldn't be enough to eliminate all the adverse effects that computer systems may have on the private lives of people. It doesn't help much for

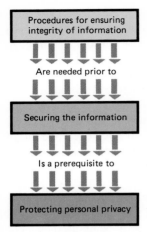

Figure 15-6 The relationship among data integrity, systems security, and personal privacy.

a person to know that the information relevant to him or her that's stored in a data bank is accurate and complete if he or she also knows that the information isn't *secured and protected* against theft, fraud, or malicious scrutiny and manipulation.

*Both* information *integrity and security* are needed to protect a person's **right to privacy**—i.e., to protect the legitimate right of an individual to limit access to personal and often sensitive information to persons authorized to use it in the individual's best interest. If a lack of integrity in a law enforcement data bank permits the arrest of an individual for driving his or her own car and then results in the creation of an arrest record that may not be purged from the system, and if a lack of systems security subsequently permits the circulation of this arrest record to prospective employers and credit agencies, these deficiencies have certainly contributed to an invasion of the individual's privacy. In short, data integrity, information security, and personal privacy are interrelated, as shown in Figure 15-6.

For our purposes, **systems security** involves:

■ The protection of stored *data* against accidental or malicious disclosure.

■ The *physical* protection of hardware and software against damage or destruction.

The consequences that an organization may face when it fails to maintain system security were outlined in Chapter 14. It's equally important from an individual's point of view that confidential records be preserved and used only for approved purposes, and that the equipment and programs needed to store and retrieve them be protected against damage or penetration.

The vulnerability of computer systems has increased in recent years, and so the security issue has become more important. Early computers were located in self-contained installations, were accessible to a relatively small number of specialists, and were used to process batches of data in a single stream. As computer systems increased in number and became more sophisticated, however, many more people had access to them, the use of shared resources and jointly used data became common, and direct interaction with a computer became a routine activity for even casual users. Such an environment has obviously increased the difficulty of maintaining security. The vulnerability of systems has also increased because:

■ The information to be found in a relatively complete and up-to-date data bank may be of sufficient value to provide the incentive for outsiders to seek access to it.

■ More people have now been trained in the skills required to program, penetrate, and manipulate computer systems.

**Lack of Control over Security.** The computer hardware in general use today was not designed with security provisions in mind. Thus, the provisions that do exist are found in the software and in the organizational policies and data processing controls that may exist in the particular system.

When it comes to security, existing software is indeed soft. Clever individuals have had no difficulty in breaking through the security provisions of those computer operating system programs that they've sought to penetrate. Its happened frequently enough, in fact, that the use of personal computers to gain unauthorized access into organizational systems is a popular story line used today by television and movie writers. Today's computer operating systems aren't completely predictable, and so there's no analytical method for proving that an operating system *isn't* performing unauthorized acts. Thus, there's no guaranteed defense against several known techniques by which a programmer can corrupt a system.

**Impact on People.** The lack of control over computer system security has resulted in undesirable consequences for people. *Economic loss, inconvenience, loss of privacy*—these are just a few of the aggravations people have suffered because computer systems weren't secure.

Individuals as well as organizations lose money to the computer thief. In one instance, a computer was used to send out phony invoices to people. The thief knew that some people pay authentic-looking bills automatically, without questioning their validity. When a phony bill was questioned, however, the thief would merely send back a form letter saying "Sorry. Our computer made an error." A person's finances can also become fouled up in other ways. For example, a Chicago woman was mailed a bank money card and a personal identification number without having requested them. Both were intercepted by a thief and used to empty a $600 account of hers and run up an additional overdraft of $1,200. The bank then froze the woman's other account because she was overdrawn. It took an attorney and 2 months of wrangling with the bank to get her money released.

A lack of control in handling input media can result in inconvenience. Suppose a shift supervisor at a computer center servicing dozens of banks processes a tape containing a day's checks and deposits but fails to properly record this processing run. The next shift supervisor may then rerun the tape with the result being that double deposits and double withdrawals may appear in customer accounts. You're delighted with your double credit, but I am really chapped by my double withdrawal. And we are both inconvenienced by the later attempts to straighten out this mess.

Finally, as noted earlier, a lack of control over systems security can lead to the invasion of an individual's legitimate right to privacy.

## The Privacy Issue

We know that for years private and public organizations have been building separate files containing "threads" of information about those with whom they come in contact. But many of these older files are incomplete and poorly maintained. Thus, the value of their contents may be such that unauthorized persons have little incentive to snoop. *The development of computer data banks, however, has changed the situation.*

**Dossiers and the Invasion of Privacy.** Files maintained in large, integrated computer data banks are more complete. Seemingly innocent data recorded and stored at one time may be retrieved and correlated quickly and inexpensively by the computer with other data collected from different sources and at different times to reveal potentially damaging information about individuals. It might then be possible to bring pressure to bear on people to make them do things they might otherwise not have done.

As every man goes through life, he fills in a number of forms for the record, each containing a number of questions. There are thus hundreds of little threads radiating from each man, millions of threads in all. If these threads were suddenly to become visible, people would lose all ability to move.

Alexander Solzhenitsyn

Thoughtful opponents of consolidated data banks acknowledge that such banks can help public and private organizations provide individuals with many of the benefits discussed earlier in the chapter—e.g., better and more efficient service and greater safety. But they are concerned about the threat that these banks might eventually present to an individual. This concern is perhaps summarized in a *Saturday Review* cartoon which shows a distressed executive listening to a telephone message. The message is: "This is the Computer Data Bank. Leave $100,000 in small bills in Locker 287 at the Port Authority Bus Terminal or I'll print out your complete dossier and send it to your wife."

Electronic banking, like all systems, is liable to potential abuses. Consumer education and computer literacy maintain an informed public, which is vital to a free society. (Courtesy NCR Corporation)

**Impact on People.** A few examples and speculations here should be sufficient to demonstrate how a computer system or network may be used for surveillance, for the creation of a climate that restricts individual freedom, and for other abuses.

*EFTS Surveillance Possibilities.* Although the electronic funds transfer systems (EFTS) being implemented by banks and other financial institutions aren't intended for *surveillance,* they could be easily adapted to this purpose in the future. The use of *cash* in a transaction reveals little or no information about the parties to the transaction. When a *check* is written, a record is created of the payer, the payee, and the transaction amount. And when a *money card* is used, all this information, along with the transaction time, location, and nature of the transaction, is recorded. Thus, if all your transactions were normally to be processed through EFTS computers, a *daily record* of much of *what* you do and *where* you do it could be prepared. A few years ago, a group of computer, communications, and surveillance experts was gathered and given the following hypothetical problem: As advisers to the head of the KGB (the Russian secret police), they were to design an *unobtrusive* surveillance system to monitor the activities of all citizens and visitors inside the U.S.S.R. As one of these experts testified in Congressional hearings, ". . . [T]his group decided that if you wanted to build an unobtrusive system for surveillance, you couldn't do much better than an EFTS."

Of course, EFTS proponents maintain that adequate laws can be passed to prevent surveillance abuse. But critics aren't so sure. They point out that existing check authorization systems can "flag" accounts so that if a "flagged" individual tries to cash a check someone (police perhaps?) can be notified of the individual's exact location. They are fearful that future operators of EFTS networks would be unable to resist the pressures from governments to allow the EFTS to be used for surveillance purposes.

*List-Compiling Abuses.* Mailing lists giving details about people are regularly compiled and sold by both private and public organizations. State auto licensing agencies, for example, sell lists to auto equipment suppliers. There's probably not much harm in this if it results only in your receiving literature that tries to persuade you to buy seat covers a few weeks after you've registered your new car. But what about the case of the computer dating service that sold its list of female clients to a publishing organization that printed and sold through local newsstands lists of "Girls Who Want Dates"? Try to tell one of those women that her privacy hasn't been invaded!

*Freedom Restrictions.* Consider the following facts:

■ Thousands of law enforcement officers and bank, employment agency, and credit company clerks have easy access to networks containing information on millions of people. Many of these officers and clerks without any real "need to know" may while away the time browsing through the records of friends and acquaintances just to see what they can uncover.

■ Most categories of personal information gathered for legitimate research purposes by reputable social, political, and behavioral scientists don't enjoy any statutory protection. Thus, sensitive personal information gathered by these researchers may be obtained through a subpoena issued by a court or other government body and put into data banks for future use. If the researchers, who may have assured the respondents that their replies would be kept in strictest confidence, refuse to honor the subpoena and turn over the data, they may be cited for contempt and be made to suffer the consequences. Given that alternative, they generally surrender the data.

Being aware of such facts and of the possible uses of large computerized data banks may have a sobering effect on people. It may restrict their actions even when the data are accurate, the use of the data is authorized by law, and controls on the use of the data are imposed. You may be in favor of the use of computers to curtail crime, but you may also resent being listed with felons in an unsecured data bank. And you may believe that a university professor should conduct a study that requires the gathering and analyzing of personal data, but you may not feel free to personally participate in that study. In short, you may now tend to behave differently (and less freely) than you once would have because of your increasing awareness that what you say and do may become part of some computer record.

**Privacy Controls.** We've been discussing an individual's "right" to privacy, but the word *privacy* doesn't appear anywhere in the Constitution. What, then, is the legal status of privacy? An early consideration of privacy as a legal concept was presented in 1890 by Louis Brandeis and Samuel Warren in an article entitled "The Right to Privacy." In 1928, after being appointed to the Supreme Court, Justice Brandeis again took up the concept when he wrote in a minority opinion: "The right to be let alone is the most comprehensive of rights and the right most valued by civilized men."

Of course, what one person may consider to be a privacy right may be judged by others to be an item of genuine public concern. For example, if a newspaper reporter unearths the fact that a member of Congress has put a number of relatives on the government payroll for no good purpose, and if the reporter then reveals this fact and prints the names and salaries of the relatives, she has undoubtedly infringed on their privacy. But she has also used rights guaranteed to her in the Bill of Rights (the First Amendment's freedom of speech and freedom of the press) to perform a public service. Thus, there may be legitimate rights operating against privacy in some situations. In short, since privacy is not one of the specific constitutional rights, and since a balance has to be struck between the need for privacy on the one hand and society's need for legitimate information on the other, *the extent to which individuals are given privacy protection must depend on judicial and legislative decisions.* That is, the *continuous* task of balancing human rights against basic freedoms in order to establish privacy controls is the responsibility of the judicial and legislative branches of government.

Lawmakers have been busy in recent years in an effort to restore some balance in favor of privacy. The result has been that numerous federal statutes and about 150 state bills have been passed over a brief time span to control the invasion of privacy. Some *examples of existing* **privacy laws** *are:*

- *Fair Credit Reporting Act of 1970.* This federal law gives people the right to know what information is kept on them by credit bureaus and other credit investigation agencies. People also have the right to challenge information they consider to be inaccurate.

- *State "Fair Information Practice" Laws.* The California Fair Information Practice Act of 1974 (and similar laws in many other states) spells out the rights of people when dealing with state government data banks. Individuals have the right to know what information is kept on them in the various data banks, and to contest the "accuracy, completeness, pertinence, and timeliness" of the stored data.

- *Privacy Act of 1974.* This federal law became effective late in September 1975. It's aimed at some of the uses and abuses of federal data banks. Some of its provisions are:
  *(a)* With the exception of classified files, civil service records, and law enforcement agency investigative files, people have the right to see their records in federal data banks.
  *(b)* They may point out errors in their records, and if these errors aren't removed, they may ask a federal judge to order the correction.
  *(c)* Unless specifically authorized by law, federal agencies cannot sell or rent personal data bank information, nor can they monitor a person's religious or political activities.

- *State Cable Television Privacy Acts.* In the early 1980s, Illinois, Wisconsin, California, and other states passed laws prohibiting cable TV companies from monitoring subscribers' sets or their selection of programs.

## Feedback and Review 15-1

The subject of artificial intelligence has been discussed in this chapter. And some of the benefits available to people from computer usage, along with some of the possible dangers associated with the use of computer systems, have also been outlined. To test and reinforce your understanding of these subjects, match the letter of the appropriate term to the definition or concept to which it belongs: a) know, b) finance, c) heuristic, d) identifier, e) EFTS, f) privacy, g) service, h) displace, i) robots, j) productivity, k) animation, l) videotex, m) AI, n) Turing, o) judicial. (Place the correct letter in the space provided.)

___**1.** The amount of goods or services possessing economic value that people and machines can produce in a given time period is their _____ .

___**2.** Computers can help organizations provide higher-quality products and better _____ .

___**3.** Computer _____ is being used to give the illusion of movement to inanimate objects.

——**4.** A _____ system can be used by individuals to retrieve information from dozens of data banks.

——**5.** Personal _____ benefits are one of many categories of benefits that can be obtained through the use of personal computers.

——**6.** An acronym for the use of computers to solve relatively unstructured problems such as programming computers to play chess is _____.

——**7.** The author of a test to determine if a computer program might be considered to possess intelligence.

——**8.** A word used to describe the judgmental part of problem-solving.

——**9.** Studies have shown that computers can _____ large numbers of clerical workers.

——**10.** A serious displacement problem is likely to result from the use of _____ in assembly operations.

——**11.** Data have been gathered about people in the past when there was no valid "need to _____" basis for doing so.

——**12.** The social security number is being used as the personal _____ in numerous large data systems.

——**13.** Both data integrity and system security are needed to protect a person's right to _____.

——**14.** It would be possible to use an _____ as an unobtrusive surveillance system.

——**15.** Privacy protection depends on _____ and legislative decisions.

# LOOKING BACK

**1.** Computer chess programs can now defeat 99.5 percent of all human chess players. Experiments are being conducted by researchers in the field of artificial intelligence to improve the machines' heuristic capabilities. One result of this research is the development of a number of expert systems. But humans still remain far superior to computers in this area of intellectual work. The potential of an alliance between humans and computers, however, cannot be restricted in any way we can now anticipate.

**2.** Some managers and employees in organizations have found their jobs more rewarding because of computer systems, and consumers have received benefits from the ways in which organizations use computers. Increased efficiency, higher quality, and better service are three benefits described in the chapter. Without computers many recreational and educational benefits wouldn't be feasible, handicapped persons would be denied tools that make their lives more meaningful, and retrieving needed information would be a more tedious task.

**3.** Although some managers and employees have benefited by the use of computers on the job, others haven't been so fortunate. Some have lost their jobs or have suffered a loss of status and prestige when computer systems were installed. Clerical employees, for example, have often been displaced by computers, and production employees are being threatened by the rapidly growing use of computer-controlled robots.

**4.** In private life some people (who may have been helped on the job by computers) have been inconvenienced and confused by computer information systems employing questionable

data processing practices. In some systems there seems to be a lack of control over the data originating/recording step. Data are sometimes gathered without a valid reason; when a valid reason does exist, gathered facts are sometimes used in ways that were not originally intended. A number of people have also been the casualties of systems errors of commission and omission and/or the victims of a cold, impersonal, and remote computer system that classifies, sorts, and treats them as depersonalized numbers.

**5.** Information integrity and security are needed to protect a person's legitimate right to privacy. Systems security involves the protection of both the data and the hardware and software used to process the data. Computer security difficulties are caused by the fact that many skilled people may have access to the system, and by the fact that the value of the stored data may warrant the attempt to penetrate the system. Although there are hardware and software security provisions in a typical system, these provisions are seldom capable of blocking the attempts of a skilled penetrator. The lack of control over computer systems security has resulted in economic loss, inconvenience, and a loss of privacy for people.

**6.** There are many benefits to be obtained from the creation of data banks, but there's also a concern about the threat these data banks might present to an individual. Ways in which computers are used (or could be used) for surveillance, for the creation of a climate that restricts individual freedom, and for other abuses are presented in the chapter, along with an overview of several laws passed to restore some balance in the favor of privacy.

## KEY TERMS AND CONCEPTS

artificial intelligence (AI) 392
Turing's test 394
heuristic 395
synergy 396
productivity 399
computer animation 401

computer photography 401
resistance to system change 403
unemployment 404
displacement 404
standard 408
standardization 408

data integrity 409
right to privacy 410
systems security 410
privacy laws 414

## TOPICS FOR REVIEW AND DISCUSSION

**1.** Why does controversy surround the question of whether computers can be programmed to "think"?

**2.** Robert Jastrow, Director of NASA's Goddard Institute for Space Studies, has written that the alliance between humans and computers will not last very long. He states that: "Computer intelligence is growing by leaps and bounds, with no natural limit in sight. But human evolution is a nearly finished chapter in the history of life." Jastrow believes that a new kind of intelligent life will probably emerge on the earth, and this life "is more likely to be made of silicon." (a) What's your reaction to this opinion? (b) Are your views changed by the fact that Jastrow believes the evolution of the new silicon species will take about a million years?

**3.** (a) How have managers of organizations benefited from computer usage? (b) Identify employees of organizations who have benefited, and explain how they've been helped.

**4.** Discuss how the following individuals in organizations may benefit from computer usage: (a) law enforcement officers, (b) members of Congress, (c) school teachers, (d) nurses, and (e) district office managers.

**5.** Identify and discuss four ways in which consumers may benefit from the use of computers (a) by businesses, (b) by public organizations, and (c) in the home.

**6.** (a) How have managers been the victims of computer usage? (b) How have employees been victimized?

**7.** Westinghouse Electric Corporation has a grant from the National Science Foundation to experiment with the use of robots to replace people in low-volume or batch-manufacturing operations—the types of operations that account for about 75 percent of all U.S. manufacturing. According to a Westinghouse spokesperson, "complex assembly tasks will continue to be per-formed by people, but many repetitive, boring tasks, and those performed in an unpleasant environment can and should be automated." Discuss this statement.

**8.** How may a lack of control over data originating/recording lead to undesirable results for people?

**9.** "Data integrity, information security, and personal privacy are interrelated." Define these terms and discuss this statement.

**10.** Explain how a lack of data security and physical security can lead to undesirable consequences for people.

**11.** (a) Discuss the EFTS surveillance possibilities. (b) How may questionable activities by government organizations create a climate that restricts personal freedom?

**12.** In George Orwell's *1984*, Big Brother controls individuals through sensors housed in the two-way (send-receive) TV screens located in all homes, offices, and public squares. The sensors tune in on people and monitor their heartbeats. Recently, a young physiologist, seeking to measure the physiological activities of salamanders, created a delicate instrument that can detect and record from a distance an animal's heartbeat, respiration, and muscle tension. In all, Orwell described 137 "futuristic" devices in *1984* (which was published over 30 years ago). About 100 of these devices are now practical. Do you think that a democratic society has anything to fear from such technology?

**13.** "What one person may consider to be a privacy right may be judged by others to be an item of public concern." Discuss this statement.

**14.** Identify and discuss some of the legal controls that are available to restore some balance in favor of privacy.

## PROJECTS TO LOOK INTO

**1.** Identify a topic of interest in the field of artificial intelligence—e.g., game-playing programs, "thinking" computers, Turing's test, expert system packages, AI pioneers—and research the topic you've selected. Present your findings to the class.

**2.** Visit your library and identify an activity by a government or private organization that you believe may threaten an individual's right to privacy and prepare a report about it.

## ANSWERS TO FEEDBACK AND REVIEW SECTION

**15-1**

| | | |
|---|---|---|
| 1. j | 6. m | 11. a |
| 2. g | 7. n | 12. d |
| 3. k | 8. c | 13. f |
| 4. l | 9. h | 14. e |
| 5. b | 10. i | 15. o |

# Careers in Computing

In considering the impact of computers on people in Chapter 15, we've considered both the benefits and potential dangers of computer usage. One group that should obviously benefit are those hundreds of thousands of people who are working in computer installations.

Every issue of *Computerworld,* a weekly newspaper for the computer industry, contains many pages of "help wanted" ads with enticing captions (see Figure 15-A). These ads are aimed at finding people to fill the occupational categories presented in the following sections. As you read these sections, perhaps you'll find a path that will lead to future opportunities.

## Information System Managers

Like all managers, a *manager of a department* such as system analysis/design or program preparation must perform the functions of planning, organizing, staffing, and controlling. To be able to plan effectively and then control his or her department activities, such a manager must possess technical know-how in addition to managerial ability. But too much emphasis on technical competence at the expense of management skills should be avoided. Too often in the past, the most skilled technician was promoted to group manager only to demonstrate, very soon, a lack of competence in management techniques. It's likely that the larger the department, the more important managerial skills become in the total mix of skills required by a manager (Figure 15-B).

The *management information system (MIS) director* must also possess technical knowledge, for he or she is responsible for planning and controlling the information resources of an organization. In addition, however, the MIS director must:

### IBM has career openings in

**SYSTEMS PROFESSIONALS...
ADVANCE YOUR CAREER WITH
A DYNAMIC LEADER!**

**CAREER OPENINGS**
With
**World-Wide Travel Opportunity**

**CHALLENGING CAREER
OPPORTUNITY
IN
OPERATING SYSTEM
SOFTWARE SUPPORT**

**PHOENIX, ARIZONA
MIS OPENINGS**

The City of Phoenix has immediate openings in the MIS Department for well qualified persons in the following key areas.

Figure 15-A A small sampling of ads from an issue of *Computerworld.* Scores of ads covering dozens of pages were included in this issue.

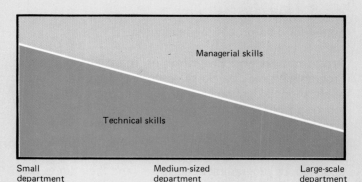

Managerial skills

Technical skills

Small department     Medium-sized department     Large-scale department

**Figure 15-B** Total mix of skills required by an information systems manager.

- Clearly understand the organization's purpose and goals, and its unique data processing needs.
- Be able to communicate with, motivate, and lead a number of highly skilled people.
- Possess the poise and stature to command the respect of other company executives as well as data processing employees.

People planning to seek a career in information system management should acquire a college degree. Courses in business administration, economics, personnel management, data processing, and statistics are desirable. And practical experience is also required to attain the maturity that's needed.

## Data Base Administrators

The data base in an organization and some of the functions of those who administer it are discussed in Chapter 13. The role of a *data base administrator (DBA)* is to:

- Establish a data dictionary that records company-wide data definitions and standards.
- Coordinate the data collection and storage needs of users.
- Act as a file design and data base consultant to others in the organization.
- Design the data base security system to guard against unauthorized use.

To perform these duties, a DBA must have a high degree of technical knowledge. He or she must also have the political skills needed to balance conflicting user needs, and the ability to communicate effectively with users who have dissimilar backgrounds.

Given this job description, it's not surprising that the DBA has sometimes been called the "superperson" of the data processing installation. Educational backgrounds vary, but a college degree that emphasizes data processing, management, and communications skills is appropriate. In large organizations, there can be several DBAs working under the direction of a manager of data base administration.

## Systems Analysts

The title of *systems analyst* is given to those who are responsible for analyzing how computer data processing can be applied to specific user problems, and for designing effective data processing solutions. Although there are often several grades of systems analyst (lead, senior, junior), the job consists of:

- Helping users determine information needs.
- Gathering facts about, and analyzing the basic methods and procedures of, current information systems.
- Designing new systems, integrating existing procedures into new system specifications as required, and assisting in the implementation of new designs.

Senior systems analysts are often chosen to act as leaders of system study teams (discussed in Chapter 12) and systems development project teams (mentioned in Chapter 14).

Analysts must usually be very familiar with the objectives, personnel, products and services, industry, and special problems of the organizations that employ them. They must also know the uses and limitations of computers as well as other types of data processing equipment, for they are the interpreters between users and other data processing specialists. They must understand programming basics and be able to determine which jobs are candidates for computer processing. In addition to logical reasoning ability, they must also have initiative and the ability to plan and organize their work since they will frequently be working on their own without much direct supervision. And they must be able to communicate with and secure the cooperation of operating employees and supervisors. Educational backgrounds vary, but a college degree or the equivalent is generally needed. Courses that have proven valuable to the types of

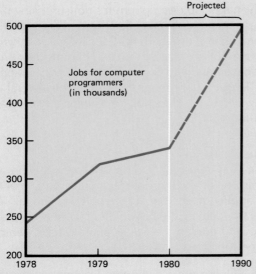

**Figure 15-C** Jobs for trained programmers are expected to double from their 1978 level of a quarter million to half a million by 1990. Others in high demand will be software engineers, systems analysts, and management-level personnel with computer knowledge, including data base managers and managers of information service systems. (Source: Bureau of Labor Statistics)

system analysts described above are the same ones mentioned for data processing managers.

## Programmers and Programmer Team Personnel

Programmers may be classified here into two categories: applications programmers and systems programmers. The job of an *applications programmer* is often to take the systems specifications of analysts and transform them into effective, efficient, and well-documented programs of instructions for computers. However, there are different applications programmer categories, and their duties can vary in different organizations. In some companies, for example, the duties of system analyst and applications programmer are combined into an *analyst/programmer* job. In other organizations, some applications programmers work primarily on new program development while others devote their time almost exclusively to maintaining existing programs. A single programmer may be assigned to develop a new program, or a team of programmers may be given the task. As Figure 15-C shows, job opportunities for programmers will continue to grow throughout the 1980s.

The organizing of programmers into *chief programmer teams* and *"egoless" programming teams* is discussed in Chapter 19. When chief programmer teams are used, a highly skilled *lead* or *"chief" programmer* is in charge of the team, another senior programmer acts as the chief's *backup programmer,* and a *team librarian* is assigned to gather and organize the records and documents associated with the project. Other applications programmers are assigned to the project team as needed.

The job of a *systems programmer* is to select, modify, and maintain the complex system software packages described in Chapter 13. Systems programmers thus perform a support function by maintaining the system software environment in which applications programmers and computer operators work. They also participate in decisions involving hardware/software additions or deletions.

Since programmer job descriptions vary, the educational requirements for these jobs also vary. A systems programmer is likely to need the courses offered in a computer science degree program or the equivalent in professional training. The educational background needed by applications programmers depends on such factors as:

■ The degree of separation between the systems analysis and programming functions.

- The complexity of the data processing systems in the organization.
- The industry in which the organization operates.

Completion of a 4-year college program isn't an absolute condition for employment in most applications programming groups, but the skills required from a 2-year college program are often needed.

Regardless of the educational background requirements, however, all programmers need the following basic skills:

- Analytical reasoning ability, and the ability to remember and concentrate on small details.
- The drive and motivation to complete programs without direct supervision.
- The patience and perseverance to search for small errors in programs, and the accuracy to minimize the number of such errors.
- The creativeness to develop new problem-solving techniques.

## Telecommunications Personnel

*Telecommunications specialists* are responsible for the design of the local-area and external data communications networks described in Chapter 10. They work with others such as systems programmers to evaluate and select the communications processors to be used in the network. The analysis of network traffic and the preparation of data communications software are included in their duties. They may also establish the standards for network operation. Nondata communications links used for voice and picture transmission are also likely to be included in their responsibilities. Like systems programmers, telecommunications specialists perform a support function. And also like systems programmers, they need a strong technical background.

## Computer Operations Personnel

As Figure 15-D shows, about 40 percent of the people in a typical MIS division in a large company perform computer operations functions. The duties of *computer operators* include setting up the processor and related tape and disk drives, starting the program run, checking to ensure

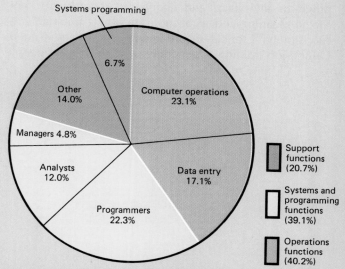

**Figure 15-D** How people are classified in a typical MIS division in a larger company. (Source: International Data Corporation)

proper operation, and unloading equipment at the end of a run. Some knowledge of programming is needed. Programs at some 2-year colleges are designed to train computer operators. But on-the-job training and experience are often all that's required to hold operating jobs.

*Data entry operators* transcribe data from source documents into a paper or magnetic media form that's suitable for input into a computer system. Skill at a keyboard is usually needed, and intelligence and alertness is required to recognize and correct errors. A formal educational background is usually not necessary, but careful on-the-job training is needed to minimize data entry errors. Data entry operators may be grouped together at a centralized site or dispersed at remote terminal locations. The demand for data entry operators at central sites is likely to decline in the future.

*Program and media librarians* are often found in the computer operations section. They have the very important task of maintaining and protecting the installation's programs and data. The documentation of programs and procedures is controlled by a librarian. Magnetic tapes and disks are cataloged, stored, and supplied to authorized people by a librarian. Computer operators and programmers must get a librarian's approval to check out programs and data, and charge-out records are kept. Media cleaning and inspection are also a librarian's responsibility. Clerical record-keeping skills are needed. On-the-job training is generally used to prepare people for librarian jobs.

Figure 15-E summarizes some of the possible career paths for those who choose opportunities in data processing.

**Figure 15-E** Some of the possible career paths in data processing. (Courtesy Honeywell, Inc., and General Electric Information Systems Company)

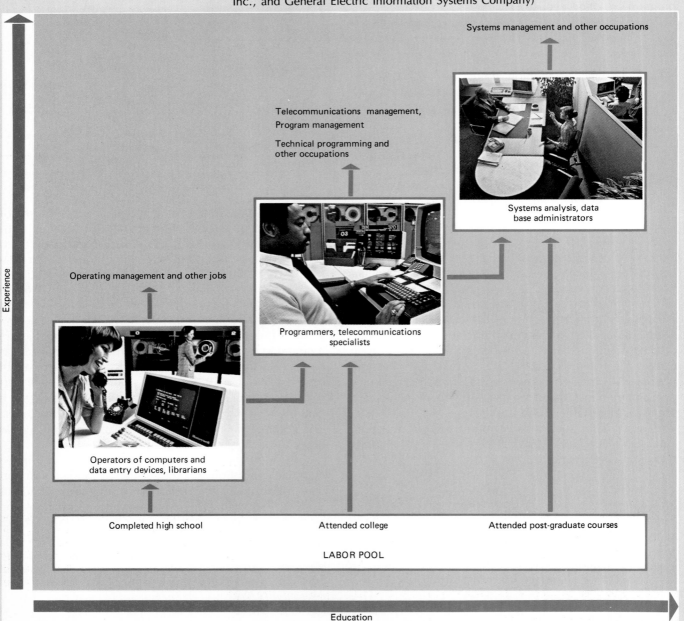

Experience

Systems management and other occupations

Telecommunications management, Program management

Technical programming and other occupations

Systems analysis, data base administrators

Operating management and other jobs

Programmers, telecommunications specialists

Operators of computers and data entry devices, librarians

Completed high school        Attended college        Attended post-graduate courses

LABOR POOL

Education

# The Impact of Computers on Organizations

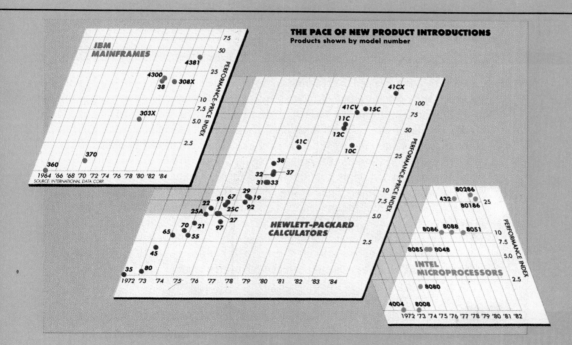

**THE PACE OF NEW PRODUCT INTRODUCTIONS**
Products shown by model number

IBM MAINFRAMES — PERFORMANCE-PRICE INDEX

HEWLETT-PACKARD CALCULATORS — PERFORMANCE-PRICE INDEX

INTEL MICROPROCESSORS — PERFORMANCE INDEX

SOURCE INTERNATIONAL DATA CORP.

## Product Life Cycles Just Aren't What They Used to Be

The challenge that managers face from technological innovation is apparent in these three products. From 1964 to 1976 IBM introduced only two families of mainframe computers. When the technology began to change rapidly, birth announcements came more frequently: four in the next four years. Hewlett-Packard did not begin selling calculators until 1972. But the technology evolved so quickly (23 models in eight years) that calculators entered their mature phase by 1980. Intel's microprocessors have been coming along so steadily that no life cycle has yet emerged. The performance-price index is a ratio of processing speed to introductory price for IBM mainframes. For the Hewlett-Packard calculators, performance is judged by the amount of memory and number of functions the model can perform. Intel's microprocessors are plotted according to performance (speed) alone because prices have fallen so sharply that if a performance-price index were used, some would have to be plotted off the page.

—FORTUNE Art Department, © 1984 Time Inc. All rights reserved.

423

In this chapter you'll see how organizations react to and may be affected by computer usage. We'll discuss the impact on businesses in the information processing industry itself and the effects of computer systems on other industries and organizations. The information in this chapter will enable you to:

▪ Discuss the rapid changes taking place in the information processing industry

▪ Outline how computer systems can affect productivity and security in organizations

▪ Explain how computers can be used in planning, decision-making, and control operations in the fields of government, health care, and education

# THE INFORMATION PROCESSING INDUSTRY

Computers have created a dynamic industry which produces and maintains the machines and supplies much of their software. The growth curve has been climbing so rapidly in the information industry that sales statistics and other measuring data become outdated almost as soon as they are gathered and published. Even during economic recessions, information industry sales have continued to expand. This is because computer systems can boost productivity in offices and factories and so customers of these systems continue to buy them to reduce their costs.

The latest figures available at this writing show that industry sales had grown nearly 20 percent from the preceding year, and total revenues for just the top 100 U.S.-based firms were over $80 *billion*. The revenues of Japanese and European businesses added additional billions to these figures. The industry leader is IBM with revenues of about $40 billion. The next 10 U.S. firms in the industry also had data processing revenues that topped the $1 billion mark.

## Chapter Outline

**Rapid Change Is the Rule**

Since it is technology-driven and subject to short product cycles and rapid obsolescence, the information processing industry is one in which *rapid change is the rule*. To illustrate:

- Company rankings in the top-100 group can change dramatically in a single year. In the latest year for which figures are available, 12 new companies replaced a dozen others on the top-100 list. The most notable upward movement in the rankings came from the makers of personal computers (one pc supplier jumped past 22 other top-100 companies).

- Tiny companies producing micro- and minicomputers have grown almost overnight into large $100 + million operations. And the fall of some of these firms has been even faster than their growth. For example, Osborne Computer Corporation was started, grew to 1,000 employees who were unable to keep up with the demand for its portable pc, achieved an annual sales rate of nearly $100 million, and then filed for bankruptcy—all in a period of just $2\frac{1}{2}$ years! The fortunes of the home computer division of Texas Instruments followed a similar roller-coaster ride in the early 1980s before TI decided to abandon the home market. Industry analysts expect that only a few of the more than 150 firms still in the pc market at this writing will be around by 1990. And some expect that IBM will account for half of the world pc market after 1986—and an additional 25 percent of this market, they say, will belong to firms making machines that will run the programs written for the IBM-PC family. But several newcomers don't believe these analysts and have formed new firms in just the past year.

- Large department store chains, independent computer retail stores, and software outlets are now stocked with products produced by the smaller pc vendors and software houses (Figure 16-1). But in addition, these stores are also selling pc products made by leading mini- and mainframe suppliers—a development that would have been considered most unlikely just a few years ago. Since stores typically stock only a few of the brands that are available, it's difficult for small manufacturers to acquire the shelf space they need to display their products.

- Competitive pressures aren't limited to the pc market. Large and well-financed companies such as General Electric, RCA, and Xerox have tried to compete in the mainframe market sector and have failed. Some smaller "plug-compatible" vendors of mainframes that run IBM software have been successful, but others have folded. And several companies that bought mainframes to meet the specifications of users and then leased these systems to the users have gone broke because technological change drastically reduced the value of the used computers they owned.

- Entrepreneurs with technical and managerial skills have started many small companies with money supplied by venture capitalists, have nursed these start-up operations into thriving businesses, have sold out to larger organizations at attractive prices, and have then started a second, third, or even fourth high-technology company. For example, Gene Amdahl left IBM to

**Figure 16-1** These days, buying a computer can be easier than buying a car. Several models are under one roof at your local computer store. (Courtesy ComputerLand)

form Amdahl Corporation, and his son Carlton was a founder of Magnuson Computer Systems. Father and son then worked together at Trilogy Systems Corporation—the second plug-compatible mainframe start-up venture for both of them. Similar examples are numerous.

■ Makers of integrated circuits are putting the mainframes of a few years ago on one or a few silicon chips. New semiconductor companies are regularly formed, and a premium is placed on innovation and being the first to reach the market with a new device. A "long" lead over the competition is often measured in a few months. And "silicon spies" quickly obtain new chips and analyze them for the competition.

■ Barely in existence a decade ago, the independent software sector of the industry is experiencing explosive growth. Software houses are now selling billions of dollars of off-the-shelf applications packages and operating system programs each year.

■ The merging of data processing, word processing, and data communications technologies has made competitors out of those firms that a few years ago were not considered to be included in the "computer industry." For example, the American Telephone and Telegraph Company has split off its Bell Telephone operating companies in response to a federal government antitrust action. Thus, AT&T and other previously regulated telecommunications organizations have now moved into the unregulated and competitive information processing industry.

■ Competition from Japanese and European companies is growing. The Japanese, for example, are aggressively promoting their pc systems and small peripheral devices. And they have embarked on an ambitious "Fifth Generation" national development effort to build the supercomputers that will run the expert system software they expect to create (see Chapters 9, 14, and 15 for more discussion of supercomputers and expert systems). To meet overseas competition, U.S. computer, communications, and semiconductor firms have launched a wave of joint ventures, research cooperatives, technology exchanges, and ownership agreements. For example, IBM has bought stakes in Intel (semiconductors) and Rolm (telecommunications), NCR has acquired an interest in Ztel (telecommunications), and Control Data has invested in Centronics (peripherals) and Source Telecomputing (telecommunications). In addition, a number of companies are supporting the Semiconductor Research Cooperative and the Microelectronics & Computer Technology Corporation (MCC).

**Summarizing the Effects of Change**

As you can see from the above examples, competition is strong in the information processing industry. Some small firms have become overnight successes in one sector of the industry. Some large businesses such as RCA have retreated almost totally from the industry. And some businesses such as Xerox have failed in one sector and have come back strong in others.

The speed with which new technology is being applied produces a complex and challenging competitive environment. The reaction time available to a firm to take advantage of new discoveries is constantly shrinking. The rewards are great for those that respond quickly and accurately to the information needs of users, but the penalties are also severe for those who fall behind. (The latest figures show that one company in the top-100 firms in U.S. industry was passed by 24 others in just one year.)

# SOME EFFECTS OF COMPUTERS ON OTHER INDUSTRIES

Computers are used in organizations to improve the quality and accelerate the flow of information, and thus to speed up and improve the performance of planning, decision making, and control activities. In many businesses, the planning and decision process begins with the setting of business strategies and long-term goals based on product and economic assumptions. These strategies and goals are then tested through the use of *market forecasting* techniques. The expectation of how many goods or services can be sold then becomes the basis for *production plans* (how and when to acquire materials and make the items) and *financial plans* (how and when to have the money on hand to pay for the items produced). This overall business planning and decision process is discussed in more detail in Chapter 14.

## Effects on Productivity

Economists tell us that the amount of goods or services possessing economic value that individuals can produce in a given time period—i.e., their *productivity*—is dependent on such factors as:

- The attitudes, health, and training of people.
- The abundance of natural resources.
- The amount of capital equipment available and the technological sophistication of this equipment.

Computers are sophisticated tools that can significantly improve productivity. And productivity gains, in turn, can lead to a stronger competitive position in the world. During the 1970s and early 1980s, the overall increases in productivity in U.S. businesses trailed the gains made in many other industrial nations. Thus, a concerted effort is now under way to apply computers in design and production processes in order to improve productivity. Let's consider here how **flexible manufacturing systems (FMS)** and **computer-aided design (CAD)** improve productivity.

**Flexible Manufacturing Systems.** Unlike a **fixed automation system** which follows a preordained series of steps to produce a product, a flexible manufacturing system can be programmed to alter its procedures to suit different production needs. For example, an FMS can produce several parts simultaneously, and it can also be quickly reprogrammed to handle design changes and produce new items. Since the robots used in an FMS can be switched from the production of one item to another simply by changing programs, it's feasible to keep FMS equipment busy by having

## ROBOTS AND LASERS

Of all the technological advances now boosting American manufacturing, no two are more exciting or potentially more versatile than robots and lasers. All the excitement stems from potential applications for these new tools.

Robots are moving from their initial uses on the factory floor literally into your living room—or kitchen (A). In fact, it's not at all farfetched to imagine a personal robot one day taking up residence in your home alongside—and perhaps controlled by—your personal computer (B). And while most robots, especially industrial robots, hardly look human (C), more and more robots are taking on a lifelike look. Remember watching *Star Wars* for the first time and meeting C3PIO and R2D2 (D)?

Today robots have been "hired" to perform thousands of factory jobs and programmed to perform tasks that are dangerous or boring for humans. Demand for increased robotics technology will continue to expand as scientific applications, such as undersea exploration or satellite repair, broaden into the realm of commerce. And who knows, someday you may be able to call on a robot helper to do your dishes or clean the house.

—Photos courtesy D&M Computing; Androbot, Inc.; and Cincinnati Milacron. © Lucasfilm Ltd. (LFL) 1977. All rights reserved.

**D**

**A**

**B**

**C**

**A**

**B**

**C**

Lasers are many and varied in their color, intensity, and usefulness. Since the development of a synthetic laser in 1960, potential uses for this awesome tool have multiplied endlessly.

Surgeons use lasers in the operating room (A); lasers weld car parts on assembly lines; the police use lasers to detect fingerprints where none could be recovered before. Lasers are precise measurement tools (B) and can assist in restoring fine art (C). There's no doubt too that lasers make the best light shows, entertaining people in some unusual places (D).

Since lasers harness light, which is a basic form of energy, their potential seems boundless. Consider the Industrial Revolution, which was made possible by the harnessing of another form of energy—steam—and think of what the future might bring.

—Photos © Chuck O'Rear/West Light.

**D**

it produce small quantities of a number of different customized and individualized items. Thus, small-lot manufacturing may become nearly as economical as mass production is today. In fact, computers and robots may reduce overall costs in small-lot manufacturing by more than 50 percent between 1980 and 1990. Many future "parts-on-demand" FMS production facilities may be able to turn out different products on different days or even different hours. The need to mass-produce large quantities of products in a single location may be reduced. But since the machines that will be used in future mass production operations will themselves be produced in small lots, the net effect is that they will be relatively less expensive, and so may be the prices of the items they produce.

**Computer-Aided Design.** Certain steps are generally required in the development of a wide range of items. These steps are (1) preliminary design, (2) advanced design, (3) model development, (4) model testing, (5) final testing, and (6) production and construction. All these steps are being facilitated by the use of computers. In the past, preliminary sketches, design drawings, and engineering drawings were usually prepared early in the design and development of new products and projects. When designers or engineers had a new thought, they would make some preliminary sketches to get the idea down on paper so that it could be analyzed more thoroughly. As the design was modified, additional drawings would be required. When the design was finally approved, further detailed production drawings were prepared. Thus, the preparation of drawings could occupy a substantial portion of the designers' time. And time spent at the drafting board was time that couldn't be devoted to considering other (perhaps better) alternative designs.

If you've read Chapter 6, you know that special electronic pens and graphic display devices now make possible quick changes and modifications in the sketches of an engineer. Once the initial drawings are finished and displayed to the engineer's satisfaction, the computer may then be instructed to analyze the displayed design and report on certain characteristics. Interactive communication between designer and computer may continue until a design with a desirable set of characteristics is produced. Such interaction between designer and machine is now relatively common. In addition, it may be common in the near future to have the computer prepare (1) detailed engineering blueprints from the stored design, and (2) control tapes that program automatic machine tools and robots to precisely produce component parts of new products according to the blueprint specifications. In other words, in such a **computer-aided design/computer-aided manufacturing (CAD/CAM)** environment, it may be common for the computer to interact with the engineer from the time of the initial idea until the final production step is completed.

Some current applications of CAD are in:

■ *Electronic circuit design.* Computers are now being used to assist engineers in designing circuits for other computers. Several hundred programs are available to help electronic engineers in their circuit design work. An engineer may define the circuit requirements, and then the computer develops, analyzes, and evaluates trial designs that may meet the requirements. A trial design may be modified by the engineer as required. The computer then analyzes and evaluates the modification. Computer-aided design is also used to plan the layout of integrated circuits, the location of circuit boards in the computer, and the ways in which these boards will be interconnected.

■ *Ship design.* Computers may do much of the detailed design work such as determining the positioning of hull reinforcing members, determining welding requirements, and generating numerical control programs to control the flame cutting machines that are used to shape steel plates.

■ *Aircraft design.* Aircraft designers working at a display can draw the shape of a fuselage and have the computer analyze the physical characteristics of the shape. They can also vary the position, angle, and length of the wings and have the computer report on structural strength and life characteristics.

■ *Highway design.* The Ohio Highway Department has a computer system that enables design engineers to quickly determine the social and economic impact of proposed road construction. The system permits engineers to consider factors such as alternate routes, amount of earth to be moved or added, number of citizens that will be forced to relocate, and construction costs of alternate routes. Aerial photographs are converted by computer into three-dimensional topographical maps. Proposed routes are then plotted on these maps, and a computer is used to evaluate the alternatives.

■ *Automobile design.* Automobile manufacturers are using computers to evaluate the structural characteristics of alternative designs. Engineers can "assemble" models of the components in a car and then "road test" the proposed car design on a simulated drive route. A chassis cross-member, for example, can be redesigned to reduce weight, and the effects of the change can be determined by a computer program. This design approach significantly reduces the costly and time-consuming process of making and testing a series of prototype parts until the desired results are obtained.

**Threats to Security**

If you've read Chapter 14, you know that businesses can be vulnerable to computer systems that aren't adequately controlled. In fact, there are organizations whose very existence has been threatened by computer system control problems. They have failed to design adequate controls to prevent theft, fraud, espionage, sabotage, accidental erasure of vital records, and/or physical destruction of important files. In one reported case, for example, an organization received a long-distance call from a computer operator who had failed to report for work. The operator was calling from a European city with disturbing news: He claimed to have the only tape of a vital master file and announced that he would return it only when the organization had deposited a large amount in a numbered Swiss bank account. His claim was quickly checked and found to be correct, and the ransom was reluctantly paid. Other organizations have been equally vulnerable, as you can verify in Chapter 14.

**Computer Systems and National Borders**

International airlines have reservation systems that cross many national boundaries, and international news agencies have worldwide information and retrieval networks. Stock quotation services have expanded to provide their customers with

"There's never a computer around when you need one."

up-to-the-minute quotations from the major securities exchanges in the free world. And engineering, extracting, and manufacturing companies link multinational facilities by computer-communications networks for planning and control purposes. Such broad networks may be expected to improve decision making and efficiency for the multinational businesses, but they may also increase the tension among nations and the companies that operate within their boundaries.

Nations claim sovereignty over the types of changes that occur within their borders, but rapid cultural, social, and economic changes may result from the operations within their jurisdictions of powerful multinational corporations using global technology. These organizations have found that computer usage has brought them into greater conflict with national governments. In the mid-1970s, for example, *The Reader's Digest* was denied permission by the Swedish government to process a large file containing information on Swedish households at a data center located in another country. Invoking their Data Act of 1973, which restricts the creation and use of data files on their citizens, the Swedes reasoned that permitting *The Reader's Digest* to export a large amount of information about Swedish citizens might invade their personal privacy and might also compromise Swedish national security.

At this writing, **transborder data flow** is a hot issue in Europe. Austria, Denmark, West Germany, and Norway have followed the Swedish example by passing their own data protection laws, and most other European countries are working on similar legislation. Many multinational businesses and many other organizations in the United States feel that these barriers to international data transmission are a form of trade restriction and an obstacle to the free exchange of scientific and cultural information.

# COMPUTERS IN GOVERNMENT, HEALTH CARE, AND EDUCATION

**Computers in Government**

Many of the public concerns of modern nations have become so intertwined with computer technology that the two areas are virtually inseparable. Computers are used in federal, state, and local governments for *planning/decision making, control,* and *law enforcement* purposes. For example, government agencies such as the Internal Revenue Service and the Social Security Administration have such large volumes of data to process in repetitive fashion that they *must* use computers (Figure 16-2). And law enforcement agencies and government space and missile laboratories need the quick-responding and accurate information systems made possible by computers. Let's look at how these and other applications are having an impact on government organizations.

**Planning and Decision Making.** Government planners have a mandate to effectively use public funds and resources in ways that best serve the needs of society. Unfortunately, policy makers have often been required to function in settings where the data available for planning are inadequate and/or inaccurate. They have thus turned to computer usage in the hope that higher-quality information will enable them to make better plans and decisions. Some examples of how computers are now being used for planning and decision-making purposes are discussed below.

*Environmental Planning.* **Technology assessment** is a phrase used in the federal government to refer to the evaluation of the consequences of technological change beyond short-term economic costs and benefits. Because many of the problems of environmental quality are the result of changes in technology, use of the technology-assessment concept has become increasingly important in **environmen-**

Figure 16-2 Computers are indispensable for processing the vast stores of data collected by government agencies. (Courtesy Social Security Administration and Internal Revenue Service)

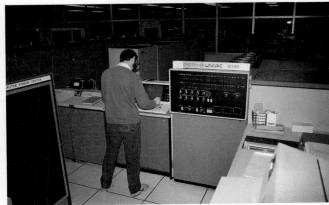

**tal planning** and in the protection of our natural resources. The National Environmental Policy Act requires federal agencies to include a detailed statement in every proposal for legislation or other action that significantly affects the quality of the environment. As a result of this act, greater emphasis has been given to the use of computers for ecological and environmental research and planning. To cite just two examples:

1. The Department of Health, Education, and Welfare has sponsored the development and use of a highly sophisticated computer simulation to predict the life-sustaining ability of rivers. In addition to analyzing existing river conditions, the model can also be used by planners to gain insights into the cause-and-effect relationships of water pollution so that preventive action can be taken to protect a river.

2. The Soil Conservation Service of the Department of Agriculture uses radio signals reflected from ionized meteor trails in the earth's atmosphere to relay data on snowfall and rainfall from sensors located at 160 remote stations in 10 Western states to central data-collection sites in Boise, Idaho, and Ogden, Utah. The data are processed by minicomputers at these sites, forwarded to the Conservation Service's Portland, Oregon, center, and then distributed to farmers, ranchers, and government irrigation agencies in the 10-state area. The data on the amount of snowfall in the mountains are particularly important to these agricultural planners because about 85 percent of the annual water supply in the 10-state area comes from melting snow.

This Navy fire control trainer system simulates realistic combat conditions including targets, coastal outlines, land masses, weather effects, and electronic counter-measures. (Photo courtesy Gould, Inc.)

*Military Planning.* Computers are being used increasingly by military planners. For example, they are used to *simulate wars*—i.e., to sharpen analytical skills and gain experience in decision making through the use of "war games." They are also used by military leaders for planning and controlling logistics—i.e., for managing the procurement, storage, and transportation of needed supplies and equipment.

*Planning Research Examples.* Computers are used by the federal government for research purposes in many agencies and for many types of applications. The Federal Reserve System is the nation's central banker. A member of its board of governors may use a computer in researching the tradeoffs between inflation and unemployment at given times prior to making monetary policy judgments. Or the governor may use the computer to research the concentration of banks in a particular market area prior to making a decision on a merger application.

By classifying, sorting, and manipulating census data, the Census Bureau can assist planners in weighing the needs and problems of whole groups or any segment of the population. For example, information about families living in poverty areas can be analyzed. Also, the computers can pigeonhole the massive national census data by state, county, or even city block if research and planning needs are served by such information.

The Department of Agriculture, in a joint effort with the National Oceanic and Atmospheric Administration (NOAA) and the National Aeronautics and Space Administration (NASA), is using *Landsat* earth-orbiting satellites to view the crop-

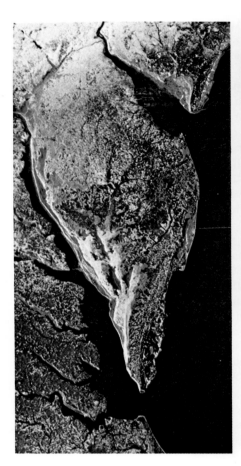

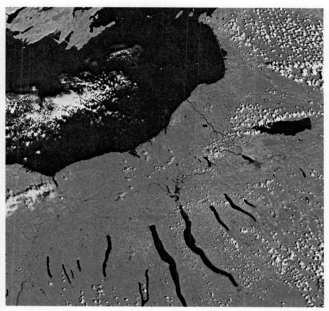

**Figure 16-3** Data from satellite photos are fed into computers and analyzed for planning and research purposes. *(left)* Two Landsat satellite photos are combined to show the ice patterns that have formed along the western shore of the Delmarva Peninsula. Factory smoke from the northeastern shore of the peninsula is also visible as the winds drive the pollution eastward. *(above)* An infrared photo of the Finger Lakes region of New York was taken from an altitude of over 500 miles by NASA's Earth Resources Technology Satellite. Healthy crops and vegetation show up bright red. Areas with sparse vegetation appear light pink. Clear water is black. Lake Ontario is at the top left of the picture, and the Finger Lakes appear at the bottom of the image. (Courtesy National Aeronautics and Space Administration)

lands planted in wheat and other grains in such important growing regions as the United States, the Soviet Union, Canada, Australia, and India. The satellite photos (Figure 16-3) allow planners to estimate the acreage under cultivation, and the worldwide weather data supplied by NOAA during the growing season permit them to develop computer-based crop yield models and make harvest predictions. A better foreign crop assessment capability is important to those who must make decisions about domestic agricultural policy.

At NASA's Goddard Space Flight Center at Greenbelt, Maryland, the Telemetry Data Processing Facility reduces telemetry data from over a dozen orbiting scientific satellites into proper form for study and analysis by scientists. Instruments in satellites perform experiments and transmit the results to earth. The data are received from worldwide tracking stations, are processed, and the information is forwarded to scientists located throughout the United States, Canada, and Europe. This information, in turn, adds to the storehouse of scientific knowledge, leads to plans for additional space experiments, and serves to reinforce or change existing scientific theories.

And scientists at the Laboratory for Applications of Remote Sensing at Purdue University have used a computer to analyze the multispectral scanner data obtained by *Landsat* satellites while passing over the Great Lakes region of the United States and Canada. Maps produced as a result of the analysis pinpoint industrial and agricultural areas that may be dumping pollutants into the lakes. Once pollution sources are identified, plans can be made to minimize further environmental damage.

***Congressional and Legislative Data Systems.*** Members of Congress and the state legislatures are expected to perform in at least three capacities: as *lawmakers* deciding on important legislation; as *responsible representatives* of their states or districts; and as *public servants* who will try to assist their constituents on both important and trivial matters. To perform these roles, they need accurate and timely information. Even though much substantive work is performed by working committees, each lawmaker must still do research, form opinions, and make decisions on scores of bills each session. It's not surprising, then, that representatives have voted on bills in the past without understanding all the implications of the legislation. In fact, it's a difficult task for lawmakers and their staff aides to maintain even the most rudimentary knowledge of the content and status of "major" legislation.

In Congress, a system called LEGIS records, stores, and provides prompt computer response to inquiries about the current status of all bills and resolutions. A SOPAD system provides members with an up-to-the-minute "summary of proceedings and debates" taking place on the floors of the House and Senate, and FAPRS (Federal Assistance Program Retrieval System) helps members determine what federal loans and grants can be used by their constituents.

And a number of state legislatures—New York, Washington, Florida, Pennsylvania, Hawaii, and North Carolina, to name just a few—make effective use of computers to index, store, process, and retrieve statutory material; draft bills; prepare roll-call vote reports; provide census population data for planning purposes; address mailing labels; and provide other information and services to legislators and their staffs.

***Social Welfare Planning.*** In social welfare agencies, as in other organizations, computer usage can be of value in administrative planning. For example, in the administration of one social welfare agency—Family Service of Metropolitan Detroit—computer-processed data have speeded up administrative analysis and improved program planning. Caseloads of social workers, median income of the families served, size and composition of families (presence of young children, aged dependents, etc.), family stress caused by such factors as divorces and unemployment—all this information is used by Detroit administrators to analyze the effects of possible changes in agency policies and services.

***Urban Planning.*** It's no secret that many urban planners are currently facing an explosion of problems. Traffic congestion, pollution, tensions within and between racial, ethnic, and economic groups, deteriorating public housing and other facilities—all these problems are facing many areas. Attempts have thus been made to develop more comprehensive urban information systems that would provide planners with the information needed to cope with these difficulties. For example, *traffic congestion* problems have been tackled by planners using computers to simulate traffic flow patterns. Variables such as the expected distribution of trips, the type of travel modes used, and the routes traveled are used to estimate the flow of persons and vehicles on transit facilities and roads. Various alternative transportation systems can be evaluated through computer simulation. In evaluating alternative traffic systems, however, the planner must take into consideration the interactions which exist between transportation systems and other aspects of urban life. All too often in the past, traffic planners have begun road construction without considering recreational, housing, and other alternative land-use needs.

The need to consider alternative uses of land as a vital input of detailed traffic models has, in fact, resulted in the development of local and regional **land-use models.** Included in land-use simulation equations are future expectations of population, employment, number of households, income, and distribution of available land for commercial and residential purposes. These data, in turn, can be used as input into traffic planning simulations. In the Washington metropolitan area, a computer land-use data system is used for planning. This system receives data from continuously updated files and is of value to satellite governments as well as Washington planners.

**Control Applications.** Computers are used by many government agencies for control purposes. The Internal Revenue Service, for example, uses computers to monitor the returns of individual and corporate taxpayers. Filed reports of interest paid to individuals by banks may be compared against interest income reported by the taxpayer. Without computers, such comparisons would probably not be possible. Computers may also be used by the IRS in randomly selecting and making preliminary audits of tax returns.

Computers are used for **environmental control** purposes. Federal agencies processing environmental data with the help of computers include the Air Pollution Control Office and the Water Quality Office of the Environmental Protection Agency, the National Center for Health Statistics, the U.S. Geological Survey, and the Department of Agriculture. States and cities are also using computers to evaluate and control the levels of pollution. To cite just one example from the many that exist, the Empire State System of New York collects water and air data from monitoring stations located at critical sites around the state. Data from the stations are automatically forwarded to a central computer. Each air-monitoring station reports every 15 minutes, and each water station transmits once every hour. Upon receiving transmitted data, the computer edits the message, sends any necessary operating instructions to the station, compares edited information to acceptable environmental standards, and, if standards are not met, sends an appropriate alarm message to either the Air Resources or Pure Waters Division of the Department of Environmental Conservation. Corrective action may then be taken.

Computers are also helping to *conserve* natural resources. California's State Water Project, for example, is designed to conserve water by moving it from surplus areas in northern California to needy areas in the south and west. Water is moved hundreds of miles through a network of canals, tunnels, gates, pipelines, pumping stations, and power plants. All these facilities are monitored by computers located at five remote control centers. In the event of emergency, a control center will quickly shut down the affected part of the system. For example, should a canal be broken by an earthquake, check gates in the affected section would be closed immediately to prevent serious loss of water.

**Figure 16-4** The FBI's National Crime Information Center network provides online access to law enforcement agencies throughout the United States. (Courtesy Federal Bureau of Investigation)

**Computers in Law Enforcement.** The Federal Bureau of Investigation makes extensive use of computers (Figure 16-4). The FBI's computerized National Crime Information Center (NCIC) is an automated nationwide **police information network.** Online terminals installed at local police stations are connected to central police computers in the states and to the NCIC computers in Washington. The central state computers are, of course, also connected to the NCIC network. Electronic direct access to the arrest records of people is thus possible in a short period of time. Obtaining such information can help federal, state, and local law enforcement officers make decisions about detaining, interrogating, and arresting those suspected of having committed crimes. The NCIC computers also store information on stolen property and wanted persons. More than 260,000 transactions involving fugitives, stolen property, and criminal history records are handled daily, and an average of over 1,000 positive responses (''hits'') involving wanted persons and stolen property are produced daily. Of course, as we saw in the last chapter, some concerned citizens question whether the issues of *individual freedom* and the *right to privacy* are being given proper consideration in the use of systems such as NCIC.

Three examples of the many law enforcement computer systems located at the state and local levels are:

1. Los Angeles County's Automated Want and Warrant System (AWWS) keeps track of those wanted by the police. In one case, a University of Southern California student was stopped for making an illegal left turn.

Law-enforcement agencies are finding lasers an improvement over dusting for fingerprints. Prints can now be detected on materials that used to be print-proof—human skin, leather, and even Formica. (© Chuck O'Rear/West Light)

Upon inquiry, the police officer found that 48 traffic violations covering a 3-year period were charged against the student and fines totaling $555 were unpaid. (But the use of AWWS has also resulted in some innocent people being arrested because they had the same names as those wanted for violations.)

2. The Law Enforcement Information Network (LEIN) at Michigan State Police headquarters contains online information about wanted persons, stolen cars and other property, and revoked or suspended drivers' licenses. A patrol officer can radio the license number of a car he or she has stopped or is chasing and can be warned to exercise extra caution if the car is stolen or if the occupant is believed to be dangerous. Police in Michigan cities are using terminals connected to the state system to see if arrested individuals are also wanted elsewhere. In one 24-hour period, Detroit police found that 17 persons they were holding were wanted in other jurisdictions. Of course, LEIN is tied into NCIC.

3. The New York Statewide Police Information Network (NYSPIN) has a central computer complex that serves hundreds of online terminals located in state and municipal agencies, criminal justice departments, the FBI, the National Auto Theft Bureau, and the Federal Bureaus of Narcotics and Customs. NYSPIN is also linked with a number of other computers including those at the NCIC, the National Law Enforcement Telecommunications System in Phoenix, Arizona, and the Department of Motor Vehicles in Albany. Most of the functions performed in the systems described above are available with NYSPIN.

## Computers in Health Care

You don't have to look far to discover reasons for the accelerating use of computers in health fields:

- There's a serious shortage of doctors, nurses, and medical technicians. By relieving scarce people of routine tasks, computers can help increase their effectiveness.

- Computers may make it possible for physicians and health scientists to conduct research that will extend the frontiers of medical knowledge. Without computers, some promising research couldn't be explored.

- Computers can help improve the quality of a physician's diagnoses on the one hand, and can help improve the control of important medical processes on the other.

- Medical knowledge is advancing rapidly. The ability to acquire and quickly apply new information may mean the difference between life and death. Computers are needed to retrieve relevant information rapidly.

Let's look now at a few *planning/decision-making* and *control* applications that are having an impact on health-care professionals and organizations.

**Computers in Medical Planning/Decision Making.** Applications of computers which have medical planning and decision-making implications include *computer-assisted diagnosis and research,* and *medical history preparation and retrieval.*

*Computer-Assisted Diagnosis and Research.* Some doctors are using the computer as a **diagnostic tool** in hospitals and clinics (Figure 16-5, left). At a number of "multiphasic" screening centers around the country, for example, patients are given physical exams consisting of a series of basic tests. Data from the tests may be fed into a computer in a separate operation, or the testing equipment may be linked directly to a computer for an automatic transfer of results. Once the data are received, the computer can compare test measurements against the standards established in the program. Within a few minutes after the examination procedures are completed, the computer output is ready. The test results are reported, and if they fall outside prescribed limits, procedures that should be repeated and/or additional tests that should be conducted may be indicated. The computer may also be programmed to suggest tentative diagnoses to explain abnormal test results. The patient's physician, of course, is responsible for the final diagnosis. The Kaiser Foundation Hospital in Oakland, California, is processing about 4,000 people per month through its 19-step physical exam, and Good Samaritan Hospital in Cincinnati has a successful multiphasic testing program. If you've read Chapters 14 and 15, you know that research in artificial intelligence has produced *expert system* software packages capable of diagnosing medical problems.

Computers are also being used for such diagnostic purposes as (1) displaying heart function on a terminal screen from motion-picture x-rays and calculating the volume and width of the patient's left ventricle—the heart's pump, and (2) deter-

**Figure 16-5** *(left)* Diagnostic testing aided by computer systems in a hospital. *(right)* Graphic display of a brain scan produced by a CAT scanner. (Courtesy Picker International; Dan McCoy from Rainbow)

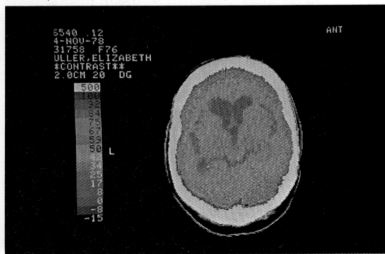

mining by means of a **computer-aided tomography (CAT) scanner**—a device that x-rays tiny slices of body structures and then combines the thousands of shots into a single picture—the area in the brain that has been damaged by a stroke so that the proper medication can be given right away (Figure 16-5, right).

In addition to being a diagnostic tool, the computer is also a *research tool* that's providing insights into:

1. *Causes and prevention of stroke.* A stroke usually occurs suddenly and is due to a disruption in the normal flow of blood in the brain. Statistical research to correlate many of the factors suspected of causing stroke is being conducted by the Iowa Heart Association. By isolating the most important causes of stroke, the researchers plan to educate the public on possible preventive measures and contribute information of value in stroke diagnosis and treatment.

2. *Patterns of drug addiction.* There's currently no agreement on the causes of drug addiction, nor is there any consensus on what constitutes a cure. However, the National Institute of Mental Health has a research program under way at 16 treatment agencies that will, it's hoped, shed new light on the causes of addiction and its treatment. Each of the 16 agencies assesses the effectiveness of its own efforts, and each agency supplies information to a data bank established at Texas Christian University. Data on addicts are obtained when they are initially admitted for treatment and at 2-month intervals thereafter. Computer analyses of the data gathered on several thousand addicts and their responses to different treatment approaches may lead to future plans for combatting the addiction problem.

*Medical History Preparation and Retrieval.* In developing a record of a patient's medical history, a usual practice is for the doctor or nurse to ask the patient a series of questions about past illnesses or health problems. This history-taking is a time-consuming aspect of the patient-physician relationship. Computers can be used to reduce the time involved and to tailor the questions to the patient's situation.

At the Mayo Clinic in Minnesota, Dr. John Mayne has developed a system that displays medical history questions and multiple-response choices on the screen of a terminal. The patient answers the questions by pointing to the appropriate response with a light pen. Medidata Sciences, Inc., in Massachusetts also uses a display terminal to project questions for patient response. The patient answers by pressing one of the five buttons opposite the most appropriate answer to the question. The computer is programmed to follow certain question paths depending on the answers received. For example, if the question is "Do you smoke?" and the answer is yes, several additional questions will be asked. If the answer is no, these questions will be omitted. After the patient has answered all relevant questions, the medical history can be printed out for the doctor's use, or it may be stored on magnetizeable or microfilm media.

Once the patient's history and medical records are available in machine-accessible form, they may be retrieved by the doctor as necessary for review and updating. Although the records of most people are currently maintained in file cabinets in doctors' offices, it's possible that in the future this record-keeping function will increasingly be handled by a computer data bank. With available technology, this data bank need not be located in a large computer complex. Any doctor could enter patient data into an office personal computer system for rapid online retrieval. These data could include type of ailment, level of severity, results of most recent examination, etc. When a patient moves, personal health records may be transferred to a new data bank, alleviating the need for completing a new medical history. Since the patient is often a poor transmitter of personal health data, the new doctor would probably have a more complete and accurate record available than would otherwise be possible.

**Health Control.** Control of the *physiological status of patients* and *laboratory tests* are among the many applications of computers in medicine.

*Physiological Monitoring.* Several real time computer systems are being used for patient monitoring. For example, patients who have just had major surgery and those who have recently suffered heart attacks are connected to computer-monitored sensing devices capable of immediately detecting dangerously abnormal conditions. If necessary, the system flashes a warning signal to doctors and nurses. At the Pacific Medical Center in San Francisco, the body functions of patients in the cardiopulmonary intensive care unit are continuously checked. And the heartbeat, respiration, temperature, and blood pressure of premature infants placed in the neonatal intensive care unit at New York Hospital–Cornell Medical Center are constantly being monitored by two minicomputer systems.

*Control of Laboratory Tests.* Some of the more successful applications of computers in hospitals are found in the laboratory. From the doctor's initial request for a test to the printing of test results, a computer may be used to monitor each step in the process. Automated testing may lead to greater accuracy and faster reporting of findings. Also, the information reported may be in a more useful format—e.g., abnormal results may be emphasized for special attention and compared with normally expected readings for those in the patient's age and sex category.

One example of a computer-controlled laboratory program is IBM's Clinical Laboratory Data Acquisition System, which enables hospitals to link dozens of lab instruments directly to a computer for automatic monitoring and reporting of test results. The system may, for example, collect, analyze, and verify data extracted from blood specimens by an automatic blood-testing device. At the same time, it can monitor the operation of the device to make sure that it's calibrated correctly. At the end of each test run, the computer prints the results for the patient's physician, for lab records, for administrative reports, and for patient-billing purposes. In addition to providing information that's accurate and timely, the system also reduces the time that technicians must spend on paperwork and instrument checking.

## Computers in Education

It's possible to consider the subject of computers in education in at least two ways. From the contents of this book, it's obvious that computer hardware and software can first be considered as *subjects for study.* Colleges have offered computer courses for many years. And the introduction of millions of personal computers into elementary and high schools in recent years has enabled those schools to also offer computer courses. The second way to view the computer in education is as a *tool to be used in the educational process,* which we'll consider now.

Computers can bring to the educational process such attributes as untiring patience, around-the-clock availability, and individualized and student-paced instruction programs. And their use *can* lead to improved student performance in thinking logically, formulating problem solution procedures, and understanding relationships. A look at a few applications in the areas of planning/decision making, control, computer-assisted instruction, and simulation can show us how computers are affecting educational organizations.

**Planning and Decision Making in Education.** Operating on the reasonable assumptions that differences exist between students, and programs tailored to the needs of individuals are educationally more effective than those aimed at "average" groups, some schools are seeking to plan and implement more individualized programs of instruction. Up to now, individualized instruction programs have been used primarily with gifted or handicapped students, and separate facilities and special teachers have often been employed. But the computer is a tool that may now permit teachers in conventional classroom settings to manage individual instruction programs. **Computer-managed instruction (CMI)** is a name sometimes given to this use of the machines. A properly programmed computer may help teachers manage a student's schedule of activities as the student progresses through a program of instruction. Educational research centers at such schools as the University of Pittsburgh and Florida State University are working on CMI projects.

At one elementary school participating in a University of Pittsburgh project, a computer is being used to make required day-to-day instructional plans and decisions. In the science curriculum, for example, a student may specify a particular subject he or she wishes to study. The computer may then be used to evaluate the student's background in order to determine any needed prerequisite lessons prior to beginning the study of the specified topic. Control Data Corporation's PLATO system (Figure 16-6) has extensive capabilities for implementing CMI in an industrial training setting as well as in public and private academic institutions. Sales training courses, for example, may be offered to salespersons through the use of PLATO.

Computers are also speeding up the scheduling of classes every term in hundreds of schools. Improved class scheduling procedures make it possible for school administrators to make better plans and decisions about the use of such resources as teachers, textbooks, and classroom space.

**Control in Education.** Two control applications of computers in education are found in the areas of testing and error analysis. In one area of *testing*—interactive **computer-assisted testing**—student progress can be determined quickly, students can get immediate feedback, and instructors can be relieved from having to grade the tests. To illustrate, at Dartmouth College randomized vocabulary tests in Latin may be taken by students. Sitting at an online station, students select the Latin lesson or lessons they wish to be checked on. The computer program may randomly select Latin words from the indicated lesson, and the students must then respond with the English meanings. If the students miss on the first try, they are given one more chance before the correct response is supplied. If they have no idea what the correct response should be, they can type a question mark and the proper word will

Figure 16-6 The PLATO system pioneered the use of computers in education. (Courtesy Control Data Corporation)

be presented. Of course, the computer is keeping track of the students' success (or lack of success) during the exercise. The stored results of computer-assisted testing may also be used for *error-analysis* purposes. The types of errors being made by students during testing can be analyzed, and suggestions for eliminating detected deficiencies may be supplied to the student and/or the teacher at the end of the session.

**Computer-Assisted Instruction. Computer-assisted instruction (CAI)** is a term that refers to a learning situation in which the student interacts with, and is guided by, a computer through a course of study aimed at achieving certain instructional goals. In a typical CAI setting, the student sits at a personal computer or an online terminal and communicates with the program in the CPU. Interaction may take place in the following way: (1) The computer presents instructional information and questions; (2) the student studies the information or instructions presented, answers the questions, and, perhaps, asks questions of his or her own; and (3) the computer then accepts, analyzes, and provides immediate feedback to the student's responses, and it maintains records of the student's performance for evaluation purposes.

The simplest and most-used form of CAI is the **drill-and-practice approach** that's designed to complement instruction received from teachers, printed materials, and other noncomputer sources. Student responses are given to factual questions presented by the computer (Figure 16-7). Learning is facilitated because the computer can quickly supply correct answers as feedback to student mistakes. However, new material is generally not introduced, and the student-computer interaction is highly structured so that little or no deviation from a programmed sequence of steps is allowed. The drill-and-practice approach has been found useful in learning areas such as mathematics, statistics, languages, reading, spelling, etc., where substantial memory work is required.

Figure 16-7 *(left)* Schoolchildren working in the computer lab. *(right)* Educational software called "Rocky's Boots" is an electronic erector set. The learner can explore basic computer circuitry and learn formal logic processes. (Courtesy Radio Shack, A Division of Tandy Corporation and The Learning Company)

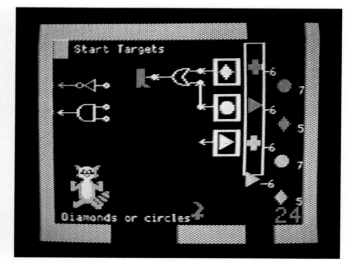

A second and more complex level of interaction between a student and a CAI computer program is found in the **tutorial approach.** With this approach, the program assists in presenting new material to the student. The intent of the tutorial approach, of course, is to have the computer program approximate the actions of a private and very patient tutor working with an individual student. Numerous branching opportunities in the CAI program permit a choice of materials to be presented, depending on how a student responded to the previous question. However, the student-computer interaction is still structured. The sequence in which information is presented is prescribed, and the expected student responses must all be anticipated by the program author. Tutorial CAI programs have been developed by Stanford University researchers for reading and elementary mathematics courses.

Two interesting applications of the CAI concept are:

1. The University of Illinois's use of the PLATO system at its Champaign-Urbana campus to help teach 150 subjects ranging from physics to Swahili. The PLATO system was developed at Illinois with the help of Control Data Corporation, and it's now being marketed by Control Data Education Corporation. PLATO delivers instructional materials in the form of text, drawings, and animated graphics. Users communicate with the lesson materials through the keyboard or by touching the screen. PLATO terminals are available on a number of other campuses.

2. The University of California at Irvine's Physics Computer Development Project, which enables students to control the timing of their progress through the introductory physics course. Different CAI modes are selected by students, and a management system keeps a record of student progress.

Some educators have resisted using computer-based instruction approaches that are new to them. And the demand for good, inexpensive CAI software always tends to exceed the supply available at any given time. But new and innovative software packages appear daily, and resistance has melted away because of these advantages:

■ Individual help is available to a student who might otherwise be ignored in a classroom.

■ By being able to privately move at their own pace, gifted children are not bound, slower students are not rushed, and shy students are not embarrassed.

■ The computer is impartial, patient, and objective, and the student gets immediate feedback to answers given.

**Simulation as a Teaching Aid.** Computers are being used for **educational simulation** in various fields.

*Physics.* High school physics students in Lexington, Massachusetts, have written a program that simulates an Apollo moon landing. The object of the program is to have a physics student land the spacecraft safely—an operation requiring the student to apply information that she or he has learned about gravitational effects and Newton's laws of motion. The simulation begins with the spacecraft traveling at a velocity of 3,600 miles per hour and at an altitude of 120 miles above the moon. Every 10 seconds a "radar" check is made and measurements are taken of velocity and remaining fuel. At this time, the student must tell the computer the amount of fuel to use during each of the following 10 seconds. A safe landing requires a touchdown at a speed of a tenth of a mile per hour or less, with an exhausted fuel supply. Most students "crash" on their first landing attempt and must go back and make calculations to support the decisions they will make on the next attempt. These calculations, of course, reinforce the physics concepts being taught.

Similar lunar lander simulation programs are now available for personal computers at most computer retail stores. In addition to its ASTRO lunar lander simulation, the Talcott Mountain Science Center in Connecticut has programs named POLLUTE (a water pollution simulation) and WEATHERWISE (a simulation to help students learn how to interpret weather data so that they can pilot a ship safely across the Atlantic Ocean from New York to Iceland).

*History.* History students may be paired up (one representing the North, the other the South) to make decisions about the tactics, troops, supplies, etc., prior to the beginning of a specific Civil War battle. The object of the simulation is to win the battle. Since the simulation program is based on actual Civil War conflicts, the history student is motivated to learn about the clashes because he or she will be "participating" in them. It's possible for an informed "Southern General" to defeat an uninformed Northern opponent at the Battle of Gettysburg. Elementary students in Yorktown Heights, New York, are also encouraged to take a greater interest in history by being placed in the role of the king of ancient Sumer. The "king" makes decisions about ruling the kingdom, and the computer acts as the king's prime minister and chief adviser.

*Forestry.* The School of Forestry at the University of Georgia uses a program to simulate a forest and the effects on the forest of various cutting practices. Students make decisions about tree harvesting and are thus able to test and put into practice concepts in forestry management that they've been taught.

## Feedback and Review 16-1

To test and reinforce your understanding of the impact that computer systems may have on organizations in society, place a T or F in the space provided in the following true-false questions:

___1. Sales in the information processing industry are growing at a rate that exceeds 100 percent per year.

___2. The information processing industry is technology-driven and is subject to short product cycles and rapid product obsolescence.

___3. In a reaction to overseas competition, U.S. computer, communications, and semiconductor firms have launched a wave of joint ventures, research cooperatives, and ownership agreements.

___4. Analysts in the computing industry believe that the total number of personal computer makers will expand significantly each year until 1990.

___5. Computers are used in organizations to improve planning, decision-making, and control activities.

___6. Productivity is dependent, in part, on the amount of sophisticated capital equipment that's available for use.

___7. A flexible manufacturing system (FMS) cannot be reprogrammed to alter its procedures.

___8. It's feasible to keep an FMS busy by using it to manufacture small lots of products.

___9. Computers can be used to help engineers design circuits for newer computers.

___10. An organization's existence can be threatened by the inadequate control of its information systems.

___11. Transborder data flow is a strong issue in the United States, but is of little concern to other nations.

___12. Computers are commonly used for ecological research and environmental planning and control.

___13. Computers are seldom used by the federal government for research purposes.

___14. Congressional and legislative data systems are designed primarily to print mailing labels for lawmakers.

___15. Land-use models are used by the National Park Service, but are of little use in urban areas.

___16. Law enforcement computer systems are located at fed-

eral, state, and local levels and are tied together by telecommunications networks.

___17. Computers and expert system programs are used to help doctors diagnose human disease.

___18. A CAT scanner is used primarily in research on the cause of strokes in animals.

___19. Computers are commonly used to monitor patients in critical condition and to control laboratory tests.

___20. CMI permits teachers to manage individual instruction programs.

___21. The simplest and most-used form of CAI is the tutorial approach.

___22. CAI usage has suffered in recent years with the development of personal computers.

___23. Simulations can be used to put students into challenging and entertaining learning situations.

# LOOKING BACK

**1.** Computer systems are obviously having a profound impact on the dynamic information processing industry that produces them. This industry is technology-driven, and its products are subject to rapid obsolescence. The competition can be fierce, and company positions in the industry can change dramatically in a year's time.

**2.** A concerted effort is now under way in industrial nations to apply computers in design and production processes in order to improve productivity. Computer-aided design techniques are used to speed up product development, and robots and flexible manufacturing systems are used during production. Several applications of computer-aided design are discussed in the chapter.

**3.** In addition to productivity and other benefits, however, the use of computer systems can also lead to difficulties. Organizations can be vulnerable to computer systems that aren't adequately controlled. And multinational corporations have found that computer usage has brought them into conflict with governments in some of the nations where they operate.

**4.** Government planners at all levels have a mandate to efficiently use public funds and resources in ways that best serve the needs of society. High-quality information is needed by planners to achieve their objectives, and thousands of computer

applications have been developed to supply planners with better information. Federal government decision makers are actively using computers in such areas as environmental planning, military planning, and research. State and municipal planners are concerned with such areas as social welfare planning and urban planning. Members of Congress and legislators are finding legislative data systems to be of value. The control function is being performed at all levels of government by computer systems. Conservation and environmental control applications by federal, state, and municipal agencies are discussed in the chapter. Millions of dollars have been channeled into the development and use of law enforcement computer systems. Many of these systems are tied together at the state levels, and the state systems are, in turn, linked to the FBI's NCIC system. Thus, a nationwide network of police data banks is now operational.

**5.** Computers and expert system programs are being used to assist doctors in diagnosing illnesses, and computer-assisted research is providing new insights into the way the body functions and into the causes and cures of disease. By placing the medical history of a patient in a data bank, one or more doctors can retrieve and update it as needed. Better information about a patient's medical background should enable doctors to do a more effective job of preventing potential health problems and detecting illnesses. Control of the physiological status of patients and control of laboratory tests are also important applications of computers.

**6.** Computers can bring to the educational process such attributes as patience, around-the-clock availability, and individualized and student-paced instruction programs. In computer-managed instruction, computers assist teachers in the administration of individual instruction programs. Computer-assisted instruction refers to situations where students themselves interact with computers and where instruction is presented or reinforced. Control applications of computers in education are found in the areas of testing and error analysis. In some subjects, CAI methods are well suited for testing student progress. The simplest and most-used form of CAI is the drill-and-practice approach. Computer simulations may be used as teaching aids. Students learn by making decisions and by learning of the consequences of those decisions. Theories can be put into practice, and valuable experience can be gained in a safe and inexpensive way.

## KEY TERMS AND CONCEPTS

**flexible manufacturing system (FMS) 427**
**computer-aided design (CAD) 427**
**fixed automation system 427**
**computer-aided design/computer-aided manufacturing (CAD/CAM) 430**
**transborder data flow 432**

**technology assessment 433**
**environmental planning 433**
**land-use models 437**
**environmental control 437**
**police information network 438**
**diagnostic tool 440**
**computer-aided tomography (CAT) scanner 441**

**computer-managed instruction (CMI) 443**
**computer-assisted testing 443**
**computer-assisted instruction (CAI) 444**
**drill-and-practice approach 444**
**tutorial approach 445**
**educational simulation 445**

## TOPICS FOR REVIEW AND DISCUSSION

**1.** "The information processing industry is one in which rapid change is the rule." Explain why this statement is true and give examples to illustrate your points.

**2.** (a) How may computers be used in market forecasting and planning? (b) In production planning and scheduling?

**3.** (a) Identify three factors that help determine productivity. (b) How can computer-aided design (CAD) improve productivity? (c) Identify and discuss four CAD applications.

**4.** Why do multinational corporations object to transborder data flow legislation?

**5.** (a) Discuss and give examples of how computers have been used for planning and decision making at the federal government level. (b) At state and local levels.

**6.** (a) What's a legislative data system? (b) For what purposes are such systems used?

**7.** (a) Give examples of ways in which computers are used by the federal government to perform the control function. (b) Give examples of state and local government control activities.

**8.** (a) What's the NCIC? (b) What functions does it perform? (c) Identify two other systems that are tied into NCIC.

**9.** Why is there an accelerating use of computers in health fields?

**10.** "Some doctors are now using the computer as a diagnostic tool in hospitals and clinics." Discuss this statement.

**11.** How can a computer be of value in physical examinations?

**12.** (a) How can a computer be used to take a medical history? (b) Would there be any advantages to a medical record data bank? (c) Would there be any possible disadvantages to such a data bank?

**13.** (a) How can a computer be used for physiological monitoring? (b) Discuss the use of computers in controlling laboratory tests.

**14.** In the 1970s, doctors found that the radiation therapy used to treat certain thyroid diseases in the 1950s actually caused thyroid tumors to occur at a later time in a patient's life. Similarly, high doses of diethylstilbestrol were later found to produce uterine tumors. (a) How could a computerized medical record retrieval system be of help in these cases? (b) Do the possible advantages of such a retrieval system outweigh the potential dangers?

**15.** (a) What is meant by computer-managed instruction? (b) What is meant by computer-assisted instruction?

**16.** Identify and discuss the two CAI approaches.

**17.** What are the advantages of CAI?

**18.** Discuss ways in which computer simulation can be used for instructional purposes.

## PROJECTS TO LOOK INTO

**1.** Consider the following case: A Decision Information Distribution System (DIDS)—a low-frequency radio network to warn people quickly of impending attack—has been under development in the Pentagon. If this system ever materializes, all citizens would be expected to buy a specially designed unit capable of receiving DIDS warning broadcasts. The DIDS would also warn listeners of impending floods, hurricanes, and similar emergencies, and would provide other services. Because of the warning functions of DIDS, the receiving units in the homes could be turned on *automatically* by the message-sending agency (the circuitry to do this is available). Under questioning by a congressional subcommittee member, a Pentagon delegate admitted that the DIDS receiver could also be converted into a *transmitter*. A subcommittee staff member has commented: "They'll ultimately decide to go ahead with DIDS because they'll be evaluating only its *technical* performance, not its *political* possibilities." Plans have been made to seek funds to install DIDS units on new radio and TV sets. A coast-to-coast network could be in operation in a few years. *Question:* On balance, is DIDS a good idea? Defend your answer to this question in a class presentation.

**2.** Visit your library and/or a computer retailer and identify three educational software packages. Prepare a report describing the purpose and characteristics of each package.

## ANSWERS TO FEEDBACK AND REVIEW SECTION

**16-1**

| | | |
|---|---|---|
| 1. F | 9. T | 17. T |
| 2. T | 10. T | 18. F |
| 3. T | 11. T | 19. T |
| 4. F | 12. T | 20. T |
| 5. T | 13. F | 21. F |
| 6. T | 14. F | 22. F |
| 7. F | 15. F | 23. T |
| 8. T | 16. T | |

# Micros Flood Campuses

Microcomputers are pouring onto campuses across the U.S. in rapidly increasing numbers. These powerful machines are being offered either at deep discounts or even free by manufacturers eager to get a generation of prospective future customers used to working with their equipment. Many educators see great potential in networking micros as well as in using them to enhance learning. If used well, they believe micros can change the way students learn; they can show how complex processes work, allow new kinds of lectures and interactive discussions, greatly improve writing skills, and encourage creativity. But the software—or courseware, as it is sometimes called—needed to tap the potential educational power of these systems is only beginning to appear. At the same time, even though many schools, especially the more prestigious ones, are paying bargain prices for systems, total costs can be quite high. Over the next five years, MIT and Brown will be spending over $70 million each.

The educators leading the way recognize that the success of these costly microcomputer experiments will depend on integrating the systems into a school's curriculum, rather than simply providing sophisticated toys for students. And that's "the most painful and difficult aspect of setting up a workstation system," says Dick Phillips, head of the Computer-Aided Engineering Network at the Univ. of Michigan.

Because techniques for teaching with micros need considerable development, each school experimenting with the systems is taking a different route, and will concentrate on different parts of its curriculum. Many are beginning with engineering and science courses, because it is easier to see potential applications of computers in these fields. The engineering college at the Univ. of Mich-

Some students come to college with a computer, and most schools are creating their own "electronic environment" on campus.

igan—one of the best in the U.S.—is leading the university in making advanced workstations available to all its students. A task force will study engineering core courses to decide how best to teach with micros. Producing software for liberal arts courses may prove even more difficult, and only a few institutions are concentrating on humanities. Brown is one pioneer; "The best way to ensure the systems' applicability to liberal arts is to participate in development," says William Shipp, director of Brown's Institute for Research, Information, and Scholarship.

The essential feature of new educational software will be interactivity, made possible by the speed and power of advanced micros. Any school that settles for traditional drill-and-practice routines may find that micros are simply new tools for memorizing. Interactive courseware, however, can change the way students think and work. Sophisticated word processing programs, for which micros are most commonly used, have improved students' ability to write. And other new software packages have far more innovative uses. They can demonstrate abstract concepts in such areas as physics and math. They can allow a student to experiment with several solutions to a problem. Lectures can be more interactive. Simulations can be run in real time, permitting a student to observe a process repeatedly or see the effect of variations.

One interactive program enables students to use on-screen windows to experiment with parts of the computer programs they're writing in a class at Brown. While students work, the professor is available to answer questions. Using the same technique, students in a poetry class supplement lectures by discussing poems via graphics-based workstations. A student can annotate a poem, read the instructor's comments on his work, see other students' responses, or retrieve related poems. And while watching a professor run a model on an IBM PC, economics students at U. Cal. Berkeley can suggest changes and see the results in real time.

Some of the most exciting applications, though, may arise from the development of interactive programs with artificial intelligence capabilities. Computer tutors incorporating AI techniques have been proposed at Drexel Univ. (Philadelphia) and MIT. These expert systems would be programmed to assist students who need extra help. The EE department at Carnegie-Mellon Univ. (Pittsburgh) is working on a program that will assist students in analyzing circuits. Creating such sophisticated software for the entire curriculum will require years of development as well as advances in artificial intelligence, says Jean Dexheimer, of CMU's Center for the Design of Educational Computing.

The electronic environment won't come cheaply. Although MIT and Brown are among those with the most extensive programs, all schools face steep expenses for microcomputer projects. Therefore students, universities, and manufacturers will share costs. Computer use fees, increased tuition, and even required purchases of micros will pass costs to students. Universities will seek grants

The next step is the electronic classroom where students use advanced technology to enhance their learning experiences.

and donations from outside to supplement their budgets. Manufacturers are offering discounts or even donating equipment.

University officials believe that micros are worth the price. Student demand for computer time and courses has been mushrooming; networks of microcomputers will give more of them access. And using micros should make students more productive, as well as improve the quality of their work. . . .

Most students have responded positively to the use of micros in courses. In fact, the micros give students a common experience that tends to draw them together instead of isolating and alienating them as some educators had predicted. Micros have spurred student creativity. In the poetry class at Brown, they increased students' writing output up to three times. Outside classes, the micros can foster entrepreneurship; students at Clarkson have bought printers, which they rent to classmates who don't want to go to central printing locations. Meanwhile social scientists at several universities are studying the impact of micros on social relations, learning, and scholarly habits.

Although most college micro projects are only beginning, the computers seem to be here to stay.

—Margie Ploch, "Micros Flood Campuses," reprinted with permission, *High Technology* magazine, March 1984. Copyright © 1984 by High Technology Publishing Company, 38 Commercial Wharf, Boston, Mass. 02110. Photos courtesy Apple Computer, Inc. and Tandem Computers, Inc.

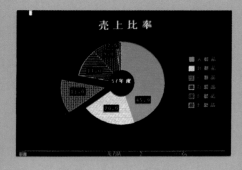

## Japan's Closing In

Japanese gains in the U.S. information processing market are advancing as aggressively as in the camera, automobile, and stereo industries, according to a recent research report. . . .

The report forecasts enormous gains in market share by Japanese exporters in certain segments. For example, among central processing units, the micros will jump from a 1 percent share of the U.S. market for Japanese manufacturers in 1983 to 30 percent in 1987.

Already, nearly half of the U.S. market for advanced memory chips are supplied by three Japanese companies: Fujitsu, Nippon Electric, and Hitachi. The Japanese have gained an understanding of the market through computer experts working and based in this country for years.

By 1987, Japan also will capture 45 percent of the floppy disk drive U.S. market and 35 percent of the dot matrix printer business, both up from present 10 percent levels. The copier market will go from 80 to 95 percent, and facsimile machines, from 54 to 85 percent in the next four years.

In PBX, the share will rise from 15 to 32 percent, and in software, from 0.5 to 23 percent.

—"Japan's Closing In," excerpted from *Office Administration and Automation,* copyright © October 1983 by Geyer-McAllister Publications, Inc., New York. Photo courtesy Fujitsu Microelectronics, Inc., Professional Microsystems Division.

In this chapter we'll speculate briefly on some of the computer—and computer-driven—developments that may be possible by the 1990s. We'll survey some possible applications of future computer systems. And we'll examine the technological outlook for computer hardware, software, and information systems, as well as their possible impact on people. The information in this chapter will enable you to:

■ Identify some of the possible applications of future computer systems

■ Discuss some of the possible developments in hardware, software, and information systems that you expect by the 1990s

■ Present the optimistic and pessimistic views about the future impact of computer systems on people

■ Form some opinions of your own on the future impact that computer systems are likely to have on society

# TOMORROW'S APPLICATIONS

Imagine this: Most families own computers, most doctors have installed computer-assisted diagnostic systems in their offices, and microelectronic implants have restored the sight and hearing of many handicapped persons. As Figure 17-1 shows, these are just a few of the technological developments and applications effects of computer systems that are expected before the turn of the century. We'll highlight some of these applications areas in this section. The applications presented here seem to be *technically* possible by the 1990s; whether they are all *socially desirable*, however, is another matter. Most of the applications that we've speculated on in

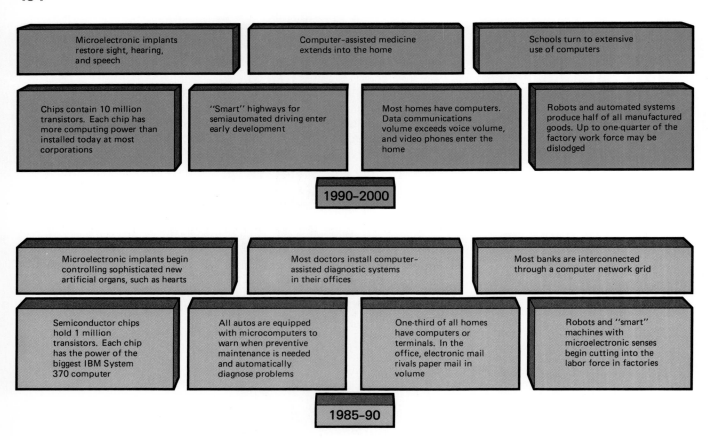

Figure 17-1 The coming impact of microelectronics. (Source: Adapted from "The Microchip Revolution: Piecing Together a New Society," *Business Week,* Nov. 10, 1980, p. 96.)

earlier chapters aren't repeated here. (Throughout this chapter, there may be terms that are unfamiliar to you that have been introduced and discussed in earlier chapters. You can locate unfamiliar terms by using the index at the back of the book.) The applications we'll consider have been arbitrarily classified into those which may affect people in *private life* and those which may have an impact on people in *organizations.*

**Applications That Will Affect People**

**Home and Hobby Possibilities.** A flood of microprocessors on small chips will have entered most homes by the 1990s. They will be used to control home appliances. Television sets will use them to perform automatic fine tuning and color-regulating operations. And inexpensive typewriters will duplicate the functions of some of today's stand-alone word processors by incorporating them for

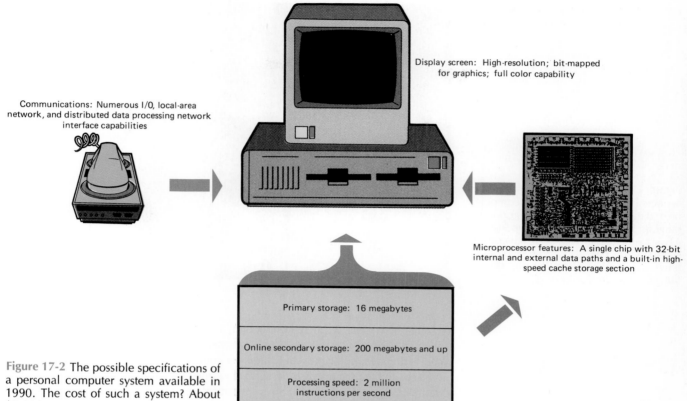

Display screen: High-resolution; bit-mapped for graphics; full color capability

Communications: Numerous I/O, local-area network, and distributed data processing network interface capabilities

Microprocessor features: A single chip with 32-bit internal and external data paths and a built-in high-speed cache storage section

Primary storage: 16 megabytes

Online secondary storage: 200 megabytes and up

Processing speed: 2 million instructions per second

**Figure 17-2** The possible specifications of a personal computer system available in 1990. The cost of such a system? About $7,500.

control, storage, and duplication purposes. The millions of personal computers found in homes today will have been discarded by the 1990s. In their place will be tens of millions of pc systems possessing the processing power and storage capabilities of many of the small mainframes in use today. These powerful systems (Figure 17-2) will be used for home recreation, education, and countless other applications (see Chapter 8).

For example, we've seen that videodisk players attached to television sets currently may use optical disks to provide viewers with up to an hour's worth of television programming for approximately the price of a phonograph record. Future home systems will *merge* videodisk players and powerful personal computers into a combination that can either include a television screen or be attached to a TV set. Videodisks for this "visual computer" will be sold in stores and may contain complete *interactive* entertainment, hobby, and educational sequences including computer programs, audio segments, and video materials. In short, an exciting environment designed to simultaneously stimulate the user's senses will be created. Home-delivered videodisks could someday supplement or replace newspapers and magazines with a more versatile product.

A more immediate impact on the print media, however, may come from the *videotex home system* that will emerge in the 1980s. Massive data bases including

Figure 17-3 Videotex home information systems link home terminals to computerized data banks to provide information ranging from stock market reports and news to theater reviews and advertising. Most systems can also be used for shopping and banking from home. (Reproduced with permission of AT&T)

the latest news and weather information, airline schedules, tax information, etc., will be stored in central computer systems. A page of this information will be requested from a home personal computer connected to a telephone or cable television line, and the requested page will be returned over the line to a receiving screen (Figure 17-3). If the viewer wants a permanent copy, the page can be printed by the home computer system. In short, users can browse through the electronic newspaper/magazine/encyclopedia, select the sections that interest them, and thus tailor the information to their individual needs.

In later years, a much higher percentage of the population may use their personal computers as *telecommuting stations* and may thus avoid the need to travel to central offices each day. Still later, the home pc system may be used to submit specifications to manufacturing facilities. Consumers may thus order their own custom-made clothes, cars, and appliances. And the more powerful pc systems that will be available in the years ahead will support what is likely to be an explosion of low-cost *expert system software packages* for consumers. As the user supplies input facts, the expert system responds as an intelligent assistant (or as a consultant with specialized knowledge) by giving advice and suggesting possible decisions. Thus, a consumer could receive expert guidance in personal finance, accounting, healthcare, legal, and many other areas.

**Telemedicine Applications.** Satellite communications between ill or injured persons in remote areas and specialists in urban areas should be in widespread use by the 1990s. Medical aides in remote areas can administer the emergency treatment recommended by a specialist backed up by diagnostic computing resources. Instrumented hospital beds in remote clinics may regularly be linked with computers and/or intensive-care monitors at an urban hospital.

**Applications That Will Affect Organizations**

**Computer-Assisted Manufacturing.** As we saw in Chapter 16, flexible manufacturing systems and computer-controlled robots are being developed rapidly. Tens of thousands of robots will be installed in worldwide assembly operations by the 1990s. Automobile workers will be working alongside robots capable of assembling components such as carburetors and alternators. In fact, in studies conducted jointly by the University of Michigan and the Society of Manufacturing Engineers, it's predicted that in just a few years:

- Half the human labor in such small-component assembly will be replaced.

- Production control will be automated to the point that 80 percent of all in-process technology will be computer-controlled.

- The 50 percent of the workforce remaining on the production floor will be the highly skilled and trained engineers and technicians needed to keep the automated plants operating.

**Automatic Meter Reading.** Many telephone companies have now installed computer-controlled testing equipment to check on the condition of telephone lines. By the 1990s, gas, electric, and water meters may be connected to these telephone lines so that as the system automatically tests line condition, it will also read the meters for the utility companies.

**Attending Meetings Electronically.** The material presented in Chapter 11 showed how an *electronic mail/message system* (EMMS) can now be used to permit "conferences" to be held at the convenience of the participants (Figure 17-4). Telephone and/or cable TV lines may be combined with computers in a future

**Figure 17-4**   This experimental videoconferencing system uses communications satellite circuits to link widely separated locations. (Courtesy GTE Corporation, Stamford, Conn.)

extension of this EMMS concept to provide an integrated voice-data-picture communication system for some organizations.

Witnesses could testify at government hearings without leaving their hometowns. They could go to a local courthouse and be sworn in; their testimony could be recorded and transmitted to the hearings room at the state or national capital. And if the increase in telecommuting activities expected by many analysts becomes a fact, the need to crowd together into cities may be reduced. Communities of interest and interaction may be linked electronically rather than by geographic boundaries.

**Educational Applications.** The same low-cost computer/television systems that will entertain and educate in the home by the 1990s will also be used in schools. More importantly, perhaps, these low-cost systems will lead to the development of innovative and much-needed educational software. Bright students will learn the subject matter and will help teach other students by writing educational programs at home and at school. Hobbyists (including teachers) with home computers will write programs with high educational value for their own children and will then share these programs with others. And clubs of computer hobbyists may make the preparation of good educational programs a club project. Future homework may consist of a student taking a floppy disk or videodisk home and playing it on the family system. Computerized educational systems will also play an important role in upgrading the skill levels of workers on the job. Control Data Corporation's PLATO computer-based teaching system is currently used by schools, but it's also used by many corporations. William Norris, CDC Chairman, believes that PLATO will be CDC's biggest and most profitable division sometime in the 1990s.

# TOMORROW'S TECHNOLOGY

Although the explosion in electronics technology is having a profound effect on such things as the way time and other variables are measured (with digital display devices), food is cooked (with microwave devices), and people are entertained (with home videotape recorders), we'll limit our discussion in this section to the outlook for computer hardware and software.

## Computer Hardware

**I/O Equipment.** In the *data entry* field, most keypunches and stand-alone data entry systems will be replaced by *multifunction online stations* that capture data at the point of transaction. By the 1990s, most of these stations will be able to perform *both* word processing and data processing functions. Of course, many organizations cannot convert overnight to online stations for transaction-oriented processing. Thus, *optical character recognition* (OCR) equipment will often be used to avoid the need to rekey data captured by nonelectronic data entry devices such as typewriters. The use of offline *multistation keyboard-to-disk-storage devices* for data entry purposes is therefore likely to decline gradually over the next decade. *Speech recognition* will become the preferred means of supplying input data to future com-

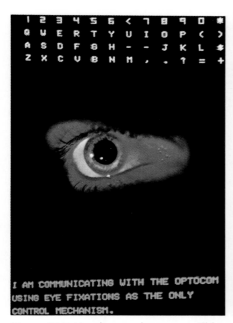

I AM COMMUNICATING WITH THE OPTOCOM
USING EYE FIXATIONS AS THE ONLY
CONTROL MECHANISM.

**Figure 17-5** Handicapped persons will be able to supply input data via systems such as OPTOCOM, which produces characters in response to eye movements. (Dan McCoy from Rainbow)

puters in a growing number of applications. And Figure 17-5 shows a system which permits severely handicapped people to control data entry solely by eye movements.

The speed of *impact printers* will not change much in the next few years. A booming market for the low-speed line and character impact printers used with personal- and minicomputers is assured. Improvements in dot-matrix character printers will result in output that's of full-strike typewriter quality. Multicolor graphics capabilities will be found in most of these printers, and their prices will continue to fall. *Nonimpact character printers and plotters* using inkjet and laser technology will be inexpensive and will give pc users the ability to produce variable typefaces and excellent graphics. New nonimpact printers in the 1,000-line-per-minute speed range will appear to challenge chain, drum, and band-type impact machines. Since these new printers will be much less expensive, they'll succeed in replacing many of the older "workhorses."

New systems requiring a great deal of archival storage will bypass printing altogether and make greater use of lower-cost *computer-output-to-microfilm* (COM) equipment. There should also be some cost reduction in *magnetic tape drives* in the next few years, and there should be a doubling in transfer speeds as the amount of data packed in an inch of tape doubles or even triples. Overall, however, the life cycle of magnetic tape may have peaked.

*Direct-access storage devices* will continue to be a hotbed of research activity for years to come. Such devices will be developed to provide virtually unlimited online secondary storage at a very modest cost. *Storage hierarchies* will continue— i.e., the fastest auxiliary storage utilizing the latest technology will be more expensive and may have less storage capacity than slower and less expensive alternatives. Mass storage approaches being considered by equipment designers include:

■ *Higher-density magnetic direct-access systems.* **Perpendicular recording techniques** (Figure 17-6) and other approaches that will significantly increase the density of data storage on a given disk surface are expected to be developed in the near future. It will not be long before the contents of over 600 books of this size can be stored in a disk device occupying the space of two small present-day floppy-disk drives. Over 15 million bits of data are currently being stored on a square inch of some disk surfaces. In the next six or seven years, there may be a tenfold improvement—to 150 million bits or more. The costs of disk storage will also drop dramatically. A 100-million-character hard-disk drive for personal computers will soon be available for less than $1,000.

■ *Optical direct-access systems.* Information may be regularly stored on a special optical disk (Figure 17-7). A beam of laser light is used to burn tiny holes or pits into a thin coating of metal or other material deposited on a spinning disk. Visible only under a powerful microscope, these holes are used in commercial television *videodisk systems* to represent images and sounds. A less-powerful laser light beam in a *videodisk player* is used to read the hole patterns and convert these patterns into audio-visual signals that can be fed to a television set. The same technology that's used to record and play back sound and images can also be used to store and

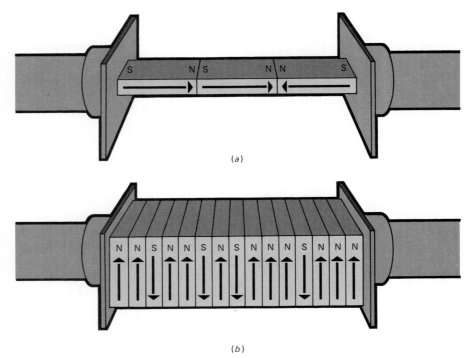

Figure 17-6 The perpendicular recording techniques now being introduced promise to significantly increase the density of data storage on a disk surface. *(a)* When the conventional horizontal recording approach is used, the bits of stored data resemble bar magnets lying end to end. *(b)* In contrast, the perpendicular recording technique stands the recorded bits upright in a crystal structure made from cobalt and chrome. (Copyright 1982 by CW Communications, Inc., Framingham, Mass. 01701. Reprinted from Computerworld.)

(a)

(b)

Figure 17-7 Optical videodisks have both industrial and commercial applications for storing and retrieving massive volumes of data. (Courtesy 3M)

retrieve data. The storage density of optical disks is enormous, and the storage cost is extremely low. Laboratory systems with the potential to store on a single disk the contents of a library of several thousand volumes have already been demonstrated. In the next decade, it's likely that many permanent archives now stored on microfilm and magnetic tape will be placed on optical disks. One small inexpensive disk will be able to replace 25 reels of magnetic tape.

Analysts expect that the nearly 8 million online terminals that were installed in 1983 will have tripled in number by 1990. Much of this growth is expected to be in the categories of *typewriterlike terminals* (or *teleprinters*), *intelligent visual display terminals* with graphics capabilities, and *specialty terminals* (see Figure 17-8).

Many of the teleprinters of the late 1980s, however, will have undergone considerable change. They'll be "intelligent" portable devices containing microprocessors and memory chips, and they'll be used in organizations to meet both word and data processing needs. As data entry stations, they'll be used to capture and relay facts to a distributed or host computer; as *communicating word processors*, they'll be used by people on the move to distribute (and receive) electronic mail and messages. And they'll also be used by participants in computerized conferences.

Intelligent visual display terminals will also be used for word processing and data entry applications. These terminals will often have color screens, and plug-in modules will be available to easily convert many of them into full-fledged personal computers. Personal computers are the *executive workstations* of choice in many

**Figure 17-8** "Traveling" terminals are among the millions of online devises in use today. (Courtesy Motorola, Inc.)

"Since 1962 the number of components per chip has increased by a factor of 100,000. We have learned that fundamental physical limits will not retard progress through this decade, and that we will continue to see near-exponential growth for at least another decade. In fact, I have no doubt that silicon integrated circuits will ultimately exceed tens of millions of components per chip . . ."

John S. Mayo, Executive Vice-President, Bell Laboratories

organizations today, and they usually are found lacking in one way or another. But the capabilities of these professional stations will have improved dramatically by 1990 with the development of *integrated applications software packages* and expert system programs. The proliferation in the number of these workstations will be accompanied by the creation of new internal *local-area networks* and new external *distributed processing networks* in many more organizations. Better *micro-to-main-frame linkages* will be a component of the improved communications infrastructure that may be expected.

Sales of such specialized data stations as *POS terminals* and *teller terminals* will grow rapidly in the 1980s, but by 1990 market saturation may cause a tapering off of sales to replacement levels. However, other specialized terminals such as those used in (1) security systems to read industrial and office badges, and (2) manufacturing data entry systems are poised for rapid growth. Hand-held portable terminals that will be linked to a computer by radio transmission will also probably experience enormous growth.

**Central Processors.** There will continue to be substantial reductions in the *size* of electronic circuits. The average number of components packed on advanced integrated circuit chips has grown tremendously every year since 1962. In the 1960s, for example, there were about 50 transistors on a chip. Then in the 1970s, 1,000 transistors occupied the same space. Now, the number is 500,000, and by 1990 each chip may contain up to 20 million transistors.

As suggested in Figure 17-2, many of tomorrow's *microprocessor chips* will be 32-bit devices with the processing capability of some mainframe models currently in service (Figure 17-9). By 1990, tens of thousands of bytes of high-speed cache storage may also be fabricated on a microprocessor chip. Personal computers employing such chips will be able to use the same powerful instruction sets as present-day mainframe models. And they'll be able to accept without modification the large libraries of software written for these mainframe families. The future pc storage and processing specifications outlined in Figure 17-2 describe many of today's mainframes. But by the 1990s, a typical mainframe processor will have much greater storage capacity, may execute over 70 million instructions per second, and may be packaged in a cubic foot of space!

*Greater speed* will accompany further size reductions. Scientists and engineers are working on several *primary storage approaches* that promise to be much faster than anything in current use. It has been found, for example, that if conventional storage devices can just be made small enough they'll enter an ultra-high-speed conducting state called *ballistic transport*. Some experiments with ballistic transport are replacing silicon with a semiconductor material called *gallium arsenide*. Supercomputer designers in the United States and Japan expect that these experiments and other breakthroughs will enable them to produce systems by 1990 that are 1,000 times faster than present models.

Regardless of the primary storage approach selected, tomorrow's supercomputers will also achieve higher speeds through the use of *new architectures*. You've seen in the "Architectural Differences" section in Chapter 1 and on many other pages that most of today's computers have *single* control, primary storage, and arithmetic-logic sections. Such computers are sometimes called **von Neumann**

**Figure 17-9** Processor size shrinks as capacity grows: a single chip smaller than a dime *(above)* may contain the comparable capacity of one of today's mainframe processors *(right)*. (Courtesy Motorola, Inc.; IBM Corporation)

**machines** (Figure 17-10*a*) because they follow the design approach developed by John von Neumann and others in the mid-1940s. (See the Closer Look reading following Chapter 1.)

A problem with the von Neumann machine is that instructions are interpreted and data are processed and stored in a single sequential stream. Since there's only a single channel to carry instructions from primary storage to the control section, and since only one data path is available between primary storage and the arithmetic-logic section, the processing speed is limited by the speed of the circuits in these channels. Like constrictions in the pipes feeding crude oil to a refinery, these channels can limit the amount of processing achieved.

But scientists are working now to produce faster, smarter, and cheaper alternative designs that will eliminate the **von Neumann bottleneck.** New supercomputers now have several powerful arithmetic-logic/storage systems under the control of a central computer (Figure 17-10*b*). And future supercomputers will be able to execute thousands of millions of instructions per second by harnessing tens of thousands (millions?) of micro-sized processors in *parallel assemblies* (Figure 17-10*c*). For example, Columbia University scientists are working on a ''Non Von''—i.e., non von Neumann—project to arrange a million processors in a branching, treelike structure.

In the meantime, instead of wiring individual chips together to build future computers, some designers have worked to densely pack the equivalent of 100 chips on a single $2\frac{1}{2}$-inch *wafer* of silicon. Such packaging could significantly reduce the costs and problems associated with chip interconnections. Although **wafer scale integration** was attempted and then abandoned at Trilogy Systems Corporation, the concept still has some appeal.

What about the *cost* of future central processors? You already know the answer to this question: For a given level of computing power, cost will continue to drop

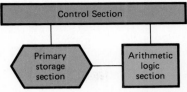

(*a*)  The von Neumann machine has single control, primary storage, and arithmetic-logic sections. Instructions and data flow over single channels, which limit processing speed.

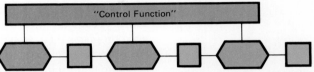

(*b*)  The new supercomputers that Cray Research Inc. and Control Data Corp. are building have several powerful arithmetic-logic/storage systems under the control of a central computer (the "control function" box shown here).

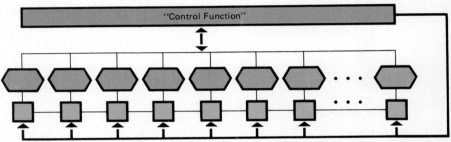

(*c*)  Future supercomputers will use huge numbers of processors in a parallel assembly, but it's likely that the overall control of these processors will reside in a von Neumann machine (the control function box) that performs like the conductor of an orchestra.

**Figure 17-10** The look of future computers.

| Year | Bits/Chip | Retail price/MB |
|------|-----------|-----------------|
| 1975 | 1K | $95,000. |
| 1977 | 4K | 37,000. |
| 1979 | 16K | 15,000. |
| 1981 | 64K | 6,000. |
| 1983 | 256K | 2,500. |
| 1985 | 1M | 1,000. |
| 1987 | 4M | 450. |
| 1989 | 16M | 200. |
| 1991 | 64M | 80. |

**Figure 17-11** Cost trends for 1 million characters of primary storage capacity in the central processor.

like a brick. The cost of primary storage in a CPU represents a significant part of the total cost. Figure 17-11 shows the cost trends for 1 million bytes (a *megabyte* or MB) of primary storage. As you can see, the retail price per MB was $95,000 in 1975, but it's expected to be $80 by 1991! We're likely to see similar trends for other components in the CPU.

*Microprograms.* The subject of *microprograms* was introduced in Chapter 5. Such microprograms stored in *read-only memory* (ROM) devices are used to interpret the problem-solving instructions written by a programmer and to translate these instructions into steps that the hardware can accept. For years, microprograms have also been used to permit one computer to interpret and execute instructions written for a different machine. In other words, the microprograms (also called *stored logic* and *firmware*) will analyze and decode foreign instructions into the elementary operations that the particular CPU is designed to execute (Figure 17-12).

In addition to permitting one computer to *emulate* another, it's also feasible to use various combinations of plug-in microprograms with *generalized* central pro-

**Figure 17-12** A use of microprograms, or firmware, which is software substituted for hardware and stored in read-only memory.

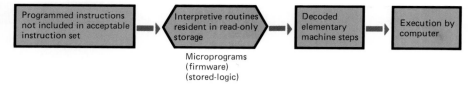

Programmed instructions not included in acceptable instruction set → Interpretive routines resident in read-only storage → Decoded elementary machine steps → Execution by computer

Microprograms
(firmware)
(stored-logic)

cessors to create custom-built systems for specific users. This "computer within a computer" approach can facilitate standardized CPU manufacturing and maintenance operations. It also makes it possible to convert software routines into microprograms that can be executed in a fraction of the time previously required. Furthermore, it's possible for vendors and users to *permanently* fuse important microprograms into ROM chips and thus, in effect, convert important software into hardware. Figure 17-13 illustrates how a computer manufacturer or user can create a customized computer system. Unlike the special-purpose computers of earlier years, however, the same processor can now be adapted to different functions by a simple change of microprograms.

Computer technology will probably make greater use of firmware in the future. By converting functions currently being performed with software into circuit elements (which are becoming less expensive), the need for some of the detailed programming currently being done may be reduced. For example, in performing its functions of scheduling, control, etc., the *operating system* (OS) software discussed in Chapter 13 uses storage space in, and the time of, the CPU—space and time resources that might otherwise have been used for data processing tasks. To reduce this OS overhead, resident microprograms operating at hardware speeds may be substituted for some of the tasks currently being accomplished at relatively slow speeds with a series of OS program instructions. Also, specialized microprocessors and microprograms are likely to be used frequently in the future in place of software for language translation, data security, and data manipulation and control. Chapter 10 shows how "front-end" processors are used to relieve a host CPU of data communications functions. In the future, "back-end" processors may also be commonly used to handle *data base management functions* (Chapter 13), and to control the movement of data between various storage elements in a storage hierarchy.

Instead of using microprograms and ROM chips to create custom-built systems for specific users, several chipmaking firms are now producing specialized hardwired chips that meet the exact specifications of their customers. In the past, the design of custom-made chips was a time-consuming and expensive operation that could be justified only when a large number of chips were needed. But in the future, new computer-based *design-automation systems* will allow customers to select the exact combinations of circuit patterns needed (logic gates, storage components, microprocessors) from a library of functional circuit blocks or **standard cells.** Since these specified cells will be automatically arranged and interconnected by the design-automation system, the design cost will be low and it will be economical to produce customized chips in small quantities. During the late 1990s, the design-automation systems in these "silicon foundries" will be using software programs called **silicon compilers.** The silicon compilers may enable a designer to enter a customer's functional specifications at one end of a small machine room and then go to the other end of the room to pick up the fabricated chips.

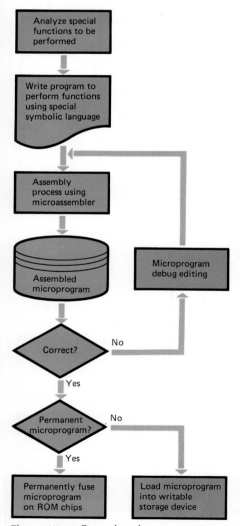

Analyze special functions to be performed

Write program to perform functions using special symbolic language

Assembly process using microassembler

Assembled microprogram

Microprogram debug editing

Correct? → No

Yes

Permanent microprogram? → No

Yes

Permanently fuse microprogram on ROM chips

Load microprogram into writable storage device

**Figure 17-13** Procedure for customizing a computer with microprograms.

We've seen that the traditional and still very popular von Neumann machine will give way in the future to *multiprocessor* systems in larger installations. Of course, the component micro- and mini-sized systems dedicated to performing the specialized functions such as data base management and security are likely to be smaller than those reserved to process user jobs in multiple and simultaneous streams. But future users—connected to such a multiprocessor system, perhaps, by intelligent workstations that further distribute and decentralize the computing power of the network—may expect faster, more reliable, and more secure service.

## Computer Software

There are numerous technical articles being published that predict with confidence the course of hardware development over the next decade. But you won't find this confident tone in the articles dealing with the future of software development. Perhaps this is due to the fact that the development of software will continue to be slower, more expensive, and more painful than hardware development because the functions performed by software are now (and will continue to be) more complex than the operations performed by hardware. Of course, as we saw in the preceding section, many of the functions now being performed by system software packages may be taken over by future hardware elements. And the future use of multiprocessor systems may *reduce* the need for complex *multiprogramming* software (Chapter 13) that permits instructions from several programs to be interleaved and executed on a single processor. In short, the cost trends for information systems will encourage the replacement of expensive software with cheap hardware whenever possible.

Don't interpret these comments to mean that there will be no progress in software development. On the contrary, existing *languages* such as BASIC, COBOL, FORTRAN, Pascal, etc., will be enhanced and improved to accommodate the *structured programming* approach discussed in Chapters 18, 19, and 21. Furthermore, new very-high-level software packages will be developed to solve particular types of problems so that nonprogrammer users can conveniently make use of computing capabilities. From the users' standpoint, the vocabulary of such packages will be more like their native English (or German, French, Spanish, etc.), and the packages will be *conversational*. That is, the computer itself will keep track of the acceptable vocabulary of a package, and it may display permissible alternate terms and statements to users in a "question and answer" format until the problem is satisfactorily formulated. The machine will then compute the answer to the problem. Thus, the users' major skill will be in their ability to state problems, and they will be assisted by a "dialogue" with a "user-friendly" computer system as it seeks to find out what they want to say. This is essentially the approach that will be followed by users as they interact with the *expert system software packages* discussed in Chapters 14, 15, and 16.

Conversational "fourth-generation" programming tools are a feature of some of the *data base management software* packages described in Chapter 13. The availability of such tools, and the creation of the *information centers* discussed in Chapter 14, gives end users a direct online path into an organization's data bases. In 1974, there were only about 1,500 true data base management systems in worldwide use. By 1990, however, there will be tens of thousands of these software systems in operation. They will be more comprehensive, and they will enable end users of the information to bypass the services of applications programmers and produce their own output to support their planning and decision-making activities.

Some managers will continue to use terminals in information centers to access the data bases. But a larger number may use *micro-to-mainframe linkage software* to call up data base information from their desktop personal computers. With many more pc systems linked to organizational data bases, additional provisions to ensure the *integrity* and *security* of stored information will be incorporated into future data base software as well as future hardware.

*Program development aids* such as structured programming will result in higher programmer productivity, shorter program development times, and more understandable and error-free program modules. And the trend toward the greater use of packaged programs will have to accelerate because of the shortage of the experienced and highly skilled in-house programmers needed to develop tomorrow's custom systems.

Many of the new packages will be written to perform *single* functions on personal computers and larger machines. But the development of more powerful pc systems will be accompanied by the creation of more flexible *integrated software packages* of the type discussed in Chapters 4 and 8. Combining several different functions (e.g., processing words, manipulating spreadsheet data, preparing graphical presentations) in a single package can help increase the productivity of pc users. In some of today's integrated pc packages (e.g., Lotus Development Corporation's *1-2-3* and *Symphony,* and Ashton-Tate's *Framework*), all of the function programs are built into the package by the designers of the package. In other pc packages (e.g., Apple Computer's Lisa/Macintosh Software, VisiCorp's VisiOn, and Quarterdeck Office Systems' *DesQ*), an *electronic desktop environment* is created that permits the user to transfer and integrate the data files created by several different programs written by one or more firms for a particular operating system. Both of these integration approaches will result in future packages that are much more powerful and also much easier to use. In addition, future pc users may not need to search for separate packages to perform graphic and external interface operations because such functions will be built into the pc's operating system.

The electronic environment is one approach to software integration. (Courtesy Apple Computer, Inc.)

# TOMORROW'S INFORMATION SYSTEMS

We're now in a period of transition between an existing industrial society that emphasizes standardized mass production and distribution and an emerging information/communications society that will carefully fit standard components together to produce highly customized and individualized configurations of products and services. The traditional batch processing computer installations used to good advantage in a standardized setting are economical, are well suited to many types of routine applications, and are going to continue to be used to process large volumes of information. But the trend toward a customized and individualized society will require future systems that will be *quicker responding* and *broader in scope* than these traditional installations.

**Quick-Response Systems**    We've seen that emphasis is currently being given to the development of:

- Distributed computer networks with logic and storage capability moved to the point of origin of transactions.

- User-oriented interactive software packages and tools designed to enable operating personnel to get information quickly without having to wait for the help of an applications programmer.

- New direct-access storage devices, online stations, and multiprocessor computer configurations.

These developments, in turn, signal a definite trend in the direction of quick-response systems that will give remote users immediate access to very powerful computing facilities. *Real time processing* will become increasingly common in those applications where immediate updating of records is justifiable. When the time limitations are not so severe, *online processing,* with periodic updating of those records which affect other users of a distributed network, will often replace traditional batch processing methods. Source data will frequently be keyed directly into the computer system, thus eliminating the need for input media in many applications. As we've seen, the same stations used to enter data will also be used as communicating word processors to distribute (and receive) electronic mail and messages.

With increased emphasis being placed on quick-response systems, there will obviously be greater use of *data communications* facilities. In fact, the transmission of data is expected to continue to increase by at least 35 percent *each year* between now and 1990. New data communications services will be established, and the current services offered by data carrier organizations will be expanded to meet this demand. Satellites will be used more extensively in space, and the *fiber optic* and *laser* technology discussed in Chapter 10 will be used in land-based transmission channels. When compared to costs at the beginning of this decade, telecommunications costs will be reduced by over 50 percent by 1990. When the use of fiber optic/laser channels becomes widespread, this technology will reduce enormously the cost of communications (Figure 17-14). At that point, an individual will be able to utilize transmission resources that only the largest organizations can now afford.

**Broader Systems**    Many of the quick-response systems that will be developed in the next few years will take a broader data base approach (Chapter 13) to the needs of the organization. Given the rapid growth expected in data base management software, this isn't a surprising prediction. The data base approach can be flexible: It may be used by organizations combining large centralized computers and a centralized data base with terminals located at the operating level; it may be used by organizations with a smaller central processor to maintain a centralized data base for a network of distributed personal computers and outlying intelligent terminals; or it may be used by organizations adopting some other alternative.

Regardless of the technical approach used, the trend in many organizations will be to define, classify, and store certain types of basic data commonly so that better

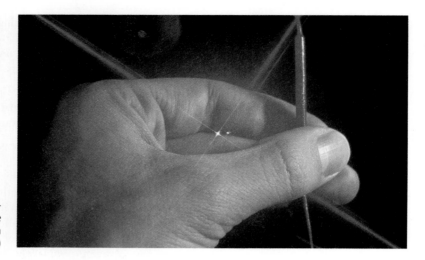

**Figure 17-14** Advancing optics technology will make telecommunications more powerful and much less expensive in coming years. (Photo courtesy Gould Inc.)

integration will be possible. The development efforts to produce data banks that will replace a multitude of the independent files maintained at the present time will probably continue at a more rapid pace in spite of the potential dangers to individual privacy. Why will this happen? It will probably happen because managers will have to respond to future changes that may occur at a much faster rate than in the past. Therefore, decision makers forced to make quicker choices involving greater risks will press for relatively complete information rather than settle for information in bits and pieces located in scattered files.

# TOMORROW'S OUTLOOK

### The Optimistic View

Optimistic forecasters believe that computer usage will result in greater freedom and individuality and a more human and personalized society. They point to many of the computer applications we've described here and in earlier chapters to prove their contention that the benefits to be obtained far outweigh any temporary difficulties and inconveniences.

For example, the computer-assisted manufacturing trends described in this chapter and elsewhere, and the resulting outlook for productivity gains, they are convinced, will lead to a higher standard of living, a shorter work week, and increased leisure time. And personal computers may be used to stimulate the analytical and intellectual abilities of people and add to their enjoyment of this increased leisure time. Of course, these optimistic views don't go unchallenged.

### The Pessimistic View

The pessimistic view of the future is that the effects of computer usage will not lead to greater freedom and individuality. On the contrary, pessimists can examine many of the same applications as optimists and come to the opposite conclusion that computer usage will:

■ Dominate our lives as a society and as individuals.

■ Sweep us along in a tide over which we—the harassed and exposed victims of a depersonalized and dehumanized process that places greater value on efficiency than on the more noble qualities of life—shall have little control.

Pessimists do agree with optimists, however, that computer-assisted manufacturing techniques will result in enormous gains in productivity. But the pessimists argue that when humans must compete with robots the humans will lose—they'll lose their jobs, they'll lose their security, and they'll lose their personal dignity. And pessimists can also see dangers in educational applications. For example, research has been conducted on the feasibility of installing voice-print analyzers into future computerized teaching systems. These analyzers would be able to determine the student's identity and also his or her mental stability and emotional state. Optimists say that this voice analysis will enable the system to determine if a student is unhappy, angry, nervous, or cheerful so that a teaching program may be selected automatically to respond in a more personal way to the student's mood. But pessimists are convinced that such monitoring of individuals, with the concomitant danger to privacy, is truly an Orwellian prophecy come true.

**A Final Note**     Is it possible in this last section to draw any conclusions from the many different viewpoints that have so often been presented in the pages of this Social Impact Module? Perhaps. We can conclude, for example, that there are at least three different contemporary views of computers and technological change:

1. *Computers and technology are an unblemished blessing.* This uncritical, optimistic view holds that technology is the source of all progress for the individual and society, that social problems will inevitably be solved through the application of technology, and that every new technological possibility will automatically be beneficial.

2. *Computers and technology are an unbridled curse.* This pessimistic view holds that technology increases unemployment, leads to depersonalization and bewilderment, threatens an individual's right to dignity and privacy, and threatens to pollute and/or blow up the world.

3. *Computers and technology are undeserving of special attention.* This unconcerned view holds that technology has been with us forever, and we are now better educated and more able than ever before to adapt to the new ideas and changes which it has brought and will bring.

Each of these views is deficient, although each probably contains an element of truth. The optimists are correct when they conclude that new technology often creates new opportunities for society. The pessimists are correct when they conclude that new problems are often created by new tools. And the unconcerned are correct when they conclude that social institutions (e.g., schools) can, and often do, play an important role in tempering the effects of technology.

## COMPUTER BEGINS A NEW ERA

The entire industrial era ran its course without the aid of the computer. This new organizing mechanism didn't come "on-line" until the mid-1960s. It didn't begin to exert a commanding presence until the early 1980s. The computer only caught the tail end of the industrial era. While it will no doubt be used in a myriad of ways to stretch out the remaining years of the industrial epoch, its real import has yet to be gleaned by the future forecasters.

The computer is the organizing mechanism for the age of biotechnology, just as the industrial machine was the organizing mechanism for the industrial revolution. Whereas the machine transformed nonrenewable resources into economic utilities, the computer will transform biological material into economic products and processes.

The computer is also the language of the biotechnical age. Every great economic period brings with it a unique form of communication. Hunter/gatherer societies relied on sign and oral language, while every advanced agricultural society had some form of written language. The printing press was used during the early stages of the industrial revolution. No self-respecting anthropologist, however, would refer to the Paleolithic period as an oral economy, or the Neolithic period as a written economy, or the Industrial Age as a print economy. Yet today's futurists believe that what lies ahead is the computerized information economy. They fail to understand that the computer and information sciences do not in and of themselves comprise the new economy. Rather, they comprise the organizing language for the new economy. They are the means of communication that humankind will use to reorder living material in the biotechnical age.

In 1981, the first computerized gene machine made its debut. One need only type out the genetic code for a particular gene on the computer's keyboard and within a matter of a few hours "the machine delivers a quantity of synthetic gene fragments that can be spliced together and put into the DNA of living organisms." With the gene machine it is possible to begin transforming living material into new designs and products in large enough volumes and with sufficient speed to provide a cost-effective starting point for the biotechnical economy. This, however, is only the beginning stage of the coming economic revolution. Eventually scientists hope to mesh living material and the computer into a single mode of production. Already, corporate funds are being channeled into research designed to replace the microchip with the biochip and the microcomputer with the biocomputer. According to James McAlear, president of EMV, one of the firms pioneering in this research: "Our aim is to build a computer that can design and assemble itself by using the same mechanism common to all living things. This mechanism is the coding of genetic information in the self-replicating DNA double helix and the translation of this chemical code into the structure of protein."

Within the coming decade, the computer industry and the life sciences are expected to join together in a new field—molecular electronics. Companies like Japan's Mitsui Corp. are already planning for the day by acquiring "a large stake in both biotechnology and microelectronics." The grand objective is to turn living material into biocomputers and to use these biocomputers to further engineer living materials. In the future, biocomputers will be engineered directly into living systems, just as microcomputers are engineered into mechanical systems today. They will monitor activity, adjust performance, speed up and slow down metabolic activity, transform living material into products, and perform a host of other supervisory functions. Scientists even envision the day when computers made of living material will automatically reproduce themselves, finally blurring the last remaining distinction between living and mechanical processes.

According to Dr. Zsolt Harsanyi, vice president of DNA Science, the day of the biocomputer is within grasp. He predicts that by the time today's babies reach adulthood, the biocomputer will be commonplace. The biocomputer represents the ultimate expression of the biotechnical age. By successfully engineering living material into an organic computer that can think, reproduce itself, and transform other living material into economic utilities, humanity becomes the architect of life itself in the coming age.

—Jeremy Rifkin, "The Other Half of the Computer Revolution," *Datamation*, May 1983, p. 262. Reprinted with permission of *Datamation®* magazine, © Copyright by Technical Publishing Company, A Division of Dun-Donnelley Publishing Corporation, A Dun & Bradstreet Company, 1983. All rights reserved.

No one is sure about the future effects on employment of technology advances. Computers have caused displacement. But has the development of the computer caused a larger number of people to be unemployed than would otherwise have been the case? In other words, have computers reduced the total number of jobs available in the total labor market? Two decades ago, Professor Yale Brozen, University of

Chicago economist, expressed the views of many of today's authorities when he wrote:[1]

> The reigning economic myth is that automation causes unemployment. It has only a slight element of truth—just enough to make the proposition plausible. Automation does cause displacement. A few become unemployed because of it. However, it does not create unemployment in the sense that a larger number are unemployed than would have been if no automation had occurred. . . . Many persons point to specific persons unemployed as a result of automation. What they fail to do is point to the unemployed who found jobs because of automation or to those who would have joined the jobless if new technology had not appeared.

A majority of economists today probably believe that (1) displacement must not be prevented, and (2) unemployment is best avoided by high levels of capital investment, unhampered mobility of capital and labor, and a continuing high level of technological progress. But a growing number of these same economists are joining Nobel Prize winner Wassily Leontief in wondering if investment in high technology can replace the number of industrial jobs likely to be lost in the years ahead. In spite of the growing uneasiness, though, the concensus seems to be that since other nations are committed to the concept of factory automation and the goal of higher productivity, our alternative to technological progress is apt to be economic stagnation and a declining standard of living.

Pessimists have definitely pointed out influences and possibilities that the concerned citizen should keep in mind. Many pessimists *don't* disagree with the optimistic position that computer technology *could* increase freedom, individuality, social justice, and well-being. But the pessimists doubt that the effort to increase social awareness and give adequate attention to necessary safeguards will be made.

The predictions of optimists or pessimists will become facts or fables if people make them so. We cannot know what people will do in the future. They *could* achieve the optimistic vision. But if in using computers they choose procedures that are impersonal and coldly efficient, they should not be surprised if the results are inhumane and inflexible. Thus, in the years ahead, it will be up to concerned and informed citizens who have an awareness of the potential dangers to see that the optimistic view prevails.

[1] Yale Brozen, "Putting Economics and Automation in Perspective," reprinted from *Automation* (now *Production Engineering*), April 1964, p. 30.

## Feedback and Review 17-1

In spite of the profound warning contained in an old proverb—"Prediction is difficult, particularly when it pertains to the future"—we've attempted in this chapter to briefly summarize some of the computer—and computer-related—developments that you may expect in the next few years. Topics relating to applications, hardware/software, systems, and social impact have all been considered. These topics, of course, represent the main themes of *Computers Today*.

Charles McCabe of the San Francisco *Chronicle* has noted that "Any clod can have the facts, but having opinions is an art." Since this chapter deals primarily with opinions rather than certain facts, there are no objective questions for you to answer here. After all, is the statement "A Non-Von supercomputer with one-million micro-sized processors will be offered for sale in 1995" true or false?

# LOOKING BACK

**1.** Dramatic developments are expected in the next few years in computer hardware. Some of the likely changes have been outlined in this chapter. For example, it's expected that central processors will become much smaller, faster, and cheaper. Personal computers available early in the 1990s will have the processing capabilities of many of the mainframes in service today. There's likely to be a tenfold improvement in the storage capacity of disk surfaces in the next few years. Distributed processing networks using intelligent terminals and pc workstations will gain rapidly in popularity. Some powerful future systems are likely to harness tens of thousands of microprocessors in a parallel architecture. And automated systems should make it possible for designers to select the exact combinations of circuit patterns needed to produce customized chips from a library of standard cells.

**2.** In the software area, new conversational packages and data base management software will receive greater emphasis. Much of the new software will be developed using structured programming concepts. And the sale of packaged software will grow at a rapid rate.

**3.** Future information systems will be quicker responding and broader in scope than the average installation in operation today. Data communications services will have to be expanded to handle the rapid increase in data transmission. A network of distributed processors and a broader data base approach will be frequently used to respond to the needs of organizations and decision makers.

**4.** The future uses of computers are viewed by some people with optimism, while others believe that computers and technology are likely to be the curse of humanity. Which view— optimism or pessimism—will prevail? No one knows. Predictions of each group will become facts or fables only if people make them so. An enlightened citizenry, aware of the dangers, can help bring about the optimistic version.

## KEY TERMS AND CONCEPTS

perpendicular recording techniques 459

von Neumann machines 461

von Neumann bottleneck 462

wafer scale integration 462

standard cells 464

silicon compiler 464

## PROJECT TO LOOK INTO

**1.** Select either a hardware/software topic identified in this chapter or a computer application topic of interest to you. Using recent periodicals and/or interviews with knowledgeable people, develop your own opinions about future developments in the field you've selected. Share your opinions and predictions with the class.

## TOPICS FOR REVIEW AND DISCUSSION

**1.** Discuss the changes that may be expected in the next decade in I/O equipment.

**2.** What changes may be expected in future central processors?

**3.** How will future hardware developments support (a) distributed processing networks? (b) Quick-response systems? And (c) data base systems?

**4.** Discuss how microprograms may be used in the future.

**5.** What changes may be expected in software in the next decade?

**6.** "We are now in a transition between an old industrial society and a new information/communications society." Discuss this statement.

**7.** (a) Are you an optimist or a pessimist about the future impact of computer systems on people? (b) Defend your answer.

# The CAD/CAM Revolution

What do shoes, bulldozers, artificial limbs, and airplanes all have in common? Answer: they are among the hundreds of items now being modeled by computer-aided design (CAD). Once merely an adjunct to the engineer's drafting board, CAD now enables manufacturers to build solid models of engines, to road-test automobiles, and to gauge the stability of offshore drilling platforms—all on a computer screen. But this is just the beginning. CAD, along with its companion discipline, computer-aided manufacturing (CAM), is advancing to the point where computers will soon handle nearly every aspect of a product's development from conception to production line.

CAD systems have come a long way from the original versions of 25 or so years ago. These were little more than computer-controlled plotting pens. Later the computers were linked to display terminals where a model of a part's shape could be used to make a drawing. Today's CAD units include an expanding array of software that permits such functions as geometric modeling, simulation, engineering analysis, testing, and interfacing with manufacturing, as well as automated drafting.

—John K. Krouse, "Automation Revolutionizes Mechanical Design," reprinted with permission, *High Technology* magazine, March 1984. Copyright © 1984 by High Technology Publishing Company, 38 Commercial Wharf, Boston, Mass. 02110. Photos reprinted with permission from Computervision Corporation, Bedford, Mass.

**The next stage.** CAD/CAMs baby cousin, computer-aided engineering (CAE) combines high-powered software with computerized workstations for the design of microprocessor chips and electronic systems. CAE is helping engineers conceive and develop electronic products, right up to chip diagrams and final production runs. Analysts predict a $1 billion market by 1988. (Photo courtesy Honeywell, Inc.)

# Programming

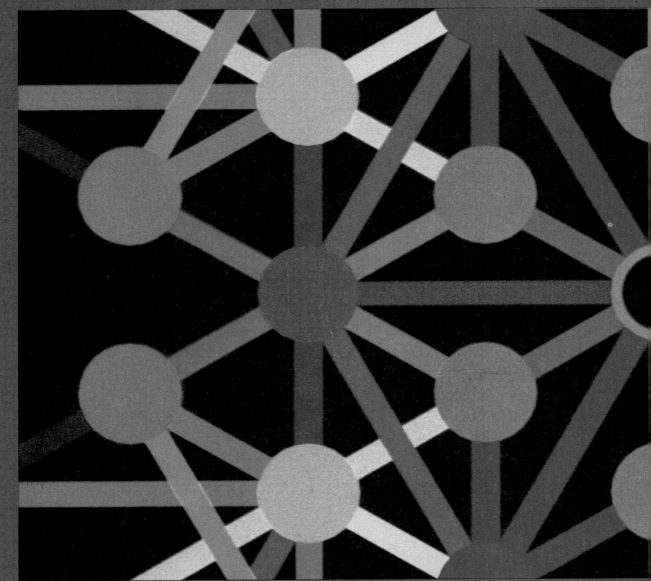

# module 5

In the Background Module, computer hardware was shown to be just one element in a computer-based data processing system. Hardware components and system development concepts are discussed in earlier modules. The focus of this module is on software development: the analysis and preparation of computer applications programs. The chapters included in this Programming Module are:

## chapter 18

# Programming Analysis

## Structured Systems Design and Development

The major advantage of this approach to software development is that the user is involved throughout the entire process. His participation ensures that his desires will be met and that there will be an understanding of what the system's capabilities are.

The next advantage is that this methodology affords great control over the software development process. Every step has certain outputs expected and the step is not considered completed unless the outputs have been presented and approved by the users and peers in the systems and programming group. And if someone should leave the staff, the project will not be substantially delayed. The new person can review the documentation of the previous steps and continue the project.

Finally, by following the methodology, one is assured of achieving a high-quality software product. This result will pay repeated benefits as it becomes necessary to maintain and enhance the software over its lifetime.

The major disadvantage of structured system development is that one is still developing systems from scratch. All the high costs associated with this kind of effort will be experienced. Also, there is a heavy time commitment required by the user. In many projects, the user must assign people full time to participate in the development effort.

The methodology has to be performed by trained, experienced people. Valuable staff members may have to be taken away from other projects and a good deal of money spent on training. Even with all the training, there is no assurance that the people will understand and adopt the concepts involved.

Finally, since the system will be built in-house, it will have to be maintained in-house.

—Mike Ruggera, "Four Tools to Build Systems Synergy," *Computerworld*, Oct. 31, 1983, p. 17. Copyright 1983 by CW Communications, Inc., Framingham, Mass. Photo courtesy ITT Information Systems.

This chapter is the first of four that deal with analyzing and preparing computer applications programs—the actual software development process. After a brief introduction to some program development concepts, you'll see how problem specifications are broken down into the steps that computers are able to perform. Program flowcharts are used to analyze a series of applications problems—all of which were introduced in Chapter 2. (Solutions for all these problems are coded later in Chapter 20.) The final pages of the chapter then give you a summary of the logic structures used in programs, and introduce you to two other programming analysis tools. The information in this chapter will enable you to:

■ Define the programming process and understand program development

■ Identify the basic symbols used in program flowcharts, construct a simple chart to meet a set of problem specifications, and outline the benefits and limitations of flowcharts

■ Create the logic needed to process multiple records and understand the use of accumulators and counters

■ Summarize the structured logic patterns used to solve problems

■ Identify and discuss alternative analysis tools that may be used to replace or supplement program flowcharts.

## Chapter Outline

# SOFTWARE DEVELOPMENT: AN ORIENTATION

You'll recall from Chapter 3 that to perform useful work with a computer, people must generally follow a specific series of steps:

1. ***Define the need.*** The particular problem(s) to be solved, or the tasks to be accomplished, must be clearly defined. A personal computer (pc) user may work alone to complete this step and others in the software development process. But in organizations, managers, employees, and data processing specialists often work together to identify the need and set goals.

2. ***System analysis.*** Data pertaining to the problem(s) must be gathered and analyzed. In organizations, a study team comprised of information system users and one or more data processing specialists often collaborate to gather and analyze data about current data processing operations.

3. ***System design.*** The next step is to design any new systems or applications that are required to satisfy the need. Personal computer users and organizational study teams often prepare design specifications that include the output desired, the input data needed, and the general processing procedures required to convert input data into output results. As you saw in Chapter 3, it's often possible at this point for computer users to identify and select an available software package that will meet their needs. If a suitable package is found, steps 4 and 5 can be bypassed.

4. ***Programming analysis.*** If custom-made software is needed, programmers must break down the design specifications into the input/output, calculation, logic/comparison, and storage/retrieval operations required to satisfy the need.

5. ***Program preparation.*** The specific operations identified in step 4 must then be translated or coded by programmers into a language and form acceptable to the personal, mini, or larger computer system.

6. ***Implementation and maintenance.*** The coded program(s) must be checked for errors and tested prior to being used on a routine basis. Maintenance of program(s) refers to their periodic modification and improvement.

The **system analysis and design process** includes the *first three* of the six steps listed above. Further system analysis and design details are left to Chapter 12 in the Systems and Software Module. For our purposes in this module, **programming** is defined as the **process** of converting broad system specifications into usable machine instructions that produce desired results. But as Figure 18-1 shows, programming isn't just the program preparation or coding step. Rather, programming consists of the *last three* of the six listed steps. It's a challenging process that doesn't begin and end with the writing and/or keying of lines of code.

## A Program Development Approach

Part of the challenge of programming is that different programmers can, and do, use different strategies to develop solutions for programming applications. Regardless of the **program development approach** used, however, a programmer must answer a number of questions. The following checklist of these questions should be helpful to you as you develop your own programs:

1. ***Have the problem specifications been spelled out clearly and completely?*** A specification to "Write a program to prepare customer bills" is not enough. Before the programmer can make any significant progress, the specifics must be available:

   ■ The program must print a number of bills.
   ■ Each bill must contain the customer's name, street address, city, state, Zip code, and net amount owed.
   ■ For each bill, the input data to be processed are customer name, street address, city, state, Zip code, quantity of a single product purchased, and unit price of the product.

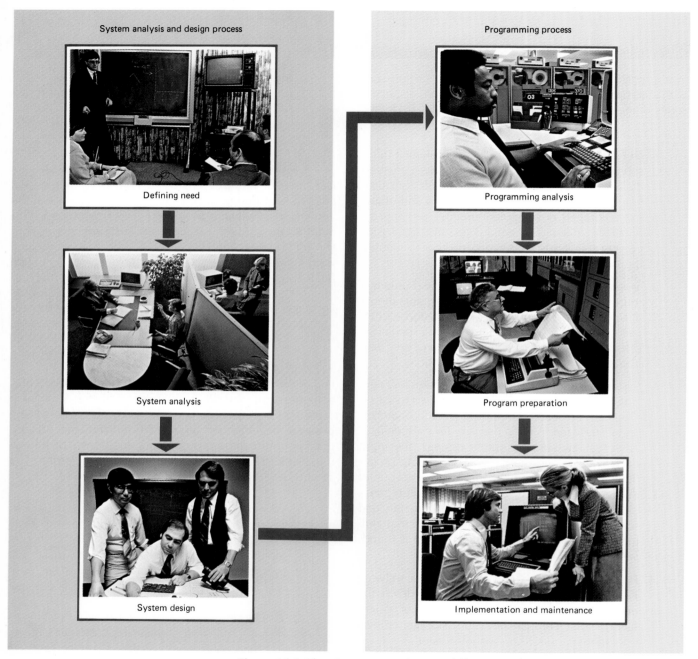

System analysis and design process

Defining need

System analysis

System design

Programming process

Programming analysis

Program preparation

Implementation and maintenance

**Figure 18-1** The six steps people must follow in order to use computers for useful purposes may be classified into system analysis/design and programming stages. The chapters in this module deal with the three steps in the programming process. Details of system analysis/design are presented in the Systems and Software Module. (Photos courtesy Hewlett-Packard Company; Honeywell, Inc.; Teletype Corporation; General Electric Information Systems Company; Edith G. Haun/Stock, Boston; and Control Data Corporation)

2. *Am I familiar with a solution method that will solve the problem?* An **algorithm** is a finite number of step-by-step directions that are sure to solve a particular type of problem. The algorithm to compute the acreage in a rectangular lot, for example, consists of the following steps: *(a)* Multiply the length (in feet) of the lot by the width (in feet) of the lot to get the square footage of the property, and *(b)* divide this square footage figure by 43,560—the number of square feet in an acre—to get the acreage of the property. When a programmer has personal knowledge of an algorithm or procedure that will solve the problem at hand, the solution may then be coded in a selected language. If this isn't the case, the next question should be considered.

3. *Can I locate a solution method to solve the problem from other people or from books or journals?* Full or partial solutions to problem situations are often available. After all, the programmer who's given the task of writing a billing program today is certainly not the first one to have faced that problem. If other resources can provide the solution method, the necessary program may then be coded in a selected language. If a solution method is unavailable, the next question must be considered.

4. *How can I develop an algorithm or procedure that will solve this problem?* This is the creative problem-solving question that often challenges programmers. An effective approach to follow in the programming analysis stage of program development is to *break down a large* (and seemingly unmanageable) *problem into a series of smaller and more understandable tasks* or subproblems. Each of the above questions in the checklist can

then be applied to the individual subproblems. For example, the revised billing program specification listed in question 1 can be broken down into the following major tasks:

**(a)** Enter customer name, local address, city, state, Zip code, quantity purchased, and unit price into the CPU.

**(b)** Compute net amount owed by customer.

**(c)** Print customer name, local address, city, state, Zip code, and net amount owed.

**(d)** If there's another bill to process, branch program control back to **a.** Otherwise, continue to next task.

**(e)** Stop processing.

In many (perhaps most) cases, it will be desirable to break some of the initially identified tasks into still smaller units. For example, task **b** must be refined as follows:

**(b)** Compute net amount owed by customer.

**(b1)** Compute net amount owed by the formula $A = Q \times P$ (where A is net amount, Q is quantity purchased, and P is unit price).

The programming analysis stage continues until *every* small task or subproblem has been reduced to the point that the programmer is confident he or she does have a solution method that will solve the task. Effective program coding can begin only after the programmer has this confidence. Note that it's not necessary that the first solution method be *the* best possible method. Improvements can often be added to functioning programs, and the best possible method may never be discovered.

A number of programming analysis tools are available to help the programmer break a problem down into smaller tasks in order to arrive at a solution method. One frequently used tool is the program flowchart.

# GENERAL FLOWCHARTING CONCEPTS

You'll recall from Chapter 3 that a *system flowchart* provides a broad overview of the processing operations that are to be accomplished, but it doesn't go into detail about how input data are to be used to produce output information. A **program flowchart,** on the other hand, *is* a detailed graph that represents steps to be performed within the machine to produce the needed output. Thus, as Figure 18-2 shows, the program flowchart evolves from the system chart.

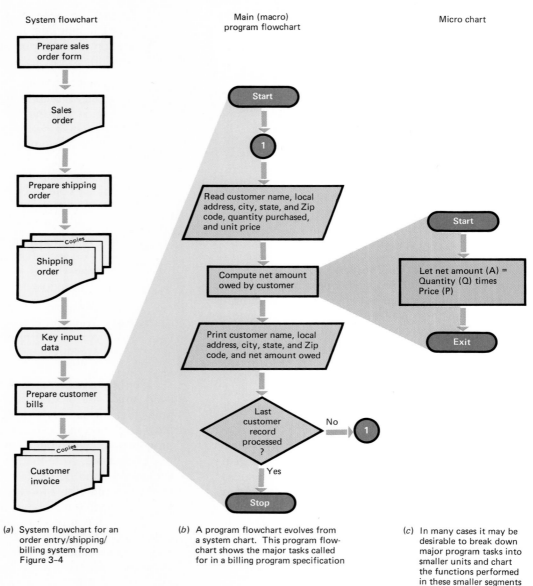

System flowchart      Main (macro) program flowchart      Micro chart

(a) System flowchart for an order entry/shipping/ billing system from Figure 3-4

(b) A program flowchart evolves from a system chart. This program flow- chart shows the major tasks called for in a billing program specification

(c) In many cases it may be desirable to break down major program tasks into smaller units and chart the functions performed in these smaller segments

**Figure 18-2** A program flowchart evolves from a system chart. In many cases, a main (or macro) program chart identifies the major tasks or modules to be performed, and then detailed micro charts are used to show the processing steps within specified modules. Thus, programmers may prepare one macro program chart and several micro charts during programming analysis.

## Levels of Program Flowcharts

There are no set standards on the amount of detail that should be provided in a program chart. The billing pro- gram outlined in Figures 18-2b and 18-2c could easily have been shown in a single chart. But as you've seen, it's often desirable in more complex situations to break major **program** segments or **modules** into still smaller and more manageable units. Figure 18-2c illustrates how a smaller chart can evolve from a higher-level chart. A chart that outlines the main segments of a program is called a **main-control, modular,** or **macro chart.** One that details the steps in a module is called a **micro chart.**

## Symbols Used in Program Flowcharts

Only a few symbols are needed in program charting to indicate the necessary operations. These symbols, which have been adopted by the American National Standards Institute (ANSI), are shown here and their descriptions follow. (Most of them have already been used in Figure 18-2, and many have been used throughout the book).

**Input/Output.** The basic **input/output symbol** used in system charts is also used in program charts to represent any I/O function. The special symbols designating disks, tapes, documents, etc., that are used in system charts are generally not used with program diagrams. In the program flowchart section of Figure 18-2, the same I/O symbol designates:

- The *input data* to be read into the CPU (customer name, address, quantity purchased, and product price).

- The *output information* to be printed on the customer's bill (customer name, address, and amount owed).

**Processing.** The rectangle used in system charts is again used in program charts to represent processing operations. Of course, the processing described in the rectangle of a program chart is only a small segment of a major processing step called for in a system chart. Arithmetic and data movement instructions are generally placed in these boxes. A **processing symbol** is shown in the micro chart in Figure 18-2c. The net amount of a customer's bill is computed by multiplying the quantity of a product purchased by the unit price of the product.

**Terminal.** The **terminal symbol,** as the name suggests, represents the beginning (START) and the end (STOP) of a program. It may also be used to signal a program interruption point when information may enter or leave. For example, to detect certain errors in input data, the programmer may provide a special program branch ending in a terminal symbol labeled "HALT."

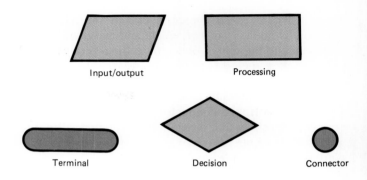

Input/output  Processing

Terminal  Decision  Connector

**Decision.** The I/O and processing symbols have two flow lines (one entry and one exit), while the terminal has a single entry or exit line. The diamond-shaped **decision symbol,** on the other hand, has one entrance and at least two exit paths or branches. This symbol indicates logic/comparison operations, and was used several times in Chapter 2. As shown there and in the macro program chart in Figure 18-2b, exit paths are generally determined by a yes or no answer to some **conditional statement** written in the form of a question. In Figure 18-2b, the condition to be determined is whether or not the last customer record has been processed. As you'll recall from Chapter 2, a dummy record can be placed at the end of the customer file so that the computer program will know when the last valid record has been processed. So long as valid records remain, program control will exit from the conditional branch of the decision symbol labeled "NO." When the last valid record has been processed and the dummy record is then read, the "YES" branch is followed and processing stops.

**Connector.** A circular **connector symbol** labeled "1" is encountered in Figure 18-2b when program control exits from the decision symbol along the "NO" branch. This connector symbol is used when additional flow lines might cause confusion and reduce understanding. Two connectors with identical labels serve the same function as a long flow line. That is, they show an exit to some other chart section, or they indicate an entry from another part of the chart. How's it possible to determine if a connector is used as an entry or an exit point? It's very simple: If an arrow *enters but doesn't leave* a connector, it's an exit point and program control is transferred to the identically labeled connector that does have an outlet.

Thus, in Figure 18-2*b*, the connector to the right of the decision symbol is an exit point, and program control loops back to the entry connector at the top of the chart when another record is to be processed.

**Offpage Connector.** Some programmers prefer to substitute an **offpage connector symbol** for the circular connector to show that program flow is entering from or going to a separate flowchart page. (This symbol isn't included in the ANSI standards.)

**Preparation.** And some programmers also prefer to use the **preparation symbol** rather than the general-purpose processing symbol to control, initiate, or perform some other operation on the program itself. For example, the processing symbol is used to present the initial values for accumulators and counters in Figures 18-9, 18-10, 18-11, and 18-13. But the preparation symbol could also have been used to present these initial values.

**Predefined Process.** Programmers frequently find that certain kinds of processing operations are repeated in their programs. Instead of rewriting a module each time it's needed, the programmer can prepare it once and then integrate it into other programs as required. Libraries of these predefined processes, or **subroutines,** are often maintained to reduce the time and cost of programming. Thus, a single **predefined process symbol** replaces a number of operations that need not be detailed at that

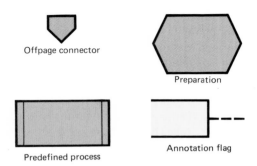

Offpage connector

Preparation

Predefined process

Annotation flag

particular point in a chart. (Of course, a detailed micro flowchart of the subroutine should be available if needed.) In short, the subroutine is a commonly used module that receives input from the main-control program, performs its limited task, and then returns the output to the primary program.

**Annotation. Annotation flags** are used to add clarifying comments to other flowchart symbols. They can be drawn on either side of another symbol.

We'll use most of these flowchart symbols in the next section to analyze a number of program applications. Beginning with several very simple problem situations, we'll gradually develop these situations into more realistic examples. The problems that are charted in this chapter are coded in the BASIC programming language in Chapter 20.

# PROGRAMMING ANALYSIS USING FLOWCHARTS

You learned in Chapter 2 that applications such as billing customers, paying employees, analyzing sales, controlling inventories, and preparing mailing labels account for the greatest use of business computing resources. Many of these same applications are processed regularly by schools, hospitals, and government agencies. These, then, are the types of applications that we'll analyze and chart in this section. And all our applications will apply to a single organization—R-K Enterprises, which was introduced in Chapter 2.

## Simple Input/Process/Output Charts
You know that programming analysis involves converting problem specifications into the I/O, calculation, logic/comparison, and storage/retrieval operations needed to solve the problem. (You also know, of course, that not every type of operation may be needed for every problem solution.) Let's now begin to analyze some problem specifications to see how the use of flowcharts can be of value.

**Problem 1: Simple Billing, Single Customer.** Let's assume that right after R-K's partners, Rob and Kay, decided to grant credit to selected customers of their mosquito bird tee shirts, they drew up the following specifications for a program to prepare customer bills:

■ Input data to be processed are customer name, quantity of shirts purchased, and unit price of the shirts.

■ The net amount owed by the customer should be computed.

■ The printed output should be a bill giving the customer's name and net amount owed.

The flowchart shown in Figure 18-3 satisfies these specifications, and illustrates a simple input/process/output procedure. You'll notice that convenient abbreviations have been assigned by the programmer to identify the input data and the result of processing. The programmer has considerable freedom in selecting abbreviations, but, as we'll see in Chapters 20 and 21, the selections must conform to the rules of a programming language. As you saw earlier, the net amount owed by a customer is found by multiplying the quantity purchased times the

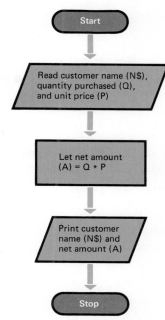

Figure 18-3 Program flowchart for problem 1: Simple Billing, Single Customer.

unit price. In flowcharts and programs, the asterisk is generally used to indicate multiplication. Other operation symbols include + (addition), − (subtraction), and / (division).

## Feedback and Review 18-1

Let's assume that the procedure charted in Figure 18-3 will give an accurate figure of the amount owed by out-of-state customers. Let's further suppose, however, that a sales tax of 6 percent of the net amount owed must be charged on bills sent to customers within the state. To test your understanding of the program development and flowcharting concepts you've just read, *prepare a program flowchart* for bills sent *within* the state. Your chart should reflect the following specifications:

■ Input data to be processed are customer name, quantity of shirts purchased, and unit price of the shirts.

■ The net amount owed by the customer should be computed.

■ The sales tax amount should be computed using a tax rate of .06.

■ The sales tax should be added to the net amount to get the total amount of the bill.

■ The printed output should be a bill giving the customer's name, net amount owed, sales tax amount, and total amount owed.

## Gaining Flexibility with Decision Symbols and Loops

You've probably already noticed what Kay and Rob quickly found out: Their initial billing program would compute one customer bill and then stop! After each bill was printed, the program would have to be reloaded into the computer before the next bill could be processed—hardly an efficient use of the partner's valuable time.

**Problem 2: Simple Billing, Multiple Customers.** In order to modify the program charted in Figure 18-3, the partners prepared the following revised specifications:

■ Input data to be processed are customer name, local address, city, state, and Zip code, quantity of shirts purchased, and unit price of the shirts.

■ The net amount owed by the customer should be computed.

■ The printed output should be a bill for each customer giving the customer's name, local address, city, state, and Zip code, and net amount owed.

■ The program should be able to process bills for any number of customers!

The flowchart shown in Figure 18-4 satisfies these requirements. The I/O operations and the net amount computation are similar to those shown in Figure 18-3. But this program is much more flexible. It can follow a controlled loop, repeat processing steps, and print any number of bills. A **loop** consists of a body made up of a sequence of instructions that can be executed repeti-

**Figure 18-4** Program flowchart for problem 2: Simple Billing, Multiple Customers.

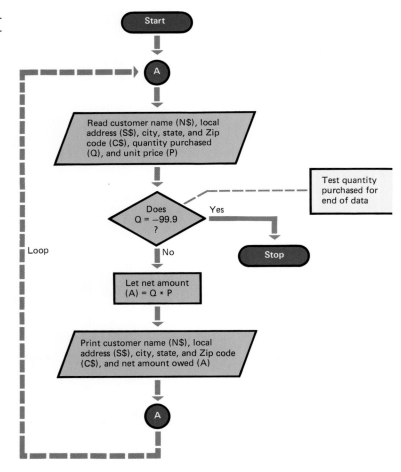

tively, a test for exit condition, and a return provision. Without the ability to execute loops, computers would be little more than toys.

The **body of the loop** in our example that makes repetition possible is found between the two connector symbols labeled "A." The repetitive processing of bills continues until the last valid bill has been printed and a "sentinel value" is encountered. This value is the quantity purchased amount of −99.9 that's shown in the decision symbol in Figure 18-4. It will appear in a last dummy record at the end of the customer file. A **sentinel value**, then, is simply some *arbitrary* data item that's placed at the end of a file to indicate that all valid data have been processed. (In our example, the sentinel could have been a unit price of −999.9 rather than a quantity value of −99.9). Of course, the sentinel must have a value that *couldn't possibly occur* as a valid data item. A negative number consisting of a string of 9s is often used as the sentinel value because the 9s stand out and are generally understood to be artificial or "dummy record numbers."

In summary, then, as long as valid records are being processed, the answer to the **test for exit condition** shown in the decision symbol in Figure 18-4 will be "NO." The bill amount will then be calculated, the bill will be printed, and program control will loop back to read the next record to be processed. When all bills have been printed and the dummy record is read, the answer to the conditional statement is "YES." The exit path out of the loop is then followed and processing stops. Such an exit path must, of course, exist when loops are used. **Endless** or **infinite loops** (Figure 18-5) result from failure to provide an exit path and are a common and troublesome problem that programmers often run into.

**Problem 3: Preparing Mailing Labels.** You'll recall from Chapter 2 that Kay and Rob mail promotional material to the prospective customers on their mailing list. The following specifications were set up to prepare a program to print the names and addresses of these prospects on gummed labels:

■ Input data to be processed are prospect name, local address, and city, state, and Zip code.

■ The printed output should be a gummed label for each prospect giving the prospect's name, local address, city, state, and Zip code.

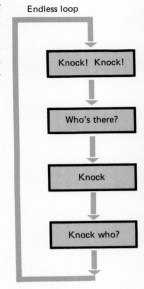

**Figure 18-5** An irrelevant example of an endless loop. (From Stan Kelly-Bootle, *The Devil's DP Dictionary*, New York, McGraw-Hill Book Company, 1981. Used with the permission of the McGraw-Hill Book Company.)

■ The program should be able to process labels for any number of prospects.

Figure 18-6a shows a chart drawn to these specifications; Figure 18-6b shows the mailing label output. In this case, the dummy record inserted at the end of the prospect file has "END OF DATA" as the prospect's name. The exit path out of this loop will be followed only when the dummy record satisfies the exit condition test.

**Problem 4: Sales Compensation, Single Commission Rate.** Every four weeks Rob and Kay receive a sales compensation report that's used to evaluate salesperson performance and prepare paychecks (see Figure 2-5, page 43). During the preparation of the sales compensation program, they drew up the following specifications for the report:

■ The report should have headings indicating the name, sales amount, and earnings.

■ Input data to be processed are the name and weekly sales data for each salesperson.

■ The four-week total sales amount should be computed for each salesperson.

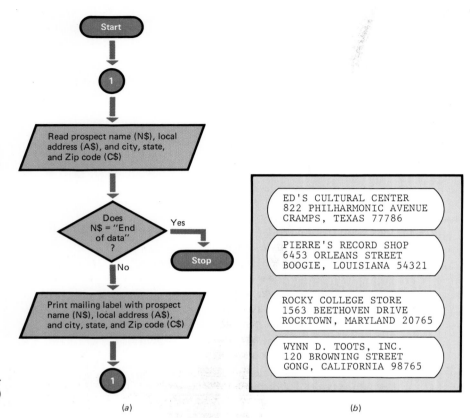

Figure 18-6 *(a)* Program flowchart for problem 3: Preparing Mailing Labels. *(b)* Mailing label output.

*(a)*

*(b)*

■ The total sales amount for each salesperson should be multiplied by a 10 percent commission rate to get the earnings of each salesperson.

■ Under the report headings should be printed the name, total sales amount, and earnings for each salesperson.

■ The program should be able to include any number of salespeople in the report.

The flowchart in Figure 18-7 meets these specifications. The report headings are printed first. The body of the loop that processes the data for each salesperson is then located between the connector symbols labeled "1." If the printing of the headings had been included in the loop, there would be a separate—and redundant—heading for each salesperson. The exit path out of the loop is followed after the computer reads a record—the last dummy record—that has a sales value of −99.9 for week number 1.

## Feedback and Review 18-2

Let's assume once again that the billing procedure shown in Figure 18-4 will only produce accurate results for bills sent to out-of-state customers. And let's suppose once more that a sales tax of 6 percent of the net amount owed must be charged on

bills sent to customers within the state. Using the concepts presented in Figure 18-4, *update the program flowchart you prepared in Feedback and Review 18-1* to meet these specifications:

■ Input data to be processed are customer name, local address, city, state, and Zip code, quantity of shirts purchased, and unit price of the shirts.

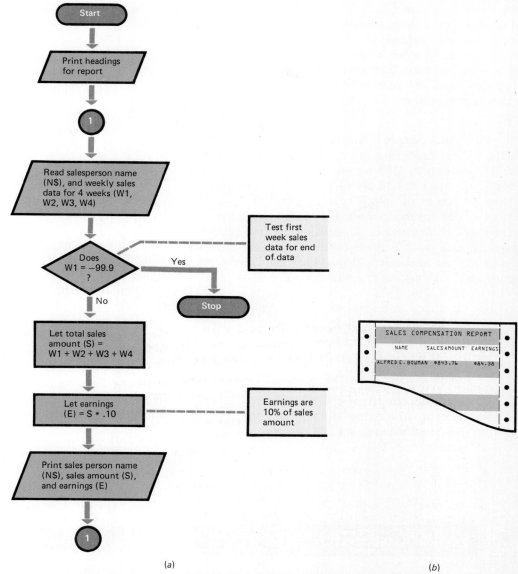

**Figure 18-7** *(a)* Program flowchart for problem 4: Sales Compensation, Single Commission Rate. *(b)* Sales compensation report from Figure 2-5.

■ Compute the net amount owed by the customer.

■ Compute the sales tax amount using a tax rate of .06.

■ Add the sales tax to the net amount to get the total amount of the bill.

■ Print a bill for each customer giving the customer's name, local address, city, state, and Zip code, net amount owed, sales tax amount, and total amount owed.

■ The program should be able to process bills for any number of customers.

## Multiple-Decision Charts

It has been possible to chart each of the preceding problems using only a *single* decision symbol. But the intricate logic needed to solve more complex problems requires that *many* decision paths be available. The following problem gives an example of the use of multiple decisions. Later problems will also use a series of logic decisions.

**Problem 5: Simple Billing with Discount.** We'll now add a second logic/comparison operation to the partners' billing application. Let's assume that to encourage large shipments, Kay and Rob decide to offer a 15 percent discount on purchases with a quantity equal to or greater than ($\geq$) 100 dozen tee shirts. Let's also assume that the customers who receive bills processed with this program must be charged a 6 percent sales tax on the amount owed after any discount is deducted. The following program specifications are drafted:

- Input data to be processed are customer name, local address, city, state, and Zip code, quantity purchased, and unit price.

- The amount owed before any discount should be computed.

- If quantity purchased is $\geq$ 100 (dozen tee shirts), allow a 15 percent discount on the amount owed. Otherwise, set the discount amount at zero.

- A sales tax amount equal to 6 percent of the amount owed should be computed after the discount is deducted.

- The sales tax amount should be added to the amount owed by the customer after the discount is deducted to get the total amount owed.

- A bill should be printed for each customer giving customer name, local address, city, state, and Zip code, quantity purchased, unit price, amount owed before discount, discount amount, sales tax owed, and total amount owed.

- The program should be able to process bills for any number of customers.

The flowchart for this program is shown in Figure 18-8. Since the first several steps are similar to those in Figure 18-4, we don't need to consider them here. The conditional statement in the second decision symbol—IS Q $\geq$ 100?—requires that the quantity purchased field of the input record be compared to 100. If the quantity is 100 dozen or more, a discount of 15 percent is computed. If the quantity is *less* than 100, a discount amount of zero is supplied. The last two processing symbols in the chart compute the sales tax and the total amount owed by the customer. Finally, a customer's bill is printed and program control branches back to read another customer record.

 ## Feedback and Review 18-3

Here's your chance to update the sales compensation report program produced for problem 4 and charted in Figure 18-7. Let's suppose that Rob and Kay decided to pay salespeople a 12 percent commission if their total sales for a period are equal to or greater than $100. If total sales are less than $100, however, the commission rate will remain at the 10 percent value used in problem 4. You should thus *prepare a revised sales compensation report flowchart* to meet these specifications:

- The report should have headings indicating the name, sales amount, and earnings.

- Input data to be processed are the name and weekly sales data for each salesperson.

- The 4-week total sales amount should be computed for each salesperson.

- If this total sales amount is $\geq$ $100, a 12 percent earnings commission should be computed. Otherwise, a 10 percent earnings commission should be calculated.

- Under the report headings should be printed the name, total sales amount, and earnings for each salesperson.

- The program should be able to include any number of salespeople in the report.

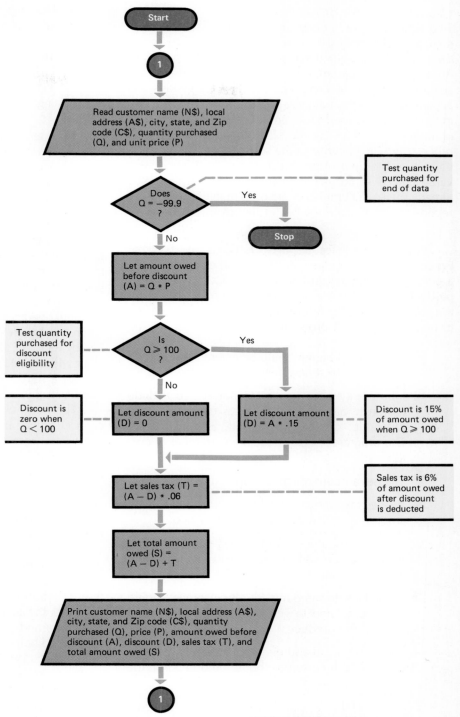

**Figure 18-8** Program flowchart for problem 5: Simple Billing with Discount.

## Charting the Use of Accumulators

Two sales analysis reports are used by the partners to manage their business. (These reports were discussed in Chapter 2 and presented in Figures 2-13a and b, page 55.) An important programming technique—the use of an accumulator—is used to prepare both these reports. An **accumulator** is a programmer-designated storage location in the CPU that's used to accept and store a *running total* of individual values as they become available during processing. The contents of the storage location *must* initially be set to zero. After this first step, each successive value placed in the accumulator is added to the value already there. Accumulators are used in the sales analysis reports to accumulate total sales figures.

**Problem 6: Sales Report Classified by Type of Product.** This report classifies the purchases made during a period by a named customer according to the type of product shipped. There are different reports for each of the products sold. The following specifications were used to prepare the report program:

■ The product name should be entered and printed as part of the report heading.

■ Input data to be processed should also include customer name, local address, city, state, and Zip code, quantity purchased, and unit price. The program should process any number of customers.

■ The net amount purchased should be computed.

■ A sales tax amount equal to 6 percent of the net amount purchased should be calculated.

■ The sales tax amount should be added to the net amount purchased to get the total sales amount for the customer.

■ The total sales amounts for all customers should be accumulated to get a grand total amount of sales of the product.

■ The name, local address, and city, state, and Zip code of each customer should be printed on the report.

■ "QUANTITY," "UNIT PRICE," "NET AMOUNT," "SALES TAX," and "TOTAL" sub-headings should be printed below the name and address of each customer.

■ The quantity purchased, unit price, net amount, sales tax, and total amount figures for each customer should be printed below these subheadings.

■ After all valid customer records have been processed, a "GRAND TOTAL" subheading and the accumulated grand total amount should be printed at the bottom of the report.

The chart in Figure 18-9 was produced to these specifications. You'll notice that the first operation is to set a grand total sales accumulator (G) to zero. The product name is then read, and a report heading is printed. As you'll see in the programming language used in Chapter 20, characters that are bounded by quotation marks in a printing operation are reproduced in exactly that way when a program is run. Thus, if the product name identified by P$ is TEE SHIRTS (DOZ), the heading set up by our chart will be SALES REPORT FOR TEE SHIRTS (DOZ). (Of course, if P$ is some other product, that product will be printed in the heading.)

The body of the loop to process the input data for each customer begins at the connector labeled 1. The input data from each customer record are read, the net amount purchased is computed, the sales tax is figured, and the total amount purchased is calculated. The next processing symbol then reads LET $G = G + S$, where G equals the value in the accumulator and S is the total purchases made by a customer. If the *first* customer's total purchases are $500, then $500 will be added to the initial value in the accumulator (0), and the new total of $500 will now be stored in the accumulator. If the next customer's purchases are $350, the total in the accumulator will then be $850 ($500 + $350).

After the accumulator has been updated, the customer's name and address are printed. Several subheadings are printed below each name and address to highlight the output that's produced for each customer. After the last customer record is processed, the grand total of all purchases is stored in the accumulator. Once the exit condition has been met, a GRAND TOTAL subhead and the amount in the accumulator are printed.

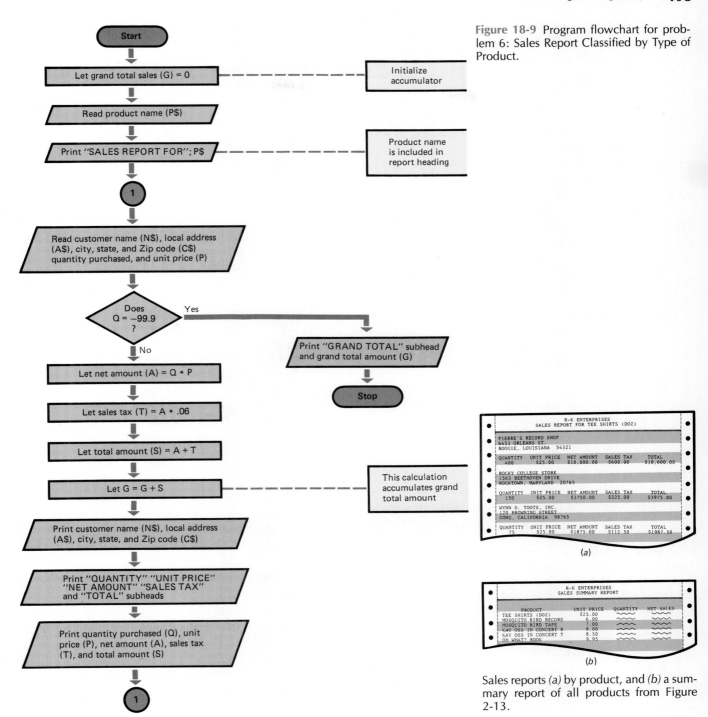

Figure 18-9 Program flowchart for problem 6: Sales Report Classified by Type of Product.

Sales reports (a) by product, and (b) a summary report of all products from Figure 2-13.

**Problem 7: Sales Summary Report.** This report summarizes the sales of *all* products sold by the partners' business for a period. As you know, their first product was the mosquito bird tee shirt. You'll also recall from Chapter 2 that "The Mosquito Bird Song" is being sold as a record and a tape cassette. Capitalizing on her sudden fame as the creator of this song, Kay has also given a concert on campus. This concert was recorded by Rob and is now being offered as a "Kay Oss in Concert" record and tape cassette. To round out their product line, Rob has just published (over Kay's objections) a book of poems written by Ms. Fitt, his English teacher. Since these poems include such biggies as "Oh What Is the Meaning of Life?" "Oh What Is the Meaning of Truth?" and "Oh What Is the Meaning of Fast Food Franchises?" the book's title is *Oh What?*

The following specifications were used to prepare this summary report program:

■ The report should be prepared with a "SALES SUMMARY REPORT" heading followed by a line of "PRODUCT," "UNIT PRICE," "QUANTITY," and "NET SALES" subheadings.

■ Input data to be processed should include the name of each product, its quantity sold, and its unit price. The program should process all products sold.

■ The net sales of each product should be computed.

■ The total sales of all products should be accumulated.

■ The product name, unit price, quantity sold, and net sales of each product should be printed on the report below the appropriate subheadings.

■ After all products have been processed, a "TOTAL NET SALES" subheading and the accumulated total sales amount should be printed at the bottom of the report.

The chart used to prepare the summary report program is shown in Figure 18-10. Report headings are printed and the accumulator is set to zero. The body of the loop then begins with the reading of input data about a particular product. The net sales of this product are computed, and the amount is added to the total in the accumulator. The product name, unit price, quantity sold, and net sales amounts are then printed, and the program loops back to read the data for the next product. When all products have been processed, the total of their sales is stored in the accumulator. Once the condition needed to exit the loop is met through the reading of a last dummy record, a "TOTAL NET SALES" subheading and the accumulated total sales are printed.

## Feedback and Review 18-4

How about making some changes to the sales compensation report program chart that you worked on in Feedback and Review 18-3? (Don't tell me your answer, it might depress me.) Anyway, that's what we're going to do. Let's suppose this time that the program should meet these specifications:

■ The report should have a heading line indicating "NAME," "SALES AMOUNT," and "EARNINGS."

■ Input data to be processed are the name and weekly sales figures for each salesperson. The program should be able to include any number of salespeople.

■ The 4-week total sales amount for each salesperson should be computed.

■ The total sales amount for each salesperson should be multiplied by a 10 percent commission rate to get the earnings of each salesperson. (We'll not use multiple commission rates in this exercise.)

■ The total sales for all salespersons should be accumulated.

■ Under the report heading line should be printed the name, total sales amount, and earnings for each salesperson.

■ After all salespeople have been processed, their total earnings should be computed by multiplying their accumulated total sales by .10.

■ Print "TOTAL SALES" and "TOTAL EARNINGS" subheadings, and the amount of total sales and total earnings for all salespersons at the bottom of the report.

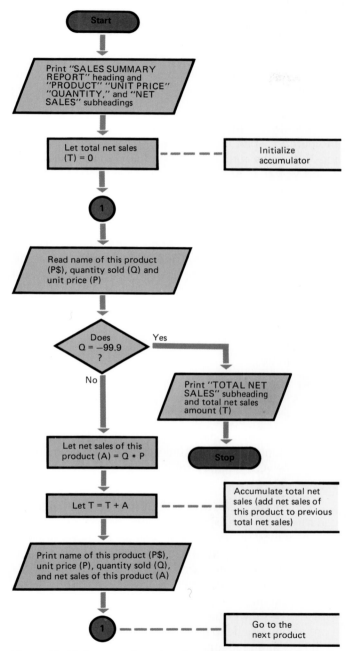

**Figure 18-10** Program flowchart for problem 7: Sales Summary Report.

## Charting the Use of a Counter

You've now seen how accumulators may be used. Another important programming technique is the use of a counter. A **counter** is a special type of accumulator that's often used to record the number of times a loop has been processed. For example, if a programmer wants to process the procedure in a loop a fixed number of times, that number can be specified in the program. A counter can then be used to keep track of the number of passes through the loop. When the counter value reaches the predetermined number, an exit condition based on the value of the counter is satisfied, and an exit path out of the loop is followed.

**Problem 8: Simple Billing with a Counter.** The following specifications can serve to show how a counter is used to control a loop:

- Input data are the number of customer records to be processed, and the name, quantity purchased, and unit price data for each customer.

- The net amount owed by each customer should be computed.

- The printed output should be a bill for each customer giving the customer's name and net amount owed.

- Processing should stop after all customers have been billed.

The chart in Figure 18-11 shows how these specifications can be met. A counter is *initialized* (or initially set) at 1 in our example, and the number of records to be processed is entered. After the first customer record has been processed, a test for exit condition is made. The initial value of the counter (1) is compared to the number of records to be processed. Since the counter value does not yet equal this number of records, program control moves to the next operation. In this step, the counter is *incremented* (or added to) by a value of 1, and so the counter's value is now 2. When the last customer record has been processed, and when K = N, the exit path out of the loop will be followed without any need for a dummy record at the end of the file.

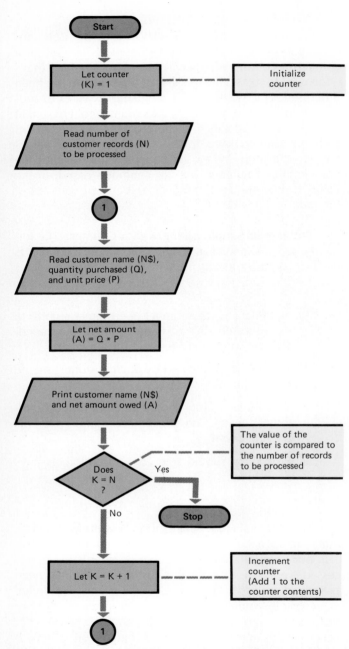

**Figure 18-11** Program flowchart for problem 8: Simple Billing with a Counter.

## Additional Charting Examples

You'll be pleased to know that we're only going to look here at two more charts that analyze programs used in the partners' business. Since no major new programming or charting techniques are introduced in these two examples, we'll be able to move through them quickly.

**Problem 9: Inventory Control Report.** We discussed the purpose of an inventory control application in Chapter 2. And the format of the partners' inventory control report was shown in Figure 2-12, page 55. The essential specifications for this report are:

- ■ Report headings are needed, and the input data consist of the name of each product and the beginning inventory, quantity received, and quantity sold figures for each product. Any number of products can be processed.

- ■ The inventory available for sale during a period is found by adding the quantity received during the period to the inventory at the beginning of the period.

- ■ The inventory at the end of the period is found by subtracting the quantity sold from the available inventory.

- ■ The name of each product is printed on the report along with its beginning inventory, quantity received, quantity sold, and ending inventory.

Figure 18-12 shows the flowchart for this inventory control report. The body of the loop begins after the report headings shown back in Figure 2-12 are printed. Input data are entered, a test is made to see if all valid records have been processed, and the inventory available for sale is determined. The available inventory *should* be found by adding receipts (R) to the beginning inventory. If a data error shows quantity received to be less than zero, a provision is made to keep the available inventory equal to the beginning figure. The ending inventory *should* be found by subtracting sales from the quantity available. But if a data error shows quantity sold to be less than zero, no change is made to the available inventory. (Sales returns are treated as quantity received.) The output shown in the chart is then printed under the report headings.

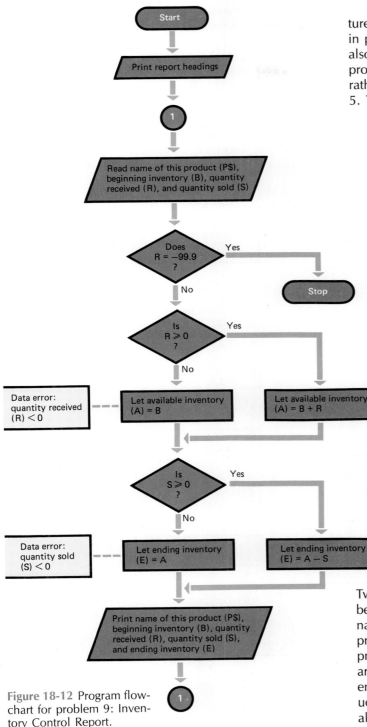

Figure 18-12 Program flow-chart for problem 9: Inventory Control Report.

**Problem 10: Final Billing Program.** Many of the features of this final billing procedure were discussed earlier in problem 5. But a number of additional features have also been added. In this billing version, for example, the program must accommodate all possible products sold rather than just the single product processed in problem 5. The specifications for this billing procedure are:

■ Input data include the names and addresses of multiple customers, and the quantity and price of the multiple products they've purchased.

■ A heading line should be printed on each customer's bill. The total amount billed to all customers before and after discounts should be accumulated and printed after all bills have been prepared.

■ The amount owed before any discount should be computed for each product.

■ If the quantity purchased of a product is $\geqslant$ 100, a 15 percent discount is allowed. Otherwise, no discount is permitted.

■ A 6 percent sales tax should be computed after the discount is deducted, and this tax should be added to the after-discount amount to get the total amount owed for the product.

■ Each printed bill should give the customer's name and address. The name, quantity purchased, price, amount owed before discount, discount amount, sales tax, and total amount owed for *each product* should also be listed.

The chart in Figure 18-13 satisfies these conditions. Two accumulators are set up to total the amounts billed before and after discounts have been computed. The name and address of the first customer are then read and printed. A heading line for the customer's bill is also printed. The name, quantity, and price of the *first* product are entered next. The test in the first decision symbol is an end-of-record test designed to determine if *all* valid products in a customer's record have been processed. If they all *have* been processed, a dummy price field with a value

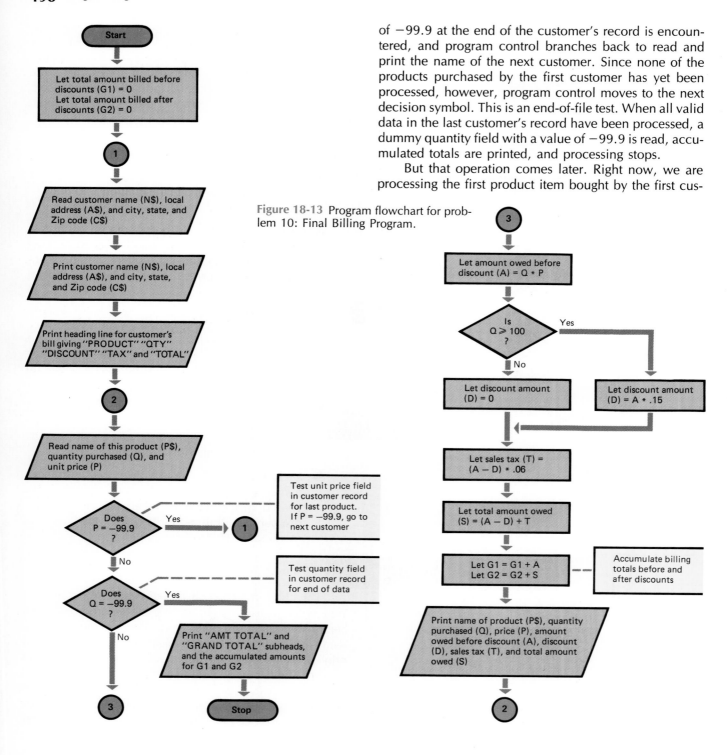

of −99.9 at the end of the customer's record is encountered, and program control branches back to read and print the name of the next customer. Since none of the products purchased by the first customer has yet been processed, however, program control moves to the next decision symbol. This is an end-of-file test. When all valid data in the last customer's record have been processed, a dummy quantity field with a value of −99.9 is read, accumulated totals are printed, and processing stops.

But that operation comes later. Right now, we are processing the first product item bought by the first cus-

Figure 18-13 Program flowchart for problem 10: Final Billing Program.

tomer. Since the next several steps in the chart are identical to those explained in problem 5, we can skip them here. You'll notice, however, that the before and after discount amounts for the first product are added to the accumulators. The totals of all successive products will also be accumulated. The name of the first product and other pertinent facts are then printed on the first customer's bill. Program control now branches back to the connector labeled 2 and the next product is processed. This continues until the last product bought by the first customer has been accounted for. Then, as we've seen, the exit test condition for the first decision symbol will be met and processing will begin on the next customer's record.

## A Summary of Structured Logic Patterns

A number of different problems have now been analyzed and charted. As you examined the logic of these problems, you may have noticed that a few patterns were frequently repeated. What you probably didn't realize, however, is the rather surprising fact that *any* problem can be solved through the repeated use of just a few basic logic structures. These patterns are shown in Figure 18-14. The **simple sequence structure** (Figure 18-14a) merely consists of one step followed by another. The **selection structure** (Figure 18-14b) requires a test for some condition

followed by two alternative program control paths. As you know, the path selected depends on the results of the test. This pattern is sometimes referred to as an IF-THEN-ELSE structure. The **loop structure** involves doing one or more operations *while* a condition is *true* (Figure 18-14c). When the condition becomes false, the looping process is ended. If the condition is initially false, the operation(s) found in this DO WHILE structure aren't executed. A variation of this third basic pattern is one in which the operation(s) is (are) repeated *until* a condition is found to be true (Figure 18-14d) after which the exit path is followed. This variation is called a DO UNTIL structure.

These three basic logic structures are all that are necessary to prepare any program. Supporters of a programming approach built around the use of these three structures believe that the use of any additional patterns generally causes needless complexity and confusion. The **branch structure** shown in Figure 18-14e, for example, causes control to branch away from a sequence and GO TO operation K if the condition test is false. Adherents of the structured programming approach believe such a pattern is counterproductive. But it's included here since many programmers still use it today. A thesis of structured programming is that although the basic patterns can be combined and/or "nested" in actual practice as shown in

**Figure 18-14** Basic coding structures.

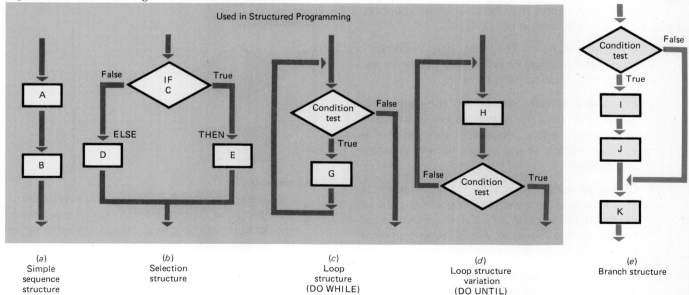

(a)
Simple sequence structure

(b)
Selection structure

(c)
Loop structure (DO WHILE)

(d)
Loop structure variation (DO UNTIL)

(e)
Branch structure

Figure 18-15, each pattern has a single entry and exit point, and each is readable from top to bottom. This inherent simplicity can lead to more understandable problem logic. Structured programming concepts have gained rapid acceptance. We'll discuss them in more detail in Chapter 19.

## Benefits and Limitations of Flowcharts

The following benefits may be obtained when flowcharts are used during programming analysis:

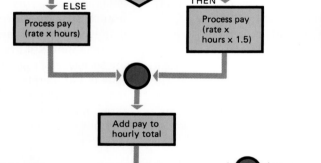

**Figure 18-15** Partial payroll program showing structure combinations.

1. **Quicker grasp of relationships.** Current and proposed procedures may be understood more rapidly through the use of charts.

2. **Effective analysis.** The flowchart becomes a model of a program or system that can be broken down into detailed parts for study.

3. **Effective synthesis.** Synthesis is the opposite of analysis; it's the combination of the various parts into a whole entity. Flowcharts may be used as working models in the design of new programs and systems.

4. **Communication.** Flowcharts aid in communicating the facts of a problem to those whose skills are needed in the solution. The old adage that "a picture is worth a thousand words" rings true when the picture happens to be a flowchart.

5. **Proper program documentation.** Program **documentation** involves collecting, organizing, stor-

ing, and otherwise maintaining a complete historical record of programs and the other documents associated with a system. Good documentation is needed for the following reasons: (a) Documented knowledge belongs to an organization and does not disappear with the departure of a programmer; (b) if projects are postponed, docu-

**A LITTLE-KNOWN CONTRIBUTION FROM GRACE M. HOPPER**

Long recognized and honored for her pioneering work in compilers and programming languages, Captain Grace Murray Hopper was also present when one of the famous words of "computerese" was coined. In an interview with *Computerworld*, she reminisced about working on the Mark I computer at Harvard in the days following World War II.

"In 1945, while working in a World War I-vintage non-air-conditioned building on a hot, humid summer day, the computer stopped. We searched for the problem and found a failing relay—one of the big signal relays," she recalled.

"Inside, we found a moth that had been beaten to death. We pulled it out with tweezers and taped it to the log book," Hopper continued. "From then on, when the officer came in to ask if we were accomplishing anything, we told him we were 'debugging' the computer."

—Marguerite Zientara, "Capt. Grace M. Hopper and the Genesis of Programming Languages," *Computerworld*, Nov. 16, 1981, p. 50. Copyright 1981 by CW Communications, Inc., Framingham, Mass.

mented work will not have to be duplicated; and (c) if programs are modified in the future, the programmer will have a more understandable record of what was originally done. From what we've seen of the nature of flowcharts, it's obvious that they can provide valuable documentation support.

6. *Efficient coding.* The program flowchart acts as a guide or blueprint during the program preparation phase. Instructions coded in a programming language may be checked against the flowchart to help ensure that no steps are omitted.

7. *Orderly debugging and testing of programs.* If the program fails to run to completion when submitted to the computer for execution, the flowchart may help in the "debugging" process. That is, it may help in detecting, locating, and removing mistakes.

In spite of their many obvious advantages, flowcharts have several *limitations:*

1. Complex and detailed charts are sometimes laborious to plan and draw, especially when a large number of decision paths are involved.

2. Although branches from a *single* decision symbol are easy to follow, the actions to be taken, given certain specified conditions, can be difficult to follow if there are *several* paths.

3. There are no standards determining the amount of detail that should be included in a chart.

# OTHER PROGRAMMING ANALYSIS TOOLS

Because of such limitations, flowcharts may be replaced or supplemented by alternative analysis tools.

## Decision Tables

A **decision table** can be a powerful tool for defining complex program logic. The basic table format is shown in Figure 18-16a. The table is divided into two main parts: The upper part contains the *conditions* and questions that are to be tested in reaching a decision, and the lower part describes the *actions* to be taken when a given set of conditions is present. The contents of the condition stub correspond to the conditions contained in the decision symbols of a flowchart, and the condition entries correspond to the paths leading out from decision symbols. Action statements corresponding to the statements located in nondecision symbols of a chart are listed in the action stub.

A decision table version of the inventory control report problem charted in Figure 18-12 is shown in Figure 18-16b. Each decision rule column is the equivalent of

| Table heading | | Decision rules | | | | |
|---|---|---|---|---|---|---|
| Condition | If | | | | | |
| | And    stub | entries | | | | |
| | And | | | | | |
| Action | Then | | | | | |
| | And    stub | entries | | | | |
| | And | | | | | |

(a)

| Inventory control report | | Decision rule number | | | | |
|---|---|---|---|---|---|---|
| | | 1 | 2 | 3 | 4 | 5 |
| Condition | Quantity received = −99.9 | N | N | N | N | Y |
| | Quantity received ⩾ 0 | Y | N | Y | N | |
| | Quantity sold ⩾ 0 | Y | N | N | Y | |
| Action | Let available inventory = B + R | X | | X | | |
| | Let available inventory = B | | X | | X | |
| | Let ending inventory = A − S | X | | | X | |
| | Let ending inventory = A | | X | X | | |
| | Print line on report | X | X | X | X | |
| | Read next record | X | X | X | X | |
| | Stop | | | | | X |

(b)

**Figure 18-16** (a) Decision table format. (b) Decision table for problem 9: Inventory Control Report.

one path through the flowchart. Decision tables may thus be used in place of program flowcharts for the following reasons:

▪ Tables are easier to draw and change than charts, and they provide more compact documentation (a small table can replace several pages of charts).

▪ It's also easier to follow a particular path down one column than through several flowchart pages.

But tables aren't as widely used as charts because:

▪ Charts are better able to express the total sequence of events needed to solve a problem.

▪ Charts are more familiar to, and are preferred by, many programmers.

## Structured Pseudocode

Another programming analysis tool is pseudocode. Since *pseudo* means "imitation" and *code* refers to instructions written in a programming language, **pseudocode** is a counterfeit and abbreviated version of actual computer instructions. These pesudoinstructions are phrases written in ordinary natural language (e.g., English, French, Spanish). A pseudocode version of the inventory control report problem that we've now charted and put in a decision table format is shown in Figure 18-17.

As you can see in Figure 18-17, pseudocode is compact and is thus easy to revise. A few terms or "keywords" are often written in uppercase letters in a pseudocode problem solution. These keywords identify the *sequence, selection,* and *loop structures* discussed a few pages earlier. Figure 18-18 presents some of these common keywords, and shows you how they identify the three structured logic patterns. Figure 18-19 summarizes the concepts outlined in Figure 18-18 and shows a pseudocode solution for the billing problem charted in Figure 18-8.

Computer professionals who use a structured programming approach in their work often prefer to use pseudocode in preparing a detailed plan for a program. However, there are no standard rules to follow in using pseudocode, and, of course, a graphic representation of program logic isn't available.

**Figure 18-17** Pseudocode for problem 9: Inventory Control Report.

```
Print report headings
Read first product record
DOWHILE there are more records
    IF quantity received ⩾ 0
        Let available inventory = beginning inventory + receipts
    ELSE
        Let available inventory = beginning inventory
    ENDIF
    If quantity sold ⩾ 0
        Let ending inventory = available inventory − sales
    ELSE
        Let ending inventory = available inventory
    ENDIF
    Print line on report
    Read next record
ENDDO
Stop
```

## SEQUENCE STRUCTURE:

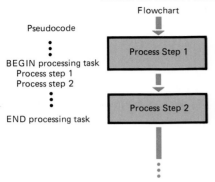

Pseudocode    Flowchart

BEGIN processing task
  Process step 1
  Process step 2

END processing task

Although steps in sequence are usually written in lowercase letters, the BEGIN and END keywords may be used to identify a well-defined block of these steps.

## SELECTION STRUCTURES:

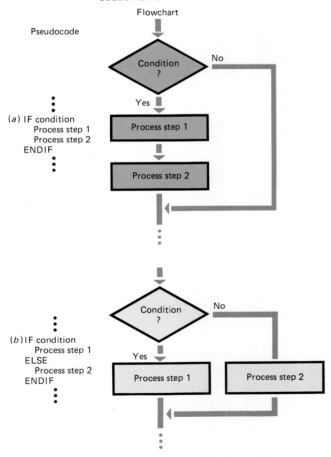

Pseudocode    Flowchart

(a) IF condition
  Process step 1
  Process step 2
ENDIF

(b) IF condition
  Process step 1
ELSE
  Process step 2
ENDIF

In the IF-THEN structure (a), steps 1 and 2 are processed if the specified condition is true. If the condition isn't true, both of these steps are skipped. The IF-THEN-ELSE selection structure (b) is different. If the condition is true, then step 1 is processed; else (if it isn't true) step 2 is completed. The keywords (IF, ELSE, and ENDIF) are capitalized, and the processing steps are indented as shown.

## LOOP STRUCTURES:

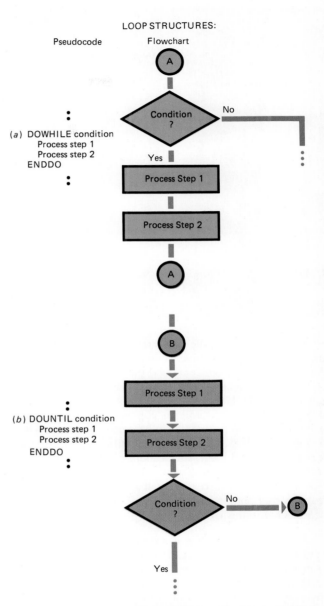

Pseudocode    Flowchart

(a) DOWHILE condition
  Process step 1
  Process step 2
ENDDO

(b) DOUNTIL condition
  Process step 1
  Process step 2
ENDDO

In the DOWHILE loop structure (a), steps 1 and 2 are processed while the condition is true. When the condition becomes false, the looping stops. The looping in the DOUNTIL structure (b) continues so long as the condition is false and until it is found to be true. The condition test is at the beginning of a DOWHILE loop and at the end of a DOUNTIL loop. The pseudocode keywords to identify these structures are DOWHILE, DOUNTIL, and ENDDO.

**Figure 18-18** Pseudocode keywords and concepts.

```
Read first customer record
DOWHILE there are more records
     Let amount owed before discount (A) = quantity purchased
          (Q) * unit price (P)
     IF quantity purchased ≥ 100
          Let discount amount (D) = A * .15
     ELSE
          Let D = 0
     ENDIF
     BEGIN tax/total computation and record printing
          Let sales tax (T) = (A - D) * .06
          Let total amount owed (S) = (A - D) + T
          Print customer name, address, Q, P, A, D, T, and S
     END tax/total computation and record printing
     Read next record
ENDDO
Stop
```

**Figure 18-19** Many of the concepts outlined in Figure 18-18 are shown in this pseudocode solution for problem 5 (Simple Billing with Discount). This problem is flowcharted in Figure 18-8.

# LOOKING BACK

**1.** People must usually follow six steps in order to put computers to work. The first three (defining the need, gathering and analyzing data, and designing and preparing specifications to solve the problem) are included in the systems analysis and design process. The last three steps (programming analysis, program preparation, and program implementation and maintenance) are found in the programming process. Included among the questions that must be considered during program development are: *(a)* Are problem specifications clear and complete? *(b)* Is a solution method now known? *(c)* If not, can such a method be obtained from other sources? *(d)* If a solution method must be created, what approach should be used? Each of these questions is considered in this chapter.

**2.** A program flowchart is a detailed picture of how steps are to be performed within a CPU to produce the needed output. A single chart may be used to represent a problem solution, or the major program modules in a main-control chart can be drawn separately in a series of micro charts. The standardized symbols used in program flowcharts are introduced and explained in this chapter.

**3.** Ten problem situations dealing with such popular applications as billing customers, paying employees, analyzing sales, controlling inventories, and preparing mailing labels are analyzed and charted in this chapter. These same applications are coded in the BASIC language in Chapter 20. The specifications for each of the problems was presented, and a flowchart was drawn to meet these specifications. After examining a simple input/process/output chart, we moved to problem situations that

required the flexibility made possible by the use of decisions and loops. Charts with multiple decision symbols were presented, and then the use of accumulators and counters was discussed.

**4.** Only a few logic structures were used in all our charting examples. In fact, the logic of all programs written for computers can be described using just the simple sequence, selection, and loop structures. A fourth branch structure is used by many programmers today, but some professionals believe that its use leads to needless complexity and confusion.

**5.** Flowcharts enhance communication and understanding, contribute to effective problem analysis and synthesis, provide good documentation, and are useful during program coding and debugging. However, complex and detailed charts can be hard to draw, and following the actions to be taken in specified situations can be difficult when many decision paths are available.

**6.** Other programming analysis tools such as decision tables and pseudocode are sometimes used to replace or supplement program flowcharts. A decision table is compact and is easy to draw and change. It's a powerful tool for defining complex program logic because a single table column can represent a maze of lines through several pages of flowcharts. Charts are more frequently used, however, because they are better able to express the total sequence of events needed to solve a problem. Pseudocode is a counterfeit and abbreviated version of actual computer instructions. It's compact, easy to change, and popular with programmers who use a structured approach. But there are no standard rules governing its use.

## KEY TERMS AND CONCEPTS

system analysis and design process
   479
programming process 479
program development approach
   479
algorithm 481
program flowchart 481
program modules 482
main-control (modular or macro)
   flowchart 483
micro flowchart 483
input/output symbol 483

processing symbol 483
terminal symbol 483
decision symbol 483
conditional statement 483
connector symbol 483
offpage connector symbol 484
preparation symbol 484
subroutines 484
predefined process symbol 484
annotation flag 484
loop 486
body of the loop 487

sentinel value 487
test for exit condition 487
endless (infinite) loop 487
accumulator 492
counter 495
simple sequence structure 499
selection structure 499
loop structure 499
branch structure 499
documentation 500
decision table 501
pseudocode 502

## TOPICS FOR REVIEW AND DISCUSSION

**1.** *(a)* What are the steps in the system analysis and design process? *(b)* What are the steps in the programming process?

**2.** "Although different programmers use different strategies to develop program solutions, certain questions must usually be considered regardless of the strategy used." Identify and discuss these questions.

**3.** In computer science, the term "stepwise refinement" is given to the process of breaking down a large problem into a series of smaller and more understandable tasks. How can the use of program flowcharts help in this process?

**4.** *(a)* What's the purpose of a program flowchart? *(b)* How does it differ from a system flowchart? *(c)* What symbols are used in program charts?

**5.** "A loop consists of a body, a test for exit condition, and a return provision." Discuss this statement.

**6.** *(a)* What's a sentinel value? *(b)* Why must the sentinel be a value that couldn't occur as a valid data item?

**7.** *(a)* What's an accumulator? *(b)* How is an accumulator initialized and then updated to compute a running total?

**8.** *(a)* What's a counter? *(b)* How can a counter be used to keep track of the number of times a loop has been executed?

**9.** Problem 10 is referred to as the "Final" Billing Program. Can you see any deficiencies in this program that might call for further modifications?

**10.** Using the chart for problem 5 in Figure 18-8, identify the simple sequence, selection, and loop structures in the program logic.

**11.** Discuss the benefits and limitations of flowcharts.

**12.** Why is proper documentation required?

**13.** What are the advantages and limitations of decision tables?

**14.** *(a)* What is pseudocode? *(b)* Prepare a pseudocode solution for the Sales Report problem charted in Figure 18-9. *(c)* Prepare a pseudocode solution for the Sales Summary Report charted in Figure 18-10.

**15.** Review the chart for problem 2 in Figure 18-4. How could you modify it so that the partners could interact with the program and supply the input data at the time of processing?

**16.** After reviewing the chart for problem 4 in Figure 18-7, how could you modify it so that Rob and Kay could interact with the program and supply the input data at the time of processing? Let's assume that the program should print instructions on how to enter the input data, and it should print a heading line for each salesperson showing "NAME," "SALES AMOUNT," and "EARNINGS." It should also print an "END OF DATA" message after each record has been processed to allow the partners to stop processing or to continue with another record.

**17.** After reviewing the chart for problem 8 in Figure 18-11, how could it be changed so that the total amount billed to each customer could be accumulated and then printed with a "TOTAL AMOUNT" subheading at the end of the billing run?

**18.** Let's assume that you need to prepare a program that will compute the number of acres in any number of rectangular lots. The program should interact with the user and request the length (in feet) and width (in feet) of each lot prior to computing its acreage and printing out the result. There are 43,560 square feet in an acre. After computing the acreage in a first lot, the program should then determine from the user if there are any additional lots to process. When the processing is completed, the program should print a "GOOD-BYE" message. Draw a flowchart for this program.

**19.** Now let's assume that Ms. Fitt, Rob's English teacher, has found a student guilty of chewing gum in class. The punishment is to write "I will not chew gum in class" 10 times. Prepare a flowchart for a program that will *(a)* accept any "naughty student" message, and *(b)* reproduce this message any designated number of times.

**20.** Rob has recently bought a new Firebelch V/8 and has decided to use his computer to keep a record of the car's gasoline mileage during his sales trips. Prepare a flowchart that will reflect the following program specifications: *(a)* Input data to be processed are the odometer readings at the beginning and end of a trip, and the gallons of gasoline used. *(b)* The gasoline mileage—the miles-per-gallon—should be computed. *(c)* The printed output should be a mileage report showing the input data and the computed gasoline mileage.

**21.** As a continuation of question 20 above, what if Rob makes several trips in his Firebelch in a week and wants to compute the gasoline mileage for each trip? He could repeatedly rerun the program prepared from the flowchart for question 20, but this would be a tedious process. Rob wants to modify the question 20 program so that it can handle the processing of multiple trips. Prepare a flowchart that will accommodate the following program specifications: *(a)* The program should compute and then print as output the miles-per-gallon for any number of trips. *(b)* The program should "converse" with Rob and ask him to supply it with the necessary input data for each trip. *(c)* After computing the miles-per-gallon for a trip, the program should ask Rob if data from another trip are to be processed. *(d)* Finally, as a nice gesture, Rob would like the computer to print a polite sign-off message when the processing has been completed.

**22.** Let's now assume that Rob's state decided to impose a one-time tax on new cars in an effort to (1) raise additional revenue, and (2) encourage citizens to buy more fuel-efficient cars. (Alas, this tax went into effect the day before Rob bought his new Firebelch.) The tax on each car is based on its current overall Environmental Protection Agency (EPA) mileage rating. The EPA mileage rating categories and the tax payment due on purchase are indicated below:

| EPA mileage rating | Tax due |
| --- | --- |
| Less than 15 mpg | $450 |
| 15 and less than 20 mpg | 250 |
| 20 and less than 25 mpg | 100 |
| 25 mpg and over | 5 |

Prepare a flowchart for a program that meets the following specifications: *(a)* It should produce the amount of tax due, given a car's EPA mileage rating as input. *(b)* It should interact with the user by requesting the necessary input data.

**23.** While Rob is out hot rodding, it's fallen to Kay to close down shop for the holidays. To give R-K customers ample warning of this decision, Kay plans to print a message on gummed labels that can then be attached to the bills and correspondence sent to customers. Prepare a flowchart for a program that achieves the following objectives: *(a)* The number of labels to be printed is specified in the program. *(b)* The message to be printed on each label is:

"R-K ENTERPRISES WILL BE CLOSED FROM DECEMBER 20 TO JANUARY 4. PLEASE KEEP THIS IN MIND WHEN PLANNING YOUR NEXT ORDER. THANK YOU."

**24.** Rob has owned his Firebelch V/8 for 6 months now, and the car has been in the shop for numerous repairs. Suspecting that he may have a "lemon," Rob is thinking of trading it for another model. The price of the Firebelch was $9,875, and Rob has been offered $9,295 for the car. He would like to know the annual rate of depreciation on the Firebelch before making a decision. The annual rate of depreciation is calculated by the following formula:

$$\text{Depreciation rate} = 1 - \left( \frac{\text{resale price}}{\text{original price}} \right)^{1/\text{age in years}}$$

Prepare a flowchart for a program that will *(a)* request that the user supply it with the original and resale prices, and the age of the investment in years, *(b)* compute the annual depreciation rate and convert it into a percentage, and *(c)* be able to repeat these operations as needed.

**25.** Let's suppose that Kay and Rob have decided to produce their own "Mosquito Bird" and "Kay Oss in Concert" tapes. This production is carried out by other students who use their tape recorders to duplicate the R-K products. (The quality and fidelity of the sound thus produced leaves something to be desired, but that fact seems to enhance the appeal of the tapes.) The students are supplied with blank tapes and receive $0.50 for each "Mosquito Bird" and $1.00 for each "Kay Oss in Concert" tape they record. A recent production compensation report looked like this:

| EMPLOYEE | MOSQUITO BIRD TAPES PRODUCED | KAY OSS CONCERT TAPES PRODUCED | EMPLOYEE EARNINGS |
| --- | --- | --- | --- |
| C. HEAD | 50 | 60 | $85 |
| A. MUNDAY | 120 | 200 | $260 |
| J. TAYLOR | 110 | 300 | $355 |

Prepare a flowchart for a program that will create this output by *(a)* accepting the input data given in the first three columns of this report, and *(b)* produce the employee earnings amounts shown in column 4.

**26.** How would you modify the flowchart you prepared for question 25 above to produce the following production compensation report?

| EMPLOYEE | MOSQUITO BIRD TAPES PRODUCED | KAY OSS CONCERT TAPES PRODUCED | EMPLOYEE EARNINGS |
|---|---|---|---|
| C. HEAD | 50 | 60 | $85 |
| A. MUNDAY | 120 | 200 | $260 |
| J. TAYLOR | 110 | 300 | $355 |
| | | | TOTAL EMPLOYEE COMPENSATION |
| | | | $700 |

**27.** Kay wants to be prepared in case R-K Enterprises becomes a big success. To facilitate the financial planning she hopes to do in the future, Kay has decided to prepare a "Savings Accumulation Simulator" program. She wants this program to print messages requesting input data on an initial savings amount, an expected interest rate to be earned, and the number of years to be simulated. She also wants the program to run one simulation and then ask the user if more data are to be processed. A number

of "what if" simulations can thus be processed by the user for financial planning purposes. The output of the program should look as follows if the user supplies an initial savings figure of $20,000, an interest rate of 6 percent, and a simulation period of 10 years:

```
INITIAL SAVINGS? 20000
INTEREST RATE ON SAVINGS (PERCENT)? 6
NUMBER OF YEARS? 10

SAVINGS ACCUMULATION MODEL
```

| YEAR NO. | SAVINGS BALANCE |
|---|---|
| 1 | 21200 |
| 2 | 22472 |
| . | . |
| . | . |
| . | . |
| . | . |

```
MORE DATA (YES, NO)?
```

Prepare a flowchart for the program needed to produce this output.

## PROJECT TO LOOK INTO

**1.** Contact an organization of interest to you and determine the programming analysis approach used by the organization. Also, inquire about the procedures used to acquire software applications packages. Present your findings to the class.

## ANSWERS TO FEEDBACK AND REVIEW SECTIONS

Possible flowcharts for Feedback and Review sections 18-1 through 18-4 follow. Your versions may differ in some respects and still be correct.

A possible flowchart for Feedback and Review 18-2. (Note that the programmer has exercised his or her freedom to use some different abbreviations for input data and processing results.)

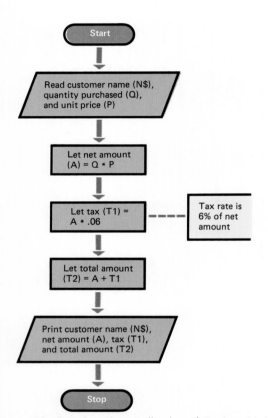

A possible flowchart for Feedback and Review 18-1.

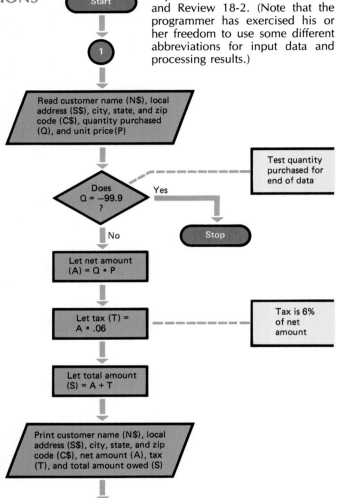

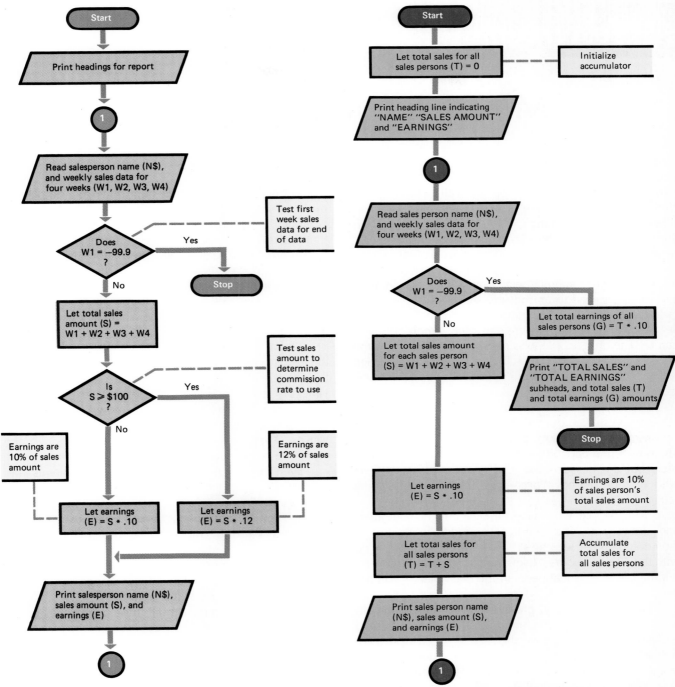

A possible program flowchart for Feedback and Review 18-3.

A possible program flowchart for Feedback and Review 18-4.

# Making Software "Easy"

Steven Jobs points to a slide on the wall behind him. It shows a typical bell curve, a small fraction of which is filled in. That, the chairman of Apple Computer tells his audience, represents the 5% of the "knowledge workers" in this country who own and use personal computers.

Two days later a front-page story in the *Wall Street Journal* describes in great detail how a "glut of computer software may lead to an industry shakeout."

Can a mere 5% penetration of the potential pc market cause a shakeout? The answer, quite simply, is that it can't. "The only people who get shook are the ones who deserve to be," says Esther Dyson, president of Rosen Research, New York, and editor of the RELease 1.0 newsletter. . . .

The key problem—the mistake that most vendors about to be shaken out will make—is that current applications software is about as easy to use as a sports car. The power and capabilities are there for the experienced user, but the novice—the 95% of knowledge workers who do not yet have pcs—may find the early going rough.

"The people who have already bought computers and software are the technically minded innovators at their companies," Jobs says. "They were willing to put up with the 20 to 40 hours it takes to master current software, but their less technical peers in the mass market will not be."

Thomas J. Gregory, president of Boston-based software vendor Ovation Technologies, notes that "today's professional does not have the time or interest to learn complicated technical terminology or extensive commands. Over and over we hear users ask for 'easy to operate,' 'user friendly,' 'logical English commands,' and 'true integration.' In essence, users want a system that acts human and performs computer."

For many users, the issue boils down to a simple cost justification. "A company that buys $400,000 of microcomputer software may have to spend $1.5 million to train users," says Martel Firing, a founder of Noumenon Inc., an Alameda, Calif., software vendor. "Most companies can't afford to take the time or the money to train people, and the software may not make the company any money or reduce its costs. Those will be the only criteria and if the software falls short the whole pc market will go down the tubes." . . .

Unfortunately, some vendors note, understanding the needs of the users and being able to meet them are not the same thing. "Industry people are alert to new advances in technology, but new users have expectations of glory far beyond what we can do now," says Kenneth Scott, senior vice president of Microrim Inc. in Bellevue, Wash. "They saw HAL in *2001* over 15 years ago and figure we're way past that today." . . .

Even the current emphasis on windows, menus, and data swapping applications falls short of the mark, vendors admit. "Windows are a pacifier to the naive," Scott says. "They are transitional vehicles that just get in the way later. We don't mess around with menus, for the same reason."

Firing tends to be more sympathetic to windows, arguing that they "are fundamentally very good," but that the current technology is just a gimmick." . . .

The basic problem with all these approaches is that the software is still one step removed from the user's way of thinking.

## chapter 19

# Preparing Computer Programs
## *an overview*

### The High Price Of Compatibility

The more than 200 computer languages make up a diverse lot. As with spoken languages, each has its own history, evolution, color, nuances, special characteristics, and quirks.

Such individuality has created a system compatibility nightmare. *Science News* recently reported that the U.S. Navy currently uses about "50 million unique lines of software" written in a variety of computer languages. The magazine goes on to quote Navy Captain David Boslaugh, who estimates that to redo these lines of code to achieve software compatibility among its computer systems "would take years, considerable expertise, and at least $85 billion."

The fact is that so-called outdated computer languages are self-perpetuating because of the enormous investment in existing programs. Take COBOL, for example. Originally developed on mainframes and rewritten for micros, it has been criticized as being slow, ponderous, and anachronistic. Yet COBOL is especially well suited to business applications, where the name of the game is software maintenance.

A prime reason for COBOL's continued popularity is that its code reads like an English sentence. In fact, there are more help-wanted ads today for COBOL programmers than for any other computer language. So much for dead languages.

Each computer language, obviously, has its strengths and weaknesses. BASIC is easy to learn but Pascal admirers say BASIC's loose format encourages sloppy programming habits. Artificial-intelligence researchers will settle for nothing but LISP while a growing body of successful professionals and midnight hackers claim FORTH is the "best" and most "serendipitous" computer language.

—From "The High Price of Compatibility" by Rich Friedman appearing in the September 1983 issue of *Popular Computing* magazine. Copyright © 1983 Byte Publications, Inc. Used with permission of Byte Publications, Inc. Photo courtesy Texas Instruments Incorporated.

In this second chapter dealing with the programming process, you'll learn about some of the issues that must be considered during the program preparation stage. The different categories of programming languages are then identified and discussed. Next, you'll be introduced to some of the major high-level languages used in program coding. And the implementation and maintenance of coded applications programs are presented in the final pages of this chapter. The information in this chapter will enable you to:

◼ Identify and discuss several of the issues and options involved in program preparation

◼ Outline the features and uses of machine languages, assembly languages, and high-level languages

◼ Summarize the steps that are taken during program implementation and maintenance

# ISSUES AND OPTIONS IN PROGRAM PREPARATION

After programming analysis as discussed in Chapter 18 has been completed, the second step in programming is to code the specific instructions needed to process an application into a language and form acceptable to a computer system. And the third step in the process is to then implement and maintain these coded instructions.

## Issues and Options in General
Preparing computer programs has historically been a painstaking art. It still is. Whether programming for an organization or a personal application, programmers generally share similar objectives:

## Chapter Outline

1. To serve user needs.

2. To reduce the time and money needed to develop and implement programs.

3. To produce programs with minimal errors.

4. To produce programs that are easy to implement and maintain.

In trying to achieve one desirable goal, however, programmers are often faced with tradeoffs: *Should we reduce development time at the risk of producing programs that are more error-prone and harder to maintain?* And in any case, programmers must usually deal with a number of issues involving methodology and the use of resources: *Should we create a new program or should we buy a packaged program from a vendor? How should programming tasks be assigned? What program design methods should we use?* One reason programming is still an art rather than an exact science is that reasonable people with essentially the same types of problems to solve have chosen different options when answering these and other questions.

In the next few pages we'll look at a few of the issues and options facing those who prepare programs. The field of **software engineering** has emerged in the last decade to address some of these issues by applying scientific principles to the development of computer programs. As a result, it's likely that professional programmers will follow a more scientific approach in dealing with programming issues in the years ahead.

## Make or Buy?

Perhaps the first issue to be considered is the "make or buy" question. Should a new custom-made program be created within an organization, or should an existing applications package be purchased from a supplier of such software? You'll recall from Chapter 4 that applications packages or **packaged programs** are programs written by outside vendors that are available for specific applications (Figure 19-1). No one knows how many packages are available today in this multibillion-dollar market. One software searching firm has compiled descriptive information on more than 30,000 packages for its clients, but this number isn't a complete listing and the total is growing daily. Generally speaking, the make or buy decision involves tradeoffs. The packaged program usually

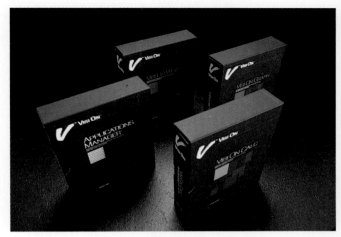

**Figure 19-1** Microcomputer software packages include extensive documentation manuals as well as floppy disks. (Courtesy Visicorp. Photographs by Anderson and Carry Studios)

achieves the goals of lower cost (development costs are shared by many customers), faster implementation, and reduced risk of error (the package is available for testing). The in-house, custom-made program has the possible advantages of greater operating efficiency and the ability to more effectively satisfy the unique needs of users (in trying to appeal to many potential users the packaged program may sacrifice processing performance in areas important to a particular organization).

Whenever feasible, however, the use of an appropriate application package should always be considered as an alternative during program development. The following listing summarizes some of the factors that should be examined in evaluating package alternatives (more detailed information is given in Chapter 8 on identifying and selecting personal computer software packages):

- *Package quality.* A check of current users should be made to evaluate the suitability, ease of use, performance, and reliability of the software.

- *Vendor reputation.* The vendor should be financially strong, and should be able to provide the technical support needed to install, maintain, and update the package.

- *Documentation.* Those in the organization who must work with the package should have adequate documentation available to meet their needs.

## Programmer Organization

The output of a program preparation project should be an effective product at an economical price. Programmers are currently assigned to such program preparation projects in various ways. Each option for organizing programmers differs in significant ways from the others. There's no agreement on which approach is best. Some organizations are trying to develop other options for organizing programmers that combine some of the features of the three presented here:

**Traditional Hierarchical Grouping.** A programming manager assigns tasks to programmers, and exercises overall control over the project. But the manager does not normally participate in the actual coding. Rather, individual programmers code, test, and document the programs to which they are assigned. They may be shifted from project to project as the workload dictates.

**Chief Programmer Teams.** In the **chief programmer team** approach, each project is assigned to a team con-

## GAINING A COMPETITIVE EDGE WITH SOFTWARE

Software used to be invisible. Programmers worked deep in the corporate backrooms of accounting or data processing departments. But the proliferation of microcomputers being used by individuals within companies has lent software a sudden surge of popularity. With the micro handling an ever-increasing variety of management tasks, the spotlight is truly on software for the first time, and programs are gaining prominence in business.

One insurance company executive draws an analogy between the software packages used to run his business and "the tools an auto maker puts in place to manufacture auto parts. Our 'plant' is our data processing system."

Executives are now engaged in refining the art of using information as a tool to increase their organization's competitive position within its industry. Since the same hardware, in essence, is available to everyone, the obvious advantage of effective customized software can give a company a real competitive edge.

Of course, there is another major area of impact, and that's the corporate budget. Estimates range up to half the yearly budgets of some data processing departments spent either on writing software or on buying packages from independent vendors.

On an individual level, the story is more dramatic. *Business Week* estimates that over the life of a microcomputer, an owner will spend $2 on software for every $1 spent on hardware.

In many companies, it's becoming more and more difficult to produce effective programs from scratch. Users have come to expect regularly to wait for programs for as long as a year and a half. They recognize that their companies simply do not have sufficient resources to hire enough programmers to write all the software they need in house.

Writing software is a time-consuming process, and new applications spring up constantly in many industries. Companies with heavy data processing needs have found that although they *want* to use their computers to handle more applications, their resources prohibit full employment of their hardware.

The solution has been to compromise: companies are buying more ready-to-run packaged software all the time. While users do give up the aura of customized programs by buying packages, they gain the advantage of saving time and money, and this factor often outweighs the advantages of uniqueness.

For instance, packaged software can cut program development costs in the range of one third to three quarters over starting from scratch, and packages can cut the time it takes to get a system up and running by more than half. In many cases where a customized solution is required, companies can save time by modifying an existing package for their own use.

All these approaches make sense because of the immense variety of commercial software available today. The make-or-buy decision now requires close evaluation by managers, but the right decision can give a company that vital competitive edge.

—Source of data: *Business Week*, Feb. 27, 1984.

sisting of a senior-level *chief programmer,* a skilled *backup programmer,* and a *librarian.* Applications programmers and other specialists are added to this nucleus as needed. In many ways, this team is like a surgical team in a hospital. The chief programmer (surgeon) has responsibility for the project and is the key coder of the program(s) being prepared. The backup programmer (assisting doctor) is ready to take the chief programmer's place if necessary, and is expected to develop important elements of the program. Other team members (like nurses and an anesthesiologist) perform special tasks for the chief programmer. The librarian, for example, gathers and organizes the records and documents associated with the project. And applications programmers code modules that have been mapped out by the chief programmer.

**"Egoless" Programming Teams.** We've seen in the traditional approach that a programmer may often be responsible for coding and implementing an entire program. This close association with the program may serve to make it an extension of the programmer's ego. If errors are then discovered in the program (and they often are), the programmer may consider the discovery to be a personal attack. To avoid this situation, an **"egoless" programming team** is assigned to a project. Membership in the close-knit team seldom changes, and there's no designated chief. Assignments are determined in a democratic way with each member doing that part of the work for which he or she is best suited. During coding, team members check the work of each other to help locate and correct errors. The completed code is then not the responsibility of a single person but is rather the product of the entire team.

## Program Construction Techniques

Different program construction techniques have been developed to help achieve the four goals listed at the beginning of this section. Again, different organizations often use a varying mix of the following program construction options:

**Modular Program Design.** You'll recall from Chapter 18 that a **main-control program** may be used to outline the major segments or *modules* needed to solve a program. The main-control program specifies the order in which each module (or subroutine) in the program will be processed. When the **modular program design** technique

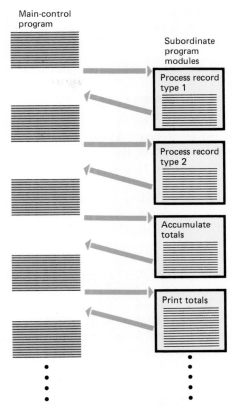

Figure 19-2 The modular programming option.

is used, an instruction in the main-control program branches control to a subordinate module. When the specific processing operation performed by the module is completed, another branch instruction may transfer program control to another module or return it to the main-control program. Thus, the modules or subroutines are really programs within a program. Each module typically has only one entry point and only one exit point. Many programmers believe that modules should be limited in size to about 50 lines of code—the amount that can be placed on one page of printer output. Figure 19-2 summarizes the modular technique. Some of the advantages of using this construction option are:

1. Complex programs may be divided into simpler and more manageable elements.

2. Simultaneous coding of modules by several programmers is possible.

3. A *library* of modules may be created, and these modules may be used in other programs as needed.

4. The location of program errors may be more easily traced to a particular module, and thus debugging and maintenance may be simplified.

5. Effective use can be made of tested subroutines prepared by software suppliers and furnished to their customers. All these advantages help programmers realize their goals.

**The Use of Basic Coding Structures.** A clever programming "artist" can write programs containing a maze of branches to alter the sequence of processing operations. These programs may work at first. But since the artist may be the only one who understands the convoluted logic that was used, they can represent a nightmare for the person(s) responsible for their maintenance. To counter such artistic tendencies, many organizations specify that programmers stick to the use of the simple sequence, selection, and loop structures presented in Chapter 18. These organizations have found that when programs are so structured, and when modular techniques are used, programs can be read from top to bottom and are easier to understand. This greater clarity can help reduce (1) program errors, (2) the time spent in program testing, and (3) the time and effort spent on program maintenance.

**Peer Reviews.** The technique of holding a **peer review** during program construction to detect software errors is called a **structured walkthrough.** Each review is initiated by the programmer whose work is to be checked. Materials are handed out in advance of the review session, and the objectives of the session are outlined to participants. (Programmer managers are not invited.) The role of the participants is to detect errors, but no attempt is made during the session to correct any errors that are discovered.

A walkthrough session will typically include three to five of the programmer's colleagues. (These colleagues will have their own work reviewed in other similar sessions.) During the session, the reviewee will walk through, step by step, the logic of the work. One participant will keep a record of any errors that are uncovered so that proper corrective action can be taken by the

reviewee. The tone of the session should be relaxed, and there should be no personal attacks.

The possible advantages of the peer review technique are:

1. Fewer errors are likely to get through the development process.

2. Faster implementation, a reduction in development costs, and greater user satisfaction may then be possible.

3. Better program documentation may be obtained.

4. Later program maintenance efforts may be easier and less expensive.

5. Higher programmer morale may result from the spirit of cooperation that can exist.

These same advantages, of course, are possible when programmers are organized into the egoless programming teams described earlier.

**Structured Programming Environment.** The term **structured programming** has been compared to a snowman after a day in the warm sun—both may originally have been distinctly formed, but both are now rather vaguely defined. Originally, the term was defined to be the disciplined use of the three basic coding structures mentioned above. Care was taken to allow only one entrance and one exit from a structure and to minimize the use of branching instructions such as GO TO. Rules on indenting the coding structures written on coding sheets were also established to give a clearer picture of the coding logic. Since this original use of the term, however, a number of *other* techniques have also been added under the structured programming banner. Thus, many now expand the definition of structured programming to include the use of:

- A "top-down" approach to identifying a main function and then breaking it down into lower-level components for analysis and modular program design purposes.

- Structured walkthroughs.

- Chief programmer teams.

Combining these program construction and programmer organizing techniques into a disciplined structured programming environment can lead to improvements in programming efficiency and in software quality.

But an organization must carefully weigh the possible benefits to be obtained from the use of structured programming techniques against its own needs and resources.

# PROGRAMMING LANGUAGE CLASSIFICATIONS

A language is a system of communication. A **programming language** consists of all the symbols, characters, and usage rules that permit people to communicate with computers. Some programming languages are created to serve a *special purpose* (e.g., controlling a robot), while others are more flexible *general-purpose* tools that are suitable for many types of applications. However, every programming language must accept certain types of written instructions that will enable a computer system to perform a number of familiar operations. That is, every language must have instructions that fall into the following familiar categories:

1. *Input/output instructions.* Required to permit communication between I/O devices and the central processor, these instructions provide details on the type of input or output operation to be performed and the storage locations to be used during the operation.

2. *Calculation instructions.* Instructions to permit addition, subtraction, multiplication, and division during processing are, of course, common in all programming languages.

3. *Logic/comparison instructions.* These instructions are used to *transfer program control,* and are needed in the selection and loop structures that are followed to prepare programs. During processing, two data items may be compared as a result of the execution of a logic instruction. As you know, program control can follow different paths depending on the outcome of a selection test (IF R > 0, THEN A, ELSE B). And a loop can be continued or terminated depending on the outcome of an exit condition test (does Q = −99.9?). In addition to the instructions in languages that set

up tests or comparisons to effect the transfer of program control, there are also *unconditional* transfer instructions available that are not based on the outcome of comparisons.

4. *Storage/retrieval and movement instructions.* These instructions are used to store, retrieve, and move data during processing. Data may be copied from one storage location to another and retrieved as needed.

But even though all programming languages have an instruction set that permits these familiar operations to be performed, there's a marked difference to be found in the symbols, characters, and syntax of machine languages, assembly languages, and high-level languages.

## Machine Languages

A computer's **machine language** consists of strings of binary numbers and is the only one the CPU directly "understands." An instruction prepared in any machine language will have at least two parts. The *first part* is the *command* or *operation,* and it tells the computer what function to perform. Every computer has an **operation code** or "op code" for each of its functions. The *second part* of the instruction is the **operand,** and it tells the computer where to find or store the data or other instructions that are to be manipulated. The number of operands in an instruction varies among computers. In a *single-operand* machine, the binary equivalent of "ADD 0184" could cause the value in address 0184 to be added to the value stored in a register in the arithmetic-logic unit. In a *two-operand* machine, the binary representation for "ADD 0184 8672" could cause the value in address 8672 to be added to the number in location 0184. The single-operand format is popular in the smallest microcomputers; the two-operand structure is likely to be available in most other machines.

By today's standards, early computers were intolerant. Programmers had to translate instructions directly into the machine-language form that computers understood. For example, the programmer writing the instruction to "ADD 0184" for an early IBM machine would have written:

00010000000000000000000000010111000

In addition to remembering the dozens of code numbers for the commands in the machine's instruction set, a programmer was also forced to keep track of the storage locations of data and instructions. The initial coding often took months, was therefore quite expensive, and often resulted in error. Checking instructions to locate errors was about as tedious as writing them initially. And if a program had to be modified at a later date, the work involved could take weeks to finish.

## Assembly Languages

To ease the programmer's burden, *mnemonic* operation codes and *symbolic* addresses were developed in the early 1950s. The word mnemonic (pronounced ne-mon'-ik) refers to a memory aid. One of the first steps in improving the program preparation process was to substitute letter symbols—mnemonics—for the numeric machine-language operation codes. Each computer now has a **mnemonic code,** although, of course, the actual symbols vary among makes and models. Figure 19-3 shows the mnemonic codes for a few of the commands used with some IBM mainframe computers. (The complete instruction set has about 200 commands.) Machine language is *still* used by the computer as it processes data, but **assembly language** software first translates the specified operation code symbol into its machine-language equivalent.

And this improvement set the stage for further advances. If the computer could translate convenient symbols into basic operations, why couldn't it also perform other clerical coding functions such as assigning storage addresses to data? **Symbolic addressing** is the practice of expressing an address *not* in terms of its absolute numerical location, but rather in terms of symbols convenient to the programmer.

In the early stages of symbolic addressing, the programmer assigned a symbolic name and an actual address to a data item. For example, the total value of merchandise purchased during a month by a department store customer might be assigned to address 0063 by the programmer and given the symbolic name TOTAL. The value of merchandise returned unused during the month might be assigned to address 2047 and given the symbolic name CREDIT. Then, for the remainder of the program, the programmer would refer to the *symbolic names rather than to the addresses* when such items were to be processed. Thus, an instruction might be written "S CREDIT, TOTAL" to subtract the value of returned goods from the total amount purchased to find the amount of the customer's monthly bill. The assembly language software might then translate the symbolic instruction into this machine-language string of bits:

| Command name | Mnemonic (symbolic) operation code | Command name | Mnemonic (symbolic) operation code |
|---|---|---|---|
| *Input/Output Commands* | | Compare Logical Character | CLC |
| Start I/O | SIO | Branch on Condition Register | BCR |
| Halt I/O | HIO | Branch on Condition | BC |
| *Calculation Commands* | | Branch on Count | BCT |
| Add | A | *Storage/Retrieval and Movement Commands* | |
| Subtract | S | Load Register | LR |
| Multiply | M | Load | L |
| Divide | D | Move Characters | MVC |
| *Logic/Comparison Commands* | | Move Numerics | MVN |
| Compare Register | CR | Store | ST |
| Compare | C | Store Character | STC |

Figure 19-3 Partial instruction set for some IBM mainframe computers.

<u>011111</u>        <u>011111111111</u>  <u>000000111111</u>

Mnemonic op code      2047        0063

(S)        (CREDIT)    (TOTAL)

Another improvement followed. The programmer turned the task of assigning and keeping track of instruction addresses over to the computer. The programmer merely told the machine the storage address number of the *first* program instruction, and the assembly language software then automatically stored all others in sequence from that point. So if another instruction was added to the program later, it was not necessary to modify the addresses of all instructions that followed the point of insertion (as would have to be done in the case of programs written in machine language). Instead, the processor automatically adjusted storage locations the next time the program ran.

Programmers no longer assign actual address numbers to symbolic data items as they did earlier. Now they merely specify where they want the first location in the program to be, and an assembly language program takes it from there, allocating locations for instructions and data.

This **assembly program,** or **assembler,** also enables the computer to convert the programmer's assembly language instructions into its own machine code. A program of instructions written by a programmer in an assembly language is called a **source program.** After this source program has been converted into machine code by an assembler, it's referred to as an **object program.** It's easier for programmers to write instructions in an assembly language than to prepare instructions in machine-language codes. But two computer runs may be required before source program instructions can be used to produce the desired output. These separate *assembly* and *production* runs are outlined and discussed in Figure 19-4.

Assembly languages have *advantages over machine languages.* They save time and reduce detail. Fewer errors are made, and those that are made are easier to find. And assembly programs are easier for people to modify than machine-language programs. But there are *limitations.* Coding in assembly language is still time consuming. And a big drawback of assembly languages is that they are *machine oriented.* That is, they are designed for the specific make and model of processor being used. Programs might have to be recoded for a different machine.

## High-Level Languages

The earlier assembly programs produced only one machine instruction for each source program instruction. To speed up coding, assembly programs were developed that could produce a *variable* amount of machine-language code for *each* source program instruction. In other words, a single **macro instruction** might produce *several* lines of machine-language code. For example, the programmer might write "READ FILE," and the translating software might then automatically provide a detailed series of previously prepared machine-language instructions which would copy a record into primary storage from the file of data being read by the input device. Thus, the programmer was relieved of the task of writing an instruction for every machine operation performed.

The development of mnemonic techniques and macro instructions led, in turn, to the development of **high-level languages** that are often oriented toward a particular class of processing problems. For example, a number of languages have been designed to process problems of a scientific-mathematic nature, and other languages have appeared that emphasize file processing applications.

Unlike assembly programs, high-level language programs may be used with *different makes of computers* with little modification. Thus, reprogramming expense may be greatly reduced when new equipment is acquired. Other advantages of high-level languages are:

- They are easier to learn than assembly languages.

- They require less time to write.

- They provide better documentation.

- They are easier to maintain.

- A programmer skilled in writing programs in such a language is not restricted to using a single type of machine.

**Compiler Translation.** Naturally, a source program written in a high-level language must also be translated into a machine-usable code. A translating program that can perform this operation is called a **compiler.** Compilers, like advanced assembly programs, may generate many lines of machine code for each source program statement. A *compiling run* is required before problem data can be processed. With the exception that a com-

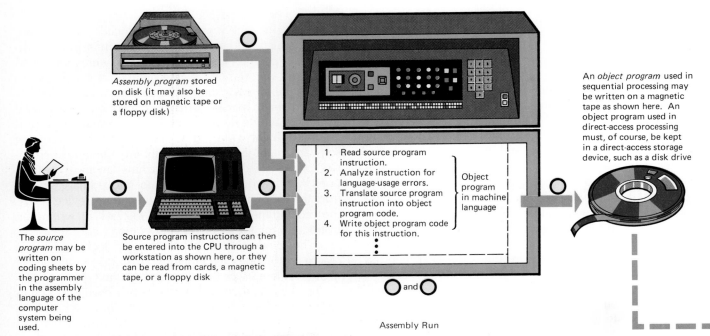

Assembly program stored on disk (it may also be stored on magnetic tape or a floppy disk)

The source program may be written on coding sheets by the programmer in the assembly language of the computer system being used.

Source program instructions can then be entered into the CPU through a workstation as shown here, or they can be read from cards, a magnetic tape, or a floppy disk

1. Read source program instruction.
2. Analyze instruction for language-usage errors.
3. Translate source program instruction into object program code.
4. Write object program code for this instruction.

Object program in machine language

An object program used in sequential processing may be written on a magnetic tape as shown here. An object program used in direct-access processing must, of course, be kept in a direct-access storage device, such as a disk drive

and

Assembly Run

**Figure 19-4** Assembly language source program instructions are translated into machine-language code during the assembly run (steps 1–4). The machine-language object program is then used to process problem data during a production run (steps 5–7).

## Assembly Run

**1.** The *assembly program* or *assembler* is read into the computer, where it has complete control over the translating procedure. This program is generally supplied by the manufacturer of the machine, or by an independent software house. It's usually stored online on a disk or on secondary storage media such as a magnetic tape or a floppy disk.

**2.** The *source program* instructions are written by the programmer on coding sheets in the assembly language of the machine being used. These instructions can then be keyed into the CPU from a workstation or entered through the use of input media such as magnetic tape, or floppy disks.

**3.** During the assembly run, the source program is treated as data and is read into the CPU, one instruction at a time, under the control of the assembler.

**4.** The assembler translates the source program into a machine-language *object program,* which may be stored on-line or recorded on a secondary storage medium as the output of the assembly run. It's important to remember that *during the assembly run no problem data are processed.* That is, the source program is *not* being executed. It's merely being converted into a form in which it can be executed by the CPU.

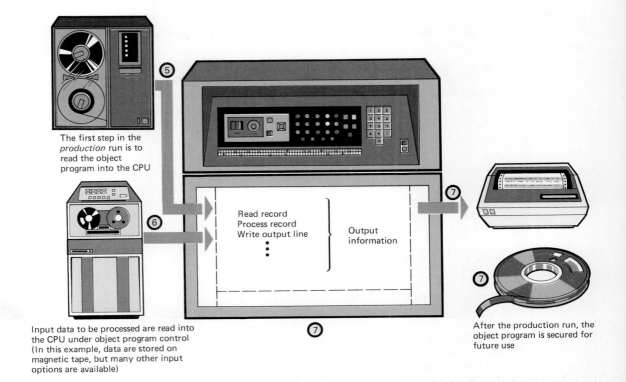

The first step in the *production* run is to read the object program into the CPU

Read record
Process record
Write output line
$\vdots$

Output information

Input data to be processed are read into the CPU under object program control (In this example, data are stored on magnetic tape, but many other input options are available)

After the production run, the object program is secured for future use

### Production Run

**5.** The object program is read into the CPU during the first step in the *production run*. The frequently needed object programs used in direct-access processing are kept in an online storage device. The object programs used in sequential processing applications are usually stored on magnetic tape, cards, or floppy disks.

**6.** Input data, which may be recorded on a suitable input medium or entered from an online terminal, are read into the CPU under object program control.

**7.** The data are processed, information output may be produced, and the object program is secured for future use.

piler program is substituted for an assembly program, the procedures are essentially the same as those shown in Figure 19-4. The production run follows the compiling run.

**Interpreter Translation.** An alternative to using a compiler for high-level language translation is often employed with personal computers. Instead of translating the source program and permanently saving the object code produced during a compiling run for future production use, the programmer merely loads the source program into the computer along with the data to be processed. A permanently hardwired **interpreter** program located inside the computer then converts each source program statement into machine-language form as it's needed during the processing of the data. No object code is saved for future use.

The next time the instruction is used, it must once again be interpreted and translated into machine language. For example, during the repetitive processing of the steps in a loop, each instruction in the loop will have to be reinterpreted every time the loop is executed. The interpreter eliminates the need for a separate compiling run after each program change to add features or correct errors. But a previously compiled object program should obviously run much faster than one which has to be interpreted each step of the way during a production run.

# MAJOR HIGH-LEVEL LANGUAGES USED IN PROGRAM CODING

Early work on high-level languages began in the 1950s. UNIVAC's Dr. Grace M. Hopper, for example, developed a compiler (named A-2) in 1952. Since then, many other high-level languages have been produced. A closer look at some of the people responsible for developing these languages is presented at the end of Chapter 1. Let's take a look now at a few of the most popular high-level languages.

## BASIC

**BASIC** (Beginner's All-purpose Symbolic Instruction Code) is a popular interactive language that has wide appeal because it's easy to use. An **interactive language** permits direct communication between user and computer system during the preparation and use of programs. A problem-solver with little or no knowledge of computers or programming can learn to write BASIC programs at a terminal or personal computer keyboard in a short period of time. Entering data is easy, and the problem-solver need not be confused about output formats because a usable format may be automatically provided. It's also easy to insert changes and additions into a BASIC program.

Because of its simplicity, BASIC was used in the first microcomputer to gain commercial success. It's now by far the most popular high-level language used in personal computer systems. This fact makes it one of the most widely installed computer languages in the world. Interpreters are frequently used in personal computer systems to translate BASIC instructions into machine-language code. But BASIC language compilers are also available for these systems. Recreational and educational programs are published in many of the personal computing magazines listed in Figure 8-6, page 221, and these programs are usually documented in BASIC.

BASIC was developed between 1963 and 1964 at Dartmouth College under the direction of Professors John Kemeny and Thomas Kurtz. Their purpose was to produce a language that undergraduate students in all fields of study (1) would find easy to learn, and (2) would thus be encouraged to use on a regular basis. BASIC was a success at Dartmouth on both counts. The Dartmouth computer system used General Electric equipment, and BASIC was implemented on this equipment with the assistance of GE engineers. Recognizing the advantages of BASIC, GE then quickly made the language available for the use of their customers who were buying time on GE's commercial timesharing systems. And Hewlett-Packard and Digital Equipment Corporation offered early versions of BASIC to run on their timeshared computer systems.

By 1974, BASIC was available for most computers, and it's now offered by virtually all computer manufacturers. Although the original BASIC had a well-defined syntax, numerous extensions to the language were written in the decade after 1964. Little thought was given to making these extensions compatible with other versions of the language. And so it is today that "BASIC" is really a generic name for a group of dialects with many similar features. There's an American National Standards Institute **(ANSI) standard** for a minimal version of BASIC that was published in 1978. But this standard is so simple that it has been extended in virtually every available BASIC dialect.

Users of BASIC range from public school students to aerospace engineers to business managers. After studying the next two chapters, you may also be included in this group because we'll be coding a number of applications in these chapters using the BASIC language. A BASIC version of a simple billing program designed to process bills for multiple customers is shown in Figure 19-5. This is the program for problem 2 that was discussed in Chapter 18 and charted in Figure 18-4, page 486.

## FORTRAN

A FORTRAN program listing for this same simple billing problem is shown in Figure 19-6. When supplied with the data shown in the BASIC program, this FORTRAN version will produce the same output, as you can see in Figure 19-6. We can trace the origin of **FORTRAN** (FORmula TRANslator) back to 1954 when an IBM-sponsored committee headed by John Backus began work on a scientific-mathematic language. The result of this effort was FORTRAN, which was introduced in 1957 for the IBM 704 computer. It's estimated that the cost of producing the 25,000 lines of detailed machine instructions that went into the first FORTRAN compiler was $2.5 million. FORTRAN is noted for the ease with which it can express mathematical equations. It has been widely accepted and has been revised a number of times. Several of its features were later incorporated into the first BASIC language.

The vast majority of all computers now in service—from small micros to the largest number-crunchers—can use FORTRAN. Compilers rather than interpreters are used. Because of its early widespread acceptance, work began in 1962 on FORTRAN standard languages. Two standards—a basic or minimal version of FORTRAN and a "full" or extended version—were approved by ANSI in 1966. FORTRAN thus has the distinction of being the first standardized language. The current FORTRAN standards were published by ANSI in 1978.

As you can see in Figure 19-6, a FORTRAN program consists of a series of *statements*. These statements supply input/output, calculation, logic/comparison, and other basic instructions to the computer. The words READ, WRITE, GO TO, and STOP in the statements mean exactly what you would expect. FORTRAN programs are executed sequentially until the sequence is altered by a transfer of control statement.

FORTRAN has the *advantage* of being a compact language that serves the needs of scientists and business statisticians very well. Huge libraries of engineering and scientific programs written in FORTRAN are available to scientists and engineers. The language is also widely used for business applications that don't require the manipulation of extensive data files. Because there are established FORTRAN standards, programs written for one computer are usually easily converted for use with another. *However*, it may be more difficult to trace program logic in FORTRAN code than in some other high-level languages. And FORTRAN is not as well suited for processing large business files as the next language we'll discuss, COBOL.

## COBOL

As its name indicates, **COBOL** (COmmon Business Oriented Language) was designed specifically for business-type data processing. And it's now the most widely used language for large business applications. The group that designed the language gathered at the Pentagon in Washington, D.C., in May 1959, with the official sanction of the U.S. Department of Defense. Members of the COnference of DAta SYstems Languages (**CODASYL**) represented computer manufacturers, government agencies, user organizations, and universities. The CODASYL Short-Range Committee, which prepared the COBOL framework, consisted of representatives from federal government agencies and from computer manufacturers. From June to December 1959, this committee worked on the language specifications. Its final report was approved in January 1960, and the language specifications were published a few months later by the Government Printing Office.

Since 1961, COBOL compilers have been prepared for virtually all processors used in business data processing. And they are available now for use with small personal computers. Other CODASYL committees have continued to maintain, revise, and extend the initial specifications. An ANSI COBOL standard was first published in 1968, and a later version was approved in 1974. A new standard is scheduled to appear in the 1980s.

```
10  REM *BILLING PROGRAM
20  REM *
30  REM *VARIABLE NAMES
40  REM * N$   NAME
50  REM * S$   ADDRESS
60  REM * C$   CITY AND STATE
70  REM * Q    QUANTITY PURCHASED
80  REM * P    UNIT PRICE
90  REM * A    NET AMOUNT
100 REM *
110 REM *READ NAME,ADDRESS,QUANTITY PURCHASED AND PRICE
120     READ N$,S$,C$,Q,P
130 REM *TEST QUANTITY FOR LAST INPUT
140     IF Q=-99.9 THEN 400
150 REM *COMPUTE NET AMOUNT
160     LET A = Q*P
170 REM *PRINT NAME,ADDRESS AND NET AMOUNT
180     PRINT N$
190     PRINT S$
200     PRINT C$
210     PRINT TAB(3);"NET = ";A
220     PRINT
230     PRINT
240     GO TO 120
260 REM *INPUT DATA
270     DATA "PIERRE'S RECORD SHOP"
280     DATA "6453 ORLEANS STREET"
290     DATA "BOOGIE,LOUISIANA 54321"
300     DATA  300.0,25.00
310     DATA "ROCKY COLLEGE STORE"
320     DATA "1563 BEETHOVEN DRIVE"
330     DATA "ROCKTOWN,MARYLAND 20765"
340     DATA  3.25,25.00
350     DATA "WYNN D.TOOTS,INC."
360     DATA "120 BROWNING STREET"
370     DATA "GONG,CALIFORNIA 98765"
380     DATA  2.00,25.00
390     DATA "L","L","L",-99.9,0.
400     END
```

Computer listing of the BASIC program

**Figure 19-5** An example of a BASIC program. At the top of this figure is a computer listing of a simple billing program designed to process bills for multiple customers. (The flowchart for this program was shown in Chapter 18, Figure 18-4.) At the bottom of this figure is the output produced by the computer when the program is run. Each step of this example is discussed in the next chapter.

```
PIERRE'S RECORD SHOP
6453 ORLEANS STREET
BOOGIE,LOUISIANA 54321
  NET =    7500


ROCKY COLLEGE STORE
1563 BEETHOVEN DRIVE
ROCKTOWN,MARYLAND 20765
  NET =    81.2500


WYNN D.TOOTS,INC.
120 BROWNING STREET
GONG,CALIFORNIA 98765
  NET =    50
```

Output produced by the computer as the program is executed

```
C ...BILLING PROGRAM
      INTEGER ADDR1,ADDR2
      DIMENSION NAME(20),ADDR1(20),ADDR2(20)
C...READ NAME,ADDRESS,QUANTITY PURCHASED AND UNIT PRICE
   10 READ(5,70) NAME
      READ(5,70) ADDR1
      READ(5,70) ADDR2
      READ(5,75) QTY,PRICE
C ...TEST QTY FOR LAST CARD
      IF(QTY.EQ.-99.9) GO TO 20
C ... COMPUTE NET PRICE
      ANET = QTY*PRICE
C ...PRINT NAME,ADDRESS AND NET PRICE
      WRITE(6,80) NAME,ADDR1,ADDR2
      WRITE(6,85) ANET
      GO TO 10
   20 STOP
C ...FORMAT STATEMENTS
   70 FORMAT(20A4)
   75 FORMAT(2F10.2)
   80 FORMAT(//3(/3X,20A4))
   85 FORMAT(6X,6HNET = ,F10.2)
      END
```

Computer listing of the
FORTRAN Program

```
PIERRE'S RECORD SHOP
6453 ORLEANS STREET
BOOGIE,LOUISIANA 54321
   NET =     7500.00




ROCKY COLLEGE STORE
1563 BEETHOVEN DRIVE
ROCKTOWN,MARYLAND 20765
   NET =       81.25




WYNN D. TOOTS,INC.
120 BROWNING STREET
GONG,CALIFORNIA 98765
   NET =       50.00
```

Output produced by computer as
program is executed. The same
input data used in the BASIC
Program were punched on cards
and read into the computer under
program control.

Figure 19-6 A computer listing of the simple billing program written in the FORTRAN
language.

Figure 19-7 shows a computer listing of a COBOL program. This program is a COBOL version of the BASIC and FORTRAN simple billing programs illustrated in Figures 19-5 and 19-6. If the same input data used in the earlier language examples are read into a computer under the control of this COBOL program, the output results will be essentially the same as you can see in Figure 19-7.

COBOL is structured much like this chapter. *Sentences* (analogous to statements in FORTRAN) direct the processor in performing the necessary operations. A varying number of sentences dealing with the same operation are grouped to form a *paragraph*. Related paragraphs may then be organized into a *section*. Sections are then grouped into a *division*, and *four divisions* complete the structural hierarchy of a COBOL program.

The *first* entry, line 1 in Figure 19-7, is IDENTIFICATION DIVISION—the first of the COBOL divisions. A required paragraph identifies the program, and additional optional paragraphs are included for documentation purposes. The *second* division, line 7, is the ENVIRONMENT DIVISION, which consists of two required sections that describe the specific hardware to use when the program is run. If the application is to be processed on different equipment, this division will have to be rewritten, but that usually presents no problem.

The DATA DIVISION (line 17 in Figure 19-7), the *third* of the four divisions, is divided into file and working storage sections. The purpose of this division is to present in detail a description and layout of:

■ All the *input data* items in a record, and all the records in each file that's to be processed.

■ All *storage locations* that are needed during processing to hold intermediate results and other independent values needed for processing.

■ The format to be used for the *output* results.

The *last* COBOL division, the PROCEDURE DIVISION (line 52), contains the sentences and paragraphs that the computer follows in executing the program. In this division, input/output, calculation, logic/comparison, and storage/retrieval and movement operations are performed to solve the problem.

One *advantage* of COBOL is that it can be written in a quasi-English form that may employ commonly used business terms. Because of this fact, the logic of COBOL

programs may often be followed more easily by the nonprogrammers in business. Thus, there may be less documentation required for COBOL programs. COBOL is better able to manipulate alphabetic characters than FORTRAN, and this is important in business processing where names, addresses, or descriptions are frequently reproduced. Also, a standard version exists; the language is relatively machine-independent; and it's maintained, updated, and supported by its users. Finally, there are large libraries of COBOL business applications modules and packages available today from vendors. To give just one example, Raytheon's ReadyCode system offers customers a library of reusable modules and logic structures that can significantly reduce the time required to code and test new COBOL programs. A *limitation* of COBOL, however, is that it's obviously not a compact language. It's not the easiest high-level language for most of us to learn, and it's not as well suited for complex mathematical computations as FORTRAN.

## PL/I

We've seen that early languages such as FORTRAN and COBOL were written to solve *either* scientific or business data processing problems. But in the early 1960s, IBM and a committee of users of the IBM System/360 family of computers began development work on what was promoted as a "universal language." This **PL/I** language (Programming Language/"One") was implemented in the mid-1960s to solve all types of business and scientific problems. As a scientific language, PL/I was designed to include some of the features of FORTRAN; however, COBOL-type file processing techniques are also used. An ANSI committee produced a PL/I standard in 1976. A "Subset G" of this full standard is also available for use with personal computers.

Since it has features found in both FORTRAN and COBOL, PL/I is a flexible and sophisticated language. A portion of a PL/I program to average test grades is shown in Figure 19-8. Although this program was written on a general-purpose coding sheet, PL/I programs can be prepared in a rather free-form way. The basic element in PL/I is the *statement* which is concluded with a semicolon. Statements are combined into *procedures*. A procedure may represent an entire small program or a "building block" or module of a more complex program.

Because of its modular structure, a novice programmer need only learn a small part of the language in order

```
00001                          IDENTIFICATION DIVISION.                             BILLING
00002                          PROGRAM-ID.   BILLING PROGRAM.                        BILLING
00003                          AUTHOR.       CRAIG ELDERS.                           BILLING
00004                          REMARKS.      THIS PROGRAM PRODUCES A PRINTOUT CONTAINING:  BILLING
00005                                        NAME, ADDRESS, AND NET PRICE.           BILLING
00006                                                                                BILLING
00007                          ENVIRONMENT DIVISION.                                 BILLING
00008                          CONFIGURATION SECTION.                                BILLING
00009                          SOURCE-COMPUTER.   XEROX-SIGMA-9.                      BILLING
00010                          OBJECT-COMPUTER.   XEROX-SIGMA-9.                      BILLING
00011                                                                                BILLING
00012                          INPUT-OUTPUT SECTION.                                 BILLING
00013                          FILE-CONTROL.                                         BILLING
00014                              SELECT CARD-INPUT ASSIGN TO CARD-READER.          BILLING
00015                              SELECT PRINTOUT   ASSIGN TO PRINTER.              BILLING
00016                                                                                BILLING
00017                          DATA DIVISION.                                        BILLING
00018                          FILE SECTION.                                         BILLING
00019                          FD  CARD-INPUT                                        BILLING
00020                                  RECORD CONTAINS 80 CHARACTERS                 BILLING
00021                                  LABEL RECORD IS OMITTED                       BILLING
00022                                  DATA RECORDS ARE CARD-NAME-ADDRESS-RECORD     BILLING
00023                                                 CARD-QUANTITY-PRICE-RECORD.    BILLING
00024                          01  CARD-NAME-ADDRESS-RECORD.                         BILLING
00025                              05  CARD-NAME-ADDRESS          PICTURE X(30).      BILLING
00026                              05  FILLER                     PICTURE X(50).      BILLING
00027                                                                                BILLING
00028                          01  CARD-QUANTITY-PRICE-RECORD.                       BILLING
00029                              05  CARD-QUANTITY              PICTURE 999V99.     BILLING
00030                              05  CARD-PRICE                 PICTURE 999V99.     BILLING
00031                              05  FILLER                     PICTURE X(70).      BILLING
00032                                                                                BILLING
00033                          FD  PRINTOUT                                          BILLING
00034                                  RECORD CONTAINS 132 CHARACTERS                BILLING
00035                                  LABEL RECORD IS OMITTED                       BILLING
00036                                  DATA RECORD IS PRINTER-RECORD.                BILLING
00037                          01  PRINTER-RECORD.                                   BILLING
00038                              05  FILLER                     PICTURE X(10).      BILLING
00039                              05  PRINT-AREA                 PICTURE X(30).      BILLING
00040                              05  FILLER                     PICTURE X(92).      BILLING
00041                                                                                BILLING
00042                          WORKING-STORAGE SECTION.                              BILLING
00043                          77  NET-COST                       PICTURE 99999V99.   BILLING
00044                          77  END-OF-DATA-FLAG               PIC X(3)  VALUE 'NO'.  BILLING
00045                          77  MISSING-CARD-FLAG              PIC X(3)  VALUE 'NO'.  BILLING
00046                          01  NET-COST-PRINT-LINE.                              BILLING
00047                              05  FILLER  VALUE SPACES       PICTURE X(10).      BILLING
00048                              05  FILLER  VALUE IS 'NET = '  PICTURE X(6).       BILLING
00049                              05  PRINT-NET-COST             PICTURE $$$,$$$.99. BILLING
00050                              05  FILLER  VALUE SPACES       PICTURE X(106).     BILLING
00051                                                                                BILLING
00052                          PROCEDURE DIVISION.                                   BILLING
00053                          OPEN-UP-FILES.                                        BILLING
00054                              OPEN INPUT  CARD-INPUT.                            BILLING
00055                              OPEN OUTPUT PRINTOUT.                              BILLING
```

**Figure 19-7** The computer listing of the simple billing program written in the COBOL language is numbered from 1 to 102. The four required divisions in any COBOL program are shown. The same input data used in the BASIC and FORTRAN examples were punched in cards and read into the computer under the control of this program. The output results are similar.

```
00056                                                                    BILLING
00057                    PERFORM READ-LOOP THRU READ-LOOP-EXIT           BILLING
00058                        UNTIL END-OF-DATA-FLAG = 'YES'.             BILLING
00059                                                                    BILLING
00060                    CLOSE CARD-INPUT.                               BILLING
00061                    CLOSE PRINTOUT.                                 BILLING
00062                    STOP RUN.                                       BILLING
00063                                                                    BILLING
00064            READ-A-CARD.                                            BILLING
00065                    READ CARD-INPUT                                 BILLING
00066                        AT END MOVE 'YES' TO END-OF-DATA-FLAG.      BILLING
00067                                                                    BILLING
00068            READ-LOOP.                                              BILLING
00069                    PERFORM READ-A-CARD.                            BILLING
00070                    IF END-OF-DATA-FLAG = 'NO'                      BILLING
00071                        MOVE ALL SPACES TO PRINTER-RECORD           BILLING
00072                        MOVE CARD-NAME-ADDRESS TO PRINT-AREA        BILLING
00073                        WRITE PRINTER-RECORD AFTER ADVANCING 2 LINES BILLING
00074                        PERFORM READ-A-CARD                         BILLING
00075                        IF END-OF-DATA-FLAG = 'NO'                  BILLING
00076                            MOVE CARD-NAME-ADDRESS TO PRINT-AREA    BILLING
00077                            WRITE PRINTER-RECORD AFTER ADVANCING 1 LINES BILLING
00078                            PERFORM READ-A-CARD                     BILLING
00079                            IF END-OF-DATA-FLAG = 'NO'              BILLING
00080                                MOVE CARD-NAME-ADDRESS TO PRINT-AREA BILLING
00081                                WRITE PRINTER-RECORD AFTER ADVANCING 1 LINES BILLING
00082                                PERFORM READ-A-CARD                 BILLING
00083                                IF END-OF-DATA-FLAG = 'NO'          BILLING
00084                                    COMPUTE NET-COST =              BILLING
00085                                        CARD-QUANTITY * CARD-PRICE  BILLING
00086                                    MOVE NET-COST TO PRINT-NET-COST BILLING
00087                                    WRITE PRINTER-RECORD FROM       BILLING
00088                                        NET-COST-PRINT-LINE AFTER ADVANCING BILLING
00089                                        1 LINES .                   BILLING
00090                                ELSE                                BILLING
00091                                    MOVE 'YES' TO MISSING-CARD-FLAG BILLING
00092                            ELSE                                    BILLING
00093                                MOVE 'YES' TO MISSING-CARD-FLAG     BILLING
00094                        ELSE                                        BILLING
00095                            MOVE 'YES' TO MISSING-CARD-FLAG.        BILLING
00096                                                                    BILLING
00097                    IF MISSING-CARD-FLAG = 'YES'                    BILLING
00098                        DISPLAY 'THERE ARE NOT ENOUGH DATA CARDS TO BE PROCESSED'BILLING
00099                            UPON PRINTER.                           BILLING
00100                                                                    BILLING
00101            READ-LOOP-EXIT.                                         BILLING
00102                    EXIT.                                           BILLING
```

PIERRE'S RECORD SHOP
6453 ORLEANS STREET
BOOGIE, LOUISIANA 54321
NET =  $7,500.00

ROCKY COLLEGE STORE
1563 BEETHOVEN DRIVE
ROCKTOWN, MARYLAND 20765
NET =      $81.25

WYNN D. TOOTS, INC.
120 BROWNING STREET
GONG, CALIFORNIA 98765
NET =      $50.00

Output produced by the
computer as the program
is executed

GENERAL PURPOSE CARD PUNCHING FORM

PUNCHING INSTRUCTIONS

| JOB | AVERAGE OF TEST SCORES |
| BY JOHN Q PROGRAMMER | DATE 1/26/99 |

WRITTEN AS:

PUNCH AS:

NOTES: PL/I

FIELD IDENTIFICATION

| | 1-10 | 11-20 | 21-30 | 31-40 | 41-50 | 51-60 | 61-70 | 71-80 |
|---|---|---|---|---|---|---|---|---|

```
1   AVERAGE: PROCEDURE OPTIONS (MAIN);
2   DECLARE
3     N FIXED (2),
4     NAME CHARACTER (15),
5     SCORE FIXED (3),
6     TOTAL FIXED (4),
7     AVE FIXED (3),
8     SWT FIXED (1),
9     WORK FILE,
10    NWORK FILE PRINT;
11  TOTAL = 0;
12  N = 0;
13  SWT = 0;
14  OPEN FILE (WORK) INPUT, FILE (NWORK) OUTPUT;
15  READ: GET FILE (WORK) EDIT (NAME, SCORE) (X'
16  ON ENDFILE (WORK) GO TO OUTPUT;
17  IF SWT = 1 THEN GO TO CONTIN
```

Figure 19-8 A portion of a program written in PL/1.

to prepare applications programs of a particular type. Also, modular procedure blocks and other features of the language support the use of structured programming concepts. And a PL/I compiler has built-in features—called *default options*—that can detect and correct common programming errors. But a *limitation* of PL/I is that it's more difficult to learn in its entirety than either FORTRAN or COBOL.

## RPG

**RPG** (Report Program Generator) was introduced in the 1960s as a language that could readily duplicate the processing approach used with punched card equipment. Its use is still limited primarily to business applications processed on small business computers. As the name suggests, RPG is designed to generate the output reports re-

sulting from the processing of such common business applications as accounts receivable and accounts payable. But RPG can also be used to periodically update accounts receivable and accounts payable files.

In spite of its file-updating capabilities, RPG is a *limited-purpose* language because object programs generated by the RPG compiler follow a basic processing cycle without deviation. The general form of this cycle is shown in Figure 19-9. Since the processing logic is built into the language and never varies, the RPG programmer is concerned only with *file description* and with specifications about *input, calculations,* and *output.* Very detailed coding sheets are used by programmers to write these specifications.

One *advantage* of RPG is that it's relatively easy to learn and use. Since program logic is fixed, there are

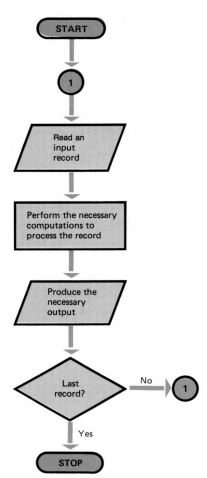

**Figure 19-9** The processing logic built into the RPG language.

fewer formal rules to remember than with many other languages. RPG is well suited for applications where large files are read, few calculations are performed, and output reports are created. It has been an important language of small business-oriented computers for years.

Of course, the limited purpose for which it was designed is also a *disadvantage* of the language: RPG has restricted mathematical capability and cannot be used for scientific applications. Finally, RPG is not a formally standardized language and so programs written for one processor may require modification before they will run on a different make of machine. However, the RPG versions produced by IBM have tended to become "de facto" standards.

## ALGOL, Pascal, Ada, and Some Others

**ALGOL** (<u>ALGO</u>rithmic <u>L</u>anguage) was introduced in 1958. It was designed by an international group of mathematicians, and developed by groups in Europe and the United States. John Backus of FORTRAN fame assisted in this development. As you might expect, ALGOL was intended for the use of those involved in scientific and mathematical projects. Several versions of the language have been created, and the current version is ALGOL 68. FORTRAN has generally been used instead of ALGOL in the United States, but ALGOL is very popular in Europe. Like PL/I, ALGOL is a block-structured or modular language that's well suited for use in a structured programming setting.

An offspring of ALGOL is **Pascal.** Named in honor of Blaise Pascal, a seventeenth-century French mathematician, philosopher, and inventor, this language was developed in the late 1960s and early 1970s by Professor Nicklaus Wirth at Switzerland's Federal Institute of Technology. Pascal was the first major language to be created after the concepts associated with structured programming became widely disseminated.

A Pascal version of a simple billing program similar to those presented earlier in other languages is shown in Figure 19-10. The output produced by this program when three input records are supplied is also shown. Like ALGOL, Pascal is block-structured. Programs are composed of *blocks* starting with BEGIN and terminating with END. Program *statements* proceed in a logical flow from start to finish. All variables are identified at the beginning of the program. The three basic logic structures are supported by statements in sequence separated by semicolons, IF . . . THEN . . . ELSE selection statements, and WHILE . . . DO loop statements.

Pascal can be used for both scientific and file processing applications. A growing number of college instructors are using it to teach programming to their computer science majors. And Pascal is now one of the major languages running on mini- and microcomputer systems. Professor Kenneth Bowles of the University of California at San Diego has pioneered the use of Pascal on small machines.

Another language in the ALGOL/Pascal lineage is **Ada.** This language is named in honor of Lord Byron's daughter Ada Augusta, the Countess of Lovelace. Ada worked with Charles Babbage on the concepts for an "Analytical Engine" in England during the first half of the

```
(* BILLING PROGRAM
   VARIABLE NAMES:

   Q:  QUANTITY PURCHASED
   P:  UNIT PRICE
   A:  NET AMOUNT *)


PROGRAM PROGRAM1 (INPUT,OUTPUT);
VAR CH:CHAR; Q,P,A:REAL; I:INTEGER;
BEGIN
WHILE NOT EOF (INPUT) DO
BEGIN
FOR I:= 1 TO 3 DO
     BEGIN

        (*  READ AND WRITE NAME AND ADDRESS *)

        WHILE NOT EOLN DO
        BEGIN READ (CH);
        IF NOT EOF THEN WRITE (CH);
        END;
        IF NOT EOF (INPUT) THEN
             BEGIN READLN; WRITELN;
             END
     END;
     IF NOT EOF (INPUT) THEN
     BEGIN
                     (* READ QUANTITY AND PRICE *)
        READ (Q,P);
        A := Q * P;
        WRITE ('  NET = ',A);
        READLN;
        WRITELN;
        FOR I := 1 TO 2 DO WRITELN;
     END
END
END.
```

Computer listing of
the PASCAL program

```
PIERRE'S RECORD SHOP
6453 ORLEANS STREET
BOOGIE, LOUISIANA  54321
  NET =        7500


ROCKY COLLEGE STORE
1563 BEETHOVEN DRIVE
ROCKTOWN, MARYLAND  20765
  NET =        81.25


WYNN D. TOOTS, INC.
120 BROWNING STREET
GONG, CALIFORNIA  98765
  NET =             50
```

Output produced by the
computer as the program
is executed

**Figure 19-10** A computer listing of the simple billing program written in the Pascal
language.

nineteenth century. Because of her writings, she is considered by many to be the first programmer.

The Ada language is sponsored by the U.S. Department of Defense (DOD) for use by the military services. In 1975, the DOD began a series of studies for the purpose of specifying and designing a new common language to be used by computer vendors and military programmers. The new language—Ada—was presented by the design team late in 1980. Critics called it unwieldy and inefficient, while supporters labeled it a breakthrough in software technology. It's still too early to know which view will prevail. Since the DOD will require military computers to have Ada capability, however, the language will endure. And announcements of powerful microcomputer chips supported by an Ada compiler have been made by Intel Corporation.

Dozens of other programming languages have been developed. Some of the more important examples are summarized in alphabetical order in Figure 19-11.

### The Programming Language Issue

As you've seen by now, many languages are available that will permit the programmer to write instructions to control the computer during the processing of an applica- tion. Which language should be used? Obviously, a selection must be made prior to program coding, but several factors may combine to make language selection difficult. Obtaining answers to the following questions will generally help in the selection process:

1. **Are programmers familiar with the language?** In many cases, the language used is simply the one that's best known to the programmers. If a language is not familiar, can it be learned quickly? Is it easy to use?

2. **What's the nature of the application?** Does the language perform well in applications of this type?

3. **Does the language support structured programming concepts?** COBOL, PL/I, ALGOL, and Pascal are better able to support structured programming than most BASIC or FORTRAN dialects.

4. **Is satisfactory translating software available?** There's an important distinction between a language and a compiler. A language is a humanly convenient set of rules, conventions, and representations used to convey information from

**Figure 19-11** A summary of additional major programming languages.

*APL* (*A* *P*rogramming *L*anguage) is a powerful interpreted language that's used with personal computers and larger systems. It uses many curious symbols such as squashed squares and bent arrows, but it can often perform complex arithmetic/logic operations with a single command.

*APT* (*A*utomatically *P*rogrammed *T*ooling) is used in manufacturing applications to control machine tools.

*C* was developed at Bell Laboratories and was used to produce the Unix operating system discussed in Chapter 13. It is a favorite of systems programmers and others who develop software packages for small computer systems. It is also used to create graphics and special effects in films (e.g., *Star Trek II* and *Return of the Jedi*). Code that approaches machine language in density and efficiency may be written, but C also offers some high-level language features.

*FORTH*, like C, resembles a high-level assembly language. It's used by systems programmers for in-house software development projects. It's also used to control astronomical telescopes in observatories around the world.

*Fourth-Generation Languages* is a term that's often applied to the sophisticated software packages that permit end-users to query data bases and extract the information needed to solve problems and prepare reports. These *application generators* allow people to specify the results desired, but users don't have to outline the approach required to achieve the results.

*LISP* (*LIS*t *P*rocessing Language) was developed by John McCarthy in 1959–1960 to support research in the field of artificial intelligence (AI). It's designed to manipulate nonnumeric data, and has remained the language of choice among AI researchers in the United States.

*Logo* was developed as an offshoot of LISP and has been popularized by Seymour Papert and others as a first instructional language for children. Although it's used in universities for serious scientific work, young children are able to write Logo programs in a short period of time. For example, they can use an on-screen "turtle" to create drawings and animated cartoons.

*Modula-2* is a new language developed by Nicholas Wirth, the creator of Pascal. Although it retains the advantages of Pascal, Modula-2 is expected to be more powerful and easier to use. It's relatively easy to translate Pascal programs into Modula-2 code.

*PILOT* (*P*rogrammed *I*nquiry *L*earning *O*r *T*eaching) is used by the developers of computer-assisted instruction materials to prepare programs that emphasize drills, tests, and dialogs.

*PROLOG* is a relatively new AI language that has been chosen by the Japanese to be the standard language for their "fifth-generation" computer project. (See Chapters 9, 14, and 15 for more details on this Japanese effort.)

*SNOBOL* (*StriNg O*riented *SymBOl*ic Language) is a text-manipulating and information retrieval language used by researchers in the humanities.

human to machine. A compiler is a translator written by one or more programmers. It's entirely possible that a good language, when used with an inefficient compiler, will yield unsatisfactory results.

5. *How often will the application be processed?* An assembly language program written by a clever programmer usually has a shorter production run time and takes less storage space than does a program of the same application written in a high-level language. If the job is run often enough, the value of the operating time saved may be more than enough to offset the cost of additional time spent in program preparation. For limited-life jobs, however, the faster the possible programming time is (with high-level languages), the more economical the approach.

6. *Will the program be changed frequently?* The ease of program modification varies with different languages. A high-level language is typically easier to modify than an assembly language.

7. *Is a hardware change anticipated during the life of the application?* Conversion of standardized high-level language programs is easier and faster. Machine-oriented programs may have to be completely rewritten.

8. *Is the language being supported, improved, and updated?* Are resources being committed to the support of the language? Will new computers continue to accept the language source programs? Who's sponsoring the language, and what's their commitment to it?

# PROGRAM IMPLEMENTATION AND MAINTENANCE

So far we've looked at some of the issues and options facing programmers during program preparation. We've also considered programming language categories and discussed several major high-level languages. All these topics occupy an important place in the program preparation stage. But this stage culminates with the actual writing (or coding) of the instructions needed to process an application into a language and form acceptable to a computer. **Program coding** is too important to be dismissed with a few paragraphs, and so Chapters 20 and 21 are devoted exclusively to writing instructions in the BASIC language. As you'll see, you must follow specific rules with respect to punctuation and statement structure.

Once a program has been written, the final step in the programming process is to see that it's implemented and then maintained. The time and effort required for these activities will often be determined by the options selected during the program preparation phase. For example:

■ The use of tested applications packages may make it possible to bypass many implementation problems.

■ The use of modular program design to divide complex programs into more manageable elements may make it easier to trace errors and to insert tested and proven subroutine modules into the program as needed.

■ The use of basic coding structures can lead to programs that are easier to understand, and that are thus easier to test and maintain.

■ The use of peer reviews can result in fewer errors, faster testing, better documentation, and easier maintenance.

## Program Implementation

The first step in **program implementation** is to *debug* the program—i.e., to detect and correct errors that prevent the program from running. *Testing* the results produced by the program to see if they are correct is the next implementation step. And ensuring that a complete *documentation* package is available for the application is a third implementation step.

**Debugging.** There are days when things never seem to go quite right. Such days may be more common for programmers than for other mortals. *Bugs* are the clerical mistakes and errors that crop up in programs. These bugs or "glitches" (bugs have also been defined as "sons of glitches") just seem to occur even under the best of circumstances and even when matters are not being helped along by our natural human tendency to screw things up. It's unusual for complex programs to run to completion on the first attempt. In fact, the time spent in **debugging** and testing often equals or exceeds the time spent in program coding. Failure to provide for a possible program path, keying errors, mistakes in coding punctuation, transposed characters—these are but a few of the bugs that can thwart the programmer.

To reduce the number of clerical and logical errors, the programmer should carefully check the coding for accuracy prior to its entry into the computer. This **desk-checking** process should include an examination of program logic and program completeness. Furthermore, typical input data should be manually traced through the program processing paths to identify possible errors. In short, the programmer attempts to play the role of the computer.

After programs have been desk-checked for accuracy, an attempt is made to convert the source program into object-program form. Compiler programs and interpreters contain error-diagnostic features, which detect (and print messages about) mistakes caused by the incorrect application of the language used to prepare the source program. In many organizations, a programmer can sit at a workstation and key in the program code from his or her coding sheets. The programmer can then call up an online compiler program to immediately convert the source code into object code. Next, a listing of the detected language-usage (or **syntax**) **errors** may be displayed on the screen of the workstation. The programmer may interact with program development software and use the editing features of the workstation to correct detected errors. When changes have been made in response to detected errors, a new compilation can be ordered. This process may continue until all detected syntax errors have been remedied.

You should realize, however, that compiler/interpreter diagnostic checks will *not* detect the presence of **logical errors** in a program. If an instruction should be "LET A = B*C" but has been coded "LET A = B + C," this error will not be noticed since no language rules have been broken. Thus, an "errorless" pass of the program through the compiler or interpreter *does not* mean that the program is perfected or that all bugs have been eliminated. But it usually does mean that the program is ready for testing.

**Testing.** A program to be tested has generally demonstrated that it will run and produce results. The purpose of **testing** is to determine whether the results are correct. The testing procedure involves using the program to process input test data that will produce known results. *The items developed for testing should include:*

- Typical data, which will test the generally used program paths.

- Unusual but valid data, which will test the program paths used to handle exceptions.

- Incorrect, incomplete, or inappropriate data, which will test the program error-handling capabilities.

A testing procedure that's often followed is to separately test different portions of a program. This helps to isolate detected errors to a particular program segment. The use of a modular programming approach, of course, eases this procedure. Another technique that's often used is to entrust much of the testing to someone other than the programmer who wrote the code. A fresh outlook is often helpful, and errors that are missed by a programmer who is "too familiar" with the code may be easily picked up by someone else. There are also many specialized software packages available today that are designed to help people test applications programs. For example, Softool's INSTRUMENTER packages may be used to test COBOL programs, and Boole & Babbage's XPF is used for online, interactive testing.

If the program passes the tests, it may be released for use. It should be noted here, however, that errors may still remain. In complex programs there may be tens of thousands of different possible paths through the program. It simply isn't practical (and maybe not even possible) to trace through all these paths during testing. For example, the flowchart in Figure 19-12 looks rather simple, but the number of different possible paths is an astounding $10^{20}$. If we could somehow check out one path per nanosecond, and if we had started our testing in the

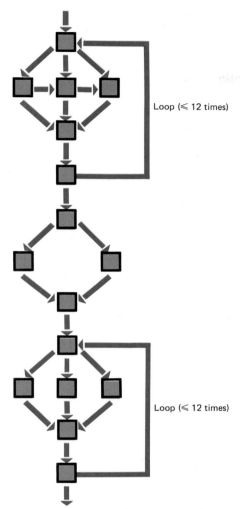

Loop (≤ 12 times)

Loop (≤ 12 times)

**Figure 19-12** Errors can remain hidden in an obscure path in a program for years without even being detected. This is possible because complex programs contain billions of possible paths. In this simple-looking flowchart, for example, there are $10^{20}$ possible paths.

year 1, we would only be about half done today! This is why programs may suddenly produce nonsense months after they've been released for use. Some unique and unanticipated series of events has produced input or circumstances that turn up an error for the first time. The error was always there; it simply remained undetected. It's thus impossible to certify that very complex systems are error-free.

If the program does not pass a test, the programmer may do the following:

1. Call for a **trace program** run. The trace program prints out the status of registers after each operation. Errors may be discovered by noting register contents after each program step.

2. Call for a **storage dump** when the program "hangs up" during a test run. That is, obtain a printout of the contents of primary storage and registers at the time of the hangup. The programmer can then study this listing for possible clues to the cause of the programming error(s).

After the program appears to be running properly and producing correct results, there's frequently a transitionary cutover period during which the job application is processed both by the old method and the new program. The purpose of this period, of course, is to verify processing accuracy and completeness.

**Documentation. Documentation,** as we've seen, is the process of collecting, organizing, storing, and otherwise maintaining on paper (or on some relatively permanent medium) a complete record of *why* applications were developed, for *whom, what* functions they perform, and *how* these functions are carried out. Producing documentation is an important—but often neglected—activity of programmers. A number of special programs are available to help people carry out this function. (Softool's DOCUMENTER A, and CGA/Allen's DCD II are just two examples of these documentation tools.)

The *documentation package* for a program used in an organization should include:

1. *A definition of the problem.* Why was the program prepared? What were the objectives? Who requested the program and who approved it?

2. *A description of the system.* The system or subsystem environment in which the program functions should be described (systems flowcharts should be included). Broad systems specifications outlining the scope of the problem, the form and type of input data to be used, and the form and type of output required should be clearly stated.

3. *A description of the program.* Program flow-charts, program listings, test data and test results, storage dumps, trace program printouts—these and other documents that describe the program and give a historical record of difficulties and/or changes should be available.

4. *A recitation of operator instructions.* Among the items covered should be computer switch settings, loading and unloading procedures, and starting, running, and terminating procedures.

5. *A description of program controls.* Controls may be incorporated in a program in a number of ways. For example, programmed controls may be used to check on the reasonableness and propriety of input data. A description of such controls should be a part of the documentation.

## Program Maintenance

Changing business conditions, the revised needs of personal computer users, new laws—these and other factors require that production programs be continually *maintained* and modified. **Program maintenance** is an important duty of programmers and may involve all steps from problem definition through analysis, design, and program preparation. In some installations there are programmers who do nothing but maintain production programs. It generally takes less time for these programmers to make a change than it does to find the program location(s) where changes are needed.

When an organization first acquires a computer,

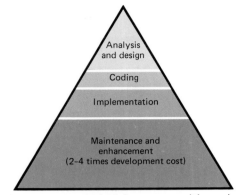

Figure 19-13 Cost pyramid of the program life cycle.

much of the programming effort goes into the development of new applications. But as the number of installed programs in the organization grows, it's not unusual to find that more programming time is being spent on maintenance than on new development work. In fact, in many organizations well over half the total programming effort is spent on maintenance. And it's estimated that over the life cycle of a typical application, the maintenance and enhancement costs that are incurred may be two to four times larger than the initial development costs (see Figure 19-13). To reduce maintenance costs and improve programmer productivity, many organizations have invested in software packages that can automatically go through programs and identify poorly written or unnecessary lines of code. (Catalyst Corporation's Structured Retrofit, and SAGE Software's Maintenance Programming System are examples.)

## Feedback and Review 19-1

You should now have an understanding of some of the decisions that must be made during program preparation. You should also be aware of some of the general characteristics of programming languages. And you should be able to outline the steps followed during the implementation and maintenance phase of the programming process. To test and reinforce your understanding of the material presented in this chapter, fill in the *crossword puzzle* form presented below.

### Across

**1.** A computer's _____ language consists of strings of binary numbers and is the only one it directly understands.

**2.** One of the first high-level languages designed for scientific applications, and still one of the most popular, _____ was designed in the mid-1950s by an IBM-sponsored committee headed by John Backus.

**5.** The _____/I language was designed to solve all types of business and scientific problems. It includes features found in both FORTRAN and COBOL, and it facilitates the use of structured programming concepts.

**7.** The _____ division is the third of the four divisions required in a COBOL program. This division presents a detailed description of the input data to be processed, the working storage locations that are needed, and the format to be used for the output results.

**9.** After a program has demonstrated that it will run and produce results, the next step is to _____ it to see if the results are correct.

**10.** The first part of a machine-language instruction is called the command or operation, and it tells the computer what function to perform. Every computer has an _____ code for each of its functions.

**13.** A _____ review is also called a structured walkthrough. The purpose of this review is to allow a programmer's colleagues to check his or her work in order to detect errors.

**15.** A block-structured scientific language that's very popular in Europe. Pascal is considered an offspring of this language.

**18.** _____ languages use mnemonic operation codes and symbolic addressing, and they are designed for a specific make and model of computer.

**21.** A program that translates the source code of a high-level language into the machine-language object code of a computer is called a _____. Unlike the object code produced by an interpreter, the object code produced by this program is saved for repetitive use.

**22.** Whenever feasible, the purchase of an appropriate _____ program should be considered as an alternative to the creation of an in-house custom-made program.

**23.** Changing conditions require that production programs be continually _____ and up-

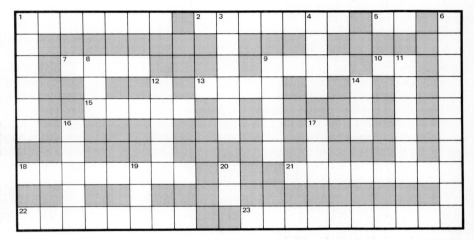

dated. The effort spent on this activity can easily exceed the time spent on new program development.

### Down

**1.** In a modular program, a main-control program specifies the order in which each _____ (or subroutine) in the program will be processed.

**3.** An assembler or compiler is used to translate a source program written in the language used by the programmer into a machine-language _____ program that the computer can understand.

**4.** An acronym for the organization that publishes programming language standards.

**6.** There can be little doubt about the existence of a _____ programming setting when programs are written using only a few basic logic structures, when program functions are broken down into lower-level components, and when peer reviews and chief programmer teams are used.

**8.** Named after Lord Byron's daughter, this recent language in the ALGOL/Pascal line is sponsored by the U.S. Department of Defense.

**9.** If a program fails to pass a test, the programmer can call for a _____ program run to check on the status of registers after each program operation.

**11.** The first major language to be created after structured programming concepts became widely disseminated, _____ is an offspring of ALGOL and is now running on many micro- and minicomputers.

**12.** Designed specifically for business-type data processing applications, _____ is a standardized language that requires the use of four divisions in every program. Programs can be written in a quasi-English form, and the language is suited to manipulating large files.

**14.** _____ is a nonstandard language used with small business computers to generate output reports. These reports result from the processing of common business applications.

**16.** The most popular language used with microcomputers and timeshared minicomputers, _____ is an easy-to-use high-level language that was originally developed at Dartmouth for the use of undergraduate students.

**17.** When a programmer is responsible for coding an entire program, the program may become an extension of the programmer's _____.

**19.** The inelegant term used to describe a clerical mistake or logical error that crops up in programs.

**20.** RPG is a language that uses built-_____ processing logic.

**1.** Programmers generally want to write programs that meet user needs, are produced on time and with a minimum cost, are accurate, and are easy to implement and maintain. In trying to achieve these goals, however, they must usually deal with a number of issues involving methodology and the use of resources. Included among these issues are: Should a new program be written or should an existing program package be purchased? How should programming tasks be assigned? What program design methods should be used? Which programming language(s) should be selected?

**2.** When compared with custom-made programs, packaged programs are generally less expensive and are likely to contain fewer errors. But the custom-made program can be designed to better fit the unique needs of users. The responsibility for preparing a program can be assigned to a programmer who codes and implements the task. Or a programming project can be assigned to a chief programmer or to egoless programming teams. Each of these options for organizing programmers differs from the others, and there's no agreement about which approach is best.

**3.** Different organizations also use different program construction techniques. Modular program design, the use of basic coding structures, the use of peer reviews, and the application of structured programming concepts—a mix of these and other techniques is often followed.

**4.** Assembly and/or high-level programming languages are selected for program coding. Most applications are coded in a high-level language. Before the source program instructions written in the programmer's language can be used by the computer, however, they must be translated into the machine-language object code that the computer understands. This machine language consists of strings of binary numbers. An assembly program (used with assembly languages) or a compiler or interpreter (used with high-level languages) is used to translate source programs into object programs.

**5.** An overview of some of the most popular high-level languages in use today is presented in this chapter. These languages include BASIC (an easy to use, general-purpose language), FORTRAN (a popular language for scientific-mathematic applications), COBOL (the most widely used language for large business applications), PL/I (a language suitable for both business and scientific applications), RPG (a limited-purpose language used to prepare business reports), ALGOL (a scientific-oriented language that's popular in Europe), Pascal (a general-purpose language that supports the structured programming approach), and Ada (a new language sponsored by the U.S. Department of Defense). Other important languages are summarized.

**6.** After a program has been coded, the final step in the programming process is to see that it's implemented and then maintained. Implementation consists of debugging the program, testing the results produced by the program to see if they are correct, and preparing a complete documentation package for the program. Maintenance consists of revising and updating production programs in light of changing conditions. Much of the programming effort in organizations with mature data processing operations is spent on maintenance.

## KEY TERMS AND CONCEPTS

## TOPICS FOR REVIEW AND DISCUSSION

**1.** "During program preparation, programmers must usually deal with a number of issues involving methodology and the use of resources." Discuss this statement and identify three of the possible issues.

**2.** What are the possible advantages and limitations of packaged programs?

**3.** Identify and discuss three ways that programmers can be assigned to program preparation projects?

**4.** (a) What is a modular program? (b) What advantages might there be to the use of modular programming techniques?

**5.** What advantages might there be in requiring that programmers use only simple sequence, selection, and loop structures in their programs?

**6.** (a) What's a peer review? (b) What advantages may there be to the use of this technique?

**7.** Identify the program preparation techniques that have often been included under the term "structured programming."

**8.** "Every programming language has instructions that fall into four categories." Identify and discuss these categories.

**9.** "An instruction prepared in any machine language has at least two parts." Identify these parts and discuss the function of each.

**10.** (a) How does an assembly language differ from a machine language? (b) How is an assembly language source program translated into a machine-language object program?

**11.** (a) What advantages do high-level languages have over assembly languages? (b) Discuss two approaches used to translate high-level languages into machine languages.

**12.** (a) What is BASIC? (b) Where did it originate? (c) How is it used today?

**13.** (a) What is FORTRAN? (b) How did it originate? (c) How is it used today?

**14.** (a) What is COBOL? (b) How did it originate? (c) How is it used today?

**15.** (a) What is PL/I? (b) What advantages does it possess?

**16.** (a) What is RPG? (b) How is it used? (c) Why is it a limited-purpose language?

**17.** Discuss the development and current use of (a) ALGOL, (b) Pascal, and (c) Ada.

**18.** What questions should be considered in determining the programming language to use in given situations?

**19.** What steps can be taken during debugging and testing to locate and remove program errors?

**20.** What should be included in a program documentation package?

**21.** Why is program maintenance needed?

## PROJECT TO LOOK INTO

**1.** Visit a computer center in your area and identify the programming languages supported by the center. Prepare a report that (a) lists these languages, (b) describes the reason for their selection in given applications, and (c) outlines the extent to which each language is used.

## ANSWERS TO FEEDBACK AND REVIEW SECTION

**19-1**
The solution to the crossword puzzle is shown at right.

# A Primer on Programming Languages

Programming a computer to solve a problem involves two chores. First, the problem must be broken down into a sequence of operations that the computer can perform. Then, instructions telling the computer how to perform the operations must be encoded. In most computers, instructions are encoded as binary numbers—strings of 0s and 1s—that specify such information as the type of operation (for example, addition or subtraction), the location of the operands in memory, and the place to store the result. Determining and encoding all the instructions required to perform even the simplest task on a computer is tedious and time-consuming. Moreover, programs expressed as a series of binary codes (machine language) are difficult, if not impossible, for humans to read.

To simplify programming, computer scientists have developed programming languages that express operations in terms more familiar to people. In addition, they have developed programs that translate these higher-level languages into machine language. To translate a source program (one written in a higher-level language), a user typically loads the translation program into computer memory. The computer then reads and translates the source program under the translation program's control. The result, called the object program, is stored on magnetic disk for later use.

Two types of programming languages are in common use: assembly languages and high-level languages. In assembly language, alphanumeric symbols represent the instruction contents. For example, ADD X,Y might tell a computer to add the contents of storage location X to those of Y. An assembler program does the source-to-object program translation. As a labor-saving feature, many assemblers allow a programmer to define "macro instructions"—instructions that designate a sequence of machine instructions. Whenever an assembler encounters a macro instruction, it substitutes the appropriate sequence of machine instructions as previously defined by the programmer.

A high-level language allows a user to express problems as a series of English-like or algebraic statements, each of which may stand for numerous machine instructions. In FORTRAN, a typical high-level language, the statement X = SIN(THETA) stands for "compute the sine of the number stored in the memory location symbolized by THETA and store the result in the location symbolized by X." The operation defined by this statement might require several hundred machine instructions on a typical computer. A program called a compiler determines and encodes the appropriate sequence of machine instructions required to perform a high-level statement. The compiler also performs other functions such as checking for errors and allocating memory space.

Assembly languages are simply alphabetic representations of numeric machine language. Each assembly-language statement corresponds to a single machine-instruction statement (except in the case of macros). The assembler does not figure out the instructions required to perform a task. Assembly-language programmers must do this themselves. By contrast, high-level languages justify their name by enabling a programmer to express a problem compactly in mathematical or quasi-natural language. The computer determines (via a compiler) the detailed sequence of instructions required to do the tasks expressed in the high-level language. High-level languages are thus tremendous labor-savers.

In addition, high-level languages are machine independent: A program written in a high-level language can run on any computer. This is because high-level languages express problems in terms appropriate to the problem rather than to a particular method of solution on a particular computer. The FORTRAN statement X = SIN(THETA) expresses a problem—not a solution. Most computer manufacturers supply FORTRAN compilers that will determine and encode the instructions necessary to perform this operation on their computers.

Despite their advantages, high-level languages are not a panacea. They have a significant drawback: inefficient translation. Compilers approach, but do not match human programmers in choosing the fastest or smallest instruction sequence required to perform a specific task—a key compilation objective. Moreover, the proliferation of high-level languages and dialects has negated the advantage of machine-independence. A program written for one manufacturer's machine often will not run on another's because no compiler is available for the language or dialect in which the program is written.

High-level languages dominate in programming big computers. There, programmer productivity is a paramount consideration because programs are large, and inefficient translation is a minor drawback because memory space and processing power are abundant. Because of its efficiency, assembly language is still widely used in microprocessor applications. But as memory prices fall and processor speeds soar, even the microprocessor world is expected to yield to high-level languages because of their programmer productivity advantage.

—James Fawcett, ''Ada Tackles Software Bottleneck,'' reprinted with permission from the February 1983 issue of *High Technology* magazine. Copyright © 1983 by High Technology Publishing Corporation, 38 Commercial Wharf, Boston, Mass. 02110.

# Programming in BASIC

### Forty Days and Forty Nights

When Michael Wise sits down at a keyboard, he never knows when he will get up. The plump, bearded computer programmer often works twelve, 24, even 36 hours without a break, filling a green screen at the San Rafael, Calif., offices of Broderbund Software with words and numbers that only he and his computer completely understand. Since December, Wise has written 40,000 lines of instructions for a video game he calls Captain Goodnight, after the old *Captain Midnight* radio series. By the time the program is ready for release, it will have grown to 50,000 lines and swallowed up some 900 hours of programming time, or nearly 40 days and 40 nights. . . .

Wise's first task in writing his program was to create the objects displayed on the screen. These are actually just patterns of colored dots, with each dot controlled by an individual on-off switch. Wise sketched the images on an electronic drawing tablet that translated his lines into patterns of ones and zeros, where one represents a dot of color and zero a blank space. . . .

After the objects were drawn, Wise began creating a series of small, self-contained miniprograms called subroutines. One subroutine, for example, moves the captain's jet. Another controls the enemy planes. A third fires a missile. In all, the finished program will have 400 different subroutines. Wise writes it one subroutine at a time, making sure that each new one works before continuing . . .

As the pieces of the program fall together, their interrelationship becomes maddeningly complex. Even one letter misplaced in 10,000 lines of code is enough to throw the whole program out of kilter. At one stage in the game's development, the computer had the captain walking in mid-air because one subroutine was inadvertently modifying another subroutine's instructions. "I almost went blind trying to find that bug," Wise recalls.

# LOOKING AHEAD

The purpose of this chapter is to give you an introduction to BASIC—a popular programming language that makes it relatively easy for terminal and personal computer users to interact with their machines. After you've mastered the language rules and programming techniques presented in this chapter, you'll have the tools needed to write programs that can solve complex problems. BASIC is a rich and powerful language and Chapter 21 contains additional instruction in using it. The information in this chapter will enable you to:

- Identify and discuss the general elements found in a BASIC statement

- Understand and use the BASIC statements discussed in the chapter to prepare programs

- Write programs that may incorporate input operations, calculations, decisions, loops, counters, accumulators, and output operations to achieve specified goals

## Chapter Outline

# THE BASIC PROGRAMMING ENVIRONMENT

In the early 1960s, computer use was generally restricted to groups of people in large organizations with specialized tasks to perform. For example, people in accounting used computers to prepare payrolls and bills, and aeronautical engineers used the machines to analyze aircraft designs. Computing hardware was expensive. The languages and operating system programs of the time often seemed geared to satisfying the needs of machines rather than the needs of people. And those who could have benefited from computer usage were often denied access to the machines. But as time passed, the access problem was relieved through the use of timesharing. In the mid-1960s, as you'll recall, Dartmouth professors Kemeny and Kurtz were motivated to create a programming language (BASIC) that would make it easy for people at timesharing terminals to *interact* with computers.

It didn't take long for BASIC to become popular. Over the years, millions of people have quickly learned to use BASIC, which is now the primary language used by the millions who own personal computers (Figure 20-1). Since its inception, BASIC has been improved and its scope has been extended. We've seen that there are many different versions or dialects in existence today. Unfortunately, this means that a BASIC program prepared for use on one manufacturer's equipment may not run without

Figure 20-1 BASIC is a second language that millions have now learned. Classes are given by schools, computer clubs, and even by retailers. (Courtesy ComputerLand)

modification on another system. In the pages that follow, we'll discuss certain BASIC program statements that permit the computer to perform such activities as input, data movement, and output. The use of these statements in the example programs found in the chapter follow the rules of many BASIC dialects. The differences that may exist between the BASIC version that your computer system uses and the version used in this chapter should be relatively easy to resolve.

## The Equipment
Since BASIC is a language that's meant to be used for interactive computing, the user typically writes programs and enters some or all of the necessary data from the *keyboard* of a terminal or personal computer (pc) system. Data may also be entered through magnetic tape cassette units, and floppy- and hard-disk drives that are attached to terminal/pc systems. The *output* information used by humans is usually obtained from a visual display or character printer. Output may also be recorded on magnetic tapes or disks through the use of appropriate terminal/pc attachments.

## Sign-On Procedures
Let's assume that you glanced ahead in this chapter to get an idea of what's involved in preparing a BASIC program. Since we are supposing, let's also assume that at the first opportunity you then rushed to an available keyboard to try your hand at writing a program. Alas, banging on the keyboard produced no results—you neglected to turn the computer on, or you were unable to follow the proper sign-on (or "log-on") procedure required to get access to the CPU.

In a *personal computing environment,* the sign-on "procedure" may simply involve turning on the power. The BASIC interpreter may be permanently stored in integrated circuit chips inside the CPU, instantly ready for use. In a *timesharing environment,* the terminal must be turned on first. A procedure is then required to establish communication between the terminal and the central processor. This procedure may involve typing specified words—e.g., HELLO or LOGIN—and/or pressing specified keys on the terminal. It may also involve dialing a number on a phone next to the terminal and using a communications device called a modem to make a connection with the CPU.

Once hooked up, the computer may automatically send a sign-on request to the terminal in the form of a message or special character. The user must then follow a prescribed sign-on procedure. Typically this involves supplying one or more of the following: an account or project number, a user name or identification, and/or a password. After this information has been supplied, some systems that support multiple languages also require that the user indicate the programming language that will be used. Thus, it may also be necessary to type BASIC so that the computer can call up the BASIC translating software.

To illustrate these comments, in several Digital Equipment Corporation systems, the sign-on procedure is to turn on the terminal and type HELLO. The computer responds with an information line and then prints #. The user types in a project number and programmer number, and the computer responds with PASSWORD. After the password is supplied, the system is ready. In a Hewlett-Packard 3000 system, the terminal is turned on, and the user presses the RETURN key and types HELLO followed by an identification number. The computer responds with an information line and then types the colon (:). The user then types BASIC, and when the system replies with the > character, the system is in BASIC and ready to be used.

Obviously, there's no standard sign-on procedure. But there are no difficult ones either. The procedures for signing on the particular system you'll be using are easy to learn and are available from local sources.

### System Commands and Program Statements

System commands and program statements are both found in a BASIC programming environment, and both make use of certain designated words. Let's make sure we know the difference between these two categories. We've seen that some computer systems may require the user to type key words like HELLO or LOGIN as a part of the sign-on procedure. Such words are referred to as **system commands.** They are entered by the user into the system, and they direct the computer to take immediate action to accomplish a specific task. A number of system commands are found in every BASIC programming environment, but the words vary with the system being used. Some typical system commands found in most settings are:

- RUN (to execute the user's program of current interest).
- LIST (to list the contents of a current program).
- SAVE (to store a current program—which must be given a name—in online secondary storage for later access).
- NEW (deletes program from memory).

As with sign-on procedures, the system commands for the particular equipment you'll be using are available from local sources.

Designated words such as READ, INPUT, LET, and END are also found in the sequence of numbered individual instructions or **program statements** that make up a BASIC program. We'll discuss the meanings and uses of these key words later in the chapter.

You've seen that when a system command is entered, it causes the computer to take *immediate action*. When a program statement is initially keyed in, however, the computer may take *no apparent action at all*. Of course, the machine is probably checking the statement for syntax errors and storing it with other statements, but the program instruction in the statement is not immediately executed at the time of entry. Rather, the individual statements are stored until a complete program is formed and until the user turns the control of the computer over to the program through the use of a RUN command. The statements are then executed to process the input data and produce the output results.

## SOME BASIC NECESSITIES

We are about ready to write the programs needed to solve the problems discussed (and flowcharted) in Chapter 18. Only a few *program entry, arithmetic,* and *error-correcting* necessities stand in our way.

### Program Entry Elements

Key words are used in constructing program statements, and statements are then put together to form a BASIC program. A BASIC statement may take the following form:

line number    type of statement    value(s)

Let's look at each of these statement elements.

**Line Numbers.** Each statement in a BASIC program begins with a **line number (ln).** Depending on the equipment used, the ln can be any integer (whole number) beginning at 1 (and going to 4 or 5 digits) that *you* select. The *order* of these line numbers is used by the computer during the execution of the program. Beginning with the lowest ln, statements will be processed in ascending order until conditional or unconditional transfer statements are encountered that cause a change in the sequence. It's generally desirable to number your statements in increments of 5 or 10. That way you'll have room later to include any additional instructions or modifications that may be needed, and you won't have to renumber the lines that follow the insertion. For example, let's assume that you've written a BASIC program that looks like this:

```
10   LET A = 5
20   LET B = 8
30   LET C = A + B
40   END
```

This program will add the values of A and B, but since you've forgotten to tell the computer to print out the result of this tough computation, it will forever remain a mystery. To remedy this oversight, you can type the following statement at the bottom of the program:

```
35   PRINT C
```

The computer will then know that you want to print the value of C after line 30 has been executed. If you should later enter a system command to LIST the program, you'll see that ln 35 has been correctly positioned between statements 30 and 40.

**Types of BASIC Statements.** Every statement in BASIC has a *statement type,* and learning the language is mainly a matter of learning the rules that apply to these statement types. As you'll recall from the last chapter, computer instructions are found in all languages to permit input/output, calculation, logic/comparison (to permit transfer of program control), and storage/retrieval and data movement operations. In the simple program we've

just encountered, the LET statement was used to initially *assign* values to storage locations labeled "A" and "B" in the computer. The LET statement was also used to look up the values of the contents of A and B, calculate the sum of those values, and assign the total to a storage location labeled "C" (30 LET C = A + B). Thus, the LET, or *assignment,* type of statement can be used to assign input values to locations, perform calculations, and move processed results to other locations. The PRINT type of statement, of course, is used for *output.* An END statement is the highest-numbered statement in any program and simply indicates the completion of the program. In the pages that follow, we'll examine a number of other types of BASIC statements.

**Values in BASIC.** BASIC deals with values that may be constants or variables. A *constant* is a value that is provided explicitly by the program and *cannot* be changed by the computer at any time during program execution. Valid **numeric constants** include such values as 55, $-16.5$, 3.14159, and $1.09E + 8$. The 55 could represent a constant rate of speed, that is, 55 miles per hour. The $-16.5$ could represent the constant amount of dollars to be deducted from paychecks for a group insurance plan. And the 3.14159 could be the approximation of pi used in calculations.

The E (exponential) notation used in the constant $1.09E + 8$ is needed because there's only a limited amount of space available to store a value in the computer's memory. Thus, $1.09E + 8$ can be used to represent $1.09 \times 10^8$ or 109000000. Also, $1.26E - 6$ can be used to represent $1.26 \times 10^{-6}$ or .00000126. (Don't worry too much about this E notation shorthand for expressing very large or very small quantities. It's mentioned here so that if you should receive some output in E notation form, you'll understand what it means). Valid constants may also include strings of alphanumeric characters. **Character string constants** may be any string of characters enclosed in quotation marks, e.g., "4009 SARITA DRIVE" or "KAY OSS."

Unlike a constant, a **numeric variable** is a quantity that can be referred to by name and that *can* change values at different stages during the running of a program. Although it's true that the *location* in storage that holds the variable (and the *name* given by the programmer to that location) *doesn't change,* the *contents* of the storage location (like the contents of a post office box) may be altered many times during the program's processing of the available data. For example, you may recall from Chapter 18 that a counter can be used to record the number of times that a loop has been executed. To do this, a storage location with the **variable name** K can be established by the programmer and assigned an initial value of 1. An appropriate BASIC statement to do this is

    10   LET K = 1

where K names a variable. After each pass through the loop, the contents of the counter will change or be incremented by a value of 1. That is,

    100   LET K = K + 1

Obviously, in this BASIC statement the equals sign (=) does not mean the same as it does in algebra. Rather, the numeric variable value stored at the location identified by "K" is retrieved from storage, a value of 1 is added to it, and the new variable quantity replaces the previous contents in the location named "K." Thus, if a loop is executed 30 times, there will be 30 different values for K.

*It will be up to you to name the variables that are needed* in the programs you write. The rules in BASIC that govern the naming of variables are easily remembered, but they're often more restrictive than the rules that apply to other languages. This is a shortcoming of some BASIC dialects. For example, in many established versions of the language a numeric variable is restricted to a name that consists of a single letter or a single letter followed by a single digit. Thus, in these dialects A, X, B1, and T2 are all valid numeric variable names, but 7G, AB, RATE, and

B24 are not. Note, however, that newer versions of BASIC allow much longer numeric variable names. For example, the version of Microsoft BASIC used with the IBM Personal Computer permits these names to have up to 40 characters, but the first character must still be a letter. We'll use one- or two-character numeric variable names in our examples because they are accepted by all BASIC dialects.

In addition to numeric variables, there are also **string variables**—i.e., strings of alphanumeric and special characters—that can be referred to by name and that can change during the running of a program. For example, the contents of the storage space that contains a customer's name will change constantly during the processing of a billing program. When naming a string variable in many established versions of BASIC, people must choose a single letter followed by a dollar sign ($). In those dialects, E$, B$, and N$ are all valid, but AB$, $X, and XYZ$ are not. Some other BASIC systems also allow a string variable name to be any valid numeric variable name followed by a dollar sign. Thus, A1$ and C2$ are valid examples in such systems. But newer versions of BASIC are less restrictive—e.g., the Microsoft BASIC used with the IBM-PC permits string variable names to have up to 40 characters, but the first character must still be a letter and the last character must still be a dollar sign. We'll use the two-character string variable names in our examples that are accepted by all BASICs.

## Arithmetic Operations

You'll be concerned with five arithmetic operations in writing BASIC programs: addition, subtraction, multiplication, division, and exponentiation (raising to a power).

Figure 20-2 Arithmetic operations: Symbols and examples in the BASIC language.

| Operation | BASIC Symbol | BASIC Examples | Algebraic Equivalent |
|---|---|---|---|
| Addition | + | A + B<br>2 + 8 | A + B<br>2 + 8 |
| Subtraction | − | B − C<br>6 − 3 | B − C<br>6 − 3 |
| Multiplication | *<br>(asterisk) | D * E<br>4 * F | DE or D(E) or D × E<br>4F or 4(F) or 4 × F |
| Division | /<br>(slash) | G/H<br>8/2 | $G \div H$ or $\frac{G}{H}$<br>$8 \div 2$ or $\frac{8}{2}$ |
| Exponentiation | ∧ or ↑ | J ∧ 2 (or J ↑ 2)<br>3 ∧ 3 | $J^2$<br>$3^3$ |

The symbols used to indicate these operations (and examples of their use) are shown in Figure 20-2. Note that in BASIC the multiplication symbol must be present, even though it can be omitted in algebra. Failure to use the asterisk is a common error, and the computer will probably send you an error message if you forget it.

A formula in a program may include several operations. You must understand the order in which the computer handles these operations so that you may avoid errors. What value will be assigned to A, for example, when the computer encounters this statement that you've written?

50    LET A = 4 + 6 ∧ 2/10 − 2

If the computer simply started at the left and performed operations in sequence, the result would be 4 plus 6 (or 10), raised to the second power (giving 100), divided by 10 (10), minus 2, giving a value of 8 to assign to A. But the computer follows a different set of rules in determining the order of operations. Moving from left to right in a formula *without parentheses:*

1. All exponentiation is performed first.

2. All multiplication and division operations are then completed.

3. Finally, all addition and subtraction takes place.

Following these priority rules, then, what value would the computer assign to A in our example? The *first*

## HOW TO "WRITE" PROGRAMS

Programs, like television scripts, are "written"—not in English, but in English-like commands that vary from machine to machine. BASIC, for example, is a "language" most desktop computers are wired to understand.

In the past, computer owners had to write their own software. Today thousands of prewritten programs are on the market, ranging from games to accountants' tools. Running these software packages, as opposed to writing them, is no more difficult than playing a record or a videotape. Just find the appropriate disc, put it in a disc drive and push a button. In a matter of seconds the computer is programmed and set to do the job at hand—from balancing the books to finding misspelled words to playing a video game.

Making the programs, however, involves grueling and painstaking work, most of it done by a software engineer, also known as a programmer. Just what is it that a programmer does and how does he do it?

The first step is to decide what you want the computer to do—play blackjack, manipulate text, juggle figures? Once the task is clearly defined, the programmer lays out a step-by-step procedure for executing that task. Think of these procedures as roughly akin to cookbook recipes. The recipe for playing blackjack, for example might go something like this: "Get a deck of cards. Shuffle the cards. Deal two cards to each player. Ask the first player if he wants another card. Did the face value of that third card put his total over 21? If not, ask if the wants another card . . . "

Once the task is set and the recipe spelled out, the programmer sits down at a computer and translates each step into commands that the machine can understand. A typical command might say: PRINT "DO YOU WANT ANOTHER CARD?" . . .

Even a program for playing blackjack can quickly grow to be hundreds of lines long, each line densely packed with convoluted commands and alphanumerical characters. If there is even one character out of place in those hundreds of lines, chances are the program will not work properly. These software "bugs," as programming mishaps are called, can take weeks to find. One bug in an AT&T program knocked out all long-distance telephone service to Greece in 1979. It was months before Ma Bell's programmers pinned down the problem.

When the programmer has thoroughly tested and corrected his work he stores it on a magnetic tape or disc, much as someone might use a tape recorder to store a noteworthy speech. A particularly useful or entertaining computer program might be accepted by one of the growing number of software publishers. They will copy the program onto blank discs and send them to computer stores around the country.

When a user slips his brand-new blackjack program into a disc drive and turns on his computer, the drive starts spinning the disc at a rate of hundreds of revolutions per minute. As the disc spins, a record-playback head moves across its surface, picking up the original programmer's typed instructions and loading them into the computer's memory. When the disc stops spinning—presto!—an exact replica of the program will be imprinted on the machine's temporary memory, all debugged and ready to deal the cards. Or, depending on the disc, proofread the term paper, balance the books or tell you to sell the hogs.

operation performed would be to square 6 (6 $\wedge$ 2), giving 36. *Next,* the value of 36 would be divided by 10, giving 3.6. Your formula now looks like this:

$$4 + 3.6 - 2$$

*Finally,* moving from left to right, 4 is added to 3.6, giving 7.6, and 2 is then subtracted from 7.6 to give the final value of 5.6 to assign to the variable name A.

*If parentheses are used,* the computations within the parentheses are handled first, using the above order rules. If several sets of parentheses are nested within one another, the operations in the innermost group are performed first. For example, suppose your assignment statement had looked like this:

50    LET A = (8 + (6*4)/2)/2

The first part of the formula evaluated is (6*4) in the innermost set of parentheses. The result is

50    LET A = (8 + 24/2)/2

Within the remaining set of parentheses, the division operation is performed first, and the resulting value of 12 is then added to 8. This total of 20 is then divided by 2 to get a value of 10 to assign to A.

## Correcting Errors

In entering your program statements at the keyboard, you'll probably make errors that will have to be corrected. A very common error, of course, is to strike the wrong key or keys during program or data entry. If, as is often the case, you immediately detect your mistake, you need correct only one or two characters and then continue on with the line you are typing. For example, let's assume that the correct entry should be

50    LET A = (4*G)/2

but you type

50    LEG A

and then catch your error. How can you "erase" the G and enter the T? Different BASIC systems use different approaches, but generally a special correction key (such as RUBOUT, DELETE, or ← key) is used for this purpose. Each time you strike this **correction key** (CK), you erase one character in the typed line and move to its left. Thus, to change the G to a T, you would need to press the CK 3 times: once to erase A, once to erase the blank character, and once to erase the G. You could then enter the T and complete the line.

Suppose, however, you discover that you've typed

50    LTE A = (4*G)/2

*before* you press the RETURN key that will cause the computer to analyze the statement. In this case you *could* backtrack with the correction, but it would probably be easier to delete the *entire line* and start over. The method to do this varies with the system being used, but on many systems the procedure is to hold down the CONTROL or CTRL key and then press either the U or the X key.

Finally, let's assume that you've typed

50    LTE A = (4 + G)/2

instead of

50    LET A = (4*G)/2

and you *have pressed* the RETURN key. In this case, the computer will probably detect the *syntax error* in the spelling of LET, reject the statement, and send you an error message. You'll then have to reenter the statement. If in retyping the statement you repeat the mistake of *adding* 4 to the quantity stored in G rather than *multiplying* these values, the computer will accept the statement because it contains no syntax errors, but, of course, a *logical error* still remains. To correct this statement that has now been stored in the computer, you need only reenter the same line number with the correct information, and this second entry will completely erase the previous contents of the line (a very nice feature). If you should want to delete from a program a line that has already been stored, you simply type the line number and then hit the RETURN key, and the previous entry will be deleted.

Now that you have a grasp of some of the details associated with program entry, arithmetic operation, and error correction, it's time to look at some example programs that illustrate the use of various types of BASIC statements.

# SIMPLE INPUT, PROCESSING AND OUTPUT PROGRAMS

Several example problems were analyzed and flow-charted in Chapter 18. As you know, all these examples apply to R-K Enterprises. Let's now see how programs for these examples can be prepared in BASIC.

## Program 1: Simple Billing, Single Customer

The billing program to compute the net amount owed by a single customer, along with the output bill produced by this program, is shown in Figure 20-3. (The flowchart for this program is shown in Figure 18-3, page 485.) You'll notice that this program was written earlier and stored or saved under the arbitrary name of GDS1. In response to the LOAD and LIST system commands used by the R-K

Enterprises computer, the machine has printed a listing of the program. In response to the RUN command, the computer has executed the program to produce the output results shown.

Before we examine the program in Figure 20-3 in more detail, we should digress briefly for a few words about **programming style.** "Style" may be defined as the way in which something is said or done, as distinguished from its substance. An objective of this chapter is to present the programs in a style that will make them *easier to read and understand*. For this reason, you'll see a lot of program statements in this chapter that begin with REM— a BASIC abbreviation for REMark. A **REMark statement** is

```
>LOAD GDS1
>LIST
    10 REM *BILLING PROGRAM
    20 REM *
    30 REM *VARIABLE NAMES
    40 REM * N$ NAME
    50 REM * Q  QUANTITY PURCHASED
    60 REM * P  UNIT PRICE
    70 REM * A  NET AMOUNT
    80 REM *
    90 REM *READ NAME,QUANTITY PURCHASED AND PRICE
   100      READ N$,Q,P
   110 REM *COMPUTE NET AMOUNT
   120      LET A = Q*P
   130 REM *PRINT NAME AND NET AMOUNT
   140      PRINT N$,A
   160 REM *INPUT DATA
   170      DATA "ROCKY COLLEGE STORE",3.25,25.00
   180      END
```

Computer listing of the program

```
>RUN

14:01   MAR 26  GDS1...
ROCKY COLLEGE STORE              81.2500

      180 HALT
```

Output produced by the computer in response to the system command RUN

**Figure 20-3** BASIC Program 1: Simple billing, single customer.

used for program documentation and is provided *solely* for the benefit of people who want to read and understand the program. As far as the computer is concerned, as soon as it encounters the letters REM, it ignores the rest of the statement and moves on to the next line number!

Every program in this chapter (and in Chapter 21) uses REM statements to (1) identify the program, (2) define the variable names used in the program, (3) place explanatory headings throughout the body of the program, and (4) add spacing within the program to aid readability. Indentation of statements is also used to aid readability. Of course, the disadvantages of these stylistic features are that they add to program length, are harder to type, and take up more storage space. After all, 12 of the 17 lines in the program in Figure 20-3 are "unnecessary" REM statements. Usually, though, the merits of REM documentation will outweigh their inconvenience in the programs you write.

The first nine lines in Figure 20-3 are self-explanatory REMark statements. The program is identified, variable names used in the program are defined, and a heading explains the purpose of line number (ln) 100. The statement in ln 100 is an input **READ statement** that *must be combined* with a **DATA statement.** The general form of these statements is

| ln READ | list of variable names | ln DATA | list of data values |
|---------|------------------------|---------|---------------------|

where the values to be assigned to the variable names identified in a READ statement are found in a DATA statement. Thus, when the computer encounters

   100   READ N$, Q, P

it looks for a DATA statement (which it finds at ln 170) and reads the first three data values it finds. In other words, it "uses up" the data by assigning them to the variable names, as follows:

| 100 | READ | N$, | Q, | P |
|-----|------|-----|-----|-----|
| 170 | DATA | "ROCKY COLLEGE STORE", | 3.25, | 25.00 |

You'll notice that since the customer's name is a string variable, it's referred to as N$ in the program to conform to the rules for naming string variables discussed

earlier. The numeric variable names given to quantity purchased (Q) and unit price (P) also follow these rules. These variables are named by the programmer and are arbitrary choices. The customer name variable, for example, could just as easily have been C$ (or A$, B$, . . .) as N$.

Each of our data items could have been placed in a separate DATA statement. It's common, however, to compress multiple data items into a single statement as shown here. But the data must always be typed in the DATA statement(s) in the *order indicated by the READ statement*. The computer doesn't care how many DATA statements there are because before it executes the program it will arrange in order, in a single long list, all the values contained in all the DATA statements. A *pointer* is set internally in the system at the *first* value in the list, and, as we've seen, the first variable name encountered in a READ statement during program execution is assigned the value indicated by the pointer. The pointer then shifts to the next value, which will be "used up" by the next variable name encountered in a READ statement. And so it goes throughout the entire data list. Although DATA statements may be typed anywhere in the program except after the END statement, it's common practice to locate then near the end of the program, as shown in Figure 20-3.

Once the *data-input* operation has been accomplished, the next step in the program is to compute the amount owed by the customer. This *processing* is carried out by using the **LET statement** in ln 120. The amount owed is found by multiplying the 3.25 dozen tee shirts purchased (Q) by the unit price of $25.00 per dozen (P). The net amount owed is assigned the variable name A.

The *output* bill produced by the program consists of one printed line (ln 140). A **PRINT statement** is used to display program results. (Such commands, when found at the end of very long programs, may account for the expression "Some day your PRINTs will come.") The PRINT statement in ln 140 causes the computer to produce the output line shown in Figure 20-3. You'll notice that the N$ and A variable names shown in ln 140 are not printed in the output. Rather, the contents of the storage locations given these names are printed.

*Commas* in PRINT statements serve a specific function. A statement that reads

   015   PRINT A,B,C,D,E

will cause the values of the five variable names to be printed across the page, with A beginning at the left margin, B beginning (perhaps) 14 spaces to the right, C beginning 28 spaces to the right, etc. The width of many terminal/pc printers is 72 or 80 characters, and the use of commas in the PRINT statement may *automatically* establish a format of five columns or zones. The automatic spacing can vary from one system to another. This implicit-specification feature of BASIC is especially appreciated by problem-solvers who are not professional programmers. In our example, the customer name is printed beginning at the left margin. Since the customer name exceeds the spacing of the first zone and extends into the second zone, the comma causes the net amount of the bill ($81.25) to be printed beginning at the third zone.

*Semicolons* are also used in PRINT statements to cause items to be printed close together. Although a small amount of space may be automatically placed before and after a variable quantity in some systems, the spacing is much closer than when commas are used. Suppose, for example, the following statement is written in a program:

195　PRINT "NET = ";A

The first thing you'll notice is that quotation marks are used. Characters (including blank spaces) that are bounded by these marks in a PRINT statement are printed exactly as they appear in the statement when the program is executed. The marks themselves, however, aren't printed. Thus, NET = is printed, beginning at the left margin, when this program is run. The value of the variable name A following the semicolon is then printed with little additional spacing.

A print statement can be used to produce *vertical spacing* in the output. If, for example, you write the following statement:

25　PRINT

the computer will follow your wishes—it will fill a line with blank spaces and advance the output page to the next line. Any number of empty PRINT statements can thus be used to control output line spacing.

The last program statement in Figure 20-3 is the **END statement.** It's the last statement in a BASIC program, and it includes only a line number. Some versions of BASIC don't require an END statement. But it's a good idea to use it because you might someday want to run your programs on other systems that do require its use.

## Feedback and Review 20-1

You may remember that in Feedback and Review 18-1, page 485, you were asked to modify problem 1 in that chapter by preparing a program flowchart for customer bills that included the computation of a 6 percent sales tax. It was specified that the output of the modified program should be a bill giving the customer's name, net amount owed, sales tax amount, and total amount owed. A possible flowchart of this program is shown at the end of Chapter 18. The variable names used in that flowchart are:

N$　Customer name
Q　Quantity purchased
P　Unit price
A　Net amount owed
T1　Sales tax amount
T2　Total amount of bill

Using these names (or other variable names of your own choosing), write a BASIC program to process the following input data:

Customer: WYNN D. TOOTS, INC.
Quantity purchased: 5.50 dozen tee shirts
Unit price: $25.00 per dozen

The output should be a two-line bill. The *first* line should be the customer's name. The *second* line should be in this format:

NET = (net amount) TAX = (sales tax) TOTAL = (total amount)

# DECISIONS AND LOOPS IN BASIC PROGRAMS

As we saw in Chapter 18, Rob and Kay quickly learned that using a program that would compute one customer bill and then stop was the pits. And so, they revised it.

## Program 2: Simple Billing, Multiple Customers

The program shown in Figure 20-4 was written so that bills could be processed for any number of customers. (The logic of this program was charted in Figure 18-4, page 486.) This added flexibility is achieved through the use of a loop controlled by a logic/comparison statement.

The REMark statements from ln 10 through ln 110 are similar to those in Program 1. Since Program 2 will also process a customer's local address (S$) as well as a city and state address (C$), names have been supplied for these variables. (The Zip code is included in C$.)

The READ statement in ln 120 is combined with the DATA statements in ln 270 through ln 390 to provide the program with the input data to be processed. The first time the READ statement is executed in our example, the input data in ln 270 ("PIERRE'S RECORD SHOP") are assigned to N$, the data in ln 280 ("6453 ORLEANS STREET") are assigned to S$, the data in ln 290 ("BOOGIE, LOUISIANA 54321") are assigned to C$, and the data in ln 300 (300 dozen tee shirts and $25.00 per dozen) are the quantity and price assigned to Q and P.

On ln 140 we find a new statement type—the **IF . . . THEN conditional branching statement.** IF . . . THEN statements take the following form:

ln IF (logical assertion) THEN ln

For example, in

120   IF A <10 THEN 30

the computer is told that if the logical assertion is *true*—i.e., if A is *less* than 10—program control is transferred to line number 30. If, however, the condition expressed in the assertion isn't met, the program moves to the next statement in the line number sequence. Other examples of logical assertions are:

$A = B$
$B > C$
$D < = 0$   (D is less than or equal to 0)
$M > = N$   (M is greater than or equal to N)
$S < > T$   (S is not equal to T)
$3*Z > X/T$

As you can see, a "logical assertion" consists of a first expression (a constant, a variable name, or a formula), a relational ($=$, $<$, $>$, or some combination of these), and a second expression.

In the statement on ln 140 of our example program,

140   IF Q = −99.9 THEN 400

the value assigned to the quantity purchased field (Q) of the input record is compared to a sentinel value of −99.9. (A *sentinel value*, you'll recall, is an arbitrary data item placed at the end of a file to indicate that all valid data have been processed.) Since the value of Q during the first pass through the loop is the 300 dozen tee shirts purchased by Pierre's Record Shop, the logical assertion is false and the program moves on to ln 160. You'll notice, however, that a last dummy record has been placed in ln 390 with a sentinel value of −99.9 for Q. When this record is finally read, the logical assertion will be true, the exit condition will be met, program control will be transferred to ln 400, and processing will END.

The statement in ln 160 computes the amount of the bill for Pierre's Record Shop. And the three PRINT statements in ln 180 through ln 200 cause the system to print the customer's name, local address, city, state, and Zip code on the bill as shown in the output section of Figure 20-4. These three lines of print begin at the left margin of the page.

The **PRINT TAB function** in ln 210 is a little different. In this statement,

210   PRINT TAB(3);"NET = ";A

the TAB(3) part of the instruction controls the *spacing on the print line* much as a tabulator setting controls the

```
>LIST
    10 REM *BILLING PROGRAM
    20 REM *
    30 REM *VARIABLE NAMES
    40 REM * N$   NAME
    50 REM * S$   ADDRESS
    60 REM * C$   CITY AND STATE
    70 REM * Q    QUANTITY PURCHASED
    80 REM * P    UNIT PRICE
    90 REM * A    NET AMOUNT
   100 REM *
   110 REM *READ NAME,ADDRESS,QUANTITY PURCHASED AND PRICE
   120     READ N$,S$,C$,Q,P
   130 REM *TEST QUANTITY FOR LAST INPUT
   140     IF Q=-99.9 THEN 400
   150 REM *COMPUTE NET AMOUNT
   160     LET A = Q*P
   170 REM *PRINT NAME,ADDRESS AND NET AMOUNT
   180     PRINT N$
   190     PRINT S$
   200     PRINT C$
   210     PRINT TAB(3);"NET = ";A
   220     PRINT
   230     PRINT
   240     GO TO 120
   260 REM *INPUT DATA
   270     DATA "PIERRE'S RECORD SHOP"
   280     DATA "6453 ORLEANS STREET"
   290     DATA "BOOGIE,LOUISIANA 54321"
   300     DATA  300.0,25.00
   310     DATA "ROCKY COLLEGE STORE"
   320     DATA "1563 BEETHOVEN DRIVE"
   330     DATA "ROCKTOWN,MARYLAND 20765"
   340     DATA  3.25,25.00
   350     DATA "WYNN D.TOOTS,INC."
   360     DATA "120 BROWNING STREET"
   370     DATA "GONG,CALIFORNIA 98765"
   380     DATA  2.00,25.00
   390     DATA "L","L","L",-99.9,0.
   400     END
```

Computer listing of the program

```
>RUN
PIERRE'S RECORD SHOP
6453 ORLEANS STREET
BOOGIE,LOUISIANA 54321
  NET =    7500


ROCKY COLLEGE STORE
1563 BEETHOVEN DRIVE
ROCKTOWN,MARYLAND 20765
  NET =    81.2500


WYNN D.TOOTS,INC.
120 BROWNING STREET
GONG,CALIFORNIA 98765
  NET =    50


    400 HALT
```

Output produced by the computer in response to the system command RUN

Figure 20-4  BASIC Program 2: Simple billing, multiple customers.

spacing on a typewriter. When the computer encounters this part of the statement, it knows that it's to move three spaces *from the left margin* and then begin printing the heading enclosed in quotes. After NET = is printed, the amount of Pierre's bill is also supplied, as you can see in the output of Figure 20-4. (Mosquito bird tee shirts are obviously selling well in Louisiana!) Suppose the following PRINT statement had been encountered:

180    PRINT TAB(18);M;TAB(28);N

The value of the variable name M would be printed beginning 18 spaces from the left margin, and the value of N would be printed starting at 28 spaces *from the left margin* (not from M).

The two empty PRINT statements in ln 220 and ln 230 cause the output page to advance two lines before printing the next customer's bill. On ln 240, we find another new BASIC statement type. There's nothing difficult about this **GO TO unconditional branching statement.** It simply transfers program control to the line specified in the statement. Thus,

240    GO TO 120

causes program control to branch back to the READ statement on ln 120 to begin processing the next customer's bill.

duced as output. In this case, the output messages are requesting input data from the program user. As you'll notice in Figure 20-5, when the program is run, these two message lines are printed immediately.

Line number 130 is

130    INPUT N$,S$,C$,Q,P

This is a new type of BASIC statement that causes the computer to (1) print a question mark (?), and (2) stop executing the program until the user supplies it with the necessary input data for the variable names listed in the **INPUT statement.** INPUT is always followed by one or more variable names separated by commas. Therefore, the *first* result of ln 130 is to cause a ? to be printed as shown in the output of Figure 20-5. The *second* result of the INPUT statement is to halt the program until Rob or Kay types in the customer's name (N$), complete address (S$ and C$), quantity purchased (Q), unit price (P), and then presses the RETURN. The first output is produced as shown below:

ENTER NAME, ADDRESS, QUANTITY, AND PRICE
(ENTER −99.9 FOR QUANTITY AMOUNT TO INDICATE END OF DATA)

Produced by the PRINT statements on ln 115 and ln 120

?       "PIERRE'S RECORD SHOP", "6453 ORLEANS STREET", . . . .

caused by INPUT statement on ln 130       keyed in by user

## An Alternative to Program 2

Let's assume (have you noticed that we do a lot of assuming in this book?) that instead of using READ . . . DATA statements, Rob and Kay would rather *interact* with the computer and give the necessary input data in the form of responses to questions and messages supplied by the program. The program in Figure 20-5 shows us how this might be done. The first eleven line numbers in this program are about the same as those in Figure 20-4.

In the PRINT statements in ln 115 and ln 120, however, things start to change. As you know, the messages enclosed in quotes in these PRINT statements will be pro-

Before moving on, let's consider one other aspect of PRINT and INPUT statements. Suppose a program contains the following statements:

100    PRINT "ODOMETER READING AT START OF TRIP";
110    INPUT M

The effect of placing a semicolon *at the end of a PRINT statement* is to suppress the automatic printer carriage return that usually takes place when the computer reaches the end of a PRINT instruction. Thus, the printing (or display) mechanism does not return to the left margin. So when the computer encounters the INPUT statement in ln 110, the ? caused by this statement will be printed to the

```
>LIST
    10 REM *BILLING PROGRAM
    20 REM *
    30 REM *VARIABLE NAMES
    40 REM * N$  NAME
    50 REM * S$  ADDRESS
    60 REM * C$  CITY AND STATE
    70 REM * Q   QUANTITY PURCHASED
    80 REM * P   UNIT PRICE
    90 REM * A   NET AMOUNT
   100 REM *
   110 REM *INPUT NAME,ADDRESS,QUANTITY PURCHASED AND PRICE
   115      PRINT "ENTER NAME,ADDRESS,QUANTITY AND PRICE"
   120      PRINT "(ENTER -99.9 FOR QUANTITY AMOUNT TO INDICATE END OF DATA)"
   130      INPUT N$,S$,C$,Q,P
   140      IF Q=-99.9 THEN 250
   150 REM *COMPUTE NET AMOUNT
   160      LET A = Q*P
   170 REM *PRINT NAME,ADDRESS AND NET AMOUNT
   172      PRINT
   174      PRINT
   180      PRINT N$
   190      PRINT S$
   200      PRINT C$
   210      PRINT TAB(3);"NET = ";A
   220      PRINT
   230      PRINT
   240      GO TO 115
   250      STOP
   400      END
```

Computer listing
of the program

```
>RUN
ENTER NAME,ADDRESS,QUANTITY AND PRICE
(ENTER -99.9 FOR QUANTITY AMOUNT TO INDICATE END OF DATA)
?"PIERRE'S RECORD SHOP","6453 ORLEANS STREET","BOOGIE,LOUISIANA 54321",300.00,25.00

PIERRE'S RECORD SHOP
6453 ORLEANS STREET
BOOGIE,LOUISIANA 54321
  NET =    7500

ENTER NAME,ADDRESS,QUANTITY AND PRICE
(ENTER -99.9 FOR QUANTITY AMOUNT TO INDICATE END OF DATA)
?"ROCKY COLLEGE STORE","1563 BEETHOVEN DRIVE","ROCKTOWN,MARYLAND 20765",3.25,25.00

ROCKY COLLEGE STORE
1563 BEETHOVEN DRIVE
ROCKTOWN,MARYLAND 20765
  NET =    81.2500

ENTER NAME,ADDRESS,QUANTITY AND PRICE
(ENTER -99.9 FOR QUANTITY AMOUNT TO INDICATE END OF DATA)
?"WYNN D. TOOTS, INC.","120 BROWNING STREET","GONG,CALIFORNIA 98765",200.0,25.00

WYNN D. TOOTS, INC.
120 BROWNING STREET
GONG,CALIFORNIA 98765
  NET =    5000

ENTER NAME,ADDRESS,QUANTITY AND PRICE
(ENTER -99.9 FOR QUANTITY AMOUNT TO INDICATE END OF DATA)
?L,L,L,-99.9,0.0

    250 HALT
```

Output produced by the
computer in response to
the system command RUN

Figure 20-5 An alternative to Program 2 using the INPUT statement.

right of the message produced by ln 100. The output would then look like this:

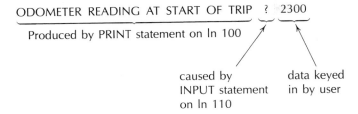

ODOMETER READING AT START OF TRIP  ?  2300

Produced by PRINT statement on ln 100

caused by INPUT statement on ln 110

data keyed in by user

Once the user has supplied the input data for a customer record in our example and has pressed the RE-TURN key, the program takes over to print the customer's bill as shown in the output of Figure 20-5. There are only slight differences in the remainder of this program from the one shown in Figure 20-4. One difference is that a new **STOP statement** in ln 250 has been included here to halt the execution of the program. Commonly used in more complex programs that incorporate subordinate program modules or subroutines, the STOP statement works exactly like a GO TO the END statement. Thus, the statement in ln 140 could just as easily have been

140   IF Q = −99.9 THEN 400

which would have branched program control to the END statement.

## Program 3: Preparing Mailing Labels

You know that R-K Enterprises mails promotional materials to the prospective customers on its mailing list. The program in Figure 20-6 is used to prepare the gummed labels for these mailings. (The logic for this program was charted in Figure 18-6, page 488.) Since there are no new types of BASIC statements used in this program, you should be able to follow most of the coding steps to see how the output labels are printed.

You'll notice that the last customer in the mailing list file is WYNN D. TOOTS, INC. If there had been no DATA statement in ln 380, the computer would first try to READ more data after processing the TOOTS record. Since no more data are present, some message such as "OUT OF DATA" would probably be printed, and the execution of the program would stop automatically. Perhaps terminating the program with such a message would be satisfac-

tory in this example, but provision is made in our program to avoid that message. An exit path out of the program loop is established in ln 130. This path is followed when the prospect's name (N$) is equal to "end of data." Then, as you can see in ln 380, a dummy record at the end of the prospect file gives this sentinel value to the string variable N$.

## Program 4: Sales Compensation, Single Commission Rate

You'll remember from Chapter 18 that Kay and Rob receive a sales compensation report every four weeks that's used to evaluate salesperson performance and prepare paychecks. In problem 4 outlined in Chapter 18 (and charted in Figure 18-7, page 489), it was specified that a single 10 percent commission rate be used to compute the earnings for each salesperson. The BASIC program for this application is shown in Figure 20-7.

The first nine REMark statements in this program are self-explanatory. In ln 100, however, we come to a new type of **PRINT USING function** that's used here to prepare a heading for the sales compensation report. The statement

100   PRINT USING 225

is used to align the output of the computer according to a *specified format*. In ln 100, the computer is instructed to PRINT the headings found in ln 225 in the exact format shown on the *image line* in ln 225. An image line for a PRINT USING statement is identified by a colon immediately after the line number. Thus, the output headings in Figure 20-7 are reproduced exactly as specified in ln 225. Another PRINT USING statement found in this program

190   PRINT USING 230, N$,S,E,

uses the format specified in image line 230 to print the values located in the variable names N$, S, and E. In the dialect of BASIC used here, the # characters can be thought of as "place holders" for the alphanumeric data contained in N$, S, and E. Thus, there are 20 spaces allocated for the salesperson's name (N$). The periods in the spaces allocated for sales amount (S) and earnings (E) figures indicate exactly where the decimal point will be printed. You can see the effect of using the format specified in ln 230 in the output report. The advantage of the

```
>LIST
   10 REM *MAILING LIST PROGRAM
   20 REM *
   30 REM *VARIABLE DEFINITIONS
   40 REM * N$ NAME
   50 REM * A$ ADDRESS
   60 REM * C$ CITY AND STATE
   70 REM *
  100 REM *READ NAME,ADDRESS,CITY AND STATE
  110      READ N$,A$,C$
  120 REM *TEST NAME FOR END OF DATA
  130      IF N$="END OF DATA" THEN 500
  140 REM *PRINT MAILING LABEL
  150      PRINT
  160      PRINT
  170      PRINT TAB(3);N$
  180      PRINT TAB(3);A$
  190      PRINT TAB(3);C$
  200      GO TO 110
  210 REM *INPUT DATA
  220      DATA "ED'S CULTURAL CENTER     "
  230      DATA "822 PHILHARMONIC AVENUE "
  240      DATA "CRAMPS, TEXAS 77786      "
  250 REM *
  260      DATA "PIERRE'S RECORD SHOP     "
  270      DATA "6453 ORLEANS STREET      "
  280      DATA "BOOGIE, LOUISIANA 54321 "
  290 REM *
  300      DATA "ROCKY COLLEGE STORE      "
  310      DATA "1563 BEETHOVEN DRIVE     "
  320      DATA "ROCKTOWN, MARYLAND 20765"
  330 REM *
  340      DATA "WYNN D. TOOTS, INC.      "
  350      DATA "120 BROWNING STREET      "
  360      DATA "GONG, CALIFORNIA 98765  "
  370 REM *
  380      DATA "END OF DATA","DUMMY","DUMMY"
  500      END
```

Computer listing of the program

```
>RUN

ED'S CULTURAL CENTER
822 PHILHARMONIC AVENUE
CRAMPS, TEXAS 77786

PIERRE'S RECORD SHOP
6453 ORLEANS STREET
BOOGIE, LOUISIANA 54321

ROCKY COLLEGE STORE
1563 BEETHOVEN DRIVE
ROCKTOWN, MARYLAND 20765

WYNN D. TOOTS, INC.
120 BROWNING STREET
GONG, CALIFORNIA 98765

  500 HALT
```

Output produced by the computer as the program is executed

Figure 20-6 BASIC Program 3: Preparing mailing labels.

```
>LIST
    10 REM *SALES COMPENSATION REPORT
    20 REM *
    30 REM *VARIABLE NAMES
    40 REM * N$     NAME
    50 REM * W1-W4 SALES DATA FOR WEEKS 1 TO 4
    60 REM * S      SALES AMOUNT
    70 REM * E      EARNINGS
    80 REM *
    90 REM *PRINT HEADING
   100      PRINT USING 225
   110 REM *READ NAME AND SALES
   120      READ N$,W1,W2,W3,W4
   130 REM *TEST W1 FOR END OF DATA
   140      IF W1=-99.9 THEN 320
   150 REM *COMPUTE SALES AMOUNT AND EARNINGS
   160      LET S = W1+W2+W3+W4
   170      LET E = S*.10
   180 REM *PRINT NAME,SALES AMOUNT AND EARNINGS
   190      PRINT USING 230, N$,S,E
   200      GO TO 120
   220 REM *FORMAT STATEMENTS
   225:NAME                      SALES AMOUNT        EARNINGS
   230:##################      #######.##        #######.##
   240 REM *INPUT DATA
   250      DATA "ALFRED E. BOWMAN"
   260      DATA  50.00,80.00,33.50,680.26
   270      DATA "R. GOLDBERG"
   280      DATA  2.00,4.00,8.00,16.00
   285      DATA "C. MACARTHY"
   287      DATA  10.52,20.36,15.30,50.00
   290      DATA "C. NATION"
   300      DATA  35.26,18.50,52.30,758.50
   310      DATA "END OF DATA",-99.9,0.,0.,0.
   320      END
```

Computer listing of the program

```
>RUN
NAME                      SALES AMOUNT        EARNINGS
ALFRED E. BOWMAN              843.76            84.38
R. GOLDBERG                   30.00             3.00
C. MACARTHY                   96.18             9.62
C. NATION                    864.56            86.46

    320 HALT
```

Output produced by the computer as the program is executed

Figure 20-7 BASIC Program 4: Sales compensation, single commission rate.

PRINT USING statement is that it gives the programmer strict control over the output format. However, not all dialects of BASIC have a PRINT USING statement, and the details of usage in those which do can vary. You should check the operating manual of your particular system for possible differences.

The remaining statements in Figure 20-7 should be easy to follow. Each salesperson's name and weekly sales amounts are READ (ln 120) from the DATA statements (ln 250 through ln 310). After a test for exit condition is made (ln 140), the weekly sales amounts are added (ln 160), the 10 percent sales commission amount is computed (ln 170), and a line is printed on the output report (ln 190). These steps are repeated until the last dummy record in ln 310 is read and the processing stops.

## Feedback and Review 20-2

Using what you've now learned of the BASIC language, update Program 2 to take into account the changes outlined in Feedback and Review 18-2, page 488, and shown in the flowchart for Feedback and Review 18-2 presented at the end of Chapter 18. These changes involve computing a 6 percent sales tax on the net amount owed by a customer, and then adding this tax amount to the customer's net amount to get the total amount owed. The same *input data* used in Program 2 should be processed, and the same variable names can be used. Additional variable names for tax amount (T) and total amount owed (S) are also needed.

The *output* of the first bill should look like this:

PIERRE'S RECORD SHOP
6453 ORLEANS STREET
BOOGIE, LOUISIANA 54321
    NET = 7500.00    TAX = 450.00    TOTAL = 7950.00

There should be two line spaces between each output record.

# MULTIPLE DECISIONS IN BASIC PROGRAMS

Only a single logic/comparison statement was used in the preceding programs. But we know that many decision paths are needed to solve more complex problems. Although the following program isn't particularly complex, it does illustrate the use of multiple decisions. Later programs will also use a series of logic decisions.

## Program 5: Simple Billing with Discount

Let's assume that to encourage large shipments, Rob and Kay decide to offer a 15 percent discount on purchases with a quantity greater than or equal to 100 dozen tee shirts. A 6 percent sales tax must be charged on the amount owed after any discount is deducted. The flowchart outlining in detail the logic of this program is shown in Figure 18-8, page 491.

Figure 20-8 shows the program for this billing application example. Since there are no new types of BASIC statements used in this program, you should be able to follow it without too much trouble. The first 14 lines are self-explanatory REMark statements. Input data contained in ln 460 through ln 580 are read, a record at a time, by the READ statement in ln 150. The *first* decision, found in ln 170, is an IF . . . THEN statement that controls the program loop. The exit condition is satisfied when the dummy record in ln 580 is read. The *second* decision on ln 210

    210   IF Q > =100.0 THEN 240

sets up a selection structure. If quantity purchased (Q) is greater than or equal to 100, program control goes to ln 240 and the discount amount (D) is computed. If Q is less than 100, however, control moves to ln 220 and the discount amount is set at zero.

After the appropriate discount path has been selected and the discount amount has been computed or assigned, the 6 percent sales tax (T) is computed on the amount owed after the discount is deducted (ln 260). The total amount of the bill (S) is then computed (ln 280), and the output results shown in Figure 20-8 are prepared using the PRINT and image line statements shown on ln 300 through ln 440. After an input record has been processed and a bill has been printed, program control branches back to read another record (ln 390).

```
>LIST
    10 REM *BILLING PROGRAM
    20 REM *
    30 REM *VARIABLE NAMES
    40 REM * N$ NAME
    50 REM * A$ ADDRESS
    60 REM * C$ CITY AND STATE
    70 REM * Q  QUANTITY PURCHASED
    80 REM * P  UNIT PRICE
    90 REM * A  AMOUNT BEFORE DISCOUNT
    95 REM * D  DISCOUNT
   100 REM * T  SALES TAX
   120 REM * S TOTAL
   130 REM *
   140 REM *READ NAME,ADDRESS,QUANTITY AND PRICE
   150       READ N$,A$,C$,Q,P
   160 REM *TEST QUANTITY FOR END OF DATA
   170       IF Q=-99.9 THEN 590
   180 REM *COMPUTE AMOUNT BEFORE DISCOUNT
   190       LET A = Q*P
   200 REM *COMPUTE DISCOUNT
   210       IF Q>=100.0 THEN 240
   220       LET D = 0.
   230       GO TO 260
   240       LET D = A*.15
   250 REM *COMPUTE SALES TAX
   260       LET T = (A-D)*.06
   270 REM *COMPUTE TOTAL
   280       LET S = A-D+T
   290 REM *PRINT RESULTS AND RETURN
   300       PRINT N$
   310       PRINT A$
   320       PRINT C$
   330       PRINT
   340       PRINT USING 420, Q,P
   350       PRINT USING 430, A,D,T
   355       PRINT USING 440, S
   360       PRINT
   370       PRINT
   380       PRINT
   390       GO TO 150
   410 REM *FORMAT STATEMENTS
   420:QUANTITY = ######.##    PRICE    = ######.##
   430:AMT      = ######.##    DISCOUNT = ######.##    TAX = ####.##
   440:TOTAL    = ######.##
   450 REM *INPUT DATA
   460       DATA "PIERRE'S RECORD SHOP"
```

Figure 20-8 BASIC Program 5: Simple billing with discount.

```
470         DATA "6453 ORLEANS STREET"
480         DATA "BOOGIE,LOUISIANA 54321"
490         DATA  300.00, 25.00
500         DATA "ROCKY COLLEGE STORE"
510         DATA "1563 BEETHOVEN DRIVE"
520         DATA "ROCKTOWN,MARYLAND 20765"
530         DATA  3.25,  25.00
540         DATA "WYNN D. TOOTS,INC."
550         DATA "120 BROWNING STREET"
560         DATA "GONG,CALIFORNIA 98765"
570         DATA  50.00 25.00
580         DATA "END OF DATA","X","X",-99.9,0.
590         END
```

Computer listing of the program

```
>RUN
PIERRE'S RECORD SHOP
6453 ORLEANS STREET
BOOGIE,LOUISIANA 54321

QUANTITY =       300.00   PRICE    =       25.00
AMT      =      7500.00   DISCOUNT =     1125.00   TAX =  382.50
TOTAL    =      6757.50



ROCKY COLLEGE STORE
1563 BEETHOVEN DRIVE
ROCKTOWN,MARYLAND 20765

QUANTITY =         3.25   PRICE    =       25.00
AMT      =        81.25   DISCOUNT =        0.00   TAX =    4.87
TOTAL    =        86.12



WYNN D. TOOTS,INC.
120 BROWNING STREET
GONG,CALIFORNIA 98765

QUANTITY =        50.00   PRICE    =       25.00
AMT      =      1250.00   DISCOUNT =        0.00   TAX =   75.00
TOTAL    =      1325.00

     590 HALT
```

Output produced by the computer as the program is executed

**Figure 20-8** *continued*

## Feedback and Review 20-3

Here's your chance to update the sales compensation report shown in Figure 20-7. Let's assume that the partners decide to pay salespeople a 12 percent commission if their total sales for a period are greater than or equal to $100. If total sales are less than $100, however, the commission rate remains at the 10 percent value used in Program 4. The *input data* should be the same as in Figure 20-7. The *output report* format should also be the same as in Figure 20-7. A possible flowchart for this updated program is the one shown for Feedback and Review 18-3 at the end of Chapter 18.

# THE USE OF ACCUMULATORS

Two sales analysis reports are used to help manage R-K Enterprises. An important programming technique—the use of an accumulator—is used to prepare both reports. As you saw in Chapter 18, an *accumulator* is a programmer-designated storage location that's used to accept and store a running total of individual values as they become available during processing. The contents of the accumulator location must initially be set to zero. Each successive value placed in the accumulator is then added to the value already there. Accumulators are used in the R-K sales analysis reports to accumulate total sales figures.

### Program 6: Sales Report Classified by Type of Product

Figure 20-9 shows a listing of the program used to prepare this sales report along with the output produced when the program is executed. As you can see, this report classifies the purchases made during a period by a named customer according to the type of product shipped. Different reports can be prepared for each of the products sold by Kay and Rob. The logic of this program was discussed in Chapter 18, and the flowchart for the program is shown in Figure 18-9, page 493.

The first 15 lines are REMark statements. In ln 160,

LET   G = O

the location that's used to accumulate the grand total sales figure (G) is set to zero. The name of the particular product being considered is READ (ln 180) from DATA line 555, and the appropriate heading is printed on the output report using the PRINT and format statements found in ln 190 and ln 490. Since we've examined similar statements in other programs, you should have no diffi-culty now in understanding the effects of ln 195 through ln 270.

In ln 290,

LET   G = G + S

the value of G is the grand total sales in the accumulator, and S is the total amount of the sales made to a customer. In processing the first record for Pierre's Record Shop, we can see from the output results in Figure 20-9 that Pierre's total purchases for the period amounted to $7,950.00. When ln 290 is executed, this amount is added to the previous amount (0) in the accumulator. The new total of $7,950.00 is then assigned to the accumulator thereby erasing the previous value of 0. When the next record for Rocky College Store is processed, the $86.12 total for this customer will be added to $7,950.00 now in the accumulator to get a new total of $8,036.12 ($7,950.00 + $86.12). And so the process of updating the accumulator continues until all records have been processed.

The name and complete address of each customer is printed on the output report by the PRINT statements in ln 310 through ln 330. After spacing a line (ln 335), a row of subheadings is printed for each customer using the statements in ln 350 and ln 500. The sales figures for each customer are then printed using the statements in ln 370 and 510. The program then loops back at ln 380 to read the next customer record. When the last valid record has been processed, the exit condition in ln 230 is satisfied, and program control branches to ln 400. The PRINT USING statements in ln 410 and 420, and the image line statements in ln 520 and 530 establish the GRAND TOTAL subheading at the bottom of the report. The statements in ln 430 and ln 540 then cause the printing of the grand total sales amount stored in the accumulator. Pro-

```
>LIST
   10 REM *SALES REPORT PROGRAM
   20 REM *
   30 REM *VARIABLE NAMES
   40 REM * N$  NAME
   50 REM * A$  ADDRESS
   60 REM * C$  CITY AND STATE
   70 REM * P$  PRODUCT NAME
   80 REM * Q   QUANTITY SOLD
   90 REM * P   UNIT PRICE
  100 REM * A   NET SALES
  110 REM * T   TAX
  120 REM * S   TOTAL SALES
  130 REM * G   GRAND TOTAL SALES
  140 REM *
  150 REM *INITIALIZE ACCUMULATOR
  160     LET G = 0.
  170 REM *READ PRODUCT NAME AND PRINT HEADING
  180     READ P$
  190     PRINT USING 490, P$
  195     PRINT
  200 REM *READ NAME,ADDRESS,QUANTITY AND UNIT PRICE
  210     READ N$,A$,C$,Q,P
  220 REM *TEST QUANTITY FOR END OF DATA
  230     IF Q=-99.9 THEN 400
  240 REM *CALCULATE NET AMOUNT,SALES TAX AND TOTAL
  250     LET A = Q*P
  260     LET T = A*.06
  270     LET S = A+T
  280 REM *ACCUMULATE GRAND TOTAL
  290     LET G = G+S
  300 REM *PRINT NAME AND ADDRESS
  310     PRINT N$
  320     PRINT A$
  330     PRINT C$
  335     PRINT
  340 REM *PRINT SUBHEADING
  350     PRINT USING 500
  360 REM *PRINT QUANTITY,UNIT PRICE,NET AMOUNT,SALES TAX AND TOTAL
  370     PRINT USING 510, Q,P,A,T,S
  373     PRINT
  375     PRINT
  377     PRINT
  380     GO TO 210
  390 REM *PRINT GRAND TOTAL AND STOP
  400     PRINT
  410     PRINT USING 520
  420     PRINT USING 530
  430     PRINT USING 540, G
  470     STOP
  480 REM *FORMAT STATEMENTS
  490:SALES REPORT FOR ###################
  500:QUANTITY   UNIT PRICE   NET AMOUNT    SALES TAX       TOTAL
  510:#####.##    #######.##   #######.##    ######.##    #######.##
  520:                                                       GRAND
  530:                                                       TOTAL
  540:                                                    #######.##
  550 REM *INPUT DATA
  555     DATA "TEE SHIRTS(DOZ)"
  560     DATA "PIERRE'S RECORD SHOP"
  570     DATA "6453 ORLEANS STREET"
  580     DATA "BOOGIE,LOUISIANA 54321"
  590     DATA  300.00,25.00
  600     DATA "ROCKY COLLEGE STORE"
  610     DATA "1563 BEETHOVEN DRIVE"
  620     DATA "ROCKTOWN,MARYLAND 20765"
  630     DATA  3.25,25.00
  640     DATA "WYNN D. TOOTS,INC."
```

Computer listing
of the program

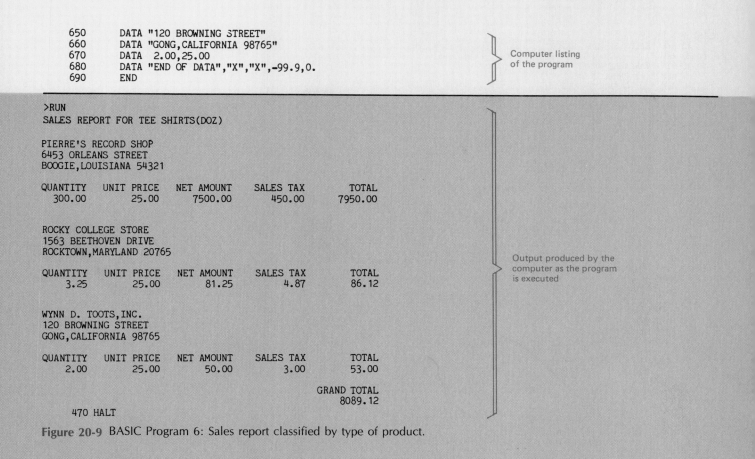

```
650    DATA "120 BROWNING STREET"
660    DATA "GONG,CALIFORNIA 98765"
670    DATA  2.00,25.00
680    DATA "END OF DATA","X","X",-99.9,0.
690    END
```

Computer listing
of the program

```
>RUN
SALES REPORT FOR TEE SHIRTS(DOZ)

PIERRE'S RECORD SHOP
6453 ORLEANS STREET
BOOGIE,LOUISIANA 54321

QUANTITY    UNIT PRICE    NET AMOUNT    SALES TAX       TOTAL
  300.00         25.00       7500.00       450.00     7950.00


ROCKY COLLEGE STORE
1563 BEETHOVEN DRIVE
ROCKTOWN,MARYLAND 20765

QUANTITY    UNIT PRICE    NET AMOUNT    SALES TAX       TOTAL
    3.25         25.00         81.25         4.87       86.12


WYNN D. TOOTS,INC.
120 BROWNING STREET
GONG,CALIFORNIA 98765

QUANTITY    UNIT PRICE    NET AMOUNT    SALES TAX       TOTAL
    2.00         25.00         50.00         3.00       53.00

                                          GRAND TOTAL
                                             8089.12
    470 HALT
```

Output produced by the
computer as the program
is executed

**Figure 20-9** BASIC Program 6: Sales report classified by type of product.

gram control then moves to ln 470, and the STOP statement halts the processing.

## Program 7: Sales Summary Report

The purpose of this report is to summarize the sales of all products sold by R-K Enterprises during a period. A listing of the program used to prepare this report, along with the output produced by the program, is shown in Figure 20-10. The flowchart outlining the specifications and logic of this program is shown in Figure 18-10, page 495.

After the headings shown on the report are printed (ln 110–115, and ln 320–325), the accumulator is set to zero (ln 130). Input data are read (ln 150), a test for exit condition is made (ln 170), the net sales for a product are computed (ln 190), and the sales amount is accumulated (ln 200). A line on the output report is printed for the product (ln 220 and ln 330), and the program loops back to read another record (ln 230).

After all valid records have been processed, the exit condition in ln 170 is satisfied, and program control branches to ln 250. The same procedure discussed in the preceding program is then followed to print the TOTAL NET SALES subheading at the bottom of the report. The accumulated total net sales figure is then printed below the subheading and the processing stops.

```
>LIST
    10 REM *SALES SUMMARY REPORT
    20 REM *
    30 REM *VARIABLE NAMES
    40 REM * P$ PRODUCT NAME
    50 REM * Q   QUANTITY SOLD
    60 REM * P   UNIT PRICE
    70 REM * A   NET SALES
    80 REM * T   TOTAL NET SALES
    90 REM *
   100 REM *PRINT HEADING
   110     PRINT USING 320
   115     PRINT USING 325
   120 REM *INITIALIZE ACCUMULATOR
   130     LET T = 0.
   140 REM *READ PRODUCT,UNIT PRICE AND QUANTITY SOLD
   150     READ P$,Q,P
   160 REM *TEST QUANTITY FOR END OF DATA
   170     IF Q=-99.9 THEN 250
   180 REM *COMPUTE NET SALES AND ACCUMULATE TOTAL NET SALES
   190     LET A = Q*P
   200     LET T = A+T
   210 REM *PRINT PRODUCT,PRICE,QUANTITY AND NET SALES THEN RETURN
   220     PRINT USING 330, P$,P,Q,A
   230     GO TO 150
   240 REM *PRINT TOTAL NET SALES AND STOP
   250     PRINT
   260     PRINT
   270     PRINT USING 340
   280     PRINT USING 350
   290     PRINT USING 360, T
   300     STOP
   310 REM *FORMAT STATEMENTS
   320:                SALES SUMMARY REPORT
   325:PRODUCT                 UNIT PRICE    QUANTITY      NET SALES
   330:#######."###########    #######.##    #######.##    #######.##
   340:                                                    TOTAL
   350:                                                    NET SALES
   360:                                                    #######.##
   370 REM *INPUT DATA
   380     DATA "TEE SHIRTS(DOZ)"
   390     DATA  35.75, 25.00
   400     DATA "MOSQUITO BIRD R"
   410     DATA  300.0, 6.00
   420     DATA "MOSQUITO BIRD T"
   430     DATA  50.00, 7.00
   440     DATA "KAY OSS IN CONCERT R"
   450     DATA  200.0, 8.00
   460     DATA "KAY OSS IN CONCERT T"
   470     DATA  70.00, 8.50
   480     DATA "OH WHAT? BOOK"
   490     DATA  2.00, 9.95
   500     DATA "END OF DATA",-99.9,0.
   510     END
```

Computer listing
of the program

**Figure 20-10** BASIC Program 7: Sales summary report.

```
>RUN
               SALES SUMMARY REPORT
PRODUCT                 UNIT PRICE    QUANTITY      NET SALES
TEE SHIRTS(DOZ)             25.00        35.75         893.75
MOSQUITO BIRD R             6.00        300.00        1800.00
MOSQUITO BIRD T             7.00         50.00         350.00
KAY OSS IN CONCERT R        8.00        200.00        1600.00
KAY OSS IN CONCERT T        8.50         70.00         595.00
OH WHAT? BOOK               9.95          2.00          19.90


                                                    TOTAL
                                                    NET SALES
                                                    5258.65

    300 HALT
```

Output produced by the
computer as the program
is executed

## Feedback and Review 20-4

It's time once again for you to become a maintenance programmer! Your assignment is to update the sales compensation report program you prepared for Feedback and Review 20-3. You'll use the same *input data,* and the same general output format. However, you should modify the program so that the *output* looks like this:

| NAME | SALES AMOUNT | EARNINGS |
|------|-------------:|---------:|
| ALFRED E. BOWMAN | 843.76 | 84.38 |
| R. GOLDBERG | 30.00 | 3.00 |
| C. MACARTHY | 96.18 | 9.62 |
| C. NATION | 864.56 | 86.46 |
| | TOTAL SALES | TOTAL EARNINGS |
| | 1834.50 | 183.45 |

As you can see from the output, only a 10 percent commission rate is applied to each person's sales amount to get their earnings. Multiple commission rates aren't used for this exercise. What *is* being emphasized here, however, is the use of an accumulator to total the sales made by each salesperson. The flowchart for Feedback and Review 18-4, shown at the end of Chapter 18, should help you prepare this program.

# THE USE OF COUNTERS

Another important programming technique discussed in Chapter 18 is the use of a counter. A *counter,* you'll recall, is a special type of accumulator that's often used to record the number of times a loop has been processed. The counter is incremented with each pass of the program through the loop. When the counter value reaches a predetermined number, an exit condition based on the value of the counter is satisfied, and an exit path out of the loop is followed.

### Program 8: Simple Billing with a Counter

The listing in Figure 20-11 shows how a counter can be used to control a loop. The flowchart for this program is found in Figure 18-11, page 496.

The counter (K) is initialized at 1 in ln 120, and the number of records to be processed (and thus the number of passes to be made through the loop) is read in ln 130. In our example, the number of records to be processed (N) is set at 4 by the first DATA item in ln 300. After the first customer record has been processed (ln 150 through ln 210), a test for exit condition is made in ln 230. In the first pass through the program loop, this statement

```
230   IF K = N THEN 410
```

compares the initial value of the counter (1) to the number of records to be processed (4). Since the counter value obviously doesn't equal 4, program control moves on to ln 250. In this step,

```
250   LET K = K + 1
```

the counter is incremented by a value of 1, and so its new value is 2. When the last customer record has been processed, and when K = N, the exit path out of the loop will be followed to ln 410, and processing will END without any need for a dummy record at the end of the file.

### Built-in Looping with an Automatic Counter

Since using a counter to control a loop is such a useful technique, most programming languages have instructions that can be used to establish an automatic counter. The program listing in Figure 20-12 shows how an automatic counter can be set up in BASIC. This program represents an alternative to Program 4 shown in Figure 20-7.

```
>LIST
     10  REM *BILLING PROGRAM
     20  REM *
     30  REM *VARIABLE NAMES
     40  REM * N$ NAME
     50  REM * Q   QUANTITY
     60  REM * P   UNIT PRICE
     70  REM * A   NET AMOUNT
     80  REM * N   NUMBER OF RECORDS TO BE PROCESSED
     90  REM * K   COUNTER
    100  REM *
    110  REM *INITIALIZE COUNTER AND READ NUMBER OF RECORDS
    120      LET K = 1
    130      READ N
    140  REM *READ NAME,QUANTITY AND PRICE
    150      READ N$,Q,P
    160  REM *COMPUTE NET AMOUNT
    170      LET A = Q*P
    180  REM *PRINT NAME AND NET AMOUNT
    190      PRINT USING 280, N$,A
    200      PRINT
    210      PRINT
    220  REM *TEST FOR END OF DATA
    230      IF K=N THEN 410
    240  REM *INCREMENT COUNTER AND RETURN
    250      LET K = K+1
    260      GO TO 150
    270  REM *FORMAT STATEMENT FOR OUTPUT
    280:##################   NET = ######.##
    290  REM *INPUT DATA
    300      DATA   4
    310      DATA "ED'S CULTURAL CENTER "
    320      DATA   3.50,    25.00
    330      DATA "PIERRE'S RECORD SHOP "
    340      DATA   5.75,    25.00
    350      DATA "ROCKY COLLEGE STORE  "
    360      DATA  10.00    25.00
    370      DATA "WYNN D. TOOTS, INC.  "
    380      DATA   6.00,    25.00
    410      END
```

Computer listing
of the program

```
>RUN
ED'S CULTURAL CENTER   NET =      87.50


PIERRE'S RECORD SHOP   NET =     143.75


ROCKY COLLEGE STORE    NET =     250.00


WYNN D. TOOTS, INC.    NET =     150.00


    410 HALT
```

Output produced by the
computer as the program
is executed

Figure 20-11   BASIC Program 8: Simple billing with a counter.

```
>LIST
    10 REM *SALES COMPENSATION REPORT
    20 REM *
    30 REM *VARIABLE NAMES
    40 REM * N$      NAME
    50 REM * W1-W4 SALES DATA FOR WEEKS 1 TO 4
    60 REM * S       SALES AMOUNT
    70 REM * E       EARNINGS
    80 REM * N       NUMBER OF RECORDS TO BE PROCESSED
    90 REM *
   100 REM *READ NUMBER OF RECORDS TO BE PROCESSED
   110      READ N
   120 REM *PRINT HEADING
   130      PRINT USING 260
   140 REM *PROCESS DATA USING LOOP
   150      FOR K=1 TO N
   160 REM *READ NAME AND SALES DATA
   170      READ N$,W1,W2,W3,W4
   180 REM *COMPUTE SALES AMOUNT AND EARNINGS
   190      LET S = W1+W2+W3+W4
   200      LET E = S*.10
   210 REM *PRINT NAME,SALES AMOUNT AND EARNINGS THEN RETURN
   220      PRINT USING 270, N$,S,E
   230      NEXT K
   240      STOP
   250 REM *FORMAT STATEMENTS
   260:NAME                    SALES AMOUNT        EARNINGS
   270:##################     ######.##       ######.##
   280 REM *INPUT DATA
   290      DATA  4
   300      DATA "ALFRED E. BOWMAN"
   310      DATA   50.00,  80.00,  33.50, 680.26
   320      DATA "R. GOLDBERG"
   330      DATA    2.00,   4.00,   8.00,  16.00
   340      DATA "C. MACARTHY"
   350      DATA   10.52,  20.36,  15.30,  50.00
   360      DATA "C. NATION"
   370      DATA   35.26,  18.50,  52.30, 758.50
   380      END
```

Computer listing of the program

```
>RUN
NAME                    SALES AMOUNT        EARNINGS
ALFRED E. BOWMAN              843.76           84.38
R. GOLDBERG                   30.00            3.00
C. MACARTHY                   96.18            9.62
C. NATION                    864.56           86.46

    240 HALT
```

Output produced by the computer as the program is executed

Figure 20-12 An alternative to Program 4, Figure 20-7, showing built-in looping with an automatic counter.

The number of input records is specified in Figure 20-12, but otherwise the input data and output results are the same for both programs.

The statements from ln 10 through ln 140 are familiar types. But this program then uses a pair of statements—the **FOR statement** on ln 150 and the **NEXT statement** on ln 230—that you're not familiar with. These FOR and NEXT statements must always be used together. The FOR statement *opens* a loop, and the loop is *closed* with the NEXT statement. That is, a FOR statement sets up a loop and is placed at the beginning of the loop, while the NEXT statement is located at the end of the loop. The program line or lines that are *between* the FOR and NEXT statements are executed repeatedly and form the *range,* or *body,* of the loop.

The general form of these statements is

```
ln   FOR v = i TO t STEP n
ln    ·
ln    ·
ln    ·
ln   NEXT v
```

where ln is a line number, v is a variable name acting as an automatic counter or index, i is the initial value or expression given to the counter, t is the terminal value or expression of the counter when the looping is completed, and n is the amount by which the counter should be stepped up or down after each pass through the loop. (If the step value is omitted in the FOR statement, the computer will automatically use a step size of 1.) Some examples of valid FOR . . . NEXT statements are:

```
150   FOR K = 1 TO N

230   NEXT K

130   FOR J = 5*N TO A/B STEP 2

180   NEXT J

160   FOR P =  25 TO 1 STEP − 1

260   NEXT P
```

The first of these FOR . . . NEXT examples is found in our program in Figure 20-12. In our example, the automatic counter (K) is initially set at 1 in the FOR statement (ln 150), a salesperson's record is read and processed (ln 170 through ln 200), an output line is printed (ln 220 and ln 270), and the end of the loop is reached at the NEXT statement (ln 230). An automatic test is made to determine if the counter value (K) is greater than N (in this case 4). Since K is now 1 and obviously isn't greater than N, the counter is automatically stepped up by 1 and the next pass through the loop occurs. When the records of the four salespeople have been processed, the value of K *will* be greater than N, the processing will stop, and program control will exit from the FOR . . . NEXT loop structure to the next executable line number in sequence. In our example, this is the STOP statement on ln 240. As this example illustrates, the built-in looping capability available through the use of FOR . . . NEXT statements gives the programmer a relatively simple and powerful repetitive processing tool.

# ADDITIONAL BUSINESS DATA PROCESSING IN BASIC

Only two more R-K Enterprises programs remain to be considered in this chapter—a final billing program and an inventory control program. The flowchart for the billing program is shown in Figure 18-13, p. 498, and the inventory control flowchart is found in Figure 18-12, page 497. Since there are no new programming techniques and no new types of BASIC statements to consider in these programs, we'll move through them quickly.

### Program 9: Final Billing Program

Many of the features found in the program listed in Figure 20-13 were shown earlier in Program 5, Figure 20-8. But a number of additional features have also been added. For example, this program accommodates all possible products sold by Rob and Kay rather than just the single product discussed in Program 5. In addition, accumulators are set up (ln 180 and ln 190) to total the amounts

```
>LIST
    10 REM *BILLING PROGRAM
    20 REM *
    30 REM *VARIABLE NAMES
    40 REM * N$ NAME
    50 REM * A$ ADDRESS
    60 REM * C$ CITY AND STATE
    70 REM * P$ PRODUCT NAME
    80 REM * Q  QUANTITY
    90 REM * P  UNIT PRICE
   100 REM * A  AMOUNT BEFORE DISCOUNT
   110 REM * D  DISCOUNT
   120 REM * T  TAX
   130 REM * S  TOTAL
   140 REM * G1 GRAND TOTAL AMOUNT BEFORE DISCOUNT
   150 REM * G2 GRAND TOTAL AMOUNT AFTER DISCOUNTS
   160 REM *
   170 REM *INITIALIZE ACCUMULATORS
   180      LET G1 = 0.
   190      LET G2 = 0.
   200 REM *READ CUSTOMER NAME AND ADDRESS AND PRINT HEADING
   210      READ N$,A$,C$
   220      PRINT
   230      PRINT
   240      PRINT
   250      PRINT N$
   260      PRINT A$
   270      PRINT C$
   280      PRINT
   290      PRINT USING 590
   300 REM *READ PRODUCT,QUANTITY AND PRICE
   310      READ P$,Q,P
   320 REM *TEST QUANTITY FOR END OF DATA AND PRICE FOR LAST PRODUCT
   330      IF P=-99.9 THEN 210
   340      IF Q=-99.9 THEN 530
   350 REM *COMPUTE AMOUNT BEFORE DISCOUNT
   360      LET A = Q*P
   370 REM *COMPUTE DISCOUNT BASED ON QUANTITY SOLD
   380      IF Q>=100. THEN 410
   390      LET D = 0.
   400      GO TO 430
   410      LET D = .15*A
   420 REM *COMPUTE TAX AND TOTAL
   430      LET T = .06*(A-D)
   440      LET S = A-D+T
   450 REM *ACCUMULATE TOTALS
   460      LET G1 = G1+A
```

Figure 20-13 BASIC Program 9: Final billing program.

Computer listing
of the program

```
470        LET G2 = G2+S
480 REM *PRINT PRODUCT,QUANTITY,PRICE,AMOUNT BEFORE DISCOUNT,DISCOUNT,
490 REM *       TAX AND TOTAL THEN RETURN
500        PRINT USING 600, P$,Q,P,A,D,T,S
510        GO TO 310
520 REM *PRINT GRAND TOTALS THEN STOP
530        PRINT
540        PRINT
550        PRINT USING 610, G1
560        PRINT USING 620, G2
570        STOP
580 REM *FORMAT STATEMENTS
590:PRODUCT                    QTY PRICE     AMT DCOUNT   TAX   TOTAL
600:################### ####.## ###.## #####.## ####.## ###.## #####.##
610:AMT TOTAL   = #######.##
620:GRAND TOTAL = #######.##
630 REM *INPUT DATA
640        DATA "ED'S CULTURAL CENTER"
650        DATA "822 PHILHARMONIC AVENUE"
660        DATA "CRAMPS,TEXAS 77786"
670        DATA "MOSQUITO BIRD R    ", 200.00,  6.00
680        DATA "MOSQUITO BIRD T    ", 300.00,  7.00
690        DATA "LAST PRODUCT", 0.,-99.9
695 REM *
700        DATA "PIERRE'S RECORD SHOP"
710        DATA "6453 ORLEANS STREET"
720        DATA "BOOGIE,LOUISIANA 54321"
730        DATA "TEE SHIRTS(DOZ)    ",   3.00, 25.00
740        DATA "MOSQUITO BIRD R    ",  50.00,  6.00
750        DATA "MOSQUITO BIRD T    ",  60.00,  7.00
760        DATA "KAY OSS IN CONCERT R", 110.00,  8.00
770        DATA "KAY OSS IN CONCERT T", 200.00,  8.50
780        DATA "OH WHAT? BOOK      ",  30.00,  9.95
790        DATA "LAST PRODUCT", 0.,-99.9
795 REM *
800        DATA "ROCKY COLLEGE STORE"
810        DATA "1563 BEETHOVEN DRIVE"
820        DATA "ROCKTOWN,MARYLAND 20765"
830        DATA "TEE SHIRTS(DOZ)    ",   6.25, 25.00
840        DATA "MOSQUITO BIRD R    ",   6.00,  6.00
850        DATA "MOSQUITO BIRD T    ",   5.00,  7.00
860        DATA "KAY OSS IN CONCERT R",   2.00  8.00
870        DATA "KAY OSS IN CONCERT T",   2.00  8.50
880        DATA "OH WHAT? BOOK      ",   4.00  9.95
890        DATA "LAST PRODUCT", 0.,-99.9
895 REM *
900        DATA "WYNN D. TOOTS,INC."
910        DATA "120 BROWNING STREET"
920        DATA "GONG,CALIFORNIA 98765"
930        DATA "OH WHAT? BOOK      ",   5.00, 9.95
940        DATA "END OF DATA", -99.9, 0.
950        END
```

Figure 20-13 *continued*

Computer listing
of the program

```
>RUN

ED'S CULTURAL CENTER
822 PHILHARMONIC AVENUE
CRAMPS,TEXAS 77786

PRODUCT                QTY   PRICE      AMT  DCOUNT     TAX    TOTAL
MOSQUITO BIRD R     200.00    6.00  1200.00  180.00   61.20  1081.20
MOSQUITO BIRD T     300.00    7.00  2100.00  315.00  107.10  1892.10


PIERRE'S RECORD SHOP
6453 ORLEANS STREET
BOOGIE,LOUISIANA 54321

PRODUCT                QTY   PRICE      AMT  DCOUNT     TAX    TOTAL
TEE SHIRTS(DOZ)       3.00   25.00    75.00    0.00    4.50    79.50
MOSQUITO BIRD R      50.00    6.00   300.00    0.00   18.00   318.00
MOSQUITO BIRD T      60.00    7.00   420.00    0.00   25.20   445.20
KAY OSS IN CONCERT R 110.00   8.00   880.00  132.00   44.88   792.88
KAY OSS IN CONCERT T 200.00   8.50  1700.00  255.00   86.70  1531.70
OH WHAT? BOOK        30.00    9.95   298.50    0.00   17.91   316.41


ROCKY COLLEGE STORE
1563 BEETHOVEN DRIVE
ROCKTOWN,MARYLAND 20765

PRODUCT                QTY   PRICE      AMT  DCOUNT     TAX    TOTAL
TEE SHIRTS(DOZ)       6.25   25.00   156.25    0.00    9.37   165.62
MOSQUITO BIRD R       6.00    6.00    36.00    0.00    2.16    38.16
MOSQUITO BIRD T       5.00    7.00    35.00    0.00    2.10    37.10
KAY OSS IN CONCERT R  2.00    8.00    16.00    0.00    0.96    16.96
KAY OSS IN CONCERT T  2.00    8.50    17.00    0.00    1.02    18.02
OH WHAT? BOOK         4.00    9.95    39.80    0.00    2.39    42.19


WYNN D. TOOTS,INC.
120 BROWNING STREET
GONG,CALIFORNIA 98765

PRODUCT                QTY   PRICE      AMT  DCOUNT     TAX    TOTAL
OH WHAT? BOOK         5.00    9.95    49.75    0.00    2.98    52.73


AMT TOTAL   =   7323.30
GRAND TOTAL =   6827.78

     570 HALT
```

billed before and after discounts have been computed.

After the name and complete address of the first customer are read and printed (ln 210 through ln 280), a heading line for the customer's bill is printed (ln 290 and ln 590). The name, quantity, and price of the *first* product are entered next (ln 310). An *end-of-record test* is then made

330   IF P = −99.9 THEN 210

to see if all products in a customer's record have been processed. If they all *have* been processed, a dummy price field with a value of −99.9 at the end of a customer's record is encountered (see ln 690, 790, and 890), and program control branches back to ln 210 to read and print the name of the next customer. Since none of the products purchased by the first customer have yet been processed, however, program control moves to the next statement.

This statement

340   IF Q = −99.9 THEN 530

is an *end-of-file test*. When all valid data in the last customer's record have been processed, a dummy quantity field with a value of −99.9 is read (ln 940), program control moves to ln 530, accumulated totals are printed (ln 550 and 610, and ln 560 and 620), and processing stops (ln 570).

But that operation comes later. Right now, we are processing the first product item bought by Ed's Cultural Center in Cramps, Texas. The statements from ln 360 through ln 440 are identical to those explained in problem 5, so we can skip them here. You'll notice in ln 460 and ln 470, however, that the before and after discount amounts for the first product (mosquito bird record) are added to the accumulators. The totals of all successive products will also be accumulated. The name of the first product and other pertinent facts are then printed on the first customer's bill (ln 500 and ln 600). Program control then branches from ln 510 back to ln 310, and the next product is processed. This continues until the last product bought by the first customer has been accounted for. Then, as we've seen, the exit test condition for ln 330 will be met and processing will begin on the next customer's record.

## Program 10: Inventory Control Report

Figure 20-14 shows a listing of the program for the inventory control report along with the output produced when the program is executed. The body of the program loop begins after the report headings are printed (using ln 115 through ln 126, and ln 340 through ln 360). Input data are entered (ln 150), a test is made to see if all valid records have been processed (ln 170), and the inventory available for sale is determined (ln 190 through ln 220). The ending inventory is then found (ln 240 through ln 270). An output line for a product is printed (ln 300 and ln 370), and program control then branches from ln 310 back to ln 150 to read and process another record.

The output produced by this inventory control program shows some distressing figures. We'll interpret these figures at the end of Chapter 21 after you've had the opportunity to study a program that helps explain these inventory results.

```
>LIST
     10 REM *INVENTORY CONTROL REPORT
     20 REM *
     30 REM *VARIABLE NAMES
     40 REM * P$ PRODUCT NAME
     50 REM * B  BEGINNING INVENTORY
     60 REM * R  QUANTITY RECEIVED
     70 REM * S  QUANTITY SOLD
     80 REM * A  AVAILABLE INVENTORY
     90 REM * E  ENDING INVENTORY
    100 REM *
    110 REM *PRINT HEADING
    115     PRINT USING 340
    118     PRINT
    122     PRINT USING 350
    126     PRINT USING 360
    130 REM *READ PRODUCT,BEGINNING INVENTORY,QUANTITY RECEIVED
    140 REM *AND QUANTITY SOLD
    150     READ P$,B,R,S
    160 REM *TEST QUANTITY RECEIVED FOR END OF DATA
    170     IF R=-99.9 THEN 320
    180 REM *COMPUTE AVAILABLE INVENTORY
    190     IF R>=0. THEN 220
    200     LET A = B
    210     GO TO 240
    220     LET A = B+R
    230 REM *COMPUTE ENDING INVENTORY
    240     IF S>=0. THEN 270
    250     LET E = A
    260     GO TO 300
    270     LET E = A-S
    280 REM *PRINT PRODUCT,BEGINNING INVENTORY,QUANTITY RECEIVED
    290 REM *QUANTITY SOLD AND ENDING INVENTORY THEN RETURN
    300     PRINT USING 370, P$,B,R,S,E
    310     GO TO 150
    320     STOP
    330 REM *FORMAT STATEMENTS
    340:                INVENTORY CONTROL REPORT
    350:PRODUCT           BEGINNING     QUANTITY     QUANTITY     ENDING
    360:                  INVENTORY     RECEIVED     SOLD        INVENTORY
    370:################### -#######.##   #######.##    #######.## -#######.##
    380 REM *INPUT DATA
    390     DATA "TEE SHIRTS(DOZ)    ",  50.00,   10.00,    30.75
    400     DATA "MOSQUITO BIRD R    ",  30.00,   20.00,    20.00
    410     DATA "MOSQUITO BIRD T    ",  20.00,   20.00,    30.00
    420     DATA "KAY OSS IN CONCERT R",  10.00,    6.00,  5000.00
    430     DATA "KAY OSS IN CONCERT T",  10.00,    5.00,  5000.00
    440     DATA "OH WHAT? BOOK      ",   5.00, 6000.00,    00.00
    460     DATA "END OF DATA        ",   0.00,  -99.90,    00.00
    470     END
```

Figure 20-14 BASIC Program 10: An inventory control report.

```
>RUN
                INVENTORY CONTROL REPORT

PRODUCT             BEGINNING   QUANTITY   QUANTITY   ENDING
                    INVENTORY   RECEIVED   SOLD       INVENTORY
TEE SHIRTS(DOZ)        50.00      10.00      30.75       29.25
MOSQUITO BIRD R        30.00      20.00      20.00       30.00
MOSQUITO BIRD T        20.00      20.00      30.00       10.00
KAY OSS IN CONCERT R   10.00       6.00    5000.00    -4984.00
KAY OSS IN CONCERT T   10.00       5.00    5000.00    -4985.00
OH WHAT? BOOK           5.00    6000.00       0.00     6005.00

    320 HALT
```

Computer listing of the program

Output produced by the computer as the program is executed

# LOOKING BACK

**1.** BASIC is a popular timesharing and personal computing language that makes it easy for people to interact with computers. Sign-on procedures, the key words used in systems commands, and other details of language usage vary from one system to another.

**2.** Key words are used in constructing BASIC statements, and these statements are then put together to form a program. Each statement in a BASIC program begins with a line number, and each type of statement has certain rules that must be followed. A number (but certainly not all) of these rules have been discussed in the chapter for the following types of statements and functions:

| | |
|---|---|
| REM | IF . . . THEN |
| READ . . . DATA | GO TO |
| LET | STOP |
| PRINT | FOR . . . NEXT |
| INPUT | PRINT TAB |
| PRINT USING | END |

**3.** The values used in BASIC statements may be constants or variables. There are numeric constants and character string constants, and there are also numeric variables and string variables. Specific rules for naming and using these numeric and string values must be followed.

**4.** The computer handles arithmetic operations in a specific order. The rules used in determining the order of these operations have been spelled out in the chapter. Some common procedures for correcting errors that may occur during program and data entry have also been discussed.

**5.** Solutions have been written in BASIC for all the problems analyzed and flowcharted in Chapter 18. All programs have been written in a programming style that may make them easier to read and understand. Beginning with some short programs to accomplish simple input, processing, and output, we have moved on to more detailed examples that use decisions, loops, counters, and accumulators. The language rules and programming techniques that have been considered during the discussion of these programs can be used to solve very complex problems. Of course, BASIC has many additional features that are not considered in this chapter. Some (but again not all) of these additional features are presented in Chapter 21.

## KEY TERMS AND CONCEPTS

system commands 545
program statements 545
line number (ln) 546
numeric constants 546
character string constants 546
numeric variable 546
variable name 547
string variables 547

correction key 549
programming style 550
REMark statement 550
READ. . . .DATA statements 551
LET (assignment) statement 551
PRINT statement 551
END statement 552
IF . . . THEN conditional branching
    statement 553

PRINT TAB function 553
GO TO unconditional branching
    statement 555
INPUT statement 555
STOP statement 557
PRINT USING function 557
FOR . . . NEXT statements 570

## TOPICS FOR REVIEW AND DISCUSSION

**1.** Explain the procedures required to sign on the system you are using.

**2.** (a) What is the difference between a system command and a program statement? (b) Which typically causes the computer to take immediate action?

**3.** Identify and discuss the elements that may be found in a BASIC statement.

**4.** "BASIC deals with values that may be constants or variables." Discuss this sentence.

**5.** Define and give examples of a (a) numeric constant, (b) character string constant, (c) numeric variable, (d) variable name, (e) string variable, and (f) string variable name.

**6.** (a) Why is it important to understand the order in which the computer handles the arithmetic operations in a formula?

(b) What is this priority order in a formula without parentheses? (c) What changes are made in this order when parentheses are used?

**7.** Explain the procedures required by the system you are using to correct the errors that may occur in program and data entry.

**8.** "Diagnostic messages detect syntax errors but not logical errors." Discuss this statement.

**9.** What will the computer do in executing the following BASIC statements:

| | | |
|---|---|---|
| **(a)** | 010 | READ A,B,C,D,E |
| | 200 | DATA 025,200,300 |
| | 210 | DATA 060,150,175, . . . . . , 125 |
| **(b)** | 120 | PRINT A,B,C |
| **(c)** | 020 | PRINT TAB(10);"HELP" |
| **(d)** | 050 | IF N <=50 THEN 100 |
| **(e)** | 130 | FOR J = 1 to 10 STEP 2 |
| | 170 | NEXT J |
| **(f)** | 60 | INPUT S$ |
| **(g)** | 20 | REM GIVE THE USER A SHOCK |
| **(h)** | 40 | LET A = (K*P/G)/2 |
| **(i)** | 60 | PRINT "WHAT IS YOUR AGE"; |
| | 70 | INPUT A |
| | 80 | PRINT |
| **(j)** | 210 | PRINT USING 440, A,B,C |
| | 440: | ###.##    ####.##    ##.# |
| **(k)** | 150 | PRINT TAB(20); "HOW DO I GET OUT?" |

**10.** Program 9 is referred to as the "Final" Billing Program. Can you see any deficiencies in this program that might call for further modifications?

**11.** After reviewing Program 4 in Figure 20-7, how could you modify it so that Rob and Kay could interact with the program and supply the INPUT (hint) data at the time of processing? Let's assume that the program should print instructions on how to enter the input data, and it should print a heading line for each salesperson showing "NAME," "SALES AMOUNT," and "EARNINGS." It should also print an "END OF DATA?" message after each record has been processed to allow the partners to stop processing or to continue with another record.

**12.** After reviewing Program 8 in Figure 20-11, how could it be changed so that the total amount billed to each customer can be accumulated and then printed with a "TOTAL AMOUNT" subheading at the end of the billing run?

**13.** After reviewing Program 8 in Figure 20-11, make the following modifications so that data may be entered for each customer by the use of INPUT statements: (a) Print a message asking the user to enter the number of customer records to be processed. (b) Print a message asking for the user to supply a customer's name, quantity purchased, and unit price. The output produced for each customer should be in the same format used in Figure 20-11, but, of course, the messages instructing the user to supply the needed facts will also be printed.

**14.** After reviewing the possible program for Feedback and Review 20-4 shown on page 581, write a program using two accumulators to total both the SALES AMOUNT and EARNINGS columns in the output. Then, instead of using TOTAL SALES and TOTAL EARNINGS subheadings at the bottom of the report, use the following format:

| | | | |
|---|---|---|---|
| C. NATION | ⋮ | 864.56 | 86.46 |
| | | 1834.50 | 183.45 |

Finally, process the data within the program loop using FOR . . . NEXT statements.

**15.** Write a program for the specifications outlined in question 18 at the end of Chapter 18 (page 505).

**16.** Write a program for the specifications outlined in question 19 at the end of Chapter 18 (page 505).

**17.** Write a program for the mileage report problem outlined in question 20 at the end of Chapter 18 (page 506). Use READ . . . DATA statements in your program.

**18.** Write a program for the mileage report problem outlined in question 21 at the end of Chapter 18 (page 506).

**19.** Write a program for the tax payment problem outlined in question 22 at the end of Chapter 18 (page 506).

**20.** Write a program for the mailing label problem outlined in question 23 at the end of Chapter 18 (page 506).

**21.** Write a program to solve the depreciation problem outlined in question 24 at the end of Chapter 18 (page 506).

**22.** Write a program to solve the production compensation report problem outlined in question 25 at the end of Chapter 18 (page 506).

**23.** Write a program to solve the production compensation report problem outlined in question 26 at the end of Chapter 18 (page 507).

**24.** Write a program to solve the simulation problem outlined in question 27 at the end of Chapter 18 (page 507). Use INPUT and FOR . . . NEXT statements in your solution.

**25.** Modify the simulation program prepared for question 24 above to produce the following output information: [The figures of 2000 (yearly deposit), 20000 (initial savings), 6 (interest rate), and 10 (number of years) are supplied by the user, but, of course, the program should be able to process other input data.]

```
YEARLY DEPOSIT? 2000
INITIAL SAVINGS? 20000
INTEREST RATE ON SAVINGS(PERCENT)? 6
NUMBER OF YEARS? 10
```

SAVINGS ACCUMULATION MODEL

| YEAR NO. | YEARLY DEPOSIT | INTEREST EARNED | SAVINGS BALANCE |
|---|---|---|---|
| 1 | 2000 | 1200 | 23200 |
| 2 | 2000 | 1392 | 26592 |
| ⋮ | ⋮ | ⋮ | ⋮ |

MORE DATA (YES,NO)?

**26.** Modify the program prepared in question 17 above to use INPUT statements rather than READ . . . DATA statements.

## ANSWERS TO FEEDBACK AND REVIEW SECTIONS

Possible programs for Feedback and Review sections 20-1 through 20-4 follow. Your versions may differ in several ways and still be correct. For example, PRINT statements using various TAB functions, quotation marks, commas, and semicolons can easily be substituted for the PRINT USING statements and image lines presented in the following programs. And, of course, different REM statements and different variable names will cause a difference in appearance without any significant difference in content.

A possible BASIC program for Feedback and Review 20-1.

```
>LIST
     10 REM *BILLING PROGRAM
     20 REM *
     30 REM *VARIABLE NAMES
     40 REM * N$ NAME
     50 REM * Q  QUANTITY PURCHASED
     60 REM * P  UNIT PRICE
     70 REM * A  NET AMOUNT
     80 REM * T1 TAX
     90 REM * T2 TOTAL AMOUNT
    100 REM *
    110 REM *READ NAME,QUANTITY PURCHASED AND PRICE
    120     READ N$,Q,P
    130 REM *COMPUTE NET AMOUNT
    140     LET A = Q*P
    150 REM *COMPUTE TAX AND TOTAL PRICE
    160     LET T1 = A*.06
    170     LET T2 = A+T1
    180 REM *PRINT NAME,NET AMOUNT,TAX AND TOTAL
    190     PRINT N$
    195     PRINT "NET = ";A;"TAX = ";T1;"TOTAL = ";T2
    210 REM *INPUT DATA
    220     DATA "WYNN D. TOOTS,INC.",5.50,25.00
    230     END
```

Computer listing of the program

```
>RUN
  WYNN D. TOOTS,INC.
  NET =    137.500  TAX =     8.25000  TOTAL =      145.750

      230 HALT
```

Output produced by the computer in response to the system command RUN

```
>LIST
    10 REM *BILLING PROGRAM
    20 REM *
    30 REM *VARIABLE NAMES
    40 REM * N$   NAME
    50 REM * S$   ADDRESS
    60 REM * C$   CITY AND STATE
    70 REM * Q    QUANTITY PURCHASED
    80 REM * P    UNIT PRICE
    90 REM * A    NET AMOUNT
   100 REM * T    TAX
   110 REM * S    TOTAL AMOUNT
   120 REM *
   130 REM *READ NAME,ADDRESS,QUANTITY AND PRICE
   140      READ N$,S$,C$,Q,P
   150 REM *TEST QUANTITY FOR LAST INPUT
   160      IF Q=-99.9 THEN 440
   170 REM *COMPUTE NET AMOUNT,TAX AND TOTAL AMOUNT
   180      LET A = Q*P
   190      LET T = A*.06
   200      LET S = A+T
   210 REM *PRINT NAME,ADDRESS,NET,TAX AND TOTAL
   220      PRINT N$
   230      PRINT S$
   240      PRINT C$
   250      PRINT USING 298, A,T,S
   260      PRINT
   270      PRINT
   280      GO TO 140
   295 REM *FORMAT STATEMENT FOR OUTPUT
   298:   NET = ####.##   TAX = ###.##   TOTAL = ####.##
   300 REM *INPUT DATA
   310      DATA "PIERRE'S RECORD SHOP"
   320      DATA "6453 ORLEANS STREET"
   330      DATA "BOOGIE,LOUISIANA 54321"
   340      DATA  300.0,25.00
   350      DATA "ROCKY COLLEGE STORE"
   360      DATA "1563 BEETHOVEN DRIVE"
   370      DATA "ROCKTOWN,MARYLAND 20765"
   380      DATA  3.25,25.00
   390      DATA "WYNN D.TOOTS,INC."
   400      DATA "120 BROWNING STREET"
   410      DATA "GONG,CALIFORNIA 98765"
   420      DATA 200.0,25.00
   430      DATA "L","L","L",-99.9,0.0
   440      END
```

A possible BASIC program for Feedback and Review 20-2. If in place of your equivalent of ln 250 shown here, you had something like this:

```
250   PRINT TAB(3);"NET = ";A;"TAX = ";T;"TOTAL = ";S
```

then your output spacing might look slightly different, and you might have more or less digits in some of your output values, but that doesn't make your program wrong. In fact, it shows that you're learning this language!

Computer listing of the program

```
>RUN
PIERRE'S RECORD SHOP
6453 ORLEANS STREET
BOOGIE,LOUISIANA 54321
   NET = 7500.00   TAX = 450.00   TOTAL = 7950.00


ROCKY COLLEGE STORE
1563 BEETHOVEN DRIVE
ROCKTOWN,MARYLAND 20765
   NET =   81.25   TAX =   4.87   TOTAL =   86.12


WYNN D.TOOTS,INC.
120 BROWNING STREET
GONG,CALIFORNIA 98765
   NET = 5000.00   TAX = 300.00   TOTAL = 5300.00


   440 HALT
```

Output produced by the computer as the program is executed

A possible BASIC program for Feedback and Review 20-3. (Other PRINT statements can easily be substituted for the PRINT USING and image line statements shown here. Other variations are, of course, also possible.)

```
>LIST
    10 REM *SALES COMPENSATION REPORT
    20 REM *
    30 REM *VARIABLE NAMES
    40 REM * N$     NAME
    50 REM * W1-W4 SALES DATA FOR WEEKS 1 TO 4
    60 REM * S      SALES AMOUNT
    70 REM * E      EARNINGS
    80 REM *
    90 REM *PRINT HEADING
   100      PRINT USING 280
   110 REM *READ NAME AND SALES DATA
   120      READ N$,W1,W2,W3,W4
   130 REM *TEST W1 FOR END OF DATA
   140      IF W1=-99.9 THEN 500
   150 REM *COMPUTE SALES AMOUNT
   160      LET S = W1+W2+W3+W4
   170 REM *CALCULATE EARNINGS AS 12 PCT FOR SALES GREATER THAN OR EQUAL
   180 REM *TO 100 AND AS 10 PCT FOR SALES LESS THAN 100
   190      IF S>=100. THEN 220
   200      LET E = S*.10
   210      GO TO 240
   220      LET E = S*.12
   230 REM *PRINT NAME,SALES AMOUNT AND EARNINGS THEN RETURN
   240      PRINT USING 290, N$,S,E
   250      GO TO 120
   270 REM *FORMAT STATEMENTS
   280:NAME                     SALES AMOUNT        EARNINGS
   290:###################     #######.##        #######.##
   300 REM *INPUT DATA
   310      DATA "ALFRED E. BOWMAN"
   320      DATA   50.00,  80.00,  33.50, 680.26
   330      DATA "R. GOLDBERG"
   340      DATA    2.00,   4.00,   8.00,  16.00
   450      DATA "C. MACARTHY"
   460      DATA   10.52,  20.36,  15.30,  50.00
   470      DATA "C.NATION"
   480      DATA   35.26,  18.50,  52.30, 758.50
   490      DATA "END OF DATA", -99.9,0.,0.,0.
   500      END
```

Computer listing
of the program

```
>RUN
NAME                    SALES AMOUNT        EARNINGS
ALFRED E. BOWMAN            843.76          101.25
R. GOLDBERG                 30.00            3.00
C. MACARTHY                 96.18            9.62
C.NATION                   864.56          103.75

    500 HALT
```

Output produced by the
computer as the program
is executed

```
>LIST
      10 *SALES COMPENSATION REPORT
      20 REM *
      30 REM *VARIABLE NAMES
      40 REM * N$     NAME
      50 REM * W1-W4 SALES DATA FOR WEEKS 1 TO 4
      60 REM * S     SALES AMOUNT
      70 REM * E     EARNINGS
      80 REM * T     TOTAL SALES
      90 REM * G     TOTAL EARNINGS
     100 REM *
     110 REM *INITIALIZE ACCUMULATOR
     120      LET T = 0.
     130 REM *PRINT HEADING
     140      PRINT USING 340
     150 REM *READ NAME AND SALES DATA
     160      READ N$,W1,W2,W3,W4
     170 REM *TEST W1 FOR END OF DATA
     180      IF W1=-99.9 THEN 280
     190 REM *COMPUTE SALES AMOUNT AND EARNINGS
     200      LET S = W1+W2+W3+W4
     210      LET E = S*.10
     220 REM *ACCUMULATE TOTAL SALES
     230      LET T = T+S
     240 REM *PRINT NAME,SALES AMOUNT AND EARNINGS
     250      PRINT USING 350, N$,S,E
     260      GO TO 160
     270 REM *COMPUTE TOTAL EARNINGS AND PRINT TOTAL SALES AND EARNINGS
     280      LET G = T*.10
     290      PRINT
     300      PRINT USING 360
     310      PRINT USING 370
     320      PRINT USING 380, T,G
     330 REM *FORMAT STATEMENTS
     340:NAME                   SALES AMOUNT        EARNINGS
     350:####################    ######.##          ######.##
     360:                        TOTAL              TOTAL
     370:                        SALES              EARNINGS
     380:                        ######.##          ######.##
     390 REM *INPUT DATA
     400      DATA "ALFRED E. BOWMAN"
     410      DATA  50.00, 80.00,  33.50, 680.26
     420      DATA "R.GOLDBERG"
     430      DATA   2.00,  4.00,   8.00,  16.00
     440      DATA "C. MACARTHY"
     450      DATA  10.52, 20.36,  15.30,  50.00
     460      DATA "C. NATION"
     470      DATA  35.26, 18.50,  52.30, 758.50
     480      DATA "END OF DATA",-99.9,0.,0.,0.
     490      END
```

Computer listing
of the program

```
>RUN
NAME                   SALES AMOUNT        EARNINGS
ALFRED E. BOWMAN          843.76             84.38
R.GOLDBERG                30.00               3.00
C. MACARTHY               96.18               9.62
C. NATION                864.56             86.46

                       TOTAL              TOTAL
                       SALES              EARNINGS
                       1834.50            183.45

   490 HALT
```

Output produced by the
computer as the program
is executed

# True BASIC versus Street BASIC

Not since Polish oculist L. L. Zamenhof invented Esperanto has an artificial language attracted as many adherents as Basic, a computer language.

The language has helped make many computer entrepreneurs rich, but the two Dartmouth College professors who invented it have only benefited by writing a Basic textbook. Now, they want to perfect their language and, they hope, make some substantial money as well. So, John G. Kemeny and Thomas E. Kurtz are rewriting Basic and plunging into the vibrant computer marketplace they helped create.

The two first wrote Basic to help undergraduates pick up computing experience quickly without having to master intricate computer languages. "We envisioned even a below-average college student being able to program," says Mr. Kemeny. Dartmouth copyrighted Basic, but made it available free to anyone interested.

Basic has grown with the personal-computer industry, partly because it comes free with most personal computers, often embedded in the memory of the machine, and partly because it's easy. Dozens of youthful programmers have become millionaires by parlaying their knowledge of the language and their sense of the market into profitable programs. Hundreds of thousands, maybe millions, of people around the world program in Basic.

To cash in on Basic's business, the two professors have organized True Basic Inc., with financing from a group of Dartmouth alumni, offices over a campus tavern, three professional programmers to do most of the actual coding and plans to bring out a product by the fall.

Mr. Kemeny, who is the chairman, says textbook publishers are already interested because the rewritten language will run on most popular personal computers, eliminating the need for a different textbook for each machine. And even though True Basic plans to keep prices low for the education market, Mr. Kemeny predicts that sales may reach $1 million a year.

But while the Dartmouth duo may be revered by computer scientists and historians for their seminal work, they face the same marketing hurdles as any computer newcomer. "I'm sure they deserve success, but I wouldn't say the market is crying for an improved Basic," says William F. Zachmann of International Data Corp., a Framingham, Mass., computer industry market-research concern.

Mr. Kemeny concedes, too, that the new company needs marketing expertise. The 57-year-old math professor was a research assistant to Albert Einstein, served for 11 years as Dartmouth's president and was chairman of President Carter's commission on the Three Mile Island nuclear-plant accident. He hasn't any business experience, though, and neither has Mr. Kurtz, 55, a computer science professor.

Mr. Kurtz and Mr. Kemeny developed Basic because they believed, back in 1964, that every educated person should have computer experience. To make computers accessible, the Dartmouth professors did two things. They developed one of the first time-sharing systems, a method for letting people at hundreds of computer terminals use a main computer at the same time, dividing up valuable computer time.

And they developed Basic—Beginners All-purpose Symbolic Instruction Code. Computer languages of the era, principally Fortran, were frustrating to learn because even simple ideas required complex instructions. For example, to print out a number, a programmer had to type in a series of codes. In Basic, the programmer could simply type PRINT followed by the number, and the computer would do it.

Basic consists of about 200 words that can be used to tell a computer to perform almost any imaginable task. When the computer recognizes a certain one-word instruction, it must perform a particular operation within its electronic circuits. For example, if a command contains INT, the computer knows it must deal only with integers in that operation.

Basic was easy to use partly because the programmers and professors constantly received feedback from users. "It was an unusual sociology," says John M. Nevison, an undergraduate of that era who has written several books on Basic programming. "You'd have a student coming to class and complaining to the author that he'd had trouble with some command. It would get fixed that night."

Dartmouth's Basic was widely adopted by companies that rented computer time. And when personal computers came along, starting in 1975, Basic was the language that was condensed to fit in their small memories. William Gates, the chairman of Microsoft Corp, of Bellevue, Wash., who wrote the first Basic for a personal computer, says that for beginners "Basic is great." His company has made tens of millions of dollars adapting Basic for most personal computers.

Despite its popularity, Basic is widely criticized by computer scientists. While it works well for short programs, lengthy Basic programs are generally confusing. Unlike modern structured computer languages, Basic can't easily be broken up into discrete parts that can then be assigned separately to different members of a team collaborating on a long, complicated program. A command called GOTO enables programmers to write programs that tell computers to jump from one section of the program to another, making it difficult to follow the logic of the program or correct defects. A well-written program in a structured language such as Pascal will be divided into logical blocks, like chapters in a textbook, while a Basic program is likely to interweave ideas with almost Faulknerian complexity.

Mr. Kurtz, who heads a committee of computer scientists and professionals who are developing a set of standards for all versions of Basic, says that True Basic will overcome those problems.

He blames many of Basic's problems on the many revisions it has gone through. "We don't recognize our own grandchild, as it were," he says. "We're concerned because people are learning street Basic."

Mr. Kemeny predicts that once a better Basic is developed, it will be able to both become a universal language and help users to think logically.

But many computer professionals believe advocates of a universal computer language will fare no better than promoters of Esperanto. They predict a continuing proliferation of languages. For example, the special commands that thousands of users of the program VisiCalc use daily could be considered a language.

Moreover, as computers become more powerful, increasing amounts of money will be able to be used to make it easier for humans to deal with them in our own languages. Robert M. Frankston, president of Software Arts Inc., Wellesley, Mass., and an author of VisiCalc, argues that "designing computer programs to understand English will be more useful than improving Basic."

—William M. Bulkeley, "Originators of Basic Computer Language Seek to Profit from Success of Their Work," *The Wall Street Journal*, Dec. 16, 1983, p. 25. Reprinted by permission of *The Wall Street Journal*, © Dow Jones & Company 1983. All Rights Reserved.

# More About BASIC

### DEC Smites April Fools

Several years ago, Digital Equipment Corporation installed a number of Decmate II microcomputers at selected test sites. The customers at these sites, who had the machines before they were available to the rest of the public, were given special deals as incentives to keep DEC informed about system bugs.

Because the Decmate II has proved to be one of the better word-processing systems around, the word-processing software provided to the test sites was of particular interest—especially to people who wanted to pad their incomes by selling bootleg copies to their friends or hoped to save some money by keeping a copy of the software for their own use.

But DEC had a surprise in store for these thieves. In a unique software protection scheme, DEC had embedded into the word-processing source code the statement IF DATE$ = APRIL 1, 1983 THEN DELETE ALL FILES.

All across the country, people with pilfered software were happily writing and editing away until the morning of this year's April Fools' Day. Then, CRASH! Down came the systems like houses of cards—and, of course, a phone call to DEC's customer-support hotline would have been tantamount to an admission of piracy.

It brings to mind the old saying about the last laugh being the best.

Our study of the BASIC language continues here with example programs that demonstrate its additional features. Once again, all our examples apply to R-K Enterprises. The information in this chapter will enable you to:

■ Write BASIC programs using nested FOR . . . NEXT loops and selected library functions

■ Create one- and two-dimensional arrays, and use these arrays in BASIC programs

■ Follow the program logic used to sort data items into a predetermined order

■ Explain the use of the additional BASIC statements presented in the last section

## NESTED FOR . . . NEXT LOOPS

### FOR . . . NEXT Loops: A Review

You saw in Chapter 20 how a FOR statement is used to open a loop and establish an automatic counter, and how the loop is then closed with a NEXT statement. The program lines located between the FOR and NEXT statements are executed repeatedly and form the range or body of the loop. A simple example

of the FOR . . . NEXT structure is shown in the program in Figure 21-1. Rob and Kay have decided to close R-K Enterprises and take a vacation during the mid-term holidays, and Kay has prepared this program to print a message on gummed labels. These labels can then be attached to bills and correspondence to give customers ample notice of the temporary closing.

```
LIST


10   REM *MESSAGE LABELS PROGRAM
20   REM *
30   REM *VARIABLE NAMES
50   REM * N NUMBER OF LABELS TO BE PRINTED
60   REM *
70   REM *READ NUMBER OF LABELS TO BE PRINTED
80       READ N
90   REM *PRINT MESSAGE
100      FOR K = 1 TO N
110      PRINT TAB(5);"R-K ENTERPRISES WILL BE CLOSED FROM"
112      PRINT TAB(5);"DECEMBER 20 TO JANUARY 4.  PLEASE"
114      PRINT TAB(5);"KEEP THIS IN MIND WHEN PLANNING YOUR"
116      PRINT TAB(5);"NEXT ORDER.  THANK YOU."
118      PRINT
120      PRINT
130      NEXT K
135 REM *LABELS TO BE PREPARED
140      DATA 4
150      END
READY
>
```

Computer listing
of the program

```
RUN
     R-K ENTERPRISES WILL BE CLOSED FROM
     DECEMBER 20 TO JANUARY 4.  PLEASE
     KEEP THIS IN MIND WHEN PLANNING YOUR
     NEXT ORDER.  THANK YOU.


     R-K ENTERPRISES WILL BE CLOSED FROM
     DECEMBER 20 TO JANUARY 4.  PLEASE
     KEEP THIS IN MIND WHEN PLANNING YOUR
     NEXT ORDER.  THANK YOU.


     R-K ENTERPRISES WILL BE CLOSED FROM
     DECEMBER 20 TO JANUARY 4.  PLEASE
     KEEP THIS IN MIND WHEN PLANNING YOUR
     NEXT ORDER.  THANK YOU.


     R-K ENTERPRISES WILL BE CLOSED FROM
     DECEMBER 20 TO JANUARY 4.  PLEASE
     KEEP THIS IN MIND WHEN PLANNING YOUR
     NEXT ORDER.  THANK YOU.


READY
>
```

Output produced by the
computer as the program
is executed

Figure 21-1 An example of a FOR . . . NEXT loop.

The REMark statements in line number (ln) 10 through ln 70 of Figure 21-1 are clear enough. In ln 80, a READ statement determines from the DATA statement in ln 140 that four labels are to be printed. The FOR statement in ln 100 opens the loop and specifies that N (or 4 in this case) labels are to be printed. The message repeated on each label tells customers that R-K Enterprises will be closed for the mid-term holidays. The PRINT statements on lines 110–120 form the body of the loop. These lines produce the message and control line spacing. The loop is closed with the NEXT statement on ln 130. With each pass through the loop, an automatic test is made to determine if the counter value (K) is greater than N. When four labels have been printed, the value of K will be greater than N, printing will stop, and program control will exit from the FOR . . . NEXT loop structure to the next executable line number in sequence. In our example, this is the END statement in ln 150.

### Flowcharting FOR . . . NEXT Loops: A Dilemma

It's a simple matter to prepare a flowchart for the program given in Figure 21-1. In fact, *each* of the three charts in Figure 21-2 presents the logic of Kay's message label program. But the dilemma illustrated in Figure 21-2 is that there's little agreement on the approach to use in charting FOR . . . NEXT loops. Version (a) uses standard symbols but is somewhat more tedious to prepare than versions (b) and (c). Version (b) is compact and convenient, but it uses a rather cryptic and nonstandard symbol. Since version (c) uses standard symbols and is also relatively com-

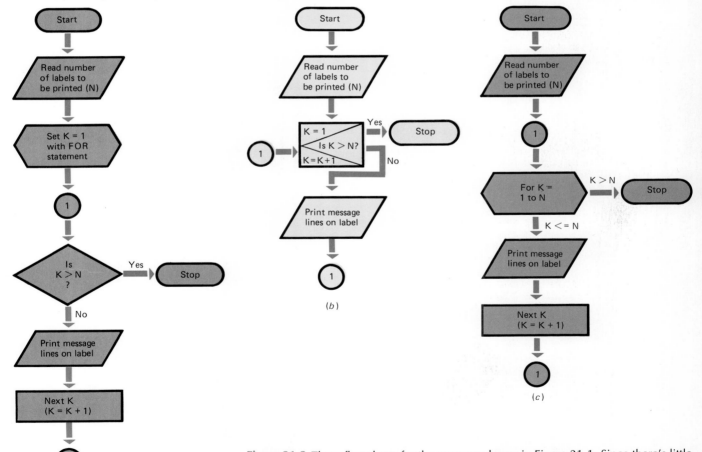

**Figure 21-2** Three flowcharts for the program shown in Figure 21-1. Since there's little agreement on charting FOR . . . NEXT loops, we'll use the approach shown in version (c). The other versions are equally correct.

```
LIST

10    REM *REMINDER LABELS PROGRAM
20    REM *
30    REM *VARIABLE NAMES:
40    REM * A NUMBER OF REMINDER LABELS TO BE PRINTED
50    REM * B NUMBER OF "HAPPY HOLIDAY" GREETINGS ON EACH LABEL
60    REM *
70    REM *READ NUMBER OF LABELS AND NUMBER OF GREETINGS ON EACH LABEL
100        READ A, B
105   REM *SET UP OUTER LOOP TO CONTROL NUMBER OF LABELS
110        FOR X = 1 TO A
115   REM *SET UP INNER LOOP TO CONTROL NUMBER OF GREETINGS
120        FOR Y = 1 TO B
130        PRINT TAB(15);"HAVE A HAPPY HOLIDAY!"
140        NEXT Y
145   REM *MESSAGE PRINTED ON EACH LABEL AFTER INNER LOOP IS PROCESSED
150        PRINT TAB(5);"BUT PLEASE REMEMBER THAT R-K ENTERPRISES"
152        PRINT TAB(5);"WILL BE CLOSED FROM DECEMBER 20 TO
154        PRINT TAB(5);"JANUARY 4."
156        PRINT
158        PRINT
160        NEXT X
165   REM *NUMBER OF LABELS AND GREETINGS
170        DATA 3, 4
180        END
READY
>
```

Outer loop

Inner loop

Computer listing
of the program

```
RUN
                    HAVE A HAPPY HOLIDAY!
                    HAVE A HAPPY HOLIDAY!
                    HAVE A HAPPY HOLIDAY!
                    HAVE A HAPPY HOLIDAY!
        BUT PLEASE REMEMBER THAT R-K ENTERPRISES
        WILL BE CLOSED FROM DECEMBER 20 TO
        JANUARY 4.


                    HAVE A HAPPY HOLIDAY!
                    HAVE A HAPPY HOLIDAY!
                    HAVE A HAPPY HOLIDAY!
                    HAVE A HAPPY HOLIDAY!
        BUT PLEASE REMEMBER THAT R-K ENTERPRISES
        WILL BE CLOSED FROM DECEMBER 20 TO
        JANUARY 4.


                    HAVE A HAPPY HOLIDAY!
                    HAVE A HAPPY HOLIDAY!
                    HAVE A HAPPY HOLIDAY!
                    HAVE A HAPPY HOLIDAY!
        BUT PLEASE REMEMBER THAT R-K ENTERPRISES
        WILL BE CLOSED FROM DECEMBER 20 TO
        JANUARY 4.


READY
>
```

Output produced by the
computer as the program
is executed

(a)

Figure 21-3 *(a)* A program, and *(b)* a flowchart showing a nested FOR . . . NEXT loop.

pact, we'll use this flowcharting approach to represent FOR . . . NEXT loops. But the other versions are equally acceptable.

## Inner and Outer Loops

It's often desirable to include one or more **inner loop** structures within the body of an **outer loop.** That is, it's common to find one or more **nested FOR . . . NEXT loops** within the range of an outer FOR . . . NEXT structure. Consider the example in the next column:

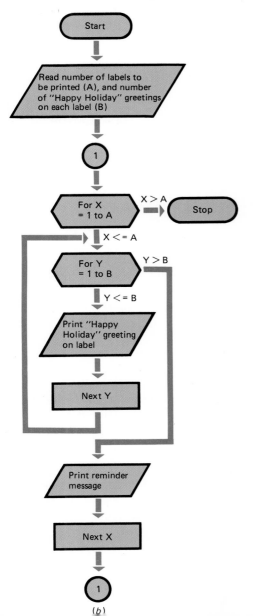

(b)

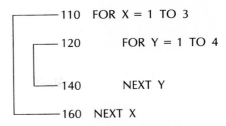

In this example, the *Y or inner loop* is executed four times each time there is a pass through the *outer or X loop.* That is, when program control first moves to ln 110, the X loop is established and the first pass through the X loop begins. In ln 120, the inner Y loop is created and is then executed four times. After the fourth pass through the Y loop, program control moves in sequence to ln 160 to complete the first of three passes through the X loop. In the second iteration through the outer loop, the Y loop is again executed four times. Thus, when the three passes of the outer loop have been completed, the inner loop has been executed a total of 12 times.

It's desirable during programming to *indent inner loops* to make them easier to identify and understand. The indentation of inner loops also helps to prevent the creation of **crossed loops**—a logic error that prevents the computer from correctly executing the program. Examples of valid and invalid loop structures follow:

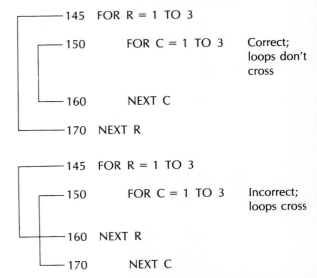

Let's take a look now at a simple program that illustrates the use of nested loops. The purpose of the program shown in Figure 21-3*a* is once again to print a message on gummed labels. The message is to wish customers a happy holiday and to remind them once more that R-K Enterprises will be closed for the mid-term holidays. A flowchart showing the logic of this program is presented in Figure 21-3b.

Following the initial REMark statements, the READ statement in ln 100 and the DATA statement in ln 170 determine the number of labels to print and the number of "Happy Holiday" greetings to produce on each label. The outer (or X) FOR . . . NEXT loop is established on ln 110 to control the number of labels to print. In this case, A is 3, so the outer loop will be executed three times, and three labels will be printed. The inner (or Y)

FOR . . . NEXT loop is created on ln 120, and this loop is programmed to PRINT "HAVE A HAPPY HOLIDAY!" B (or 4) times on each label. After the inner loop has been executed four times on the first pass through the outer loop, program control passes to line numbers 150–158 and a reminder message is printed on the first label. The first label is now printed, and the first pass through the outer loop is completed on ln 160. Program control is then automatically transferred back to ln 110 to begin another execution of the outer loop. As the output in Figure 21-3a shows, the outer loop is executed a total of three times, and the inner loop is executed a total of ($3 \times 4$ or) 12 times.

# THE USE OF LIBRARY FUNCTIONS

Since there are a number of common computing tasks that are frequently needed in BASIC programs, these tasks have been *preprogrammed* and are available to the BASIC user as built-in **library functions.** Among them are sophisticated trigonometric and exponentiation functions and three functions which we'll consider now: SQR (square root); INT (integer); and RND (randomize).

**The SQR Function**

We can illustrate SQR simply; for example,

100   LET Y = SQR(X)

tells the computer to look up the value of X, take the *square root* (**SQR**) of that value, and then assign the result to the variable name Y. If X has a value of 36, then 6 is the result that will be assigned to Y.

Let's look now at a more challenging example. The **economic order quantity (EOQ)** is a term often encountered in inventory management. It refers to the order size for some item in inventory (e.g., tee shirts) that results in the lowest total inventory cost for a period. Managers often use an EOQ model to plan inventory levels and make ordering decisions. If the assumptions underlying the model are valid, then the following formula will produce the economic order quantity:

$$Q = \sqrt{\frac{2\,A\,P}{U\,I}}$$

where:

Q = economic order quantity
A = quantity of inventory required for a period
P = cost of placing one order
U = unit cost of item ordered
I = inventory carrying costs expressed as a percentage of the unit cost

Instead of writing a detailed sequence of instructions to perform the square root function, the programmer can use the SQR function to determine the EOQ value with a single line:

420   LET Q = SQR((2*A*P)/(U*I))

You'll need to use this SQR function to write one of the programs outlined in the questions at the end of the chapter. In most BASIC dialects, the SQR function must be used with positive values.

**INT and RND Functions**

**INT** ("integer") and **RND** ("randomize") **functions** are presented in the program shown in Figure 21-4a. The flowchart to help you trace through the logic of this program is shown in Figure 21-4b.

The program in Figure 21-4a was devised by Rob Brooks to screen applicants for sales positions at R-K Enterprises. Since salespersons are paid only if they make

```
LIST


10   REM *PERSONNEL TEST PROGRAM FOR R-K ENTERPRISES
20   REM *
30   REM *VARIABLE NAMES:
40   REM * N$ APPLICANT NAME
45   REM * A  FIRST FACTOR
50   REM * B  SECOND FACTOR
60   REM * C  CORRECT RESPONSE
70   REM * P  APPLICANT RESPONSE
80   REM * Q1 NUMBER OF CORRECT RESPONSES
90   REM * Q2 NUMBER OF INCORRECT RESPONSES
100  REM * S  TEST SCORE
110  REM *
112  REM *INITIALIZE ACCUMULATORS
114      LET Q1 = 0
116      LET Q2 = 0
120  REM *OBTAIN APPLICANT'S NAME AND SUPPLY TEST INSTRUCTIONS
130      PRINT "    APPLICANT TEST DRILL"
140      PRINT
145      PRINT "WHAT IS YOUR NAME";
147      INPUT N$
148      PRINT
149      PRINT "PLEASE PAY ATTENTION, ";N$;"."
150      PRINT "THIS IS A TEST OF YOUR KNOWLEDGE OF THE"
160      PRINT "MULTIPLICATION TABLES.  YOU'LL BE ASKED"
170      PRINT "TO MULTIPLY 20 PAIRS OF NUMBERS.  CONSIDER"
175      PRINT "YOUR ANSWERS CAREFULLY.  YOUR FUTURE AT"
177      PRINT "R-K ENTERPRISES DEPENDS ON HOW YOU DO ON"
179      PRINT "THIS TEST.  A SCORE OF 85 IS REQUIRED FOR"
180      PRINT "EMPLOYMENT."
190      PRINT
240  REM *LOOP THROUGH SEQUENCE OF TEST QUESTIONS
250      FOR K = 1 TO 20
260  REM *GENERATE TWO RANDOM INTEGERS IN INTERVAL FROM ZERO TO NINE
270      LET A = INT(RND(0)*10)
280      LET B = INT(RND(0)*10)
290  REM *COMPUTE CORRECT RESPONSE
300      LET C = A*B
310  REM *OBTAIN APPLICANT RESPONSE
315      PRINT
320      PRINT "WHAT IS ";A;" TIMES ";B;
330      INPUT P
340  REM *
350  REM *TEST APPLICANT RESPONSE
360      IF C = P THEN 420
370  REM *INCORRECT RESPONSE MESSAGE:
380      PRINT "SORRY, THE CORRECT ANSWER IS ";C;"."
390      LET Q2 = Q2+1
400      GOTO 440
410  REM *CORRECT RESPONSE MESSAGE:
420      PRINT "CORRECT."
430      LET Q1 = Q1+1
440      NEXT K
450  REM *COMPUTE TEST SCORE, EVALUATE PERFORMANCE, AND STOP.
460      LET S = (Q1/(Q1+Q2))*100
470      IF S < 85 THEN 510
475  REM *PASSING SCORE MESSAGE:
480      PRINT "GOOD WORK, ";N$;", YOU PASSED.  YOUR SCORE"
490      PRINT "WAS ";S;", AND 85 IS CONSIDERED PASSING."
500      STOP
505  REM *FAILING SCORE MESSAGE:
510      PRINT "TOO BAD, ";N$;", YOU FAILED.  YOU NEEDED AN"
520      PRINT "85 TO PASS, AND YOUR SCORE WAS ONLY ";S;"."
540      STOP
550      END
READY
>
```

Computer listing
of the program

Figure 21-4a Personnel test for R-K Enterprises.

```
    RUN
        APPLICANT TEST DRILL

WHAT IS YOUR NAME? DON

PLEASE PAY ATTENTION, DON.
THIS IS A TEST OF YOUR KNOWLEDGE OF THE
MULTIPLICATION TABLES.  YOU'LL BE ASKED
TO MULTIPLY 20 PAIRS OF NUMBERS.  CONSIDER
YOUR ANSWERS CAREFULLY.  YOUR FUTURE AT
R-K ENTERPRISES DEPENDS ON HOW YOU DO ON
THIS TEST.  A SCORE OF 85 IS REQUIRED FOR
EMPLOYMENT.


WHAT IS  0  TIMES  4 ? 0
CORRECT.

WHAT IS  2  TIMES  0 ? 0
CORRECT.

WHAT IS  9  TIMES  3 ? 27
CORRECT.

WHAT IS  1  TIMES  8 ? 8
CORRECT.

WHAT IS  9  TIMES  9 ? 81
CORRECT.

WHAT IS  5  TIMES  0 ? 5
SORRY, THE CORRECT ANSWER IS  0 .

WHAT IS  3  TIMES  0 ? 0
CORRECT.
                .
                .
                .
                .
                .
                .
                .

WHAT IS  9  TIMES  2 ? 18
CORRECT.

WHAT IS  4  TIMES  5 ? 20
CORRECT.

WHAT IS  1  TIMES  0 ? 0
CORRECT.

WHAT IS  5  TIMES  8 ? 40
CORRECT.

WHAT IS  5  TIMES  4 ? 20
CORRECT.
GOOD WORK, DON, YOU PASSED.  YOUR SCORE
WAS  85 , AND 85 IS CONSIDERED PASSING.
Break in 500
READY
>
```

The *first* output produced by the computer as the program is executed

```
RUN
     APPLICANT TEST DRILL

WHAT IS YOUR NAME? ROB BROOKS

PLEASE PAY ATTENTION, ROB BROOKS.
THIS IS A TEST OF YOUR KNOWLEDGE OF THE
MULTIPLICATION TABLES.   YOU'LL BE ASKED
TO MULTIPLY 20 PAIRS OF NUMBERS.   CONSIDER
YOUR ANSWERS CAREFULLY.   YOUR FUTURE AT
R-K ENTERPRISES DEPENDS ON HOW YOU DO ON
THIS TEST.   A SCORE OF 85 IS REQUIRED FOR
EMPLOYMENT.


WHAT IS  4   TIMES  0 ? 4
SORRY, THE CORRECT ANSWER IS  0 .

WHAT IS  2   TIMES  8 ? 10
SORRY, THE CORRECT ANSWER IS  16 .

WHAT IS  3   TIMES  2 ? 6
CORRECT.

WHAT IS  3   TIMES  9 ? 27
CORRECT.

WHAT IS  4   TIMES  3 ? 12
CORRECT.

WHAT IS  2   TIMES  7 ? 9
SORRY, THE CORRECT ANSWER IS  14 .

WHAT IS  0   TIMES  4 ? 4
SORRY, THE CORRECT ANSWER IS  0 .
               •
               •
               •
               •
               •
               •
               •
               •
               •

WHAT IS  0   TIMES  9 ? 0
CORRECT.

WHAT IS  8   TIMES  0 ? 8
SORRY, THE CORRECT ANSWER IS  0 .

WHAT IS  5   TIMES  6 ? 30
CORRECT.

WHAT IS  6   TIMES  2 ? 12
CORRECT.
TOO BAD, ROB BROOKS, YOU FAILED.   YOU NEEDED AN
85 TO PASS, AND YOUR SCORE WAS ONLY  65 .
Break in 540
READY
>
```

The output produced when Rob Brooks tried his own program

Figure 21-4a  The personnel test program.

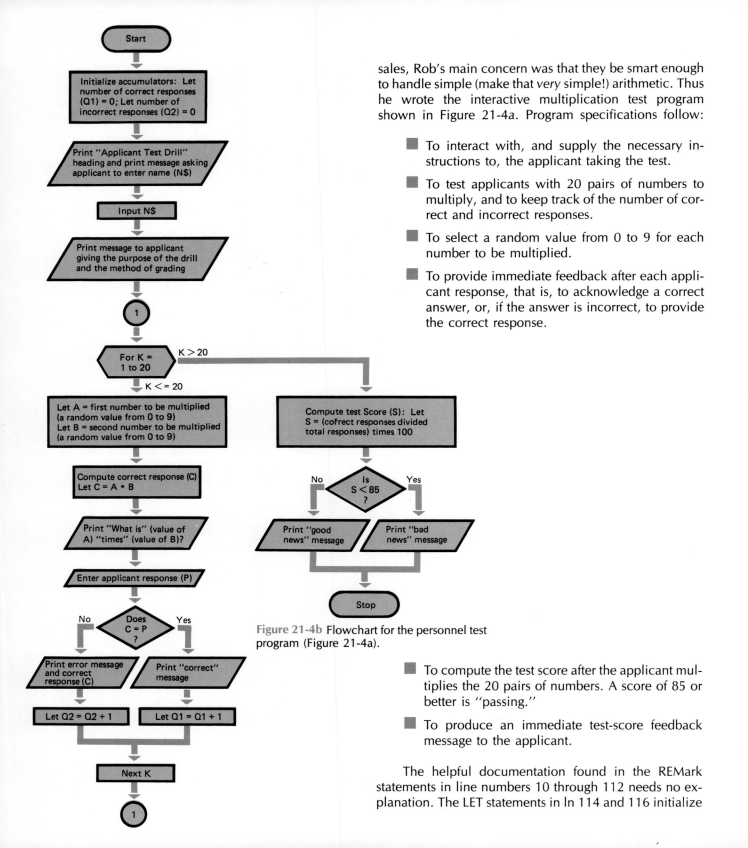

sales, Rob's main concern was that they be smart enough to handle simple (make that *very* simple!) arithmetic. Thus he wrote the interactive multiplication test program shown in Figure 21-4a. Program specifications follow:

- To interact with, and supply the necessary instructions to, the applicant taking the test.

- To test applicants with 20 pairs of numbers to multiply, and to keep track of the number of correct and incorrect responses.

- To select a random value from 0 to 9 for each number to be multiplied.

- To provide immediate feedback after each applicant response, that is, to acknowledge a correct answer, or, if the answer is incorrect, to provide the correct response.

**Figure 21-4b** Flowchart for the personnel test program (Figure 21-4a).

- To compute the test score after the applicant multiplies the 20 pairs of numbers. A score of 85 or better is "passing."

- To produce an immediate test-score feedback message to the applicant.

The helpful documentation found in the REMark statements in line numbers 10 through 112 needs no explanation. The LET statements in ln 114 and 116 initialize the accumulators that will be used to total the number of correct (Q1) and incorrect (Q2) applicant responses during a test. PRINT statements giving instructions to the applicant, along with an INPUT statement requesting the applicant's name so that applicant-program communication can be more "personalized," occupy the line numbers from 130 through 190.

The FOR . . . NEXT loop initiated in ln 250 causes the program to process 20 pairs of random numbers. (The NEXT statement to close this loop is found on ln 440.) The random numbers from zero to 9 are generated in line numbers 270 and 280 and are assigned to the variable names A and B.

The mathematical methods used to produce such random numbers are complex. Different manufacturers use different approaches. It's enough for us to know that vendors have prepared programmed sets of instructions that will produce sequences of numbers that appear to have no pattern or relationship. These numbers are generated randomly, are equally likely to occur, are generally in a range from 0.000000 to 0.999999, and are available for use in a BASIC program when the RND library function is called up by the programmer. In our example,

```
270   LET A = INT (RND(0)*10)
```

the RND(0) segment will give a sequence of random numbers each time the program is used.[1] Unfortunately, these numbers would not be in the decimal fraction range given above. To get around this problem, we multiply each random number generated by 10. Thus, .106471 becomes 1.06471. Finally, the INT (INTeger) function simply deletes everything following the decimal point. Thus, 1.06471 simply becomes 1. (The value .681732 called

up by the RND function would first become 6.81732 and then simply 6 in Rob's program.)

Once random integers from zero to 9 have been assigned to A and B in line numbers 270 and 280, the program performs the following steps:

1. The pair of random numbers are multiplied, and the result is assigned to C (ln 300).

2. The applicant is asked to multiply A times B, and the applicant response is assigned to P (ln 320 and ln 330).

3. If the applicant response is *correct,* a reinforcement message is printed, the "correct response" accumulator (Q1) is incremented, and the loop is repeated (line numbers 360, 420, 430, and 440).

4. If the applicant response is *wrong,* the correct answer is given, the "incorrect response" accumulator (Q2) is incremented, and the loop is repeated (line numbers 360, 380, 390, 400, and 440).

When the loop has been executed 20 times, program control passes to ln 460, which computes the applicant's test score. If the test score is "passing"—*not* < 85 in ln 470—line numbers 480 through 500 are executed; if a "failing" grade is made, line numbers 510 through 540 are executed.

In Figure 21-4a, the first applicant to use Rob's program was Don. As you can see, Don passed (barely) with a score of 85. The second output run was the result of a demonstration Rob gave to his partner Kay Oss—a classic case of being hoisted on one's own petard!

## ONE-DIMENSIONAL ARRAYS

An **array** may be thought of simply as a collection of data items that are generally related in some way and are stored in a computer under a *common name*. If the array consists of a single *list* of items, it's called a **one-dimensional array.** You may recall from Chapter 20 that the products sold by R-K Enterprises, and the prices of these products, are as follows:

| PRODUCT | UNIT PRICE |
|---|---|
| TEE SHIRTS(DOZ) | $25.00 |
| MOSQUITO BIRD R | 6.00 |
| MOSQUITO BIRD T | 7.00 |
| KAY OSS IN CONCERT R | 8.00 |
| KAY OSS IN CONCERT T | 8.50 |
| OH WHAT? BOOK | 9.95 |

The list of R-K products is a one-dimensional array, and this array can be stored in the computer under a com-

[1]Some systems require a preliminary statement before the RND usage such as 265 RANDOM or 265 RANDOMIZE to make sure that the sequence of random numbers produced each time the program is run is not a repeating sequence.

mon variable name. The same rules that govern the naming of simple variables also apply in naming arrays. Since the product list consists of character string values, an **array name** of P$ may be selected. Each item (or *element*) in this P$ array is then identified by a *subscript* as shown below:

| P$ ARRAY | SUBSCRIPT |
|---|---|
| TEE SHIRTS(DOZ) | (1) |
| MOSQUITO BIRD R | (2) |
| MOSQUITO BIRD T | (3) |
| KAY OSS IN CONCERT R | (4) |
| KAY OSS IN CONCERT T | (5) |
| OH WHAT? BOOK | (6) |

Each subscript merely identifies one element or product in the array. Thus, P$(1) identifies the first product in the P$ array which in this case is TEE SHIRTS(DOZ). The identification needed by the computer to locate the OH WHAT? BOOK item in the P$ array is P$(6). This product array is called *one-dimensional* because only a *single* subscript is needed to locate an element in the array.

Another one-dimensional array can be set up to store the unit price list for the R-K products. This array may be named P, and the elements of this array may be identified as follows:

| P ARRAY | |
|---|---|
| $25.00 | P(1) |
| 6.00 | P(2) |
| 7.00 | P(3) |
| 8.00 | P(4) |
| 8.50 | P(5) |
| 9.95 | P(6) |

## KILLER DOS STALKS SOFTWARE

When I was in Arlington Heights, Illinois, recently, I heard a story that at first I thought was pretty funny—then I realized that this funny story will result in not-so-funny tragedies and maybe some genuine horrors.

The story was about how some devilish young programmer genius created a version of Apple DOS called Killer DOS. It is reminiscent of a kind of program called a worm. Worm code is specialized programming usually found on mainframe computers. It is designed to act independently of the operating system and somehow worm its way through the system and pop up here and there on various terminals with snide messages.

If well written, it is impossible to trace and sometimes impossible to get rid of. Just as a herpes virus attaches itself to a nerve cell and lies dormant for awhile, so too will worm code hide in a backed-up file, ready to sneak back into the operating system at any time. Killer DOS works like a worm. The contaminated DOS is booted on an unsuspecting computer, then it copies itself into RAM and any other DOS found on any other disk.

In the case of Killer DOS, the program waits for a fixed number of disk accesses and then (after maybe a whole day's work passes) goes to work. First, it locks up the keyboard; second, it erases all disks in the system; and finally, puts a message on the screen: "Killer DOS strikes again!"

At first glance this may seem like an innocuous prank. But what happens if the disks contain important medical information on someone? Or worse, what if the machine is monitoring medical instruments keeping someone alive? While I may seem melodramatic about this, let's face it—this is simply a new high-tech version of juvenile delinquency, and it's going to get worse before it gets better. I've always suspected that the high-tech punks I know urge the implementation of the Unix operating system for the simple reason that it is easier to sabotage than a more simple, compact operating system.

The first worm program was done on the Department of Defense ARPAnet system in the late 60s. At the time, the program was called a creeper. Countermeasures were taken by systems programmers to rid the network of the creeper program. The antidote was called a reaper. The term *worm* was first introduced in a John Brunner book, *Shockwave Rider*. It is a story about a futuristic, fascist society run by a computer network. The hero created a worm program to destroy the social structure and bring back democracy.

The most notorious real-life worm program was injected into the UCLA system. It was called Pinball. It hung around the operating system for months and then would pop up with a message on the system console that said, "Let's play pinball!" The screen would go crazy as the program took over the computer and moved the heads on the hard disks back and forth as fast as they'd go—all the while erasing files.

It's best not to use the same name for both an array and a simple variable in a program even though BASIC will permit this confusing practice. Why? Because P1 and P(1) in a BASIC program look alike but they refer to different variables. The P1 name is given to a simple variable found in a single storage location while the P(1) variable refers to the first item in an array named P.

## Entering Data into Arrays

FOR . . . NEXT loops are a convenient way to enter data into arrays. *Character string items* can be entered as shown below:

```
125   FOR H = 1 TO 6
130      READ P$(H)
135   NEXT H
140   DATA "TEE SHIRTS(DOZ)", "MOSQUITO BIRD R"
142   DATA "MOSQUITO BIRD T", "KAY OSS IN CONCERT R"
144   DATA "KAY OSS IN CONCERT T", "OH WHAT? BOOK"
```

In ln 125, the FOR statement sets up a loop and creates an index (H) to control the reading of six data items. In the first pass through the loop, the value of H is 1. When the READ statement in ln 130 is executed for the first time, the computer reads TEE SHIRTS(DOZ) from the DATA statement in ln 140 and stores it in P$(1), the first location in the array named P$. The NEXT statement on ln 135 is then encountered and the next loop begins. This time, the value of H is 2, and MOSQUITO BIRD R is read into the P$(2) location in the array. And so it goes until all six data items have been entered into the array.

*Numeric values* are entered into an array in the same way. The following program segment shows how the unit price list for the R-K products may be entered:

```
155   FOR I = 1 TO 6
160      READ P(I)
165   NEXT I
170   DATA 25.00, 6.00, 7.00, 8.00, 8.50, 9.95
```

In this case, the $25.00 price of a dozen tee shirts will be identified by P(1), the first item stored in the array named P. The value of P(2) will be $6, and the other prices will be stored in sequence as P(3), P(4), P(5), and P(6).

## Printing Arrayed Data

How can we get the computer to print the items that we've now entered into the arrays named P$ and P? It's very simple:

```
215   FOR N = 1 TO 6
225      PRINT P$(N); TAB(25); P(N)
230   NEXT N
```

As the loop index (N) goes step by step from 1 to 6, the PRINT statement on ln 225 prints the elements stored in locations 1 to 6 in both the P$ and P arrays. The following output is produced when all the program segments listed above are executed:

```
RUN

TEE SHIRTS(DOZ)            25
MOSQUITO BIRD R            6
MOSQUITO BIRD T            7
KAY OSS IN CONCERT R      8
KAY OSS IN CONCERT T      8.5
OH WHAT? BOOK              9.95
READY
>
```

## The DIM Statement

A computer must know how many elements there are in an array so that provision can be made to store and properly manipulate these elements. When the size of an array is *not* specified in a program, the BASIC interpreter or compiler will usually contain instructions that will automatically provide storage space for 10 elements. This automatic feature of BASIC was used when the six elements in the P$ and P arrays mentioned above were entered into the computer. It would *not* be possible, however, to enter an array of 20 products without reserving space in advance for 20 elements.

Space is reserved for a specific number of elements in an array by the use of a **DIM** (for DIMension) **statement.** It's good programming practice to use DIM statements in all programs regardless of the size of the arrays. And since these DIM statements must precede any other program statements that deal with the arrays they describe, it's also good practice to place the DIM statements immediately after the introductory REM statements.

The general form of the DIM statement is:

ln   DIM   array name1(limit 1), array name2(limit 2), . . .

Each limit is an integer (whole number) that specifies the *maximum* number of storage locations to be reserved for the preceding array name. (A subscript of zero is possible in some BASIC dialects, and this will add one additional element to the maximum number that can be stored.) Thus, in the following statement,

    90    DIM   P$(20)

space is reserved for 20 elements in an array named P$. Fewer than 20 elements can be read into P$, but element P(21) cannot be stored. A single DIM statement can also be used to specify the number of elements to be stored in multiple arrays. Thus,

    97    DIM   P$(6), P(6), Q(6), A(6)

identifies P$, P, Q, and A as array names and specifies that six is the maximum number of elements that can be stored in each array.

## Example Programs Using One-Dimensional Arrays

Figure 21-5a presents a program that incorporates the array concepts that we've now covered. The flowchart in Figure 21-5b will help you trace through the logic of this program. The program produces a report that summarizes the sales of all products sold by R-K Enterprises during a period. Another program approach to produce this report was flowcharted in Figure 18-10, page 495, and a listing of this alternative program is shown in Figure 20-10, page 566. (Since PRINT USING statements found in Figure

---

### HOW THE PROS WRITE COMPUTER GAMES

*Have you ever admired a computer game, and wondered how it was programmed? Where the programmer got the idea or what programming tools were used? Or how long it took? Here's the inside story on how professional game programmers work.*

So there you are at one o'clock in the morning, nodding over your computer keyboard with bloodshot eyes, trying to program your first computer game in BASIC. "Space Weirdos" seemed like a good idea at first, but it isn't turning out that way. The Weirdos keep flying off the screen and causing errors. Even when the Weirdos are on the screen, they move so slowly that they could be zapped by a sleeping zombie. And now you realize that there's no way for the game to keep track of scores.

Obviously, there must be some trick to programming games that you don't know about. . . .

Actually, of course, there is no "trick" to programming a top-notch computer game. Like most other skills, game programming is an art which usually requires years to develop . . .

Good game programming requires a high level of mastery of the computer, and the ability to constantly push the machine to its limits—or even beyond established limits. It is safe to say that some of the most innovative microcomputer programming going on today is in the field of entertainment. Techniques discovered and sharpened by game programmers spread to educational programs and even business software . . .

Not only is there no "trick" to game programming, but there is also no single style. Although many people think of programming as a primarily technical task, it is really a highly creative pursuit. As a result, professional programmers tend to be a very individualistic bunch. The game programmers we contacted advocate several different styles. . . . For example, some programmers work everything out on paper before they ever touch a keyboard. Others sit down at the keyboard and start hacking away without ever touching paper.

On the other hand, professional game programmers also have some characteristics in common. . . . Many were introduced to computing as teenagers. They tend to specialize on one particular computer, often the one on which they learned. Surprisingly, few professional game programmers have computer-related college degrees, or even any formal education in programming. Virtually all of them write their games 100 percent in machine language.

Computer games have a lot in common with novels. They begin life as an idea in someone's mind, an idea that is then developed into a "scenario," or plot. When the idea has matured or solidified to a certain point, work begins. As things progress, parts of the original idea may be dropped, and subplots may be added. . . . Often, the work is declared "done" only because the author is too spent to carry it any further, or because a deadline looms. Then, like a novel, the computer game hits the market and lives or dies on the effectiveness of its promotion, the reactions of reviewers, and the response of consumers. Only a few rise to the top and become best sellers.

—Tom R. Halfhill, "How the Pros Write Computer Games," *Compute!* February 1983, p. 34.

```
LIST

10   REM *SALES SUMMARY REPORT
20   REM *
30   REM *VARIABLE NAMES:
40   REM * P$ PRODUCT NAME
50   REM * Q  QUANTITY SOLD
60   REM * P  UNIT PRICE
70   REM * A  NET SALES
80   REM * T  TOTAL NET SALES
90   REM *
95   REM *SPECIFY STORAGE SPACE FOR ARRAYS
97        DIM P$(6), P(6), Q(6), A(6)
100  REM *PRINT HEADINGS
110       PRINT TAB(20);"SALES SUMMARY REPORT"
115       PRINT "PRODUCT";TAB(22);"UNIT PRICE";TAB(38);"QUANTITY";TAB(50);"NET SALES"
120  REM *ENTER LIST OF PRODUCT NAMES
125       FOR H = 1 TO 6
130         READ P$(H)
135       NEXT H
140       DATA "TEE SHIRTS(DOZ)","MOSQUITO BIRD R"
142       DATA "MOSQUITO BIRD T","KAY OSS IN CONCERT R"
144       DATA "KAY OSS IN CONCERT T","OH WHAT? BOOK"
150  REM *ENTER UNIT PRICE LIST FOR PRODUCTS
155       FOR I = 1 TO 6
160         READ P(I)
165       NEXT I
170       DATA 25.00, 6.00, 7.00, 8.00, 8.50, 9.95
180  REM *ENTER QUANTITY SOLD
185       FOR J = 1 TO 6
190         READ Q(J)
195       NEXT J
200       DATA 35.75, 300.00, 50.00, 200.00, 70.00, 2.00
210  REM *COMPUTE NET SALES AMOUNTS AND PRINT OUTPUT RESULTS
215       FOR N = 1 TO 6
220         LET A(N) = Q(N) * P(N)
225         PRINT P$(N);TAB(25);P(N);TAB(40);Q(N);TAB(52);A(N)
230       NEXT N
240  REM *INITIALIZE ACCUMULATOR AND COMPUTE TOTAL NET SALES
245       LET T = 0
250       FOR K = 1 TO 6
255         LET T = T + A(K)
260       NEXT K
265  REM *PRINT TOTAL NET SALES AMOUNT AND STOP
267       PRINT
270       PRINT TAB(50);"TOTAL"
275       PRINT TAB(50);"NET SALES"
280       PRINT TAB(51);T
290       END
READY
>
```

Computer listing
of the program

```
RUN

                  SALES SUMMARY REPORT
PRODUCT                 UNIT PRICE      QUANTITY       NET SALES
TEE SHIRTS(DOZ)             25            35.75          893.75
MOSQUITO BIRD R             6             300            1800
MOSQUITO BIRD T             7             50             350
KAY OSS IN CONCERT R        8             200            1600
KAY OSS IN CONCERT T        8.5           70             595
OH WHAT? BOOK               9.95          2              19.9

                                                    TOTAL
                                                    NET SALES
                                                    5258.65
READY
>
```

Output produced by the
computer as the program
is executed

Figure 21-5a Use of one-dimensional arrays to produce a sales
summary report for R-K Enterprises.

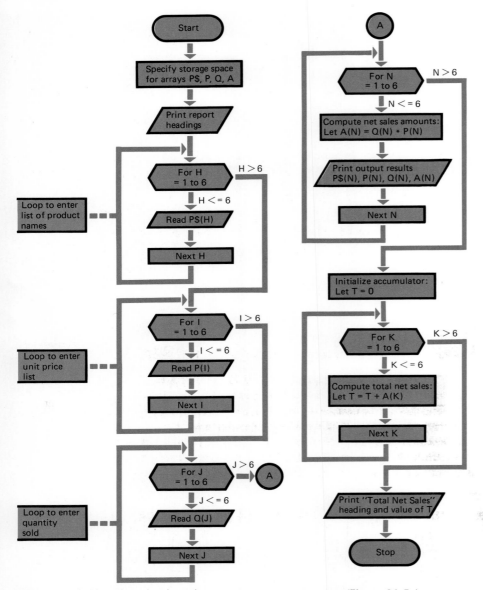

**Figure 21-5b** Flowchart for the sales summary report program (Figure 21-5a).

20-10 are not used here, the output of Figure 21-5a differs somewhat from the program output shown in Figure 20-10.)

Following the preliminary REMark statements, you'll notice in ln 97 that a DIM statement is used to specify the storage space needed for the arrays named P$, P, Q, and A. Report headings are then printed (ln 110–115), and the list of R-K product names is read into the P$ array using lines 125–144. The unit price list for these products is stored in the array named P in lines 155–170. (Do you get the feeling that you've seen this program before?) And the quantities of each product sold during the period are stored in array Q in lines 185–200.

The net sales amounts for each product are com-

```
LIST

10   REM *LORD BYRON
20   REM *
25   REM *VARIABLE NAMES:
30   REM * T$ ARRAY OF TITLES
35   REM * N$ ARRAY OF NOUNS
40   REM * V$ ARRAY OF VERBS
45   REM * A$ ARRAY OF ADJECTIVES
50   REM * P  NUMBER OF POEMS
60   REM *
65   REM *SPECIFY STORAGE SPACE FOR ARRAYS
70        DIM T$(20), N$(30), V$(22), A$(20)
75   REM *ENTER NUMBER OF POEMS TO BE COMPOSED
80        PRINT "NUMBER OF POEMS";
85        INPUT P
90   REM *READ IN STRING DATA
100       FOR B=1 TO 20
110       READ T$(B)
115       NEXT B
125       FOR C=1 TO 30
130       READ N$(C)
140       NEXT C
142       FOR D=1 TO 22
144       READ V$(D)
150       NEXT D
152       FOR E=1 TO 20
154       READ A$(E)
156       NEXT E
160  REM *COMPOSE THE TITLE
165       FOR J=1 TO P
170       PRINT TAB(3);"OH WHAT IS THE MEANING OF ";T$(RND(20))
180       PRINT
190  REM *WRITE A FOUR LINE MASTERPIECE
200       FOR K=1 TO 4
210       PRINT A$(RND(20));N$(RND(30));V$(RND(22));
220       PRINT A$(RND(20));N$(RND(30))
230       NEXT K
232       PRINT
234       PRINT
235       NEXT J
300  REM *INPUT DATA
310       DATA "NIGHT ","PLEASE ","NO" ,"MAUDE","STRIFE"
320       DATA "NEVER","BEAUTY","RAPTURE","WOOL","LOVE"
322       DATA "HELL","SNOW","YES","MUSIC","LIFE"
324       DATA "WATER","FAST-FOOD FRANCHISES","MILK","TIME","DREADFUL"
330  REM *
340       DATA "YEAR ","FIRE ","TREE ","TIME ","TOWN "
345       DATA "CHILDREN ","SUMMER ","BRIDE ","FLOWER ","HEART "
348       DATA "MIND ", "BODY ", "BED ","KEY ","DEW-DROPS "
350       DATA "BEAR ","SAND ","PATH ","PLACE ","HOUR "
352       DATA "SOLDIER ","COMRADES ","GRAVES ","DEVIL "
354       DATA "VINE-CLAD HILLS ","BIG BAD WOLF ","ANGELS "
356       DATA "THREE LITTLE PIGS ","BEASTS ","GODS "
360  REM *
370       DATA "RUNS ","SWIMS ","DIES ","TALKS ","WORKS "
380       DATA "PLAYS ","WALKS ","FEELS ","SEES ","NODS "
382       DATA "MOURNS ","ENTANGLES ","GASPS ","EBBS "
384       DATA "FLOWS ","FADES ","BURIES ","BEATS "
386       DATA "RETURNS ","THREATENS ","BREAKS ","LIVES "
390  REM *
400       DATA "A BIG ","A FISHY ","THE HUNGRY ","THE LOST ","A LONELY "
410       DATA "THE STRONG ","PLAYFUL ","THE SPRY ","A LIVELY ","ONE LAZY "
420       DATA "A HAIRY ","THE FAT ","THE SAD ","A TINY ","CHEERFUL "
430       DATA "THE BOLD ","YOUNG ","A GALLANT ","ONE BRAVE ","DELICATE "
440       END
READY
>
```

Computer listing of the program

**Figure 21-6a** The Lord Byron poetry generator program.

```
RUN

NUMBER OF POEMS? 10
     OH WHAT IS THE MEANING OF MAUDE

A LIVELY TREE NODS ONE BRAVE TREE
THE SAD FIRE WALKS THE SPRY HOUR
THE HUNGRY SAND WALKS THE SAD TIME
THE HUNGRY PATH FADES CHEERFUL BRIDE


     OH WHAT IS THE MEANING OF YES

A GALLANT SOLDIER RETURNS A LIVELY CHILDREN
THE FAT COMRADES EBBS THE SPRY YEAR
A FISHY BODY ENTANGLES CHEERFUL GODS
THE SAD HEART GASPS A HAIRY PATH


     OH WHAT IS THE MEANING OF PLEASE

A BIG VINE-CLAD HILLS SEES THE FAT PLACE
ONE LAZY SUMMER GASPS ONE BRAVE FLOWER
A LIVELY TOWN EBBS A LONELY TIME
A TINY VINE-CLAD HILLS FEELS THE BOLD GRAVES


     OH WHAT IS THE MEANING OF LIFE

THE SAD SUMMER ENTANGLES THE FAT TOWN
THE HUNGRY BRIDE MOURNS A HAIRY TREE
THE HUNGRY TREE FADES CHEERFUL CHILDREN
DELICATE DEW-DROPS FEELS ONE BRAVE SOLDIER

                    .
                    .
                    .
                    .
                    .

READY
>

 RUN
NUMBER OF POEMS? 10


     OH WHAT IS THE MEANING OF LIFE

A LONELY FIRE BEATS DELICATE CHILDREN
YOUNG PLACE BURIES ONE BRAVE MIND
CHEERFUL DEW-DROPS FEELS A FISHY COMRADES
THE HUNGRY BIG BAD WOLF ENTANGLES A LONELY DEW-DROPS


     OH WHAT IS THE MEANING OF PLEASE

THE SAD MIND PLAYS THE FAT DEW-DROPS
THE FAT ANGELS TALKS A BIG BODY
A BIG TIME MOURNS DELICATE BIG BAD WOLF
THE BOLD PATH WALKS A LONELY BEAR


     OH WHAT IS THE MEANING OF LOVE

A FISHY BRIDE BURIES THE SPRY PATH
A FISHY FLOWER RETURNS A LONELY FIRE
A FISHY HEART MOURNS THE BOLD ANGELS
A TINY SUMMER THREATENS THE FAT TREE
```

Output produced by the computer as the program is executed

Figure 21-6a *continued*

```
     OH WHAT IS THE MEANING OF STRIFE

YOUNG HEART FEELS CHEERFUL SOLDIER
PLAYFUL SUMMER FADES CHEERFUL SAND
THE HUNGRY GRAVES BREAKS A FISHY BEASTS
ONE BRAVE KEY RUNS ONE LAZY TIME

                    •

                    •

                    •

                    •

                    •

                    •


READY
>

 RUN
NUMBER OF POEMS? 15
     OH WHAT IS THE MEANING OF WOOL

THE FAT BODY NODS THE LOST BEAR
THE HUNGRY BEASTS SEES ONE LAZY SAND
PLAYFUL FLOWER NODS A LONELY BODY
A TINY BRIDE ENTANGLES PLAYFUL FIRE


     OH WHAT IS THE MEANING OF FAST-FOOD FRANCHISES

THE SAD BEAR ENTANGLES A FISHY HEART
THE BOLD BEAR BURIES THE FAT DEW-DROPS
THE STRONG BEASTS LIVES A LIVELY ANGELS
THE LOST KEY NODS A LONELY MIND


     OH WHAT IS THE MEANING OF RAPTURE

CHEERFUL DEVIL RETURNS ONE BRAVE BEASTS
A GALLANT SAND NODS A LONELY YEAR
THE SPRY BEAR EBBS THE FAT TIME
THE BOLD KEY RETURNS PLAYFUL BODY

                    •

                    •

                    •

                    •
```

Output produced by the computer as the program is executed

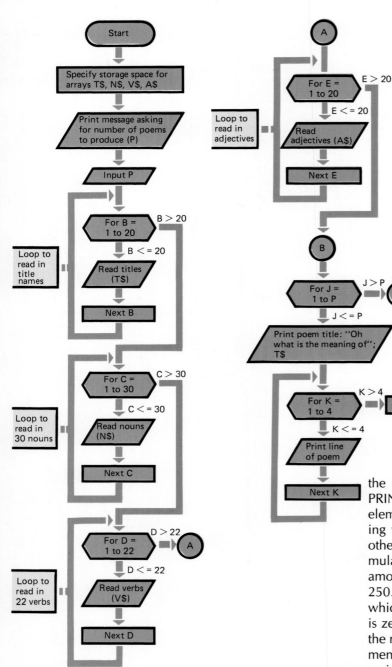

**Figure 21-6b** Flowchart for the Lord Byron program (Figure 21-6a).

the net sales amount assigned to A(1) is $893.75. The PRINT statement in ln 225 is then used to print the first element in arrays P$, P, Q, and A. In each of the remaining five passes through the loop in lines 215–230, another line will be printed on the output report. An accumulator is then established in ln 245 to total the net sales amounts stored in array A. Another loop is initiated in ln 250. In the first execution of this loop, the value of A(1), which is $893.75, is added to the initial value of T which is zero, to produce a new total for T (ln 225). In each of the remaining five passes through this loop, the other elements in array A are added to the accumulator. The remaining program lines (267–280) then print a "TOTAL NET SALES" heading and the amount accumulated in T.

You'll find another example program that uses a number of one-dimensional arrays in Figure 21-6a, and the flowchart for this program is shown in Figure 21-6b.

puted in lines 215–220. In the first execution of the loop initiated in ln 215, the net sales for the first product—TEE SHIRTS(DOZ)—are determined by multiplying Q(1) times P(1). Since Q(1) is 35.75 dozen, and P(1) is $25.00,

As you know, R-K Enterprises has published a book with the title of *Oh What?* This book of poems was written by Ms. Fitt, Rob's English teacher. During the preparation of the *Oh What?* manuscript, Ms. Fitt was inspired to produce many selections by using the poetry generator shown in Figure 21-6a. After editing many of the "poems" produced by the program to correct gross errors in grammar, Ms. Fitt then added them to her manuscript. Let's take a look now at the "Lord Byron" program (named in honor of Ada's father).

The variable names assigned to the arrays are shown in the early REMark statements, and the storage spaces for these arrays are assigned by the DIM statement in ln 70. The number of poems to be produced is entered (ln 80–85), and the arrays of title names (T$), nouns (N$), verbs (V$), and adjectives (A$) are loaded by the four FOR . . . NEXT loops in lines 100–156. Another FOR . . . NEXT loop is used to compose the title of a poem (ln 165–180). The number of titles and poems generated is determined by the value the user assigns to P in

## Feedback and Review 21-1

A portion of a program that produces a weekly production report for R-K Enterprises, and the output produced by this program in a recent period, is shown below:
Explain the purpose of lines 80–140 in this program.

```
10   REM *WEEKLY PRODUCTION REPORT
15   REM *
20   REM *VARIABLE NAMES:
30   REM * N$ ARRAY OF EMPLOYEE NAMES
40   REM * W  ARRAY OF WEEKLY PRODUCTION TOTALS
60   REM *
70   REM *SPECIFY STORAGE SPACE FOR ARRAYS
80       DIM N$(8),W(8)
90   REM *READ IN NUMBER OF WORKERS
100      READ N
110  REM *READ WORKER'S NAME AND WEEKLY PRODUCTION TOTALS
120      FOR I=1 TO N
130      READ N$(I),W(I)
140      NEXT I
```
Program segment

| EMPLOYEE NAME | WEEKLY PRODUCTION TOTAL |
|---|---|
| U. BROWN | 10 |
| A. COLWELL | 15 |
| D. GARCIA | 21 |
| C. HEAD | 8 |
| K. KARR | 25 |
| L. LONDON | 21 |
| A. MUNDAY | 11 |
| J. TAYLOR | 16 |

```
READY
>
```
Program output

the INPUT statement in ln 85. In ln 170, the first part of the PRINT statement produces the "OH WHAT IS THE MEANING OF" part of the title. The last word in the title is then selected at random from one of the 20 elements in the T$ array. (The RND function your system uses to perform this operation may differ from the one shown here.)

Once the title of a poem has been generated, a nested FOR . . . NEXT loop (ln 200–230) randomly selects items from the A$, N$, and V$ arrays to produce the first line of the poem. Since the FOR . . . NEXT loop in ln 200–300 is executed four times, a four-line masterpiece is created. After the four lines are produced, program control loops back to ln 165 and a test is made to see if the specified number of poems has been prepared. If J is < = P, another poem is generated; if J > P, then the program stops.

Some of the poems produced by this program are shown following the program listing in Figure 21-6a. You can see why Kay Oss opposed the publication of the *Oh What?* book! You might also want to modify this program (use more arrays with larger and better vocabularies) to create a superior poetry generator—a "William Shakespeare" perhaps?

# TWO-DIMENSIONAL ARRAYS

We've been discussing arrays consisting of lists of items. But an array can also be a *table,* or *matrix.* Let's suppose, for example, that the R-K Enterprise partners want to analyze the tee shirt sales made in different types of retail outlets in different regions of the country. Let's also assume that the following table presents the available sales data for a particular period:

(row ↓ column→) SALES OF TEE SHIRTS(DOZ)

| SALES DIVISION | CAMPUS STORES | SPECIALTY SHOPS | DEPARTMENT STORES |
|---|---|---|---|
| EASTERN | 195 | 40 | 85 |
| CENTRAL | 185 | 25 | 60 |
| WESTERN | 155 | 65 | 45 |

As you can see, this table consists of data organized into rows and columns. Each row gives the sales data for a region of the country, and each column shows the sales made to a particular type of retail outlet. Thus, you can see that 65 dozen tee shirts were sold to specialty shops in the Western Division (third row, second column).

You'll notice that there are a total of nine elements in the table (3 rows × 3 columns). A particular element in a table is identified by a *pair* of subscripts. Thus, the 65 dozen tee shirts sold to specialty shops in the Western Division are indicated by the subscript (3,2), where the *first number indicates the row* and the *second the column.* This table is called a **two-dimensional array** because two numbers (row, column) are needed to locate the element.

A two-dimensional array is named just like other BASIC variables, but the same name can't be used in the same program to identify both one- and two-dimensional arrays. If the array name S is used in our example to store the table data in the computer, then the sales made to the different retail outlets can be identified by the subscripts shown below:

S ARRAY

| | | |
|---|---|---|
| S(1,1) 195 | S(1,2) 40 | S(1,3) 85 |
| S(2,1) 185 | S(2,2) 25 | S(2,3) 60 |
| S(3,1) 155 | S(3,2) 65 | S(3,3) 45 |

We can also store the names of the sales divisions and the retail outlets in the following one-dimensional arrays:

| D$ ARRAY | | S$ ARRAY | |
|---|---|---|---|
| EASTERN | D$(1) | CAMPUS STORE | S$(1) |
| CENTRAL | D$(2) | SPECIALTY STORE | S$(2) |
| WESTERN | D$(3) | DEPARTMENT STORE | S$(3) |

The BASIC interpreter or compiler will usually also contain instructions that will automatically provide storage space for a two-dimensional array with up to 10 rows and 10 columns. But as noted earlier, it's good practice to use DIM statements in all programs regardless of the size of the arrays. The following statement

60 DIM B(15,8)

```
LIST


10   REM *RETAIL SALES ANALYSIS FOR TEE SHIRTS
15   REM *
20   REM *VARIABLE NAMES:
25   REM * D$ SALES DIVISIONS
30   REM * S$ TYPES OF RETAIL STORE OUTLETS
35   REM * S  SALES DATA FOR TEE SHIRTS
40   REM * R  SUBSCRIPT TO CONTROL TABLE ROWS
45   REM * C  SUBSCRIPT TO CONTROL TABLE COLUMNS
50   REM * T1 ROW TOTALS
55   REM * T2 COLUMN TOTALS
60   REM * T3 TOTAL SALES FOR THE PERIOD
70   REM *
75   REM *SPECIFY STORAGE SPACE FOR ARRAYS
80        DIM D$(3), S$(3), S(3,3)
85   REM *ENTER LIST OF SALES DIVISIONS
90        FOR L = 1 TO 3
95           READ D$(L)
100       NEXT L
105       DATA "EASTERN DIVISION", "CENTRAL DIVISION"
107       DATA "WESTERN DIVISION"
110  REM *ENTER TYPES OF STORE OUTLETS
115       FOR M = 1 TO 3
120          READ S$(M)
125       NEXT M
130       DATA "CAMPUS STORE", "SPECIALTY SHOP"
135       DATA "DEPARTMENT STORE"
140  REM *ENTER SALES DATA FROM TABLE.  THE R LOOP CONTROLS
141  REM *THE TABLE ROWS AND THE C LOOP CONTROLS THE TABLE
142  REM *COLUMNS.
145       FOR R = 1 TO 3
150         FOR C = 1 TO 3
155            READ S(R,C)
160         NEXT C
165       NEXT R
170       DATA 195, 40, 85, 185, 25, 60, 155, 65, 45
180  REM *PRINT HEADINGS
185       PRINT TAB(22);"R-K ENTERPRISES"
190       PRINT TAB(12);"SALES OF TEE SHIRTS(DOZ) BY DIVISION"
195       PRINT TAB(12);"----- -- --- ------ ---  -- --------"
200  REM *INITIALIZE ACCUMULATOR AND COMPUTE DIVISION SALES
205       FOR I = 1 TO 3
210       LET T1 = 0
215         FOR C = 1 TO 3
220            LET T1 = T1 + S(I,C)
225         NEXT C
230       PRINT D$(I);" SALES = ";T1
235       NEXT I
240  REM *PRINT HEADING
245       PRINT
250       PRINT TAB(12);"SALES OF TEE SHIRTS(DOZ) BY OUTLET"
255       PRINT TAB(12);"----- -- --- ------ ---  -- ------"
260  REM *INITIALIZE ACCUMULATOR AND COMPUTE RETAIL OUTLET SALES
270       FOR J = 1 TO 3
275       LET T2 = 0
280         FOR R = 1 TO 3
285            LET T2 = T2 + S(R,J)
290         NEXT R
295       PRINT S$(J);" SALES =";TAB(25);T2
300       NEXT J
```

Computer listing
of the program

Figure 21-7a Retail sales analysis program using two-dimensional array.

```
310 REM *COMPUTE TOTAL SALES OF TEE SHIRTS(DOZ) FOR PERIOD
320       LET T3 = 0
325       FOR R = 1 TO 3
330         FOR C = 1 TO 3
335           LET T3 = T3 + S(R,C)
340         NEXT C
345       NEXT R
350 REM *PRINT SUMMARY LINE AND STOP
355       PRINT
360       PRINT TAB(10);"**TOTAL SALES FOR PERIOD =";T3;"(DOZ)."
370       END
READY
>
```

```
RUN


                      R-K ENTERPRISES
              SALES OF TEE SHIRTS(DOZ) BY DIVISION
              ----- -- --- ------ --- -- --------
EASTERN DIVISION SALES =   320
CENTRAL DIVISION SALES =   270
WESTERN DIVISION SALES =   265

              SALES OF TEE SHIRTS(DOZ) BY OUTLET
              ----- -- --- ------ --- -- ------
CAMPUS STORE SALES =        535
SPECIALTY SHOP SALES =      130
DEPARTMENT STORE SALES =    190

        **TOTAL SALES FOR PERIOD = 855 (DOZ).
READY
>
```

Output produced by the computer as the program is executed

Figure 21-7a *continued*

will reserve storage space for a two-dimensional array named B that has 15 rows and 8 columns. And this statement

    80   DIM   D$(3), S$(3), S(3,3)

will provide space for the one- and two-dimensional arrays discussed above.

## Example Program Using Two-Dimensional Array

Let's assume that the partners want a program that will compute tee shirt sales by division and by sales outlet. These results will then be printed in a report, and the total sales of tee shirts for the period will also be accumulated and printed. Figure 21-7a is a program to produce this report, and the flowchart presented in Figure 21-7b will help you trace through its logic.

Following the initial REMark documentation, the DIMension statement in ln 80 specifies the storage space needed for the arrays. Then the D$ (sales divisions) and S$ (store outlets) arrays are entered into storage (line numbers 85–135). Lines 145 through 170 employ a nested FOR . . . NEXT loop structure to enter the sales data from the table into the two-dimensional array named S. The outer (or R) loop initiated in ln 145 controls the table rows, and the inner (or C) loop set up in ln 150 controls the table columns. In the first pass through the outer loop, R has a value of one, and the inner loop is executed three times. In these three executions of the C loop, the values of 195, 40, and 85 are read from the DATA statement in ln 170 and are assigned to storage as array elements S(1,1), S(1,2), and S(1,3) by the READ statement in ln 155. The six remaining elements in the S array are stored in the second and third executions of the R loop.

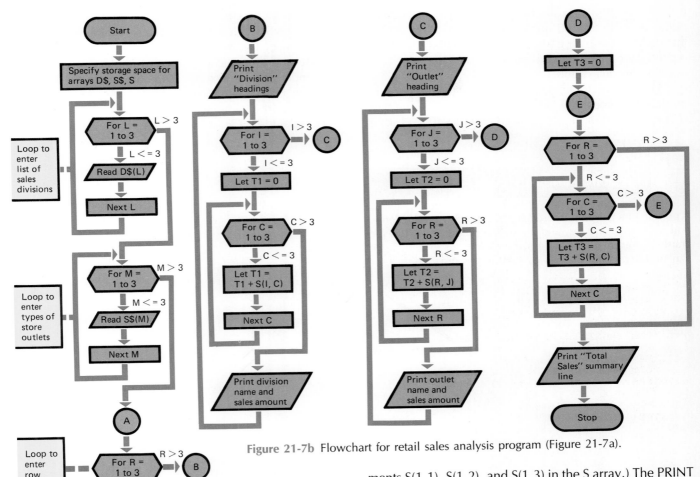

**Figure 21-7b** Flowchart for retail sales analysis program (Figure 21-7a).

After report headings are printed in lines 180–195, another nested FOR . . . NEXT loop structure accumulates and prints the sales of each division. Lines 205–210 set up the outer (I) loop and initialize the "row total" accumulator (T1). The first execution of the inner (C) loop in lines 215–225 adds the sales data in the three columns of row 1 of the table to the accumulator. (These are ele-

ments S(1,1), S(1,2), and S(1,3) in the S array.) The PRINT statement in ln 230 then prints (1) the name of the first sales division stored in the D$ array (EASTERN), and (2) the total sales (T1) for that division. In the second iteration through the outer loop, the accumulator is reset to zero and the procedure is repeated for the next sales division.

After division sales have been computed and printed, another heading is printed on the output report (lines 240–255). Program control then moves to the nested FOR . . . NEXT structure in lines 270–300. The purpose of this structure is to accumulate and print the sales of each type of retail outlet. Lines 270–275 set up the outer loop (J) and initialize the "column total" accumulator (T2). The first execution of the inner (R) loop in lines 280–290 adds the sales data in the three rows of column 1 of the table to the accumulator. (These are elements S(1,1), S(2,1), and S(3,1) in the S array.) The PRINT statement in

In 295 then prints (1) the name of the first type of retail outlet stored in the S$ array (CAMPUS STORE), and (2) the total sales (T2) for that type of outlet. This procedure is repeated for the other retail outlets in the next two executions of the outer loop.

Finally, the total sales of tee shirts for the period is produced in lines 320–345. A "total sales" accumulator (T3) is initiated in ln 320, and an outer loop (R) is set up by the FOR statement in ln 325. The elements S(1,1), S(1,2), and S(1,3) are added to the accumulator in the first execution of the inner (C) loop in lines 330–340. The second and third passes through the outer loop add the remainder of the elements in the S array to the value of T3. The PRINT statement in ln 360 then prints on the output report a summary line and the total sales amount accumulated in T3.

## Feedback and Review 21-2

A portion of a program that generates a monthly production report for R-K Enterprises, and the output produced by this program in a recent period, is shown below:
Explain the purpose of lines 80–140 in this program.

```
10    REM *MONTHLY PRODUCTION REPORT
15    REM *
20    REM *VARIABLE NAMES:
30    REM * N$ ARRAY OF EMPLOYEE NAMES
40    REM * W  ARRAY OF WEEKLY PRODUCTION DATA
50    REM * M  ARRAY OF MONTHLY PRODUCTION TOTALS
60    REM *
70    REM *SPECIFY STORAGE SPACE FOR ARRAYS
80         DIM N$(8),M(8),W(8,4)
90    REM *READ IN NUMBER OF WORKERS
100        READ N
110   REM *READ WORKER'S NAME AND WEEKLY PRODUCTION DATA
120        FOR I=1 TO N
130        READ N$(I),W(I,1),W(I,2),W(I,3),W(I,4)
140        NEXT I
```

Program segment

| NAME | W1 | W2 | W3 | W4 | TOTAL |
|------|----|----|----|----|-------|
| ---- | -- | -- | -- | -- | ----- |
| U. BROWN | 10 | 16 | 12 | 19 | 57 |
| A. COLWELL | 15 | 18 | 16 | 21 | 70 |
| D. GARCIA | 21 | 25 | 19 | 22 | 87 |
| C. HEAD | 8 | 10 | 12 | 9 | 39 |
| K. KARR | 25 | 22 | 27 | 19 | 93 |
| L. LONDON | 21 | 24 | 22 | 29 | 96 |
| A. MUNDAY | 11 | 9 | 13 | 16 | 49 |
| J. TAYLOR | 16 | 22 | 19 | 25 | 82 |
| READY | | | | | |
| > | | | | | |

Program output

# LET'S SORT THIS OUT

You learned way back in Chapter 1 that people often prefer to work with data that have been arranged in some logical sequence. The sequence may be from first to last, from largest to smallest, from oldest to newest. Arranging data in such a predetermined order is called **sorting.** Names are often put in alphabetical order, and numeric data are often sorted into an ascending or descending sequence. In fact, you've seen in Chapter 2 that the records in sequential files must be stored in an ascending or descending order determined by a record key before sequential (batch) processing can be carried out. When there are only a few data items to deal with, people can quickly examine these items and then mentally place them in a desired order. But what if there are hundreds, thousands, and even millions of items to consider? Fortunately for people, the computer easily handles these large sorting tasks.

*Example.* Before we examine one way that a computer can be used to sort data items, let's first look at an example program. There's nothing new in the Weekly Production Report program shown in Figure 21-8. (In fact, you may recognize part of it from Feedback and Review 21-1.) Rob and Kay have decided to produce their own "Mosquito Bird" and "Kay Oss in Concert" tapes. This production is carried out by other students who use their personal tape recorders to duplicate the R-K products. The FOR . . . NEXT loop in ln 120–140 is used to load two arrays with worker names and production totals for a recent week. You should now be able to trace through the rest of this program to see how the program output is produced.

## Bubble Sorts

You'll notice that the output produced in Figure 21-8 is in an alphabetical name order because that's the way the input data file is organized. However, Kay believes that the production report would be more useful if the program sorted and then printed the weekly production totals in a *descending order.* That way, it would be easier to identify the top producers.

Although there are several approaches that we could use to accomplish this sorting assignment, we'll only consider one here. This **bubble sort approach** compares two adjacent elements in an array and then immediately interchanges them if they aren't in the desired ascending or descending sequence. The program shown in Figure 21-9a is a modified version of the one presented in Figure 21-8. This new version uses a bubble sort to arrange the weekly production totals in a descending order. The flowchart presented in Figure 21-9b will help you trace through the logic of this program.

Although two new variable names have been defined in the early REMark statements in Figure 21-9a, there are no other differences between this program and the one you've just studied in Figure 21-8 until you get to the REMark statement in ln 230 that announces the beginning of the sorting procedure. In ln 270, a variable named F$ is set up as a "flag." This variable—initially set to "DONE"—will be used later to determine if the entire sorting process has been completed.

The *first sorting pass* through the array of weekly production totals (W) is established with the FOR statement in ln 290. You'll notice that this FOR . . . NEXT loop (ln 290–490) will be executed N-1 times during this first sorting pass. Since N is 8 in our example, the FOR . . . NEXT loop will be executed 7 times to complete one sorting pass. In the first execution of this loop I = 1, and in ln 300 the first item in the W array of production figures is compared to the second item in that array. Since the value of W(1) is 10, and since the value of W(1+1) is 15, the IF . . . THEN statement in ln 300 causes program control to branch to ln 330. The F$ flag is set to "NOT DONE" in ln 330 to indicate that the sorting hasn't been completed, and lines 340–360 are used to interchange the weekly production values of W(1) and W(1+1). This exchange is accomplished by first creating a working storage space (S) so that the switch can be made. In ln 340, the value of W(1), or 10 at this time, is stored in the location named S. In ln 350, the value of W(1+1), or 15 at this time, is transferred to W(1), thereby erasing the value of 10 previously stored there. And the switch is completed in ln 360 when the previous value of W(1) that's stored in S is assigned to W(1+1), thereby erasing the value of 15. Thus, W(1) now has a value of 15 and W(1+1) contains a value of 10. The same procedure is then followed in the next

```
    LIST

    10   REM *WEEKLY PRODUCTION REPORT
    15   REM *
    20   REM *VARIABLE NAMES:
    30   REM * N$ ARRAY OF EMPLOYEE NAMES
    40   REM * W  ARRAY OF WEEKLY PRODUCTION TOTALS
    60   REM *
    70   REM *SPECIFY STORAGE SPACE FOR ARRAYS
    80        DIM N$(8),W(8)
    90   REM *READ IN NUMBER OF WORKERS
    100       READ N
    110  REM *READ WORKER'S NAME AND WEEKLY PRODUCTION TOTALS
    120       FOR I=1 TO N
    130       READ N$(I),W(I)
    140       NEXT I
    512  REM *PRINT REPORT HEADING
    514       PRINT TAB(25);"WEEKLY PRODUCTION"
    515       PRINT "EMPLOYEE NAME";TAB(30);"TOTAL"
    517       PRINT "-------------";TAB(25);"------------------"
    520  REM *PRINT OUT REPORT
    530       FOR I=1 TO N
    540       PRINT N$(I);TAB(30);W(I)
    560       NEXT I
    580  REM *INPUT DATA
    590       DATA 8
    600       DATA "U. BROWN      ",10
    610       DATA "A. COLWELL    ",15
    620       DATA "D. GARCIA     ",21
    630       DATA "C. HEAD       ",8
    640       DATA "K. KARR       ",25
    650       DATA "L. LONDON     ",21
    660       DATA "A. MUNDAY     ",11
    670       DATA "J. TAYLOR     ",16
    700       END
    READY
    >
```

Computer listing of the program

```
    RUN


                              WEEKLY PRODUCTION
    EMPLOYEE NAME                   TOTAL
    -------------             ------------------
    U. BROWN                         10
    A. COLWELL                       15
    D. GARCIA                        21
    C. HEAD                          8
    K. KARR                          25
    L. LONDON                        21
    A. MUNDAY                        11
    J. TAYLOR                        16
    READY
    >
```

Output produced by the computer as the program is executed

Figure 21-8 An R-K Enterprises program that produces a report giving the weekly production of tape products.

```
LIST

10   REM *WEEKLY PRODUCTION REPORT
15   REM *
20   REM *VARIABLE NAMES:
30   REM * N$ ARRAY OF EMPLOYEE NAMES
40   REM * W  ARRAY OF WEEKLY PRODUCTION TOTALS
45   REM * F$ FLAG INDICATING COMPLETION OF SORTING
50   REM * S  WORKING STORAGE SPACE--EMPLOYEE PRODUCTION TOTAL
55   REM * S$ WORKING STORAGE SPACE--EMPLOYEE NAME
60   REM *
70   REM *SPECIFY STORAGE SPACE FOR ARRAYS
80        DIM N$(8),W(8)
90   REM *READ IN NUMBER OF WORKERS
100       READ N
110  REM *READ WORKER'S NAME AND WEEKLY PRODUCTION DATA
120       FOR I=1 TO N
130       READ N$(I),W(I)
140       NEXT I
230  REM *SORT EMPLOYEES ON BASIS OF PRODUCTIVITY
250  REM *
260  REM *SET FLAG TO "DONE" INITIALLY
270       LET F$="DONE"
280  REM *EXAMINE DATA TO SEE IF THEY ARE IN ORDER
290       FOR I=1 TO N-1
300       IF W(I)<W(I+1) THEN 330
310       GOTO 490
315  REM *IF DATA ARE NOT IN ORDER THEN
320  REM *SET FLAG TO "NOT DONE" AND INTERCHANGE ORDER
330       LET F$="NOT DONE"
340       LET S=W(I)
350       LET W(I)=W(I+1)
360       LET W(I+1)=S
370  REM *
380       LET S$=N$(I)
390       LET N$(I)=N$(I+1)
400       LET N$(I+1)=S$
480  REM *
490       NEXT I
500  REM *IF FLAG INDICATES "NOT DONE" THEN REPEAT
505       IF F$="NOT DONE" THEN 270
510  REM *PRINT REPORT HEADING
512       PRINT TAB(25);"WEEKLY PRODUCTION"
514       PRINT "EMPLOYEE NAME";TAB(30);"TOTAL"
517       PRINT "-------------";TAB(25);"------------------"
520  REM *PRINT OUT REPORT
530       FOR I=1 TO N
540       PRINT N$(I);TAB(30);W(I)
560       NEXT I
580  REM *INPUT DATA
590       DATA 8
600       DATA "U. BROWN    ",10
610       DATA "A. COLWELL  ",15
620       DATA "D. GARCIA   ",21
630       DATA "C. HEAD     ",8
640       DATA "K. KARR     ",25
650       DATA "L. LONDON   ",21
660       DATA "A. MUNDAY   ",11
670       DATA "J. TAYLOR   ",16
700       END
READY
>
```

Computer listing of the program

**Figure 21-9a** An R-K Enterprises program that sorts the weekly production of tape products in a descending order.

```
       RUN

                               WEEKLY PRODUCTION
       EMPLOYEE NAME                  TOTAL
       -------------           ------------------
       K.  KARR                        25
       D.  GARCIA                      21
       L.  LONDON                      21
       J.  TAYLOR                      16
       A.  COLWELL                     15
       A.  MUNDAY                      11
       U.  BROWN                       10
       C.  HEAD                         8
       READY
       >
```

Output produced by the computer as the program is executed

Figure 21-9a *continued*

three program lines (ln 380–400) to interchange the employee names so that they correctly match the data in array W. Note that an S$ working storage space has been created in ln 380 to permit this switch.

Having now switched the first two values in the W and D$ arrays, the computer encounters the NEXT statement in ln 490, and program control is transferred back to ln 290 for a second iteration through the FOR . . . NEXT loop. Note that we *haven't* completed the *first sorting pass* through the data. All we've done is complete the *first iteration* through the loop in lines 290–490. In the *second iteration,* the value of W(2) is compared to W(2+1) in ln 300. Since W(2) was changed to a value of 10 in the first iteration, 10 is now compared to W(2+1) which now has a value of 21. Since 10 < 21 in ln 300, program control branches to ln 330 and the values of W(2) and W(2+1) are switched in lines 340–360. The employee names in N$(2) and N$(2+1) are also switched in lines 380–400.

Figure 21-10 shows the results of the comparisons made by the FOR . . . NEXT loop in lines 290–490 during the *first sorting pass* through the arrays. As you can see, N-1 or 7 comparisons were made as specified by the FOR statement in ln 290. (If the FOR statement had read FOR I = 1 to N, the computer would have tried to compare item 8 to item 9 in ln 300, and the W array doesn't have an item 9!) When the first sorting pass through the W array is completed, the order of the W array will be as shown in column 4 of Figure 21-10. Program control then

branches to ln 505, and a test is made of the contents of the F$ storage location. If F$= "NOT DONE", then program control branches back to ln 270, F$ is set to "DONE", and another sorting pass is processed. Since F$ was changed to "NOT DONE" by the sorting carried out in the first pass discussed above, there will be a second pass. The values of the W array at the end of this *second sorting pass* are shown in column 5 of Figure 21-10. Since additional sorting took place in this second pass, the F$ flag is once again set to "NOT DONE", a *third pass* is carried out, and the results are shown in column 6 of Figure 21-10.

At the end of each sorting pass, the largest value of 25 in the W array has "bubbled up" by one position (see columns 4–7 of Figure 21-10). Thus, after the *fourth pass,* the value of 25 is at the top of the array and all the other values are in a descending order. (If 25 had been the last value in the original W array, N-1 or 7 sorting passes would have been required to put the array in a descending order.) At the end of the fourth pass, the F$ flag is set to "NOT DONE" so a fifth pass is made. In this pass, the computer goes through the entire array and makes no switches. Thus, the value of F$ remains set to "DONE" at the end of the pass. Program control then moves to ln 512, and the production report headings are printed. The contents of the sorted N$ and W arrays are then printed by the FOR . . . NEXT loop in lines 530–560 and the processing stops.

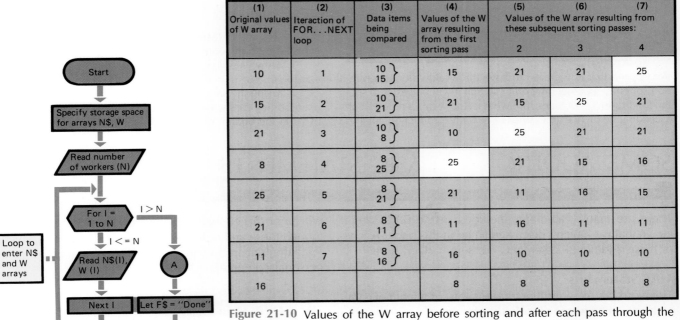

| (1) Original values of W array | (2) Iteration of FOR...NEXT loop | (3) Data items being compared | (4) Values of the W array resulting from the first sorting pass | (5) Values of the W array resulting from these subsequent sorting passes: 2 | (6) 3 | (7) 4 |
|---|---|---|---|---|---|---|
| 10 | 1 | 10 15 | 15 | 21 | 21 | 25 |
| 15 | 2 | 10 21 | 21 | 15 | 25 | 21 |
| 21 | 3 | 10 8 | 10 | 25 | 21 | 21 |
| 8 | 4 | 8 25 | 25 | 21 | 15 | 16 |
| 25 | 5 | 8 21 | 21 | 11 | 16 | 15 |
| 21 | 6 | 8 11 | 11 | 16 | 11 | 11 |
| 11 | 7 | 8 16 | 16 | 10 | 10 | 10 |
| 16 | | | 8 | 8 | 8 | 8 |

**Figure 21-10** Values of the W array before sorting and after each pass through the sorting loop.

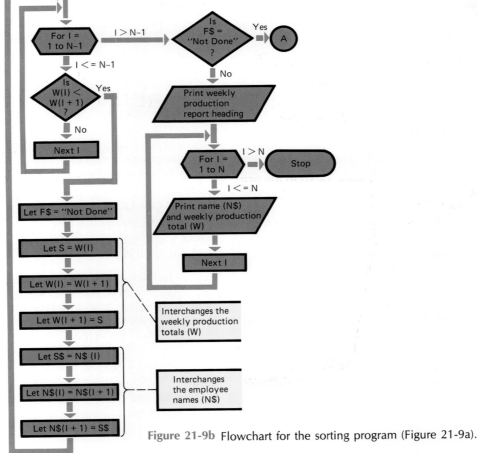

**Figure 21-9b** Flowchart for the sorting program (Figure 21-9a).

## Feedback and Review 21-3

We've seen that Kay prefers to have the weekly production report sorted in a descending order so that it will be easier to spot the top producers of tapes. But what if Rob wants a report in an ascending sequence (the smallest weekly production total is printed first and the largest total is printed last) so that the "laggards" are prominently displayed at the top of the report?

**1.** How would you modify the program in Figure 21-9a so that the output is sorted in an ascending order?

**2.** Using the same input data shown in Figure 21-9a, how many sorting passes would be needed to place the largest value of 25 at the bottom of the W array?

# SOME ADDITIONAL BASIC STATEMENTS

There are many statements included in the BASIC language that we haven't discussed so far in this book. A few of these additional statements are summarized here.

### MAT Statements
The word *matrix* is another term for a list or a table of data elements, and some BASIC dialects have a number of **MATrix statements** to carry out array activities. For example, this statement

```
150   MAT A = ZER
```

stores zeros in all the elements of an array named A. And these line numbers

```
100   DIM A(2,2)
110   MAT READ A
120   DATA 15.00, 6.25, 8.00, 5.00
```

will read the data items indicated into a two-dimensional array named A. Thus, the element in A(1,1) is 15.00, the A(1,2) element is 6.25, and the A(2,1) and A(2,2) elements are 8.00 and 5.00.

The following statements will permit a user to interact with the program and enter data into a two-dimensional array from a keyboard:

```
100   DIM A(3,4)
110   MAT INPUT A
```

Of course, the first four data items entered must be in the proper row order. That is, they must be the elements in the first row of the array. The next four elements must be those in the second row, and so on.

Finally,

```
200   MAT PRINT A
```

will print the elements in the array in a row order. Although these and other MAT statements are very convenient, they are not available for use with many popular personal computers.

### ON GOTO Statement
This statement serves as a multiway branching instruction. In this example,

```
100   ON B GOTO 150, 180, 210
```

if the variable name B has a value of 1, program control is transferred to ln 150. If the value of B is 2, program control branches to ln 180. And control goes to ln 210 if B equals 3. There could have been additional line numbers specified in our example statement to accommodate B values of 4, 5, etc. If B isn't one of the values provided for, control may move to the next executeable statement in the program sequence or an error message may be printed.

The **ON GOTO statement** is useful in routing program control to different parts of a program in response to a user's selection of option 1, 2, 3, 4, etc. in a menu of possible alternatives. Thus, this program segment

```
100   PRINT "ENTER 1 TO COMPUTE TEE SHIRT SALES"
110   PRINT "ENTER 2 TO COMPUTE MOSQUITO BIRD R SALES"
120   PRINT "ENTER 3 TO COMPUTE MOSQUITO BIRD T SALES"
130   PRINT "WHAT IS YOUR SELECTION";
140   INPUT C
150   ON C GOTO 200, 300, 400
         .
         .
```

will enable the R-K partners to choose the part of a program they wish to have executed.

## GOSUB/RETURN Statements

The **GOSUB** and **RETURN statements** are used to (1) transfer control from the main program sequence to a subroutine, and to then (2) return program control back to the main program location after the subroutine has been executed. For example,

```
100   GOSUB 450
110      .
120      .

450   LET A = B + C
460      .
470      .
480      .
500   RETURN
```

In 100 transfers program control to the subroutine beginning in In 450. After the steps in this subroutine are executed, control is returned from In 500 to In 110 in the main program.

GOSUB and RETURN statements are often used by professional programmers who work in a structured programming environment, and who prefer to follow the "top-down" approach (discussed in Chapters 12 and 19) to identify a main function and to then break it down into lower-level modules or subroutines for analysis and program design purposes.

## RESTORE Statement

As you know, when the first READ statement is encountered in a BASIC program, the computer looks for the first DATA statement and assigns the first data value(s) it finds in the DATA statement to the variable(s) specified in the READ statement. And subsequent READ statements "use up" the values found in the later DATA statements. But it's sometimes desirable to *reuse* the same data items several times during the execution of a program. When this is the case, duplicate DATA statements *could* be entered on different lines as needed. But there's an easier way.

The **RESTORE statement** can be used to reset the internal data pointer to the *first item* found in the *first DATA statement* in the program. Thus, when the READ statements following the RESTORE statement are encountered, the computer reassigns the data values beginning with the first DATA statement.

In this program segment, for example,

```
110   READ N$, R
         .
         .
         .
430   RESTORE
435   READ P$, X
         .
         .
         .
620   DATA "ROB BROOKS", 25
         .
         .
```

the first READ statement in In 110 looks to the first DATA statement in In 620 and assigns "ROB BROOKS" to the variable named N$, and 25 to the location named R. Later in the program, the RESTORE statement is used to reset the internal data pointer once again to the DATA statement in In 620. Then "ROB BROOKS" and 25 are reassigned by In 435, but this time to the variable names P$ and X.

## IF-THEN-ELSE Statement

Many newer versions of BASIC have an **IF-THEN-ELSE statement** to facilitate the use of a selection structure in solving problems. (See the discussion of structured logic patterns and structured pseudocode in Chapter 18.)

If the following statement is encountered

```
220   IF J = N THEN LET B = 20   ELSE LET B = 10
```

the action to be selected is determined by the condition following the IF part of the statement. If the condition is *true*—i.e., if J *does* equal N—then the computer carries out the activity prescribed by the THEN part of the statement (LET B = 20). But if the condition is *false,* then the computer selects and processes the ELSE part of the statement (LET B = 10). In this example, program control will move to the next line number in sequence after B is set to either 20 or 10.

## WHILE/WEND Statements

Newer versions of BASIC may also incorporate **WHILE** and **WEND statements** to control loops. These statements make it possible to process the DOWHILE loop structure discussed in the structured logic patterns and structured pseudocode sections of Chapter 18. For example,

```
360    WHILE Q <> −99.9
370      LET A = Q*P
380      LET T = A + T
390      PRINT P$,P,Q,A
400      READ P$,Q,P
410    WEND
```

A DOWHILE loop structure is established by the WHILE statement in ln 360. Such a loop must always end with a WEND (While END) statement (ln 410). The steps to be processed within the loop are located between the WHILE and WEND statements (ln 370 through ln 400 in our example). The condition expressed in the WHILE statement may be any condition that's valid in an IF statement.

In our example, the condition is that Q isn't equal to −99.9—i.e., it is < or > −99.9. Assuming that this condition is true when program control passes to ln 360, the steps in ln 370 through 400 are executed. When the WEND statement in ln 410 is encountered, control then branches back to ln 360 and another test of the WHILE condition is made. This looping process will continue until the WHILE condition becomes false—i.e., until Q = −99.9. Program control then exits the loop and goes to the first instruction following the WEND statement.

## A Final Sad Note

They said it couldn't be done
So he went right to it.
He took that thing that couldn't
be done. . . .
And couldn't do it.

You may recall that some distressing figures were revealed in the R-K Enterprises' inventory control report shown back in Figure 20-14, page 575. For one thing, there's a great demand for "Kay Oss in Concert" records and tapes, but R-K Enterprises has none in stock. The report shows a severe "backorder" condition for these products. Even more distressing is the fact that a huge inventory of the *Oh What?* book of poems written by Rob's English teacher, Ms. Fitt, is available, but absolutely no one is buying it. Since you've now examined the "Lord Byron" poetry generator, you *know* why the book isn't selling. But Rob cannot understand this lack of market interest. After all, Ms. Fitt is noted for her motto of "Write it right, write it good." Thus, we have this tragic situation: The R-K products in demand cannot be reordered because all the partners' capital is tied up in a bomb of a book that Rob has published. And so, like this chapter, R-K Enterprises has come to an end. We won't have Rob and Kay to kick around anymore.

 **LOOKING BACK**

**1.** We've considered several example programs that show additional features of the BASIC language in this chapter. Some new programming techniques—e.g., using arrays and sorting data—have also been demonstrated. We've reviewed loops and seen how one or more inner FOR . . . NEXT loops may be nested within the body of an outer FOR . . . NEXT loop. And we've seen how preprogrammed library functions such as SQR, INT, and RND may be called up and used in BASIC programs.

**2.** An array is a collection of data items or elements that are generally related in some way and are stored in a computer under a common array name. A one-dimensional array consists of a single list of items, and only a single subscript is needed to identify a particular item. A two-dimensional array, on the other hand, consists of data arranged in columns and rows. An item in an array with three columns and two rows is identified by the array name and two subscripts. Thus, N(1,2) identifies the item located in row 1 and column 2 of the N array. Example programs have been presented to show you how to enter alphanumeric data into one- and two-dimensional arrays with the help of DIM statements, how to call up and manipulate array elements during processing, and how to print the contents of arrays.

**3.** An example program that uses the bubble sort technique has also been presented. A bubble sort approach compares two adjacent elements in an array and then immediately interchanges them if they aren't in the desired ascending or descending sequence.

**4.** Finally, a few additional BASIC statements (MAT, ON . . GOTO, GOSUB/RETURN, RESTORE, IF-THEN-ELSE, and WHILE/WEND) are briefly summarized in the last section of the chapter.

## KEY TERMS AND CONCEPTS

inner loop 589
outer loop 589
nested FOR . . . NEXT loops 589
crossed loops 589
library functions 590
SQR function 590
economic order quantity (EOQ) 590

INT function 590
RND function 590
array 595
one-dimensional array 595
array name 596
DIM statement 597
two-dimensional array 606
sorting 611

bubble sort approach 611
MATrix statements 616
ON . . GOTO statement 617
GOSUB/RETURN statements 617
RESTORE statement 617
IF-THEN-ELSE statement 618
WHILE/WEND statements 618

## TOPICS FOR REVIEW AND DISCUSSION

**1.** "It's common to find one or more nested FOR . . . NEXT loops within the range of an outer FOR . . . NEXT structure." What is meant by the term "nested loop"?

**2.** In the following program segment,

```
180   FOR M = 1 TO 10
190      FOR N = 1 TO 5
         .
         .
         .
220      NEXT N
240   NEXT M
```

how many times will the N loop be executed?

**3.** (a) Is it necessary to indent the inner loops in a nested structure? (b) Is it desirable to indent the inner loops? Why or why not?

**4.** (a) What is a BASIC library function? (b) Give three examples of these functions and explain the purpose of each.

**5.** (a) What is an array? (b) How are arrays named?

**6.** (a) What is a one-dimensional array? (b) What is a two-dimensional array?

**7.** (a) How may data be entered into arrays? (b) How may arrayed data be printed?

**8.** Explain the purpose of this line in a BASIC program:

```
80   DIM  N$(8), M(8), W(8,4)
```

**9.** "Since the BASIC interpreter or compiler will usually contain instructions that will automatically provide storage space for arrays, the use of the DIM statement is generally a waste of time." Discuss this sentence.

**10.** Why must computers be able to sort data into predetermined sequences?

**11.** (a) What approach is followed when the bubble sort technique is used to place data items in a predetermined sequence? (b) How does this technique get its name?

**12.** When the bubble sort approach is used, what's the maximum number of sorting passes that would be needed before eight items are put in a descending sequence?

**13.** Summarize some of the functions of the following BASIC statements: MAT statements; ON . . GOTO statement; GOSUB/RETURN statements; RESTORE statement; IF-THEN-ELSE statement; WHILE/WEND statements.

**14.** After reviewing the "Lord Byron" poetry generator in Figure 21-6a, write your own version (a "William Shakespeare"?) to produce four-line masterpieces.

**15.** Write a program that (1) uses INPUT statements to receive data, and (2) employs the SQR function to produce the following economic order quantity results: (Hint: see "The SQR Function" section in the chapter.)

```
RUN

QUANTITY OF INVENTORY REQUIRED FOR PERIOD? 12000
COST OF PLACING ONE ORDER? 300
UNIT COST OF ITEM? 100
INVENTORY CARRYING COST FOR ITEM FOR PERIOD? 10

          EOQ OUTPUT

ECONOMIC ORDER QUANTITY = 848.528
MORE DATA(YES,NO)?
```

**16.** The R-K partners have developed an "Accounts Payable" program to help them determine their weekly cash requirements. By promptly paying their bills, the partners are able to take advantage of the 2 percent discounts offered by their creditors. The output of this Accounts Payable program for a recent week is shown below. Write a program that will accept as input the data in the first four columns of this report (pay date, vendor name, invoice number, and gross amount), and will then generate output results that are similar to those in the table below.

R-K ENTERPRISES
ACCOUNTS PAYABLE REPORT
CASH REQUIREMENTS FOR WEEK

| PAY DATE | VENDOR NAME | INVOICE NUMBER | GROSS AMOUNT | DISCOUNT AMOUNT | PAY AMOUNT |
|---|---|---|---|---|---|
| 6/06 | SPEAR SHIRT CO. | 12615 | 424 | 8.48 | 415.52 |
| 6/07 | BLACK PUBLISHERS | 6010 | 649.49 | 12.9898 | 636.5 |
| 6/07 | FIDELITY RECORDS | 616 | 886.44 | 17.7288 | 868.711 |
| 6/08 | METRO TRUCK LINES | 68660 | 191.12 | 3.8224 | 187.298 |
| 6/10 | LONGHORN NEWS | 181 | 24.95 | .499 | 24.451 |

TOTAL DUE FOR WEEK 2132.48

**17.** Modify the program produced in question 16 above by using the INT function to round the discount amount computed to the nearest cent.

**18.** The Monthly Production Report for R-K Enterprises that was introduced in Feedback and Review 21-2 is a monthly summary of the Weekly Production Report shown in Figure 21-8. After reviewing Figure 21-8 and the program segment shown in Feedback and Review 21-2, prepare a program that will produce the Monthly Production output shown in Feedback and Review 21-2.

**19.** Modify the Monthly Production Report program prepared for question 18 above so that the monthly production total is sorted into a descending order as shown below:

| NAME | W1 | W2 | W3 | W4 | TOTAL |
|---|---|---|---|---|---|
| L. LONDON | 21 | 24 | 22 | 29 | 96 |
| K. KARR | 25 | 22 | 27 | 19 | 93 |
| D. GARCIA | 21 | 25 | 19 | 22 | 87 |
| J. TAYLOR | 16 | 22 | 19 | 25 | 82 |
| A. COLWELL | 15 | 18 | 16 | 21 | 70 |
| U. BROWN | 10 | 16 | 12 | 19 | 57 |
| A. MUNDAY | 11 | 9 | 13 | 16 | 49 |
| C. HEAD | 8 | 10 | 12 | 9 | 39 |

**20.** Let's suppose that the R-K partners are trying to select the fabric to use for their next batch of tee shirts. They decide to conduct a marketing survey with some sample shirts made of five fabrics—silk, wool, cotton, nylon, and burlap. They ask some student friends to try the shirts and rank them in order of preference from 1 to 5. The input data for a "marketing survey" program is shown below. (The numbers refer to the rankings of the materials in the order mentioned above—i.e, the first number is for the ranking of silk, the second is for wool, and so on.)

```
1260   REM *SURVEY DATA
1280      DATA "U. BROWN    ",1,2,3,4,5
1300      DATA "A. COLWELL   ",4,2,1,5,3
1320      DATA "D. GARCIA    ",2,3,1,5,4
1340      DATA "C. HEAD      ",1,3,2,4,5
1360      DATA "K. KARR      ",3,5,4,1,2
1380      DATA "L. LONDON    ",5,3,1,2,4
1400      DATA "A. MUNDAY    ",3,5,1,2,4
1420      DATA "J. TAYLOR    ",5,4,3,2,1
1440      DATA "END OF DATA",0,0,0,0,0
```

Using the input values given, prepare a marketing survey program to produce the following output:

R-K ENTERPRISES
MARKETING SURVEY

RANKING BY FIRST PREFERENCE

| | |
|---|---|
| SILK | 2 |
| WOOL | 0 |
| COTTON | 4 |
| NYLON | 1 |
| BURLAP | 1 |

**21.** Since the output for the program prepared in question 20 above lists the "first place" votes but doesn't give an overall ranking, the R-K partners feel that it would be better if the program gave an overall ranking value to each fabric. They thus decided to assign a value of 5 to each first choice, 4 to each second choice, 3 to a third choice, and so on. Using the same input data found in question 20, modify the program prepared for question 20 so that it produces the following output results:

R-K ENTERPRISES
MARKETING SURVEY

RANKING BY FIRST PREFERENCE

| | |
|---|---|
| SILK | 2 |
| WOOL | 0 |
| COTTON | 4 |
| NYLON | 1 |
| BURLAP | 1 |

OVERALL RANKING

| | |
|---|---|
| SILK | 24 |
| WOOL | 21 |
| COTTON | 32 |
| NYLON | 23 |
| BURLAP | 20 |

# ANSWERS TO FEEDBACK AND REVIEW SECTIONS

**21-1**

Line 80 sets up two one-dimensional arrays named N$ and W, and reserves storage space for eight items in each of these arrays. Line 100 reads the number of production workers (N) from a DATA statement located later in the program. As you can see from the output, the value of N is 8 for this period. The FOR . . . NEXT loop in lines 120–140 is used to load the N$ and W arrays with data taken from later DATA statements. In the first pass through this loop, the first employee name (N$) encountered in a DATA statement (we see it's "U. BROWN" from the output) is assigned to storage location N$(1), and the first weekly production total found in a DATA statement (we can see that it's 10) is assigned to storage location W(1) in the W array. This process continues until the other names and production totals are loaded into the N$ and W arrays. By the way, this segment comes from Figure 21-8, a program considered later in the chapter.

**21-2**

Line 80 sets up two one-dimensional arrays named N$ and M, and reserves storage space for eight elements in each of these arrays. A two-dimensional array (W) is also specified for a table with eight rows and four columns (see output). Line 100 reads the number of production workers (N) from a later DATA statement. The FOR . . . NEXT loop in lines 120–140 is used to load the N$ and W arrays with data items found in later DATA statements. For example, if ln 130 reads the following DATA line

600   DATA "U. BROWN ", 10,16,12,19

it will assign U. BROWN to N$(1), 10 to W(1,1), 16 to W(1,2), 12 to W(1,3), and 19 to W(1,4). This process continues in lines 120–140 until the other names and production figures are loaded into the N$ and W arrays. As you can see in the output, the program later adds these weekly production figures to produce a monthly total. (One of the questions at the end of the chapter asks you to complete the program steps needed to produce the output shown.)

**21-3**

1. A small portion of the modified version of Figure 21-9a that produces a production report sorted in an ascending order is shown below. The output of this version is also presented. To save you some eye strain, look at ln 300 in this program. In Figure 21-9a, this line was

300   IF W(I)<W(I+1) THEN 330

And in the modified version this line is

300   IF W(I)>W(I+1) THEN 330

That's it. Changing < to > is all it takes to convert the sorting program from a descending order to an ascending sequence.

2. After the first sorting pass, the item with the largest value will always be in the last position in an ascending sequence.

```
            .
            .
            .
280 REM *EXAMINE DATA TO SEE IF THEY ARE IN ORDER
290        FOR I=1 TO N-1
300        IF W(I)>W(I+1) THEN 330
310        GOTO 490
            .
            .
            .
```

A partial computer listing of the program

```
RUN


                        WEEKLY PRODUCTION
EMPLOYEE NAME                 TOTAL
-------------           -----------------
C. HEAD                        8
U. BROWN                      10
A. MUNDAY                     11
A. COLWELL                    15
J. TAYLOR                     16
D. GARCIA                     21
L. LONDON                     21
K. KARR                       25
READY
>
```

Output produced by the computer as the program is executed

# "Computer People": Yes, They Really Are Different

Computer people, for the most part, can be quite different from corporate managers. A Columbia University study sponsored by BUSINESS WEEK reports that the innovative specialists who help companies develop and use their computer systems effectively often bring to their jobs different work standards, definitions of status, and criteria for success than those of most managers.

Columbia researchers surveyed 117 managers and 624 computer specialists—including hardware designers, software designers, and corporate management information systems and data processing employees—at 10 companies. These companies, which participated on the condition that they would not be identified, included four computer companies, four manufacturers, one insurance company, and a financial services company. Eight of the 10 are among the 500 largest U.S. corporations.

"Overall, the respondents were a well-educated, rather young sample of fairly recent entrants into the labor force," notes Laurie M. Roth, the research associate who completed the study last year at the Center for Research in Career Development at Columbia's Graduate School of Business. About 40% of those who participated were 33 years old or younger, and the same percentage reported less than six years of work experience. "Many of the computer professionals who have recently entered the work force are part of the post-World War II baby boom and have been educated and socialized in an affluent society," Roth notes. As a result, she says, computer people "tend to have acquired especially high expectations for meaningful work and job satisfaction, which are often not met by the traditional opportunity structures within companies."

In some respects, technical computer people and managers are alike. For instance, in rating the factors that led them to take their first jobs with their current employers, both groups said they were primarily motivated by "the opportunity to learn new skills, use more skills, and advance one's career." Less important were "better hours and working conditions and job title."

But the differences between the two groups show up in the relative degree of importance that each placed on the various factors. While 83% of the managers rated "responsibility" as very important, only 51% of the computer professionals gave it such a high ranking. On the other hand, 81% of the computer people said that "opportunity to learn new skills" was very important, compared with 63% of the managers.

## 'DUAL LADDER'

The differences were especially striking between computer people and managers from noncomputer companies. That was the only group in which a majority—70%—rated salary as very important. This managerial group was also much more likely than all others to rate "job title" as very important, suggesting that they were more interested than the other groups in classic bureaucratic rewards.

"The implications for recruiting computer specialist talent is clear," Roth says. "Organizations that solely depend on the more traditional rewards of pay, title, and promotion to attract computer specialists are overlooking one critical ingredient: these professionals' desire to develop their specialist skills with challenging work."

Overall, the respondents expressed a good deal of satisfaction with their jobs. But they were not as optimistic about their chances for advancement inside their companies as they were on the outside. Perhaps as a result, a "rather substantial minority"—27%—said that they would probably look for a job next year.

The survey findings support a solution already adopted by some companies: the creation of separate but equally respected career paths and reward systems for technical specialists and managers, Roth says. Such a "dual ladder" approach provides for "alternative definitions of career success for different employee groups," she says. That "should be basic to managerial philosophy and practice in companies that must manage technical and/or professional people."

—"When Money and Rank Are Not Enough," *Business Week,* Feb. 20, 1984, p. 72. Reprinted by special permission, © 1984 by McGraw-Hill, Inc., New York, NY. All rights reserved.

# GLOSSARY

The communication of facts and ideas in any field is dependent on a mutual understanding of the words used. The purpose of this section, then, is to present definitions for some of the terms that are often used in the field of computers and data processing.

**access**  To locate the desired data. See *direct-access, random access, remote access, serial access*.

**access time**  The elapsed time between the instant when data are called for from a storage device and the instant when the delivery operation is completed.

**accumulator**  A register or storage location that forms the result of an arithmetic or logic operation.

**ACM**  Acronym for Association for Computing Machinery, a professional group dedicated to advancing the design, development, and application of information processing.

**acoustic coupler**  A type of modem which permits data communication over regular telephone lines by means of sound signals.

**acronym**  A word formed from the first letter(s) of the words contained in a phrase or name.

**Ada**  A high-level programming language developed by the Department of Defense for use in military systems.

**address**  An identification (e.g., a label, name, or number) that designates a particular location in storage or any other data destination or source.

**ADP**  Automatic Data Processing.

**ALGOL**  (ALGOrithmic Language)  An algebraic, high-level language similar to FORTRAN that is widely used in Europe.

**algorithm**  A set of well-defined rules for solving a problem in a finite number of operations.

**alphanumeric**  Pertaining to a character set that includes letters, digits, and, usually, other special punctuation character marks.

**analog computer**  A device that operates on data in the form of continuously variable physical quantities.

**analyst**  See *system analyst*.

**annotation symbol**  A symbol used to add messages or notes to a flowchart.

**ANSI**  (American National Standards Institute)  An organization that develops and approves standards in many fields.

**APL**  (A Programming Language)  A mathematically oriented high-level language frequently used in timesharing.

**application program**  Software designed for a specific purpose (such as accounts receivable, billing, or inventory control).

**architecture**  The organization and interconnection of computer system components.

**arithmetic-logic unit**  The part of a computing system containing the circuitry that does the adding, subtracting, multiplying, dividing, and comparing.

**artificial intelligence** (AI)  A computer science branch that's involved with using computers to solve problems that appear to require human imagination or intelligence.

**ASCII**  (American National Standard Code for Information Interchange)  A standard code used to exchange information among data processing and communications systems.

**assembler program**  A computer program that takes nonmachine-language instructions prepared by a programmer and converts them into a form that may be used by the computer.

**assembly language**  A means of communicating with a computer at a low level. This language lies between high-level languages (such as BASIC and COBOL) and machine language (the 1s and 0s the computer understands).

**automated office**  A general term that refers to the merger of computers, office electronic devices, and telecommunications technology in an office environment.

**auxiliary storage**  A storage that supplements the primary internal storage of a computer. Often referred to as *secondary storage*.

**back-end processor**  A computer that serves as an interface between a larger CPU and data bases stored on direct-access storage devices.

**background processing**  The automatic execution of lower-priority (background) computer programs during periods when the system resources are not required to process higher-priority (foreground) programs.

**backup**  Alternate programs or equipment used in case the original is incapacitated.

**bank switched memory**  The use of software-controlled switches that allow a central processor to switch between memory locations in primary and supplementary memory banks so that the apparent size of primary storage is increased.

**BASIC**  (Beginners All-Purpose Symbolic Instruction Code)  A high-level interactive programming language frequently used with personal computers and in timesharing environments.

**batch processing**  A technique in which a number of similar items or transactions to be processed are grouped (batched) and processed in a designated sequence during a machine run. Often referred to as *sequential processing*.

**baud**  A unit for measuring data transmission speed.

**BCD**(Binary-Coded Decimal)  A method of representing the decimal digits zero through nine by a pattern of binary ones and zeros (e.g., the decimal number 25 is represented by 0010 0101 in 8-4-2-1 BCD notation).

**binary digit**  Either of the characters 0 or 1. Abbreviated ''bit.''

**binary number system**  A number system with a base or radix of two.

**bit**  See *binary digit*.

**block**  Related records, characters, or digits that are grouped and handled as a unit during input and output. A section of program coding treated as a unit.

**branch**  An instruction that transfers program control to one or more possible paths.

**broadband channels**  Communications channels such as those made possible by the use of laser beams and microwaves that can transmit data at high speed.

**buffer**  A storage device used to compensate for the difference in rates of flow of data from one device to another—e.g., from an I/O device to the CPU.

**bug**  An error in a system or program.

**bus**  Circuits that provide a communication path between two or more devices, such as between a CPU, storage, and peripherals.

**byte**  A group of adjacent bits, usually eight, operated on as a unit.

**cache**  A very high speed storage device.

**CAD/CAM** (Computer-Aided Design/Computer-Aided Manufacturing)  A general term applied to the efforts being made to automate design and manufacturing operations.

**CAI** (Computer-Assisted Instruction)  A general term that refers to a learning situation in which the student interacts with (and is guided by) a computer through a course of study aimed at achieving certain instructional goals.

**call**  A transfer of program control to a subroutine.

**canned programs**  Programs prepared by an outside supplier and provided to a user in a machine-readable form.

**cathode ray tube**(CRT)  An electronic tube with a screen upon which information may be displayed.

**central processing unit** (CPU)  The component of a computer system with the circuitry to control the interpretation and execution of instructions. The CPU includes primary storage, arithmetic-logic, and control sections.

**channel**  (1) A path for carrying signals between a source and a destination. (2) A track on a magnetic tape or a band on a magnetic drum.

**character string**  A string of alphanumeric characters.

**chip**  A thin wafer of silicon on which integrated electronic components are deposited.

**clock**  A device that generates the periodic signals used to control the timing of all CPU operations.

**COBOL** (COmmon Business-Oriented Language)  A high-level language developed for business data processing applications.

**code**  A set of rules outlining the way in which data may be represented; also, rules used to convert data from one representation to another. To write a program or routine.

**collate**  To combine items from two or more sequenced files into a single one.

**COM** (Computer Output Microfilm)  A technology that permits the output information produced by computers to be stored on microfilm.

**common carrier**  A government-regulated organization that provides public communications services.

**communications channel**  A medium for transferring data from one location to another.

**compiler**  A computer program that produces a machine-language program from a source program that's usually written in a high-level language by a programmer. The compiler is capable of replacing single source program statements with a series of machine-language instructions or with a subroutine.

**computer**  An electronic symbol manipulating system that's designed and organized to automatically accept and store input data, process them, and produce output results under the direction of a detailed step-by-step stored program of instructions.

**computer network**  A processing complex consisting of two or more interconnected computers.

**computer operator**  One whose duties include setting up the processor and peripheral equipment, starting the program run, checking on processor operation, and unloading equipment at the end of a run.

**concentrator**  A communications device that receives input from many low-speed lines and then concentrates and transmits a compressed and smooth stream of data on a higher-speed and more efficient transmission channel. Multiplexers also perform this function.

**conditional transfer**  An instruction that may cause a departure from the sequence of instructions being followed, depending upon the result of an operation, the contents of a register, or the setting of an indicator.

**connector symbol**  Used in a flowchart to represent a junction in a flow line, this symbol is often used to transfer flow between pages of a lengthy chart.

**console**  The part of a computer system that enables human operators to communicate with the computer.

**constant**  A value that doesn't change during program execution.

**control program**  Generally part of an operating system, this program helps control the operations and management of a computer system.

**control unit** The section of the CPU that selects, interprets, and sees to the execution of program instructions.

**counter** A device (e.g., a register) used to represent the number of occurrences of an event.

**CPU** See *central processing unit*.

**crash** A hardware or software failure that leads to an abnormal cessation of processing.

**CRT** See *cathode ray tube*.

**cursor** A symbol on a visual display screen that highlights the location(s) to be affected by the next character or command that is entered.

**cybernetics** The branch of learning which seeks to integrate the theories and studies of communication and control in machines and living organisms.

**cylinder** All tracks on magnetic disks that are accessible by a single movement of the access mechanism.

**DASD** Acronym for Direct-Access Storage Device.

**data** Facts; the raw material of information.

**data bank** See *data base*.

**data base** A stored collection of the libraries of data that are needed by organizations and individuals to meet their information processing and retrieval requirements.

**data base administrator** The one responsible for defining, updating, and controlling access to a data base.

**data base management system** (DBMS) The comprehensive software system that builds, maintains, and provides access to a data base.

**data communications** The means and methods whereby data are transferred between processing sites.

**data entry operator** One who transcribes data into a form suitable for computer processing.

**data processing** One or more operations performed on data to achieve a desired objective.

**debug** To detect, locate, and remove errors in programs and/or malfunctions in equipment.

**decision support system** (DSS) A computer-based system that backs up and assists those engaged in planning and decision-making activities.

**decision symbol** This diamond-shaped symbol is used in flowcharts to indicate a choice or branch in the processing path.

**decision table** A programming analysis tool that shows all the conditions to be considered in a problem as well as the actions to be taken when a given set of conditions is present.

**diagnostics** Error messages printed by a computer to indicate system problems and improper program instructions.

**digital computer** A device that manipulates discrete data and performs arithmetic and logic operations on these data. Contrast with *analog computer*.

**digital PBX** A private branch exchange system that may be used to automatically manage thousands of communications lines without human assistance. Both voice and data transmissions can be handled simultaneously over telephone lines, and no modems are needed for local data exchanges.

**direct-access** Pertaining to storage devices where the time required to retrieve data is independent of the physical location of the data.

**disk** A revolving platter upon which data and programs are stored.

**disk pack** A removable direct-access storage medium containing multiple magnetic disks mounted vertically on a single shaft.

**diskette** A floppy disk. A low-cost magnetic medium used for I/O and secondary storage purposes.

**distributed data processing** (DDP) A general term describing the processing of a logically related set of information processing functions through the use of multiple, geo-

graphically separated, computing and communications devices.

**documentation** The preparation of documents, during system analysis and subsequent programming, that describe such things as the system, the programs prepared, and the changes made at later dates.

**DOUNTIL loop structure** A control structure in which one or more operations in a loop are repeated until a condition is found to be true, after which the exit path out of the loop is followed.

**DOWHILE loop structure** A control structure in which one or more operations in a loop are continued while a condition is true. When the condition becomes false, the exit path out of the loop is followed.

**downtime** The length of time a computer system is inoperative due to a malfunction.

**EBCDIC** (Extended Binary-Coded Decimal Interchange Code) An 8-bit code used to represent data in modern computers.

**edit** To correct, rearrange, and validate input data. To modify the form of output information by inserting blank spaces, special characters where needed, etc.

**editor** A program used to interactively review and alter text materials and other program instructions.

**EDP** Acronym for Electronic Data Processing.

**EEPROM** An electrically erasable and programmable read-only memory chip that can be reprogrammed with special electrical pulses.

**electronic funds transfer** (EFT) A general term referring to a cashless approach used to pay for goods and services. Electronic signals between computers are often used to adjust the accounts of the parties involved in a transaction.

**electronic mail** A general term to describe the transmission of messages by the use of computing systems and telecommunications facilities.

**electronic spreadsheet program** A software package that permits users to quickly create, manipulate, and analyze data organized in columns and rows.

**emulator** A stored logic device or program that permits one computer to execute the machine-language instructions of another computer of different design.

**EPROM** An erasable and programmable read-only memory chip that can be reprogrammed under limited conditions.

**executive routine** A master program in an operating system that controls the execution of other programs. Often referred to as the executive, monitor, or supervisor.

**executive workstation** Special desktop computer-based units designed for busy people who may not like to type. They have special function keys, and may accept input through the use of a mouse or a touch screen. They have the ability to perform word/data processing, manage data bases, produce graphics, and support many other activities.

**expert system** A software package that includes (1) a stored base of knowledge in a specialized area, and (2) the capability to probe this knowledge base and make decision recommendations. Expert systems are the products of research in the field of artificial intelligence.

**facsimile system** A system used to transmit pictures, text, maps, etc., between geographically separated points. An image is scanned at a transmitting point and duplicated at a receiving point.

**fiber-optic cable** A data transmission medium made of tiny threads of glass or plastic that is able to transmit huge amounts of information at the speed of light.

**field** A group of related characters treated as a unit—e.g., a group of adjacent card columns used to represent an hourly wage rate. An item in a record.

**file** A collection of related records treated as a unit.

**file processing** The updating of master files to reflect the effects of current transactions.

**floppy disk** See *diskette*.

**flowchart** A diagram that uses symbols and interconnecting lines to show (1) a system of processing to achieve objectives (system flowchart), or (2) the logic and sequence of specific program operations (program flowchart).

**FORTRAN** (FORmula TRANslator) A high-level language used to perform mathematical computations.

**front-end processor** A CPU programmed to function as an interface between a larger CPU and assorted peripheral devices.

**full-duplex transmission** The simultaneous sending and receiving of data over a communications path.

**generator** A computer program that constructs other programs to perform a particular type of operation—e.g., a report program generator.

**graphic display** A visual device that is used to project graphic images.

**half-duplex transmission** The sending and then receiving of data over a communications path during alternating periods of time. Data may not be sent in both directions at the same time.

**hard copy** Printed or filmed output in humanly readable form.

**hard disk** A rigid metal platter coated with a magnetizeable substance. Contrast with *floppy disk*.

**hardware** Physical equipment such as electronic, magnetic, and mechanical devices. Contrast with *software*.

**heuristic** A problem-solving method in which solutions are discovered by evaluating the progress made toward the end result. A directed trial-and-error approach. Contrast with *algorithm*.

**hierarchical data structure** A logical approach to structuring data in which a single-root data component or "parent" may have subordinate elements or "children," each of which, in turn, may "own" one or more other elements (or none). Each element or branch below the parent has only a single owner.

**high-level language** A programming language oriented toward the problem to be solved or the procedures to be used. Instructions are given to a computer by using convenient letters, symbols, or English-like text, rather than by using the 1s and 0s code that the computer understands.

**HIPO charts** (Hierarchy plus Input-Process-Output charts) Charts used in the analysis, design, and programming of computer applications.

**Hollerith Code** A particular type of code used to represent alphanumeric data on 80-column punched cards.

**host computer** A main control computer in a network of distributed processors and terminals.

**hybrid computer** A data processing device using both analog and discrete data representation.

**IF-THEN-ELSE selection structure** A basic program control structure that requires a test for some condition followed by two alternative program paths. The path selected depends on the results of the test.

**indexed sequential access method** See *ISAM*.

**information** Meaning assigned to data by humans.

**information retrieval** The methods used to recover specific information from stored data.

**input/output** (I/O) Pertaining to the techniques, media, and devices used to achieve human/machine communication.

**input/output symbol** A figure in the shape of a parallelogram that's used to indicate both input and output operations in a flowchart.

**instruction** A set of characters used to direct a data processing system in the performance of an operation—i.e., an operation is signaled and the values or locations of the instruction operands are specified.

**integrated software package** A software product that combines several applications—e.g., word processing, spreadsheet operations, the creation of graphs—into a single package so that it's possible to share data and move material among these functions.

**intelligent terminal**  A terminal with a built-in CPU that can be programmed to perform specific functions such as editing data, controlling other terminals, etc.

**interactive system**  One that permits direct communication and dialog between system users and the operating program in the CPU.

**interface**  A shared boundary—e.g., the boundary between two systems or devices.

**internal storage**  The addressable storage in a digital computer directly under the control of the CPU.

**interpreter**  A computer program that translates each source language statement into a sequence of machine instructions and then executes these machine instructions before translating the next source language statement. A device that prints on a punched card the data already punched in the card.

**I/O**  See *input/output.*

**ISAM**  (Indexed Sequential Access Method) A method whereby records organized in a sequential order can be referenced directly through the use of an index based on some key or characteristic.

**item**  A group of related characters treated as a unit. (A record is a group of related items, and a file is a group of related records.)

**job**  A collection of specific tasks constituting a unit of work for a computer.

**job-control language**  (JCL) A language that permits communication between programmers and an operating system. A job-control program written in this language can be translated into requests for action that can be executed by the computer.

**jump**  A departure from sequence in executing instructions in a computer. See *conditional transfer.*

**K**  An abbreviation for a value equal to $2^{10}$ or 1,024.

**key**  A unique item that's used to identify a record.

**label**  One or more characters used to identify a program statement or a data item.

**language**  A set of rules and conventions used to convey information.

**library routine**  A tested routine maintained in a library of programs.

**light pen**  An electrical device that permits people to provide input to computers by writing or sketching on the screen of a cathode ray tube.

**local area network**  (LAN) A privately owned communications system that links computers, terminals, word processing stations, and other devices located within a compact area such as an office building or a campus.

**logic diagram**  See *flowchart.*

**LSI**  (Large Scale Integration) The process of integrating a large number of electronic circuits on a single small chip of silicon or other material.

**machine language**  A language used directly by a computer.

**macro instruction**  A source language instruction that's equivalent to a specified number of machine-language instructions.

**magnetic ink character recognition**  (MICR) The recognition of characters printed with a special magnetic ink by machines.

**magnetic storage**  Utilizing the magnetic properties of materials to store data on such devices and media as disks, drums, cards, cores, tapes, chips, and films.

**main control module**  The highest level in a hierarchy of program modules. This module controls others below it.

**mainframe**  A large computer system that has the capability to support many powerful peripheral devices.

**maintenance programming**  The act of changing and modifying existing programs to meet changing conditions.

**management information system**  (MIS) A computer-based information system de-signed to supply organizational managers with the necessary information needed to plan, organize, staff, direct, and control the operations of the organization.

**master file**  A file containing relatively permanent data. This file is often updated by records in a transaction file.

**memory**  Same as *storage.*

**menu**  A set of programmed choices provided to a computer user.

**message switcher**  A communications processor that receives messages and forwards them to appropriate locations.

**MICR**  See *magnetic ink character recognition.*

**microcomputer**  The smallest category of computer, consisting of a microprocessor and associated storage and input/output elements.

**microfiche**  A sheet of film (usually 4 by 6 inches) that may be used to record the results of computer processing.

**microprocessor**  The basic arithmetic, logic, and storage elements required for processing (generally on one or a few integrated circuit chips).

**microprogram**  A sequence of elementary instructions that is translated by a micrologic subsystem residing in the CPU.

**microsecond**  One-millionth of a second.

**micro-to-mainframe linkage**  A hardware/ software product that permits communication between a mainframe system and the personal computer systems located on the desks of users.

**millisecond**  One-thousandth of a second.

**minicomputer**  A relatively fast but small and inexpensive computer with somewhat limited input/output capabilities.

**MIS**  See *management information system.*

**mnemonic**  Pertaining to a technique used to aid human memory.

**modem**  A device that modulates and demodulates signals transmitted over voice-grade communication facilities.

**modular approach** Dividing a project into segments and smaller units in order to simplify analysis, design, and programming efforts.

**monitor routine** See *executive routine.*

**mouse** An input device about the size of a tape cassette that rolls on a small bearing and has one or more buttons on the top. When rolled across a flat surface, the mouse guides the cursor on a visual display screen in the direction of the mouse's movement.

**multiplex** To simultaneously transmit messages over a single channel or other communications facility.

**multiplexer** A communications device that receives messages from low-speed lines and then sends these messages along a single high-speed transmission channel. Concentrators also perform this function.

**multiprocessing** The simultaneous execution of two or more sequences of instructions by a single computer network.

**multiprocessor** A computer network consisting of two or more central processors under a common control.

**multiprogramming** The simultaneous handling of multiple independent programs by interleaving or overlapping their execution.

**nanosecond** One-billionth of a second.

**narrow bandwidth channels** Communications channels that can only transmit data at slow speeds—e.g., telegraph channels.

**natural language** A human language such as English, French, German, etc.

**network** An interconnection of computer systems and/or peripheral devices at dispersed locations that exchange data as necessary to perform the functions of the network.

**network data structure** A logical approach to structuring data that permits network nodes to be connected in a multidirectional manner. Each node may have several "owners," and may, in turn, own any number of other data units.

**node** An end point of a branch in a net-work, or a common junction of two or more network branches.

**nonvolatile storage** A storage medium that retains its contents in the absence of power.

**object language** The output of a translation process. Contrast with *source language.*

**object program** A fully compiled or assembled program that's ready to be loaded into the computer. Contrast with *source program.*

**OCR** (Optical Character Recognition) The recognition of printed characters through the use of light-sensitive optical machines.

**octal** Pertaining to a number system with a base of eight.

**offline** A term describing persons, equipment, or devices not in direct communication with the CPU.

**off-page connector symbol** A flowchart symbol used to show that program flow is entering from or going to a separate flow-chart page.

**online** A term describing persons, equipment, or devices that are in direct communication with the CPU.

**operand** The data unit or equipment item that's operated upon. An operand is usually identified by an address in an instruction.

**operating system** An organized collection of software that controls the overall operations of a computer.

**operation code** The instruction code used to specify the operations a computer is to perform.

**overlapped processing** An approach that permits the computer to work on several programs instead of one.

**parallel interface** An electrical interconnection that permits 8 or more bits of data to be moved in the same instant in time. Contrast with *serial interface.*

**parity check** A method of checking the accuracy of binary data after those data have been transferred to or from storage. The number of 1 bits in a binary character is controlled by the addition or deletion of a parity bit.

**Pascal** A popular high-level programming language that facilitates the use of structured programming techniques.

**patch** The modification of a program in an expedient way.

**peripherals** The input/output devices and auxiliary storage units of a computer system.

**personal computer** (pc) A single-user-oriented and general-purpose microcomputer processing system that can execute program instructions to perform a wide variety of tasks.

**picosecond** One-thousandth of a nanosecond.

**pixel** A picture element on the screen of a visual display used for graphics work that is controlled by the contents of a specific location in storage. By turning each pixel on or off, the CPU is able to paint a graphic image.

**PL/I** (Programming Language I) A high-level language designed to process both scientific and file processing applications.

**plotter** A device that converts computer output into a graphic, hard-copy form.

**pointer** A data item in one record that contains the location address of another logically related record.

**point-of-sale (POS) terminal** An I/O device capable of (1) immediately updating sales and inventory records at a central CPU, and (2) producing a printed sales transaction receipt.

**port** An electrical interconnection. See *parallel interface, serial interface.*

**preparation symbol** A flowchart symbol used to indicate the control, initiation, or performance of some other operation on the program itself.

**primary storage section** Also known as *internal storage* and *main memory,* this section of the CPU holds program instructions, input data, intermediate results, and the output information produced during processing.

**printer** A device used to produce humanly readable computer output. A wide range of impact and nonimpact printers is currently available.

**processing symbol** A rectangular figure used in flowcharts to indicate a processing operation—e.g., a calculation.

**program** (1) A plan to achieve a problem solution; (2) to design, write, and test one or more routines; (3) a set of sequenced instructions to cause a computer to perform particular operations.

**program flowchart** See *flowchart*.

**program library** A collection of programs and routines.

**programmer** One who designs, writes, tests, and maintains computer programs.

**programming language** A language used to express programs.

**PROM** (Programmable Read-Only Memory) A read-only storage device that can be programmed after manufacture by external equipment. PROMs are usually integrated circuit chips.

**pseudocode** A programming analysis tool. Counterfeit and abbreviated versions of actual computer instructions that are written in ordinary natural language.

**radix** The base number in a number system—e.g., the radix in the decimal system is 10. Synonymous with base.

**RAM** (Random Access Memory) A storage device structured so that the time required to retrieve data is not significantly affected by the physical location of the data.

**random access** See *direct-access*.

**real time** Descriptive of online computer processing systems which receive and process data quickly enough to produce output to control, direct, or affect the outcome of an ongoing activity or process.

**record** A collection of related items of data treated as a unit.

**register** A device capable of storing a specific amount of data.

**relational data structure** An approach to structuring data in such a way that the logical relationships are represented in interrelated tables.

**relational symbols** Symbols such as > (''greater than''), < (''less than''), or = (''equal to'') that are used to compare two values in a conditional branching situation.

**remote access** Relating to the communication with a computer facility by a station (or stations) that is distant from the computer.

**report program generator** (RPG) Software designed to construct programs that perform predictable report-writing operations.

**robotics** The study of the technology of programmable manipulators that are designed to move materials, parts, tools, or other specialized devices through a series of programmed steps.

**ROM** (Read-Only Memory) Generally a solid-state storage chip that's programmed at the time of its manufacture and may not be reprogrammed by the computer user.

**routine** An ordered set of general-use instructions. See *program*.

**run time** The time required to complete a single, continuous execution of an object program.

**scratchpad storage** A memory space used for the temporary storage of data. Typically, scratchpad memories are high-speed integrated circuits. See *cache*.

**semiconductor storage** A memory device whose storage elements are formed as solid-state electronic components on an integrated circuit chip.

**sequential processing** See *batch processing*.

**serial access** Descriptive of a storage device or medium where there is a sequential relationship between access time and data location in storage—i.e., the access time is dependent upon the location of the data. Contrast with *direct-access* and *random access*.

**serial interface** An electrical interconnection that permits data to be moved one bit at a time over a single path. Contrast with *parallel interface*.

**simplex transmission** The movement of data along a path that permits communication in only one predetermined direction.

**simulation** To represent and analyze properties or behavior of a physical or hypothetical system by the behavior of a system model. (This model is often manipulated by means of computer operations.)

**software** A set of programs, documents, procedures, and routines associated with the operation of a computer system. Contrast with *hardware*.

**solid-state** Descriptive of electronic components whose operation depends on the control of electric or magnetic phenomena in solids, such as transistors and diodes.

**sort** To arrange data into a predetermined sequence.

**source language** The language that is an input for statement translation.

**source program** A computer program written in a source language such as BASIC, FORTRAN, COBOL, etc.

**spooler program** Software that allows the CPU to alternate between processing a user's ongoing activity and controlling another activity such as printing.

**spreadsheet program** See *electronic spreadsheet program*.

**statement** In programming, an expression or generalized instruction in a source language.

**storage** Descriptive of a device or medium that can accept data, hold them, and deliver them on demand at a later time. Synonymous with *memory*.

**structured programming** An approach or discipline used in the design and coding of computer programs. The approach generally assumes the disciplined use of a few basic coding structures and the use of top-down concepts to decompose main functions into lower-level components for modular coding purposes.

**supercomputer** Computer systems characterized by their very large size and very high processing speeds. Generally used for complex scientific applications.

**supervisor** See *executive routine.*

**system** (1) A grouping of integrated methods and procedures united to form an organized entity; (2) an organized grouping of people, methods, machines, and materials collected together to accomplish a set of specific objectives.

**system analysis** A detailed step-by-step investigation of related procedures to see what must be done and the best way of doing it.

**system analyst** One who studies the activities, methods, procedures, and techniques of organizational systems in order to determine what actions need to be taken and how these actions can best be accomplished.

**system commands** The means by which programmers communicate with the operating system of the computer.

**system design** The creation of alternative solutions to the problems uncovered in system analysis. The final design recommendation is based on cost effectiveness and other factors.

**system flowchart** See *flowchart.*

**systems programming** The development and maintenance of operating system software.

**telecommunications** Transmission of data between computer systems and/or terminals in different locations.

**telecommuting** Substituting work performed on computer-based workstations and telecommunications networks in homes and neighborhood work centers for tasks performed in central office locations.

**teleconferencing** The electronic linking of geographically scattered people who are all participating at the same time.

**terminal** A device that performs I/O operations in a computer system.

**terminal symbol** An oval-shaped figure used in a flowchart to indicate starting and termination points.

**throughput** The total amount of useful work performed by a computer system during a given time period.

**timesharing** The use of specific hardware by a number of other devices, programs, or people simultaneously in such a way as to provide quick response to each of the users. The interleaved use of the time of a device.

**top-down methodology** A disciplined approach to organizing complexity by identifying the top-level functions in a system and then decomposing these functions into a hierarchy of understandable lower-level modules.

**unconditional transfer** An instruction that always causes a branch in program control away from the normal sequence of executing instructions.

**UPC** (Universal Product Code) A machine-readable code of parallel bars used for labeling products found in supermarkets.

**user-friendly software** A phrase that presumably describes a program or system that people with limited computing backgrounds will find easy to learn and/or use.

**utility routine** Software used to perform some frequently required process in the operation of a computer system—e.g., sorting, merging, etc.

**value added network (VAN)** A communications network operated by an organization that leases the facilities of a common carrier and then offers additional services to its customers.

**videotex systems** A general term used to describe personal computing/communications networks that permit interaction between people and stored data bases.

**virtual storage** Descriptive of the capability to use online secondary storage devices and specialized software to divide programs into smaller segments for transmission to and from internal storage in order to significantly increase the effective size of the available internal storage.

**visual display terminal** A device capable of displaying keyed input and CPU output on a cathode ray tube.

**VLSI** (Very Large Scale Integration) The packing of hundreds of thousands of electronic components on a single semiconductor chip.

**voice-grade channels** Medium-speed data transmission channels that use telephone communications facilities.

**volatile storage** A storage medium that loses its contents in the event of a power interruption.

**von Neumann bottleneck** A reference to the fact that processing speed in a von Neumann machine is limited by the speed of (1) the circuits in the single channel used to carry instructions from primary storage to the control section, and (2) the circuits in the single data path between primary storage and the arithmetic-logic section.

**von Neumann machine** A computer system whose CPU has a single control, primary storage, and arithmetic-logic section. Such a machine follows the design approach developed by John von Neumann and others in the mid-1940s.

**Winchester technology** The name given to those types of rigid magnetic disk storage systems that are permanently housed (along with their access arms and read/write heads) in sealed, contamination-free containers. Winchester disk systems come in many sizes and storage capacities.

**window** A portion of the visual display screen used to show the current status of an application of interest. The display screen can be separated into several windows to simultaneously show the status of the different applications in an integrated software package.

**word** A group of bits or characters considered as an entity and capable of being stored in one storage location.

**word length** The number of characters or bits in a word.

**word processing** The use of computers to create, view, edit, store, retrieve, and print text material.

**zone bits** Used in different combinations with numeric bits to represent alphanumeric characters.

# Index

From the time of Marco Polo until the late eighteenth century the stability and wealth of the Chinese Empire were regarded with awe by the nation-states of Europe. When Marco Polo returned from his journey to the Far East in 1295 he described a place of mythic wealth, beauty, and harmony called Xanadu — the summer retreat of the Emperor of China, the Great Kublai Khan. The Empire of the Great Khan extended from the Mediterranean to the China Sea, and along the fabled Silk Road, European and Arab merchants shipped the exquisite products of Chinese civilization. Not only were China's luxury goods exported, but its technologies as well, for scientific discovery and technological innovation have long been regarded as the source of wealth and power.

*Roads to Xanadu* is a journey through world history that follows the different roads taken by nations to achieve wealth and power. It traces the differing roads of social and technological change that have been followed in east Asia and in the west. It looks at why technological innovations first developed in China should have had such different social and economic impacts when they were eventually taken up in Europe, and the different roads Japan and China were to take in the nineteenth and twentieth centuries as they attempted to come to terms with the threat of European imperialism.

# ROADS TO XANADU

### EAST AND WEST IN THE MAKING OF
### THE MODERN WORLD

# ROADS TO
# XANADU

Bodleian Library, Oxford

## EAST AND WEST IN THE MAKING OF
## THE MODERN WORLD

## JOHN MERSON

**Weidenfeld and Nicolson**
**London**

For Gwynedd, Emily & Francis

First published in Great Britain by
George Weidenfeld & Nicolson Limited
91 Clapham High Street, London SW4 7TA

© 1989 John Merson and Associates Pty Ltd

ISBN 0 297 79707 7

Produced by Weldon Owen Pty Limited
43 Victoria Street, McMahons Point NSW 2011, Australia
Telex 23038; Fax (02) 929 8352
A member of the Weldon International Group of Companies
Sydney • Hong Kong • London • Chicago • San Francisco

Printed in Australia by The Griffin Press

A Weldon Owen/ABC production

Endpapers: Chang Tse-Tuan, Chhing-Ming Shang Ho Thu (returning up the River to the City at the Spring Festival) (1125), Su Song scroll.

Page 2: Wang Hui (1632–1717) and his assistants, *From Tsinan to Tai-an, with Performance of Ceremony at Mount Tai.* (Detail no 4 "Arrival at Mount Tai.") Handscroll: The K'ang-hsi Emperor's Second Tour of the South. Scroll no.3 from series of 12. Ink and colors on silk, Ch'ing Dynasty (1691–98). The Metropolitan Museum of Art, Ourchasem The Dillon Fund Gift, 1979

Page 3: In response to China's growing wealth and power, the merchant-adventurer Marco Polo left his native Venice in the late thirteenth century and travelled to Kublai Khan's summer retreat, known in the west as Xanadu. Bodleian Library, Oxford

# CONTENTS

# PREFACE

During the past decade, some scholars and journalists have asked if the shift of economic power from the Atlantic to the Pacific would continue and would change the shape of the world in the twenty-first century. The question is not as speculative today as it was ten years ago. And thirty years ago, the question itself would have been considered absurd. But asking the question of the present will yield little profit if we do not go further and ask a few questions of the past, even though these may seem old, familiar ones. For example, why did a scientific civilization not emerge in the Pacific in the first place? After all, China had a brilliant start and remained creative for two thousand years. And why did this scientific revolution occur in a corner of Western Europe? That was a most remarkable circumstance, which made it possible for the west to transform and dominate the world. Yet, less than two centuries later, there are new questions about how long that dominance will last.

Of the old questions, one still baffles us. Why did China succumb so easily to the aggressive drives of the upstart powers of northwestern Europe in the nineteenth century? Another old question remains important. Why did Japan succeed in responding to the western challenge where China failed? Now, surprisingly, the question is, will China follow the rest of East Asia into new forms of capitalism, and will this usher in "the Pacific century" in a few decades' time?

John Merson has set out to bring both old and new questions together in a fresh way. He has asked similar questions before. As an experienced science journalist and historian he has personally pursued answers to these questions for several years. Those about China intrigued him most of all. They aroused his curiosity and led him, not only into China's scientific past, but also into history, culture and the nature of Chinese society. He produced a major series for the Australian Broadcasting Corporation and published a book, *Culture and Science in China,* in 1981. But China continued to change after 1981, so too did Japan's position as an economic superpower, and even more so the "four small dragons" of East Asia, which glowed like satellites around the brightest star. So questions were reframed and reexamined. Advances in the region's economy, and new attitudes in China towards science and progress were recorded on film. And, not least, John Merson wrote this book to capture his odyssey through world history and through the events that mark the latest shifts in technology and culture.

I have known John Merson for more than ten years. His keen and retentive mind, his infectious enthusiasm and his feel for the adventures in science that the Chinese people have experienced qualify him to tell this imaginative and fast-moving story. I commend this book to all who enjoy the sweep of history and love the juxtaposition of chance and genius, discovery and loss, catastrophe and rebirth that make the human condition so enduringly interesting. Today this story has become increasingly important.

WANG GUNGWU

Vice Chancellor
University of Hong Kong
September 1988

Unidentified artist, *Family Group,* Hanging scroll, colors on silk. Late Ming Dynasty (1368–1644).

The Metropolitan Museum of Art, Anonymous Gift, 1942

# INTRODUCTION

*In Xanadu did Kubla Khan*
*A stately pleasure-dome decree:*
*Where Alph, the sacred river, ran*
*Through caverns measureless to man*
*Down to a sunless sea.*
*So twice five miles of fertile ground*
*With walls and towers were girdled round:*
*And there were gardens bright with sinuous rills*
*Where blossom'd many an incense-bearing tree;*
*And here were forests ancient as the hills,*
*Enfolding sunny spots of greenery.*

Samuel Taylor Coleridge

On a summer evening in 1797 the English poet Samuel Coleridge took his regular draft of laudanum, a mixture of opium and alcohol. He had been reading of Kublai Khan and the palace he commanded to be built. In the drug-induced reverie that followed, he composed his poem on Xanadu (Shangdu), the summer retreat of the Emperor of China. First described by Marco Polo in his account of his journey to the Far East in the late thirteenth century, Xanadu became an ideal place of mythic wealth, beauty and harmony. Ironically, it was opium, smuggled illegally into China by the same European merchants who were supporting Coleridge's habit, that led in 1840 to a devastating war between Britain and China; a war in which the Chinese were to see the return, on board British gunboats, of gunpowder and the cannon, which they had invented a thousand years earlier, their destructive power now tempered and refined in the highly competitive industrial environment of nineteenth century Europe. The obvious superiority of British military technology revealed China's profound vulnerability and, by 1900, the Celestial Empire was in ruins.

In the thirteenth century, however, China was not only the richest and most powerful country in the world but, according to Marco Polo, the most civilized as well.

> ...equally opposite to preconceived ideas, was the polish, courtesy, and respectful familiarity, which distinguished their social intercourse. Quarrels, blows, combats, and bloodshed, then so frequent in Europe, were not witnessed, even amid their deepest potations. Honesty was everywhere conspicuous: their wagons and other property were secure without locks or guards. Notwithstanding the frequent scarcity of victuals, they were generous in relieving those in greater want than themselves.

From Marco Polo's time until the late eighteenth century the stability and wealth of the Chinese empire were regarded with awe and envy by the tiny nation-states of Europe. The empire of the Great Khan, which stretched from the Mediterranean to the China Sea, had enabled direct links to be made between the civilizations of the Far East and those of Europe. Along the fabled Silk Road and sea routes from the Persian Gulf, European and Arab merchants shipped the exquisite products of Chinese civilization. Silks and porcelain of such refinement that few, if any, European craftsman could match them until well into the eighteenth century. But China's influence on the development of Europe came not only from the export of luxury goods; its technology also had a profound influence.

In the sixteenth century the English philosopher and statesman Francis Bacon, reflecting on the forces that were transforming European society on the eve of the scientific and industrial revolutions, identified three inventions that he believed had changed the world — paper and printing, gunpowder and the compass. Paper and printing rapidly expanded access to scientific and technical knowledge. The compass enabled merchants to navigate the globe and to bring back to Europe the riches of the east. Gunpowder, and the arms race it spawned, allowed the highly competitive European nation-states to inflict their will upon the rest of the world. At the time when these key innovations were introduced in Europe, few Europeans had any idea that they had been invented in China, or that they had been in common use there for at least five hundred years. This raises some interesting questions. If these technologies were already available in China, why did the Chinese not sail their junks, bristling with guns, into European ports and demand trade? This they could easily have done in the early fifteenth century, for not only was the Chinese navy the largest in the world but China's trading and financial networks were as extensive as those of European merchants. The Chinese were trading with paper money as early as the eleventh century, using mechanical clockwork in the twelfth century, and spinning with water-power-driven machines in the fourteenth century. Yet these inventions did not have the significant social and economic impact in China that they later had in Europe.

In the modern industrialized world we have come to regard technological and social change as linear and driven by inexorable economic forces. Once an invention has proved its usefulness it will continue to develop irrespective of the cultural context. For example, the European matchlock rifle, introduced in Japan in the sixteenth century, was widely used and developed to a high level of technological sophistication; yet it had virtually disappeared from Japanese society by the early seventeenth century and did not reappear until the nineteenth century. Computer-controlled industrial technology and robotics were developed in the United States in the 1950s but this technology was taken up and developed more effectively by the Japanese in the 1960s and 1970s so that, by the 1980s, Japan had eclipsed the United States in key industrial fields to become one of the world's leading economic powers.

*Roads to Xanadu* explores why the full potential of scientific discovery and technological invention, now regarded as the source of wealth and power, is often not realized in its country of origin. The reason, paradoxically, lies not in failure but in success — in the tendency of cultures and civilizations to ossify around those economic institutions and ideologies that, at some stage, provided maximum stability and wealth. These institutional structures are often retained by bureaucracies and the power elites who are their beneficiaries long after they have become redundant. Economic growth and cultural development do not stem merely from technological innovation but from social and political change. However, the motivation for such change rarely comes from within. Often, it has been the competitive threat from outside that has forced societies to come up with new and innovative social, economic and political structures.

*Roads to Xanadu* is a journey through world history that follows the different roads taken by nations to achieve their wealth and power. It traces the transfer of technology, ideas and even social institutions from east to west and west to east. In the process it explores some of the reasons why the centers of economic power, intellectual creativity and technological innovation have shifted in the course of the last thousand years from China to Europe and the United States and now perhaps to Asia again .

JOHN MERSON
November 1988

9

U.S.S.R.

□ Urumqi

XINJIANG

PAKISTAN

KUNLUN MOUNTAINS

GANSU

QINGHAI

Xining □

Lanzhou

XIZANG

Nu Jiang
(Salween R.)

SICHUAN

Chengdu

□ Lhasa

NEPAL

BHUTAN

Zig

INDIA

BANGLADESH

Kunming

YUNNAN

BURMA

VIETN
(CHA

LAOS

One of the most important ritual functions of the emperors of China was to begin the agricultural year by turning the first sod of earth, as shown in this painting by Guiseppe Castiglione.

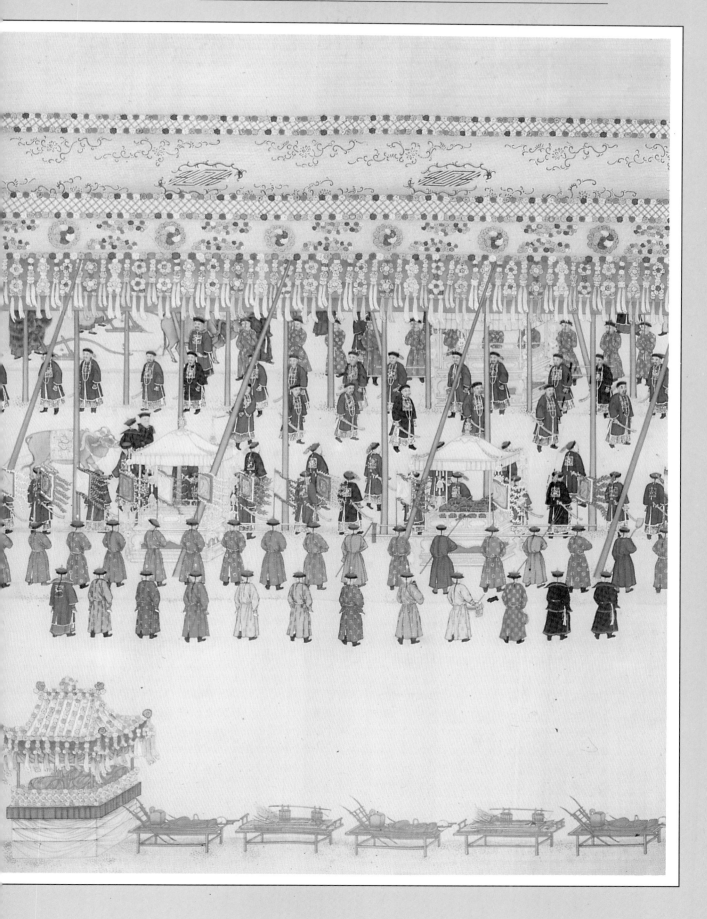

# THE CELESTIAL EMPIRE

*China is a sea that salts all rivers that flow into it*

Marco Polo, 1275

When Marco Polo arrived in China in the thirteenth century he was astounded by what he saw. China under the Yuan (Mongol) dynasty consisted of a vast empire that extended from the Yellow Sea to the Mediterranean, from the Steppes of Siberia to northern India. China was the jewel in this empire. Not only were the Chinese producing salt on an industrial scale — 30,000 tons a year in Sichuan (Sze-ch'uan) alone — but their internal economy dwarfed that of Europe. Iron production was in the vicinity of 125,000 tons a year, a level not reached in Europe until the eighteenth century. Metal-casting techniques and mass production could deliver standardized military and agricultural equipment anywhere in the empire. A canal-based transportation system linked cities and markets in a vast commercial network in which paper money and credit facilities within the merchant community were highly developed. As an employee of the Great Khan, Marco Polo passed through cities in the rich Yangtze valley with populations of more than a million inhabitants, which astounded even a sophisticated Venetian:

> At the end of three days you reach the noble and magnificent city of Kin-sai [Hangzhou], a name that signifies "the Celestial City" and which it merits from its pre-eminence to all others in the world, in point of grandeur and beauty, as well as from its abundant delights, which might lead an inhabitant to imagine himself in paradise . . . According to common estimation, this city is an hundred miles in circuit. Its streets and canals are extensive, and there are squares, or market places, [these] being necessarily proportioned in size to the prodigious concourse of people.

Not only Hangzhou, but also Suzhou and Nanjing (Nanking), dwarfed Marco Polo's native Venice, then the most powerful city in Europe. In China, people were able to buy paperback books in market stalls and paper money was in common use as were tissues. The rich ate from fine porcelain bowls and wore fabrics of silk that no European craftsman could match.

From the coastal cities of Quanzhou (Ch'uanzhou and Marco Polo's Zaitun) and Guangzhou (Canton) merchant fleets carried these commodities throughout Southeast Asia and to the Persian Gulf and from there to the Middle East and Europe, where they set the standard in refinement and luxury. These fleets of Chinese junks that traversed the Indian and Pacific Oceans in the thirteenth century were equipped with watertight bulkheads, stern-post rudders and compasses. They were manned by sailors with a knowledge of navigation by the stars, and were far advanced in size to any ships built in Europe until the sixteenth century. In the early fifteenth century the

The fabled Silk Road through Central Asia is depicted in this fourteenth century manuscript. Along this route passed not only the riches of the east, but Arab and European merchant-adventurers. In the late thirteenth century most of Central Asia was under the control of the Mongol empire and, with a "passport" in the form of a seal issued by the great Kublai Khan, Marco Polo and his uncle were free to travel unhindered from the Mediterranean to the Yellow Sea.

Ming emperor was able to send a fleet of 60 ships or more carrying 40,000 troops to the east coast of Africa and India to wave the flag. Between 1405 and 1433 the Great Three Jeweled Eunuch, Admiral Zheng He (Cheng Ho), settled a succession dispute in Sumatra and also brought back the King of Ceylon to Beijing (Peking) as a disciplinary measure for his failure to show due respect to the representatives of the Son of Heaven. In short, China at this time was the most cosmopolitan, technologically advanced and economically powerful civilization in the world.

To understand why China failed to maintain this technological lead over the west and why the priorities of the Chinese emperors were so different from those of the European monarchs, it is necessary to go back to the beginning of the Celestial Empire and the source of China's wealth — the land.

\* \* \*

The Emperor Kublai Khan and his entourage on a hunting trip. Kublai Khan completed the conquest of China begun by his grandfather, the remarkable Mongol leader, Genghis Khan. The Mongols were prepared to employ foreigners, such as Marco Polo, since they were initially unsure of the loyalty of the traditional Chinese scholar-officials.

If you fly across the great plains of China, you can still clearly see the economic foundations of its ancient civilization. The great rivers wind down from the mountains in the far west and meander through the huge alluvial plains that make up the country's heart. Running off from these can be seen a network of canals interlinked like the fine veins on the surface of the human skin. These carry the life-giving energy, the rich silt and water that still allow this land to support an extraordinary density of people. China, after all, has the largest population in the world, more than one billion people, around 80 per cent of whom still live in villages in the countryside. These villages can also best be seen from the air. They radiate like a web that covers the landscape. Within what appears to be reasonable walking distance, there is a larger market town that dominates a region. If you take a wide-angled view, you will see that these towns also cluster in a web around a major city. But the essential and most basic element in this economic system remains the village with its surrounding agricultural land. It has formed, over the millennia, the basic social unit of traditional China.

From ancient times these villages were more or less self-governing production units, which were taxed in the form of grain and corvée labor. This labor was demanded each year to support public works, such as the maintenance of the canal system and the building of roads or even walls to defend the provincial capital. What is most striking is the extent to which this is a human-made landscape. The structure of this remarkable economic enterprise was built up over thousands of years by generations of peasants and government officials — a structure that for more than two thousand of those years supported the most stable empire the world has ever known, one that existed, with minor breakdowns, from 221 B.C. to A.D. 1911.

China's agriculture was able to support such a vast population because geography and Chinese culture came together to transform the land into an extraordinarily

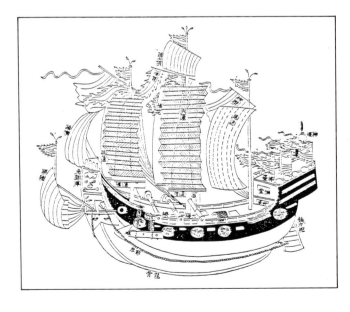

It was on a Chinese junk like this that Marco Polo, after ten years in the service of the Great Khan, traveled on his return journey to Europe. Such vessels regularly made their way from China to the ports of Southeast Asia, India and the Middle East. These boats featured a number of important nautical innovations such as the stern-post rudder and watertight bulkheads, which were later to be taken up by Arab and European shipbuilders.

productive agricultural system. One of the key elements was the control of water.

China is dominated by two great river systems, the Yangtze and the Yellow rivers. Known as "China's Sorrows," they and their numerous tributaries originated in the foothills of the Himalayas and the Kunlun Mountains in the far west. The Yellow River, (Huang He in Chinese), gets its name from the rich loess silt that, since the last ice age, was blown from the plateaux of central Asia and now covers much of northern China.

The perennial flooding of these great rivers renewed the productivity of the land but the destructive power of these rivers was such that they would not only inundate fields but would also wipe out all trace of human habitation. The Yellow River, over its 2,700 miles from the western mountains, has changed course on a number of occasions, devastating vast areas of agricultural land. The coastal plains are essentially flat and any significant rise in water levels can flood hundreds of thousands of acres. Because the Yellow River carries and deposits so much fine silt, it therefore frequently silts up and breaks its banks. Today, the Yellow River flows within dykes high above the surrounding land. Over the centuries these dykes have been built up to control flooding while also providing access to river water for irrigation.

Efforts to control the Yellow River date back to before the founding of the Chinese empire in 221 B.C. From these very early times, the independent kingdoms that made up "China" were of necessity concerned with the control of water, not just to prevent flooding, but also to increase agricultural productivity and thereby the surplus wealth that could be taxed by the kingdoms. Growth in output allowed small kingdoms to support larger and larger armies with which they could subdue their neighbors and thus increase their territory, power, wealth and prestige. It is a familiar story.

Waterways also provided a means of transport, not only for troops in their efforts to command wide regions, but also for merchants and their wares. The canal networks encouraged commerce, and thus increased the size and complexity of the market and led to craft specializations in specific regions. The division of labor required a large market system with good communications linking villages to towns, which in turn were linked to provincial capitals.

An interesting example of water control is to be found in the great water conservancy system at Dujiangyan, which still serves the Chengdu plains and the capital of Sichuan, Chengdu itself. This remarkable system of canals and dams was started about 250 B.C. by the Governor of Sichuan, Li Bing. The system still irrigates an area of around two million acres, supporting about five million people.

Li Bing had the Minjiang River divided into two channels. This was done at Dujiangyan because of a natural island and sandbar in the center of the river. The outer channel carried the fast-flowing flood water downstream to join the Yangtze; the inner channel carried water into the irrigation canals. In ancient times, it was found that by building up the sandbar in the center of the river (called the "fish's snout") it was possible to keep a fairly constant level of water flowing into two canals. These canals carry silt-rich water through a network of smaller and smaller canals that intersect the Chengdu plains and finally rejoin the Yangtze River further downstream. During periods of drought it was possible to block off the outer

*Above:* The building and maintenance of the dykes that held "China's Sorrows" — the great Yangtze and Yellow rivers — on their course was a major responsibility of the imperial state. This section of a seventeenth century scroll depicts the massive earthworks carried out by corvée labor on the dykes that had to be maintained to stop the Yellow River from breaking its banks.

*Left:* This nineteenth century representation of water conservancy shows how dykes were built up using the silt and sand deposited on the bed of the rivers. Without such dredging, river courses would shift with devastating consequences.

channel (with barriers made up of long baskets of stones), forcing more water to flow through the canals; in times of flood the main stream was opened up and a shallow bar or spillway would allow the bulk of the water to be channeled down river.

At Dujiangyan today there is still a temple dedicated to Li Bing and his sons, one of whom was supposed to have been killed during the construction of the project. It is a beauty spot for tourists but local people still come to make offerings to this great public benefactor as they have done for the past two thousand years. It is quite understandable for contemporary Chinese to pay such respect, not just to Li Bing the good public official whose modern plaster image still gazes heroically over the river, but to the water control system that he established; one that continues to provide them with the water essential for intensive farming. Intensive irrigation systems like that at Dujiangyan have allowed the population of China to grow to its present size. From Li Bing's time onwards, the maintenance of the water control systems was one of the central responsibilities of the state. If the canal systems were not maintained, the people starved.

The engineering significance of Dujiangyan is matched by other equally remarkable hydraulic works carried out at the same time. The Zheng Gou Canal was begun in 221 B.C., the first year of the reign of Qin Shi Huangdi (Ch'in Shih Huang-ti), who was the first emperor of China. It was designed by a hydraulic engineer, Zheng Gou, after whom the canal is named. This canal, 93 miles long, directs the water of the Jingshui River across the Guanzhong plain, irrigating around 350,000 acres. This system was designed not just for irrigation but for fertilization as well. The canal runs off the river at a point where maximum silt can be drawn, allowing the alkaline soils of central Shaanxi (Shensi) to become fertile.

When the Minjiang River flooded, a weir on the inner channel at Dujiangyan allowed excess water to be spilled back into the main stream, keeping the water in the canals at a constant level.

In terms of sheer audacity, the Dragon Head Canal in Shanxi (Shansi) province is perhaps the most remarkable. This canal, which passes three and a half miles under the Shangyan Mountains, was built on the orders of the Emperor Wu Di of the Han dynasty (206 B.C.– A.D. 220) that followed the short-lived Qin dynasty. Because of the scale of the imperial state, Wu Di was able to marshal the labor of 10,000 soldiers to redirect water to irrigate the dry Zhongquan region of Shanxi province.

These are just a few early examples of a tradition that became a major responsibility of the Chinese imperial state for the next two thousand years. Men such as Li Bing and Zheng Gou are significant in Chinese history because they represent the ideal public official or bureaucrat. One of the distinguishing characteristics of traditional Chinese culture was the importance of what we would call public servants. This is true of most civilizations dependent on large-scale water control systems. In Persia and Egypt, at different times, they produced equally complex administrative systems. Like them, China's culture developed in response to the economic realities of maintaining an increasingly large and centralized kingdom. Between 230 and 221 B.C. the kingdoms of Han, Zhao, Wei, Chu, Yan, and Qi fell in rapid succession to the king of Qin, Shi Huangdi, who became the first emperor of China.

The unification of the empire was of profound significance. It made peace possible after centuries of warfare, but it also permitted a unique form of bureaucratic feudalism to replace the feudal kingdoms of the earlier period. The creation of a class of administrative and bureaucratic officials, operating throughout the length and breadth of China on behalf of the emperor, meant that technological innovations developed in one part of the country could be spread easily to all parts of the empire. In addition, a unified empire allowed for a high level of technological specialization, for example, iron and steel production rose to meet the demands of the empire for standardized products. Shi Huangdi introduced a system of common coinage, weights and measures. He even standardized the width of the axles on carts and chariots to prevent damage to the empire's highways. Military technology was also standardized, allowing for large-scale mass production of cast-iron weapons.

Although the empire brought peace within its borders, there remained the constant threat from nomadic tribes to the northwest. This threat necessitated large standing armies, which had to be supported by the state. By the time of the western Han dynasty, government monopolies in key commodities such as salt and iron, along with the traditional resources from agriculture, provided the revenue with which to support this large military and the imperial administration. As early as 119 B.C. there were at least 46 state-run iron-casting centers throughout China. In Henan (Honan), the scale of cast-iron production was massive by any standards. The core or salamander left from one of the damaged crucibles used in smelting was found to weigh 20–25 tons, a capacity not reached in Europe until well into the eighteenth century. In A.D. 806 China was producing 13,500 tons of iron a year but by 1078, during the Song (Sung) dynasty, this had risen to 125,000 tons. This period also marked a high point in Chinese industrial development, which could be described as an industrial revolution of sorts.

Chinese iron masters working in state-owned foundries had developed remarkably sophisticated techniques for iron and steel production. They had even discovered the principle of blowing air through molten iron as a means of gaining the increased heat necessary to produce fine steel — the same principle that was used in the blast furnace developed by Henry Bessemer in the nineteenth century.

Making state monopolies of essential commodities such as salt and iron, like the contemporary practice of "nationalizing" strategic industries, occurred early in Chinese history. It allowed for the standardization of products needed, for example, by the army and also provided a source of revenue. In 1083 the production of iron farm implements was turned into a state monopoly. This meant that hoes, plows, mold boards and scythes were produced on an enormous scale. The demand for cast-iron implements and the scale of the Chinese market rewarded specialization and technological innovation. At two government arsenals at this time 32,000 suits of armor in three standardized sizes were produced each year. Iron and steel were also being used for the construction of bridges and even for the building of a cast-iron pagoda, 70 feet high.

In northern China the widespread use of the iron-tipped plow and the mold board, which turned the earth, allowed for deep plowing, which significantly increased the productivity of the land. In the northern provinces where the crops were mainly wheat and millet, the mechanical seed drill, which may have come from India, was in use allowing farmers to sow in even rows. This was of enormous importance since it permitted weeding between the rows as well as easier irrigation.

A contemporary statute of Li Bing who, as Governor of Sichuan in 250 B.C., had the water control system built at Dujiangyan. A temple dedicated to him still overlooks his project and, even to this day, people come to light joss sticks in his honor. As a dedicated government official, Li Bing embodied the Confucian ideals of selfless service to the welfare of others and was the subject of a recent feature film in socialist China.

Prior to this the technique had been to broadcast grain by hand, which was both wasteful and inefficient. (This seed drill, or at least the concept, may well have come into Europe from China in the eighteenth century when it was introduced into common use by the famous British agricultural innovator, Jethro Tull.)

The most significant revolution in Chinese agriculture came with the population shift from the north to the rich rice-growing areas south of the Yangtze delta from the ninth century onwards. By 1380 the south had two and a half times the population of the north: 38 million in the south compared with 15 million in the north, according to official statistics. This profound demographic change involved not only the migration of people but also a change in diet from wheat and millet to rice.

Wet-rice agriculture was given an enormous stimulus in China with the introduction of a new variety known as "Champa rice" from Vietnam in about 1012. This rice ripened faster than local varieties, allowing for the production of two and even three crops a year. Like other innovations this one was sponsored by imperial officials and, in turn, encouraged investment in more widespread land reclamation and water control systems. Because of the obvious benefits to the state of this eleventh century "green revolution," officials promoted the use of these new farming techniques through tax relief, credit facilities and through the establishment of a system of model farms. Books were also published to inform government officials of the benefits. For the new variety to be fully productive it required paddy-field cultivation and new water control techniques. Water loaded with fine silt provided the essential nutrients for an enormous increase in the yield per acre, but it also allowed more people to be supported on far less land than in Europe, as the French economic historian, Fernand Braudel, has argued:

# SALT OF THE EARTH

Approaching the city of Zigong in western Sichuan province, as Marco Polo may well have done on his tour of inspection as an imperial bureaucrat in the service of the Great Kublai Khan, Emperor of China, you immediately notice the towering derricks, which still stand out against the skyline as they did in the thirteenth century. For this is one of the oldest salt-producing areas in the world.

Salt was essential for the preservation of food, and in China, as in all other ancient civilizations, people starved in winter unless they could store sufficient salt meat, fish and vegetables. Starving people also threatened the stability of the empire and it was therefore not surprising that salt should become a state monopoly and was not left to the vagaries and greed of merchants. This monopoly by the state meant that production techniques developed in one area were rapidly spread by imperial officials throughout the country.

One of the most impressive things about this ancient technology was not so much its size but the ingenious use of local materials.

The traditional derricks were timber structures, some as high as 200 feet and made up of three upright poles like a tripod. From a massive capstan, turned by bullocks, a rope lifted and dropped a ten-foot long iron bit. This form of percussion drilling was used to sink the well. The rope used was made of twisted strips of bamboo and had a tensile strength equal to that of steel wire. This rope would manipulate the iron bit 2,000 feet below the surface. The wells were also fitted with bamboo linings. From the wellhead, bamboo pipes joined together by tarred cloth carried off the brine and natural gas to the processing room. The brine was drawn off into a tank and the natural gas used to boil off the water in large woks (vats) leaving behind the high-quality salt. This was the world's first industrial use of natural gas and also of drilling wells.

Methane gas struck at levels of 2,000 feet was dangerous unless mixed with the right amount of oxygen. The Chinese solved this problem by covering the wellhead with a large wooden barrel into which air was drawn to achieve the right balance, as in the carburettor of an automobile. From one wellhead it was possible to heat 600–700 reducing vats; one well was reported to have run as many as 5,000 vats. This

was salt production on an industrial scale not seen in Europe until the eighteenth century.

Sealed bamboo pipes and leather bags were also used by travelers to carry the gas around the countryside (as we use gas cylinders when camping) to provide light and heat. There is even an account of gas being used to provide street lighting.

As early as the sixteenth century at Leshan, not far from Zigong, these same techniques were also used to drill for oil, which came into common use in that region as a form of fuel. The lack of the chemical knowledge to refine the oil meant that its discovery in China did not have the revolutionary economic impact it was to have in the west in the late nineteenth century. In the 1850s it was, however, these Chinese techniques of drilling that were used to open up the Pennsylvania oil fields.

Courtesy Film Australia

Courtesy Film Australia

The rice-field is thus a factory. In Lavoisier's time [the eighteenth century] one hectare of land under wheat in France produced an average of five quintals [1 quintal = 220.46 pounds]; one hectare of rice-field often bears thirty quintals of rice in the husk. After milling this means twenty-one quintals of edible rice at 3500 calories per kilogram, or the colossal total of 7,350,000 calories per hectare, as compared with 1,500,000 for wheat and only 340,000 animal calories if that hectare were devoted to stock-raising and produced 150 kilograms of meat.

Unlike the agricultural revolution that was to occur in Britain in the seventeenth and eighteenth centuries, that of Song dynasty China did not lead to the same loss of people to the cities. Wet-rice agriculture by its nature is labor intensive. What the new varieties and greater sophistication of production meant was that more people could be employed on the same area of land and still produce a surplus. Rural villages were able to absorb more and more people as double cropping spread throughout the rich river delta of the Yangtze.

Wet-rice agriculture also required a high degree of social discipline and co-operation. In both China and Japan, the five-month turnover of rice crops required enormous amounts of labor at key times such as harvests in June and November, and

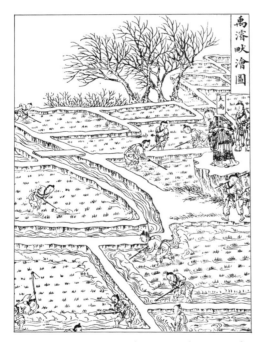 

*Left.* The extraordinary productivity of wet-rice agriculture meant that more and more land was turned over to this form of cultivation. It required sophisticated hydraulic engineering and considerable social organization, as this late Qing woodblock illustrates.

*Right.* Encyclopedias on agriculture were widely circulated among the scholar-bureaucrats to promote the use of new technology. The square-mallet chain pump, more commonly known as the "dragon's backbone pump," was introduced to lift water from one paddy field to another, and a more modern version is still widely used throughout the countryside.

Until the eighteenth century European agriculture was rarely as productive or as labor-intensive as that of wet-rice cultivation in China. The system of broadcasting grain by hand, shown here, was both inefficient and wasteful with birds often taking a good deal of the seed before it could even germinate.

planting in January and July. Failure to get one crop in could mean starvation for a family. Social organization at the village level was also needed to see that the water was available to each paddy field when needed. The coercive power of the village community over the individual was enormous. It was at the level of the village, which was often an extended family with most people in some way related, that the Confucian hierarchy of relationships served to maintain order and discipline. It should also be appreciated that under the legal practices that existed in China throughout the imperial period, any family member was liable to be punished for the wrongdoing of any other member of the family, if the perpetrator could not be found. This too had a powerful effect on encouraging social conformity.

Ironically, the very success of Chinese agriculture was in a sense a trap. While productivity per acre went up enormously with the widespread adoption of wet-rice cultivation, making it the most productive agriculture in the world, there was a price to be paid. Wet-rice cultivation was extremely vulnerable to natural disasters. Any breakdown in the flow of water because of drought, flood or simple neglect could lead to widespread famine and a consequent breakdown in social order and, thus, the harmony of the state. This meant that the government was locked into the development and maintenance of complex water control systems and was forced to stockpile grain to quell potential uprisings of starving peasants.

With so many people engaged in paddy-field cultivation and living in the warmer regions of the south, new parasitic diseases became widespread throughout the population. Schistosomiasis, a disease carried by tiny snails that lived on the edge of slow-flowing water courses, and malaria both became endemic. These parasitic diseases do not lead to immediate death but sap energy and shorten life expectancy. The productivity of the individual may well be significantly reduced by these diseases, as was the case in southern Europe when malaria was endemic. It therefore meant that more people were required to achieve the same levels of output.

Interestingly, the pressure to bring more and more land under paddy-field cultivation also meant that there were fewer grazing and draft animals than before. Fortunately for Europe, the large number of draft animals required for farming the larger acreages needed to support an average family not only freed peasants from back-breaking labor but also provided an additional source of protein and an alternative source of blood for the malarial mosquito — a source of blood in which the malarial parasite cannot live. Thus the spread of such diseases was kept in check by the different ecology of northern Europe and the draining of fen and swamp lands for use as dry-land farming greatly reduced the breeding grounds of mosquitoes.

The increasing dependence on rice and the complex, interlocked water control system needed to maintain China's dense, rural population meant that the needs of agriculture became the imperial administration's central and constant concern. With productivity so high there was little room or reason for change. In China, therefore, it made sense to be conservative. In Europe, with an agricultural system much less dependent on one type of crop and the control of water, and with far fewer people to be supported per acre, there was scope for change and development through the application of labor-saving technology.

# SCHOLARS AND BUREAUCRATS

*To enrich your family, no need to buy good land:*
*Books hold a thousand measures of grain.*
*For an easy life, no need to build a mansion:*
*In books are found houses of gold.*
*Going out, be not vexed at absence of followers:*
*In books, carriages and horses form a crowd.*
*Marrying, be not vexed by the lack of a good go-between:*
*In books there are girls with faces of jade.*
*A boy who wants to become a somebody*
*Devotes himself to the classics, faces the window, and reads.*

Song Emperor, Renzong (Jen Tsung)

The system of imperial government that developed in China was different from that of Europe or Japan. It was not based on the power of feudal clans but was organized around a centralized bureaucratic structure. In fact, the Chinese could be said to have invented the idea of a meritocratic civil service. In China power and status were based on scholastic merit, as determined by results in the world's oldest written examination. The empire was actually run by a relatively small number of scholar-bureaucrats, not by a hereditary, warring caste bound by ties of blood and clan loyalty, as was the case in both Europe and Japan.

The use of public examination as a means of deciding who should occupy the top positions in the imperial administration had its beginnings in the sixth century. Although the formation of new dynasties was basically dependent upon military power, the Chinese emperors soon realised that, once having gained imperial power, they needed more than military strength to maintain the vast empire. Military men too close to the center of power might also threaten the stability of the empire. From the time of Shih Huangdi, the first emperor, there was a systematic effort to destroy the roots of feudal and aristocratic power in the previous existing kingdoms, now under the control of the rulers of the state of Qin. Throughout the following centuries, and with a good deal of bloodshed, aristocratic feudalism disappeared in China and the tradition of rule by an administrative bureaucracy was established. The military was given low status and kept, as much as possible, under the control of the scholars — on tap but not on top.

Each year up to 30,000 students would gather at the local provincial capital. Here they would spend an average of five days locked in tiny cells. They would enter the examination compound at about 5 A.M. each morning and after being verified by a known teacher or local official (to prevent substitution) they would be given a number and a cell. The examination paper, like those used internationally today,

*Above:* The Song Emperor Renzong, whose poem extolling the benefits of study was criticized by later generations as giving a false impression of the real objectives of scholarship.

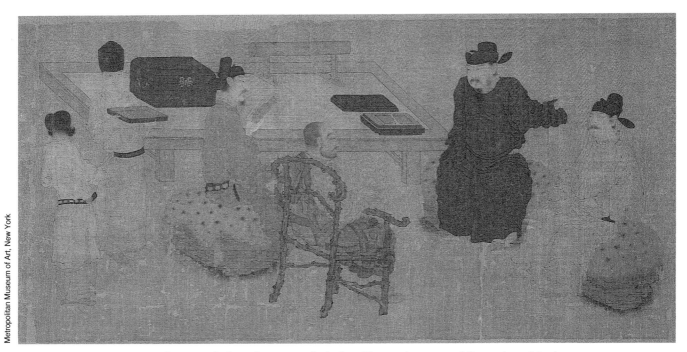

A Song dynasty painting of a group of scholars. Those who successfully graduated in the imperial examination system ran the empire. By gaining even an elementary degree one was exempt from doing corvée labor or receiving corporal punishment, and was given a small state pension.

would have on it only the student's number. Even the written work completed by each student would be copied out by a scribe so that favored students could not be identified by their calligraphy.

The students' future careers, social status and even the prosperity of their family depended on the results of this examination. The pressure was enormous. Even to be able to sit for the first of three levels of examinations, the student would have had to spend at least six years studying the Confucian classics and memorizing long texts, which he would be expected to quote accurately. It is little wonder that, despite great security precautions, some students reverted to the time-honored tradition of cheating. Silk crib sheets containing key passages of text and model essays were hidden in food, in clothing or anywhere else the wit of man could devise. One ingenious student had a silk inner lining made for his jacket, which he had covered with a vast amount of text. There were even cases where an official was bribed and a student used a code to identify himself, but the consequences of being caught were extremely serious, with some corrupt officials losing their heads.

If you were able to pass this first, county-level exam *(xian)* you had a foot on the first rung of the ladder to a career as an imperial official. This qualified you to sit for the prefectural examination *(fu)*. If you passed this exam you would be given the lowest level qualification, a licentiate or bachelor degree known as *juren* or "flowering talent." You were now part of the "literati," which meant you were exempt from doing corvée labor, could not be given corporal punishment and were entitled to a small state pension. Above this were two more levels. At the highest level, an examination was held in the Forbidden City (during Ming and Qing dynasties) and supervised by the emperor himself. By passing this exam you became a *jinshi* or "presented scholar." From this group would be chosen the officials who administered the provincial and central organs of government. These men were expected to be as adept in law as they were in art, poetry, mathematics or engineering. These scholar-officials were generalists, men of integrity and sound judgment that made them good civil servants. They were also extremely conservative, regarding themselves as guardians of the Confucian ideals of harmonious government.

In the late eighteenth century this Chinese system of examination, described in glowing terms by Jesuit missionaries working in China, was introduced in France and, later, in Britain, as a means of selecting public servants. The education in classics offered by the universities of Oxford and Cambridge, which became the primary intellectual training for nineteenth century civil servants, aimed at producing the same sort of all-rounders who, as judges and administrators in the far-flung regions of the British empire, performed the same role as the Chinese scholar-bureaucrats.

One of the consequences of the Chinese examination system was that it encouraged a conservative and often narrow intellectual orthodoxy, particularly as access to the top positions of power in the bureaucracy was dependent on years of study for examinations set by bureaucrats who were themselves the products of the system.

Courtesy Film Australia

This is a reproduction of the tiny cells used by students sitting for the imperial examinations. Over a number of weeks students would come to such cells to sit for their exams. As many as 30,000 students would put themselves through the grueling county exams in the hope of becoming officials. Through the doorway of these cells lay the only legitimate path to power and status throughout the empire.

Courtesy Film Australia

*Above:* As early as the twelfth century printed books made on woodblocks like these were being sold in market places throughout the empire.

*Left:* In imperial workshops, using movable type, encyclopedias of useful knowledge on agriculture, medicine, engineering and military affairs were produced and circulated among scholar-officials.

Another interesting aspect of this written examination was that it was made possible because of the development of paper in China in the second century. The early development of printing also allowed the basic texts used in the examinations to be widely available, even though the time needed by students to study them was dependent upon their families having the means to support them for many years; a simple economic fact that excluded a large number of people from gaining access to power, despite the system's avowed intention of being open to all.

\*    \*    \*

To support and legitimate the imperial government there also evolved a cosmology and ideology that drew on a wide range of philosophical schools, which blossomed in the period just prior to the unification of the empire. During the Han dynasty (206 B.C.–A.D. 220) something of a synthesis of ideas occurred. Although always evolving and changing with new influences such as Buddhism (which came to China in the second century) there were nonetheless a number of basic principles that remained remarkably intact right up until 1911, when the Chinese imperial system was finally abandoned. These ideas, embodied in the Confucian "four books and five classics" shaped the intellectual, scientific, aesthetic and political perspective of generations of Chinese. They also formed the all-important basis of the imperial examination that

A Song dynasty painting entitled "The Return of Lady Wen." The family lay at the heart of all Confucian values — filial piety and respect for seniority in the large extended family provided the basis for all relationships. Those in seniority, including the emperor , were expected to devote themselves to the well-being of their dependents.

selected those who, in the final analysis, would rule the country.

The two dominant schools of thought, which came together in the Han, were Confucianism and Taoism. Confucius (Kong Fuzi in modern transliteration), or Master Kung, is often described as the patron saint of Chinese bureaucracy. Confucius (551– 479 B.C.) lived in a time known as the Spring and Autumn period, when kingdoms were battling for control of territory, each trying to absorb its weaker neighbors. For Confucius, the violence and destructiveness of this form of military adventurism proved that it was no way to run a civilized society. If one wanted to categorize his approach to government and to morality, Confucius could be described as a radical traditionalist. He believed that China had gone downhill since the relatively peaceful dominance of the kingdom of Zhou came to an end in 771 B.C. He therefore endeavored to change society and government according to the values that he believed had existed in the past. He did this in his role as a government official in the kingdom of Lu and as a teacher within his own school.

For Confucius the primary model of social harmony was the family, but a family in which the status and role of each individual was clearly defined and formalized. He argued that if each individual was brought up to show the correct respect and deference within the family then respect and deference for the greater order of society at large would be possible. He believed that society should not be governed by military power or legalistic rules but by officials, men of learning like himself, who had been inculcated with the five essential virtues — benevolence (*ren*), righteousness (*yi*) propriety (*li*), wisdom (*zhi*) and trustworthiness (*xin*). He did not believe that such virtues were innately part of any aristocratic, religious or military caste but believed that human nature was capable of being molded. It was the duty of the state to inculcate these principles into its citizens. For this reason, he placed great emphasis on education since he believed that all men were equally capable of becoming sages given the right training and example. The place where this was to be done was within the family.

This humanistic philosophy bears some resemblance to that developed in Greece at a similar time (fifth century B.C.) by Socrates and Plato who promoted the idea that society should be governed by a group of benign intellectuals, or "philosopher kings." In Greece and even in Italy during the Renaissance, when such ideas had great appeal, they were rarely to become embodied in social institutions. In Europe aristocratic or military elites were to remain dominant well into the eighteenth and

Courtesy Film Australia

A Taoist monk from the White Cloud Temple in Beijing.

early nineteenth centuries. In China, on the other hand, these humanistic ideas, embodied in the examination system, were to be the dominant social and political values of generations of scholar-officials who ran the empire for most of its 2,000 years of existence. But these highly rational and ethical concerns were to be tempered by another powerful influence in Chinese intellectual and cultural life — Taoism.

Taoism developed in China as something of an antithesis to the purely social and ethical concerns of the Confucian school. Taoism, like Confucianism, had its roots in the ideas of a particular teacher or sage, Laozi (Lao Tzu). He was a somewhat anarchistic figure who believed that social harmony was not to be found through the rational ordering of society but through the achievement of inner harmony on the part of the individual — a harmony and balance that paralleled that which governed cosmic forces and underpinned the ecological balance of the natural world.

Taoist philosophy formed a rich intellectual tradition that played with philosophical paradoxes as a means of pointing to the limitations of purely rational systems of thought. Taoist religion on the other hand was infused with ideas that date back to the animistic and pantheistic world of ancient Chinese culture. So while the Confucians had little interest in investigating natural phenomena, the Taoists were concerned with understanding the *dao* (*tao*) or "way" of nature through contemplating its myriad manifestations and cycles. It would be wrong to make too much of the separation of these two schools since, in practical terms, they complemented each other, as can be seen in the classics. This corpus of learning included both Confucian texts and books like the *Yijing* (*I ching*), which is Taoist in origin. Therefore the scholar-bureaucrats who espoused Confucian ideas in their capacity as public officials could well, on returning home, take up esoteric contemplative practices that were clearly Taoist.

This eclecticism, common throughout much of Asia, is due in part to the fact that China was spared the dogmatic obsessions of the credal religions of the Middle East and Europe — Judaism, Christianity and Islam. By postulating a supreme and single creator-god whose "will" or plan for the world and humanity was revealed only to a select few, these religions could claim that they not only had a monopoly on the truth but also a mission to convert all of humanity to the truth of their revelation. This has led throughout the history of Europe and the Middle East to a high degree of religious intolerance and persecution. Either you are on the side of the truth or you are against it, so "off with your head." In Chinese culture, a wide range of religious and philosophical beliefs have been tolerated at different times, including Buddhism, Christianity, Judaism and Islam. Muslim communities in the southern and western provinces were, by the time of Marco Polo's arrival, large and prosperous.

Confucianism is not a religion in the western sense. It is primarily a system of ethics. The respect for ancestors or ancestor worship, often associated with Confucianism, was no more than an extension of respect for the achievements of the elders in the family. Given the reliance of all Chinese on the vast water control systems and other public works on which civilized life depended, it made sense to show reverence for men like Li Bing and other, similar, social benefactors.

# THE MANDATE OF HEAVEN

*The first month [February in Gregorian calendar]*

*Biological phenomena: hibernating insects wake up; wild geese fly north; pheasants drum and call; fish rise beneath the ice; leeks appear in the garden; field rodents emerge; otters seek for fish as food; hawks become turtle doves [turtle doves, which came in spring, were mistaken for hawks]; catkins burst forth on the willow; the plum, apricot and mountain peach blossom; the cypress flowers; hens begin to lay.*

*Meteorological phenomena: in this season sweep gentle breezes; though chilly still, they melt the frozen soil.*

*Celestial phenomena: Ju star is seen; at dusk Shen [Orion] culminates; Doubling [the "handle" of the seven stars of the Great Bear] hangs downwards.*

*Farm tasks: [Farmers maintain their] implements for tilling; the farming inspector proceeds to mark off the fields; yellow rape is picked as sacrificial flowers for the ancestors.*

From the *Xia xiao zheng* (Xia dynasty calendar), c. 2100 –1600 B.C.

The Chinese imperial system of government evolved over a long period and it would be misleading to write about its institutions as if they were somehow static and immutable. Nevertheless, there were some basic assumptions embodied in the Confucian classics, which, because of the examination system, shaped the outlook of those who governed and therefore the course of Chinese history.

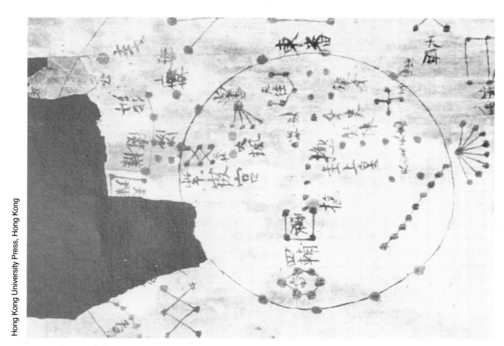

This eighth century star map depicts the constellations of Ursa Major around the North Pole. The stars representing the emperor, his army, the imperial household, and even the imperial kittens are contained within the area circled. A number of stars have represented the emperor over the long history of Chinese imperial astrology, but he has most consistently been associated with the pole star.

While the imperial system was built around maintaining and taxing the surplus of the world's most productive agriculture, there were strict limitations imposed on those who wielded imperial power. The Chinese emperor did not rule by "divine right" like many European monarchs. The right to rule or the "mandate of heaven" was conditional upon the emperor fulfilling the functions laid down by tradition: a tradition established by the Confucian scholars and bureaucrats who gradually came to dominate the management of the empire. The right to rule was dependent on maintaining social, economic and cosmological harmony. The Son of Heaven (the emperor) was the mediator between the people and the forces of nature. He was responsible for seeing that the water conservancy system was kept in order, that relief was provided in times of famine or when natural disasters struck (as they often did with devastating effect) and, more importantly, that the population was adequately forewarned of these disasters (a drought, flood or famine occurred in one of China's provinces every year). He was also expected to predict eclipses and other unusual astronomical events, for it was believed that events in the sky were directly related to events on earth. For this reason, one of the major institutions of government was the department of astronomy and mathematics.

From earliest times Chinese astronomers documented the events of the night sky in their constant search for these portents or warnings. However, while their initial concerns were primarily astrological, they developed in the process a very advanced understanding of astronomy, sufficient to predict eclipses and to apply mathematical techniques to the analysis of the movement of the planets.

There was another important reason why accuracy of observation was important and this was the requirement for the emperor to publish a calendar each year. This calendar specified the day on which the winter and summer solstices would occur, enabling imperial bureaucrats around the country to co-ordinate essential agricultural events such as the release of water for irrigation, the celebration of public festivals or the arrangement for corvée labor to be set to work on major public projects, such as the building of the Great Wall or a new water conservancy system. Corvée labor required all men, apart from scholars and Buddhist monks, to give a percentage of their time every year to carrying out public works — a system similar to the requirement in feudal Europe for peasants to work their lord's lands in exchange for military protection. The calendar also provided a precise astronomical catalogue of the most auspicious days and times for carrying out all sorts of functions, from getting married to fixing and painting the house.

The institution of this imperial calendar dates back to the beginning of the empire itself. It served to affirm the emperor's role as the intermediary between his subjects and the cosmos. By understanding, and thereby predicting the ways of heaven, apparently inauspicious events such as eclipses or the arrival of comets could eventually be accommodated into a cosmological status quo and thereby lose some of their doom-laden character.

Each evening, on the city walls of Beijing or earlier centers of imperial government, astronomers would record with meticulous detail the events in the night sky. With these records, kept within the department of astronomy, they were

*Above:* An armillary sphere used to calculate the position and predict the movement of stars. This instrument, which still stands on the old city wall in Beijing, was built with the help of Jesuit missionaries in the seventeenth century.

*Left:* Chinese scholar – bureaucrats contemplating an armillary sphere, similar to that used in the Su Song astronomical clock of 1088.

able to recognize and predict the periodic arrival of at least 40 comets before A.D. 1500, among them Halley's comet, first identified in Europe in the seventeenth century. These records have also provided contemporary astronomers with an invaluable resource, allowing them to confirm the dates of past astronomical events such as the birth of new stars or supernovae.

What is astounding is the detailed empirical approach taken by these Chinese astronomers. Though not "scientific" in the modern sense, they possessed a sophisticated understanding of the causes of astronomical phenomena. For example, as early as the end of the first century the astronomer Zhang Heng, in his book *The Spiritual Constitution of the Universe,* was able to explain accurately the cause of lunar eclipses ". . . since the moon reflects the sunshine, it will be eclipsed when it travels into the shadow cast by the earth."

Star maps of considerable accuracy were being produced and recorded on stone tablets by the eleventh century. One of the most famous of these is the Suzhou planisphere of 1247, which records a total of 1,434 stars. At this time mathematicians such as Guo Shoujing who built the famous gnomon near Kaifeng (the capital of the Northern Song dynasty) were measuring the length of the year as 365.2425 days. The gnomon measured the length of the shortest and longest day in the year, relating this date to the position of stars.

The Chinese gained this understanding of astronomical processes, not from any belief in the intrinsic value of scientific knowledge but because it fulfilled important functions for the imperial state by improving the accuracy of the calendar and allowing the emperor to fulfill his cosmological responsibilities. The cosmology itself was clearly pre-scientific, as its major use was not astronomical but astrological. Everything on earth was believed to have its counterpart in heaven and this included the emperor, the imperial palace and the various government ministries. A cluster of stars at the head of Scorpio were believed to represent the emperor, the imperial palace and a number of senior government ministries. In A.D. 340, the minister of justice, who also held the post of attorney general, was a man by the name of He. It was reported that the planet Mars was approaching the star that represented his ministry. On hearing the news he immediately petitioned the emperor to allow him to resign and take a lower government job, that of keeper of the imperial seal, in order to avert what might well be a disaster for him or his department. His request was granted by the emperor and disaster averted.

It is interesting to note that the reporting of unlucky portents in the vicinity of the stars representing the emperor and the imperial household increased dramatically during unpopular dynasties. In other words, the department of astronomy was in a politically strategic position to make veiled or, at times, quite pointed criticism of the behavior of the emperor. After all, his "mandate of heaven" was dependent on support from the bureaucracy and there were always many contenders for the position waiting in the wings. Events that had not been predicted were interpreted as heaven's warning. For this reason, many emperors treated the findings of this department as a state secret. Leaks, which might get into the hands of the opposition, were regarded with as much concern as official secrets are by contemporary governments. Given the importance of the department of astronomy, it is no wonder that the Chinese should have calculated the precise orbit of at least 40 comets.

A late Qing illustration showing the use of a small gnomon. With this instrument, which measured the length of the shadow cast by a perpendicular rod, it was possible to measure the shortest and longest days of the year — the summer and winter solstices — with great accuracy. This knowledge was essential for maintaining the accuracy of the imperial calendar.

# CELESTIAL CLOCKWORK

Perhaps the most remarkable achievement of the scholar-officials, and the imperial workshops they maintained, was the invention of clockwork.

Understanding both the motions of the planets and the cyclic nature of the position of the fixed stars led Zhang Heng in the second century to apply water power to drive astronomical instruments. This description of Zhang's water-driven armillary sphere was given in an official history of A.D. 132:

"Zhang Heng made his bronze armillary sphere and set it up in a closed chamber, where it rotated by the force of flowing water. The order having been given for the doors to be shut, the observer in charge of it would call out to the watcher on the observatory platform, saying the sphere showed that such and such a star was just rising, or another star just culminating, to yet another star just setting. Everything was found to correspond with the phenomena like the two halves of a tally."

The device was further developed by the Buddhist mathematician and astronomer Yi Xing in the eighth century, who added a clock to it. The best known model of this astronomical clock was the one produced by Han Gonglian at Kaifeng (the Northern Song capital) under the direction of Su Song, Minister of Personnel, in 1088. Though knowledge of this form of clock disappeared at the end of the Northern Song dynasty, Su Song's directions for its construction remained in a book, *Xin yi xiang fa yao* (New Design for an Armillary Clock). From the description contained in this book, Professor Yang of the Beijing Historical Museum was able, in the 1950s, to construct a model of this remarkable clock — remarkable because it included the first use of the escapement mechanism, "the soul" of all mechanical clocks.

The Su Song clock was housed in a wooden tower 39 feet high. On the top was a platform with an armillary sphere similar to that developed by Zhang Heng, which was covered by a movable roof, like that of a modern observatory. This sphere, when aligned through a sighting tube, kept time with the motion of the planets. It was connected by gears to the driving mechanism of the clock, which was worked by water filling wooden buckets. When one bucket was full, the weight would lift a lever allowing the next bucket to move forward; with a constant flow of water the motion produced would be precise and regular.

*Constructed in the 1950s by Professor Yang, this model of Su Song's clock is housed in the Beijing Historical Museum.*

The first floor housed a celestial globe also geared to move time with the natural cycles of the heavens. On the ground floor was the clock mechanism and a series of windows at which 24 puppet figures announced the *shichen* by ringing a bell. The *shichen* or *shi* was a measure of time equivalent to two European hours. At another window a figure beat a drum at each *ke* (equivalent to approximately 15 minutes). Additional to the 12 *shi* in each Chinese day, there were 100 *ke* — the first beginning at midnight and the fiftieth at noon. Another series of puppets would emerge to play stringed instruments for each *geng* and *chou*. A *geng* was one-fifth of the length of the night and a *chou* was one-fifth of the length of a *geng*. The length of the night, varying with each season, meant that these measurements were constantly being adjusted.

One of the most important functions of this astronomical clock for the imperial household was the setting up of imperial horoscopes. In China these were calculated from the moment of conception not from the moment of birth, as is the case in European tradition. Where the destiny of a future Son of Heaven was concerned, the moments of imperial ecstasy with empress or concubine had to be recorded and correlated with the rising and setting of the planets, whether the sky was visible or not.

The intriguing thing is that such an important discovery — the regulation of motion through the use of precise clockwork mechanisms — should have been discovered in China and then allowed to disappear from use altogether, two centuries before it was developed independently in Europe. When the Song emperor was driven out of Kaifeng by the invading Jin Tartars in 1127 the clock was allowed to fall to pieces. For the scholar-officials who governed the empire such technology was not relevant to the needs of ordinary people. The celestial clock at Kaifeng provided information appropriate only to the needs of the emperor and his court. Being made largely of wood, the mechanism must have been notoriously inaccurate, which made it more of a novelty than genuinely useful for it was never rebuilt.

Mechanical clocks, so fundamental to the later technological and industrial development of the west, did not reappear in China until the arrival of Jesuit missionaries in the sixteenth century.

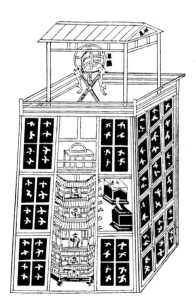 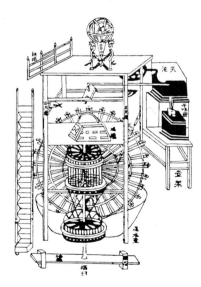

*These illustrations were taken from Su Song's original plans for the great astronomical clock he set up for the Emperor in 1088.*

# SELF-CULTIVATION AND THE COSMOS

*By studying the organic patterns of heaven and earth a fool can become a sage. So by watching the times and seasons of natural phenomena we can become true philosophers.*

Li Chuan, *Yin fu jing,* A.D. 735

*The sage can rival the skill of the shaping forces;*
*Raising his hand, he plucks the sun and moon from the sky*
*To put in his pot.*

A Chinese alchemic verse

The power of the imperial bureaucrats was considerable, for it was through them that the emperor ruled and was himself ruled. For he too was educated in the Confucian cultural values that they espoused. Any propensity to autocratic power and radical action was checked by traditional precedents and limited by bureaucratic inertia.

Scholar-officials were posted from the imperial capital, on passing their final exams, to junior positions in a provincial bureaucracy. From here, by dutiful service, they would begin to climb, as officials do today, to the top of the greasy pole becoming, if they possessed the "right stuff," ministers and eventually close advisers to the emperor himself. As scholars they would be expected to conform to the behavior expected of a Confucian gentleman, which, like the nineteenth century European ideal of the gentleman, embodied many patronizing assumptions of superiority.

At its best, however, this bureaucratic tradition encouraged the spread of knowledge and learning throughout the empire. These imperial civil servants were not allowed to govern in the province in which they were brought up or had close family ties and they were transferred regularly to prevent the forming of corrupt relationships with the powerful local landowners or gentry, who held local administrative posts. Corruption did, of course, occur and a blind eye was often turned to the profiteering carried out by members of the civil service. By tax farming and squeezing local merchants' profits bureaucrats were able to make a comfortable livelihood, well above that allowed by their modest imperial salary.

To regard all officials as corrupt would, however, be wrong. Many were genuinely imbued with Confucian ideals and were dedicated to improving the lot of the people they served. Together with the local gentry, officials established medical temples such as the Yao Wang Mountain Medical Temple in Shaanxi province. Here there are sculptures celebrating the great medical figures of the past, particularly Su Simao, a physician of the Sui and Tang dynasties, to whom one section of the temple was dedicated during the Ming dynasty. Throughout the courtyards they set up steles (granite slabs) on which were carved medical texts containing recipes and methods of treatment for a wide range of common ailments. These were carved in the form of

*Above:* The Yao Wang Mountain Medical Temple in Shaanxi; for a thousand years people have come here to obtain medical advice and the ingredients to make up prescriptions.

*Left:* Su Simao, a physician of the Tang dynasty, is still venerated at the Yao Wang Mountain Medical Temple for his pioneering work in cataloging the medicinal properties of plants. Though a brilliant scholar, he is reported to have consistently declined the offer of an official position in the imperial bureaucracy on the grounds that it would interrupt his medical research. He must have got something right for he lived to be over 100 years old.

pages and, by taking rubbings on rice paper, could be cut to form books.

The local community could come to this temple and not only get the necessary ingredients for the medicines — the herbs that were collected and stored in the temple — but also take rubbings from the steles. These were the libraries and photocopiers of the ancient world.

In the famous forest of tablets at the Confucian temple in Xi'an (Hsi-an) there is a vast hall of such granite slabs that provided students and the general public with access to the Confucian classics needed to pass the imperial examination. These were, in effect, public printing presses, which allowed useful knowledge to be dispersed. However, one had to be able to read and basic literacy was not available to everyone in China, any more than it was in Europe until the twentieth century. Literacy was confined, for the most part, to public officials and the landowning gentry, from which class most students came.

One of the important functions of these officials posted to the far reaches of the empire, was the collection of information and knowledge that might be useful in other regions of China. With governors and officials moving regularly from one area to another this meant that any knowledge of medical, agricultural and industrial techniques invented in one province was soon dispersed elsewhere. This dissemination was augmented by the official publication and distribution among these bureaucrats of technical encyclopedias. These covered useful knowledge from agriculture and irrigation to medicine and military defense.

In 1057 the Song emperor Renzong (Jen Tsung) instructed Su Song (who had the

Courtesy Film Australia

The forest of tablets at the Confucian temple in Xi'an on which are carved the Confucian classics. These tablets were the public libraries and photocopiers of ancient China.

famous astronomical clock built) and the naturalist Zhang Dong (Chang Tung) to gather together all knowledge about medicinal plants within the empire. In 1082 this was published under the title *Bencao tujing* (Pharmaceutical Natural History). This encyclopedia was then circulated throughout China and significantly expanded the common knowledge of a wide range of medicinal plants and their uses.

To standardize medical practice within the imperial household a college of medicine was established in the Tang dynasty from which students graduated after a proper training and examination. This, however, was not a prerequisite for medical practice outside the court. A book on forensic medicine, the first in the world, was published by a Chinese judge, Song Ci (Sung Tz'u) in 1247 and circulated among magistrates throughout the empire.

Public health was a matter of prime concern. By the thirteenth century China had many large cities of more than a million people, far larger than any cities in Europe. In the Southern Song capital of Hangzhou the population density was extremely high. The outbreak and spread of epidemics was a constant problem causing appalling death tolls. One of the reasons why Chinese medicine was so highly developed at this time was that the imperial scholar-officials had to cope with the epidemics and other health problems that came with crowded urban living, long before this became a problem in the west.

One remarkable Chinese discovery in the tenth century was the technique known as "variolation," a form of inoculation used against smallpox. Doctors took swabs from smallpox pustules, dissolved them in water and kept them at body temperature

Courtesy Film Australia

*Above:* Ginseng, found in the mountains of the north and west, was used widely as a medicinal plant throughout China and was made an imperial monopoly.

*Left:* These statues of medical heroes at the Yao Wang Mountain Medical Temple were made in the Ming dynasty. Chinese scholars and physicians such as these developed the world's first method of inoculation and started forensic medicine.

for a few weeks to allow for detoxification. The inoculum was then placed on cottonwool balls in the nose of a healthy person. The patient would get a mild dose of the disease allowing the body to develop immunity. This technique later spread to Russia and Turkey where, in the eighteenth century, it was used by Lady Mary Wortley Montagu, the wife of the British ambassador to Turkey, to provide her family with immunity during an outbreak of smallpox, which occurred in Constantinople in 1718. Details on the use of the technique had already been published in the *Philosophical Transactions of the Royal Society* in London in 1714. In all probability Jenner, who developed his method of vaccination in the second half of the eighteenth century, was aware of this Chinese technique.

Medical knowledge and discovery were not necessarily the exclusive prerogatives of the scholar-officials. For the most part medicine was in the hands of medical practitioners independent of the official examination system. In fact, medicine was one of the fields that a Confucian scholar could enter. It was considered a respectable profession because it served the people and was in the public interest. In this respect, the Confucian tradition succeeded in establishing an intellectual orthodoxy, endowing some professions with respectability while others were deemed to be heterodox and inappropriate for a scholar or gentleman.

Alchemy was one of these heterodox fields, which, nonetheless, was to have a considerable influence on medicine, metallurgy and the military. There were in fact two traditions or schools of alchemy, which were dominated, for the most part, by Taoist ideas. There was an outer or *wai tan* school that was concerned with studying chemical processes and an inner or spiritual school called *nei tan*. The alchemists of the *wai tan* school aimed at understanding the cosmological processes by studying the transformation of metals and chemicals when heated. By contemplating the changes from one state or phase to another they believed they would not only understand the cycles that govern all change but could even produce elixirs of immortality.

These ideas were also associated with a commonly held view that all natural phenomena were divided into two polarities of *yin* and *yang*. *Yin* represented elements such as water, dark, cold, the feminine and the yielding, while *yang* represented the sun, heat, the masculine, dominance and so on. The elements of *yin* and *yang* were believed to be present in all phenomena. The energy that drove the universe and animated biological life was called *qi* (*chi*). This could take either a *yin* or *yang* form.

The Chinese also recognized that all things were in a stage of flux or transformation from one state to another. Both the animate and inanimate worlds were seen to be in one of five phases that moved in cycles. For example, the phases known as wood and fire were associated with spring and summer and were *yang* parts of the year; the phases of metal and water, autumn and winter were the *yin* phases representing increasing slowness and receptivity. Apart from these four, there was earth representing the balancing of these opposites and the completion of the cycle. This passage from *Inner Writings of the Jade Purity* gives some sense to this view of the world:

Taoist sages contemplate the symbol of *yin* and *yang*. The unity of *yin* and *yang* is expressed by a light *yang* dot inside the dark *yin* half of the circle and vice versa.

In the great *tao* of heaven and earth, what endured of the myriad phenomena is their primal and harmonious *qi*. Of the things that exist in perpetuity, none surpass the sun, moon and stars. *Yin* and *yang,* the five phases [elements], day and night, come into being out of earth, and in the end return to earth. They alter in accord with the seasons, but that there should be a limit to them is also the *tao* of nature. For instance when pine resin imbibes the *qi* of mature *yang* for a thousand years it is transformed into fungus. After another thousand years of irradiation it becomes spirit; in another thousand it becomes amber and in another thousand years crystal quartz. These are the seminal essences formed through irradiation by the floriated *qi* of sun and moon.

The alchemists believed that they could produce these cycles of change artificially. One by-product of this tradition was the conviction among some alchemists (who seemed to mix their metaphors as often as their chemicals) that, by heating and reheating a mixture of mercury and sulfur (to produce cinnabar), they could make immortality pills from the compound. However, the mercury they contained, taken over a long period of time, led to the poisoning of numerous emperors, princes and high officials, particularly during the Han and Tang dynasties. The reddish gold color of cinnabar was associated with gold, and since gold was a stable substance immune from decay, it was clearly a metaphor for permanence or immortality.

This poetic analogy to gold became lost over time and, when these alchemic ideas spread to Europe, the object of the exercise was thought to be the production of gold from base metals. However, despite the abuse of this early form of chemistry, by the tenth century the Chinese were using a wide range of metals as part of compound

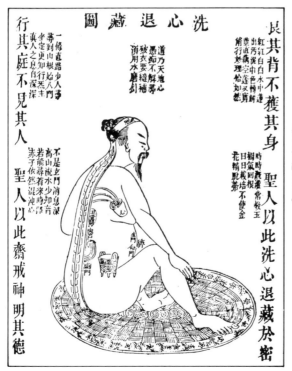

*Above:* A small burner used by alchemists during their experiments.

*Left:* This illustration from a *nei tan* alchemic text (1615) shows the *qi* flowing up the spinal column and feeding through to the heart. The cauldron in the abdomen is where the energy is transformed and immortality formed.

medicines. Chinese physicians eventually understood that mercury, used in very small quantities, could be used to kill bacteria. And as early as the Tang dynasty (618–906) the Chinese were using silver-tin amalgams for filling holes in teeth. It was not until the time of Paracelsus in the sixteenth century that the idea that the function of alchemy was to make better medicine gained currency in Europe.

It is ironic that out of the efforts of Chinese alchemists to understand the harmony with the cosmos came the discovery of the most destructive compound known — the mixture of sulfur, saltpeter and charcoal to produce gunpowder. Interestingly, even gunpowder was first used as a medicine to treat skin diseases and as a fumigant to kill insects long before it was taken up by the military in the tenth century.

The second school of alchemy, *nei tan,* was concerned with the internal transformation of the individual, the final goal being the achievement of spiritual immortality by the refinement and transformation of the body's basic energy. As in the *wai tan* school this involved heat as the transforming agent. This heat was produced by the breathing exercises involved in meditation, which fanned the fires of sexual energy at the base of the spine and lifted them to the higher mental centers. In some writings this process gave birth to a "homunculus" or new embryonic but immortal being within the body. The meditative practices and ideas associated with this *nei tan* school have a great deal in common with Tantric Buddhism and the esoteric yogic practices of India, and there may well have been shared origins. In India the idea was that the awakening of the forces of Kundalini (the twin serpents dormant at the base of the spine) and their movement up the spinal column would bring higher and higher levels of spiritual awareness, detachment and ecstasy.

Among Chinese scholars and physicians, these esoteric practices were often taken up as a means of achieving a psychic and physical balance between *yin* and *yang.* Illness was the result of an imbalance in these basic forces within the body and psyche. The role of the doctor was to restore this balance and create harmony. In acupuncture, needles were used to stimulate the circulation of the *qi* or life energy into areas that would increase the *yin* or *yang* elements. There was also the common belief that, in the act of sex, *yin* passed from the female to the male and vice versa. Sex was, therefore, regarded as a means of restoring psychic and physical balance — an idea perhaps drawn originally from Tantric Buddhism.

Sex in China was not associated with the sort of puritanical obsessiveness found in the west, where the separation of spirit and body was a fundamental assumption of Christian dogma: the escape from the corruption of the body requiring its denial as a means of elevating the spirit. In China there was no such split. The idea of another world or creator-god outside this one pulling the strings like a grand puppeteer never took hold. Although Buddhism had a considerable influence in China during the Sui and Tang dynasties, its other-worldly concerns meant that it was, for the most part, the religion of the poor and disadvantaged.

Despite the influence of some of these religious ideas, the dominant values that shaped Chinese culture were the rational and humanistic values of Confucianism. As Master Kung himself wrote: "It is man that can make the *tao* great, not the *tao* that can make the man great."

# BOMBARDS AND CATHAYAN
# FIRE ARROWS

The properties of saltpeter (potassium nitrate) were known and used by Chinese alchemists from the second century to dissolve metals. It was often known as "solve stone." In the west, the first record of its use is to be found under the name of "Chinese Snow" in *The Book of the Assembly of Medical Samples* by Ibn al-Baitar published in 1240.

Arab traders had been operating out of the southern Chinese cities of Guangzhou (Canton) and Quanzhou since the Tang dynasty (618–907). In both these cities there were large Islamic communities who were engaged in international trade and who acted as the conduit for ideas and technologies transmitted between the two cultures. Through the Arab world Chinese alchemic ideas and technology reached Europe.

By A.D. 300 the alchemist Ko Hung (Ge Hong) was mixing sulfur, saltpeter, mica hematite and clay, and heating them to produce a purple powder, which was supposed to turn mercury into silver when heated. Sulfur was the common ingredient in all recipes for elixirs. Its poisonous properties were well known and a technique of "subduing the toxicity and volatility of sulfur by fire" was adopted by alchemists and could well have led to the development of gunpowder itself.

Cathayan fire arrows, as they were known in the west, represented the first use of rocket propulsion in warfare. By the eleventh century these arrows were often fired from rocket launchers loaded on wheelbarrows. Many had explosive warheads, which, although not of great destructive power, could cause mayhem among cavalry.

Alchemists would mix sulfur and saltpeter then ignite it until there was no longer any flame. This was the subduing process. One of the earliest alchemic texts (which dates from around 850) referring to the inflammable properties of sulfur and saltpeter was the *Classified Essentials of the Mysterious Tao of the True Origin of Things:*

> Some have heated together sulfur, realgar [arsenic disulfide] and saltpeter with honey; smoke and flames result, so that their hands and faces have been burned, and even the whole house where they were working burned down. Evidently this only brings Taoism into discredit and Taoist alchemists are thus warned clearly not to do it.

However, despite all the warnings, knowledge of the incendiary properties of gunpowder were to move out of the domain of alchemists and into the hands of the military. The significance of its use in the military field was clear by 1067, when the emperor banned the sale of sulfur and saltpeter to foreigners and turned their production and use into a state monopoly. Twenty-three years earlier, in 1044, Zeng Gongling (Tseng Kong-ling) compiled his *Collection of the Most Important Military Techniques* in which he described many kinds of gunpowder weapons and gave a number of instructions for making them. One such instruction provides the first

As Chinese military strategy was primarily defensive these new gunpowder weapons were to play a significant role as the Song dynasty came under siege from northern invaders throughout the eleventh and twelfth centuries. Here, fragmentation bombs are seen doing their all too familiar work among the invaders.

account of a bomb producing poisonous gas. To produce a *du you yan qiu* the following ingredients were mixed:

| | |
|---|---|
| 30 liang of saltpeter | Arsenic |
| 15 liang of sulfur | Roots of langdu |
| 5 liang of charcoal | Bamboo and hemp fibers |
| Croton seeds | Wood oil and tar |

[1 liang = 1.75 ounces]

Within a period of less than two hundred years the Chinese were to field a vast number of gunpowder-based weapons, including cannons or bombards, bombs that were lobbed on invading troops, two-stage rockets and fire arrows, land mines and even submarine mines. The reason for this proliferation of new weapons was not just the knowledge of the explosive properties of gunpowder, but the fact that the Song emperors were constantly under siege from invading armies of the Jin Tartar from the northwest. The production of gunpowder weapons was to be taken over by a special government bureau, which established 11 large workshops employing more than 40,000 workers. In *Xinsi qi qi lu* (Tearful Records of the Battle of Qizhou) Zhao Yurong wrote of the output of these imperial factories in 1221:

This late Qing illustration shows imperial officials surveying one of the imperial workshops where a variety of weapons were made.

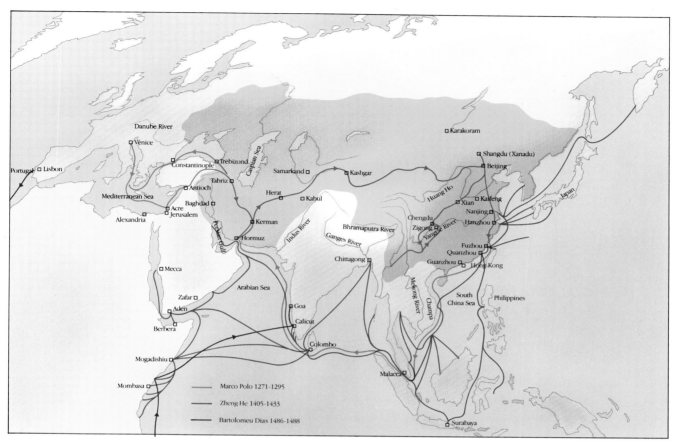

This map traces the complex routes by which gunpowder, silk, porcelain, paper, printing and the compass were transferred from China, through Central Asia, to Europe where they were to play a crucial part in the breakdown of feudalism. A technological arms race was set in motion, which would not only transform and refine gunpowder weapons, but would return them to the gates of the Celestial Empire with quite devastating consequences.

On the same day there were produced 7,000 gunpowder crossbow arrows, 10,000 gunpowder longbow arrows, 3,000 barbed gunpowder bombs and 20,000 ordinary gunpowder bombs.

By this time the Chinese were producing fragmentation bombs (*zhentian lei*) that could devastate an area the size of a house. A graphic description of its destructive power is found in *Jin shi* (History of the Jin Dynasty) 1126:

When it went off it made a report like sky-rending thunder. An area of more than half a mu [one-twelfth of an acre] was scorched on which men, horses and leather armor were shattered. Even iron coats of mail were riddled.

The scale of the Chinese army was enormous by European standards. By 1040 the regular army comprised about 1.25 million men. The cost of maintaining such an army was also enormous. Quite apart from the production of gunpowder weapons, the traditional bow and crossbow departments were producing 16.5 million arrowheads a year. By 1160, the yearly output of the imperial armaments office came to 3.24 million weapons. Iron production during the eleventh century reached 125,000 tons a year.

The troops were stationed primarily on the northwestern borders. They lived in fortress towns, which extended in an arc from the Great Wall in the north to the Kunlun Mountains that run up to the high Tibetan plateau. The strategy was defensive, with the armies acting as self-sufficient frontier communities, growing their own food wherever possible. The military strategy was to create an impenetrable barrier against the highly mobile armies of the nomadic Mongol peoples of central Asia.

Despite enormous efforts to limit the spread of their advanced military technology to the enemy beyond China's borders, there was a constant dispersion of knowledge as traders and captured soldiers provided the Khitan and Jin Tartar kingdoms, to the northwest, access to crossbows, methods of making armor plating and, finally, to gunpowder weapons. So that, despite China's technological superiority and enormous resources, the Jin Tartars were able to occupy the north of China and take the Northern Song capital of Kaifeng in 1127. The spread of military technology to the west was to be greatly increased with the Mongol invasion in 1279, which in turn displaced the Jin.

Under the Emperor Kublai Khan, China was reunited and a loose imperial structure of kingdoms established throughout central Asia that extended Mongol power and influence from the Pacific to the Mediterranean. It was this vast Mongol empire that allowed European merchants such as Marco Polo to travel, with passports bearing the seal of the Great Khan, along the famous silk route from Constantinople to Xanadu, the emperor's summer residence. Along this highway camel trains carried the exquisite industrial products of China — porcelain, silk and even silkworms smuggled in bamboo poles, which were used to found the silk industry in Europe. Accounts, like those of Marco Polo, of the fabulous wealth and power of China were to fire imagination and greed.

By this same route that brought gunpowder weapons to the west, came the "black death" (the bubonic plague) the other great scourge that was to devastate Europe in the fourteenth century. These two imports from the east were to play a significant part in breaking down the feudal social and economic structures of medieval Europe.

# MERCHANTS, ARTISANS AND BUREAUCRATS

*I assure you that this river runs for such a distance and through so many regions and there are so many cities on its banks that, truth to tell, in the amount of shipping it carries and the total volume and value of its traffic, it exceeds all the rivers of the Christians put together and their seas into the bargain. I give you my word that I have seen in this city fully five thousand ships at once, all afloat on this river. Then you may reflect, since this city, which is not very big, has so many ships, how many there must be in the others. For I assure you that the river flows through more than sixteen provinces, and there are on its banks more than two hundred cities, all having more ships than this.*

Marco Polo, on passing through the city of I-ching on the Yangtze
in the thirteenth century.

To maintain the vast Song and Mongol armies, the imperial workshops as well as the state monopolies in iron and salt required economic organization and technology of considerable sophistication. By the Song dynasty (960 –1279) merchant guilds were involved in large-scale internal and international trading

Despite the low social status of merchants, government revenue generated from trade became increasingly important. Along the waterways of the rich rice-growing regions of the Yangtze delta, depicted in this Song dynasty scene, prosperous cities such as Suzhou, Hangzhou and Nanjing grew up. Here, rich merchant families were employed to manage the trade in government monopolies, such as salt, tea, iron, porcelain and even silk.

operations. As Marco Polo observed, the volume of trade through the waterways of the Yangtze delta was clearly greater than that of Europe. Craft specialization and increasingly wide markets for industrial products allowed for a division of labor that was not achieved in Europe until the eve of the Industrial Revolution in the late eighteenth century. Paper money was being used, in part, to alleviate the growing demand for metal currency, which was always in short supply. In fact, China at the time that Marco Polo was employed by the Great Khan seems to have been on the threshold of a mercantile and even an industrial revolution.

The Industrial Revolution in Britain in the eighteenth century was essentially built around the factory system of production, particularly in the spinning industry where water power was combined with the mechanical skills of instrument makers who were able to automate the spinning of thread. Economic historians have pointed to the silk and cotton spinning factories established by John Lombe and by Richard Arkwright as forming the "leading edge" of technological and industrial innovation, which was to spread to other industries such as the potteries of Staffordshire and the iron foundries of Derby. Yet, as early as 1313, the scholar Wang Chen in his *Treatise on Agriculture* described the mechanical spinning of hemp, which was used widely throughout northern China. Wang was so delighted by this example of industrial innovation that he wrote the following poem in praise of mechanical spinning:

> There is one driving belt for wheels both great and small.
> When one wheel turns, the others all turn with it.
> The rovings are transmitted evenly from the bobbin rollers.
> The threads wind by themselves on to the reeling frame.

But this technology was not to have the same impact on China as it was to have on Europe.

In ceramics, Chinese porcelain was not only one of the most sought after commodities for trade but was actually produced on commission for Arab merchants or their agents living in the ports of Guangzhou and Quanzhou. The skill of the craftsmen and the quality of the glazes were not matched in Europe until the late eighteenth century. Large quantities of Chinese porcelain were shipped throughout Southeast Asia and the Middle East, and the scale of production was enormous. Silk and cotton weaving, despite being essentially "cottage" industries, used complex two-man draw looms, which allowed for the weaving of rich and magnificent patterns sought after throughout the world.

Despite this large-scale trade, the status of merchants in China up until the Song dynasty was low. They were at the bottom of the social hierarchy, as they were in the same period in Europe. In cultures relying primarily on agriculture for their wealth, the trader was often regarded as a parasite who failed to contribute to the productive well-being of the state. Until the advent of money as the dominant mode of economic exchange, taxes were collected in the form of grain, cloth or other domestic produce but with traders constantly on the move, taxing them on the basis of a percentage of productive output was, to say the least, difficult. Even when taxes

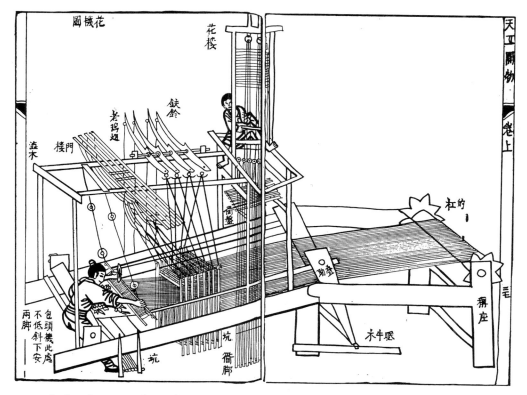

Craft industries such as silk and porcelain had reached remarkable levels of technological
sophistication. The two-man draw loom allowed for the weaving of intricate patterns,
which made Chinese silk a prized luxury throughout the ancient world.

could be extracted, the actual extent of a merchant's wealth was never easy to verify.
In China, from the time of the Han dynasty, laws had been enacted restricting the
commercial activities and the power of merchants.

In *Five Evils,* Han Fei had this to say on the issue of merchants and artisans:

> An enlightened administrator causes the number of merchants, artisans and vagrants to
> be few and places them in a humble post in order to make them desire to engage in the
> basic occupation [agriculture] and to reduce the numbers engaged in the subsidiary
> occupation [commerce].

As late as the Yuan (Mongol) dynasty (1279–1368), Wang Chen in his book *Nong
shu* extolled the activities of the farmer and criticized the inability of the wandering
merchant to fulfil his moral obligation as seen from the Confucian perspective:

> In his public relations he [the farmer] pays his tax and does his corvée service; at home
> he feeds his parents and rears his wife and children. In addition he concludes marriage
> relationships and has social contact with his neighbors. In the field of social customs
> nobody is better than the farmer. Craftsmen on the other hand rely on their skill and
> merchants manipulate surpluses. They move around and are without a definite place to
> live. They cannot be perfect in the fulfillment of their duties of caring for their parents
> and their feelings of friendship.

Such moralizing about the virtues of the farmer and the turpitude of the merchant and artisan did not prevent some Chinese merchants from becoming both rich and influential. However, traditional Confucian attitudes clearly affected the merchants' official status. For example, the sons of merchants were, at times, banned from sitting for the imperial examinations. For a wealthy merchant to gain social status he had to give up trade, buy a rural estate and become one of the gentry. He might thereby be able to get his children into the imperial civil service and through them achieve high social standing. Only scholars and Buddhist monks were free from the humiliation of corporal punishment and the obligations of corvée labor. (A similar attitude towards trade continued in Europe well into the nineteenth century. Trade or manufacture were considered to be of sufficiently low status, particularly in Britain to cause rich industrialists to retire, buy rural estates and send their children to Oxford or Cambridge, so allowing them to join the elite who manned the British imperial service as governors of Bengal, New South Wales or Canada — a possible factor in Britain's industrial decline in the late nineteenth century.)

Chinese merchants were also seen to be making immoral profits by buying cheap and selling dear, and from usury — lending money and obtaining wealth from interest. Given human nature's propensity for envy, the capacity to accumulate wealth was regarded by the Chinese Confucian scholars (as it was by Church fathers in Europe) as disruptive to social harmony — a social harmony that was primarily designed to allow *them* to control the surplus from agriculture and with it to maintain their own power and privileges.

Until the Tang Dynasty (618–907) the major challenge to the power and

The Art Institute of Chicago

Merchants were, for the most part, treated as necessary parasites by the Confucian scholars who ran the empire. In the Confucian social hierachy scholars were at the top followed by farmers, while merchants and artisans were at the very bottom.

prerogatives of the Confucian scholar-bureaucrats had been the threat from military and aristocratic families intent on establishing a feudal structure similar to that which existed in Europe and Japan. But by the Song dynasty the meritocratic imperial examination had become accepted as the normal route to political power by the dominant rural gentry. It also provided an avenue, however indirect, by which merchants with talent could gain social mobility. Merchant wealth, or an alliance with such wealth, could also provide the means by which poor officials and gentry could support a son through the arduous examination system, which took a minimum of six years even to be ready to sit for the qualifying examination.

A change in both the status and power of merchants in Europe and China occurred as rulers came to rely increasingly on money, despite the fact that laws aimed at keeping merchants separate from the rest of the community remained in the statute books. Sumptuary laws controlling all aspects of consumption were common in both cultures with the same intention of preventing merchants from using their wealth to achieve social status and, in some cases, were designed to make them look ridiculous. In China, in the Tang dynasty, no merchant was permitted to ride on a horse or wear rich clothes. (One of the factors creating a demand for luxuries in Europe was the relaxing of these laws there in the fourteenth century. With social mobility new craft industries grew up to cater for the demands of socially mobile merchants and artisans.) In China, by the twelfth century, merchants were nonetheless being employed to manage many of the great state monopolies, as well as to control the supplies that kept the border armies functioning.

In Song China the transition to a money economy was to happen much earlier

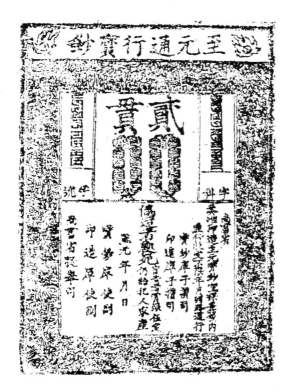

The world's first paper money; the rings towards the top of the note represent the number of strings of "cash" (100 copper coins) it represented. Throughout the eleventh and twelfth centuries trade grew at such a rate that a cash economy began to emerge. To cope with the demand for currency the Song emperors printed paper money, and suffered the inevitable consequences of rampant inflation.

than in Europe. For example, in 749 less than 4 percent of taxes and revenue were collected in money but by 1065 this had risen to over 50 percent. There were, however, a number of crucial changes during the Song dynasty that led to a marked increase in commerce and, particularly, in international trade. The financial and military plight of the Song empire was to change, briefly, the status of merchants and to shake the Chinese Confucian bureaucrats out of their traditional conservatism.

The empire was saddled, not only with an army four times the size of that required in the earlier Tang dynasty (because of the significantly greater military threat on the northern borders), but also with an equally large increase in the number of bureaucrats needed to serve it. To meet the consequent need for extra revenue the Song took measures to stimulate foreign trade. They established a maritime trade commission to supervise and tax merchant ships. In 987 four separate missions or trade delegations were sent to other Southeast Asian countries carrying a selection of Chinese goods, including silk and porcelain. These delegations offered special licenses to foreign merchants and also issued them to Chinese merchants going abroad. During the Tang dynasty there was only one port — Guangzhou — that was allowed to trade with foreigners. The maritime trade commission opened up seven more points along the Guangdong (Kwantung) and Fujian coasts, as well as a dozen naval bases from which armed vessels patrolled the coast protecting merchant fleets from Japanese and other pirates.

With the splitting of the empire after the successful invasion of northern China by the Jin Tartars, the Song emperor was forced to turn his attention to building a navy to hold the invaders at the Yangtze River.

60

The strategy seems to have worked. In 1098 foreign trade represented 0.82 percent of the gross cash income of the Song government; 13 years later, in 1111, it had doubled to 1.7 percent. However, the pressure to raise more and more revenue to support almost constant warfare with the Jin Tartars on the northern borders forced the Song into the classic response of printing more money. By 1107 the value of paper currency in China had dropped to 1 percent of its face value, perhaps one of the first examples in history of inflation caused by too much money circulating in the economy. Prices soared and the necessary financial stringency, coupled with the famines and internal disarray led to the Jin Tartars overrunning northern China in 1127 and driving the Song south of the Yangtze River. Here they could hold their own against the northern armies of the Jin whose strength lay in the mobility and skill of their cavalry. Among the waterways of the rich rice-growing areas of southern China they were no match for the Song navy.

The need to rely on naval power led to a new emphasis on boatbuilding and the creation of a vast array of vessels. Innovation was rewarded by the administration. The world's first paddle boat was designed, and used to move troops through the shallow waterways and canals that intersect the countryside south of the Yangtze. Huge boats designed like fortresses were sent into battle, equipped with cannon, rockets and bombs of all descriptions. Explosive rockets, which would shoot across the surface of the water, were developed along with submarine mines. But perhaps the greatest long-term impact of this new emphasis on naval defense was its effect on overseas trade.

With the agricultural land upon which the southern Song could draw for revenue reduced enormously, the income from trade in state monopolies and excise duties on trade made up 50 percent of total government revenue. By 1131 overseas trade alone had grown to 20 percent of the total cash revenue. With this change in the basic balance of the Chinese imperial economy there was a subsequent shift in the attitude of the bureaucracy towards merchants. The two merchants who were largely responsible for the increase in overseas trade in 1131, Cai Jinfang (Ts'ai Chingfang) and a Muslim, Pu Luoxin (Abu al-Hassan) were both given honorary official rank in 1136. The Song court also announced that any merchants whose overseas trade figures for the year amounted to more than 50,000 strings of cash would be given official rank, and that any government official in charge of commercial affairs who supervised more than one million strings of cash would be promoted one grade. (Chinese paper currency represented so many strings of copper cash. The Chinese copper coin had a hole in the middle allowing a thousand of them to be threaded on to one piece of string to represent a single unit.)

It is significant that the second of these two merchants should be a Muslim. In both Guangzhou and, later, Quanzhou large Muslim communities had established themselves during the Song, for, as the overland silk routes that linked the Middle East with China became impassable because of constant warfare on the Chinese borders, the sea routes to the Red Sea became correspondingly more important. By this route silk, porcelain, tea and spices reached the Arab world and from there the growing markets of Europe.

The scale of this trade was considerable: nearly 10,000 pieces of broken Chinese porcelain have recently been found at Fustat near Cairo, one of the factory bases used in this trade since the Tang dynasty. Similar sites have been discovered in Oman and other centers of trade in the Red Sea.

Not only trade goods reached the west via this route; the transfer of Chinese technology was to be equally or more important than the luxuries that found their way into the hands of kings, feudal lords and the great monasteries. Of greater long-term significance were Chinese navigational techniques. The compass and Chinese boat designs were taken up by Arab traders and transferred from there to Europe. The south-pointing compass was adapted for navigation at sea during the Song dynasty. The compass had been used in China for centuries by geomancers for the laying out of buildings so that they would conform to *fengshui,* the earth's vital energy, which the Chinese believed flowed through the surface of the earth like blood through the veins of the human body. Often referred to as the forces of "wind

Courtesy Film Australia

The descendants of the Arab traders who established themselves at Guangzhou during the Song dynasty still gather at their ancient mosque.

and water," they governed the correct positioning of buildings in relation to landscape, which was considered crucial for the harmony of humanity and the environment. The compass was also soon to be taken up by the military and by miners who used it to find direction underground. Its arrival in Europe came at a crucial time and was essential for navigation out of sight of land. Before this sailors hugged the shore, a dangerous practice but the only means they had of knowing where they were going.

Another important Chinese device to be taken up by European boatbuilders was the stern-post rudder. Hitherto, European ships had depended upon the use of an oar extending from the back of galleys. The stern-post rudder allowed for the construction of much larger boats whose direction could be controlled by a wheel. The addition of more than one mast and the use of lateen sails, derived from the Arab dhow, allowed European sailors to extend radically the scale and scope of maritime trade. The adoption of this new fore-and-aft rig enabled mariners to tack effectively into the wind. It removed the need to have oarsmen, a basic feature of the medieval galley. This had two results: it lightened the boats, providing more room for cargo, and it also allowed boats to sail at any time of the year, not just when the winds were blowing in the required direction. Ships from the eastern Mediterranean could now travel in all seasons to northern Europe and the Baltic States.

\*   \*   \*

The European Crusades to retake the Holy Lands from the Islamic infidels from the eleventh century onwards also exposed many northern Europeans to the luxuries and sophistication of Islamic culture, art and technology. With the improvement in shipping, new commodities once only accessible to aristocrats began to turn up in the market places of Bruges, Antwerp, London and Hamburg. Apart from the pepper,

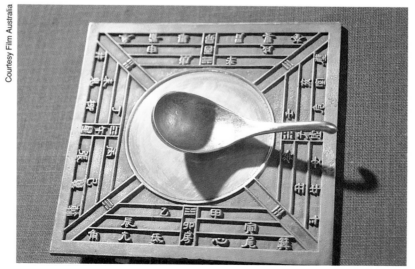

Courtesy Film Australia

An early form of the Chinese south-pointing compass, which was brought to the west by Arab traders in the thirteenth century.

63

cinnamon, cloves and nutmeg that were increasingly in demand to disguise the flavor and taste of bad food, there were new commodities and, with them, new words entered the languages of Europe. Cotton from the Arab *cotone,* damask from Damascus, baldachin from Bagdad, muslin from Mosul, gauze from Gaza, along with divan, bazaar, artichoke, spinach, tarragon, tariff, orange, alcove, arsenal, jar, magazine, syrup, taffeta, tea and porcelain.

The new all-weather ships, first developed in the Italian city-states between 1280 and 1330, linked Europe in a coherent commercial web as never before, despite the almost constant political and military conflicts. Salt, for example, from southern Europe could be shipped to the Baltic where it was used to preserve fish and cabbage, and markedly improved the diet and the capacity of people to sustain themselves through the harsh northern winters. In return, timber, metals, cloth and wool were shipped back. The trade in these commodities led to a closer commercial interaction in a Europe-wide market.

Credit facilities, bills of exchange and the greater circulation of money began to lubricate the wheels of trade. The access to wider markets allowed, as it had so much earlier in China, for greater specialization on the part of artisans based in towns and in traditional rural industries. It also precipitated a shift in the centers of wealth and power from feudal aristocratic estates into the hands of the merchant princes of the Italian city-states.

# POWER, PROFITS AND THE ARMS RACE

*At the end of five days' journey, you arrive at the noble and handsome city of Zaitun [Quanzhou], which has a port on the sea coast celebrated for the resort of shipping, loaded with merchandise, that is afterwards distributed through every part of the province of Manji [Fujian]. The quantity of pepper imported there is so considerable, that what is carried to Alexandria, to supply the demand of the western parts of the world, is trifling in comparison, perhaps not more than the hundredth part. It is indeed impossible to convey an idea of the number of merchants and the accumulation of goods in this place, which is held to be one of the largest ports in the world. The Great Khan derives a vast revenue from this place, as every merchant is obliged to pay ten per cent. upon the amount of his investment. The ships are freighted by them at the rate of thirty per cent. for fine goods, forty-four for pepper, and for sandalwood and other drugs, as well as articles of trade in general, forty per cent. It is computed by the merchants, that their charges, including customs and freight, amount to half the value of the cargo; and yet upon the half that remains to them their profit is so considerable, that they are always disposed to return to the same market with a further stock of merchandise.*

*The Travels of Marco Polo*, Book II

In 1271 China was overwhelmed by the Mongol armies of the Great Khan. The northern capital of Beijing was established and Kublai Khan ruled the greatest empire the world has ever known. The Yuan dynasty, which he founded, extended the policies of maritime expansion adopted by the Song. The European end of the trade with China was controlled largely by Venice and Genoa. These city-states were a new and unique phenomenon. They contributed to the rise of Europe as an economic and military power and were eventually to challenge the might of imperial China. However, at the end of the thirteenth century when Marco Polo had returned to his native city of Venice, the Venetians and the Genoese were at war over the control of the trade in Asian luxuries flowing into the ports of Egypt and the Middle East. In fact Marco Polo was to write his account of his journey to the east in a Genoese jail after being captured at the famous Battle of Curzola in September 1298.

The Venetian fleets were funded and maintained by powerful merchant families. The power and influence of the merchants in these cities was in marked contrast to those of Song China. Venice and Genoa were city-states whose major source of revenue and wealth was maritime trade conducted by merchants whose economic fortunes had grown with the power of these city-states. They shipped Asian spices and luxuries such as porcelain and silk to the market places of northern Europe and, in return, they brought salt fish, grain and woolen textiles from the north to the market places of southern Italy. In the republican structure, which underpinned the rule of the doge (the head of the Venetian state and maritime empire), the influence of these merchants had grown to challenge the traditional patrician and aristocratic power.

Venetian merchants trading bolts of cloth, usually woolen, in exchange for pepper and spices from Java or silk and porcelain from China.

Throughout feudal Europe aristocratic lords were concerned with the control of agricultural surplus and the Church itself was one of the great landowners and supporters of this feudal system. The towns of medieval Europe grew up outside this enclosed rural economy. They were the domain of craftsmen and merchants and were the market centers that offered a new freedom. Here, merchants challenged the laws of the Church by using Jews as bankers to escape the prohibition on usury. Here too, new ideas, fashions and tastes were evident; in marked contrast to the Chinese towns, which, however rich, remained administrative centers governed by imperial bureaucrats.

There was another important difference in the position of merchants operating out of the city-states. Florence, Genoa, Milan and Venice were all constantly in competition with one another, each trying to absorb part of the territory of the other. In these predominantly money economies taxes on merchant wealth provided the means for defense and paid for mercenary armies or condotieri (contractors), which were in common use by the thirteenth century. The technological arms race, which

A fourteenth century siege of a stronghold showing the use of primitive cannons and crossbows introduced from China.

this competition spawned, provided new careers for artisans and craftsmen in Europe.

First, crossbows entered the arsenals of Europe from China and then gunpowder and cannons. Between Milan and Genoa there was a race to see which one would produce stronger armor to withstand arrows from increasingly powerful crossbows. The arrows were originally made of wood and then of laminated metal, making previous armor redundant. The crossbow also helped to shift the balance of power away from the arbitrary power of those masters of the "feudal blitzkreig," the knight in armor. The longbow took a strong man and ten years of training to shoot accurately. The crossbow, on the other hand, could be fired, like the gun, by almost anyone who could point a stick straight. It therefore provided townspeople with an easily mastered means of defending themselves. The Catalan Company, using crossbows in Sicily in 1282, for example, destroyed an army of French knights. It is little wonder that at the Second Lateran Council (1139) the pope should decree this weapon too lethal to be used by Christians against one another.

There was another import from Asia that was to have an equally profound impact on the fabric of feudal Europe — the black death. In 1346 when the bubonic plague first began its appalling sweep through Europe, it killed about a third of the population within one generation. The source of peasant labor to work the feudal lords' lands was in many areas completely wiped out. There was an acute labor shortage, which provided those peasants who survived with a new mobility. Before the plague they were neither permitted to leave their lord's domain or "hundred" nor to sell their labor. Now there was such an acute shortage of labor that even to plant and bring in the harvest it was necessary to poach labor from neighboring regions and to pay cash wages as an inducement. The corvée labor system of many areas of medieval Europe was broken down. Money wages in the hands of the rural peasantry linked them more closely than ever before to the market place of the town and the mercantile values it embodied.

\*   \*   \*

It is interesting to speculate on what would have happened in Europe had the efforts of Pope Innocent III (1198 –1216) and Boniface VIII (1295–1303) to create a Holy Roman Empire (like that of China) embracing all of Europe been successful. Within the Catholic church there existed many parallel institutions to those that provided the Chinese empire with its great stability and continuity. First, there was the

Bibliothèque Nationale, Paris

The taking of Rouen by Henry V, 1418 –19. Cannons were becoming increasingly more powerful and were employed to attack the once invulnerable bastion of feudal power — the castle. By the end of the Hundred Years War between England and France, the King of France's artillery train was knocking down English castles in Normandy at the rate of one a month.

cosmology provided by the Bible; second, there was the clergy, linked by a common language, Latin, and an administrative hierarchy based, in part at least, on education. There is little reason to believe that the bureaucracy surrounding the thirteenth century popes could not have been extended effectively to the management of an imperial structure, had the geographical, cultural and economic circumstances of Europe been different. However, the marriage of ecclesiastical and temporal authority, embodied in the emperor of China, eluded popes and princes alike, and Europe was to remain fragmented in competing city- and nation-states, with all the consequent violence and rivalry.

For example, when the Hundred Years War between France and England began in 1337, it was little more than a squabble between two families over succession and inheritance. By the time it ended it was a full-scale war between nation-states. In the Battle of Crécy in 1346 it was the English longbow men who brought the flower of French chivalry to their knees and gave Normandy to the English, despite the fact that the French had 24 cannons at their disposal. But in 1453 it was the artillery train of Louis XI that was able to take back this same territory by blowing down the walls of the English castles in Normandy at the rate of one a month. The constant pressure of warfare and the demand for new and better cannons was soon to sweep away the security and political power that was once embodied in the feudal castle and the knight on horseback.

With remarkable speed, new variations on the cannon emerged. Primitive devices made on the same principle as wooden barrels (laying strips of iron side by side and binding them together with metal bands) were soon to be replaced by fully cast bombards of considerable size.

At the other extreme, handguns, known as Hakenbüchse, were being produced in the fourteenth century in Germany. These initially required two men to operate: one aiming and the other lighting the fuse. By the mid-fifteenth century these had evolved into the matchlock, with a trigger allowing one man to aim and fire. At the Venetian-controlled armaments factory at Brescia, matchlock guns — arquebuses or harquebuses — were being produced for the arsenals of monarchs throughout Europe. It was from here that Henry VIII ordered his handguns. The demand required founding and metalwork skills of a high order. The production of the trigger mechanism, in particular, demanded the precision engineering of clock-makers, combined with the steel-making capacities of the finest swordsmith. To cast the massive cannons also demanded metallurgical skills of an extremely high order.

In Venice, the arenali or arsenal (from the Arab word for workshop) was established, which provided a virtual production line in boatbuilding and fitting out. At its peak 16,000 craftsmen and workers were employed. As boats moved down the canal, workshops producing guns, rigging, sails and provisions fitted them out. With these warships the Venetian state protected its maritime empire. A significant element in the struggle for economic power was the control of the lucrative trade in Asian goods and between them the Venetians and Genoese had cornered the market. However, the trade was severely threatened by the collapse of the Mongol empire, and the rise of the Ottoman Turks. The capture of Constantinople by the Turks in

# LEONARDO'S LETTER

In the highly competitive environment of fifteenth century Europe the demand for skilled artisans and engineers grew as monarchs competed to attract them to their courts, especially those whose inventive powers might give the monarch a military or economic advantage. Many of these skilled engineers were educated men familiar with the Greek sciences that flourished during the Renaissance. New careers and social status came as they hawked their talents around the courts of Europe. Leonardo da Vinci wrote the following letter to Duke Ludovico Sforza (Duke of Milan) in 1482 selling his services, not as a painter, but as a military engineer:

"Having seen, most Illustrious Lord, and considered to my own satisfaction the specimens of all those who proclaim themselves skilled contrivers of instruments of war, and observing that the invention and operation of such instruments are no different from those in common use, I shall endeavour, meaning no insult to anyone else, to make myself known to your Excellency, revealing my secrets, and offering them as it may please you and at an opportune time, and to put into operation all those things which are briefly described below:

Item 1. I have a method of constructing bridges, both strong and extremely light, so as to be easily carried, whereby you may pursue and at other times fly from the enemy; and others, safe and indestructible by fire or battle, easy and convenient to lift and place in position. Also methods of burning and destroying those of the enemy.

Item 2. I know a way, during the conduct of a siege, to take water out of the trenches, and to make an infinite variety of bridges, corridors and ladders, and other machines pertaining to such expeditions.

Item 3. Furthermore, if, by reason of the height of the defences, or by the strength of the building and its situation, it is impossible to take by bombardment, I have a method of destroying any rock fortress or other stronghold, even if it be founded in solid stone.

Item 4. I also have a method of constructing a kind of cannon, most convenient and easy to carry, that may hurl a small storm of missiles; and the smoke will greatly frighten the enemy to his great harm and confusion.

Item 5. And should the fight be at sea, I have many kinds of instruments for both attacking

and defending ships, which will resist the greatest bombardment, and powder, and smoke.

Item 6. I have a means whereby, by the use of secret and winding passages and paths, and without making any sound, you may reach whatever place you choose, even if it is necessary to pass under a trench or river.

Item 7. I will make covered chariots, safe and impregnable, which may enter among the enemy and his artillery, and so defeat any body of men, however great, and behind them may come infantry without risking hurt or setback.

Item 8. If there should be need, I will make cannon, mortars and lighter ordnance of a fine and useful kind, and quite unlike those in common use.

Item 9. If bombardment should fail, I will contrive catapults, mangonels, *trabocchi* and other machines of marvellous efficacy and uncommonness. And in short, according to the circumstances, I can contrive varied and infinite means of offence and defence.

Item 10. Also, in time of peace, I believe I can satisfy very well, and as much as any other, in architecture, in the composition of buildings both public and private, and in bringing water from one place to another.

Further, I can execute sculpture in marble, in bronze or in clay, and likewise painting, in which I will do whatever is wanted and as well as any other.

And I would be able to fashion the bronze horse, which will be to the immortal glory and the eternal honour of the happy memory of the Lord, your father, and of the great house of Sforza.

And if it should seem to any man that the things described herein are not possible, I offer most freely and openly to make trial of them in your park, or in whatever place it may please your Excellency, to whom, with the utmost humility, I commend myself."

Photo: Scala

This detail from Carpaccio's "Return of the Ambassadors" depicts the new merchant class who, in Venice and other Italian city states, had not only gained enormous wealth but had won political control of the state itself. This would have been unthinkable in Confucian China despite the prosperity of its own merchants.

1453 cut European access to the overland trade routes to the east. Though Chinese and other Asian commodities continued to arrive, taxes and commissions demanded by the Turks, Egyptians and other intermediaries forced up prices.

Other European monarchs had looked on with envy at the profits being made by the Venetians and Genoese in this eastern trade, and the possibility of finding a direct route to its source, thereby eliminating the Arab and Turkish intermediaries, inspired some heroic efforts. In 1291 the Vivaldi brothers from Genoa attempted to find a sea route around Africa but were never heard of again. Mythical stories of the mighty kingdom of Prester John, a knight who went to the Crusades but continued east, kept alive a vision of Christian kingdoms in the east of unbelievable luxury and wealth.

While much of Europe was torn by internecine warfare throughout the fourteenth century, Portugal was a united kingdom and largely untouched by civil disturbance. In 1385 King John I (known as John the Great or John the Bastard depending on one's view of history) seized the Portuguese throne and founded the Aviz dynasty. He was able to defeat the King of Castile, primarily with the aid of English archers. To cement his ties with the English throne, and to help secure his country's independence from Spain, he married Phillippa of Lancaster, the daughter of John of

Gaunt. She bore him six sons, the third of whom was to become known as Henry the Navigator. Henry was to make possible the global expansion of European maritime power and trade.

Like other European princes, Henry and his brothers were expected to prove their manhood by participating in the Crusades and "washing their hands in the blood of the infidel." Henry's father assigned him the task of building an armada at Oporto to invade the Muslim stronghold of Ceuta, opposite Gibraltar on the north African side of the Mediterranean. In 1415 the armada took Ceuta and, apart from the satisfaction of massacring infidels, the loot, consisting of pepper, cloves and other spices from the Far East along with other Asian riches, obviously impressed Henry. He returned to Portugal and established at Sagres, Portugal's most southerly promontory, a court devoted to maritime exploration. At the nearby port of Lagos, Henry began to experiment in shipbuilding. He adopted the design of the Arab dhows that plied the Mediterranean and Indian Oceans and whose lateen sails gave them superb maneuverability. The name of these boats was *caravos* in Arabic and they became known as caravels. They were about 70 feet long, 25 feet in the beam and displaced about 50 tons. These small boats, with crews of around 20 sailors, were equipped with Arab charts and the Chinese compass. Henry was to establish one of the most extensive libraries of charts and maps in Europe. His brother, on a tour to Venice, even acquired charts and an account of Marco Polo's travels for Henry. With as much knowledge as was possessed by Europeans at this time, he sent his tiny fleets on missions to explore the southern African coast and perhaps even to discover the source of oriental trade and riches. When Vasco Da Gama finally succeeded in reaching India in 1498 he provided the Portuguese with direct access to the markets of the east. As a consequence, the Portuguese forced down the taxes levied by the Egyptian, Turks and Italian middlemen to one eightieth of their former level.

Biblioteca Nacional, Lisbon

Henry the Navigator, son of the King of Portugal who, in the early fifteenth century, financed a revolution in boat design incorporating Arab and Chinese techniques, which ultimately enabled the European merchants to find a direct sea route to the east.

# ZHENG HE AND THE LAST OF THE TREASURE SHIPS

*The ships, which sail the southern seas and south of it, are like houses. When their sails are spread they are like great clouds in the sky. Their rudders are several tens of feet long. A single ship carries several hundred men and has in the stores a year's supply of grain. Pigs are fed and grain fermented on board. There is no account of dead or living, no going back to the mainland when once the people have set forth upon the caerulean sea.*

Zhou Chufei, 1178

*Among the inhabitants of China there are those who own numerous ships, on which they send their agents to foreign places. For nowhere in the world are there to be found people richer than the Chinese.*

Ibn Batuta, 1347

Had Vasco da Gama arrived in the Indian Ocean just 70 years earlier he might well have met the vast Chinese fleet of the Three Jeweled Eunuch, Admiral Zheng He, whose huge treasure ships were five times the size of the Portuguese caravels. Between 1405 and 1430 this great admiral led seven armadas each consisting of as many as 62 ships and carrying around 40,000 soldiers. His journeys of discovery and diplomacy had taken him along the east coast of Africa, to Mecca (he was, in fact, a Muslim) and to the ports of India, Ceylon and Sumatra. He may well have explored the coast of Australia, but most of the accounts of his voyages and his charts were lost or destroyed.

The Ming emperor who approved his journeys was continuing the policy of maritime expansion begun by the Song dynasty and continued by the Yuan (Mongol) dynasty. The Mongol emperors had engaged in an extensive policy of shipbuilding in preparation for the invasion of Japan and Southeast Asia. For his abortive invasion of Japan in 1281 the Great Khan had 4,400 junks constructed. Equally impressive fleets were used in the invasion of Tonking and Champa (Vietnam) in 1283–88 and of Java in 1293. When the Mongol dynasty fell, to be replaced by the Ming, there was an initial continuation of the policy of supporting maritime exploration.

There were two significant aspects of Zheng He's voyages for the Ming government: they were to represent the emperor of the Middle Kingdom to the tributary states of Southeast Asia in order to bring previously unknown kingdoms into the appropriate relationship to the source of all civilization and they were to collect tributes of pepper, sapanwood, and exotic plants and animals in exchange for gifts of silk and porcelain. Zheng He even brought back a giraffe from Africa, as well as several disrespectful monarchs, notably the King of Ceylon.

Then, suddenly, in 1433 the Ming emperor banned Chinese merchants from going abroad. The great treasure ships of Zheng He's fleet, the largest seagoing vessels in

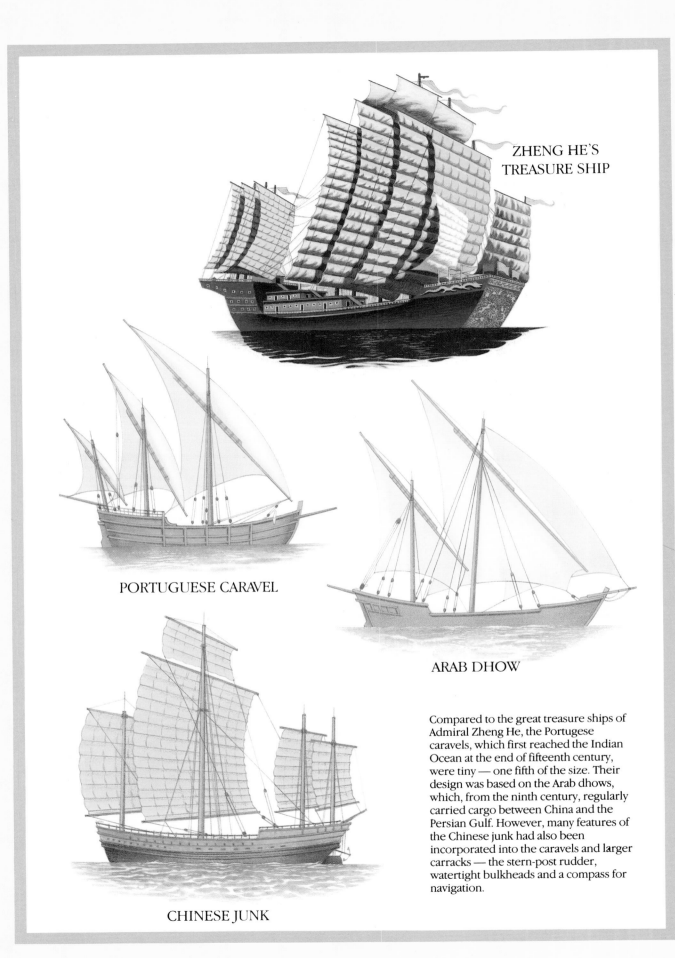

ZHENG HE'S
TREASURE SHIP

PORTUGUESE CARAVEL

ARAB DHOW

CHINESE JUNK

Compared to the great treasure ships of
Admiral Zheng He, the Portugese
caravels, which first reached the Indian
Ocean at the end of fifteenth century,
were tiny — one fifth of the size. Their
design was based on the Arab dhows,
which, from the ninth century, regularly
carried cargo between China and the
Persian Gulf. However, many features of
the Chinese junk had also been
incorporated into the caravels and larger
carracks — the stern-post rudder,
watertight bulkheads and a compass for
navigation.

the world at that time, were simply put out of commission. By 1550 a Ming scholar commented that knowledge of how to build these boats had been completely lost. The Ming navy shrunk into insignificance and China withdrew from the world. It is extraordinary that this should happen at the very time when on the other side of the Eurasian continent, Europeans were just beginning a period of massive overseas expansion and colonization that was to change the world fundamentally. There were in fact good economic reasons for the Ming withdrawal from foreign trade.

As a result of the earlier Song policy of encouraging shipbuilding and overseas trade, Chinese merchant fleets had, by the eleventh century, begun to displace the Arabs in the shipping of goods between Southeast Asia, the Middle East and China. Chinese merchant colonies had also grown up throughout Southeast Asia in the wake of this trade. However, the pepper and sapanwood brought back by Zheng He were an imperial monopoly and no one but the Chinese government could trade in them. Because of its traditionally high value, Ming emperors from 1407 began to use pepper and sapanwood to pay their troops and civil servants. Their monetary value was artificially held 10 times above the actual market value and was considered a better means of payment than paper money, which suffered the constant problem of hyperinflation. By 1424 there were such massive stores of pepper and sapanwood in the imperial warehouses that when the Emperor Renzong ascended the throne, residents and low-ranking officials were given them as part of the celebrations:

> To each banner bearer, horse keeper, soldier and guardsman one catty [1.33 pounds] of pepper and two catties of sapanwood; to each first-degree literary graduate and licentiate, district police chief, prison warder, astronomer and physician, one catty of pepper and two catties of sapanwood; to each resident of the city and the environs of Beijing, each Buddhist priest or Taoist priest, artisan, musician, professional cook, yamen [government ministry] runner and yamen cook, one catty of pepper and one catty of sapanwood.

However, despite the use to which these trade commodities were to be put in the early stages of the Ming dynasty, the economic realities were that revenue from foreign trade as a proportion of total government income had dropped from 20 per cent during the Southern Song to 0.77 per cent in the Ming, due simply to the fact that the area of land now controlled by the Ming was, with reunification, vastly increased. The cost–benefit of maintaining a large navy was losing its economic rationale. The need to protect the grain shipments from the south to the northern capital of Beijing and the armies on the northwestern frontier meant that the early Ming emperors had to maintain the strong navy, which in the 1400s consisted of a fleet of about 6,450 vessels. Of these, 2,300 ships were used as a coastal defense fleet to protect this transport and other merchant shipping from Japanese pirates; the largest of these ships could carry 500 men, cannon and other arms. It was without doubt the most powerful navy in the world. However, with the reopening and expansion of the Grand Canal in 1411 and the abolition of the use of sea transport to ship essential supplies to the north in 1415, the need for this extensive navy was far less obvious.

There was also the fact that the real threats to China were, as they had always been, from the north and west. It was the need to strengthen the armies on these borders and to maintain the security of the empire that obsessed the Ming government. No force, at that time at least, could conceivably have threatened China from the sea. The only threat would come from the Steppes of central Asia and Manchuria. With the Ming, relative peace and harmony were to return to the empire. There was even a movement of population back to areas in the north and west.

The Ming emperors were also of a very different temper and type from the cosmopolitan and highly cultured rulers of the Song and Yuan. The first Ming emperor had been a peasant turned bandit who had been able to gather enough support to seize control of the empire. The Ming were from the heartlands of rural China and, after almost two centuries of foreign Mongol rule, a mood of xenophobia seemed to overcome both the court and the scholars who served it.

Obviously the reduced economic importance of foreign trade did not justify

Courtesy Australian National University Library, Canberra

A giraffe from Africa, one of the gifts for the Ming emperor brought back to China by the Three Jeweled Eunuch, Admiral Zheng He, from one of his great voyages of discovery and diplomacy.

continued state support. The Ming Emperor Gaozong summed up the issue in the following terms: "China's territory produces all goods in abundance, so why should we buy useless trifles from abroad?"

In 1433, and again in 1449 and 1452, imperial edicts banning overseas trade and travel, with savage penalties, were issued. Any merchant caught attempting to engage in foreign trade was defined as a pirate and executed. For a time even learning a foreign language was prohibited as was the teaching of Chinese to foreigners.

On the one hand, this policy was designed to eliminate piracy, which had increased along the southern Chinese coast, but it was also designed to control and tax merchant trade more effectively. Sea transport was regarded by many officials as a means of avoiding levies. A Ming account of the process of taxation gives some idea of the constraints on merchants who often complained that the taxes they were forced to pay were greater than the value of the goods themselves, for each province and each market town levied its own duties:

> All goods, whether personal or professional, whether traded or used, were always taxed . . . in a few square miles there will be at least three official posts, which will levy duties on all merchandise. All along the canals the goods will be taxed every time a boundary is passed, that is, every few dozen miles or even few miles and when one reaches the market itself the official flag will immediately be hoisted and duties levied for opening the hold, for boarding the ship and for bringing up the cargo. If goods are transported overland the duties are just as bad.

Transport by sea avoided all these levies, and costs were therefore around 70–80 percent lower than land or canal transport. The effect of the Ming ban on overseas trade was devastating for merchants and the prosperous cities along the southern coastal provinces. It is little wonder that so many turned to piracy to survive. Compared with the situation in Europe where piracy was an equally serious problem a century later the Ming emperors seemed quite uncompromising. It should not be forgotten that between 1573 and 1580, Francis Drake captured treasure from Portuguese and Spanish vessels worth £1.5 million. Elizabeth I, instead of prosecuting Drake, attended a banquet on his ship, knighted him and took a share of his booty, which was used to pay off foreign debt. The rest was invested and formed the capital with which the East India Company was eventually formed. In Europe, piracy came to be regarded as a legitimate state enterprise. In China, even when European pirates joined the Japanese in the seventeenth century, the Ming and later dynasties did little to protect their merchants even after earlier prohibitions on overseas trade were lifted. In order to deny Ming loyalists and pirates supplies and support along the Chinese coast, Qing dynasty officials in the seventeenth century actually cleared a strip of land — 700 miles long and up to 30 miles wide — along the southern coast by moving the population and burning villages.

So completely had the Ming turned from the sea that not only the art of building the massive treasure ships was completely lost but even the constant motif of the sea disappeared from Ming porcelain as if by imperial decree. The oceans and all they meant were to be excluded from Chinese consciousness. What was lost with it was

A Song dynasty lighthouse, which guided the great twelfth century Chinese and Arab trading fleets into the port of Quanzhou on the coast of Fujian. Past this lighthouse came Marco Polo, and Zheng He on one of his many voyages. It stands as a legacy to the course China might have taken had the Ming emperors not turned from the sea, repressed the merchants and abandoned the policy of maritime expansion being pursued by European nation states.

the essential stimulus that comes from trade and contact with the rest of the world: the stimulus of new ideas and discoveries, which were to play such an important role in the later development of Europe. Had China become fragmented into small kingdoms, as seemed possible during the Southern Song, then the subsequent history of east Asia may well have been more like that of capitalist Europe. However, the enormous size of the Ming and later Qing empires and the primacy of maintaining social control meant that the traditional Confucian values were never seriously challenged. Merchants and artisans wielded too little economic power compared with the traditional rural gentry, whose priority was, as it had always been, the maintenance of traditional agricultural practices, which, after all, remained the most productive in the world well into the twentieth century. Without economic and political change, there was little opportunity for the promotion of new social institutions to take advantage of Chinese inventive genius.

There had been significant technological inventions and industrial innovations, for example, the mechanical spinning of hemp, the Su Song clock, and the discovery and use of natural gas and oil, but there was no great advantage in displacing the cheap rural labor that already adequately supplied local demand. In manufacturing, labor-saving machines would only have made sense if there was a sudden and massive expansion of markets to justify the introduction of new systems of production. Without the option of wide-scale international trade providing such a demand, the stimulus for social and economic change in Ming China was limited.

This is not to suggest that the social harmony, stability and peace maintained by the Ming government were not desirable or wise choices. However, in the conservatism of Ming policies lay a vulnerability, a potential Malthusian trap of an ever-increasing rural population struggling to live on a finite area of land whose productivity was almost as high as it could be without modern scientific and technological input. This weakness was to become acutely apparent as western maritime fleets and colonial empires shrank the world and confronted China in the nineteenth century with the terrible irony of seeing military technology they had first developed centuries earlier returning to haunt them with gunpowder-based weapons, transformed and refined in the aggressive and highly competitve environment of the European nation states.

Although most European monarchs would have loved to have the level of social control possessed by the Ming emperors, they had no choice but to risk the social disorder caused by the rising power of merchants for the sake of the wealth that it generated. This wealth was essential for the viability of the nation-state. In Europe there was no alternative but to make merchants respectable by allowing them entry into the establishment. In so doing, money and the values of the market place were allowed to change the nations' economic, cultural and intellectual institutions. The price the European monarch had to pay for this was increased social mobility, greater individual freedom and the loss of social control. But for the Ming dynasty the price of harmony was the absence of this new social dynamic. Foreign contact, the only stimulus that might have provided change had been cut off and China's economic and cultural institutions were to remain, refined and perfected but, ultimately, out of step with what was taking place on the other side of the globe. For, as China closed its gate on the world, European nations began to build a new and very different road to Xanadu.

In the late sixteenth century, Jesuit missionaries on board Portuguese merchant fleets arrived in Japan. The merchants went for profits; the Jesuits wanted souls.

# THE TRANSMISSION OF KNOWLEDGE

*Those who labor with their mind rule while those who labor with their physical strength are ruled by others.*

Meng-tse (Mencius)

*We should note the force, effect and consequences of inventions which are nowhere more conspicuous than in those which were unknown to the ancients, namely, printing, gunpowder and the compass. For these three have changed the appearance and state of the whole world.*

Francis Bacon, *Novum Organum,* Aphorism 129, 1620

Many of the ancient universities of Europe bear a remarkable similarity to the Islamic Madrassas or schools of the Middle East. In the ancient centers of Islamic civilization — Bagdad, Damascus, Cairo and Istanbul — beside each mosque there is a large rectangular building with an open courtyard in the center, which has broad walkways of arched columns providing shelter from the intense heat. In the tenth century one would have found, in various positions around the courtyard, teachers who specialized in different fields of study gathered with their students in small groups. Some would be teaching Greek logic, others geometry, astronomy, physics, metaphysics, grammar, law and of course the Koran. The teaching method these students were being exposed to was that of the seminar or *halqa,* where ideas were discussed and debated.

In the late Middle Ages the Madrassas were the crucial junction points in the transmission of knowledge from the ancient world of Greece and China to the west. Here the works of classical Greek mathematicians, physicians and scholars were studied. Books saved from the famous library of Alexandria, which was destroyed with the collapse of the Roman empire, included Euclid's geometry, Pythagoras' mathematics, Galen's medical theories and, perhaps most important of all, Aristotelian logic. Here too, Chinese ideas on medicine, alchemy and astronomy mingled with the cosmology and poetry of the Islamic mystics Attar, Rumi and Al Ghazali.

In the Dark Ages, which overwhelmed Western Europe with the fall of Rome in the third century, the cultivation of learning and inquiry became centered in the Madrassa's and the libraries of the Arab world. When Pope Urban III ordered the first Crusade to the Holy Land in 1095 he could not have known that, in the retaking of Jerusalem in 1099, his pure Christian knights would be contaminated with ideas and tastes that, in the long term, were to help undermine the power and credibility of the Catholic church, the very institution he was concerned to strengthen and preserve. New tastes for refined food, clothing, and the music and ideas of the east were brought back to Europe with the completion of each campaign. The Holy Roman

This painting by Gentile Bellini shows the official reception for the Venetian ambassador to Cairo in 1512. The Arab world was not only the conduit for exotic commodities and technology from the east, it was also a source of classicial Greek learning, which until the fifteenth century was inaccessible to all but a handful of European scholars.

Emperor Frederick II, for example, returned with an entire band of Arab musicians, who not only changed the character of western music, but introduced new instruments such as the lute (from the Arabic *l'oud*) as well as a whole family of reed and stringed instruments.

These are perhaps trivial examples, but they reflect a characteristic of European culture as it began to emerge from the Dark Ages. By the end of the fourteenth century almost all the classical Greek and Arab books on science and medicine had been translated into Latin. There was an enormous appetite for novelty and a willingness to adopt the technology and cultural institutions from the east that could qualitatively improve the basic conditions of life. Of the latter, perhaps one of the most significant was the transformation of cathedral schools into universities along the lines of the Islamic Madrassa. In this the Italian city-states, those "republics of merchants," were to lead the way.

The Madrassa, which formed the model for the University, was not an isolated community like a Christian monastery, but aimed to provide a broad religious education to the community at large. It was usually funded through a property trust or *wakf* set up by wealthy merchants, very much like the system of endowments that continues to support the ancient English universities such as Oxford and Cambridge.

The style of education carried out in the Madrassa, also adopted in European universities, gave primary emphasis to argument and debate. In contrast to China at this time, printed books were not available in the west, and those made of vellum were costly and were locked away in monastic and university libraries. Written examinations such as those common in China were technically impossible until the advent of papermaking in the thirteenth century.

Perhaps the greatest influence on European intellectual life, which came with the establishment of universities, was the discovery of Greek philosophy and science, particularly that of Aristotle and Plato. The impact of these new ideas was as much a revelation to the scholars of medieval Europe, as was the impact of western science on China and Japan in the eighteenth and nineteenth centuries. At first the Church

*The Ambassadors* (1533) by Hans Holbein the Younger. These Renaissance men are surrounded by the mathematical instruments that gave them not only new insights into nature but also the navigational skills and military power to expand the known world far beyond Europe to the Americas and to the Celestial Empire.

attempted to repress this influence. In 1210 the ecclesiastical authorities in Paris condemned Aristotle's ideas and particularly his scientific works. To teach them either publicly or privately would lead to excommunication. However, the ban was lifted in 1234 and Dominican scholars, such as Albertus Magnus, began to write outlines of Aristotle's essential ideas, spelling out where they contradicted Church dogma. This provided an added stimulus to debate and to a concern with the refinement of the tools of argument, logic and investigation. So keen were medieval universities on the principles of dialectical thinking that students were often divided into positive and negative groups to discuss specific topics. Students were also expected to pass an oral exam that required them to put forward propositions and to argue for and against them.

These European universities were not just teaching institutions. By the early years of the Renaissance they had become the new centers of intellectual life. At the University of Paris, in the fourteenth century, it was commonplace for such heretical notions as that the earth turned on its own axis to be debated with senior scholars taking opposing views. This encouraged a tradition of critical thought and helped to reinforce the tradition of debate as a means of reaching the truth, which was to be introduced later into other European political and legal institutions.

At its worst, this emphasis on argument ended in a shallow scholasticism with debates about how many angels could fit on the head of a pin. However, an appeal to the real world, to nature and natural law soon began to emerge as the ultimate arbiter of truth. Even Christian theology was to be drawn out of the sanctity and mystery of the Church and monastery, and submitted to the rigors of Aristotelian logic.

It was St Thomas Aquinas, a fellow Dominican and student of Albertus Magnus, who first championed this cause, though perhaps not its consequences. Aquinas, like other intellectuals within the Church, was concerned to reconcile the writings of Aristotle with that of Christian dogma, which was based on faith rather than reason. He argued that Christian teachings should be subject to logical reasoning. This in reality opened a theological "can of worms." The more traditional Church fathers, nurtured in the Augustinian tradition of faith and revelation, were horrified. However, the new passion for logic and "the light of reason" was to be applied not only to theological issues, but to the analysis of the underlying principles governing God's creation — in many cases simply to try to justify the Bible and disprove Aristotle's scientific and social theories.

As Christian scholars increasingly accepted Greek mathematics and logic as a road to ultimate truth, revelation and faith, the traditional foundations of their religion came to play a secondary role. As a consequence, metaphysics, the spiritual dimension of Christianity, was kept securely within the confines of the monastery and the Church, while philosophers were now concerned, not with trying to find God's "hidden hand" in biblical texts, but in his creation and in laws governing the natural world. In this search for an understanding of God in the mathematical principles that governed the universe lay the seeds of the scientific revolution of the seventeenth century.

In China, by contrast, education consisted primarily of learning by rote a vast body of classical literature. This became standardized in the seventh century with the establishment of the imperial examination system, which fostered the establishment of a class of scholar-officials who were important for the collection and dissemination of knowledge. Primarily this examination system encouraged an intellectual tradition in which memorization and documentation rather than disputation and debate were encouraged. After all, the object of the system was the creation of bureaucratic generalists familiar with an accepted ethical outlook and body of knowledge, not with the growth of knowledge or with academic specialization. As the Japanese historian Shigeru Nakayama notes:

> The explicit purpose of the system lay neither in education nor in the promotion of learning but in choosing a limited number of men for official posts from among a large pool of candidates seeking to improve their lot in the world by rising through the ranks of public service . . .
>
> . . . The founding of schools and the creation of an education system does not necessarily lead to the growth of learning. As an institution, the school incorporates and maintains knowledge that has been developed from a given paradigm. A vessel that shields the lamps of learning from the winds of external pressure, it also serves to check and control explosive internal developments.

British Library, London

All things were measurable. "The book of nature," Galileo wrote, "cannot be understood unless one first learns to comprehend the language and read the letters in which it is composed. It is written in the language of mathematics."

In China it was assumed that "those who worked with their heads rule, those with their hands serve." The Confucian scholar who dominated intellectual life in China had little involvement in experiment or practical investigations. Because so much emphasis was placed on memory and documentation there was significantly less attention given to logical reasoning than in the west. Take, for example, the common use of circular arguments exemplified by this passage from *Great Learning,* one of the principle works to be studied and memorized:

> The ancients who wished to be illustriously virtuous throughout the kingdom, first ordered well their own states. Wishing to order well their states, they first regulated their families. Wishing to regulate their families, they first cultivated their persons. Wishing to cultivate their persons, they first sought to rectify their hearts. Wishing to rectify their hearts, they first sought to be sincere in their thoughts. Wishing to be sincere in their thoughts, they first extended to the utmost their knowledge. Such extension of knowledge lay in the investigation of things.
>
> Things being investigated, knowledge became complete. Their knowledge being complete, their thoughts were sincere. Their thoughts being sincere, their hearts were then rectified. Their hearts being rectified, their persons were cultivated. Their persons being cultivated, their families were regulated. Their families being regulated, their states were rightly governed. Their states being rightly governed, the whole kingdom was made tranquil and happy. From the Son of Heaven down to the mass of the people, all must consider the cultivation of the person the root of everything besides.

# TIME

Two developments in particular — the clock and perspective drawing — embodied the new emphasis on rationality and quantification, which began in Europe with the Renaissance of classical learning in the fourteenth century.

The first mechanical clocks in Europe were a response to the concern of monastic religious orders to regulate the time of prayer both day and night. The Christian monastic communities of the Middle Ages lived in the expectation of the second coming of Christ, which in principle could occur at any time, day or night. Their responsibility was to be spiritually prepared for this event.

There were no fixed times for prayer in the early Christian Church, as there were in both Judaism and Islam. Only with the establishment of the monasteries were strict times for religious observances established. In these communities they took seriously the gospel parable of the bridegroom coming at midnight (Matt. 25:6) and the admonition "Watch therefore: for ye know not what hour your Lord doth come" (Matt. 24:42). After all, with the second coming, as predicted in the Bible, the world would end and only those spiritually prepared would be among the elect. The rest of benighted humanity would be condemned to damnation. Time was of the essence. One's spiritual duty was to rise above the demands of one's body and to feed one's immortal soul through prayer and meditation. The body was of this world — the world of death, corruption and destruction. The soul was nurtured by God's grace, in return for unflinching devotion and preparation for his Son's final coming.

Time in the Christian world was, therefore, unquestionably linear, moving from the creation to the second coming. As the millennium (the year 1000) approached, time was seen to be running out for mankind. Attention to the things of this world was a false and mistaken investment of one's time. In the ninth century the Cluny and Benedictine monasteries adopted a relay of almost continual prayer, while monks engaged in many extraordinary forms of ascetic behavior to induce grace and hallucinations.

This, of course, was in marked contrast to time as experienced by the peasantry, who made up the bulk of the population. Most of them, although nominally Christian, had a way of life that was governed by the cycles of nature and the more animistic religious values of pre-Christian times. They were, for the most part, outside the world of monastic religious communities and did not share their sense of cosmological urgency. Like their Chinese counterparts, the peasants' primary concerns were with survival and this meant working closely with the cycles of nature. Work and leisure were governed by the demands of the land, not religion. They could not afford the luxury of such unworldly asceticism.

The mechanical clock, when it was first developed, offered to the monks the security of being able to keep up their grueling observance throughout the night. It was also to provide a new concept of time — time that was abstract, broken up into mathematically precise units and independent of nature. This was God's time.

Bibliotheque Nationale, Paris

*Solomon and a Clock* from a fifteenth century Flemish manuscript. The time measured by the first mechanical clocks set up in the churches and monasteries of late medieval Europe was God's time; for, like the deity, its mathematical precision transcended the crude cycles of nature.

# COSMOLOGY AND THE CLOCK

Prior to the advent of the clock, time was measured by reference to the familiar cycles of nature and the patterns of work required throughout the agricultural year. Time was approximate and relative — the cycles of the planets and the seasons provided the only manifestation of regularity. Estimates of how long something would take were measured in terms of events familiar to everyone; so there were "paternostra whiles" (the time it took for the paternostra to be recited in church) as well as the more prosaic "pissing whiles." However, with the advent of the clock, time became a mathematically precise entity. For astronomers, using the new geometry of Euclid and the mechanical clock, it was possible to measure both time and space with new precision. It was also possible to understand the actual motion of the planets, which Copernicus, by the fifteenth century, was forced to conclude did not behave in the way that Ptolemy, Aristotle or the Church authorities claimed. The earth went around the sun, and it could be proven by observation, logic and mathematics.

The first European clocks were either sundials or water clocks like those of the Chinese. However, as the metalworking and mechanical skills of European craftsmen developed in the early fourteenth century, the first mechanical clocks began to appear in monasteries and on church spires, to control the ringing of bells. The mechanical clock in Europe may have been invented, Joseph Needham argues, as a result of hearing accounts of the famous Su Song clock in China, but the early devices produced in Europe bore little relation to the Chinese clocks. The escapement mechanism, often described as the "soul" of the clock, was developed in the west quite independently.

The first clocks, situated in belfries, simply rang bells on the hour. Later, a clock face was added. Within a remarkably short time other mechanical devices were included showing astronomical phenomena such as the cycles of the moon and the planets. The clock then passed from the monastery to the towns, and its use grew rapidly with the expansion of trade in the fourteenth and fifteenth centuries. Among the Protestants of northern Europe, who had adopted many of the religious values of the monasteries and brought them into the everyday life of the towns, the clock was used to reinforce the virtues of work and time discipline.

Courtesy Sydney College of the Arts

*The skilled clock and instrument makers were to form a new class of craftsmen. They combined engineering and metallurgical skills with the mathematical precision promoted by the new sciences.*

The millennium came and went without the apocalypse or Christ's reappearance. Living conditions in the world outside the monastery walls began to improve. With increasing political stability populations grew, and increased production from agriculture was encouraged by new farming techniques developed in and disseminated through Cistercian monasteries. However, it was in the growing towns and, particularly, the centers of textile manufacture that mechanical clocks took on their now familiar role. As the workforce in the towns was employed for wages, the length of hours worked, the starting times and finishing times needed to be set by something more reliable than natural light, which varied according to season. No longer were the masters' claims taken on face value. Soon clocks began to appear, not only on cathedral spires, but in specially constructed clocktowers on large public buildings, such as town halls.

The Protestant Reformation of the sixteenth century, which in England led to the dissolution of the monasteries, resulted not in a decline in religious discipline but in its extension into the wider community. The humanistic ideas fostered during the Italian Renaissance shifted the cultural emphasis from a concern with the end of the world to the possibility of improving this one, if only to make it more acceptable for a second coming. This required discipline and the clock was necessary to regulate not only prayer, but also work. Among the merchants and independent artisan-manufacturers of the new towns — the bourgs from which the word bourgeoisie is derived — time mattered. In a money economy the familiar nexus between cost and time determined profit or loss. For the Calvinists, God's grace was manifested by his providence. To the honest, hardworking and pious would come wealth and

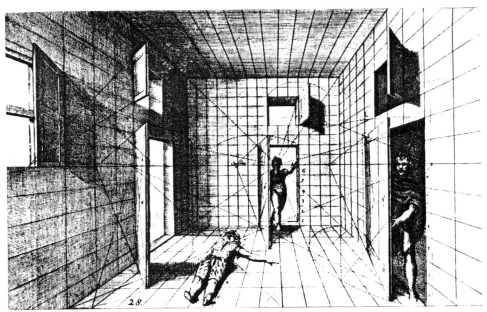

With perspective, not only could an accurate representation of an object be made, but by using the technique of chiaroscuro or shadowing it was also possible to represent a three-dimensional image.

A wire grid allowed artists to represent an object in space from the perspective of the viewer. It also allowed the object to be represented in precise mathematical detail.

prosperity. Among the new middle class of the towns, wealth was not to be disposed of in the form of conspicuous consumption but to be husbanded, saved and invested. Like God's time it could be saved, wasted or lost. Time like money was also always "running out." Time *was* money and both were now essential elements in the growth of international trade.

# SPACE

Perspective drawing was pioneered by the Italian artist Brunelleschi in 1425. An attempt to explain its use was put forward by Leone Battista Alberti in his book *Della Pittura* in 1435. In the spirit of Aquinas, Alberti stated the principle that the most basic requirement for the painter was an understanding of geometry. Like other humanist scholars of the Renaissance, Alberti believed that nature could best be understood through mathematics; behind all phenomena there were structures with precise mathematical dimensions. Just as Aristotelian logic became the tool for exploring and expressing philosophical and theological ideas, so too was mathematics the tool by which the natural world could be understood. Given that these were aspects of the human mind, God must have created them for a reason: to know him and his creation better. Man, made in God's image, was the point from which the world was to be viewed and measured. The strange cosmological and mystical perspective that underpinned earlier art gave way to the centrality of the individual viewer.

In the introduction to the *Trattato della Pittura,* Leonardo da Vinci writes "let no one who is not a mathematician read my works." For him painting was a science, a means of exploring the nature of the world:

> . . . for no human inquiry can be called science unless it pursues its path through mathematical exposition and demonstration. . . . The man who discredits the supreme certainty of mathematics is feeding on confusion, and can never silence the contradictions of sophistical sciences, which lead to eternal quackery.

What perspective offered was not only the capacity to see objects in relation to the field of vision of the artist himself, but it also allowed objects to be represented in precise mathematical detail.

We are probably most familiar with the revolution of perspective drawing in terms of its impact on the arts where, along with the rationalistic spirit initiated by Aquinas, it led to a tradition of didactic painting and illustration. However, the attempt to reproduce on paper the precise proportions of an object in three-dimensional form was to become equally important in the growth of technological drawing and the spread of technical books, for example, Vesalius's *Fabric of the Human Body* which for the first time showed the actual structure of the organs of the human body in realistic and accurate proportions. The use of woodblock and copperplate engravings printed on paper was to have a profound effect on education, especially after the development of movable-type printing by Gutenberg (c.1437) made books cheaper and available outside the confines of the monastery and university libraries:

> A man born in 1453, the year of the fall of Constantinople, could look back from his fiftieth year on a lifetime in which about eight million books had been printed, more perhaps than all the scribes of Europe had produced since Constantine founded his city in 330.

As can be seen from the technical drawings of Leonardo da Vinci, the representation of objects and technological processes, from the anatomy of the

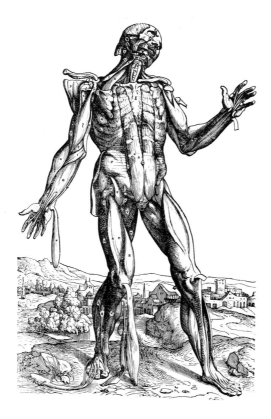

An illustration from Vesalius's *Fabric of the Human Body* published in 1543. This illustrated book was to apply the new perspective-drawing techniques to provide precise images of the "architecture" of the human body. It was to form the model for educational books, which applied these same techniques to mechanical drawing.

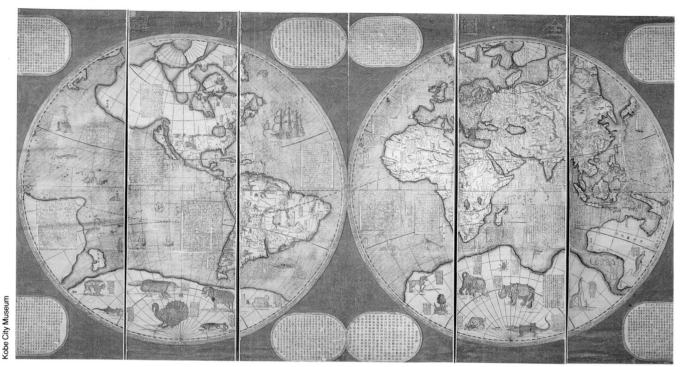

A world map, using Mercator's projection, drawn for the Chinese by the Jesuit missionary
Ferdinand Verbiest in 1674.

human body to the trajectory of a cannon ball could be analyzed and understood in
precise geometrical terms. This facility applied not only to the small and domestic
but to the depiction of the globe and earth's place in the cosmos. For the perspective
screen held before the nude by Dürer is, in its function, little different to the latitude
and longitude screen that cartographers began to hold over the image of the earth
itself. Gerardus Mercator (1512–94), a Flemish cartographer, was the first to devise a
map of the globe that took into account the problem of its spherical shape and came
up with Mercator's projection, a technique for dividing the earth into precise
measures of time and space without distorting the perspective by reducing it to a
two-dimensional image. For the powerful merchant-adventurers of Portugal, Spain
and Holland whose livelihood depended on such navigational aids, this was the
perspective that really counted.

In the Ming court, on the other side of Eurasia, the image of the world was still
governed by a geopolitical fantasy that placed the Middle Kingdom in the center of a
flat earth with peripheral states decreasing in importance and levels of cultural
development as they radiated out from the imperial capital, the epicenter of the
universe and of human civilization.

# THE JESUITS AND THE EMPEROR

*Coming into contact with barbarian peoples you have nothing more to fear than touching the left horn of a snail. The only things one should be anxious about are the means of mastery of the waves of the sea and, worst of all dangers, the minds of those avid for profit and greedy for gain.*

From a Qing dynasty treatise on navigation

*It was a star that long ago led the Three Kings to adore the true God. In the same way the science of the stars will lead the rulers of the Orient, little by little, to know and to adore their Lord.*

Jesuit Missionary Ferdinand Verbiest, Beijing, 1674

The response of the Church to the great voyages of discovery initiated by Henry the Navigator of Portugal, was to send forth missionaries to convert the poor benighted heathens discovered in the "new worlds" of the Americas and the east to Christianity. While merchant-adventurers attempted to capture the economic resources of east Asia on behalf of mammon, new religious orders such as the Society of Jesus, founded by St Ignatius of Loyola in 1540, took it upon themselves to capture souls for Christ and the Catholic church: "to garner into the granaries of the Catholic Church a rich harvest from this sowing of the gospel seed."

In 1488 the Portuguese Bartolomeu Dias had found the route to the Indian Ocean around the Cape of Good Hope. Four years later in 1492 the Spanish, trying to beat the Portuguese to the source of eastern wealth, sponsored Christopher Columbus to find a western route. The competition between Portugal and Spain had grown so intense that, by the end of the fifteenth century, Pope Alexander VI was forced to intervene with his famous Papal Bull of 1493. This remarkable document divided the world between Portugal and Spain, with Portugal taking Brazil and most of the east, and Spain taking most of the Americas and the Pacific, including the Philippines. The assumption that the world could be carved up in such a fashion reflected a Eurocentric arrogance, which was to reach its height later in the nineteenth century, when European nations did carve up the world.

With papal support, Vasco da Gama arrived in India in 1498, and set the scene for the first European maritime empire in Asia. In 1510 Alfonso de Albuquerque captured the Indian city of Goa, and a year later Malacca, thus giving Portugal control of the rich spice trade with Europe. In 1517 the king of Portugal had sent a mission with eight ships, and Tome Pires as ambassador, to China. After being joined by the mayor of Goa, Fernao de Andrade, the mission arrived at Guangzhou in September. From the start the Portuguese made a poor impression. The letting off of a thunderous salute of guns terrified the Chinese who were not accustomed to their tributary missions behaving with such a fundamental lack of decorum. However, the governor-general received them and allowed them to stay while Pires made his long journey to Beijing. Unfortunately, a year later Simao de Andrade, Fernao's brother, arrived and forcibly occupied the island of Tamao where he built a fort without the permission of the Chinese governor. Their behavior was so highhanded that the Chinese came to regard Europeans as little better than Japanese pirates, and proposed to expel them all. Pires was thrown into prison where he died, while the Portuguese fort of Tamao was besieged and taken by Chinese troops. Despite these unfortunate beginnings, the Chinese permitted the Portuguese merchants to establish a trading base at Macao, which, over time, was treated as a colonial territory by the Portuguese but in reality was leased in return for annual custom dues.

In 1564 while the Portuguese were establishing their trading base near Guangzhou, the Spanish from their base in Acapulco on the west coast of Mexico took the island of Luzon in the name of Philip II; it became known as the Philippines. From here they began to trade with Fujian. From the ports of Quanzhou (Zaitun), Fuzhou and Xiamen (Amoy), Spanish trade routes to the west opened up via the Philippines and Mexico, and began to challenge the dominance of Portugal.

*　*　*

In the wake of all this overseas expansion, the Church was not idle. The Jesuit order sent Francis Xavier to the east in 1541 to begin the great task of converting Asia to Christianity. He established his base at the Portuguese fort in Macao, and from here Xavier began his first assault on Japan. He met a young Japanese, Yajiro, who had killed a man and escaped on a Portuguese merchant ship that was moored in the

Kobe City Museum

Francis Xavier as portrayed by Jesuit missionaries in Japan.

southern port of Kagoshima. The captain of the ship introduced him to Xavier in Malacca, and it was this meeting that persuaded the Jesuit to begin his mission in Japan. On 15 August 1549 Xavier arrived in Kagoshima with Yajiro as an interpreter.

He was impressed by what he found as he recorded in a letter back to the missionaries in Goa:

> The people whom we have met so far, are the best who have yet been discovered, and it seems to me that we shall never find amongst heathens another race to equal the Japanese. They are a people of very good manners, good in general and not malicious . . . There are many who can read and write, which is a great help to their learning quickly prayers and religious matters.

However, his fellow missionaries as they came to understand Japanese culture were to confront a society far stranger and more challenging than the one for which Xavier had prepared them. Alessandro Valignano, an Italian Jesuit, wrote in 1583:

> They also have rites and ceremonies so different from those of all the other nations that it seems they deliberately try to be unlike any other people. The things which they do in this respect are beyond imagining and it may be truly said that Japan is a world the reverse of Europe . . .

A Spanish Jesuit, Luis Frois, writing two years later in 1585 was equally perplexed by the cultural differences of these otherwise highly civilized people:

> Most people in Europe grow tall and have good figures; the Japanese are mostly smaller than we in body and stature.
> The women in Europe do not go out of the house without their husbands' permission; Japanese women are free to go wherever they please without the husband knowing about it.
> With us it is not very common that women can write; the noble ladies of Japan consider it a humiliation not to be able to write.
> In Europe the men are the tailors and in Japan the women.
> Our children first learn to read and then to write; Japanese children first begin to write and thereafter to read.
> We believe in future glory and punishment and in the immortality of the soul; the Zen bonzes deny all that and avow that there is nothing more than birth and death.

This first experience of the Far East for the Jesuits, transmitted through their letters to Europe, stimulated a growing sense of cultural relativity, an awareness of cultural differences that provided a new perspective from which to view their own social institutions — an awareness that was to reach its peak in the eighteenth century and form the basis of what were to become the social sciences.

Xavier, although entranced by the manners and cultivation of the Japanese, soon became aware that their cultural roots were to be found in China, and came to the conclusion that if he was to convert Asia to Christianity, then he would have to confront the Celestial Empire itself. He therefore left the Japanese mission in the hands of others and set out for China.

Musée Guimet, Paris (Photo: Cliché Musées Nationaux)

A Japanese view of the European missionaries and merchants who began to arrive at southern ports such as Kagoshima and Nagasaki in the mid-sixteenth century.

St Francis Xavier died before he could establish his mission in China. The task was to fall to a remarkable Italian Jesuit and scholar Matteo Ricci (1552–1610). Ricci, like most of the Jesuits in the Asian mission, was well educated in mathematics and the new sciences that were so much the focus of the humanistic movement then dominant in Europe. After spending four years studying and teaching at the Jesuit mission in Goa, Ricci was transferred in 1582 to the mission headquarters at Macao to take up the task left incomplete by Xavier. Along with a fellow Jesuit, Michele Ruggieri, he established a mission house in the town of Zhaoqing (Chao-ch'ing) west of Guangzhou. Here he spent seven years learning about Chinese culture and its language, with which he became thoroughly conversant. However, he was able to make little headway in his primary objective of wide-scale conversion. The townspeople were extremely suspicious and stoned the mission, believing that Ricci's presence would bring Portuguese pirates to sack the town. He made just as little headway with the local literati who regarded the religion of the Jesuits, in their long and simple monks' robes, as little better than Buddhism, a religion practiced by the poor and underprivileged and hence of extremely low status.

Bayerische Verwaltung der Staatlichen Schlösser, Gärten und Seen, Munich

This eighteenth century tapestry shows the Jesuits teaching the Chinese about western astronomy and science.

Staatsbibliothek Preussischer Kulturbesitz, Berlin (West)

*Le Pere Matthieu Ricci.*     *Le Pere Adam Schaal.*     *Le Pere Ferdinand Verbiest.*

Matteo Ricci, Adam Schall, and Ferdinand Verbiest, the three Jesuits who penetrated the Chinese imperial bureaucracy and attempted to convert the emperor to Christianity.

With these seven frustrating years behind him Ricci came to the conclusion that the only way to convert China was to start from the top, and that he would have to approach his task, not through the conversion of the "blessed poor and humble," but through the powerful scholar-official class whose power and influence spread out from the emperor in Beijing. In a masterly stroke Ricci abandoned his humble monk's robe, adopted the guise of a scholar and set off for Beijing for what he hoped would be an audience with the emperor. On approaching the imperial capital, in 1601, he and his companions were arrested and his possessions seized. They carried with them the marvels of European culture: clocks, maps and religious paintings using European perspective and illustrated books on mathematics and science — objects which in Guangzhou had so impressed the officials with whom he had made contact. After six months in jail Ricci was released and his gifts delivered to Emperor Wanli. The emperor was so delighted by one of Ricci's remarkable chiming clocks, which "struck all Chinese dumb with astonishment," that officials were persuaded to allow Ricci the almost unprecedented favor (for a foreigner) of being allowed to remain in Beijing.

With his fluent Chinese and remarkable knowledge of the Confucian classics he made a considerable impact among some of the high-ranking scholars in the capital. But his object was to reach the emperor himself. This was no easy task. The emperors of China, by tradition, lived aloof from the world within the Forbidden City, surrounded by the imperial household of wives, concubines and eunuchs who, essentially, managed the imperial household. Audiences with the emperor were for ministers of government, high-ranking scholars and the heads of visiting tributary delegations. The prospects of this solitary Jesuit priest making his way through the labyrinthine hierarchy that surrounded the Son of Heaven, were slim. What finally got him to his goal were his clocks. When one of them stopped chiming, the emperor was so upset that he demanded that Ricci be called to the Forbidden City to repair it and to train four of his mathematicians to repair and maintain the clocks.

This was the first foot in the door, which was to lead to the Jesuits establishing a church and working their way into the structure of the imperial bureaucracy. Not since the time of Marco Polo, three centuries earlier, had any European come so close to the center of imperial power. What made this possible was Ricci's subtle intellect and his familiarity with mathematics and astronomy. For it was these skills that impressed the Chinese, not any interest in what they regarded as his somewhat absurd religious beliefs. As Ricci himself noted:

> These globes, clocks, spheres, astrolabes and so forth, which I have made and the use of which I teach, have gained for me the reputation of being the greatest mathematician in the world. I do not have a single book on astrology [astronomy], but with only the help of certain ephemerides and Portuguese almanacs I sometimes predict eclipses more accurately than they do.

Ricci was familiar enough with the imperial structure to know that what the emperor needed from him were more accurate systems, both for predicting astronomical events such as eclipses and for setting the imperial calendar. It was for this reason that he insisted that the missionaries sent to him from Rome should be well versed in astronomy, mathematics and the sciences. He was playing a difficult cat-and-mouse game. His object was clearly to win converts to Christianity, but he could not afford to alienate himself from the Confucian officials in the powerful ministries who could easily have him expelled if he was seen as a threat. As Ricci noted in his journals: "In order that the appearance of a new religion might not arouse suspicion amongst Chinese people, the Fathers did not speak openly about religious matters when they began to appear in public."

Instead, they attempted to impress upon the Chinese the superiority of European science and of the intellectual world view the Jesuits professed. Like the bait in a carefully constructed intellectual trap they hoped to capture Chinese souls with the very sciences that, ironically, back in Europe were beginning to threaten the very foundations of traditional Church dogma. It was a dangerous game, as Ricci recalled in his journals:

> We must mention here another discovery which helped to win the good will of the Chinese. To them the heavens are round but the earth is flat and square, and they firmly believe that their empire is right in the middle of it. They do not like the idea of our geographers pushing their China into one corner of the Orient. They could not comprehend the demonstrations proving that the earth is a globe, made up of land and water, and that a globe of its nature has neither beginning nor end. The geographer was

Adam Schall in the robes of a Chinese scholar-official. The insignia on the front of his gown indicates his status in the imperial bureaucracy. As director of the bureau of astronomy, he hoped to have more direct influence over the Confucian scholars who surrounded and advised the emperor.

State Library of New South Wales

100

therefore obliged to change his design and, by omitting the first meridian of the Fortunate Islands, he left a margin on either side of the map, making the kingdom of China to appear right in the center. This was more in keeping with their ideas and it gave them a great deal of pleasure and satisfaction. Really, at that time and in the particular circumstances, one could not have hit upon a discovery more appropriate for disposing this people for the reception of the faith. . . .

Because of their ignorance of the size of the earth and the exaggerated opinion they have of themselves, the Chinese are of the opinion that only China among the nations is deserving of admiration. Relative to the grandeur of empire, of public administration and of reputation for learning, they look upon all other people not only as barbarous but as unreasoning animals. To them there is no other place on earth that can boast of a king, of a dynasty, or of culture. The more their pride is inflated by this ignorance, the more humiliated they become when the truth is revealed.

The Jesuits in China were always on thin ice. Hostility towards them from officials in the department of astronomy led to many efforts to have them ousted. Six years after Ricci's death in 1610, Jesuit priests were arrested and their churches closed. Those that did not leave the country went into hiding. This did not, however, stop Johann Adam Schall von Bell.

Adam Schall was a young German Jesuit who, in 1611, met Father Nicholas Trigault who had worked with Ricci in Beijing. Trigault brought to Rome Ricci's journals, which were widely circulated and read. He was so impressed by Schall's enthusiasm and intelligence that in 1618, after finishing his studies, Schall was allowed to join the mission in Macao. It was Schall who was to fulfill one of Ricci's long-term objectives — to penetrate the bureaucratic hierarchy and thus gain direct access to the emperor. Schall was a capable mathematician and astronomer, familiar with the revolutionary astronomical ideas and methods of Kepler and Galileo. Accompanying Schall was a Swiss Jesuit, Father Johann Schreck, who had studied astronomy and mathematics under Galileo at the University of Padua and held a medical degree. The two Jesuits were not able to go to Beijing until 1623 when the ban on Jesuits was lifted. In the meantime they studied Chinese at the mission headquarters in Macao. Here the Jesuit fathers applied their practical knowledge to the casting of cannon, and even participated in the defense of Macao when it was invaded by the Dutch in 1622. The accuracy of the cannons fired from the Jesuit fort of St Paul, which hit the powder from a keg in the Dutch army ranks, turned the invasion into a rout. Three hundred Dutch soldiers were beheaded in honor of St John the Baptist. These were not the retiring ascetics of the ancient monastic tradition, these were men of Renaissance polymaths in every sense.

When Schall and Schreck finally arrived in Beijing they were to attack the Chinese bureaucracy at its weakest point: Chinese pride in the accuracy of their calendars, which Ricci had already observed. In 1623, and again in 1625, Schall was able to accurately predict the occurrence of an eclipse. In 1629 the first real breakthrough came when Xu Guangqi (Hsü Kuang-ch'i), one of Ricci's Christian converts, became vice-president of the board of rites, one of the top positions in the imperial bureaucracy. He was commissioned to head a new calendrical department and to staff it with men of his own choice. He chose, among others, two Jesuits Schreck and Longobardi and initiated western techniques. Schreck attempted to elicit the help of his old professor Galileo but in 1616 the Inquisition in Rome had forced Galileo to recant his belief in the heliocentric astronomy of Copernicus. He was therefore not inclined to provide his services to the Church's missionaries, much to the disappointment of the Jesuits in Beijing. Kepler, the other great astronomer of the time, however, provided help in the reform of the Chinese calendar.

In 1630 Schreck died suddenly, and Schall was called upon to take his place. This was the first step on a ladder that was to lead the Jesuits to the very heart of Chinese power. The Church could now claim several thousand converts, many from the imperial household itself. In April 1644 the Ming dynasty fell before the invading Manchus from the north. The last Ming emperor committed suicide in his palace. Realising that the new Manchu dynasty would have to be governed along the lines established by tradition, Schall petitioned the emperor concerning an eclipse expected the following September: "Your subject humbly begs from Your Highness a decree to the Board of Rites to test publicly the accuracy of the prediction of the solar eclipse at a proper time." The request was granted and Schall had the opportunity to prove, publicly, the superiority of western astronomy over what he knew to be the less precise techniques of the Chinese or Muslim astronomers who had previously dominated the bureau of astronomy. On the appointed day Schall's gamble paid off. He was right and the Chinese wrong. For his success Schall was now offered the directorship of the bureau and was thereby promoted to the fifth grade in the ninth

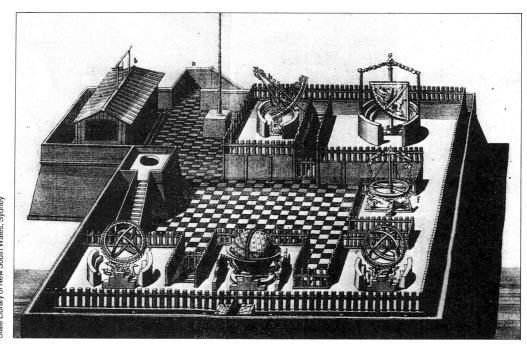

The observatory on the city wall in Beijing has been preserved as a museum with the instruments that were designed and cast by Verbeist for Emperor Kangxi.

tier of the upper echelons of the Chinese bureaucracy. Jesuit patience, persistence and scientific knowledge had, eventually, paid off.

Now in a powerful position within the bureaucracy, one might have expected the influence of the Jesuits to spread more widely throughout the Chinese governing class. In fact, the Jesuits were to remain confined within this specific domain. While they saw science as their means to gain access to power and influence for the sake of their primary objective — the conversion of the imperial court — the emperors of China were far more astute. The Jesuits were useful for their knowledge, which was all that interested the emperors. The knowledge that Schall and his successor in the bureau, Ferdinand Verbiest, brought to the Chinese court was useful as long as it conformed to the central objective of maintaining the Chinese imperial state. The Chinese only took what was useful — the clocks, the mathematical techniques and, especially, the techniques for casting better cannon. Verbiest cast 132 heavy cannon and 320 light cannon at the imperial workshops as well as a range of western astronomical instruments. As for Christianity, there was no real use for it. Even though Verbiest was, in the late seventeenth century, to achieve Ricci's goal in becoming both tutor to the brilliant young Emperor Kangxi (K'ang-hsi) and vice-president of the board of works, the clocks, astrolabes, telescopes, mathematics and other scientific techniques he introduced were of interest and useful but had little real impact on the Middle Kingdom.

In his journals Kangxi (1662–1722), the emperor most influenced by and interested in western science and technology, made the following observations:

Courtesy Film Australia

With instruments like these, modeled on the latest designs developed by the great Flemish astronomer, Tycho Brahe, the Jesuits were able to guarantee the emperor more accurate predictions for the imperial calendar.

I realized, too, that western mathematics has its uses. I first grew interested in this subject shortly after I came to the throne, during the confrontations between the Jesuit Adam Schall and his Chinese critic, Yang Guanxian, when the two men argued the merits of their respective techniques. . . . Schall died in prison but, after I learned something about astronomy, I pardoned his friend Verbiest in 1669 and gave him an official position, promoting him in 1682. . . . For even though some of the western methods are different from our own, and may even be an improvement, there is little about them that is new. The principles of mathematics all derive from the *Book of Changes,* and the western methods are Chinese in origin: this word algebra — a-erh-chu-pa-erh — springs from an eastern word. And though it was indeed the westerners who showed us something our ancient calendar experts did not know — namely how to calculate the angles of the northern pole — this but shows the truth of what Zhu Xi arrived at through his investigation of things: the earth is like the yoke within an egg. . . . I did praise their work, saying "the 'new methods' of calculating make basic errors impossible" and "the general principles of western calendrical science are without error." But I added that they still could not prevent small errors from occurring, and that over the decades these small errors mount up. After all, they know only a fraction of what I know.

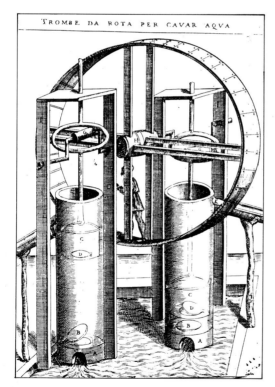 

The Jesuits' library in Beijing offered Chinese scholars access to western scientific books illustrated with the new perspective drawings of technical detail. However, it was difficult to translate this illustrative technique into the Chinese style. The crucial mechanical detail is almost completely unintelligible in the Chinese copy of seventeenth century mechanisms for lifting water. Traditional Chinese encyclopedias were designed by and for the use of scholar-officials not craftsmen or artisans.

Even with an enlightened emperor such as Kangxi there remained a tendency, which was to become a habitual response of Chinese scholars for the next two hundred years, to regard western learning as no more than a refinement of what was already present in the traditional Chinese classics. A century after Kangxi, in the 1782 edition of the *Siku quanshutiyao* (The Index to the Grand Library) there was this entry regarding the uses of western learning:

> In regard to the learning of the west, the art of surveying the land is most important, followed by the art of making strange machines. Among these strange machines, those pertaining to irrigation are most useful to the common people. All the other machines are simply intricate oddities, designed for the pleasure of the senses. They fulfill no basic needs.

Within the priorities of Chinese culture, from the perspective of an eighteenth century scholar-bureaucrat, these sentiments were probably right. It would be equally arrogant of us to dismiss the Chinese literati for showing little interest in western science and technology, given the values in which they were educated and the stability and harmony of the imperial culture they maintained. After all, in Europe too the scientific revolution was greeted by the Church and its aristocratic patrons with little enthusiasm. The treatment of Galileo is but one example of numerous efforts at repression. The appeal of the new sciences came from the advantages they provided in the highly competitive battles for economic and military power, which dominated the relationships between the expanding nation states of Europe: they appealed to necessity and greed.

The Jesuit mission proved, eventually, to be a failure. Kangxi was, understandably, to lose his patience with the Jesuits who, though accepting official positions in the Chinese imperial service, were in the final analysis accountable to the pope in Rome. Torn apart by the famous "rites controversy," where competing Catholic orders criticized the Jesuit policy (begun by Ricci) of bending Christian dogma to conform to the Confucian view of the world, the Jesuit order was disbanded by papal decree in 1773 and the emperor formally restricted the activity of Christian missionaries throughout the country.

# TIME'S CHARIOT — NEW HORSES AND NEW COURSES

*The skill originated in the west*
*But by learning, we can achieve the artifice:*
*Wheels move and time turns round,*
*Hands show the minutes as they change.*
*Red-capped watchmen, there is no need to announce the dawn's coming.*
*My golden clock has warned me of the time.*
*By first light I am hard at work,*
*And keep on asking, "Why are the memorials late?"*

"Lines in praise of a self-chiming clock," Emperor Kangxi, c. 1705

Kangxi was clearly enthusiastic about his clocks. He is reported to have had over two thousand in the imperial palace alone, including clockwork globes and elaborate mechanical toys of great ingenuity given as tributary gifts by European states, usually in the hope of gaining more favorable conditions of trade. They were regarded largely as curiosities in the same way that we might regard a Chinese gnomon or armillary sphere today, ingenious but largely irrelevant. In Chinese culture and economy there was no great need for them except as collectors' items among the imperial bureaucrats and gentry.

This was due to the fact that the contemporary generation of scholars' interest in technology was extremely limited, compared with that of earlier dynasties such as the Song. From the time of the Ming dynasty's withdrawal from the world in the fifteenth century, the intellectual horizons of the scholars had become similarly introverted, concerned essentially with maintaining traditional Confucian values and the agricultural economy on which it was built.

Meanwhile, in Europe there was to be little or no stability. By the early seventeenth century Holland and Britain had supplanted Portugal and Spain, largely through their dominance of international maritime trade. It was a time of almost constant warfare between the Protestant north, centered on the northern Dutch provinces and the Catholic south dominated by Spain and France. The repression of Protestants and particularly the Huguenots in France benefited the Dutch and the English. Many of the most entrepreneurial merchants and artisans were driven out, bringing with them their skills and capital. They included skilled weavers and potters, clockmakers and educated merchants. The Protestant movement was a focus, not only for religious reformers but also for those rebelling against the repressive remnants of the old feudal order. The Protestant emphasis on the freedom of individual conscience, frugality and on popular literacy (ostensibly so that all would be able to read the Bible in their own language) provided this new and increasingly powerful class with a religion that expressed their values. Wealth was nothing to be ashamed of, it was an expression of God's providence and individual diligence. With

*Return from the Second Voyage to the East-Indies* by H.C. Vroom (1566 – 1640). The Dutch East India Company, which dominated sixteenth century trade with Asia, became the model for other European powers who were to enter the China trade.

wealth one was better able to benefit society as a whole and demonstrate one's Christian charity by endowing orphanages, hospitals and schools.

With the growth in wealth that came from an expansion in international and local commerce, new economic and scientific institutions were created, which, in turn, stimulated both economic growth and technological innovation.

Holland, that great "republic of merchants," had by the end of the sixteenth century eclipsed Genoa and Venice as the financial capital of Europe. This was partly because of its proximity to Antwerp, the clearing house in Europe both for Asian goods and for gold and silver coming in from the Spanish colonies in South America. Antwerp, unlike the earlier tightly controlled trading centers in the Italian city-states, was perhaps the first city in Europe to match the cosmopolitan character of Quanzhou in the twelfth and thirteenth centuries. From here Italian and Jewish bankers, and English and French merchant guilds established their trading networks that covered northern Europe. Here vast loans were negotiated on behalf of monarchs like Henry VIII of England.

An example of the importance of the new freedoms that the Netherlands offered can be seen in the decline of Antwerp after 1558 when the Spanish occupied the city together with much of southern Holland and Flanders. The repression of Calvinists and other Protestants led to a mass exodus north to the city of Amsterdam, which as a consequence took over Antwerp's role as the center of international trade throughout the early seventeenth century.

Amsterdam and other cities of the United Provinces offered merchants unprecidented political and economic freedom. Here they were to establish three new commercial institutions essential to the growth of capitalism. The Amsterdam deposit bank which stabilised the currency and made commercial transactions more secure. The stock exchange or Bourse which provided a new source of capital and where shares in the great trading companies could be bought and sold on an open market. Linked to both the Bourse and the bank was the joint stock company now independent of the state and beholden primarily to its investors. The difference with these new joint-stock companies was that their profits could not simply be drawn off by the state or the monarch to be used for conspicuous consumption or for waging war. The profits could be used as capital for further investment by the directors of the company, who acted on behalf of the investors.

As Adam Smith argued in *Wealth of Nations*, this new financial institution became the foundation stone of western capitalism. It had the advantage of avoiding "the agency risk" common in all bureaucratic organizations, where those in power within the hierarchy use the organization to serve their own private interests, at the expense of its ostensible purpose; financial corruption being the perennial problem especially where accountability was in the hands of those easily bought off. In both

Amsterdam Historical Museum

This painting by Job Berkcheyde shows the courtyard of the Amsterdam exchange in 1668. The Dutch pioneered the most essential institutions of European capitalism — the joint-stock company and the bourse or stock exchange where shares could be traded. This provided the capital that allowed Dutch merchants to build the great fleets, which enabled them to dominate trade with the east.

State Library of New South Wales, Sydney

Dutch naval architecture in the sixteenth and seventeenth centuries was the most developed in the world . . . and it needed to be. It took anything up to three grueling years to complete the round trip to China, and few ships survived more than two or three trips.

China and Europe the "squeezing" of large surplus profits from merchants and their enterprises was a quick method for governments to gain much-needed revenue or for officials to gain personal wealth.

The capacity to buy and sell shares in an enterprise allowed investors to put their money into other companies if their interests were not being served. This form of financial accountability became centered on the bourse in Amsterdam, the clearing house for such investment and the prototype of the modern stock exchange. The operation of this financial market system was to have profound consequences. Perhaps the greatest of these new companies was the Dutch East India Company or VOC (Verenigde Costindische Compagnie), which controlled and managed Dutch interests in the east. Its power was enormous. It has been described as a "state within a state" and was rather like the modern multinational corporation. As merchant fleets were armed with cannon and marines to protect themselves from piracy, they tended to run their trading settlements like states, with the cost of garrisons being included in the overall cost of trade. In Java, their main base in the East, they established plantations and enslaved native people, repressing the traditional economy and culture. These companies, which were to be duplicated in Britain, France and elsewhere in northern Europe, had the virtual capacity to make war or peace anywhere in the world, supported by their government. As many of these merchant-adventurers were raised in the tradition of European piracy, best exemplified by the exploits of Sir Francis Drake a century earlier, they now pursued their more legitimate commercial interests with equal ruthlessness.

# FROM GUNPOWDER TO THE STEAM ENGINE

At the Académie des Sciences in Paris the great Dutch scientist Christiaan Huygens, one of its founding members, had encouraged the experiments of Denis Papin, a French mathematician and physicist. Huygens had been fascinated by Leonardo da Vinci's idea that if gunpowder could drive a cannon ball down a shaft why could it not be used to drive an engine. Papin had been experimenting with gunpowder testers, which were needed by the military in order to test the most appropriate mixtures of saltpeter, charcoal and sulfur for the great array of new weapons being developed — from massive cannon to small handguns. The tester worked by placing a specific amount of gunpowder in a small cylinder; on the top of the cylinder was placed a cap attached to a ratchet or spring; the gunpowder was ignited forcing up the cap and the explosive force then measured on a calibrated gauge.

Papin took this idea a step further. If the amount of gunpowder and the explosive power within the cylinder could be controlled, then the movement up and down of the cap within the cylinder could be used as the driving force for an engine. He made several designs and even attempted to produce such a machine. However, gunpowder was impractical and he turned to steam. He was never actually to develop a working machine himself but he did

*James Watt and one of his steam powered beam engines.*

Courtesy Powerhouse Museum, Sydney

lay down the principle that was later to be taken up by Thomas Newcomen, an ironmonger from Dartmouth in Devon. Papin did, however, produce the world's first "digester" or pressure cooker, which incorporated the most essential device later used in the steam engine — a valve that could control the pressure within a vacuum or cylinder.

Newcomen, aware that one of the major problems in mining was flooding, designed what he called an "atmospheric engine" to pump water out of the mines. This was first used at a colliery near Dudley in Staffordshire in 1712. In 1763 a working model of this engine was given to an instrument maker at Glasgow University, James Watt, for repair. The consequences of Watt's repairs and his further development of this machine would help turn Great Britain into the industrial powerhouse of Europe.

*Dionysius Papin M. D., Anno (1689)*

# POWER IN NUMBERS

The merchant empires established by the East India companies in far-flung parts of the east (the Dutch in Batavia, the British in India, the Portuguese in Macao, the Spanish in the Philippines) provided a stimulus to the intellectual ferment that was occurring in Europe. As the world of the Europeans expanded, so did the boundaries of knowledge. Prior to the sixteenth century and reinforced by the Italian Renaissance, the intellectual world view of scholars was confined to rediscovering what was known to the ancients, the Greek philosophers and mathematicians. This, along with the Bible, provided all that was needed. However, it was soon discovered, as reports of strange animals, plants, people and places circulated through the libraries and universities, that this knowledge was not complete.

The Dutch merchant-adventurers were to establish great collections of these animals and plants. In their libraries there were journals and accounts of the societies with which they came into contact. It was becoming obvious that knowledge was not static but, like wealth, was capable of growing. Societies too were changing as new customs, from the smoking of tobacco to the drinking of tea and coffee, and eating off china plates, were taken up with extraordinary enthusiasm. But more significant were the possible sources of wealth that might exist in remote and unexplored parts of the world. Thus, the scientific interest in the exotic and the accumulation of new knowledge were clearly tied up with a concern for profit.

This link was not lost on the monarchs of Europe. They were soon to become the patrons of new scientific institutions whose broad interest in the growth of knowledge were predicated on the benefits of providing solutions to economic and military problems. In 1662 the Royal Society of London was founded to advance scientific knowledge with King Charles II as its patron. In 1666 the Académie des Sciences was established in Paris under the patronage of Louis XIV. In order to solve the problems of longitude that made accurate navigation impossible, the Royal Greenwich Observatory was set up in 1675, under royal patronage.

Isaac Newton, as President of the Royal Society, was as acutely aware of the importance of this issue as anyone else. In his *Principia Mathematica* and other publications in which he was to explore his theory of gravity and the mechanics of planetary motion, there is the underlying assumption that the universe works like some giant clockwork device, which, having been set in motion by God, follows its own inexorable course. This course was none other than that determined by the laws of mechanics, which, in turn, could be understood with an increasingly high level of mathematical certainty. The predictive power of Newton's mathematical methods was to be passed on to the other experimental sciences emerging under the umbrella of the Royal Society. If God had made a universe that worked on the basis of mathematically precise mechanisms and could be understood in terms of laws, which operated like clockwork, could not the rest of nature be understood in the same terms? It was in the investigation of natural phenomena not in sacred texts that the "hidden hand" of God would be revealed.

But the problem for devout Christians such as Newton was that if the universe ran

The impact of Asia and the exploration of the New World undertaken by the seventeenth century Dutch merchant fleets were to expand intellectual horizons. The Dutch began making vast collections of zoological and botanical curiosities, which, in turn, stimulated scientific interest in species and their origins.

like a giant clockwork machine, how was it possible that God could intervene in his creation as the Bible stated? Such metaphysical issues, however, are beyond the scope of this book and, possibly, beyond most of the natural philosophers who took up Newton's question.

With new institutions that could sponsor scientific research, new careers began to emerge. The demand for scientific instruments, to investigate the inner workings of nature and the universe, meant that the natural philosophers had to leave their libraries in order to work closely with craftsmen. Clockmakers like John Harrison were to turn their precision-engineering skills to the design of new instruments; instruments that were to be as important for navigation as they were for astronomy. As finer microscopes and telescopes, electrical gauges, orreries and sextants were required, mathematicians and instrument makers worked closely together. Of the instrument maker George Graham, the Astronomer Royal James Bradley had this to say in 1747:

> I am sensible, that if my own Endeavours have, in any respect, been effectual to the Advancement of Astronomy; it has principally been owing to the Advice and Assistance given me by our worthy member Mr George Graham; whose great skill and judgment in mechanicks, join'd with a complete and practical knowledge of the use of Astronomical Instruments, enable him to contrive and execute them in the most perfect manner.

An engraving from Thomas Sprat's *The History of the Royal Society of London for Improving Natural Knowledge* published in 1667, five years after the founding of the Society. The bust is of Charles II the Society's founder; on his right is Francis Bacon whose writings promoting science led to its foundation, and on the left is the Society's first president.

113

# TIME, SPACE AND THE LONGITUDE PROBLEM

The problem of establishing longitude had occupied the best minds of Europe for more than a century. As early as 1567 Philip II of Spain had offered a prize of 9,000 ducats to anyone who could come up with a solution; the States General of Holland offered 30,000 florins and the Venetians and Portuguese also offered prizes.

Even Galileo set his mind to the problem. Having first applied the telescope to the observation of the moons of Venus, he proposed that the regular rotation of these moons could be used as a celestial clock. In 1616 he submitted his proposal to the Spanish with tables listing the times of eclipses. However, the Spanish were not impressed, first because it required a telescope and good weather to take a reading at sea, and also, they argued, the eclipse occurred too slowly to allow for the precision needed to measure longitude. Galileo presented his idea to the Dutch but without any success. He did, however, come up with the idea that the regular oscillations of a pendulum could be used to drive a clock, without the cumbersome system of the traditional weights. This he developed into a mechanism in 1642, the last year of his life.

The Dutch scientist Christiaan Huygens knew of Galileo's work and, in 1657, he tried to produce a pendulum clock that would work at sea. Experiments and trials were made but the movement of the boat produced such huge errors that the project was abandoned. The Académie des Sciences in Paris pursued the problem as did other scientific institutions throughout Europe. In 1668 Louis XIV offered a prize of 60,000 livres to a German inventor who came up with an ingenious form of nautical odometer, which he hoped would record precise distances at sea, but this too was a failure.

The Royal Observatory at Greenwich was established in 1675 primarily to resolve the problem of longitude. It was here that many of the major advances in observational astronomy were to be made over the next two centuries. Here too, using a clock with a four-metre long pendulum, designed on the principles developed by Galileo and Huygens, John Flamsteed the first British Astronomer Royal was able to determine the precise time it took for the earth to complete one rotation, the first step for fixing longitude.

This did not stop other astronomers from coming up with novel ways of using the regular motions of planets, including the moon, as a celestial clock capable of being read from anywhere on the globe, and especially at sea.

In 1714 the British parliament received the following petition from a group of London merchants calling for a prize to be established for anyone who could solve the problem of longitude. It was subsequently published in the *House of Commons Journal*:
"A Petition of Several Captains of Her Majesty's Ships, Merchants of London, and commanders of merchantmen, on behalf of themselves, and all others concerned in the Navigation of Great Britain, was presented to the House, and read; setting forth, That the Discovery of the Longitude is of such consequence to Great Britain, for Safety of the Navy, and Merchant

*The famous Octagon Room at the Greenwich Observatory designed by Sir Christopher Wren. The clock faces at the end of the room were controlled by a giant pendulum designed by the instrument maker Thomas Tompion for the Astronomer Royal, John Flamsteed.*

*The Royal Greenwich Observatory was established in 1675 with the basic purpose of improving astronomical knowledge for the purposes of navigation.*

Ships, as well as Improvement of Trade, that, for want thereof, many ships have been retarded in their voyages, and many lost; but if due Encouragement were proposed by the Publick, for such as shall discover the same, some Persons would offer themselves to prove the same, before the most proper judges, in order to their satisfaction, for the Safety of men's Lives, her Majesty's navy, the increase of trade, and the Shipping of these Islands, and the lasting honour of the British Nation."

In response to this request a Committee was formed and the proposal passed on to Isaac Newton who discounted the possibility of using either the "eclipses of Jupiter's satellites" or the "place of the Moon" and argued that what was needed was a "watch regulated by a spring, and rectified every visible sunrise and sunset." Parliament accepted Newton's recommendations and the House of Commons passed a Bill on 17 June 1714 "Providing a Publick Reward for such Person or Persons as shall Discover the Longitude at Sea." The commission set up to manage the prize money — £20,000, more than $1 million in today's terms — was the Board of Longitude.

The man who was to win most of this prize money was typical of the craftsmen and instrument makers who were to play a significant role in the early stages of the Industrial Revolution. John Harrison (1693 – 1776) was the son of a country carpenter from Yorkshire. He and his brother, although originally carpenters, turned to clockmaking when the family moved to Lincolnshire. Harrison showed early talent and, in 1730, was able to gain the support of Edmond Halley, the Astronomer Royal, and George Graham, one of the most influential clock and scientific instrument makers in London. They, in turn, approached the East India Company for funds to allow Harrison to devote his time exclusively to the problems of developing a spring-controlled maritime clock. Over the next thirty years, with the support of the Board of Longitude and the British Navy, Harrison perfected his famous marine clock, an early version of which Captain Cook was to take with him on his voyages to Australia and the Pacific in 1770. For his efforts he received most of the Board of Longitude prize money and the Copley Medal from the Royal Society. For a craftsman and artisan this financial reward and public recognition from the highest institutions in the land, and the social mobility they entailed, was unprecedented.

Until the sea routes to the east were established in the sixteenth century, Chinese porcelain had the rarity value of precious treasure. Nowhere in Europe could anyone produce anything to match it. The word "porcelain" in Italian means "shell-like," which indeed some of the best pieces were — fine translucent bowls and cups, richly decorated with glazes in subtle colors that did not easily chip or break like traditional European clay-based pottery. This Chinese porcelain clearly belonged to a culture of great refinement — an impression that was supported by the writings of the Jesuit missionaries. This impression was reinforced by many other products from the east, especially silk fabrics, which were also far superior to anything being produced in Europe. To Marco Polo the porcelain he came across throughout his journeys was not only of exquisite beauty but extremely cheap by European standards.

This was not lost on either Portuguese or Dutch merchants. By the early seventeenth century the Dutch had established trading bases at Batavia in Java and at Nagasaki in Japan, and huge boatloads of Chinese porcelain began to arrive in the port of Amsterdam. From here it was either distributed to local markets or transhipped to ports throughout northern Europe. The trade was enormous as was the demand. However, in 1644, when the Ming government fell to the invading armies of the Manchus, production in and export from China ground to a standstill for nearly 30 years.

The town of Delft, situated in the center of Holland, about 60 kilometres from Amsterdam, is connected by canal to the port of Rotterdam. In the early part of the seventeeth century Delft was a major center for brewing beer, having achieved something of a monopoly in the surrounding region. This monopoly was challenged by other brewers and, by the middle of the seventeenth century, Delft's major industry was in decline, with many breweries closing down.

The response of the brewers was to convert their breweries into pottery works. They could see there was a demand for Chinese porcelain so they moved their capital to where potential profits were to be found. They began to make imitation porcelain out of clay, taking advantage of the high prices and limited supply of the original. The famous blue and white pottery, for which Delft has for centuries been famous, is in

fact no more than a copy of Chinese blue and white porcelain.

By 1660 there were at least 32 pottery works employing around one quarter of Delft's population of 24,000. What is remarkable is that it was possible to mobilize capital, and import and train skilled craftsmen in so short a time. The availability of capital was an advantage the Dutch had over many other European countries at the time; money was available from Dutch banks at interest rates of 3–6 per cent, half the interest rate of other European countries.

However, the quality of delftware in the early years could not possibly compare with that of Chinese porcelain. Some firms even went so far as to put imitation Chinese characters on the bottom of their pieces to make them appear like the genuine article. In the twentieth century, European consumers have often scoffed at the poor imitations of well-known European brand names manufactured by the Japanese and Chinese as if such imitation was an admission of cultural inferiority. It should not be forgotten, however, that Europe in the seventeeth and eighteenth centuries pioneered this course of action, with flagrant efforts to produce cheap imitations not only of Chinese and Japanese porcelain but also of Asian silk and cotton fabrics.

Spectators gathered in 1783 to catch a glimpse of the Montgolfier brothers' demonstration
of their hot-air balloon.

The expansion of public education among the sons of craftsmen and merchants
allowed the revolution in quantification and precise measurement to be applied
broadly to a wide range of craft industries. The competitive demands for new
technology and the rewards being offered for innovation created a climate in which
experimentation could flourish.

The application of mathematical principles to the design of new technology and
instruments was to become widespread as the new scientific and economic
institutions mediated fashion, status and wealth. The use of precision instruments in
drawing plans and the ability to analyze structural possibilities on paper was a
stimulus to the creativity of engineers. The work of the seventeenth century French
hydraulic engineer, De Beladoir, provides a good example of this.

From Jesuit descriptions and drawings, the idea of the "dragon's backbone pump"
was introduced to Europe. A small portable example may well have been brought
back on a merchant ship. The pump was a simple wooden chain pump, which was
used to lift water from one paddy field into another. There was a long rectangular
box, like a gutter, along which a chain of pallets moved lifting the water. The whole
device was pedal-driven, the source of energy being strong leg muscles. It was an
extraordinarily efficient and practical machine. In China there were, however, only
two sizes. The dimensions remained essentially the same for thousands of years. In

Popular science was promoted throughout the eighteenth century by lectures and demonstrations of scientific principles. Creating a vacuum in a glass jar, and rendering a bird momentarily unconscious, provided a graphic, and fairly sensational, demonstration of the importance of oxygen.

Europe, when the machine finally arrived, it was deemed to be ideal for lifting water to help firefighting in Strasburg. De Beladoir, however, was not satisfied with the models he had received from China. Applying the methods of differential calculus devised by Newton and the other great European mathematician and philosopher, Gottfried Leibnitz, he began to design a whole array of different sizes and systems to cope with different scales of lift, some involving large numbers of people all pedalling at the same time. This method of lifting water was superseded by the suction pump and the "dragon's backbone" had only a brief period of glory. Its passing reflected the widening gap between the technologies of China and Europe.

This was also the case with hot-air ballooning, first developed in eighteenth century France by the Montgolfier brothers. The Chinese already used the principle in their floating paper lamps. These were simply paper globes in which a candle was placed, the hot air causing the lantern to float in the air. These were used in festivals

118

throughout China and yet the principle behind the phenomenon was never investigated nor was its potential as a means of flight ever seriously considered.

It is interesting to note that the Montgolfier brothers were from a family of papermakers from Annonay near Lyon. Both were well educated in the new sciences and were aware of the debates about the nature of air and the effect of heat upon gases. A common experiment in the eighteenth century involved putting a bird and candle in a sealed jar to show that when an animal is denied oxygen it becomes unconscious and will eventually die. Experiments to discover the constituents of air engaged some of the best scientific minds in eighteenth century Europe — Priestley in England, and Charles and Lavoisier in France.

The issue here is not so much why the Chinese did not go in for ballooning, after all why should they, but why the Europeans did. What was the impetus for experimentation and invention that seems to have been such a dominant feature of European culture in the seventeenth and eighteenth centuries? Money is one part of the answer but there was also a recognition that progress through technological and social change was a "good" thing and that society as a whole was moving towards some ideal end. This was to be found in earlier visions of the future put forward in popular literature such as Thomas More's *Utopia* and Francis Bacon's *The New Atlantis* (1620). Bacon was the first European thinker to put forward seriously the notion of a society led by a high priesthood of scholars and engineers — a vision, paradoxically, not unlike the Chinese Confucian ideals. However, rather than being concerned with ethical and philosophical issues, Bacon's bureaucrats were practical men imbued with the ethos and methods of science, and committed to the goal of material rather than moral progress.

What perspective drawing and the new mathematical techniques offered was the ability to play on paper with three-dimensional models and extend the possibilities of the known world. It was a perspective, in a sense, that saw people not only as the center of the world, in the humanistic sense, but also as creators. As God's chosen agents they were here to fulfill his will. Thus the new scientific prophet would lead humanity to the promised land. It was this faith in social and intellectual progress that was one of the driving forces of the remarkable technological and scientific creativity of seventeenth and eighteenth century Europe.

# CHINOISERIE AND THE CHINESE MIRROR

Interestingly enough while all this was going on there was, among the aristocracy and the wealthy, a fashion for all things eastern. It was not just the flood of Chinese and Japanese porcelain and textiles, which were obviously important, but a recognition that China had perfected a form of benign autocracy; an imperial system whose stability and longevity was the envy of European monarchs and aristocrats. The Jesuits were largely responsible for the generation of this image. The journals, letters, and translations of Ricci, Schall and Verbiest were widely read and translated. They painted a picture of Chinese culture as seen from the imperial perspective — a somewhat idealized view.

For this reason it could be said that the Jesuit mission probably had more long-term impact on Europe than it did on China, although this was certainly not the Jesuits' intention. In a sense China provided eighteenth century Europe with a mirror with which to view their own social institutions. As early as 1621, in Robert Burton's *The Anatomy of Melancholy* there are passages that compare the example of China's meritocratic system of government to the traditions of aristocratic privilege still common in Britain:

This painting by Cu Liu Peng shows a traditional group of scholars gathered in a rock garden.

Out of their philosophers and Doctors they [the Chinese] choose Magistrates; their politick Nobles are taken from such as be *moraliter nobiles,* virtuous noble, as in Israel of old, and their office was to defend and govern their country, not to hawk, hunt, eat, drink, game alone, as too many do. Their Mandarins, Litterates, Licentiaters, and such as have raised themselves by their worth, are their noble man, only thought fit to govern the state.

China was held up as the mirror against which the institutional inadequacies of Europe could be paraded in the hope of encouraging reform. Du Halde's *Description de la Chine,* published in Paris in 1735, was widely circulated and translated into numerous languages. From Jesuit sources and with illustrations taken from drawings done by artists attached to the Jesuit mission, China was presented to Europe as a model of civilization.

For social critics such as Voltaire and Montesquieu in France, China was a society with no Christian Church and no aristocracy, run by a class of bureaucratic officials who owed their position in the vast imperial hierarchy to their scholastic achievement, to merit, and not to birth. This for Voltaire was a revelation and was used to good effect in his polemics against the privileges and corruption of both the Church and the aristocracy.

The human mind certainly cannot imagine a government better than this one where everything is to be decided by the large tribunals, subordinated to each other, of which the members are received only after several severe examinations. Everything in China regulates itself by these tribunals.

Courtesy Film Australia

A passion for chinoiserie swept through eighteenth century Europe, with architects and designers attempting to incorporate Chinese motifs into their work. This wallpaper in the Chinese room at Woburn Abbey, came with additional flowers and birds, which could be attached to the wallpaper if a more ornate effect was desired.

At Woburn Abbey the Duke of Bedford had this dairy built in the Chinese style to keep up
with the eighteenth century fashion for chinoiserie.

These sentiments were to be echoed by enlightened intellectuals, from the encyclopedist Diderot to the economist Quesnay. By the end of the eighteenth century, even before the French Revolution in 1789, Talleyrand had adopted the Chinese system of a written examination for civil servants, a practice which was later taken up elsewhere in Europe.

In many respects, China's distance from Europe made it a suitable mirror in which reformers could project their hopes and ideals. The fact that many of these were half-truths did not detract from their potency. This was complemented by a corresponding taste for Chinese decor and even clothes. Rooms were decorated in the Chinese style. Furniture such as that produced by Chippendale reflected this new vogue for things Chinese. Wallpaper from China was introduced into Europe for the first time. At Woburn Abbey the fourth Duke of Bedford, who had financial interests in the China trade through the East India Company, had a whole room hung with wallpaper specially ordered from China. The notion of "hanging" wallpaper dates from this time when the paper panels of an original painting were far too expensive to stick to the wall and so were hung. (Only much later when printed wallpaper was being produced in Europe in large quantities was it stuck to rather than hung on the wall.)

The vogue for chinoiserie extended further: at Woburn a Chinese dairy was built; pagodas were put up in Royal Kew Gardens and, at Brighton, an extraordinarily lavish and vulgar mixture of Asian designs was put together in the Brighton Pavilion. On the continent, the vogue was the same, with magnificent rooms being created in the Louvre and the Potsdam Palace.

The English habit of taking tea in the afternoon is attributed to the Duchess of Bedford who made it fashionable in the late eighteenth century. With a family stake in the East India Company, whose major import from China at this time was tea, it made good sense, although tea drinking was not greeted with universal enthusiasm. Some like Jonas Hanway in his "Essay of Tea" railed against this pernicious habit:

> We have abundance of milk; beer of many kinds; lime which we import from countries in Europe near at hand; infusions of many salutary and well-tasted herbs; preparations of barley and oats; and above all, in most places, exceedingly good water. . . . Tea when it is genuine it hurts many, when adulterated or dyed, it has been found poisonous. . . . The young and old, the healthy and infirm, the superlatively rich, down to vagabonds and beggars, drink this enchanting beverage, when they are thirsty and when they are not thirsty.

In respect of water, Hanway was not altogether correct. The quality of drinking water in many of the crowded cities, especially London, was downright dangerous,

The Duchess of Bedford, who was said to be responsible for initiating the English habit of taking tea in the afternoon.

This late Qing painting shows the emperor granting an audience in the imperial gardens. China was portrayed in idealized form, with the emperor presented as the embodiment of a philosopher king or benign autocrat — positions of power to which European aristocrats aspired though rarely achieved.

with open drains, carrying sewage, polluting wells and spreading diseases like cholera. The boiling of water for tea, although few were aware of it at the time, prevented the spread of disease. It was also an alternative to drinking beer and other alcoholic beverages. Among the sober merchants and gentry tea provided a social habit appropriate to clear thinking and hard work. With this new habit came new demands for "China" cups, teapots and plates.

China, because of its inaccessibility and exotic character, was to represent all things to all people. For the radicals and reformers it was to be used as a lever for change whereas, for the aristocrat, its benign and stable despotism offered a model and a future, in a political climate that was growing increasingly democratic and republican. It is amusing to find Louis XVI of France and Frederick the Great of Prussia both imitating the Chinese emperors' ritual of plowing the first furrow to open the spring plowing season. Such affectations, however, were not to hold back the floodgates of political and social reform.

# DESPERATION AND SKULDUGGERY IN THE CHINA SHOP

The power of this new spirit of inquiry is perhaps best seen in the manner in which the Europeans went about trying to "reverse-engineer" or copy the Chinese method of making porcelain. Nowhere, except perhaps in the Japanese postwar takeover of the international automobile industry from the Americans, has there been such a systematic effort made at industrial imitation, eventually leading to innovation.

The raw materials for European ceramics were natural clays covered with a heavy white glaze. Despite their achievements, the Dutch could not match the translucence and hardness of the Chinese originals. As supplies of Chinese porcelain came on to the European market, the local industries were pushed to the limits of their technological ability in trying to produce ceramics that could compete with the Chinese originals. The Chinese kept the production process a carefully guarded industrial secret.

It was a German alchemist by the name of Johann Friedrich Böttger (1682–1719) who was to make the first breakthrough, but in a most surprising manner. European alchemists were believed to be able to produce gold by chemical transformations. Eastern European monarchs, concerned with maintaining revenue, were in the habit of imprisoning or putting under house arrest anyone claiming to be an alchemist. These unfortunate souls were kept by the state for ten years and, if they did not produce gold in that time, they were executed.

Böttger was one such character who was imprisoned by the Elector of Saxony, Augustus the Strong, who had just become King of Poland and badly needed revenue to pay his armies. Böttger was no fool and, while desperately trying to come up with the gold the Elector wanted, he had to think of some way of saving his neck. For heating metal, he required crucibles that could withstand extremely high temperatures. In experimenting with materials that could be used for this purpose he noticed that, in applying high temperatures to a mixture containing crushed kaolin and quartz he came up with crucibles that markedly resembled Chinese porcelain. The penny dropped and Böttger abandoned the futile task of trying to produce gold by chemical processes. With the help of an eminent scholar, Ehrenfried Walter von Tschirnhaus, he turned to the problem of making "hard-paste" porcelain. In 1711 he was able to announce to the Elector that he had been able to produce, not gold, but a very good source of it. As a result he was released and given the title of Baron. At the chateau of Albrechtburg at Meissen the Elector of Saxony established the first porcelain workshop in Europe and began to produce fine porcelain bowls and "objets d'art" of extraordinary beauty that were the equal of anything produced in China.

However, while the Elector of Saxony was establishing his works at Meissen, in Paris the French were busily engaged in industrial espionage to achieve the same ends. Orrey, a senior government official, who was eventually to become minister of finance, had interests in a ceramics works established at Vincennes in Paris. He contrived through a relative, who was head of the Jesuit order in Paris, to have Father

D'Entrecolles, a French Jesuit missionary in Beijing, visit the famous porcelain center of Jingdezhen. The purpose of his visit was to try to discover the Chinese method of making porcelain and, if possible, to smuggle back samples of the materials used. D'Entrecolles did his father superior's bidding and visited Jingdezhen, an industrial city unparalleled in the world until the Industrial Revolution in the north of England. Here the imperial workshops produced porcelain for export and for the imperial palace. The fire from the kilns was said to light the night sky, and the general atmosphere was one of great industry. In 1712 there were around 18,000 families associated with porcelain production in the city. D'Entrecolles reported that there were 3,000 kilns in operation (300 of them in the imperial factory) and that 80 per cent of all export porcelain was manufactured there.

D'Entrecolles achieved his task of getting samples without getting caught and, with accompanying descriptions of all he had observed, sent the lot back to Paris. There was one problem, however. He got the labels confused and no one could make sense of his descriptions. The Académie des Sciences was brought in to help with chemical analysis, one of the first examples of their direct involvement in the application of science to industrial research. Even eminent savants of the Académie could make no sense of the letters from D'Entrecolles. With a round trip from Paris to Beijing, without any mishaps, taking about three years, the frustration must have been enormous. However, one researcher, Réamur, who had carefully studied the letters and misunderstood their meaning, accidentally invented an entirely new form of "soft-paste" porcelain, which could be molded like clay. In this way the French porcelain industry was established. It became a royal monopoly and the workshop was moved to Sèvres on the outskirts of Paris.

Courtesy Film Australia

Left: The figure of Emperor Quianlong reproduced at Sevres from the original eighteenth century molds. This figure made of "soft-paste" porcelain was sent to the Emperor as a gift to encourage him to take an interest in French manufacture.

Right: Porcelain production in China was depicted in eighteenth century illustrated volumes as a romantic, pastoral process when, in reality, the major center of production at Jingdezhen was far more like the crowded industrial cities that were just beginning to emerge in Europe. Many of the labor-intensive stages in Chinese porcelain production have changed little since that time . . . and the west still comes to buy.

Courtesy Film Australia

Courtesy Film Australia

127

In 1768 Henri Bertin, a trade minister in the French government, commissioned a statue of the Emperor Quianlong (Ch'ien Lung), taken from a drawing by the Jesuit missionary Panzi, to be made out of this porcelain. The gift was sent back to China with two young Chinese Jesuits who had been studying in Paris. The statue was part of a package of goods, including silk tapestries, clocks and other automata sent in the hope of encouraging trade. To the Chinese it must have seemed the height of impudence.

Important though this achievement was in dispelling some of the mystique attached to Chinese industrial technology, the development of a porcelain industry also encouraged original designs and techniques, which made European porcelain increasingly different from that of China. By the end of the eighteenth century European porcelain was preferred to the Chinese original. However, porcelain was always a luxury in Europe. It was to remain the "china" of the aristocrat and the rich. It was to be in England that the real revolution in the production of crockery for everyday use was to occur.

Josiah Wedgwood was representative of a wholly new craft tradition. He was an industrialist and entrepreneur with close ties to the scientific community and, more important perhaps, equally close ties with the growing middle class who were demanding access to luxury goods hitherto only accessible to the aristocracy. Like

This illustration, from de Milly's *L'Art de la Porcelaine,* of 1771, shows techniques of production that are still used to make this most refined of luxuries. Genuine porcelain remains extremely expensive and labor intensive.

Thomas Edison in the nineteenth century, Wedgwood was both an inventor and businessman, with an acute awareness of what the market needed and he set his considerable talents to meeting it.

Wedgwood was born into a Staffordshire family, which for four generations had worked in the pottery trade. He began school at the age of six but when he was nine years old his father died and he had to take up an apprenticeship as a potter. However, poor health kept him from work, allowing him time to study, particularly the sciences. With connections in the trade and with an obvious entrepreneurial flair Wedgwood opened up a small pottery works of his own in 1754 in partnership with a successful manufacturer Thomas Whieldon.

In England, by the mid-eighteenth century, there was not only a significant growth in population (due in part to the waning of the plague) but also a significant rise in wealth from improvements in agriculture and growing trade. The habit of drinking tea, for example, had become widespread among the new middle class, and there was a great demand for good quality crockery at modest prices.

Wedgwood was fully aware of this as he noted in his experiment book: "I saw the field was spacious, and the soil so good as to promise ample recompense to any who should labor diligently in its cultivation." Wedgwood applied his efforts to developing a form of earthenware pottery that would have all the characteristics of

Josiah Wedgwood and his family as portrayed by George Stubbs in 1780. Wedgwood was typical of the new northern English industrialists, most of whom began as humble craftsmen but were to achieve a status and influence unthinkable for craftsmen in China.

129

porcelain but would be cheap. The ingredients for porcelain were expensive, and the time and labor involved too great to be able to manufacture it cheaply enough for ordinary people. So in a laboratory in the basement of his house Wedgwood set about systematically experimenting with different mixtures of clays and glazes, all faithfully recorded in his experiment book. He was to apply the methodology of the new sciences and seek the advice of many of the leading figures of his day. He was a member of the Luna Society, a group of like-minded experimentalists who met every full moon to discuss scientific matters. Joseph Priestley, one of the most famous chemists of his day, and Erasmus Darwin, grandfather of Charles, were both members of this group.

In 1763 Wedgwood described what was to be one of his major achievements:

[A] species of earthenware for the table, quite new in appearance, covered with a rich and brilliant glaze, bearing sudden alterations of heat and cold, manufactured with ease and expedition, and consequently cheap, having every requisite for the purpose intended.

This cream-colored earthenware made from a mixture of Cornish China clay, China stone, ground flint and Devon ball clay covered with a tough lead glaze, was to become known as queen's ware — an order was placed by Queen Charlotte and Wedgwood was astute enough as a businessman to realize the commercial advantage of that. What he had produced was the stuff of the commonplace: "china" to be used

The Staffordshire potteries where Josiah Wedgwood established his factory. Here he experimented with clays and glazes, which were to lead to the mass production of basic crockery for everyday use.

Mary Evans Picture Library, London

in daily life. Because of its low price and the demand created by large-scale marketing, Wedgwood was able to establish a factory at Etruria on a truly industrial scale. This factory was on a canal linking the Trent and Mersey Rivers, allowing the clays and flints needed by the Staffordshire potteries to be brought in by barge and the chinaware to be shipped out to the markets of London. Here Wedgwood opened his own shop and engaged agents to handle his overseas exports. One shipment from his Etruria works to continental Europe was worth £20,000. He was a leading figure in the local chamber of manufacturers, and was the model of the new wealthy industrialist. He was to continue, for the rest of his life, to pursue practical scientific experiments to improve methods and techniques used in his works: improvements that were later adopted by the many other pottery works established in Staffordshire. He even met some Chinese potters in London in 1775 through a friend, John Blake, a member of the East India Company. He recorded in detail their conversation and methods used for firing and kiln construction.

Perhaps his most important scientific achievement was the development of the pyrometer — an instrument for determining the precise heat of a kiln. In his "commonplace book" there is the following entry:

In the long course of experiments for the improvement of the manufacture I am engaged in, some of the greatest difficulties and perplexities have arisen from not being able to ascertain the heat to which the experiment pieces had been exposed.

Josiah Wedgwood & Sons Limited, Barlaston, Stoke-on-Trent, England

Wedgwood was probably the first manufacturer in Europe to engage in scientific research and development. He operated a laboratory in the basement of his house and was a leading member of the Luna Society, which was concerned with promoting scientic methods in industry. Shown here is just one of the 3,000 trials he carried out and documented in trying to perfect his jasper ware.

He set his mind to the problem and came up with a simple but ingenious method of measurement. Like any potter, he realized that clay shrinks at a fairly uniform rate according to the heat of the kiln. However, existing methods using thermometers could only handle temperatures to a maximum of 300 degrees Celsius. Wedgwood needed to know the precise temperature of kilns to 1,000 degrees or more. He therefore constructed a calibrated brass gauge (narrower towards one end) in which a square groove had been cut. A cylinder of clay was placed on one end and would gradually move down the gauge as it shrank in the heat of the kiln. With the pyrometer it was possible to get a precise temperature measurement. This was not only important for his experiments but was to be adopted widely within the industry, not only to achieve more uniform products, but also to minimise loss. For the invention of this simple but useful device, Wedgwood was made a member of the Royal Society in 1783.

The differences between the English and the Chinese ceramics industries were interesting. In China, the knowledge of how to fire a kiln and measure its temperature was a carefully guarded secret kept within the families of craftsmen and taught only to apprentices who were taken into the business. It was considered and remained a trade secret. In China a tradition of observational methods using subtle changes of color and atmosphere in the kilns had evolved over the centuries. These methods had allowed the Chinese to produce some of the finest porcelain in the world. As with the great violins of Italy, few craftsmen even to this day can match the quality of some of the finest pieces. This secrecy prevailed in all the craft guilds in China. There was no tradition of recording techniques or producing technical manuals, except by scholar-officials who did it as part of the amassing of technological information for the great imperial encyclopedias. However, these books were never meant to be read by craftsmen and were usually circulated only among scholars and bureaucrats. Although they contained woodblock illustrations showing the processes, these were never plan drawings. The end result was that this knowledge was never disseminated.

European craft industries in the Middle Ages were also governed by secretive guilds like China's but, by the seventeenth and eighteenth centuries, it had become widely recognized that the growth of scientific and technological knowledge was a public asset. This had been acknowledged as early as the reign of Elizabeth I, when the first British royal patent was given to a stained-glass maker on condition that the knowledge of his techniques be made readily available to other glass makers. The patent system was to be very important in this regard, for it rewarded invention and innovation by giving an individual a limited monopoly while, at the same time, allowing technological knowledge to be widely disseminated. In the highly competitive European climate this obviously made sense. For this dissemination the capacity to make geometrically precise three-dimensional drawings was to play an important role. In China no such development occurred, in part, because there was neither the competitive environment nor the rapid change in taste and demand that there was in Europe. After all, many of the craft industries were imperial monopolies and produced in bureaucratically managed state factories, with little competition.

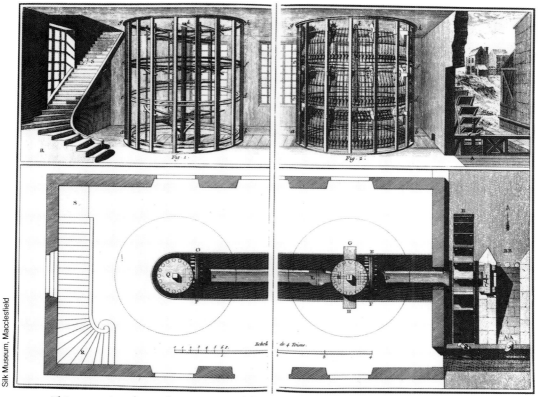

This engraving shows the operation of the Piedmont "silk-throwing" machine, the secret of which John Lombe, an early industrial spy, was to bring back to England.

Craft traditions were established and knowledge of techniques kept a carefully guarded secret, an attitude that was commonplace in China until very recently. The danger of this was that important technological knowledge could be completely lost, for example, the methods of construction of the great treasure ships used by Zheng He and the methods of building water-powered spinning wheels or mechanical clocks. It would be fair to say that institutional innovations were as important as the more obvious technological innovations to the growing industrial power of Europe. This is nowhere more evident than in the silk and textile industries where, for centuries, the Chinese led the world.

## SILK STOCKINGS AND COTTON SOCKS

From the thirteenth century, when silkworms were supposedly smuggled in bamboo poles from China to Europe, Piedmont in northern Italy was the center of the silk weaving and spinning industry. The region kept a monopoly on the industry by maintaining draconian laws governing the practice of the trade. This was especially true of the spinning of the powerful warp threads used in the weaving of silk fabric. The Italians had developed what was called a "silk-throwing" machine to spin these threads, for which they held a virtual European monopoly. The industry was centered around the city of Lucca and the technology was a carefully guarded secret. In 1308 there was even a guild statute that stated that any man practicing the craft outside the city would be hanged and any woman burned. By 1589 the Piedmontese were so concerned about losing control of this industry that they were even prepared to offer a 50 ducat reward to anyone who killed an artisan practicing their method of silk throwing outside the province.

In 1714 a young Englishman, John Lombe, left London for Piedmont with the sole purpose of stealing the secret of the Lucca "throwing machine." The reason was simple, there was a growing demand in England for silk fabric but a major factor affecting the cost of production was the Piedmont monopoly on the production of the essential warp thread, which, throughout the seventeenth and eighteenth centuries, had to be imported. Try as they might with other methods the English did not seem able to match the quality achieved by the Italians. John Lombe had been apprenticed into the silk trade at an early age and was from a family with a long association with silk and wool weaving. At the age of 20 he joined Thomas Cotchett, a retired solicitor who had established a silk-spinning mill in Derby.

There were four processes involved in the making of the strong warp thread. The first involved the winding of the silk filament from the cocoon on to a bobbin; the thread was then cleaned and twisted to form a standard thread. The final process was called "doubling" and involved the twisting of this thread to make the strong warp thread. It was this last process that Cotchett and Lombe were unable to achieve satisfactorily, in spite of importing Dutch machinery, and, as a consequence, English silk made from local thread was inferior to that made from the expensive Italian warp thread.

Lombe, in an act of extraordinary bravado, decided to become an industrial spy. For this task he learned Italian, draftsmanship and mathematics, and left for Italy with the support of his half-brother, Thomas, who ran the Lombe family business. Lombe was able to enlist the help of a Jesuit priest who, so the story goes, on the payment of an "oblazione" or bribe secured him a position in a Lucca mill as a machine winder. He would wait behind in the evenings and make detailed plan drawings of the throwing machine and its various parts. He smuggled the drawings back to his brother, hidden inside bales of silk thread. However, he was discovered and had to flee Piedmont. If he had been caught he would have been hung by one leg from the gallows "until dead," a gruesome end. Fortunately, he was able to get to the coast and on to a British merchant ship that was leaving for London. On finding out he had escaped in this manner, gunboats were sent in hot pursuit but the British ship succeeded in escaping them.

On his return to London in 1716, John Lombe immediately took out a patent on the machine and, with money from his half-brother Thomas, set up England's first water-powered textile factory in Derby. This was to be the prototype of the modern textile factory whose widespread adoption throughout northern England was to form the foundation for the Industrial Revolution. It was powered by a single undershot water wheel, which, by means of gearing, drove a whole battery of throwing machines tended by 300 factory workers. This was mechanization on an unprecedented scale.

Derbyshire County Council

Above: Lombe's water-powered silk spinning factory, built in Derby in 1720, was the prototype for the factory system of production. The factory system was to provide England with the industrial wealth and power that would shake the foundations of the Celestial Empire in the east.

Right: A scale model of Lombe's "silk-throwing" machine built for the Silk Museum in Derby. The original was three times the size, and was driven by water power.

Courtesy Film Australia

# NUMERICAL CONTROL — FROM LOOMS TO COMPUTERS

In the early eighteenth century at Lyon, the center of the French silk industry, weavers were confronted with increased competition both from Chinese imports and from other centers within Europe. The master weavers of the town began to look for technological solutions to the problems of quality and cost. Basil Bouchon, one of these master weavers, was impressed by the engineering skills of craftsmen making the ingenious clockwork dolls or automata, which were then in vogue. These automata, which played the harpsichord or performed complex acrobatic movements, were controlled by sophisticated clockwork gearing driven by a cylindrical drum with jacks, the same method as used in musical boxes that played melodies. The jacks on the cylinder were arranged to trigger different movements, in sequence, as the cylinder turned.

It struck Bouchon that the same principle could be applied to the weaving of the complex new designs required for silk fabric (given the increased competition in the silk industry it was necessary to be able to change patterns to suit changing tastes). With traditional techniques, changing the pattern was difficult and very laborious. The traditional loom used in silk production required two men, one doing the actual weaving and the other, the drawboy, controlling the pattern by holding up various combinations of the warp threads. This technique, originally developed in China, was satisfactory if a standardized product was required and if labor costs were low. However, unless the drawboy was very skilled, inaccuracies in design were inevitable.

Bouchon decided to encode the design on to a roll of paper (the same principle still used in the pianola or player piano), which would control the movement of the warp threads. Bouchon never got the idea to work effectively and it was another Lyon silk weaver, Jean-

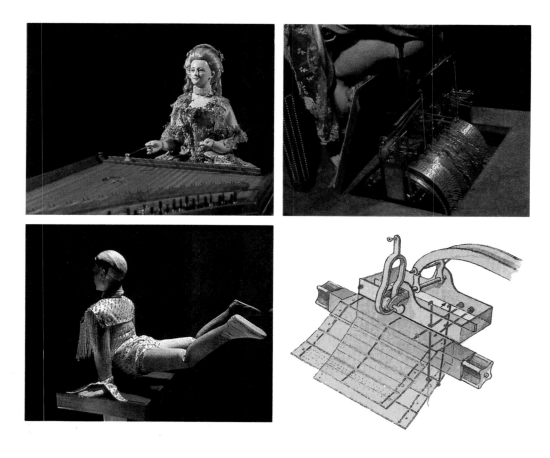

Marie Jacquard, who was to perfect the system. Jacquard exchanged the continuous roll of paper for a chain of cards, each card representing one movement of the shuttle. As many as 30,000 of these cards could be used in the production of one piece of silk fabric. Jacquard's loom caused a sensation when he finally perfected it in the early 1800s. In 1806 he was awarded the Chevalier de la Legion d'Honneur by Napoleon and given a state pension of 3,000 francs for his efforts.

Not all the reactions to his invention were as appreciative. In 1810 drawboys went on the rampage through the streets of Lyon, smashing Jacquard's looms; Jacquard himself was lucky to escape with his life. However, the economic advantages of his machine were obvious to every silk weaver. Even those who may not have wished to change to the new methods had to, or be forced out of business. Drawboys were but one of a number of craft skills that were to disappear overnight in the momentum of technological change. By 1812 there were 11,000 Jacquard looms operating in France alone.

This method of encoding information or sequences of instructions on to punched cards, developed by Jacquard and the other weavers of Lyon, was to have profound consequences far beyond the silk industry. These same Jacquard cards were to be used in the early development of computers, first by Babbage in Britain and later by Hollerith in the United States. The cards were eventually used to encode data in the first electronic computer, the ENIAC, developed at the end of World War II and used by John von Neumann to perform the mathematical calculations necessary to make the first atomic bomb. In the 1950s IBM would turn these same cards into an international symbol of efficiency and innovation.

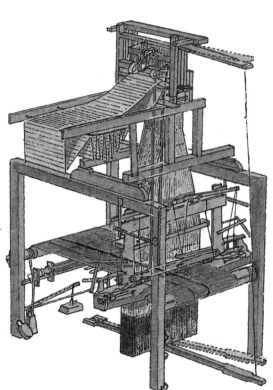

The story has a dark ending. In 1722 John Lombe died suddenly at the age of 29, only six years after his return to England. A mysterious Italian woman who arrived in Derby soon after the establishment of his factory was employed there and it was later believed by many that she had been sent by the Piedmontese to seek revenge, presumably by slowly poisoning him; she disappeared soon after his death. The factory was not a huge success but it was to become the model for the use of water-powered gearing to drive spinning machines and was soon taken up in the cotton industry.

If there was a growing demand for silk in England in the second half of the eighteenth century, the demand for cotton cloth was even greater. The industry had grown out of the demand stimulated by the East India Company's import of cotton cloth from India and China. The center of the local cotton industry was on the damp side of the Pennines around the city of Manchester. The major problem was the supply of yarn. Traditional hand-spinning techniques could not meet the demand. Supplies of cotton were readily available from North America and the West Indies, and flax from Ireland. In 1733 John Kay had invented the flying shuttle, which meant that the weavers were able to work at much greater speed, with the shuttle being thrown by springs from one side of the loom to the other. This increased the speed of weaving and therefore the demand for thread.

In 1761 the Society for the Encouragement of Arts, Commerce and Manufactures offered a reward of £50 to anyone who could invent a spinning machine. James

Popular science was promoted throughout the eighteenth century by a new class of instrument makers and scientists who gave popular lectures and demonstrations of scientific principles. Here, a lecture is being given on pneumatics.

Derby Art Gallery

Richard Arkwright's cotton spinning mill, established at Cromford in 1771. In this remote valley he built a massive factory complex and established an entire industrial community. Many of these communities, which grew up around the factories of Lancashire, were run with a benign paternalism; the conditions in others were appalling.

Hargreaves came up with the spinning Jenny, a machine that would allow eight cotton spindles to work at the same time, but it was difficult to operate. It was the youngest son of an impecunious barber and wigmaker, Richard Arkwright, who solved the problem. In conjunction with a clockmaker, John Kay (not to be confused with the inventor of the flying shuttle), Arkwright developed a spinning machine known as the water frame, which he patented in 1769. Arkwright continued to experiment with the water frame and debated whether to market it for domestic use. However, he had seen what the Lombe brothers had been able to achieve in their factory at Derby. By applying water power, geared by engineers familiar with clockwork mechanisms, it was possible to drive a whole army of machines. He therefore decided to set up a factory but had the difficult task of finding the capital.

While continuing in the family's profession of wigmaking, he traveled the countryside collecting hair. In Nottingham he made contact with a hosier (stocking maker) Jedediah Strutt who was impressed with the strength and fineness of the yarn produced on Arkwright's water frame, which was ideally suited for the hosiery industry. In 1770 Arkwright, Strutt and another man, Samuel Need, set up in partnership.

In 1771 Arkwright and his partners, with investment from bankers in Nottingham, set up a mill at Cromford, then a small village near Matlock north of Derby. The virtue of this site was its good supply of water to drive the water wheels, and it was also sufficiently far from the center of the textile industry where riots had begun to break out as machinery began to displace labor. In the *Derby Mercury* of 13 December 1771 this advertisement appeared:

> Wanted immediately, two Journeymen Clock-makers, or others that understands Tooth and Pinion well: Also a Smith that can forge and file — Likewise two wood turners that has been accustomed to Wheelmaking, Spoleturning etc. Weavers residing at the Mill may have good work. There is Employment at the above Place for Women, Children, etc. and good Wages.

In order to set up an entire industrial community, Arkwright built not only a large factory, but also houses for weavers, a school, a church and other essential amenities. Here, we begin to see the formation of the industrial community, and the breakdown of the production process like the cogs in a giant machine. Skills were no longer embodied in people but in machines; machines that could be owned by those with the capital to invest in their invention and the establishment of a factory. Thus the independence of small craftsmen, who had been engaged, usually with their entire families, in the production of cloth, was eroded. The benefits went to the new industrialists and to consumers who now had access to better and cheaper cloth. The cost was borne by the displaced artisans who now had little alternative but to give up their cherished independence and become wage-earning workers in the new factories. It is little wonder that some ran amok breaking looms and industrial machinery.

So successful was Arkwright's first mill and so large the demand that a second mill, 125 feet long and seven-stories high, was put up at Cromford in 1776. As Arkwright's original patent expired, other mills were opened up on the basis of his success at Cromford. Throughout the Midlands the factory system with its use of water power, geared to drive increasingly sophisticated machinery, led to the mechanization of all aspects of textile manufacture. This was made possible by the application of engineering skills first developed by the earlier clock and instrument makers — skills that had been evident in the great astronomical clock of Su Song and in the elaborate robotic devices such as musical boxes, which had so entertained the Chinese court and the European aristocracy.

# GOD AND THE NEW FACTORY

*Religion must necessarily produce both industry and frugality, and these cannot but produce riches. But as riches increase, so will pride, anger, and love of the world . . . How then is it possible that Methodism, that is, a religion of the heart, though it flourishes now as a green bay tree, should continue in this state. . . . So, although the form of religion remains, the spirit is swiftly vanishing away.*

John Wesley, founder of Methodism

The new factory system was built on the driving force of water (and later steam power) and on machines that could break down the production process into rational units or tasks. But these technological developments were not enough in themselves to account for the phenomenal growth of output, which was to be such a feature of the British Industrial Revolution. After all, the Chinese 500 years earlier had had water-powered spinning. The difference in eighteenth century Europe was that new economic institutions supported by international trading networks had vastly increased the size of the market that was available; a market far larger than was possible within the Chinese empire, which was vast by any national standards.

The new emphasis on free trade, which was being demanded by merchants frustrated by state monopolies, led to the articulation of economic theories that provided a philosophical rationale for free-market capitalism. Adam Smith in his

Styal Mill at Quarry Bank, near Manchester, was established by the Greg family in 1790, after Richard Arkwright's original patent on the water frame expired. The clocktower and the chimney were the two potent symbols of the new discipline demanded by the factory system. With the application of machinery for spinning and weaving, the cost of producing simple cotton cloth was to fall to levels that would make Manchester synonymous with cotton fabric throughout the world.

Courtesy Film Australia

*Wealth of Nations* provided a completely new concept of national wealth, based, not on the control of trade (the traditional mercantilist theory), but on production. Smith saw in the rational division of labor the economic advantage of producing better and cheaper goods. His famous example was the pin factory. If one man was to make a whole pin by himself he would produce fewer pins than if the process was broken up into discrete tasks with one worker specializing in each. He also believed that, if manufacturers were left to compete freely with each other in the market, the price of goods would be regulated, and the cheapest and most efficient production techniques automatically encouraged. For the British utilitarian philosophers such as Bentham and Mill this freedom was seen to "provide the greatest happiness for the greatest number." In this market mechanism Smith saw what he, along with new industrialists such as Arkwright and Wedgwood, believed to be "the hidden hand of Progress." The new market system would find the correct balance between the factors of production — labor, capital and land.

What was not taken into account in this unbridled enthusiasm for the free market was the position of those who sold their labor and who were to become its unquestioned victims. No one could deny the benefits of increased productivity or that the freedom of the individual to pursue his or her "enlightened self-interest" was an advancement, but at what cost. The legacy of Aquinas and the Calvinists was to be restated for the new working class by the fire-and-brimstone preachers of the

Mary Evans Picture Library, London

"While the engine runs people must work — men, women, and children are yoked together with iron and steam," commented Dr J.P. Kay in 1832 on the work discipline demanded in the cotton mills of the north of England.

Methodist Church. The almost monastic discipline of the Protestant middle class had centered on the virtue and urgency of work and its rewards of grace and providence. This was now to be extended to the new factory workers, the displaced weavers, spinners and potters forced to abandon their independent semi-rural existence to become wage laborers in the rapidly growing cities of northern England. For as the price of the cotton cloth produced in the new factories halved and halved again in a matter of years, the small weaver was put out of business.

The rigorous discipline demanded by the factory owners was alien to many of their employees' traditional way of life. Much of the early factory labor was supplied by women and children who were pliable and more able to withstand the monotony of 12–14 hour days tending machines. Traditionally, the weaver worked at his craft between periods of agricultural labor, work followed the pattern common to rural life of following the cycles of nature, with its seasonal demands and numerous holidays. The weavers had been, above all else, moderately independent as they owned and controlled the means of production — their looms and spinning wheels.

The factory system demanded that they be cogs in a giant machine, whose interdependent parts operated like clockwork. Dr Andrew Ure in *The Philosophy of Manufactures* (1835) described it in the following words:

> [The factory]... involves the idea of a vast automation, composed of various mechanical and intellectual organs, acting in uninterrupted concert for the production of a common object, all of them subordinated to a self-regulated moving force....
>
> To devise and administer a successful code of factory discipline, suited to the necessities of factory diligence, was the Herculean enterprise, the noble achievement of Arkwright. Even at the present day, when the system is perfectly organized, and its labor lightened to the utmost, it is found nearly impossible to convert persons past the age of puberty, whether drawn from rural or from handicraft occupations, into useful factory hands. After struggling for a while to conquer their listless or restive habits, they either renounce the employment spontaneously, or are dismissed by the overlookers on account of inattention.

Apart from rationalizing the use of child labor in factories, Ure was probably accurate in his observations about the difficulties with which rural workers came to terms with the conditions of employment in the new factory system, which had its beginnings in the cotton mills of Lancashire and, by the early nineteenth century, had spread to other industries throughout England. Ure realised that an inner change had to take place in individual workers, and the most powerful weapon to use to inculcate this internal work and time discipline was fear. The chapels and Sunday schools constructed by the millowners were a source of conditioning, as important as the clocks and bells that governed the working day and towered above the factory roofs like the spires of the ancient monasteries. The fire-and-brimstone preaching of the early Methodist chapel, along with the puritanical sexual repression it demanded, gave to the rural workforce the sense of urgency that the factory system demanded. For Ure this was part of what he described as the "moral economy of the factory system":

It is, therefore, excessively the interest of every millowner to organize his moral machinery on equally sound principles with his mechanical, for otherwise he will never command the steady hands, watchful eye, and prompt cooperation, essential to excellence of product. . . . There is, in fact, no case to which the Gospel truth, "Godliness is great gain", is more applicable than to the administration of an extensive factory.

The fear of losing work or money was not sufficient to inculcate the virtues that Ure envisaged. These virtues had to come from a sense of almost revolutionary zeal; a self-discipline that would make individuals abandon their traditional values for those of the industrial system in which they now worked.

However, the missionary zeal with which the Methodists approached the inculcation of work discipline among the recalcitrant working class of England was nothing to the efforts that were to be expended on behalf of the heathens in the rest of the world. It was with very different eyes that Protestant missionaries regarded Asia and the culture of imperial China. Compared with the Jesuits two centuries earlier, the Protestant merchants and missionaries of the early nineteenth century who arrived at the ports of Guangzhou and Nagasaki regarded the culture they saw as decadent, corrupt and lacking the dynamic character embodied in the European drive for progress. Having mastered and even surpassed the Chinese in many of the industrial arts and technology that had for centuries inspired awe, respect and emulation, the European merchants now came to promote their own versions of the porcelain, cotton textiles and guns in the very market places where they had first appeared a thousand years earlier.

# THE CHINA TRADE, TRIBUTES AND THE OPIUM WAR

*It may be perhaps supposed that the sight of the masterpieces of art, which the Chinese receive annually from Europe, will open their eyes and convince them that industry is here carried further than amongst themselves and that our genius surpasses theirs; but their vanity finds remedy for this. All those wonders are included in the class of superfluities and by placing them behind their wants they place them at the same time beneath their regard.*

Van Braan, leader of a Dutch mission to the court of Emperor Qianlong, 1792

On 26 September 1792 the "Ambassador Extraordinary and Plenipotentiary from the King of Great Britain to the Emperor of China," Lord Macartney, left England. The primary objective was to win from the aging Emperor Qianlong trading concessions and the lifting of the severe restrictions on foreigners, who were forced to operate only through the port of Guangzhou where all overseas trade was conducted. Above all, Lord Macartney was to promote British manufac-

James Gillray's prophetic caricature of Lord Macartney's reception in China was published a week before Macartney left London for the east.

tured goods, which could be traded in exchange for tea and other Chinese products. At that time 90 per cent of Chinese imports to Europe had to be paid for in bullion, which was apparently all the Chinese would accept.

Trade had expanded greatly throughout the latter part of the eighteenth century. In 1751, 19 foreign ships arrived at Guangzhou; by 1797 this had increased to 81. In the first quarter of the eighteenth century the East India Company was importing, on average, 400,000 pounds of tea; by the end of the century this had grown to 23.4 million pounds, such was the demand not only in Britain but also in her American colonies. American merchants were not allowed to trade directly with Guangzhou for Chinese commodities but had to deal through the East India Company in London. This meant that the price of tea in the American colonies was significantly higher than it would have been if they had traded directly. Dutch merchants were constantly smuggling tea to the New England coast, much to the chagrin of the British colonial government.

The Boston Tea Party of 1773 — when boxes of tea shipped from London were thrown into Boston harbor by colonists and merchants protesting at the duty on tea and frustrated by their lack of freedom under British rule — was the first incident in what was finally to lead to the War of Independence and the formation of the United States. The arrival of the *Empress of China* from New York in 1784 was the first from a country that was to become a major new player in the China trade.

Conditions in Guangzhou for foreign merchants were severely restricted. The trading season was short, lasting from October to January, and they were required to deal only with officials sanctioned by the Chinese government. This was equally difficult for the Chinese merchants who were forced to ship tea, silk and other products over 800 miles from the production centers in Fujian, Anhui (Anhwei) and Jiangxi (Kiangsi) to Guangzhou in the far south. No foreign merchants were allowed at any other port. The rules of behavior laid down by the Governor-General Li Siyao

Courtesy of the Board of Trustees, Victoria & Albert Museum, London

In the eighteenth and nineteenth centuries idealized pictures of the production of tea, porcelain and silk were produced for the west. There was great curiosity about these products, and methods of production were obviously of interest to the growing number of consumers of Chinese goods in the west, particularly in the United States.

Hong Kong Museum of Art, Hong Kong

Conditions at the foreign trading bases at Guangzhou were unduly restrictive. The arrival of American merchants resulted in further crowding, and it was, in part, to change these conditions by allowing greater freedom of trade that George III sent his Ambassador Extraordinary, Lord Macartney, to China.

(Li Ssu-yao) in 1759, designed to minimize conflict and contact between Chinese and Europeans, were considered demeaning and insulting by many of the European and American merchants forced to wait for as long as three months for the turn round in their cargoes:

1. No foreign warship may sail inside the Bogue [the entrance where the Pearl River reaches the South China Sea].
2. Neither foreign women nor firearms may be brought into the factories [the name given to the warehouses used by the merchant companies].
3. All pilots and compradores [Chinese middlemen who assisted in negotiations] must register with the Chinese authorities in Macao [the first point of entry]; foreign ships must not enter into direct communication with Chinese people and merchants without the immediate supervision of the compradore.

A Chinese view of the procession of gifts brought by Macartney to China. Included were the traditional objects, which Europeans assumed were of interest to the Chinese emperors — astronomical and scientific instruments, and elaborate clocks. However, what interested the court most were pieces of Wedgwood's jasper ware.

4. Foreign factories shall employ no maids and no more than eight Chinese male servants.

5. Foreigners may not communicate with Chinese officials except through the proper channel of the co-hong [officially recognized association of merchant middlemen].

6. Foreigners are not allowed to row boats freely in the river. They may, however, visit the Flower Gardens (*Hua-ti*) and the temple opposite the river in groups of ten or less, three times a month — on the 8th, 18th and 28th. They shall not visit other places.

7. Foreigners may not sit in sedan-chairs, or use the sanpan boats with flags flying; they may ride only in topless small boats.

8. Foreign trade must be conducted through the hong merchants. Foreigners living in the factories must not move in and out too frequently, although they may walk freely within a hundred yards of their factories. Clandestine transactions between them and traitorous Chinese merchants must be prevented.

9. Foreign traders must not remain in Guangzhou after the trading season; even

The Emperor Qianlong arriving to meet with Lord Macartney at Jehol, his summer residence to the north of Beijing. Here, the Manchu emperors could return to the nomadic traditions of their forefathers. This picture was painted by Alexander who accompanied Macartney on his journey as the recorder of events.

during the trading season when the ship is laden, they should return home or go to Macao.

10. Foreign ships may anchor at Whampoa but nowhere else.
11. Foreigners may neither buy Chinese books, nor learn Chinese.
12. The hong merchants shall not go into debt to foreigners.

With the intention of changing all this, Lord Macartney arrived off Guangzhou on 19 June 1793 and immediately sailed north to Tianjin (Tientsin) for his meeting with Qianlong. As tradition demanded, Macartney's mission was to be treated as any other tributary mission. He had come prepared with presents costing around $30,000 including a planetarium, globes, mathematical instruments, chronometers, a telescope, measuring instruments, chemical and electrical instruments, window and plate glass, carpets, goods from Birmingham, goods from Sheffield, copperware and some of Wedgwood's latest jasper ware. Of all the goods, this new pottery most amazed and delighted the Chinese who had seen nothing like it before.

As the emperor was at his summer retreat north of the great wall at Jehol, Macartney traveled there for his audience on 14 September. He was expected to do the usual kowtow, numerous bowings and prostrations lying flat on the ground, but Macartney refused. He considered it to be beneath his dignity. There was some contention over this break with tradition but, as it was Qianlong's eighty-third birthday and he was said to have been in a good mood, Macartney was allowed to sink to one knee as he would before his own king.

Alexander's portrait of the Emperor Qianlong. Despite Lord Macartney's appeals, Qianlong saw no reason to break with tradition and grant the British, or any other European nation, rights other than those of a tributary state to trade in the customary manner from Guangzhou.

Gifts were exchanged and a letter from King George III was presented to the emperor. The event was seen to have been a great success and Macartney and his mission were treated with great courtesy. But to Qianlong, the ambassador of George III was doing no more than showing the appropriate respect of a tributary state on the occasion of the emperor's birthday. The event so inspired Qianlong that he composed the following poem:

Formerly Portugal presented tribute;
Now England is paying homage.
They have out-traveled Si-hai and Heng-zhang;
My ancestors' merit and virtue must have reached their distant shores.
Though their tribute is commonplace, my heart approves sincerely.
Curios and boasted ingenuity of their devices I prize not.
Though what they bring is meager, yet,
In my kindness to men from afar I make generous return,
Wanting to preserve my good health and power.

Macartney remained with the emperor until 9 October and left with the following edict addressed to George III, rejecting all requests for a relaxation in the conditions at Guangzhou or any extension of the terms of trade, which would allow British goods to be sold in China:

Yesterday your ambassador petitioned my Ministers regarding your trade with China, but his proposal is not consistent with our dynastic usage and cannot be entertained. Hitherto, all European nations including your own country's barbarian merchants, have carried on their trade with our Celestial Empire at Guangzhou. Such has been the procedure for many years although our Celestial Empire possesses all things in prolific abundance and lacks no product without our borders. There was therefore no need to import manufactured goods of the outside barbarians in exchange for our own products. But as the tea, silk and porcelain which the Celestial Empire produced are absolute necessities to European nations and to yourselves, we permitted, as a mark of favor, that foreign business houses should be established at Guangzhou. . . . It behoves you, O King, to respect my sentiments and to display even greater devotion and loyalty in future so that, by perpetual submission to our Throne, you may secure peace and prosperity for your country thereafter.

The mission was a complete failure. Macartney was, as one wit in the East India Company observed, "received with the utmost politeness, treated with the utmost hospitality, watched with the utmost vigilance and dismissed with the utmost civility." The whole exercise had cost the British government more than $150,000. Although in 1816 they were to send another mission, led by Lord Amherst, in the hope of persuading Qianlong's son Jiaqing (Chia-ch'ing) to open the country to greater trade, nothing was achieved.

Despite this, the China trade through the port of Guangzhou was to grow enormously, particularly as New England merchants began to play an increasingly important role during the Napoleonic Wars when much of European shipping was tied up. By the 1830s in many of the coastal ports of New England such as Salem, Boston and Mystic as much as 20 per cent of domestic furnishings were being imported from China. Chinese merchants acted as commission agents for porcelain, crockery, furniture, silverware, wallpaper, cotton and silk fabrics as well as tea. Hauqua, one of the Chinese compradores who handled these commissions and controlled much of the tea trade out of Guangzhou, was reputed to be the richest man in the world. In 1834 he was reported to have a fortune of $47 million. When traditional designs fell out of favor, Chinese artisans proved adept at copying western products and producing them to order. In 1833, for example, imports from China to the United States were worth about $7.5 million. In the same year, customs duties made up $29 million of the $34 million total treasury receipts. The expansion of international trade was clearly a significant issue for the United States government.

In Britain, the East India Company had grown so powerful that it virtually ruled India on behalf of the British government. The shift in interests from purely trade concerns to economic power was to be seen in the ruthless destruction of the traditional cotton spinning and weaving industry in Bengal in order to provide a market for cotton cloth manufactured in Manchester. The Company was soon exporting raw cotton from India and importing cotton cloth from factories in Britain. It is little wonder that Mahatma Gandhi should use the spinning of cotton as a symbol of defiance to British rule during the independence movement of the 1920s and 1930s.

For both the East India Company and the British government the situation in

Jardine Matheson & Co. Ltd, Hong Kong

Hauqua, a compradore merchant in Guangzhou, was considered to be the richest man in the world in the early nineteenth century, with a personal fortune of $47 million. His money came from acting as a middleman between foreign merchants and Chinese producers.

China was intolerable. From 90 to 98 per cent of all trade was conducted with gold or silver; no other import being considered acceptable. But by the mid 1820s this was to change and the agent of change was opium. The East India Company had, in 1770, gained a monopoly on opium production in Bengal. The Chinese had banned its use and sale from as early as 1729 when the Portuguese had begun to import the drug. But as contraband it had become, by the 1830s, the major item of trade, with deals being arranged with Chinese merchants at the foreign factories in Guangzhou, and delivery taking place at sea, outside Chinese waters. The illicit trade was large, with American ships transporting the drug from Turkey and the Levant, and the British from India. Private trading companies such as Jardine Matheson and Sassoons from Britain, Robert Forbes from Boston and Wilcocks & Latimer from Philadelphia were involved in the trade. Although the East India Company had nothing to do with the trade in China, it was the major supplier of the drug through its factories in India.

It was not just with China that opium was traded. The drug was also being imported into Britain and Europe where it was mixed with alcohol and sold under the name of laudanum. There, the consequences of addiction were not as severe as they were in China although many writers, such as De Quincy and Coleridge, became addicts. It is ironic that Coleridge should write his famous poem "Kubla Khan" after taking the drug and while looking out through the gloomy smog of industrial London at the dome of St Paul's. He ends the poem with an oblique warning:

And all should cry,
Beware! Beware!
. . .
For he on honey-dew hath fed,
And drunk the milk of Paradise.

In the land of Xanadu itself the economic consequences of the opium trade were disastrous. The addiction to the drug was widespread and affected all classes. The human cost was great with an estimated two million people using opium, many of them becoming addicts. Around 20 per cent of government officials used the drug. The economic consequences were to be equally harmful. While, between 1800 and 1810, large amounts of silver flowed into China as a result of foreign trade; between 1828 and 1833 the British alone shipped out $29.6 million in hard currency. For the East India Company the situation was ideal. In 1836, for example, they sold opium in China, worth $18 million, which was traded for tea and silk worth $17 million. The parliamentary debates, which failed to ban its sale in Britain, were prepared to condone the trade, regarding the social consequences as a Chinese problem. The more important issue, it was argued, was the right of free trade. In 1834 parliament repealed the monopoly held by the East India Company on British trade with China and a bill was passed allowing all merchants the right to trade wherever they wished. The system of trade in Guangzhou was therefore challenged by a new and far less respectful body of merchants buoyed up by the unquestioned moral virtues of free trade and Britain's obvious international naval and military supremacy.

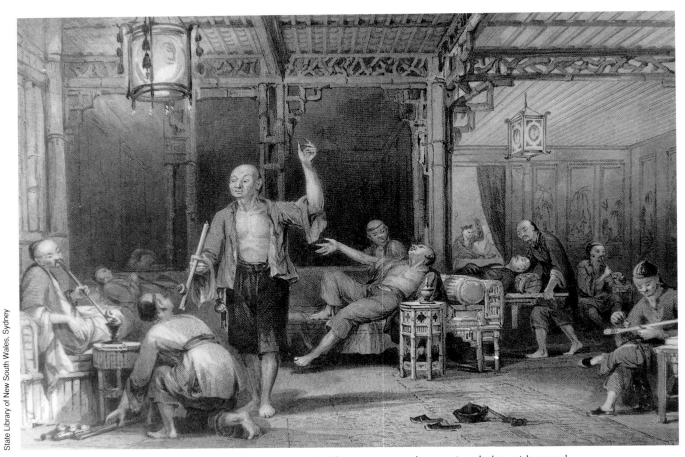

Although opium was officially banned in China, access to cheap opium led to widespread addiction, with scholars as well as laborers falling prey to the habit. Because of a high level of corruption the trade was able to flourish under the very noses of officials.

This confrontation with recalcitrant foreign merchants was unprecedented for the Chinese. Because of the lack of interest in international trade shown by the imperial government, the institutions to deal with the situation had not evolved as they had in Europe. The Chinese navy was ineffectual and there was no customs system to control illegal imports. Smuggling along the southern coast had gone on for centuries under the very noses of government officials who were usually the beneficiaries.

The Chinese government was, however, determined to do something about this insidious trade in opium. After a long debate, the emperor decided to send an experienced and incorruptible scholar-official Commissioner Lin Zexu (Lin Tse-hsu) to Guangzhou to stamp out the trade. Lin's approach was, initially, to avoid confrontation and to research the problem carefully, even consulting western books on international law to develop a case to be put to Queen Victoria to stop the trade:

I have heard that smoking opium is strictly forbidden in your country. Why do you let it be passed on to the harm of other countries? Suppose there were people from another country who carried opium for sale to Britain and seduced your people into buying and smoking it; certainly your honorable ruler would deeply hate it and be bitterly aroused. . . . Naturally you would not wish to give others what you yourself do not want. . . . May you, O Queen, check your wicked and sift your vicious people before they come to China, in order to guarantee the peace of your nation, to show further the sincerity of your politeness and submissiveness.

The climate in Britain was not responsive to such moral reasoning. First, the letters probably did not even reach the Queen herself and, second, the idea that moral arguments of this sort should be allowed to undermine the mechanism of the free market and of free trade — the principle of laissez-faire to which the dominant political groups within the British government were now committed — was perhaps too much to expect. British wealth and prosperity depended on free trade and the idea of the government acting as an international moral censor as the Chinese demanded was not possible.

Lin received no response to his appeals. On 18 March 1839, like the head of a modern drug-enforcement agency, he got tough. He demanded that all opium should be surrendered and that merchants should sign a pledge forgoing such trade in the future under threat of death. He confined 350 foreign merchants to their factory compounds, stopped all trade out of Guangzhou and withdrew the services supplied to the foreign factories, leaving them without any resources until the merchants complied. The Superintendent of Trade, Captain Charles Elliot, took on the negotiations on behalf of the British government, which shifted the incident to a new political level. On 18 May he delivered 21,306 chests of opium to Lin. Three large trenches were dug, 150 feet long, 75 feet wide and 7 feet deep; the opium balls were crushed with lime and salt and, when dissolved, were flushed into a nearby creek.

The situation escalated, with demands for reprisals coming from powerful merchant groups in London, Manchester and Liverpool. Lord Palmerston sent an expeditionary force to blockade the port of Guangzhou. On 3 November Admiral Guan (Kuan) leading 29 Chinese war junks engaged the British fleet and the first Opium War began.

The British then began to blockade all Chinese ports in the hope that a show of strength would lead to the Chinese backing down. Over a period of almost two years negotiations were attempted, with the British making demands for territorial rights to Hong Kong Island and trading rights throughout China as well as compensation for their opium, all of which were completely unacceptable to the Qing court. Finally, in the spring of 1842, with 25 warships carrying 668 guns, 14 steamships carrying 56 guns and 10,000 men, Sir Henry Pottinger led the British forces up the Yangtze taking strategic cities: Wusong on 16 June, Shanghai on 19 June, and Jinjiang (Chinkiang) on 21 July. Jinjiang was a major port on the Grand Canal, which carried grain supplies to the imperial capital of Beijing. The threat of a blockade on essential food supplies moving north and the threatened destruction of Nanjing forced the Chinese to concede to all the British demands.

The Chinese confronted the reality of European industrial power for the first time.

The Opium War, which followed the confinement of foreign merchants and the destruction of opium stocks by Commissioner Lin, confronted the Chinese with a military machine refined by centuries of conflict in Europe and the colonial territories. The relative peace and social harmony that the Chinese had been able to maintain within their borders had not prepared them for the firepower of British gunboats.

The fall of their forts, which were helpless against the superior fire power of the British gunboats, was to bring home a vulnerability for which there was no precedent. In the past no power could seriously have threatened China from the sea. The fort of Wusong had fallen in a matter of hours. Of the three hundred cannons captured by the British most were made of bamboo, and many of the Chinese soldiers were still using crossbows as they had done at the time of Marco Polo. The Chinese governor of Shanghai described the siege as the city's defenses fell:

> . . . cannon balls innumerable, flying in awful confusion through the expanse of heaven, fell before, behind and on either side . . . while in the distance [I] saw the ships of the rebels, standing erect, lofty as the mountains. The fierce daring of the rebels was inconceivable. Officers and men fell at their posts. Every effort to resist and check the coast was in vain and a retreat became inevitable.

The emperor had no alternative but to sue for peace on any terms. On 29 August 1842, Chinese officials were taken from the city of Nanjing to the gunboat *Cornwallis*. Here the Treaty of Nanjing was formally signed, ending the first Opium

War. The Chinese agreed to pay the British $21 million in reparations, including the cost of the opium destroyed; to open up five ports for international trade; to lease the island of Hong Kong to the British as a base and, above all, to accept that communications between the British and the Chinese would be carried out under conditions of equality as befitted sovereign states. This last point was an interesting one for, in the view of John Quincy Adams, United States Secretary of State at the time, the war with China was not over the importation of opium any more than the American War of Independence was over the throwing of tea into Boston harbor:

> The cause of the war is the Kowtow — the arrogant and insupportable pretensions of the Chinese, that she will hold commercial intercourse with mankind not upon terms of equal reciprocity, but upon the insulting and degrading forms of relations between lord and vassal.

The idea that the Chinese might have a right not to engage in international trade or relations with the outside world was not regarded as a serious proposition. On the other hand, the concept that China was merely a nation state on an equal footing with others was contrary to the traditional Chinese world view, and one that was to prove extremely hard to change.

In the calculations of the British government, the moral issue of the opium trade was clearly to take second place to the higher principle of free trade and international commerce. Like the steam engines that now powered the cotton looms of Lancashire and drove the new gunboats on the Yangtze, the market was seen as a self-regulating mechanism. Driven by the forces of supply and demand, it would serve everyone's interests as long as the government allowed the individual consumers and producers maximum freedom to do what they liked, even, some would argue, to consume opium. This was regarded as enlightened self-interest. In this concept of a market running as a self-regulating mechanism, like Newton's clockwork universe, the political economists of the day believed that they had discovered the hidden hand of progress, the secret of unlimited wealth and power.

For the Chinese the British justification for the war, in terms of the sanctity of free trade, was only to reaffirm the widely held opinion in the imperial capital that the western barbarians were morally bankrupt, and that their traditional policy of keeping them out of the Celestial Empire had been entirely justified. But, however reassuring this sense of moral superiority might have been, it provided little consolation as the Chinese reviewed their battered forts and hopelessly inadequate means of defending themselves against the obvious technological superiority of the British gunboats.

Contemptuous though many Confucian officials were about the European preoccupation with "mere ingenious technology," they, like the Japanese and other Asian nations, now had no alternative but to try to come to terms with the alien values and economic institutions, which allowed these Europeans their remarkable industrial wealth and overwhelming military power.

*The Prosperity of an English Trading Firm in Yokohama in 1871* by Ochiai Yoshiiku. Having for centuries looked
to China as the centre of civilization the Japanese in the late nineteenth century turned to the west, avidly
adopting not just European military and industrial technology but their cultural and economic institutions.

# DREAMS OF WEALTH AND POWER

# ON THE WINGS OF CHANGE

*Win the War*
*And Japan will be denounced as a yellow peril*
*Lose it,*
*And she will be branded as a barbaric land.*

Mori Ogai, on the Russo-Japanese War, 1905

*The great questions of the day will not be settled by*
*resolutions and majority votes but by iron and blood.*

Otto von Bismarck

The Opium War of 1839–42 sent shock waves, not just through China, but through all of Asia. The vast Chinese empire had been brought to its knees by the power of the European gunboats, which meant, in effect, that the traditional tributary relationship offered by China to the smaller countries in the region had been fundamentally devalued. China, for the first time in two thousand years, was no longer the dominant military power in east Asia.

This reality was not lost on the Japanese. For centuries they had operated uneasily within the Chinese sphere of influence; uneasily, despite the fact that from the eighth century their written language, art, music and technology were offshoots of Chinese culture. During the Tokugawa shogunate (1603–1868) there was even a self-conscious effort to introduce Confucianism as a means of gaining stability and peace after centuries of clan warfare.

Both Japan and China were now confronted with an external threat to their sovereignty more serious than any internal rebellion. Their different responses to this threat from the west illustrate some of the important economic and political differences that separate them despite their shared cultural heritage. It is also an intriguing story; one that is essential for an understanding of the extraordinary re-emergence of east Asia as a center of industrial innovation and economic power over the past two decades.

When Commodore Perry turned up in Edo (Tokyo) harbor in 1853, his iron ships bristling with cannon, his mission for the United States government was to open Japan to international trade in the same way that the Opium War had opened China — by sheer might of arms.

The gifts brought by Perry to convince the Tokugawa shogun of the advantages of trade were of more than symbolic significance. They were not just the products of the Industrial Revolution, but lay at the heart of the United States' growing wealth and power — guns, pistols, a telegraph and a miniature steam locomotive along with tender and passenger cars. There were even some crates of champagne to jolly the proceedings along.

The Japanese, for their part, offered the traditional luxury goods that had formed the basis of their trade with the west — silk, porcelain and lacquer ware — cultural

Kurofunekan

One of the "black ships" of Commodore Perry as seen by a Japanese artist. These ships were not just a military threat, they also confronted the Japanese with the industrial and technological power of the west in the mid-nineteenth century.

products still sought after but no longer the sole monopoly of east Asia as they were when the Portuguese first arrived in the sixteenth century.

For the Japanese the objects on Perry's ships were a source of endless fascination. Artists were employed, not only to depict the gifts they brought, but also every product, weapon, utensil, machine and item of clothing on the ships. Their attention to detail was extraordinary.

The American account of the Japanese response to the model train, telegraph and armaments has all the smug self-satisfaction of the trader bringing beads and axes to a primitive tribe. The image of Japanese samurai going round and round on model trains, like children at a fairground, must have reinforced this impression.

When Commander John Rodgers, in 1855, visited the island of Tanega-shima 20 miles off the coast of the main southern island of Kyushu, he was amazed to find the Japanese almost completely ignorant about the use of firearms:

> It strikes an American, who from his childhood has seen children shoot, that ignorance of arms is an anomaly indicative of primitive innocence and Arcadian simplicity. We were unwilling to disturb it.

Rodgers' romantic ignorance of Asian history, though understandable, was common among nineteenth century Europeans and Americans, who were inclined to regard civilization as synonymous with technological power. In reality the people of Tanega-shima had known about guns well before European colonies were established in the Americas. In 1543 Portuguese merchants, en route to China, were blown off course by a typhoon and drifted ashore on the island. The merchants were Antonio da Mota, Francisco Zeimoto and Antonio Peixoto — the first westerners to be encountered by the Japanese.

The feudal ruler, or daimyo, of Tanega-shima was Tokitaka who, when confronted with the matchlock muskets brought ashore by the Portuguese, immediately bought two of them for 2,000 ryo; a very high price equivalent to about $1 million in today's terms. He then gave them to his swordsmith to reproduce, or reverse-engineer. There is an apocryphal story associated with the craftsman, Kimbei, who was given the task of producing a Japanese version of the musket. He was able to reproduce all the parts except for the spiral grooves cut on the inside of the barrel and the safety cap at the end. With his lord and master having invested a large amount of money in this new technology, Kimbei was confronted with a real dilemma. It was resolved, however, when another Portuguese vessel arrived at Tanega-shima and Kimbei was able to find someone who knew how to make these crucial parts. The condition on which the Portuguese merchant would impart this knowledge was that Kimbei should give him his only daughter, Wakasa, as a wife — an appalling notion for a Japanese father. Kimbei was confronted with a dreadful choice, which he resolved in classical Japanese fashion by sacrificing his daughter to the foreign barbarian in the interests of serving his feudal lord Tokitaka.

Tokyo Communications Museum

The telegraph brought from the United States as a gift for the Tokugawa Shogun — a sophisticated device for its time, operating as it did on an early form of ticker tape.

Saga Prefectual Museum

The miniature train, which was included among the gifts designed to lure the Japanese out of their self-imposed isolation, actually worked and was to be the source of endless amazement and fascination.

This story, though mythical, is important in two respects. It shows something of the loyalty that the Japanese feudal lord commanded and the power that the daimyo had over his domain — a level of power and independence that no provincial governor in China would ever have been permitted. With regard to the Tanega-shima gun, Tokitaka was soon able to manufacture matchlock muskets, which he then began to sell all over Japan. There was a huge demand, for Japan was in a state of almost continual clan warfare, and these guns, along with Portuguese military advisers, were to become of ever-increasing importance.

By the late sixteenth century the quality of matchlock muskets was equal to anything that was being produced in Europe at the same time. The Japanese capacity for the reverse-engineering of foreign technology had been a long-established tradition. The Japanese had, after all, derived much of their basic technology from Korea and China and so imitating what the west had to offer had a precedent.

With the aid of these superior firearms, the Tokugawa clan by 1603 was able to achieve dominance over the entire country and to take on the role of shogun, or military dictator, governing a loose confederation of clans, many of whom were fiercely independent, particularly those in the south.

Having gained control of the country, the Tokugawa then systematically set about getting rid of guns. First, they centralized gun production at Nagahama in 1609, requiring that gunsmiths produce weapons only for the state. They then gradually reduced orders to the point where, by 1673, only 53 matchlocks and 334 small guns were produced in one year. With over half a million samurai, or knights, to be armed the gun ceased to be an important military weapon, and the gunsmiths of Tanega-shima, most of whom had previously been swordsmiths, returned to making swords.

There was also a good cultural reason for the Tokugawa shogun's actions. The gun, like the crossbow in Europe five hundred years earlier (which had been banned by the Catholic church for similar reasons), threatened the traditional feudal order. It did so by democratizing military power. A peasant could easily be taught to draw a crossbow or fire a gun; it did not take years of training and both were lethal against sword-wielding samurai or knights no matter how well they might be protected by armor. The codes of behavior of the dominant military castes in such a culture would also be undermined. Single combat with a sword was the acceptable mode of doing battle. The gun clearly challenged this crucial element of traditional Japanese culture and was not to be encouraged in times of peace. It was hard enough for the Tokugawa to control the activities of half a million samurai armed with swords, let alone the threat posed by the wide-scale adoption of such undignified weapons as guns. It was to prevent such subversion that the Tokugawa also banned contact with foreigners and ordered the Portuguese advisers, merchants and missionaries out of the country. Foreign contact was restricted to the small island of Deshima in Nagasaki harbor, which was a base for Dutch merchants, who dominated trade with Japan for the next two hundred years. Such then was the power and social control possessed by the shogun.

Tokugawa Art Museum, Nagoya

One of the decisive battles that allowed the Tokugawa clan to unify Japan and take over the role of shogun in the early seventeenth century. The Tokugawa relied, not only on their own capable gunsmiths, but also employed European weapons and military advisers.

# THE TAIPING REBELLION

In China the impact of the Opium War was extremely destabilising to the Qing (Manchu) government. Having to give way to European military pressure and trading demands was regarded as a sign of weakness, and of dynastic decline.

In 1852 the Huang He (Yellow River) also broke its banks, shifting its route to the north of the Shandong (Shantung) peninsula. This was to have disastrous economic consequences for millions of people and blame was laid at the feet of the Manchu government. In traditional terms, to maintain the dykes, dredge the great rivers and keep the canals operating was one of the primary imperial responsibilities. The fact that the Yellow River broke its banks' was taken as another clear sign of dynastic decline.

As a consequence, rebellions broke out throughout the empire. These were often led by secret societies such as the Triads, The Heaven and Earth Society and the Hung League, which had come into existence as a focus for opposition to Manchu rule during the seventeenth century. Between 1850 and 1878 there was some form of rebellion going on continuously.

The most disastrous of these uprisings was the Taiping rebellion, which between 1850 and 1864 raged through 16 provinces and tied up much of southern China. It was led (as were many such rebellions in Chinese history) by a failed and disillusioned scholar by the name of Hong Xiuchuan (Hung Hsiu-ch'uan). Hong came from Guangzhou and had therefore been exposed, not only to the traditional values and expectations of the scholar, but also to those of Protestant missionaries. Through an early convert, Liang Afa (Liang Ah-fa), Protestant religious tracts were widely circulated in Guangzhou. Hong came into contact with these in 1836. Perhaps as a consequence of the arduous nature of the traditional exams and the disappointment of his constant failures, Hong went through a period of severe psychological stress. He saw visions and entered a delirious state. He claimed to have seen God and to be the younger brother of Jesus Christ. He ended up with an odd mixture of Christian fundamentalism and Confucianism. The former gave him an acute concern for social justice with a consequent need to reform Chinese society; the latter gave him a traditional form into which to channel his revolutionary zeal.

In 1840 he organized himself and his followers into the "God Worshippers' Society" and was soon attracting members from the old Triad societies, the poor and the landless, as well as other disaffected opportunists such as pirates. By 1851 his army of misfits and idealists captured the city of Yongan (Yung-an) in Guangxi (Kuang-hsi) province, which gave him sufficient strength to challenge the imperial government under the title *Taiping tianguo (Tai-ping t'ien-kuo)* — the Heavenly Kingdom of Great Peace. In 1853 his power and following had grown to the point where he was able to capture and hold the southern capital of Nanjing. From here he was to dominate much of southern China and to represent the most serious challenge yet to the beleaguered Qing dynasty.

Hong's challenge was consistent with Chinese tradition. Many of his ideas for reform were drawn from the Confucian classics but they were coupled with Christian ideas. He offered communal ownership of land and equality of the sexes. The

# THE TOKUGAWA AND RANGAKU

*Dutch letters*
*running sideways*
*like a row of wild geese*
*flying in the sky.*

Eighteenth century Japanese
description of European writing

Until the nineteenth century and the arrival of western gunboats, the center of civilization for the Japanese was China. From the sixth century, when the country was unified, students were sent to the Celestial Empire to learn the arts of civilization. From that time on, a self-conscious effort was made to introduce Chinese social and economic institutions — Buddhism and Confucianism, the written language, craft industries like silk and porcelain, as well as Chinese art and music.

Though deriving much of its early culture and technology from China, Japanese society, nonetheless, had much in common with that of medieval Europe. Unlike China, with its vast imperial bureaucracy, Japanese society was organized around powerful feuding clans who controlled their domains from fortified castles. These clans were dominated by a military caste of samurai who served their feudal lord or daimyo like European knights.

In the sixteenth century, when contact was first made with Europeans, the Tokugawa shoguns were keen to use western military technology and advisers to help them win control of the country. However, to manage the

Yokohama Archives of History

peace, they turned, as Japanese rulers had always done, to the model of Confucian China.

To control his feudal lords and to prevent revolt the shogun forced his daimyo to house their wives and families at Edo, the center of Tokugawa power. Ming Neo-Confucianism was introduced in the hope of turning the sword-wielding samurai to more civilized pursuits. Schools were established where children were taught the Confucian classics, and the five virtues of benevolence, wisdom, propriety, righteousness and trustworthiness. As in Ming China, these Confucian ideas were used to reinforce a strict social hierarchy with shogun, daimyo and samurai on the top, farmers next, and merchants and artisans at the bottom.

The samurai class, freed from the preoccupation with constant warfare, was now concerned with managing agriculture and craft industries in the domains, in order to maintain the daimyo (and their considerable households) at the capital of Edo. This resulted in greatly

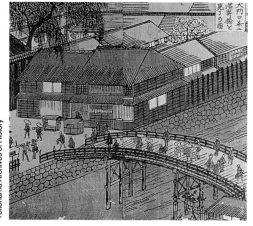

Yokohama Archives of History

increased commerce and improved communications. In order to ship supplies from the domains to Edo, roads were improved and large commercial networks established, particularly at Osaka. Here, many of the great merchant families, such as the Mitsui, established their trading houses. Urban life grew rapidly and the Japanese were bound in a unified culture as never before.

In 1639, over two hundred years after the Ming emperor had cut China off from the rest of the world, the Tokugawa shogun adopted a similar policy of isolation. The large Japanese merchant fleets, which had been found in ports throughout Southeast Asia between 1600 and 1639, suddenly disappeared from the scene — this at a time when Japan was producing a third of the world's silver.

Not only were Japanese merchants restricted but foreigners as well. In 1634 the Shogun Tokugawa Ieyasu decided to restrict all movement of foreign merchants to Deshima, a small artificial island he had built in Nagasaki harbor, connected to the mainland by a narrow bridge. Initially, both Portuguese and Dutch merchants were forced to take up residence on this tiny island, 180 metres by 60 metres. However, in 1637, after a riot involving Catholics broke out at Shimabara, the Portuguese were expelled from the country and the Dutch gained a virtual monopoly of trade with Japan.

The German physician Engelbert Kaenpfer, who was employed at Deshima at the end of the seventeenth century had this to say about the place:

"So great was the covetousness of the Dutch, and so strong the alluring power of Japanese gold that, rather than quit the prospect of a trade (indeed most advantageous), they willingly underwent an almost perpetual imprisonment — for such, in fact, is our residence in Deshima."

Despite extreme restrictions, the Dutch settlement was to have a considerable influence, not only on the economy of southern Japan, but as a conduit by which western science, astronomy, medicine and industrial technology found their way into Japan.

As the restrictions on contact between the Dutch merchants and Japanese scholars lessened, a school of Dutch learning, Rangaku,

arose. Its impact, however, was limited to a relatively small group of enthusiastic scholars. Honda Toshiaka, a leading eighteenth century Rangaku scholar observed:

"In recent years European astronomy has been introduced into Japan. People have been astonished by the theory that the earth is actually whirling about, and no one is ready to believe it. In Japan even great scholars are so amazed by this notion that they assert, 'If the earth were in fact spinning about, my rice bowl and water bottle would turn over and my house and storehouse would be broken to bits. How can such a theory be true?' "

Apart from useful technology such as the musket, the telescope, the mechanical clock and the camera obscura, which helped to introduce perspective into Japanese art, European influence on Japan was limited, and certainly secondary to the influence of China, which for most Japanese remained the center of civilization. It was not until China's power in the region declined in the face of European expansion in the nineteenth century, that it occurred to the Japanese leaders that they would have to take seriously the culture and technology of the "hairy barbarians of the west."

crippling custom of binding women's feet, first begun under the Ming, was banned, as was opium smoking, slavery, alcohol and tobacco. Economic activity was carried out by groups of 25 families who formed a unit with a church and a treasury, which distributed wealth equally.

Their religious devotions included the worship of God, Jesus and Hong. What the Taiping offered was some hope to the landless and poor, at a time when China's traditional economic and political institutions seemed incapable of stemming the rising tide of rural poverty. Economic decline was a result of an extremely rapid increase in population without an equivalent increase in productivity. The population rose from 143 million in 1741 to 430 million in 1840. This was a gain of around 200 per cent while the amount of arable land grew by only 35 per cent. In other words there were 3.86 *mu* (one *mu* = one-sixth of an acre) per person in the 1750s and only 1.86 *mu* in the 1850s. Of this arable land 50–60 per cent was in the hands of rich gentry, another 10 per cent in the hands of government officials and the remaining 30 per cent was divided among the 400 million who made up the rest of the population; 60 per cent of these had no land at all. The Opium War had resulted in the drug being sold in China without government controls. The foreign and Chinese merchants had, by 1850, almost doubled the amount being brought into the country and, as a consequence, there was a massive outflow of silver currency, matched by a decline in the demand for Chinese exports of silk, porcelain and tea. There were, therefore, purely internal economic reasons why China was in serious difficulties, quite independent of the imperialist pressures on the coast. The Europeans were, however, now to play a significant role in determining how Chinese reformers were to go about trying to solve the difficulties.

\*   \*   \*

To cope with the Taiping rebellion the Qing government was to bring to the fore some remarkable, traditional scholar-officials who were to set China on the first tentative steps towards institutional reform.

The first was Zeng Guofan (Tseng Kuo-fan) (1811–72), a graduate of the highest imperial exam who, in 1852, was sent to Hunan by the Qing government to raise an army to fight the Taiping. Zeng was a committed Confucian who was to apply its basic principles to raising an army with a sense of morals and commitment sufficient to meet the revolutionary forces of Hong. For Zeng this was not a war in which the issue was to be decided by superior technology; this was a challenge to the very credibility of Confucian culture, which had sustained the Chinese empire for two thousand years. With the support of the local gentry, and a commitment to three cardinal principles drawn from the Confucian classics — respect for superiors, concern for the common people and cultivation of good habits — Zeng's Hunan army was to be a formidable force. In 1853 they were able to retake Wuhan (Wuchang). In the rest of the country there was neither the same success nor the same commitment.

The second scholar-official to emerge was Li Hongzhang (Li Hung-chang) (1823–1901) who also came from a long tradition of scholars. His father had been a

This painting depicts imperial troops in battle against the Taiping rebels. For almost fifteen years China was engulfed in an enervating civil war in which it is estimated that around forty million people lost their lives.

student with Zeng Guofan in Beijing. On graduating, Li went to the imperial capital to continue his studies under the direction of Zeng who became his patron and friend. When Zeng was sent to Hunan to combat the challenge of the Taiping, Li and his father returned to their native province of Anhui where, on Zeng's recommendation, the governor employed Li to organize recruits and to lead them against the rebels. (Li was to become a close ally of Zeng and was eventually made governor of Jiangsu province.)

In the meantime, European attitudes towards the Taiping vacillated. Because they were at least a quasi-Christian movement concerned with social reform, they appealed to Protestant missionaries and foreign diplomats who saw advantages in supporting what might become a new dynasty, for, in the 1850s, there was considerable doubt as to whether the Qing government could withstand this challenge. However, when the Taiping moved against the treaty port of Shanghai, sympathy began to swing behind the government. A brigade mounted with funds raised by European and Chinese merchants, and led by an American, Frederick Townsend Ward, successfully pushed the Taiping back up the Yangtze. This force was to be given honors and the title of the "Ever Victorious Army" by the emperor.

However, in September 1862 Ward was killed trying to take the town of Tseki.

His position was eventually taken by a British army officer, Charles ("Chinese") Gordon who, with Zeng's and Li's armies, eventually took back the territories controlled by the Taiping and, finally, their capital at Nanjing in July 1864.

This rebellion (civil war would be a more apt description) dwarfed the American Civil War and any European war in its destructiveness and dislocation. At least 20 million people lost their lives and the imperial government was further impoverished by the lack of revenue with which to build up its defenses and to withstand further foreign undermining of its sovereignty.

# NARIAKIRA'S DREAM

While the impact of the Opium War on China was to stimulate a challenge to dynastic power, in Japan the arrival of Commodore Perry's "black ships" was to have equally shattering consequences for the power and status of the Tokugawa shogun.

The authority of the shogun had, by the 1850s, been eroded to the point where the southern daimyo were openly disobeying almost all of the traditional rules about isolation from foreigners and trade. After all, these were not imperial civil servants like the governors of Chinese provinces. The Japanese daimyo was similar to a medieval European feudal lord in the sense that he was the head of an independent clan whose primary loyalty was to him and not to the shogun or the emperor. He also owned the lands of his domain and was directly responsible for their development and exploitation. A prime example was the Satsuma clan whose domains covered the eastern side of the southern island of Kyushu. The Satsuma had a long tradition of foreign trading through their port of Kagoshima with the Ryukyu Islands (Okinawa), with the Chinese and with the Portuguese. As the European presence in the region increased throughout the early nineteenth century these southern daimyo became interested in the superior European technology. Initially, this interest was confined to military and naval matters but soon extended to making more thorough investigations of European industrial methods and institutions.

It was to fall on the head of the twenty-fifth lord of Satsuma, Nariakira Shimayu, to try to come to terms with all of this. Nariakira took over the position of daimyo in 1857 at the age of 42. He had, by dint of his own enthusiasm for western learning, become well versed in some of the achievements of the European Industrial Revolution. To gain greater access to western science and technology, Nariakira secretly sent some young members of the clan to study in London, despite the shogun's prohibition. These students also acted as agents, buying cotton-spinning machinery from Platt Brothers of Oldham, the leading textile-machinery producer in Europe.

In 1856 on a portion of his estate on the outskirts of Kagoshima, he had constructed a reverberatory furnace in order to produce iron for cannons. The design was taken from a Dutch textbook he had studied for six years. He was able to produce about fifty 200-pound cannons, which he placed in batteries around Kagoshima Bay. Not satisfied with this he built a stone British-style factory and began to manufacture farm implements and glass. Across the harbor on the shores of the

This is the European-style stone factory Nariakira Shimayu had built overlooking Kagoshima Bay.

volcanic island (which lit up during its occasional bursts of volcanic activity) he established Japan's first modern shipyards. By 1857 the factory and shipyards were employing some 1,200 people producing telegraphic equipment, gas lamps, ceramics and swords.

The shipbuilding began at Kagoshima with the arrival of John Franjiro in 1851. Franjiro had, some years earlier, been picked up while drifting at sea by an American whaler. He was taken back to the United States where he worked in a large shipbuilding yard. Nariakira soon had him on his payroll and, four years later, he produced Japan's first steam-driven boat. In the same year construction began on a western-style warship, which, when it sailed into Tokyo harbor, was to cause almost as much amazement as Perry's ships had a few years earlier. Flying from the mast was a flag Nariakira had designed: the red sun of Japan's rising power against a white background of purity and integrity. A flag that less than a century later was to be flying all over Southeast Asia and the Pacific.

Nariakira was well known for his fascination with pyrotechnics. At his villa he would arrange demonstrations of torpedoes and land mines, detonating them out in

# THE TREATY PORTS

The Treaty of Nanjing in 1842, which ended the Opium War with Britain, forced China to abandon her traditional policy of restricting international trade to the southernmost port of Guangzhou. Four new ports — Shanghai, Xiamen (Amoy), Fuzhou and Ningbo — were opened. In these ports an entirely new system was introduced giving the British unprecedented freedom and rights within China. The three crucial elements of this Treaty were a fixed tariff of 5 per cent on all goods, extraterritoriality and most-favored nation status. Perhaps the most significant of these three clauses for the sovereignty of China was that of extraterritoriality. This meant that, although living in China, British subjects would be governed by their own laws, and responsibility for their behavior rested with the British government representative. Foreigners were also able to acquire land on which to establish their own businesses, factories and residences. At the time, it made some sense to the Chinese for it meant that the onus of managing the foreigners lay with the British government. However, as soon as the Treaty became public knowledge, the other western powers demanded to have similar rights and, in 1844, the Americans and French signed similar treaties.

As the foreign settlements grew they had the effect of undermining the Chinese government's control of the economy. These treaty ports, controlled by foreign interests, were to become the dominant economic and industrial centers in the country. As further conflicts erupted, the Chinese were forced to accept even more humiliating backdowns, and more ports and inland cities were opened up to western trade and influence. It was the thin end of the wedge of western imperialism, which ultimately reduced China to semi-colonial status. By 1907 foreign domination of the modern sector of the economy was such that 84 per cent of shipping, 34 per cent of cotton spinning and 100 per cent of iron production were under foreign control. By 1911, 93 per cent of railways (of vital strategic importance) were also in foreign hands.

Japan too was to be subject to these "unequal treaties." Perry's blockade of Edo harbor led to an American demand for conditions similar to those achieved by Britain in China, with two and then six Japanese ports being opened up for trade. Britain, Russia and Holland immediately followed suit, gaining similar unequal rights of fixed tariffs and extraterritoriality. The port of Yokohama near Tokyo, and Kobe, across the bay from Osaka, eventually took on many of the same characteristics as Shanghai and Guangzhou. The second-class status that this conferred on both the Japanese and Chinese was galling.

The quest to regain national sovereignty was to become a central preoccupation for both countries. Japan's size and the simple-minded commitment of the Meiji government to emulating western social and economic institutions, allowed it a level of economic growth sufficient to build its own industrial base. Thus, unlike China, key areas of technological development such as railways, shipping and textile production were in Japanese hands. This made the presence of western imperialist powers far less damaging than it was in China.

Unlike the Chinese, who had always regarded their country as the center of the universe and their traditional Confucian culture as superior to that of any other nation, the Japanese had seen themselves as being on the periphery of China's great civilization from which they had derived most of their early technology, written language and cultural institutions. When the west appeared on the scene and exhibited its far greater wealth and power, it was easier for the Japanese pragmatically to accept a different model and turn to the west as the new center of civilization. There was even a policy developed during the Meiji of "de-Asianization." The sociologist Sugimoto Toshio has argued that much of the hostility and racism exhibited by the Japanese towards their Asian neighbors resulted from an acute feeling of inferiority in relation to Europeans and Americans. For Japan, therefore, the passion to catch up with the west was both an economic and a psychological necessity.

Kagoshima Bay and all round the harbor by pulling an electric switch in a special pavilion he had had constructed for staging such spectacles. These displays astounded visitors and may well have given the twenty-sixth daimyo a false sense of security after Nariakira died at an early age.

In 1862 on the road from Edo to Kyoto an Englishman, Lennox Richardson, was killed by Satsuma guards for failing to show sufficient and customary respect for their lord. As a consequence, the British government demanded that the perpetrator of the act be brought to justice and that £25,000 be paid in compensation. While the shogun was prepared to accede to the demands, the young daimyo and his clan were not. On 11 August 1863 the British declared war on the Satsuma and sent seven warships to Kagoshima harbor. In spite of Nariakira's fortifications and cannon, the superior fire power of the latest British Armstrong guns left the city devastated and the daimyo in no doubt that he must find out the real secret of the Europeans' economic and military power; acquiring their technology was obviously not enough.

The Japanese were, in the 1860s, in a state of profound uncertainty about how to deal with the foreign incursion, with western merchants establishing prosperous businesses operating out of the ports of Yokohama and Nagasaki. These foreign merchants and the embassies that were established to represent European and American interests were governed, not by Japanese law, but by their own — the same conditions that prevailed in the Chinese treaty ports. The unequal nature of these treaties under which Europeans operated galled both the Chinese and the Japanese. In Japan a group of southern reformers who had greater exposure to western influence took command of government when both the shogun and emperor died in quick succession. In 1868 the young Emperor Meiji was established as a European-style constitutional monarch, and a new focus of loyalty and nationalism was created.

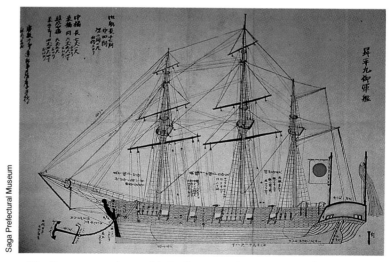

Saga Prefectural Museum

The European-style warship built at Kagoshima in 1855. Flying from its mast is the flag that Nariakira designed, which, when taken up by the Meiji reformers in 1868, was to become the new symbol of Japanese nationalism.

# SELF-STRENGTHENING WITH TI AND YONG

In China reformers like Li Hongzhang and Zeng Guofan were confronted with a far more difficult situation. While the reunification of the country in 1865, after the disastrous decade of the Taiping rebellion, was described as the Tongzhi (T'ung Chih) restoration, any comparison to the Japanese Meiji restoration is limited indeed.

While reformers in both countries perceived the need to understand the west and "learn the superior technology of the barbarians in order to control them," the political and economic circumstances of China were profoundly different to those of Japan. For a start, Japan was the size of one Chinese province.

A significant ally of the reformers in China was Prince Kung, the brother of the Emperor Xianseng (Hsien-feng). As head of the grand council and the *zongli yamen,* the newly created office concerned with foreign affairs, Kung had considerable power and influence. With his support Zeng and Li set up a number of arsenals and shipyards at Shanghai, Nanjing and Fuzhou. In his diary of June 1862 Zeng notes the following concerning the self-strengthening movement:

Royal Geographical Society, London

Li Hongzhang one of a new generation of Confucian scholar-officials who was to play an important part in the suppression of the Taiping rebellion. He was also to become one of the leaders of the self-strengthening movement, which attempted to adapt western technology to traditional Chinese culture.

If only we could possess all their [the barbarians'] superior techniques, then we would have the means to return their favors when they are obedient, and to avenge our grievances when they are disloyal.

To justify their policy among conservative officials, the reformers put forward the policy of *ti* and *yong* — "Chinese spirit and western means." What China needed to do was simply to graft western technology on to its traditional political and economic institutions.

To this end the Jiangnan arsenal was established at Shanghai in 1865, with machines purchased in the United States. This arsenal had a multiplicity of functions. It was to produce ships and guns, but also to act as a conduit for western science and technology. The arsenal was to set up an entire department devoted to the translation of western books, and for this Zeng Guofan employed a number of Europeans, including John Fryer, a Protestant missionary. By 1868 they had produced their first ship and, by 1872, had produced five additional 400-horsepower gunboats each carrying 26 guns. In seven years they had translated 98 western books; 47 were in the fields of natural sciences and 45 on military tactics and technology. At Fuzhou they had produced 40 ships under the guidance of two French engineers Giguel and d'Aiguebelle.

A number of other Europeans were employed at this time. Perhaps the most influential was the Englishman Robert Hart. Hart was employed by the Chinese government to set up and run the department of maritime customs. He staffed the department with a mixture of Chinese and European officers, and ran it with the utmost firmness and with a genuine commitment to the interests of the Chinese government. Prior to this, the administration of the collection of customs duties was a shambles. In a circular dated 21 June 1864 Hart spelled out a code of behavior for all the foreigners he employed:

> . . . it is to be distinctly and constantly kept in mind that the Inspectorate of Customs is a Chinese and not a Foreign Service, and that, as such, it is the duty of each of its members to conduct himself towards the Chinese, people as well as officials, in such a way as to avoid all cause of offence and ill feeling. . . . It is to be expected from those who take the pay and who are the servants of the Chinese Government, that they, at least, will so act as to neither offend susceptibilities, nor excite jealousies, suspicion, and dislike.

However, this code was not followed by many of the other Europeans who operated out of the treaty ports.

Resources raised by Hart provided the Chinese with an important new source of revenue with which to carry out their policy of modernization. But despite the efforts of Prince Kung and the other reformers there remained a basic mistrust of westerners on the part of conservative officials who were prepared, grudgingly, to accept the need for western military technology but believed that was the extent of what was needed. The basic assumption, which bordered on blind arrogance, was that China could afford to ignore the changes that were taking place in the world around them. The notion that they could continue to retreat into the self-sufficent complacency of Qianlong was not only being challenged by the presence of the imperialists on their doorstep but by the reality of their own internal economic conditions. The reformers were acutely aware of this but, unlike their counterparts in Japan, their ability to unify the country behind genuine reforms was limited. China was an empire not a nation-state. Its vast size meant that, apart from those living on the coast and in direct contact with foreigners, there was little appreciation of the threat that China faced. Li Hongzhang, however, clearly did appreciate the situation:

> Chinese scholars and officials have been indulging in the inveterate habit of remembering stanzas and sentences and practicing fine model calligraphy, while our warriors and fighters are, on the other hand, rough, stupid and careless . . . In peace time they sneer at the sharp weapons of foreign countries as things produced by strange techniques and tricky craft, which they consider it unnecessary to learn. In wartime, then, they are alarmed that the effective weapons of western countries are so strange and marvellous, and regard them as something the Chinese cannot learn about. They do not know that for several hundred years the foreigners have considered the study of firearms as important as their bodies and lives . . .

In response to such arguments the conservatives continually played upon the moral shallowness and untrustworthiness of foreign barbarians to deflect the arguments of the reformers for widespread reform of education and institutional practices. Prince Kung's suggestion that western professors of mathematics and

The Jiangnan arsenal established in 1865 at Shanghai. The arsenal was run with the help of European advisers who not only helped with technical matters but translated western books on science and engineering. From here the Chinese launched their first steam-powered gunboat in 1872.

astronomy be invited to teach in traditional institutions was greeted by the grand secretary Wo-Jen with a restating of the traditional Confucian attitude that China had no need to learn from barbarians:

> If we seek trifling arts and respect barbarians as teachers regardless of the possibility that the cunning barbarians may not teach us their essential techniques — even if the teachers sincerely teach and the students faithfully study them — all that can be accomplished is the training of mathematicians. From ancient down to modern times, your servant has never heard of anyone who could use mathematics to raise the nation from a state of decline or to strengthen it in times of weakness. The empire is so great that one should not worry lest there be any lack of abilities therein.

The problem facing the traditional scholar elite of China was that, if they were to accept more than the very minimum from the west, they would begin to invalidate the very basis of China's claim that its culture was the essence of civilized existence. To adopt western cultural institutions would be to admit the inadequacy of their own. This tended to eliminate any inclusion of western social or economic institutions in the process of reform. The old bureaucratic institutions in China were, however, not well suited to take the graft of European systems of technological innovation and industry. Among the Japanese there was no such inhibition, having in the first place adopted many of their institutions from China.

In trying to sow the seeds of industry the efforts of the reformers were considerable for, apart from arsenals, Li established foreign language schools and machine factories. However, the enterprises that were set up by officials were run as government-owned but merchant-managed concerns. This made them vulnerable to the long-established practice of government officials drawing off capital without consideration of the need to provide for expansion or reinvestment. There was also a tendency to have a misplaced faith in foreign experts; these foreigners were often completely inexperienced. Halliday McCartney who ran the Nanjing arsenal was a medical doctor; the two Frenchmen who ran the Fuzhou (Foochow) arsenal and dockyards had never built a ship in their lives.

The first problem was that, while the new arsenals could build adequate boats, there were few locally trained engineers or the industrial infrastructure to allow for much local innovation. Even the scholars who accepted the necessity of military improvement for the sake of defense, had no idea of the scientific and technological training that was needed to support and keep them abreast of the ever-changing international arms race. This meant that even though they had produced warships at Fuzhou and Shanghai, they could not seriously compete with those being produced in the west. To keep abreast the government was forced to invest in buying expensive military technology direct from Europe.

There was a second problem that resulted from the fact that most of the industrial enterprises were set up and owned by the government, either through direct financing or on the basis of investment by wealthy merchants and landowners. As was traditional in China these industries became state monopolies and were to become the victims of nepotism and inefficiency. In other words, the agency cost was too high as the function of the organization was lost in the self-interest of those who controlled its operation and purse strings. The fate of the Chinese Merchants' Steam Navigation Company, which was set up by Li Hongzhang, is but one example of profits that should have been reinvested being channeled out of the company into the hands of government officials. Although initially successful, it could not compete with the lines run out of the treaty ports by foreign firms. There was a long-standing mistrust of merchants and a lack of interest in providing new institutional structures that would foster entrepreneurial activity. A visitor to the busy port of Shanghai in 1870, who might have formed the impression that China was on the brink of leaping into the industrial age, would only have had to go 50 miles inland to find that the impact of European industry was superficial. Much of the resistance came from the powerful and conservative families who dominated local politics at the regional level, and whose support imperial officials required in order to govern.

The conflict between the interests of the gentry and the increasing demands of the Europeans and Americans in the treaty ports came to a head in 1876 when Jardine Matheson built a short railway line from Shanghai to the port of Wusong on the main channel of the Yangtze River.

There had been many proposals put forward by foreign firms and governments to build railway networks and to set up telegraph lines throughout China but these had been firmly resisted. For example, in 1863 Sir MacDonald Stephenson came to China in the hope of persuading the government to let him build an entire network connecting China through to India where railways had already been installed by the British. The Russians also applied considerable pressure but the Chinese government consistently refused. In this, paradoxically, they were supported by Li Hongzhang and other supporters of westernization.

In July 1863 Li Hongzhang, in his position as governor of Jiangsu province, was petitioned by 27 foreign firms working in Shanghai to allow a railway line to be built from Shanghai to Wusong. His reply was to the point: " . . . he would consider it his duty to oppose the attempt on the part of foreigners to gain such an undue degree of influence in the country as the concession sought for would confer upon them." The policy of self-strengthening was to use technology to contain foreign influence not to expand it. Railways in foreign hands would give them direct access to China's rural heartland. In this there was common agreement among reformers and conservatives within the government.

Jardine Matheson attempted to force the issue and eventually went ahead and built the line, claiming at first that they were actually building a road. The road company, set up in 1865, was run by Jardine Matheson with a number of western and Chinese merchants as shareholders; it must be appreciated that Chinese merchants and some compradores (commercial agents) living in the treaty ports were inclined to support the greater freedom and access to resources that railways would have brought. The Wusong line was completed in June 1876 and ran very successfully despite official opposition. However, on 5 August a Chinese was killed on the line, perhaps run over, although the precise details have been lost. The governor of Nanjing was called in to negotiate a settlement, which had the gentry up in arms. They argued that the railway

Through the arsenal in Nanjing Chinese officials and soldiers learned to use the latest European weaponry, in this case a Gatling gun. Unfortunately the Chinese had to rely on advisers of very limited experience — Halliday McCartney who ran the Nanjing arsenal was a medical doctor.

not only extended foreign powers but that it offended *fengshui,* the veins of energy or *qi* that ran through the natural contours of the landscape. Straight roads or even telegraph lines, which were also opposed, were believed to cut across the flow of this energy and could cause natural disasters — floods, famines, droughts and even earthquakes.

This was a persuasive argument for it was to prevent such calamities that the Son of Heaven was given his mandate. For officials who had just restored the empire after the Taiping and other rebellions, there was an obvious need to be responsive to the local gentry on whose support the whole imperial system of government depended. It should be pointed out, however, that the appeal to the offended *fengshui* was also an appeal to traditional economic interests. The gentry and the compradores in the treaty ports had an obvious interest in maintaining their control over the countryside. Railways not only cut across the earth's vital lines of energy but across their own lines of control and financial interests. It also threatened to displace large numbers of people working in the traditional transport systems, thereby driving more families into poverty and providing more potential fuel for revolt.

At the Chepo Convention when Li Hongzhang met with Sir Thomas Wade, the

Mary Evans Picture Library, London

One of the problems of establishing either railways or telegraph lines in China was the opposition from the peasantry and rural gentry who were opposed to them on the grounds that cutting straight across the landscape would disturb ancestral graves and upset the fengshui. Unstated, however, was the fact that such development also cut across the well established traditional transport systems and, therefore, conservative rural interests.

British Ambassador, to resolve the issue, Li argued that the railway should be in the hands of the Chinese government and offered to buy it back. The railway was eventually sold to the Chinese government who promptly ripped it up and sent it to Taiwan where it could not cause trouble. This was not an irrational act but a highly logical one under the circumstances.

Seen in the broader perspective this was only one of many setbacks to the modernization of the Chinese economy and a reinforcement of the power of the conservative landed gentry, for at this time railways were helping to create new economic networks throughout the world. They were opening up the vast resources of Russia and the American west. They linked the rich grazing lands of Australia and Argentina to the markets and industrial centers of Europe. With the advent of steam-powered ships, the world was being linked into a vast market network, which, for all China's desire to ignore it, was encroaching increasingly on the vulnerable Celestial Empire.

# STRONG ARMY, RICH NATION

*King Leopold thus spoke to the Prince [Prince Mimbu], "A nation that uses iron is strong, and a nation that produces iron is wealthy. It is necessary for Japan to become powerful by using iron. This means that Japan should import iron from a foreign country, and I hope that that country will be no other than Belgium." The King presented the case in an interesting manner. But to me who was raised according to the teachings of Confucius and Meng-tse and in an atmosphere thick with* bushido *spirit, which scorns material interests, the King's words appeared very strange, and made me question in my mind whether it is kingly for a royal personage to act like a merchant.*

Shibusawa Eichi, 1867

In Japan, in the early years of the Meiji government, there was social chaos as the traditional policy of isolation ended. With extraordinary speed the new government demolished Japan's ancient feudal institutions. Many of the samurai were devastated when, in 1871, the government abolished the feudal system of domains and the annual stipends on which they depended. Now, loyalty, once focused on the daimyo and the clan, was to be redirected to the nation, as embodied in the person of the emperor. The Meiji reformers created a new cult of emperor worship in order to build a nation out of the fiercely independent clans. Their task was in many ways similar to Germany's under Bismarck, or Garibaldi's in Italy.

The breakdown of the system of feudal domains also meant that the samurai, who

Yokohama Archives of History

Collection of H. Kwan Lan, New York

The Emperor Meiji as a young man in traditional clothing, and in the new uniform of a European-style constitutional monarch. He became the focus of a somewhat contrived cult of emperor worship that was used as a means of shifting loyalty from the old feudal clans to the new nation state for which he became the symbol.

This nineteenth century woodblock print *Salesroom in a Foreign Business Establishment* is by Sadahide Hashimoto. Western merchants in Yokohama, like their counterparts in Shanghai, provided access to western manufactured goods and shipped local silk and porcelain to Europe and the United States.

depended on their yearly stipends for survival, were suddenly forced to find new careers. Some profoundly resented the change and with quixotic spirit attacked both foreigners and the Meiji government. In 1877 there was a last-ditch stand by the samurai when 40,000 took on the government's conscript army, whose western guns were to completely outclass the samurai with their swords. (Ironically, this battle took place in Nariakira's old domain of Satsuma, and was led by one of his sons.)

Others, like the self-strengtheners in China, were aware of the need for fundamental change and embraced it with enthusiasm. The difference for the Japanese reformers was that they had behind them a powerful and united government committed to their aims, in spite of much public opposition. The students and missions sent to Europe and the United States had, by the 1870s, returned with accounts, not just of the west's technological achievements, but of the cultural and economic institutions that made them work.

Because the Japanese were less tied to the cultural institutions that had been introduced from China (particularly neo-Confucianism during the Tokugawa era) it was easier to abandon them when they ceased to serve their needs. They were, unlike the Chinese, also used to borrowing pragmatically from others.

\* \* \*

In a small wooded corner of Keio University campus stands one of the few buildings in Tokyo from the Meiji era that withstood the appalling firebombing of World War II. It survived not because it was particularly strong or well built (quite the opposite, it is timber); it was luck that preserved Fukuzawa's "Speaking Hall." Coming across it on a stroll around the campus you might mistake it for some postwar gift from the United States since the building looks like an eighteenth century Quaker meeting hall or New England church. It was built in 1875 by Fukuzawa Yukichi, one of Japan's great educational reformers who established the first private university and school at Keio, and was also one of the most popular writers and newspaper editors of his day.

Fukuzawa was born in 1835 into a low-ranking samurai family, as were many of the early reformers. His father was something of a scholar and encouraged his son in the study of the Confucian classics that made up the educational curriculum of the samurai class. After an early education in Osaka, he left there at the age of 19 to study "Dutch learning" or Rangaku in Nagasaki. This was in 1854, a year after Perry's arrival at Edo, but even at this time the only official place to make contact with foreigners and their ideas was in Nagasaki. With the new foreign threat posed by the United States, Fukuzawa decided in 1858 to learn English. In the following year he was asked to sail with the *Kanrin-Maru,* a Japanese boat purchased from the Dutch, which was to accompany a Japanese delegation to the United States to sign a treaty opening Japan to foreign trade. With limited English, he set out on the journey to San Francisco. The impression the west made on this young 23 year old must have been overwhelming, as he was to write later:

> Foreign countries are not only novel and exotic for us Japanese, everything we see and hear about these cultures is strange and mysterious — a blazing brand has been thrust into ice-cold water, not only are ripples and swells ruffling the surface of men's minds but a massive upheaval is being stirred up at the very depth of their souls.

Fukuzawa Yukichi as a young samurai during a visit to Paris in 1862. He was a translator on various missions sent by the Tokugawa government to the United States and Europe, an experience that had a profound impact on his outlook and development.

Keio University Library, Tokyo

Fukuzawa was to travel on a number of foreign missions as a translator for the Tokugawa government. With the establishment of the Meiji government he reached the conclusion that what the Japanese needed most from the west was education. He therefore set up a small school on the site of what is now Keio University. Here he had the Speaking Hall built, based on designs sent to him from the United States. The Japanese, he believed, needed to learn public speaking. A seemingly insignificant thing though this might appear, to Fukuzawa it was one of the characteristics of western culture that most impressed him. In feudal Japan there was no such tradition of public debate on issues of social concern. Because of the authoritarian character of feudal relationships, those in power had no tradition of rationally justifying their behavior nor were they accountable in any democratic sense.

In the Speaking Hall a new generation of Japanese students were to confront a teacher who encouraged them, not only to absorb new western ideas and concepts, but to express themselves and their ideas publicly. A new domain of national public life was to come into existence to replace the autocratic ways of feudal Japan.

It was not simply as an educationalist, introducing a western-style school system, that Fukuzawa was to have an impact on Japanese intellectual life, but as a liberal and democratic editor and as a popular author. His book *Conditions in the Western World* (1866) was extremely influential, as was *The Encouragement of Learning* (1872) which sold 20,000 copies. In *Conditions in the Western World,* Fukuzawa described, in great detail, every aspect of European life and behavior:

> The bed linens are extremely clean. The sheets are white as snow, and you never find any fleas or lice. The container that you see under the bed . . . is a chamber pot. You always find this thing underneath the bed when you stay in a westerner's house. You should be careful not to mistake this container for something else when you visit a western country as some Japanese actually did.

Some of Fukuzawa's companions, on their first mission to the United States, mistook the chamber pot for pillows since, in Japan, a hard porcelain block was used instead of a soft pillow to support one's head.

In his enthusiasm for western learning Fukuzawa was clearly not alone. Another young reformer who was to join one of the many missions to Europe was Shibusawa Eichi. Shibusawa (1840–1931) had been brought up, like Fukuzawa, on the Chinese Confucian classics, although he was not born of the samurai class but was to be adopted into it. He was, for a time, a member of an anti-foreign terrorist movement whose aim was to rid the country of westerners. However, after being chosen to accompany the Tokugawa mission to the Paris Exhibition in the early 1850s he changed his mind completely. With remarkable pragmatism, he came to the conclusion that if the Japanese were to be successful in these efforts at modernization they would have to adopt, not only the technology of the west, but also the cultural and political institutions that underpinned them. As a gesture of liberation Shibusawa abandoned his samurai garb for the frock coat and tie of a European gentleman.

In the two years Shibusawa was to spend abroad he studied European social and economic institutions. Europe's strength, he believed, was built upon an industrial system that rewarded innovation and individual enterprise but also led to great social inequalities.

On returning to Japan he was employed in the ministry of finance, whose primary task was to support and encourage the establishment of western-style industrial enterprises. The return of students and fact-finding missions sent abroad to study the ways of the west provided the Meiji government with a number of models from which to choose — one of the advantages of being a late developer. Like shoppers in a world supermarket, the reformers went about systematically choosing their new institutions. They adopted a German public health system, a French–American education system, a British navy and financial institutions, and a Prussian army and constitution. Apart from modeling their institutions on the best that the west had to offer, they also brought to Japan large numbers of foreign experts, often referred to as "live machines," who were to act as technical advisers.

While working for the ministry of finance Shibusawa was involved in setting up Japan's first western-style factory. He was to confront many of the same problems as Li Hongzhang in China.

A remarkable historical accident was to benefit the Japanese at this time. In the 1860s a blight hit the French and Italian silk industries, which prevented them from meeting the growing demand for silk thread. This provided an opening for the traditional Chinese and Japanese silk industries. However, the quality of the silk thread produced in the local "cottage industry" was neither sufficiently standardized nor of the quality required by European manufacturers.

It was therefore decided to establish a European-style silk spinning factory at Tomioka in Gumma prefecture, about 100 miles from Tokyo. For the design of the factory the government went to Lyon in France, one of the centers of the European silk industry. They employed Paul Brunot to manage the plant and brought out a

Courtesy Film Australia

The Speaking Hall that Fukuzawa had built at his school (now Keio University) in 1875. Modeled on an American Quaker meeting hall, it was used to encourage public speaking. Fukuzawa believed that if the Japanese were to catch up with the west they needed a western-style education system to inculcate "the spirit of number and reason." In Japan's traditional feudal culture those in power had never had to justify their actions through rational argument, which Fukuzawa saw as one of the great virtues of the western liberal and democratic tradition. At the far end of the Speaking Hall, Professor Eiichi Kiyooka stands beneath a portrait of his grandfather Fukuzawa Yukichi.

whole range of European advisers. The factory was begun in the early 1870s and immediately ran into local opposition for, while the Meiji bureaucrats might have been enthusiastic for all things western, local people brought up on the xenophobic policies of the Tokugawa found the presence of foreign barbarians, and their proposed industry, unacceptable. Even getting the factory built was extremely difficult and frustrating. First, the French architects and engineers designed it as they would in France, to be built of brick, but in Japan such building materials were not used, so they had to set up their own kiln and import cement. Second, there was a basic conflict with the Japanese carpenters employed. Local contractors would not, at first, supply timber for the project, and then the carpenters argued that the European design was unsafe and refused to work on it unless it conformed to the traditional timber structure that had been proven, over centuries, to withstand earthquakes. A compromise was finally reached and what emerged was a traditional Japanese wooden structure faced with brick to make it look like a European factory.

In 1872 the plant was finally ready but again there were serious problems. The French could not get a sufficient number of girls to apply to work in the plant. They were forced to try to bring employees to the factory from other areas. However, there was no tradition of moving to another area to accept work, particularly when this involved living and working with another and alien clan. When the factory finally went into production it was understaffed and the discipline of the workers suffered many of the same problems exhibited by European factory workers in the eighteenth century.

The silk spinning factory at Tomioka was set up by the Meiji government as a model factory in 1872.

The demand for Japanese silk thread and fabric in the west provided the impetus for small private factories to set up in business. This factory, in Tokyo, shown using silk-reeling technology imported in 1872. Experience gained in the state-run factories like Tomioka provided trained workers for the growing private sector, which was funded through new commercial banks established by the Shibusawa and Mitsui families.

For the government this was to be a model factory, which it was prepared to support. It had set up a somewhat idealized European model of a factory and left the running of it to the French manager. He, of course, took no account of the indigenous culture and ran it as he would have in Lyon. There were eight-hour days and a holiday on Sunday, despite the fact that the notion of the European week was completely alien to the staff, who were housed in dormitories and were even expected to attend church.

Despite such setbacks, the Meiji government plowed ahead with its policy of western-style modernization. The Gregorian calendar was adopted in 1873, along with European dress and social habits, much to the contempt of Chinese visitors. The enthusiasm for all things western was such that in Tokyo there was even a European-style reception hall built where, dressed in the latest European fashion, Japanese officials would hold charity concerts and balls to entertain foreigners. It was known as the Rokumeikan, or Deer Cry Pavilion, and was extremely popular among the new Japanese leaders. One Japanese observer of this new cultural institution, Okura Kihachiro (1837–1928), described a remarkable scene on the floor of the ballroom:

The partners were both men, one with the huge build of a sumo wrestler, the other an especially skinny fellow; the couple was dancing in all seriousness but since their contrast was peculiar it created a commotion among the spectators, who were trying to determine their identity. On closer observation the huge man turned out to be Oyama, Japan's Minister of War, and the skinny man was the then Governor of Tokyo. . . . Now

At the Deer Cry Pavilion or Rokumeikan, the new Japanese leaders could meet and entertain the growing western community living in Tokyo and nearby Yokohama. Here, the Japanese would learn ballroom dancing and hold charity concerts, in an imitation of upper class groups anywhere in Europe or the United States. In this way the Japanese hoped to be accepted as being civilized, and equal with the west.

on this occasion Oyama was in formal western military attire while his companion was in Japanese kimono and hokama, and they were earnestly engaged in dancing, at which neither was very good.

This activity was brutally satirized by European visitors such as the French cartoonist, George Bigot, which offended and bewildered the Japanese who expected that such an endorsement of Europe as the new center of civilization would have been applauded. (There was even a "civilization ball game" invented in the late 1870s to help educate children in the virtues of western technology: as a child bounced or threw a ball, he or she would name desirable western inventions — gas lamps, steam engines, cameras, telegraphs, lightning conductors, newspapers, schools, post boxes and so on.) Although many government-sponsored model factories were to be financial disasters they did provide an important training ground in industrial management with staff going from Tomioka to other smaller private firms, bringing to them new skills and ideas. The demand for silk was sufficiently great that Japan was able to gain the lion's share of the European market by the late 1870s. However, the real impetus for growth was not to come from government. The industries they established were often run by ex-samurai with little business experience and with wage structures unrelated to profitability.

Shibusawa, aware that such enterprises were doomed to failure, left the ministry of finance and, with the support of the Mitsui family, established Japan's first commercial bank. Through this bank he provided financial support for new firms outside government control — firms modeled on the joint-stock companies, which, he believed, formed the basis of European and American wealth.

In this he was, initially, up against some deep-seated cultural prejudices. The dominant samurai class had absorbed from Confucian China a distrust of and disdain for merchants, who were believed to be concerned only with private gain and were therefore of very low social status. The ideal of a samurai was selflessly to serve the interests of his traditional lord, and in this he was governed by a rigorous code of discipline. While the Meiji government had tried to shift the focus of loyalty to the nation they had failed to find a role for this largely dispossessed and very influential military class. Shibusawa, from his studies of European institutions, realised that what Japan needed was the entrepreneurial spirit that was at large in the west. However, without an indigenous bourgeoisie and an equivalent of Adam Smith to sanctify the market system, he had to find a new way of making commerce acceptable to the samurai educated in and inculcated with a Confucian world view.

Like his contemporary, Fukuzawa, he was to argue that the west offered a model of efficient economic management of the nation's resources. As Japan now faced a crisis affecting its very survival as a sovereign state, the object of industrial enterprises was to build a rich nation. The efficient management of commercial industry was

Samurai, the once dominant caste in Japan, lost their guaranteed state stipend and social role in Meiji Japan. They remained powerful but largely ineffectual after the suppression of a Satsuma-led rebellion in 1877 when an army of samurai challenged the Meiji reformers and the direction they were taking towards ever-greater westernization. It was Shibusawa, himself a ex-samurai, who was to present the argument that working to build Japan's new industries was not merely a matter of trade or the pursuit of personal gain but was of service to the state and therefore, consistent with the Samurai code of bushido.

東京横濱蒸氣鐵道之圖

横濱ステーシ

Railway companies set up with capital made available through the new banks, began
to take over many areas previously dominated by government. The first railway line
ran from Tokyo to Yokohama and was opened in 1872.

therefore a task consistent with the code of service to the state promoted by the
samurai. The new nationally sponsored industries could be regarded as social
organizations like the old feudal domains. The dedication of the businessman to the
social and economic goals of the new firms was similar to the Confucian concern for
the interests of the clan, rather than that of the selfish merchant concerned simply
with private profit.

Shibusawa believed in the idea of a moral economy: "all sorts of industrial work
and the existence of co-operative systems are conducted on moral reasons and
mutual confidence." So while the Japanese were to adopt both the technology and
institutions of the west, they were to mold them effectively on to their existing social
systems. While in Europe and the United States aggressive merchants and bankers
used their capital to build industrial empires, which were ends in themselves, and
were accountable only to shareholders, the enterprise in Japan as it emerged under
the new ideology of Japanese nationalism was an extension of the government policy
of "strong army, rich nation."

With the money raised by his bank Shibusawa was to invest in a wide range of
activities. First, the Osaka Cotton Spinning Company and then paper, gas, railway and
shipping companies. His firms, like his bank, were to be supported by the old
merchant family, Mitsui. In the same way that the Protestant Reformation was to take
the time discipline of the medieval monasteries and apply it to the demands of the
market place, so too did Shibusawa and other early Meiji industrialists take the values
of the samurai and apply them to the economic goals of building powerful

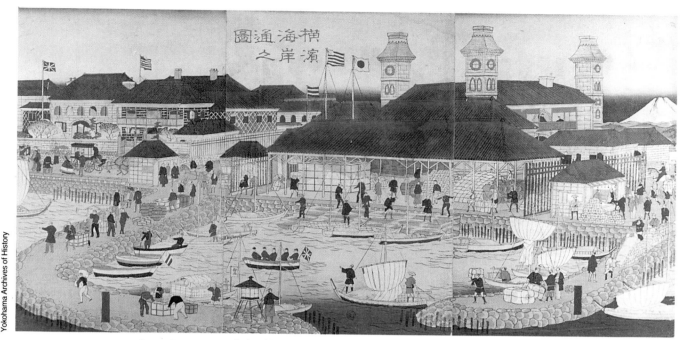

横濱海岸通之圖

Large European-style buildings were erected to house the new public schools, banks, insurance companies and business houses that flourished on the back of the silk industry centred in Yokohama.

corporations and industrial enterprises. The function of these firms was to manage the essential transfer of western technology and adapt it to the problems of production in Japan.

Linking the commercial interests of private firms with national goals allowed capitalist economic rationalism to be squared with Confucian notions of loyalty and service to the collective good of society. As the new industries were responsible for training the essentially unskilled rural workers who made up the growing industrial labor force, there was a high priority on not losing this investment — a labor market operated to a very limited extent. The firms tended to function like extended families or clan enterprises, and notions of loyalty and commitment, similar to those that existed in the feudal domains, were expected. The idea of private property rights sanctioned by law, which were so basic to western capitalism, did not exist. (The wealth of the feudal domains was regarded as a collective asset with rights based on clan and caste associations.)

After a decade of rapid growth the new private sector was to be further enhanced in 1881. The international demand for silk had provided new wealth in some rural areas, and also provided the capital for the building of better transport systems based on railway networks, which gradually linked the whole country, providing new markets and increased demand. It also led to rampant inflation, forcing the government to intervene in the economy. The finance minister, Matsukata Masayoshi, once a leading samurai of the Satsuma clan, began to divest the government of their draining and unprofitable enterprises such as the Tomioka silk mill.

191

Shipyards at Nagasaki and Hyogo, established by the government as part of its efforts to improve transportation and to support the navy, were sold off to Iwasaki Yataro (the founder of the firm Mitsubishi) and Kawasaki Shoya respectively. (Kawasaki was a supporter of the Meiji who, although not a samurai, had started a small shipping firm.) Not all government-sponsored enterprises were even capable of being sold off. The Kamaishi steel mill set up in 1874 with the aid of British engineers was, by 1882, declared a complete failure due to the poor quality ore and smeltable coke and, equally important, the incompetence (or inexperience) of the workforce. When put on the market in 1882 there were no buyers.

The sale of many strategic industries into private hands was to create a close bond between the government and the large trading and industrial conglomerates or *zaibatsu,* which were formed at this time.

There was another and increasingly important factor in the remarkable speed with which Japan was able to build up its industrial base. This was the connection between government-owned arsenals and the rest of industry. Like those established in China, these arsenals were the earliest centers of industrial training and large-scale production. For example, in the 1880s arsenals and government shipyards employed around 10,000 people, compared with 3,000 employed in private firms. These government arsenals were also to apply the latest iron and steel casting techniques to produce better guns, and, indirectly, better machine tools for private industry. Six of the ten private cotton textile firms, which began operation in the 1880s using spindles imported by the government, relied on steam engines produced at the Yokosuka arsenal. The military were also to play an important role in modernizing private industry, as the suppliers of essential technological components.

The Osaka arsenal provided a large number of machines, such as lathes, planers and grinders operated by steam engines, for private firms. The congruence of interests of government and private institutions was to be a characteristic of Japanese industrial success; as important an element in postwar Japan as it was in the Meiji. It was, however, to be a factor fundamentally lacking in China.

Connections established with the major armament makers of Europe, such as Krupp of Germany and Armstrong of Britain, gave the Japanese an immediate awareness of the arms race and the crucial role of industrial innovation in that process. From the numerous students sent abroad and the advisers brought to Japan, they had become aware of the spread of technological change in Europe and the United States, from which they could not afford to isolate themselves.

# WINDOWS ON THE WORLD

*Whatever happens we have got the Maxim gun and they have not.*

Hilaire Belloc

The Japanese and Chinese students and missions that went abroad to learn from the west were to confront a culture and industrial system in the process of rapid transformation. The problem was to understand what within that apparent anarchic chaos was the key to its success and the secret of its growing wealth and power. Cheap steel clearly had something to do with it.

In 1851 in a small Kentucky town, William Kelly who cast the reducing vats for sugar production began to experiment with the production of a more economical method of making steel. The basic problem was that the normal methods of burning off the excess carbon from pig iron to produce mild steel required very large amounts of fuel. It was both slow and very expensive; sufficiently economic for the production of knife blades and fine mechanisms but not available on an industrial scale. Kelly was believed to have employed a number of Chinese at his foundry. It is possible that it was they who suggested to him the method of blowing air through molten iron to produce the heat required to transform it into fine steel; the oxygen burning off impurities such as sulfur and carbon. This ingenious method had been used in China for centuries and was now to transform western industry.

Kelly was to spend a great deal of time and effort getting the process to work on an industrial scale. In 1857 he took out a patent on the process but went bankrupt the following year. However, it was not Kelly but an Englishman, Henry Bessemer, who was to build his reputation as the inventor of the blast furnace.

Bessemer was a classic nineteenth century inventor. His first achievement was to produce European gold lacquer that could compete with the Japanese product, which at that time was extremely fashionable in Europe. Bessemer's reputation was such that, in 1854, Louis Napoleon of France offered him unlimited credit for access to his latest invention. Bessemer had come up with a shell that spun on its axis as it left the barrel, giving it greater stability in flight and, ultimately, greater accuracy. The problem was that the traditional iron and bronze cannon could not handle the additional pressure the shell produced and would split. So to make the invention practicable it was necessary to find some stronger material for the cannon. Steel was the obvious choice but at that time was much too expensive. Bessemer, therefore, set about trying to find a means of producing cheap steel.

There is some controversy surrounding the issue of whether he knew of Kelly's earlier work since he came up with the same solution. But, whereas Kelly was unable to gear his process to operate on an industrial scale, Bessemer was to design a blast furnace that could reduce the time taken to transform pig iron into steel from hours to minutes — saving energy, time and money. In 1856 he was to outline this process in a paper, "On the Manufacture of Malleable Iron and Steel without Fuel," which he presented to the British Association for the Advancement of Science.

Great exhibitions, the first of which opened in Paris in 1853, promoted the technological inventiveness of European industry. It also presented to bewildered Japanese and Chinese visitors a specter of constantly changing military and industrial technology.

It took a decade to perfect this method of steel production but it was increasingly clear throughout the latter half of the nineteenth century that applied scientific research enabled existing industrial products to be made more cheaply and therefore to be more readily available.

Metallurgists in Germany were soon to take Bessemer's original blast furnace and adapt it to cope with wider ranges and qualities of iron ore. In 1864 the Siemens-Martin open-hearth furnace was being used by Alfred Krupp in the Ruhr valley to produce steel for massive cannon, which were to be used to pound the outskirts of Louis Napoleon's Paris when Germany invaded France in 1870.

In the United States the Bessemer revolution was to see a fall in the cost of steel from around $100 a ton in the 1870s to $12 in the 1890s. Andrew Carnegie in Pittsburg was producing 1,200 tons of iron and steel a week by 1880. Carnegie was one of the first to recognize the benefits of employing scientists in industry. The competitive demands of providing more durable steel railway lines and steel for the growing machine-tools industry led Carnegie to employ a German chemist by the name of Fricke. In a letter, Carnegie made the following comments on the benefits that were to flow from this decision:

We found . . . a learned German, Dr Fricke, and great secrets did the doctor open to us. [Ore] from mines that had a high reputation was now found to contain ten, fifteen, and even twenty per cent less iron than it had been credited with. Mines that hitherto had a poor reputation we found to be now yielding superior ore. The good was bad and the bad was good, and everything was topsy-turvy. Nine-tenths of all the uncertainties of pig iron making were dispelled under the burning sun of chemical knowledge. What fools we had been! But then there was this consolation: we were not as great fools as our competitors [who] years after we had taken chemistry to guide us [the steel industry] said they could not afford to employ a chemist. Had they known the truth then, they would have known they could not afford to be without one.

This realization was to be reinforced frequently as apparently insignificant resources were to become valuable assets overnight through the application of scientific knowledge to the problems of industrial production. This was the case with crude oil. In 1854 Professor Silliman at Yale University discovered that by heating and distilling crude oil it was possible to produce two new and more functional products — kerosene and petroleum. This discovery was to make oil, a resource known by the Chinese for a thousand years, accessible for widespread industrial and domestic use.

Edwin L. Drake, who first discovered oil in Pennsylvania in 1859, used Chinese-style drilling rigs, which were soon popping up all over the United States. Refineries provided the fine oils needed for industry and for the railway locomotives that now linked the United States' vast internal market to that of Europe and the rest of the world. In 1880 Standard Oil was in a position to open three large-scale refineries bringing the price of kerosene down from $1.50 a gallon in 1882 to $0.45 in 1885. The greater efficiency of production that came with applying science to industry was clearly seen by the end of the nineteenth century and had profound economic implications.

The work of German chemists had forced down the price of blue dye from DM 200 in 1870 to DM 6 by 1886. New methods of refining aluminum saw the price fall from Fr 39.8 per pound in 1888 to Fr 1.70 in 1895. This pattern of price reductions made new products possible, which, in turn, fueled a revolution in domestic technology. Singer sewing machines came on the market along with steel-framed bicycles and Remington typewriters. The scale of the market for these new consumer goods was also greatly expanded by mail-order firms, which used the railways and fast international shipping.

This second industrial revolution, based on scientific discovery, allowed the formation of new institutions and opportunities for ingenuity and invention. In 1876 an inventor like Thomas Edison was able to establish his research laboratory at Menlo Park employing trained scientists and engineers in what he described as an "invention factory." The Edison Company not only invented the electric lamp, or light bulb, but also the entire distribution and delivery system for domestic lighting. The General Electric Company that was to grow out of Edison's original firm had as its basis a tradition of industrial research and development, which increasingly held the key to industrial innovation. This was to be taken up by the new German-style universities, springing up throughout the United States, whose research departments

Within a few years of the illumination of New York in 1882, the Tokyo Electric Company
had lit up the Ginza area of Tokyo, to the amazement of all. Through licensing agreements
between the Edison Company and firms such as Toshiba, Japanese enterprises gained
access to the western technology vital for both industrial and military purposes.

were increasingly linked to the needs of local industrial enterprises.

All this was absorbed by the Japanese and Chinese students sent abroad to study
science and engineering. However, when they returned home, the political response
to their new knowledge was to be markedly different. Japanese students returned,
not just to academic jobs in institutes of learning, but to positions in the new
industrial enterprises being funded by people like Shibusawa and his Dai-Ichi Bank.
The Japanese students were often sent by their companies to learn specific industrial
applications of new technology. Within a few years of New York being illuminated by
the Edison Company in 1882, the Tokyo Electric Company (later Toshiba) switched
on street lights in Tokyo. Through the international patent system Japanese firms
were, by license, able to gain access to the new technology as it emerged in the west.
More often than not they reverse-engineered what they could not license and
adapted it to their own requirements. This was to be particularly true of textile
technology. For example, the heavy metal looms introduced into Japan from Europe
presented serious problems. They were extremely expensive and, when broken,
parts had to be sent from Britain, France and Germany. Toyoda Sakichi in 1896 took
the heavy European power loom and rebuilt as much of it as possible in wood. He

also made it small so that it would take the standard width of cloth used in kimonos throughout Japan. These he was able to sell at around Y93 each as opposed to Y872 for a German machine or Y389 for a French machine. At this price the Toyoda loom was accessible to small-scale cottage industries. This simple innovation was to play an important part in the modernization of the Japanese textile industry and was to provide a model for the adapting of western methods to Japanese conditions, which was to occur in a number of technological fields. The adaptation and refinement of this original Toyoda loom was to lead to the Platt Brothers in England, the world's leading supplier of textile machinery, buying the patent to it in 1929 for £25,000.

In the fields of heavy industry, firms like Mitsubishi were able to diversify from shipbuilding into locomotive and armaments manufacture. Government and military contracts under the "strong army, rich nation" policy meant that Japanese industrialists, many trained in universities in Europe and the United States, recognized the importance of research and were prepared to carry the costs of sending capable engineers abroad for training. These overseas-trained students and observers provided access to what was being done in industrial and military fields.

There was, therefore, by the 1880s an industrial context in which innovation could occur, especially as the Meiji government's comprehensive western-style education system in the 1870s now turned out well-trained technicians and engineers able to take on the new roles defined by the growing industrial base. The demand for western-style consumer goods, and the money with which to pay for them, provided the basis for new industries and new careers.

\*　　\*　　\*

Chinese students returning from abroad were increasingly frustrated in their efforts to bring about change. With the possible exception of the European-dominated treaty ports of Shanghai and Guangzhou, the basic ambivalence of government officials towards western values and institutions meant that industrial growth and change were slow and often inhibited. Even in Guangzhou, for example, when a Chinese textile mill was burned down, government officials would offer no help or support to the local entrepreneur, arguing that such an industry was basically immoral because it simply made the factory owner rich, and undercut the economic viability of the traditional handicraft industry.

In this they were quite right but the cost of maintaining their traditional rural-based craft industries was unrealistic in the face of overseas competition. British and American textiles sold through the treaty ports undercut this local craft industry and placed increasing strain on an already depressed economy. Even the modern manufacturing and transport systems set up by reformers like Li Hongzhang were constantly in difficulties. The state-owned but merchant-run firms had many of the same failings as the early Meiji enterprises. Without the support of the Chinese government, to protect and nurture these fledgling industries, they had little opportunity to compete with those European-owned enterprises in the treaty ports whose power and influence over the coastal economy continued to grow.

# CARVED UP LIKE A RIPE MELON

*[Such scientific subjects as] electricity, heat, astronomy, air, light, dynamics, and chemistry are what the English call real knowledge, while they consider the teaching of our Chinese sages as empty and useless talk. Chinese officials who are deceived by their words often agree with them. I argue against these beliefs, saying that their real knowledge consists only of petty, miscellaneous tricks, which can be used to make "a utensil" of but limited capacity . . . They concentrate on such miscellaneous tricks, using boats and vehicles made to bring in profit, and firearms made for killing, trying to produce more and more of such things to become wealthy and strong. How can we call all this useful, real knowledge? Since the beginning of history, China has endured longer than any other civilization, and has produced a hundred and several dozen sages one after another, daily refining and completing their [social and moral] institutions. The depth of our philosophical discussions greatly exceeds those of the west. Foreigners consider material wealth as true wealth; western nations think brute force is strength: China takes deference as strength. This is the real truth. It cannot be explained in a few hurried words.*

Liu Xihong, Chinese envoy to London, 1877

*Just as good iron is not made into nails, so good men do not become soldiers.*

Popular Chinese saying

While traditional Chinese scholar-officials like Liu Xihong, one of the first Chinese ambassadors to London, had confidence in the Confucian moral virtues that had sustained Chinese imperial culture for 2,000 years, others were increasingly concerned for the very survival of China as a sovereign entity. In the late nineteenth century the forces of western economic imperialism were reaching a pitch that even the Celestial Empire could not ignore. The scrabble for colonial territories in Africa and much of Southeast Asia confronted China with the prospect of being next on the agenda. In fact the view expressed in the capitals of Europe was that it was ready to be "carved up like a ripe melon."

The failure of self-strengthening to unite the government and empire in the sorts of change embarked upon by the Meiji government in Japan was understandable. The price of China's commitment to its traditional world view was that it was increasingly out of kilter with what was actually happening around it. The tragic double bind faced by the Chinese governing elite was not merely a consequence of having a group of intransigent and xenophobic mandarins in power: they were genuinely caught between two stools for which their culture and education had not prepared them. They had to affirm the traditional cultural values that legitimized their power and held the empire together. They were also forced to contain the European influence that increasingly threatened to split up the empire as had happened in India, with the British playing one state off against another to divide and rule.

Too much change could destabilize the whole empire, too little made it

198

vulnerable to attack and foreign encroachment. In 1874, for example, the Japanese under a pretext took over Formosa (Taiwan) and five years later annexed the Luich'iu Islands; the British became involved in trying to take over Yunnan in 1875, and the Russians successfully occupied Ili in Xinjiang (Sinkiang) in 1871–81. In 1884–85 the French seized Annam (now Vietnam), which was regarded as a part of China, and the resulting war ended in a humiliating backdown on the part of the Chinese government, and large payments in reparation. Above all else these wars, like the disastrous Taiping rebellion, cost the Chinese government dearly, weakening both the credibility of the Qing dynasty and the government financial reserves.

The financial plight of the empire had never been worse. In the late eighteenth century the government of Quianlong had surplus reserves of around 70 million taels ($7 million). One hundred years later China had an annual budget deficit of 10 million taels.

It was only by taking foreign loans that the Chinese were able to purchase the increasingly sophisticated military technology needed for defense — cannon from Krupp and battleships from Britain — despite the establishment of their own arsenal. The problem was that Chinese military production had little connection with the sources of innovation and, without a modern education system, was unable to keep abreast of scientific and technological advances. This was to be most painfully revealed in 1894 in the humiliating confrontation with the Japanese over Korea.

Korea had, until the 1880s, been one of the most loyal of China's traditional tributary states. Intensely xenophobic it was, however, like many other Asian

China and Japan fish for control of Korea, once a tributary state loyal to China but, by the 1890s, under pressure from reformers to follow the path of social and economic reform taken by Japan; Russia looks on eager to increase its territory and power in the east. The competition between them came to a head in 1894.

On 17 September 1894 the Chinese and Japanese fleets confronted each other off the coast of Korea. Although numerically stronger, the Chinese ships were older and much slower than the Japanese, which gave the Japanese a tactical advantage.

With the fall of their forts to the Japanese army, the Chinese were forced to sue for peace. At Shimonoseki in Japan, the Chinese delegation, led by Li Hongzhang, had no alternative but to concede to terms that gave Japan territorial rights within China, similar to those won by the European imperial powers, as well as a hefty indemnity payment.

cultures, divided into those loyal to the traditional Confucian values of the past and those drawn to the pragmatic modernization of Japan.

Inevitably these political factions called on support from their respective mentors. The conflict over the position of Korea and its independence or lack of it was to lead to a head-on military confrontation between the brashly self-confident Japan and imperial China. This was, in a sense, to be a test of the achievement of the two approaches to self-strengthening. In reality it was Japan's final step in its efforts to join the exclusive club of imperialist powers. The Japanese had clearly learned the principles of western industrial production and, as good students, had learned the other essential lesson of nineteenth century western political economy — controlling colonial territories whose resources could feed the expansion of industrial power.

The extension of the United States westward beyond Mexico and the west coast to Hawaii and the Philippines in the late 1880s provided the model for what the Japanese could only come to perceive as a global game of chess.

In a subtle political move the British were prepared to encourage Japanese expansionism in northeast China as a bulwark against imperial Russia whose expansion into Afghanistan and the Crimea had threatened British interests. The construction of the trans-Siberian railway also gave Russia direct access to the east. So with what seemed to be the tacit support of the British, Japan began to extend its sphere of influence to include Korea. In China this challenged the traditional tributary relationship, which had to be honored, and the die was cast. Li Hongzhang, as governor to the northern provinces was at the heart of the negotiations with the Koreans to try and head off a confrontation with the Japanese. His success with the Taiping, and in numerous other foreign conflicts, made him eminently suitable in the eyes of the imperial government in Beijing.

In August 1894 the Japanese army occupied the capital P'yongyang on the pretext of preserving its independence. They sank a Chinese boat in the harbor and China sent in its navy. China had twice the naval strength of Japan: 65 ships as opposed to 32 ships. But lack of centralized control over this navy meant that two of the three Chinese fleets available remained in harbor in the south, due to the fact that they were under the control of the provincial authorities whose bureaucratic mechanism was not designed for rapid decision making.

On 17 September 1894 a Chinese Peiyang fleet of 25 ships led by Admiral Ting met the Japanese fleet of 21 ships near the Yalu River in Korea Bay. There was one essential difference between the two forces. The Japanese navy was equipped with newer battleships, which could travel at speeds of up to 23 knots, while the Chinese ships were much slower, heavier and older, and could travel at only 15 knots. The consequence was that the Japanese navy could easily outmaneuver the Chinese and, within four hours, the Chinese had lost four ships and about a thousand officers and men. The Japanese lost one ship. The Chinese fleet retreated to Port Arthur where they had established powerful fortifications, only to find that the Japanese had captured the forts from the landward side, and were able to turn the 70 Krupp cannons, which Li had installed there and at Weihaiwei, upon the helpless Chinese navy. Admiral Ting committed suicide and the Japanese captured seven Chinese warships.

The repercussions of these events were enormous. Li Hongzhang was severely criticized and lost the right to wear the yellow jacket, the mark of imperial favor. He was also forced to go to the negotiation table with the Japanese who, like the Europeans before them, were to demand large economic concessions and reparations.

At the city of Shimonoseki, Li confronted the Japanese negotiating team of Ito and Mutu — Li dressed in the gown of an imperial court official, Ito and Mutu in European military uniforms. All three were of a generation concerned with self-strengthening. (Ito had been one of the early students who was smuggled into Europe in the 1860s with the help of Thomas Glover, an English merchant and entrepreneur living in Nagasaki.)

Li was to open the negotiations with an appeal to their shared Confucian heritage and the common threat, which should unite them against European expansion throughout Asia, but his words fell on deaf ears. The Japanese had for centuries suffered from the superiority and condescension of Chinese imperial officials to a tributary state; now the tables were turned.

However, in the middle of these negotiations a Japanese fanatic shot Li, hitting him just below the left eye. Suddenly, public opinion, as expressed in the press and by the negotiators, softened a little out of acute embarrassment over the incident. Sympathy was to be shortlived.

In April 1895 a treaty·was drawn up that forced China into accepting Korea's "independence" (under Japanese domination). China was forced to pay an indemnity of 200 million taels ($20 million) to Japan; to secede Taiwan, the Pescadores and the Liaodong Peninsula, and to open the ports of Chongqing (Chungking), Suzhou and Hangzhou to international trade. Finally, and perhaps most importantly, Japanese nationals had the right to open factories within China on the same basis as other imperialist powers. The Chinese had little option but to accede to these demands now or suffer the possibility of having to give up more the next time.

For Japan the benefits of the engagement were encouraging. The reparations from China represented 15 per cent of Japanese gross national product in 1895. The success of the military was to strengthen their hand in government and their call for government-sponsored steel production was now to have some effect. Twenty-five million yen went to the establishment of a new steel mill to supply material, particularly for the navy. German engineers, experienced in the Krupp steelworks, helped to set up the massive Yawata steelworks, later to become Nippon Steel. The foundry ensured that this most fundamental material, the key to nineteenth century military and industrial power, was readily available.

There was, however, to be one major and bitter setback amid all this triumph. Japan was, for the most part, to be blackballed by the imperialist club. This parvenu in their midst had the Germans, French and Russians up in arms, largely because of the territorial concession of the Liaodong Peninsula in southern Manchuria, which Ito and Mutu were able to extract from the Chinese. Under considerable pressure the

Japanese were forced to back down on their claims to the territory only to find that three years later these same European powers made similar territorial claims, with Russia gaining the Liaodong region.

With all this came a torrent of racist invective directed against the Japanese by European states concerned that Japan might be moving in on territories they wished to control themselves. The German Kaiser, Wilhelm II, whose interests in Shandong (Shantung) were threatened by Japan, even invented the term "yellow peril," while the United States and Australia adopted exclusionist policies directed against Asians, in particular, the Japanese. A German political commentator, Baron Von Falkenegg, was to whip up anxiety within Europe:

> The European powers should have realized in good time that the cunning, skilled and valiant Japanese people would soon be uttering the slogan "Asia for the Asians"... [that] is directed at all those Europeans who want to take political and commercial advantages in Asia. But for the Japanese, "Asia for the Asians" has the obvious implications "Japan dominates Asia, and Asia dominates Europe."

In France best selling novels such as the *The Yellow Invasion* by Emil Driant fictionalized the threat of oriental hordes sweeping across central Asia like Gengis Khan and his army. Rene Pinon, a French writer of the time, had this to say about the hysteria of the "yellow peril," which was used in some quarters to draw attention to European decadence:

> Whether one likes it or not, the "yellow peril" has entered already into the imagination of the people... Japanese and Chinese hordes spread out over all Europe, crushing under their feet the ruins of our capital cities and destroying our civilizations, grown anaemic due to the enjoyment of luxuries and corrupted by vanity of spirit.

Yokohama Archives of History

Japan's success in taking on the might of imperial China meant that they had finally qualified for membership of the exclusive imperialist club. However, Japan was not admitted; the reaction of the Europeans was to succumb to racist paranoia and to invoke the specter of the "Yellow Peril" rising in the east.

The racist assault upon the Japanese at this time cut deep, and brought about an inevitable swing against Europe, and against western values and institutions in general. Although not slowing the pace of modernization, ballroom dancing at the Rokumeikan was to come to an abrupt end. An imperial edict on education promoted the virtues of Confucian values and Japanese traditions. Racism was to be fought with racism.

Ten years later, in 1905, the unthinkable was to happen. The Japanese, smarting from the insults and maneuvers to limit their access to the mainland of China, finally came to a showdown with imperial Russia over the control of Manchuria. Both at sea and on the plains of Manchuria they were to drive the Russians out of the Liaodong Peninsula and gain their rightful status as an imperialist power. They had joined the club despite the "whites only" sign above the door. Some European commentators were more honest about the events taking place in the Orient. The French novelist Anatole France wrote:

> What the Russians are paying for at this very moment in the seas of Japan and in the gorges of Manchuria is not just their avid and brutal policy in the Orient, it is the colonial policy of all the European powers... It would not appear to be the case, however, that the yellow peril terrifying European economists is comparable to the white peril hanging over Asia. The Chinese do not send to Paris, Berlin or St. Petersburg missionaries to teach Christians *feng-shui* and cause general chaos in European affairs . . . Admiral Togo did not come with a dozen battleships to bombard the roadstead of Brest in order to help Japanese commerce in France. . . . The armies of the Asiatic powers have not taken to Tokyo or Peking the paintings of the Louvre or the china of the Élysée.

In an editorial in the influential science journal *Nature* in June 1905, this perceptive comment appeared, drawing the attention of complacent Europeans to the relevance of what the Japanese had achieved in less than fifty years:

> The operations of the present war with Russia have clearly demonstrated the importance of the introduction of the scientific spirit into all the national activities. . . . The lesson, which our educationalists and statesmen have to learn from Japan is that the life of a modern nation requires to be organized on scientific lines in all its departments, and that it must not be directed chiefly to personal ends, the attainment of which may, to a large extent, intensify many of our problems, but that it be consciously used for the promotion of national welfare.

*     *     *

In China the response to the debacle over Korea and the conditions of Shimonoseki was to bring home as never before the empire's critical vulnerability. Clearly the attempt to simply graft military and industrial technology on to existing imperial institutions was not working. In the wake of this a new group of reformers emerged with a far more radical approach, one which was based very much on the Japanese model.

One of the leading intellectual figures, who was to lash out at the failings of earlier reformers such as Li Honzhang was Yan Fu (Yen Fu). At the time of the war with Japan

Yan Fu had been superintendent of the Peiyang Naval Academy and it was many of his students and colleagues who went with the ill-fated Peiyang fleet to meet the Japanese off Yalu.

Yan Fu was one of the early students sent from China to study naval engineering in Britain. He was a contemporary of Japanese students such as Ito and Togo who were to rise rapidly to positions of power and influence in Meiji Japan, while returned students such as Yan Fu were to have little influence on the conservative Confucian scholars surrounding the Qing court.

Yan Fu (1854–1921) came from a scholar family from Fujian and he was brought up with a thorough grounding in the Confucian classics. He was an extremely capable student and, instead of following the traditional career path into the bureaucracy, Yan Fu was sent at the age of 14 to Li Hongzhang's Fuzhou naval dockyards, to study English, mathematics and science. In 1876 he was sent to study at Greenwich Naval Academy.

Britain in the 1870s was in the midst of the great Darwinian debate on the nature of evolution. The social and cultural implications of Darwin's theories of natural selection were not explored by Darwin himself but by his most ardent disciples, Thomas Huxley and Herbert Spencer, who were to popularize his ideas. The young Yan Fu, like Ito of Japan, was to fall under the spell of this intellectual movement. (Spencer was to become an adviser to the Japanese government after Ito became prime minister.) In essence the crude social Darwinists, as they were known, justified the intense competitiveness of the capitalist market place, as well as the conflict between nation-states on the basis that it conformed with the natural order of "survival of the fittest." This notion of "survival of the fittest" was taken from Darwin's biological examples and elevated to an economic and moral virtue. Why were the Europeans apparently "fitter" than the Chinese? This was what concerned Yan Fu.

It was not only Darwin, but writers such as John Stuart Mill and Adam Smith, who were to provide him with some of the answers to the secret of the west's wealth and power. It also provided him with a position from which to see the limitations and strengths of his own cultural and economic institutions. With the support of renegades in the London embassy, such as Guo Songdao who believed that China must reform its traditional institutions, and quickly, Yan Fu began to translate into classical Chinese the works of Huxley, Smith, Darwin, Spencer and Mill. In these annotated translations Yan Fu was to provide Chinese scholars with their first real understanding of the roots of western economic and political institutions, as well as its cultural values. The failure of Confucian culture to release the creative and dynamic potential of the individual was to be one of the recurring themes that Yan Fu was to derive from Mill and Adam Smith. For while Adam Smith convinced him of the virtues of the free market regulated by individuals pursuing their own "enlightened self-interest," John Stuart Mill provided an extension of this to cultural and intellectual freedom. The growth of knowledge was possible only in a "free market of ideas." This was the key to the growth of Europe's liberal-intellectual tradition. What Yan Fu also emphasized was the need for European-style individualism, as well as the legal and political institutions, to protect enterprising individuals from the arbitrary power of the state — in China's case the imperial bureaucracy. He came to regard the refined, isolated and contemplative Confucian mandarins as effete. His call for educational and democratic reforms was to have a considerable influence on the thinking of a whole generation of scholars, particularly those who were not able to travel abroad and who otherwise had only official prejudices to guide them.

With the military debacle at the hands of the Japanese forcing conservative officials to look for some real solutions, Yan Fu and other returned scholars demanded fundamental reforms; reforms that would strike at the very heart of the Chinese imperial system. Kang Youwei (K'ang yu-wei) and Liang Qichao (Liang Ch'i-ch'ao) were scholar-officials close to the center of imperial power and both were profoundly influenced by the writings of Yan Fu. With clear examples of what Japan's Meiji reformers had achieved they began to work within the government structure to bring about radical change. After three years of agitating for reform, and with some adroit political maneuvers against conservative government officials, Kang was finally to get the support of the Emperor Guangxu (Kuang Hsü). A famous meeting on 16 June 1898 was recorded by Liang Qichao:

> After the emperor had asked about his [Kang's] age and his qualifications:
>
> KANG: The four barbarians are all invading us and their attempted partition is gradually being carried out: China will soon perish.
>
> EMPEROR: Today it is really imperative that we reform.
>
> KANG: It is not because in recent years we have not talked about reform, but because it was only a slight reform, not a complete one, we change the first thing and do not change the second, and then we have everything so confused as to incur failure, and eventually there will be no success. The prerequisites of reform are that all the laws and the political and social systems be changed and decided anew, before it can be called reform. Now those who talk about reform only change some specific affairs, and do not reform the institutions.

The emperor was impressed and asked Kang to provide a more detailed outline of his proposals. He was appointed secretary of the *zongli yamen* and produced a radical manifesto that, with the emperor's approval, was promulgated as a series of decrees, which over the next hundred days were designed to transform education, administration, political institutions and industry. These institutional reforms were very much along the lines of those adopted not only in Meiji Japan but in Germany and Russia as well:

> In revitalizing the various administrative departments our government adopts western methods and principles. For, in a true sense, there is no difference between China and the west in setting up government for the sake of the people. Since, however, westerners have studied [the science of government] more diligently, their findings can be used to supplement our deficiencies. Scholars and officials of today whose purview does not go beyond China [regard westerners] as practically devoid of precepts or

principles. They do not know that the science of government as it exists in western countries has very rich and varied contents, and that its chief aim is to develop the people's knowledge and intelligence and to make their living commodious. The best part of the science is capable of bringing about improvements in human nature and the prolongation of human life.

This resolution on the part of the emperor to take decisive action to bring about institutional reforms in China could have changed the course of Asian history. However on 21 September, conservative government officials staged a coup. Supported by the aging, though extremely powerful, Empress Dowager Zixi (Tzu-hsi), they were able to take over the reins of government and, after putting the emperor under house arrest on a small island in the imperial gardens, they began to persecute those who were responsible for the reforms. Kang was able to escape to Shanghai and Liang Qichao to Japan; others were not so successful. Four reformers in the Grand Council along with Kang's brother were executed without trial. Twenty-two senior officials and scholars were jailed or banished for their involvement in the reform movement. All the edicts issued by the emperor were rescinded except, surprisingly, the one establishing an imperial university in Beijing. The Empress Dowager had now become the de facto ruler of China, and any hope of reform had been lost.

The powerful Empress Dowager Zixi whose support for conservative officials led to the coup that stopped the young Emperor Guangxu's efforts at institutional and economic reforms along the lines taken by Meiji Japan.

With the obvious success of the conservative element in government, a popularist anti-foreign movement, known as the Boxers, gained both confidence and official support. As with the Taiping rebellion it was spurred on by increased economic hardship. Foreign domination of local trade through the treaty ports meant that imported manufactured goods were driving out local craft industries. The Boxers or the "Righteous and Harmonious Fists" got their name from the form of martial arts they practiced. They also held Taoist magical beliefs, which supposedly endowed the practitioners with protection from western bullets after a hundred days of training. In this they were very similar to the Sioux Indian ghost dancers in their last-ditch stand to drive Europeans from their lands in the 1890s.

The Boxers became a focus of anti-foreign feelings. In May 1900 they were able to take over most of the imperial capital and to hold the foreign legations under siege until relief armies, consisting of British, German, American, French and Japanese troops, arrived to suppress the revolt.

The empress and the newly triumphant conservative forces within the Chinese government had tacitly supported the rebellion in the vain hope that they could in fact drive the Europeans out and reassert their traditional cultural values. But, yet again, the Chinese government was humiliated and forced to pay massive reparations to the foreign powers. The possibility of modernizing the old imperial order was a lost cause.

European missionaries and their schools had been one of the main targets of the anti-foreign movement. They were now given even greater access and rights throughout China to offer their corrosive western-style education. Within six years the Empress Dowager was dead, and the ancient imperial examination system, which for 1,500 years had provided the ideological gateway to power and wealth within China, was abandoned. In its place a western-style curriculum was introduced. Students were sent abroad in increasing numbers to gain higher education, with over 40 per cent going to Japan. A new ministry of education was set up and missions sent to Japan to study their system, which formed the model. But all this was too late to save the empire. Ten or fifteen years earlier there might have been some hope of holding the Qing empire together, but the constant repression of those idealists and reformers of earlier years had resulted in disillusionment, which now turned to revolution. It was therefore no coincidence that it should be a western-trained doctor, Sun Yat-sen, with the support of political refugees in Japan, who was to bring the empire to an end and found the first Chinese Republic in 1911.

# COMPRADORES AND WARLORDS

*Mr Science and Mr Democracy, only these two gentlemen can cure the dark maladies in Chinese politics, morality, learning and thought.*

Chen Duxiu, 1919

Sun Yat-sen, known in the Chinese-speaking world as Sun Zhong-shan, brought to Chinese politics an idealism almost unmatched by any reform movement in the twentieth century. From the point of view of his European and Japanese supporters he had gleaned the best political models from the west. His revolutionary ideas were based on the concept of "three people's principles" — people's national consciousness or nationalism, people's rights or democracy and people's livelihood or socialism (in other words "of the people, by the people, for the people"). These ideals had the broad support of progressive intellectuals, scholars and the new (and increasingly powerful) class of compradore merchants and industrialists in the treaty ports.

The reality was, however, that as the Qing dynasty went into its final years of decline, power fell back into the hands of provincial warlords. Within five years of the declaration of the Republic the warlords were battling among themselves, each trying to gain sufficient support to claim imperial power and perhaps even found a new dynasty as tradition allowed. In this the European powers were to perform a mischievous role, playing one warlord off against the other with offers of support and funds. Even the President of the Republic, Yuan Shikai (Yüan Shih-k'ai), was to use his position to pursue his own imperial aspirations in the north. Without the

Dr Sun Yat-sen in exile in Japan where he was supported in his revolutionary political efforts both by liberal Japanese and by the large number of Chinese students sent there to gain a western-style education in medicine, engineering or science.

imperial structure, it would seem that no amount of idealism could hold China together. This was a lesson not lost on later revolutionaries.

Despite this political chaos, the fragmentation of power did not prevent the introduction of some long overdue institutional reforms. By 1914 China had 17 modern banks, and chambers of commerce were set up to support local entrepreneurs. However, despite the 200,000 members throughout China, and the success of the international treaty port cities of Shanghai, Guangzhou and Nanjing, the modern industrial sector of the economy remained dominated by foreign capital and firms. Little of this capital was to spread to the great bulk of the population who remained in rural villages, increasingly impoverished and only marginally affected in their day-to-day life by the economic activities in the coastal cities. Although ideals of public education and land reform were basic planks in the republican agenda there was neither the political will nor the money to carry them out effectively. The failure of the efforts at modernization to reach the common people was to be a lasting dilemma for liberal reformers trying to introduce into China the sort of democratic institutions that they believed lay at the heart of western culture.

Profound changes were happening among the traditional educated elite. Instead of being put through the imperial examination en route for the bureaucracy, they now went to missionary schools and colleges in the hope of gaining access to an overseas university. As had occurred in Japan, earlier in the Meiji, Chinese students returning from abroad were now able to take influential positions in government and in the new universities.

For example, Cai Yuanpei (Ts'ai Yüan-p'ei), a traditional Confucian scholar who had studied philosophy in Germany and France, returned to become Minister for Education in the Sun Yat-sen government. In 1917 he became Chancellor of Beijing University, which he transformed from a "bureaucrat-ridden school that prepared officials to hold sinecures" into a radical center of learning.

The Dean of Letters was the journalist Chen Duxiu (Ch'en Tu-hsiu) who had also been a student in France and who was a passionate proponent of the ideals of the French Revolution — the ideals of "liberty, equality and fraternity." Like Fukuzawa in the 1870s, Chen founded a radical journal, *New Youth*. This provided a forum and a focus of identity for a whole new generation attempting to throw off the "mind-binding" character of the traditional Neo-Confucian ideas and values that had dominated China since the Ming dynasty. Chen exhorted his students to give up their passivity and concern with self-cultivation; to "be independent not servile, progressive not conservative, dynamic not passive, cosmopolitan not isolationist, scientific not merely imaginative"; to break the traditional notion that it was somehow demeaning for a scholar to be practical and get his hands dirty. Even physical fitness was promoted, perhaps as a consequence of the "healthy minds and bodies" policy of the missionary schools. (It should not be forgotten that one of the first articles written by Mao Zedong (Mao Tse-tung) was on the importance of physical fitness and strength.)

Chen's major ally at Beijing University was another young Confucian scholar Hu Shi. Hu had been sent to study at Cornell University in New York and had come under the influence of the philosopher and educationalist John Dewey. Hu Shi's relationship with him brought Dewey to Beijing for a lecture series, at about the same time that the British philosopher Bertrand Russell was also giving lectures there. While Dewey tried to convince an eager generation of Chinese students of the virtues of individualism and science, Russell was promoting socialism and a healthy distrust of western imperialism. All this was to provide enormous intellectual stimulus.

In an article in *New Youth*, Hu Shi denounced the classical Chinese that had served as the language of scholars and the imperial government for over two thousand years. He regarded it in much the same way that Reformation scholars regarded Latin, as "a dead language, which could not produce a living literature." What he campaigned for was a language capable of expressing the new values that had been discovered in the revolutionary social movements of the west and, above all, the concepts of modern science.

These frustrations were expressed in popular slogans "Down with Confucius and Sons. Long live Mr Science and Mr Democracy." However, while radical social and political reforms were being aired in the new intellectual forum of the universities and colleges, there was still little link between these erudite intellectuals and the large mass of impoverished and largely illiterate peasants and industrial workers. For many this was to change suddenly and quite remarkably on 4 May 1919.

At the Versailles conference following the Allied victory against Germany in 1918, the German concessions in Shandong were to be given to Japan, with the tacit approval of Yuan Shikai's warlord government in Beijing. (He had been prepared to trade Shandong for the promise of Japanese support for his imperial aspirations.) This betrayal on the part of the Allied Powers, which China had supported throughout the War, brought an immediate and unprecedented response.

Three thousand students from 13 institutions in Beijing assembled in Tiananmen Square to demonstrate. This was the first time such a demonstration had been seen in China. The movement was to spread like wildfire to other major cities such as Shanghai and Guangzhou. The students were soon joined by the workers from the newly formed labor unions, the press and even merchants. In Shanghai workers in some thirty factories went on strike. There was a call for a boycott of Japanese goods. The cabinet in Beijing resigned and the Chinese delegation at Versailles refused to sign the treaty. In some senses Chinese nationalism was to emerge from this final injustice. It was also to turn many students away from the seemingly impractical liberal and democratic ideals put forward by Sun Yat-sen, and those calling for gradual reform such as Hu Shi.

The 1917 Bolshevik revolution in Russia provided some hope for radical Chinese students: hope that the socialist ideal first espoused by Sun Yat-sen might be realized by a backward agricultural country like China and that the laws of human economic and political development, put forward by Hegel and Marx, might not be as absolute as was claimed. Lenin had obviously demonstrated that it was not necessary to go through the phase of fully developed capitalism before one could achieve the goal of socialism. Chen Duxiu, disillusioned by the failure of republican reforms to come to terms with the extraordinary inequalities within China or to provide a force that would give the country some unity of purpose, turned to the Russian example. His enthusiasm for the Russian revolution and its achievement was shared by another scholar from Beijing University, Li Dazhao (Li Ta-chao), who devoted an entire edition of *New Youth* to "The Victory of Bolshevism." One of Li Dazhao's assistants working in the library at the University was a young scholar from Hunan, Mao Zedong.

In September 1920 Chen and Li decided to form a Chinese communist party and in Shanghai in June the following year, with the support of the Soviet Union, the First Congress of the Chinese Communist Party was held with representatives from Beijing, Wuhan, Guangzhou and Jinan. Heading the delegation from Changsha was Li's library assistant, Mao Zedong.

For many who were to subsequently join the Party it was to offer an all-inclusive ideology and clear targets to blame for China's prolonged poverty and underdevelopment. The imperialist powers who exploited the venality of warlords, and the compradores who acted as their agents provided a focus for Chinese nationalism. Marxism-Leninism had the appearance of being scientific and progressive in its social values. It also offered perhaps that most basic and important requirement of traditional Chinese policy, an ideology that could provide an ethical system to fill the vacuum left by Confucianism and the empire. But this all-embracing ideology came at a price, that of intellectual freedom of which Hu Shi was to remind his more romantic colleagues:

> There is no liberation *in toto*, or reconstruction *in toto*. Liberation means liberation from this or that institution, from this or that belief, for this or that individual; it is liberation bit by bit, drop by drop.

However, it seems that time was running out for such subtleties. China was not only to be fragmented by foreign concessions and feuding warlords, but was now confronted with an ideological and civil war between the remnants of Sun Yat-sen's republican movement, the Kuomintang, and the communists; a battle for the hearts and minds of the Chinese people.

# *ZAIBATSU* AND THE ZERO-SUM GAME

*We are no longer ashamed to stand before the world as Japanese. . . . The name "Japanese," like the names Satsuma and Choshu after the Boshin War, like the name of the returned explorer Stanley and the name of Wellington after Waterloo, now signifies honor, glory, courage, triumph, and victory. Before, we did not know ourselves, and the world did not yet know us. But now that we have tested our strength, we know ourselves and we are known by the world. Moreover, we know we are known by the world.*

Tokutomi Soho, 1894

The "May 4" boycott of Japanese goods in China represented a watershed in the souring of relations between the two countries. In commercial terms it represented only a temporary setback. Japan had done well out of World War I. Not only had it gained German concessions in China, but also, while the Europeans had been busily disemboweling each other, Japanese manufacturing firms had gained access to many of the traditional European markets throughout east Asia.

The stimulus to industry that this provided brought fundamental changes to Japanese society. In 1880 Japan was a predominantly agrarian society with small-scale rural industries; by 1920, 50 per cent of the population lived in cities. Many were employed in the small workshops that had sprung up to supply components for the large corporations known as *zaibatsu* or "money cliques." These *zaibatsu* were set up along the lines developed by Shibusawa in the 1880s, with strong connections to government. They were organized around a central bank and trading company. The largest of these are still household names around the world — Mitsui, Mitsubishi, Sumitomo and Nissan.

The power of these massive companies was extensive, not only because of their wealth and the number of people dependent on them, but also because of their ability to influence political life, now centered on the Diet (the German parliamentary system that was introduced with the Prussian constitution in 1889). The capacity of these large firms to buy politicans became a national scandal by the 1920s and was the cause of a good deal of disillusionment with the government on the part of those liberals who believed that the European model of democratic government was the best means of catching up with the west. (Liberty in both China and Japan was never accepted as an end in itself. It was, for the most part, like other political ideas, adopted because of its promise to deliver a rich and powerful state.)

The *zaibatsu,* though large in terms of the diverse industries they controlled, contracted out a great deal of their work to small workshops with 10–100 employees. These small firms could not offer the job security or the conditions of employment enjoyed by the well-educated and highly skilled workers in the head offices. The workshops often provided seasonal work and employment for those unable to gain a living from agriculture. For example, in 1929, there were two million families engaged in silk production. For the large *zaibatsu* one of the great advantages of this system of contracting out work was that it was much easier for firms to expand, contract and readjust as the market demanded. This was to become evident in 1929 when the demand for Japanese goods virtually dried up, with disastrous consequences.

The Great Depression hit Japan more severely than it did any other industrialized country, with the possible exception of Germany. The large market for Japanese silk in the United States and Europe disappeared overnight, throwing as many as 10 million people out of work. The impact was not restricted to rural industries such as silk; the small workshops contracted by the *zaibatsu* had their contracts terminated and large numbers of semi-skilled workers were forced on to the streets.

The consequent resentment and despair led right-wing groups, particularly in the countryside, to direct their aggression against what they saw as a foreign conspiracy working in league with the old *zaibatsu* companies. From the point of view of those thrown out of work, the destruction of their livelihood was yet another example of foreign greed and malevolence. After all, the *zaibatsu* had, in large part, been set up as a means of gaining foreign technology. There had been close collaboration with foreign firms through licensing agreements for electrical firms such as Toshiba (linked to General Electric in the United States) and Nippon Electric (linked with Western Electric); in heavy engineering the pattern was the same.

This relationship with foreign companies led to the old *zaibatsu,* such as Mitsui, coming under political attack from the new ultra-nationalist forces. As in Germany and Italy in the 1930s, it was the disadvantaged rural communities in Japan who formed the political base for national socialist or fascist movements. They were supported by large sections of the military, which was made up of conscripts also from the countryside. They saw the westernized leaders of industry as traitors because they had corrupted the political institutions to support their own financial interests. By the late 1930s the balance of power in the Diet had begun to shift. The power once exerted by the large *zaibatsu* had begun to give way to the ultra-nationalists and the military. Central to this shift was Japan's expansion into Manchuria and its rise as an imperial power. The mass education system established by the Meiji government had now created a literate urban population, who were increasingly well informed about world events and acutely aware of Japan's disadvantaged position and unequal status as an imperial power.

The Japanese delegation to the Versailles peace conference argued for a clause on "racial equality" but this was rejected by the United States, Britain, Australia and Canada. The myth of the "yellow peril," fostered by hysterical journalism in the west, remained strong. So much so that in 1924 the United States Congress passed an Exclusion Act directed specifically at Asian immigrants. The Japanese, in particular, took this insult very much to heart and it helped to boost support for those among the military and the ultra-nationalists seeking to promote the policy of "Asia for the Asians."

In 1930 the London Naval Conference attempted to set artificial limitations on

Japan's construction of heavy cruisers. This so incensed nationalist sentiment that violent protests broke out and a fanatic shot the prime minister. A spate of assassinations followed with the head of Mitsui also being shot.

The sense that Japan was being relegated to second-class status by the western powers was acute. Japanese citizens were denied the right to emigrate to either Australia or the United States, the last regions with open lands. Japanese manufactured goods were also disadvantaged by European colonial control of the markets in Southeast Asia.

Increasingly boxed in, the Japanese military looked to Manchuria as the only avenue for expansion. Their position in the government had always been a powerful one, enshrined in fact in the Prussian-style constitution. They were also increasingly regarded as patriotic in a way that the leaders of industry and business were not.

Japan already held concessions in Manchuria, won from Russia in 1905, but in 1931 Japanese military officers staged a mock sabotage of the south Manchurian railway. On the pretext of defending their interests the Japanese army occupied Manchuria. By January 1932 the army had established the puppet state of Manchuko, with the last (Qing) Manchu Emperor of China, Pu Yi (P'u-i), as its official head.

In 1934 the support for the military in the Japanese government was such that they were able to take control of Manchurian affairs from the ministry of foreign affairs. The greater centralization of power and the deficit financing of military expansion in Manchuria provided an early solution to the Depression, as did Hitler's similar policies in Germany.

The army, however, was not equipped to engage directly in industrial development but they were openly mistrustful of the old *zaibatsu* such as Mitsui and Mitsubishi whom they saw as being dominated by "greedy capitalists," linked to corrupt politicians and committed to internationalism. The success of fascism in Italy and Germany gave them additional support.

To manage the industrial development of Manchuria the army used a number of the large trading companies. Nissan was encouraged to shift its operation to the new colonial territory with the new name of "Japan Industry Company." Like the British and Dutch East India Companies in the eighteenth century these new *zaibatsu* — the Japan Industry Company and the South Manchuria Railway Company — provided the organizational structure for managing the Manchurian economy.

Through these two companies the Japanese government began to build up the industrial infrastructure in Manchuria as a colonial showpiece; building railways, harbors, and opening mines and chemical plants. By 1938 the Japan Industry Company was the second largest corporation in Japan with 18 subsidiary companies specializing in mining, chemicals and electronics. Many of these subsidiaries were also engaged in armaments manufacture.

The economic benefits of Manchuria were to be more psychological and strategic than economic. In fact the Japanese poured more capital into their colonial territory than they ever got out of it. The benefit was essentially the economic stimulus created by the demand for manufactured goods, and military hardware and machinery.

However, Japan was faced with increasing isolation and prejudicial economic exclusion from markets in the rest of the world. This was partially in response to their takeover of Manchuria but also to prevent cheaper Japanese goods (textiles in particular) from competing on equal terms with European manufactured goods. The Depression called forth protective measures in every country and Japan was no different to others in erecting tariff barriers. Yet the destruction of the bonds of economic interdependence and the mutual necessity of international trade played into the hands of the military.

The Smoot-Hawley tariff established in the United States in 1931, and barriers restricting the import of Japanese goods into the Dutch colonial empire (now Indonesia) in 1933, were seen as hostile to Japan. The Ottawa conference of 1932 at which Britain, with the agreement of its colonial governments and dominions, inaugurated a new system of tariffs and imperial preference, was all part of an "economic offensive" to prevent Japanese goods undercutting British goods anywhere in the empire.

From this perspective it is perhaps understandable that the ultra-nationalists in the military should begin to propose not just "Asia for the Asians" but the concept of "the greater east Asian co-prosperity sphere" — in other words, an economic zone covering most of Asia and the Pacific in which Japan would play the dominant industrial role, with the rest of the region benefiting by being freed from European colonial domination. There were many nationalist movements in the smaller countries that saw the Japanese as a potentially liberating force; China, however, was not one of them.

The occupation of Manchuria was of profound concern to China, as was the possibility of further Japanese expansion. On 7 July 1937 fighting broke out between Japanese and Chinese troops near Beijing. Despite years of appeasement the Chinese government in the north was not prepared to accept the Japanese military commander's terms, which as usual were prejudicial to China.

The nationalist armies led by Chiang Kai-shek (Jiang Jieshi in modern transliteration), after decades of fighting an ideological and civil war with the communist guerilla forces led by Mao Zedong, were not going to accept further humiliation. On 14 August they bombed Japanese warships in Shanghai. Given the control that the army and navy had over the Japanese government, a decision was made to invade northern China, despite the opposition of the Japanese emperor who, by this stage, was no more than a symbol of patriotic fervor.

By late August the Japanese had occupied most of northern China and the treaty port cities along the southern coast. With appalling savagery and brutality, the southern capital of Nanjing on the Yangtze was taken. It was almost as if the centuries of racism on the part of the European powers had been internalized and turned, with sadistic hatred, against the Chinese. Thousands of men, women and children were senselessly massacred and a long, and ultimately disastrous, war with China had begun.

Despite Japanese hostility towards the west, commercial relations continued. The transfer of technology was as important as ever, especially with the demands of the

Despite Japanese hostility towards the west, commercial relations continued. The transfer of technology was as important as ever, especially with the demands of the military. Access to components for aircraft design and construction meant that the links between the major *zaibatsu* firms and those in the United States and Europe were even more crucial, although at times strained by the political climate. In March 1938 an Airplane Manufacturing Industry Law was passed by the Diet. A technical sub-committee with strong representation from the military licensed 15 companies. The two leading firms were Mitsubishi Heavy Industries and Nakajima Airplane Manufacturing Company. Top engineers from these firms had studied at Massachusetts Institute of Technology, Stanford University and California Institute of Technology, the leading engineering schools in the United States. Many production workers had been apprenticed to Douglas, Boeing and Lockheed, with licensing agreements having been established early in the 1930s.

The demands of the navy for an all-purpose fighter aircraft capable of being used from aircraft carriers presented the Mitsubishi engineers in Nagoya with the necessity of coming up with a totally new design. The Zero aircraft, which were to accompany the Japanese bombers to Pearl Harbor in 1941, were perhaps the best fighter aircraft in the sky. In dogfights in the Pacific war they could outmaneuver the best that others could put up against them. As the British discovered in Singapore months later, the assumption of the technological superiority of the west was no longer a foregone conclusion. In less than a hundred years Japan had been transformed from a small, isolated country on the periphery of China into an industrial power to be reckoned with. The extent of this transformation was not to be fully appreciated in the west for another thirty years.

United States Air Force

The artist Shari-arai's impression of Zero fighters on an aircraft carrier during the Pacific War. This was the first example of Japanese designed technology to have an impact on the west.

*Today's "Foolish Old Men" Create New Scenes* by Cheng Minsheng and Chang Lin, peasant artists from Hunsien country. The scrolls painted in the early 1970s depict the inspiring bounty and cornucopia that would be possible through collective effort.

# THE COLOR OF THE CAT

# THE DRAGONS AWAKE

*Black or white, if cats catch mice they are all right.*

Deng Xiaoping, 1962

*In the article "Devote every effort to running successfully a socialist research institute of science," "the arch-unrepentant capitalist roader in the party, Deng Xiaoping," should read simply, "Deng Xiaoping."*

Notice attached to *Scientia Sinica,* November 1976

During the decade 1966 – 76 China entered a phase of ideological and political conflict unprecedented in contemporary history. This "great proletarian cultural revolution" began as an effort to purify the Communist party of what Mao Zedong believed to be the corrupting influence of capitalist ideology.

In the long battle between the leftists, who supported Mao, and the more pragmatic or "scientific Marxists" Deng Xiaoping was to argue that it did not matter what color the cat was as long as it caught mice. In other words, the primary responsibility of social and economic institutions was that they work and the primary responsibility of the Party leadership was to improve the material and social well-being of ordinary people.

History has been kind to this small but amazingly resilient survivor of the Long March, and of the equally long and at times tortuous road, which the Chinese Communist party has followed since liberation in 1949. Over the past 10 years, Deng has deftly guided China from an isolation matched only by that of the Ming emperors, back into the international arena. He has also released economic forces within the country that could, in the next century, see China, like Japan, becoming a major economic power, and perhaps once again becoming a center of technological creativity and innovation. China, however, cannot be understood in isolation. What is happening there is related to the extraordinary re-emergence of east Asia, in particular Japan, as an economic and industrial powerhouse. To understand the reason for the rise of what some have described as the "Pan-Confucian" culture of the east, it is necessary to go back to 1945 and the end of the Pacific War.

The dropping of the atomic bombs on Hiroshima and Nagasaki, to American minds, brought the war in the Pacific to a close. It was the culmination of a massive conventional bombing campaign on Japanese cities, which, in reality, caused far more destruction than either of the two atomic bombs. The presence of Soviet forces in Manchuria, poised to occupy the northern islands in the Japanese archipelago, was probably as important a factor in Japan's capitulation. The Japanese already knew what had happened in Europe with the partitioning of Germany and saw a similar fate for their own country if the Soviet Union invaded the north and the United States took the south.

In 1945 Japan lay shattered after its defeat in World War II. The Mitsubishi steel works (shown here) was unrecognizable after the dropping of the atomic bomb on Nagasaki.

The occupation of Japan by the Allied Forces was to bring some immediate and obvious changes in the power structure. The objective of the United States State Department was to rebuild Japan as a model democracy. This was undertaken by a remarkable collection of idealists who surrounded General Douglas MacArthur, the United States Viceroy.

Many of these "missionaries for democracy" who surrounded him were brought up with the New Deal idealism of the Roosevelt era. They saw the causes of Japanese militarism as flowing from a conspiracy between big business and the military who, between them, were able to undermine the country's fledgling democratic institutions. To foster democracy they began to rebuild Japan in the image of their own ideals of what the United States should be. The new Japanese constitution was written by these men.

One of their early acts was to break up the *zaibatsu,* which supported Japan's military government. In late 1946 officials, on orders from MacArthur, raided the head offices of Mitsui and Mitsubishi, and confiscated all documents and stocks. The family control of these massive combines was broken up, along the lines of the "trust-busting" that had occurred in the United States in the 1920s and 1930s.

The numerous subsidiaries were separated from the central trading company, becoming independent enterprises with new and younger men brought in to head them. Three hundred *zaibatsu* firms were earmarked but the program proved difficult to implement and was never completed.

The next step in the process of reform was to re-establish trade unions, which had been illegal in Japan since the 1930s. These were set up along western lines and became a powerful force for political resistance to the reintroduction of the traditional power elite. By 1949, 6.5 million workers had joined unions. In the late 1940s and early 1950s Japan was rocked by a series of strikes and occupations of factories. It was in this environment of industrial confrontation that new approaches to management began to be worked out. The behavior of the trade union movement had become so demanding that MacArthur, ironically, had to intervene to break up strikes, which were banned in the public sector. Many "leftists" were also purged as the cold-war politics that dominated the thinking of the State Department led to the great fear that Japan might turn to communism.

Perhaps the most important role that the United States was to take — almost equivalent to the Marshall Plan that helped to rebuild Europe — was to allow the Japanese easy access to American technology on favorable terms. This was not done out of altruism but as a consequence of the victory of the communist forces of Mao Zedong in China against the Nationalists of Chiang Kai-shek backed by the United States. The fear was that, if Japan was not supported, all of Asia might fall to communism. The "yellow peril" had now been replaced by the "red peril." With the intervention of the United States and her allies, Britain and Australia, in Korea in 1950, Japan was soon to become a production base for military equipment and

Courtesy Film Australia

General Douglas MacArthur leaving his office in Tokyo. As head of the allied occupation forces he attempted to reshape Japanese society into a model of capitalist democracy.

supplies. Within a few years of promulgating constitutional rules to prevent Japan from rearming, the Japanese were churning out trucks, jeeps and armaments under license for the United States government. Large amounts of capital in the form of government loans and contracts flowed into the country and were to play a major part in the rebuilding of the Japanese economy. Nonetheless, throughout the 1940s and 1950s, Japan was poor and under profound economic restrictions.

One of the key institutions in the rebuilding and restructuring of Japanese industry at this time was the Ministry of International Trade and Industry (MITI). This was in fact the reconstituted wartime ministry of munitions, which had been responsible for military contracts and for accessing foreign military technology for the army and navy. Its new role was to vet the licensing arrangements between Japanese companies and foreign firms for new technology. MITI could provide or withhold precious foreign exchange and was therefore able to define the industrial priorities of Japan's domestic and export industries. One of MITI's most important functions was to plan the introduction of new industries and, even more importantly, the phasing out of old or uncompetitive ones. This was demonstrated in the way MITI helped to establish the iron and steel industry in the immediate postwar period, then phased it out gradually to replace it with high-value industries such as consumer goods, electronics, and pharmaceuticals. The early recognition that Japan must export to survive meant that restrictive licensing agreements (common elsewhere in the world) were not entered into. The licenses taken up were for technology and products that Japan could realistically produce for the international market. Therefore, very early in the postwar reconstruction, Japanese firms were looking for overseas markets and sales to make their industries viable.

Japan was too poor, too small and had too many people to be able to withdraw into its own economic and cultural boundaries to lick its wounds as China was capable of doing after 1949. However, Japan had one great advantage in the young and well-trained body of engineers and scientists who emerged from World War II with a good understanding of the processes of industrial production and innovation. Between 1955 and 1961 the Japan Productivity Center sent 2,500 business people, engineers and researchers to the United States to investigate advanced technology and its possible application in Japanese industry.

# SONY AND THE TRANSISTOR

In 1948 a remarkable breakthrough in electronics was announced by three researchers at Western Electric's Bell Laboratories in New Jersey. Shockley, Bardeen and Brattain had made the first transistor. The potential of this tiny conductor to eliminate the cumbersome valves of the past was obvious to electronics engineers around the world.

In Japan the news was greeted by physicists and electronics engineers with equal enthusiasm, but few believed that they were in any position to profit from this discovery. However, Ibuka Masaru and Morita Akio, two war-time electronics engineers who had formed the company Totsuko — the Tokyo Telecommunications Engineering Corporation — were prepared to act. Ibuka and Morita had already designed and built Japan's first tape recorder, which was, by 1950, being widely used in broadcasting by NHK. They were so impressed by the reports of the American breakthrough that Ibuka flew to the United States in 1952 in an attempt to get a licensing agreement from Western Electric to produce transistors in Japan. To his amazement, senior executives agreed to give Totsuko the Japanese license for $25,000

Then Ibuka and Morita had to convince the bureaucrats at the Ministry of International Trade and Industry that the transistor was a useful and desirable product on which to spend valuable foreign exchange. At the meeting their proposal was greeted coolly, and it was only after considerable lobbying that they were given access to the foreign exchange needed to enter into the agreement. At the final meeting with Western Electric, the executives handling the contract offered the advice that the best possible use for the transistor would be in the manufacture of hearing aids.

Two years later, under the now international brand name of Sony, Totsuko was to produce Japan's first fully transistorized radio. By 1960 it had manufactured the world's first transistorized television and was fast becoming one of the most innovative electronics companies in the world, with huge sales in the United States and Europe. Sony transistors were to enable other Japanese electronics firms to enter the consumer-electronics field where, by the 1970s, Japan was an international force to be reckoned with.

# PERMANENT REVOLUTION

*Historical experience has proved that only by first creating revolutionary public opinion and seizing political power, and then changing the relations of production is it possible to greatly develop the productive forces.*

Mao Zedong

W hile the United States was placing its cultural and political stamp on Japan in the late 1940s, the Soviet Union had again occupied much of Manchuria. Here they came across industrial plant and equipment of considerable value, which, as traditional spoils of war, were shipped home to help in the postwar reconstruction of the Soviet Union. Meanwhile they were offering support to the Chinese "red army" in its war against the Nationalists. In an extremely short time, following World War II, the cold-war politics of the superpowers was to draw every country into its bipolar antagonisms.

The victory of Mao Zedong's army in October 1949 and the declaration of the People's Republic of China was to bring about a profound reorientation of Chinese culture and institutions. China's education and industrial structure had been modeled on those of the United States and Europe. Now the new Chinese leadership turned to the Soviet Union not only for aid to rebuild and reform its tortured economy, but as a model of how to build a socialist culture and economy.

Library of Congress, Washington D.C.

In 1946 Soviet troops, once again in control of Manchuria, dismantled Japanese industrial plant and equipment for shipment back to the Soviet Union.

Mao Zedong and the People's Liberation Army entered Beijing in January 1949. In October of that year, Mao announced the formal establishment of the People's Republic of China.

In 1950 Mao Zedong flew to Moscow to meet Stalin. After pledging fraternal loyalty as communist states and after making the appropriate obeisance to Marx and Lenin, they got down to the business of Mao's mission. China needed capital and assistance in its "socialist reconstruction." Capital was not easy to come by, after all the Soviet Union was itself still in the process of rebuilding its war-ravaged economy. Mao succeeded in extracting a loan of $300 million from Stalin but, perhaps more significant, the offer of Soviet personnel — engineers and specialists — who would help construct 50 major projects essential for the building of China's industrial base. Within a year literally thousands of Soviet technicians, scientists and economic planners, with all the enthusiasm of nineteenth century missionaries carrying forward the gospel of Marxism-Leninism, were being shipped off to China. Soviet technicians were to be found working on bridge, dam and factory constructions from Manchuria to Sichuan. By 1952 the number of industrial projects using Soviet technology and technicians had grown from 50 to 141. By 1955 there were around ten thousand Soviet advisers and technicians working in China. They brought with them 63 machine-tool plants, 24 electrical power plants and three large iron and steel plants. By 1957, 50 per cent of all Soviet exports to China was industrial machinery and equipment.

The traffic was not only one way. While Soviet advisers were arriving to help the Chinese to restructure their education system along Soviet lines, 37,000 undergraduates, graduates and technicians were sent to the Soviet Union for education and training. This was one of the largest transfers of technology and personnel ever seen. The educational problems facing the new Chinese government were enormous. In 1949, because of decades of war, 90 per cent of the population was illiterate; by 1956 this had dropped to 78 per cent. Compared with the Japanese, labor skills available to the Chinese were limited. The priority was to raise the educational level as rapidly as possible with the widespread establishment of schools and universities on the Soviet model.

In 1950 Mao Zedong met Soviet leaders, Stalin and Bulganin, to request assistance with China's "socialist reconstruction."

For many of China's leading scholars, scientists and engineers this reorientation of education and academic life was to present real problems. They were confronted with a new, harsh ideological environment. Under Stalin, for example, classical genetics had been categorized as a pseudo-science and was not taught. The reasons for this lay in the deeply held assumption among the ideological commissars in the Kremlin, that human nature and behavior were the product of political and economic circumstances. The idea came from Lenin's response to the Marxist notion that culture was an outcome or by-product of economic structures. Change the economic relationships between people and you would automatically change their world view and behavior. Lenin's "reflection theory" was accepted as the basis of Soviet psychology — the mind was simply a reflection of the objective reality of the political and economic institutions in which the individual was brought up — and the emphasis of the socialist revolution was therefore on changing social relations and creating "new people." According to this argument, society could not be changed simply by changing mental outlook as religious groups and idealists believed.

In the late 1930s an agricultural technician, Lysenko, took these same ideas and applied them to plant breeding. His assumption was that if you changed the plants' physical environment it would be possible to permanently change the characteristics of the plants themselves in one or two generations. Traditional genetics held that such changes were superficial and that effective crossbreeding had to be done over a long period of time.

In the desperate economic circumstances of the war-torn Soviet Union any ideas that promised a rapid increase in agricultural yields were greeted by the leadership with jubilation, especially if they conformed to current ideological thinking. Stalin placed his support behind Lysenko who rose rapidly in the ranks of researchers and was made head of an agricultural research institute. However, his findings were dismissed as nonsense by the great Soviet geneticist Vavilov. The ensuing scientific controversy was resolved with Vavilov being sent off to one of Stalin's labor camps, where he died, and classical genetics being defined as bourgeois and reactionary. Plant breeding and biology in the Soviet Union declined in direct relationship to the rise of Lysenkoism and his "revolutionary" biological ideas.

In the early 1950s the Soviet advisers restructuring Chinese science and education brought this dogma with them and, as a result, affected the work and lives of a number of Chinese academics, among them, the plant physiologist, Professor Cao Zongxun, from Beijing University and the geneticist, Tan Jiazhan, from Fudan University who were both trained in the United States. They had worked with the leading western researchers in what was to be a crucial field for China — the development of new grain and plant varieties that could, potentially, lift the levels of agricultural production. Both scientists were extremely patriotic and, although they could have stayed on in the United States in academic posts, both decided to return to China after 1949 to help rebuild the country. On their return to China they were forced to learn Russian and to teach from Soviet textbooks. As Professor Cao, one of the few women in prewar China to have gained a scientific education, noted:

I had to pretend to accept it. One had to make oneself simple minded and not think about other possibilities. . . . I had to learn how to criticize all the American and European principles. . . . I had to abandon my English for a long time.

A new intellectual strait jacket was to be placed on Chinese scholars, as "mind bending" as the earlier Confucian tradition that Hu Shi's generation had tried to throw off. However, even at the level of the less advantaged — the rural peasantry — a basic problem was to arise that was to set Chinese and Soviet planners and advisers on a collision course.

The basic assumption of the Soviet-style development masterminded by Lenin and Stalin was that highly centralized planning was needed and that the priority had to be the building up of heavy industry — iron and steel works, and electricity grids to cover the whole country — before turning attention to agricultural development. To pay for this, not only had agriculture to be neglected, but revenue from the land had to be used to support the development of city industry. For Mao this represented a basic problem — a betrayal. The Chinese red army had been built on the commitment and blood of peasants, in contrast to the city-based industrial proletariat that had supported the Russian revolution in 1918. Mao himself was the son of a rich peasant. He had not studied abroad, unlike most of the other leading cadres in the Chinese Communist party, such as Zhou Enlai and Deng Xiaoping who had both studied in Paris. Mao's roots lay deep in the Chinese countryside.

By the time Stalin died in 1953 Mao had grown disenchanted with both the policies and ideological leadership provided by Moscow. The attempt to apply Soviet

Courtesy Film Australia

Professor Cao Zongxun, one of China's leading biologists, was one of the few women to gain a scientific education in the 1930s. She studied and taught in the United States during the 1940s, then, like many patriotic Chinese, returned to China in the 1950s to help rebuild her country. During the cultural revolution she was sent, like many leading scientists, to the countryside for re-education.

solutions to Chinese problems was perhaps as vain an endeavor as the earlier efforts to introduce European liberalism in China in the 1920s.

Mao was concerned that China should follow a course that would allow development of both sectors at once — what he called "walking on two legs." One "leg" being the commitment to heavy industry and the other pursuing rural development. Perhaps the central importance of agriculture in Chinese culture played a part. The maintenance and improvement of the water control systems could not have been ignored by Mao any more than it could be by the emperors of the past. Stalin could ignore the needs of his peasants; Mao could not. The disproportionate attention given to industry in China's first five-year plan was reflected in the statistics — industrial production grew at a rate of 18 per cent a year compared with 4.5 per cent for agricultural production.

By 1957 the relationship between China and the Soviet Union had passed from the honeymoon to the divorce court, as it were, without there ever having been a marriage. Mao and Kruschev could not get on and in late 1956, when Moscow called on China to repay its loans and the interest bill on the massive amounts of heavy industrial technology, relations rapidly deteriorated. By 1960 many of the engineers and technical advisers sent from Moscow began to leave, taking their blueprints and plans with them. China was left with half-constructed factories, half-trained personnel and partially built bridges, such as the massive structure spanning the Yangtze River at Nanjing, which the Chinese were to complete themselves without plans.

The Sino-Soviet split was also to encourage Mao and the other leaders to return to the spirit of self-reliance they had gained in Yan'an (Yennan) during the long guerilla war with both the Japanese and the Nationalist forces. Mao accepted the Soviet withdrawal as an opportunity to reassert the revolutionary ideals and commitment that had given the Chinese communists their victory — the spirit of the Long March.

In 1957 the "great leap forward" was announced. This was to be a mass movement drawing on the revolutionary achievements of the Chinese people themselves, not on foreign advisers. Its aim was to keep alive at the local level the initiative of the revolution; this was later to be described by Mao as continual revolution. It was also a reaction to the emergence of the bureaucratic structures established under Soviet influence — structures that no doubt seemed to allow the old Confucian scholar-bureaucrats to re-emerge in the guise of party cadres or administrative officials.

The slogan of the "great leap forward" was "industrialize every corner of the country," and the party faithful in each region took the command quite literally. Labor was diverted from agriculture to small open iron and coal mines; backyard or village iron production was undertaken, often using traditional methods that had died out in most of China 50 years earlier.

The enthusiasm took China by storm. Mao's hope of extending to the countryside the benefits of industrial growth seemed to be working. By the end of 1958, 100,000 coal pits were in operation, engaging the labor of some twenty million peasants. According to official figures coal production rose from 7.5 million tons in 1957 to more than 50 million tons in 1958. The only problem to cast a cloud over this remarkable achievement was the report by some officials that the quality of the coal and iron being produced was so low that it was almost completely useless. However, this did not dampen the enthusiasm. The local officials who were now given control of regional planning were able to command labor to achieve public works on a scale not seen in China since the days of Li Bing and the building of his great water control system.

Mao had demonstrated, he believed, that it was possible to motivate people by social ideals and to inspire them to work for the common collective good, once the barriers of the social and economic oppression of the past had been removed. These were the same ideals that had been expressed in Russia in 1919 and by the eighteenth century French revolutionaries. He had seen examples of these ideals at work in the red army during the war with the Nationalists, and afterwards when the revolution was carried into the Chinese countryside.

Using the language of a military campaign Mao exhorted the masses. In some areas extraordinary things were achieved, for example, in the campaign against schistosomiasis, a disease that was endemic in China. It was discovered that tiny snails, which accumulate in the waterways and canals of the southern provinces, were the carriers, and a campaign was then mounted to get rid of the snails. Hundreds of thousands of peasants combed the canal banks and the waterways collecting snails; analogous to the ancient tradition of corvée labor, directed to carry out public works by imperial bureaucrats, which had constructed the basic network of canals in the first place. Now there was something different at work, a form of idealism and participation in the building of a new China — there was nationalism.

In many areas the campaign worked. The snail population virtually disappeared and the disease went with it. Encouraged by such success a new campaign was planned to improve other areas of public health by the same methods. In 1958 the country was mobilized against the "four pests" — sparrows, mice, mosquitos and fleas. These campaigns were systematically organized by party officials at the local level, after receiving directives from the Central Committee. A Soviet scientist, Mikhail Klochko, working in China at the time, described what happened:

> On Sunday, 20 April, I was awakened in the early morning by a woman's bloodcurdling screams. Rushing to my window I saw that a young woman was running to and fro on the roof of the building next door, frantically waving a bamboo pole with a large sheet tied to it. Suddenly, the woman stopped shouting, apparently to catch her breath. . . . I realized that in all the upper stories of the hotel, white-clad females were waving sheets and towels that were supposed to keep the sparrows from alighting on the building. This was the opening of the anti-sparrow campaign.

All over China people took to the streets, banging gongs, firing guns and generally making an enormous racket. The effect was to frighten the sparrows from their nests in buildings and to keep them in the air until they collapsed exhausted on the ground (sparrows can only stay in the air for three or four hours) and were then collected.

The campaign, however, had unforeseen consequences. With the sparrows gone,

Revolutionary idealism and selfless enthusiasm for the Party's campaigns were promoted. Working collectively, some remarkable results were achieved. Commune members rebuilt landscapes, turning previously useless areas into highly productive land. Above all, there was a sense of being freed from the fatalism and powerlessness that had dominated the lives of Chinese peasants for centuries.

Against conservative advice, Mao pushed ahead in 1958 with the full collectivization of agriculture and the creation of 26,000 vast communes responsible for 98 per cent of agricultural production.

insect numbers increased in plague-like proportions and devastated the crops. The Chinese were then forced to revert to insecticides like DDT to control the insects. In turn the insecticides got into the water of canals and rivers and poisoned the fish. Ecological campaigns were clearly not as simple as military ones.

*    *    *

Land reforms introduced by 1950 had redistributed almost 120 million acres of agricultural land among 300 million poor peasants. The old landlord class had either been killed or driven from the land. Agricultural production had begun to rise but there was still rationing of grain in 1957. Mao, against the advice of his former Soviet economic planner, forged ahead with the collectivization of agriculture. By 1957 agricultural production was organized in socialist collectives of around 800,000 co-operative farms. Each farm had around a hundred families or 700 people. Buoyed by the extremely high production levels achieved by these collectives, and by the 600,000 backyard furnaces that had sprung up throughout the countryside, Mao announced the formation of even larger collectives — the people's communes. By November 1958 the co-operative farms had been amalgamated into 26,000 vast

# "LET A HUNDRED FLOWERS BLOOM"

In the euphoric period following the Sino-Soviet split, Mao and the Party received continual requests for greater freedom from leading intellectuals and scientists, who felt unduly fettered by the ideological limits that came with the adoption of the Soviet models in education and research. Many, educated in the United States and Europe, argued that only with the free airing of criticism would it be possible for the Party and the country to achieve rapid economic and cultural development. In 1957 Mao declared in a speech that "a hundred flowers should bloom and a hundred schools of thought contend." This was taken by many intellectuals and writers to mean that they were free to criticize the Communist party and its policies. With the tacit encouragement of the Party many came forward.

One of the most important critics was the economist and demographer, Ma Yinchu, from Beijing University. In an attempt to get some long-term perspective on China's economy, Ma had been looking at the relationship between population growth and the possible increase in the yields from agriculture and outputs from industry. At the time, China's population had reached some 700 million people. According to Ma's estimates, China had to take action immediately to curb population growth if it was to achieve its goal of a steadily rising standard of living.

To the alarm of the Party, the criticism of its policies unleashed by Mao's "hundred flowers" speech went, like the production figures, far beyond their expectations. But the criticism cut too close to the bone, challenging many of the basic tenets of Marxism-Leninism. In a sudden reversal of policy the Party bureaucrats organized a savage anti-rightist campaign to counter the assault. Across the country those who had had the temerity to come forward with criticism of the party's policies were declared "rightists" and "anti-revolutionaries." Thousands of intellectuals and workers lost their jobs.

Among them was Ma Yinchu who was savagely attacked as a Malthusian and a reactionary because he did not believe that the new socialist system would be capable of transcending the productive capacities and contradictions of capitalism. Ma was hounded from the University, and China had to wait for another twenty years before the Party would accept the reality of the problem. By then China's population had grown to one billion.

communes of around 25,000 people and representing 98 per cent of farm production.

The commune system was to prove extremely effective in the introduction of new agricultural technology and methods of production. With limited capital resources, the communes provided the means for shared access to tractors, gasoline-driven pumps, electricity and new chemical fertilizers. In economic terms the communes allowed for an enormous increase in productivity and the standard of living of rural communities. The scale of this achievement was incredible — one estimate of the labor-intensive construction carried out on the communes between 1957 and 1960 suggests it was equivalent to the building of 960 Suez Canals.

Party enthusiasm for the ideals and achievements of "the great leap forward" were intoxicating in 1958. There was a sense that anything could be achieved with enough commitment on the part of the Party and by mobilizing the energy and revolutionary zeal of the masses — the liberated energies of previously repressed peasants and workers. Throughout 1958 reports were coming into the Party's Central Committee of record production figures. In July the government announced that miracle targets had been reached and by September it was reported that grain production had doubled and that it was possible to abandon grain rationing. Industrial production had exceeded 1956 figures by 65 per cent. With the conviction that food production was under control, efforts at local industrialization were stepped up. Millions of peasants left the countryside for local towns to participate in the industrial boom. Crops were not being planted in some areas, and in others there was insufficient labor to harvest what had been sown.

By early 1959 alarm bells had begun to ring in Party headquarters in Beijing. It was becoming clear that the figures for grain production on the part of over-enthusiastic Party bureaucrats had been grossly overestimated. Over a quarter of the steel being produced in the local backyard furnaces (3 million of the 11 million tons produced in 1958) was unfit for industrial use. Worst of all, as the harsh winter of 1960 approached, grain stocks were found to be far lower than imagined. Suddenly, with the unusually bad climatic conditions in 1960 – 61, many areas of the country were hit with famine, unseen since well before liberation. It has been estimated that around ten million people died as a consequence. Mao, aware of the chaos brought to the country's economy by his policies, retired to a back seat and left the running of the economy to men of a more pragmatic disposition — Liu Shaoqi, Zhou Enlai and Deng Xiaoping.

# MADE IN JAPAN

*The nail that sticks up is nailed down.*

Japanese proverb

*In a Confucian society, each individual must strive to demonstrate his loyalty to the society to which he belongs. The extent of his loyalty is measured in terms of the degree to which he is prepared to sacrifice himself. . . . In this sort of society the freedom of the individual is often regarded as treachery or a challenge to society or to the majority, and anyone who dares to assert his freedom will probably become completely isolated.*

Morishima, 1982

As China gradually hauled its economy back on to a more even keel during the early 1960s, Japan was also beginning to step out of the shadow of its wartime ignominy and was beginning to challenge the assumption that "made in Japan" was synonymous with all that was cheap and trashy. This attitude was typified in a scene in the Hollywood movie *The Princess and the Pirate* made in the late 1950s where Bob Hope draws a pistol and tries to shoot at an oncoming troop of pirates. The pistol fails to fire, he tries again and again and then gives up, turns to the camera and with a shrug says, "Made in Japan!" This film was made at a time when increasingly large numbers of people around the world were discovering that Nikon cameras, Kawasaki and Honda motor bikes, and Seiko watches were not only cheaper than any of those produced locally but also better. Myths and stereotypes die slowly, not only those held about other cultures but those one holds about oneself. In this the complacency of the west and, in particular, the United States was pervasive and myopic. One of the technological myths in the postwar United States was that "either you did things the American way or it did not work."

Another pervasive myth at this time concerned the relation of government to the economy. While American advisers in Japan in the late 1940s were promoting the abolition of *zaibatsu* and the need to limit the power of big business, back home Eisenhower was railing against the growing power of the military-industrial complex, a nexus of interests similar to that of the old Japanese *zaibatsu*. This conspiracy of interests between the government, big business and politicians arose from World War II when very large contracts to supply military equipment were being tendered. Because of the importance of these defense contracts in providing employment, and in fostering industry and development in whatever region they were placed, politicians lobbied in conjunction with local firms to get the orders. It was encouraged by liberals as a form of Keynesian economics. John Maynard Keynes, in the 1930s, had first put forward the principle of government spending as a means of pulling western economies out of the Depression. Administrations wanting to win support could promise to give contracts to firms who would locate themselves in economically depressed regions.

During wartime this made sense. However, the process did not stop after 1945. In fact it increased with the cold war and the arms race to a degree where, even in the view of conservatives, the tail of military expenditure was beginning to wag the political dog. The demands of the military for a larger and larger slice of government expenditure were supported by the wide range of industries that had grown fat on these lucrative contracts. They, in turn, were capable of putting enormous pressure on politicians to vote for increased military budgets and to bargain for greater expenditure going to their state.

The problem with these political deals was that the normal checks and balances of the market were not able to work. Overpricing, inefficiency and waste were accepted and absorbed by the government. This at a time when the United States was presenting itself to the world as the embodiment of free-market capitalism. With their increasing military involvement throughout the world, in the belief that they were saving it from communism, the United States was falling into the trap that Great Britain and other once-powerful military powers had fallen into. In reality, the

The ENIAC was a useful recruitment device for the United States Army. However, the application of computer-controlled manufacture in the United States was relatively slow except in the machine-tools industry, where it was adopted by larger companies for military production. There was considerable opposition from labor unions who saw increased automation as a threat to the jobs of skilled machinists.

government and bureaucratic mechanisms fostered by ever-growing military expenditure were cutting across the free market as effectively as in many socialist countries. This was to have significant consequences for the United States economy and the industrial competitiveness that had made it the world leader in the 1920s.

Take, for example, the development and use of computer-controlled technology or what is more commonly called robotics, the key industrial technology of the late twentieth century. This technology was developed, as was the first electronic computer — the ENIAC — under military sponsorship. This computer was built during World War II and was used by the mathematician Von Neumann to carry out the calculations essential for the completion of the Manhattan Project, which built the atomic bombs that flattened Hiroshima and Nagasaki. Without this computer, it has been argued, the atomic bombs could not have been dropped before the Japanese capitulation. Ironically, the Japanese were to return the favor by taking this technology and using it to undermine the industrial lead of the United States.

The application of numerical data on punched cards to control the complex movements of machines was first realized by the clock and mechanical doll makers of France in the eighteenth century, and taken up by Jacquard later in the century. The next step in developing the computer to the control of industrial processes was in making the machine tools used in aircraft production. This was carried out by researchers at Massachusetts Institute of Technology in the early 1950s, with support from the Pentagon.

The goal from the military point of view was to get greater standardization and therefore a more reliable product. Once developed, the cost of adopting this new computer-controlled technology was enormous and often uneconomic compared with other alternatives. However, a condition of gaining lucrative military contracts was the use of this technology. The contracts therefore went to larger firms that could afford the massive capital investment and they, in turn, passed the increased cost of production back to the military. Many smaller firms in the machine-tools industry went out of business and, with less competition, prices rose rapidly.

A second factor that affected the spread of this revolutionary technology to other industries in the United States was the nature of industrial relations. Labor unions saw the increased automation of factories as a strategy to wrest control of the factory floor from skilled machinists. In the paranoid atmosphere of the McCarthy era, alleged "communist conspirators" were to be found among the working class. Labor unions, and organizations of industrial workers generally, were regarded as hotbeds of socialism. Class antagonism, which had governed industrial relations in both Europe and the United States since the nineteenth century, with labor treated as just a factor of production, meant that those firms that did invest in the new technology saw the advantages of the automated factory as a means of weakening the power of labor or at least their capacity for industrial disruption. Where military production was concerned this was an important consideration, and was promoted as a benefit of computer-controlled systems.

The attitude of workers in other industries where robotic technology could have been introduced was often hostile and unco-operative. Companies looking at introducing the new technology were confronted with a double bind: first, the cost of the technology was very high because military contracts had inflated its price and, second, industrial relations made their introduction difficult. There was a third factor — things were going very well in the United States and the need for change and innovation was not as obvious as it now appears in hindsight.

In Japan, where class-based industrial relations were not a dominant characteristic, the problem of introducing new technology hardly existed. Because of the commitment of the large firms to their staff — offering them lifetime employment and retraining as opposed to making them redundant when new technology was introduced — there were few industrial problems associated with the introduction of robotics. Instead of being displaced, skilled workers were taught computer-related skills and were expected to participate in the effective introduction of the new technology. These workers were also extremely important in making the new systems more productive since their commitment was to the firm rather than to a specific job or craft skill.

Throughout the 1960s and 1970s the effectiveness of the Japanese production system was to make them more and more competitive with firms in the United States. In 1979 when computer-controlled technology had been available for 20 years, only 2 per cent of American firms had taken it up. At this time Japan was producing 14,000 of these new computer-controlled machining centers a year compared with less than half that number in the United States. Firms like Fujitsu Fanuc in Japan, which had first produced robotic machines under license for General Motors in the United States, were now the world leaders. By 1981 Japan was supplying 40 per cent of the computer-controlled machining centers used by industries in the United States.

The consequence of this for other Japanese industries was to become increasingly obvious. Japanese firms were able to produce basic consumer goods — automobiles, electronic goods and other mass-produced commodities — that were cheaper and better than those produced in the United States and most European countries.

By the late 1960s, as the Japanese began to make inroads into traditional American markets in a whole range of consumer goods the American business and academic elites were still making the same old observation that the Japanese were not creative but were just imitators. This is, ironically, exactly what the Europeans, particularly the British in the late nineteenth century, had said about the Americans as they captured their markets using European technology but applying new methods of production.

In 1977 the number of American patents taken out in Japan made up more than 43 per cent of the total; this had dropped to 41 per cent by 1979. Conversely, in the same period, Japanese patents in the United States rose from 25 per cent to 28 per cent, making Japan the largest foreign source of patents. While OECD countries declined in overall patent rates during the latter part of the 1970s, Japan increased its level of technological innovation to the extent that, between 1977 and 1980, Japanese technological imports increased by only 3 per cent while exports increased by 42 per cent. This increase was particularly marked in fields such as precision instruments,

Survey Japan

"Motoman," Yaskawa's welding robot comes off the production line.

micro-electronics and robotics.

The myopic inability to recognize the importance of continued innovation in industrial processes as well as in the creation of new products left the United States as vulnerable as Great Britain had been fifty years earlier. While the Europeans and Americans would continue to come up with the technological and scientific knowledge from which individual reputations, fame, and Nobel prizes were to be gained, the stress in Japan was on improving the productive efficiency of firms.

For their success the Japanese owed a great deal to an American authority on quality control, Edwards Deming. Deming was a statistician and one of the postwar specialists sent to Japan to help improve the functioning of its census bureau. His major obsession was, however, with quality control. For the Japanese, losing the War had made it necessary to rethink and rebuild. The lack of certainty meant that they were prepared to look for new ways to improve their economic competitiveness and their share of world markets. It was in fact an area where Japan could not only gain immediate benefit but also redeem wounded national pride.

Deming had made a study of quality control and was profoundly disillusioned with what he found at home in the United States. The postwar boom had bred an acceptance of waste and an arrogant disregard for the quality of products, which affronted his common sense and set him at loggerheads with the prevailing assumptions.

Deming's ideas grew out of the work of the physicist, Walter Shewhart, from Bell Laboratories who had pioneered the use of statistical methods to improve quality in industrial products and processes. During World War II his ideas were taken up by the department of defense. But in the postwar boom such concerns seemed less important.

The Japanese, on the other hand, in attempting to rebuild their shattered wartime industries, were looking for the secret of American success; a success that had defeated them both on the battlefield and in the quality of their military technology.

Deming's ideas were basic. Senior engineers had to be on the shop floor and integrally involved with the production process. From the managing director down there had to be a commitment to quality and to the improvement of the production process. In the postwar antagonism between labor and capital in the United States, with automation being seen largely as a means of displacing shop-floor workers, commitment to improving the quality of goods was hard to achieve. When the Americans left Japan in the early 1950s their trade-based union system was replaced with a company-based system — one that was more congenial to the Japanese clannish approach to enterprise.

In this environment, the influence of Deming was to be profound. His first major lecture on the subject of quality control in 1950 was organized by Ichiro Ichikawa who had not only been a professor of engineering but was the head of Keidanren, the most powerful business organization in Japan.

Deming was amazed by the Japanese response; at home he had been largely ignored. In the ruthlessly competitive economic market that the Americans had

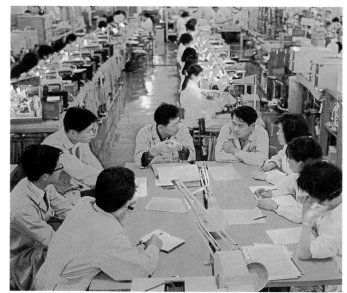

Quality control, one of the keys to Japan's industrial success, was promoted by an American, Edward Deming, in the 1950s. The commitment to quality, from the manager of the company down to the manual worker, allowed the Japanese to dispel the notion that Japanese goods were shoddy. At Nissan and NEC, quality-control circles became an essential feature of production throughout the 1960s and 1970s.

Paul Fusco/Magnum/John Hillelson Agency

241

fostered in postwar Japan, the younger managers were looking for the means to capture the local market and to free Japanese goods from their reputation for being shoddy. Deming provided these means.

Deming's ideas worked; a wire company executive announced a 30 per cent increase in production within months of applying Deming's methods. Other firms reported similar success. Soon an annual Deming Prize was announced for the firm that achieved the greatest improvement in quality control, and Deming was to be turned into something of an industrial guru in Japan where his books were widely studied and applied. In the west, his message largely fell on deaf ears — everything seemed to be going too well so why bother.

The reason for the success of quality control in Japan was that it complemented the Japanese ability to work together in teams. Having a culture that emphasized conformity, as opposed to the individualism of the west, was an unexpected advantage. The family orientation of their Confucian past worked in their favor. Shop-floor workers, like executives, were expected to stay with the company all their working lives and therefore identified with the firm and were committed to its goals. In a Japanese company the heads of sections were not found in their own private offices removed from subordinates. They sat in the middle of a large room surrounded by their workers.

The Japanese sociologist Nakane, when discussing the distinction between Japan and the west, focused on the group orientation of the Japanese as a major feature. She emphasized the very limited significance given to kinship relations in Japan, compared with China, other Asian countries and even Europe. The primary attachment in Japanese society is to "the corporate group based on work, in which the major aspects of social and economic life are involved." This is observed when Japanese are forced to define themselves to an outsider. Rather than identifying themselves by their professional qualifications, for example, "I am a doctor" or "I am an engineer," they will identify themselves by the corporation or institution for which they work — "I am a Sony san [man]" or "I am a University of Tokyo man."

The notion of a labor market where an individual sells his or her labor, or has a purely contractual relationship with a corporation is still alien to the Japanese; professional identity is not based on skill acquisition as it is in the west. Morishima also stressed the all-embracing aspect of the social group or economic enterprise:

> The company is not just a profit-making organization; it is a complete society in itself, and frequently it is so all-embracing that all the activities of the daily lives of the company's employees can take place within the company framework.

In the feudal period prior to the Meiji restoration, clan organizations were concerned with military and economic power in the region but were easily transformed into modern economic organizations. The commercial and mining conglomerate, Sumitomo, is an interesting example of this. The Sumitomo clan built up their resources and organization from the 1850s onwards. The organization still retains the feudal crest as its symbol, and the employees still refer to themselves as

"Sumitomo men" as they would have done during the Tokugawa period.

This sort of loyalty and commitment to the operation of firms has clearly been an important ingredient in the success of Japan as an industrial power, but there are other features of Japanese society that are equally important.

Lifetime employment, until recently, was offered by all major (and some small) companies, and by the government to their employees, including scientists. On graduation, the young person will have the option, depending on which university he or she attended, of applying for a job in a major company or government institution. On gaining entry, they start on an upward path that will provide them with incremental increases in salary and status as their seniority increases. Seniority is determined by length of service and is consistent with Confucian notions of respect for elders. The individual is thereby bound by a complex pattern of vertical relationships, which he or she is expected to honor and reciprocate, for built into the relationship with the group is a very basic dependence and fear of rejection. The psychiatrist Doi Takeo has described this as *amae,* a Japanese word not easily translatable into English, but which means a childlike need to be loved and accepted by others. This dependency, and the guilt associated with it, are inculcated in children from an early age. Devitt described the process:

> . . . the child is taught to be interdependent, rather than individually independent; to be calm, quiet and passive, rather than aggressive and articulate; to be trusting, to fear loneliness; to respond to subtle, implicit methods of discipline, rather than overt definable methods; to respect relative status within the family; to conform to the requirements of the role he is to play within the family group; to have a sense of his own family group versus other family groups and outsiders.

This form of upbringing leads to individuals with relatively weak egos, but with a corresponding sensitivity and responsiveness to the requirements of the social group to which they belong, and a strong fear of rejection. This, Doi argues, has led to a tendency to conformity and compliance, "Just as betrayal of the group creates guilt, so to be ostracized by the group is the greatest shame and dishonor." This has therefore made it difficult for western concepts of individual freedom to gain great currency within Japanese society.

Although such generalizations about national characteristics can be taken too far, nonetheless observations suggest that such qualities as creativity and originality would be held in lower esteem in Japan than in western cultures. A revealing statement was made by Yasuo Kato, assistant general manager of Nippon Electric's Systems Research Laboratories:

> We are not so creative because the creative mind is peculiar, and we Japanese do not like anything peculiar. We believe that everyone should be the same.

\*     \*     \*

The dream of Shibusawa and the early Meiji reformers was to adapt their country's traditional Confucian value system to the productive powers of western capitalism.

# WALKING TRACTORS

In the mid 1960s Japanese industry was not only producing consumer goods for the European and American markets but was manufacturing machinery and equipment to meet local demand. One of these machines was a small tractor designed to work in the tiny paddy fields used for wet-rice cultivation. This tractor, a variation of what was known in the west as a rotary hoe, was extremely popular and was marketed throughout Southeast Asia.

In 1965 at the Sichuan tractor factory at Jianyang, not far from the provincial capital of Chengdu, two young engineers, Zeng Xiuliang and Chen Wanxiong, had begun to look at the possibilities of this small tractor for China. Previously they had been trying to adapt the large Soviet and East European machines to the needs of communes in their region. These tractors, designed for the broad-acre farming of the Russian Steppes, were inappropriate for the needs of the small fields and irrigation systems used in Chinese farming. They also had the great disadvantage of being extremely expensive. A large commune could, perhaps, afford one or two, and, on top of that, there were the costs of maintenance, which required skilled engineers and mechanics to be on hand.

The government policies of self-reliance and rural mechanization remained firm commitments, despite the excesses of the "great leap forward." Chen and Zeng, who at this stage were part of the large factory-commune, decided to join forces with a similar tractor factory in Shanghai and seek the help of the agricultural machinery research institutes in Shanghai, Luoyang and Sichuan. They began to design what has come to be known as the "walking tractor," the "grasshopper" or the "iron cow." The starting point was the Japanese tractor. They needed to produce a machine that was profoundly versatile — able to maneuver in and out of small fields (unlike the Russian tractors), able to be used as a small truck to get produce to market and with the capacity to drive other machinery and equipment, such as small electrical generators.

By reverse-engineering the Japanese model and making some adaptations, such as increasing the engine's capacity from seven to ten

he would "fry fish on his hand if it worked." With considerable emotion, Chen and Zeng recounted how they took the tractor to the commune, uncertain themselves whether a locally built and designed tractor would match up to the Soviet and East European machines then in use.

The walking tractor was a remarkable success. By early 1966, 10,000 a year were produced. The tractors provided, for the first time, a form of mechanization appropriate to the needs of the majority of Chinese farmers. Now China produces each year more than one million of these small tractors, which are exported throughout Southeast Asia and Latin America to similar peasant communities in need of cheap, simple and small-scale technology.

In China the "walking tractor" is now one of the most common forms of transport in the countryside. Even the canal barges that ply the vast inland waterways of the Yangtze delta are now driven by the same small engines used in the tractors. If this is what Mao Zedong aimed to achieve with his policy of "walking on two legs" he was clearly on the right track.

horsepower and giving the tractor rubber wheels and a detachable chassis, the Sichuan team began to build their prototype. As Chen and Zeng discovered, there was considerable scepticism about whether the odd-looking machine would actually work in practice. The leader of one commune, when confronted with it, claimed that

They were able to retain the sense of collective commitment embodied in the samurai tradition and transfer this loyalty to the large corporations, which by the late 1960s were beginning to spread their operations overseas to become transnational or global institutions. Mitsubishi, Nissan, Toyota, Hitachi, Honda, Sony — these were the new domains. They were not just joint-stock companies in the western sense; they were Japan. Ownership structures as they emerged at this time were markedly different from western corporations. Not only was there a very limited labor market, there was also a limited capital market. Private shareholding remains extremely low; investment in the large companies comes from post-office saving banks, union funds and the giant insurance companies. Perhaps because of the hardships endured after the War, the frugality of the Japanese was in marked contrast to the growing consumerism in the postwar west. In the 1960s the average Japanese would have one year's salary in savings; in the United States, Australia and Europe it would be more common to be one year's salary in debt. This massive pool of savings, held by banks, provided the capital that was invested in the large industrial firms. The heads of major banks were on the boards of these great companies and were concerned with stable long-term investment not short-term return on investment as the capital market in the west demanded. This gave to Japanese firms an ability to engage in long-term planning and to act in conjunction with powerful government departments such as MITI, to take on long-term commercial strategies. It was this that led more paranoid observers in the west to coin the term "Japan Inc." in the 1970s. The success of Japan was not lost on the rest of east Asia, even China.

# BETTER RED THAN EXPERT

In May 1966 Mao Zedong launched his "great proletarian cultural revolution." He was clearly frustrated by the back-seat role to which he had been relegated since the failure of the "great leap forward." He also believed that the Communist party was falling into the hands of technocrats, planners and intellectuals who were quite prepared to be openly critical of his views and who, he believed, were not imbued with the correct revolutionary consciousness. However, in calling upon the youth of China to "bombard the headquarters," in other words to attack the Party and the "capitalist roaders" within it, he had little idea of what he was unleashing on his country.

Revolutionary zeal, fostered by almost twenty years of rhetoric and military-style campaigns against supposed counter-revolutionaries, provided a new channel for personal frustration. Now this energy was to be unleased indiscriminately and often against totally inappropriate targets. Frustration at the lack of personal advancement or achievement allowed disgruntled individuals to seek revenge on those further up the bureaucratic hierachy. However, the cultural revolution went far further than McCarthyism in the United States, although there were some superficial similarities such as the attacks on intellectuals.

Mao and his close supporters — including those who, ten years later, were to become known as the "gang of four" — gave their blessing to the formation of bands of young red guards many of whom were no more than 13 or 14 years old. Because Mao believed that the revolutionary leadership of workers and peasants had been usurped by intellectuals, particularly those who had been educated overseas, he saw his task as preventing the formation of a new technocratic and self-interested bureaucratic elite like the Confucian scholar-class who had dominated Chinese culture for much of its history. He was also smarting from attacks from scholars against the shortcomings of his policies during the "great leap forward." Under the catch phrase "better red than expert," schools, universities and colleges across the country were closed. Campaigns against reactionary and bourgeois teachers were mounted. The *Little Red Book* of Mao Zedong's thoughts was turned into virtual holy writ. One of the major sins to be accused of was that of "separating theory from practice."

The botanist Professor Cao Zongxun was dragged from her laboratory at Beijing University and paraded through the streets of Beijing with a tall dunce's hat on her head because she was found to be experimenting with small cucumbers as part of her research on pollination. Professor Cao now recalls, with some amusement, the grounds given for her being attacked:

> I could not continue my plant physiology research because it was divorced from practice. Cucumbers like mine were too small to be eaten. That is how they criticized me. They said that even kindergarten children knew that cucumbers were grown in fields and I was just crazy to grow them in test tubes.

She and many of her scientific colleagues were sent off to be re-educated in special "May 7" cadre schools in the countryside where they worked with the peasants so that they would come to appreciate the correct revolutionary consciousness. Professor Cao did not fare as badly as many other scholars, teachers and artists who ended up being beaten to death, while others committed suicide rather than endure the continual persecution and torture meted out to them. It is not certain how many people died as a result of this most ambitious of all Mao's campaigns to change irrevocably the consciousness of the Chinese people. Ken Ling, a student at Xiamen No. 8 Middle School, witnessed the violence unleashed against scholars:

> Greatly emboldened by the instigators, the other students also cried, "Beat them!" and jumped on the teachers, swinging their fists and kicking. The stragglers were forced to back them up with loud shouts and clenched fists.
>
> There was nothing strange in this. Young students were ordinarily peaceful and well-behaved but, once the first step was taken, all were bound to follow.
>
> The Principal was the most savagely beaten. He was also forced to kneel on the edge of a vertical drop on the campus. If he had allowed himself to lean slightly forward, the heavy pail around his neck would have toppled him over the edge. He knelt for 15 minutes and was visibly about to collapse. Then he was pulled to his feet and punched in the abdomen; the sound was like that of a basketball bouncing off a wall.
>
> But the heaviest blow to me that day was the killing of my most respected and beloved teacher, Chen Kuteh.
>
> Teacher Chen, over 60 years old and suffering from high blood pressure, was dragged out at 11.30 A.M., exposed to the summer sun for more than two hours, then paraded about with the others, carrying a placard and hitting a gong.
>
> He passed out several times but was brought back to consciousness each time with cold water splashed onto his face. He could hardly move; his feet were cut by glass and thorns. But his spirit was unbroken. He shouted, "Why don't you kill me? Kill me!" This lasted for six hours, until he lost control of his bowels. They tried to force a stick into his rectum. He collapsed for the last time.

One 14-year old red guard, Liang Heng, later described in his book *Son of the Revolution* how he observed musicians and composers at the Beijing Conservatorium of Music being beaten and tortured because they were accused of being more concerned with personal and professional excellence than with working for the socialist revolution. Even highly trained engineers such as Professor Zheng Wei from Beijing's Qinghua University were forced to work as janitors for years while the University was turned over to political consciousness raising by various factions of the red guard.

Lui Shaoqi, the Communist Party Chairman, was killed and members of his family imprisoned. Deng Xiaoping was branded as an "arch-unrepentant capitalist roader" and was forced from office. Mao, "the great helmsman," again took control of the Party. Supporters of the cultural revolution were brought into key positions in all public institutions to see that the Party's new policies were carried out. Any form of material incentive was removed from commune and factory life. Rigorous

In 1966 Mao Zedong called on the youth of China to attack the "capitalist roaders" in the Communist party and the "great proletarian cultural revolution" was born. China, as it had often done in the past, turned in on itself and away from western cultural influences — western books, classical music and films were banned.

ideological consciousness-raising sessions were held, in which anyone not from a worker or peasant background was expected to engage in endless public confessions of their capitalist tendencies and reactionary thoughts in the hope of gaining political redemption. This sort of activity seemed to replace much formal education on the assumption that real knowledge only came from practice. It was the workers and peasants who "knew," not "reactionary academic authorities," as Mao was inclined to call sceptical intellectuals and scientists. On this basis an illiterate abattoir worker was put in charge of the Shanghai Institute of Biochemistry, which only the previous year had been the first in the world to synthesize insulin. In effect, all serious education and research stopped in China for almost a decade.

As the red guards ran out of more obvious targets to attack they began to fight among themselves. In many major cities, such as Changsha, virtual civil war broke out with rival factions each claiming greater ideological purity as the true heirs of Mao Zedong's revolutionary ideals. The military were increasingly forced to intervene as bands of armed youths held pitched battles throughout the city. China, as it had done on other occasions, withdrew into itself, this time in the confident assumption that once the revolutionary forces of peasants and workers were in command, the Party would prove, once and for all, the superiority of socialism over the degenerate capitalism of the west. With universities closed, large numbers of teachers, graduates and even those just about to enter higher education were shipped off to the countryside in their thousands to work on communes. Some brought with them skills that were of some use to the peasants, others had nothing to offer and were more of a burden to the commune . . . and felt it.

The assumptions that peasants and workers knew best was probably true in many cases and there were many remarkable achievements. The "learn from Dazhai movement" was based on an extraordinary commune in northwestern China. In the late 1960s, by sheer determination and collective organization, the members of the commune rebuilt the landscape, terracing the mountain slopes and redirecting the flood rains into dams for irrigation. They achieved collectively what could not have been achieved in any other manner. They proved that, with genuine idealism, it was possible to overcome centuries of passive acceptance of their fate. They were to turn the arid and mountainous terrain into a highly productive region. However, while this approach worked in some instances, with examples of remarkable small-scale industrial development, in the wider perspective China was falling behind in the essential development of a nationwide infrastructure — communication systems, energy, power grids to support growing industrial demands, and sources of basic commodities such as iron, coal and oil. In the centrally planned model adopted from the Soviet Union this was the responsibility of state planning, and at this level most of the trained people had been removed from office.

With the Chinese population growing at an unchecked rate, the remarkable increases in production achieved on the communes were offset by more and more people demanding their socialist rights. In many areas this led to serious environmental problems. In order to lift grain production, commune leaders increased the demands on the land, breaking away from the traditional methods used for centuries by the peasants. Without any scientific monitoring, large amounts of pesticides, particularly DDT, were used to control insects and other pests. The unchecked use of such insecticides on a large scale resulted in high levels accumulating in the canals and waterways. Fish died, but DDT also passed through the food chain threatening human health. In many rivers, by the late 1960s, fish populations had been virtually killed off, reducing the availability of one of the most important forms of protein in the Chinese diet.

While "barefoot doctors" with elementary training were able to bring basic health care to those in rural areas who would otherwise have had no access to modern medicines, they could not deal with public health problems of this type. With scientific and technical specialists regarded as "reactionaries" and in no position to warn that short-term gains might have even greater long-term costs, there was little check on the enthusiasm of revolutionary cadres to lift production outputs at all costs. In some areas three crops of rice were planted each year even though total yields were lower, labor costs higher and the environmental balance threatened. Because of the power of the revolutionary cadres whose "redness" clearly outshone their "expertise," the common-sense of the peasants was often overridden.

It was not, however, until the death of Mao in 1976 that any real challenge could be made to the political opportunists who had come to power on the shirt tails of Mao's last drive to keep his vision of China's socialist revolution alive. The cost of his cultural revolution was to be enormous; an entire generation was denied proper education and, without adequate leadership, China's fledgling industrial and economic development fell increasingly behind that of other countries in the region, notably Japan, Taiwan, Korea, Hong Kong and Singapore.

*   *   *

In 1976 devastating earthquakes hit northern China. Many old peasants whose memories were long and whose ancient heritage had not been completely eroded by the cultural revolution saw this event as a portent. In the past such events were seen as heralding the death of emperors or the fall of dynasties. In this case they were right; within weeks Mao Zedong, the great helmsman, was dead. Almost immediately a bitter struggle began in the Party to find a successor, a new chairman. The more important issue, however, was whether the leaders of the cultural revolution could hold power without Mao there to protect them.

In the end the issue was decided by the army, which put its considerable weight behind the pragmatists in the party led by Deng Xiaoping. The notorious "gang of four" — Jiang Qing, Zhang Chunqiao, Wang Hongwen and Yao Wenyuan — were arrested. Maoist policies had achieved an amazing transformation of the country, but at a cost that was becoming increasingly obvious. Basically, it was impossible to maintain a country in a state of permanent revolution. While small-scale industrial development could make an enormous difference locally, without proper economic planning at a national level, erratic supplies of essential commodities made for great inefficiency and, after a certain point, economic stagnation.

The radical swings in policy had left most people either profoundly confused or downright cynical about the ideological leadership offered by the Communist party. The problem for the Party was to find another means of motivating people. Above all else, they had to reinstate some respect for expertise and to overcome the cultural and intellectual narrowness caused by the hothouse experiment of the cultural revolution.

In 1978 Deng reaffirmed the "four modernizations," designed to overcome China's backwardness in agriculture, science and technology, defense and industry. This was the first major step in the restructuring of the Communist party's (and therefore the nation's) priorities. In many respects the direction in which Deng was to take the country in the next decade was to be almost as radical a shift as that first set in motion by Mao Zedong in the early 1950s.

Deng Xiaoping's view of socialism differed from Mao's in one crucial respect — Deng believed that the primary objective of socialism and of the Communist party was to improve the economic well-being of the people. Once the means of production were in the hands of the people, represented by the Communist party, there was nothing wrong with using whatever methods worked. If the use of capitalist economic institutions, such as the markets, could further this goal then it

251

ABC/Warren Duncan

During the Cultural Revolution, communes like that of Taichai in the northern province of Shansi were held up as models for emulation. By mobilizing the enthusiasm and labor of the peasants, local party officials were able to transform the landscape, turning what had been barren eroded hills into productive agricultural land.

was legitimate, as long as political control remained in the hands of the Party. This was the foundation of Deng's pragmatism and it was with this open-minded approach that he began to rebuild the country's tattered institutions of higher education and the bodies concerned with mapping China's future economic course.

The great fear among the military was that China's technological backwardness would make it increasingly vulnerable. They had become acutely aware that the arms race had left them behind, as it had done so tragically in the nineteenth century.

The opening of diplomatic and economic relations with the capitalist world, particularly with Japan, provided access to much-needed technology for both defense and the civil sector. To build up their industrial and technological capacity the Chinese needed knowledge, communications and energy systems, all of which had gone into decline over the past decade.

In many areas of the country the electricity supply was so primitive that it was impossible to run the local factory when the lights went on at night. What was needed, the Party believed, were modern "turnkey" plants — complete factories or

252

electrical generating systems that could be bought "off the shelf" in the international high-tech market.

The problem with this strategy was that China had very limited supplies of foreign exchange with which to purchase the technology it needed. To pay for the new military and industrial technology China needed to export and, therefore, to turn its attention to the world market. However, much of what the Chinese had to sell was too poorly designed and manufactured to appeal to the sophisticated western consumer market. In an effort to get access to overseas markets and to industrial technology, Deng put forward perhaps one of the most radical suggestions of his stormy career — joint ventures with foreign firms. Within a very short time foreign businesses were flocking to Beijing hoping to make direct sales of technology or to enter into joint ventures producing goods for the Chinese market. The Japanese were in a particularly strong position to take advantage of this change of policy. Although memories of their brutal occupation during the war remained a cause of popular hostility, they were an Asian culture and familiar with many of the Chinese ways of doing business. They were also able to offer deals to the Chinese that seemed attractive. During 1976–78 the Chinese government signed contracts worth over $3 billion for the importation of industrial technology, 88 per cent of which were with Japan.

In 1978 the Chinese government signed an agreement with Nippon Steel for a massive $2 billion steel plant to be constructed at Baoshan outside Shanghai. This ambitious scheme to simply transplant an ultra-modern Japanese steel plant met with considerable setbacks. For a start, the Chinese had not done a proper feasibility study of the site before construction started. When they began to sink the piles to support the blast furnace, they found the site completely unsuitable to take the enormous weight. Not only was it extremely difficult to build, but there was little co-ordination of other elements such as railway lines, electricity and water supplies. It was to be almost a decade before the Baoshan steelworks was running to full capacity. Although problems like those faced in Baoshan dampened enthusiasm for buying in high-technology plants, the determination to catch up with the west and with Japan, Korea and Taiwan had caught hold of popular imagination.

With this came more visible signs of a change in priorities. The universal military-style uniforms ("Mao suits" as they have been called in the west) gave way to more individualistic self-expression — colorful blouses and skirts, and American blue jeans became the height of fashion. China turned suddenly from the dark winter of the puritanical cultural revolution, with its stultifying and mind-numbing ideological strictures, to something approaching tolerance of diversity. Even locally bottled Coca-Cola was being sold in the Peace Hotel in Beijing, and China opened its doors to increasing hordes of tourists eager for some new world to discover.

Tourist dollars, although important, were not going to pay for the foreign technology China needed for modernization. Foreign firms were loath to enter into contracts when there was no consistent code of commercial law in China. To meet this need, and with the intention of reassuring Chinese businesspeople, as well as scientists and other scholars so badly treated during the cultural revolution, a new legal system was developed. In 1980 one of its most important functions was to provide some notion of minimum legal rights for the individual, which until then had not existed. For many survivors of the excesses of the cultural revolution this constitutional right to a fair trial and legal representation gave some hope that the kangaroo courts of the past, which had allowed the brutal political persecution of the 1960s, would never reconvene. By degrees new social institutions were providing unheard-of freedoms.

As the bamboo curtain was gradually drawn back, not only did the west begin to gain a more realistic understanding of China, but the Chinese began to gain a more realistic impression of the west.

The restrictions on travel to and from Hong Kong were relaxed and Cantonese eager to make contact with their relatives crossed the borders, and Hong Kong Chinese began to re-establish relations with their families in Guangdong. The consequence was that the ordinary Chinese discovered that relatives in the west or in Hong Kong, Singapore and even Taiwan lived in material conditions far better than their own. Having been told for decades of the superiority of socialism in delivering an ever-increasing standard of living, those of the younger generation who had not known the abject poverty and deprivation of pre-liberation times had little to go on but their own eyes. They were not convinced and wanted what others had — televisions, radios and better consumer goods.

It was this demand that provided the economic planners with one practical means of stimulating the economy — consumerism. By turning their attention to the production of consumer goods, money stored under the bed, out of fear produced by the political instability and the lack of anything much to buy, was circulating once more in the economy.

Regional markets were reopened after decades of state-controlled distribution and production of basic foods. These markets soon stimulated peasants to sell the surplus from their small private plots, allowed within the commune system. Food production increased suddenly, and money began to pulse through the economy with a new energy.

The problem of how to make industry more competitive and economically efficient remained. The state factory-communes were still dominated by Party officials who had been given power during the cultural revolution, on the basis of "better red than expert." The problem with these factories, and what gave them some similarity to Japanese factories, was the fact that labor was not disposable as it was in the west. The factory-commune was a social and political as well as an economic institution. To sack workers was unthinkable.

In the periods of high revolutionary idealism during the "great leap forward" and the cultural revolution when the commune system was set up, the factory-communes were conceived of as being the incubators out of which the new socialist consciousness was to be born. But as Lysenko's adherents were to find out, nature and particularly human nature is less easily transformed. The lazy and corrupt simply exploited the system for what it was worth. These communes came to operate like small fiefdoms, linked to vertically integrated ministries, which, in turn, behaved like

The commune was the center of economic and social life. There was little or no opportunity to leave. As an individual, your destiny was linked to that of the collective.

small states and jealously guarded their resources. This developed to the extent of hoarding valued resources often needed in other industries nearby. If a local factory required steel from the local mill, the manager would have to apply via the appropriate ministry in Beijing — the process could take a long time, and was bureaucratic and cumbersome. Apart from satisfying the state's quotas there was little reason to increase production or improve efficiency through innovation. There was little or no tangible reward for the individual who put in more than the most basic amount of effort; anything more risked an accusation of "bourgeois individualism," or "capitalist roader."

Essential to the new market-orientated reforms introduced by Deng was the idea that industrial enterprises were now allowed to make profits, and to pass the benefits on to their workers. An economic think-tank of scholars brought back from the countryside was established under the auspices of the newly formed Academy of Social Sciences. In 1978 Hu Qiaomu, the president of the Academy, in an address to the State Council argued that productivity had stagnated in China compared with its east Asian neighbors because, for the past 20 years, China had ignored "objective economic laws." Since these objective laws applied in both capitalist and socialist societies, and as capitalist economies had more experience in applying such laws in enterprise management, China should learn from that experience. These so-called "objective laws" were no more than the acceptance that the pursuit of profit by an individual firm was a legitimate aim, and the use of market forces was the best means of determining the price of goods and of controlling supply and demand. If China was to be competitive in the international market then it would have to accept the priority of economic efficiency even at the cost of egalitarianism and social welfare. The driving force of individual greed or enlightened self-interest would have to take precedence over the selfless service to the state that had been the ideal of the revolutionaries. There was still the problem of how to achieve the right balance between capitalist economic mechanisms and the centrally planned elements enshrined in the model China had adopted from the Soviet Union. The agency cost in most of China's highly bureaucratic industries was high. However, to turn these industries around in order to reach the levels of efficiency and productivity being achieved in Japan, Korea and Taiwan was no easy matter.

The economic rationalists in the planning agency began to argue that firms should be allowed to lay off workers and that the "iron rice bowl" (guaranteed employment) should be smashed. For example, a truck factory in Changchun, had 40,000 workers of whom only 12,000 were actually engaged in production; the factory-commune had, however, to support the rest. Underemployment was widespread. But if the factory did lay off their excess workers where would they go,

Society for Anglo-Chinese Understanding, London

Trucks awaiting dispatch at the Changchun No.1 Motor Vehicle Factory in the late 1970s. Despite high production levels the Changchun factory-commune had to support 40,000 people, although only 12,000 were directly engaged in production.

and how could they survive? The commune provided not only work but also food, housing, schooling and hospitals. Planners attempting to make the factory more efficient recommended that 12,000 workers should be laid off.

But there was no market for labor at this stage, and the state and provincial authorities strictly controlled the movement of people from the country to the cities, and from one region to another. The situation was clearly critical. Unchecked population growth had resulted in a 25 per cent rise in population since Mao's rejection of Ma Yinchu's warnings in the 1950s. The children of the communes had to be absorbed into the workforce, fed and housed, and yet productivity was not rising at a rate sufficient to provide any hope of an equal rise in living standards. This was becoming not only an embarrassment but a threat to the viability of the whole system. What was taking place outside China's borders in the rest of Asia could not be ignored indefinitely.

China's economy had, for all the political turmoil of the previous decades, been gradually restructured. This was evident in the shift away from a reliance on agriculture. In 1949–53 agriculture provided 50 per cent of China's gross national product (GNP); by 1983 this had fallen to 27 per cent. Over the same period, the proportion of GNP from industry had risen from 30 per cent to 57 per cent, and the growth in the industrial sector between 1962 and 1980 was twice that of any other country. China's industrial base was now in a far stronger position. However, it was not sufficiently strong to solve the problems facing China's economy.

To help chart a course out of this quagmire the Party brought Zhao Ziyang (now Party Chairman) to Beijing to take over the post of Premier of the State Council. Zhao had been First Secretary of the Party in Sichuan, Deng Xiaoping's home province. In this role he had transformed the province's industry into a model of economic reform. One of the key policies developed in Sichuan was to allow a high degree of self-management and freedom for industry, particularly the capacity to produce beyond state quotas. For example, at the Chongqing Iron and Steel Works when state demand for steel plate fell below the annual quota and the plant's capacity, the firm was allowed to sell directly on the open market, both within China and also overseas. The profits were then available to be returned to the workers in the form of bonuses. This was an example of the "market socialism" that Hungary and Yugoslavia had pioneered in Eastern Europe. Material incentives were clearly the only thing that was going to work in the climate of increasing disillusionment with the Party and its revolutionary policies; the Party had no alternative but to accept this.

In close collaboration with Deng, Zhao now began to apply these policies across the entire country. The impediments to rapid economic development were not just to be found within the structure of the economy but in the role of the Party itself.

Because of the inflexibility of the system, corruption had become commonplace. The "backdoor" was almost the only way to get around the bottlenecks in the system or to gain any measure of personal freedom or advantage for one's children. *Guanxi* (connections) is the Chinese term for the system of favors and obligations that, by the late 1970s, had become so prevalent that it was almost a medium of economic exchange. In a society where power and privilege is associated with position in the

# THE CHINESE COMMUNIST PARTY

The structure of the Chinese Communist party descends in approximately eight levels from the Central Committee at the top, through six regional bureaux, 26 provincial or large city committees, 256 special district committees, 2,200 county committees and some 26,000 communes to more than one million branch committees in villages, factories, the army and other economic/social units. This structure has been the means by which policies developed by the Party's Central Committee could be passed down through the system to be implemented at the commune or factory level. It was also a structure that was intended to allow the feelings of the people to be communicated back up the hierarchy to the planners in the Central Committee. One of the problems with such a system is that information and instructions have to be interpreted as they move down the line. With the rapid shifts in Party policy, which occurred throughout the cultural revolution in particular, middle-level bureaucrats, fearful of the consequences of being identified as "capitalist roaders" or "ultra leftists" simply ceased to implement policies. It was a traditional bureaucratic response, but one that could effectively undermine even the most worthwhile reforms.

## ORGANISATION OF THE CHINESE COMMUNIST PARTY

▼ *Elects Central Committee*　　　　**NATIONAL PARTY CONGRESS**

▼ *Elects Politburo and its*　　　　**CENTRAL COMMITTEE**
　*Standing Committee*

　　　　**POLITICAL BUREAU OF THE**　　　▲ *Convenes plenary sessions of*
　　　　**CENTRAL COMMITTEE**　　　　　　*Central Committee*
　　　　**(POLITBURO)**

　　　　**STANDING COMMITTEE**　　　　　▲ *Politburo and Standing*
　　　　**OF THE POLITBURO**　　　　　　　*Committee fulfill powers*
　　　　　　　　　　　　　　　　　　　　　*of Central Committee*
　　　　　　　　　　　　　　　　　　　　　*when it is not in session.*

MILITARY
CHAIN OF COMMAND

**REGIONAL AND LOCAL BUREAUS**　　　　　　　　　　**MILITARY**
*Entire Party subordinate to Central Committee*　　　　**COMMISSION**
*under principle of democratic centralism.*

| 26 Provincial and Autonomous Region Party Committees; 3 Municpal Party Committees | Sub-municipal (district) and Commune-level Primary Party Committees and Primary Party Committees at Larger Industrial Enterprises, Major Worksites or Educational Institutions | Party Branches at Medium-Sized Industrial Enterprises and at Other Places of Work, Education, or Residence, and at Brigade Levels in Communes | Party Branches at Small Indus-trial Enterprises, within Larger Industrial Enterprises, and at Other Places of Work, Education, or Residence, and at Team-levels in Communes | General Political Department of the PLA |
| --- | --- | --- | --- | --- |
| Municipal and County-level Party Committees | | | | Party Committees at Military Region Level |
| | | | | Party Committees at Military District Level |
| | | | | Party Committees at Regimental Level |
| | | | | Party Committees at Company Level |

bureaucracy and Party hierarchy, this influence can be lucratively farmed.

An interesting play, *Impostor* or *If I were Real,* was written in 1978. It was based on the true story of a young intellectual who had been sent off to the country during the cultural revolution and his attempts to get back to his home in Shanghai. In the play Li Xiaojiang has run away from the commune where he was sent, but to reside in the city he has to be officially transferred back; this he cannot do since he is unable to pull the necessary strings. He has a passionate interest in the theater, but is unable to get in. He waits outside theaters in the hope of being able to buy a ticket, until one night he notices that the theater manager has a bundle of spare tickets. He sees a young girl come up to the ticket office and being given a ticket immediately, even though he has been told that there are none left.

> Li: If these are unused tickets, why can't you sell them?
> Zhao: (*Theater manager*): Because they're reserved for high-level cadres [party officials].
> Li: What about that girl who just went in? Is she a high-level cadre?
> Zhao: Her father is. Is yours?

This gives Li an idea. Having heard that Ma, the head of the Propaganda Department, is not going to be able to come to the play, he goes to a public telephone nearby and rings the theater.

> Li: Hello? I want to speak to backstage. I'm from the Propaganda Department of the Municipal Committee, my name is Ma. . . . That's right. . . . I want to speak to the theater manager Zhao. . . . Yes. . . . Yes. . . . It's me. . . . Is that the theater manager Zhao? I'm going on an overseas trip tomorrow, so I won't be able to come to your play tonight. . . . Can I ask you a favor. The son of my only comrade-in-arms in Beijing would like to see your play very much. He just rang me to say he was unable to get a ticket. Could you help him? No problem? Good, he only needs one ticket. His name is Jiang Xiaolin . . . . You'll wait for him at the door? . . . Good. He's in the vicinity of the theater right now. So I'll tell him to come and see you.

The upshot of all this is that Li, having discovered the key to the backdoor, in the guise of the son of a high official, manipulates the system to have himself officially transferred back to the city from the countryside so that he can marry his girlfriend. The play caused an immediate scandal when it was put on in Shanghai and was banned after a week. It was definitely too close to the bone in the late 1970s.

However embarrassing the play might have been to the Party, it presented the system's rigidity all too clearly. Zhao Ziyang now had to cope with the growing number of these displaced and disillusioned citizens, particularly educated young people sent to the country. They had no future on the land, and little in the city of their birth. The State Planning Council set up new enterprise guidelines allowing those people without official work units or communes to form co-operative companies and to operate as independent traders within the growing free markets. They had the right to produce whatever the market would sustain and could keep the profits after paying a tax to the state. To the purists of the cultural revolution, this was as near to heresy as it was possible to get, but it was only the beginning.

259

# THE OPEN DOOR

*Closer ties with the outside world broaden people's minds, and this is conducive to overcoming feudal ideas and eliminating backwardness. . . . open wide, help speed the breaking down of the inert elements in the traditional culture, inject new blood into the national culture and achieve cultural modernization.*

An Zhiguo, *Beijing Review*, 1978

The train from Hong Kong to the new Chinese city of Shenzhen often looks like a commuter service for businesspeople. In fact, when you cross the border into the People's Republic of China there is little sense of ever having left Hong Kong. Shenzhen is one of the fastest growing cities in the world. In the 1970s it was a tiny village; now it has a population of 250,000 drawn from all over China. Shenzhen, some have argued, is no more than an expensive showpiece; a political stunt to reassure rich Hong Kong merchants that there will be economic life after 1997, when Hong Kong and the New Territories are reabsorbed into China. In reality this city is a window on the world for the new Chinese economic planners; a hothouse in which new technology and methods of production are tried out under conditions that would be politically dangerous in the heartland of China. Shenzhen

Courtesy Film Australia

Shenzhen, one of China's new economic zones, is one of the fastest growing cities in the world. It is also a costly experiment in gaining access to foreign investment and technology

260

has an environment in which western-style consumerism, market forces and profit are the determining characteristics. Subsidiary factories of backward Chinese industries have opened up here. So too have Japanese, Hong Kong, Australian, European and American firms.

In the hope of tapping the technological advances taking place elsewhere in east Asia, the Chinese throughout the early 1980s set up a number of these "new economic zones." These, at first sight, seem to be the recreation of the old nineteenth century treaty-port system, by which the Qing government hoped to contain European influence, while perhaps gaining some benefits from increased trade and access to advanced technology. The crucial difference with the new economic zones is that they serve China and not foreigners. Here the Chinese have allowed legal and business conditions, familiar elsewhere in Asia, to flourish. The object is to attract overseas investment by multinational firms who set up production in Shenzhen and provide access both to new technology and to foreign markets.

When they were first established in the late 1970s, the new economic zones were primarily seen as means of gaining foreign exchange. Contracts specified that the bulk of what was produced must be exported. For foreign firms taking the opportunity to set up their factories in Shenzhen and the other economic zones, the attraction was not merely the cheap labor but the prospect of ultimately gaining access to the vast Chinese market. With the growing costs of production forcing Japanese firms to look for offshore bases, China, despite the bureaucratic irritations, offers some very great attractions.

In 1981 Hitachi set up production in Fuzhou under a fifty-fifty joint venture deal, producing television sets, the bulk of which were sold in China to meet growing consumer demand and dissatisfaction with local products. In 1984 Sanyo Electric set up a similar deal in Shenzhen. The Japanese Otsuka Pharmaceutical Company set up production in Tianjin in 1979 shifting an entire production system and capital worth $7.9 million from Japan. This represents only a fraction of Japan's direct investment in China. The impact of this competition on the Chinese market has meant that state factories are placed under increasing pressure to perform.

For the new generation of engineers and executives freed from many of the Maoist ideological and economic constraints, the new priorities of profitable firms and economic efficiency have forced them to adopt a more pragmatic approach to industrial production. What was desperately needed was some training in management; this the new joint ventures are providing.

The electronics industry is an interesting example of the changes brought about by the opening up of the Chinese economy — changes that are having a profound impact on social values. The Metto factory in Shenzhen was set up in 1986, as a subsidiary of Shanghai No. 3 Radio Factory, to produce transistors and tape recorders for export. The workforce are all on short-term contracts and the majority are young girls aged between 16 and 20. The productivity that is achieved in Shenzhen is about two-thirds higher than that of the parent company in Shanghai. The reasons are obvious to the manager Chen Gaofu. The bonuses he can pay his workers often amount to twice their weekly income. Average wages run at around 38 yuan ($10.20) a week; bonuses range from 50–150 yuan ($13.40–$40.30). The factory is also an interesting institution in itself. Like the factories set up by Arkwright and other textile manufacturers in eighteenth century England, and the Tomioka silk spinning mill in Japan in the nineteenth century, Metto must house and look after the welfare of the young people it employs. This industrial paternalism in Shenzhen is as pragmatic as it was in the early industrialization of England and Japan. The young workers come to the factory from rural communities throughout the region. The turnover is very high: on average 30 per cent leave each year. The onerous work discipline of the production line is alien but compensated for by the high wages offered. There is considerable competition for skilled labor in Shenzhen and to keep the workforce contented the manager of the factory has even taken to providing entertainment, as well as looking after their moral and material welfare.

Once a month Chen Gaofu, a cheerful middle-aged man, can be seen dancing at the latest Shenzhen disco, surrounded by forty or fifty of his young employees. The reason for this paternalism is simple: if he does not provide them with some ancillary benefits they will leave in ever greater numbers and the cost of training and recruitment will be lost to another firm eager to pick up trained factory workers.

Each week Hong Kong businesspeople and their agents arrive with orders for the Metto factory. They bring with them the latest Japanese-designed transistors and tape recorders. They meet with Chen, his engineers and design staff to discuss orders and costs. The models are then sent to the head office in Shanghai to be reverse-engineered, and the production equipment designed and geared up. A year or so later, under a variety of international brand names, they will turn up in supermarkets anywhere from Amsterdam and New York to Rio and Prague. In 1988 the Metto factory began producing three million Walkman radio cassettes for General Electric in the United States.

The scale of industrial development that is going on makes Shenzhen look more like one of the "four dragons" — Singapore, Taiwan, Korea and Hong Kong — than the People's Republic of China. The question that every visitor to the new economic zones inevitably asks is whether China's flirtation with capitalism is just a hothouse experiment to achieve its short-term financial and technological objectives, or whether the freedoms permitted in the new economic zones are to be extended throughout the rest of China. If they are, could China in the twenty-first century begin to do what Korea and Japan have done in the late twentieth century? There is little doubt that the Chinese government's economic planners would like to achieve the economic success seen elsewhere in east Asia, the question is whether the Communist party and the bureaucratic power structure that has been built up around it can be convinced to let go, and risk the social consequences of granting even greater economic and cultural freedoms.

The economic rationalists do seem to be winning the day. Even in centers not designated as new economic zones, such as Shanghai and Chengdu there is increasing independence for firms, which are expected to operate in a more competitive domestic market. Managers are no longer merely supervisors of a socialist commune in which ideological rectitude is all-important, but executives in a business that is expected to make profits or, in the final analysis, go to the wall. For some years, it has been argued that factories and state enterprises that are not run efficiently should be allowed to go bankrupt and be closed down, although this has happened rarely. Managers are now expected to offer bonuses to workers based on productivity.

At Shanghai No. 20 Radio Factory they make circuit boards for the large Shanghai-based electronics industry. Around the walls of the factory's conference room are framed the awards won for being a model factory. These awards no longer have the currency they once had. The profitability of the factory is a matter of much greater concern, despite the reassurances of the managers that socialist values continue to prevail and that "workers are not just working for themselves but for the collective interests." Given that these are now measured in terms of the profitability of the firm, they seem little different from the type of commitment achieved in Japanese or Korean firms. The factory still looks after the basic welfare of its 1,300 workers. However, those who do not work can be fired, although this has never happened. The commercial success of the factory makes it an attractive place to work. Its capacity to pay high bonuses is linked directly to its profitability, a fact certainly not lost on the employees.

Courtesy Film Australia

The production line at the Metto radio factory in Shenzhen. Here, contract workers, mostly young girls from outlying rural villages, assemble transistor radios and cassette players. Gone is the "iron rice bowl." Wages are pegged to a bonus system based on productivity, along the lines of bonus schemes operating in Japan and the west.

Many of the systems adopted in the last decade have come from Japan; these include the quality-control circle and the use of competing production teams with a prominent notice board showing the relative achievements of the teams. The production line itself was introduced in the late 1970s from Matsushita in Japan. Now this production line operates alongside two other Chinese copies built by the factory's engineers. In May 1988 a large new complex was built within the factory compound to house their latest joint venture with the Australian firm Printronics. The joint venture will allow Shanghai Printronics to sell 80 per cent of its new computer circuit boards internationally, providing them with much sought after foreign exchange.

The big question for innovative firms like Shanghai No. 20 is whether it is to be allowed the independence to pursue its commercial interests like any other international company. At present it has stiff competition from Taiwan and Singapore, which will inevitably provide a test of the extent of the pragmatism that Deng Xiaoping is prepared to allow, especially when this independence cuts across the principles of state planning. Already, small private electronics firms in Shanghai are providing serious competition to the large state-owned enterprises; a phenomenon that is widespread and one that has also had profound consequences in other industries.

Courtesy Film Australia

Shanghai's No. 20 Radio Factory runs its own school, with selected students being given technical training that will allow them to take up more senior positions on the production line or to pursue tertiary studies at the local technical college.

# TROUBLE IN STOVE CITY

*If we do not carry out reform [political and economic] now, our cause of modernization and socialism will be ruined.*

Deng Xiaoping 1978

*As economic reform progresses, we deeply feel the necessity for change in the political structure. The absence of such change will hamper the development of productive forces.*

Deng Xiaoping 1986

The ancient port city of Quanzhou on the Fujian coast has provided foreign merchants with access to porcelain for a thousand years. The Fujian merchants themselves, despite the Ming suppression of mercantile activity in the fifteenth century, had built up trading networks throughout Southeast Asia, Taiwan, the Philippines and Japan.

Even in the 1930s and 1940s the pottery and porcelain works of the region were major international suppliers of roofing, floor and bathroom tiles; the fine porcelain for which the area was once renowned having given way to more prosaic wares. In the 1950s with the Nationalists in Taiwan just off the coast, and the restructuring of the domestic economy foremost in the minds of the new communist government, this trade went into a steep decline. In some of the towns surrounding Quanzhou small state-run pottery works were maintained to meet the local demand for roofing tiles.

One of these small towns is Jinjiang, known locally as "Stove City" because its skyline consists almost exclusively of smoke stacks — giant chimneys, most made out of forty-four gallon drums welded together. In 1978 there was just one state-run pottery and tile works; now there are 581. This area, set in the denuded hills that look like a permanent quarry, has the atmosphere that Staffordshire in the north of England must have had in the late eighteenth century, when the pottery works of Wedgwood and others were beginning to mass produce common crockery.

What is astounding is the speed with which these changes came about and their effect on the political and social life of the surrounding community. When Deng Xiaoping at the Seventh Party Congress in 1978 announced the economic and political reforms he could have had no idea of the forces he was unleashing. At "Stove City" families who either worked in the ceramics industry or had been associated with it in the past began to set up small backyard furnaces and rented stalls in the town's main street to sell their wares. Many who were only making a subsistence living through agriculture found that this traditional industry could add appreciably to the family income.

These small-scale pottery works had become so successful that, by 1984, the state factory was in serious financial difficulty. The conditions of employment that it was forced to offer its employees made it simply uncompetitive compared with the small private firms. The "iron rice bowl," which guaranteed workers a basic wage whether

# FANG LIZHI AND THE ENGINEERS OF THE SOUL

*All our workers fighting on the ideological front should serve as "engineers of the soul" . . . they are charged with the heavy responsibility of educating people.*

Deng Xiaoping, 1983

Fang Lizhi, an astrophysicist of international standing, has often been described as China's Sakharov. He is perhaps the most outspoken and articulate critic of China's politics and culture, of the Communist party and of his fellow scientists. Until 1986 he was the Vice-Chancellor of China's Science and Technology University, a post he had held since 1984. During December 1986 and January 1987 students demonstrated in Beijing and Shanghai, demanding greater democracy and freedom. This demonstration led to a campaign against so-called "bourgeois liberalism" within the Communist party. Fang Lizhi was sacked from his position at the University, and from the Party. He was not alone; liberal leaders in the Communist party, such as Hu Yaobang, known to be sympathetic to democratic reforms were demoted, and numerous intellectuals and writers were expelled from the Party. The fate of Fang Lizhi has not, however, followed the course of past critics of the Party. He is still free to work, travel and express his views — clearly a reflection of the greater tolerance and pluralism in China today.

Although there was no direct connection between the student demonstrations and Fang Lizhi, his outspoken criticisms and uncompromising honesty were seen to be partly responsible. In November 1986 Fang gave a series of speeches to students in Shanghai. The following are excerpts, translated by Orville Schell, and published in *The Atlantic,* May 1988:

"Human rights are fundamental privileges that people have from birth, such as the right to think and be educated, to marry and so on. But we Chinese consider these rights dangerous. Although human rights are universal and concrete, we Chinese lump freedom, equality and brotherhood together with capitalism and criticize them all in the same terms. If we are the democratic country we say we are these rights should be stronger here than elsewhere, but at present they are nothing more than an abstract idea."

"I feel that the first step towards democratization should be the recognition of human rights . . . but [in China] democratization has come to mean something performed by superiors on inferiors — a serious misunderstanding of democracy. Our government does not give us democracy simply by loosening our bonds a bit. This gives us only enough freedom to writhe a little. Freedom by decree is not fit to be called democracy because . . . it fails to provide the most basic human rights."

"In a democratic nation democracy flows from the individual, and the government has responsibility towards him . . . We must make our government realize that it is economically dependent on its citizens, because such is the basis of democracy. But feudal traditions are still strong in China; social relations are initiated by superiors and accepted by inferiors."

"People of other societies believe that criminal accusations arising from casual suspicion harm human dignity and privacy. In China, on the other hand, it is not only normal for me to inform on you . . . but considered a positive virtue. I would be praised for my alertness and contribution to class struggle in spite of my disrespect for democracy and human rights."

On the role of the intellectual and the university in China he had this to say:

"To liberate oneself from the slavery of governmental and other non-intellectual authorities, one need only view knowledge as an independent organism. But this is not so in China. Our universities produce tools, not educated men. Our graduates cannot think for themselves. They are quite happy to be the docile instruments of someone else's purposes. China's intelligentsia has still not cleansed itself of this tendency . . . Knowledge should be independent of power. It must never submit, for knowledge loses its value as soon as it bows to power."

At the campus of Shanghai's Tongji University Fang recounted the following story, which was later published in *China Spring* and, no doubt, helped to seal his fate:

"I have often said that a university needs science, democracy, creativity and independence. A reporter later wrote to me saying that this spirit was very good but that I should supplement the transcript of my talk, lest people think that my

*Fang Lizhi with his wife Li Shuxian.*

opinions are slighting the 'four cardinal principles' [Deng Xiaoping had enunciated these as socialism, the people's democratic dictatorship, the leadership of the Communist party, and Marxism-Leninism and Mao Zedong thought]. Since I had also proposed four principles, he said, people might think this a little dangerous. I wrote back to him and said that I could add a section saying that if science, democracy, creativity, and independence conflicted with the 'four principles' then it was only because the 'four principles' advocate superstition instead of science, dictatorship instead of democracy, conservatism instead of creativity, and dependency instead of independence . . . The editor responded that perhaps the clarification would be unnecessary."

Fang Lizhi should not be mistaken for a promoter of capitalism; he is more in the mold of George Orwell, a socialist attacking the failure of its practitioners. His model of socialism is that of the northern European countries, such as Sweden, where a high level of state ownership coexists with a vigorous market economy and, above all, with intellectual freedom. For Fang, Marxism and

the Communist party have become little more than surrogates for the traditional feudal structure of China, Confucianism and the conservative scholar-bureaucrats who ran the empire. Reform requires the genuine acceptance of the values of science, which, he argues, are innately democratic and pluralist in nature.

However, in what many see as a quixotic campaign to promote democratic values in China (not unlike the "Mr Science and Mr Democracy" movement of the 1920s) he is clearly up against a powerful body of conservative Party technocrats whose proposals for reforming China are truly Orwellian, as the following extract from an article by Dr Qian Xuesen entitled "From Social Science to Social Technology" shows:

"We definitely must set up the field of moral education, which is a social science. Moral education belongs to modernized social science and ought to be on the agenda of modernization of social science. Given this science of moral education, we can organize the use in socialist propaganda work of modern science and technology. The executive leadership in propaganda work needs a communications network for liaison with all regions, to give an up-to-date picture of the ideological tendencies of the popular masses. This intelligence must on the one hand be stored in an information bank and displayed on command display screens. Propaganda staff officers use the theory of moral education to analyze the situation, and may also use electronic computers and similar instruments with analytical models to estimate the effects and functioning in the thinking of the masses of various propaganda activities. The staff officer corps following propaganda-executive decisions transmits these to lower level units, and at the same time to newspapers, periodicals, radio and television transmitters all the way to cultural and artistic units for implementation. The conditions of implementation are reported back to the propaganda executive via the communications network. The executive is thus just like a military command. It commands operations in ideological and political work, and the entirety of workers in the propaganda departments are staff members of an operational command. Is not this then another field of engineering for the reconstruction of society. Hence ideological and political work can become a social technology."

they worked or not, had led to serious overstaffing.

It was at this point that the Director of the state factory, Wu Wendian, and the Communist party Secretary Wu Yongxin came up with an entirely new system of operation, which has transformed the factory and its productivity. They broke the workforce up into six teams that operated as independent enterprises, buying materials and renting the facilities, such as kilns, owned by the factory. Each unit was expected to pay 10 per cent of its profits to the government as tax, the rest was divided among members of the unit on the basis of their work and productive output. The units were given considerable freedom to seek markets outside the province and overseas. The factory's overheads were also drastically reduced and the pre-1984 managerial staff of 60 was reduced to 17. In 1984 the factory's output was worth 700,000 yuan ($188,066). By 1987 it had more than tripled to 2.4 million yuan ($644,797).

The profits and new wealth from this production explosion were plowed back into the community in the form of a building boom. One of the new legal code's provisions, which was to fundamentally change the standard of living of many of the most industrious of "Stove City's" ceramics entrepreneurs, was the right to own property and to pass it on to children. This concession to the Chinese family system means that the wealth of the region is now beginning to show itself in the large and spacious stone houses being erected all over the city. These houses are richly decorated with the source of their wealth — gaudy porcelain tiles. "Stove City" is taking on the appearance of a boom town similar to those in Australia or California.

The people of Lin Banchen village were organized as a production brigade in

Courtesy Film Australia

Ten years ago "Stove City" had one state-owned ceramics factory; now there are over five hundred private producers.

Mao's times, now the village is a prosperous suburb of "Stove City." Across the river from the rows of elaborate three-storied stone mansions are the ancient step-kilns that have brought the new-found wealth. The families that make up the old brigade now have rights to, but not ownership of, the surrounding farm land; rights that can also be passed on to family members. Their houses are richly furnished, with televisions, videos, refrigerators and other luxuries, which one would not expect to find in rural areas. It is this wealth in the hands of such communities that is creating the demand for the consumer electronics being produced, in increasing volumes, in the factories of Shanghai. Here there is none of the jaded cynicism about materialism common in the west. The new freedom to make money and to spend it on the items most people in the west take for granted is a powerful driving force in the new Chinese economy. Like the postwar boom in domestic consumer demand, which fuelled the remarkable growth in the United States, European and Japanese economies, China with a population of more than one billion people has now discovered the dynamic economic benefits of consumerism. Already there are widespread fears among the older members of the Communist party that the Pandora's box opened by Deng in the late 1970s cannot be controlled. This issue of control is of central concern to those senior cadres, in Beijing and in the provinces, who now find that the market mechanism — "the idol" of economic rationalism — might well displace them from their once commanding role over the direction of China's social, political and economic life. Expectations as to what is possible within the system have clearly been raised and these expectations are a potent reality that neither ideology nor rhetoric can easily force back into Pandora's box.

\* \* \*

Courtesy Film Australia

China's new consumerism — a "ghetto blaster" takes pride of place before the more traditional gods.

Courtesy Film Australia

The wealth generated by the ceramics industry has led to a building boom. Fine stone houses are going up all over the area, as a consequence of the government's policy of allowing property to be passed on to heirs.

Stuck on the wall of a small nondescript building, facing a dusty street some ten minutes walk from the center of Beijing, there is a brass plate, which in English and Chinese reads "Scientific and Technological Entrepreneurs' Association of the West City District." This is the umbrella organization for a number of independent consultants who operate completely outside the state system. They own their own companies and pay taxes to the Chinese government, but apart from that they are free to go about their business. Their role is to bridge the gap between China's growing scientific-research capacity and industry.

The problem for the new industrial entrepreneurs of China is not just to gain access to overseas technology but to tap the creativity and talent of their own young and highly trained scientists and engineers. Although there remains a large hole in the education curve as a result of the "ten lost years" of the cultural revolution — when scientists were despised and technological knowledge dismissed as bourgeois — an increasing number of Chinese students are now returning from overseas training with advanced knowledge. What is in question is whether this knowledge can be effectively applied.

The Academy of Sciences and the universities and ministries that employ trained scientists and engineers have a limited relationship to industry, except for the large-scale state enterprises. The problem in the past has been that academic research was operating at a much higher level of sophistication than most of Chinese industry. Even where industry saw the need for scientific consultants from research institutions, there were too many bureaucratic obstructions and little real incentive for such relationships to work effectively.

There was one celebrated case in the early 1980s when a scientist was attacked by colleagues for acting as a consultant and gaining what they jealously believed were inappropriate financial benefits. The scientist was charged and threatened with dismissal from his university post. Had it not been for the issue being taken up publicly he would probably have lost his job.

Following this case it was agreed by the new State Science and Technology Commission and the Academy of Sciences that consultancies, for which academic staff were paid by state and private enterprises, were not only legitimate but highly desirable. They decided, there and then, to set up the Scientific and Technological Entrepreneurs' Association under the joint direction of Fang Yi, the retired head of the Academy of Sciences, Zhang Jingfu the Deputy Director of the State Economic Commission and the eminent sociologist Professor Fei Xiaotong. This body was to act as an official organization to encourage engineers and scientists who were prepared to set up as independent consultants. Although extremely small in scale the Scientific and Technological Entrepreneurs' Association is beginning to have an impact.

Zhou Hongji is an engineer who, until a few years ago, worked for the Iron and Steel Institute in Beijing. Zhou is an enthusiast and a man of considerable initiative. When the opportunity presented itself he decided to set up on his own, giving up his job, along with the fringe benefits and security that come with bureaucratic and institutional position in China. (A position in a research institute or in one of the large ministries had, in the past, offered the only career path for engineers.) Despite this Zhou set up his own consultancy — the Hua Ye Company — and began business in 1986.

His first major project was to take the research on smelting techniques on which he had been working at the Iron and Steel Institute and convince industry of its benefits. At a steel and iron mill, some three hours drive from Beijing, he was able to save the company an average of 1.5 million yuan ($402,998) a year by introducing a better smelting technique. From this his reputation has grown into that of a major independent "trouble shooter." In a country where the old Soviet ministerial and academic structures still inhibit the easy flow of information, the role of consultants like Zhou is going to be increasingly important. He is, however, not alone. At any meeting of the Association an unusual mixture of well-qualified enthusiasts, who have responded to the option of independent consultancy, attend.

But it is not only in the private sector that efforts to break down the institutional barriers to the flow of knowledge are taking place. The entrepreneurial spirit is being fostered in most state factories where rewards, in terms of bonuses, are going to innovations introduced by employees at all levels. This system was first introduced into the Japanese company structure in the 1950s. In both countries workers aim to spend a lifetime of employment committed to the collective goals of their companies. These institutions continue to act more like extended families than like western firms. In Japan the input of shop-floor workers was an essential component in quality control and in productive efficiency, and the more innovative of the new Chinese companies have introduced similar systems. This fact is still not fully appreciated by managers in the west.

At the Shanghai No. 20 Radio Factory a young trainee engineer Wu Ketong was able to earn 1,500 yuan ($403), more than double his yearly income, for inventing a new water purification system he set up for the factory. It has been so successful that it is now being introduced to other factories by the municipal government, which is concerned with the high levels of industrial pollution in Shanghai. In developing his system Wu collaborated with industrial chemists at the local institute of technology where he studies.

What is obvious from this brief review of some of the consequences of China's reforms is that, given sufficient freedom and incentives, technological innovation is possible even within a centrally planned economy like that of China.

However, without innovation within the dominant political and economic organizations, no amount of technological change will induce economic growth — for all the tinkering on the margins of power. While the cases presented here have been selected to demonstrate what can and is being done outside the more traditional institutions, they remain like vulnerable flowers that have poked their heads up between the cracks in the concrete of an otherwise inflexible bureaucratic state.

In 1987 a Shanghai firm offered a sale of shares in their company, the first case of stocks being sold in China for at least fifty years. People queued up all night so as to be able to invest in the firm. By 9 A.M. on the day of the sale the offer — more than 3 million yuan ($805,997) worth of shares — had been sold out. This specter of capitalism rearing its head in China would have had Mao leaping from his mausoleum. However, the ideal of the moral society, controlled and ordered around a single unifying ideology, does not die easily, whether it be the Confucian imperial state or the Maoist revolutionary state. There are still many senior officials within the Communist party who would happily shut out the materialistic western world and return China to its rightful concerns with social order and economic self-reliance, as the Ming emperors did in the fifteenth century and Mao tried to do in the 1960s.

# SUPERCOMPUTERS

In March 1980 Richard Anderson, a general manager at Hewlett-Packard, one of the largest computer firms in the United States, announced at a Washington conference the findings of a comparative survey on the reliability of computer chips: the best American products had a failure rate six times that of the lowest quality Japanese product.

In the late 1970s the Japanese began their assault on the global computer market, the last bastion of American technological dominance. It seemed set to be a repeat story of the rise of the Japanese automobile industry a decade earlier. By 1983 the Japanese had not only gained 70 per cent of the world market for 64k RAM (random access memory) chips, an American invention, but had embarked on a most audacious project designed to leapfrog a generation of computer technology and to come up with a supercomputer to challenge the most powerful American machines. With the support of Japan's influential Ministry of International Trade and Industry, a $100 million National Superspeed Computer Project and a $500 million fifth generation Computer Institute (ICOT) were set up in 1981–82. Involving 40 researchers from government research laboratories and eight leading computer firms — Fujitsu, Hitachi, Nippon Electric (NEC), Mitsubishi, Matsushita, Oki, Sharp and Toshiba — this 13-year project is an example of the long-term planning approach to technological development that has allowed the Japanese to dominate in a number of key high-technology fields.

Japanese computer firms belong to *kieratsu,* an association of interlinked companies ranging from semiconductor producers to robot manufacturers. Unlike American firms, the Japanese companies also had access to relatively cheap long-term finance, which made it easier for them to invest in new technology and new production processes. In the United States, because of the differences in the operation of the money market, the need for short-term return on investment made long-term technological planning more difficult. In other words the Japanese could "hold their breath for a long, long time."

The announcement of Japan's supercomputer and fifth generation project brought a new response from both government and the private sector in the United States. They began to look seriously at what the Japanese were doing and how they were doing it. The tables had finally turned. In 1982 a number of leading American semiconductor and computer companies came together to form a non-profit consortium, the Semiconductor Research Corporation. With a $30 million annual budget the Corporation was designed "to assure long-term survival in the market", according to its first director Larry Sumney. A similar research and development group — the Microelectronics and Computer Technology Corporation (MCC) — was established by Control Data and 12 other companies to follow the Japanese model of pooling resources for long-term planning.

It was the military who were most concerned about the possibility of losing dominance in such a strategically sensitive area. This led to the Pentagon announcing its $1 billion Strategic Computing and Survivability Project, which set out to do everything the Japanese had done and more. However, by late 1988 Japan's lead in the application of micro-electronics and computer systems was such that the world's most advanced fighter aircraft — the FSX — will be built at Mitsubishi's Nagoya aircraft and armaments factory. The United States will supply the body and frame but Japan will supply the remaining 65 per cent, including the engine, and the sophisticated radar and electronics. Both countries will have access to the technology developed in the final product. What is perhaps most ironic is that it was at the same Mitsubishi Nagoya plant that the Zero fighter was developed. Built from components taken from American designs and initially using American parts, it had played a decisive role in the destruction of the Pacific fleet in Pearl Harbor in 1942.

# THE PRICE OF PROGRESS

The dilemma facing Deng and Zhao Ziyang is acute. With the population growing at a still dangerous rate, rapid economic growth is not just a debatable luxury but a necessity, if living standards are not to decline. There is also the expectation, created by the promises of the Communist party leadership, that China will be able to catch up, or at least not fall further behind, her east Asian neighbors — Japan, South Korea, Taiwan and Hong Kong. The open-door policy of the last decade has forced many state enterprises to compete with foreign joint ventures, and with small privately owned companies, and in so doing they have had to adopt business practices dictated by the market. In this process greater freedom and responsibility have had to be given to individual firms and their managers, and to local officials at the provincial level.

Despite much rhetoric to the contrary on the part of senior Communist party officials, China since 1983 has started on a path of fundamental restructuring of its economic and political institutions — restructuring that, in the long term, will allow for the adoption of business practices common throughout the rest of east Asia. There is an interesting analogy here to the internationalization of military technology. Whether they like it or not, countries are forced to achieve technological parity in conventional arms if they are to defend themselves; in a similar way, the economic pragmatists argue, it is necessary to adopt the most efficient international system of industrial production if one is to compete effectively. For this reason the Chinese have welcomed joint ventures with the Japanese as have the Americans and Europeans (for example, the laser-controlled compact disk was jointly developed by Philips of Holland and Sony of Japan).

It is also interesting to observe the speed with which Japanese management approaches have been tried and in many cases adopted in the United States in the hope of regaining its lost manufacturing lead. The capacity to adopt the Japanese approach has obviously been limited by cultural and economic differences. However, there is every reason to believe that competition within the United States market from Japanese-run firms will begin to change the American industrial ethos. The Japanese have brought to industrial production new international standards of efficiency and quality control that other countries are forced to match or risk going out of business.

One has only to look at the number of failing firms in Europe and the United States that have been taken over by Japanese companies and turned around to become profitable to realise that their approach is not limited to the Japanese environment. The Dunlop tyre company in Great Britain was bought by the giant Sumitomo corporation in the early 1980s. Within 18 months, and after a major injection of capital, a net annual loss of about $40 million was turned into a modest profit. The firm had been run on traditional British class lines for decades. There were six different dining rooms, with managers and staff eating separately. Worker incentives were low as was morale. This, however, was to change radically. Under the new management 300 middle managers and ancillary staff were redeployed. There was only one canteen for everyone; there was standard dress, which eliminated the distinction between managers and workers; employees were encouraged to come up with suggested improvements in the production process and were given bonuses for doing so; levels of participation in the goals of the company increased as did bonuses based on increases in productivity and on improvements in quality.

A General Motors plant in California had an industrial relations record so bad that it was basically undermining the plant's viability. It was taken over by Toyota in the early 1980s and, by changing the production process and system of management, it was to become one of the most profitable factories in the United States. Deming's ideas were finally to be accepted back home, but via a most unexpected route.

The problem for the older industrial powers is that they, in turn, have become ossified around the institutional structures that gave them their early success. In this sense, the success of the United States in the first part of this century, like that of Britain in the previous century, provided them with little reason for change or need to innovate until a latecomer like Japan set new standards of efficiency and productivity, which challenged their domestic and overseas markets. Now change has become imperative. The only question is whether there is sufficient flexibility or pragmatism to allow the old ideological assumptions and priorities to be discarded and new approaches to be taken.

In an economy as large and complex as that of the United States there is evidence of an insularity reminiscent of the Middle Kingdom. In this respect, China and the United States face parallel problems in coping with a new international economic order in which Japan and other smaller countries (such as South Korea, Sweden and Germany) are taking the lead in key industrial fields (such as electronics, shipbuilding and automobiles). The consequences of falling behind Japan in electronics, in particular, could mean that industries in the United States have limited access to new systems of production affecting both the quality and cost of goods manufactured there. This happened to Great Britain in the late nineteenth century when Germany virtually took over the chemical industry, undercutting British firms and thus reducing the stimulus for industrial research and development. The military in the United States are particularly concerned about Japan's dominance in the electronics industry. There is a fear that the United States could fall behind and, if so, the lack of industrial innovation could affect the quality of military technology. The economic threat from Japan is not imaginary: by 1985 Japan accounted for 10 per cent of the world's economic output and in the same year average annual income in Japan was $17,000 compared with $16,000 in the United States.

The claims that the Japanese and other Asian cultures were merely imitators and could never really threaten the scientific and technological lead held by the west has encouraged complacency for more than a century. It is true that Great Britain and the United States still gain the majority of Nobel prizes and Japan, considering its present industrial power, has a woeful record in making major scientific breakthroughs. Asian cultures, many western commentators have observed, have not nurtured great or original thinkers. The emphasis on conformity and collective endeavors, it is often argued, gives east Asian cultures advantages in industrial production or process innovation, but not in invention or product innovation. In this latter area it is the more individualistic and intellectually orientated cultures of the west that will come up with original scientific and technological developments as they have done so successfully over the past two centuries.

However, as this study has, I hope, shown, such arguments take too short a historical perspective. China, long before the rise of the capitalist economies of Europe and the United States, proved itself capable of high levels of innovation, within a very different culture and economy. Also invention, although important, is not necessarily the crucial issue if one is looking for wealth and power. Many early Chinese innovations, such as mechanical spinning, had no significant economic impact in China, while in Britain with the development of the factory system it was one of the basic stimuli for the Industrial Revolution. Micro-electronics and computer-controlled production lines, although developed in the United States, were to be taken up in Japan with such success that within a decade the Japanese were to dominate the world in their use and application. Such examples prove that the benefits of invention and discovery do not necessarily accrue to the inventor.

Despite their cultural homogenity, the Japanese have proved sufficiently flexible to change their cultural institutions in the past. If greater freedom and encouragement of originality is clearly perceived to be in their economic interests, there is no reason to believe that they will not be developed. This may well be the virtue of Japanese pragmatism. An interesting issue is whether the United States, Europe and China can demonstrate similar levels of pragmatism. The cost, however, is that culture becomes subservient to economic priorities.

This is not a dilemma for the Japanese alone. The values and demands of the global market place now set the economic priorities for all countries, from the most highly developed to the smallest third-world nation. Although it was possible because of its vast size for Mao, like the Ming emperors, to insulate China from the polluting effects of the capitalist world, in the long run even China has been drawn into the global economy in order to acquire the technology it so desperately needs to keep up with its capitalist neighbors.

It would appear that, whether we like it or not, a degree of cultural and political convergence is taking place at a global level. As giant multinational corporations and international joint ventures extend national interests to a global perspective, leaders in countries as idealogically opposed as the Soviet Union, the United States, China and Australia are forced to confront the requirements of efficient industrial production and economic planning based on international demand. Modern science and technology are clearly a major force in this process. The universality of science and its embodiment in commonly used technology link human societies as never before. As basic literacy in science becomes the educational heritage of people throughout the world, it will come to represent a strong countervailing force against the traditional religious and cultural values that have fed racial and cultural bigotry for most of human history.

All this is not, however, before time, as the noted Canadian biologist and commentator on science, Professor David Suzuki, has pointed out. The price of progress, which the European economic and scientific revolution fostered, has been a double-edged sword. While progress has allowed a massive increase in our capacity to exploit the global environment and to lift standards of living to unprecedented levels, we are now, for the first time, confronted with problems that transcend the powers and capacities of individual nation-states to deal with them. The biological diversity of the globe is fast disappearing, as world population rises, demanding increased economic growth and leading, in turn, to vastly increased consumption of energy and resources. As the remaining small areas of the earth's tropical forests in the Amazon, Africa and Southeast Asia are being destroyed, and the pollution of the biosphere threatens the earth's subtle climatic balance, the idea of unlimited economic and industrial growth becomes a dangerous myth.

The global economy increasingly homogenizes consumer tastes, supposedly offering to the developing world standards of consumption achieved in the west. If this is to be successful, unprecedented levels of scientific and technological innovation will have to be achieved. While the competitive efficiency of industrial and agricultural production within a world market will determine the technology, products and cultural artifacts that are promoted or discarded, there is also the need for balance and ecological harmony, as traditional Confucian China was concerned to promote. The dynamic mechanism of the market and consumerism can, as the Chinese have recently discovered, stimulate the economy and individual initiative, but unchecked economic growth can, in an extreme case, look more like the growth of a cancer than a road to Xanadu.

In this respect the success or otherwise of China — representing as it does one-fifth of the world's population — is crucial. Considering where they were starting from, their achievements since 1949 are as impressive as Japan's, but the task of managing this vast and growing population without crushing the individual, and thus destroying the essential wellspring of innovation and creativity, is no mean task.

There is clearly not any one road to Xanadu, as many economic planners of varying ideological persuasions have tried to argue. Each country discussed in this study has been able to exploit its unique cultural and economic potential, which at different times throughout history has given it enormous economic power and influence, but this does not last, for success is so often its own worst enemy.

As we all move towards a global society, perhaps the Xanadu we should be heading for is not some place of static perfection, dreamed of in the past, but a more dynamic balance between the need to provide maximum freedom for creativity, industrial innovation and growth, and the need to preserve the earth's finite resources and natural wealth. This will require the acceptance of continued technological change, but equally important will be the capacity to accept change within our cultural, economic and political institutions. If we do not achieve this balance the price of continued growth will be a world impoverished by nationalistic greed and environmental short sightedness.

## Notes on Chinese Names

Unfortunately, there is no simple way to indicate the sounds of the Chinese language faithfully in English. In *Roads to Xanadu* we have adopted the contemporary standard offered by the People's Republic of China, known as pinyin. The older form of the name is indicated in brackets after the pinyin when it first occurs in the text, for example, Li Hongzhang (Li Hung-chang).

However, a number of names and expressions, entering English from a variety of sources, have become so familiar to generations of readers — Confucius, Chiang Kai-shek, Taoism, Yangtze and so on — that these have been retained.

# Endnotes

## The Price of Harmony

### THE CELESTIAL EMPIRE

14  Marco Polo's quotes were taken from Marsden's revised translation in Manuel Komroff, ed., *The Travels of Marco Polo (The Venetian)* (New York: Liveright, 1986), xiii.

18  For a useful article on China's early water control systems, see the article by Song Zhenghai in Chinese Academy of Sciences, ed., *Ancient China's Technology and Science* (Beijing: Foreign Languages Press, 1983), 239.

21  For more information on the Chinese iron and steel industry see Joseph Needham, *Science and Civilisation in China* (Cambridge: Cambridge University Press, 1954–62), vols. III and V. For the military implications see William McNeill, *Pursuit of Power* (Oxford: Blackwells, 1984).

22–3  For further information on Chinese agriculture see Francesca Bray, "The Chinese Contribution to Europe's Agricultural Revolution: A Technology Transformed," in *Explorations in the History of Science and Technology in China* (Shanghai: 1982) and Francesca Bray, *The Rice Economies: Technology and Development in Asian Societies* (Oxford: Blackwells, 1986). Also see Needham, *Science and Civilisation in China*, vol. VI. There is an extremely interesting chapter on China's agricultural revolution in Mark Elvin, *Patterns of the Chinese Past* (Palo Alto, Calif.: Stanford University Press, 1973). In addition, see Dwight Perkins, *Agricultural Development in China 1368–1968.* (Chicago: Aldine, 1969).

26  The quote on the rice field as factory was taken from Fernand Braudel, *Civilization and Capitalism,* vol. 1 (London: Collins, 1984), 151.

28  William McNeill, *Plagues and People* (Oxford: Blackwells, 1976) provides a good comparative account of the impact of parasitic diseases on the development of European and Asian societies. Elvin, *Patterns of the Chinese Past*, gives a useful account of the economic and social impact of the agricultural revolution in the Song dynasty.

### SCHOLARS AND BUREAUCRATS

29  Renzong's poem as quoted in Ichisada Miyazaki, *China's Examination Hell* (New Haven, Conn.: Yale University Press, 1981), 17.

30–1  For a more detailed account of the Chinese examination system see Miyazaki, *China's Examination Hell*. For an interesting discussion on the impact of this examination system on China's intellectual culture see Shiheru Nakayama, *Academic and*

*Scientific Traditions in China, Japan and the West* (Tokyo: University of Tokyo Press, 1984).

36  The extract from *Xia xiao zheng* is found in Cao Wanru, "Phenological Calendars and Knowledge of Phenology", in Chinese Academy of Sciences, *Ancient China's Technology and Science,* 230.

37  For a more detailed account of the Chinese calendar see the article by Chen Jijin in Chinese Academy of Sciences, *Ancient China's Technology and Science.* See also Needham, *Science and Civilisation in China,* vol. III.

38–9  For further details on the links between astronomy and astrology see Ho Pengyoke's article in *The Proceedings of the 4th International Conference on the History of Chinese Science* (Sydney: University of Sydney, 1985). For a review of Chinese astronomy see Nathan Sivin, *Cosmos and Computation in Early Chinese Mathematical Astronomy* (Leiden: E.S. Brill, 1969). In addition, a good general work on Chinese science is Nathan Sivin, ed., *Chinese Science: Explorations of an Ancient Tradition* (Cambridge, Mass.: MIT Press, 1973).

39  For the reference to secrecy see the quote by Christopher Cullen in John Merson, *Culture and Science in China* (Sydney: Australian Broadcasting Commission, 1981), 25.

42  The second century quote on a water-driven armillary sphere is from Robert Temple, *China: Land of Discovery and Invention* (London: Patrick Stephens, 1986), 37. For a more detailed account of the Su Song clock see David Landes, *Revolution in Time* (Cambridge, Mass.: The Belknap Press, Harvard, 1983); The article in Joseph Needham, *Clerks and Craftsmen in China* (Cambridge: Cambridge University Press, 1970); and the article by Bo Shuren in Chinese Academy of Sciences, *Ancient China's Technology and Science.*

### SELF CULTIVATION AND THE COSMOS

42  The quote from Li Chuan and the Chinese alchemic verse are from Needham, *Science and Civilisation in China,* vol. V.

44–5  Joseph Needham, "Progress in Science and its Social Conditions", in *Nobel Symposium 58* (Pergamon Press, 1983) provides a good short review of how imperial priorities set the agenda for science in China. More details on this issue can be found in Needham, *Science and Civilisation in China.*

48  The quote from *Inner Writings of the Jade Purity* is cited in Needham, *Science and Civilisation in China,* vol. V: 4, 235.

### BOMBARDS AND CATHAYAN FIRE ARROWS

51  The quote on the properties of sulfur and saltpeter is from a useful short account of the development of gunpowder in Temple, *China: Land of Discovery and Invention.* See also Zhou Jiahua's article on gunpowder and firearms in Chinese Academy of Sciences, *Ancient China's Technology and Science.* For a more detailed investigation see the sections on alchemy and gunpowder in Needham, *Science and Civilisation in China.*

52–3  Zhao Yurong's quote from *Xinsi qi qi lu,* written in 1221, is found in Chinese Academy of Sciences, *Ancient China's Technology and Science,* 188.

### MERCHANTS, ARTISANS AND BUREAUCRATS

55  Marco Polo's quote comes from R. Latham, trans., *The Travels of Marco Polo* (London: 1958), 180 and is cited in Elvin, *Patterns of The Chinese Past.*

56  Wang Chen's poem describing a spinning machine is quoted in Elvin, *Patterns of the Chinese Past*, 198. Elvin also provides a good discussion (pp. 194–99) on why the development of water-powered spinning in thirteenth century China did not have the same impact that it did in Europe. This is further developed in Elvin, "The High-Level Equilibrium Trap: The Causes of the Decline of Invention in the Traditional Chinese Textile Industries", in W. Willmott, ed., *Economic Organization in Chinese Society* (Palo Alto, Calif.: Stanford University Press, 1972).

56–7    Jacques Gernet, (H.M. Wright, trans.) *Daily Life in China on the Eve of the Mongol Invasion 1250–1276* (London: George Allen and Unwin, 1962) provides wonderful insights into social life in Song China.

57    The quote on merchants and artisans in ancient China comes from Han Fei, *Five Evils (Han Fa-Tzu Chi-Shih)*, vol. 2, 1075–76 cited in Theodore de Berry, ed., *Source of Chinese Tradition* (New York: Columbia University Press, 1960).

The quote extolling the virtues of the farmer compared with those of the merchant is from Wang Chen, *Nong shu* cited in de Berry, *Source of Chinese Tradition.*

60    For a fascinating and detailed discussion of the emergence of China's international trade and maritime commerce during the Song, see Jung-pang Lo, "Maritime Commerce and its Relation to the Sung Navy", in *Journal of Economic and Social History of the Orient,* Part 1, 1969, 57–101. See also the chapter "The Revolution in Money and Credit", in Elvin, *Patterns of the Chinese Past.*

61    For further details on the elevation of merchants during the Southern Song dynasty see *Song shi (History of the Song Dynasty),* as quoted in Lo, "Maritime Commerce," in *Journal of Economic and Social History of the Orient.*

64    For a more detailed discussion of the growth of the European economy in the medieval period see the three volumes of Braudel, *Civilization and Capitalism;* E.L. Jones, *The European Miracle* (Cambridge: Cambridge University Press, 1985); and Henri Pirenne, *Economic and Social History of Europe* (London: Routledge and Kegan Paul, 1972).

## POWER, PROFIT AND THE ARMS RACE

65    Marco Polo's description of Quanzhou is from Komroff, *The Travels of Marco Polo (The Venetian),* 254–55.

70    Leonardo da Vinci's letter comes from Carlo Maria Franzero, *Leonardo* (London: W.H. Allen, 1969), 54–56.

72    Daniel Boorstin, *The Discoverers* (U.S.A.: Dent, 1984) contains an excellent general discussion on Henry the Navigator and the impact of European voyages of discovery from the fifteenth century. For a more detailed account of the impact of Asian commodities and ideas on medieval and Renaissance Europe see Donald Lasch, *Asia in the Making of Europe* (Chicago: University of Chicago Press, 1970).

## ZHENG HE AND THE LAST OF THE TREASURE SHIPS

73    The quotes from Zhou Chufei and Ibn Batuta come from Needham, *Science and Civilisation in China,* vol. IV:3.
For an interesting discussion on maritime expansion see Jung-pang Lo, "The Emergence of China as a Sea Power during the Late Sung and early Yuan Periods", in *Far Eastern Quarterly,* vol. 4:14, 1955, 489–503.

75    The quote referring to the gifts of pepper and sapanwood is taken from Tian Rukang, "Zheng He's Voyages and the Distribution of Pepper in China", in *Journal of the Royal Asiatic Society,* No. 2, 1981.

77    The quote by Emperor Gaozong and the quote (following) on the levying of duties are from Tian Rukang, "The Causes for the Decline in China's Overseas Trade between the Fifteenth and Eighteenth Centuries", in *Papers in Far Eastern History* (Australian National University), vol. 25, 1982, 38. See also the chapter "China and the Ming and Manchu Empires", in Jones, *The European Miracle.* For a more thorough analysis, the chapter "The Turning Point in the Fourteenth Century", in Elvin, *Patterns of the Chinese Past,* should be consulted.
See John Maynard Keynes, *A Treatise on Money,* vol. 1 (London: 1930) 156–57, and J.B. Black, *The Reign of Elizabeth 1558–1603* (Oxford: 1952), 210. These are both cited by Tian Rukang in "The Causes for the Decline in China's Overseas Trade", in *Papers in Far Eastern History.* The consequences of the contraction of trade and commerce during the Ming dynasty is dealt with in the chapter on China in Jones, *The European Miracle.*

# THE INVENTION OF PROGRESS

82    The quote by Mencius' is taken from Immanuel Hsü, *The Rise of Modern China* (Oxford: Oxford University Press, 1977), 95.

82–3    Francis Bacon's quote comes from Elizabeth Eisenstein, *The Printing Revolution in Early Modern Europe* (Cambridge: Cambridge University Press, 1983), 12.

86    For an excellent discussion on the re-emergence of Greek science in medieval Europe and the importance of the Crusades in opening up Europe to new ideas see Lynn White, Jr., "The Medieval Roots of Modern Technology and Science", in Warren Scoville and J. Clayburn, La Force, ed., *The Economic Development of Western Europe — The Middle Ages and the Renaissance* (Lexington, Massachusetts: Heath and Co., 1968).

87    The quotes on education are taken from Nakayama, *Academic and Scientific Traditions,* 63–64. Also see the Maurice Keen chapter "Universities and the Friars" in *History of Medieval Europe* (Middlesex, England: Pelican 1986).

The quote from *Great Learning,* one of the principal works to be studied by Confucian scholars, is from John Fairbank, *The United States and China,* 4th ed., (Cambridge: Harvard University Press, 1983), 77. For a succinct argument on why China did not develop modern science see Fairbank's chapter, "The Confucian Pattern".

For a detailed account of the religious origins of European development and use of clocks see David Landes, *Revolution in Time* (Cambridge: Harvard University Press, Belknap Press, 1983) Chap. 3. Note that Joseph Needham, the famous historian of Chinese science, would argue that the idea for the mechanical clock passed to the west from accounts of the famous Su Song clock. However, the Harvard historian David Landes argues that there is no necessary relationship between the two.

88    For an interesting book on the notion of the millenium and its influence on western thought see Norman Cohn, *The Pursuit of the Millenium* (Oxford: Oxford University Press, 1970). For a scholarly discussion on the relationship between Protestantism and Capitalism see Max Weber, *The Protestant Ethic and the Spirit of Capitalism* (London: Unwin Paperback, 1985) and R.H. Tawney, *Religion and the Rise of Capitalism* (Middlesex: Penguin, 1972).

91    The quote from Leonardo da Vinci is taken from the excellent chapter "Painting and Perspective," in Morris Kline *Mathematics in Western Culture* (Middlesex: Pelican, 1972). Samuel Edgerton "The Renaissance Artist as Quantifier," in Margaret Hagen, ed., *The Perception of Pictures* (New York: Academic Press, 1980), 179–212, provides an interesting comparison to China where neither perspective nor plan drawing was used.

92    For an account of the impact of paper and printing on western culture see Eisenstein, *The Printing Revolution.* On the issue of the impact of increasing literacy in Europe see Carlo Cipolla, *Literacy and Development in the West* (Middlesex: Pelican 1969).

94    The quotes from the Qing dynasty treatise and Jesuit missionary Verbiest come from Jonathan Spence, *To Change China: Western Advisers in China 1620–1690* (Middlesex: Penguin, 1980).

The quote ". . . to garner into the granaries . . ." is from Matteo Ricci as quoted in Boorstin, *The Discoverers,* 56.

95    A good historical account of the early establishment of foreign relations between China and the West is to be found in Hsü, *The Rise of Modern China.*

96    Francis Xavier's quote is taken from C.R. Boxer, "The Christian Century in Japan," cited in *Kagoshima: a Brief History of Overseas Exchange* (Kagoshima: Public Relations Division, Kagoshima Prefectual Government, 1984), 14.

The quote on Jesuit impressions of Asia are taken from Endymion Wilkinson, *Japan versus Europe: A History of Misunderstanding* (Middlesex: Penguin, 1983), 32–33. As the title suggests this book reviews the relationship between Japan and Europe in contemporary economic terms. The earlier

99–101    The quotes from Ricci appear in Boorstin, *The Discoverers,* 333, 57. For an excellent short review of the efforts of the Jesuit mission to China see the first chapter in Spence, *To Change China.*

102    Schall's petition as quoted in Spence, *To Change China,* 3.

104    The quote from Kangxi's journal is taken from Jonathan D. Spence, *Emperor of China: Self-Portrait of K'ang-Hsi* (New York: Vintage Books, 1975), 72.

105    The quote on the uses of western learning is taken from Carlo Cipolla, *Clocks and Culture, 1300–1700* (New York: Norton, 1979), 89.

106    "Lines in praise of a self-chiming clock," as translated in Spence, *Emperor of China,* 63.

106-09    Like the chicken-and-the-egg argument, or the nature versus nurture debate, the issue of whether Protestantism led to capitalism, or vice versa has absorbed economic historians since Tawney and Weber. The argument will no doubt absorb many student seminars but need not concern us here.

113    The quote on the instrument-maker George Graham comes from Olivia Brown, "The Instrument-Making Trade," in *Science and Profit in 18th-Century London* (Cambridge: Whipple Museum of the History of Science, 1985).

117–18    The account of De Beladoir is drawn from Mark Elvin's remarks in Merson, *Culture and Science in China,* 55.

119    There is a good discussion of the role of the new high priesthood of science as put forward by Bacon, in I.F. Clark, *Patterns of Expectation* (London: Jonathan Cape, 1978).

121    The quote on tribunals is from Ssu-yu Teng "Chinese Influence on the Western Examination System," in Ssu-yu Teng and Biggerstaff *An Annotated Bibliography of Selected Chinese Reference Works.* (Cambridge: Harvard University Press, 1950). This work provides a very good review of the history of the adoption in the west of civil service exams.

123    The quote from "Essay on Tea" is taken from Richard Thames, *Josiah Wedgwood* (Shire, Albums–Aylesbury, 1972), 6–7.

125    For an extremely instructive and entertaining account of industrial imitation see David Halberstam, *The Reckoning* (New York: Bantam Books, 1986).

129    This account of Wedgwood is drawn from two very useful small books: Thames, *Josiah Wedgwood* and Alison Kelly, *The Story of Wedgwood* (London: Faber and Faber, 1975). Additional insights have been drawn from Gaye Blake Roberts, *Mr Wedgwood and the Porcelain Trade,* paper delivered at the English Speaking Union, 1983.

130–1    The two quotes from Wedgwood can be found in Kelly, *The Story of Wedgwood,* 16, 18.

140    The advertisement in the Derby Mercury is taken from Richard Hill, *Richard Arkwright and Cotton Spinning* (Wayland, Hove, England: 1973), 41. This is an excellent brief biography.

141    John Wesley's quote on religion is cited in Thompson, *The Making of The English Working Class,* 391.

143–4    The quotes on the factory system in industrial England and the moral economy of the factory system are taken from Thompson, *The Making of the English Working Class,* 395, 397.

145    Van Braan's quote is cited in Landes, *Revolution in Time,* 49.

146–9    These figures on the East India Company and the rules of behavior for foreigners are taken from Hsü, *The Rise of Modern China,* 200, 202.

151    Qianlong's poem and the edict addressed to George III are as translated by J. L. Cranmer-Byng in "Lord Macartney's Embassy to Peking," in *Journal of Oriental Studies,* vol. IV, 1–2, 117–83. They are also quoted in Hsü, *The Rise of Modern China,* 210, 183.

153    Coleridge's famous poem comes from *The Penguin Book of English Verse* (Middlesex: Penguin, 1958).

154–5    Commissioner Lin's statement to Queen Victoria comes from Teng and Fairbank, *China's Response to the West: Documentary Survey 1839–1923* (Cambridge: Harvard University Press, 1954), 24–27.

156    A very good outline of the American involvement in the opium trade is found in Jonathan Goldstein, *Philadelphia and the China Trade* (Philadelphia: Pennsylvania State University Press, 1978).

157    The cause of the Opium War is as quoted in Brian Inglis, *Opium War* (London: Hodder and Stoughton, 1976).

# DREAMS OF WEALTH AND POWER

## 'ON THE WINGS OF CHANGE'

160    Mori Ogai's quote is taken from Wilkinson, *Japan versus Europe,* 117. Otto von Bismarck's quote is cited in Peter Mason, *Blood and Iron* (Melbourne, Penguin, 1984).

161    The comment by Commander Rodgers is quoted in Noel Perrin, *Giving Up the Gun* (Boulder, Shambhala, 1980) in which Perrin provides an extensive review of the history of the Japanese use and abandonment of the gun 1543–1879.

163    For a good general account of Tokugawa Japan see Edwin Reischauer, *Japan: The Story of a Nation* (New York: Alfred A. Knopf, 1981) and Richard Storry, *A History of Modern Japan* (Middlesex: Pelican, 1960).

164    Donald Keene, *The Japanese Discovery of Europe 1720–1830* (Palo Alto, Calif.: Stanford University Press, 1969) deals with the impact of the west on Japan and provides a good account of the development and impact of Rangaku or "Dutch learning."

168    The statistics on population and productivity come from Hsü, *The Rise of Modern China,* 178. An additional general reference that covers this period is John K. Fairbank and Edwin O. Reischauer, *China: Tradition and Transformation* (Sydney: George Allen and Unwin, 1979).

175    The quote from Zeng's diary is cited in Hsü, *The Rise of Modern China,* 345.
       Hart's code of behavior is taken from Hsü, *The Rise of Modern China,* 339.

176    The quote from Li Hong Zhang is cited in Hsü, *The Rise of Modern China,* 347.

177    Wo-Jen's restating of the Confucian attitude comes from Hsü, *The Rise of Modern China,* 349.

178–9    A good general explanation of the complex issue of *fengshui* is found in Ernest Eitel, *Fengshui: The Science of Sacred Landscape in Old China* (London: Synergetic Press, 1985). This book, however, was first published in 1873 around the time of the Shanghai-Wusong railway controversy.

## STRONG ARMY, RICH NATION

181    Shibusawa's quote is from Kyugoro Obato, *An Interpretation of the Life of Viscount Shibusawa* (Tokyo, Bijutsu Insatsusho, 1937, 48).

183    To get some insight into Fukuzawa's thinking see Kiyooka Eichi, ed., *The Autobiography of Fukuzawa Yukichi* (Tokyo, Hokuseido Press, 1981). Fukuzawa's most influential book *Things Western* is also well worth reading.
       Fukuzawa's quote comes from Wilkinson, *Japan Versus Europe,* 107.

184    Fukuzawa's quote on western customs is from his essay "Western Clothing, Food and Homes" written in 1866 and cited in Julia Meech-Pekarik, *The World of Meiji Print* (Tokyo, Weatherhill, 1986), 70.
       See Johannes Hirschmeier, "Shibusawa Eichi: Industrial Pioneer", in William W. Lockwood, ed., *The State and Economic Enterprise in Japan* (Princeton, N.J., Princeton University Press, 1969), 209–47.

185    A good account of how foreigners were employed in Japan can be found in Hazel Jones, *Live Machines* (University of British Columbia Press, 1980).

185–6    For a very readable account of the transformation of Meiji Japan see Reischauer's biography of her grandfather, Finance Minister

Matsukata Mosoyoshi, in Haru Matsukata Reischauer, *Samurai and Silk* (Cambridge, Mass.: The Belknap Press, Harvard, 1986).

187–8    Okura Kitvachiro's description of western dance is from Meech-Pekarik, *The World of Meiji Prints.*

190    *Shibusawa's quote on a moral economy is from Marshall Byronk, Capitalism and Nationalism in Prewar Japan: The Ideology of the Business Elite, 1868–1941* (Palo Alto, Calif.: Stanford University Press, 1967), cited in Gregory, "The Logic of Japanese Enterprise," in the *Institute of Comparative Culture Business Series,* Bulletin No. 92.

190–1    For a good short review of Meiji Japan and, specifically, Shibusawa's approach to the fostering of private enterprise, see Gregory, "The Logic of Japanese Enterprise," in the *Institute of Comparative Culture Business Series,* Bulletin No. 92.
For a more detailed account of the impact of technological innovation on the industrial development of Europe in the nineteenth and early twentieth centuries see David Landes, *The Unbound Prometheus,* (Cambridge: Cambridge University Press, 1968).
The quote comes from Yamamura, "Success Illgotten?" in *Journal of Economic History,* 117.

## WINDOWS ON THE WORLD

193    Belloc's quote is cited Mason, *Blood and Iron.*

195    The quote from Carnegie's letter was taken from Nathan Rosenberg and Birdzell, *How the West Grew Rich* (New York: Basic Books, 1985). This is a very accessible account of the role of economic institutions in fostering technological change and the application of science to industry in the nineteenth and early twentieth centuries.

197    This quote is from Rosenberg and Birdzell *How the West Grew Rich,* 213.
There are numerous accounts of the events surrounding the Shanghai Wusong railway controversy and Li Hongzhang's Chinese Merchants' Steam Navigation Company, however, Hsü, *The Rise of Modern China,* and Fairbank and Reischauer, provide good general reviews. Jardine Matheson's own recent history ed., Maggie Keswick, *The Thistle and the Jade* (London: Jardine Matheson & Co. Ltd, 1982) gives a good picture of the treaty ports and their economic impact on China in the late nineteenth century.

## CARVED UP LIKE A RIPE MELON

198    The quote from Liu Xihong is taken from J.D. Frodsham, *The Chinese Embassy in the West* (Oxford: Clarendon Press, 1974, 136).

203    The quote by Baron Von Falkenegg comes from Wilkinson, *Japan versus Europe,* 59.
The quotes by Rene Pion and Anatole France are both taken from Wilkinson, *Japan versus Europe,* 59 and 61. This book offers a very good and moving account of the complex relationship between Japan and the west.

204–5    One of the best biographical studies of Yan Fu and his efforts to adapt western ideas to Confucian China is Benjamin Schwartz, *In Search of Wealth and Power* (Cambridge, Mass.: The Belknap Press, Harvard, 1964).

206    The dialogue between Kang and Emperor Guangxu, and Kang's comments on institutional reforms come from Hsü, *The Rise of Modern China,* 452, 455.

207    Marina Warner, *The Dragon Empress* (London, Weidenfeld and Nicolson, 1972) provides a good account of court life in China during the final decades of the Qing dynasty.

## COMPRADORES AND WARLORDS

209    Chen Duxiu's quote on Mr Science and Mr Democracy comes from Fairbank and Reischauer, *China: Tradition and Transformation,* 434.

210    For a discussion on the issue of western influence on education in China see Merson, *Culture and Science in China,* chaps. 4 and 5.

212    Hu Shi's thoughts on liberation are as quoted in Fairbank and Reischauer, *China: Tradition and Transformation,* 436.

## ZAIBATSU AND THE ZERO-SUMGAME

213    Tokutoini's comment on the Japanese in the eyes of the world is as quoted in Meech-Pekarik, *The World of Meiji Prints.*

214    Reischauer, *Japan: The Story of a Nation,* 186, provides details of the development of the idea of "Asia for the Asians".

217    For an account of how the Zero Fighter was built Jiro Horikoshi, its designer, provides a good account in Shojiro Shindo and Harold N. Wantiez, *Eagles of Mitsubishi* (London: Orbis, 1981).

# THE COLOR OF THE CAT

## THE DRAGONS AWAKE

220–1    For a good account of United States policies in Japan after 1945 see Reischauer, *Japan: The Story of a Nation.* Reischauer was United States Ambassador to Japan in the early 1960's and provides a very perceptive account of United States-Japanese relations in his autobiography, Edwin Reischauer, *My Life between Japan and America* (New York: Harper and Row, 1986).

223    Chalmers Johnson, *MITI and the Japanese Miracle* (Palo Alto, Calif.: California University Press, 1982) provides one of the best studies available in English of the role of MITI in Japan's postwar development.

224    For a personal account of the history of Sony see Akio Morita, *Made in Japan* (London, Collins, 1986). For Ibuka's account of the company's meteoric rise see *Sony Challenge, 1946–1968,* (Tokyo: Sony Corporation, 1986). Makoto Kikuchi, the present chief of research at Sony provides a perspective on the Japanese approach to research and development in Makoto Kikuchi, *Japanese Electronics* (Tokyo: Simul Press, 1983).

## PERMANENT REVOLUTION

225    Mao Zedong's quote is from *Miscellany of Mao Zedong 1949–1968* (Arlington, 1974), 269.

227    For further details on Sino-Soviet relations in the 1950's see Bill Brugger, ed., *China: Liberation and Transformation 1962–1979* (London: Croom Helm, 1981). Also see Wang Gungwu, *China and the World since 1949* (London: Macmillan, 1977).

229    The quote by Professor Cao Zongxun is taken from Merson, *Culture and Science in China,* 126.

232    The quote on the "four pests" campaign comes from Mikhail Klochko, *Soviet Scientist in China* (Hollis and Carter, 1964), 72. This book provides an excellent account of the experiences of a Soviet scientist sent to China in the 1950's.

233    For further statistics on the "great leap forward" see Hsü, *The Rise of Modern China,* 787.

234    Re the Box "Let A Hundred Flowers Bloom" – Thomas Malthus (1766–1834) was the economist who first put forward the theory that poverty was the result of population growth outpacing the rise in food production. A natural check on this population increase was the regular occurrence of natural disasters, war and disease. It was largely Malthus who earned for economics the title of the "dismal science."

## MADE IN JAPAN

236    Morishima's quote comes from M. Morishima, *Why Japan Succeeded,* 117.
For a good general account of the west's misunderstanding of Japan, see Wilkinson, *Japan versus Europe.* Robert Christopher,

*The Japanese Mind* (London, Pan Books, 1984) is also worth reading on this subject.

238    For a good popular history of the development of computer technology Stan Augarten, *Bit by Bit: An Illustrated History of Computers* (Unwin Paperbacks, 1984) is worth reading.

On the issue of American failure to realize fully the potential of computer technology in manufacture see Seymour Mellman, "How the Yankees lost their Know-How", in *Technology Review*, October 1983. (Mellman is Professor of Engineering at Columbia University, New York.) Also see David Noble, *America by Design: Science, Technology, and the Rise of Corporate Capitalism*, (New York: Knopf, 1977).

239    For a detailed account of the rise of the Japanese electronics industry see Gene Gregory, *Japanese Electronics Technology: Enterprise and Innovation* (Tokyo: Japan Times, 1984).

240–1    Halberstram, *The Reckoning,* provides a good short account of the impact of Deming's ideas on the Japanese. It also provides an excellent account of how the Americans lost out to the Japanese in the automobile industry.

242    Nakane's arguments about the group orientation of Japanese society are found in Chie Nakane, *Japanese Society* (Middlesex: Pelican, 1974).

The quote by Morishima is taken from M. Morishima, *Why Japan Succeeded.* The Confucian character of Japanese society is also dealt with in some detail.

243    The quote on Japanese interdependence is taken from Jane Devitt, "Changing Social Values in Contemporary Japan," unpublished paper, (Japanese Economic and Management Centre, University of New South Wales, Sydney.)

The quote by Yasuo Kato comes from *Business Week*, 14 December, 1981. On the issue of creativity in Japan see J. Bester, *Heidiki Yukawa Creativity and Intuition: A Physicist looks at East and West* (Kodansha International, 1973). Heidiki Yukawa was one of Japan's early Nobel prize-winning physicists.

243–4    Richard Pascale and Anthony Athos, *The Art of Japanese Management* (London: Allen Lane, 1981) was one of the popular books that showed American audiences just why the Japanese were doing things better than they were. Ezara Vogel, *Japan as Number One* was also written as a warning to American industry. Lester Thurow, ed., *The Management Challenge: Japanese Views* (Cambridge, Mass.: MIT Press, 1985) is a more recent work providing the Japanese perspective on how and why they have been so successful. For a critical study of the relevance of Japan as a model for other countries see Ian Inkster, *Japan as a Development Model* (Brokmeyer Bochum, 1980).

### BETTER RED THAN EXPERT

247    The quote by Professor Cao Zongxun comes from Merson, *Culture and Science in China,* 157.

248    The account of violence at a school in Xiamen comes from Ken Ling, *The Revenge of Heaven: Journal of a Young Chinese* (New York: G.P. Putnam, 1972).

Liang Heng and Judith Shapiro, *Son of the Revolution* (Aylsbury, Bucks.: Fontana, 1983) is one of a number of books written by witnesses of the cultural revolution. Others worth reading are Bao Ruowang, *Prisoner of Mao* (New York: Coward McCann and Geoghagen, 1973) and Ken Ling, *The Revenge of Heaven.*

251    An interesting perspective on the events of the cultural revolution and its links to China's past is found in Donald Munro, *The Concept of Man in Contemporary China.* (Ann Arbor, Mich.: University of Michigan Press, 1977). Bill Brugger, ed., *China: The Impact of the Cultural Revolution* (Canberra: Australian National University Press, 1978) also provides a good review of the events and the consequences of the cultural revolution.

For a detailed account of the new emphasis given to science see Tong B. Tang, *Science and Technology in China* (London, Longmans, 1984).

259    The quote from the play *The Impostor,* was translated by Danny Kane and comes from Merson, *Culture and Science in China,* 174.

### THE OPEN DOOR

260    For an account of the massive transfer of technology now going from the west to China, and its consequences see E.E. Bauer, *China Take Off: Technology Transfer and Modernization* (Seattle: University of Washington Press, 1986). Fingar et al., "Science and Technology in China," in *Bulletin of the Atomic Scientists,* October 1984, provides a detailed review of China's efforts to catch up with Japan and the west. See also Simon, "The Challenge of Modernizing Industrial Technology", in *China Asian Survey,* vol. XXVI, No. 4, April 1986.

### TROUBLE IN STOVE CITY

265    On the issue of demands for greater intellectual freedom and democracy called for by Fang Lizhi see David Kelly, "The Chinese Student Movement of December 1986 and its Intellectual Antecedents", in *Australian Journal of Chinese Affairs,* March 1988.

269    On the more general issues of world history and the reasons for the shift in centers of economic power and creativity there is an excellent study in Kennedy, *The Rise and Fall of the Great Powers* (New York, Random House, 1988).

# Notes on Illustrations

## The Price of Harmony

**Pages 12 & 13**: Guiseppe Castiglione (1662–1722), *L'emperor ouvre un siffon a l'occasion de la fête de l'agriculture* (The Emperor uses a plough at the agriculture fête) from "Voyages de L'emperor Kangxi". Code 72E239 Musée Guimet, Paris (Photo: Cliche des Musées Nationaux).

**Page 15**: *The Catlan Map* from a fourteenth century manuscript. The Mansell Collection Ltd, London.

**Page 16**: Attributed to Liu Kuan-Tao, *Kubla Khan Hunting,* (Yuan dynasty — 1279–1368). Collection of the National Palace Musuem, Taipei, Taiwan, Republic of China.

**Page 17**: "The Ocean Going Junk" in the *Liu-Chhiu Kuo Chih Lueh* of 1757. This is one of the best pictures of a Chinese ship in the Chinese style to be found in the literature. Courtesy of Joseph Needham, *Science and Civilization in China,* Vol. V1:3, (Cambridge, Cambridge University Press, 1971) 405, Fig. 939.

**Page 19**: Guiseppe Castiglione (1662–1722), *Southern Inspection Tour by Emperor Kangxi of the Building of the Dykes,* scroll number 4 (Mulan IV) from seventeenth century scroll titled "Tour of The South." Musée Guimet. (Photo: Cliche des Musees Nationaux, Paris).

**Page 19**: A late Qing (1840–1911) representation of river conservancy work from *Chin-Ting Shu ching Thu Shou* (Imperial illustrated edition of the "Historical Classic") 1905, ch 6, Yu Kung. Courtesy of Joseph Needham, *Science and Civilization in China,* Vol.IV:3, 233, Fig 865.

**Page 22**: Woodblock of iron foundries from a Chinese encyclopedia. Courtesy of Canton University Library, Canton (Guangzhou).

**Page 24**: Woodblock of salt drilling from a Chinese encyclopedia. Courtesy of Canton University Library, Canton (Guangzhou).

**Page 26** (*left*): "Rice paddies" woodblock from a Chinese encyclopedia. Courtesy of Canton University Library, Canton (Guangzhou).

**Page 26** (*right*): "Dragon's back bone pump" from *Thien Kung Khai Wu* (1637), Ch 1, 19a. Courtesy of Joseph Needham, *Science and Civilization in China,* Vol.IV:2, 340, fig 579.

**Page 27**: Paul de Limbourg and Colombe (1415–16), October *Très Riches Heures,* fol. 10v. Musée Condé, Chantilly.

**Page 29**: *Portrait of Emperor Renzong,* Song Dynasty (960–1279). Collection of the National Palace Museum, Taipei, Taiwan, Rupublic of China.

**Page 30**: Chou Wen-Chu (active 940–975), *Scholars of Liu-Li Hall,* Song Dynasty (960–1279), hand-painted scroll, detail 5 — right hand side: three scholars; two servants and Buddhist monk in front of raised platform. Ink and colors on silk. Metropolitan Museum of Art, Gift of Mrs Sheila Riddell, in memory of Sir Percival David, 1977.

**Page 32:** (*left*): "Compositors setting a book in wooden movable type." Illustration from *Chin Chien Wu ying tien chu chen pan ch'eng shih,* a manual on movable type printing written in 1777 by Chin Chien.

**Page 32** (*right*): *The Return of Lady Wen,* (28.62–65), Museum of Fine Arts, Boston.

**Page 36:** "Eighth century star map," Hong Kong University Press, Hong Kong.

**Page 38:** (*left*): "Painting of Armillary Sphere," Qing Dynasty (1644–1911). Collection of the National Palace Museum, Taipei, Taiwan, Republic of China.

**Page 39:** A late Qing representation of the measurement of the sun's shadow using a gnomon. From *Chin Ting Shu Ching Thu Shuo,* chapter 1, Yao-Tien Karlen 12, 3. Courtesy of Joseph Needham, *Science and Civilization in China,* Vol.III, 285.

**Page 45:** (*right*): Woodblock of ginseng. From a Chinese encyclopedia. Courtesy of the University of Canton, Canton (Guangzhou).

**Page 47:** "Chinese of all ages standing around the ying and yang symbol," seventeenth century painting. British Museum, London.

**Page 48:** (*left*): "Washing the heart and storing inwardly (the secretions)" From a nei tan alchemic text: *Hsing ming Kuei Chih. Hsi Hsin Thui Tsang (1615).* Courtesy of Joseph Needham, *Science and Civilization in China,* Vol.IV:2.

**Page 51:** Woodblock of wall and battle. From a Chinese encyclopedia. Courtesy of the University of Canton, Canton (Guangzhou).

**Page 53:** Gunpowder map drawn by Mike Gorman. Details courtesy of Joseph Needham, *Science and Civilization in China.*

**Page 55:** Chang Tse-Tuan, *Chhing-Ming Shang Ho Thu (Returning up the River to the City at the Spring Festival),* (1125), Su Song scroll.

**Page 57:** Woodblock of silk weaving loom. From a Chinese encyclopedia. Courtesy of the University of Canton, Canton (Guangzhou).

**Page 58:** "Merchants," Art Institute of Chicago, Chicago.

**Page 59:** Printing block for a Mongol bank note of the Chih-yuan period. Courtesy of Denis Twitchett, *Printing and Publishing in Medieval China* (London, Wynkyn de worde Society, 1983).

**Page 60:** The Battleship (Lou Chhuaan) in 1510 edition of *Wu Ching Tsung Yao* (1044). Courtesy of Joseph Needham, *Science and Civilization in China,* Vol.IV:3, 426, fig 949.

**Page 66:** "Venetian merchants Trading Bolts of Silk". from Marco Polo, *Book of Marvels, P.N. Paris MS 2810. Bibliothèque Nationale, Paris.*

**Page 67:** "Medieval siege of a stronghold in Africa" from *Chroniques de Froissart,* fourteenth century manuscript. British Museum Library Board, London.

**Page 68:** "The Taking of Rouen by Henry V (1418–19)" from *Vigiles de Charles VII,* fifteenth century manuscript. Bibliothèque Nationale, Paris.

**Page 70:** Leonardo da Vinci, *Chariot with Scythes,* Courtesy British Museum, London.

**Page 71:** Vittore Carpaccio (1460–1526), *Return of the Ambassadors* from the Cycle of the Scuola di Sant'Orsola. Accademia, Venice. (Photo: Scala).

**Page 72:** Prince Henry the Navigator from Gomes Eanes de Zurara (1410–1473) (*Cronica da Tomada*). Biblioteca Nacional, Lisbon.

**Page 74:** Illustrations by Mike Gorman.

**Page 76:** Shen Tu, *The Giraffe of Bengal,* (copied by Ch'en T'ing-pi), from the book *T'oung Pao* Vol. XXXIV, 5. Courtesy of the Australian National University Library, Canberra.

## THE INVENTION OF PROGRESS

**Page 83:** Gentile Bellini, *Audience d'une ambassade Venitienne dans une ville orientale,* (1512), Venice, school of Bellini. Musée du Louvre, Paris.

**Page 84:** Hans Holbein the Younger, *The Ambassadors* (1533). National Gallery, London.

**Page 86:** Peter Apian, *Introductio geographica Petri Apiani in*

*Doctissimus Verneri Annotationes,* Inglostadt (1533). British Library, London.

**Page 88:** *Solomon and the Clock,* Flemish mid-fifteenth century, Fr 455, fol 9. Bibliothèque Nationale, Paris.

**Page 89:** (*left*): "General views of Su Sung's clock tower", from Hsin I Hsiang Fa Yao (1092). Courtesy of Joseph Needham, *Clerks and Craftsmen in China and the West,* (Cambridge, Cambridge University Press, 1970), Figs. 62a and 62b, 211.

**Page 89:** (*right*): Stradanus of Antwerp, *Horologia Ferrea.* Courtesy of Sydney College of the Arts, Sydney.

**Page 90:** Jan Vredeman De Vries, perspective diagram. Engraving from *Perspective* (Leiden 1604–5), plate 28.

**Page 91:** Albrecht Dürer, "Perspective Device," wood-cut from *Underweysung der Messung,* (Nuremberg 1525).

**Page 92:** Andreas Vesalius, *Quinta Musculo,* from *Fabric of the Human Body* (De Humani Corporis Fabrica), (Basel 1543).

**Page 93:** Matteo Ricci, "A world map using Mercator's projection." Kobe City Museum.

**Page 95:** *St Francis Xavier* (1506–1552), by a Japanese Jesuit at Macao (1623). No 36 in the catalog. Kobe City Museum.

**Page 97:** Kano Naizen, *Nambon Screen,* late sixteenth century–early seventeenth century, six fold screen. Musée Guimet, Paris (Photo: Cliche des Musées Nationaux).

**Page 98:** (*top*): A Beauvais tapestry, *Die Astronomen,* (The Jesuits as Astronomers), Late seventeenth century. Bayerische Verwaltung der Staatlichen Schlösser, Garten und Seen, Munich.

**Page 98:** (*bottom*): "Matteo Ricci, Adam Schall and Ferdinand Verbiest", from Jean Baptist Du Halde's *Description of the Empire of China and Chinese Tartary* (London, 1738–1741, translated from 1708 work). Staatsbibliothek Preussischer, Kulturbesitz, West Berlin.

**Page 100:** Jean Baptist du Halde, "Pere, Adam Schaal", from Du Halde's *Description of the Empire of China and Chinese Tartary.* 269. State Library of New South Wales, Sydney.

**Page 102:** Jean Baptist du Halde, "Observatory on the City wall in Peking," from *Description of the Empire of China and Chinese Tartary.* State Library of New South Wales, Sydney.

**Page 104:** (*left*): Zonca, "Trombe Da Rota per Cavar Aqua" from Zonca's engineering treatise of 1607. It appears first in the mss of Francesco di Giorgio (1475). Courtesy of Joseph Needham, *Science and Civilization in China,* Vol IV:2, 214.

**Page 104:** (*right*): "The eighth diagram" from *Chhi Thu Shuo* (1627). Courtesy of Joseph Needham, Ibid.

**Page 107:** V.C. Vroom (1566–1640), *Return from the Second Voyage to the East Indies* (1599). Amsterdam Historical Museum.

**Page 108:** Job Berckheyde (1630–63) *The Courtyard of the Amsterdam Exchange* (1668). Amsterdam Historical Museum.

**Page 109:** Sieuwert van der Meulen, *The Planks Rise all around the Ship* (etching). State Library of New South Wales, Sydney.

**Page 110:** (*left*): Dionysius Papin M.D., *Anno 1689.* From George Williamson, *Memorials of the Lineage, Early Life, Education, and Development of the genius of James Watt,* (Thomas Constable, London, 1856).

**Page 110:** (*right*): James Watt and one of his steam powered beam engines. Courtesy of Powerhouse Museum, Sydney.

**Page 112:** Jan van Kessel, *Asien,* (1664–66), oil on canvas. Alte Pinakothek, Munich.

**Page 113:** Thomas Sprat, frontispiece to *The History of the Royal Society of London for Improving Natural Knowledge,* (1667).

**Page 114:** "Octagon Room at Greenwich Observatory" (engraving). National Maritime Museum, London.

**Page 115:** Unidentified Artist, "Greenwich Observatory from Croom's Hill" (about 1860). National Maritime Museum, London.

**Page 116:** Gerrit Paape, "Operations in a Delft faience factory" (copperplate). Courtesy of Gröninger Museum, The Netherlands.

**Page 117:** *Gate Crashing at the Tuileries* (1783) Montgolfier brothers' demonstration of the hot-air balloon. Courtesy of Colonel Richard Gimbel, Aeronautics History Collection, US Airforce Academy Library, USA.

**Page 118:** Joseph Wright of Derby, *An Experiment on a Bird in the*

*Airpump*, (1767–1768). National Gallery, London.

**Page 120**: Painting by Cu Liu Peng. Sydney L. Moss Ltd, London.

**Page 123**: Catterson Smith, *Anna Maria, Seventh Duchess of Bedford*. Courtesy of Woburn Abbey, Bedfordshire.

**Page 124**: "Emperor's Audience in the Imperial Garden," late eighteenth century. Hong Kong Museum of Art, Hong Kong.

**Page 127**: A contemporary painting illustrating the manufacture, transport and sale of export porcelain in China during the eighteenth century. "Perfecting the Interior" from Walter A Staehelin, *The Book of Porcelain* (1965). Collection from the Benteli Publishers, Switzerland.

**Page 128**: "Scene in a porcelain factory: painters; muffle-kiln; preparing the paste; repairers, from de Milly's *L'Art de la Porcelaine*, (1771). State Library of New South Wales, Sydney.

**Page 129**: George Stubbs, *Josiah Wedgwood and his Family* (1780). Josiah Wedgwood and Sons Limited, Barlaston, Stoke-on-Trent, England.

**Page 130**: Staffordshire potteries (engraving). Mary Evans Picture Library, London.

**Page 131**: Photo of Josiah Wedgwood's 3,000 trials carried out when trying to develop his jasper-ware. Josiah Wedgwood & Sons Limited, Barlaston, Stoke-on-Trent, England.

**Page 133**: Engraving of Piedmontese throwing mill", (1607). Macclesfield Sunday School Heritage Centre Silk Museum.

**Page 135**: (*top*): M.J. Starting, *John Lombe's Water Powered Silk Spinning Factory built in Derby in 1720*. Mary Evans Picture Library, London.

**Page 136**: Diagrams courtesy of Macclesfield Sunday School Heritage Centre Silk Museum.

**Page 138**: James Gillray, *Scientific Researches! – New Discoveries in Pneumatics! – or – an Experimental Lecture on the Powers of Air*. British Museum, London.

**Page 139**: I.M. Booth, *Arkwright's Cotton Mills, by Night*, (1782–83), 34 x 45 inches. Derby Art Gallery.

**Page 142**: Cotton mill (engraving). Mary Evans Picture Library, London.

**Page 145**: James Gillray, *The Reception of the Diplomatique and his suite, at the court of Peking*, (1792). British Museum, London.

**Page 146**: Idealized picture of the production of tea (1780). Number 6 or 7 of the catalog Craig Clunas *Chinese Export Watercolours*. Far Eastern Series, Victoria & Albert Museum, London.

**Page 147**: Canton waterfront and the European factories in 1794 (chinese scroll). Hong Kong Museum of Art, Hong Kong.

**Page 148**: A Chinese representation of the bringing of astronomical instruments as gifts by the embassy of Lord Macartney (1793), silk K'o-ssu. National Maritime Museum, London.

**Page 149**: William Alexander, *Approach of the Emperor of China to his tent in Tartary, to receive the British Ambassador* (September 1793). British Museum, London.

**Page 150**: William Alexander, *Portrait of Qianlong, Emperor of China in the Eighty Fourth Year of his Age, and Fifty Seventh of his Reign*. British Museum, London.

**Page 152**: George Chinnery (1774–1852), *Hauqua II* (1769–1843). Jardine Matheson & Co. Ltd, Hong Kong.

**Page 154**: Thomas Allom, "China Opium Smokers," from *China in a Series of Views*, (1843), 55. State Library of New South Wales, Sydney.

**Page 156**: Thomas Allom, "The Hon. East India Company's steamer *Nemsis* and the Boats of Sulphur, Calliope, Larne and Starling," *The Chinese Empire Illustrated* (1858). National Library of Australia, Canberra.

## DREAMS OF WEALTH AND POWER

**Pages 158–159**: *The Prosperity of an English Trading Firm in Yokohama*. Yokohama Archives of History, Yokohama.

**Page 161**: "One of the Black Ships" as seen by a Japanese artist (1853). Yokohama Archives of History, Yokohama.

**Page 162**: A photo of the telegraph brought from the United States. Tokyo Communication Centre, Tokyo.

**Page 163**: "Samurai watching a model train." Courtesy Saga Prefectural Museum, Saga.

**Page 164**: Anonymous, *The Battle of Nagashino*, (Edo period, seventeenth century), six fold screen, ink and color on paper. Tokugawa Art Museum, Nagoya.

**Page 166**: Woodblocks from Yokohama Archives of History, Yokohama.

**Page 169**: Anonymous, *The Taiping Rebellion*. A painting commissioned by the Qing dynasty court (1860s). Courtesy of Wango Weng, New Hampshire.

**Page 173**: "The European–style Warship." Courtesy Saga Prefectural Museum, Saga.

**Page 174**: Photo by John Thomson of Li Hongzhang. From Thomson, *Illustrations of China and its People 1868–1874*, Vol.4. Royal Geographical Society, London.

**Page 176**: "The Jiangnan arsenal" from *Tien-Shih Chai Huo Pao* (Shanghai Picture Magazine), (1884–1894). National Library of Australia, Canberra.

**Page 179**: Photo by John Thomson of Nanking Arsenal (1868–1872). From J. Thomson, *Illustrations of China and its Peoples 1868–1874*, Vol.3. Royal Geographical Society, London.

**Page 180**: "Early Chinese railway." Mary Evans Picture Library, London.

**Page 181**: (*left*): Photo of Emperor Meiji in Court Robes (1860s). Albumen print. Yokohama Archives of History, Yokohama.

**Page 181**: (*right*): Uchida Kuichi, *Emperor Meiji (1872)*. Albumen print. Collection of H. Kwan Lan, New York.

**Page 182**: Hashimoto Sadahide, *Picture of the Salesroom in Foreign Business Establishment in Yokohama*, (1861). The Lincoln Kirstein Collection, Metropolitan Museum of Art, New York.

**Page 183**: Fukuzawa Yukichi as a young samurai in Paris (1862). Albumen print. Keio University Library, Tokyo.

**Page 186**: "Silk spinning factory at Tomioka." Tomioka Museum.

**Page 187**: Utagawa Yoshitora, *An Imported Silk Reeling Machine at Tsuuiji in Tokyo* (1872). Lincoln Kirstein Collection, Metropolitan Museum of Art, New York.

**Page 188**: Hashimoto Chikanobu, *A Concert of European Music* (1889). Lincoln Kirstein Collection, Metropolitan Museum of Art, New York.

**Page 189**: Photo of samurai. Courtesy of University of Nagasaki Library, Nagasaki.

**Page 190**: "Yokohama Station" (woodblock). Yokohama Archives of History, Yokohama.

**Page 191**: "Large European–style buildings" (woodblock). Yokohama Archives of History, Yokohama.

**Page 194**: "Les Ponts Roulants in the Galerie des Machines, Paris 1889" from *Illustrated London News* (1889).

**Page 196**: "The First Electric Street Light in Tokyo's Ginza Street" (1883 woodblock). Courtesy of the Ministry of Foreign Affairs, Tokyo.

**Page 199**: George Bigot, "China and Japan fish for control of Korea" (1890s). Yokohama Archives of History, Yokohama.

**Page 200**: Anonymous woodblock. A contemporary recording of the Sino-Japanese War, (1894).

**Page 203**: George Bigot, "Japan is excluded from the Club". Yokohama Archives of History, Yokohama.

**Page 207**: Yu (court photographer), *The Empress Dowager Posed as Goddess of Mercy*, Yuan-Yin, Peking, (1902–08). Freer Gallery of Art, Smithsonian Institution, Washington.

**Page 209**: "Dr Sun Yat-sen in exile in Japan." Radio Times Hulton Picture Library, London.

**Page 217**: Contemporary painting of the zero aeroplane. Courtesy of United States Army.

## THE COLOR OF THE CAT

**Page 221**: The hypocenter of the atomic bomb and Mitsubishi steel works seen from a hill in Matsuyama-machi. Nagasaki International Culture Center. (Photo: Yosuke Yamabata, August 1945)

**Page 224**: (*top*): Ibuka standing next to a stereo speaker. Photo courtesy of Sony Corporation, Tokyo.

**Page 224**: (*bottom*) Photo taken in the Sony factory 1946. Courtesy of Sony Corporation, Tokyo.

**Page 225**: Soviet troops remove heavy industrial equipment from a Manchurian factory in 1946. Library of Congress, Washington D.C.

**Page 226**: Mao Zedong and the People's Liberation Army entering Peking, January 1949. (Chinese wall poster). Granger Collection, New York.

**Page 227**: Mao Zedong in the Soviet Union with Soviet leaders Bulganin and Stalin. Popperfoto.

**Page 237**: The *Eniac* was an enticing recruitment asset. *Popular Science.*

**Page 240**: Motoman from Kuni Sadamoto, "Robots in the Japanese Economy — facts about robots and their significance," *Survey Japan,* (Tokyo, 1981).

**Page 241**: From Richard Tanner Pascale and Anthony G. Athos. *The Art of Japanese Management,* (Allen Lane).
*(Photo)* Paul Fusco, Magnum/John Hillelson Agency.

**Page 256**: "Trucks awaiting despatch at Changchun No. 1 Motor Vehicle Factory in late 1970s." Society for Anglo- Chinese Understanding, London.

# ACKNOWLEDGMENTS

This book has evolved over some years, and its history is inexorably intertwined with a television series produced at the same time. This is not however a "book of the series." It was written with the intention of exploring a great deal more than was possible in a four-hour television series.

Many of the ideas for both the book and the television series grew out of discussions with my friend and colleague at the University of New South Wales, Professor Ian Inkster, whose encouragement and criticism were invaluable. I am also indebted to Professor Wang Gungwu, Dr Stephen Fitzgerald, Professor Nathan Sivin, Professor Ho Peng Yoke, Professor Shigeru Nakayama, Dr Mark Elvin, Professor Ko Tsun, Professor Eric Jones, Dr Tim Cheek and Dr David Kelly for the help they have given me. Above all I am indebted to the Needham Institute in Cambridge, and Dr Joseph Needham whose monumental work *Science and Civilization in China* first raised many of the issues of world history that this book attempts to address. I would also like to thank my colleagues at the School of Science and Technology Studies, University of New South Wales, and the Australian Broadcast-ing Corporation's Science Unit for their encouragement and support.

This book has also benefited greatly from access to photographs and illustrations gathered for the television series, and for the new insights that were gained in the process of making that series. For this I owe a great deal to Film Australia and, in particular, to Robin Hughes for the support she has given to this project over its long, and sometimes tortuous, history. Thanks are due also to the film production team whose capacity for demanding simple answers to problems that one would rather ignore kept me honest — in particular to David Roberts, Geoff Barnes, Tom Levenson, and Dick Gilling. For photographic material taken on location I am indebted to Tony Gailey, David Roberts, Greg Low, and Jane Castle. A special thanks to Emma Gordon whose help in picture research and in getting the manuscript ready for the publisher were essential, and to the book's editors Lesley Dow and Kim Anderson for their patience and enthusiasm.

# INDEX